Global Connections: Politics, Exchange, and Social Life in World History

VOLUME II

JOHN COATSWORTH
JUAN COLE
MICHAEL P. HANAGAN
PETER C. PERDUE
CHARLES TILLY
LOUISE TILLY

CAMBRIDGE
UNIVERSITY PRESS

CAMBRIDGE
UNIVERSITY PRESS

University Printing House, Cambridge CB2 8BS, United Kingdom

Cambridge University Press is part of the University of Cambridge.

It furthers the University's mission by disseminating knowledge in the pursuit of education, learning, and research at the highest international levels of excellence.

www.cambridge.org
Information on this title: www.cambridge.org/9780521145190

© John Coatsworth, Juan Cole, Michael P. Hanagan, Peter C. Perdue, Charles Tilly, and Louise Tilly 2015.

First published 2015

Printed in the United States of America by Sheridan Books, Inc.

A catalog record for this publication is available from the British Library

ISBN 978-0-521-76106-2 Hardback
ISBN 978-0-521-14519-0 Paperback

CONTENTS

ILLUSTRATIONS

*Source information for all illustrations in this textbook can be found online
at www.cambridge.org/globalconnections2.*

MAPS

Source information for all map in this textbook can be found online at www.cambridge.org/globalconnections2.

INTRODUCTION: THE HUMAN STORY SINCE 1500

In the years after 1500, the whole human family came into contact for the first time in thousands of years. For millennia Amerindians, Eurasians, and Polynesians had developed separately from one another with no knowledge of the existence of other members of the human race. Then in a few decades around 1500 long-lost peoples rediscovered one another. Amerindians and Europeans who had existed independently for at least 14,000 years suddenly came into contact. This same encounter occurred at many points throughout the world.

Within decades Europeans, Americans, and Asians were involved in a gigantic exchange that forever affected their menus and their agricultural life. Mineral and agricultural products crossed both the Atlantic and the Pacific in massive quantities, transforming production methods and daily consumption. From the Americas, Europeans imported turkeys, cranberries, potatoes, tomatoes, and tobacco. Asians obtained maize, peanuts, chili peppers, and most important, silver and gold in exchange for porcelain, silk, and tea. From Europe, Amerindians learned about horses, apples, barley, coffee, and wheat. Not all exchanges were productive. Crab grass comes from Europe as well as measles, malaria, cholera and bubonic plague, while smallpox devastated previously unexposed populations of the New World and Asia. From America came syphilis and hepatitis.

The sudden presence of new visitors from distant continents exposed both natives and newcomers to new diseases and increased mortality. Many Europeans succumbed within months of arrival. But in the end, in most of the world, the European diseases proved far more murderous than the American. In most places Europeans perished from new diseases, but the Eurasian Plain had already introduced many diseases to its inhabitants, who had developed immunities. Areas with smaller populations and less intimate contact lacked such wide exposure and died in catastrophic numbers. In North America whole Indian tribes were wiped out and dazed survivors had to consolidate with other groups in order to preserve any collective life at all. Massive deaths among native populations were the typical results of the age of discovery.

The exchange of foods and livestock that followed the landing of Europeans in the Americas reminds us that globalization has never been a one-way process. Globalization occurs when actions, events, and relations at an increasingly greater distance from the locality affect community life. The expansion of diseases across continents is an example of globalization. Contrary to some common usages, globalization does not mean that a process encompasses the entire globe. It refers to the *expanding* of processes and movements across territory. Deglobalization is its opposite: It refers to the *shrinking* geographic influence of processes and movements.

In the case of the encounter between Europeans and Amerindians, sometimes referred to as the Columbian Exchange, at any given time and place globalization and deglobalization were usually happening simultaneously. The utter devastations among Amerindian peoples and the destruction of Amerindian cultures that forced peoples to reorganize their collective life on a smaller scale is deglobalizing. To decide whether a region is globalizing or deglobalizing, it is the net balance that counts. Is the society globalizing *more* than it is deglobalizing? Is it territorially expanding? Do distant groups or happenings increasingly influence important events or actions?

If somehow we could measure the geographic frequency and territorial consequences of all these decisions in any one period for a given region and add them up we would be able to provide a definitive response to the question of whether globalization or deglobalization was occurring. Alas, we can seldom provide a precise answer to this question but informed estimates of main trends are possible.

The so-called Columbian Exchange should also remind us that there is nothing intrinsically good or bad about globalization. The great deaths in the Americas and elsewhere that followed European contact involved a catastrophic loss of life and human culture and the European rule that followed was murderous and oppressive. European settlers saw a land of hope and promise but others had different perspectives. Africans suffered a huge expansion in the slave trade, while Chinese and Indians gained enormous supplies of silver to fuel their commercial economy. Globalization never hits all peoples equally.

Humans connect in many different ways. For example, they can kill each other, trade with each other, or have sexual relations with each other. They can dance and sing together, worship the same gods, or build monuments together. Each kind of connection creates a different kind of relationship, and on the collective scale, a different kind of social process. As the philosopher Karl Marx put it, "Society does not consist of individuals but expresses the sum of inter-relations [between them]."

Our story features the development of politics, exchange, and social life and the changing relationships among them. In war, the most extreme form of political domination, for example, one group of human beings tries to exert power over another group through the threat of force. In less extreme form, unequal power relations pervade societies at all times. Even in peaceful times, political elites dominate their subjects first of all by threatening them with punishment. For better or worse, on our planet some people have always exercised power, military or political, over others. Coercion is one central theme of human history; it seems unlikely to disappear soon. You will read about a lot of wars in this book. Unfortunately, they mattered.

And yet, humans also contact each other on more equal terms. When one person exchanges what he doesn't need for something he wants, both sides gain. As the economic theorist Adam Smith said, "The propensity to truck, barter and exchange one thing for another . . . is common to all men, and to be found in no other race of animals." Markets, where humans gathered to exchange their goods, probably began as soon as humans learned to speak. Over time, they expanded in scale from small trading centers to large continental networks. Small markets could link themselves to larger markets in a hierarchy, bringing the products of farmers and herders from the countryside into towns and from there into large urban centers. The products of the cities likewise flowed downward through the market hierarchy into the countryside, tying producers and consumers together with continuous flows of goods.

In theory, these exchanges were equal: if no one interfered, no one had to sell anything except at a price that gave him what he needed. Real markets, however, had fewer equal exchanges. Rulers "sold" their product – protection of life – to their subjects in return for taxes and tribute, but usually the subject had no choice of whom to serve. This monopoly market in protection supported the state and protected the subject, but the ruler set the price. Sometimes, subjects could run away, look for another ruler, or revolt against unjust rulers: then they had more leverage over the terms of their trade. Still, most markets never really created truly equal relationships. They, too, never escaped the effects of power.

It was the same for merchants: some were always richer than others. The perceptive Adam Smith also said, "People of the same trade seldom meet together, even for merriment and diversion, but the conversation ends in a conspiracy against the public, or in some contrivance to raise prices." Powerful merchants tried to control markets by excluding competitors, fixing prices, or selling shoddy goods. At the same time, their rivals tried to find new customers, new sellers, and new products. The drives of consumers looking for cheaper goods and merchants looking for new sources of profit kept the engine of commercial expansion going. The expansion of commerce around the globe is our second central theme. Like war and political power, trading routes connected people across large expanses of land and sea. They did not have to speak the same language, or have very much in common; they did not even have to like each other. They could still see the advantage of selling what they had for what they wanted.

If all humans were clones, we might have no war, no political structures, no trade, and no cultural clashes. Life would be peaceful, but very boring. Human difference created the inequalities of power, possessions, and beliefs that have generated both our highest triumphs and our most terrible tragedies. Since we are not all the same, and very few of us can live entirely alone, we work with others to help us survive. Humans have always formed groups in order to devote their varied talents to a common cause. Men and women marry and raise families because few of them can do it on their own. Farmers, herders, artisans, traders, and even scholars join together to produce food, shoes, markets, and ideas. These communities are the core of social life, our third central theme. In these groups, from the families to great civilizations, humans have defined who they are, what they care about, and where they direct their most intensive efforts.

Communities ranged in size from families of two to five people to the hundreds of millions who shared one of the great world religions, like Christianity, Confucianism, or Islam. These communities expanded and contracted by different methods: families grew by reproduction or adoption, craft guilds brought in new members by recruiting apprentices, while religions spread by converting new believers. Each of them constructed rituals, like marriage, initiation, or baptism, to single out those who belonged from those who did not.

Communities rested on both similarity and difference, on equality and inequality. Most of the time, people tended to join with those like themselves, in language, religion, social status, or wealth. Yet even families contained people of different ages and genders, with different statuses. Usually, the eldest male ran the household. The domination of men over women has been a central fact of world history, which has not disappeared today.

Also, the larger a collective group grew, the more varied its members became. As communities expanded and linked with each other, they faced the challenge of keeping their members attached to shared values while accepting the inevitable diversity of human experience. The great religious traditions tried to distill out a few simple truths – the Four Noble Truths of Buddhism, the Islamic or Christian professions of faith – that summed up the essence of their creed for all believers. And yet, millions of believers in one religion did not practice their faith identically. The gap between universal ideals and diverse social practice is a constant theme of our story.

Each of these themes serves as a short description of a major global process. *Politics* describes the formation and breakdown of states, empires, and federations; *commerce* or exchange indicates the expansion and contraction of trading networks; *social life* means the formation and dissolution of communities. These processes could go in different directions at the same time. We are not describing a single, linear evolution from simple to complex societies. The world suffered major periods of catastrophic breakdown as well as growth. Even today, we have certainly advanced in our ability to control nature and improve the standard of living of many fortunate people, but have we advanced morally, aesthetically, or spiritually too? Let's leave this question open for now.

Politics, exchange, and social life did not develop in isolation from each other. Each of these processes affected the others, sometimes in concert, sometimes in contradiction. Warriors invoked religious ideals to justify their battles, and many priests supported them, but other religious figures attacked warfare and promoted peace. Local communities resisted state efforts to extract taxes and people as often as they supported state-builders. Merchants gave loans to rulers, and patronized monks and saints, but often did business in violation of moral injunctions, like those against lending money at interest, or avoided the taxes they owed to the state. This three-way tug of war between political power, private interest, and social solidarity often defined how civilizations and societies developed.

Two other central themes join with the three outlined above: technology and gender relations. Technology is the use of human power augmented by animal and mechanical forces over the non-human world, for human ends. Humans have always had to get their food, clothing, and shelter from the natural world, and they have constantly tried to improve the conditions under which they live. Superior productive power created goods that were profitable for trade, and often (in the form of weaponry) superior in war. How people gain their living from nature defines a significant portion of their culture, uniting them around a common mode of existence and separating them from others.

The use of technology thus shapes relations of power, exchange, and community, but it does not totally determine them. Although the environment has strongly affected how humans live, we should avoid assuming that natural changes directly determine their development: human social decisions have always inflected the way in which the natural world's processes make an impact on the collective whole.

Of all the ways of acting on nature that humans use for their benefit, communication and transportation technology deserve special attention. The movement of messages and goods between peoples separated by large distances is the key theme of this story of interconnections. Whether by speech, smoke signals, writing, the telegraph, or the internet, people have always sent information to each other in order to co-ordinate their activities for mutual gain, to warn their enemies, or just to express their love for each other. How fast the messages travel, how far, how often, and in what medium (oral or visual, handwritten or printed) certainly affect the density and quality of communication, but all express the underlying, irrepressible urge to tie one person to another. Contrary what you might have heard, global communication did not begin with the internet; networks of trade and information have covered the globe since the human story began. Likewise, the movement of commodities over distances short and long, on human backs, on animals, on carts, railroads, or airplanes, serves the goals of commerce and community. All things have social lives.

Gender relations have shaped the human story in the most intimate way. Humans, like other mammals, belong genetically to two biological sexes, but gender, which means the social expression of biological sex, has varied greatly over time and space. Men and women have taken on highly diverse roles depending on their relationship to hierarchies of power, relationships of exchange, and social structure. Still, in general, men have dominated power hierarchies through all of human history, as they still do. Males originally dominated because of their superior physical strength, but ideologies of rule that justified male supremacy through reference to divine power, and the fact that men wrote nearly all the histories, kept domination going over the long term.

In commercial relations, women had more nearly equal positions. Although they did not become the richest people in a society, they often controlled small-scale trade, and as artisans or textile producers they took on important economic roles within the household. In small communities like the family, women usually held subordinate but vital positions: they did the cooking, the housekeeping, and childrearing that made it possible for human social life to continue.

We cannot avoid the fact that during most of human history, men have had more social and political power than women, and they have written most of the sources historians rely on. One reason why men's activities dominate this story is that the lives of most women are nearly invisible to us. Sometimes powerful women emerged in the historical records at the top of their societies; then we can tell their stories in more detail. Until recent times, most individual women have remained nearly invisible, but they were an essential part of the processes that enable humans to survive. We can tell their collective story even if we cannot find out much about their individual lives.

Recently, historians have made great efforts to recover the lives of women, reconstructing the size of families and the life experience within them, while paying tribute to the few women who have held positions of high social power. Women often were key parts of maintaining political power, as wives and mothers of powerful men; they often ran important business operations; and most important of all, they held societies together by carrying on the crucial work of reproduction of the family. One of the most revolutionary developments of the modern world, beginning in the nineteenth century, was the entrance of women in large numbers into active political life, as voters, demonstrators, fighters, agitators, and world leaders. Whenever possible, we highlight the significant role of women and relations of gender in directing the major processes we describe.

In sum, from the migration of humans out of Africa and the spread of agriculture across the Eurasian Plain to contemporary transnational migration and the spread of electronic communication, rock, rap, and "world" music, human history has always been world history. Of these global processes, three stand out: demography, economic production and exchange, and armed conflict. Here are a few examples of how they affected regional change around the world during the sixteenth to eighteenth centuries.

Human population growth, like every other global process, varied by region. Until very recent times, more people meant more power. In the sixteenth and seventeenth centuries the high death rates of indigenous American populations exposed to European diseases, combined with the migration of Spanish, Portuguese, and British peoples to the Americas, gave the new colonists great control over the natives. At the same time, Chinese who migrated into Southeast Asia changed social arrangements in that region not by taking political control, but by dominating the economy. The devastation of Central African populations paved the way for a massive restructuring of societies by both provoking armed conflicts and migration within Africa as well as opening the continent to European conquest and colonization. Around the late eighteenth to mid nineteenth century, the connection of high population to strong power began to reverse itself. Just at this time, the political economist Thomas Malthus and the Chinese statesman Hong Liangji both predicted that societies with rapidly growing populations would soon doom themselves to endless famines, disease, and poverty. As it turned out, they were only half right. European nations and North America kept on growing, but they also industrialized, allowing them to gain wealth and power. The non-European world, except for Japan, did not industrialize in the nineteenth century, and found itself backward and poverty-stricken in the twentieth century. Population growth, in short, worked in different ways in different parts of the world, in interaction with technology and economic development.

In every epoch new techniques of production have fundamentally transformed social relations, from chipping stone for tools or arrowheads to the smelting of iron right up to the Industrial Revolution and the most recent development in electronic communications. The development of new processes of production continually increased human control over the environment. The expansion of commerce likewise linked and transformed regions. Throughout the Eurasian continent the growth of inter-regional trade put pressure on established regional social institutions and provoked intra-regional conflicts. In Southeast Asia, growing mercantile links helped the spread of Islam, which in turn undermined the claims to legitimacy of traditional rulers and favored those who converted. In sixteenth-century China, scholars lamented that commercial expansion had eroded moral values, remarkably echoing our own concerns. As one of them said:

> *Human disposition is such that people pursue what is profitable to them, and with profit in mind they will go up against disaster. They gallop in pursuit of it day and night, never satisfied with what they have, though it wears down their spirits and exhausts them physically. Since profit is what all people covet, they rush after it like torrents pouring into a valley: coming and going without end, never resting day or night, never reaching the point at which the raging floods within them subside.*

In other parts of the world, like the vast spaces of Central Eurasia, Russia, and Central Africa, commercial networks spread more slowly and sparsely. In the densely populated cores of India, China, Japan, and Western Europe, commercial and technological relations acted differently from the ways they acted in less densely populated regions with more difficulties of transportation and communication.

Finally, innovations in warfare affected the destiny of contested marginal regions on the edges of world regions, while also altering political and social life within regions and relations between them. Europe, the Ottoman empire, China, and India frequently had to respond to military threats from their neighbors. Each region had borderlands that generated powerful military threats: for Europeans, the border could be in Scotland, Spain, Russia, or the Balkans; China saw its most powerful enemies arise in the Mongolian steppes; the Ottomans faced incursions from Russia, Europe, and Persia; Turkish invaders from Central Eurasia founded the Mughal empire of India. Each region also expanded into the borderlands with military, economic, and cultural power, causing its neighbors to respond in kind. The sixteenth to eighteenth centuries were a time when many borderlands across Eurasia filled up with advancing armies, merchants, and missionaries. This global process left little space for smaller, mobile, tribal peoples in between the great empires. Preparation for war drove state-making across the Eurasian continent. As Charles Tilly has pithily put it: "States made war, and war made states." These powerful "Gunpowder Empires" needed to pay for their new technologies; in response, rulers pressed for cash developed more efficient methods for raising taxes and encouraged revenue-yielding trade. They paved the way for the nation-state system of our modern world.

Although war, trade, and religious conversion were the most common styles of large-scale intercultural contact, it's actually hard to separate these phenomena from each other, since trade, war, and religion often went hand in hand. Islam spread to both Central Eurasian and Southeast Asian regions along with the caravans of the Silk Road and the ships of the Indian Ocean. Trade routes also followed patterns of conquest. When Chinese rulers led great military campaigns, or the Mongols swept across the entire Eurasian continent, they opened the way for merchants to develop vast commercial networks in their wake. In the sixteenth and seventeenth centuries, the slave trade, based on alliances between European money, local West African power holders, and European colonists in the New World, carried Africans across the entire Atlantic world. The slave-based economies of the African diaspora in the Mediterranean, the Americas, and the Caribbean also became nodes of cultural exchange.

Clever religious entrepreneurs linked their belief systems to existing power structures. Jesuit missionaries in China, in order to attract imperial support, demonstrated their ability to cast good cannon, while also trying to bend the Catholic doctrine to accommodate local Chinese beliefs in ancestral rituals. Subject peoples often tried to preserve elements of their own cultures while adopting elements from colonial cultures that could be used to combat or resist them. Mesoamerican Indians, after the Spanish conquest, sought to blend Catholic imagery with their own traditional religious practices. On other hand, religious convictions often gave conquered peoples the passion to rebel against their oppressors. Religious beliefs could serve established power relations or resist them.

Military successes in one geographic region had an impact on trade and commerce in other regions. Ottoman rulers fought with Venetian merchants for control over the slave trade in the Caspian Sea as well as for dominance of the trade routes to China and India. All of them wanted to seize control of the trade in the precious spices of Southeast Asia. The success of the Ottomans in gaining control over these trade routes set the West on its fateful quest to circumvent Islamic domination by sailing around the Horn of Africa and, eventually, due west across the Atlantic.

Wars always changed power relations, but seldom did civilizations clash as neatly opposed wholes. Some rulers even built their empires on the basis of combining different cultures. In sixteenth-century India, the tolerant Mughal ruler Akbar sought to synthesize elements of Islamic and Hindu culture and religion to accommodate his diverse subjects. The Ottoman rulers claimed to be militant defenders of Islam, but they allowed Christian and Jewish communities within their empire to survive by practicing their own laws. The Manchu rulers of China tolerated and even encouraged diverse faiths, including Confucian rituals, Tibetan Buddhism, Daoism, Islam, and, for a time, Christianity.

In many ways, then, the connections between coercion, commerce, and community created the world we live in today. Different parts of our modern world come from different depths of historical time: We have pretty much the same bodies as our Paleolithic ancestors, only somewhat bigger; we grow the same plants, eat most of the same foods, and live in cities as post-agricultural transformation people did; whenever we write a letter, a novel, or a history, we do what scribblers of five thousand years ago did, even if we use computer screens and they used clay tablets. But our industrial civilization, based primarily on the use of underground organic energy (coal and oil) to drive machinery, is only two hundred years old, and our ability to alter the human genome, thus fundamentally changing the species, has only developed in the last decade. Our ability to destroy all life on the planet, since the invention of the atomic bomb, is very recent, as is our global environmental awareness that we share responsibility for all living things, not just ourselves. (Although even here, Buddhists anticipated the ideas, if not the technology, of universal destruction and compassion.) Sorting out what is really new and what is old is a historian's central task. In this story, we point to revolutions, crucial turning points, and conceptual breaks as well as continuities and structural constraints. Our goal is to help the student place her personal experience alongside millions of other ordinary people who lived through great changes, so as to better understand herself and the world.

Global map, 1600

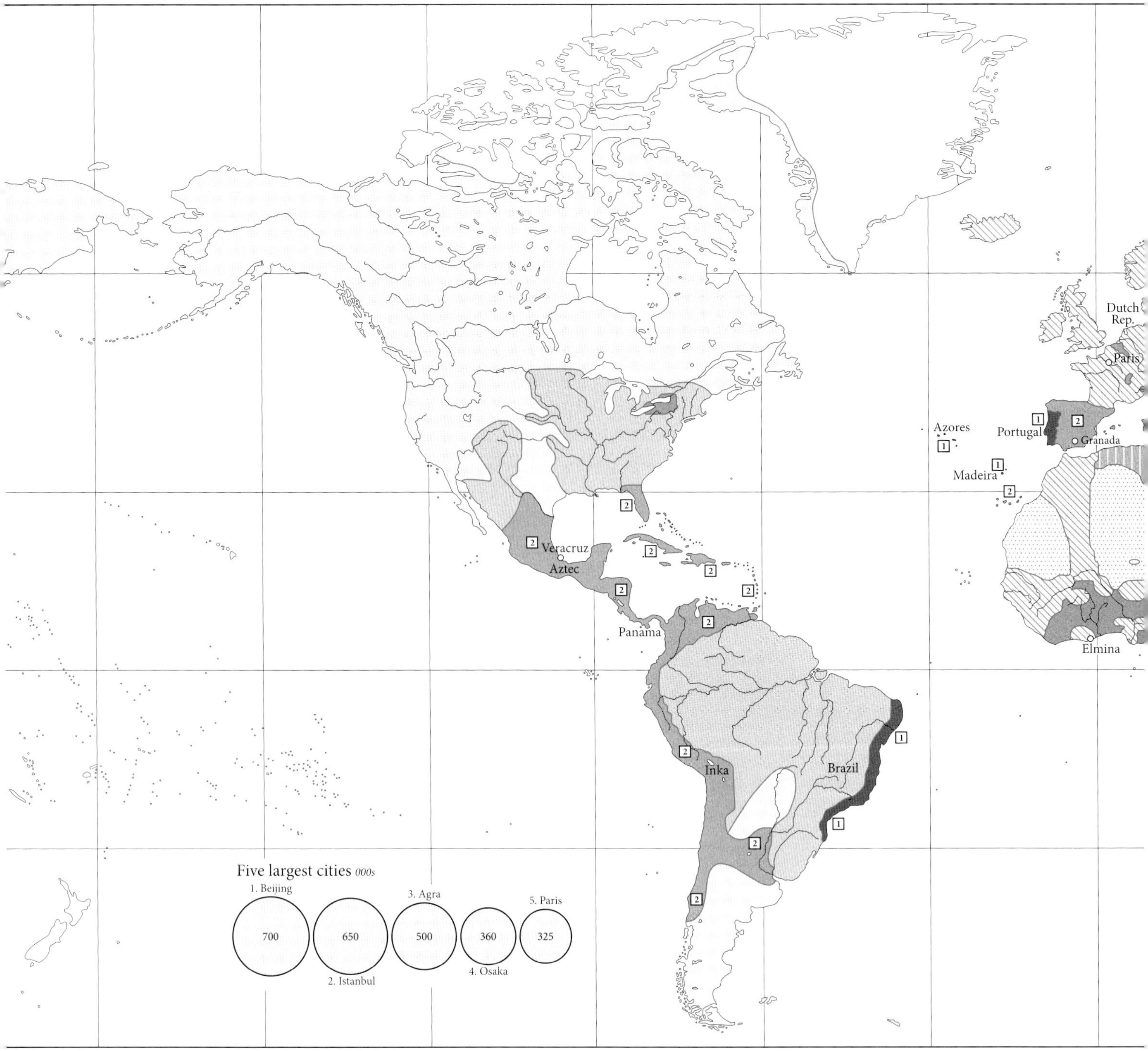

Dutch
Rep.

Paris

Azores
Portugal [1] [2]
[1]
Granada

Madeira [1]
[2]

Elmina

Veracruz [2]
Aztec

[2]

[2]

Panama [2]

[2]

[2]

[2]

Inka [2]
Brazil [1]

[1]

[2]

[2]

Five largest cities *000s*

1. Beijing
3. Agra
5. Paris

700
650
500
360
325

2. Istanbul
4. Osaka

PART I

1500–1700: The early modern world

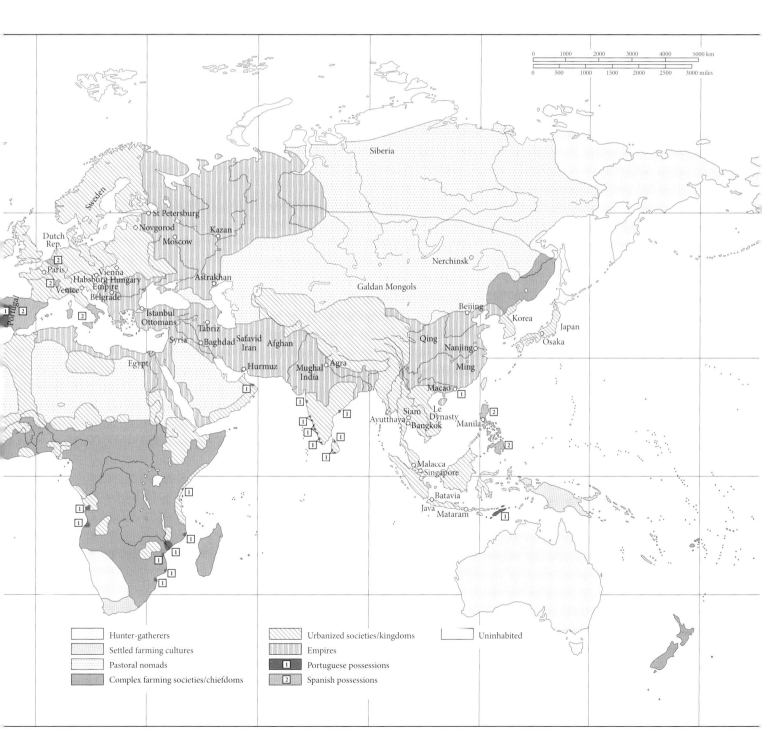

Hunter-gatherers	Urbanized societies/kingdoms
Settled farming cultures	Empires
Pastoral nomads	1 Portuguese possessions
Complex farming societies/chiefdoms	2 Spanish possessions

Uninhabited

Middle East	
1453	Ottomans conquer Constantinople.
1501	Shah Isma`il conquers Iran and establishes Safavid state.
1520–66	Reign over Ottoman empire of Suleiman the Magnificent.
1526	Babur conquers India and establishes Mughal empire.
1556–1605	Reign of Akbar in Mughal India.
1571	Venice defeats Ottoman navy at Lepanto.
1596–1610	Celali peasant revolts in Ottoman empire.
1658–1707	Reign of Awrangzeb in Mughal India.
1683	Ottoman siege of Vienna defeated.
1722	Fall of Safavid Iran to Afghan tribal armies.

China	
1368–1644	Ming dynasty.
1557	Portuguese permanent settlement at Macao.
1582	Jesuit mission in China begins under Matteo Ricci.
1592–93,1597–98	Japanese invasions of Korea repelled.
1636	Manchus declare Qing dynasty at Mukden (but it does not succeed the Ming dynasty in China proper until 1644).
1644	Conquest of Beijing by Manchus.
1644–1912	Qing dynasty.
1697	Kangxi emperor defeats Galdan.
1722	Yongzheng emperor ends Jesuit mission.

Russia	
1547	Ivan IV is crowned tsar.
1552, 1556	Muscovy's conquests of Kazan and Astrakhan open a door to the East.
1565–72	Time of oprichnina.
1582	Yermak begins conquest of Siberia.
1598–1613	Time of Troubles.
1613	Michael Romanov elected tsar by zemsky sobor.
1649	Law code enforces serfdom.
1670–71	Stepan Razin revolt.
1682–1725	Reign of Peter the Great (b. 1672).
1689	Treaty of Nerchinsk with China.
1703	St. Petersburg founded.
1709	Battle of Poltava breaks Sweden.

Japan	
1543	First arrival of Portuguese, with firearms, in Japan.
1600	Battle of Sekigahara defeats rivals to Tokugawa Ieyasu.
1603	Ieyasu claims shogunate.
1637	Shimabara Rebellion; final suppression of Christianity; restriction of foreign trade.

The Americas and Africa	
1487	Bartolomeu Dias rounds the Cape of Good Hope; first Portuguese traders arrive in Indian Ocean in 1497.
1492	Granada captured by Castile, completing the Reconquest of Spain from the Moors; Columbus sails toward Asia, finds the Caribbean, and returns.

1494	Treaty of Tordesillas divides the New World between Spain and Portugal.
1496	Henry VII of England, who had turned Columbus down two years earlier, finances the North Atlantic voyage of John Cabot.
1513	Balboa and Pizarro cross the Isthmus of Panama.
1518	First shipment of slaves directly from Africa to the Americas.
1519–22	Ferdinand Magellan's crew completes the first circumnavigation of the globe.
1519	Hernán Cortés lands at Veracruz, Mexico.
1521	Fall of the Aztec empire.
1532	Pizarro captures Atahualpa and defeats Inka army at Cajamarca.
1619	First slaves imported to the territory that would become Virginia.
1630s–1660s	Great Britain seizes Jamaica from Spain (1655); French, Dutch, and others grab territory for slave plantation colonies.

Europe

1454	Gutenberg and others develop printing press in Europe.
1517	Luther's ninety-five theses demand radical reform of the church.
1524–25	Peasant War in Germany.
1536	*Institutes of the Christian Religion* published by John Calvin.
1540	Founding of Jesuit order.
1568–1648	Dutch War of Independence, ending with Netherlands gaining independence from Spain as United Provinces.
1588	Defeat of Spanish Armada by English.
1598	Edict of Nantes ends religious war in France and guarantees Protestant rights.
1618–48	Thirty Years' War, concluded by Treaty of Westphalia
1642–49	English Civil War.
c. 1650–*c.* 1700	Peak of witchcraft trials in Europe.
1685	Revocation of Edict of Nantes ends religious toleration in France.
1692	Witchcraft trials in Salem, Massachusetts; twenty-two executed.

Southeast Asia

1351	Founding of Ayutthaya kingdom.
1427	Founding of Le dynasty of Vietnam.
1511	Portuguese seize Malacca.
1571	Manila in Philippines is center of Spanish power in Asia.
1600–02	Establishment of British East India Company and Dutch East India Company (VOC).
1641	Dutch take Malacca from Portuguese.
1677	Sultan of Mataram gives monopoly trade rights to Dutch.
1740	Massacre of Chinese in Batavia.
1767	Burmese capture and loot Ayutthaya.
1771–1802	Tayson Rebellion in Vietnam overthrows Le dynasty.
1782	Rama I founds new Siamese dynasty at Bangkok.
1788	Chinese invasion of Vietnam is beaten back.
1795	British take Malacca from Dutch.
1799	VOC trade monopoly abolished; Dutch state takes control of Java.
1819	Founding of Singapore.

These two centuries initiated the true unification of the globe. The voyages of European explorers to North and South America began a continuous process of engagement between the Eurasian, African, and New World continents. The exchanges begun by Columbus' voyage of 1492 included military conquest, migration and settlement, the construction of new empires, the exploitation of tropical lands for valuable commodities, enslavement of much of the African population and extermination of much of the indigenous American population, as well as religious expansion, new trade rivalries, and imperial competition. All of these processes had already worked themselves out in each of the continents independently – the Americas had their empires as well as the Eurasians and Africans – but now they were inexorably tied to each other. The scale of political, commercial, and social exchange widened to include the entire globe.

Equally important, however, were developments in Asia itself. Asia's riches were the original goal of the European explorers looking for a shortcut to the fabulous East. In Asia, five massive empires expanded dramatically until they ran into each other's frontiers. The Qing in China, the Mughals in India, the Safavids in Iran, and the Ottomans in the Middle East each conducted vigorous military campaigns, conquering territories on an unprecedented scale. Russia spanned Europe and Asia with its vast territorial reach. Each of them combined techniques of military organization derived from Central Eurasian pastoral nomads with the civil administrative techniques of the settled urbanized regions they ruled. Southeast Asian states also increased their territorial control and administrative integration, like their European counterparts, without uniting into a single empire. The combined effect of European and Asian expansion was to bring a large portion of the earth's surface under the control of a small number of huge imperial formations. The world shrank in the 1500s because of the interaction of global maritime networks woven by Europeans and the great system of unified empires erected in Asia.

All of these conquerors relied heavily on that ancient Chinese chemical invention: gunpowder. Artillery, the central new source of power, made it possible to besiege large cities successfully, and slowly the infantryman with his musket began to replace the mounted horseback warrior as the central military force of the era. Gunpowder, the most destructive technology of the modern era, sparked intense military competition among the European states and the Asian empires alike, as well as bringing about the unification of Japan. The small armed sailing ships of Portugal were the other key technical advance. The Portuguese pioneered the art of rapid maneuver in battles at sea, allowing them to seize coastal footholds across African and Asian coasts. Then they negotiated trading rights with the large empires around them and seized the opportunity to promote Christianity. In their wake came the Spanish, the Dutch, the English, and the French, all competing for the new profits of this maritime Asian trade.

Supporting expeditions and armies required a great deal of money. The large quantities of silver and gold discovered in the New World supported rapid growth of the commercial economies of all these regions. Precious metals flowed out of the Spanish colonies across the Atlantic into Europe and across the Pacific into China. Silver and gold, portable commodities of high value, easily divisible into lumps or coins, stimulated convenient collection of taxes and large-scale trade. The movements of silver, more than any other commodity, caused economies over vast distances to move in tandem. Besides silver, other global commodities, especially the addictive stimulants from the tropics – tea, sugar, coffee, cocoa, and opium – generated worldwide consumer demand and great accumulations of wealth.

Although the world economy prospered, not everyone did well. Most unfortunate were the native inhabitants of the New World, severely hit by epidemic diseases and driven to starvation by overwork under colonial plantation owners. Africans sold into slavery replaced the dying natives, in conditions almost as bad. Mobile peoples, like the free nomads of the steppes and the forest peoples of upland villages, lost their independence under constant assault by expanding states supporting agrarian settlement.

Religious warfare also generated vicious waves of persecution and massacre. The Protestant Reformation and its aftermath threw Europe into civil wars lasting over a century. The Muslim conquest of India brought both toleration under the enlightened ruler Akbar and persecution under more rigid Islamic believers like Awrangzeb. The Manchu conquerors of China massacred Han Chinese and Mongols in the course of their campaigns. Jews suffered pogroms across Eastern Europe and Russia, and poor marginal women found themselves accused of witchcraft in Europe and North America.

With some exceptions democracy and popular rule did not flourish. The English Revolution of the mid seventeenth century did limit the king's power, and the Netherlands created a wealthy, powerful federation of commercial cities, strong enough to fight off Spanish domination. Most other states, however, reinforced the absolutist power of their rulers in order to obtain security in war and wealth in economic competition. A new kind of economic organization, the chartered trading company, united merchant adventurers with the English and Dutch states, while Russia and China also gave official charters to their merchants. Most merchants happily supported the new autocrats with loans, even if sometimes they went bankrupt when the rulers canceled their obligations.

On the positive side, the introduction of printing to Western Europe promoted the growth of written native languages over classical Latin, fostering diversity of thought and closer contacts between elite writers and their people. Shakespeare in England and Rabelais in France demonstrate the vigorous use of popular idioms in literary culture. Something similar happened in China. Mass printing in vernacular Chinese created the first Chinese novels out of tales told by street-corner storytellers. The vibrant cultural life of Mughal India produced spectacular architecture, vivid painting, lively stories, and popular religious activity. The European humanist Renaissance and scientific revolution, by contrast, was mainly a product of small elites who wrote in Latin. They had little impact at the time on religious repression and popular beliefs, but they laid the groundwork for an immense boom in philological, scientific, and technological research in the following centuries.

Most peasant agriculturalists did not improve their lives much in Europe, where productivity remained low, but Asians probably made slow and steady progress. The new unification of the world took a long time to penetrate remote agricultural regions, but it began the process of globalization that continues today.

1 New empires in Asia and the Middle East

Timeline	
1453	Ottomans conquer Constantinople.
1501	Shah Isma`il conquers Iran, establishes Safavid state, and declares Shi`ite Islam the state religion of Iran.
1503	Ottomans defeat Venice at Lepanto.
1514	Battle of Chaldiran between Ottomans and Safavids sets border.
1515–20	Reign over Ottoman empire of Selim I.
1516	Ottomans conquer Syria.
1517	Ottomans conquer Egypt.
1520–66	Reign over Ottoman empire of Suleiman the Magnificent.
1521	Ottomans conquer Belgrade.
1524–87	Shah Tahmasp rules Safavid Iran.
1526	Babur conquers India and establishes Mughal empire.
1530	Babur dies, succeeded by son Humayun.
1538	Ottomans under Suleiman take Baghdad.
1556–1605	Reign of Akbar in Mughal India.
1571	Venice defeats Ottoman navy at Lepanto.
1596–1610	Celali peasant revolts in Ottoman empire.
1605–27	Jahangir's rule in Mughal India.
1607	Shah Abbas of Safavid Iran retakes Tabriz.
1622	Iran expels Portuguese from Hormuz in Persian Gulf.
1624	Shah Abbas takes Baghdad for Iran.
1628–58	Shahjahan's rule in Mughal India.
1638	Ottomans retake Baghdad from Iran (and keep it until World War I).
1639	Treaty of Zuhab establishes peace between Safavids and Ottomans.
1658–1707	Reign of Awrangzeb in Mughal India.
1680	Hindu leader Shivaji dies.
1683	Ottoman siege of Vienna defeated.

1694–1722	Reign in Safavid Iran of religiously strict Shah Sultan Husayn.
1699	Treaty of Carlowitz: Ottomans cede Hungary to Habsburg empire.
1722	Fall of Safavid Iran to Afghan tribal armies.

Nur Jahan (1577–1645) was born Mihr al-Nisa. Her extended family was from Tehran, in Iran, and they emigrated to Mughal India. When she turned 17, she was married to a Mughal military man of Iranian heritage. He became involved in political intrigue and backed the wrong candidate for the throne, and was executed. He left her a daughter, Ladli.

A widow, Nur Jahan came to the court in 1607 to attend on one of the great women of Emperor Jahangir's harem. The imperial harem comprised some 5,000 women, most of whom were neither wives nor slave-girls of the emperor, but rather servants and artisans attending on the ladies. It was a complex small city, wherein brilliant, accomplished women played a special sort of politics, and could use it as a base to gain power even in the male-dominated world outside. In 1611 Emperor Jahangir held a large celebration of the Persian New Year, **Now-Ruz**, which falls on the first day of spring, and there he first saw Nur Jahan. She was reputed to be gorgeous, and he soon decided to marry her. It was he who gave her the name Nur Jahan ("light of the world"). Nur Jahan proved an energetic queen and hostess, taking charge of palace affairs. Jahangir was not a great emperor, and struggled with addiction to alcohol and drugs that often left him weak and shaking. He may have made a match with an older widow because he was looking for a mother figure who would take care of him. If so, Nur Jahan rose to the challenge.

She ensured that large numbers of her relatives from the Tehrani clan were advanced to high government positions, both at the court and in the provinces. Her father, I`timad al-Dawlah, and her brother, Asaf Khan, became powerful ministers at court. She employed this network of male relatives to become directly involved in running the empire, a task in which her often drunken husband had little interest. Emperor Jahangir specifically named her his queen, and not just his wife. Nur Jahan benefited from a substantial court allowance, but became enormously wealthy through her own enterprise. Under Islamic law, unlike most law codes common in Europe at that time, women could freely own and dispose of property. Nur Jahan built up vast personal estates of her own and had revenues carefully collected from them. When her father died in 1622, the emperor bestowed his huge estate on her, angering her brother. She endowed magnificent buildings, including mosques and mausoleums. She invested in private business, including the shipping of indigo and embroidered textiles, and developed a special relationship with British merchants in a bid to outflank the powerful Portuguese. She even joined in with two other court women to finance a trading journey to England, playing a role like that of the East India Company in reverse (unfortunately for her the Europe-bound ship fell victim to Portuguese piracy). Women of great property in the Mughal empire employed substantial teams of accountants and revenue officers that were modeled on the finance ministry of the empire itself.

Nur Jahan's ascendancy was challenged in the 1620s from two directions. Jahangir's energetic son Shahjahan, a successful warrior, went into rebellion from 1622–25, but he then made up with his father and would have to wait until Jahangir's death in 1627 to succeed. In 1626, in a bizarre episode, the powerful courtier Mahabat Khan put the emperor and empress under house arrest for a time, but ultimately repented and released them. When Shahjahan came to the throne, Nur Jahan was forced to retire to the northern city of Lahore, where she lived with her daughter from her first marriage, Ladli, until her death. Nur Jahan's beautiful mausoleum still stands in Lahore. Her story shows the ways in which upper-class Muslim women of her era could become the equivalent of twenty-first-century billionaires, engaging in commerce on a global scale and even emerging as de facto rulers of some estates or territories. This kind of female power was rare in Europe at that time, with the major exception of England, where succession laws allowed queens to come to power. Ordinary British women, however, were far less likely to enjoy property rights than ordinary Muslim women in these centuries.

Nur Jahan prospered in the largest and richest of the three great Middle Eastern empires of the sixteenth and seventeenth centuries. This chapter focuses on these themes of imperial expansion and rivalry among them:

- The Mughal empire, founded by a Central Asian Muslim prince, was among the largest and most populous empires in the world in 1600–1700, rivaled only by China. Practicing religious tolerance, it expanded over most of South India, trading with Arabs, Portuguese, and Southeast Asians across oceans and continents.
- In the late 1600s and early 1700s, it faced enthusiastic religious movements and political resistance among the Hindus whom they ruled.
- The Safavid empire, founded by Turkmen (Qizilbash) from eastern Anatolia in 1501, declared Shi`ite Islam the

religion of state and was intolerant of other sects. It fought wars in the east against the Uzbeks and in the west against the Ottoman empire. Its economy depended heavily on sales of silk to Europe.

- The Ottoman empire expanded rapidly in the 1500s, into the Balkans and into the Arab world, but Europeans beat them back in 1683. It encouraged trade with Italian city-states and Arab and Indian merchants in the Mediterranean and Red Sea. Trading in a new drug, coffee, gave it as much wealth as silk gave Iran.

1.1 THE AGE OF THE GUNPOWDER EMPIRES

The early modern period, around 1500–1700, was marked by the rise and flourishing of three major Muslim-ruled land empires in Asia and North Africa, two of them enormous in their geographic spread. They consisted of the Mughals in India, the Safavids in Iran, and the Ottoman empire in what are now Turkey, the southern parts of Eastern Europe, and the Arabic-speaking world. The elites ruling these empires were self-consciously Muslim in their social and religious ideology, but they all experimented with various mixes of religious and civil law and administration, and the mix changed over time. The majority of Ottoman and Safavid subjects were also Muslim, but Mughal India was largely Hindu despite being Muslim-ruled. Although by this time most of the Middle East was fairly Islamized, during this period there were further conversions from Christianity in places like Egypt and Anatolia, and Islam spread vigorously in the Balkans and in South and Southeast Asia. A major split developed, insofar as the Safavids promoted Shi`ite Islam in Iran, whereas both of the other empires were Sunni-ruled (and, indeed, most other, smaller Muslim states were Sunni, as well).

Slave Armies

All three of these empires were ruled by absolute monarchs, though the Ottomans increasingly had powerful **viziers** (first ministers). They were characterized by the development of large bureaucracies and agrarian taxation systems. They were among the first major Muslim powers to use gunpowder systematically for military purposes. The organization of their armies derived from a steppe tradition of emphasizing a heavy horse cavalry along with irregulars drawn from allied pastoral nomads. Over time some depended more on slave-soldiers, an institution long known in the sedentary Middle East. They began to make more use of a standing army and an infantry armed with handheld firearms, since the proliferation of artillery and the

matchlock both helped make the infantry more important in the early modern period. In these empires, however, the cavalry retained its centrality despite the inability of warriors to fire early harquebus firearms while on horseback. Although most of their income derived from heavy taxation of the agricultural produce grown by the peasantry, they benefited as well from the growth of world trade that came with the rise of both indigenous and European maritime trading companies. They also felt the impact of New World silver and crops, as well as newly important indigenous plants such as coffee from Yemen.

Population Growth

All three realms witnessed the sort of population growth that indicated these states were providing basic security and other services to their subjects. It is true that after 1600 Europe increasingly out-gunned and economically out-performed the Muslim empires, despite being smaller in both area and population. Measured in their own terms, however, the sultans probably provided slowly increasing prosperity until they were weakened in the eighteenth century, a century that was as dark and disastrous for the Middle East and South Asian political scene as it was momentous for Western Europe.

1.2 THE MUGHALS IN INDIA

The Mughal empire ruled over the largest population and the largest land area of the three, and it was among the richest states of its day. For this reason it will be given the most coverage. The population of the Indian subcontinent in 1600 has been estimated at as much as 145 million, and at that time the Mughal empire encompassed some 70 to 100 million subjects in its north. By 1700 the all-India population had probably risen to about 170 million, and by that time the empire had advanced south to claim sovereignty over nearly all of them – encompassing what are now Pakistan, India, Bangladesh, and southern Afghanistan, or more than a million and a half square miles. In the early modern period the subcontinent accounted for about a fifth of the world population. Map 1.1 gives an indication of the extent of Mughal rule. The other two Muslim-ruled states were much smaller in population in 1700, the Ottomans ruling around 18 million. The Ottoman empire covered a great deal of territory, over a million square miles, though often it exerted significant influence only in settled regions – cities and along coastlines – rather than in rough interiors dominated by pastoral nomads or fiercely independent peasants. The arid conditions of its Middle Eastern possessions limited the empire's population. The same was true for the Safavid empire in Iran and northern

Map 1.1 The Mughal empire

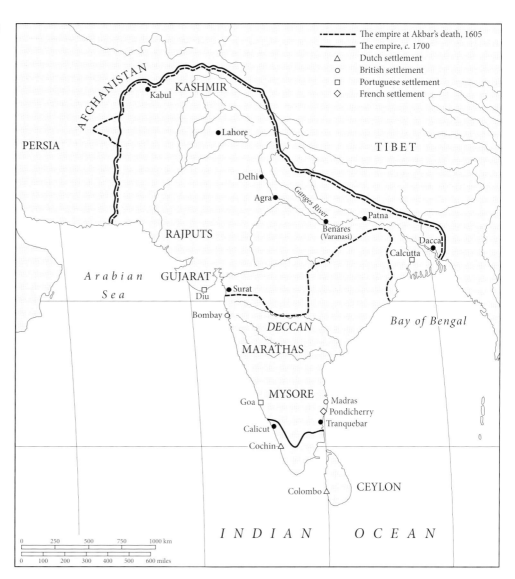

Afghanistan, which claimed rule over some 750,000 square miles, most of it desert or mountain, inhabited by something in the order of 5 million or so in 1700.

Climate and Climate Change

India's huge population advantage derived in large part from its warm, wet climate, which allowed rainfall agriculture and, with irrigation, two growing seasons. The more populous Ottoman possessions, such as Eastern Europe and some of Anatolia, also received enough rain to farm without extensive irrigation, though two growing seasons were rare in the Middle East, except in fertile watered regions like the Nile Delta. During the Little Ice Age that lasted from about 1300 to 1850, the climate of India and the Middle East was more temperate than it is now for long periods, aiding agricultural productivity and relieving the population of the torrid summers that sap human energy. The

Little Ice Age did not mean only colder temperatures, however, for summers could be hot even in Europe, and there were both heat waves and cold waves. It was a period of weather instability and extremes. We know of great weather disturbances in the eighteenth century, and it appears to have been particularly cold in South Asia, with extended drought in North India and a deadly alternation of low and high Niles in Egypt.

Population

The population of all of Europe outside Russia and the Ottoman empire in 1650 was around 75 million, and that of the then icy British Isles was only about 5.5 million in the same year. Europe thus at that time had a population about half the size of India, and several of its major countries were then less populous than the Ottoman empire. Indeed, the British Crown in the mid seventeenth century ruled over a population about the size of

Safavid Iran, the smallest of the Muslim states at which we are looking. The story of the rise of these great Asian land powers is among the more important ones we can tell about world history concerning the period 1500–1700.

Babur Founds a New Empire

The founder of the Mughal dynasty in India was Zahir al-Din Muhammad Babur (1483–1530), a young notable of the Chaghatai Turks in Ferghana Valley, Central Asia, who claimed descent from tribal conquerors Chinggis Khan and Tamurlane. He attempted and failed to subdue his own homeland, but then headed south to Kabul in what is now Afghanistan, where he had great military success. He ruled harshly there, since he did not have the ties of kinship and patronage in his new kingdom that would bind the people to him in a positive way. Babur was interested in India right from this time, but only in 1519 did he seriously consider attacking it. As a prospective conqueror, Babur knew Afghanistan was rugged and relatively poor, whereas India was green and rich.

India was somewhat protected by the high Hindu Kush mountain range that separated the Afghan highlands from the fertile plains of the **Panjab** province ("the land of five rivers"). This range gave a strategic advantage to strong Indian governments in guarding against invasion. But when the Indian state happened to be weak or divided, pastoral nomadic cavalrymen from Central Asia had repeatedly demonstrated an ability to cross the Khyber Pass and other passes that cut through the Hindu Kush. They could then conquer Indian peasants and their leaders, using their heavier Central Asian horses and excellent bows. Heavy warhorses from the steppe did not thrive in India's warmer climate, tending to lose weight and to die off. These deaths required that they be constantly imported from Central Asia and Arabia at great cost – whereas Central Asian tribespeople maintained large herds of them.

Babur mobilized his allies and 12,000 troops, marched them extraordinary distances each day, and demonstrated tactical brilliance in defeating larger armies. By 1526 he had conquered North India. Babur was the first ruler in his region to organize artillery as a special unit in his armed forces, and had not only light field artillery, but a mortar with a range of 1,600 paces. Artillery probably did not play a decisive role in the conquest of India, though it was important to the later Mughal state. Artillery began being significant in European warfare in the 1400s, and was employed, as we shall see, by the Ottomans in their conquest of Constantinople in 1453. By the early 1500s knowledge of this technology had spread to the Turkic warriors of Central Asia. Babur won a decisive victory over the Muslim Lodhi state then ruling Delhi at the first Battle of Panipat in 1526. He thus became the ruler of the Gangetic Plain.

Ironically enough, as he reveals in his priceless autobiography, the *Baburnama*, Babur rather disliked tropical India. He died in 1530. Babur's son was expelled from India for fifteen years, returning with Iranian help.

Akbar Brings New Greatness to the Mughals

Babur's grandson Akbar (r. 1556–1605) became emperor at the age of 13. He inherited not an empire but a fight, since his father had not overcome resistance to his rule. A joint Afghan and Hindu revolt in Delhi challenged the new child-emperor's power, and many Central Asian Turkic advisors to the young ruler counseled him to withdraw back to Kabul. Akbar, however, made a stand, defeating his challengers and retaking Delhi. Akbar was physically strong and courageous to the point of foolhardiness (a motif in his court paintings is his battle with an enraged elephant – see Figure 1.1). Despite his vigorous military activity, he tolerated many forms of belief. In so diverse a country as India, Akbar's tolerance attracted the allegiance of Hindu subjects better than the strict, legalistic Sunni Islam the Mughals brought with them from Central Asia.

The Rajput Connection

Looking for local groups who would support him militarily, Akbar found favorable responses among the Hindu **Rajput** people of India's northwest. The Rajputs, who lived in an arid region similar to the Middle East, and practiced some pastoral nomadism, found it easier to understand the Turkic Muslim style of life than an ordinary Hindu villager. When Akbar was 19, he accepted an offer of marriage with a Rajput princess. Soon thereafter Akbar abolished Mughal taxes on Hindu pilgrimage sites, and ceased collecting the poll tax mandated by classical Muslim law on Hindus as non-Muslims. Akbar also accepted the Rajput cavalry into his military, thus reducing distinctions between Muslim and Hindu fighting men. He incorporated Hindus into his empire as subjects rather than as a demilitarized conquered population. He abolished the slave trade, which sent thousands of Hindus every year north to Central Asia to pay for horses and other goods. India had earlier lacked much silver or gold but had a relative surplus of human beings, and previous Muslim-ruled Indian states had treated their Hindu subjects as mere property, a source of profit. The influx into India of New World silver in the early 1600s made it easier to pay for Central Asian goods in money, and thus easier to continue the ban on the slave trade.

Box 1.1 Babur on India

The Mughal emperor Babur (1483–1530) describes India here in his autobiography, the *Baburnama*.

Hindustan [India] … a wonderful country. Compared with our countries it is a different world; its mountains, rivers, jungles and deserts, its towns, its cultivated lands, its animals and plants, its peoples and their tongues, its rains, and its winds, are all different. In some respects the hot-country that depends on Kabul, is like Hindustan, but in others, it is different. Once the water of Sind is crossed, everything is in the Hindustan way, land, water, tree, rock, people and horde, opinion and custom …

The greater part of the Hindustan country is situated on level land … Rivers and, in some places, standing-waters are its "running-waters." Even where, as for some towns, it is practicable to convey water by digging channels, this is not done … To young trees water is made to flow by means of buckets or a wheel. They are given water constantly during two or three years; after which they need no more. Some vegetables are watered constantly … To some crops needing water, men and women carry it by repeated efforts in pitchers …

The towns and country of Hindustan are greatly wanting in charm. Its towns and lands are all of one sort; there are not walls to the orchards, and most places are on the dead level plain. Under the monsoon-rains the banks of some of its rivers and torrents are worn into

deep channels, difficult and troublesome to pass through anywhere. In many parts of the plains thorny jungle grows, behind the good defence of which the people of the pargana [district] become stubbornly rebellious and pay no taxes … In Hindustan hamlets and villages, towns indeed, are depopulated and set up in a moment! … if they fix their eyes on a place in which to settle, they need not dig water-courses or construct dams because their crops are all rain-grown, and as the population of Hindustan is unlimited, it swarms in. They make a tank or dig a well; they need not build houses or set up walls – grass abounds, wood is unlimited, huts are made, and straightway there is a village or a town!

The elephant, which Hindustanis call hathi, is one of the wild animals peculiar to Hindustan. It inhabits the borders of the Kalpi country, and becomes more numerous in its wild state the further east one goes. The elephant is an immense animal and very sagacious. If people speak to it, it understands; if they command anything from it, it does it … It is much relied on by Hindustanis, accompanying every troop of their armies. It has some useful qualities: It crosses great rivers with ease, carrying a mass of baggage, and three or four have gone dragging without trouble the car of the mortar it takes four or five hundred men to haul. But its stomach is large; one elephant eats the corn of two strings of camels …

Most of the inhabitants of Hindustan are pagans; they call a pagan a Hindu. Most Hindus believe in the transmigration of souls. All artisans, wage-earners, and officials are Hindus. In our countries dwellers in the wilds (i.e. nomads) get tribal names; here the settled people of the cultivated lands and villages get tribal names. Again: every artisan there follows the trade that has come down to him from forefather to forefather …

Peasants and people of low standing go about naked. They tie on a thing called lunguta, a decency-clout which hangs two spans below the navel. From the tie of this pendant decency-clout, another clout is passed between the thighs and made fast behind. Women also tie on a cloth (lung), one-half of which goes round the waist, the other is thrown over the head.

Pleasant things of Hindustan are that it is a large country and has masses of gold and silver. Its air in the rains is very fine. Sometimes it rains 10, 15 or 20 times a day; torrents pour down all at once and rivers flow where no water had been … Not only in the rains, but also in the cold and the hot season, the airs are excellent …

Another good thing in Hindustan is that it has unnumbered and endless workmen of every kind. There is a fixed caste for every sort of work and for every thing, which has done that work or that thing from father to son till now.

Multicultural Elite

Akbar laid the foundations for a truly multicultural ruling elite, combining Turks, Persians, Afghans, and Indian Muslims and Hindus. By the seventeenth century, about a sixth of the nobles and high officers derived from Turkic Central Asia. Over a quarter were from neighboring Iran. The Iranians had special advantages in the Indian government, since the bureaucratic language of the Mughals was Persian, their native tongue.

Figure 1.1 Conquerors of India such as Akbar liked to display their power by commissioning paintings which portrayed them fighting with elephants. Processions of these huge animals under the control of court riders showed the emperor's subjects that he held supreme power over humans and animals alike.

monarchy. In England at the same time, Thomas Hobbes promoted the theory, in his famous book *Leviathan*, that an absolute sovereign is required to prevent a war of all against all. Akbar's court also endorsed this theory in the classic text *Akbarnama*, the main chronicle of his reign.

Akbar put theory into practice by his conquests and firm rulership. He needed weapons as well as books to make it work. The Mughals had effective light bronze field artillery, mortars, grenades, and even rockets with a range of 1,000 yards. Heavy horse cavalry were their central striking force. As late as 1647 the Mughal army had 200,000 horsemen and 40,000 infantry (the latter including matchlockmen, gunners, and cannoneers).

Akbar Confronts Portuguese

In Gujarat Akbar encountered the Portuguese, who had navigated their way around southern Africa and had constructed garrison ports on India's west coast. He decided to allow them to retain these enclaves and their control of the sea. Compared to his huge agrarian empire, the Portuguese offered little threat. Most Mughal revenues came from agriculture, with only a small proportion deriving from taxes at port cities, and Akbar as a man of landlocked Central Asian heritage had no knowledge of or particular interest in the sea. Portugal was then merely a small country of about a million poor peasants. It only dominated the seas because its large, sturdy, fast ships, with their long-range mounted cannon, could beat smaller, less powerful Indian Ocean craft. This small relative advantage allowed the Portuguese to establish what we might call a "protection racket" on the high seas. They did not really promote the growth of trade, only the diversion of it into their own hands. The Portuguese maritime empire probably did not even increase the volume of trade in pepper, its major commodity.

Akbar's Administration

Akbar established consistent administrative divisions in India, consisting of what we might in English call provinces, counties, and localities. Akbar also established civil service and military ranks on a comparable grid. Akbar insisted that each man in his service had to maintain troops for the empire's use. His decimal scale tied the number of troops a notable could raise to his salary. A commoner vassal might be responsible for only 10 or 100 men, whereas a noble would command at least 500 and be eligible to serve under the more high-ranking nobles. By analogy, similar ranks were created in the civil service.

The earlier Central Asian conqueror Tamerlane had in the 1300s often paid his troops mainly in booty, which is a good strategy for a marauder but a poor one for a settled empire.

Another quarter consisted of local Indian Muslims and other Muslims. Yet another quarter was made up of Hindus, with Rajputs and **Marathas**, another martial Hindu group hailing from the country's south, about equal to one another in numbers. Afghans on average made up 7 percent of the Mughal nobility in the seventeenth century. Under Akbar a little over a third of noble office-holders were children of state servants, and later the proportion rose to half. The Mughal elite, unlike the European nobility, was not based on bloodlines. It became in part hereditary, but remained in part open to talent.

Akbar believed in the idea of "universal peace" but only when he could rule by his own iron hand. Compulsive and tirelessly dedicated to expansion, he invented a new kind of absolute

But the extensive Mughal bureaucracy was in part made possible by increased use of money, especially silver coins. The influx from the early 1600s of New World silver made cash payments possible.

Like many other conquerors, Akbar confiscated a good deal of land, centralizing its administration, and parceling it out to his high nobles as temporary grants. The nobles could not put down roots and gain local political support. In name, the Mughal state demanded half of the agricultural goods produced by the peasants. In fact, it seems highly unlikely that it really collected anything like that tax rate. The state usually collected taxes through local landholders, each of whom took a share for themselves. In return for those taxes, the Mughal state provided fair security and investments in agrarian infrastructure. Their most important contribution was the maintenance of irrigation canals. These were an imported Middle Eastern technology that allowed two growing seasons in wet, fertile India.

The Muslim Mughals Must Accept India's Religious Diversity

India's religious diversity and its Hindu majority bothered strict Muslims in the ruling elite. Muslim scriptures had thunderously denounced idolatry and paganism since the birth of Islam in Mecca. Most Middle Eastern Muslims could not help but feel that Hinduism was even more objectionable, because it had more idols and more myths. Yet a few thousand Muslims from Central Asia could never survive if they forced tens of millions of Hindus into a choice between conversion or death. Instead, even strict Muslim rulers in India tended to treat Hindus as members of a "protected minority" on analogy with Jews and Christians. Muslims did often target Hindu places of worship for effacement or destruction, and even under Akbar some Hindu temples were torn down. After tearing down a temple, he had mosques built atop the site to signal greater honor for the religion of the Muslim sultan.

Religious Tolerance

Indian Muslims and Hindus influenced and borrowed from each other religiously, even though their high culture tended to be quite strict and orthodox on both sides. Muslim clerics in India wrote extensively on Islamic law, and produced monumental books of jurisprudence, but said little about Hindu beliefs. Hindu **Brahmins** (the priestly caste) writing in Sanskrit about Hindu theology likewise did not so much as acknowledge Islam's existence.

Akbar himself gradually moved away from his Sunni Muslim roots to experiment with other religious traditions. He learned

of Hindu ideas during pillow talk with his Rajput wife, and during his conquest of Gujarat he encountered Zoroastrian or Parsi thinkers, with whom he engaged in long conversations. In the 1570s he established a debating hall, or House of Worship, calling on Muslim learned men to engage each other on controversial issues in the interpretation of Islam. In 1578 a powerful mystical experience caused Akbar to cancel his large royal hunt, saving the lives of dozens of animals. He thereafter increasingly leaned toward vegetarianism. This concern with animal life and avoiding meat probably shows the influence of his conversations with **Jains** (a sect devoted to non-violence to all creatures) or perhaps strict Brahmin Hindus.

Akbar opened the debates at the House of Worship to the learned men of all religions, including Christians, Hindus, Jains, and Zoroastrians. Portuguese Jesuits also spoke at his court. This multicultural engagement shows how the world was shrinking in the 1500s owing in part to the global maritime networks being woven by Europeans and in part to the great system of unified empires erected in Asia by the three Muslim powers. Akbar gave the Friday sermons in the capital himself, replacing the Muslim cleric, and developed personal rituals such as bowing toward the sun. He was not unique in such an engagement with India's religious pluralism, since many Muslim **Sufis** or mystics did much the same. What was unusual was for the ruler to sample the religious scene so widely. By giving up the strict Islam of his origins, Akbar dramatically changed the religious policies of the Mughals in India.

Akbar's Successors Face Tension and Resistance

When Akbar died in 1605 he left behind a large, unified state that encompassed most of North India, with a uniquely organized bureaucracy and army and a thriving economy. His son and successor, Jahangir, was an alcoholic and drug addict who did not contribute anything substantial to the administration of the empire. Jahangir's formidable queen, Nur Jahan, who was from an immigrant clan of Iranian nobles, was more directly influential than most Mughal ladies of the imperial harem, and her relatives often served as high ministers or governors. She also joined with other noblewomen in investing in trading ventures to Europe. Jahangir's religious policy gradually shifted away from that of Akbar, in which he had been raised, and toward a more orthodox Sunni Islam. He disliked and punished sectarian conflict among the Sunni and Shi`ite branches of Islam, and also punished a mystical Sufi leader for claiming too high a station for himself. A challenge came to Jahangir on his accession from his son, Khusrau, who was supported by the leader of the Sikh religion in the Panjab. Khusrau was defeated, and relations were thereafter strained between the Mughals and the Sikhs. The **Sikhs**, who claim as their founder Guru Nanak (1469–1539), had begun as an enthusiastic (bhakti) wisdom religion that drew on Hindu and Muslim mysticism, but as clans of Jat Panjabis converted to it they brought with them a feuding ethos that began making the religion more sectarian and militant.

Among the first acts of Jahangir's successor, Shahjahan (r. 1628–58), was to expel the Portuguese from Bengal. He had feared that they were preparing to attempt to conquer it away from the Mughal empire. In 1633 he annexed the entire region of Ahmadnagar, which Jahangir had coveted, in Southwest India. An attempt to expand north into Central Asia was blocked by the Uzbeks. Shahjahan sent his son Awrangzeb to conduct military campaigns in South India, seeking further conquests in that region, with little decisive success – though he did manage to make the Muslim-ruled kingdoms of Bijapur and Golconda his tributary vassals.

In religious policy Shahjahan moved even further away from Akbar's liberal tolerance. Most conversion to Islam in India, however, was not by force but rather because of the attractiveness of the Muslim religion, its egalitarian appeal for lower-caste Hindus, or the material advantages that conversion brought with it given that Muslims were the ruling elite. Shahjahan did not have the means actually to enforce most of his strict decrees against Hinduism, and even his own son, Dara Shikuh, continued to study and translate the Hindu scriptures and to commission Persian translations by Muslim scholars of the Sanskrit classics. Architectural historians have suggested that the Taj Mahal tomb complex, with its gardens, is not so much a monument to his dead wife as a representation on earth of the mystical Muslim notion of paradise. Some 20,000 men labored full-time for about sixteen years to build the complex, designed by an architect from Shiraz, at a cost of between 5 and 20 million rupees.

Awrangzeb

The most energetic of Shahjahan's generals had been his son Awrangzeb, a strict Sunni Muslim, a popular leader, and a sly and single-minded pursuer of his objectives. Awrangzeb marched north from his campaigns against Shi`ite-ruled Golconda, encountering the imperial army still loyal to his father, and using guns and cavalry expertly to rout it. He then fought the defensive forces of Dara Shikuh at Delhi, using artillery, disciplined cavalry, and a flanking attack to defeat his brother. Awrangzeb gradually had his brothers executed, and his ailing father put under house arrest in Agra until his death, consolidating power in his own hands. On coming to power, Awrangzeb (r. 1658–1707) imposed strict discipline on the Mughal bureaucracy, and moved Mughal legal practices closer to those mandated by Sunni orthodoxy. He ordered Hindu temples to be demolished and reimposed the poll tax on Hindus, reacting to Hindu protests with harshness. His attempt to install only Muslims in some posts, like revenue collectors on Crown lands, however, failed because of lack of qualified Muslim candidates and the specialization of some Hindu castes in such bureaucratic tasks. Despite Awrangzeb's dedication to Islam, the number of Hindus, including Hindu nobles, at his court actually increased over time. Many Hindu temples survived him or were rebuilt, and Hinduism continued to be widely and openly practiced.

Maratha Resistance

Awrangzeb repeatedly and unsuccessfully attempted to deal with the Maratha leader Shivaji (d. 1680), who raided Mughal cities, by offering him a high rank, or part of the tribute of Bijapur, or even by imprisoning him (he escaped). Shivaji established a small, self-consciously Hindu Maratha kingdom that, while it did not entirely escape the Mughal framework, boded ill for the great empire's hopes of controlling the entirety of the subcontinent. The Marathas were never entirely absorbed into the Mughal state the way the Rajputs had been, and their clan organization and rugged territory gave them a base to revolt against Mughal interference and taxation.

Maratha revolts against Bijapur, a Muslim-ruled state in southeast India, and renewed Hindu Brahmin political influence in Golconda, another Muslim-ruled state, in southwestern India, caused Awrangzeb in the mid-1680s to reverse the long-time policy of accepting those states as tributary vassals. He conquered them and brought them under direct Mughal rule. The Mughal empire was not a highly centralized structure, but rather a series of loose alliances among local elites and medium landlords, who often were both part of the empire and resistant to its embrace. The Marathas in this sense were just like intermediary elites elsewhere in India. But the Maratha leaders, despite their partial incorporation into the Mughal system, had special advantages in being able to count on the loyalty to them of the Hindu peasantry. They built in the southwest a large sub-imperial unit which had more solidarity than most other such local political structures, and which was much further away from the Mughal centers in the north than were the Rajputs. A grim and relentless old man, Awrangzeb spent the last years of his life fruitlessly attempting to defeat the Marathas decisively, but they used guerrilla tactics to outwit him. At the same time, the empire faced peasant revolts among the Jats near Delhi and the Sikhs of the Panjab, which were expensive to put down.

European Traders Arrive in India

In the course of the seventeenth century the Dutch and British trading companies became most important in India, though mainly in the south beyond the then Mughal borders. These specialized not only in primary commodities like spices and pepper, but increasingly dealt in Indian textiles, which became a major part of their trade. Probably only about 8 to 10 percent of India's population was urban in this period, but Mughal rule was good for cities and for trade, providing security and a common political framework, and some cities grew to be among the largest in the world at that time. Whether the Mughal economy actually expanded much over time is impossible to calculate with any assurance, given the lack of firm statistics. The image we get from the sources seems to indicate that Indians were relatively well off in world terms, but this is a subjective judgment. (And most people in the world then were not all that well off.) Many families invested what surplus they had in ornaments for women, and even poor women often wore large numbers of bangles, anklets, and ear and nose rings. The rich among the Mughal nobility dressed in silk and other fine materials, funding entire artisanal settlements with their demands for accoutrements such as belts, boots, buckles, tunics, saris, saddles, armor, and other goods. Cities suffered the most from periodic outbreaks of disease. Nevertheless, Lahore and Delhi are both estimated by historians to have had a population of around 400,000 in 1700, putting them nearly on a par with London and Paris, Europe's largest cities.

The large size of the Mughal empire and the lack of effective rival states may have had some negative consequences for key elements of Indian development. Mughal bronze cannon and other firearms made advances under Akbar, but by the early eighteenth century no further progress was being made in India in military technology and many armies were content to purchase cheap, inferior weaponry from European merchants. At the same time, the high end of the European weapons industry saw constantly improved firepower, ease of use, and accuracy. The constant competition with one another of a number of relatively small (from an Asian point of view) European states probably contributed to European inventiveness with firearms.

Even Without Printing, the Mughals foster a Cultural Renaissance

Communications were controlled by various specialists – court news writers and spies writing in Persian, Muslim jurists writing in Arabic, Hindu Brahmins writing in Sanskrit, Hindu castes specializing in trade or bureaucracy employing special mathematical notation, popular bhakti poets working in new regional languages like Hindi and Panjabi, and South Indian Shi`ite poets writing in the new mixture of Hindi and Persian that came to be known as Urdu. News traveled not only through professional news writers for the courts, but also through popular gossip, spread by long-distance merchants and others. Transportation in the empire was easiest on the great rivers, such as the Ganges, the Brahmaputra, and the Godavari, or along the coasts on the ocean. Some castes specialized in transporting goods by river. Travel over land was in contrast slow and expensive.

The Mughals, like other Muslim states, did not adopt the printing press. All governments (and most religious institutions) from the mid-1400s were at least a little afraid of the decentralizing potential of the printing press, which made it much cheaper to spread knowledge around to fair numbers of persons. But where one government in Europe might put restrictions on printing, another, smaller and poorer government, might allow it for the promise of an extra source of revenue. A political or religious rival might permit the printing of material another state would find offensive. Once books were printed, they were easy to transport and smuggle across European borders. The plurality of closely neighboring and religiously diverse states in early modern Europe contributed to the ability of print culture to survive and flourish. But if the extensive and influential Mughal state did not want something printed, it could exclude that material from the entire subcontinent. For whatever reason, the printing revolution did not occur in the early modern period in South or West Asia or North Africa (nor for that matter on any large scale in Russia, another large, authoritarian empire). Scribes continued to copy books in Persian, Sanskrit, and regional languages out by hand in the Mughal era.

The lack of a print revolution had implications for science and technology. The printing revolution in Europe enabled astronomers like Copernicus to make a widespread case for the heliocentric theory that the Earth revolves around the sun. The advances in medicine, physics, chemistry, metallurgy, and astronomy we associate with the Renaissance and Reformation period in Europe, then, simply did not occur in the early modern period as public, institutionalized knowledge and practice in the Mughal empire or the rest of the Muslim world. Individual scholars might learn of them through correspondence with a European colleague, but find it difficult to pass the knowledge on. The scholars of Istanbul were likely to be current with European advances, but then the Ottoman empire was partially a European one. The relatively slow pace of Mughal scientific and technical progress, which derived in part from the lack of access to printing technology for scientists and artisans, in turn contributed to the slowing pace of innovation in military weaponry.

Muslims and Hindus in Mughal Society

The Mughal period was a time of great intellectual and religious ferment, when Muslim civilization and Hindu civilization encountered one another in a very serious and sustained manner over centuries. Many literate Indian Muslims knew far more about Hinduism and Hindus than their counterparts among the Ottoman elite tended to know about Christianity and Christians. And, likewise, Hindu scribes who knew Persian often were intimately informed of Persian literary history, Muslim philosophy and religious thought, and Muslim history. The encounter could produce polemics, persecution, and revolt, but it also produced translations, dialogue, understanding, and mutual admiration among many.

Hinduism for its part proved highly resistant to Muslim proselytizing, in part because it is a decentralized religion (indeed, it would be fair to say that what we call "Hinduism" is a very diverse set of religious practices rather than one religion in the Western sense). Large temples do not survive from before the 1600s in most northern Hindu holy cities, unlike the case in South India, so the Mughal decrees against them were effective. But Hindus could worship their deities at home when temples were under attack. One Mughal miniature painting shows a peasant girl cupping a brazier in her hand, appearing to be worshipping the fire. Mughal concentration on hampering the infrastructure of rival religions reflected tactics developed in the Middle East to combat Christianity and Zoroastrianism. The decentralized form of Hinduism under Muslim rule allowed the proliferation of lower-class enthusiastic sects, called bhakti, which taught divine love, encouraged worshipful dancing and singing, and tended to de-emphasize the caste system in favor of a more egalitarian ethos. Special attention was paid by these groups to Krishna, the god to whom the teachings of the Bhagavad Gita (Divine Song) were attributed. Poets such as the weaver Kabir (1440–1518) and teachers such as Guru Nanak gave expression to these sentiments, often criticizing both the Hindu priest caste (the Brahmins) and the Muslim clerics or **ulama**.

In the Mughal period bhakti movements sometimes influenced and came under the influence of Muslim mystical orders, called Sufi brotherhoods. As late as the nineteenth century, British ethnographers reported Hindu castes that specialized in telling the stories of Muslim sacred history or mourning Muslim martyrs. On the other hand, Muslim mystics in India often recognized Hindu figures like Ram and Krishna as prophets from God on a par with Muhammad, or attempted to reconcile monistic Hindu philosophy like that of the Upanishads with the Sufi theory of the unity of being. We have seen that even Muslims from the ruling strata like Akbar and Dara Shikuh were attracted by such mixing of religious ideas. Members of some Sufi orders adopted fasting, meditation, and posture and breathing techniques from Hindu yoga, allowing them to enter alternative mental states.

Mughal Art and Architecture

The artisans of the Mughal period produced some of the world's most magnificent art and architecture. Royal tombs like that of Humayun in Delhi, as well as mosques, palaces, and court buildings, and the unique Taj Mahal, attest to the brilliance of Mughal architects and to the fertile mixture of Persian, Central Asian, and Indian themes and techniques. The Mughal period was important as a chapter in the development of not only Persian literature but other Indian literatures. Safavid Iran, with its dour Shi`ite rulers, was inhospitable to the often sensual and profane practice of Persian poetry, so that many of the best Persian poets left Iran and set up in Agra, Delhi, and Lahore. The movement to translate Sanskrit works, including moral tales and fables, into Persian, encouraged Persian writers to imitate these classical Indian models. Painting also flourished as an art, along with poetry, in the Mughal period. Royal ateliers supported the production of hundreds of fine miniatures, depicting scenes from classical Persian romances and epics, events from Mughal history, India's flora and fauna, and increasingly recording the styles of life of most of the Indian social classes. Hindu paintings also were produced in great numbers, depicting stories of the mischievous god Krishna and his dalliances with the cow girls, and other scenes from Hindu tales and mythology. The Muslim tradition of miniatures (initially influenced by Mongol and Chinese painting) had an influence on, and was influenced by, the Rajput and other Hindu styles. Some Muslim painters also came under European influence, adopting Renaissance techniques such as perspective.

1.3 THE SAFAVIDS CONQUER IRAN

A new empire in Iran melded the Middle East's two great sources of social and cultural power: pastoral nomads and urban Sufi orders. Pastoral nomads, as we have seen, formed a formidable natural cavalry and could often establish new states where they conquered settled regions and decided to hunker down themselves to tax them. But pastoralists founded fewer large, long-term states than they might have because their organization into often competing tribes, sub-tribes, and clans tended to open them to internal feuding and impeded their making a united stand for any period of time. Only when a successful, charismatic chieftain managed to transform himself into the founder of a dynasty of monarchs with a bureaucracy and regular military could such states hope to become long-term concerns. The Turkmen tribespeople of eastern Anatolia in the mid-1400s found themselves under pressure from the expanding Ottoman state, which was becoming a settled empire that found pastoralists an impediment to regular farming and taxation. The Turkmen tried to move east into the Caucasus, but encountered fierce resistance from the Christian tribes there, who could employ their knowledge of the rugged local terrain to ambush and defeat invaders.

Isma`il

Nearby, in the shrine city of Ardabil on the Caspian Sea, a venerable Sufi order existed, the Safavi. It was initially a Sunni order. Gradually its leaders made contact with the lightly Islamized Turkmen, probably at first in hopes of proselytizing them. These tribes were known as **Qizilbash**, or "red heads," because of their red caps, often pierced with twelve holes, probably a shamanic symbol that came to be interpreted as symbolizing the Shi`ite Imams. The tribespeople with unusual beliefs came to idolize the Safavi leaders, even to consider them divine. The main state in northwestern Iran or Azerbaijan at this time

was that of the White Sheep tribal federation. In the late 1400s and the opening years of the 1500s the young Safavi leader Isma`il (1487–1524) and his regents and supporters defeated both princes in the Caucasus and the White Sheep armies, taking the large and important city of Tabriz in 1501. Isma`il was crowned the first monarch of the Safavid dynasty, moving from the status of Sufi leader and adopted tribal chieftain to that of king. His forces then overran what is now Iraq, and also the Iranian plateau, which had been ruled mainly by weak, fragmented states that were successors to the disintegrating empire founded by Tamerlane. As Box 1.2 points out, Isma`il's accession was the beginning of a great Shi`ite revival.

Isma`il came under the influence of Shi`ite Islam from two directions. The first was the folk adoration of the family of the Prophet and the tendency to theological extremism characteristic of the illiterate Turkmen tribespeople among whom he was in part raised. The other was the tradition of urban, literate Shi`ite Islam, as exemplified in one of his most beloved tutors. He proclaimed Shi`ite Islam the official religion of his newly conquered realm, instituting widespread attacks on Sunnis who declined to convert to the rival branch of Islam. Sunni mosques were burned, Sunni lands confiscated, and steadfast Sunni communities opened to pogroms.

Box 1.2 The Shi`ite Revival of the Sixteenth Century

Shi`ite Islam had all along been a minority branch of Islam. By the 1400s, it had declined to a small set of communities in Syria, Bahrain, and Eastern Arabia, in addition to quarters in some Iranian cities. The central theme of Shi`ism is devotion to the family of the Prophet Muhammad and conviction that just rule can only come from one of his descendants. The Turkmen nomads of eastern Anatolia came to hold these beliefs in the late 1400s. When they accepted the leadership of the Safavid Shah Isma`il, and conquered Iran, they changed the religious landscape of the Middle East.

Shah Isma`il (r. 1501–24) made Shi`ite Islam the state religion of the Safavid empire. Some of his followers harshly persecuted Sunnis, confiscating their wealth and their mosques and forcing them to convert. Sunnis held that the prophet was rightly succeeded by caliphs not from his immediate family, in accordance with community consensus. The group that became Shi`ites favored the direct descendants of the Prophet as leaders of the Muslims. Over time, a majority of Iranians adopted the Shi`ite branch of Islam.

The rise of Safavid Shi`ism had a big impact elsewhere, especially in India. The Adil Shah dynasty of Bijapur in southwest India imitated the Safavids in declaring Shi`ite Islam the religion of state in 1502. A Shi`ite dynasty ruled Kashmir briefly in the 1500s. The Qutb Shah dynasty in Golconda, South India, was devotedly Shi`ite and ruled from 1518 to 1687. Most Indians remained Hindus, and most Indian Muslims remained Sunnis. Unlike the case in Iran, the Shi`ite dynasties in India did not impose Shi`ism on their subjects. But as an aristocratic religion, it deeply influenced literature, poetry, and official rites. The Sunni-ruled Mughal empire gradually conquered and absorbed most of the Indian Shi`ite-ruled states.

Safavid Shi`ism also gave encouragement to the Shi`ite communities in the eastern Arab world, including those of what is now South Lebanon, southern Iraq, Bahrain, and Eastern Arabia. Many Arab Shi`ite scholars studied in Iran and some settled there permanently, helping the Safavid kings to convert the population from Sunnism to Shi`ism.

Isma`il was aided in making Iran Shi`ite by Sunni clerical families who did convert to Shi`ism, the "clerical notables," and at least in some part by immigrant Arab Shi`ite clergy from what are now Lebanon, Iraq, and the Persian Gulf. Many of the Arab Shi`ite thinkers, however, saw Isma`il's state as illegitimate in the absence of the hidden Twelfth Imam, and declined to support it. Only the absent Imam, they believed, could authorize state functions such as the collection of religiously ordained taxes, or the appointment of Muslim court judges. Other Shi`ite thinkers, mainly of the scholastic and rationalistic **Usuli** school, came to believe that the Shi`ite clergy themselves could in a general way substitute for the Imam in authorizing such state actions. These Usuli clergymen were rapidly promoted into important religious positions in the Safavid empire, and their school became predominant until the late 1600s. It taught, as well, that all the laity had to choose an upright and knowledge-able clergyman whose rulings they had to follow. This doctrine of lay 'emulation' of the Shi`ite clergy differentiated this school from Sunni Islam and gave the clerics more ideological control.

A Safavid Ruler Turns Iran into a Shi`ite Society

Isma`il ultimately succeeded in his goal. Iran had been majority Sunni before 1501, but by the eighteenth century it was solidly Shi`ite. Folk Shi`ite practices grew up involving the ritual cursing of Sunni holy figures, and extensive mourning ceremonies, processions, and plays were staged for the martyred early Shi`ite Imams or descendants of the Prophet Muhammad, which were distinctive and were denounced by Sunnis. The Shi`ite move-ment in Iran looks something like the Protestant Reformation in Europe. Both movements split up a large cultural region that had previously been more homogeneous. Safavid Shi`ism, how-ever, was if anything more like Catholicism than Protestantism. It elevated a scholarly elite and venerated the lives of earlier imams, not unlike the priestly hierarchy and the veneration of saints in the Latin church. Isma`il's religious policy derived from his deep faith in Shi`ism, not from any desire to create a religious barrier between Iran and the neighboring Muslim states of the Ottoman empire and the Uzbek principalities to his east. Sunnis continued to travel and communicate through Iran, and to conduct diplomacy with the Safavids, so that the lands of Islam were not decisively cut off from one another by the schism.

After its first century Safavid Iran was still not firmly estab-lished, and it faced continuing and dire challenges to political stability. One such menace came from the Shaybanid rulers of Central Asia to the east, who claimed much Safavid territory, including the eastern areas of Khurasan. Isma`il fought them to a standstill in 1513, seeking to make the Oxus River the border between Safavid and Uzbek domains. Isma`il's son and successor, Tahmasp I (r. 1524–87), had to face five invasions of his territories in Khurasan by the Uzbeks, all of which were beaten back, and in some battles artillery bought by the Safavids from the Portuguese was decisive (the Uzbeks could not yet cast their own cannon and did not have a reliable supplier of such arms). Sometimes overtaxed commoners in the eastern parts of the Safavid empire even co-ordinated with the Uzbeks to rise up and take over cities like Herat. In the end, the Safavids always prevailed, however. In the seventeenth century, the Uzbek state posed no further threat to eastern Iran, even though inhab-itants of that part of Iran suffered from continual raids by Turkic tribespeople.

The Ottomans Strongly Challenge the Safavid State

A somewhat more substantial challenge to Safavid sovereignty and even survival was mounted by the Ottoman empire (see Map 1.2). Those Qizilbash who did not emigrate to Iran dwelled in Ottoman domains in eastern Anatolia, and massive Turkmen revolts in that area in 1511 and 1512 convinced the Ottomans that they were a threat to the integrity of the state. Their brethren's conquest of neighboring Iran was thus all the more alarming to Istanbul. Further, the adherence of the new state and its Qizilbash supporters to Shi`ite Islam dismayed the staunchly Sunni Ottomans, who saw Shi`ism as a conspiracy to undermine the true Islam. Selim I, the "Grim," came to the throne in Istanbul amidst this turmoil, and immediately enacted harsh measures against the Turkmen in eastern Anatolia. Thou-sands were forcibly moved elsewhere, some even to the Balkans. Selim then marched on the Safavids themselves, facing the army of Shah Isma`il at Chaldiran in 1514. The Ottoman army was larger than the Safavid force, and Selim had brought along field artillery. The Safavids had used artillery and harquebus muskets in some battles, but these weapons were not ideally suited to a tribal cavalry used to fighting from horseback, and their use was not consistent. They did not have an artillery unit present at Chaldiran, depending instead on archers on horseback, and they lost the battle very badly.

Up until then many Qizilbash tribesmen had thought Isma`il infallible and invulnerable, a manifestation of God. This defeat made him begin to resemble more a simple king, though many of his followers stubbornly insisted on seeing him and his successor as divine. Although his army was crushed, Isma`il escaped and regrouped. The Ottomans briefly occupied Tabriz, the Safavid capital, but then withdrew, perhaps for logistical reasons, and Isma`il was able to move back in. The Battle of Chaldiran fixed the Safavid–Ottoman border, a border that con-tinues to be drawn in virtually the same way between modern Turkey and Iran.

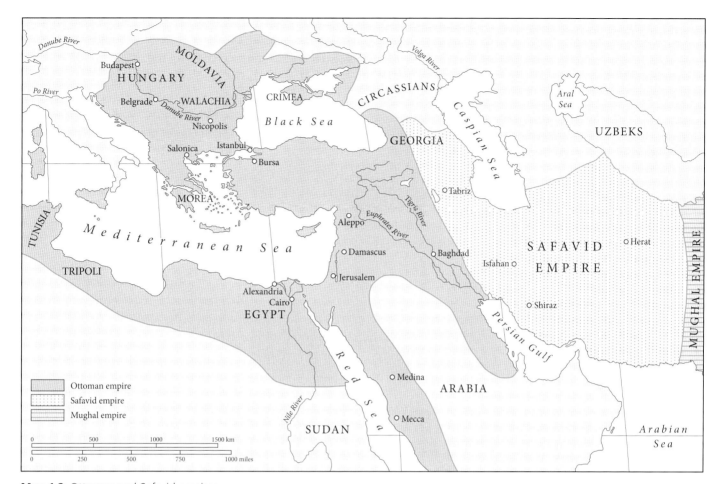

Map 1.2 Ottoman and Safavid empires

The struggle between the Ottomans and the Safavids was not over, however. In 1534, flush with victories in Europe, the Ottomans invaded and occupied Tabriz once more, then Sultan Suleiman the Magnificent marched on Baghdad, taking it. The Safavid ruler Tahmasp regained Tabriz, but the Ottoman hold on Arab Iraq was thereafter nearly permanent, save for a relatively brief period under the later Shah `Abbas the Great. In 1578–90 the Ottomans fought another series of wars for Tabriz, which they took. In 1603–07 Shah `Abbas mounted a war against the Ottomans that succeeded in driving them out of Tabriz and back across the border set by Chaldiran. He imported harquebuses from Russia and England, and his infantry put them to good use, though the Safavid infantry remained low in status and not the leading edge of the army. In the early 1620s Shah `Abbas now went on the offensive, taking Ottoman Diyarbakr and Baghdad itself away from the Ottomans.

In 1629–38 the Ottomans riposted, taking back territory in Anatolia and reconquering Baghdad, which they then kept till World War I. There were no further major Ottoman–Iranian military confrontations until the eighteenth century. The

1639 Peace of Zuhab between the two, however, may have contained hidden dangers for Iran. Thenceforth the Safavids had less incentive to innovate in military technology or to keep up with their powerful western neighbor. They were in any case hampered in manufacturing muskets and cannon by the difficulty of obtaining sulfur, saltpeter, iron, copper, and tin in Iran. These raw materials existed there but were often found in remote areas where it was difficult to mine them. The Safavids, being a steppe dynasty with relatively little interest in defending cities, seldom built major fortresses in theirs, and were less and less involved in warfare that required them to reduce enemy fortresses. This lack of need to contend with early modern fortifications retarded military innovation. Finally, the tribal groupings along Iran's peripheries, such as Uzbeks, Kurds, and Baluchis, were relatively slow to adopt handheld firearms, instead tending to field cavalry archers. The Safavids found these most effectively opposed by another army of better cavalry archers. Harquebuses actually required the warrior to dismount before firing, and only the later invention of the flintlock made it possible for cavalry to fire from horseback. Cannon were clumsy, inaccurate, and difficult to transport over Iran's extensive mountains and deserts. A rapid adoption of flintlocks by Afghan tribesmen in the early 1700s took the Safavids by surprise, and by then it was too late.

Tribal Armies Undermine Safavid Cohesion

The third threat to Safavid stability was internal, since the Safavid monarchs in the 1500s did not have a strong standing army of their own, depending instead on tribal levies from their vassals among the various Qizilbash chieftains, who were divided into seven great tribes. The advantage of the Turkmen forces was that they were excellent natural cavalrymen and had proved their ability to conquer the settled population of Iran and, generally speaking, to face down external invasions. Along with the largely Persian-speaking bureaucracy, the Turkic soldiery was one of the two pillars of the Safavid state in the sixteenth century. They had the disadvantage that the seven tribes tended to fight amongst themselves, and sometimes a chieftain intrigued against the shah himself, seeking to take his place. Such internal, tribally-based turmoil frequently became an invitation for Uzbek or Ottoman invasions.

Shah `Abbas I attempted to resolve this problem of the tribes by capturing Christians from Georgia and other regions of the Caucasus, converting them to Islam, conscripting them, and making them into a slave army (**ghulams**). Thereafter the Safavid shahs depended less on the tribal cavalry of the Qizilbash for their military forces. The slave-soldiers used traditional weaponry and cavalry tactics on the whole, although some were armed with firearms. Shah `Abbas also relocated a large Armenian merchant community from Armenia to his new capital of Isfahan, encouraging them to pursue their international trading activities for Iran's benefit. To pay for the new standing army of slave-soldiers, the shahs began usurping land that had previously been awarded as tax farms (a sort of fief) to Qizilbash chieftains for their military service, creating them as directly taxed and administered Crown lands. The amount of Crown land in Iran grew enormously in the seventeenth century.

The Silk Trade Helps the Safavids Prosper

Iran in the 1600s was frequently at peace, and its borders were seldom threatened after 1638. It was no longer a state seeking expansion, and many of its rulers suffered from alcoholism. Shah `Abbas I began a custom of killing or blinding most of the potential heirs to the throne, and of raising the remaining princes in the harem. This latter custom may not have harmed the monarchy. The harem, a complex social setting with many rivalries and often with external property and investments, was a perfectly good place to be trained for kingship. Beyond farming products like grains and pastoral ones like meat, dairy goods, and wool, some of the surplus that supported the Safavid state was generated by taxes on long-distance trade and by Iran's own production and sale of silk. Important "trading diasporas" such as the Sindhis and Armenians operated throughout South Asia and the Middle East, with extensive establishments in Iran. In addition, this was the period of the great European East India Companies. Iran stood to benefit from its position dominating the Persian Gulf, through which trade to and from India flowed as part of a route that employed the Tigris and Euphrates rivers, with an overland leg through Syria to the Mediterranean. In 1622 Iran recovered the key Persian Gulf trading entrepôt of Hormuz from the Portuguese with British help.

Shah `Abbas brought under state control key silk-producing regions, and made many of these Crown lands, ensuring that the Safavid monarchy would benefit directly from the important Iranian silk trade. Silk revenues helped pay for the wars against the Ottomans and the measures taken to weaken the Qizilbash. It was an important chip in the diplomacy he pursued with the Spanish, Russians, British, and Dutch in his search for allies against the Ottomans and for profits. But the European trading companies were used to paying for goods with other goods, and the Safavid insistence on being paid in silver specie, as well as the constantly changing terms of trade offered by the shahs as monopolists, discouraged them. Iranian silk was not as high in quality as what was available in the Far East, and was only interesting to the Europeans because it was nearer and less expensive.

The frustrations of dealing with the shahs caused the the merchants to look elsewhere, even to Italy, a possibility the shahs appear to have discounted. The Armenians based in Julfa emerged as the most important traders of Iranian silk, using overland routes to the Levant and to Russia. Whereas in the 1670s a majority of silk traded by the Dutch East India Company in Amsterdam derived from Iran, by the 1690s most was coming from Bengal, with the Iranian share reduced to only 6 percent. It is not clear whether the overall volume of Iranian silk exports declined, though, or whether the total volume of silk traded simply increased with the advent of new suppliers in India and elsewhere, within which Iranian silk took a smaller proportion of the market. What does seem clear is that the shahs did not manage their silk production for the world market as intelligently as they could have, and that for various reasons the income of the Safavid state appears to have declined in the period 1690–1720.

The End of the Safavid Dynasty

This era coincided with the reign (1694–1722) of Shah Sultan Husayn, an ineffectual and somewhat bigoted ruler who bowed to the wishes of his main Shi`ite clerical official in expelling thousands of Hindu Indian and other foreign merchants from the country, in persecuting Jews, Christians, and even Shi`ite nonconformists, and in treating the Sunni minorities in the east of the Safavid domains harshly. The Baluchi and then Afghan tribes increasingly revolted in the teens of the eighteenth century, and the Safavid state lacked the military and financial resources to defeat them. The Afghan tribal leader Mahmud of the Ghilzais took Kerman and then marched ultimately on Isfahan, defeating the shah's army outside the capital in 1721. A long siege followed, with the city finally falling to the Sunni tribesmen, who sacked and looted it, reducing this great metropolis of several hundred thousand inhabitants to a small town of 20,000–50,000 persons.

The Afghans by this time had flintlocks (which could be fired from horseback), and used them to defeat the better-supplied and larger Safavid forces. Just as artillery had aided the rise of large, centralizing states, so the spread to ordinary folk of handheld firearms had a centrifugal effect, benefiting separatists, pastoralists, and peasants in the face of the central state. A decade of turmoil followed, in which several major Iranian cities were sacked. In 1736 an adventurer named Nadir crowned himself shah, having put together an unstable coalition of Afghan and Qizilbash tribal armies (the one fierce Sunnis, the other deeply committed Shi`ites). He conquered all of Iran for his new, short-lived Afsharid dynasty, paying his tribesmen with booty. He then conquered North India, including Delhi, as we saw in the previous section on the Mughals, leaving that city and Lahore devastated and bringing their treasures, including the fabled peacock throne, back to Iran. His mixed Sunni–Shi`ite army increasingly fought with one another, and he was assassinated in 1747. A twenty-year gap followed in which political power was fragmented in Iran, and economic life ground to a virtual standstill.

Safavids and Mughals Compared

The Safavid state presided over a small population (an average of perhaps 4 or 5 million) compared to that of Mughal India, though its geographic extent was about half that of the latter. It remained in important respects a tribal state, where pastoral nomads probably constituted some 2 million of the 4. That such a large proportion of the population was mobile, could form natural cavalries, and was politically fragmented into clan rivalries, introduced a constant element of instability into Safavid affairs. The ambitions of the Uzbeks in the east and the Ottomans in the west presented further continual challenges to state-making in Iran, at least until 1639 or so. The silk and to a lesser extent wool trade helped support the central state, but its insistence on being paid in cash for silk, the relatively inferior quality of the product, and the changing terms of trade demanded by the overconfident shahs all encouraged European trading companies to go elsewhere, in the end, for their silk. The Safavid state had few incentives in the seventeenth century to improve its armaments or military, and did not. It did succeed in entrenching Shi`ite Islam on the Iranian plateau. But the intolerant religious policies of Shah Sultan Husayn, the new military vitality gained by the Afghan Sunni tribes from their adoption of the flintlock, the lack of cash in the imperial coffers, and the dilapidated state of the Safavid army all contributed to the dynasty's overthrow in 1722. The Safavid period did not produce truly great literature in Iran, though there are some impressive Persian miniatures from the period and schools of Neoplatonic philosophy and mysticism were extraordinarily vigorous. The Safavid great mosque and other buildings along the central Square of Isfahan are breathtakingly beautiful, with their blue tile mosaics and imposing facades.

1.4 THE OTTOMANS

The dynamic Ottoman empire brought a vast set of regions together, from eastern Europe as far north as Hungary and parts of Poland to the Persian Gulf and from Baghdad to Algiers. Map 1.3 shows the pace and extent of Ottoman expansion. The Ottomans, a Turkish dynasty originally based in Asia Minor or Anatolia, fostered a flourishing trade and commercial life in this new single market. In the first part of their reign, up to about 1600, they were among the more militarily advanced powers in the world, and regularly defeated European armies. Even after the Ottomans stopped expanding their territories around 1600, they continued to flourish in many ways. Ottoman population probably increased between 1500 and 1800 by about 40 percent. There are some Ottoman censuses for a few provinces such as Aleppo, and these bear out this long-term trend. This number is an average, and some regions in some eras did suffer population declines, or grew even more quickly for a while. While this sort of population growth was exceeded by some European states in the same period, it certainly suggests that the Ottomans were providing basic security and amenities to their subjects. Jews and Christians, though not equal to Muslims and subject to some disabilities, were treated better, on the whole, in the Ottoman empire than were religious minorities in Europe right up to the eighteenth century. Most of the Jews expelled from Spain found refuge in Ottoman domains, where on the whole they were welcomed. After 1600 the Ottomans did not make the same sort of advances in technology and military, economic, and social organization as did Europe. But that conclusion does

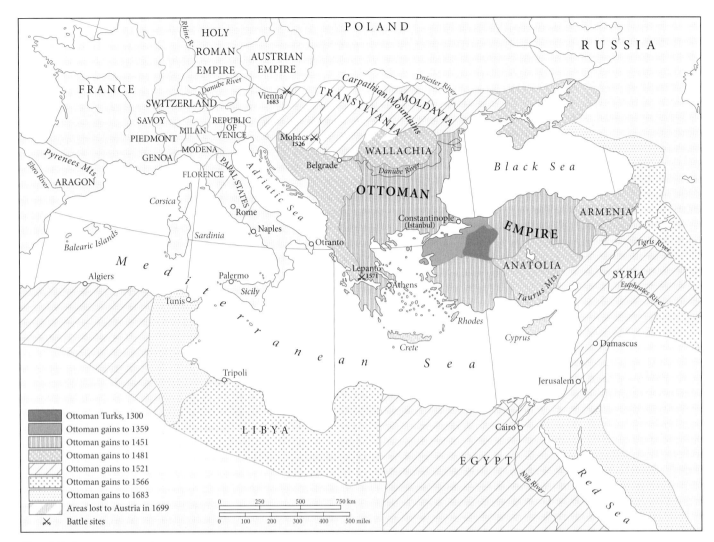

Map 1.3 Ottoman expansion

not require that they declined in any absolute sense. They may have advanced, but just not as quickly as did Western Europe.

The Ottomans developed a bureaucratic administration, and the sultan was advised by its head, the vizier or first minister, who gained great power. Most personal status law was administered by the Muslim court judges, who became state employees and ruled according to classical Islamic jurisprudence. Some administrative and criminal law, however, was made by the sultan, who claimed powers of legislation based on Turco-Mongol custom. The Ottomans also developed their military and built up a powerful navy that was able to dominate the Black Sea and even the eastern Mediterranean, defeating Venice in the first battle for Lepanto in 1499–1503. They used their navy to transport heavy artillery, and employed artillery to good effect in that war. At Modon in 1500, they fired an average of 165 shots per day from 22 cannon and 2 mortars. The Ottomans encouraged trade, allowing merchants from the great Italian city-states of Venice and Florence to operate in Ottoman cities such as Bursa and Aleppo, and declining to attack these Italian centers even though they did mount assaults on their neighbors on the other side of the Adriatic Sea. The Italian Renaissance occurred very much in the shadow of Ottoman power, and in some ways was made possible by Ottoman complaisance toward the city-states.

We have seen that Selim I (r. 1515–20) defeated Shah Isma`il in Iran in 1514, again using firearms and artillery. His great victories, however, were in the Arabic-speaking lands. In 1516 his forces defeated the Mamluks in Syria, and, attracted by the Nile Valley's grain-producing potential, took Egypt in 1517, ending the Mamluk regime. The Ottomans also took the Hijaz, or western coast of Arabia, and so became guardians of the Muslim holy cities of Mecca and Medina, as well as coming to control the commerce of the Red Sea. Selim's successor, Suleiman the Magnificent (r. 1520–66), as we saw above, took Baghdad and ultimately Basra and the Arabian coast along the Persian Gulf. He thus sought to gain access to the lucrative trade route running from the Indian Ocean through the Persian Gulf and the Fertile Crescent to the Mediterranean.

The Ottomans Confront Europe

The Ottomans were opposed in this strategy by the Portuguese, who wished to divert the spice trade around the Cape of Good Hope to Lisbon, away from the Middle East and the Mediterranean, and therefore away from Venice. The Ottoman navy, despite its earlier strength against Venice, was defeated by the Portuguese in the Arabian Sea in the mid sixteenth century. Ottoman shipbuilding technique was forged in the Mediterranean, so that their vessels were smaller than the big Portuguese ships developed to ply the Atlantic, which could be mounted with more powerful cannon. Nevertheless, the Persian Gulf–Mediterranean route was revived in the second half of the sixteenth century, and Portuguese attempts to maintain a monopoly on the spice trade failed. The Ottomans were more successful in keeping the Portuguese out of the Red Sea, and they captured most of the North African coast east of Morocco.

In Europe, Suleiman took Belgrade, defeated the Hungarians, besieged Vienna, and forged an alliance of convenience with the Protestants. Although Luther had seen the Ottomans as a dire enemy of Christendom, the Protestant Reformation had the ironic effect of helping consolidate Ottoman rule in Eastern and Central Europe by giving it allies against the Catholic powers. Ottoman rule had the unexpected effect of helping the Protestants survive there in the face of hostility from those same powers. Internally, Suleiman reorganized the laws and government of the Ottoman empire, so that in Turkish he is not known as "the Magnificent," as in the West, but rather as "the Lawgiver."

Trade and Agriculture Flourish under Ottoman Rule

The sixteenth century appears to have been a time of great prosperity in the Ottoman empire. This huge area had no internal trade barriers, allowing a prosperous commercial life, and the security provided by the state permitted agriculture to flourish as well. At the base of Ottoman society were the peasants, whether they toiled in Middle Eastern river valleys like the Nile or the Tigris–Euphrates, on plateaus like Anatolia, or on the plains of Eastern Europe. In the southern stretches of Eastern Europe or the Balkans, most of these peasants were Christian, including those in Romania, Serbia, Greece, and most of Bulgaria, though some populations there converted to Islam, and some Muslims immigrated into this region. In Anatolia and the Arabic-speaking regions, the peasants were predominantly Muslim, though the Levant, Egypt, and Iraq had significant Christian minorities. Peasants for the most part produced

grains, vegetables, and fruit, though some regions did specialize in cash crops, as with coffee in Yemen or dates in the southern Iraqi city of Basra. The introduction of American maize in the 1600s probably increased agricultural productivity for Egyptian and other peasants who grew that crop. Although peasants were for the most part nominally Muslim, peasant religiosity tended to focus on Sufi mystics, whose shrines they felt bestowed blessings.

In the Middle East, there were large numbers, as well, of pastoral nomads. It is difficult to know their proportion of the Ottoman population in the early modern period, but as late as the mid nineteenth century, a third of the inhabitants of what is now Iraq were pastoralists. Significant numbers of pastoralists also lived in greater Syria, Anatolia, and North Africa. They lived in felt tents thrown over temporary frames of branches, which they dismantled regularly, rolling them up and packing them on camels for transport to the next grazing ground. The nomads produced key goods such as horses, camels, meat, dairy products, wool, rugs, and felt, but they were very difficult to rule or tax, often raided the peasants, and formed a constant element of potential political disruption for the central state. Pastoralists were usually better off than peasants, since all of them had some property in the form of livestock. The Ottoman elite viewed both peasants and pastoralists as "sheep" needing a shepherd, and often needing a shearing as well.

The empire contained many important cities, and urban dwellers constituted between 10 and 20 percent of the population. The larger cities in the empire were Cairo, Damascus, Aleppo, Baghdad, and Istanbul, with the last, the imperial capital, having a huge population of perhaps half a million by the mid-1600s. Most of the empire was illiterate, being largely rural and lacking printing technology, but cities were more likely to have literate individuals. Urban dwellers were stratified into slaves, day laborers, skilled craftsmen (who were members of guilds or organizations that tried to keep craft wages high by establishing monopolies), shopkeepers, small merchants and peddlers, and great long-distance merchants. Most slaves in the Ottoman empire were household slaves, the women often serving as concubines for the master and giving birth to free children who had inheritance rights. The slaves came mainly from the Caucasus and from the Sudan. Middle Eastern slave-trading networks and practices formed a background for the rise of the Atlantic slave trade. Still, there was very little plantation slavery in the Ottoman empire, and slaves' position, while servile and coerced, was very unlike that of slaves in the Americas. Women were hardly free but they possessed a wider array of freedoms than their Western counterparts. (See Box 1.3.)

Most workers in the Ottoman empire were free day laborers and artisans. Ottoman women, unlike those in Europe, could

Box 1.3 Women and Property in the Ottoman Empire

Recent scholarship has shown that Ottoman women played an active role in public life. They show up in Ottoman Islamic court archives as plaintiffs, defendants, and witnesses. Because Islamic law, unlike most European law of the early modern period, allowed women to inherit, own, and deal in property, they became involved in legal disputes over it. In one rural city in Anatolia, a scholar found that women were involved in 40 percent of all the property transactions.

In other cities, as well, they appear in the records as actively involved in selling, buying, and leasing real estate and farms. They often owned shops, vineyards, and orchards. Since they sometimes left such properties to their heirs even when they were married, some of them, at least, must have owned the properties apart from their husbands. A few were involved in commerce, as in buying silk in Iran for import, or in other commercial partnerships. They also took out substantial loans from lending institutions, and clearly were trusted to repay them. They even sometimes loaned money to their own husbands. Some may even have been moneylenders as an informal profession.

Throughout the empire, women pursued court cases against males, even against their own family members, and were accepted by the courts as equal in the law in this regard. They sold real property to other family members, and bought it from them. In one case in the city of Bursa, a woman angrily sued her husband for having built an addition onto a house that she owned. She demanded that it be demolished, and the court ruled in her favor. Although women were sometimes disinherited by the machinations of their brothers, some of them, at least, recovered their rights by going to court.

In the larger cities, women were involved in cottage industries such as bleaching and spinning silk. In the large commercial center of Bursa, women owned half of the silk-spinning equipment in the city in the late 1600s. Poor women produced textile goods at home, and perhaps as many as a sixth of women in some cities owned simple looms.

Although Islamic law technically allowed polygamy, where men take more than one wife, estate records from Ottoman times show that this practice was in reality rare. Ottomanist Haim Gerber looked at 2,000 estates records in the city of Bursa and found only 20 of the men to have had more than one wife.

own property, including shops, and they made investments in trading journeys. The greatest of the merchants in the Ottoman empire may have been the coffee magnates of Cairo, who marketed coffee grown in Yemen. Coffee initially grew popular in the sixteenth century as a sort of drug for enhanced energy, and was taken in concentrated doses. As a result, it was viewed with disfavor by some governments, including the Ottoman, which tried to ban it and even executed some coffee traffickers. In time it came to be brewed as a drink and became widely accepted, as well as very lucrative. Only Yemenis had coffee beans that could be used to plant this crop, giving them a monopoly on a beverage that was increasingly popular throughout Europe and Asia, and which also underpinned the spread of the new institution of the coffeehouse. It was marketed by the great merchants of Cairo. Coffee was to Ottoman Egypt, in short, as silk was to Iran.

The Ottomans Embrace a Diverse Elite

The ruling stratum of the Ottoman empire was quite diverse, though dominated by Turkish-speaking emirs from Anatolia. This elite included many Muslim notables from Baghdad, Syria, Cairo, Crete, Albania, and Bulgaria as well. These were bound together by loyalty to the sultan, by the Ottoman (Osmanli) language (a melding of Turkish grammar and basic vocabulary with high-flown Persian and Arabic words), by Islam, by common economic interests as great landholders, and by Ottoman military and administrative practice. The elite also included subject Christian princes and lords in the Balkans. The women of the elite included both well-born Muslim ladies and Caucasian and other slaves, with the latter sometimes emerging as wealthy and powerful despite servile status in law. Women owned property, ran businesses through male agents, and endowed mosques. A final element in this elite was the slave-soldiers. These were boys taken in war or simply conscripted from Christian or Jewish families in Ottoman Eastern Europe, who were converted to Islam and trained for military or administrative service. They ultimately gained their freedom. The Ottoman elite dominated administration, the military, and high culture. They provided the scribes and bureaucrats, the officers, and the poets, chroniclers, astrologers, and other men of culture. Ottoman poetry built on the Persian and Arabic heritage, and

Figure 1.2 The famous Blue Mosque of Istanbul is a striking demonstration of the monumental power exerted by the Ottoman rulers in both religious and secular realms.

was devoted to love lyrics, religious themes, mysticism, and praise of rulers and other patrons. It is little translated but extremely subtle and beautiful. The chronicles are rich historical documents of elite life, arranged by yearly events. The Ottoman elite also left a string of beautifully designed, monumental mosques with pencil-shaped minarets throughout the empire but especially in Istanbul. The Blue Mosque shown in Figure 1.2 is one striking example. The city of Istanbul itself was also an object of great pride.

The Ottoman military, about 100,000 regulars during the reign of Suleiman, was divided into two main forces, the cavalry, who fought with lances or bows, and foot-soldiers, who increasingly depended for their prowess on their mastery of handheld firearms. The cavalry consisted of officers who were paid by the bestowal on them of estates, called **timars**. In return, they were required to maintain a certain number of horses for the sultan's military service. Pastoralists also contributed cavalrymen as irregulars for some battles, as at Baghdad in 1638. The Ottoman cavalry continued throughout this period to be twice as large in numbers as the infantry force, despite the increased importance of the latter deriving from the rise of siege cannon and field artillery in European warfare. The foot-soldiers, some 35,000 to 40,000 strong in the 1600s, were most often **Janissaries**, from non-Muslim families. These initially were considered slaves of the sultan and subjected to almost monastic strictness, being confined to barracks when not fighting, and prohibited from marrying or owning land. At first the state simply provided them with food, uniforms, and shelter, but in the 1500s they began receiving a salary. Because matchlocks could not easily be fired from horseback, the previously despised foot-soldiers were given the task of taking up firearms when these became essential to warfare. The Janissaries did not displace the cavalry, but they did play a major role in Ottoman victories over the Safavids, Mamluks, and Habsburgs.

1.5 CRISES STRIKE IN THE SEVENTEENTH CENTURY

Most historians see the years 1596–1610 as an era of extreme crisis in the Ottoman realm. The real value of Ottoman government revenue was halved in the period 1520–63, and by

1591 the treasury had a deficit. From 1580 in particular, silver from South America began flooding into the Ottoman empire, helping provoke relatively high inflation. Inflation is caused by too much money chasing too few goods. The productivity of Ottoman farmers and workers had not increased, but suddenly the money supply had, because previously rare silver coinage was now much more available. Even mild inflation could be very unsettling to an agrarian society where ordinarily prices do not change much, and it has an especially devastating effect on persons on fixed incomes, as Ottoman cavalry officers were. This was a time before inflation was well understood, and salaries were not automatically raised by the state, so that the purchasing power of the officers declined. The state responded to this fiscal crisis by imposing new taxes.

Advances in Central Europe by the Habsburgs and in Iran and what is now Iraq by Shah `Abbas reduced the total territory held by the Ottomans and therefore reduced the number of land grants (timars) that could be awarded for the support of cavalry officers. The light cavalry officers who could not defeat the heavily armed German fusiliers of the time had to return home to Anatolia, penniless. They hoped to devote themselves to their timar estates, in order to ensure that they yielded their customary revenue. The Anatolian population (and perhaps that of some other regions) increased about 40 percent during the 1500s, as a result of the relative stability and prosperity of Suleiman's era, but by the end of the century this increase had produced a certain amount of rural unemployment. Another development of this period was the spread among the peasants of handheld firearms, despite their being officially banned. This development occurred among Anatolian peasants a full century before it happened among Safavid Afghans. The result of all these changes was a series of uprisings in Anatolia beginning in the late 1590s, called the **Celali revolts**, where as many as 20,000 irregulars were involved in some battles against the Ottoman armies. By 1610 the state had defeated and killed thousands of these rebels, while others were pardoned and brought into the state apparatus as high officials. The effort and expense involved in putting down these extensive revolts in the empire's own territory greatly detracted from its ability to pursue expansion in Europe.

Moreover, the European powers were making advances in military and other technology that put the Ottomans at a disadvantage. In 1571 the Venetians, allied in a Holy League with Austria and the papacy, took revenge for their defeat at the beginning of the century by besting the Ottoman navy at Lepanto in a rematch. This battle was not truly decisive, since the Ottomans rebuilt their navy and reasserted control of the eastern Mediterranean in subsequent decades. But Ottoman naval power was not to remain formidable for much longer.

Both Venice and the Ottomans were still using Mediterranean oar-driven galleys, whereas the Atlantic European powers were making great advances in building large, sail-driven ships that could not only navigate the turbulent Atlantic, but could face down the Ottomans in the Indian Ocean and, increasingly, in the Mediterranean and Black Sea themselves.

The Ottoman siege of Vienna in 1683 was beaten back by a coalition of Austrian, German, and Polish forces, despite Ottoman numerical superiority. The great expense involved in this Austrian campaign led to further taxation at home, causing Anatolians to rise up yet again. Even more ominously, the Russian Cossacks began attacking Ottoman territory around the Black Sea. A weakened empire could not deal effectively with Russian advances, and with revolts among the largely Christian subject population. In 1699 the Ottomans accepted the Treaty of Carlowitz, signaling their resignation to losing Hungary to the Habsburg empire.

It is only after 1680 that we can speak of Europeans gaining an edge over the Ottomans in military technology. Ottomans were slow to adopt the new flintlock musket, clinging to the older matchlock. They also for a very long time rejected the bayonet, and they did not keep up with advances in European field artillery, which produced more accurate and mobile guns that could fire both grape and canisters. Ottoman commanders paid relatively little attention to strategy and tactics, and did not use the drill in the way it was coming to be used in Europe.

The Ottomans were disadvantaged, as well, by some customs and by the social basis of their military. Their armies were supposed to be led by the sultan or grand vizier, but this belief limited them to fighting only one campaign at a time. The army lacked the option of splitting to confront an attack by two allied enemies from two different directions. Because it was too cold in the West to fight in the winter, and because the cavalry officers were also gentlemen farmers who had to supervise the harvest on their estates in the fall, the army could never fight further than it could march from April through October. As for the infantry, over time Janissary discipline became difficult to maintain. Their salaries were so low that their morale was affected, and many started working part-time as artisans in the cities when not on campaign, intermarrying with the families of other guildsmen. These relationships gave them their own social and economic interests, which were not always the same as those of the sultan. The Janissaries were not at the forefront of adopting new military technology, and they never developed the sorts of drill that European armies did. They tended to fight as an undisciplined crowd, firing at will. In contrast, Europeans developed close-order formations that fired volleys in unison.

The Ottoman state, unlike its European rivals, never created the financial instruments for deficit spending and long-term government debt. Their European enemies could borrow to pay a standing army even in bad times. The Ottomans paid for their wars out of current account balances or by bestowing land on cavalry officers, or by letting troops keep plunder. When the Ottomans could expand and maintain stability at home, they had more of all of these resources to give out. When they lost territory at the frontiers, or lost control of lands in their own interior, however, their current resources shrank rapidly, with losses producing more weakness and more losses. Unable to borrow, they were victims of a reverse snowball effect. They were probably somewhat hurt in the period 1600–1700 by the decline of long-distance transit trade overland from Central Asia and from the Indian Ocean through the Fertile Crescent and the Red Sea. The European route around Africa was in this period made even more economical by Dutch improvements in sailing ships. Although the Ottomans and the other great Muslim empires received most of their revenue from taxes on agriculturists and pastoralists, the luxury transit trade had provided some "cream" in the form of tariffs. In this period towns and trade are recorded as subject to periodic decline in eastern Anatolia, though merchants were inventive and often could come back from such disasters. Some trade continued throughout this period, it should be remembered, as with Iranian silk, Yemeni coffee, Levantine cotton, and textiles manufactured in the empire.

Conclusion Most accounts of the early modern period stress European advances and expansion. In fact, the European era had not yet begun, and Europe remained diverse. Great differences separated French from Sicilians, and the Dutch from the Irish. Between 1400 and 1700, in any case, no great advances in European agricultural productivity, or in overland travel time, were achieved. The impressive state-making achievements of the Muslim gunpowder empires must be accounted one of the more important developments in the early modern period. In sheer military and political power, no single European state was a match for either the Mughal or the Ottoman empire in the 1500s. Certainly, little Portugal, which came to control the Indian Ocean in that century, was not, despite its ability to defeat the Ottomans at sea and the way the Mughals allowed its taxation of a few ports. In a major land battle, either could have easily bested Lisbon, as was demonstrated by Shahjahan in Bengal. Even Iran succeeded in expelling the Portuguese from the Persian Gulf in 1622, albeit with British help.

Nor did the Portuguese empire's advent in the Indian Ocean really change all that much. Its attempt to establish a monopoly in the spice trade and to destroy the routes through the Middle East to the Mediterranean had some success until about 1550, but thereafter failed as the Mediterranean route revived. Portuguese trade does not appear to have actually increased total volume of trade in goods like spices, but rather simply redistributed it toward Western Europe. During the 1500s, in contrast, Akbar built a huge land empire in North India encompassing nearly 100 million persons and many key trade routes, Shah Isma`il and Tahmasp subdued the vast Iranian plateau, and Selim and Suleiman brought under their control enormous territories stretching from Belgrade to Basra and from Tunis to Aleppo. The Ottomans in this period fought the powerful Habsburgs to a standstill, raiding more than once up to their very capital.

The 1600s appear for the most part economically vigorous in India and Iran, but perhaps somewhat less so in the Ottoman empire. In the Mughal and Ottoman empires, the sort of population growth that occurred from 1500–1700 pointed to a moderately well-governed state that provided basic security to its peoples. The Mughals continued their territorial expansion, and at least up until about 1690 the silk trade gave support to the Safavid state. None of these Muslim empires developed printing technology, and so any scientific or technological discoveries their sages and artisans made remained of purely local significance and risked dying out easily. Lack of printing led to low emphasis on literacy, since manuscript reading materials were relatively expensive, and remained the concern of nobles, bureaucrats, clerics, and great merchants. The Middle East and South Asia were plagued by low literacy rates compared to Europe and East Asia from the beginning of the early modern period until fairly recently. A long period in which printing was not adopted, and stretches of colonial rule that was uninterested in universal literacy, help explain the difference.

The great Muslim land empires of about 1500–1700 were strongly shaped by the main factors that made for the early modern period generally. Gunpowder may not have been always decisive, but it certainly came to form part of their military. The low status of the infantrymen who were the first to adopt the matchlock, the continued reliance on heavy cavalry archers, and the lack of technologically advanced neighbors, all retarded Mughal and Safavid advances in weaponry. The Ottoman army was forced to adapt to greater reliance on an armed infantry, which acquitted itself quite well in the 1500s. Later on, earlier European adoption of the flintlock and European innovations in drill and strategy helped stop the Ottoman advance even though they could not roll it back. The spread of matchlocks to Anatolian peasants in the late 1500s, and of flintlocks to Afghan tribesmen in the early 1700s, both had a decentralizing effect, counteracting the earlier centrifugal forces set in motion by the advent of field artillery.

Greater use of money rather than barter trade was now possible, which allowed a bigger and more efficient bureaucracy and taxation regime. At the same time, the influx of silver probably added enough of a steady but small increment to the underlying rate of inflation to prove a source of instability in these ponderous agrarian economies. The rise of the great maritime trading companies had less impact on Mughal India and the Ottoman empire than one might have thought. Most Dutch trade in spices and textiles in the second half of the 1600s was with South India, which only gradually came under Mughal rule, and it was really after 1700 that the Mughal state saw significant benefits from the European trade. Iran did profit from trading silk to the Dutch and British, but its internal network of Armenian merchants may have accounted for a more consistent volume of trade in that commodity. The main impact on the Ottomans of the Dutch maritime empire was probably negative: the rerouting of goods to the Atlantic route rather than the overland routes that transited through Aleppo or Istanbul. Still, the contrasts between Western Europe and the Asian land powers heightened in the succeeding period. England in the eighteenth century built enormous numbers of surfaced roads, improved its naval technology and power, developed sophisticated financial instruments, and used printing technology to spread ideas, inventions, news, and schooling. The great Muslim land powers may have for a time presented a credible set of rivals to the power of seagoing European mercantilism. They were to prove no match for the Europeans of the Industrial Revolution.

Study Questions

(1) What similarities and differences do you see in the Mughal Emperor Akbar and the Ottoman Emperor Suleiman the Magnificent? Both were empire-builders, but they had different styles of rule. Explain.

(2) What were the drawbacks for the Muslim Asian land empires of not adopting printing technology? How might this policy have affected their relative power in comparison with Europe and East Asia, both of which had printing?

(3) What was the role of firearms and artillery in the early modern period? How did this new technology change warfare, conquest, and even the tradition of walled cities?

(4) What was the role of the Portuguese seagoing empire in this period? Was it a sign of European superiority? What were its economic achievements?

(5) How important was Islam as an ideology for the Mughal, Safavid, and Ottoman empires? How did Islam differ in each of the three? What was the role of non-Muslims in each?

(6) If you are a Muslim ruler of a large number of non-Muslim or heterodox Muslim subjects, why would you tolerate their heretical religious practices? Discuss the policies of the Mughals, Ottomans, and Safavids.

Suggested Reading

Mughal Empire MUZAFFAR ALAM AND SANJAY SUBRAHMANYAM (eds.), *The Mughal State, 1526–1750* (Delhi: Oxford University Press, 1998).

M. ATHAR ALI, *The Mughal Nobility Under Aurangzeb*, rev. edn. (Delhi and New York: Oxford University Press, 1997).

Shireen Moosvi, *The Economy of the Mughal Empire, c. 1595: A Statistical Study* (Delhi: Oxford University Press, 1987).

Safavid Iran Said Amir Arjomand, *The Shadow of God and the Hidden Imam: Religion, Political Order, and Societal Change in Shi'ite Iran from the Beginning to 1890* (University of Chicago Press, 1984).

Kathryn Babayan, *Mystics, Monarchs and Messiahs: Cultural Landscapes of Early Modern Iran* (Cambridge, MA: Harvard University Press, 2003).

Rudolph P. Matthee, *The Politics of Trade in Safavid Iran: Silk for Silver, 1600–1730* (Cambridge University Press, 1999).

The Ottoman Empire Halil Inalcik, *The Ottoman Empire: The Classical Age, 1300–1600* (London: Weidenfeld & Nicolson, 1973).

Halil Inalcik and Donald Quataert (eds.), *An Economic and Social History of the Ottoman Empire, 1300–1916* (New York: Cambridge University Press, 1994).

Rhoads Murphey, *Ottoman Warfare, 1500–1700* (New Brunswick, NJ: Rutgers University Press, 1999).

Donald Quataert, *The Ottoman Empire, 1700–1922* (New York: Cambridge University Press, 2000).

Glossary

bhakti: Enthusiastic, mystical form of Hinduism that stressed equality of believers and singing, dancing, and emotion.

Brahmins: Hindu priestly caste.

Celali revolts: A series of peasant revolts in Anatolia against the Ottoman empire from 1596–1610.

ghulams: Slave-soldiers in the standing army of the Safavids.

Jains: Religious sect devoted to non-violence toward all living beings.

Janissaries: Ottoman infantrymen recruited from non-Muslim families, enslaved, and raised Muslim.

Marathas: A Hindu people of southwestern India who speak Marathi and resisted complete incorporation into the Mughal empire.

Now-Ruz: The Persian New Year, adopted in eastern Muslim cultures from the old Zoroastrian calendar. It falls on the first day of spring.

Panjab: Province of India, literally "the land of five rivers." Also spelled Punjab.

Parsi: Zoroastrian community of western India. Also spelled Parsee.

Qizilbash: Turkic-speaking tribespeople who became committed Shi`ites and helped conquer Iran for the Safavid dynasty.

Rajput: War-like, pastoral nomadic Hindus of northwest India who allied themselves with Mughals.

Sikhs: Religious movement founded in the 1500s by Guru Nanak in Panjab. It has a background in Hinduism but is monotheistic like Islam.

Sufi: Mystical form of Islam that stresses morals and feelings more than law and is centered on attendance at the shrines of saints, said to bestow blessings.

Taj Mahal: Magnificent tomb built by Shahjahan for his deceased wife, laid out on the plan of paradise.

timars: Landed estates given to cavalry officers by the Ottoman sultan as a way of paying them.

ulama: Seminary-trained Muslim learned men.

Usuli: Legal school of Shi`ite Islam that stressed the duty of laypersons without a seminary education to follow the rulings of trained jurists, who use techniques of reasoning to determine the law.

vizier: First minister to the ruler or sultan in Muslim empires. Viziers often gained substantial executive power.

2 Centralization and commercialization in Russia, Central Eurasia, and East Asia

China	
1368–1644	Ming dynasty.
1555	Pirates besiege Nanjing.
1557	Portuguese permanent settlement at Macao.
1560	*The Golden Lotus* (pornographic Ming novel) published.
1582	Jesuit mission in China begins under Matteo Ricci.
1592–93, 1597–98	Japanese invasions of Korea repelled.
1616	Nurhaci declares Latter Jin dynasty.
1636	Manchus declare Qing dynasty at Mukden (but it does not succeed the Ming dynasty in China proper until 1644).
1644	Conquest of Beijing by Manchus.
1644–1912	Qing dynasty.
1661	Accession of Kangxi emperor, aged 8, personal rule 1669–1722.
1674–81	Revolt of Three Feudatories.
1693–1700	Rites controversy.
1697	Kangxi emperor defeats Galdan.
1722	Yongzheng emperor ends Jesuit mission.

Russia	
1478	Ivan III annexes Novgorod.
1547	Ivan IV is crowned Tsar.
1552, 1556	Muscovy's conquests of Kazan and Astrakhan open a door to the East.
1558	Livonian War begins.
1565–72	Time of oprichnina.
1582	The Cossack Yermak begins.
1584	Ivan IV dies.
1598–1613	Time of Troubles.
1613	Michael Romanov elected tsar by zemsky sobor.
1648	Revolt in Moscow.

1649	Law code enforces serfdom.
1666–67	Revision of church ritual, secession of Old Believers.
1670–71	Stenka Razin revolt.
1682–1725	Reign of Peter the Great (b. 1672).
1689	Treaty of Nerchinsk with China.
1700–21	Great Northern War.
1703	St. Petersburg founded.
1709	Battle of Poltava breaks Sweden.
Japan	
1467	Civil wars break out in Japan.
1543	First arrival of Portuguese, with firearms, in Japan.
1549	Arrival of Francis Xavier.
1600	Tokugawa Ieyasu defeats his rivals in the battle of Sekigahara.
1603	Ieyasu claims shogunate.
1637	Final suppression of Christianity and restriction of foreign trade begins period of isolation (*sakoku*).
1701–03	Forty-seven ronin incident.

In 1682, the boyars of Russia chose the vigorous 10-year-old boy Peter as their new tsar, with his mother Natalia as regent. Unfortunately, Peter's accession was immediately challenged by relatives of his older half-sister Sophia. A mob of dissatisfied musketeers broke into the Kremlin square, slaughtered the top boyars, murdered Peter's brother, but swore loyalty to the new tsar. Peter and his mother, still fearing for their lives, fled the capital. For the rest of his life, Peter hated Moscow, the Kremlin, and all it represented: intrigue, violence, superstition, and anarchy. He resolved to build an orderly state that insisted on honest service from all its subjects. As a youngster growing up in the suburbs of Moscow, he played with foreigners who taught him how to train his own soldiers. He learned to build his own ships. When he grew up, Peter forced the Russian people into the world of Western European states. But Russia also expanded to the borders of China, where it met the equally dynamic **Kangxi emperor**. The Kangxi emperor also came to the throne as a young man, challenged his elder relatives, and made China both strong and actively engaged with Western European powers. By 1700, these two vigorous rulers had made their states the dominant powers of Eurasia.

Despite the "discoveries" of the New World, the gunpowder revolution, and the spread of European empires to Asia, Europeans still had only marginal impacts on dense Asian trade networks, and little military power on the continent. Portuguese and Dutch superiority in naval guns guaranteed them only small

footholds. By 1700, China and Japan had ousted or blocked Christian missionaries and European merchants. The interior of Eurasia still commanded greater strategic attention than the coast.

Tribesmen from Manchuria created China's largest, most dynamic, and wealthiest empire, the Qing dynasty (1644–1912). Japan and Russia emerged from destructive civil war as powerful, pacified states. Russia, like China, built an enormous empire. Japan, by contrast, bureaucratized and commercialized without facing military competition. After a brief, humiliating intervention in Korea, Japanese rulers turned inward, but they gradually absorbed much of China's bureaucratic philosophy. Abundant flows of silver from Japan and the New World energized China's economy, while Russia plundered Siberia's furs to obtain bullion from China and the Middle East. Over these two centuries, even the most reactionary rulers had to respond to the rising importance of trade. Global silver flows linked regions together, provided resources for state-builders and merchants, but also disrupted agrarian social orders.

We shall examine four patterns of development in Eurasia during these centuries:

- Centralization of state power.
- The spread of bureaucratic techniques.
- The diffusion of a commercial economy.
- Cultural integration.

2.1 SIXTEENTH-CENTURY CHINESE TRADE

In 1600, China was unquestionably the richest and largest economy in the world. Commerce flourished on the rivers of the lower Yangtze Valley (**Jiangnan**). Here large cities stood at the top of an extensive hierarchy of market towns, extending into the highly productive countryside. China's population reached 150 to 175 million people by 1600, or 25 to 30 percent of the world. The Ming empire (1368–1644) completed the Great Wall to hold off nomadic attacks, and merchants moved out from Jiangnan to the southeast coast, the interior Yangtze Valley, North China, and the garrisons in the northwest. These merchants brought new goods to popular markets and read new literature in the vernacular language. Because commerce so decisively shaped politics and culture, we can call this period China's "early modern" era.

Nostalgic Confucian literati thought that something had gone wrong. They thought that an obsessive drive for wealth had corroded social values, as the newly rich proudly showed off "superfluous things," like exquisite collections of rocks, porcelain, gardens, and paintings. They praised the simpler life of earlier times, when peasants labored in the fields to support their families, women made clothing only for their family, merchants knew their place, and scholars only concentrated on learning, not consumption. They argued that everyone should practice restraint, the government should discourage mobility and trade, and loans should only charge low interest rates. But the backward-looking scholars could not stop change. Vigorous pursuit of monetary gain pervaded Ming China, as markets ran roughshod over official prohibitions.

Many people still have the mistaken belief that the Ming rulers shut down maritime trade after the early fifteenth century. On the contrary, Ming officials never completely banned maritime trade. They only prohibited exports of strategic goods. But the arrival of the Portuguese in the Philippines from 1500 to 1520 confirmed their worst fears about foreign traders. The Portuguese, with their long-range naval guns, plundered or sank nearly every competing trading vessel and butchered Chinese merchants in Malacca in 1511. As the regional economy connecting China and Southeast Asia fell into a slump, violent trade conflicts increased. Bans on foreign trade had no effect. The traders simply moved to offshore islands. Pirates also raided the coast in the 1540s and 1550s, when famine drove Chinese sailors, Japanese, and other foreigners to "raid where they could not trade."[1] But gradually profits overcame prejudice, and regular trade replaced piracy and suppression. In 1557 the Portuguese established a legal treaty port in Macao. In the 1560s and 1570s, coastal officials lifted the ban on overseas trade, just as the Spanish conquered the Philippines and opened the great silver mines of Potosi, Bolivia.

Silver Flows Unite the World

A great flow of silver tied together the first truly global economy. The demand for silver, the indispensable lubricant, had grown even before the New World mines opened. Chinese first obtained bullion (lumps of silver and gold) from Japan, but the arrival of Pacific silver greatly stimulated coastal exports, as tea, silk, and porcelain flowed out through Southeast Asia to European consumers. In return, the Europeans had little to offer besides bullion and guns. Anxious commentators focused on the trade deficit with Asia, but in China, by contrast, it was the influx of silver that caused concern.

Chinese villagers paid for local needs in copper cash. They paid taxes in kind and provided corvée labor to the state. But this began to change, as local officials took advantage of the spread of silver currency to begin a remarkable tax reform from the bottom up. They consolidated many small payments into lump sums in silver levied in approximate proportion to land value. **Zhang Juzheng**, the great reforming Grand Secretary, finally made silver taxes compulsory in 1582. Supplying the northwest frontier on behalf of the state turned into a profitable business for frontier merchants. Under the old system, merchants who had purchased monopoly licenses to trade in salt delivered grain and cloth to the garrisons. Now, the government simply paid them in silver to perform the task.

With these changes, silver dispersed from the southeastern and Japanese entry points into the small capillaries of rural trading systems and the underdeveloped frontiers. Chinese peasants and traders sucked up most of the world's silver, but they did not freeze it in hoarding; instead, the silver flow fueled an expansive money economy that knitted the country's regions together. Silver plus the Grand Canal ensured that China would never break apart again for long.

The Grand Canal and Great Wall Also Foster Trade

The cancellation of the early Ming ship voyages did not slow down innovation. China completed two of the world's greatest civil engineering projects – the Great Wall and the Grand Canal – in the sixteenth century. In the eighth century, rulers had a canal dug to supply their capital, and the Mongols in the thirteenth century extended it, but the Ming canal had the largest shipping volume. By 1430, 160,000 transport soldiers carried over 350,000 metric tons annually to Beijing, in barges carrying 30 metric tons of grain each. Hundreds of thousands of laborers dredged the canal bed. The canal, China's greatest

Box 2.1 Chinese Literati Lament Luxury and the Loss of Moral Values

For conservative Chinese, the early Ming preserved a simple, rural, self-sufficient economy. Taxation was light, and paid only in kind. In their idealized view, officials were revered; no one had ambitions to move, or sufferings to flee. As one local gazetteer writer put it: "Most rural residents are simple, upright folk, whereas in the city … some are fond of cheating others, dressing in fancy clothes and taking pleasure in making luxury articles."

But now, they thought, money ruled. As one scholar said, people "rush after [profits] like torrents pouring into a valley … never reaching the point at which the raging floods within them subside." They lamented change, but could not stop it. Another said, "One man in a hundred is rich, while nine out of ten are impoverished. The poor cannot stand up to the rich, who, though few in number, are able to control the majority. The lord of silver rules heaven and the god of copper cash reigns over the earth."

north–south commercial artery, also linked North China's cotton-growing regions to the mills of Jiangnan. It carried private and official letters as well as visiting foreign delegations. One could travel from Ningbo in the south to Beijing in the north in 49 days, at an average rate of over 28 miles per day. The canal brought prosperity to China's poor north and rich south, but it also fostered mobility, crime, and disease. Great epidemics in 1641–42, originating in the northwest, spread rapidly south along the canal, killing up to half the population in some southern counties.

At first, military detachments administered grain transport, but when the soldiers went to war, civilians helped out. Canal transport, a vital lifeline, gradually slipped out from under imperial control. Initially, military officials fined wealthy "grain administrators" for failing to deliver their heavy tax quotas. In response, the grain administrators illegally contracted with violent "bullies" to protect their shipments and defy officials. The only way to keep the system from collapsing was to allow private merchants to use 10 or 15 percent of the total fleet. Many of the transport soldiers deserted, turning to piracy or smuggling. A drop in shipments to Beijing alarmed officials, but piracy made sea transport too dangerous. On the other hand, higher local production of grain in North China made the canal shipments from the south less critical.

The Qing dynasty simplified canal transport radically. Merchants built the boats and civilians completely replaced soldiers. Boatmen, transport officials, and powerful merchants colluded against local people and provincial officials. The great Ming canal project, which had constructed the world's largest state-led logistical network, ended up in the eighteenth century as a flourishing, corrupt and violent network of private transport businesses.

The Great Wall, too, was a product of China's commercial society. Only a government that could pay with silver could build brick kilns and quarries, and carry materials to distant frontiers to support the corvée peasant laborers on the wall. It showed Ming China's greatest strengths – its massive commercial wealth and its great expertise in logistics – and its greatest weaknesses: its exclusion of frontier peoples and its lack of strong leadership.

New Foods Come to China

Besides silver, the southeast coastal trade brought China crops from the New World, changing the Chinese diet and helping the population to grow. Peasants left overcrowded valleys to plant them. The nutritious maize and sweet potato and spicy chili peppers could grow on poor, eroded hillsides without backbreaking labor. Fujian province in the southeast, for example, had poor soils, but prospered from tobacco exports. These imports added variety to the Chinese diet. *Gongbao jiding* (chicken with chilies and cashews), a classic dish, gets its main flavorings from the New World (see Figure 2.1).

China also exported sugar to Southeast Asia and the West. Buddhist missionaries had brought sugar from India in the eighth century CE. By the thirteenth century, doctors knew that it rotted teeth, but only in the sixteenth century did it enter the regular Chinese diet. In Fujian and Guangdong, sugarcane production grew rapidly, and by the eighteenth century China was one of the world's largest sugar producers. Sugar went well with the new foods: peanut brittle candies mixed New World nuts with Chinese cane. China's per capita consumption of about 2 pounds was comparable to that of France. Only England and the Netherlands were ahead.

Commercialization

As the sugar trade shows, Europeans did not bring global trade to Asia. they only entered as marginal actors in already thriving, large-scale, intra-Asian networks. The Dutch brought over 4 million pounds of Chinese sugar to Amsterdam in 1637, while

Box 2.2 The Great Wall: Myth and Reality

For most foreign observers in modern times, the Great Wall has always been a central image of China. You might imagine it as an ancient barrier built at immense human cost, lined with towers, beacons, and horsemen, holding off nomadic conquerors from China's heartland. In fact, most of this conventional wisdom (including the idea that it is the only man-made object visible from outer space) is myth. Nearly all dynasties built walls of varying length, and Qin Shihuangdi, the first Chinese emperor, of the third century BCE, did link together many of the walls of his time. But only in the sixteenth century did a dynasty build a continuous defensive barrier along the northwest frontier.

The distinctive characteristics of Ming China made this immense feat feasible. More aggressive dynasties, like the Tang and Qing, drove back nomads so far that there was no need for a wall. The defensive Song dynasty, after losing control of North China, kept away its enemies with river barriers and heavy tribute payments. Ming China, ruled by Han Chinese from the south who had little familiarity with the north and nothing but contempt for nomads, could never pursue aggressive military campaigns into the steppe after the fifteenth century. The expensive Great Wall strategy was only a fallback when trade and war failed. Wall-building was no one's first choice.

It ran from Jiayuguan in the west, in modern Gansu province, through Ningxia, south of the great bend of the Yellow River, in the Ordos region, across northern Shanxi, around Beijing, to meet the sea at Shanhaiguan. Nine border garrisons occupied key defensive positions. At Badaling (where most tourists visit the wall today), 40 miles northwest of Beijing, a great arch displays inscriptions in Sanskrit, Tangut, Uighur Turkish, Tibetan, Mongolian, and Chinese.

Plausible estimates of the wall's length range from 1,500 to 2,500 miles. At its best spots, men on horseback could ride on top of its wide brick paths, but in many parts it was only made of earth. Garrisons of men and horses stationed in defensive outposts along the wall ranged from several hundred to several thousand. Positions for firearms and blockhouses on the wall also helped to terrify the Mongols and to support raiding parties. The towers spaced along the wall were, however, the most important part. Because the nomads moved so rapidly, communications mattered more than defensive brickwork. Beacon fires told commanders to rush forces to a vulnerable spot to resist raids.

These layers of defensive barriers still did not stop the Mongols. In 1550 they went around the wall to the northeast, camped in the suburbs of Beijing, and looted the surrounding countryside. Costly extensions of the walls across the northeast temporarily held off Mongol raids. The Ming rulers never established peaceful diplomatic or commercial relations with their neighbors in the steppe. Like France's Maginot line, built unsuccessfully to stop German invasion in the early twentieth century, China's wall was a temporary political solution, and an inadequate strategic defense work.

---

they also sponsored cultivation in Batavia and Taiwan. The Dutch and British soon discovered that the biggest profits lay in the trade between Asian ports. In the 1630s maybe 40,000 tons of goods were transported in Chinese ships in Asian seas as compared to between 12,000 and 14,000 tons on Dutch ships. Thus China's southern and southeastern coastal regions kept up their global trade, defying official frowns.

Domestic crop production – cotton, silk, and grain – became much more highly commercialized in the sixteenth and seventeenth centuries. Plantations based on larger estates and hired labor exported raw cotton from North China to the spinning and weaving centers in Jiangnan. Although monetized taxation and the Grand Canal helped textile production everywhere, the center of specialized planting and weaving remained in the lower Yangtze Valley. Songjiang county (now Shanghai) planted as much as 90 percent of its land in cotton. No longer did one peasant household grow, spin, and weave its own cloth. Merchants bought ginned cotton, sold it to spinners, bought the yarn to distribute to weavers, and sold the cloth to wholesale dealers.

This production process looks like the "putting-out" system of early modern Europe, which many historians see as the "proto-industrial" stage leading to full-fledged capitalism. But it was not exactly the same. No one group of merchants controlled the entire production process, nor did merchant capital genuinely drive the peasant producers' activities. Instead, many merchants bought and sold in many markets; some could monopolize the peasants' output with usurious loans, but none could truly eliminate the independent peasants' control over relations of production.

Converting to commercial cropping could be risky. Lower Yangtze cloth producers now depended more heavily on grain exports from the middle Yangtze Valley. A failed harvest, or

Figure 2.1 Restaurants around the world now feature this Chinese dish, Gongbao Jiding, which contains chicken, nuts, and chili peppers, but it originated in the sixteenth century, when ingredients from the New World first entered Chinese cuisine.

floods on the Yangtze, could easily cause famine. Heavily indebted peasants could go bankrupt when prices fell. If they lost their land, they had to become hired laborers, refugees, or bandits. These were not "proletarian" rural laborers, but such insecure mobile populations caused anxiety.

2.2 POPULAR AND ELITE CHINESE CULTURE

The spread of markets expanded the distribution of printed books. The Chinese had, of course, invented printing in the eighth century CE. The first mass-produced religious literature was not the Gutenberg Bible, but Buddhist sutras. During the Ming, published materials reached a large urban population. The basic technology did not change, but the number of book-sellers and supply of paper, ink, and woodblock carvers increased. Publishing centers emerged in surprising places. Suzhou, the mercantile and artistic capital of Jiangnan, produced the highest quality books, at the highest prices, but Fujian's interior, where abundant bamboo forests made paper cheap, sent books over 600 miles north to Nanjing. Erudite gentry caught a collectors' frenzy. In the sixteenth century, famous collectors gathered 1,000 volumes in a private library; by the seventeenth century, collections of up to 5,000 volumes were not rare.

The distribution of knowledge, however, was uneven. Officials tried to educate farmers about advanced plowing techniques by publishing agricultural manuals and promoting demonstration fields. On the other hand, specialized craftsmen jealously guarded their professional secrets. Publishers of herbal manuals criticized doctors who concealed their healing techniques.

Unlike what some claim for sixteenth-century Europe, mass printing did not cause China to break through from an oral to a literate culture, nor did printing undermine the empire's unity. China's literate elite favored the wide dissemination of knowledge, thinking that vernacular literature would help to hold society together. Printing circulated the classic texts, commentaries on them, lectures, letters, and short stories throughout society. Even though only a minority could read classical Chinese, the urban publics could attend lectures, storytellers' recitals, dramas, and puppet shows putting the ancient wisdom into vernacular forms.

With a few exceptions, the emperors did not try to censor this flood of information. European printing, requiring substantial capital investment in metal presses, could be controlled, but in China, anyone could hire woodcarvers. The Chinese solution to the dangers of heterodoxy was to drown the people in more information. So the first Ming emperor had his pronouncements against evil and corruption printed on a wide scale and made required reading for examination students. Classical texts, law cases, and administrative handbooks guided officials, while morality books and stories of heroes gave models to the public. Officials printed multiple copies of blank forms for registering land. Still, the reading public wanted more than the official word. They wanted language primers, almanacs to foretell auspicious days, divination rituals, religious tracts, and erotic stories. Plenty of booksellers could satisfy their demand.

Couriers took private letters long distances, bringing ideas to scholars and deals for merchants. Scholars' letters could turn into published works. The philosopher Li Zhi (1527–1602) published his debates with his opponents before he committed suicide. Several leading philosophers, like Wang Yangming and Li Zhi, denounced the stultifying effect of memorization for exams, urging their disciples to find moral values within themselves. These networks especially helped women. They could write to fellow artists, poets, and religious believers, even if their husbands kept them secluded at home.

The official world enforced conformity through the examination system. In these "cultural prisons," students had to reproduce the orthodox version of the Song philosopher Zhu Xi's Confucianism to obtain degrees. Every three years, only a few hundred out of 50,000 to 75,000 provincial degree candidates would pass, and most of them would never get an official post. Intensive mass competition for degrees focused China's brightest minds on a single goal but inflicted immense mental strain. Frustrated scholars had rebellious dreams. Students tried desperate measures to get ahead, including cheating (inscribing characters in one's robe) and appeals to divination and magic. Examiners, as they do everywhere, condemned students' efforts to beat the system, and tried hard to remove favoritism and arbitrariness. Popular novels and advice books saw the examination system not as selection by merit, but as an arbitrary, capricious institution that raised a few to the heights of power and dashed most into despair.

The exam system, however, had considerable flexibility. Not all the questions asked for simple regurgitation. Like many of today's exams, fill-in-the-blanks or multiple choice questions dominated, but the essay questions varied over time. A surprising number of questions in the Ming asked about the natural world. Questions on astronomy, calendrical calculation, mathematical harmonics, and philology all allowed promising candidates to develop technical intellectual skills, akin to the scientific method. The exams and their examiners reflected broader intellectual trends of the sixteenth century, open to new views of the natural and human world. This openness disappeared after the Qing conquest of the mid seventeenth century, when the Kangxi emperor banned dangerous questions on heavenly portents and the calendar.

2.3 THE LAST EFFORTS AT MING REFORM

Ming China headed downhill quickly in the seventeenth century. By 1600, Ming population had grown to 150 to 175 million, but the registered population remained only a little over 60 million, the same as 1400. Clearly, many wealthy elites and peasants evaded registration. But this light taxation only caused resentment at obvious inequalities. Rent resistance movements and uprisings by bondservants tore apart rural society, while garrison soldiers deserted and commanders pocketed their rations.

Clearly, reforms were needed. Grand Secretary Zhang Juzheng was determined to enforce austerity on the court and efficiency in the provinces. Zhang told the emperor to cut back the imperial household of 20,000 eunuchs and 3,000 palace women. He also insisted on full payment of taxes and launched a national land survey to uncover concealed land, generating a storm of criticism. When scholars attacked him for refusing to leave office on the death of his father, he had them beaten. Zhang himself lived in high style and cultivated his own favorites to offset the patronage networks of his enemies. Although his harsh methods might have saved the dynasty from collapse, few grieved at his death in 1582. Instead, the young **Wanli emperor** (r. 1572–1620) released his victims and confiscated Zhang's property. The next Grand Secretaries gave in to the interests of local officials and elites.

Without a strong person at the top, factionalism tore apart the bureaucracy. Political rivalries among literati factions, eunuchs, and imperial relatives paralyzed decision-making. The sensitive, intelligent, but feckless Wanli emperor refused to enforce discipline. Defying convention, he insisted that the son of his beloved concubine succeed him to the throne. His second great interest was his own tomb, the great modern tourist site built at colossal expense outside Beijing. Bored with ceremonies, he refused to confirm appointments or give direct orders; eunuchs took care of official business. The bureaucrats themselves did not want the emperor to know too much about how the country really ran, so they kept him confined to the palace compound.

Some officials perceptively diagnosed the empire's moral and fiscal failure, sounding remarkably like critics in the Ottoman and Habsburg empires. Like the Ottoman Katib Celebi, they attacked decline and called for reform. At the **Donglin academy** in Jiangsu province, scholars insisted that high moral principles must govern public life. They conducted lectures, held annual meetings, and even sang together to reinforce their solidarity. Critics of the Donglin at court attacked them for improper interference in political affairs. The powerful eunuch **Wei Zhongxian**, the de facto policy-maker in Beijing from 1612 to 1627, had several Donglin supporters killed, purged the organization, and stripped its members of their degrees. In 1626 he ordered the academy destroyed. In 1627, however, a new emperor dismissed Wei, restoring the academy, but eliminating its political influence.

After the suppression of the Donglin, a new academy movement, the **Fushe**, tried to create a true political organization by putting private funds into national communication networks. They focused more on concrete policy issues like famine

Box 2.3 Iconoclasts, Dissenters, Rovers, and Rebels

Wang Yangming (1472–1529) shook up orthodox Chinese philosophy as radically as Martin Luther did Christianity. He was no typical student. He thought that he must examine objects in the world to discover the rational principle (*li*) behind them. But after intensive meditation in a bamboo grove for seven days, he fell ill and suffered a spiritual crisis. In 1506, serving in exile in the remote southwest, living with poor aboriginal peoples, he suddenly realized that the true source of understanding was not in the world, but in the mind (*xin*). "My own nature," he said, "is, of course, sufficient for me to attain sagehood. And I have been mistaken in searching for the *li* in external things and affairs." Wang argued that moral principles originate in the individual's mind and that scholars must put their deepest moral beliefs into practice.

Wang, unlike most philosophers, was a talented administrator and even military strategist. He defeated rebellions, relieved tax burdens, and gained fame for delivering justice. He gathered villagers together with officials at banquets for collective "self-criticism" sessions to improve local government. Hundreds of disciples spread Wang's idea of "innate knowledge of the good," and some even preached to mass assemblies. Wang also inspired followers in Japan, like Kumazawa Banzan (1619–91), arrested for attacking the *sankin kotai* system, and Nakae Toju (1608–48), who abandoned government service to teach in village schools.

His idea of "the unity of thought and action" inspired everyone from Tokugawa Japanese intellectuals, samurai, and the leaders of the Meiji Restoration to Sun Yat-sen and Mao Zedong. In the powerful influence of Wang and his followers, we can detect signs of individualism and liberalism in Confucian guise, driven by new social mobility and intellectual development.

Both Wang Yangming and Luther suffered serious spiritual crises, attacked the establishment, and spread their doctrines by the printed word. Just as Catholics attacked Luther for dividing Christendom, critics attacked Wang's doctrine as "wild Ch'an [Zen]" Buddhism and blamed him and his disciples for causing the moral degeneration that allegedly led to the collapse of the Ming dynasty. But Wang became an honored official and scholar by the end of the Ming, and the dynasty fell not because of him but because of deeper fiscal and institutional weaknesses.

The passionate, bitter skeptic Li Zhi (1527–1602) took Wang's inwardness to extremes. He had a Muslim background and came from coastal, mercantile Fujian. He hated all organized creeds and especially the examination system. Unlike Wang Yangming, Li did not serve the common people, but became a monk. In his famous work *A Book to Be Burned*, he attacked Confucian rationalist metaphysics. An angry mob burned down his temple home, while conservatives had him arrested. To protest his imprisonment, Li committed suicide by slashing his throat.

Li Zhi, like Nietzsche, insisted that heroic, strong men must defy social norms. He even admired the despotic emperor of Qin. Many modern scholars see Li as a martyr for intellectual independence, although he himself was intolerant. His books circulated widely in the late Ming atmosphere of tolerance, skepticism, and decadence.

Three men, however, who refused to serve the Qing wrote daring critiques of the autocratic state. Huang Zongxi (1610–95), in *Waiting for an Enlightened Prince* (1662), attacked the emperor for thinking that the entire realm was his personal property. Anticipating the French liberal philosopher Montesquieu, he argued for local freedoms based on the security of a hereditary elite, one closer to the "feudal" nobility of ancient China. Gu Yanwu (1613–82) looked to resist autocratic power by investigating regions suitable for guerrilla warfare. He blamed Ming philosophy for bringing down the empire. The most eccentric of all, Wang Fuzhi (1619–92), found an unbridgeable divide between barbarian Manchus and civilized Han. In his defiant, openly racialist categorizations, he rejected multicultural integration and laid the basis for virulent anti-Manchu nationalism.

---

relief, tax reform, and public works than the Donglin, and they sponsored important collections of writings on statecraft. They gained substantial regional power in Nanjing in the last years of the Ming, but most were executed or driven into exile under the Qing.

The Donglin and Fushe movements stand out as rare examples of collective political organization by the literate elite outside the official bureaucracy to promote reform. Confucian political teaching supported the right of individuals to protest improper behavior by the ruler, but discouraged "factionalism," or group dissent. These scholars were not true democrats or liberals: they advocated only moral transformation, not institutional change. But like the "individualist" followers of Wang Yangming, whom they detested, they

Box 2.4 Chinese Vernacular Literature

In the late Ming, the popular Chinese novel came into its own. Ever since Song times, fast-talking storytellers on the streets had turned sages, warriors, and statesmen into lovers, gods, and heroes. Elitists looked down on novels, but several eccentric scholars used them to write works filled with details of family life. Three of the six most famous ones were published in the sixteenth century: *The Romance of the Three Kingdoms*, *Jin Ping Mei* (or *The Golden Lotus*), and *Journey to the West* (or *Monkey*). (For a discussion of a fourth novel, *Outlaws of the Marsh*, see Chapter 13.)

The Romance of the Three Kingdoms tells about the battles and intrigues following the fall of the Han dynasty, when good King Liu Bei, a descendant of the Han royal house devoted to justice, and his blood brothers, Guan Yu and Zhang Fei, courageous, honorable strongmen, lose to the arch villain Cao Cao. Popular tradition deified the heroic warrior Guan Yu, and admired the clever schemes of Liu Bei's master strategist Zhuge Liang. As recommended in Sun Tzu's *Art of War*, Zhuge Liang defeated a superior foe while minimizing the use of force. Like Odysseus and his patroness Athena, he is the ultimate master of cunning wisdom. Mao Zedong in fact studied the stratagems of the *Three Kingdoms* as a guide to guerrilla warfare.

In *The Golden Lotus*, the upright Wu Song leaves home, and his wife Lotus is seduced by the unscrupulous Ximen Qing. Its hundred chapters describe life in a wealthy merchant household, including graphic sex scenes that until recently could only be translated into Latin. The innocent Lotus turns into a nymphomaniac whose passion literally arouses Ximen Qing to death. Then Wu Song returns, like Odysseus, to his endangered household, and sets things right by slaughter. The strange (to us) mixture of businesslike description of merchant affairs with equally clinical pornography indicates the wide-ranging tastes of Ming readers, who formed a genuine middle-class, but far from Victorian, audience.

Journey to the West unites a deep spiritual quest with magic, violence, adventure, comedy, and picaresque travel. Nominally, it portrays the historical journey of the monk Tripitaka to India to obtain sacred scriptures, but Tripitaka's two animal companions steal the story. Greedy Pigsy, a fat hog with a vicious rake for a weapon, constantly gets Tripitaka into trouble, but fights valiantly to rescue him. He represents human lust.

Mischievous Monkey, the most brilliant creation of the Chinese novel tradition, probably originates in popular stories told by Indian Buddhists and may have a connection to the Hindu deity Hanuman and the Indian Buddhist concept of *upaya*, or "skillful means." When he stole the sacred peaches from heaven, he was banished to earth to help mortals find salvation. Despite demons and seductive women, Monkey's enormous magical powers, controlled by Guanyin, the Buddhist manifestation of compassion, guide the pilgrims to their goal. This fantastic and humorous novel is much more entertaining than *The Pilgrim's Progress* and almost as rambunctious as Rabelais. Monkey's clever tricks, like those of Zhuge Liang, exalt the role of cunning. Monkey's sharp eyes, like "glinting-eyed Athena," perceive the demonic traps missed by the obtuse, blind Tripitaka. Guanyin, however, also uses deception and coercion over Monkey to convert him to a saint. Monkey is really an allegory for the "monkey-Mind": The novel exalts the creativity of human intelligence.

---

expressed hopes for change in a fluid society. Unfortunately, China's "sprouts of liberalism" soon withered under the turmoil of the last years of the dynasty.

In these troubled times, some Ming literati, inspired by Buddhist ideals of compassion and by Confucian goals of harmonious social relations, tried to improve society by practicing philanthropy. They might purchase and release birds and fishes, feed rice gruel to the starving, or sponsor orphanages, old age homes, and homeless shelters. Qi Biaojia (1602–45) wrote a 200-page diary describing his efforts to relieve a famine in his home town. Relief workers today face many of the same practical dilemmas: how to purchase grain, how to set up soup kitchens, how to regulate grain prices, and how to co-ordinate the activities of local elites.

2.4 THE COLLAPSE OF THE MING: THE EAST ASIAN SEVENTEENTH-CENTURY CRISIS

Crisis struck major states across Eurasia in the seventeenth century. The English Civil War, French religious wars, the Thirty Years' War in Europe, rebellions in Spain, Russia's Time of Troubles, and the military upheavals in China and Japan do not have one single cause, but similar patterns do appear.

The underlying factors include climatic change (the Little Ice Age), population pressure, fiscal limitations, decline in silver flows, and blocked mobility of aspiring elites. In each region, however, specific military and state formations modified the general upheaval. Ming China collapsed from a classic combination of internal unrest and external invasion on its northwest and northeast frontiers.

The revolts took different forms in different parts of Eurasia. Unemployed, unpaid soldiers touched them off in many places. In Anatolia, as in Ming China, the soldiers set up new regimes. But the Anatolian soldiers quickly surrendered to the Ottomans when they received their back pay, allowing the empire to survive. In China, by contrast, rebel leaders directly challenged the center. While the Ottoman rebels relied on soldiers, students, and provincial magnates, China's rebel armies also gathered peasant support. Ultimately, the Chinese rebels failed because of the Manchu invasion. In Russia, the Cossacks of the southern steppe rebelled against the Muscovite state, and eventually worked out a measure of independence. French peasants revolted too, against excessive rents and taxes. By the mid seventeenth century, all these agrarian empires had stabilized themselves.

Central Eurasia in the Sixteenth and Seventeenth Centuries: Rise of the Manchus

Across Eurasia, centralization, commercialization, and religious consolidation went together. Ming China reinforced Confucian orthodoxy, the Shaybanid khans of the Uzbek state had close ties to Sufi Islamic orders, and the Tibetans and Mongols relied on Buddhist lamas. Most successful of all in fusing trade, state power, and ideology, however, were the Manchus northeast of China, who conquered the Ming state and Central Eurasia together.

Ming emperors had eventually learned how to hold off Mongol attacks in the northwest. In the mid sixteenth century, Altan Khan led a Mongolian tribal alliance that repeatedly raided the Chinese frontier, then asked to open border trade, which Ming officials indignantly refused. This damaging cycle of raid, request, and refusal continued until 1570, when the astute Zhang Juzheng negotiated a truce. Altan Khan, under the title of "Submissive Prince," gained the right to "offer tribute," that is, to sell poor quality horses to the Chinese at high prices in exchange for valuable supplies of metal goods, silk, tea, and farm tools. He founded a city which became modern Hohhot, capital of Inner Mongolia. Most important, in 1578 he granted the monk Sodnam Gyamtsho, leader of the Yellow Sect of Tibetan Buddhism, the title of "Dalai Lama" (Oceanic Teacher). The Dalai Lama declared Altan Khan to be a reincarnation of Khubilai Khan, and Altan Khan declared Tibetan Buddhism the

religion of all the Mongols. Soon after, the Ming also gave the Dalai Lama a Chinese title. Thus began a triangular strategic relationship between Tibet, Mongolia, and China that affected frontier policy for the next two hundred years. The Dalai Lamas now secured control in Lhasa, the Mongols converted enthusiastically to Buddhism, and the Chinese attempted to use the Buddhist church to gain Mongolian loyalty. Upon Altan's death in 1582, the Mongols fell apart again, and the northwest frontier remained relatively quiet.

The most successful Central Asian challengers to Ming rule came not from Mongolia, but from the broad valleys of the Amur, Liao, Sungari and Yalu rivers in Manchuria. Since the twelfth century, the Jurchen tribes, predecessors of the Manchus, had lived there in scattered settlements mainly from hunting, forest products, and fishing. A Ming commander in **Liaodong** (a region in southern Manchuria, and the core of the Qing state in the early seventeenth century) defended Beijing and granted trading licenses to local chieftains. Nurhaci (1559–1626), the builder of the new Manchu state, was a chieftain who prospered from his close contacts with the Ming. Nurhaci's rise as a frontier chieftain on the border of a rich empire, with patronage from frontier commanders, recalls the methods used by Muscovy under the Mongol empire, and those of the early Ottomans in relation to Byzantium. Each of them drew on the resources of a wealthy imperial neighbor to strengthen their power in a poorer, less strictly controlled borderland. In 1583, at age 25, he took control of his clan and began to expand his control. The Ming commander gave him the rank of brigadier general, and the Mongols named him Kundulun Khan. For proposing (but not actually fighting) to help rescue Korea from invasion by the Japanese military ruler Hideyoshi in 1592, the Ming gave him the highest military title ever given to a Manchu, and Nurhaci profited from exporting ginseng, fur, and pearls to Korea and China. The Manchu state expanded its control in the remote northeast border region beyond the Ming but also profited from international trade routes.

In 1599, Nurhaci ordered his advisors to create a new phonetic script for the Manchu language. Now armed with wealth, large populations, and writing, Nurhaci created the **Eight Banners**, his most brilliant innovation. Adapted from the Mongolian military organization of thousands and ten thousands used by Chinggis Khan, each Banner had its own flag, subordinate companies ("arrows"), and commander. They included soldiers, their families, artisans, and farmers. Most important, by cutting across strong clan ties, they allowed Nurhaci to build a powerful war machine. Mongols and Chinese who joined the expanding state formed their own banner companies. The flexible banner mechanism brought the diverse ethnic groups of Manchuria under unified leadership. Along with the Ottoman *devshirme*, it was the most powerful creation of the Central Asian military state-building tradition.

The Manchus Conquer the Chinese Heartland

In 1616, with his entire population organized as a war machine, Nurhaci proclaimed himself khan of a new dynasty, the Latter Jin. His ancestors had created their own regional dynasty, the Jin, that controlled Manchuria and North China until 1234. Nurhaci at first only looked back to this regional regime, but to keep his alliance together, Nurhaci had to keep expanding. He successfully stormed the major Chinese city of Shenyang (Mukden), and made it his capital in 1625, but died soon after losing a major battle in the next year. His son, Hong Taiji, completed the autocratic centralization of the Manchu state and continued the "Great Enterprise," the conquest of China. Beijing, one of the two huge capital cities of the Ming dynasty, became the sole capital of the Qing dynasty after the Manchus conquered it in 1644. They expanded its walls and added on a separate district of the city open only to Manchus and their military supporters (see Map 2.1).

Hong Taiji rejected his father's concept of collective leadership, soon expelling his brothers from power and confiscating their banner properties. He raided North China and invaded Korea in order to grab silver supplies. Unlike Hideyoshi's invasion, no one rescued the Koreans this time, which is why they remained hostile to the new rulers of China for the next 250 years. Once replenished, he openly declared himself the emperor of a new dynasty, the Qing, in 1636 and renamed his people "Manchus." Once he had captured a seal from Chinggis Khan's Mongol dynasty, he could now claim a universal lordship that united Chinese, Manchu, and Mongol under a single

regime. He pillaged many Chinese cities, but died in 1643 before the final conquest.

As the Manchus grew, Ming power weakened. Frontier desertions depleted the garrisons and put pressure on the poor peasantry of the northwest. In the backwaters of Northern Shaanxi, a horrible famine in 1628 drove desperate farmers to form bandit gangs. Over 30 of them, with 200,000 followers, spread all over the province. Two ex-soldiers turned these gangs into large rebel armies that finally brought down the Ming regime: **Li Zicheng** (1605–45), a postal courier and skilled horseman, and **Zhang Xianzhong** (1606–47), a strong, hairy garrison soldier.

Military officers at first concealed Beijing's defeats, as rebel mobility outwitted the government's slow troops. As Li rampaged back and forth across North China, during terrible droughts, he promised tax relief to attract local gentry support. In 1641 he besieged the key city of Kaifeng. Its defenders cut the Yellow River dikes to drive him away, killing several hundred thousand innocent victims. Beijing's officials were too divided and too busy holding off the Manchus in the northeast to act. In 1644, Li marched his army into Beijing to establish a new dynasty, which would last less than two months. Meanwhile, in Sichuan, Zhang Xianzhong likewise proclaimed a new dynasty and terrorized wealthy families and Ming officials. Abandoning the province, he was killed in 1647 by Manchu troops.

The last Ming emperor called on General **Wu Sangui** of Liaodong to save the capital but abandoned his palace compound and hanged himself from a tree when Li invaded. Wu arrived at **Shanhaiguan**, the critical pass where the Great Wall joins the sea, only to learn that the emperor had died and rebels controlled the capital. **Dorgon**, the Manchu regent, told Wu that the Ming had lost the Mandate of Heaven, and only the Manchus could restore order. Wu made the fateful decision to ally with the Manchus, allowing them through the pass to drive

Box 2.5 Manchu and Central Eurasian Scripts

Manchu is an Altaic language, part of the broad family of languages that includes Turkish, Mongolian, Tungusic languages like Manchu, and possibly Japanese and Korean. Across Central Eurasia, nearly all aspiring state-builders established scripts in their native languages as their communication needs grew, or they borrowed from available trading languages. Sogdian, the primary trading language of medieval Central Asia, derived its script from Syriac, and ultimately from Aramaic and Phoenician. The Turkic Uighurs in the eighth century turned the script 90 degrees counter-clockwise, imitating the up-and-down Chinese characters, but keeping the phonetic alphabet. The Mongols adopted this script, and the Manchus then modified it to fit their language. Manchu was the last of the new phonetic scripts of the world, all of which can trace their roots back to the Phoenicians of the first millenium BCE. The Manchu alphabet thus came from ancient global communication technology.

Map 2.1 City of Beijing

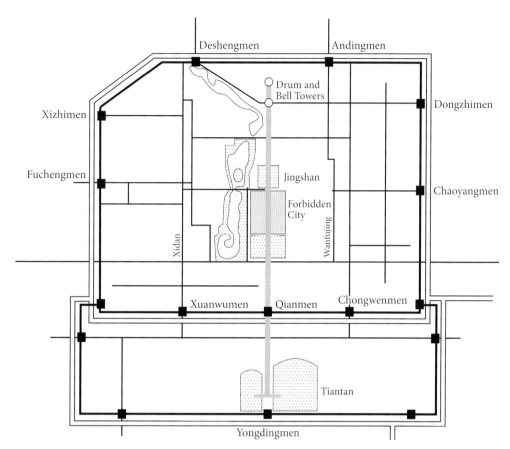

out Li from the capital. On June 6, 1644, the Manchu leaders declared the establishment of the new Qing dynasty.

Late nineteenth-century Chinese condemned Wu Sangui as a traitor for helping the barbarian Manchus, but almost no one in the seventeenth century thought in racial terms. Loyal Confucians had to decide whether to support a defeated regime or, like Wu, turn to the new conquerors. Other Ming officials followed the fleeing princes of the imperial family south, hoping to create a viable regime there. Christians in the Ming court even appealed to Pope Innocent X for aid. But this Southern Ming lasted only until 1662, when the Manchu armies drove the last Ming pretenders into oblivion in Burma. On Taiwan, meanwhile, the merchant pirate adventurer Zheng Chenggong (Koxinga) drove out the Dutch, and his son held out until 1683.

The Manchu military leaders used exemplary terror to enforce submission. At Yangzhou they massacred those who resisted. These measures were indeed barbarous, but many others perpetrated violence too. Roving bands of soldiers, refugees from famines, peasants fleeing the land, and rampant epidemics lasted for nearly a century. Ultimately, only the disciplined Manchu armies, not the ragtag Ming troops, showed any promise of being able to knit the social fabric back together.

2.5 THE KANGXI EMPEROR'S REIGN, 1661–1722

In 1661, a robust boy survived smallpox to become the Kangxi emperor. Under him, the Manchus began their "Flourishing Age." In 1667, at the age of 14, he faced his first great challenge: the power of Wu Sangui and other Chinese military leaders in the south. They had been rewarded with autonomous regional commands, called the Three Feudatories, for their support of the Manchu conquest. The young emperor, remembering how Nurhaci, his grandfather, had overthrown his benefactors, the Ming, provoked them into revolt and suppressed them vigorously.

By 1683, after capturing Taiwan, he had created a truly centralized regime, larger and stronger than the Ming (see Map 2.2). He restored the economy by investing in water conservancy and giving peasants tax breaks to cultivate wasteland. He kept taxes low but enforced equitable payment. And he welcomed Ming scholars into the new state, offering them elite privileges. These "holdover" literati wondered whether to cling to memories of the vanished Ming, or surrender to the disciplined Manchus, who promised to restore the classical order. Confucius himself, facing a similar dilemma, had provided ambiguous advice. Most chose the easier path, and convinced themselves that it was the

Box 2.6 Dorgon and Wu Sangui Negotiate the Manchu Takeover, 1644

In 1644, as the Manchus pressed close to Beijing, the emperor fled, and the rebel Li Zicheng took the capital. Wu Sangui commanded the most powerful remaining Ming army, guarding the pass at Shanhaiguan. Dorgon, the Manchu commander, offered him powerful benefits if he defected to the Manchu side.

Wu then wrote to Dorgon:

Presently our state, because of the isolation of the Ningyuan area, has ordered Sangui to desert Ningyuan and garrison the Shanhaiguan. The purpose of this order was to defend the eastern border and consolidate the defenses of the capital. Who could guess that roving bandits would commit treason against Heaven and attack the gates of the capital itself? How could such a mob of dog thieves accomplish anything?

But the minds of the people of the capital wavered; treasonous parties opened the gates and presented tribute. Our late Emperor came to an unfortunate end and the nine temples were left in ashes! Now the bandit chief has usurped the exalted title [of emperor] ... I, Sangui, have received great grace from our country and feel deep compassion for the people who are suffering from this calamity ... I beg you to consider the loyal and righteous words of this solitary official of a destroyed kingdom and immediately summon crack troops to enter the central and western zones.

Dorgon replied:

When I heard that roving bandits attacked and captured the capital and

that the Ming Emperor met a miserable end, I was unbearably angry! ... Your excellence thought to repay your [Ming] lord's graciousness toward you and refused to share the same sky with the roving bandits. This is certainly the righteousness of a loyal subject! ... If your excellence is willing to lead your troops to us, we will enfeoff you with a domain and ennoble you as a prince. Your state will then be avenged and you and your family will be protected. Your posterity will enjoy wealth and nobility as eternal as the mountains and rivers.

Wu decided to let the Manchus through the pass, and the rest is (Qing) history.

---

moral thing to do. They joined actively in projects of "statecraft," aiming to reform the system from within.

2.6 JESUITS AND CHINESE IN THE MING AND QING COURTS

Since the late Ming, European influence, brought by Jesuit missionaries, had grown. The Italian Jesuit **Matteo Ricci** (1552–1610) arrived in Macao in 1582, and after twenty years of effort, accomplished the incredible feat of learning classical Chinese to the level of top-ranking scholars, publishing works in Chinese, and gaining the right to live in the capital and see the emperor. The most brilliant cultural mediator of all time, he converted several prestigious scholars to Christianity.

Ricci succeeded because of his unique personality, not because of the innate appeal of Christian doctrine. Ricci argued that Confucian and Christian traditions shared themes of moral quest and respect for a common "Heaven." Quite a few scholars believed that Christianity only carried on the original wisdom of the sages: Confucius and Laozi had "gone West" in ancient times, and the Westerners were now bringing them back. Ricci's key tactic of "accommodation" of Christian teachings to Chinese views brought attacks from both purist Christians and suspicious Chinese. But Ricci sent back to Europe reliable, positive information about the Chinese empire.

The scholar Xu Guangqi, baptized "Paul," author of *A Complete Book of Agricultural Management* and translator of Western texts on mathematics and astronomy, was Ricci's most famous convert. Xu presided over the famous competition between Chinese, Muslim, and Western astronomers in 1629 to predict a solar eclipse. All imperial rulers carefully supervised the calendar, because the order of government had to align with the order of the heavens. The victory of the Jesuit calculators led to reforms of the Chinese calendar on Western principles.

Ricci carefully avoided stressing features of Christianity that would shock his Chinese audience, like the cannibalism of the Eucharist, or the intolerance of other gods announced in the Ten Commandments. The discovery of a tablet describing Nestorian Christianity in the Tang dynasty also helped to show that Christianity was a familiar, ancient faith. It had first come from the northwest, along the Silk Road, and now it arrived by sea, just like Islam.

The canny Jesuits knew that it would take more than philosophy to win China for Christendom. They offered practical skills, like gunpowder and navigation, to all sides during the Ming–Qing transition. Jesuit cannon helped the Ming defeat Nurhaci in 1626. Since the fleeing Ming court had written letters to the pope appealing for more aid against the Manchus, anti-Christians had good reason to suspect "foreign interference in China's internal affairs," as the modern Chinese put it. Yet the young Kangxi emperor studied mathematics and astronomy with Jesuit

Box 2.7 Massacres during the Ming–Qing transition

When the Manchus decided to massacre the Chinese of Yangzhou, eyewitnesses described "piles of corpses everywhere ... babies lay everywhere on the ground. The organs of those trampled like turf under horses' hooves ... were smeared in the dirt, and the crying of those still alive filled the whole outdoors."

One Chinese observer described another massacre, which could have been done by Manchus, Ming troops, or bandits:

[In 1649] I heard something about a massacre in Xiangtan, but I doubted that it was true ... In the middle of the second month I went with my companion to the Xiangtan market. Our feet grew feeble as we walked forward; even though we wanted to withdraw, we couldn't. Our souls left us, and our hearts chilled in fright. Traces of blood were still fresh, and the rank odor was oppressive. One could hardly remain standing, nor could one swallow any food. There was only the sight of corpses and heads strewn everywhere, too ghastly to talk about ... Over several days' time people gradually returned to their hearths in the city, and the dead bodies were either taken care of or cast away. Many were thrown into the river, and not a few were put in the scrublands outside the city. Some were cremated using firewood obtained by tearing down their houses, and others received burials paid for [by charitable survivors]. Other carcasses became nests for rats, the abdomens and chests being completely eaten out. Those who had been recognized by family members and taken in for proper burials were one or two in a hundred.

An epidemic followed.

In Xiangtan county the populace had just recovered when a pestilence ensued. As it spread from one rural area to another, nine in ten people were stricken. There being neither medicines nor doctors, it got so bad that everyone in a household would succumb to the fever, leaving no one to take care of the bodies. Or, in some villages, where it was less severe, the residents closed their doors and didn't go out. With few people on the roads and no signs of life around the houses, tigers and leopards became numerous, and hungry dogs roamed in packs ... People in the city market would chat and laugh in the morning, break out in a fever after the noon hour, become delirious in the evening, and be partly eaten by rats when found dead at sunrise ... Those who survived the disease for as long as seven days relied on medicinal plants for cures.

tutors. He used these skills when he led troops on his northwest campaigns, and the Jesuits helped him, too, to obtain cannon.

The Jesuits gave China new maps as well as weapons. Louis XIV had sponsored cartographic projects in order to give the absolutist ruler a transparent, rationalized perspective on his realm. Tax collectors, military recruiters, and administrators could now extract uniform levies unimpeded by customary practices. Kangxi had similar aims in mind when he commissioned the Jesuits to survey the entire empire, using the geometrical mapping techniques recently developed in Europe. From 1707 to 1717, the Jesuits and Chinese assistants created the "Comprehensive View of Imperial Territory," or "Jesuit Atlas," a beautiful cartographic achievement, displaying on a uniform latitude and longitude grid the administrative centers and terrain features of the whole empire.

The Chinese found Western planetary theory less impressive. In 1616 the Catholic church had condemned Galileo's teaching as heresy, so the Jesuits in China could not openly espouse the Copernican system, even though they knew it was correct. Chinese astronomers, who had no fixed views on the immobility of the Earth, appreciated the Jesuits' accurate data but were baffled by the theoretical contortions forced on them by the pope. Western religious dogmatism, revealed in the Rites Controversy of 1693 to 1700, defeated this great effort at bridge-building. When the papal legate declared in 1705 that Christian converts could not practice ancestral rituals, he undermined the evasive Jesuit efforts at accommodation. In 1722, the Yongzheng emperor, Kangxi's successor, abolished the Jesuit mission. The wrangling of rival Dominicans and Jesuits for imperial favor only ensured the suppression of Christianity as a subversive sect.

2.7 CHINESE, RUSSIANS, AND MONGOLS IN THE NORTHWEST

In the seventeenth century, three young emperors – **Peter the Great** (r. 1682–1725), Louis XIV (r. 1643–1715) and the Kangxi emperor (r. 1661–1722) – personally led military expansion and centralization, and defined absolutist rule in continental Eurasia. In the end, Louis gained little or nothing for France with his wars, but he still centralized the state. Kangxi dominated the

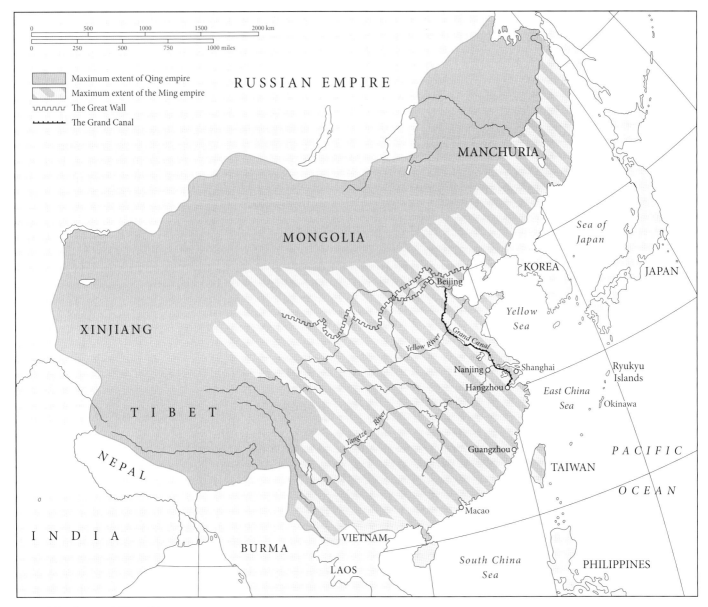

Map 2.2 Ming and Qing China

steppe partly because, as a Manchu, he knew how to manipulate Central Asians with marriages, alliances, and force. The wealthy, populous Chinese could afford imperial aims. Peter expanded his empire by savagely enforcing radical reform. Russians, a small, poorer population, paid the highest price of the three.

After restoring central power, the young Kangxi emperor turned to the vital northwestern frontier. Here he faced two strong rivals. Since 1582, Cossacks had established fortresses across Siberia to furnish valuable furs for the Russian treasury. They built Khabarovsk and Albazin on the Amur River in 1652. The Western Mongols (**Zunghars**) began to form a powerful new state under the leadership of **Galdan** (1644–97), who expanded his control into the oases of Turkestan. Galdan was the last of the great steppe conquerors of Central Eurasia. Only

the vigorous military campaigns of the Kangxi emperor, combined with a Russian choice of Chinese trade over a Mongolian alliance, ensured his defeat. Kangxi personally led four campaigns against Galdan, traveling further into the steppe than any emperor before him, with enormous logistical burdens inflicted on hundreds of thousands of troops.

Galdan, just as intransigent as the Chinese emperor, risked his fate in fixed battle twice, and was nearly wiped out. Still, his Mongols could replenish their supplies and live off the grasslands, while the Chinese troops, near starvation, depended on precarious supply routes from interior China. In 1697 Galdan died, probably killed by his remaining followers, giving the emperor an unprecedented victory. Kangxi had expanded the empire to unheard-of size and justified enormous risks, defying the cautious advice of his ministers. He could now legitimately claim to be a sage king, who best understood the will of Heaven.

Clever diplomacy supported military valor. The Treaty of Nerchinsk, negotiated in 1689 after the Chinese twice destroyed the fortress of Albazin, fixed the border with the Russians. The Treaty of Kiakhta of 1727 gave them regular trading privileges in Beijing. In these first treaties with a Western power, the Jesuits played the key role, as they used Latin to bridge Russians on one side and Manchus and Chinese on the other. Just as Latin was declining in Europe in the face of rising national languages, it served cultural mediation at the other end of Eurasia. The Russians needed to sell Siberian furs to China to fill the state treasury. The Chinese needed, most of all, Russian neutrality in the wars with Galdan. Like today, they used access to China's great markets as a diplomatic lever. The Chinese got the better of the deal in the long run. The fur trade declined, but Kangxi crushed Galdan, despite his desperate appeals for Russian aid.

By the end of his reign, Kangxi could convincingly claim to have created a larger, more stable, and more prosperous empire than any other in history, encompassing nearly 200 million diverse people. In these two centuries China, like most of the rest of Eurasia, had undergone upheaval, followed by restoration of order and extensive international economic and cultural connections. Foreigners who saw the great empire were still struck with awe. A century later, very few were impressed. Then, they saw weakness and potential decline, though not yet actual decay. By 1900, Chinese civilization itself was desperately struggling for survival. In the face of later humiliations, the glories of the early Qing still stand out as a source of pride.

2.8 MUSCOVY'S EXPANSION, COLLAPSE, AND REVIVAL

Ivan the Terrible

The strange, paradoxical figure of **Ivan IV** (the "Terrible" or "Threatening," r. 1533–84) nearly wrecked the Muscovite state established in the wake of the Mongol empire. Historians have never agreed on his character: Was he artistic, sensitive, and farsighted or psychopathic, savage, and deranged? He was the first ruler to call himself "Tsar and Autocrat," but he destroyed much of the elite and the economy. He, or his advisors, reformed the administration and conquered Kazan and Astrakhan, but ruined the country with the useless Livonian War.

Ivan grew up under the regency of his mother and leading boyar families like the Shuiskys, whose intrigues threatened his life. Muscovy's centralization was precarious. Without a strong central leader, the state apparatus dissolved into turbulent

factionalism, much like the late Ming. Ivan's first official act, at age 13, was to have Prince Shuisky thrown to the dogs. His reign began ominously. A fire during his majestic coronation ceremony caused terrified mobs to storm the Kremlin.

At first, capable administrators enacted reforms, and Ivan brought more boyars into the Duma. The first **zemsky sobor** (Assembly of the Land), convened in 1549 and 1566, brought together people from different estates to consult on public affairs. But at the same time, the new law code of 1550 almost completely eliminated the peasants' freedom to move. New special army units, supported by rationalized service obligations, learned to use firearms. Ivan established the first truly professional soldiers with fixed salaries, the sharpshooters, or **streltsy**.

After 1560, when his young wife died, Ivan struck out on his own. Threatening to abdicate the throne, he only returned when promised absolute power. His notorious **oprichnina**, established in 1565, could prosecute anyone for disloyalty. For seven years, wearing bizarre dark robes, with dogs' heads on their saddles, these young men terrorized princely families, local gentry, townspeople, foreigners, and villagers indiscriminately. Over 4,000 people lost their lives. The oprichnina sacked and burned Novgorod because of its merchants' foreign contacts. Some Russian historians have praised the oprichnina for eliminating corrupt boyars, while others have called it a merchant and lower gentry class alliance against the nobles, but the devastation showed little economic or administrative rationality. We cannot ignore Ivan's paranoid personality, exacerbated by a painful bone disease. Great (or terrible) men do change history.

Meanwhile, Ivan's foreign minister Adashev carefully moved against Kazan. He cleverly cultivated supporters within the city, but in the end Ivan had to besiege it in 1552. The fall of Astrakhan in 1556 consolidated Moscow's position on the Volga, but risked causing conflict with the Ottoman empire. Both sides avoided major conflict in order to keep their profitable commerce.

Muscovy then expanded further south and east with the help of Cossacks. The Cossacks had gathered in the southern borderlands of Russia (the modern Ukraine) from the mid fifteenth century. These freebooters included Tatars fleeing Moscow's service, peasants fleeing landlords, roving tribesmen, and unemployed soldiers. By the sixteenth century, they had created fortified self-governing communities, electing their own headmen, and living from fishing and agriculture in the Don and Dnieper valleys. Like Siberia, the Ukraine, far away from the landlord, military recruiter, and tax collector, offered freedom to the common Russian. Both Polish and Russian rulers realized that the Cossacks would serve them loyally if given rewards. The Cossack Yermak opened up the road to the Far East in 1582. The greatest beneficiaries of the Russian move east were

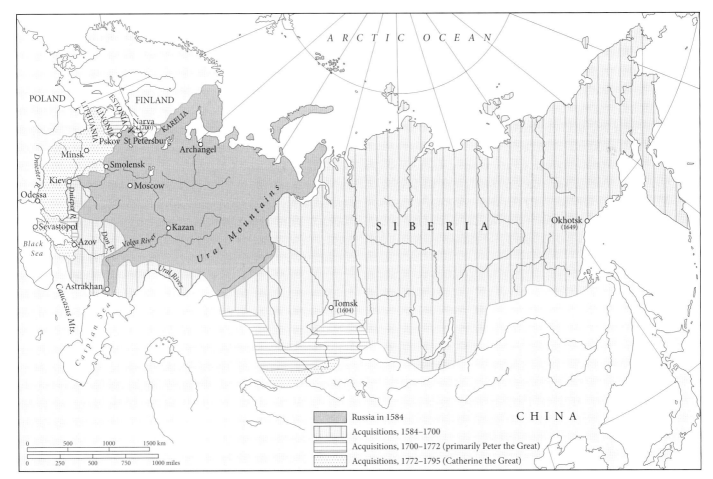

Map 2.3 Russian expansion, 1600–1750

the wealthy Stroganovs, who actively promoted Siberian expansion so as to increase their profits from furs and salt.

Muscovy's catastrophic western expansion, by contrast, squandered the profits of its eastern gains. In the Livonian War (1558–83), Ivan fought the powerful, efficiently armed states of Poland, Lithuania, Sweden, and Denmark. Taxes per acre on the peasant rose by more than ten times in monetary terms from 1530 to 1584, and 84 percent of the state budget went to the military. In sum, Ivan's oprichnina and his wars left the country economically ruined, filled with desolate villages and abandoned land.

The English found Russia during Ivan's reign, while looking for a northeast passage to China's fabled markets. In 1553 the tsar welcomed Richard Chancellor to Moscow and offered the English commercial privileges, hoping to break a blockade by the Poles, Germans, and Swedes. The English found no river passage to China but expected to reach Persia down the Volga River. They established their first chartered company, the Muscovy Company, to promote overseas trade.

English visitors provided valuable, though biased, accounts of this new "rude and barbarous kingdom." Giles Fletcher depicted "a true and strange face of a tyrannical state ... without true knowledge of God, without written Law, without common justice," the exact opposite, in his view, of the balanced constitution of Tudor England.[2] Ever since, Russia has often served as the Oriental Other for observers warning Westerners to guard their constitutional liberties. Indirectly, Fletcher's account protested royal absolutism in England. Like Chinese critics of the Manchus, and Montesquieu, who criticized the arbitrary rule of French kings, Fletcher believed that only a hereditary nobility could prevent despotism. This, he thought, was what Muscovy lacked.

The Time of Troubles (1598–1613) Tears Russia Apart

Ivan the Terrible's overextension of Russia left the country vulnerable to a new crisis in the seventeenth century, known as the Time of Troubles, during which Russians suffered social upheaval and foreign invasion. As in the Ming–Qing transition, one dynasty fell but in the end a new native dynasty, the Romanovs, restored the autocracy.

Ivan had murdered his eldest son in a fit of rage, leaving his second son Fyodor, a much weaker man, to rule. During Fyodor's life and after his death in 1598, the capable minister

Boris Godunov took charge. (Godunov is better known as the legendary usurper in Mussorgsky's opera than for his real achievements.) Godunov was elected tsar by the zemsky sobor with fervent prayers of support from the clergy and people of Moscow. But he was unlucky. From 1601 to 1603, a catastrophic famine struck the devastated country. One hundred thousand people died in Moscow alone. Soon, rumors spread that because Boris had murdered 9-year-old Dmitri of Uglich, Ivan's youngest son, Heaven was punishing the people for his sins. There is no evidence that Boris murdered the young heir, but the myth is as ineradicable as Shakespeare's tale of Richard III and the boys in the tower. A refugee monk, the "False Dmitri," invaded Russia in 1604 with an army of Cossacks and Poles. Boris Godunov died the next year. When the False Dmitri and his Polish entourage alienated the Russians, Prince Basil Shuisky led a coup and proclaimed himself tsar. Slave rebellions, a second False Dmitri, and a Swedish invasion prolonged the chaos until an army led by Minin, by profession a butcher, and the warrior Pozharsky, responding to desperate appeals from the church, freed Moscow from foreign occupation. A zemsky sobor elected as tsar 13-year-old **Michael Romanov** in 1613. The Romanovs then suppressed the common people who had rebelled against serfdom.

The Romanov Autocracy Stabilizes Russia

The Romanovs' autocracy (1613–1917) lasted for 300 years. They created a durable, though oppressive, political system. The elites followed secret but predictable patterns of conduct. Three cultural spheres held Russia together: the peasant village at the local level, the state and the bureaucracy at the center and provincial level, and smaller, more autonomous groups on the periphery. Let us briefly examine the logic of each.

The Russian state had expanded over a vast, thinly populated territory, mostly located in northern lands with low agricultural yields. To hold these lands together, the rulers focused on limited goals. They extracted enough from the population to support a basic military and bureaucratic apparatus. Centralization was the key: All resources had to be funneled to Moscow. Regional autonomy threatened to destroy the entire structure. They exploited all possible sources of revenue, in agriculture, trade, and industry. Foreigners marveled at the "greed," or business sense, of the tsars. The Chinese emperors, equally "autocratic" and expansive, could afford to leave a greater surplus among the people and ignore mercantile wealth, because they could draw on rich lands in the south. Muscovy had fewer options.

Russian peasants also faced a precarious, hostile environment with relatively few tools. The village community, or **mir** (which also means "world"), insured them against disaster. By periodically redistributing landholdings, no one could get too poor or too rich.

Land redistribution protected the most unfortunate and restrained the most aggressive. The village was hardly a collective paradise: It brutally enforced confiscation, marriages, and justice. But Russian villages, like Japanese ones, most effectively disciplined their members into serving the community. Because the state and landlords in both societies levied taxes and labor on the village as a whole, the community became tighter as state power grew. The law code of 1649 eliminated all legal options for escape from the land. Conservatism, informal customary decision-making, and isolation protected the village from hazards and blocked change.

The peak of the political structure worked the same way. Russian "autocrats" did not have total power. Historically, the Grand Princes had mainly refereed disputes among boyar clans. Ivan IV's failure to destroy the boyars with his oprichnina brought only devastation. The turmoil of the Time of Troubles inspired caution. After electing Michael Romanov tsar, most of the nobles went home to their estates, leaving a small, cohesive group of boyar families to control Moscow. Official ceremonies of autocratic power in Russia and Ming China deceived foreign observers, but many of the tsars and Chinese emperors were weak: bound by ritual activities, often excluded from real decisions. Courtiers jockeyed for positions close to the tsar through marriage alliances. Without a single person at the center, the boyars' intrigues would tear the system apart, but within this closed world the political elite had to subordinate family interest to the needs of the whole.

In addition to the bureaucrats, nobles, and village communities that comprised most of the Russian state, other groups stood outside the system. In the southern region now known as Ukraine, free-ranging farmers, horsemen, and nomads formed the military communities known as Cossacks. They lived in independent villages, and from time to time chose to serve the tsarist state. Far to the east in Siberia, peasants were also free from serfdom, and fur trappers collected resources from the vast forests. In the very far north, schismatic religious communities, like the Old Believers, established monasteries with independent moral and economic institutions. In the west, on the Polish and Lithuanian borders, Catholics, Jews, and Orthodox believers mingled together. In sum, the Russian state firmly fastened down its population in the heartland with noble rule and serfdom, but on the peripheries populations pursued more autonomous ways of life.

2.9 MERCHANTS, BUREAUCRATS, AND CHURCHMEN PROSPER UNDER AUTOCRATIC RULE

Before reaching the audience hall we passed through a vaulted chamber in which were seated, or standing at the sides, imposing old men with long gray beards, gilded clothes, and tall

Box 2.8 Olearius' Views of Russian Merchants

Olearius, in his account of his travels in seventeenth-century Russia, describes the people thus:

With regard to intelligence, the Russians are indeed distinguished by cleverness and shrewdness. However, they use these qualities not to strive for virtue and glory, but to seek advantage and profit and to indulge their appetites …

Their cleverness and shrewdness are manifested, in their commerce, among other activities; when buying and selling for profit, they resort to any expedient they can think of to cheat a neighbor …

The merchants are shrewd and eager for profit. Within the country they trade in all varieties of goods essential

for daily life. Those who have the Tsar's permission travel to neighboring countries, like Livonia, Sweden, Poland, and Persia, where they trade principally in sables and other furs, linen, flax, and Russian leather. They often buy cloth from English merchants, who carry on a great commerce in Moscow.

sable hats. They are called His Tsarist Majesty's gosti, *or distinguished merchants. Their clothing belongs to His Tsarist majesty's treasury; it is distributed for occasions such as this and then returned.*[3]

Russia's twenty or thirty wealthiest merchants, the gosti, dominated the trade of Moscow, Archangel in the far north, and much of the interior, and passed on their wealth for generations. Although the English and Dutch called them poor and backward, Russian merchants were relatively prosperous by continental standards. The Archangel trade, opened by the British, but soon dominated by the Dutch, brought Russian goods like hemp, linen, leather, and wax to Northern Europe in exchange for cloth, gold, and silver. Twenty to sixty ships arrived per year at Amsterdam. Trade along this very difficult route, frozen in the winter and dangerous at all times of year, which took at least four weeks, increased dramatically during the seventeenth century. Another trade route, centered at Astrakhan on the Volga, connected Muscovy to the south; a significant Indian merchant settlement in Astrakhan linked Russia to the East.

Russia, like Asia, was a net bullion importer but more closely tied to European markets. Russian prices followed the "revolution" of sharp rises in sixteenth-century Europe, followed by stagnation and decline in the seventeenth century. Russian merchants seldom traveled abroad, and protectionist tariffs kept out foreign competition. They profited from collecting taxes for the state. The Russian state did not suck the merchants dry; just as often the merchants squeezed the state out of its revenues. The 'subservience' of the gosti reflected their profitable use of ties to the tsar for their own benefit.

State administration developed alongside commerce. A hereditary class of literate clerks produced documents and routine procedures, but nobles resisted by petitioning the merciful tsar for aid in controlling runaway peasants. Petitions stressed

not only the tsar's unlimited power but also collective decision-making among the boyars. The apparently subservient language implied limits to the tsar's arbitrary power, much like Chinese literati memorials. The phrase "The tsar decreed and the boyars affirmed" indicated that a benevolent tsar should take advice from worthy advisors and "the land," meaning the general population which he ruled. Some petitions even implied that unresponsive tsars served the Antichrist. In 1648, when the tsar ignored numerous noble petitions, a mob stormed the Kremlin. In the 1649 law code, the nobility got their wish, at a cost. The state's officials would enforce serfdom, but personal appeals to the tsar ended. This bureaucratic growth prepared the way for Peter's radical reforms.

The religious culture of Muscovy also changed dramatically. Monks lost power to church bishops, who supported the centralizing state. As the decline of monastic influence left a spiritual vacuum, believers prayed to icons, like the Virgin of Kazan, for health, while a mostly illiterate class of village priests carried on the traditional rituals. In the mid seventeenth century, the Orthodox church split, in a dispute about the power of the religious hierarchy over popular liturgy and the power of the state over the church. Patriarch Nikon tried to create a uniform liturgy based on new interpretations of Orthodox texts. When he ordered that parishioners must not kneel but bow from the waist, and cross themselves with three fingers instead of two, the monk Avakkum attacked him as the Antichrist, and led his followers, who came to be known as **Old Believers**, in reasserting the time-honored rituals. Nikon expelled his critics, but he himself was defrocked in 1667 for resisting the tsar. Avakkum, exiled north of the Arctic Circle, continually defied the authority of both church and state. Old Believers, besieged in monasteries, committed mass suicide by fire rather than surrender. Despite repression, the Old Believers persisted for centuries as stalwart, enterprising dissenters.

Despite the schism, the church did not prevent all change. Reforming clergymen, adopting ideas from the Ukraine and Poland, began to preach sermons about moral self-improvement. In this way, Orthodox religious practice began to converge with that of Western Europe of the Reformation and Counter-Reformation. Before Peter's dramatic intervention, Russia had moved toward greater focus on individual spiritual improvement and a more legal and bureaucratically organized state. Peter accelerated reform, but he did not start from nothing.

2.10 PETER THE GREAT (R. 1682–1725)

Few rulers in history have so drastically transformed their societies as Peter I. Why did he dedicate himself so single-mindedly to the reform of Russia, and why did he have such an impact? Personal, political, military, and social influences all played a part.

As we noted, Peter's turbulent path to the throne formed his attitudes at a young age. After educating himself about the outside world, he reached out to connect with Europe and the Middle East. As always with Peter, war came first. First he turned south, where the Ottomans and the Crimean khan blocked Russian access to the Black Sea. In 1695 he besieged the important fortress of Azov at the mouth of the Don. A failure on the first try, the siege succeeded the next year under Peter's unrelenting supervision. In the Black Sea campaigns, Peter built a new fleet and a new city, and learned new methods of warfare to prepare for his campaigns in the north.

In 1697 he traveled to Western Europe to study military technology and artisanship. He ignored stultifying ceremonies, art masterpieces, and splendid Baroque churches. Instead, he worked as a carpenter in a Dutch dockyard, studied blacksmithing, and observed dissections, forcing his squeamish comrades to tear the muscles out of a corpse with their teeth (one of his little jokes). Foreigners and Russians admired his simple ways, his curiosity, his openness to people of all classes, while puzzling over his outbursts of rage, his drunken orgies, and his crude practical jokes. But no one missed the force of his will.

Peter observed open debates in the English Parliament, but after a year he rushed home to squelch more revolts by the sharpshooters. Now he took power in earnest. Two years later, in 1700, he launched the Great Northern War against Sweden, the dominant military power of the Baltic, led by the equally young and vigorous king, Charles XII.

Peter took on a formidable foe. Like Muscovy, the Swedes had built a powerful military state, despite the low yields of northern lands, but the Swedish peasant and soldier, unlike the Russian serf, was a freeholder, and the Swedes controlled important iron mines and the lucrative Baltic trade. Ivan IV had failed, but Peter tried again to break through to the Baltic. Following a disastrous Russian defeat at the siege of Narva in 1700, the victorious Swedes invaded Russia through the Ukraine. The passive, disorganized Russian army needed a complete overhaul.

In a few years, Peter created a disciplined army by supplementing the unwilling service nobility with 400,000 peasant recruits, nearly 10 percent of the male population. These men, literally branded as permanent soldiers, trained constantly for a lifetime of war. Villagers mourned their sons' departure as if they had died. New artillery and cavalry units joined the peasant infantry. Tactical training stressed meeting the enemy in the field instead of waiting for him behind fortified walls. A comprehensive code of military law influenced by the West taught the officers discipline, initiative, and responsibility. Peter's army stressed unquestioning obedience and efficient action in the service of the state. It was a model of a new society.

Peter, however, placed even more emphasis on the navy. His new fleet rose on the shores of the Baltic, as the tsar himself carved timbers with his axe and designed the keels of his ships. By the end of his reign the Russians had built over 1,100 ships, along with a huge infrastructure: nails, sawmills, rope yards, sailcloth factories, and harbors. In 1714, at the Battle of Hangö, Russia gained its first naval victory against the Swedes.

Military needs drove the industrialization of the country. All European states of this time endorsed the principles of mercantilism: countries must accumulate wealth through trade at the expense of others, and the state must direct the economy. Peter drove these principles to extremes. He directed the entire economy toward military needs. His crash industrialization programs eerily resemble Stalin's Five Year Plans. Russia first cast iron in 1702 from ore deposits in the Urals. Stalin built the huge steel town of Magnitogorsk in the same place two centuries later. Foreign specialists supervised new technologies, while the state requisitioned peasant labor and raw materials, controlling exports and distribution. The salt and tobacco monopolies sold basic necessities to the people at profits of 100 to 800 percent for the state.

The dark side was the destruction of Russia's merchant class, the gosti. Peter forcibly redirected foreign trade from Archangel to his new city of St. Petersburg, driving the old merchant lineages out of business. Only a few, like the Stroganovs, escaped by gaining lucrative imperial contracts for the exploitation of Siberia.

A famous edict of Peter stated, "Collect as much money as possible inasmuch as money is the artery of war."[4] Taxes hit the peasantry hardest. Peasants, legally bound to the land, now owed money, crops, labor, horses, and the quartering of soldiers to the state, in addition to their landlords' levies. Not surprisingly, large numbers fled to the frontier or became brigands. Once again, the Cossacks rebelled. They occupied large sections of the Don region in the midst of the grinding Northern War.

But Peter did not give up his personal campaign. Despite the fearsome reputation of Charles XII's army, Peter gained an amazing victory at Poltava, on the lower Dnieper River, in 1709, in which the Swedes lost 10,000 of 19,000 men, and the Russians lost only 1,300 out of 42,000. This victory put Russia on the map. Peace finally came twelve years later, destroying the Swedish empire and bringing new respect for Russia as the rising power in Europe. For twenty years Peter had given Russians "schooling" in the harsh ways of the modern world.

Unlike the tyrant Ivan IV, Peter did not destroy the regime he hated; instead he remade it into a thoroughly rationalized bureaucratic state. For the first time, Russia's state demanded a loyalty separate from the personal household of the tsar. The Muscovite rulers and officials saw state service as a way of supporting, or as they put it, "feeding" themselves and their families. In Peter's conception, state service meant dedication to the welfare of the entire country, not merely the imperial and noble families. Peter replaced the corrupt provincial governors with new regional units ruled by men loyal only to himself. Since the tsar left the country so often on campaigns, he needed a central executive institution. The Senate, the supreme co-ordinator of military and fiscal affairs, replaced the Boyar Duma, which had been made ineffective by autocratic tsars. The Colleges, specialized bureaus for military affairs, foreign policy, tax collection, and documentary co-ordination, regulated bureaucrats, copying the Swedish model. Peter's reforms seemed like a whirlwind, but they were piecemeal rather than comprehensive. He took Muscovy's bureaucratization to unprecedented lengths, but kept many of the old institutions alongside the new.

Cultural change likewise came suddenly. The tsar needed allies from the established courts of Europe, and to win them he needed to reshape Russia's image. He forced the boyars to cut their beards and abandon Orthodox ritual to avoid embarrassment abroad. He sent the officer corps for training in science and engineering at Europe's universities. Like Kangxi, Peter commissioned detailed maps of his realm from foreign experts. Hardly an aesthete, Peter nevertheless purchased classical paintings and statuary from Italy and Germany that became the nucleus of the Hermitage collection, and he hired the most expensive architect in Europe to design the palaces in his new city. The Pavilion at Peterhof featured views of the sea, spectacular fountains, and large gardens. He also respected theoretical science. After long correspondence with the German philosophers Leibniz and Christian Wolff, he planned Russia's Academy of Sciences, founded after his death in 1725.

Finally, and most significantly, Peter built his new city, St. Petersburg, at the mouth of the Neva in order to "open a window to Europe." Its cost was immense. As one historian said, "It would be difficult to find in military history a massacre which accounted for more men than St. Petersburg."[5] Peter compelled peasants to dig, nobles to build houses, and merchants to trade in empty forests and swamps. "Peter built his own city like a ship," carefully planning streets, palaces, and canals on regular, military lines.[6] Except for his palaces, it looked like a crude camp, but half a century later St. Petersburg had become one of the most beautiful cities in the world (see Figure 2.2).

Peter's reign highlighted the fundamental issues of Russia and of many other developing countries. Modernizers idolized him, but Slavophiles attacked him for wrenching Russia away from her native harmony. Liberals focused on the contradictions between autocracy and democracy: How can you beat people to make them free? Peter responded that English institutions were irrelevant to Russia, where the peasants were uneducated, the clergy illiterate, and the nobles stagnant. So what if the pursuit of military power came at murderous cost? Wealth and power for the state came first; the people benefited later. Under Peter, in a very short time, Russia turned from a continental, Orthodox, inward, and Eastern-oriented autocracy into a secular, modernizing bureaucratic empire. It followed Eurasian trends toward integration and consolidation in the most extreme form.

2.11 THE UNIFICATION OF JAPAN

Powerful military leaders also centralized Japan in this period. In the sixteenth century, known as the "Age of Warring States," regional lords (**daimyo**) and their military servitors (**samurai**) fought incessantly, while Westerners brought Christianity and gunpowder weaponry, domestic and foreign trade flourished, and Japanese armies intervened in Korea. By the early seventeenth century, the new Tokugawa **shogun**s (chief general and de facto ruler of Japan) had expelled foreigners, ruthlessly suppressed Christianity, and nearly shut off foreign trade, inaugurating the so-called "Period of Seclusion" (**sakoku**). This phase of Japanese history, called the Tokugawa, or Edo period (see Map 2.4), lasted until 1868. Japan was, however, not entirely cut off from the world. Its commercial change and creeping bureaucratization paralleled other Eurasian states.

In the mid fifteenth century, like Muscovy, civil wars engulfed Japan. Tens of thousands of soldiers battled in the streets of the capital, leaving it in ashes, with the emperor impoverished, the shogun insecure, and most of the country under autonomous military governors. Yet this constant violence laid the groundwork for unification. New men rose from obscurity; inferiors

Figure 2.2 Peter the Great of Russia built his capital city St. Petersburg from scratch in the middle of marshes on the Baltic Sea, at enormous cost in human life. A century later, under Catherine the Great, it had become one of the most beautiful and cultured cities in the world.

Map 2.4 Japan under the Tokugawa

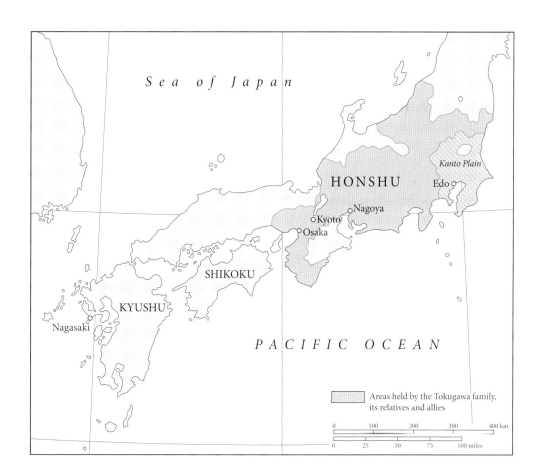

Box 2.9 Views of the Japanese by Foreigners and by Themselves

Kumazawa Banzan offers this account of his own nation:

What Japan has that is superior to [foreign lands beyond] the Four Seas are the sacred qualities of the national land and the purity of the people's hearts. [But] the reason that in recent years the spirit of the national land has become thinner, and her people have become inferior [to what they once were] is surely that [we have] not preserved the gold, silver, copper, and iron
that are the ultimate spirit of the mountains and streams [of our land], but have dug them out and . . . shipped them to foreign lands in great quantity, so that our mountains are laid waste, and our rivers become shallow.

Alessandro Valignano offers a foreign perspective:

The second defect of this nation is the meagre loyalty which the people show towards their rulers. They rebel against
them whenever they have a chance, either usurping them or joining up with their enemies. Then they about-turn and declare themselves friends again, only to rebel once more when the opportunity presents itself . . . The chief root of the evil is the fact that . . . there was a rebellion against [the emperor] and Japan was divided up among so many usurping barons that there are always wars among them, each one trying to grab for himself as much territory as he can.

overthrew their superiors. Warring lords built thousands of castles across the country, and nearly everyone was armed. Within their domains, the lords forged powerful tools for local administrative control.

Firearms were brought by the Portuguese in 1543 and first used in 1575. Foreigners and Japanese prospered in trade. Some merchants joined the pirates and smugglers along the Chinese coast; others ran important cities, like Sakai, through their guilds. After the Jesuit Francis Xavier arrived in 1549, Christianity began to take hold in the west and south, supported by lords looking for foreign aid.

Just as in Europe, foot-soldiers with muskets made the sword-wielding samurai obsolete. But gunpowder required larger resources. A brutal, powerful warrior, **Oda Nobunaga** (1534–82) began to form a winning coalition. He consolidated his position in central Japan, then marched triumphantly into Kyoto in 1568, and seized Sakai in 1569. Notoriously, he burnt to the ground 2,000 buildings in the huge Mount Hiei monastery, for the Buddhists too had large armies. But Nobunaga was killed before he could claim to be shogun of a unified Japan. **Toyotomi Hideyoshi** (1536–98) completed the unification. Hideyoshi had no family lineage at all; he lived only by the sword. At first an enemy of Nobunaga, he then allied himself with Nobunaga and expanded his base in central Japan. By 1590 he had subordinated all the major lords in the country. Hideyoshi gathered his followers into large coalitions; he fought few major battles. He had a gift for diplomacy in this treacherous age.

Hideyoshi's administrative reforms had more lasting impact than his battles. In 1588 he ordered the Great Sword Hunt, stating that "the farmers of the various provinces are strictly forbidden to possess long swords, short swords, bows, spears, muskets, or any other form of weapon."[7] All metal weapons would be melted down and cast into a Great Buddha. Daimyo and samurai gave up the gun, but kept their honorific swords. Thus he ensured that no mass army could resist him. He then froze the social order. He prohibited farmers from going into trade or leaving the villages and samurai from doing hired labor. Samurai were separated from the land, so they could not hold independent fiefdoms, and farmers were bound to the soil like serfs. Unlike Ming China, Japan's military rulers could enforce reliable registration with a comprehensive land survey. Taxes were assessed according to the productive potential of the land, measured in *koku*, a unit roughly equivalent to one year's per capita grain consumption. Of the national total of 18.2 million koku for 12 million people, Hideyoshi controlled approximately 2 million koku in his own domains, plus gold and silver mines.

Hideyoshi pressed hard on the peasantry, but he left the lords alone. Daimyo owed soldiers to the shogun in proportion to the size of their domains, but they were otherwise free. Unlike Peter of Russia, Hideyoshi stopped short of nationalizing the army; daimyo maintained their followers, but the shogun could confiscate and rearrange their fiefs. His final campaign destroyed the castles that had sprouted like mushrooms during the century of civil war. By 1615, daimyo had only one castle each. Hideyoshi feared foreigners and their Christian followers, because they supported the western daimyo. He banned proselytizing in 1587, and crucified many Japanese Christians when he became suspicious of the quarrels between the Franciscans and Jesuits. He began to put controls on foreign commerce, and strictly suppressed piracy.

Figure 2.3 Japanese in the sixteenth century were fascinated by the strange appearance of foreigners with large noses and black robes, who arrived to conduct trade and spread Christianity in the southern coastal city of Nagasaki.

Near the end of his life, Hideyoshi announced that "My wish is nothing other than that my name be known throughout the three countries [of Japan, China, and India]."[8] In 1592, he launched an almost inexplicable campaign against Korea. Was he trying to divert the attention of his domestic rivals, or was he driven by a megalomaniacal ambition to conquer East Asia? As in 1895, Japan's intervention on the continent brought disastrous results for everyone. When a Japanese army of over 200,000 men took Seoul, Hideyoshi envisaged an easy conquest of Beijing, but the Korean admiral Yi Sunsin, with his famous armada of "turtle-clad boats," the first armored ships in naval warfare, decimated the Japanese navy, while Korean guerrillas harassed the occupying troops. Chinese troops crossed the Yalu River and quickly drove out the Japanese army in 1593, inflicting a humiliating defeat. The consequences for Japan were short-lived, but Korea was devastated, and the fiscal strains on the Ming aided the expansion of the Manchu state. For the next three centuries, Koreans, the true Confucians, hated both sets of barbarians: the Japanese and the Manchu conquerors of the Ming.

Tokugawa Ieyasu (1543–1616) put the finishing touches on the structure that Hideyoshi had begun. As the Japanese proverb says: "Oda Nobunaga assembled the ingredients, Hideyoshi baked the bread, and Ieyasu ate it." Unlike his predecessors, Ieyasu came from a prestigious military family. At Hideyoshi's death he had the largest holdings in the country, 2.5 to 3 million koku. Then he carefully maneuvered to make himself the supreme leader. At the critical battle of Sekigahara on October 21, 1600, 80,000 supporters of Hideyoshi's heir faced off against Ieyasu's roughly equivalent forces for the ultimate prize: the title of shogun. Ieyasu's victory entitled him to claim the shogunate in 1603. He concluded the civil war in 1615 when he captured Osaka castle from the last holdouts. The **bakufu**, or military government, had moved its capital from Kamakura to Kyoto in the fifteenth century, but Ieyasu now moved the capital to the small fishing village called Edo (now Tokyo) in his domains in the Kanto Plain (see Map 2.5). It grew to become the largest city in the world by 1700, with over a million people, including the shogun's retainers and officials, merchants, daimyo and their attendants, artisans, and construction workers.

The extraordinary control system established by Ieyasu and his successors balanced feudal and bureaucratic elements. The **sankin kotai** hostage system required all the daimyo to maintain costly residences in Edo and to spend up to half the year there, closely watched by the shogun's inspectors and spies. When they

Map 2.5 City of Edo

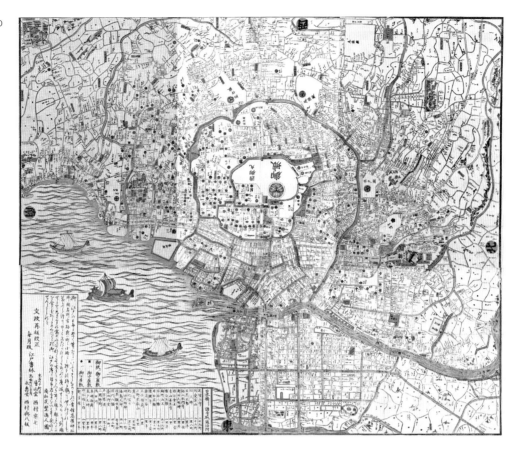

returned to their domains, they had to leave their wives and children behind as hostages to ensure their good behavior. Not only did it keep the daimyo under close watch, but traveling with their retinues to and from Edo used up much of their income. Daimyo were divided into three classes depending on their loyalty to Ieyasu. The 23 shimpan daimyo, relatives of the shogun, provided heirs when the Tokugawa line was broken; the 145 fudai daimyo, loyal but unrelated, formed the linchpin of regional administration; and the 98 tozama daimyo, mostly hostile to Ieyasu, secretly nursed their grudges. After much land confiscation and domain transfer, the shogun himself held 6.8 million koku, the fudai and shimpan 9.3 million koku, and the tozama 9.8 million koku. Two of the most powerful tozama daimyo, Satsuma and Choshu, led the Meiji Restoration movement that overthrew the bakufu two and a half centuries later.

To be a daimyo required a minimum of 10,000 koku. The peasantry gave over two thirds of their agrarian production to their lords, probably the most intensive agrarian extraction rate in the world. The disarmed and immobilized peasantry were nearly helpless in the face of the lords and their arrogant sword-carrying samurai, but thousands of peasant protests did occur. The shoguns appointed the daimyos' heirs, but within the domains, the lords had complete power over justice, tax collection, and internal affairs. Shogunal law evolved from vassal oaths into formalized codes, which emphasized strict frugality and a static, agrarian economy, much like the first Ming emperor. The emperor himself, the source of legitimacy for the shogun as military ruler, received large land grants and a lavish new palace in Kyoto, but he was kept out of any access to power.

Japan's state structure puzzles analysts accustomed to European institutions, inspiring contradictory phrases like "bureaucratic feudalism." On the one hand, the vassal oaths, independent lords, service ethic of the samurai, and military ideology evoke the European Middle Ages, but the growing bureaucratization, pervasive control measures, and commercial growth look like absolutist regimes. Yet Russia, too, baffled Western visitors with its combination of service nobility and apparent absolute power granted to the tsar. These examples ought to undermine our natural assumptions of sharp oppositions between "feudal" and "modern" (bureaucratic) society, and lead us to reconsider the real nature of state development in the West, which also blended medieval and centralizing elements.

The military leaders needed a new ideology to legitimize their rule during peacetime. Chinese Neo-Confucianism offered the most convincing answers. In its Japanese version, it stressed the strict social hierarchy dividing **shi** (scholars in China; samurai in Japan), merchants, artisans, and peasants, and the obligations of filial piety, meaning obedience of inferiors to superiors within the family and the polity. The scholar Hayashi Razan (1583–1657) identified the samurai with the Confucian "gentleman" and stressed the transformation of men of war into literate scholar-officials and loyal bureaucrats. Confucian popularizers, like Kaibara Ekken (1630–1714), explained the classical texts simply for rural people, women, and children, and wrote practical works on agronomy and childbearing. Japan's active publishers disseminated these ideas in thousands of copies. Printing and literacy spread widely, and schools proliferated, but not every rough warrior could make the transition.

From 1701 to 1703, the episode of the forty-seven ronin epitomized the changes of the century, inspiring plays, tales, and later, films. When Asano, the backwoods daimyo, was insulted by the urbane Kira, protocol officer at the bakufu, he drew his sword and slightly wounded him. It was a capital offense to draw a sword at the shogun's court, so Asano was sentenced to perform ritual suicide (**seppuku** or **harakiri**). Asano's retainers became masterless samurai (**ronin**), whose primary duty was to avenge their lord's death. They carefully bided their time, feigning dissoluteness to throw their enemies off guard. Twenty-two months later, they stormed Kira's mansion in Edo, cut off his head, and presented it to their lord's tomb. The bakufu was thrown into extensive debate. The ronin had admirably followed the traditional code of loyalty, but they had disrupted law and order. Finally, they were not condemned as criminals, but allowed to perform honorable seppuku. The courage of the ronin won them great acclaim from both samurai and commoners, at a time when the growth of commercialized pleasures led many to be concerned about the softening of the nation's moral fiber.

Such a mismatch between China's bureaucratic state and Japan's special hybrid stimulated vigorous controversy. The controversial Wang Yangming (Yomeigaku) school became especially powerful in Japan. Yomeigaku followers advocated the purity of individual will against restrictions by ceremonial codes or domain laws. The native Japanese religious cults, systematized as Shinto, as well as the Buddhist sects, offered alternatives to Chinese Neo-Confucian orthodoxy and possibilities for syncretism. The Chinese, Koreans, and Dutch who were allowed to send trade and tribute embassies kept open an important window on the outside world. Beneath the surface of the isolationist, repressive shogunal regime in the seventeenth century there bubbled an effervescent intellectual culture. Japan was never truly isolated in the so-called "sakoku" period.

The Tokugawa period created many of the conditions facilitating Japan's rapid breakthrough into the industrial age. In this way, historiography of Japan has paralleled that of Russian scholars who find in seventeenth-century Muscovy the germs of Peter's reforms. Even without the stimulus of foreign wars, extensive foreign trade, or religious controversy, Japan still had an active cultural life and growing economy, and gradually created a literate, mobile, inquisitive population. Rather than stopping halfway on a road leading from feudalism to an autocratic state, it creatively balanced local autonomy and central control.

2.12 COMMONALITIES AND CONTRASTS ACROSS EURASIA

Environment, Transportation, Communication, and Gunpowder

The agrarian environment fundamentally shaped all these societies because peasant farmers formed the vast majority of the population. Without them, the states had no taxes, the merchants had no goods, the armies had no soldiers, and the cities had no food. Climate and location set firm limits.

Russia's short growing season severely limited agricultural yields. Trees and rainfall were abundant, but soils were heavy, infertile, and difficult to plow. Travel was easiest in the summer, feasible on the frozen ground in the winter, except during blizzards, but impossible in the spring thaw, which immobilized vehicles in mud. Princes had to exert tremendous force to extract surplus from widely dispersed, self-sufficient villages. In southern Russia, Cossacks and independent farmers controlled fertile lands beyond the reach of Muscovy.

Weather fluctuations were even more severe in the steppes. Nomads, however, did not depend primarily on agriculture. For them, the critical resource was grass, and the critical variable was rainfall. They moved their herds in carefully prescribed seasonal patterns in search of the richest pastures. Scarcities forced tribes to struggle with each other, or to raid the neighboring settled societies. Historians have repeatedly suggested that desiccation drove nomadic invasions; without accurate climatic data, we cannot be sure of this, nor can we forget the role of charismatic leadership and political organization.

In Manchuria, a forest and agricultural zone, hunters and fishermen built a massive state out of primitive resources, but they also adroitly exploited their neighbors: trading with richer Korea and China, allying with nomads, and using their fairly limited cultivated fields. Limited food supplies several times put the Manchus on the brink of starvation until they won a decisive battle. The conquest of China came not a minute too soon.

North China had a more temperate climate but also faced limits to growth. The fertile loess soil needed rain, but rainfall was unpredictable and concentrated only in a few months of the year. Floods and droughts constantly threatened the overpopulated North China Plain. Northwest China, source of the rebellions that overthrew the Ming, was even more precarious, being subject to famine and Mongol raids. Only the abundant agriculture of South China held the empire together over the long run. South China's paddy rice agriculture was the most productive of calories per acre in the world, but also the most labor-intensive. Shipping its grain to the north on the Grand Canal, and shipping the population to the south, via migration, resolved the basic food problem and helped to balance the regions. New World crops allowed migrants to clear the hilly lands that surrounded South China's paddy fields, but these soils easily eroded when the forest cover was stripped.

Japan's main islands lay in a mild temperate zone, with adequate rainfall and plentiful forests. The small plains and rivers supported dense peasant populations. Valleys separated by mountain passes formed worlds of their own, leading to constant destructive warfare between the lords. Fires also constantly swept through the wooden cities. Unification under the Tokugawa finally unleashed Japan's great potential for growth, at the cost of substantial loss of forest cover and threats of erosion.

Transportation costs limited commercial networks and empires, too. Rivers, inland seas (the Baltic, the Mediterranean, the Inland Sea of Japan), land routes, and open sea stand in descending order of convenience, cost, and security. The relative importance of these different forms of transportation determined the nature of each state's linkages to its neighbors.

The great rivers of China were the core of its inland trade. China lacked an inland sea, but had coastal shipping on the southeastern harbors. On land, costs rose dramatically, for very few roads were passable year round. Only major military expeditions could afford many horse-drawn carts, but a chain of human porters could bring goods to riverbanks for bulk shipment by boat. Least attractive of all was the open sea, menaced by pirates, storms, and poor navigation.

Russia's major rivers linked it to the glittering riches of Byzantium, the Ottomans, and Persia. The British at Archangel opened a link to the West, but only Peter's forcible expansion broke through directly to the Baltic. At the same time, the Russian state drove inland east and south. When it captured Kazan and Astrakhan on the Volga, Central Asian rulers lost control of river trade, but they could still profit from luxury trade between oases: Overseas maritime trade had still not displaced the Silk Road. The Manchus took greatest advantage of

both the northwest frontier and the southeast coast of China, while the Ming had tried to seal them off. Japan's "seclusion" from the continent was not so damaging economically: Traders still went to China via Kyushu and Okinawa, but most important, internal trade networks developed rapidly. Both the Inland Sea and the **Tokaido** Road (running through central Japan) tied the Tokugawa realm together.

It is much easier to send messages rapidly than to send goods. Two technologies accelerated the transfer of information: postal couriers and mass printing. Both Russia and China adopted the Mongol postal courier system for state communications. Japan created an equivalent communication apparatus using the inns of the Tokaido Road. State and commercial communications coexisted and aided each other, as private letter deliveries in Ming China followed the same routes as government couriers. Printing spread more unevenly. Since China had long had printed books, the Ming–Qing period developed regional distribution networks for a broadly based reading public. The new Manchu script likewise served state centralization. Japan also expanded printed materials for both urban and prosperous rural readers. Russian officials and churchmen, by contrast, feared giving the people access to print. Muscovy was a much more illiterate society than East Asia; only a very small stratum of bureaucrats communicated with each other; much of the literate culture was isolated in monasteries.

Printing did have broad cultural effects in China and Japan, but they were less dramatic than Europe's, because East Asia started from a higher level of literacy. East Asian literate elites did not see printing as threatening to spread dangerous knowledge to illiterate masses, unlike some Europeans, and the printed word did not create separate states based on different spoken languages. But the East Asian societies were not linguistically homogeneous. Six or more different printed languages circulated in China, and Qing sponsorship of multilingual scriptures, dictionaries, and atlases had a powerful impact on Central Asia. Mongols, Manchus, Tibetans, and Muslims received messages of unity from state-sponsored publication projects. Cultural integration using the printing press held together a classical Chinese ecumene that expanded to include non-Han peoples.

Gunpowder weaponry significantly affected all these areas. The "military revolution" of sixteenth-century Europe did not give Europeans unquestioned superiority over Asians in continental warfare, and technology alone did not determine the fate of any of these "gunpowder empires." But Chinese gunpowder warfare, invented in the tenth century, exported across Asia by Mongols and Muslims, then reintroduced by Portuguese and Jesuits to East Asia in the sixteenth century, stimulated more efficient killing, favored those with more money, and led to reorganization of military forces along more impersonal, less class-stratified lines. Every military competitor had to respond to it. Japan and China at first eagerly adopted, and then repressed or neglected, the technology, in the interests of establishing social peace. They calculated that powerful armaments, an unfortunate necessity in times of turmoil, should be abandoned in times of peace. Japan successfully gave up the gun for nearly two hundred years, and Chinese emperors found little effective use for them after 1760. Their domestic enemies, mainly peasant rebels, were not a great enough challenge. In Russia Peter had no choice but to modernize his military against great internal opposition. One lesson we may draw is that military technologies do not progress smoothly and inevitably along a single track; most people, including generals, prefer predictability. Brutal competition forced them into an unpredictable struggle between innovation and tradition.

History is not only a story of winners, even though they dominate the written record. Let us not forget those who suffered most in this period: the independent nomads of Central Eurasia, the hill peoples of China, the enserfed Russian peasantry and Japanese community-bound villagers, and, to some extent, women everywhere. State-builders were most afraid of people who were free to move. Their empires and bureaucracies were designed to track down, register, and control their millions of subjects, whatever the wishes of the latter. The defeat of Galdan marked the end of the last serious effort by a nomadic leader to construct an autonomous state in the steppe. China had begun to incorporate eastern Central Eurasia (Mongolia, Xinjiang, Tibet), and would finish the process in the eighteenth century. In Western Eurasia, independent oasis kingdoms remained, but Russia would swallow them up in the eighteenth and nineteenth centuries. By eliminating the steppe frontier through negotiated treaties, the Chinese and Russians ensured that nomads had nowhere to flee: Both agrarian empires agreed to deport refugees, tribesmen, and deserting soldiers back home to prevent unrest. The Russian autocratic state tried to prevent the movement of its peoples by enforcing laws on serfdom binding peasants to their nobles. Serfdom, fortunately, did not encompass the entire empire; it allowed some freedom for Cossack communities and Siberian peasants at the margin. China had no institution comparable to serfdom, but its officials also attempted to control migration with a collective registration system. Tokugawa Japan succeeded even more than Russia in tying down villagers to tightly organized communities. Like Russia, the Tokugawa shoguns forbade unlicensed travel of villagers across feudal domains, and the village communities were collectively responsible for taxation. Russian villagers could flee to a sparsely settled frontier, but except in the northern island of Hokkaido, Japanese peasants had little room to move.

Dissenters mainly found space only at Russia's edges. The free Cossacks sometimes fought for the state and sometimes rebelled against it. In 1648 Bogdan Khmelnitsky led the "Ukrainian War of Liberation" against Poland, asking to unite with Moscow. Moscow took over the Ukraine in 1654. In Stenka Razin's revolt of 1670–71, Don Cossacks moved up the Volga, threatening Moscow. In the north, Novgorod tenaciously pursued its own traditions, despite repeated ravaging by Moscow in 1480 and 1570. During the Old Believer controversy of the mid seventeenth century, defiant clergy from the north rejected the imposition of new state rituals, including the foreign Gregorian calendar. Rebels in China rose up in remote, hilly areas, or in newly settled territories like Taiwan or Xinjiang. Their rebellions lasted a much shorter time once the Manchus had established firm control. In Japan, peasants could organize petitionary movements to beg for reductions of taxes in times of famine, but they had been disarmed by the Tokugawa shoguns, so they could never engage in serious armed conflict against their samurai superiors.

Gender Relations

Women's experiences remain quite obscure, but we have information at least for some elite women. Printed texts, legal cases, along with the proliferation of woodcuts and popular imagery, give us many more sources than for earlier periods. The common trends of state centralization and commercialization affected women, too.

These were all highly patriarchal societies. Russian Orthodoxy, Confucianism, Buddhism, and samurai norms all insisted on the absolute domination of men over women, and on women's duty to obey. Christian clerics saw women as weak, doomed to sin ever since Eve; Confucians located the *yin*, or weak force, predominantly in females and infants. Women were necessary for procreation, but they were feared as sexual temptresses. Most elite women were kept in seclusion for nearly all of their life. Until marriage, their families carefully sheltered them. Their most traumatic journey was on their marriage day, when they traveled from the protection of their natal family to their husband's home. Parades and ceremonial celebrated the transfer of the bride, who had never met her prospective husband. Olearius' description of seventeenth-century Russia could apply almost as well to China: "Generally, even the lesser notables raise their daughters in closed-off rooms, hidden from other people, and the groom does not see the bride before he receives her in the marriage bedroom. Thus some are deceived, and instead of a beautiful bride are given an ugly and sickly one."[9] Usually, however, the family of the groom carefully examined the bride, and especially the size of her dowry, before agreeing to a contract. It was a family contract, not up to individuals to decide.

After marriage, women remained in their husbands' houses. Russian boyar women were secluded in separate living quarters called the *terem*. They could receive visitors and manage the household, but they only went out in public to churches, in closed carriages. Because marriage politics were crucial to the status of the boyar elite, the noblemen carefully insulated their women from inappropriate contact. As wives and regents, Russian women appeared sporadically as tsar-makers on the top-level political scene, but their position was dangerous: Ousted regents and even wives could be killed, or sent to distant convents.

Chinese elite women were kept in special quarters of the family estate. Worse yet, their feet were bound, preventing them from doing more than hobbling around outdoors. This crippling custom had begun in elite circles in the Tang and Song dynasties, but made its way down the social scale in the Ming and Qing. It was another example of emulation and status-seeking: only women with dainty feet could expect to marry men of talent and means. In the ideal view, men plowed the fields and women stayed home to weave clothing.

Manchu and Mongol women were freer than women in settled societies. While the men engaged in battle on their dashing, but economically useless, steeds, the women and children performed the vital economic tasks of tending herds of sheep and cattle. They were highly mobile, accompanying the flocks to their customary pastures. As mothers, they had vital roles in arranging marriage alliances and watching over new brides. Unlike their Chinese counterparts, they did not bind their feet. The greater freedom of the non-Chinese women of the frontier was another reason for orthodox ideologists to regard these peoples as barbarian and dangerous.

The strict bonds of patriarchy were not all-encompassing. Within their separate spheres, women could exert considerable autonomy. They controlled childbirth, a process shielded from men's eyes, known to midwives alone. Once they produced children, especially male heirs, their status rose considerably. Once their sons married, they could look forward in middle age to nearly absolute power over the new brides, returning the same abuse they had suffered when they arrived in a strange household. As widows, they earned great respect, as long as they did not remarry, and could even inherit property.

Centralization of state power and commercialization transformed women's lives by imposing new obligations on the men. When Russian or Japanese men were away from home on service to the ruler or in war, women ran the estates. In mercantile households, they often balanced the books and participated actively in the business of the shop. Chinese popular literature describes men on the road whose wives were seduced while they were away, but also notes the women's considerable independence. Markets also gave Asian women some economic autonomy, when they could sell the textiles they wove outside the home. In China and Japan, a substantial fraction of women (up to 10 percent) were literate, linked to the world through letter writing and book reading. Itinerant preachers found their greatest audiences among women at home.

Male power-holders tried to repress any signs of women's growing freedom. Historians have viewed the witchcraft crazes of Western Europe and New England, in which 80 percent of the accused were women, as attacks on marginal women who seemed to threaten social order. Russia offers an interesting contrast, because only 32 percent of witchcraft cases involved women. The tightened bonds of local community inflicted by the legal imposition of serfdom constricted women, but protected them from attack. In East Asia, there was no general witch craze, but the reasserted central power of the Manchus and shoguns put the mark of Zhu Xi's highly patriarchal orthodoxy into family law, reasserting the male head's power over property and women. In Russia, the cult of family honor allowed raped women to bring suit against their abusers for "dishonor," but Chinese law allowed no such claims.

Peter's greatest contribution to women was to liberate them from seclusion. He abolished the terem as part of his attack on the boyar clans. Russia's eighteenth century brought much greater exposure to Western European norms, which favored cultivated, educated women. In China, the increasing attractions of leisure, literacy, and commerce in the sixteenth century led women to struggle against efforts of male rulers and kinsmen to confine and isolate them. By the eighteenth century, a reaction set in. Some of the fluidity and flexibility for multiple gender roles of the sixteenth and seventeenth centuries was stamped out.

Conclusion From 1500 to 1700, the opening of the early modern age, extended networks of trade connected the New and Old Worlds for the first time, and maritime routes across the great oceans came to dominate world trade. Yet it was a time of upheaval for states and empires everywhere. Climatic cooling, international war, religious strife, imperial collapse, and general suffering struck much of Eurasia and the Americas. The next century, a much more peaceful age, saw populations grow, civil arts flourish, commerce spread, and literacy grow. This time of "dappled sunshine" built on the important bases of global economic integration, state centralization, and domestic commerce established in these two violent, but dynamic centuries.

Study Questions (1) Compare how Peter the Great, the Kangxi emperor, and Louis XIV reformed their states and prepared for wars of expansion. Who had the greatest advantages, and who was the most successful in the end?

(2) Religious leaders driven by passionate spiritual concerns led much of the opposition to the autocratic states. How did they express their dissent, and how did populations respond to them?

(3) What allowed merchants to prosper in Russia, China, and Japan during this period? Which trade routes were most lucrative, and how important a position did merchants have in relation to state officials?

(4) Trace the flow of silver into Asia from Japan and the New World, and discuss its effects on commercial activity, military expansion, and urban culture.

Suggested Reading

Russia PAUL BUSHKOVITCH, *Peter the Great* (Lanham, MD: Rowman & Littlefield, 2001). Bushkovitch provides an excellent short synthesis of the politics influencing Peter's reforms.

JANET MARTIN, *Medieval Russia, 980–1584* (Cambridge University Press, 1995). This is an outstanding synthesis of the rise of Muscovy, ending with Ivan the Terrible's reign.

OLEARIUS, *The Travels of Olearius in Seventeenth-Century Russia*, ed. and trans. S.H. BARON, (Stanford University Press, 1967). Olearius offers a fascinating primary source describing Russian life from a German observer's viewpoint.

Japan MARY ELIZABETH BERRY, *Hideyoshi* (Cambridge, MA: Harvard University Press, 1982). This is a political biography of the most important founder of early modern Japan.

CONRAD TOTMAN, *Early Modern Japan* (Berkeley: University of California Press, 1993). Totman's excellent survey emphasizes environmental factors.

China TIMOTHY BROOK, *The Confusions of Pleasure: Commerce and Culture in Ming China* (Berkeley: University of California Press, 1998). Brook's work is a brilliant analysis of the role of commerce in Ming China, with many translated excerpts from primary sources.

RAY HUANG, *1587, a Year of No Significance: The Ming Dynasty in Decline* (New Haven, CT: Yale University Press, 1981). Huang uses the events of a single year to survey a broad range of personalities and issues affecting late Ming society.

JONATHAN SPENCE, *The Death of Woman Wang* (New York: Viking, 1978). This is a gripping description, part literary, part historical, of life in a remote rural area of seventeenth-century China.

Lynn Struve (ed. and trans.), *Voices from the Ming-Qing Cataclysm: China in Tigers' Jaws* (New Haven, CT: Yale University Press, 1993). These beautifully translated sources portray the horrors of seventeenth-century China.

Weiming Tu, *Neo-Confucian Thought in Action: Wang Yang-ming's Youth (1472–1509)* (Berkeley: University of California Press, 1976). This is a careful analysis of how Wang's spiritual crisis inspired his powerful philosophy.

Glossary

Altan Khan: Mongol leader (1507–82) who negotiated peace with Ming dynasty.

Cossacks: free military communities in the borderlands of the Russian empire.

bakufu: Japanese military government.

daimyo: Japanese lords, owning landed estates and supported by military followers, or samurai.

Donglin academy: Group of scholars who attempted to reform Chinese government in the late sixteenth century.

Dorgon: Representative of Manchus (1612–1650) who persuaded Wu Sangui to let Manchus take Beijing.

Eight Banners: Manchu social groups devised by Nurhaci, dividing the Manchu people across traditional clan ties.

Fushe: National organization of scholars promoting political reform in seventeenth-century China.

Galdan: Mongol leader (1644–97) who resisted expansion of Qing empire under Kangxi.

Ivan IV: Russian Tsar (the "Terrible," r. 1533–84) who nearly destroyed his state with his oppressive oprichnina.

Jiangnan: Wealthy region of China in the lower course of the Yangtze River.

Kangxi emperor: Long-lived ruler of Qing China (r. 1661–1722) during the Flourishing Age.

Li Zicheng: Unemployed soldier and rebel against Ming dynasty (1605–45). He briefly occupied Beijing and proclaimed a new dynasty.

Liaodong: region in southern Manchuria, core of Qing state in early seventeenth century.

Matteo Ricci: Italian Jesuit (1552–1610) who succeeded in spreading Christian doctrines in late Ming China.

Michael Romanov: Russian tsar (r. 1613–45) who established a long-lived Russian dynasty, after Time of Troubles ended.

mir: Russian term for the village community.

Nurhaci: Manchu tribal leader (1559–1626), founder of the Qing state.

Oda Nobunaga: First unifier of Japan (1534–82), a military man who destroyed the power of the Buddhist temples.

Old Believers: Russian Orthodox religious sect which rejected state control in the seventeenth century.

oprichnina: Special detachments of spies and police created by Tsar Ivan IV.

Peter the Great: Russian tsar (r. 1682–1725), famous for radical reforms enhancing the power of the Russian state and introducing Western European culture.

ronin: Japanese samurai who had lost their master.

sakoku: Japanese "Period of Seclusion" from 1633–1853.

samurai: Japanese warrior class, servants of feudal lords.

sankin kotai: Control system used by Japanese military rulers, requiring lords to leave hostages in the capital city.

seppuku (harakiri): terms for ritual suicide in Tokugawa Japan.

Shanhaiguan: Mountain pass controlling the route from Beijing to Manchuria.

shi: In Tokugawa Japan, term for ruling class of samurai and lords. In China, scholars who obtained degrees in the examination system.

shogun: Chief general of Japan, protector of the emperor, and de facto ruler.

streltsy: Regiments of musketeers controlling political change in Moscow.

Tokaido: Main commercial road running through central Japan.

Tokugawa Ieyasu: Third unifier of Japan (1543–1616), who declared himself shogun and established the institutions of the bakufu state.

Toyotomi Hideyoshi: Second unifier of Japan (1536–98), who completed the war of unification, and attempted unsuccessfully to invade Korea.

Wanli emperor: Ming dynasty emperor (r. 1572–1620), builder of an enormous tomb for himself.

Wei Zhongxian: Powerful conservative eunuch of the Ming dynasty (1568–1627), who suppressed the Donglin academy literati reformers.

Wu Sangui: Chinese general (1612–78) who allowed Manchus to capture Beijing.

zemsky sobor: Russian "Assembly of the Land," collecting representatives of all the people to discuss public affairs.

Zhang Juzheng: Ming Grand Secretary and reformer (1525–82).

Zhang Xianzhong: Rebel leader (1605–47), centered in Sichuan, where he massacred many gentry and landlords.

Zunghars: Western Mongolian tribes who fought against the Qing dynasty in the seventeenth and eighteenth centuries.

Notes

1 Timothy Brook, *The Confusions of Pleasure: Commerce and Culture in Ming China* (Berkeley: University of California Press, 1998), p. 123.

2 Giles Fletcher, *Of the Russe Commonwealth* [1591] (Cambridge, MA: Harvard University Press, 1966), Preface.

3 Olearius, *The Travels of Olearius in Seventeenth-Century Russia*, ed. S.H. Baron (Stanford University Press, 1967), pp. 61–62.

4 E.V. Anisimov, *The Reforms of Peter the Great: Progress Through Coercion in Russia* (Armonk, NY, and London: Sharpe, 1993), p. 94.

5 V.O. Klyuchevsky, *Peter the Great* (London: Macmillan; New York: St. Martin's Press, 1958), p. 155.

6 Anisimov, *Reforms of Peter the Great*, p. 239.

7 Mary Elizabeth Berry, *Hideyoshi* (Cambridge, MA: Harvard University Press, 1982), p. 102.

8 Berry, *Hideyoshi*, pp. 208, 213.

9 Olearius, *Travels of Olearius*, pp. 164–65.

3 The Americas and Africa in the era of conquest and enslavement

Timeline	
1249	Alfonso III expels the last Islamic states from Portugal.
1418–19	Portuguese expedition lays claim to the Madeira Islands.
1427	Portuguese colony established in the Azores.
1453	Fall of Constantinople to the Ottoman Turks; this closes the eastern Mediterranean to the West.
1469	Ferdinand of Aragon and Isabela of Castile marry, uniting Spain under two monarchs.
1479	São Tomé, a Portuguese sugar plantation using slave labor, is established.
1482	Portuguese trading post of Elmina is established on the coast of West Africa.
1487	Bartolomeu Dias rounds the Cape of Good Hope; first Portuguese traders arrive in the Indian Ocean in 1497.
1492	Granada captured by Castile, completing the Reconquest of Spain from the Moors; Columbus sails toward Asia, finds the Caribbean, and returns.
1493	Columbus' second voyage begins Spanish invasion and conquest of the Americas.
1494	Treaty of Tordesillas divides the New World between Spain and Portugal.
1496	Henry VII of England, who had turned Columbus down two years earlier, finances the North Atlantic voyage of John Cabot.
1500	Pedro Alvarez Cabral accidentally discovers Brazil.
1513	Balboa and Pizarro cross the Isthmus of Panama.
1518	First shipment of slaves directly from Africa to the Americas.
1519–22	Ferdinand Magellan's crew completes the first circumnavigation of the globe.
1519	Hernán Cortés lands at Veracruz, Mexico.
1521	Fall of the Aztec empire.
1525	Death of Huayna Capac, ruler of Inka empire; civil war between sons Atahualpa and Huascar; Atahualpa victorious.
1532	Pizarro captures Atahualpa and defeats Inka army at Cajamarca.

1536–37	Failed siege of Cusco by Manca Inka; last effective Inka resistance.
1542	"New Laws" prohibit the enslavement of Native Americans, limiting forced labor.
1549	Viceroy Antonio de Mendoza begins the *repartimiento de indios* in Mexico City.
1568	Dutch Republic declares independence from Spain; recognized by Spain in 1648.
1580–1640	Spain and Portugal united under one king.
1599–1630	Abolition of forced labor in most Spanish colonies, except for mining in Peru.
1619	First slaves imported to the territory that would become Virginia.
1630–54	Dutch occupy northeastern Brazil (sugar region), and transfer technology to the Caribbean.
1630s–1660s	Great Britain seizes Jamaica from Spain (1655); French, Dutch, and others grab territory for slave plantation colonies.

Bartolomé de Las Casas followed Christopher Columbus to the Indies as a conqueror, determined to get rich. He went first to Hispaniola in 1502 at the age of 28 to help his merchant father sell provisions to the expeditions that explored and conquered throughout the Caribbean. He received a grant of **encomienda** (from the Spanish verb "to entrust") in Hispaniola and another in Cuba. This institution had developed during the Spanish Reconquest of the Iberian peninsula from the Moors. The encomiendas allowed him to collect tribute and demand labor services from the Native Americans in his domains in exchange for supervising their conversion to Christianity. He took the work of conversion seriously and learned to communicate in several of the indigenous languages, unlike other encomenderos, who gave little thought to conversion and worked their charges to the point of exhaustion and death.

In 1514, Las Casas freed the indigenous people in his own encomiendas and demanded that other Spaniards follow his example. None did. He returned to Spain to lobby church authorities and the Spanish king to intervene. He entered the Dominican order in 1523 and began studying and writing. He played a key role in drafting the "New Laws" issued in 1542 that outlawed Indian slavery and undermined the encomienda system.

Appointed bishop of Chiapas in Southern Mexico in 1544, he promptly infuriated the local Spanish elite by announcing that no one within his jurisdiction would be granted absolution for his sins unless he first freed his indigenous servants and made restitution for all that had been stolen from them. Las Casas's parishioners responded with insults and threats; he narrowly missed death when several tried to poison him.

Las Casas's most influential work, called *The Devastation of the Indies, A Summary Account*, appeared in 1552. The book not only denounced the Spanish mistreatment of Native Americans, but condemned African slavery as well. Translated into many languages, this work formed the basis for what came to be called "the Black Legend" of the Spanish conquest. It also established Las Casas's reputation as the pioneer in struggles for human rights that continue in the Americas to this day.

Las Casas's book illustrates how dramatically the history of the world changed after Columbus' first voyage in 1492. In the short period of seventy-three years, from 1492 to 1565, explorers working for the Spanish government established regular round-trip communication and trade across the Atlantic and the Pacific Oceans. In the same era, Portuguese navigators established the first regular commerce ever between Europe and sub-Saharan Africa and between the Atlantic and the Indian oceans. Earlier navigators and explorers, like the Norsemen in the North Atlantic and seafarers in the South Pacific, had already crossed and even recrossed these oceans, but not until the voyages of Columbus, Cabral, and Magellan did regular communication and trade begin. This chapter examines this important achievement and its often tragic consequences.

Historians once recounted this history with ill-disguised Eurocentric triumphalism, emphasizing the achievements of European navigators, the Europeans' technical and military superiority, and the benefits they conferred on the people they came to dominate, such as Christianity and trade goods. In more recent times, influenced by modern ideas of democracy, human rights, and racial and ethnic equality, historians have called attention to the horrendous price paid by Native Americans and Africans, and their descendants. Though historians of these two schools disagree over many aspects of the history of this era, they are often criticized together for treating Native Americans and Africans as essentially passive and unable to influence events or trends. Contemporary historians have thus turned to studying the history of resistance to European domination as well as the persistence and adaptation of African and Native American cultures, religious practices, and patterns of social interaction into the modern era.

This chapter focuses primarily on the origins and impact of the European expansion. The main characters in these scenes are Europeans and those who helped them or suffered at their hands. For accounts of the peoples, cultures, and societies of Africa and the Americas before the arrival of the Europeans, see Volume 1, Chapters 4, 9, and 12. Resistance by Africans and Native Americans is discussed in this chapter and in Chapter 7. On the history of Africa after the slave trade, including the successful anti-colonial and anti-apartheid struggles of the twentieth century, see Chapter 15.

- Between 1500 and 1700, Africa and the Americas became the first regions to feel the full impact of Europe's expansion as European sailing vessels full of trade goods and war parties created a new international trading system, and new kinds of empire.
- Trade developed and flourished on a scale never before possible. New World plants and minerals helped to transform European societies, while European crops, domesticated animals, and technologies spread throughout the Americas.
- New forms of exploitation and domination arose simultaneously while European conquerors and settlers inadvertently spread epidemic diseases that helped them push aside Native American governments and seize control of all the commercially valuable parts of the western hemisphere.
- In Africa, the Europeans diverted and vastly expanded a pre-existing trans-Saharan slave trade into a transatlantic system that forced thousands, eventually millions, of Africans into slavery and abuse in New World plantations.
- The history of Africa and the Americas between 1500 and 1700 is thus a history of technological and commercial advance linked to conquest, domination, death, and enslavement.

3.1 TRAVEL IN THE MEDIEVAL AND EARLY MODERN ERAS

In the medieval and early modern world, travel was slow, uncomfortable, and often dangerous. Most people avoided it.

Paved roads or streets were rare, even in cities. Rain or melting snow turned highways into rivers of mud. The only sure protection against thieves was poverty. Regular stagecoach, freight, or mail services did not exist in most areas of the world. Hotels for travelers were few, expensive, and often filthy.

Transporting merchandise was both costly and risky. Bulky foodstuffs could not be shipped more than a few miles by land, so overland trade beyond local markets consisted mainly of luxury goods with a high value to bulk ratio: precious metals and gems, ivory, silk cloth, and spices. Valuable goods often moved in caravans with armed guards and plenty of provisions. Even merchandise that could walk to market, like cattle and slaves, had to be fed and protected from bandits along the way. Insurance against loss was a novelty and hardly ever available.

Despite these problems, long-distance trade developed throughout much of the ancient world. Specialized traders and merchants developed contacts (including family members) spread out along caravan routes over great distances. This helped to keep them informed about markets and road conditions. Rulers in many places learned that respecting the property of traders (even foreigners) and levying modest taxes and tolls brought in more revenues in the long run than scaring off merchants by seizing their property or taxing away their profits. Merchants developed ingenious mechanisms for ensuring that loans would be repaid and promises kept, even when local governments were corrupt and their courts unreliable.

Regular long-distance trade across large bodies of water used all of these advances, but also required:

- Detailed knowledge of weather, winds, and sea currents over huge expanses of water.
- Navigational techniques and skills that helped ships' captains to stay on course.
- Large specially designed cargo ships that could carry enough goods to make the journey profitable.
- Protection against thieves and pirates.

Merchants, sea captains and crews, specialized ship builders, and occasionally even governments accumulated knowledge, tried out new navigational aids, experimented with new ship designs and shipbuilding techniques, and devised elaborate schemes to increase safety.

Advantages of Water Transport

The inspiration for efforts to improve the technology of sea travel was much the same over many centuries in nearly every part of the world. Water transport had three great advantages over land transport. It was cheaper, faster, and safer.

Shipping by water was (and still is) much cheaper than by land, often by a ratio of ten to one or better. A cargo of grain loaded on wagons pulled by horses, mules, or oxen, cannot be carried more than a day or two (say 30 to 60 miles) before the animals and their drivers eat so much of the cargo that the journey becomes pointless. With no animals and fewer people per ton of cargo, ships could carry the same produce 300 to 600 miles and still leave a profit for the producer and the merchant.

Ships are also faster and bigger than wagons. In one day with a good wind, a medieval cog in the Baltic Sea or a dhow in the Indian Ocean could carry up to 400 tons as far as 150 miles with a small crew. Chinese junks could carry over 1,000 tons. Overland, the same cargo required hundreds of heavily laden wagons. With two good mules and a skilled driver on a good road, it took more than a week to travel the same distance, and each wagon could carry only a tiny fraction of a ship's cargo.

Ships were also safer because they were harder to ambush. Even in pirate-infested waters, a ship had a better chance of slipping through undetected than a caravan or wagon train that had to follow a fixed route along a well-known road or trail.

For all these reasons, people who lived near rivers, lakes, and seacoasts benefited from cheaper transportation since they did not have to depend for all their food on local farmers. Local producers could specialize in whatever the local soils and climate helped them to produce better or more cheaply and exchange their products for imports produced far away. From earliest times, human settlements and especially cities tended to be built near waterways, not just for drinking and irrigation but because cheap water transportation made it possible to import food, cloth, and luxuries from more distant places.

One of the earliest long-distance seagoing trading systems developed in the Mediterranean Sea beginning in the second millennium BCE. By 200 CE, the world's first trans-oceanic trading system developed in the Indian Ocean, with ships that made regular voyages of hundreds of miles out of sight of land. Scandinavian voyagers in the North Atlantic also traveled great distances, reaching Newfoundland in modern Canada (see Box 3.1 for details). Until the European voyages that began in 1492, however, there was no regular trade or communication across the Atlantic or the Pacific, nor any seaborne traffic at all between any of the world's great oceans.

3.2 WHY AND HOW DID EUROPE EXPLORE AND CONQUER?

Historians have long sought to understand why and how it was that Europeans "discovered" and eventually came to dominate most of the rest of the world. First Portugal, then Spain, England,

the Netherlands (Dutch), France, and eventually Belgium, Denmark, Sweden, Germany, and Italy all invaded and set up "colonies" in the Americas, Africa, and Asia. Europeans ruled major portions of these continents for periods as long as 500 years, from the late 1400s to the late 1900s in some cases. European colonialism changed shape and structure across time and space, as Box 3.2 points out. Even in many areas where the Europeans took longer to impose colonial rule (as in most of Africa) or did not actually displace local governments (as in China), European political and economic influence grew too powerful to resist.

The beginnings of this vast process can be found in the developments that occurred in medieval and early modern Western Europe. No one in 1500 would have predicted that this tiny, backward, war-torn region at the tip of the Eurasian landmass would emerge in the next two centuries to dominate much of the globe. The history of this process raises many questions addressed throughout the rest of this book (for example, see Chapter 6). It all began with the voyages of discovery (and profit) in the fifteenth century.

European Advantages

Here we start with two of the most basic and important of these questions. How and why did Western Europeans become the first people to explore distant oceans and engage in long-distance trade, conquest, and colonization? And why was there no Asian, African, or Native American "discovery" and colonization of Europe?

One answer to these questions may be that Europe's problems and difficulties worked to the region's long-term advantage. These included:

- An unstable and highly competitive system of small states controlling small territories pushed toward the Atlantic by waves of Asian invaders.
- Weak political and religious institutions that had difficulty controlling labor and trade and thus left seafarers, adventurers, and merchants freer to explore for plunder and profit.
- A nearly obsessive preoccupation with military technology in all its forms as a result of widespread religious, civil, and international warfare.

The first of these factors – small states pushed westward by powerful enemies – forced European governments, especially small and isolated Portugal, to look for ways to expand overseas and to use trade (a low-prestige activity in most places) to enhance the power of the king and support his dynastic and territorial ambitions. The second factor, weak institutions, made it necessary for Western European governments to contract with

Box 3.1 The Norse Colonies in America

In the North Atlantic, archaeological evidence has confirmed the tales recorded in the Norse sagas of long voyages by migrating settlers who eventually reached Newfoundland in modern Canada. The Norse peoples or Vikings of Scandinavia began raiding all over Europe in the ninth century, starting in the Baltic Sea and along the coast of England and France. Some of their war parties got as far as the Mediterranean to the south and the Volga River in Russia. In some areas, like Normandy (named for the Norsemen) in France, they pushed aside local inhabitants and established colonies of their own people. Elsewhere, they simply displaced local overlords and established themselves as the new rulers.

Small groups of Norse sailors also voyaged west into the North Atlantic, settling in Iceland as early as 874 CE. A century later in about 985, a leader known as Erik the Red led a band of settlers that established a colony in Greenland. His son, Leif Erikson, sailed further west and in about the year 1000 reached the coast of North America. The navigation skills required to sail across the North Atlantic in the small Norse ships must have been considerable, though each stage in the voyage from Europe to the islands to America measured less than 250 miles and in good weather with favorable winds took less than three days to travel – much shorter distances than those traversed by Polynesians migrating across vast stretches of the Pacific Ocean at the same time. Norse seafarers simplified their navigational tasks by sailing east and west always at the same latitude, which they calculated roughly by checking the angle of the sun or the North Star from the horizon.

Historians, archaeologists, and local politicians have debated the exact location of the Norse colony Erikson named "Vinland" (wine land), apparently because he and his followers thought the place suitable for growing grapes. The ruins of a Norse settlement at L'Anse aux Meadows in Newfoundland have been identified beyond any doubt, but Norse artifacts have also turned up on Baffin Island and the Labrador coast. Within a few years, at least three settlements had been established, but they did not last. The Norse legends, written down a century or more later, attributed the failure of these colonies to attacks by local Native Americans, and to disunity and squabbling among the colonists themselves.

They never returned to Newfoundland, no doubt because the initial failure convinced them that a new attempt would not be worth the effort. The colonists had found nothing valuable enough to trade or pillage. In the fifteenth century, during a long spell of exceptionally cold weather, the Norse also abandoned their settlements in Greenland. Their American expeditions remained unknown to all but readers of the Norse "sagas" until modern times.

Circumstantial evidence has convinced some enthusiasts that other Europeans, Africans, Egyptians, Polynesians, and travelers from Japan or China (or even Outer Space) might also have reached the Americas before Columbus. No physical proof has yet been found to support any of these hypotheses.

---

independent merchants, navigators, and mercenaries to explore and conquer. And the third factor, Europe's preoccupation with military technology, helped the Portuguese government and others to understand the value of investing in what today would be called "research and development."

Why Not Others?

By contrast, large and well-ordered states elsewhere in the world tended to look inward. Revenues came from taxing peasant harvests, sales taxes in urban markets, and plunder from conquering new lands. The only serious threats to such governments came from invasions by land or internal revolts. Wealth and power thus rested on controlling territory with loyal troops. The great land empires and states of Asia, Africa, and the Americas showed little interest in the oceans they touched.

In the Indian Ocean, the world's first trans-oceanic trading system developed after 500 CE once seafarers discovered how to make use of monsoon winds that reverse direction biannually, blowing from the east from April to August and from the west for the rest of the year. Trading ships timed their voyages to catch favorable winds. In this environment, experience and skill counted for more than navigation technology. Indian Ocean navigators and traders did explore far down the African coast, but found little of interest south of Madagascar and the Swahili coast.

Even if they had discovered a route around southern Africa and up the Atlantic to Europe, however, they would have found that the West Africans and Europeans produced little of value to trade for except slaves and precious metals, both available closer to home. And they would have lacked the support of their governments and religious institutions for a war of conquest

Box 3.2 Types of European Colony

In the two centuries after the opening of trans-oceanic and inter-ocean trade, Europeans created four different kinds of trans-oceanic colony in various parts of the Americas, Africa, and Asia.

The earliest outposts of European rule were fortified *trading posts* established by the Portuguese government (called *feitoras*), beginning with Elmina (initially called São Jorge da Mina) in 1482, along the coast of West Africa and eventually into the Indian Ocean up along the East African coast, on the coast of India, and on various spice islands.

Second came the *conquest colonies* of Spain in the Caribbean, Mesoamerica, and the Andean region. Spanish

conquistadores (conquerors) invaded, defeated, and subjugated Native American populations in these regions between 1492 and 1537. In the conquest colonies, small European and creole (people with European ancestry, but born in America) minorities controlled all high political and ecclesiastical offices, enjoyed privileges (including tax exemptions) denied others, and owned the most valuable assets – agricultural estates, mines, trading houses, and other enterprises.

Third came the so-called "true" or *settlement colonies*, like those of the Spanish in the Rio de la Plata (Argentina) and the English in New England. In these colonies, the Europeans ignored,

pushed aside, or exterminated the Native American population to make way for an expanding neo-European society.

Finally, *plantation colonies* dominated by large slave-worked agricultural estates producing tropical products like sugar and cacao constituted the fourth kind of colony established by the Europeans in the Americas.

One type of colony often evolved into another. The conquest colonies in the Caribbean became settlement colonies when the indigenous population died, and later became plantation colonies when the settlers imported African slaves to produce sugar.

and colonization so far away. If Asian explorers had reached Europe by sea before the Europeans had discovered the route round Cape Horn, they would probably have returned with little to show for their efforts.

3.3 THE PORTUGUESE IN AFRICA AND SOUTH AMERICA

The Portuguese government played a key role in accelerating the development of maritime technology, beginning in the late fourteenth century. After uniting under a single monarch, Alfonso III (r. 1248–79), Portugal's isolation at the southwestern tip of Europe helped protect the kingdom from external conquest and foreign wars. Alfonso's army cleared the last of the Islamic states from Portuguese territory in 1249. Looking for opportunities to expand the kingdom, the Portuguese government began sending ships down the African coast on voyages of reconnaissance and exploration (see Map 3.1). By 1340, Portuguese and Spanish sailors had found the Canary Islands. Portugal's overseas conquests and explorations multiplied during the reign of King John (João) I (r. 1385–1433). John's sons included the eldest, Prince Edward (Duarte), who helped organize successful expeditions against Islamic states in present-day Morocco, and Prince Henry (Henrique), "The Navigator" (1394–1460), who took charge of military expeditions and explorations south along the African coast.

Portugal's Goals

Portuguese exploration, territorial expansion, and trade promotion served many, sometimes competing goals. The king and government sought prestige and new sources of revenue from victories over traditional Muslim enemies. The Portuguese Catholic church, linked to the Pope in Rome but tied to the government as the official state religion, gained souls to save as well as income from new tithe revenues and indulgence sales. For the nobles and merchants who financed the expeditions and the navigators, sailors, and traders who participated, profit-making was the key goal. The early Portuguese conquests along the Atlantic coast of Africa hardly repaid the effort, but they eventually put Portuguese traders in touch with the areas south of the Sahara that had been supplying Muslim caravans with gold, slaves, and ivory for centuries. By the early 1500s, the Portuguese were already diverting a major portion of the trans-Saharan trade to their own ships in exchange for Portuguese trade goods, including cloth and weapons.

The long-term goal of the Portuguese expeditions down the African coast, however, was not just to circumvent the trans-Saharan camel caravans but also to find a way around Africa to the fabled riches of Asia. Western European imports of Asian luxury goods such as spices (especially pepper, cloves, and nutmeg used to flavor meat) and medicinal herbs, silks, porcelain, and other objects amounted to little more than a trickle. Most of these products came across the Indian Ocean to Red Sea ports, then overland to the Mediterranean, and then

Map 3.1 African coastline with Portuguese islands (São Tomé) and forts, ports on west and east coast

by sea to Italian city-states like Genoa, Venice, and Pisa. Shipping costs were high because each cargo had to be sold and resold, loaded and unloaded, and taxed every time it entered a new kingdom or city. Frequent land and naval wars in the Middle East and pirates throughout the Mediterranean raised the risk that cargoes would be lost or seized. In 1453, when Constantinople fell to the Ottoman Turks (who renamed the city Istanbul), trade in the eastern Mediterranean became even more expensive and risky for merchants from Christian states to the west. Shippers raised their rates even higher to compensate.

The Portuguese government's goal of finding an all-water route to the Indian Ocean that avoided the high costs and risks of the Mediterranean route made good economic sense. The profits from just a single successful voyage could be (and later proved to be) enormous. A secondary goal of the Portuguese government was to establish contact with the legendary Christian kingdom of "Prestor John" located, so the tales told, in the heart of Africa. Amazingly, the Portuguese achieved both goals, and sooner than anyone could have expected.

Prince Henry's "Research and Development"

Prince Henry put together a rudimentary but effective research and development staff that assembled maps and scientific information, tested new navigational devices, and promoted innovations in ship design. He founded a School for Navigation at Sagres on Cape St. Vincent and hired an international group of experts in map making, ship design, navigation devices, and ocean winds and currents. The Mediterranean and Indian Ocean trading systems had already stimulated the development and application of new navigation technologies. Sailors in both areas had learned to use the position of the sun and the stars to make rough estimates of their ships' positions. The magnetic compass, first used for navigation in China by 1090, spread to both areas.

The **astrolabe** was even more important. This ingenious device, probably invented by ancient Greek or Egyptian astronomers, developed into a navigational device in the late medieval era. Navigators calibrated the angle of the sun (or a specific star at night) and compared it to a table showing the sun's position at various points north or south of the equator. This made it possible to locate a ship's latitude (how far north or south of the equator) on a map.

Prince Henry's collaborators experimented with all of the new devices and improved on several of them. In addition, they collected maps, both old and new, followed debates on the shape and size of the world (and the universe), and avidly pursued and recorded information on wind and sea currents, weather, and sailing conditions.

The improvements adopted or pioneered by the Portuguese were crucial to establishing regular communication and trade between the Atlantic and Indian oceans and across the Atlantic and the Pacific. Unlike the Mediterranean, the distances across the Atlantic and especially the Pacific are enormous (1,000 to 3,000 miles). Unlike the Indian Ocean, winds in the Atlantic and Pacific Oceans do not conveniently reverse direction on schedule. Instead, they blow predictably in different directions at different latitudes. The compass, and especially the astrolabe, thus proved to be vital to the European explorers. To cross the Atlantic as well as the Pacific, seamen had to be able to calculate roughly the latitude of their ships in order to find the right winds.

One of the most important achievements of the Portuguese experiments was the development of a new kind of ship. The Portuguese **caravel** (shown in Figure 3.1) combined **lateen** (triangular) sails (used in the Mediterranean since Roman times) with a stern-mounted rudder (a feature of Chinese ocean-going ships since ancient times). The lateen sails made it much easier to tack into the wind, and the rudder, which unlike a steering oar did not interfere with the sails, made the ships much more maneuverable.

Portuguese Exploration Down the African Coast

The Portuguese government organized and subsidized exploratory expeditions of up to a dozen ships, ordered the building of forts and trading posts to protect Portuguese ships and merchants along the African coast, and installed colonists and officials at strategic points, like offshore islands along the key trade routes. To stimulate private investment in exploration, the Portuguese Crown issued **cartas de doação** granting to navigators not only the right to govern any new lands they discovered, but also to monopolize the trade of such places, control immigration and any new colonies established there, and send exports back to Portugal free of taxes – all in exchange for a royal fifth of all profits. Prince Henry invested his own money in the expeditions, using funds raised by taxing peasants on lands owned by a religious society, the Order of Christ, which he controlled.

CARAVELS OF CHRISTOPHER COLUMBUS.
(*After an Engraving published in 1583.*)

Figure 3.1 This illustration is based on a 1583 engraving showing the two caravels in the expedition to the "Indies" captained by Christopher Columbus in 1492. Caravels were preferred by explorers because of their maneuverability and ability to tack into the wind, qualities that could prove crucial in unfamiliar waters. Larger ships were preferred for voyages of conquest and invasion in already explored waters when troop numbers and supplies could be the key to success and maneuverability was less important.

Portuguese expeditions soon succeeded in planting the Portuguese flag on a series of Atlantic island groups. After capturing Ceuta and several other Muslim towns along the Saharan coast of modern Morocco, a Portuguese expedition in 1418–19 laid claim to the Madeira Islands. The government sent peasant colonists to produce food and ships' supplies (including, eventually, the famous Madeira wines). In 1425, Prince Henry attempted to seize the Canaries from Spain, but failed. Further out in the Atlantic, the Portuguese in 1427 set up a permanent colony in the uninhabited Azores, a group of rocky islands located 740 miles (1,190 kilometers) west of Lisbon, Portugal's capital and main port. Slowed by defeats in North Africa that forced them to return Ceuta to the Moors in 1437, the Portuguese resumed their efforts in 1445 by settling colonists on the island of Cape Verde further to the south. Conflict between Portugal and the Spanish kingdom of Castile in the fifteenth century, and the resulting treaties, codified Portugal's southern thrust and helped to keep Portugal's government fixed on its explorations down the African coast. War broke out in 1468 when the Portuguese king, Alfonso V (r. 1438–77) attempted to secure the Castilian throne for his son João by arranging for him to marry the Castilian princess Juana. When her father King Henry (Enrique) IV died, Juana claimed the throne. The rival claimant to the Castilian throne, Isabela, mobilized her supporters and those of her husband Ferdinand (Fernando), king of Aragon, to defeat João and Juana. In the 1479 peace agreement, João had to renounce his marriage plans and Juana was forced to enter a convent. The treaty also gave Spain uncontested title to the Canary Islands in return for recognizing Portugal's rights to the Azores, the Madeira Islands, and the Cape Verde island group along with the right to explore and trade down the coast of Africa without Spanish interference.

Portuguese navigators also managed to overcome winds and currents that pushed ships to the south. Seamen feared they would never be able to return if they sailed beyond Cape Bojador (modern Cape Boujdour). It took Prince Henry until 1434 to outfit an expedition of caravels that sailed beyond Cape Bojador for the first time. The caravels could sail against the wind by tacking, using the head winds on their lateen sails to push in a northeasterly direction, then back toward the northwest. Within a few years, ships exploring Portugal's new island possessions discovered winds running north and west further out in the Atlantic. By the 1440s, traveling down the African coast with south winds and then back by catching northerly winds further out to sea made regular trade and communication feasible.

With this discovery, it became possible to send ships much further south than ever before. At first, the African coast past Cape Bojador and around the hump of the continent did not prove inviting. The first expeditions encountered miles of mangrove swamps, beaches exposed to pounding surf, virtually no natural harbors, and either arid desert or impenetrable forest behind the coastline. In the 1470s, however, Portuguese ships made contact with African city-states on the coast of the Gulf of Guinea whose inhabitants were eager to trade. On European maps, these south-facing shorelines were named according to the export commodities the Portuguese bought: the "Ivory Coast," the "Gold Coast" (modern Ghana) and the "Slave Coast" (modern Benin and Nigeria). The Portuguese purchased locally produced gold, captured slaves, and luxury items like ivory and spices, in exchange for Portuguese weapons and cloth. With the development of this trade, Portugal redoubled its explorations down the African coast.

The Portuguese in the Indian Ocean

Finding a sea route to the Indian Ocean, Portugal's ultimate strategic goal, came sooner than anyone expected. In 1487, a Portuguese caravel captained by Bartolomeu Dias, blown off course in a terrible storm, rounded the Cape of Good Hope and sailed into the Indian Ocean. A decade later, the Portuguese government sent out a large expedition led by Vasco da Gama that reached Calicut in Southwest India. His expedition returned with a fabulous cargo of cloves and silks. (See Map 3.2)

Map 3.2 European explorations with specific voyages of Columbus, Cabral, Cabot, da Gama and Magellan

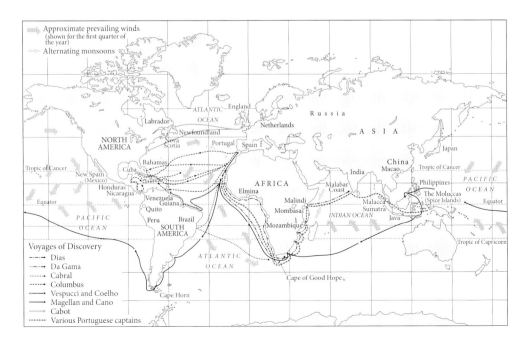

Three years later in 1500 a follow-up expedition to the Indian Ocean led by Pedro Alvares Cabral headed south along the African coast and found itself pushed off course by strong easterly winds. When the expedition found land, Alvares Cabral put it down as an uncharted island, piously named it the Island of the True Cross, and continued on his way to the riches of the East. It would be another two decades before the Portuguese realized that Alvares Cabral had "discovered" Brazil.

By this time, Portuguese trading vessels were making their long-awaited profits on the Indian Ocean spice trade. The Portuguese attacked Muslim port cities and ships all along the East African coast, seizing control of trade and trade routes. They built fortified trading posts along both coasts of Africa, and at key points on the Indian subcontinent, in the "Spice Islands" of modern Indonesia, and as far east as Macao on the south coast of China.

In 1487, a Portuguese agent reached the Christian kingdom of Ethiopia, which had developed regular contact with Italy a century earlier. Ethiopian rulers sought and eventually received Portuguese help to withstand attacks from Muslim neighbors between 1529 and 1540. But the Portuguese were disappointed; the "Prestor John" legend had led them to expect a wealthy and powerful ally, rather than a weak regime in need of aid (see Volume 1, Chapter 12).

From da Gama's voyage in 1497–99 and for more than a century thereafter, Portuguese naval vessels in the Indian Ocean fought to establish and maintain a Portuguese monopoly over the spice trade. Portuguese naval vessels attacked and sank ships that tried to evade the monopoly, bombarded ports where local rulers failed to co-operate, and intruded repeatedly in the domestic politics of states throughout the region to secure governments they could better control or influence. Though a great boon to the Portuguese Crown and the fortunes of merchants and sea captains for a time, the Portuguese empire in Africa and the Indian Ocean could not compare with the fabulous riches Spain seized in the Americas.

3.4 CONQUERING THE ATLANTIC AND PACIFIC OCEANS

Spain started later than Portugal. After the Islamic invasions of the seventh century, the territory of modern Spain fractured into a series of warring Christian and Islamic kingdoms. By the thirteenth century, shifting alliances of Christian princes had succeeded in defeating and reoccupying most of the territory, while dynastic marriages and treaties had brought most of the territory under the control of the monarchs of Aragon and Castile. The marriage of Ferdinand (Fernando) of Aragon and

Isabela of Castile in 1469 united the two remaining monarchies, but the "Catholic sovereigns" (*reyes católicos*) faced a series of revolts in Castile and a dynastic war with Portugal in 1474–79 before they could consolidate their authority. After suppressing internal resistance, the two launched a war of attrition in 1485 against Granada, the last of the Muslim states on the Iberian peninsula. In 1492, a Castilian army finally took the city of Granada itself. Spain was now united and ready to follow Portugal into the Atlantic.

"Discovering" the Americas

Four months after her victory at Granada, Queen Isabela summoned Christopher Columbus (born Cristoforo Colombo in Genoa, Italy, but known as Cristobal Colón in Spanish) and offered him modest support for a peculiar scheme he had been trying to convince various European monarchs to invest in for years. His idea was to sail west from the Spanish Canary Islands to Asia. Having defeated the Moors, Isabela was now prepared to make a risky investment, though a small one, to turn the 1479 treaty with Portugal to Spain's advantage. The Portuguese were concentrating on finding a route around Africa. Maybe Columbus could get to Asia first by sailing west.

Columbus' scheme looked dubious because, as the experts on the queen's own staff pointed out and later discoveries confirmed, Columbus' calculations of the distance from Spain to Japan were a wild underestimate. But Columbus was well connected at the Spanish court and the queen was in an expansive mood after the victory at Granada. So it was that Spain's New World empire got its start as a speculative investment by a monarch who had much more important things on her mind.

The scheme Columbus convinced Isabela to support was majestically simple. The main problem mariners faced in traveling west into the Atlantic was how to get back, since easterly winds and currents south of the Iberian peninsula all pushed to the south and west. Columbus knew this, but he also suspected from his experience sailing in more northern latitudes that westerly winds and currents to the north could be relied on to bring him home. He thus proposed to reach Asia by sailing a southerly route to the west and to return by taking a more northerly route. The expedition included ninety seamen in three small ships. They sailed first to the Canaries, the only Atlantic islands owned by Spain, located two weeks' sailing to the southwest of the Iberian peninsula. Then the expedition sailed west into uncharted waters. With easterly winds pushing the little fleet through mostly calm seas, it took only thirty-three days to reach land, a tiny Caribbean island in the Bahamas, on October 12, 1492. Map 3.3 shows the routes of all four of Columbus' voyages to the Caribbean.

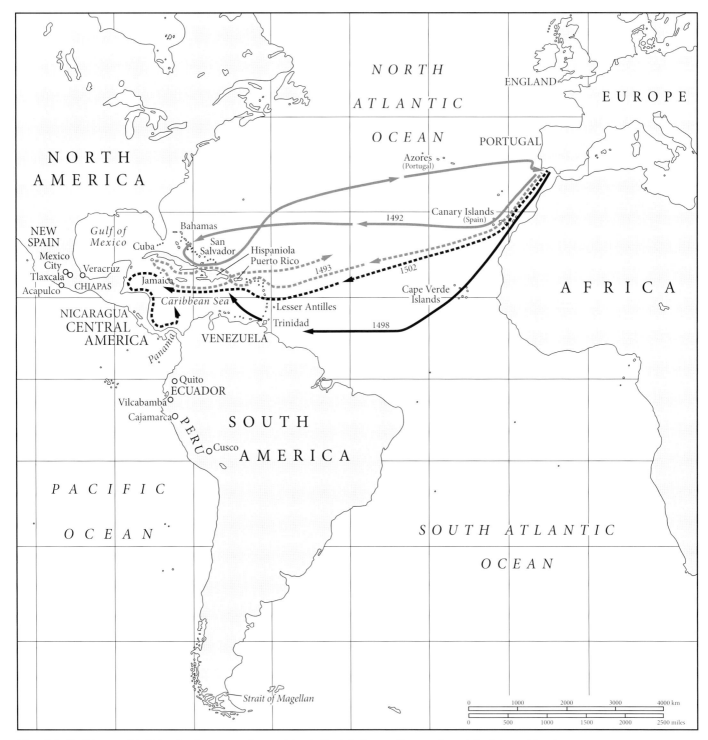

Map 3.3 Caribbean with Columbus' voyages, Canary Islands (Spain), Azores (Portugal), and Caribbean islands

The expedition's success, however, depended on the return voyage. After finding Cuba, Hispaniola (modern Haiti and the Dominican Republic), and various lesser islands, Columbus' simple scheme worked. He found westerly winds north of Puerto Rico and rode them all the way back across the Atlantic. After a brief unscheduled stop in Portugal, Columbus reached Cádiz on March 15, 1493, six months and nine days after he had departed from the Canary Islands for Asia. He insisted that the islands he had reached formed part of the (East) "Indies." He brought back with him seven "Indian" slaves, several chests full of gold trinkets and artifacts, and a sample of the plants found here and there, including sweet potatoes (most of which the crew had eaten on the stormy trip home). From this small beginning, Spain laid claim to a vast empire in what her rulers only later realized was for them a "new" world.

Crossing the Pacific and Back

The Pacific Ocean proved to be more difficult. An expedition of 5 ships and 265 sailors led by Ferdinand Magellan (Fernão de Magalhães) accomplished the first recorded crossing of the Pacific Ocean on a voyage around the world that took three years to complete (1519–22). Magellan, a Portuguese captain working for the Spanish government, sailed south and west through what later came to be called the Strait of Magellan at the southern tip of South America and then on across the Pacific Ocean to the Philippines. Magellan himself died there of wounds inflicted by local residents who attacked the expedition for meddling in their political conflicts. Magellan's crew continued on through the Indian Ocean, around the Horn of Africa and back to Spain. Only eighteen sailors and a single ship completed the voyage, the first recorded circumnavigation of the globe.

Magellan's expedition proved experimentally what most competent Arab and European cartographers already suspected: the Earth is an oblate spheroid, that is, nearly round in shape. Magellan also discovered that prevailing easterly winds could be used to cross the southern Pacific. But regular trade and communication between the Americas and Asia depended on two-way traffic. Again the key lay in finding reliable westerly winds. A Spanish expedition, financed by the colonial government of New Spain (Mexico) accomplished this feat by sailing to the Philippines and back in 1564–65. The leader of the return voyage, an Augustinian priest, Andrés de Urdaneta, had learned something about Pacific Ocean wind patterns on a previous expedition. The voyage from the Philippines back to Acapulco took four months. News of its success prompted Spain to invade and conquer the Philippine islands.

Deciding Who Gets What

Having financed the voyages of discovery, the governments of Spain and Portugal, with the pope mediating, divided up the globe. In 1494 the two countries signed the Treaty of Tordesillas. This treaty drew a line down the middle of the Atlantic Ocean, 370 leagues (about 1,430 miles) west of the Cape Verde Islands, and specified that Spain owned everything to the west of the line, Portugal everything to the east. The Spanish government thought it had achieved a monopoly on New World territories and only later discovered that the line ran through the eastern tip of South America leaving a part of what later became Brazil to the Portuguese. Finally, in 1529, the two countries signed the Treaty of Zaragoza that extended the Tordesillas line into the Pacific. Spain thus protected the Pacific coast of its newly discovered territories from Portuguese intrusion. Though the Zaragoza line left the Philippines in the Portuguese sphere, Spain kept

it on grounds that it had established a claim to it prior to the treaty.

The other Northern European powers paid no attention to the Spanish–Portuguese treaties, despite the pope's blessing, and quickly began sending out expeditions of their own. England, Holland, and France concentrated their efforts in the North Atlantic because winds and currents made it easier for them to focus there. King Henry VII of England sponsored the first of the northern expeditions. As news of Columbus' first voyage spread, the English king probably regretted having turned down Columbus' proposal to sail to Asia under the English flag some years earlier.

When another Genoese sea captain (known to history as John Cabot but probably born Giovanni Cabote or Gabote) offered in 1496 to sail to the wast in exchange for privileges like those accorded Columbus by the Spanish Crown, Henry VII accepted the proposition at once. The following year, Cabot became the first modern explorer to rediscover what the Vikings had learned 600 years before: how to use prevailing winds to sail across the North Atlantic and back.

Within a few years of the pioneering Spanish and Portuguese expeditions, explorers financed by the English, Dutch, French, and even the Scandinavian governments were sailing regularly across the North Atlantic in search of a "Northwest Passage" to Asia. Unlike the Spaniards, however, the Northern Europeans found little worth exploiting: no precious metals and a climate inhospitable to growing profitable export crops like sugar. More than a century passed after their first explorations in the early 1500s before the English, Dutch, and French established permanent colonies in North America.

3.5 THE SPANISH CONQUEST

Between 1493, when Columbus set out on his second voyage to the "Indies," and 1537, when Inka resistance effectively ended, Spain seized territories many times its own size in area and population. Amazingly, Spain did not conquer by mobilizing huge armies and great fleets of warships, like other great empires. In fact, Isabela and her heirs acquired their vast empire without sending any professional soldiers or warships to the Americas. They did it by signing approximately seventy joint venture contracts with private investors (including navigators, adventurers, merchants, and speculators of all kinds), who outfitted the expeditions and expected to profit from them. Some of these contractors were not even Spanish, like Columbus himself.

On returning from his first voyage, Columbus convinced his royal patrons that his small cargo promised vast riches. He had no trouble raising money and recruiting seamen for a second and much larger expedition. He even found a good number of relatively high-status volunteers and fortune-seekers with their employees and retainers willing to invest in his project and accompany him back to "Asia."

Columbus Conquers the Caribbean

Unlike his first expedition, which had set out to explore the unknown in three small and relatively maneuverable ships, Columbus organized his second voyage as a military expedition designed to conquer people and secure territory. Thus, the Spanish invasion and conquest of the Americas began with Columbus' departure from Cádiz on September 25, 1493 for his second voyage to the Indies with 17 well-armed ships and 1,200 seamen, soldiers, and adventurers. On reaching Hispaniola, Columbus found that the thirty-nine men he had left behind had all died, either of disease or at the hands of local people who resented their insistent appropriation of women and whatever gold objects they saw. European diseases had already begun to decimate the indigenous population as well.

Columbus' chief immediate problem was financial. He had to establish a colony that could pay for itself and turn a profit, at least enough to cover the costs of the expedition and satisfy both the investors back home and the colonists and soldiers who accompanied him. The ships of the second voyage carried livestock and seed for planting wheat and a variety of other European foods for subsistence, but nothing that could be raised and then profitably exported. The only exportable product the indigenous people possessed was gold, which they found in small quantities in streambeds, but the quantities that could be produced in this way appeared to be small. Columbus dispatched men to explore the island to find more of it, but they returned with only a few nuggets. Meanwhile, the Native Americans generally refused to work unless forced, so the Spaniards began capturing and enslaving them.

Enslaving the Native American inhabitants also solved the export problem. As slaves, they could be put to work helping in the search for gold. When they found deposits, they were forced to work extracting the ore and smelting it into metal. If they did not find gold or were captured in larger numbers than needed for gold production, the indigenous people themselves were exported. Spanish law and custom from the Reconquest, however, prohibited enslaving conquered populations unless they resisted Spanish rule, and Queen Isabela had instructed Columbus and others to avoid it. In flagrant violation of these orders, Columbus and the other Spanish colonists began sending ships back to Spain filled with hundreds of indigenous slaves.

Meanwhile, letters from disgruntled colonists to the Crown complained of Columbus' incompetence and arbitrariness as the colony's governor. When Native Americans resisted or Spanish colonists rebelled, Columbus had them hanged. Warned of trouble, Columbus returned to Spain in 1496 to defend himself. Ferdinand and Isabela treated him well, but kept him at court for months on end. It took him two years to outfit a third expedition. And this time he returned to Hispaniola with detailed instructions from the king and queen on how the colony should be run.

On his return, Columbus again ignored or invented novel interpretations of his instructions. He parceled out land and indigenous laborers to the colonists. He imposed a *tributo* (head tax) on all adult males in the indigenous population. He sent military expeditions to find, defeat, and round up indigenous people who resisted. To cover various mistakes, he sent back to Spain implausible reports of miracles and false accounts of successes. Exports of indigenous slaves and complaints from colonists again poured into Spain.

Columbus and his sons and relatives managed to accumulate a fortune from gold, slaves, and other profit-making activities, but the colony as a whole did not prosper. In 1500 the queen dispatched a new governor and had Columbus arrested and brought back to Spain in chains to answer charges of illegal enslavement and misrule. Though the queen set aside the charges against him, she rescinded the titles and privileges she had granted in the original 1492 contract. This time, the monarchs kept Columbus in Spain another two years, until the new royal governor in Hispaniola could establish his authority.

In 1502, Columbus set out on his fourth and last voyage of exploration, but was specifically forbidden to return to Hispaniola except for provisions on the way back. As usual, Columbus defied this and other instructions, but managed to explore the coast of Central America before ending up marooned on Jamaica for over a year after his ships developed leaks and had to be beached. By the time he made it back to Spain, his physical and mental health had deteriorated. He died in Spain on May 20, 1506, rich from the wealth he and his sons and relatives had accumulated from the gold and slaves of Hispaniola, but bitterly disappointed by the loss of political power and control in the Indies.

The indigenous population of Hispaniola disappeared within twenty years of Columbus' landing. Forced labor and abusive treatment lowered indigenous resistance to influenza, smallpox, measles, and other diseases introduced by the Europeans. The Native Americans did not have any "natural" immunity against these pathogens, which European and other Old World populations had acquired through constant exposure over many millennia. The Spaniards in Hispaniola responded to the death of their main export by sending slave-hunting expeditions that soon stripped the Bahamas of its population, and then set upon

Puerto Rico, Cuba, and Jamaica. Throughout the Caribbean, the indigenous populations virtually disappeared within a generation of the first contact, carried off by slave-hunters or by disease compounded by overwork and mistreatment. Spain's Caribbean conquest colonies became settlement colonies.

Cortés Finds the Aztecs

In the early 1500s, Spanish explorers sailed along the coast of the Yucatan peninsula, which they initially thought was just another big island, and traveled up the Mexican coast looking for a passage to Japan or the Chinese mainland. In 1518, an expedition led by Juan de Grijalvo returned to Cuba with enough gold to pay for the expedition and leave a substantial profit.

Since any large-scale effort to seize territory now required royal permission, the governor, Diego Velázquez, recruited Hernán Cortés, a relative and former secretary, to outfit a small follow-up expedition of three ships to set up a base and ward off rival expeditions that might be organized by Spaniards on Hispaniola or elsewhere. Cortés's instructions were to maintain peaceful contact with the local population, trade trinkets for gold and other valuables, and await the much larger invasion force Velázquez expected to assemble once he received a royal license to proceed. Cortés had other ideas.

Cortés landed on the coast of Mexico on April 20, 1519. He named the place he chose for his encampment "Veracruz" ("true cross") (see Map 3.3). Cortés and the 500 soldiers and crewmen with him were greeted courteously by the local Totonac lord who had befriended the Grijalvo expedition the year before. By this time, however, news of strangers arriving by sea had arrived at the court of the Aztec ruler Moctezuma. Soon after Cortés's landing, emissaries arrived bearing gifts and inviting the Spaniards to visit the Aztec capital at Tenochtitlán, site of modern Mexico City.

Cortés took his time getting there. He left a detachment behind in Veracruz and moved inland up mountain trails to the Central Plateau of Mexico with 300 Spanish adventurers, including 20 with **harquebuses** (the large, unwieldy, but very noisy predecessor of muskets) and 40 archers. They were accompanied by 150 indigenous servants from Cuba, 15 horses, and 800 Totonacs from Veracruz. As he marched, Cortés paused repeatedly to visit towns and meet local rulers along the way. By the time he reached Tenochtitlán, he knew enough about the Aztecs and their empire to have formulated the rudiments of a strategy for overthrowing it.

The Spaniards arrived at Tenochtitlán on November 12, 1519. Cortés and his lieutenants now understood that the Aztec state suffered from two main weaknesses. First, it could not count on the loyalty of most of its recently conquered subject peoples,

Map 3.4 Spanish and Portuguese empires in the Americas, showing the Tordesillas Treaty line and slave trade routes from Africa

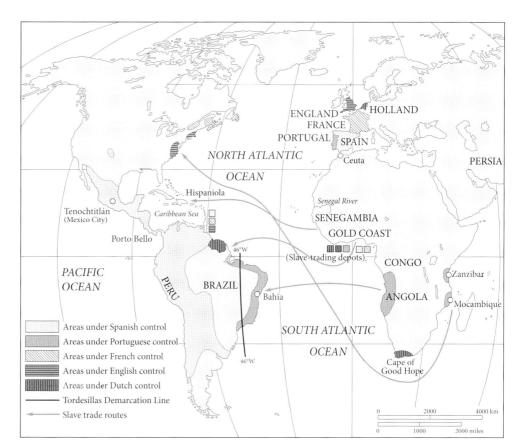

Figure 3.2 In 1978, workers for the Mexico City Electric Company were digging just off the main square (called the Zócalo) between the national cathedral and the presidential palace. Seven feet below street level, they came to a large Aztec stone disk, 11 feet in diameter, weighing over eight tons, with relief carvings of the Aztec moon goddess Coyolxauhqui dating from before the Spanish conquest. Though the Templo's approximate location was already known, subsequent excavations confirmed that the disk marked the spot of the Aztec capital's main temple. Eventually, thirteen buildings were demolished to gain access to the site.

some of whom had already secretly offered to aid the Spaniards against their Aztec oppressors. Second, it had not managed to subdue several smaller but well-armed states in the Central Plateau, of which the most important, Tlaxcala, had already offered to ally its forces to those of the Spaniards. Cortés, nonetheless, put his own life and the lives of his followers in peril by boldly marching to Tenochtitlán, a "marvelous" lake city of more than 100,000 inhabitants, built on an island and connected by causeways to the mainland. Figure 3.2 shows the excavation of the main Aztec temple (Templo Mayor) in the main square of Mexico City with the presidential palace and the city's main cathedral behind it.

Received as guests and put up in palaces, the Spaniards soon took advantage of their hosts to seize the Aztec leader Moctezuma and make him their prisoner. Shortly thereafter, Cortés ordered his men to massacre scores of leading warriors and nobles who had gathered, unsuspecting, in one of the main plazas of the city. But the Spaniards had overreached; the horrified survivors quickly replaced Moctezuma and their fallen comrades with new leaders and on what the Spaniards later dubbed "la noche triste" (the sad night) of June 30, 1520, drove Cortés and his followers from the city with many casualties.

The Fall of the Aztec Empire

Fourteen months later, Cortés returned with an army of 900 Spaniards and at least 50,000 Tlaxcalan and other indigenous soldiers, accompanied by 3 iron cannon, 100 horses, and 15 brigantines (small ships built according to Spanish design to carry troops across the lake). Tenochtitlán fell to this Spanish-led alliance of Spanish and indigenous forces on August 13, 1521. The key to Cortés's victory lay in the Spaniard's skill in exploiting the weaknesses of the Aztec state to secure massive indigenous support for what amounted to an indigenous revolt against Aztecs.

Two other factors also weighed heavily. The first was the Spaniards' technological edge. From the beginning the Spaniards had to convince potential indigenous allies that victory was possible, even inevitable. They succeeded in this by demonstrating the deadly efficiency of their steel swords. Native Americans used mainly stone weapons that seldom killed the enemy. Even disabling an opponent with a stone battle-axe took time. Aztec soldiers had lances with sharp-edged obsidian blades that could inflict a shallow gash and arrows shot from bows, but they were unable to make iron or steel and could only acquire steel swords on the battlefield. Spanish muskets and cannon helped, too, but these weapons were used mainly to instill fear. They were not very effective on the field of battle, because they took so long to load and tended to be inaccurate except at dangerously close range. Metal armor also helped, but heavy cotton padding (the "armor" developed by the Native Americans) worked just as well against Aztec arrows. Horses helped, too, but mainly as pack animals. Figure 3.3 shows some of the Spanish advantages (horses, attack dogs, and indigenous allies, but no firearms), in an indigenous painting from the era.

Figure 3.3 This mid-nineteenth-century copy of an indigenous codex depicts the conquest of Mexico that began in 1519. The painting shows indigenous (probably Tlaxcalan) allies fighting with their clubs alongside the Spanish invaders. Note that the body on the right, the only injured defender, has injuries (decapitation, limbs cut away) that could only have been accomplished by the Spaniards' swords.

The Spaniards' second advantage was disease. By the time Tenochtitlán fell, its army and inhabitants had been through a devastating epidemic that killed Moctezuma's successor and struck down many of the Aztec warriors defending the city. Spanish diseases not only weakened the Aztecs, but conveniently struck down Cortés's indigenous allies as well. The Tlaxcalans and others could have made much more trouble for Cortés after the fall of Tenochtitlán, had not so many of them ended up seriously ill or even dead in the epidemics that followed.

The Spanish conquerors followed their military victory by trying to recreate the Aztec empire, but with themselves on top. After an initial search for treasure, which yielded great quantities of silver and gold objects to be melted down and shared, according to rank, among the conquerors themselves, the new rulers used Aztec **tribute** lists to determine what each village and town should yield up to them.

Simultaneously, Spanish priests began arriving to undertake the "spiritual conquest" of the Native American population. Box 3.3 contains an account of the initial reaction of the indigenous lords and priests of Tenochtitlán, who were not at all ready to relinquish their own gods.

The Inka Empire

Cortés's victory at Tenochtitlán encouraged other Spaniards, some already living in Cuba or Hispaniola, others from Spain itself, to organize or join other expeditions. Cortés and his successors in Mexico City dispatched one expedition after another to seize control of territory throughout Central and Southern Mexico and down into Central America. Other expeditions sailed directly to Central America and the north coast of South America. In 1513, Vasco Nuñez de Balboa with Captain Francisco Pizarro crossed the Isthmus of Panama and set eyes on the Pacific Ocean. Expeditions down the Pacific coast began in 1524. One of these expeditions, led by Francisco Pizarro and his brother Gonzalo, landed and set up camp on the coast of Ecuador in 1531. The empire of the Inkas lay before them.

The Inka state, like that of the Aztecs, dominated its extensive territory from a capital in the highlands. None of the Inka cities was as large as Tenochtitlán, though the Inka capital, Cusco, had a population of 40,000 to 60,000 by the early sixteenth century. Like the Aztecs, the Inka empire was a relatively recent development. Most of the territory it occupied had been conquered by

Box 3.3 The "Spiritual Conquest" of the Americas

Spanish conquerors insisted that their militant version of Roman Catholic Christianity was the only "true" religion. They destroyed every temple or pyramid built for the worship of indigenous gods, often using the same stones to build churches atop the old foundations. In 1524, the first group of Franciscan friars arrived in Mexico City to work on converting the local population. Early in their visit, they met with the principal lords and priests of the city and explained through interpreters the religion that the defeated Aztecs were now expected to embrace. A summary account of this meeting, probably based on testimony by those who attended it or other similar meetings, was made by or for Bernardo de Sahagun in 1564. The following is an excerpt:

You have told us that we do not know the One who gives us life and being, who is Lord of the heavens and of the earth. You also say that those we worship are not gods. This way of speaking is entirely new to us, and very scandalous. We are frightened by this way of speaking because our forebears who engendered and governed us never said anything like this. On the contrary, they left us this, our custom of worshipping our gods, in which they believed and which they worshiped all the time that they lived here on earth. They taught us how to honor them. And they taught us all the ceremonies and sacrifices that we make . . .

These our gods are the source of great riches and delights, all of which belong to them. They live in a very delightful place where there are always flowers, vegetation, and great freshness, a place unknown to mere mortals called Tlalocan, where there is never hunger, poverty, or illness. It is they who bestow honors, property, titles, and kingdoms, gold and silver, precious feathers, and gemstones . . .

It would be a fickle, foolish thing for us to destroy the most ancient laws and customs left to us by the first inhabitants of this land . . . we are accustomed to them and we have impressed them on our hearts.

It is best, our lords, to act on this matter very slowly, with great deliberation. We are not satisfied or convinced by what you have told us, nor do we understand or give credit to what has been said of our gods. It gives us anguish, lords and fathers, to speak in this way. Here present are the lords charged with governing the kingdom and republics of this world. All of us together feel that it is enough to have lost, enough that power and royal jurisdiction have been taken from us. As for our gods, we will die before giving up serving and worshiping them. This is our determination; do what you will.

Inka armies after 1438. Some new areas, especially in the north (modern Ecuador) had been added to the empire after the Spaniards were already in the Caribbean. As in the Aztec lands, subject areas paid tribute to the Inka state and the Inkas severely punished resistance or rebellion. Like the Aztecs, and the Spanish conquerors later, they used massacres and gruesome tortures to impress enemies and would-be defectors.

The Inkas, however, tried to integrate their empire in ways the Aztecs never even attempted through a large bureaucracy of provincial governors and local officials that mobilized huge numbers of Andean peasants not only to make war on the Inkas' enemies but also to labor on vast public works projects, including thousands of miles of roads paved with stone. Inka colonists were settled on the periphery of the empire while large colonies of recently conquered peasants were resettled in the Inka heartland.

The uncertainty that descended on the death of each Inka ruler constituted the major weakness of the Inka state. In 1525, just before the arrival of the Spaniards, the Inka ruler Huayna Capac died in Quito, possibly from a European disease. His legitimate heir, Huascar, took the throne in Cusco. Huayna Capac, however, had already designated Atahualpa, son of a concubine, to succeed him. Atahualpa was with his father when he died and quickly took control of the court at Quito, proclaiming himself the new monarch. Civil war erupted. Atahualpa's armies, filled with recruits from Ecuador and other recently conquered provinces, descended on Cusco with a vengeance, overwhelming Huascar's smaller and less experienced forces. Atahualpa had Huascar executed along with his entire extended family. To the Inka nobility of Cusco, the victory of the usurper with his barbarian troops seemed a great disaster. Worse was yet to come.

The Collapse of the Inka State

Pizarro's band of 168 Spaniards moved south and then inland in late 1532 with a small but unknown number of black slaves and a somewhat larger number of indigenous slaves and servants captured in Nicaragua. When local people reported, through translators (actually captives from an earlier expedition), that Atahualpa could be found resting at a warm sulfur spring spa near the small town of Cajamarca, Pizarro and his men seized the deserted town and sent a small group to invite the Inka ruler to parley the next day. Atahualpa was indeed resting at a nearby palace on his way back to Cusco with an army numbering at least 40,000. He agreed to the meeting. On November 16, 1532, he arrived in the small plaza at the center of Cajamarca with a large body of lightly armed retainers in sight of the Inka army.

Pizarro had organized his men for an ambush. At the meeting, he suddenly seized Atahualpa, ordered his cannon to fire into the ruler's retinue, and set his followers to killing everyone in sight. Not a single Spaniard died that day. Estimates of the number of indigenous troops killed by cannon shot, sword, crossbow, and the lances of the 67 Spaniards on horseback start at 1,500 and run as high as 7,000. At the end of the day, after horrendous casualties and the terror-stricken flight of many thousands more, the Inka commanders retreated with what was left of their army.

The civil war among the Inkas had left bitter divisions that Pizarro and his followers now exploited with brutal effectiveness. Pizarro persuaded Atahualpa (shown in Figure 3.4 in an eighteenth-century portrait) that a huge ransom would secure his release. Messages went out to loyalist commanders to loot the temples and homes of families and towns that had supported Huascar. In many areas, small groups of Spaniards accompanied the ransom collectors. In all, the Spaniards received a ransom in statues and ornaments that, when melted down, amounted to 13,420 pounds of 22-carat gold and 26,000 pounds of pure silver. Divided according to rank among the men of Cajamarca, the ransom made all of them fabulously rich. Then they executed Atahualpa.

With Atahualpa gone, the Huascar faction of the Inka nobility offered to collaborate with Pizarro in exchange for recognition of their choice of a successor to the Inka throne. When Pizarro agreed, the Cusco nobility invited the Spaniards to come to the capital of the empire, happy to be free of Atahualpa's Ecuadorian troops. The new ruler, Manco Inka, sought to use the Spaniards against the followers of Atahualpa, but Pizarro left him little freedom. Treated with contempt by the Spaniards, who soon imprisoned and tortured him in his own palace, Manco Inka escaped Cusco with trusted aides, pulled together the two factions that had split the Inka nobility, and organized a huge army that surrounded and besieged Cusco for over a year from 1536 to 1537. In contrast to the Aztec empire, where imperial political authority melted away as soon as Tenochtitlán fell, the Inka empire was more resilient.

Nonetheless, Inka resistance failed. The siege of Cusco collapsed because the Inka soldiers fell sick or deserted to tend to crops in their home villages. The Spaniards recaptured and executed Manco Inka. Once the epidemics of European diseases began to spread and the new contingents of Spaniards arrived,

Figure 3.4 Photograph of eighteenth-century "portrait" of the Inka emperor captured by Francisco Pizarro in 1532 and executed after a ransom in gold had been collected from throughout the Inka lands. Atahualpa was the last Inka ruler to have reigned before the Spaniards arrived.

Manco Inka's successors had little chance to resume the struggle. Nonetheless, a functioning Inka state, with a new capital at Vilcabamba, continued to resist the Spaniards until the invaders finally destroyed it four decades later in 1572.

3.6 SPANISH COLONIAL SOCIETY IN THE AMERICAS

The era of great Spanish explorations and conquests in the New World lasted from 1492 through the fall of the Inka empire after 1537. Nothing comparable to the Aztec and Inka states existed anywhere else in the Americas, though new generations of Spanish adventurers continued to search for new empires to conquer, new treasures to loot, and new souls to save for the "one true faith." Each new expedition subjugated a new population, founded new towns, and extended Spanish rule to new areas. Most of the vast territory Spain claimed in the Americas, however, possessed little or no potential for enriching conquerors or generating tax revenues and so never saw a Spanish colonist or governor, evidenced by the vast spaces in the interior of South America where no Spanish or Portuguese towns or jurisdictions existed, long after these two European powers claimed "possession."

The Conquest Colonies of Mexico and Peru

The Spanish colonies of New Spain (Mexico) and Peru constituted the most important of Spain's possessions in the Americas until the empire itself fell apart in the 1820s. These colonies had two advantages over all the other Spanish possessions in the western hemisphere. First, they possessed immense mineral wealth in "mountains of silver" that soon became the envy of the entire world. Second, enough of their Native American populations survived to work and supply the mines, populate the towns with servants and craftsmen, and produce the food and fiber to feed and clothe themselves and their rulers. Other colonies became important either because of their strategic location for trade (Panama) or defense (Cuba) or because they developed taxable export crops like indigo in Central America or cacao in Venezuela. As Box 3.4 shows, food plants from the Americas influenced European diets, while foods and fibers of European origin transformed the Americas as well.

Three main trends dominated the first century of Spanish rule in Mexico and Peru. First, a political struggle developed between the Spanish government and the ambitious and often unruly men who conquered and settled the colonies. Second, though the continuous decline of the Native American population facilitated the consolidation of Spanish rule, indigenous resistance to enslavement and forced labor became more effective as Native American numbers dwindled. Third, new silver mines in the two main colonies produced immense wealth for Spanish colonists and Crown alike and made it easier to resolve both political differences and social conflicts.

The political struggle between the Spanish Crown and the **conquistadores** (the "conquerors" of the New World) and their descendants took decades to resolve. Spain's rulers, beginning with Isabela and Ferdinand, wanted to encourage seamen and adventurers along with their wealthy backers to explore and conquer new territories. So the contracts and licenses the Crown authorized for each expedition promised the explorers and would-be conquerors all kinds of privileges – the right to control

Box 3.4 The "Columbian Exchange" of Food

We have already seen two important results of European conquests in the western hemisphere: One was the migration of millions of Europeans and Africans to the Americas, and the second was the spread of diseases, especially smallpox, which decimated the Native American populations. A third effect was the reciprocal introduction of new foods. Europeans brought with them both field crops and livestock. Wheat now supplemented the indigenous maize, and citrus fruits and grapes also enjoyed local success in the Americas. On the other hand, cash crops like sugar, bananas, and tobacco (indigenous) enriched the land-owning elite in the Americas.

Before Columbus, the Native American had domesticated only dogs, turkeys, ducks, alpacas, and llamas – none of which provided much food or hauling power. Worst of all, the Native American had few animals that could turn grass into meat. The European introduction of sheep, goats, swine, cattle, and horses varied the diet of many and furnished powerful draft animals. Later, horses, cattle, and sheep became the basis of full-scale Native American herding and riding cultures among, for example, the Navajo and the Apache.

At the same time, Native American field and tuber crops had a tremendous impact in Europe after 1500. Maize and potatoes spread through the eastern hemisphere, superseding indigenous staples because they supplied more nutrients per hectare.

The potato, native to the cool valleys of the Andes, adapted very readily to temperate Northern Europe, providing the dietary mainstay from Ireland to Russia. The Dutch peasant family portrayed in van Gogh's *The Potato Eaters* could just as well have been Peruvian. Maize, native to warm Mesoamerica, was adopted in much of Southern Europe; its cultivation in Africa increased steadily till, by the 1990s, it had become the leading consumer crop on that continent. Maize and sweet potatoes became major crops in Asia, surpassed only by rice and wheat. Other Native American foods that proliferated around the world were tomatoes, squash, certain beans, and peanuts. Manioc (cassava) was an important food crop, first in Brazil and later in Africa.

Enormous economic consequences flowed from the improvement of diet ensured by maize and potato farming. In the British Isles, for example, the new crops spurred population growth, thereby furnishing both the labor and the consumer basis for the Industrial Revolution.

trade between the new colonies and Spain, the right to take prisoners and booty and to distribute both to followers and backers, positions as governors and magistrates to rule in the name of the Crown over the conquered territories and peoples, and so on.

After each successful conquest, however, the Spanish government faced three problems it could solve only by reneging on its promises to the men who did the conquering. First, most explorers and conquerors made poor governors; only Cortés in Mexico stood out as an exception to this rule. After every conquest, the Crown received numerous complaints against the leader's abuses, incompetence, and corruption. Second, the Crown wanted to avoid creating a New World aristocracy like that in Spain itself, which might challenge the Crown or even aspire to independence. For that reason and others, the Crown sought to prevent the conquerors from enslaving or enserfing the indigenous population and from stealing indigenous lands. Third, the Crown quickly became aware of the epidemics that decimated indigenous populations. Complaints sent back by some priests and administrators, like Fr. Bartolomé de Las Casas (see above), claimed that Spanish abuse of the indigenous population was largely responsible for the catastrophic indigenous mortality. The government in Spain worried that the Native American population of the mainland would completely die off, as it had in the Caribbean. This would have made it more difficult and costly to exploit the New World's resources, and incidentally cause the Crown to lose revenue from the indigenous head tax (*tributo*).

To solve the first of these problems, the Crown exploited the colonists' complaints to justify sending royal governors and viceroys to take control of each new colony from its initial leader. To solve the second, the government first enacted a series of prohibitions on enslaving the Native Americans (and incidentally recommended importing African slaves who stood up better, the Crown believed, to hard work and harsh conditions). To deal with the third issue, royal decrees defined the indigenous population as vassals of the Crown and no one else; eventually the Crown made efforts to control and regulate access to indigenous labor. All three of these problems came to a head in the 1540s.

Exploiting the Indigenous Population

In 1542, the Crown approved and sent to the colonies a set of **New Laws** that again prohibited enslaving Native Americans, but also imposed severe limits on other kinds of forced labor. The most controversial of the New Laws' provisions was the abolition of the encomienda. In the New World, the conquered populations were assigned or "entrusted" to conquistadores by grants confirmed in Madrid or later by the local viceroy or some other high royal official. The encomenderos (recipients of encomienda grants) were supposed to see to the conversion to Christianity of the Native Americans entrusted to them. In exchange, the Native Americans were obligated to pay a head tax to the encomendero, part of which went to the Crown, and to labor at the encomenderos' command. Most of the original conquistadores were granted (or granted themselves) encomiendas. They used forced laborers from their encomiendas to develop their private enterprises. As other Spaniards grabbed up lands to develop their own private agricultural estates or opened mines and other new businesses, they often used encomienda labor borrowed or rented from the encomenderos.

Not surprisingly, the Crown's decision to abolish the encomiendas provoked conflict. In Mexico, the viceroy refused to publish the law and sent it back with a plea for revision. In Lima, the viceroy published the New Laws and immediately faced an armed rebellion led by the Pizarro brothers. The Spanish government modified the New Laws to allow encomiendas to continue for a time in Mexico and Peru and even longer in more backward areas, but prohibited encomenderos from exacting personal service from their indigenous charges, imposed limitations on the amount of forced labor that could be exacted, and began eliminating encomiendas whenever they fell vacant. The encomiendas themselves lost their original value as the indigenous population declined. Encomenderos who once commanded the labor of thousands or tens of thousands of indigenous people saw these numbers fall dramatically after each epidemic.

Eventually, the Crown assumed control over allocating all forced labor, first in Mexico and then in Peru. In 1549, Viceroy Antonio de Mendoza in Mexico City began creating new courts to assign Native Americans to work on Spanish enterprises. The new institution became known as the **repartimiento de indios**. Every indigenous male head of household had a fixed obligation to work forty-five days each year wherever the court might assign him. Spanish entrepreneurs had to petition the repartimiento magistrates to get a quota of laborers for harvest labor on their estates or to work in their mines or other enterprises. In Peru, where the silver mines could not be worked without forced labor, the new system kept the old Inka name for obligatory labor drafts on public works, the **mit'a**. In the face of stiff resistance, Viceroy Francisco de Toledo in the 1560s reorganized mit'a obligations to put the allocation and enforcement in the hands of similar special courts.

Disease and Death

But still the Native American population died and kept on dying. In Mexico, large-scale epidemics in 1519, 1529–34, and

1545 brought the population down from roughly 17 million on the eve of the Conquest in 1519 to 6 million in 1548 and 2.6 million in 1568. In Peru, the indigenous population fell from perhaps 16 million to 1.8 million in the same period. By the early 1600s, Mexico's Native American population reached its lowest point at a little over a million; in Peru, less than a million remained.

Old World diseases, including influenza, plague, pneumonia, smallpox, and viral infections of all kinds, caused the catastrophic collapse of the Native American populations. Europeans, like most inhabitants of the Old World, had developed immunities, not always complete, but still effective enough to save most from death. Many acquired immunities from frequent exposure to milder forms of the diseases that proved fatal to Native Americans. Since domesticated animals act as carriers of many human diseases, the lack of domesticated animals in the Americas also protected the Native Americans from disease until the arrival of the Europeans. Contact with the Spaniards provoked what specialists call **virgin soil epidemics**, massive contagion affecting large numbers of people over three or four generations until the affected population develops sufficient immunity. Developing immunity to every one of the diseases introduced by the Spaniards probably took longer.

In the New World, the mortality from virgin soil epidemics of European diseases might have been smaller had the Spaniards treated their conquered subjects less harshly. Las Casas and other contemporaries attributed a major portion of the mortality to Spanish abuse and mistreatment. While Las Casas and others recorded numerous cases of brutality, it may be that the greatest damage to the indigenous population came from the Spaniards' insistence that the Native Americans work like Spaniards. Better-nourished Spanish peasants and laborers probably worked longer hours in a day and more days in the year than the population of Central Mexico, where protein was chronically scarce and the calories consumed by adult males probably hovered at 2,000 per day or less. At this level of what today would be considered chronic malnutrition, sustained work for more than five or six hours would have caused exhaustion and substantially reduced resistance to disease. The Spaniards probably raised the death toll among the indigenous population more by insisting on what seemed to them reasonable labor demands than by subjecting them to unusual cruelties, though cruelties there were in abundance.

The indigenous population of Mexico began to recover, though slowly at first, in the seventeenth century. The end of virgin soil epidemics, as the surviving population acquired and transmitted immunities to the European diseases, played a major role in the recovery. Two other causes were also at work: better diet and the end of forced labor for most of the indigenous population. The diet and living standards of the surviving Native American population improved slowly over the sixteenth and into the seventeenth century. Indigenous farmers abandoned marginal plots and concentrated their efforts on better land abandoned by neighbors who had died (though much good land ended up in Spanish hands). Many Native Americans turned to raising small livestock acquired from the Spaniards, especially pigs and chickens, which added protein to their diet.

Forced labor ended as indigenous resistance became increasingly effective. Indigenous villagers complained that they could not send the laborers demanded by Spanish magistrates because of population decline or other problems. They flooded the colonial courts with petitions and lawsuits, often aided by parish priests or other Spaniards who wanted to hire them for wages and did not want them dragged off to work for others. The colonial government in Mexico abandoned the repartimiento system of forced labor with a series of laws and decrees beginning in 1599. Shortly thereafter in Peru, the government abolished the mit'a for most of the indigenous population (but retained it in provinces adjacent to mining districts). The indigenous population of Mexico began to grow again by the 1630s; in Peru, the recovery began several decades later, in most areas by the 1660s to 1680s.

Spanish enterprise contracted in the seventeenth century. Silver production declined or stagnated in both Mexico and Peru, beginning in the 1630s. Trade suffered, tax revenues fell, agricultural estates languished with fewer workers and smaller harvests, and Spanish immigration to the Americas declined. Elsewhere in Spain's New World empire, stagnation had already set in. The seventeenth century belonged to Portuguese Brazil and to Spain's enemies in the Caribbean.

3.7 DEVELOPMENT OF THE TRANSATLANTIC SLAVE TRADE

In 1500, slavery in one form or another existed in most human societies, though it was relatively rare in the Americas. It had declined to insignificance in China and most of South Asia where it had never been as important as in classical Greece or Roman Italy. Household and limited contract slavery persisted in Russia, the Mediterranean, and sub-Saharan Africa, fed by endemic poverty, instability, and war.

The New Slave System

In the two centuries from 1500 to 1700, slavery re-emerged as an important institution, this time in a form far more widespread and brutal than ever before. In the same era, the world's slave population came to be composed predominantly of Africans and their descendants working on sugar plantations and other enterprises in northeastern Brazil and the Caribbean. To move African captives to these areas, a new transatlantic slave trade developed, more massive and efficient than any previous human commerce. The organization and technology employed by the New World plantations where the victims of this trade were settled had developed in the Mediterranean and the Atlantic islands, but the magnitude of this new business and its long-lasting impact on Africa as well as the Americas had no precedent.

Three inter-related developments came together to make possible this horrifying chapter in human history:

- The successful resistance of African states to European incursions, which forced the Europeans to create plantations in the Americas rather than Africa.
- The demographic catastrophe that wiped out most of the indigenous population in the Americas and sent the Europeans looking for another source of labor.
- The spread of sugar production from Asia to Iberia, and eventually to the American tropics.

These three developments were necessary for the development of the new slave system, but by themselves would not have been sufficient to initiate and sustain it. For African slavery and the transatlantic slave trade to develop on the massive scale witnessed after 1500, two powerful and partially contrasting trends in European societies had to come together: the rise of powerful nation-states and the nearly simultaneous increase in the protection of property rights of ordinary Europeans.

The governments of France, Great Britain, the Netherlands, Portugal, and Spain played critical roles in promoting (and at times monopolizing) the slave trade, establishing sugar colonies, enforcing slavery in the face of slave resistance, and providing protected markets for sugar products. In the same era in Eastern Europe and the Balkans, the Russian and Ottoman empires put an end to the invasions and raiding that had made the people in these regions easy prey for slave-hunters.

The slow emergence, mainly in Western Europe, of advances in the protection of individual rights to property against arbitrary taxation and seizure had already led to the virtual elimination of slavery within Western Europe. In the seventeenth century, this trend not only encouraged individual merchants and adventurers to engage in trade and conquer new territories, paving the way for the Industrial Revolution, but also ensured that European traders and entrepreneurs would be protected from government interference when they acquired human chattel in Africa and carried their property off to the Americas.

The Slave Trade

In the two centuries from 1500 to 1700, approximately 1,605,000 enslaved Africans are believed to have been taken on board slave ships in African ports for transport to the Americas. Since many people died after being captured and before reaching the coast, as many as half according to some estimates, the actual number enslaved may have been double this figure. Of the total sold to European traders, 1,287,000 survived the voyage and 318,000 (about one quarter) died on board ship, mostly from dehydration caused by diarrhea due to contaminated food and water. The number of enslaved people taken from Africa each year grew from 700–800 in the 1450s to over 25,000 by the late seventeenth century. More African slaves reached the Americas in this era than European immigrants, who totaled 1,176,000.

African and European immigrants to the Americas differed fundamentally because Africans were forced to migrate as slaves while most European immigrants did so voluntarily and as free citizens. Some English migrants to America in the seventeenth and eighteenth centuries came as indentured servants, agreeing to work without pay for four to seven years for employers who paid for their passage, but they retained most other rights of free men and women even during their indenture. Portugal, Spain, and England also deported convicted criminals to their colonies to serve out sentences at hard labor, but at least some of those transported agreed to go (albeit to avoid long prison terms or death sentences).

A less well-known but equally crucial difference between African and European immigrants was that Europeans generally managed to survive and multiply in the American colonies, while Africans did not. In part this was due to an imbalance in the proportion of male and female slaves in the slave trade, with men outnumbering women by a ratio of more than two to one. This imbalance, together with the high mortality rate among slaves and slave children, meant that without new imports from Africa, the slave population in Brazil and the Caribbean would have disappeared within a decade or two. In the temperate climate of the mainland colonies in British North America, however, where disease was less rampant and diet generally better, African slaves and their children lived longer and the slave population grew by natural increase throughout the slave era. As the proportion of slaves born in these colonies rose over time, the imbalance between men and women also diminished. Thus, the vast majority of the slaves imported to the Americas went not to the British colonies that later formed the United States, but to Brazil and the Caribbean.

The number of enslaved Africans exported to the Americas accelerated at the end of the seventeenth century. The total number of Africans captured, enslaved, transported across the

Atlantic and sold to European colonists in the Americas between 1518 and the last of the New World emancipations in Cuba (1886) and Brazil (1888) has been estimated at 12 to 15 million people. Map 3.4 above shows the slave-trading routes.

Sugar and Slaves in Brazil

The first African slaves to work on sugarcane plantations worked alongside Arabs, Syrians, and Ukrainians on Crete or Sicily sometime between the twelfth and fourteenth centuries. The African slaves on these sugar estates came to the Mediterranean overland across the Sahara, brought by Muslim traders. Sugar cultivation reached Muslim southern Spain by 1300 and Christian Portugal a century later. During the fifteenth century, government-sponsored colonists set up sugar plantations on the Atlantic islands of both Portugal (the Azores, Cape Verde, and Madeira) and Spain (the Canaries). African slaves worked alongside others on these plantations, but did not dominate the local labor force.

It was on the island of **São Tomé**, claimed by Portugal in 1479, that the fateful combination of sugar and African slaves first took shape. Located off what came to be called the "Slave Coast" of West Africa, São Tomé was uninhabited when the Portuguese first arrived with sugarcane plants and ambitious plans. With slaves purchased in nearby African port towns, São Tomé's plantations proved to be even more profitable than elsewhere and soon became Europe's main source of sugar. It took another half-century before Portuguese entrepreneurs carried sugarcane, along with African slaves, to Brazil, but when they did, the experiment proved so successful that it effectively condemned millions of Africans to enslavement and premature death. By the late 1540s, Brazil had become the world's largest producer of sugar and the world's largest slave importer.

After Cabral's accidental landing in 1500, it took more than twenty years for the Portuguese government to realize what a huge territory lay on the Portuguese side of the line agreed to in the Treaty of Tordesillas (see Map 3.4 above). Portuguese navigators soon began to chart the coast and explore up the Amazon River, spreading disease and looking for something valuable to trade for or plunder from the local population. Portuguese traders built small trading posts on the coast and persuaded the local Native Americans to work with Portuguese tools to cut down a species of tree whose bark contained a valuable red dye. When the local people decided they would prefer to return to other activities, the Portuguese declared them slaves and forced them to keep working. When the workers and their families began dying from European diseases or managed to escape captivity, the Portuguese sent out raiding parties to round up new captives. Eventually, the Portuguese

proudly named their colony after the tree that inspired these first settlements, called Brazil wood in English (*pau de Brasil* in Portuguese).

Brazil's transition from trading post to slave plantation colony occurred initially as a defensive response to French traders and naval vessels that began dropping anchor in Brazilian waters starting in 1504. Spanish ships were not far behind. The French even planted a short-lived colony at Rio de Janeiro, which the Portuguese did not manage to dislodge until 1565. Alarmed by new incursions in the 1530s, the Portuguese government decided to promote colonization by dividing up Brazil's vast territories into fourteen huge land grants called captaincies and awarding them to wealthy noblemen on condition that they send settlers to them. Two of the captaincies actually resulted in colonial settlements, one in Pernambuco in the northeast and the other, called São Vicente, further south near the modern port of Santos.

Only 3,500 colonists had settled in Brazil by 1549, when the Portuguese government decided to set up a single colonial administration headquartered in Bahia and took further steps to encourage colonization. In the 1550s, high sugar prices also encouraged immigration. New colonists created plantations and exploited both Native American and imported African slaves to work them. By 1585, the population of Portugal's colony had risen to over 57,000, one quarter of them African slaves. By 1600, Brazil was exporting 33,000 tons of sugar each year.

Slavery in the Caribbean and North America

In the seventeenth century, sugar cultivation and slave plantations spread to the Caribbean. Three events precipitated this momentous development. The first was the Dutch declaration of independence from Spain in 1568. The Dutch independence war dragged on in fits and starts for eighty years until Spain recognized the Netherlands as an independent state in 1648. The second event was the peaceful succession of Spain's King Philip II (1527–98, r. 1556–98) to the Portuguese throne in 1581, which unified the two countries and empires under a single monarch until the Portuguese revolted and secured their independence again in 1640. Unification made Portugal and its empire an ally of Spain against the Dutch Republic. The third event was the Dutch invasion of the sugar-growing northeastern provinces of Brazil in 1630. The Portuguese and their colonial allies fought back, but it was not until 1654 that they succeeded in expelling the last of the Dutch governors and officials from Bahia.

The Dutch took all that they had learned about making, processing, and marketing sugar in Brazil to the Caribbean, where they had already seized Curaçao and several small islands in the Lesser Antilles from Spain. Meanwhile, not to be left out in the scramble for new possessions, the British and French also began seizing islands in the Caribbean. By the time the British took Jamaica in 1655, they had already managed to seize and hold several islands in the Lesser Antilles and the Bahamas along with mainland settlements later known as Guyana (British Guiana) and Belize (British Honduras). The French occupied Guadeloupe and Martinique in the 1630s and seized the western part of Hispaniola (modern Haiti) and French Guiana later in the century. Dutch merchants helped to spread sugar technology to all of these other islands and territories. By 1700, the British, Dutch, and French colonies in the Caribbean were producing more sugar and importing more slaves than Brazil.

Slavery also spread to the North American colonies of Britain and France in the seventeenth century. The first slaves imported to the territory that would later form the United States arrived in Virginia in 1619. Though small numbers of slaves were eventually brought to Canada, New England, and the Mid-Atlantic colonies, the largest numbers went to labor on tobacco plantations in the Chesapeake area or in other British colonies further to the south. In 1700, the British colonies in North America had a total population of about 250,000, of which roughly 28,000 were slaves.

Conclusion By 1700, the focus of economic exchange and political (and military) competition among European states had shifted from the Mediterranean to the Atlantic. Navigators subsidized by the governments of five small Western European states succeeded in finding a water route to Asia. The vast continents they stumbled upon in their search proved to be far more valuable than anything they had hoped to gain from trading directly with China, Japan, India, and the South Asian Spice Islands. The Atlantic trading economy that developed after 1492 created vast new wealth for a few European governments and a tiny number of European sea captains, soldiers, officials, traders, and landowners. The conquest and colonization of the Americas helped to set in motion the economic and social changes that led to the Industrial Revolution.

The European invasion and colonization of the Americas also unleashed vast demographic and social transformations. More than 90 percent of the indigenous population of the Americas died in the century after contact began. In some areas, like the Caribbean islands, the indigenous population died off completely. The indigenous population collapsed even in huge areas in the interior of the Americas that Europeans did not explore or settle, struck down by pathogens carried by traders or refugees from infected places.

As the indigenous population died off, the European intruders repopulated their "new" world with African slaves. Between 1500 and 1700, 1.3 million Africans were captured and transported to the Americas at a rate of nearly 7,000 a year. The slave trade grew much larger *after* 1700, reaching a peak of over 100,000 slaves shipped each year in the late eighteenth and early nineteenth centuries. As a result of the slave trade, the population of some regions of sub-Saharan Africa stopped growing for three centuries and may even have declined. By 1700, more than half the population of the Americas consisted of Europeans and Africans or their descendants.

Disease and death undoubtedly helped the Europeans in their efforts to replace Native American governments and religions in the profitable areas they chose to move into. In the mainland silver colonies, where European enterprise and government weighed most heavily, Native American material culture, social organization, religious life, and cultural expression changed drastically. In the most integrated areas, a stratum of mixed-race individuals (called **mestizos** or **castas**) grew rapidly, especially in the cities. In the countryside, large estates or plantations came to dominate the landscape. Those living at the margins of European dominance or beyond European control managed to retain greater autonomy for a time, but still suffered from the epidemics.

Throughout the process of conquest and colonization, the Europeans who came to the New World encountered resistance and even rebellion, both by Native Americans and by African and creole (born in America) slaves. The complex Native American states, with their elaborate hierarchies and internal divisions, collapsed fastest. Local lords and leaders abandoned their imperial rulers and either joined the Spaniards or negotiated the best terms they could get. The Spaniards and Portuguese encountered greater resistance from bands and tribes, where class, ethnic, and political divisions did not exist. After conquest, small-scale local resistance to Spanish taxes, forced labor, and other abuses continued in various forms, including hundreds of small-scale local riots and rebellions against Spanish tax collectors and magistrates.

In the slave colonies, resistance to slavery most often appeared as acts of anonymous sabotage or retribution in response to abuse or mistreatment. In Brazil, the Guianas, and the larger Caribbean islands, runaway slaves called maroons banded together to create or recreate peasant communities (called **quilombos** in Brazil) that fought against military expeditions sent to destroy them and re-enslave their inhabitants. Hundreds of riots and small-scale rebellions, in which slaves on one or a few adjacent plantations expelled overseers, burned buildings or stores, and demanded better treatment, were commonplace. In the eighteenth century, as the Europeans imported huge numbers of new slaves from Africa, large-scale insurrections and maroon wars erupted in nearly every colony.

Out of the tense, uncertain, sometimes violent, but long-lasting and profitable exploitation that Europeans imposed on their conquered and enslaved subjects, a "New World" did emerge in the Americas between 1500 and 1700. It was not a world that anyone could have predicted. It established patterns of racial dominance and discrimination, economic exploitation and accommodation, and cultural interaction that persisted for centuries – in most areas until the late nineteenth century and in some parts of the Americas until today.

Study Questions

(1) Why did people from a few small Western European countries set out to explore, conquer, and profit from other lands? And why did such large and powerful states as China fail to do so?

(2) How did Spain organize itself to conquer the Americas? Or did it?

(3) How did so few Spaniards conquer such vast territories?

(4) Why did so many Native Americans die?

(5) Why were Mexico (New Spain) and Peru so important to the Spanish Crown?

(6) Why were African slaves taken in such large numbers to the Americas?

(7) How did Native Americans and African slaves protest against abuse and exploitation by Europeans?

Suggested Reading

Francisco Bethencourt and Diogo Ramada Curto (eds.), *Portuguese Oceanic Expansion, 1400–1800* (Cambridge University Press, 2007). This masterful study covers the creation and transformation of the Portuguese empire in Africa, Asia, and the Americas.

Alfred W. Crosby, *The Columbian Exchange: Biological and Cultural Consequences of 1492* (Westport, CT: Greenwood Press, 1972). This is a classic work on how the conquest of the Americas transformed the diet, dress, and habits of both Europeans and Native Americans.

David Eltis et al., *The Trans-Atlantic Slave Trade: A Database on CD-ROM* (Cambridge University Press, 1999). This CD-ROM contains data on over 27,000 transatlantic slave voyages, and is an excellent resource for student research.

Felipe Fernandez-Armesto, *Columbus* (Oxford University Press, 1991). This is the best biography of Columbus, by a major scholar.

Charles Gibson, *The Aztecs under Spanish Rule: A History of the Indians of the Valley of Mexico, 1519–1810* (Stanford University Press, 1964). This work is a detailed study of how conquest, disease, greed, and politics transformed the heart of the Aztec empire.

Stuart B. Schwartz (ed.), *Victors and Vanquished: Spanish and Nahua Views of the Conquest of Mexico* (Boston, MA: Bedford/St. Martin's; Basingstoke: Macmillan, 2000). This book contains a fascinating collection of primary documents, carefully translated, that provide great insight into how Spaniards and Native Americans perceived each other.

Steve J. Stern, *Peru's Indian Peoples and the Challenge of Spanish Conquest: Huamanga to 1640* (Madison: University of Wisconsin Press, 1993). Stern's highly readable major work analyzes how relations between Spanish overlords and indigenous peoples changed as epidemics spread and the Native Americans and their leaders struggled to reduce their exploitation and recover their autonomy.

John Kelly Thornton, *Africa and Africans in the Making of the Atlantic World, 1400–1800*, 2nd edn. (Cambridge University Press, 1998). This survey emphasizes the active role of Africans in shaping the societies created by their presence.

Glossary

astrolabe: Scientific instrument developed in the sixth-century Islamic world, used to reckon time and track the movement of stars. The typical astrolabe consisted of a circular base plate with a network of lines representing celestial co-ordinates, a rotating disk with a map of the stars, and a straight rule used to sight a fixed object in the sky.

caravel: Light sailing ship developed by the Portuguese for exploring the coast of Africa. Its chief value lay in its ability to sail to windward and with remarkable speed.

cartas de doação: Monopoly grants to navigators from the Portuguese Crown, these licenses gave men like Vasco da Gama important rights in territories they claimed for Portugal in exchange for a fifth of their profits.

castas: See mestizos.

conquistadores: Literally "conquerors," the Spanish adventurers who overpowered and later governed the peoples of the New World.

encomienda: Colonial institution by which conquered populations were "entrusted" to encomenderos, who agreed to supervise their conversion to Christianity. The encomenderos used the laborers granted to them by the Crown to develop private fortunes.

harquebuses: Primitive muskets with poor accuracy and firepower, but significant capacity for noisemaking.

lateen: Triangular sail that made it easier to sail against the wind by tacking (zigzagging).

mestizos: Individuals of mixed race (also known as *castas*), they rapidly became an important demographic group in the cities of the New World.

mit'a: System of reciprocal labor obligations in the Inka empire. Peasants were forced to labor on Inka public works, but many of the projects – including roads, warehouses, and irrigation canals – benefited the local population; continued under the Spaniards to supply laborers to the silver mines.

New Laws: A 1542 decree of the Spanish Crown which prohibited the enslavement of Native Americans, imposed severe limits on the kinds of labor they could be forced to do, and abolished the encomienda.

quilombos: Peasant communities formed by runaway slaves in Brazil, the Guianas, and the larger Caribbean islands.

repartimiento de indios: Institution developed in 1549 by Viceroy Antonio de Mendoza in Mexico City. Under the system, every indigenous male head of household had a fixed obligation to work forty-five days each year for a Spanish employer to whom he was assigned by a specially constituted colonial court.

São Tomé: An originally uninhabited island off the Slave Coast of Africa claimed by Portugal in 1479, São Tomé was Europe's leading source of sugar before sugar plantations were created in the New World.

tribute (*tributo*): A major source of revenue in the Spanish colonies, this head tax on Native American male heads of household declined as disease and hard labor reduced the population.

virgin soil epidemics: Massive contagions, such as those provoked among Native Americans by contacts with Europeans in the early colonial era. Surviving populations developed relative immunity to imported sicknesses only over four or five generations.

4 European and Southeast Asian crossroads

Europe	
1452–1519	Lifetime of Leonardo da Vinci, Italian artist, scientist, engineer.
1454	Gutenberg and others develop printing press in Europe.
1466–1536	Lifetime of Desiderius Erasmus, humanist scholar.
1473–1543	Lifetime of Nicolaus Copernicus, Polish astronomer.
1475–1564	Lifetime of Michelangelo Buonarroti, Italian artist.
1483–1546	Lifetime of Martin Luther, pioneer of Protestant Reformation.
1484–1531	Lifetime of Huldrych Zwingli, Swiss religious reformer.
1491–1556	Lifetime of Ignatius Loyola, founder of Jesuit order.
1509–64	Lifetime of John Calvin, religious reformer.
1509–47	Reign of Henry VIII of England.
1512–17	Fifth Lateran Council attempts reforms.
1513–21	Reign of Pope Leo X, creator of indulgences.
1516–56	Reign of Charles I of Spain, from 1519 also Charles V, Holy Roman Emperor.
1517	Luther's ninety-five theses demand radical reform of the church.
1520–66	Reign of Suleiman the Magnificent of Ottoman empire.
1521	Condemnation of Luther by Charles V.
1523	Zwingli begins Reformation in Switzerland.
1524–25	Peasant War in Germany.
1533–92	Lifetime of Michel de Montaigne, skeptical humanist writer.
1536	*Institutes of the Christian Religion* published by John Calvin.
1536	Henry VIII seizes monasteries in England.
1553–58	Reign of Mary in England.
1540	Founding of Jesuit order.
1545–63	Council of Trent.
1549	Jesuit Francis Xavier arrives in Japan.
1555	Peace of Augsburg settles German religious question.
1556–98	Reign of Philip II in Spain.

1558–1603	Reign of Queen Elizabeth of England.
1560–1640	Portugal absorbed into Spain, then freed.
1562–98	French Wars of Religion.
1564–1642	Galileo Galilei, Italian astronomer and scientist.
1568	Revolt of Netherlands begins; Declaration of Independence is made in 1581.
1571–1630	Lifetime of Johannes Kepler, German astronomer.
1581	Formation of English Levant Company.
1588	Defeat of Spanish Armada by English.
1598	Edict of Nantes ends religious war in France and guarantees Protestant rights.
1618–48	Thirty Years' War, concluded by Treaty of Westphalia.
1626	Completion of St. Peter's basilica in Rome.
1633	Galileo's trial and recantation.
1634	Assassination of Wallenstein, military entrepreneur.
1640–88	Reign of Frederick William the Great as Elector of Brandenburg-Prussia.
1642–49	English Civil War.
1643–1727	Lifetime of Isaac Newton, English astronomer and mathematician.
1648	Netherlands gain independence from Spain as United Provinces.
c. 1650–1700	Peak of witchcraft trials in Europe.
1660–1670s	English wars with Dutch.
1661–1715	Personal rule of Louis XIV in France (r.1643–1715).
1665	Great Plague and Fire of London.
1685	Revocation of Edict of Nantes ends religious toleration in France.
1688–89	Glorious Revolution of William and Mary in England; Bill of Rights in 1689.
1692	Witchcraft trials in Salem, Massachusetts; twenty-two executed.

Southeast Asia

1351	Founding of Ayutthaya kingdom.
1427	Founding of Le dynasty of Vietnam.
1511	Portuguese seize Malacca.
1514	Portuguese land in South China.
1519–22	Magellan's voyage around the world.
1571	Manila in Philippines is center of Spanish power in Asia.
1577–80	Francis Drake's voyage around the world.
1600	Establishment of British East India Company.
1602	Establishment of Dutch East India Company (VOC).
1613–46	Reign of Sultan Agung, military leader of Javanese state of Mataram.
1619	Dutch build fort at Batavia.
1641	Dutch take Malacca from Portuguese.
1664	Arrival of French missionaries in Siam.
1667	Bugis and Dutch conquer Makassar.
1677	Sultan of Mataram gives monopoly trade rights to Dutch.

1685–88	French military expedition to Siam, ending with their expulsion.
1740	Massacre of Chinese in Batavia.
1767	Burmese capture and loot Ayutthaya.
1771–1802	Tayson Rebellion in Vietnam overthrows Le dynasty.
1782	Rama I founds new Siamese dynasty at Bangkok.
1788	Chinese invasion of Vietnam is beaten back.
1795	British take Malacca from Dutch.
1799	VOC trade monopoly abolished; Dutch state takes control of Java.
1819	Founding of Singapore.

The Greek sailor Constantine Phaulkon, born to Catholic parents on a small island under Venetian control, joined the English East India Company, changed his religion to Anglicanism, and came to Siam as a merchant in 1675. A gifted linguist, he learned Thai, Malay, Portuguese, and English, becoming so skilled that he was appointed the prime counselor of King Narai. The English relied on him to promote their interests against the Dutch, with whom they had been at war. Then he converted to Catholicism, married a Christian woman of combined Japanese, Portuguese, and Bengali ancestry, and accumulated great wealth and power at the Siamese court. Aided by local Jesuits, he acted on behalf of the French against the English and Dutch. Louis XIV made him a citizen of France and a member of the French nobility, and the French had hopes of converting the king to Catholicism. Phaulkon continued to prosper in trade. He ordered jewels from the American Elihu Yale, President of the East India Company in Madras, who later founded Yale University, but returned them when he discovered that their price was too high. The French sent a military expedition to Siam in 1685, but their efforts to invade the country failed, forcing them to withdraw in 1688 in the face of intense hostility from the local population.

Members of the Siamese court, incensed at Phaulkon and the king's pro-French policy, were jealous of his power. When King Narai fell ill, his brother engineered a coup and had Phaulkon executed in 1688. The weak king died soon after, and the new king proceeded to expel most foreigners from Siam. Siam remained hostile to Western traders and missionaries for over one hundred years. Meanwhile, back in Europe in the same year, the Dutch king and queen William and Mary invaded England, creating England's "Glorious Revolution" and forging an alliance against their new common enemy, France.

This complicated episode, illustrating the entangled histories of Europe and Southeast Asia, exemplifies the themes of this chapter. Both regions consisted of multiple states contending with each other in war, trade, and religious proselytization. The competing trading companies of the Dutch, English (including Americans), and French tried to establish alliances with Southeast Asian states for their own profit, while the Southeast Asian rulers in turn used them in their own domestic political struggles. As we shall see, the two regions shared many common features, and they had close contacts with each other. They both contained many states that fought wars with each other, and traders of many different nationalities and communities with divergent religious beliefs crisscrossed the regions. The term "crossroads" applies equally well to both places. Over the long term, each region drew itself more tightly together around smaller numbers of powerful military states supporting themselves with commercial networks and more standardized cultural forms. Ultimately, however, the Europeans were the more aggressive military and commercial expansionists, and they put most of Southeast Asia under their rule until the middle of the twentieth century.

Between 1500 and 1700, Western Europe gained power and wealth both in Southeast Asia and relative to Southeast Asia. Here are this chapter's main points about the two regions and the two (or three, for Southeast Asia) momentous centuries:

- Long voyages by open sea took on extraordinary importance relative to overland movements of persons, commodities, and military forces.
- These maritime connections more closely integrated the Americas and the western Pacific into the great Eurasian system of power, trade, and belief, and established a permanent European presence in Asia.
- Although Portugal and Spain pioneered the maritime connections with Asia, other European powers – especially Holland and England – soon began to displace them.
- Southeast Asia and Western Europe stood apart from the world of large agrarian empires. Their smaller, more centralized states grew with gains from trade, while land

armies built up the power of states within their own territories.

- In Europe, competing versions of Christianity struggled to establish different relations of believers to governments, while in Southeast Asia the great text-based religions – Buddhist, Confucian, Hindu, and especially Muslim – appealed for spiritual and secular support against local animist traditions.

4.1 THE SEA VOYAGERS TO ASIA

Ferdinand Magellan and his crew were the first to sail around the world, but Magellan developed his great vision out of his experience of the spice trade with Southeast Asia. By 1506, Magellan had gone to the great port of Malacca and the Spice Islands (Moluccas). Malacca commands the narrow strait between Malaya (an extension of the Asian mainland) and the island of Sumatra. "He who is lord of Malacca," went a Portuguese saying of the time, "has his hand on Venice's throat." His effort to circumnavigate the globe, which led to his death en route, came directly out of a proposal to undermine Muslim and Venetian domination of this valuable trade by leading Portuguese ships westward across the Atlantic, around South America, then across the Pacific, to Asia.

In 1577, sixty years after Magellan set off for South America, Sir Francis Drake left England, apparently heading for the Mediterranean and the Nile. When he reached Africa, however, he informed his crews that they were actually heading for the Pacific through Magellan's strait. Since Portugal still had the best navigators, he captured a Portuguese merchant ship and commandeered its pilot. Fighting off dissension and disaster, Drake made it to South America's Pacific coast with just one ship.

England's great enemy Spain had taken over large parts of the Pacific coast. Drake's ship raided Spanish coastal towns and shipping for six months before sailing up the coast with tons of silver in his hold. After rest and repairs, Drake took his ship west across the Pacific to Indonesia, where he negotiated political and economic alliances for England while trading silver for spices. In 1580, Drake's ship crossed the Indian Ocean, rounded Africa, and worked Atlantic winds back to England. Drake, unlike Magellan, survived his voyage, going on to become a world-famous raider and scourge of the Spanish navy.

The great voyages of Magellan and Drake mark the first phase of the European sea adventures. Both Magellan and Drake played significant parts in tightening the links between Southeast Asia and Western Europe. Before the sixteenth century, Europe's main connections with Asia passed through the Middle East. European trading expeditions most often followed the Silk Road overland into Central and East Asia or left the Persian Gulf to sail the Indian Ocean. From the 1480s to 1520s, the pioneering Portuguese navigators – Dias, da Gama, Cabral, and Magellan – opened up routes westward to the Americas and the Pacific, and eastward around Africa to coastal India, establishing Portugal as a major economic and political power in South Asia.

From that base, Portuguese soldiers, administrators, priests, and merchants extended their country's influence to China, Japan, and Southeast Asia. Although the Portuguese settled in India's Goa, China's Macao, and a few other colonies, they had too few people of their own to fill distant colonies. Instead, they drew local populations into their rule through sexual liaisons, intermarriage, co-optation, and payoffs. They also made a significant share of their profits as middlemen within the Asian trade.

Across Southeast Asia the Portuguese created well-armed trading posts from which they could draw the Asian spices, herbs, textiles, and crafts Europeans prized. (Cloves, nutmeg, pepper, and other spices commanded high European prices because they added exotic tropical flavours to otherwise bland stewed meats and sauces.) In return, they shipped some European metals and textiles, but mostly gold and silver – first from Africa and Europe, then increasingly from South America. By the 1580s, Portuguese ships alone were bringing 32 tons of silver yearly to Asia. The bulk of it ended up in China, then still the world's single richest country and a great industrial power in its own right.

4.2 ENTANGLEMENTS OF TRADE, WAR, RELIGION, AND FAMILY IN EUROPE

Four Countries Fight over Trade, Religion, and Territory

The four countries of Portugal, Spain, Holland, and England had intimate ties with each other, but they fought as many families do. Portugal was even absorbed into Spain through inheritance from 1580 to 1640, but it saw Spain as a serious commercial competitor. From the later sixteenth century, furthermore, Holland and England made substantial inroads into Iberian trading territories, and broke with Spain over religious differences. The Low Countries (roughly today's Netherlands, Belgium, and Luxembourg) belonged to the Spanish royal family in 1500, the year the future King Charles I of Spain was born. In 1515, the teenaged Charles became Prince of the Low Countries, and ruled Spain from 1516 to 1556. He became

Holy Roman Emperor in 1519 with the title Charles V, the same year that he sponsored Magellan's fateful voyage. When the **Reformation** (a movement to reform or reject the Catholic church) broke out in the 1520s, large parts of the intensely commercial northern Netherlands joined the **Protestants** (who rejected the authority of the pope), while people of the southern Netherlands, Spain, and Portugal generally stuck with the Catholic church. During the 1490s, furthermore, both Spain and Portugal had forced resident Jews to choose between conversion and exile. Many Iberian Jews had fled to the prosperous northern Netherlands, where they found strong demand for their skills as merchants and artisans. In Iberian Catholic eyes, therefore, the Dutch region bore the stigma of heresy.

Under King Henry VIII (r. 1509–47), England at first defended Catholicism against Protestant advances. Henry's first wife, after all, was Catherine of Aragon, aunt of Spain's King Charles. Replying to Martin Luther in 1521 with a pamphlet of his own, Henry received from the pope the title Defender of the Faith. Henry soon broke with the Roman church, however, over the pope's refusal to authorize a divorce from Catherine. Henry also had his eye on the English Catholic church's wealth and power. By 1536, he was closing the formerly Catholic monasteries and seizing their revenues. From Henry's death in 1547 to the eighteenth century, the British Isles (England, Wales, Scotland, and Ireland) underwent repeated changes of religious regime, faced rebellion after rebellion in the name of religion, and fought several religiously polarized civil wars. Henry VIII's Catholic daughter Mary, for example, reigned as queen from 1553 to 1558. She married Charles V's son and heir Philip in 1554, precipitating a rebellion in England. The queen earned the nickname Bloody Mary for the executions of almost 300 leading Protestants during her five years of rule.

Similar struggles broke out within Spanish territories. Acting as Holy Roman Emperor, Charles condemned Luther in 1521, defeated a league of Protestant princes, and authorized extensive persecutions, including burning at the stake, in Germany and the Low Countries. He failed, however, to stem the advance of Protestantism in the Low Countries. Philip II (r. 1556–98) succeeded Charles as Spanish emperor in 1556, but by 1568 predominantly Protestant regions of the Netherlands had formed a rebellious league. In 1581 these regions (soon to be known as the United Provinces or the Dutch Republic) declared independence, and began sustained military resistance to Spanish forces. England sent troops to aid the Dutch and soon found itself in open warfare with Spain. Sir Francis Drake, by destroying a Spanish fleet near Cádiz (1587) and defeating the great Spanish Armada in the English Channel (1588), tipped the military balance toward England, protecting the Dutch from a Spanish invasion.

The Dutch war with Spain lasted formally until 1648, but the United Provinces enjoyed de facto independence after about 1609. For several decades after formal Dutch independence in 1648, England and the Netherlands warred and preyed on each other's trade. Then in 1689 Dutch Protestant prince William of Orange (cousin and husband of the English king's daughter Mary) took the English, Scottish, and Irish crowns in a new civil war later called the Glorious Revolution.

European Competition Generates a Naval Arms Race

All these struggles generated naval competition among the Portuguese, Spanish, Dutch, English, and later French. Figure 4.1 shows the number of major warships owned or maintained by each of the major maritime powers. Up to 1560 or so, Portugal predominated; then Portugal's fleet disappeared into Spain's with Philip II's inheritance of Portugal in 1580; the temporary primacy of Spain from 1590 to 1605 reflects that boost. But even Portugal's successful rebellion of 1640 did not restore it to naval pre-eminence; for the rest of the seventeenth century it had only one tenth the number of ships of the leading naval power. The Netherlands rose spectacularly after 1600 up to a peak of 141 warships in 1640. After mid-century, however, we see England, then France, putting more armed ships out to sea than even the Dutch. During the same period, the Ottoman empire – which, like Venice, had previously relied on rowed galleys, superb for coastal raiding but vulnerable in open sea cannon exchanges – also began investing in armed sailing ships. Its navy, however, did not approach the firepower of its European neighbors until well after 1700.

Figure 4.1 therefore tells one more story that is not obvious at first glance: The sheer number of warships operated by Europeans roughly doubled during the sixteenth century, then almost tripled during the seventeenth century, while the firepower of the average vessel was increasing. As the exploits of Magellan and Drake indicate, armed ships of the time shifted with relative ease among long-distance trade, raiding, exploring, and naval warfare. Warships could rapidly become freighters, and vice versa. Spain, for example, regularly kept about 60 warships under arms during the later sixteenth century, yet managed to assemble 125 vessels for the ill-fated Armada that attacked England in 1588. Naval warfare itself was becoming deadlier, and more consequential for a country's international position. For a time, commercial, political, and maritime power coincided closely within Europe.

At first, Spain gained far greater profits from South American silver than Portugal was ever able to draw from Brazil. The

Number of Warships Maintained by Major European Powers, 1500–1700

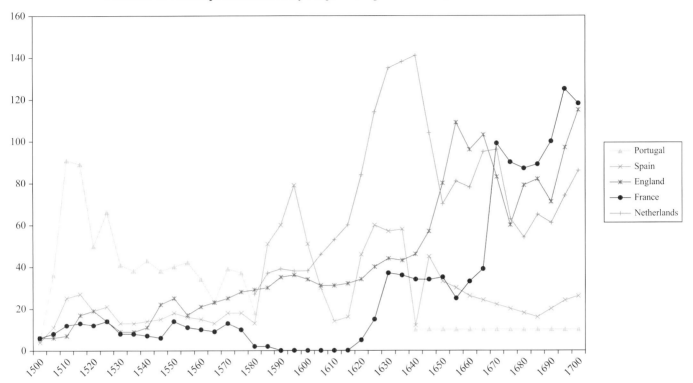

Figure 4.1 Warships of the major European maritime powers.

Dutch, however, soon proved just as enterprising as their Portuguese and Spanish predecessors. Blocked from Iberian ports by Philip II, the Dutch reached out into Asia on their own. Philip also cut the Dutch out of European distribution of Portuguese clove imports.

The Dutch Strike Back at Spain, and Create the VOC

When they were part of the Spanish empire, Dutch navigators had accumulated extensive experience in Spanish fleets. Under their own flags, they established their commercial independence with startling speed. In addition to navigational daring and military ruthlessness, the Dutch radically transformed Asian trade with a new organization adapted from England. In 1600, London merchants created an **East India Company** to pursue their interests around the Indian Ocean. The English version only temporarily made gains in Southeast Asia, but it eventually became the dominant power in India and adjacent areas of South Asia while providing the model for English enterprises in the Americas.

The **Dutch East India Company** (VOC), formed through a government-initiated merger of squabbling commercial firms in 1602, represented the great merchants of the northern Netherlands throughout Asia; it soon became a semi-independent

world power in its own right. It was a big enterprise. In 1625, the VOC had 4,500 employees serving in Asian posts and another 3,200 on board its ships. By 1688, the numbers had swollen to 16,000 stationed in Asia and 5,900 at sea. Over the seventeenth century as a whole, about 2,200 men per year lost their lives sailing, fighting, or serving for the Company; impressively, the great majority of them came from the same provinces that provided the trading company's capital. Perhaps a fifth of all boys born in those provinces died in company service.

The VOC's naval and military arms fiercely attacked Portuguese and Spanish forces wherever they found them. They not only displaced Portuguese and Spanish traders from most of their toeholds in Southeast Asia, but also beat back the English. At high cost and great profit, the VOC became effective ruler of Indonesia and a mighty presence elsewhere in the region. Despite its origins in a war against Spain, the Company traded with Spain and channeled Spain's American silver for its own profit. A VOC ship that sank near Australia in 1656, for example, carried money minted in Spain's American colonies only two years earlier.

The Dutch approach to increasingly competitive England was more hostile. The Company repelled every attempt of English merchants to enter its Southeast Asian markets. During the 1660s and 1670s, England warred repeatedly with the Netherlands and tried to exclude Dutch merchants from English markets by requiring all shipments from Asia to arrive in English or Irish ships. But prior to the eighteenth century England did not succeed in holding off Dutch competition in Asia or Europe. During the seventeenth century, profiting from its far-flung trade, the Netherlands became Europe's richest country, and by 1670 the VOC had become the world's richest firm. Profits for investors reached 27 percent a year. The VOC expanded even further, though with lower profits, during the eighteenth century, relying on the enormous wealth of the Southeast Asian trade.

Europe Moves Northwest

All these shifts in Europe's external relations altered connections and balances within the continent as well. From the thirteenth to sixteenth centuries, trade and political power had shifted toward Europe's Atlantic coasts. Commercial cities based on maritime trade extended from Spain all the way up to Scandinavia and Russia. Paris, combining commercial activity with religious and political power, had become Europe's biggest city. As of 1500, however, the Mediterranean remained Europe's richest region, Europe's Muslim-mediated links to Asia through the Middle East continued to set the rhythms of European economic activity, and Portugal's scourge Venice survived as a major power. The next two centuries changed the European map fundamentally. With one important qualification, the European center of gravity moved decisively northwest.

The qualification comes from the Ottoman empire. Ottoman expansion between 1500 and 1700 reorganized political, economic, and religious life in Southeastern Europe. Ottoman conquest of Constantinople – soon to be Istanbul – in 1453 put one of Europe's great cities and its prosperous hinterland under Muslim control. By the 1520s, under the powerful caliph Suleiman the Magnificent (r. 1520–66), the Ottomans ran most of the Balkans and were beginning centuries of military competition with the Austrian segment of Charles V's confederation of German states, the **Holy Roman Empire**. By the later seventeenth century, the still expansionist Ottomans were battling equally expansionist Poland and Russia as well. Venice, while resisting Ottoman seizure of their Mediterranean territories, survived commercially by brokering Ottoman exchanges with the rest of Europe.

Europe's major powers grudgingly acknowledged the looming Ottoman presence in their systems of diplomacy and trade. England's royally chartered **Levant Company** organized most English commercial activity in the Middle East from its formation in 1581 until its dissolution in 1825. Nevertheless, the massive presence of the Ottoman empire astride the Middle

Eastern gateway to Asia gave European kings and navigators additional incentives to discover sea routes around Africa and the Americas.

The European Urban Band: The Source of Heresy Since the Roman empire, much of the overland trade and communication within Europe went through a band of cities extending from northern Italy to the Atlantic and North Sea coasts by way of the Alps, Switzerland, the Rhine, northern Germany, the Low Countries, and northern France. The **Hanseatic League** (a trading confederation of German cities) had used these routes to build its commercial empire along the North Sea and Baltic. Within that band, a remarkable northward shift occurred between 1500 and 1700. As measured by proportions living in cities, general population density, capital accumulation, or the intensity of industrial and commercial activity, the zone running from northern France to northern Germany and southern England came to dominate urban life. The northern Netherlands led the way, with about a quarter of its population inhabiting cities of 2,500 or more inhabitants in 1500, and a full 40 percent in 1700. During the same period, England's shift from the export of wool and other agricultural products toward much more active involvement in manufacturing and international trade likewise spurred the growth of dense urban populations. These urban zones not only supported rich traders, but religious dissidents and new cultural movements. The largest of these was the Protestant Reformation.

The Reformation Splits the German Empire in Half The Protestant Reformation not only split Europe religiously but also changed relations between European churches and states. Like many earlier reform movements, it began as an internal critique of papal power. In 1500, the papacy was a wealthy and influential political institution as well as the religious center of Latin Christianity. The papacy's wealth came primarily from fees and taxes on the lands over which the church held secular power; individual endowments (bequests to monasteries, hospitals, poor funds); and rents (on lands and buildings which pious communicants had bequeathed to the church). **Tithes** (a fixed proportion of parishioners' income or crops) went to the local church to support the parish priest, the local church building, and other parish property. The papacy's growing wealth showed itself clearly in the popes' construction projects. Papal builders, for example, completed St. Peter's Basilica in 1626, after more than a century of effort. Members of the church hierarchy often appropriated ecclesiastical wealth for their own use and lived opulent lives.

Pope Leo X (r. 1513–21) expanded a moneymaking scheme called **indulgences**. Through donations, pilgrimages, extra prayers, or other pious acts, believers could obtain formal pardon of past or future sins and their punishment after death. This scheme went too far. Sale of indulgences only raised money for high church officials; they did not offer a pious path to salvation. Humanist intellectuals, members of the Dominican and Franciscan orders, lay officials, and even members of the church hierarchy called for reforms. Churchmen at the Fifth Lateran Council, meeting from 1512 to 1517, acknowledged the problems and made recommendations. Moderate bishops tried to reform their own constituencies by investigating the behavior of priests, encouraging parish priests to preach more effectively, emphasizing the spiritual side of religion, and urging their parishioners to receive the sacraments more often.

Protestant reformers, however, cared even more about doctrinal differences than about ecclesiastical extravagance and immorality. Their new doctrines challenged both papal authority and widely held Catholic beliefs. Martin Luther (1483–1546), John Calvin (1509–64), and Huldrych Zwingli (1484–1531) defined and led the major branches of sixteenth-century Protestant Christianity. The Reformation Monument in Geneva, Switzerland, today memorializes these innovators on a high, rugged wall of stone.

Luther, a German law student turned monk, developed a critique of Catholic doctrine emphasizing faith based on scripture as the key to salvation, rather than good works and prayer. He also urged the pope to end abuses (in particular the sale of indulgences) within the church. Pope Leo X rejected Luther's request as a challenge to papal authority and sought to silence him. When Luther refused to recant, the church formally labeled him a heretic. In a brave gesture, Luther burned the **papal bull** (a special order of the pope) condemning him, rejecting ever more strongly the pope's authority.

Both Henry VIII and Charles V publicly backed the pope's position, but the Elector of Saxony (a prince of the Empire, "Elector" because he had a voice in the naming of the Emperor) protected Luther against the Catholic emperor. The situation soon deteriorated, when peasants rebelled in 1525. Luther denounced them, but popular discontent escalated into religious war in Germany. Peace returned only in 1555, with a temporary settlement of the religious question by the Peace of Augsburg. That treaty announced a fateful principle for the Holy Roman Empire, **cujus regio ejus religio**: The ruler decides the country's religion. Under this principle, regional princes could decide between Catholicism and the different varieties of Protestantism. The Empire split on religious lines.

The Reformation Spreads beyond Germany and Splits Up The Protestant challenge produced very different results in France, the home of John Calvin. Calvin studied to become a priest, but switched his studies to the law before he was ordained. In 1533, in Paris, he converted to Protestantism, becoming a popular preacher, but soon left under threat of arrest. In 1534, Calvin for the first time celebrated communion in France as a Protestant. In 1535, Calvin visited Geneva, where other Protestants persuaded him to stay. In 1536 he published his *Institutes of the Christian Religion* in Latin, then quickly translated them into French as well, to make the book more accessible to ordinary people. Calvin taught that a just God predestined ignorant, sinful men to salvation or damnation; it followed, he said, that true freedom came from surrendering to God's will. In Geneva, Calvin established a theocratic state on these principles.

German Swiss Huldrych Zwingli, a former priest who had received a humanist education and had been a classics teacher, preached another version of Protestantism. Independently of the other reformers, he came to a belief in justification by faith alone, and sacred scripture as the sole source of truth. For Zwingli, good works could not ensure salvation. He greatly simplified religious ritual (substituting the Lord's Supper for the mass in 1525), materialist trappings (doing away with ornate details in churches like brass candlesticks, tapestries, and statues), and the number of sacraments (to two). Zwingli, firmly independent, publicly disagreed with Luther about the meaning of communion; he won over the people of Zurich and Bern, but when he himself instigated an attack on the Swiss cantons that objected to his doctrines, he lost his life in the battle that ensued.

Radical Protestant groups endorsed an even more literal interpretation of scripture. Consider the **Anabaptists** (those who practice rebaptism), an epithet originally applied to them by their enemies. The Anabaptists, or Mennonites (after one of their early leaders, Menno Simons), started as followers of Zwingli in Zurich. They called for a strict break from any and all Christian tenets and ceremonies that did not appear in scripture. Authorities in both Protestant and Catholic cities persecuted them for their deviation from accepted practices. Some militant German Anabaptists briefly tried to put their version of heaven on earth into practice by seizing the city of Münster in northwestern Germany, but most Mennonites simply tried to live in peace with their neighbors while exerting community control over their co-religionists.

The Counter-Reformation Responds to the Protestant Critique Those people concerned about abuses who remained in the Roman Catholic church began their own movement of internal reform. Catholic reformers worked within established institutions – parish, bishopric, papacy – to seek spiritual and moral renewal. At first, political disagreements between Charles V and the pope blocked their efforts, until the Council of Trent, meeting from 1545–63, agreed to rationalize church government, improve discipline within the clergy, and upgrade their education. To counter the Protestant belief in scriptural authority, Trent re-emphasized tradition, and the role of the church as the only legitimate interpreter of the scriptures. It condemned the Protestant assertion that faith alone is necessary for salvation, and insisted that good works were needed as well. It defined the sacraments to distinguish them strongly from Protestant practice. Finally, the Council reiterated the validity of all the non-scripturally-based Catholic beliefs and practices, such as indulgences, purgatory, and the intermediation of the saints between God and men.

At the same time, the papacy aggressively countered the Reformation's gains by issuing lists of prohibited books and putting new emphasis on the miraculous works of the saints. Secular authorities began censoring publications to exclude Protestant and other prohibited works. In Italy, the Roman Inquisition was established to control the expression of forbidden opinions in speech or in print. The Spanish soldier Ignatius Loyola (1491–1556) created the Society of Jesus, a group of highly educated men trained in rhetoric and science and absolutely obedient to the pope, who aimed to convert those who had fallen away from Catholicism, or who had yet to become Christians. Jesuits served widely as missionaries in Catholic Europe's colonial territories, including those in Asia.

Political Impacts of the Religious Wars Although the reformers themselves were divided, the attack on Catholic orthodoxy in Europe's urban band succeeded widely. It also had a broad political impact, especially when Protestantism merged with demands for popular sovereignty and national redemption. During Germany's religious wars, for example, Protestant princes battled simultaneously for freedom of (their) religion and political autonomy from a Spanish Catholic emperor.

Broadly speaking, the religious divide separated north and south, Germanic and Latin countries, and urban and rural areas. Protestantism attracted few followers in Iberia or Southern Europe. By contrast, Protestants came to dominate most urban-commercial regions north of the Alps and up the North Sea coast to Scandinavia. In many of the larger German-speaking states, sharp struggles pitted Catholic rulers against militant Protestants, but in other states rulers carried their populations with them. The Low Countries divided predictably between majority Protestantism in the urban-commercial north and greater fidelity to Catholicism in the more rural and aristocratic south. During 1566 and 1567, Protestant crowds attacked Catholic religious symbols and sacred objects so widely and furiously that Philip II sent in an army to put them down. That arrival of Spanish armed force helped precipitate the long war of the northern Netherlands against Spain. The southern Netherlands, later to become Belgium, remained Catholic. Map 4.1 displays the divisions of Europe between Protestants, Catholics, and Orthodox Christians.

In France, Protestant–Catholic divisions precipitated repeated civil wars, accompanied by competition among great lords, during the sixteenth and seventeenth centuries. Perhaps half the French nobility converted to Protestantism at one time or another during the later sixteenth century. In 1562 the Venetian ambassador to Paris, Giovanni Michieli, wrote home that:

There is no province which is not infected, and in some of them the contagion has spread even to the countryside, as in Normandy, almost all of Brittany, Touraine, Poitou, Guyenne, Gascony, a large part of Languedoc, Dauphiné, Provence, Champagne – together making almost three quarters of the kingdom. In many places, the heretics hold their meetings, which they call assemblies, wherein they read, preach, and live in the way of Geneva, without any regard for the king's ministers or his commands. The contagion extends to every class, and (a strange thing!) even to ecclesiastics ... All the harm done has not yet appeared openly.

Michieli spoke prophetically: The so-called Wars of Religion racked France most of the time from 1562 to 1598. Only when Protestant claimant to the throne Henry of Navarre capped his military victories by returning to the Catholic church (1593) and received papal absolution did the devastating civil war end. The settlement of 1598 (the **Edict of Nantes**) guaranteed Protestant political rights but confined Protestant congregations to a limited number of towns. During the next century Louis XIII (r. 1610–1643) and Louis XIV (r. 1643–1715) beat down Protestant power with military and civil action; by 1685 Louis XIV felt strong enough to repeal the Edict of Nantes and to begin military campaigns against the few remaining Protestant enclaves of southern France.

Religious changes of the sixteenth century, then, inscribed a new religious map on Europe, redistributing Christians, Muslims, and Jews alike. Over the previous two centuries considerable numbers of Jews had been moving into the expanding commercial regions of Poland and northern Germany. The expulsion of about 160,000 Jews from Iberia in the 1490s scattered them across Europe:

Ottoman empire	90,000	France	10,000
Netherlands	25,000	Italy	10,000
Morocco	20,000	Americas	5,000

The new religious map was mainly Muslim in the Balkans of the Ottoman empire, chiefly Catholic in an arc from north of that empire in Poland through Italy, Iberia, and France around

Map 4.1 Catholics, Protestants, and Orthodox Christians in Europe, 1550

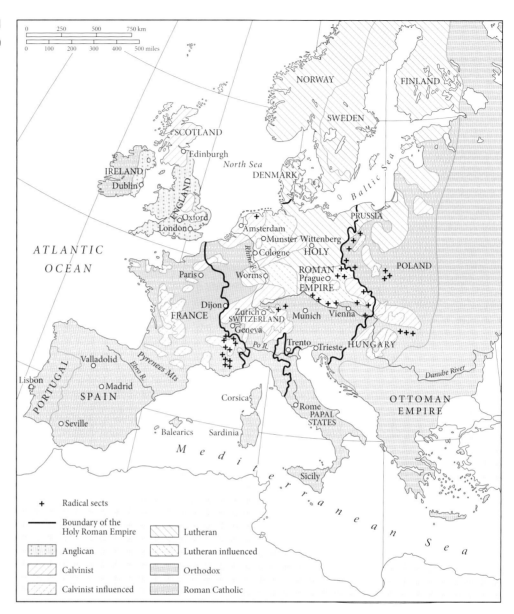

to the southern Netherlands; largely Protestant in the urban-commercial regions north of the Alps including England, Scotland, and much of the northern coast up to Finland; Orthodox Christian in Ottoman enclaves such as Greece and Serbia, and in Russia; significant Jewish clusters in the Ottoman empire, Italy, France, Poland, and the Netherlands. That religious geography stayed largely in place until the nineteenth century.

Cultural Change, Printing, and the Scientific "Revolution"

In the midst of religious strife and incessant war, small groups of scholars called **humanists** carried on the work of the Republic of Letters. They continued the active investigation of the natural world and the revival of classical learning that had begun in the

Italian Renaissance. The Dutch scholar Desiderius Erasmus (1466–1536) edited a Greek edition of the New Testament, criticized traditional interpretation of the scriptures, and in *The Praise of Folly* satirized the authorities of his time. Michel de Montaigne (1533–92), hiding from the religious wars in his private castle, took a skeptical view of all dogmatic positions; he even wondered if the cannibals of the New World were not more civilized than the Europeans who slaughtered each other for their beliefs.

It was the observers of the heavens who took the greatest step away from medieval beliefs. In 1543, the Polish astronomer Nicolaus Copernicus (1473–1543) argued that the Earth and all the planets rotated around a stationary sun. His heliocentric theory rejected the Earth-centered cosmology inherited from the Greek astronomer **Ptolemy**, and broke with orthodox church teaching. Johannes Kepler (1571–1630), relying on accurate observations by Tycho Brahe, discovered regular laws of planetary motion: that planets move in ellipses with the sun at one focus, and a line from the sun to a planet sweeps out equal areas in equal times. Galileo Galilei (1564–1642), using the newly invented telescope, confirmed the Copernican theory, but his brilliant arguments so offended the Vatican that he was put on trial and forced to recant. Even though he formally rejected his own discoveries, he supposedly said at his trial, "It [the Earth] still moves." Isaac Newton (1643–1727) explained all these phenomena and many others, from ocean tides to the fall of an apple, with the attractive force of gravity. Newton's powerful mechanical model of the universe set the new science firmly in place.

These men believed in developing new ways of justifying knowledge: through direct observation of nature and logical reasoning instead of relying on the teachings of priests or scriptural commentary. Now we call them the heroes of the "Scientific Revolution," but this new way of thinking about the world took a long time to catch on. Nearly all Europeans still followed the old ways. Witchcraft trials reached a peak of hysteria in these centuries, making victims of over 100,000, most of them helpless old women. In Salem, Massachusetts, under Puritan rule, 122 suspects were arrested and 22 executed. Box 4.1 discusses the controversies over the relationship between Protestantism, science, and printing.

Probably more influential than any of these men were the humble printers of Mainz, led by Johannes Gutenberg, who had in 1454 become the first Europeans to print with movable type. Printing changed the way everyone communicated in the early modern age, regardless of their religious beliefs: reformers and counter-reformers all quickly produced pamphlets in local languages to win over their supporters, while governments printed announcements of war and peace. As popular literacy grew, people demanded information about more immediate matters, in such forms as almanacs, medical works, and travel guides. As Box 4.2 shows, rulers and popular printers also wanted to distribute maps of the world as well as texts.

States and Empires: From 500 to 50 Sovereign Units

As of 1500, Europe's major governments fell into four main categories: city-states such as Venice that drew revenues from rich agricultural hinterlands and/or international trade; federations of formally autonomous territories such as Switzerland and the fading Hanse; kingdoms in which a single ruler prevailed; and empires combining the first three in different patterns. All of them were actually composites of different sorts of rule; even French kings, for example, ruled mainly through intermediaries and exercised their power by different rights and administrative arrangements in Brittany, Languedoc, or Normandy. The Holy Roman Empire included everything from Spain (itself still a composite of Castile and Aragon) and the Kingdom of Naples to small imperial cities along the Rhine. In fact, if we count every European political unit that had some plausible claim to independence, something like 500 different "states" divided up the European territory in 1500.

Great consolidation occurred over the next two centuries. City-states survived in 1700 – after all, Monaco, Andorra, and San Marino still enjoy nominal independence today – but occupied greatly diminished places in the European structure of power and commerce. Urban leagues and similar federations had disappeared as influential political actors. Austrian Habsburgs still operated a ramshackle – and very composite – dynastic empire, but Spanish and Portuguese empires only operated outside of Europe. By 1700, only Russia and (especially) the Ottoman empire looked much like the empires that had long dominated much of Eurasia. Consolidated states with well-defined borders, centrally co-ordinated institutions, government-controlled armed forces, and some elements of common culture were acquiring much greater weight in European affairs. France, England, Denmark, and Sweden provided the most striking models, but even Spain, Portugal, and the Dutch Republic were taking hesitant steps in the same direction.

War Causes Consolidation How and why did consolidated states begin to prevail over city-states, federations, and empires? Five words sum up the main processes: war, armies, commerce, credit, and taxes. Frequent and devastating European wars occurred almost every year between 1500 and 1700. Figure 4.2 provides a sampling for 1600 to 1650. It shows only wars in which major European powers took part, and in which at least a thousand battle-deaths resulted during each of the years listed. The wars labeled here as Bohemian, Danish, Swedish, and Swedish–French constituted different phases of the Thirty Years' War (1618–48), the most devastating war Europe had suffered up to that time. Not only did about 5 million people – only 2 million or so of them regular troops of major powers – die in the Thirty Years' War, but the fighting laid waste much of Central Europe. Map 4.2 displays the divisions of seventeenth-century Europe that resulted from these wars.

Although such wars obviously wore states down, paradoxically, mobilization for war also built them up. As the stakes of international competition rose, so did the scale of military forces. Just as warships multiplied during the sixteenth and seventeenth centuries, so did armies. During the later seventeenth century, a typical army of 60,000 men, with its 40,000 horses, consumed

Box 4.1 Protestantism, Printing, Capitalism, and Science

In Western Europe during these centuries, four new movements appeared at around the same time: religious reformation, the new communication technology of printing, expanding global capitalist markets, and the beginnings of the scientific revolution. Naturally, historians have debated their connections to each other. In 1904, the German sociologist Max Weber, in *The Protestant Ethic and the Spirit of Capitalism*, argued that the "this-worldly asceticism" of Protestantism drove the new believers, anxious about their salvation in the next world, to invest the riches they accumulated in this world in the expansion of production instead of on luxury consumption. For Protestants, according to Weber, "man is dominated by the making of money, by acquisition as the ultimate purpose of his life." English and Dutch success in commerce seemed to support his thesis; the American printer Benjamin Franklin was his prime example of a person "filled with the spirit of capitalism," "distinguished by a certain ascetic tendency." Others noted that many leading scientists were Protestant, too. Could the religious reforms begun by Luther be the real cause of Western Europe's later dominance of the world?

Not so fast. We could make three types of argument about the connection between religious belief and commercial, technological, and scientific changes: that they are (1) necessary: change in religion automatically produces the others; (2) accidental: there is no connection; or (3) contingently connected: there are some links, but they were not inevitable. The third type of argument is the most convincing. Recall that the religious changes took place while European states engaged in constant warfare and aggressive state-building. German princes supported Luther to gain autonomy from the Holy Roman Emperor; Henry VIII broke with Rome to get the marriages he wanted and to gain wealth from confiscating monastic lands. Spiritual movements were never separate from power struggles.

The same goes for science. Copernicus and Galileo were devout Catholics. Those who studied the heavens knew that if their results conflicted with orthodox doctrine, they had to move carefully. Copernicus himself argued that his model of a solar-centered system was only a revival of lost ancient ideas; even Galileo concealed his heliocentric beliefs for a long time. His primary interest was in furthering his own career as a courtier in the treacherous politics of European absolutist regimes. He was put on trial and forced to recant because he lost the political patrons who had protected him against his enemies. They were less interested in lofty theories about the stars than in political intrigue. Science, too, was not immune from politics.

Printing in vernacular languages certainly helped to spread literacy through reading of the Bible and the tracts of the reformers, but the Catholics also used it to disseminate the Counter-Reformation. The average literate person in Europe was much more likely to read tales of witches and demons than abstruse scientific or philosophical texts. Europeans did become more literate, but not more secular, during this period.

It is also hard to connect Protestantism to toleration or democracy. The Dutch did tolerate different religious creeds and philosophies, making them the intellectual center of Europe for a time; Calvin's Geneva, however, was not a tolerant place, nor was Puritan Boston. Indirectly, the incessant religious warfare backed by competitive states did in the end create a climate of greater toleration: Exhausted by conflict, the contending parties finally decided to coexist with each other.

In short, there was no necessary trend from Protestant Reformation to science, capitalism, or liberalism, but after centuries of complex political struggles, Europeans by 1700 finally sorted out their irreconcilable religious differences to create a more stable system endorsing an official state religion, but tolerating dissenting minorities.

---

almost a million pounds of food per day – some carried with the army, some stored in magazines, the great bulk procured wherever the army was located, but all of it requiring massive expenditure and organization. The sheer assembly of arms and men put unprecedented power in the hands of generals and rulers, and required vast networks of supply, communication, and command. As a result, substantial bureaucracies grew up to support and contain military activity.

Armies, however, meant more than one thing. Before 1500, four overlapping types of military organization took part in European wars: bands of personal retainers, **feudal levies**, **militias**, and **mercenaries**. Every lord great or small kept at least a few armed men at his call, and those who ran great estates could also call up their peasant serfs and tenants for warfare just so long as they did not desert their fields for long during the growing season. Thus lords could bring their own soldiers into battle to fight directly under their command. Feudal levies involved military obligations of nobles toward their overlords; a minor lord might have the duty of responding to the overlord's call by providing himself, ten armed horsemen, and a hundred armed infantrymen, plus necessary supplies, for up to a month of combat in a given year. The king himself could call on his magnates' forces in

Box 4.2 Mapping the World

All the empires and states of the early modern age realized that they needed accurate maps of the world. The sea voyages that revealed a new continent also made obsolete the medieval European "T-in-O" maps based on the sacred geography of the Holy Land. Abraham Ortelius (1527–98) of Antwerp, Belgium, published *Theatrum orbis terrarum*, the first comprehensive atlas of the world, in 1570. It was enormously popular among Europeans, who were just learning about the huge scale of the globe. Gerhard Kremer, called "Mercator," or merchant, used the accumulated European knowledge to make highly accurate maps to serve ocean traders. He made all longitude lines run parallel to each other, so that navigators could easily line up their charts from east to west. Because the spherical globe is distorted by any flat maps, Mercator's projection, still the one most commonly used today, did not give accurate representations of land areas, and, of course, he put Western Europe in the center. Each map carries cultural baggage along with its depiction of the earth. Today, for non-nautical purposes cartographers use alternative projections, like the Peters projection, that convey the sizes of continents more accurately.

Cartography, like the new astronomy and physics, was another science closely tied to political and commercial interests. The Dutch became the best map makers in seventeenth-century Europe because of their keen interest in discovering efficient trade routes, and the French sponsored large-scale projects of mapping the boundaries of Louis XIV's kingdom in great detail. In 1602, the Italian Jesuit Matteo Ricci printed a map of the world in China, but altered it to put China in the center. The emperor was so impressed that he posted the large map on the walls of his palace. A century later, the Qing emperor commissioned French Jesuits to create a large-scale map of his kingdom, entitled "A Comprehensive View of the Empire." This so-called "Jesuit Atlas," which many highly knowledgeable Chinese also worked on, gave the emperor the ability to see his entire vast empire at a single glance, and also to scrutinize local details closely. Like Louis XIV and the other absolutist kings, he embraced new cartography as a valuable tool of imperial rule.

---

specified numbers for a specified season. Cities and towns commonly created citizen militias that took responsibility for the watch in times of peace, for policing in times of local disorder, and for defense in time of war. Mercenaries were different: professional soldiers who fought for pay, and only for pay, under the command of professionals who contracted for their services. Between 1200 and 1500, European wars brought out all four types of military organization in varying combinations.

More Soldiers Fight for Pay Between 1500 and 1700, however, personal retainers, feudal levies, and militias lost ground dramatically to mercenaries. Their commanders grew rich and powerful. In 1625, Albrecht Wallenstein (of Czech origin), Duke of Friedland and governor of Bohemia for the Holy Roman Emperor, used his own domain of 2,000 square miles to supply troops at a profit on behalf of the Empire. Wallenstein became one of the leading generals of the Thirty Years' War, scoring multiple victories on behalf of Catholic forces. He operated a kind of protection racket, threatening to let his troops loose on cities for looting and raping if the city leaders did not buy him off. He also acquired so much independent power that the Holy Roman Emperor celebrated his assassination (1634) by a friend of some of Wallenstein's many victims.

Even on a smaller scale than Wallenstein, mercenaries cost a great deal of money and caused political trouble when they started using military power for their own ends. When disbanded or unpaid, furthermore, they often turned into bandits, looters, or marauders. They had, however, some powerful attractions for sixteenth- and seventeenth-century rulers: they knew how to fight, usually demanded no political rights in return for fighting, mobilized quickly when the money came, and (if paid off) did not usually stay around to make demands or cause trouble once the fighting ended. The more money a ruler could spend on war and the less he had to count on personal retainers, feudal levies, or militias, the more likely his state could win quickly and decisively by hiring mercenaries.

The Rich States Get More Soldiers, and Get Richer How well a ruler could afford to hire mercenaries depended largely on *commerce*. Commercial states gained multiply in the competition for mercenary armies because they could convert their greater monetary riches into soldiers more easily than states with land or labor, by hiring monetary specialists who had access to credit. *Credit* mattered because rulers never had enough cash on hand to buy an army or navy; the war would be lost by the time the money came in. Merchants and bankers loaned them what they needed, expecting repayment from booty, reparations,

1600-1601	Franco-Savoian	France, Savoy
1610-1614	Spanish-Turkish	Spain, Turkey
1615-1618	Austro-Venetian	(Austrian) Habsburgs, Venice
1615-1617	Spanish-Savoian	Spain, Savoy
1617-1621	Spanish-Venetian	Spain, Venice
1618-1619	Spanish-Turkish	Spain, Ottoman Empire
1618-1621	Polish-Turkish	Poland, Ottoman Empire
1618-1625	Bohemian	England, Spain, Habsburgs, Dutch
1625-1630	Danish	France, England, Spain, Habsburgs, Dutch, Sweden
1630-1635	Swedish	Spain, Habsburgs, Dutch, Sweden
1635-1648	Swedish-French	France, Spain, Habsburgs, Dutch, Sweden
1642-1668	Spanish-Portuguese	Spain, Portugal
1645-1664	Turkish-Venetian	Ottoman Empire, Venice
1648-1659	Franco-Spanish	France, Spain
1650-1651	Scottish	England, Scotland

Figure 4.2 Major European wars and their principal belligerents, 1600–50.

or taxes. As it happened, a vast increase in European commercial credit occurred between 1500 and 1700 as commerce expanded much faster than the supply of coin; merchants small and large moved away from cash settlements to paper and book transactions. (The infusion of precious metal from the Americas did not counter the trend because so much American coin ended up in Asia, exchanged for precious imports.)

That brings us to *taxes*. Rulers only kept their credit if they could reliably raise taxes to pay back debts incurred to pay for war. It is easier to levy taxes, on the average, in a monetized economy. Active markets for land, labor, and precious goods set values that tax collectors can observe. Instead of sending out squads of troops to force hidden coin from reluctant peasants, government agents can station themselves where people buy, sell, and ship, taking a share of each transaction. At the cost of encouraging fraud and smuggling, commercialization facilitates taxation to pay for war.

If the chain from war to armies to commerce, credit, and taxes completely explained military effectiveness and the consolidation of states, then obviously the intensely commercialized Dutch Republic of 1670 or so would have towered over every other European state. But in fact by 1700 France and England were beginning to compete effectively with the Dutch at sea, fielded far more extensive land armies, and had created much more centralized states. In 1705, major European land forces numbered approximately:

Spain	50,000	England	87,000
Netherlands	100,000	Sweden	100,000
France	400,000	Russia	170,000

At that point, as we saw earlier, France and England were maintaining Europe's biggest navies at about equal strength. Why did France and England surpass the Dutch? Because commerce had to be balanced by coercion. On one hand, agrarian states, like Russia and Sweden, usually had to force their peasants into their armies. On the other, in very highly commercialized states, merchants only reluctantly went to war, and they limited the power of aristocratic rulers. In the Dutch Republic, even the Princes of Orange could not grab hold of the state. England and France balanced commerce and coercion: continuing to rely on great lords to command their militaries, mixing homegrown troops with foreign mercenaries, promoting the interests of merchants only so long as they coincided with royal interests, using military force to back up their demands for domestic revenues, mostly internalizing the chain war-armies-commerce-credit-taxes rather than relying heavily on foreign creditors. In this way, they built substantial central administrations that served the rulers' interests most of the time.

Everyday Life in Sixteenth- and Seventeenth-Century Europe

How did ordinary people experience these momentous changes in European political and religious life? In short, despite the wars and contending preachers, little changed in most people's daily lives.

Sickness and health, life and death, went on as before. Birth rates continued to be high, but so were death rates. Death was more likely to come as a result of contagious illness than from old age. Sickness and hunger made the difference between life and death. Some population growth occurred during the sixteenth century, but in the seventeenth, disease and wars ended that growth. Because of malnutrition and infectious diseases, a third of a couple's children might die in their first year. Families (married

Map 4.2 Europe in the seventeenth century, after the Peace of Westphalia

couples and their surviving children) therefore remained surprisingly small. Although large households of extended family and servants prevailed in some regions of Southern and Eastern Europe, in Western Europe few households included the elderly. Since men and women married only in their mid-twenties or later, by then their parents were likely to have died. In Western Europe,

many adults never married. They might become nuns or priests, they might die before they reached marriage age, or they might not live to inherit a property or earn enough to consider marriage. Many spent their single lives as servants or hired hands.

Plague had caused a series of devastating epidemics in the late Roman empire, disappeared late in the first millennium, and re-emerged in the 1340s. It continued to return periodically in the fifteenth through seventeenth centuries. Before the seventeenth century, a plague outbreak could kill from a third to half a city's population. Although many people simply accepted plague as inevitable, some Mediterranean cities limited epidemics by imposing quarantines on infected quarters, allowing no one to enter or leave. Further north, no more plague epidemics occurred after the Great Plague and Fire of London in 1665. Plague epidemics may then have ended in Northwestern Europe because wood for building houses ran out and new housing constructed of masonry was less hospitable to the rats and lice that carried and spread plague. Around the Mediterranean, in any case, the last significant plague epidemic broke out in 1720 and 1721.

In the days before antibiotics and vaccination, highly contagious diseases such as smallpox and measles were more deadly for the very young, the very old, and people weakened by hunger or chronic illness. Congenital health problems like withered limbs and club feet could also make it difficult or impossible for an individual to work for a living. Such an individual might become a beggar. If from a more prosperous family, a handicapped person might also enter a convent or monastery, with the family paying expenses.

Commercialization, urbanization, industrialization, and modest population growth combined to increase European trade in agricultural products and to expand the number of rural Europeans working for wages in agriculture or craft production. Historians call this process **proto-industrialization**: a great expansion of rural household and small-shop production in metalworking and, especially, linen or woolen textiles. Urban merchants spun vast webs of connections that brought rural products into international trade, for example supplying cheap clothing for American slaves.

Nevertheless, the great majority of the Western European population consisted of free peasants living in rural areas and earning their livings in agricultural pursuits. By contrast, serfdom actually increased in Central and Eastern Europe, as it did in Russia. On East German and Polish estates, lords turned poverty-stricken peasants into serfs in order to export grain and ship timber to Western Europe. They ran their consolidated estates as an early modern version of agri-businesses.

Life was precarious for rural and urban residents, but in different ways. Agriculture is still a risky business, but in the early modern period it was even more so. Deep spring frosts might kill a crop still in the ground or an August hailstorm might destroy the harvest. Compared to Japan or coastal China, European agricultural yields per acre or per capita were low. No agricultural revolution arrived until after 1700.

In Western Europe many independent smallholders produced for the market. Rural debt was rising because most landholdings were modest in size, and peasants had no cushion. After a series of bad years they found it difficult to pay back their loans. In areas of large estates such as eastern England, noble landlords used overseers or leaseholders to squeeze income from their tenants. Rich city-dwellers were also buying land from impoverished peasants and prosperous large holders, contracting with landless or land-poor peasants to farm the land, and living on their estates imitating the rural lifestyle of the feudal aristocracy. These non-noble rural gentry sought to marry off their daughters to nobles to gain aristocratic status.

A large proportion of agriculture was devoted to raising grains, the main component of everyone's diet. Wheat was the most desirable and most expensive grain; poorer people ate rye, buckwheat, and others. Even in rural areas, very few people baked their own bread; instead they bought flour, and took the loaves they mixed and shaped to village bakers for cooking. People who had no access to ovens or markets typically ate porridges made of grains including oats, not so different from the oatmeal that some Europeans and Americans eat for breakfast today.

The food supply suffered all the vagaries of weather and the wars of the sixteenth and seventeenth centuries. Cities and towns took particular care to keep their populations fed, by regulating grain and bread markets, for high bread prices could lead to disorders and popular protest. Authorities commonly enforced a single market price for grain and bread within a city and its region. The prices were not arbitrary, but related to the available supply; if city authorities insisted that grain be sold at a market price particularly advantageous to consumers, grain merchants could simply go elsewhere to sell their product. Since food was expensive to ship in bulk, even by the waterways that most merchants used, cities ordinarily drew food supplies from their own immediate surroundings. In years of shortage, however, urban merchants had to go further to find supplies, and they faced competition from larger cities – especially the capital city in which the lack of grain posed the threat of social unrest. As a result, a delicate balance obtained among the urban authorities' effort to keep retail prices on bread within the reach of city-dwellers, the bakers and grain merchants who sought to profit from their enterprise, and the farmers who sold their grain in urban markets. A bad harvest easily upset the balance. An abundant harvest also had its own problems, for it meant that prices and profits would fall for growers and merchants alike.

Sharp divisions of rich and poor defined what people could eat. Besides grains, markets for wine as well as the malt and hops that went into beer were extensive. For those who could afford it, wine and beer were safer than drinking contaminated water supplies. Highly perishable food products (like fresh meat or fish, vegetables other than potatoes and onions, and fruit) became available only in season or in markets close to the producers. Burghers and nobles were more likely to increase their intake of exotic foods (peacocks or shellfish, for instance) rather than eat fruits and vegetables.

Urban Social Groups: Clergy, Artisans, and Guilds Urban life varied with a city's size, location, political function, and economic activity; religious centers, seats of governments, and textile manufacturing centers differed dramatically from each other. Most cities were filled, however, with houses several stories high whose upper floors hung out over the lower ones to cast deep shadows on narrow city streets. Water came from fountains or wells from which people fetched it in large vessels; in wealthier houses, servants fetched water; in poorer houses, women did the job. No one had central heating or plumbing. Light came from candles or oil lamps. Since both cost money, ordinary people conducted most of their lives in daylight. Filthy streets often resembled open sewers, since household wastes were often simply poured into them. Other streets had an open conduit down the middle for the purpose. Even prosperous households had little privacy for sleeping, eating, and personal relations.

In Catholic countries, priests, nuns and monks comprised what seems to modern eyes a surprisingly high proportion of urban populations, given the large number of religious institutions (convents, monasteries, churches, hospitals, schools, and orphanages) in most cities; indeed the church and its various institutions supplied many of the social services that governments provide today. Burghers were likely to be substantial male merchants or artisan-shopkeepers, lawyers, physicians, professors and teachers, city government employees, or officials in the central government's courts of justice and administrative service. For all these occupations, training was likely to consist of a formal or informal apprenticeship and progression through a guild. Smaller shopkeepers often lived more simply because their fragile economic niche required them to be on the job for long hours. They often differed little from the artisans who produced the objects they sold.

Skilled artisans working individually or in small groups carried on hand production of objects from books to shoes. Printing could, however, reach a larger scale in cities with important religious, educational, or governmental establishments. Skilled workers continued to acquire their training through apprenticeship to master artisans in small shops, in the expectation that once the worker acquired the skill he, too, could accumulate the capital to be a master. A middle-aged urban artisan could most likely support a family comfortably with his earnings, but many an artisan never succeeded in saving or borrowing the capital to start his own shop. Let us stress the *his*; although women played crucial parts in a shop's day-to-day operation, girls never became apprentices. A widow who had worked with her husband as a tailor or other artisan-shopkeeper might be able to continue the business, however, especially if she

had sons who could help her. She might also have a reliable, experienced apprentice to marry her or her daughter and take over the shop eventually.

In urban areas, crafts commonly formed their own **guilds**. Guilds were formal organizations (usually chartered by city or central governments) whose major activity was to supervise the reproduction of the skilled work they did through the institutionally controlled training of a limited number of apprentices. They also spoke for the trade in city affairs. In a university town, teachers also had apprentices. Senior students who had read and absorbed the required texts would in turn tutor younger students reading the same texts. In Western Europe, by the seventeenth century the guild system (which had sought to limit the numbers of men possessing a given skill) had passed its prime and was beginning to break down in European cities. Some artisans working outside the guild system could acquire the requisite skills and compete successfully with the guildsmen. Proto-industrial shops and households in the countryside also escaped guild control. In Central and Eastern Europe guilds kept their grip longer, disappearing completely only in the early nineteenth century.

The only skilled occupations in which women were likely to be trained were seamstress, cook, or household servant. Indeed household servants – male or female – often constituted the largest occupation in a city. Many apprentices, furthermore, were little more than servants to the master artisan by whom they were supposedly being trained. Household servant was also a position in which rural-to-urban migrants predominated; it was a place to make a beginning as a city-dweller.

European Daily Life and Mentalities During these two centuries, Europeans lived, died, grew crops, made shoes, and traded much as they had done for centuries. If we focus only on their material world, we might well call this a time of "immobile history." But their mental worlds and political structures changed dramatically because of New World discoveries, long-distance trade, religious conflict, printed texts, and the rise of consolidated states. All these changes only took effect over a long period of time: Though northwestern, Protestant states rose at the expense of southern Catholic ones, Europeans as a whole felt only gradual shifts, at best. Only tiny elites began to explore new ways of transforming and observing the world. The real material and political revolutions lay in the future.

4.3 SOUTHEAST ASIA, 1500–1800

The region we now call "Southeast Asia" includes the part of the Asian continent south of China and east of India – extending from Burma in the west to Vietnam in the east, including the modern states of Thailand, Cambodia, and Laos – Malaysia and

Singapore, plus the Philippines and the vast Indonesian archipelago. Its area of 1.5 million square miles is roughly the same as Europe without Russia. In the sea routes among the islands and along the coast, it has an equivalent to the Mediterranean Ocean. The distance from Jakarta to Canton, about 2,000 miles, is roughly the same as from the straits of Gibraltar to Istanbul.

Southeast Asia and Europe were the only two major parts of the Eurasian continent that were not under the control of large empires. Both had multiple contending polities – continental agrarian regimes and commercial city-states – linked by ties of trade and war; both faced cross-cutting allegiances created by diverse religious traditions; both had to resist and learn from the powerful empires around them. Comparing these two parts of Eurasia shows the effects of state power, commerce, and religion on political and social unification and cultural change. European expansion tied the two regions together during these centuries, but the Dutch, Portuguese, Spanish, and British formed only small parts of a complex mixture of peoples. Although all of Southeast Asia except Siam eventually became a European colony, it had its own dynamics long before the Europeans came. Map 4.3 shows the major states and regions of what we now call Southeast Asia. Map 4.4 shows the major trading posts of European powers in Southeast Asia.

The name "Southeast Asia" appeared only after World War II, but people recognized its distinctive identity much earlier. The Chinese called it the "lands of the southern seas," while Arabs and Indians called it "the lands beneath the winds." They singled out two crucial facts about the Southeast Asian lands: They could only be reached easily by sea, and their economic life depended heavily on the monsoon winds.

Favorable Climate and Sparse Population in the Tropical Zone

Compared to Europe, Southeast Asia enjoyed an extremely favorable climate. The constant high temperatures and heavy rainfall of the equatorial tropical zone supported lush vegetation, long growing seasons, and high-yielding rice paddies, and its exotic spices and rare woods fascinated Chinese, Indians, and Europeans alike. But the apparent abundance of the tropics is deceptive. Tropical soils are poor and thin. Clearing the jungle vegetation took a great deal of labor, and risked damaging the soil permanently if the nutrients were not restored. Jungle and forest still occupied most of the land area. Because the region had no grasslands and no large plains, it could not support large grazing animals. Fish and rice were the primary foods. Because of the limited area of fertile lowlands, Southeast Asia's population density of 14 people per square mile was only one sixth that of China or South Asia, and only half that of Europe.

Southeast Asian states and communities based themselves on four ecologies: two agrarian and two maritime. Intensive rice paddy agriculture vs. dispersed, mobile cultivators; port-centered trading communities vs. roving mercantile confederations: These were the poles of commercial, state, and religious organization. The continental polities, because of their primary dependence on agriculture, followed a substantially different course from the maritime ones. On land, sustained processes of territorial integration, administrative centralization, cultural homogenization, and commercialization consolidated control under three imperial systems – those of Burma, Siam, and Vietnam – by 1830. This process showed striking parallels to Western Europe in the same period. In the maritime world, however, populations scattered over vast expanses of sea did not come under unified political or cultural control until conquest by European colonialists.

The two primary modes of agricultural production – **swidden** (or slash-and-burn) agriculture, and rice **paddies** – cultivated tropical soils by radically different means. Swidden farmers burnt down the vegetation, planted seeds in the ash, and captured a crop for one year; then they moved on to another plot. Eventually, when they came back to the first plot after a decade or more, the vegetation had recovered, allowing them to plant again. Swidden cultivation took very little labor, but it only supported a very mobile, sparse population, living in the uplands. Creating a rice paddy, by contrast, required huge, long-term investments of labor to clear flat land and surround it with dikes, plus constant attention to water levels, temperature, and seedlings throughout the year. This technology supported a dense, mostly immobile population, with very high-yielding rice. China imported special early ripening rice seedlings from Champa in southern Vietnam to support its great population boom in the ninth century CE. Vietnam, whose delta was the region's most densely populated society, relied in turn on Chinese paddy techniques, while Java developed its own. A third method, in between swidden and the rice paddy, was to broadcast seeds in the mud of the rivers as they receded, and capture the harvest before the river flooded again. This required less labor than the paddy, but ran the risk of losing the crop to early floods. Still, these fields produced enough of a surplus to support Siam's large capital of Ayutthaya in the seventeenth century.

States could extract food and labor from the rice paddy populations, but they could not easily control the mobile hill peoples. The major continental states controlled small, lowland cores, surrounded by peripheries of mountains, jungles, and peoples beyond their control. Burma, Thailand, and Vietnam each built powerful state apparatuses, supporting kings, nobles, and armies, in this manner. But the lands separating these rival powers were extremely difficult to cross. Gradually, each of the states brought more of the hill peoples under their control. The states actively

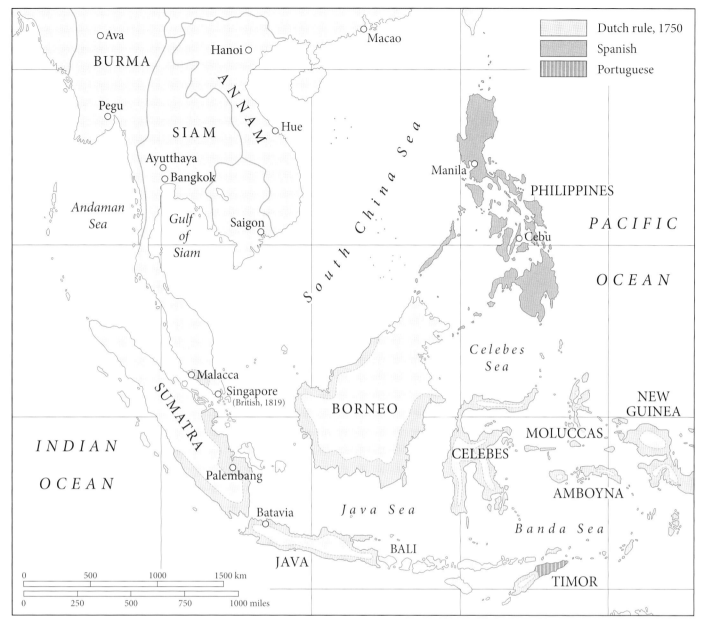

Map 4.3 Southeast Asia, c. 1750

promoted frontier expansion, but their populations grew slowly. They created densely settled central courts, acting like suns with gravitational attraction on outlying planets, or local hill lords. The gravitational pull tended to increase over time, but since the frontiers did not completely fill up with lowland settlers, despite state efforts, continental Southeast Asian military competition led to less sharply defined borders than in Europe. Negotiators resolved a border dispute between Vietnam and Cambodia, for example, by deciding that those who lived in houses on stilts belonged to Cambodia, and those who lived in houses on the ground belonged to Vietnam. The goal of invasions and raids was to capture able-bodied men, a scarce commodity, rather than to defend precise frontiers.

Two alternative states, the maritime port and the seafaring confederation, spread across the archipelago. Sultans on the north coast of Java, the city of Malacca, and the Malay peninsula profited from the cosmopolitan trading communities that collected under their rule. Another confederation, the Bugis trader-pirates, controlled many of the sea routes without holding a land base. Later, other multi-ethnic confederations tagged with insulting names by Chinese officials combined territorial bases with extensive maritime linkages from China to Sumatra. The "Japanese dwarf pirates" in the sixteenth century and "Vietnamese pirates" in the eighteenth century traded and raided along the South China coast beyond the reach of state control.

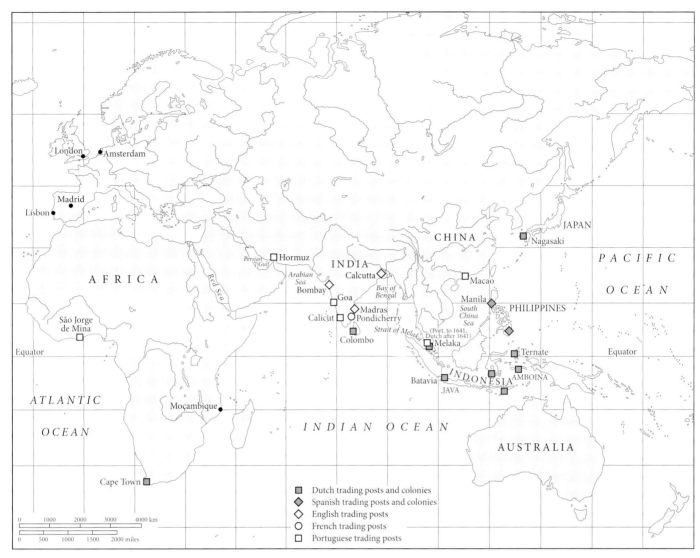

Map 4.4 European trading posts in Asia

Religions and States

Eurasia's great universal religious traditions all penetrated Southeast Asia. Hindu-Buddhist models came first, followed by Muslims, Confucian Chinese, and Christians. Each of the traditions brought concepts of political leadership linked to cosmological myths. Each great tradition, however, had to adapt to locally centered cults in order to link the villages to the central court. The Hindu-Buddhist concept of the "wheel-turning king" authorized royal authority as an essential component of cosmic evolution, but it did not support an elaborate bureaucracy or military force. In this type of "galactic polity," the ruler generated sacred space at the center while lesser nobles and beings revolved around him. By the sixteenth century, nearly all the states established on this principle, like the Khmer kings who built Angkor Wat in Cambodia, Java's Majapahit, Siam's Sukhotai, and the

Champa state of southern Vietnam had collapsed. Today, only Bali retains a strong Hindu culture.

The second religious tradition was Islam, carried by Sufi mystics and Muslim traders across the sea. Closely tied to coastal communities, Islam replenished its forces with traveling scholars, traders, and holy men moving across the archipelago. Sufi **tarekat**, or religious brotherhoods, inspired especially passionate devotion in villages, while the **haj**, or pilgrimage to Mecca, gave prestige to those who achieved it. Local rulers, or sultans, joined political and religious authority without any serious challenge from scholars or judges.

Buddhism spread in two forms, the **Mahayana** version coming south from China (which emphasized the role of bodhisattvas), and the **Theravada** (or Hinayana) form from India. Only Vietnam adopted Mahayana Buddhism, under Chinese influence. Orthodox Confucian elites remained suspicious of it,

Figure 4.3 In Ayutthaya, the capital of a powerful kingdom in Siam, or modern Thailand, large temple complexes showed off the power of the kings and their ability to sponsor Buddhist monasteries. It was one of the largest cities in the world. By the eighteenth century, after invasions from Burma, nothing but ruins remained.

but many scholars and officials endorsed and coexisted with Buddhists. The court strictly regulated the number of priests, but patronized the great Buddhist centers in Hue to conduct rituals for the souls of those who served the dynasty. Theravada Buddhism faced no substantial rivals such as the Vietnam bureaucrats, so it became much more dominant in the other Southeast Asian states. Theravada monks remained quite separate from lay society, as Theravada Buddhists held that attaining enlightenment was a rigorous, ascetic discipline open only to a few. Monks could not accept money, and they had to beg for their food from their fellow villagers. Yet they offered education in local languages, making Siam, Burma, and Cambodia remarkably literate societies, where more than half the men could read simple texts.

Christian missions established toeholds among European colonists in the Dutch and Portuguese outposts, but failed to reach deeply into the native populations. Only in the Philippines, after energetic missionary efforts, did Christianity become the dominant religion of an entire society, but the Catholic missionary effort in Indochina did attain considerable success. Let us examine three examples of continental states supported by these religious traditions: Ayutthaya (Buddhist), Vietnam (Buddhist–Confucian), and Java (Islamic–Hindu).

Ayutthaya The Ayutthaya kingdom, founded in 1351 on an island in Thailand's Chao Phraya River, lasted for over 400 years. By the sixteenth century it had expanded over much of Siam and Cambodia, placing its capital 55 miles from the sea. The Ayutthaya rulers centralized power in their capital and fought incessant wars with both of their neighbors, the Burmese and Cambodians: at least seventy-five wars during the kingdom's existence. The bitter Burmese–Ayutthaya struggles generated military competition, resource extraction, promotion of trade, and centralized bureaucracy in both states. They created a bureaucracy, patronizing craftsmen and Buddhist monasteries in the capital, building impressive monuments still visible today, a short train ride from Bangkok. Figure 4.3 shows the ruins of the great capital of Ayutthaya.

The wars seesawed back and forth from the sixteenth through eighteenth centuries, as the Burmese first besieged Ayutthaya, and then the Siamese attacked Burma's capital. Finally, in 1767, the Burmese sacked the city, leaving it in ruins. They ended the Ayutthaya kingdom, but King Rama founded a new dynasty in Bangkok, which remains to this day.

Besides warring with their neighbors, the Ayutthaya kings engaged with powers from around the world. Merchants came there from China, the Middle East, and Europe. They paid tribute to China, but kept their autonomy. Ayutthaya was a valuable stopping place for ships bringing porcelain and silk from China, and it prospered from its own exports of animal hides. Its rice exports fed the Dutch settlement at Batavia. Japanese trader-warriors, converted to Christianity by Jesuits, became an important military and commercial force in the capital until they were expelled after looting the city. The Dutch and the English trading companies each established **factories**, or trading colonies, in the city, and intrigued against each other to gain support from the Siamese kings. The Greek adventurer serving the East India Company, Constantine Phaulkon, described in the opening anecdote, even became the de facto Siamese foreign minister. Finally, French missionaries arrived in 1664. When they reported back to France enthusiastically about prospects for new Christian converts, King Louis XIV sent an embassy in 1687 which turned to gunboat diplomacy, occupying Bangkok and demanding trade privileges. But a year later the Siamese expelled the French, massacred the English, and put the Dutch in a less privileged trading position.

Siam's leaders ranged from militant warriors to peace-loving monks, and the kingdom constantly faced threats from struggles between brothers for the throne, hostile neighbors, unruly hill states, and European traders. Yet the kingdom centered at Ayutthaya and later Bangkok held itself together well enough to make itself the focal point of the Siamese, and later Thai people. Brilliant Siamese diplomats quickly learned how to manipulate trade benefits and military mobilization in these complex negotiations with global trading companies and states with imperial ambitions. They often used foreigners, East Asian or European, as crucial advisors. Siam/Thailand, unlike all other Southeast Asian states, was never colonized, because of its position between the major imperial powers and its adroit balancing of alliances in its own interests. Box 4.3 gives an eyewitness account, possibly reliable, of how a Siamese king introduced his heir to the throne.

Vietnam Vietnam stood out among these states, however, by virtue of its strong bureaucracy based on Chinese models. The Le dynasty (1427–1788) carried on the traditions established in Vietnam since the eleventh century: Use Chinese Confucian principles, pay homage to China, but never let yourself be swallowed by your powerful northern neighbor. The cult of

Box 4.3 The King of Siam Goes to War, and Names his Heir

Fernão Mendes Pinto (c. 1510–83), Portuguese adventurer, merchant, Jesuit, and writer, spent the years 1537–58 in Asia, engaging in trade, piracy, religious pilgrimages, and diplomacy, meeting many of the leading kings, warriors, and priests of the region – or so he claimed. He wrote a narrative of his travels, published in 1614, the details of which are so vivid that they sound convincing, but even today scholars cannot sort out fact from fiction. Yet even if Mendes Pinto did not actually go everywhere his book describes, he did have a great deal of reliable information from people he met, which is not found in other sources. He gives us a feel for life in the sixteenth century unmatched by other chronicles, and he portrays the tumultuous encounters of Europeans and Southeast Asians in this early imperial age.

Here he describes a battle conducted by the king of Siam against the king of Chiangmai, in northern Thailand:

As soon as [the king] came in sight, [the enemy troops] advanced in tight formation, divided into twelve battalions of fifteen thousand each, all fine-looking troops, marching in perfect
order. Then their vanguard, comprised of the forty thousand cavalrymen, rushed forward to meet the king of Siam's vanguard, comprised of seventy thousand foot soldiers, and routed them in less than a quarter of an hour, killing three princes who were among them. Seeing the defeat suffered by his men, the king of Siam, like a prudent man, realized that he would have to change his tactics, and he reorganized his troops into a single body composed of the seventy thousand foreign mercenaries and four thousand elephants and charged the enemy camp with such tremendous force that at the first encounter he succeeded in breaking it up, routing them completely and slaying an infinite number of men.

Mendes Pinto's numbers are not reliable, but this was clearly a large battle. Note the mention of the use of foreign mercenaries, who included Portuguese, other Europeans, and Asians. Poisoned by his unfaithful queen, the dying king crowned his eldest son, and had his prime minister give him eloquent instructions on the proper way to rule:

Holy child of tender age, in whose high and fortunate star it was written that thou shouldst now be chosen by heaven to rule this Sornau empire which God has commanded me, thy vassal, to deliver to thee. I hereby do so, upon thy oath that thou shalt always rule it in obedience to his divine will, dispensing equal justice to all the peoples, without showing favoritism to any person, whether highborn or low … for if thou shouldst, out of human considerations, deny justice to those who, in the eyes of the Lord of justice, deserve it, thou shalt be severely punished for it in the Concave Depths of the House of Smoke, that fiery and frightfully fetid lake where the wicked and the damned weep continuously, with the gloom of dark night in their hearts.

Although we cannot know whether any minister of a Buddhist kingdom ever said this to a new king, Mendes Pinto puts in his mouth ideals of justice under divine supervision that were common in Europe and Southeast Asia. His readers knew all too well that rulers all too rarely put these ideals into practice.

the ancestors, the insistence on filial piety, and the close regulation of family relations followed the Chinese example of making a disciplined, hierarchical family, where father knew best, into the model of the ideal state. The emperor, as "Son of Heaven," was not exactly like a Hindu god-king: he, too, had to obey Heaven's will, and he could lose his mandate if floods or rebellions indicated that he had mistreated the people. But he constantly asserted his authority to rule by divine right. Stability, however, came first, for the emperor, his officials, and the literate elite who took exams on the Chinese classics. Printed texts spread these basic ideals into the villages.

But despite this heavy Chinese mold, Vietnam had its own special characteristics. In its law codes, women had much higher status than in China, and some women became famous poets. Vietnamese writers attacked the corruption of Ming China and the devastation it caused with its failed invasion in the early fifteenth century. Yet like China under the Qing, Vietnam was an expansionist empire, moving south to destroy the Hindu Cham kingdom, and moving west into the uplands to control hill peoples in Laos. Vietnam also had its own style of rebellion, led by the Tayson brothers in 1771. Their main goal was to throw back control of the central court over their region, but they also preached redistribution of wealth, burned the hated tax registers, and drove back an invasion from China in 1788. The Tayson ruler even planned to invade South China, mobilizing the entire male population by requiring them to carry identity cards. He wanted to re-establish the old Nam Viet kingdom of the second century BCE. But his death in 1792 left behind an unstable, divided society that could not hold off European incursion in the nineteenth century. Vietnam in many ways repeated China's cycle of rise and fall, but with its own distinctive features.

Java and the Dutch The islands of Southeast Asia include the huge but very sparsely populated Borneo and Sumatra, and the smaller but densely populated island of Java. The Spice Islands in the east attracted most of the traders, but ports at crucial bottlenecks like Malacca, Batavia, and Makassar exerted great commercial power. Java had the largest population in the archipelago, but it had many rivals among the islands, and the island of Java itself was not unified. Across the islands, small states led by Muslim sultans acted autonomously to create trade coalitions and warrior alliances.

The first Europeans to settle in the archipelago were the Portuguese, who obtained a base in Malacca in 1511 after negotiations with the sultan. The Portuguese, however, concentrated only on their far-flung seaborne empire, and did not penetrate further into the islands. The Dutch VOC in 1619 established a permanent settlement at Batavia, on the northwest coast of Java. Portuguese and Chinese merchants had preceded them there. The Dutch extended their trading network eastward to Makassar, Ambon, and Malacca through the eighteenth century. The lure of pepper and spices had drawn them to the islands, but few Dutchmen wanted to stay there for their entire lives. The European community of Batavia numbered only about 2,000 people of a total of 27,000, living in "factories" isolated from the native population.

Meanwhile, the Javanese elites went their way independently of the Europeans. The trading states on the north coast, called **pasisir**, profited from the commerce with the Spice Islands to the east until a new Islamic state in the interior, Mataram, conquered almost the entire island in the mid seventeenth century. Spartan, militaristic Mataram looked down on trade. Sultan Agung (r. 1613–46) proudly declared that he was a warrior prince, not a merchant like the other Javanese. He recognized no limits on his power. He destroyed the eastern port of Surabaya in 1625, forbade his people to travel abroad, and told them to deliver all their surplus rice to him. Then the monopoly he controlled would deliver it to the Dutch. He tried and failed to conquer Batavia, and had thousands of Muslim clerics killed when he suspected them of rebellion.

The Mataram rulers constructed a vast complex of buildings, walls, and moats to mark their sacred power, and the leading hereditary families, the **priyayi**, practiced elaborate rituals to mark their status. They lived in large, refined urban centers. At its peak, the Mataram capital of Yogyakarta had 150,000 to 200,000 people. It was one of the three largest cities in Southeast Asia, along with Ayutthaya in Siam and Hanoi in Vietnam. The priyayi embraced an ethic of warrior knights, devoted to their lord in battle, which they expressed in the shadow puppet drama, a great performing tradition of stories derived from the Indian epics *Mahabharata* and *Ramayana*, delivering moral teachings, religious mythology, and entertainment to all Javanese. The shadow dramas and the **gamelan** orchestras that accompanied ritual dancers created an elaborate, stylized culture, derived from the sophisticated pasisir states of the east, which brought cultural unity to the island.

After initial success, the Javanese centralizers failed to create a unified regime, unlike the continental states. The military power of Mataram in reality did not match that of the glorious Hindu gods. After Sultan Agung's death, a series of internal wars drew in Javanese, the Dutch, Chinese, and Balinese into mutual competition to control the island. When the Sultan of Mataram was threatened by a rebellion in 1677, he signed a humiliating treaty with the Dutch in order to regain his throne. The Dutch gained complete monopoly rights over trade through this agreement, so they could make the sultans totally dependent on them. In the end, by the mid eighteenth century the VOC, although only a trading company, took control of many territories of Mataram, with the sultans and the priyayi elite under it as vassals. In 1799, after the abolition of the VOC monopoly, the Dutch state took control of all of Java, and later all of Indonesia. It held power over all the islands until 1945.

Trends Toward Standardization

These states followed, for a while, general trends toward integration similar to those of Europe. Economic exchanges drew more people into the market and promoted the circulation of coins; rulers tapped the economic surplus to increase their state revenues and support larger numbers of officials. The stronger states with greater military and administrative resources set out to compete with their rivals, eliminating the weaker ones and taking over their territory. As a result, the number of competing major state-like units was radically reduced: from about 500 in fifteenth-century Europe to about 25 by 1800; in continental Southeast Asia, from 25 to only 3 (Burma, Siam, and Vietnam). These larger state units then promoted further economic growth by supporting clearance of land on frontiers and giving privileges to merchants. They took control of religious institutions, making the monks and neo-Confucian literati into elite intellectual groups closely associated with the political center. They also standardized and disseminated the distinctive languages of the dominant group. The Siamese and Burmese adapted Indian scripts to their languages, while the Vietnamese created a unique mixture of Chinese characters and special Vietnamese characters, called *nom*. Writing poetry in nom, instead of classical Chinese, was one way for Vietnamese poets to display their independence of China and to use folk language in their literary tradition. In the seventeenth century, Vietnamese Christians also began to use the Western script introduced by French missionaries, so that modern Vietnamese is now the only East Asian language written in the Roman alphabet.

The progress toward integration was not smooth. Each of the states went through cycles of fragmentation and consolidation. The Ayutthaya and Burmese kingdoms repeatedly took advantage of each other's weakness to try to pull their rival apart, and the Vietnamese state remained divided between north, center, and south socially and politically. But by 1800, after centuries of upheaval, each core society had put itself back together. Siam remained independent, and even if Vietnam and Burma were not strong enough to resist colonial domination, they retained strong identities looking back to the glories of their precolonial past. When the colonial empires finally fell, the old states, with boundaries and peoples very much like their old ones, returned. Java, by contrast, made only an abortive move toward standardization. Significant moves toward cultural and economic unity stopped, as the island was pulled apart by tensions between inland states and the commercial fringe on the north.

In early modern Europe, the political story is one of the victory of medium-sized states over empires or city-states. The religious story is first that of the confrontation with the Muslim East, and then the fracturing of a unified Christian community by the Reformation. The Southeast Asian story also displays a softer version of the same narrative, with different results. The only great Asian empire that threatened the region was China, but Vietnam fiercely fought off China's southern expansion. The European empires did penetrate each society, and fought each other there, but none of them had gained more than toeholds by the end of the eighteenth century. The victories of Burma, Siam, and Vietnam represented consolidation by states based on densely populated commercialized agrarian regions against interior states without commercialized agriculture and trading enclaves on the coast. The Dutch had gone the furthest in mastering Java, but they had still left many princes independent. The religious story is one of a multi-sided competition of many organized faiths: Christian, Islamic, Confucian, and Buddhist, each of which entrenched itself as an orthodoxy in one place while remaining a tolerated alternative in others. Theravada Buddhism centered itself in Burma and Siam with royal patronage; Christianity dominated the Philippines, and made inroads in Vietnam; Islam pervaded the archipelago and Malay peninsula; while Confucian values supported a state structure in Vietnam and Chinese commercial enclaves throughout the region. Both regions were patchwork quilts of distinct religious and social communities, imperfectly stitched together by political and economic threads.

The Maritime Networks

Sea Peoples Beyond the reach of the continental states were many different peoples who spent most of their lives at sea. They formed communities dispersed across the thousands of islands, linked by family, political, and commercial interests. Each ethnic group had its own home base and its own customs, but all had to interact with each other. The trading communities included Portuguese and Dutch Christians, Malay and Javanese Muslims, Hindu Balinese, Chinese, and Indians, speaking hundreds of different languages. To communicate with each other, they used a common language, which eventually evolved from the lingua franca of the traders into the national languages of Malaysia and Indonesia. Malay words made their way into all the major languages, including English phrases like "run amok" and "sarong," and many of our most common words for Asian tropical products come from Malay

Figure 4.4 The Bugis, a seafaring people, dominated the maritime regions of Southeast Asia with their fast, efficient boats, equally useful for carrying trade goods and conducting piracy.

words drawn from Indian, Arabic, and Chinese sources. These include "curry," "bamboo," "ketchup," "gingham," "mango," "paddy" rice, "soy" sauce, and "tea."

Let us look at two examples of these diasporic communities: the Bugis and the Chinese. The Bugis had their base originally in the south of the island of Sulawesi, in a series of small kingdoms near the great port of Makassar. Converting to Islam under pressure from the Makassar ruler, they planted colonies across the archipelago, gaining a reputation as dynamic traders and fierce fighters. Their distinctive sailboats, carrying 150 to 250 tons of goods, appeared by the hundred in Batavia, Jakarta, Surabaya, the Celebes, and Sumatra. Figure 4.4 shows one of these boats. Because they had no strong state of their own, they served patrons in search of military forces as sailors and soldiers of fortune. In a way, they combined the island-centered commercial network of Venice with the soldier ethic of the Swiss. They maintained strict discipline on their ships by enforcing customary codes of fair trade for merchants and tight control over their crews.

The Bugis joined the Dutch to conquer Makassar in 1667, allowing the VOC to consolidate its monopoly over pepper trade east of Java. But in the eighteenth century they resisted the Dutch monopoly, setting up a flourishing city on the Riau island group near Sumatra and attacking Malacca unsuccessfully in 1756 and 1784. For a while they revived their commercial empire, but the Dutch expelled them from Riau in 1782, once more forcing them to disperse across the seas. They reached northern Australia in the nineteenth century. Although they never created a lasting state of their own, they still survive as one of the vigorous commercial communities of Singapore and Indonesia.

Chinese in Southeast Asia: Indonesian Separation and Siamese Assimilation The Chinese in Southeast Asia had a longer history and a bigger impact on the local societies, because of their greater population and their connections with the great empire to the north. They began to leave China in the twelfth and thirteenth centuries, and the pace of emigration picked up in the sixteenth. As the growing population along the south coast put greater pressure on the limited agricultural land, daring pioneers left for the South Seas to try their luck in trade. They arrived in Batavia before the Dutch, and joined the other trading communities scattered from Ayutthaya to Makassar and Manila. They had two advantages over many of their rivals, however: their strong patriarchal family values, and the presence of the Chinese empire. Most of those who came were not those destined for the study of the classics and elite government jobs; they were mainly peasants and artisans who brought Chinese oral and popular culture with them, not the high tradition. They concentrated their multi-storey shops and living quarters in separate areas of the cities, and built their own temples to worship a mixture of Confucian sages and Daoist and Buddhist gods. Their rivals singled them out as highly intelligent, hard-working, closed, and aggressive, and envied their riches: The Dutch were the first to call them "the Jews of Asia." It was not a compliment.

The Chinese empire itself was a mixed blessing for these overseas Chinese. On the one hand, the emperor claimed authority over all his Chinese subjects, wherever they lived, but on the other, he and his officials deeply distrusted the loyalties of these people who moved around too much and pursued degrading goals of profit instead of bureaucratic success. They were useful contacts who could aid the empire in its negotiations with important Southeast Asian states, but if they got into trouble abroad, the emperors wanted nothing to do with them. When Chinese suffered massacres in Manila and Batavia, the powerful Qing empire did nothing to protect them, and did not even cut off trade. Later, the Qing announced that merchants who did not return after three years abroad could no longer come back to China.

In practice, these regulations made little sense. The overseas Chinese always kept close family contacts in China, and their relatives constantly moved back and forth to serve the family business. They used the mainland base as a support for commerce, family, and culture, and many of them hoped to retire to their home villages. Even if they died abroad, the wealthiest Chinese had their coffins sent back home. Many Chinese kept common ties with each other abroad based on their shared native place of origin, forming distinctive communities around their own dialects and local gods. Yet others did settle down locally, marrying local women and merging into their adopted culture. In Java and the Malay states, some even converted to Islam. In the Philippines, many became Christians. Their descendants were called **peranakan** or **mestizos**, meaning people of mixed origin who straddled two worlds.

But the reaction to these new arrivals by other Southeast Asians varied drastically depending on circumstances. Siam and Java illustrate the opposite ends of the spectrum from assimilation to near apartheid. There were about 100,000 Chinese in Java by 1800, a very small percentage of the total population. Even today they are only 3.5 percent of Indonesia's total population. But then as now, they controlled a disproportionate share of the island's commercial wealth. The Dutch encouraged the Chinese to develop sugar and coffee plantations, admiring them as hard laborers by contrast with the "lazy" local people. The image of tropical "laziness" was a racist stereotype, based only on the fact that independent Southeast Asian peasants in underpopulated territories felt no urge to slave on European plantations. The Chinese, coming from hardscrabble lands of the South China coast, seized the chance to get ahead. Yet the Dutch were suspicious of Chinese as too ambitious and liable to turn to smuggling in defiance of regulations. Dutch misgovernment caused the Chinese uprising in Batavia in 1740 which led to the massacre of thousands of Chinese.

At the same time, the Chinese collected taxes for the Dutch from the Javanese peasants and made great profits as middlemen in the export trade. They tried to be as flexible as possible. So

Bing Kong (1580–1644), the captain of the Chinese in Batavia, grew rich from the island pepper trade. His brother stayed in China, but his son converted to Islam and moved to smaller cities in Java to conduct business. His junks moved goods from the islands to Java, Taiwan, and Annam, and he also traded profitably with the Dutch. He diversified his portfolio quite well. His successors were less lucky. They suffered from discrimination, economic competition, and increasing confinement to ghettoes in the cities. When the Indonesians finally became a nation in the twentieth century, they expelled the Dutch, but had to accept the presence of a small minority of Chinese among them who controlled 70 to 80 percent of the country's wealth. The very separate position of the Chinese made them power-brokers at the top, but victims once again of massacre by Javanese in the 1960s.

The Chinese experience in Siam differed sharply. There, too, the Chinese formed only about 5 percent of the population, but sparsely populated Siam welcomed Chinese as peasants, laborers, and merchants. Many Chinese male immigrants married local women, took Siamese names, and easily adopted Theravada Buddhism, which was much more familiar to them than Islam. One striking indicator of Chinese assimilation was their acceptance of cremation, a common Siamese practice viewed with horror by Confucians, for whom filial piety required preserving the integrity of the body after death. Several Siamese kings married Chinese women and learned the Chinese dialect. As in Java, Chinese prospered as middlemen between peasants and rulers, and controlled Siamese by lending them money at high interest rates. They also worked in mines, ran rice mills, and tended to look down on the Siamese as indolent. Yet tensions were never as great, and the Chinese were not sharply separated as a group until the twentieth century. The Dutch deliberately set the Chinese apart in Indonesia by creating a racialized colonial order in the cities, but no such trend occurred in Siam. Thai nationalists in the twentieth century also attacked them as Jews, or even the Yellow Peril, but the Chinese remain closely tied to the royal family of Thailand and are not viewed as enemies. Thus the different experiences of the two Chinese communities reflect the impact of colonialism, religious traditions, and relative population balances in the different states.

The one state that became a majority Chinese community was Singapore, established by Sir Stamford Raffles in 1819 as the key port of British Malaya. There the Chinese also prospered greatly as middlemen in colonial trade, but they outnumbered the Indians, Malays, and other foreigners in the city. After Malaya finally achieved independence from Britain in 1957 and Singapore separated from Malaya in 1965, its ruler Lee Kuan Yew devised a very distinctively Chinese state, both proclaiming multicultural diversity as a basic value along with tight authoritarian control and promotion of distinctive "Asian values" of obedience, hard work, and limits to dissent. Singapore is the last survivor of the many city-states that multiplied across the region in the sixteenth century, a true successor to Malacca and Makassar, but completely updated for the global high-technology world. Now that it has linked itself to mainland China, and begun to make peace with Malaysia and Indonesia, the Chinese communities of Southeast Asia are once again reknitting their long-standing ties with the mainland and the world.

Conclusion This brief overview of Southeast Asia shows how, just as in early modern Europe, a fascinating array of diverse communities and states actively participated in the formation of an increasingly integrated world. Major states of Southeast Asia, such as Siam, Burma, and Vietnam, brought their people under more centralized rule; they expanded links among each other and forged new ties with Europe, China, and India. In Europe, however, the major states of England, France, and Spain not only fought wars with each other, but also expanded empires into the non-European world, linking trade and conquest. Religious competition generated by the Reformation and Counter-Reformation in Europe generated a century of civil and international warfare. Southeast Asia had plenty of religious competition, but no religious wars. Southeast Asian states brought all the major faiths together and combined with local beliefs to create original versions of ancient creeds. Europe created stronger states with a truly global reach out of its cauldron of military and religious strife; Southeast Asia did not simply passively accept the European presence, but shared many of its processes and altered the European presence in distinctive fashion. Even as colonies, for the next century and a half, the Southeast Asian peoples used their long heritage to make their special mark on the world.

Study Questions (1) Compare forms of state-making in Southeast Asia and Western Europe. What were the goals of rulers? How did they mobilize resources? Who supported them and why? What explains the success of some and the failure of others?

(2) Europeans, Chinese, and Southeast Asians all had extensive networks of seaborne trade, but only the Europeans circumnavigated the world. Explain the role of the following factors in each region: wind and weather, military competition, mapping and knowledge creation, religious ideology, the lure of riches.

(3) In Europe and Southeast Asia, the competition of multiple religious traditions had powerful political and military implications. Why were the European religious wars so much more violent, and how were they settled?

(4) Both Europe and Southeast Asia consisted of competitive, middle-sized states which constantly warred with each other and competed in trade and religious orientation. Both had substantial coastlines and maritime trade. Yet the Europeans sailed across the Atlantic and Pacific, and ultimately colonized most of Southeast Asia, not vice versa. Why was this? Contrast the two regions' fates by 1700.

Suggested Reading

Europe ELIZABETH L. EISENSTEIN, *The Printing Revolution in Early Modern Europe*, 2nd edn. (Cambridge University Press, 2012). This work is the classic argument for the dramatic impact of printing.

STEVEN SHAPIN, *The Scientific Revolution* (University of Chicago Press, 1998). He states: "There was no scientific revolution, and this is a book about it." A refreshing new survey of the main issues.

Empires and Trade FERNAND BRAUDEL, *The Mediterranean and the Mediterranean World in the Age of Philip II* (Berkeley: University of California Press, 1995). Originally published in English in 1972, this is the masterwork of one of the twentieth century's greatest historians.

Andre Gunder Frank, *ReOrient: Global Economy in the Asian Age* (Berkeley: University of California Press, 1998). He asserts powerfully the unity of the globe and the dominance of Asia after 1500.

William H. McNeill, *The Pursuit of Power: Technology, Armed Force, and Society since A.D. 1000* (University of Chicago Press, 1982). McNeill describes the interaction between commercial and military expansion.

Charles Tilly, *Coercion, Capital and European States, 990–1992* (Cambridge, MA, and Oxford: Blackwell, 1992). Tilly offers a general theory of the formation of European states.

South and Southeast Asia   Victor B. Lieberman, *Strange Parallels: Southeast Asia in Global Context, c. 800–1830*, 2 vols. (Cambridge University Press, 2003). This is a brilliant argument for comparable processes in continental Southeast Asia and Western Europe.

Anthony Reid, *Southeast Asia in the Age of Commerce,1450–1680* (New Haven, CT: Yale University Press, 1988–93). Reid's work is a superb Braudelian synthesis over the long term.

Eric Tagliacozzo, *The Longest Journey: Southeast Asians and the Pilgrimage to Mecca* (Oxford University Press, 2013). This is a large survey of the extensive contacts of Southeast Asian Muslims with the Middle East.

Glossary

Anabaptists: Radical Protestant sects who insisted on extremely literal interpretations of scripture.

cujus regio ejus religio: Principle of allowing rulers to determine the religion of all their subjects, without external interference.

Dutch East India Company (VOC): Trading company chartered by the Netherlands to engage in trade with the Far East.

East India Company (EIC): Trading company chartered by the English to promote trade with the Far East.

Edict of Nantes: Edict (1598) of French king commanding mutual toleration of Protestants and Catholics.

factories: Trading colonies established by European companies in Asia in the early modern period.

feudal levies: Demands by European kings for troops to be supplied by their vassal lords.

gamelan: Type of orchestra in Java that accompanied performances of Hindu epic plays.

guilds: Organizations of merchants and craftsmen which controlled access to individual specialized occupations in European cities.

haj: The pilgrimage to Mecca, which all Muslims are expected to do once in their lifetime.

Hanseatic League: Group of German cities which banded together in a trading confederation around the Baltic Sea.

Holy Roman Empire: Name for a confederation of German states.

humanists: European advocates of study of the Greek and Roman classical texts, with open-minded attitudes toward Christian scriptures.

indulgences: Benefits sold by the Roman popes which allowed Catholics to buy their way out of spiritual condemnation.

Levant Company: English trading company chartered in 1581 to conduct trade with the Middle East.

Mahayana: Form of Buddhist teaching dominant in East Asia, which recognizes the role of bodhisattvas, who aid humans seeking salvation.

mercenaries: Soldiers who fight only for pay, not attached to a single nation or ruler.

mestizos: Spanish term for peoples of mixed blood, like many Asians in the Philippines, or Spanish and Native Americans in the New World.

militias: Military groups organized by local peasants and city people to defend their villages and towns.

paddies: Agricultural production of high-yielding rice using permanent cleared lands surrounded by earth dikes and regularly flooded with water.

papal bull: Special order of the Pope, marked with a lead seal, or *bulla*.

pasisir: Small trading states ruled by sultans, on the north coast of Java.

peranakan: Peoples of mixed origins in Southeast Asia, especially Chinese who intermarried with Malay and Javanese.

priyayi: Hereditary families exercising ritual and political leadership in Java.

Protestants: Religious groups which rejected the authority of the Roman pope over the Western Christian church.

proto-industrialization: Rural household and small workshop production in metals and textiles.

Ptolemy: Astronomer whose theory put the Earth at the center of the Universe.

Reformation: Movement to change practices of the Catholic church, or reject its central authority.

swidden: A form of agriculture practiced in the tropics where farmers burn vegetation, plant crops, and move to new fields every year.

tarekat: Muslim religious brotherhoods, led by Sufi mystics.

Theravada (Hinayana): Form of Buddhist teaching dominant in Southeast Asia (except Vietnam), in which residence in a monastery is considered necessary for salvation.

tithe: Portion of a peasant's or urban worker's income owed to religious institutions, usually around 10 percent.

Global map, 1763

Global map, 1763

England
London
Paris
France

Portugal

Mexico

Haiti

Colombia

Peru

Brazil

Bolivia

Chile

Five largest cities *000s*

1. Beijing
450

400

3. Edo (Tokyo)
300

200

5. Paris
175

2. London

4. Istanbul

1	Portuguese possessions
2	Spanish possessions
3	Dutch possessions
4	English possessions
5	French possessions
6	Russian possessions

PART II

1700–1850: Revolution and reform

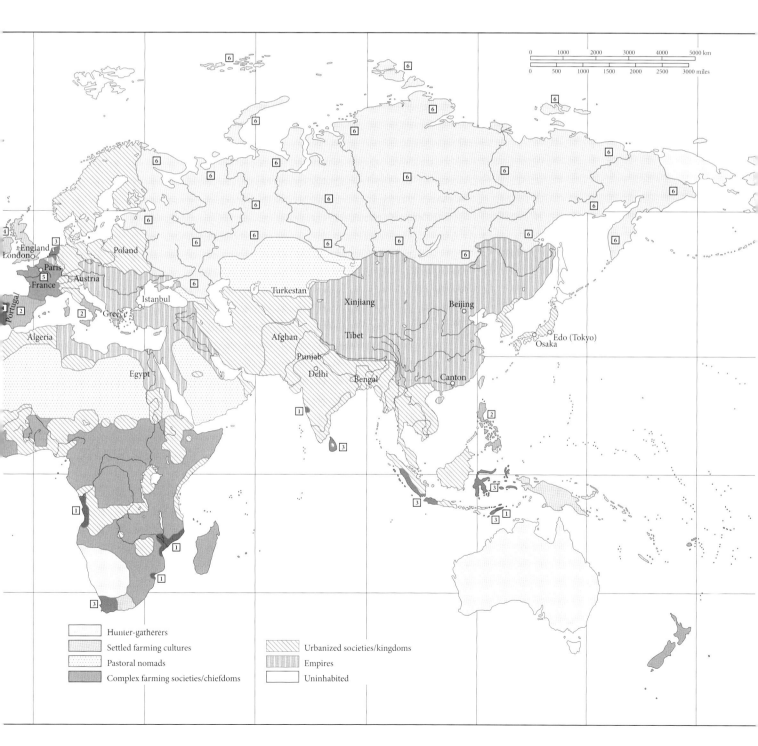

Hunter-gatherers

Settled farming cultures

Pastoral nomads

Complex farming societies/chiefdoms

Urbanized societies/kingdoms

Empires

Uninhabited

Timeline	
1644–1911	Qing dynasty in China.
1709	Abraham Darby uses coke made from coal in iron smelting; this frees metalworking from dependency on charcoal.
1712	Briton Thomas Newcomen, the inventor of the atmospheric steam engine, builds his first operating model.
1756–63	Seven Years' War in Europe (whose North American theater is the French and Indian War).
1757	Battle of Plassey. Having routed the French, Robert Clive's defeat of the nawab of Bengal marks the beginning of the British conquest of India.
1762–96	Reign of Catherine the Great of Russia.
1764	Battle of Baksar, a crucial defeat of the Mughals and their allies by the British. James Hargreaves invents the spinning jenny, making the spinning wheel obsolete.
1765	British inventor James Watt transforms the steam engine, making it much more efficient. British passage of the Stamp Act provokes widespread colonial response in British North America.
1772–95	Partition of the Polish state by Habsburg empire, Prussia, and Russia.
1773–75	Pugachev Rebellion in Russia.
1775–83	American War of Independence.
1779	Samuel Crompton's spinning mule makes it possible to produce finer and stronger thread.
1780–82	Rebellion of Tupac Amaru in Peru.
1783–84	Henry Cort introduces a new system for making wrought iron more cheaply.
1787	Northwest Ordinance in USA lays down principles for governing the lands won in revolutionary war; it forbids slavery in the new lands and provides for public education. Constitutional Convention in USA.
1789–1807	Reign of Selim III, reformist sultan of Ottoman empire.
1789	Beginning of the French Revolution: Tennis Court Oath (June 20), fall of the Bastille (July 14).
1793–94	The Terror, high point of radical revolution in France.
1795	Edmund Cartwright in Britain invents the power loom.
1796–1805	White Lotus Rebellion in China.
1798–1801	Napoleonic invasion and occupation of Egypt.
1799	Napoleon Bonaparte and others overthrow the corrupt government that followed the Terror; Napoleon becomes First Consul.
1801–25	Reign of Alexander I, a reform-minded tsar who becomes the leader of European reaction.
1803	British defeat of the Marathas and capture of Delhi marks effective end of Mughal empire.
1804	Napoleon Bonaparte becomes "Emperor of the French." Jean-Jacques Dessalines proclaims Haitian independence.
1805	Mehmet `Ali declares himself governor of Egypt.
1807	Ottoman Sultan Selim III overthrown. American Robert Fulton designs the first practical steam-driven ship. Napoleon invades Portugal; Portuguese queen flees to Brazil.

1808–39	Sultan Mahmud II continues era of reforms.
1808	Napoleon deposes Charles IV and his son and names his brother, Joseph Bonaparte, as king of Spain; Spain and Spanish America rally against Napoleon.
1810	Revolt in Mexico led by Miguel Hidalgo y Costilla begins era of colonial revolution.
1812	Napoleonic invasion of Russia fails.
1814	Briton George Stephenson adopts the steam engine to power railway wagons.
1815	Congress of Vienna ends Napoleonic Wars.
1816	Royalists appear triumphant in Spanish America.
1817–21	José de Saint-Martin's army "liberates" Chile and links up with Simón Bolívar's forces in Peru.
1819–44	Forging of the Zollverein, reducing tariff burdens among German states.
1824	Battle of Ayacucho in Peru: Simón Bolívar decisively defeats Spanish in last key battle for Latin American independence.
1825	Opening of the Erie Canal connecting the eastern states with the Midwest.
1826	Beginnings of Tanzimat reforms in Ottoman empire.
1839–42	First Opium War.
1839	Rescript of the Rose Chamber creates equality in many areas of Ottoman civil law.
1842	Treaty of Nanking ending Opium War opens China to trade on terms that heavily favor Westerners.
1848–51	Revolutionary wave sweeps continental Europe.
1868	Meiji Restoration, a period of profound reform and restructuring in Japan.

The beginning of our period, the years between 1700 and 1750, was a time of increased international commercial and political expansion. Throughout most of the world, economic growth continued almost uninterrupted until the last decades of the eighteenth century, benefiting Chinese, Indian, French, British, and Ottoman merchants alike. In addition, Chinese emperors, British monarchs, and Russian tsars all substantially enlarged their territorial possessions. Of the great agrarian empires, only Japan, in self-enforced isolation, did not benefit from the expansion of international trade, and only the Ottoman empire, beset by Russians and the Austrian Habsburgs, lost territory. Through much of the world, the early eighteenth century was a prosperous period that encouraged intellectual inquiry, intercontinental cultural interaction, and monumental architecture.

The Seven Years' War (1756–63) is one very rough marker for the beginning of an era of almost unparalleled political and social instability, aptly entitled the "Age of Revolution." Although it began in Europe, the Seven Years' War was the first modern war with genuinely global repercussions. French defeat in the Seven Years' War weakened the monarchy; the expulsion of the French from North America removed a common enemy whose presence united Britain and its colonies; and British military victories in India were the beginning of a new, violent wave of Western imperial expansion in Asia. Within less than two decades, beginning in 1776 and continuing up to 1850, revolutions swept *ancien régime* Europe and the Western colonial world. Revolution spread widely, from Massachusetts to France, from Peru to Prussia.

While the Seven Years' War marks the beginning of one cluster of political upheavals, the tempo of unrest varied around the globe. In 1763 some non-European agrarian empires were already in a state of political crisis. In the Ottoman empire, military elites, particularly in Egypt but also in much of North Africa and even in the Balkans, had already won a significant degree of autonomy. Before the large-scale entry of European armies, the revival and spread of autonomous Muslim and Hindu kingdoms had already seriously undermined the Mughal empire. In China political crisis came later; in the first half of the nineteenth century mass rebellions such as those of the White Lotus and the Triads shook the empire, foreshadowing even more serious revolts to come.

Chapters 5, 6, and 7 explore how worldwide prosperity and widespread political expansion resulted in universal unrest. They also discuss how Western states, themselves shaken by revolution, were able to gain influence over Eastern states, reeling from local challenges to their authority. Although these self-inflicted blows made possible Western military successes in Asia and the Middle East, part of the dynamism of Western success stems from the revolutions that swept *ancien régime* Europe and the Western colonial world.

Beginning in the late eighteenth century, Europe and the Americas witnessed the beginnings of a "dual revolution," a political revolution, discussed in Chapter 5, and an industrial revolution, discussed in Chapter 6. The political revolution originated in the military competition among the great European powers; the thirteen American colonies refused to support a conflict that no longer concerned them and France collapsed under the economic strain. Starting in the USA and France, continuing in Haiti, and spreading through Latin America and all of Europe, save Russia and Britain, a great wave of political revolution produced a new kind of state and a new democratic ideal. The centralized, bureaucratized, consolidated state that emerged by 1850, with a new conception of citizenship rights as well as responsibilities, represented a new form of political organization.

The consolidated state increasingly rendered obsolete the large agrarian empires that had dominated the world stage in 1700. Republics, formerly confined to city-states such as ancient Athens or eighteenth-century Geneva, now took over permanently or temporarily in large powerful states, especially the USA and France, in addition to the Netherlands, Latin America, and Britain. Already by 1850, consolidated states commanding loyal citizen-soldiers had demonstrated their superiority to agrarian empires fielding harshly disciplined subject-soldiers.

By 1850 the British empire had become the pre-eminent world power. Its Asian expansion depended on the weakening hold of agrarian empires. From a small English core, a scattered heterogeneous group of colonies, and widely scattered coal stations and fueling ports, the empire vastly swelled its territorial size and population by tightening its grip on India. The British empire represented a new kind of imperial power, a power based not merely on agrarian rents and commercial taxes but on industrial dynamism.

Almost simultaneous with the spread of political revolution, an industrial revolution had begun in England. Despite its dramatic character, this First Industrial Revolution was rooted in the worldwide economic expansion and commercial developments of the preceding period; British economic, political, and social conditions enabled that country to respond to this wave of prosperity in a new and creative way. Starting in Great Britain, the First Industrial Revolution transformed world economies like nothing since the Neolithic Revolution; the material life of a man in 1750 resembled more a Roman of Caesar's time than that of his grandchild in 1850.

The economy of the First Industrial Revolution opened a new path in human history, a path that entailed misery and pain for many but which offered a new solution to age-old problems of economic stagnation, political collapse, and overpopulation.

The chapters in Part II describe the birth of our modern world.

5 Expansion, reform, and communication in the agrarian empires of Asia

Russia	
1682–1725	Reign of Peter the Great.
1700–21	Great Northern War between Russia and Sweden.
1703	Founding of St. Petersburg.
1709	Russian victory over Swedes at Poltava.
1762–96	Reign of Catherine the Great.
1764	Catherine founds Smolny Institute for education of women.
1772, 1793, 1795	Partitions of Poland by Russia, Austria, and Prussia.
1773–75	Pugachev Rebellion.
1790	Radishchev argues for ending serfdom.
1801–25	Reign of Alexander I.
1812	Napoleon's invasion of Russia fails.
1815	Congress of Vienna reorganizes Europe.
1825–55	Reign of Nicholas I.
1825	Decembrist uprising.
1830	Polish uprising.
1851–56	Russian defeat in Crimean War.

China	
1661–1722	Reign of Kangxi emperor.
1696	Kangxi defeats Mongolian khan Galdan.
1699	First English trading post established at Canton.
1720	Qing invasion of Lhasa assures control of Tibet.
1722–35	Reign of Yongzheng emperor.
1736–96	Reign of Qianlong emperor.
1744–63	Novel *The Story of the Stone* written.
1758–60	Qing occupation of Turkestan.
1793	Macartney mission attempts to open China to trade.
1796–1805	White Lotus Rebellion.

1820	Jahangir rebellion in Xinjiang.
1839–42	First Opium War.

Japan

1716–45	Reign of reforming shogun Yoshimune.
1837	Rebellion of Oshio Heihachiro in Osaka; American ship visits Ryukyu islands.
1853	Arrival of Commodore Perry in Edo Bay.

Ottomans and India

1699	Treaty of Carlowitz ends Ottoman power in Central Europe.
1717–30	Tulip period in Ottoman empire. Upper-class Ottomans imitate European dress, court protocol, and entertainments.
1722	Fall of Safavids in Iran to invading Afghan tribesmen.
1730	Popular revolt in Istanbul.
1735–39	Russo-Turkish War. Ottomans win.
1738–46	Nadir Shah of Iran conquers Mughal India, defeats Ottomans in Iraq and the Caucasus.
1757	Clive of the British East India Company defeats Mughal nawab (governor) of Bengal, and takes control of Bengal province.
1761	Ahmad Shah Abdali of Kabul defeats Hindu Maratha armies at Panipat, preventing Mughal empire from falling into their hands.
1768–74	Russo-Turkish War. Ottomans lose.
1789	Selim III comes to the throne. Pursues civil and military reforms in the face of European challenge.
1798–1801	French invasion and occupation of Ottoman Egypt under Napoleon Bonaparte.
1799–1803	British East India Company defeats Tipu Sultan in South India and Marathas, and takes old Mughal capital of Delhi. Mughal emperor reduced to a figurehead.
1805	Albanian officer Mehmet `Ali Pasha establishes hereditary dynasty in Egypt.
1821–30	Greek struggle to secede from Ottoman empire. Ends with recognition of Greek independence.
1826	Sultan Mahmud II abolishes Janissary Corps, and begins creation of a modern Ottoman army with contemporary drill and weaponry.
1830	French conquer Algeria, which had been an Ottoman vassal state.
1831–40	Mehmet `Ali Pasha of Egypt rebels against Ottoman sultan, and is finally rolled back by European intervention.

1838–42	First Anglo-Afghan War by British Indian troops ends in British defeat and continued independence of Afghanistan.
1839	New Ottoman sultan, Abdulmecid, issues Noble Rescript of the Rose Chamber, which promises equality under the law to all Ottomans and guarantees basic civil rights and tax reforms.
1849	British in India conquer Sikh state in Panjab.

In 1712, the Manchu official Tulisen left Beijing for the shores of the lower Volga River, in Russia, to visit a Mongolian **khan**. It was a distance of over 3,000 miles, and it took him nearly three years to get there and back. The emperor of China had sent him to explore Russian territory and look for an alliance against other Mongolian rivals. He was not invited to see the **tsar** (the ruler of all Russia), but he wrote a detailed account of the topography, ethnography, and history of all the regions he had crossed.

Seven years later, John Bell, a Scotsman in the service of the Russian tsar, set out from St. Petersburg for Beijing, covering much the same route as Tulisen in the opposite direction. He, too, reported accurately on the region's geography, politics, and history, gathering scientific knowledge and military intelligence at the same time. Others followed them, like Ivan Unkovski, a Russian officer, who visited the Mongolian khan in Zungharia in 1722, and the French Jesuit Gerbillon, who accompanied the Chinese emperor on his military campaigns in the middle of the century. At the end of the century, the Englishman George Lord Macartney arrived by sea in Beijing in 1793 to negotiate the opening of formal trade relations between Britain and China.

All these men easily combined the roles of scientific investigator, diplomat, and spy. The drive for information collection made the classic imperial projects of conquest, settlement, exploration, and trade more systematic, guided by regulations of expanding bureaucracies. Science, empire, and trade supported each other. The explorers were not solitary pilgrims or missionaries; they had the backing of large institutions. They represented a new period of intensified contact between the great empires of Eurasia, as they closed in on each other. The great empires practiced similar techniques of expansion, intensified communication, regularized bureaucratic control, and active promotion of commercial integration. In some of them, the centralization increased, while in others, regional powers grew. During this period:

- Russia pushed southward against the Ottoman empire, while China advanced westward into central Eurasia.

- The Ottoman and Mughal imperial centers lost ground to regional rulers.
- The British created a permanent presence in India, and made their first advances into the China trade.
- The Industrial Revolution had not yet affected most of the world's population, but the linkages created in the eighteenth century prepared the ground for its massive influence in the late nineteenth century.
- This was the last age in world history when agrarian bureaucratic states – large empires that gained most of their wealth from peasant producers – still dominated the world.

5.1 CHINA, 1700–1850: THE FLOURISHING AGE AND ITS TROUBLED END

In the eighteenth century, the Qing dynasty of China reached its summit of prosperity and expansion. Successful military campaigns into Central Eurasia extended the empire's boundaries further than any other dynasty ruled from China's heartland. Peasant settlers followed the armies, pushing land clearance into the furthest recesses of the continent. They also engaged in trade, selling their products on markets linked by extensive transportation networks. Silver flowed in, monetizing the economy, while also generating inflation. The population grew to an unprecedented size of 300 million people by 1800, yet the standard of living remained remarkably high.

In the early nineteenth century, this prosperity began to unravel. Rebellions struck the frontiers, local officials lost control to banditry and corruption, the treasury went into deficit, and ecological crises surfaced. At the same time, the British in Canton pushed their one marketable product, opium, onto all-too-willing Chinese consumers. The Opium War of 1839–42 marked China's first major defeat by a Western power and the conventional onset of its modern history. But even by mid-century, the Western impact was small; strong internal tensions, not Western invasion, had begun to tear the empire apart.

The Qing Expands to its Limits in Central Eurasia

The Manchu rulers continued to prosecute their fundamental military goal, the elimination of an autonomous Mongolian state (see Chapter 2). The Kangxi emperor's defeat of Galdan in 1696 had not eliminated the Zunghar state; its rulers maintained their control, centered in the Ili River valley, increased revenues from Russian trade, and drafted technical advisors from as far away as Sweden. The central site of geopolitical competition with the Qing shifted to Tibet, when the Zunghars sent an army to resolve a disputed succession to the position of **Dalai Lama** (the religious and political leader of Tibet) in Lhasa. The Qing responded with an invasion in 1720 that drove out the Zunghars and put the Dalai Lama under permanent imperial supervision. The nature of Qing rule there is still hotly disputed by the Chinese and Tibetans today; the Tibetans claim that they have been substantially independent, while the Chinese claim Tibet as an inalienable part of Chinese territory. In fact, neither claim is entirely true; Tibet's semi-dependent relationship with the Qing fits neither model well.

After an embarrassing defeat in 1731, the Qing emperor stabilized borders with the Zunghars temporarily, but only two decades later, in three short campaigns over huge distances, the Qianlong emperor (r. 1736–96) exterminated the Zunghar people and their state. As the British did to the Mughals, Qianlong took advantage of internal divisions among the Mongols. By 1760, the empire had reached its maximal limits, and it had secured its Central Eurasian borders by treaty with the Russians. The Mongols were now completely under Qing domination, and so was nearly all of Turkestan. In Central Eurasia, only Kazakhs and Tatars remained as partly autonomous nomads, and small khanates like Kokand and Khiva survived, under constant pressure from Russian expansion. Box 5.1 describes the tribute offerings of subordinate peoples who recognized Qing and Russian authority. Map 5.1 shows the Qing empire during its maximum size in the eighteenth century.

Population Grows and Peasant Settlers Occupy New Lands

After the soldier came the farmer. In Northwest China, officials actively promoted peasant migration from the drought-stricken, overpopulated interior with tax breaks, tools, animals, and investment in irrigation works. At the same time, they brought up Turkic peasants from the south who knew how to use Persian underground canals to irrigate dry fields with mountain snow. Thus the Qing created a newly mixed population of Turkic Muslims, Han peasants, Manchu soldiers, and Mongolian pastoralists on their northwestern frontiers.

On these frontiers, peasant farmers from densely populated regions moved into areas containing fewer people. The migrants put pressure on the resources of fragile environments, which could not easily support the increased population. Officials were ambivalent about this migration. It freed up land, but it also created unrest. Six frontiers – Manchuria, Mongolia, Xinjiang, Tibet, Southwest China, and Taiwan – all experienced this outward push, but in different degrees. Manchuria was sealed off from Han settlement, with limited success, so as to protect the Manchu homeland. Mongolia was heavily penetrated by merchants, peasants, soldiers, and officials from North China. Like native peoples in the Americas, the Mongols died in large numbers from exposure to diseases like smallpox and syphilis; their nobles fell heavily into debt; their young men went to monasteries, deprived of the free-ranging pasturelands. Tibet remained relatively untouched, except for a small Manchu garrison. Southwest China's many hill peoples, practicing slash-and-burn agriculture in low-density tropical hills, faced a great onslaught of migrants. They could either adapt to Han ways or flee to more remote areas. In Taiwan, some local officials attempted to preserve the aboriginal populations from Han encroachment, while others actively promoted colonial development.

Unprecedented population growth drove this expansion once military force opened the frontiers. China more than doubled its population from 1650 to 1800, reaching a total of 300 million. This was a low rate of growth by modern standards, but it made China the largest single political entity in the world. On the other hand, Europe also doubled its population, as did most of the rest of the world (except for Japan and parts of the Ottoman empire). We now know that Malthus was wrong about China's demographic dynamics. Contrary to Western myth, Chinese did not heedlessly breed up to the limits of subsistence; they limited family size (by infanticide, herbal abortifacients, or abstinence) in response to food supplies. Overall life expectancy at birth of 30 to 35 compared favorably with Europe in 1800. Nearly all women married young, but they only bore an average of 6.3 children, of whom a third or more died in childhood. Extensive use of adoption provided families with male heirs, but the lopsided sex ratio in favor of males left many poor young men without brides. As "bare sticks," they were the dangerous loners of village society, excellent recruits for the army, frontier settlement, or bandit gangs.

Chinese farmers practiced the world's most intensive agriculture. In South China, where long growing seasons and water transport fostered commercial exchange, peasants labored extremely long hours to grow three crops a year, selling a substantial surplus for cash. The mulberry-silkworm-fish pond system illustrates how they made maximum use of local resources: Mulberry trees planted around fish ponds fed silkworms, whose droppings fertilized the soil and water; peasants ate the fish and sold the silk for grain. Local variations flourished: In some regions, powerful lineages bonded

Box 5.1 Rulers in Motion: Tributes, Processions, and Travels

All the imperial rulers enjoyed receiving guests. The Qing emperors graciously accepted envoys from all the countries surrounding them. In their eyes, these foreign peoples came to Beijing to pay tribute to the Central Kingdom's wealth and cultural superiority. Elaborate rituals controlled the processions that moved through Tiananmen, The Gate of Heavenly Peace, into the Forbidden City, to the heart of the empire's power. These tributary visits expressed in ritual terms the diplomatic, economic, and military relations of the Qing with the outside world. Mongolian allies, Southeast Asian trading states, Russian caravans, Korean and Vietnamese scholars, and finally, Western governments, all followed the same rules. Lord Macartney's embassy in 1793 was only one in a long series, and the emperor tried his best to "cherish visitors from afar."

The visitors themselves had other motives. They profited from trading in the capital, and they hoped to get Qing support for their own disputes. Qing China was certainly the most powerful actor in the East Asian world, but it was still only one of many players. For those who understood the system, kowtowing to the emperor was a small price to pay for economic and military alliance.

Emperors also traveled outside their palaces, to inspect their realms and to display themselves to their subjects. The Qing emperors went every year to the Temple of Heaven and the Altars of Sun and Earth to pay their respects to the natural forces that governed the universe. By sacrificing to the all-embracing sky, the Son of Heaven literally took on heavenly powers. The Manchu emperors also went north of the capital to their summer palaces in Manchuria, displaying their military prowess in huge hunting expeditions. They traveled south, to the Jiangnan region, to show their literary face to the sophisticated urban Chinese, while pretending to inspect important irrigation works. By keeping in motion, the Qing emperors made their personal and symbolic presence known throughout their vast realm.

The Russian emperors also expected tribute payments, and they, too, followed rituals of obedience and subordination. Like the Chinese, they expected loyalty from their Central Asian allies, but often they only got temporary arrangements, which were soon broken. Peter the Great, like his contemporary Kangxi, was constantly on the move, governing his never-ending military campaigns.

By the eighteenth century, emperors and empresses in both China and Russia left the palace less often, leaving administration up to local bureaucrats, and delivering orders to generals from a distance. The increased paperwork of the huge empires kept them at their desk, but also allowed local officials to deceive them. Potemkin created fake villages for Catherine to see on her tour, just as Chinese officials masked their people's suffering when the Qianlong emperor came through their county. Predictable routine replaced the violence and uncertainty of warfare.

---

their kinsmen to the soil, limiting their access to markets, or large landlords reaped the gains of trade; elsewhere, individual farmers moved into new markets without constraints. Agricultural technologies improved on traditional techniques; no radical innovations occurred, but efficiency and productivity rose. The increased output supported growing rural and urban populations; as markets became linked together in an elaborate hierarchy, prices in different regions began to move together.

The imperial state, for the most part, backed up this developing exchange economy. It was primarily interested in maintaining a prosperous peasantry, the main source of its revenue and its soldiers. About 70 percent of the imperial budget came from the land, but taxes were low in relation to production, and fixed in monetary terms. An empire-wide structure of "ever-normal" granaries bought and sold grain so as to dampen grain price fluctuations. Local elites, aided by local officials, invested in water conservancy, a key imperial concern. Elites also supported orphanages, old age homes, bridges, and other public works. Merchants created networks of native place associations, so that traveling traders had a place to stay and useful contacts away from home. Even the boatmen on the Grand Canal had their own local inns. In good times, administration and society supported each other. These multiple mixed associations between officials and local groups tied together the core of the empire with crisscrossing strands. No uniform despotism, but a loosely knit social fabric, held the core regions of the empire together.

Major cities stood at the top of the social hierarchy. Beijing, the imperial capital, gathered 750,000 to 1 million people. From the top down, these included the Imperial Clan, Manchu bannermen, Han officials and scholars, examination students, and their associated trades of book publishers, peddlers, sedan chair bearers, prostitutes, and porters. Below the imperial capital were major provincial cities, each a huge urban conglomeration with its own special character: Hankou, on the Yangtze in central China, where many urban functions were directed by merchant

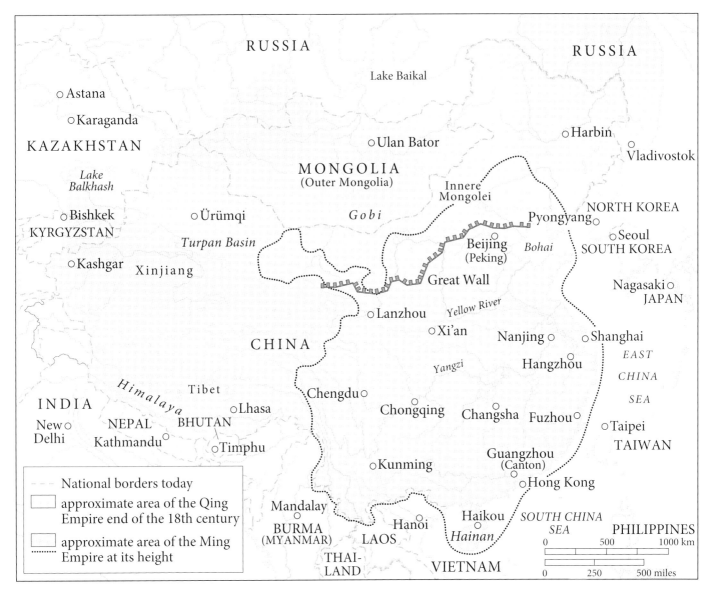

Map 5.1 The Qing empire in the eighteenth century

associations; Suzhou, center of the textile industry, drawing in silk from its hinterland to supply its thousands of looms; Yangzhou, at the base of the Grand Canal, renowned for its literary culture; and Guangzhou (Canton), in the south, the upstart center of overseas trade. Urban-commercial centers recovered from seventeenth-century devastation, and new centers spread all over the empire. Box 5.2 discusses the common features of the largest cities of the world.

Reform Efforts Attempt to Relieve Social Conflict

As before, commercial and agrarian growth created tensions. The Yongzheng emperor (r. 1722–35) made the most serious effort to address fiscal and administrative issues. The low tax rate left local government chronically underfunded, forcing officials to rely on informal levies to run their local offices. It was only a short step from essential surcharges to outright bribery and corruption. Much depended on the moral character of the official. Yongzheng instituted "nourishing virtue supplements" to official salaries, hoping that these large cash bonuses would induce local officials to reduce their informal levies. At the same time, he pushed for greater central control over local funding sources. Yongzheng had put his finger on a major structural weakness of the empire; his reform efforts partially addressed the problem, but his successor, the Qianlong emperor, failed to follow up. As commercial wealth grew, but salaries did not keep up with inflation, officials continued to expand the bounds of informal collection. Vague attacks on "corruption" became a prominent way to criticize excessive official exactions through the century. Modern Chinese use the same rhetoric.

Box 5.2 Big Cities: Beijing, Istanbul, Edo, and St. Petersburg

The great empires displayed their wealth and power in magnificent capital cities, the largest in the world. The heavy concentrations of soldiers and officials at the center naturally attracted merchants, priests, and young men on the make. Beijing was probably the largest, with over a million people. It had been a capital since 1000 CE, but it developed to its final imperial form in the eighteenth century. It had a special structure of concentric walls, with the emperor at the heart, his Manchu garrisons in the Tatar City around him, and the Han population outside. Istanbul, nearly as large, was an even more ancient capital in a perfect commercial location.

The Topkapi palace was more modest than the Forbidden City, but it contained beautiful gardens and, by the eighteenth century, wallpapered rooms influenced by Western designs.

Edo was an upstart city, created first by military conquerors as armed camps out of a fishing village, but it grew rapidly. By 1700 it had a million people, equal to Beijing, though Japan had less than one tenth of China's population. Around the shogun's castle, streets grew in a haphazard, unplanned way, completely unlike the well-ordered avenues of Kyoto. Japan divided its three central functions of military rule, imperial sovereignty, and commerce among three

separate cities, Edo, Kyoto, and Osaka, linking them with a dense road network.

St. Petersburg, the newest of all, grew out of a swamp by the order of a single ruler's will. He carried urban planning to its extreme, making it a model of rational, militarized design. Later Catherine humanized the raw city, turning it into one of the great cultural capitals of Europe.

Each of these cities focused political power, commerce, and social expression in their streets and the activities of their vibrant populations. They displayed the special characteristics of their society in the form of their buildings and streets and the life that went on in them.

Cultural tensions spread beyond the official world. The examination system was the primary source of moral training and inculcation of orthodoxy. These "cultural prisons" drilled the **Neo-Confucian** Zhu Xi orthodoxy into millions of aspirants each year, but very few would ever achieve the towering peak of an official post. Lucky ones could get posts as teachers and secretaries; less lucky ones joined the ranks of lowly clerks and runners. Others used their literacy and knowledge of the law codes to help commoners write letters and bring disputes to the magistrate's court: Attacked as "lawsuit goons" by magistrates, they still provided a useful service. Really frustrated students staged riots at examination halls, carried on smuggling rackets, or even joined bandit gangs as literate advisors.

The Manchus Need to Legitimate Their Rule

In this sea of Han, the small minority of Manchus had an even worse time. They did not assimilate easily into the Chinese mass: The **banner** institution (the military and political system devised by the Manchus to rule China in the seventeenth century) itself entitled them to privileges and walled-off quarters of every major city. Special quotas gave them a boost in the examination system, but many neglected the culture of both the pen and the sword. The Manchus did not support their entire kinship network; they cut off most of the Imperial Clan and the bannermen

with small salaries. Bannermen were the military backbone of the conquering elite, but they neglected their horsemanship and illegally joined in the lower levels of the urban economy. Imperial legitimation depended increasingly on convincing the Han majority that the Manchus not only endorsed the classical ideals, but could take them to new heights. The emperor recruited hundreds of Chinese scholars for a vast scholarly public works project, the *Complete Records of the Four Treasuries*. These men compiled and edited over 10,000 works from the classical Chinese canon with the most precise philological commentary of the newest scholarship. Concurrently, an Imperial Inquisition purged any works suspected of denigrating Manchu culture.

The Qianlong emperor did not try to argue that the Manchus had transformed themselves into "civilized" Chinese; instead, he published separate genealogies of Manchus, Mongols, and Han, giving each a lineage of equal status. By sharpening these ethnic lines, instead of merging the empire's many peoples into one civilization, he set them beside each other under the comprehensive gaze of the emperor, the only universal sovereign. Scholars developed elaborate rituals for the emperor, derived from their reading of classical texts, which demonstrated in practice his ability to link Heaven, Earth, and Man. The Temple of Heaven, shown in Figure 5.1, was located in the south of Beijing. It was the central site for imperial rituals.

Figure 5.1 The Temple of Heaven in southern Beijing was a central site of ceremonies conducted by Ming and Qing emperors to honor the cosmic forces that regulated heavenly and human affairs. The temple includes an altar for sacrifice and a large cylindrical building derived from a Mongolian tent, symbolizing the encompassing power of Heaven over all things.

Scholars Discuss Local Policy; Cao Xueqin Writes a Novel

Such a huge empire, with a limited bureaucracy and tax base, could only be held together through deft combinations of coercion and ritual. As so much of the governance of the empire relied on delegation to local powers, much of the scholarly debate of the period concerned local administration. Compilations of statecraft essays discussed how to get high quality officials to manage intricate issues of taxation, commerce, adjudication, and local order. Other scholars engaged in meticulous philological analysis of classical texts. They rejected the grand speculations of late Ming philosophers, who searched within the mind for moral insight. Qing scholars felt that finding the right pronunciation of the characters of the ancient sages, a kind of scientific philology, was a more reliable road to truth.

Emotional impulses had to seek other outlets. *The Story of the Stone* (also known as *The Dream of the Red Chamber*), written from 1744 to 1763 by the unsuccessful scholar Cao Xueqin, is the crowning glory of vernacular Chinese literature. In 120 leisurely, elegantly written chapters, it describes the maturation of Jia Baoyu, a son of a wealthy family with close connections to the Imperial court. The delicate interplay of poetic romance, bawdy humor, literary allusion, and lowdown dialogue gives us an invaluably vivid picture, drawn from Cao's own life, of the complex interpersonal relations within one wealthy household. The novel ends in tragedy, with the confiscation of the family fortune, Dai Yu's death, and Baoyu's

escape from the world into a monastery. Box 5.3 gives a comical excerpt from this vast family novel.

Disruption and Upheaval, 1800–50/60

The first half of the nineteenth century presents a different picture from the flourishing eighteenth century. There is no exact turning point, but the onset of a series of rebellions on China's peripheries in the 1790s indicates serious social tensions that challenged the empire's stability. Most dangerous was the **White Lotus** Rebellion, an outbreak by a millenarian Buddhist sect that raged in the hill regions of the central Yangtze from 1796 to 1805.

Unorthodox Believers Join In Frontier Revolts Popular religious practices beyond the orthodox ancestral rites were always of concern to the state. Outside the bounds of lineage temples and Confucian schools, many sects flourished, deriving their rituals from mingling Daoist, Buddhist, shamanist, and other local cults. Often, the officials succeeded in co-opting popular deities into the orthodox pantheon. But the White Lotus movement went further. Its adherents worshipped **Maitreya**, the Buddhist manifestation of the future, who would usher in a radically new era marked by a confrontation of the forces of light with the forces of darkness.

The sect found fertile soil in the tumultuous uplands of the Han River, north of the Yangtze, where immigrants arriving in

Box 5.3 Chinese Family Relations: *The Story of the Stone*

The Story of the Stone describes all sorts of complex relationships between the many members of a wealthy Chinese family in the eighteenth century. In this episode, Jia Rui becomes infatuated with his cousin Wang Xifeng, who lures him on and sets a trap for him:

[Xifeng says]: "Go away now and come back later when it's dark, at the beginning of the first watch. You can slip into the gallery west of this apartment and wait for me there."

Jia Rui received these words like someone being presented with a rare and costly jewel ... Having waited impatiently for nightfall, he groped his way into the Rongguo mansion just before they closed the gates and slipped into the gallery, now totally deserted – as Xifeng had promised it would be – and black as pitch ... Suddenly there was a loud slam and the gate at the east end banged shut. Alarmed, but not daring to make a sound, Jia Rui stealthily crept out and tried it. It was locked – as tight as a bucket ... this was the midwinter season when the nights are long and the bitter north wind seems to pierce into the very marrow of the bones. By the end of the night he was almost dead with cold.

Jia is beaten by his grandfather and forced to do extra homework, but is still infatuated by Xifeng. Xifeng decides that he needs another lesson:

"Only tonight," she said, "don't wait for me in that place again. Wait in the empty room in the little passage-way behind this apartment. But mind you don't run into anybody."

"Do you really mean this?" said Jia Rui.

"If you don't believe me, don't come!"

"I'll come! I'll come!" said Jia Rui. "Whatever happens I shall be there."

[He waited in the passageway at night] with the frenzied agitation of an ant on a hot saucepan ... "Surely she won't fail me? Surely I shan't be made to spend another night in the cold?" As he was in the midst of these gloomy imaginings, a dark figure glided into the room. Certain that it must be Xifeng, Jia Rui cast all caution to the winds and, when the figure approached him, threw himself upon it like a hungry tiger seizing its prey or a cat pouncing on a harmless mouse.

"My darling, how I have waited for you!" he exclaimed, enfolding his beloved in his arms, and carrying her to the kang [heated bed], he laid her down and began tugging at her trousers, murmuring "my sweetest darling" and "my honey love" and other such endearments in between kisses. Throughout all of this not a single sound was uttered by his partner. Jia Rui now tore down his own trousers and prepared to thrust home his hard and throbbing member. Suddenly a light flashed – and there was Jia Qiang holding aloft a candle in a candlestick which he shone around:

"Who is in this room?"

At this the person on the kang gave a giggle: "Uncle Rui is trying to bugger me!"

Horrors! The sight he saw when he looked down made Jia Rui want to sink into the ground. It was Jia Rong! He turned to bolt, but Jia Qiang held him fast.

"Oh no you don't. Auntie Lian has already told Lady Wang that you have been pestering her ... Come along then! Off we go!"

Jia Rui is forced to pay large sums of money to Jia Qiang to avoid being exposed; he is drenched with a slop pail of excrement while hiding from Xifeng; he falls deathly ill, and dies of sexual fever. The story contains an implicit warning against sensual indulgence, while also describing its effects in great detail.

---

the late eighteenth century found little new land to clear. They joined the new sect for collective protection with no immediate political goals. Officials at first ignored the White Lotus, but ultimately intervened to repress it as clashes increased among the settlers. Only then did the believers form armies, drive out officials, and burst into revolt. In suppressing this rebellion, the Qing troops, both banners and Han Chinese, demonstrated how much they had deteriorated since the days of conquest. Putting down the rebellion took nine years and cost 120 million ounces of silver, exhausting the treasury.

Other revolts broke out around the empire, all indicating serious loss of local control. In western Sichuan, a Tibetan cultural area, the Qianlong emperor spent huge sums trying to put down the powerful Jinchuan peoples, who held out in fortresses on high mountains. In South China, armed lineages sent their kinsman thugs to battle over land and water rights, creating landscapes marked by fortresses glowering over paddy fields. In West China, raiders known as *guolu* preyed on merchants traveling in the great Sichuan basin. Many of them were also immigrants from downstream deprived of the prospects of a livelihood. In Xinjiang in 1820, Jahangir led an uprising of Turkic Muslims to drive out infidel Han migrants. The Triads, a network of brotherhoods who swore to overthrow the Qing and restore the Ming, flourished in South China and Taiwan.

The consequences of imperial overstretch were coming home to roost, as mobile populations under limited control clashed over increasingly scarce supplies of land, water, and employment.

Britain Goes to War for Free Trade and Opium In the mid eighteenth century the British, the newly dominant European power, fresh from their incipient conquest of India, arrived on the South China coast, dreaming of huge Chinese markets. Tea had become a mass consumer good in England, necessary to keep industrial workers alert and distracted from ale, and China was its main source. What would the Chinese take in exchange? Tropical Cantonese had little use for Manchester's woolens, and their cotton and silk industries could easily outcompete Britain. As silver drained out of Britain, the East India Company merchants discovered the solution in India. Opium, grown on Bengal plantations with forced labor, became their deadly answer to the trade deficit. Although the Chinese state banned it, plenty of entrepreneurs helped the foreigners smuggle it into small ports on the southeast coast. The exchange of Indian opium for Chinese tea and silk supplied the British consumer with necessary consumption goods at low cost, financed the costs of empire in India, and thrust open the Chinese market to imperial intervention.

Of course the British manufacturers did not quite put it that way. Their main slogan was "free trade" and they viewed the Chinese mandarin class as a backward, corrupt obstacle to trade. All goods, in their view, should be allowed to flow without regulation (except in Britain, where opium use was restricted to medical purposes, such as quieting crying babies). China had confined foreign merchants to one small enclave in the port of Canton, just as it restricted Russians to two cities on the northwest border. The emperor purported to disdain foreign goods, although in fact he wanted foreign silver and military technology, and his Imperial household itself relied on commercial taxes on Canton trade. George Lord Macartney, sent to China in 1793 to open direct diplomatic and commercial contacts with the court in Beijing, represented a British king who ruled a global empire. When he refused to **kowtow** (that is, prostrate himself and knock his head on the floor) to another emperor who espoused an equal and opposite claim to a universal empire, he violated the ritual proprieties governing reception of foreign envoys (he probably did at least kneel down). Unimpressed by his gifts, the Qianlong emperor sent him away emptyhanded.

The British concluded that only military force could open China's ports. In 1839, Viceroy Lin Zexu provided the pretext when he tried to stamp out the illegal trade by burning opium publicly in front of the foreign warehouses in Canton. In 1840, sixteen British warships bombarded Chinese forts near Ningbo

in Zhejiang, then moved north toward Tianjin. The furious emperor sent Lin into exile, but he had to negotiate after British troops assaulted Canton and massacred Chinese at Ningbo. The Chinese could claim only one small victory, when a local militia force of 20,000 defeated a patrol of British and Indian troops who had raped women near Sanyuanli, a market town near Canton. This victory later served nationalists as an epochal demonstration of the power of popular mobilization against foreign oppressors.

The settlements forced on the court were humiliating "unequal treaties." Under the Treaty of Nanking, signed in 1842, China had to pay an indemnity, open five ports to trade, grant **extraterritoriality** (the right of foreigners to be tried in their own courts, indicating contempt for Chinese justice), cede Hong Kong, abolish its trade monopoly, and limit its tariffs. China now had to trade on the foreigners' terms, even though its people fought back hard to resist economic penetration. Missionaries, scholars, and more gunboats would soon follow, and the Americans and others would also charge in. Using Turkish sources, notable Boston Brahmin merchant families built their fortunes on the opium trade.

Even though the Opium War and the unequal treaties dramatically changed China's relationship with the Western powers, we should not tie too much of this giant, diverse society's development to a single external event. Like the Ottomans, Qing society was never static, and domestic drivers of change still predominated by mid-century. The major internal rebellions of the 1850s carried on the frontier turmoil of the 1790s on a much vaster scale.

5.2 JAPAN IN THE LATE TOKUGAWA PERIOD

In Japan, as in China, commercial networks spread all over the country, but unlike China, the population did not grow. Foreign trade was highly restricted, and frontier expansion was slight. By the 1790s serious tensions surfaced in the form of social unrest, foreign encroachment, crop failure, and intellectual debate, and beginning in the 1850s, disputes over foreign and domestic policy tore apart the shogunate. While Chinese reformers put the empire back together after its mid-century crisis, Japanese reformers overthrew the shogunate in 1868 and launched the Meiji Restoration that set Japan on its astonishing rise to world power. Map 5.2 shows the large landed domains owned by the shogun in Tokugawa Japan.

Japan Urbanizes, Despite the Shoguns' Intentions

The seventeenth-century unifiers had imposed a rigid military and bureaucratic structure on the country, repressed

Map 5.2 Tokugawa Japan

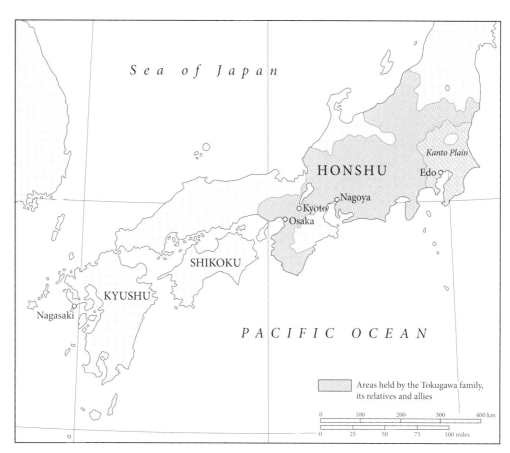

Christianity, and severely restricted foreign contact. Despite their reactionary efforts to freeze society, they unintentionally promoted change. The military rulers (shoguns), had removed the armed warriors (**samurai**) from the land, and concentrated them in castle towns, in order to watch over them. But this concentration of people made the 300 castle towns into dispersed centers of local commerce. By 1700 Osaka and Kyoto each had a population of 400,000, nearly equal to London and Paris; 5 to 7 percent of Japanese lived in cities greater than 100,000, compared to 2 percent in Europe. Japan became one of the most urbanized societies in the world.

Since the samurai living in towns had to cash in their rice stipends in order to buy urban products, Osaka became the grain-marketing center of the country, with merchants serving the shogun's agents. Three urban centers dominated the country, each with its own economic niche: Osaka as wholesaler, manufacturer, and financial center; Kyoto outstanding in fine silk and elegant crafts; Edo as the military-bureaucratic center collecting the shogun's retainers and visiting lords (**daimyo**), who demanded luxury goods and entertainment. Box 5.4 describes the life of Japanese merchants who served the shogun and court.

Because the shoguns forced the lords to leave hostages in the capital, lords and their retinues crowded the main road to Edo on Honshu island, the Tokaido, inspiring innkeepers and peddlers to supply their needs at regular stages. Figure 5.2 is a woodblock print of this vigorous commercial highway. The maritime route across the Inland Sea likewise tied Honshu, Shikoku, and Kyushu. This and other major inter-regional trade routes bound the country together economically, despite the inspection stations and custom dues at the border of each domain. There was no national currency: Edo used gold, and Osaka silver, while the countryside used copper coins, so major exchange houses dealt in sophisticated financial instruments to adjust currency rates.

New merchants, like the house of Mitsui, supplied clothing, uniforms, and household goods to the shogun, lords, and retainers. They wrote their own laws, which carefully controlled times of work, dress, food, and relations with customers so as to enforce disciplined service to the firm, described as the "main castle." In the nineteenth and twentieth centuries, they would clothe and provide ships for the Japanese military. Like Mitsui, the Sumitomo family of Osaka began as copper refiners and later developed into powerful financial cliques, called **zaibatsu**.

Box 5.4 Japanese Merchants: Work and Pleasure

The Mitsui family of Tokugawa Japan was a prosperous commercial firm with a long history. Its regulations for its employees indicate a concern for the firm's reputation displayed in strict control over their working and personal life. They must not indulge in expensive food, poetry contests, gambling, or sake drinking, associate with actors or prostitutes, or borrow money at more than 8 percent per month.

The chronicler of the pleasure quarters, Ihara Saikaku, however, saw a different side of life. He described people of all classes doing just what the Mitsuis prohibited: spending heavily on geisha, buying silk clothing, imitating samurai by studying swordsmanship, and going heavily into debt:

Ancient simplicity is gone. With the growth of pretense the people of today are satisfied with nothing but finery, with nothing but what is beyond their station or purse … Paying for his wife's wardrobe, or his daughter's wedding trousseau, has lightened the pocket of many a merchant, and blighted his hopes in business … A merchant wearing fine silks is an ugly sight. Homespun is not only more suited to his station, but he looks smarter in it.

Yet Saikaku saw that the Mitsuis' business thrived because of spendthrift customers, and he admired their skill:

In Suruga-cho … a man called Mitsui Kuroemon, risking what capital he had in hand, erected a deep and lofty building of eighteen yards frontage and eighty yards depth, and opened a new shop. His policy was to sell everything for cash, without the inflated charges customary in credit sales. There were more than forty skilled clerks in his service, constantly under the master's eye … he willingly supplied anything which his customers asked for, however trifling – a scrap of velvet an inch square, a piece of imported damask suitable for the cover of an eyebrow tweezer, enough scarlet satin to make a spearhead flag, or a single detachable cuff of ryumon silk … By such means the business flourished, and the average daily sales were said to amount to one hundred and fifty ryo. The shop was a marvel of convenience to all … He was the model of a great merchant.

Figure 5.2 From Edo (modern Tokyo) to Osaka ran this major commercial artery of Tokugawa Japan, the Tokaido Road, which provided communication, trade, and leisure activities for the samurai, merchants, and commoners who constantly moved along this bustling thoroughfare. The active life of the road inspired many woodblock print artists.

The Eighteenth-Century Population Stops Growing

The dynamic growth of the seventeenth century peaked and leveled off during the following century of "social stasis." Shoguns fruitlessly issued streams of sumptuary legislation restricting the clothing, food, and housing of townspeople, and ordered merchants not to "exceed their station," but as in Ming China, the nouveau riche, aping the superior culture of the court and lords, could buy themselves the status of connoisseurs. Despite its distinctive history, in many aspects of material life and commercial culture Japan had caught up with Ming and Qing China. Unlike China, with its vastly diversified regional economies, Japan's culture was more tightly focused on the two largest regions of Kinki (Osaka-Kyoto) and Kanto (Edo), but the mass consumer culture spread through regional and village marketing networks around the country. Cultural unification followed economic networks.

The population of Japan, however, followed a strikingly different pattern from most of the rest of the world. From 1600 to 1720, aggregate population had more than doubled, from 12 to over 30 million people. From 1720 to 1860, it hardly changed at all. The production capacities of the archipelago seemed to have run into an ecological barrier. Nearly all easily accessible trees had been cut down, and new cultivable land was scarce. Severe crop failures caused devastating famines.

Japanese village communities could enforce population controls. They were tightly bound networks of prominent families supervising dependent kinsmen, tenants, and landless laborers. The whole village paid taxes, making everyone responsible for everyone else's obligations. The government tried to enforce its ideal of a self-sufficient, harmonious community (**kyodotai**) with controls on migration and trade, as it aimed to restrict each of the four classes – samurai, merchants, artisans, and peasants – to their own profession. Lacking new land, villagers intensified production on their existing fields, but this farming system was highly vulnerable to fluctuations in the weather; households who increasingly specialized in cash cropping were at the mercy of grain markets as well. Landholdings fragmented into diverse sizes, and the uniformity of the agrarian community broke up into landlords, tenants, and landless laborers. All families practiced deliberate restriction of births to adjust their populations to limited resources. Men left home for long periods of time to labor elsewhere; induced abortions and substantial infanticide reduced fertility. Chinese practiced similar demographic controls, but the Japanese were driven to greater extremes because they lacked room to expand. The shogun's government, or **bakufu**, did try to encourage settlement of Japan's northern frontier, on the island of Hokkaido, but ran into conflicts with the native Ainu tribes there, who were offered protection by the Russians. Only fisheries offered some chance to escape land constraints.

Fiscal Crises Cause Reforms and Revolts

The bakufu and daimyo faced severe fiscal crises in the midst of these tensions between burgeoning commerce and limited agricultural production. As the samurai fell heavily into debt, merchants extended their grip over the lords' domains. Lords repudiated their obligations and the shoguns issued more coins, bankrupting many merchants and debasing the currency, but they only postponed the crisis. Shogun Yoshimune (r. 1716–45) launched a reform effort guided by the leading Confucian statecraft scholar of the day, Ogyu Sorai, but it had only modest effects. Tensions grew along with prosperity throughout the rest of the century. Rural people petitioned against heavy taxation, smashed moneylenders' shops, and in 1764 rebelled against **corvée** levies for postal stations.

Despite the shogun's conservatism, intellectual life in isolated Japan was vibrant, as scholars tried to place Japan within the East Asian order. Confucianists like Ogyu Sorai saw Japan as a society based on Chinese classical texts; Motoori Norinaga, by contrast, denounced the corrosive influence of Chinese teaching, and espoused the unique emotional linkage of the "native Japanese heart" to the Way of the Gods, as expressed in its most ancient poetry and its **Shinto** cults. Later nationalists turned his ineffable Japanese intuitions into explosive militarism. "National studies" scholars defined Japan as a unique polity (**kokutai**) superior to all others and under threat from foreign influence. By contrast, the "Dutch studies" scholars used the slim porthole of Nagasaki to obtain books on Western medicine and science. Among the general population, education spread widely through temple schools. As in China, the shoguns saw writing as useful for moral indoctrination, but Japan, unlike China, had a syllabic alphabet. Up to 50 percent of the male population and perhaps 10 percent of the female population became partially literate.

Tensions sharpened in the nineteenth century, exacerbated by new foreign contacts, another major famine and revolt, and curious popular movements. Oshio Heihachiro, an Osaka policeman inspired by Wang Yangming's dedication to the people, led an urban uprising in 1837. New religions, enthusiastic pilgrims, ecstatic dancing, and the cult of Maitreya (the same deity inspiring China's White Lotus movement) indicated a search for saviors and outlets for emotion. Ominous signs of the wider world generated more intensive debates over strengthening coastal defenses and keeping the country sealed. Learning of China's loss in the Opium War, the Japanese became even more wary of the West. Outside the central government, the still unsubdued domains of Satsuma and Choshu enacted economic reforms that made them powerful rivals of the weak shogunate. None of these tensions burst into open conflict, however, until 1853, when the American Commodore Perry steamed into Edo Bay demanding the opening of trade.

Tokugawa Japan had developed a surprisingly dense, rich, dynamic social fabric marked by intensive commerce and agriculture and creative artistic and intellectual production within a rigid institutional frame. It was communication-intensive, with a well-educated populace, and it had sophisticated financial and commercial institutions that prepared it for a new explosive outburst when the industrialized world cracked its shell.

5.3 RUSSIA, 1700–1850

While Japanese leaders debated their relations to the outside world, Peter the Great had decisively oriented Russia westward at the beginning of the eighteenth century. None of his successors could turn the clock back. Russia was now an active participant in European politics, economics, and culture, but it was still an autocratic agrarian empire based on bonded labor and a highly privileged minority. Over the next century and a half, the tensions between Russia's nobility and the tsar, and the elite and the peasantry, continued to cause its rulers to seesaw between reform and reaction. At the same time, the empire expanded to an enormous scale, fought many successful wars, and incorporated a huge variety of peoples.

Catherine the Great Turns Russia Westward Again

Between Peter's death in 1725 and Catherine the Great's accession in 1762, intrigues by lovers, palace guards, and insider families decided succession to the throne, choosing a series of weak rulers. When Catherine II, a well-educated German princess, overthrew and killed her boorish husband in 1762, Russia once again lurched toward Western Enlightenment. Catherine the Great's legacy was just as contradictory as Peter's: She corresponded with Voltaire and Diderot, but extended serfdom and brutally repressed revolt. Her Instruction of 1767 established a Legislative Commission to codify the laws of the empire, inspired by Enlightenment philosophers like Montesquieu, but the commission's goal was to make autocracy more efficient, not to limit it. She tried to create a functioning local government, as recommended by the English jurist Blackstone, and she issued a Charter to the nobility, confirming them as a legal body with special privileges, and freeing them from compulsory service to the state. Russian aristocrats became genuine participants in state administration, no longer beaten into submission to a military tsar, but dedicated to a moral mission of establishing

a cultivated, regularized administration. Russian elites came to embrace the secular, rationalizing, bureaucratic state model they saw in the West. The elite losers were the Orthodox clergy, who remained illiterate, marginalized, submissive servants of the state, incapable of providing an opposing force.

The greatest losers were, however, the enserfed Russian peasantry. Catherine extended the scope of serfdom as she expanded the empire, and she followed noble demands to put increasing restrictions on peasant freedom. Over 50 percent of the population was enserfed by 1800. The serfs could not take loans, leave the estates, or marry without their masters' permission; they paid increasingly heavy dues in labor money to support their lords' expensive tastes, and they had no recourse against abuse. Siberia and the Ukraine did offer them escape hatches, so they fled to the frontiers. The Cossacks of the Don, organized in self-governing communities, remained outside the bonds of serfdom. As Catherine moved to control them, headman Pugachev led a major rebellion in 1773 that attracted mass support from Cossacks, Bashkirs, and enserfed miners. She repressed the rebellion ruthlessly.

Russia Expands East, South, and West

Catherine continued a successful Russian foreign policy of careful encroachment on her neighbors' lands, backed by astute diplomacy and a giant military force. The Russian army, with 172,000 field troops, was one of the largest in the world, larger than the Ottoman army though much smaller than China's. A long-term alliance with the Habsburg empire, backed by a commercial treaty with Great Britain, gave Russia backing against its continental enemies: France, Prussia, Poland, and the Ottoman empire. Two wars against the weakening Ottoman empire gave Russia control of the Crimea and allowed it to fortify the shores of the Black Sea; after these victories Catherine pushed to colonize the fertile southern Russian lands with peasant settlers. Poland suffered triply, sandwiched between three aggressive empires and paralyzed by dissension among its highly independent nobility. Catherine orchestrated the progressive partition and extinction of the Polish state, dividing it between Prussia, Austria, and Russia between 1772 and 1795. In this elimination of an old neighboring state, Catherine acted from pure considerations of power politics, which we now call Realpolitik. The Poles themselves fought back in a futile national uprising led by their hero, Teodor Kosciuszko. Map 5.3 displays the expansion of Russia in the eighteenth century.

Russia was still both an Asian and European colossus. The search for furs drove its explorers across the Bering Strait (named after the Danish leader of the Kamchatka expedition of 1725–29), into Alaska, and down the northwestern American coast. Russia's population also boomed, from 13 million in

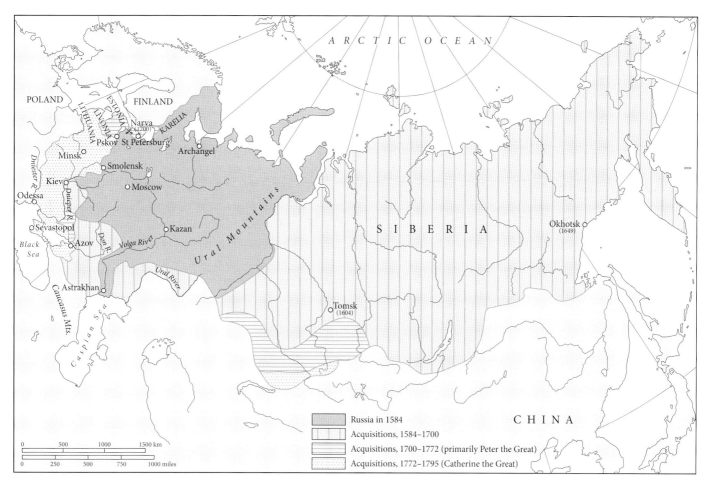

Map 5.3 From Muscovy to Russia, 1584–1796

1725 to 29 million in 1796, plus an additional 7 million added by imperial conquest. Russia's population was overwhelmingly rural, at 96 percent the most rural in Eurasia. Agricultural land nearly tripled by 1850. Russia was the part of Eurasia with the largest increase in cropland, outstripping China. Peasants moved into fertile black soil regions of the south; but they still used backward technology, and as bonded farmers, had little incentive to improve yields. Chinese and Japanese peasant smallholders intensified labor as they expanded settlement, but Russian peasants perpetuated low-yield agriculture. The Russian village community (**mir**), like Japan's, was a tightly communal organization, kept in place by collective taxation and conscription obligations to the state. It practiced, in addition, a unique method of ensuring equality, by enforcing periodic redistribution of lands, so that no family fell below a subsistence minimum, and no one could get too rich. This redistribution prevented sharp divisions within the peasant class, but the taxes levied on the commune supported a tiny landlord class who took a high percentage of the rural surplus.

The fiscal demands of the state and nobility pressed harder on the peasantry. State expenditure went primarily on war and bureaucratic administration; between 1725 and 1794 expenses quadrupled and the pressure for revenue collection mounted. Serfs owed up to five days a week of labor on their masters' lands, and in addition paid a poll tax and sales taxes on vodka and salt. There were now fewer opportunities to escape. Some local gentry did try to raise the productivity of their estates with new agronomic techniques, but they ran up against the tightly bound system of cultivation that blocked innovation.

Industry offered one outlet. Serfs worked in factories with their owners' permission and industrial enterprises proliferated, rising to 1,200 factories by the end of the century, with between 100,000 and 225,000 workers. In mining and metallurgical industries, concentrated near Moscow and in the Urals, Russia led the world. Some noble entrepreneurs emerged along with this industrial base, but the state still dominated. Russia became a major participant in international trade, exporting grain in exchange for industrial machinery. But it had no sophisticated banking or credit system, it had an unreliable currency, and the state still intervened in paternalistic fashion to control sensitive industries.

Nineteenth-Century Russia: Reform Denied, Invasion Repelled

With the outbreak of the French Revolution, Russians had to respond to Western Europe's most radical revolutionary movement. A small group of literate people, known as the intelligentsia, had been educated by the new universities under Western influence to believe in rational moral principles of government. They began to criticize autocratic institutions, but Catherine turned against her liberal French tutors and repressed dissent. She imprisoned Alexander Radishchev, who graphically described the horrors of serfdom and openly advocated a republic in his *Journey from St. Petersburg to Moscow* in 1790. Intellectuals influenced by German philosophy began to form small circles dedicated to developing the spirit of the independent thinker who attacked hypocrisy. Catherine's son Paul (r. 1796–1801), a Prussian militarist, hated his mother's indulgence, and tried to reverse her open-minded policies during his short reign. After his murder, cultivated nobles and intellectuals rejoiced at the advent of the young Alexander I to the throne in 1801. Viewed as a liberal because of his upbringing, Alexander aroused great hopes for reform, but his contradictory, irritable character only created disappointment. At first he outlined grand impractical schemes to end autocracy; more pragmatically, he supported reformist state bureaucrat Michael Speransky's effort to fulfill Catherine's project of creating a **Rechtstaat**: a German concept of a monarchy based on law and procedures, with a constitution, local self-government, and a national assembly. It did not succeed.

Napoleon's invasion of Russia in 1812 devastated the country, but revealed its people's tremendous potential for resistance. General Kutuzov's strategy was to yield ground after tenacious resistance, while mobilizing peasant guerrillas and cavalry to harass the huge French army's supply lines. Napoleon captured Moscow only after suffering over 30,000 casualties in one day at the fierce Battle of Borodino, and the city burned down. Even though the Russians had even more casualties, they refused to surrender, and Napoleon had nowhere to go, and no supplies. His catastrophic retreat back over the land he had devastated left him with only 30,000–50,000 men from his 600,000 man army. They were wiped out by hunger, disease, Russian partisan ambushes, and the notorious Russian winter.

Alexander dominated the Congress of Vienna, convened in 1815 to reshape Europe in the wake of Napoleon's defeat. He gained the co-operation of France, Great Britain, Austria, and Prussia in a concerted effort to maintain stability by preventing radical change. The wily Austrian diplomat, Prince Metternich, who masterminded the creation of this reactionary alliance, looked skeptically on Alexander's mystical vision of a Holy Alliance of Christian powers inspired by brotherly love. Yet he still relied on Russia as a gendarme to enforce peace. The rest of Alexander's reign was a period of repression, epitomized by the brutal military officer Arakcheev. His program of military colonization of new lands forced hapless peasants into a despotic system of control even worse than serfdom, and produced even worse results.

Clamping down on even the mildest critiques generated despair among the young Russian officers who had marched into Paris, where they had seen the delights of cultivated urban life. (The French *bistro*, which means "fast" in Russian, comes from the demands for service of the soldiers occupying Paris.) At Alexander's death in 1825, small circles of philosophers joined with idealistic army officers to stage the Decembrist revolt in the heart of Moscow. The mutinous officers tried to obtain the inauguration of a liberal tsar, but they got instead the even more repressive Nicholas I, who ruled with an iron hand through the middle of the century. His doctrine of "Orthodoxy, Autocracy, and Nationality" enforced a military bureaucratic regime that resisted all the changes coming from the industrializing, liberalizing world beyond Russia's borders. He repressed the efforts of the Poles to break away from the empire in 1830. His Third Department, a prime weapon against subversion, investigated all manner of personal, political, and commercial transactions in mind-numbing detail, generating pointless reports testifying only to paranoia.

Cultural Life Flourishes Despite Repression

Yet in the midst of repression, Russian cultural and scientific life flourished as never before. The University of Moscow was established in 1755. Prestigious foreign scholars, like the mathematicians Leonhard Euler and the Bernoulli brothers, came to work in St. Petersburg, and trained a small group of Russian disciples. The extraordinary genius Mikhail Lomonosov (1711–65), Russia's first great polymath scientist, rose from a peasant family to make world-class contributions to physical chemistry. Explorations of Siberia supported great projects of cartography, natural history, and descriptions of the far northern peoples; the first Western school of sinology was founded by Russians in Beijing. The century after Peter moved Russians beyond their central focus on practical skills toward genuine scientific investigation; at the same time Catherine introduced the spectacularly beautiful architecture to St. Petersburg that made it a jewel of the world.

Most important of all, the Russian language gained its modern form, casting off much of its Old Slavonic heritage and becoming a secular medium to express personal sentiment and philosophy. Alexander Pushkin (1799–1837), the greatest Russian poet, wrote in a direct, classical style that is nearly untranslatable because of his ingenious use of rhyme and phrasing. The fate of the individual overpowered by giant forces beyond his control became the central theme of the Russian literary tradition. In prose fiction, Nikolai Gogol's *Dead Souls*, sharp satires of pretentious bureaucrats, took aim at the oppressive modern state, and Lermontov's *Hero of Our Time* announced the arrival of the "superfluous man," the sensitive person aware of his society's defects but unable to find a productive role in it.

German philosophy of the Hegelian brand stimulated fierce debates between Slavophiles, who saw great moral virtues in the special features of Russia, like the egalitarian village commune, and Westernizers, who rejected Russia's enduring practices of serfdom, autocracy, and the knout. Through the middle of the nineteenth century, despite the tumultuous undercurrents of dissent among a tiny elite and occasional ferocious revolts, the surface of Russian life seemed frozen in time, compared to the West. Only stinging defeat in the Crimean War in 1856 broke open the crust, setting the empire on a dynamic new course in the second half of the century.

5.4 THE OTTOMAN EMPIRE: DEFEAT AND REFORM

From the middle of the eighteenth century the Ottoman empire entered a long period of political decentralization. Although many have referred to this process as a "decline," the empire actually continued to grow economically and demographically, on the whole. It lost territory, however, to Russian expansion, and faced revolts by the Serbs and Greeks. Local military elites took substantial power away from the center, especially in Egypt. Repeated efforts at reform aimed to strengthen central control and modernize the administration, but as the industrializing European economy penetrated the empire, local notables gained power as the sultans grew weaker.

From 1700 to 1850, the government of many provinces fell into the hands of local military elites, who were Ottoman slave-soldiers. Although the sultan could still play a role in the provinces through his governors and troops, these elites gained a good deal more local autonomy. Such slave-ruler regimes arose in Iraq, Egypt, Tunis, and Algeria. Even much closer to Istanbul, the sultan and his bureaucracy had less and less power in the Anatolian plateau, where Turkish-speaking "valley lords" or local landed elites asserted their authority. In Eastern Europe and the Caucasus, the Ottomans faced increasingly expansionist Austrian and Russian empires, whose modern militaries frequently defeated the Ottomans on the battlefield. Between 1683 and 1789 the Ottomans were forced to relinquish Hungary,

Croatia, Slavonia, and Transylvania. Map 5.4 shows the losses of Ottoman territory.

The Ottomans had been an aggressive power for centuries. Now they found the loss of their European territories to be a new and frightening experience. In response to these setbacks, some political theorists sought to revive the social and political norms of the golden age of the fifteenth and sixteenth centuries. Others sought to match the new European strength derived from advances in military technology. From the 1760s through 1789, military threats to the empire mounted. In a war with Russia that began in 1768, the Ottoman land army met defeat and the entire navy was sunk in 1770 at the Battle of Cheshme. Humiliated by these defeats, the Ottomans began making small-scale institutional changes.

From 1787–92, the Ottomans lost more territory in Eastern Europe to the Russians. The new sultan, Selim III (r. 1789–1807), was an odd combination of traditionalist and reformer. He pursued only those changes in military organization and technology he felt were essential if the empire was to compete with the Europeans. Most of his courtiers felt that bribery, corruption, and illegal taxes levied by local officials were draining money away from the central treasury. There were also concerns about rising prices, disorder in the cities provoked by increased peasant migration, and the assertiveness of non-Muslim minorities. Selim III returned many peasants to the countryside, driving them out of the cities, enforced old laws requiring that Jews and Christians wear distinctive clothes, and closed down the taverns opened by European merchants. He also tried to ensure that provincial officials and Muslim judges met a basic standard of competence. Some of his ministers, influenced by the European Enlightenment, vainly urged better adherence to the rule of law and more personal freedoms. Selim III's attempts at reform met enormous resistance, with peasants forcibly returned to the countryside turning to banditry and Muslim judges resisting the demand for better credentials.

1798: Bonaparte Invades Egypt, but Soon Leaves

The need for military reform and a tightening of imperial control was underlined in 1798 when Napoleon Bonaparte, then a promising young officer fresh from victories in Italy, invaded Egypt. Bonaparte took a huge flotilla of 50,000 men to Egypt and, taking advantage of internal divisions among the slave-rulers and their military unpreparedness, handily defeated Egypt's rulers at Alexandria and then at the Battle of the Pyramids in July 1798. The French would rule Egypt for three years, but Istanbul mobilized to regain this valuable province, making a frantic alliance with the British. The British fleet under Lord

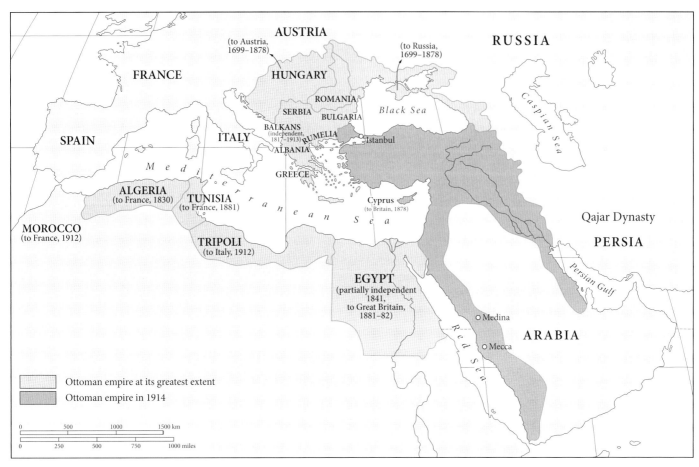

Map 5.4 The Ottoman empire, c. 1800

Horatio Nelson found the French on August 1, 1798, and destroyed their fleet in its harbor at Abukir, east of Alexandria, trapping Bonaparte and his men in Egypt. His attempts to break out of the blockade by invading Syria were defeated at Akka. Abandoning his troops, Napoleon escaped from Egypt, returning to a France that had been kept informed of his victories but not of his defeats.

Although Egyptian nationalists often attempt to trace the reforms that led to modern Egypt back to Bonaparte, in fact the French presence in Egypt was short-lived and had little impact on the lives of most Egyptians, to whom they appeared as one more contending army. The one major change they made was to defeat and weaken the caste of Ottoman slave-soldiers that had governed the province as unruly vassals. Selim III in Istanbul was determined to reform the Ottoman army in the face of such threats. He set up munitions factories. He attempted to introduce modern uniforms and drill techniques. He tried to cut the size of the slave-soldier Janissary infantry by half, to reduce the drain on imperial resources. The conservative Janissaries, resisting vigorously, derailed these reforms. The sultan also had complaints against

the elite cavalry units, whose officers were paid by being given a sort of fief. Selim attempted to keep the cavalry officers from neglecting their military responsibilities.

In the wake of a Serbian revolt, in 1807 Selim tried to reorganize the Janissaries in the Balkans, provoking a military uprising against him. He hastily cancelled all his military reforms, but it was too late. He was imprisoned and then strangled by his successor, who was in turn deposed by his brother, Mahmud II (r. 1808–39). Mahmud would become one of the more successful Ottoman rulers of the nineteenth century.

With a Sparse Population, Concentrated Settlements Grow

Around 1800 the Ottoman empire, while weakened by decentralization and under military pressure from European powers, was still a major force in the eastern Mediterranean. In the absence of official censuses we can only guess at its population, but 19 million seems plausible. Compared to other European powers, the Ottoman empire was huge but sparsely populated. It had a land area of 1.2 million square miles, while France had

25 million people on only 0.2 million square miles, and Great Britain had 11 million people on 0.12 million square miles. The majority of the population lived in rural areas, and most of these country folk were peasant farmers. Peasants predominated in those areas that could support irrigated agriculture, such as Eastern Europe, Anatolia, and the Nile River valley. Elsewhere, in arid territories such as Iraq and Iran, a third to a half of the population were pastoral nomads.

Despite the importance of agriculture, the Ottoman empire had a substantial urban sector. In 1800 perhaps 20 percent of Syrians lived in cities, 15 percent of Iraqis, and 10 percent of Egyptians. In Anatolia the huge capital city of Istanbul dominated, with some 750,000 inhabitants, alongside other substantial cities like Izmir and Smyrna (each about 100,000). Since the empire garrisoned the major cities, the people in them suffered less from bandit raids or attacks by pastoral nomads than small peasant villages. Important trade routes also fed the cities, with Iranian silk coming west through Istanbul to Europe, coffee coming from Yemen through Cairo, grain from Egypt marketed through Alexandria and Damietta to the Mediterranean, soap from Nablus, cotton from the Levant marketed through Sidon, and Indian textiles and other goods through the Persian Gulf and up the Euphrates.

Urban populations, on the other hand, were much more at risk from outbreaks of plague and, later, cholera, which struck many regions in thirty-year cycles. In 1836 a plague outbreak wiped out a third of Cairo's population. Literate Iraqis who believed in the germ theory regularly fled cities like Baghdad, Basra, and Najaf during periodic disease outbreaks. Pastoral nomads, unaffected by these epidemics, often took advantage of weakened urban structures to plunder cities in their aftermath. Still, the institution of quarantines and the central government's new firepower based on rifles and artillery gradually shifted the balance of power to sedentary groups in the succeeding century.

In the eighteenth century the population of many Ottoman provinces, including Egypt, appears to have stagnated, but in the nineteenth century most provinces doubled their population, leaving the pastoralists a much smaller proportion of the whole. If it had kept control of the territories it held in 1800, the empire would have had 42.5 million people in 1914. By comparison, France only increased its population by 40 percent in the nineteenth century, while Great Britain's population more than tripled.

Mehmet `Ali of Egypt Begins Radical Reform

A trial balloon for Ottoman reform was floated by an Albanian officer, Mehmet `Ali Pasha, who came to Egypt in the 1801 invasion force. A favorite of Ottoman army units in the country,

he attracted the loyalty of local Egyptian guilds and other popular forces, as well as prominent Muslim clergymen. In 1805 he declared himself governor, and Selim III acquiesced. Mehmet `Ali ruthlessly centralized and rationalized government in Egypt. He has been accused of over-centralizing and so defeating some of his own goals. By confiscating large amounts of land that had been put into pious endowments, he both weakened the power of the Muslim clergy and gained resources that he could bestow on his nobles and favorites. Mehmet `Ali re-established sea trade with British co-operation and cleared river pirates out of the Nile Valley. He promoted agriculture by introducing new crops, such as local long-staple cotton, and expanding the cultivation of cash crops like sugar and rice. By the 1820s he had introduced double-entry bookkeeping into government accounts, so that for the first time it was easy to tell if the budget was in surplus. He used forced labor to build dams and irrigation ditches.

Mehmet `Ali also promoted textile manufacturing. By 1840, Egypt's cotton factories employed 20,000 workers, and all Egyptian factories together employed some 200,000, as many factory workers as all of Russia in 1800. But his factories faced many problems. Without sufficient wood and coal, the steam looms could not run, and without good mechanics, they could not be fixed. European concern about the impact of Egyptian competition in the textile industry soon forced Mehmet `Ali to eliminate the high tariffs that protected his infant industries. As the rest of the developing world would discover later, backward technology and imperialist pressure severely limited their chances for growth.

Mehmet `Ali sent a number of student missions to study in European countries and learn modern sciences and languages. A new civil secondary school system was inaugurated, supplementing the Koran schools at which most boys got basic training in Arabic and mathematics.

Mehmet `Ali reorganized the army from about 1815, following in the footsteps of Selim III. The spectacular success of peasant conscription under the French revolutionary regime in the 1790s inspired him to overcome his doubts that peasants could be fashioned into fighting men. Soon the Egyptian peasant army grew to 100,000 men. This military experience helped increase the cohesion of Egypt as a province. Many peasants, however, fled or mutilated themselves to avoid conscription. In the 1810s Mehmet `Ali's New Order army acquitted itself admirably for its liege lord, the Ottoman sultan, defeating rebel tribes of the puritan Wahhabi sect in Arabia. In the 1820s the Egyptian army fought rebels in Greece after the latter had humiliated the Janissaries in trying to break away from Ottoman control. The Egyptians fought well, but were routed when the European powers, sympathetic to Greek yearning for independence, intervened in 1827 to sink the Egyptian fleet and deny supplies to Mehmet `Ali's troops.

Sultan Mahmud II Begins the Tanzimat Reforms

The Greek debacle provoked Sultan Mahmud II to take drastic action. In 1826, at the height of the Greek crisis, the sultan presented to his nobles and officials a proclamation decreeing vast reforms of the military in order to save the empire. The first minister began calling up men from each of the Janissary divisions to establish a new force. Many Janissaries, both officers and foot-soldiers, were afraid that the reforms would threaten their livelihoods. They revolted, but were put down. A military force that had been key to Ottoman affairs for centuries was suddenly abolished, replaced by a completely new military trained by Prussian officers. This new army numbered 35,000 officers and men by 1828.

Mahmud II then initiated the "reorganization" (**Tanzimat**) reforms. He moved to abolish venality, the practice (also common in early modern Europe) of allowing officials to buy their offices from the state. The buying of offices encouraged officials to raise taxes once they got in power to recoup on their investment. Now officials began to receive regular salaries. The military fiefs that supported cavalry officers were also phased out, and the income on these lands now went to the sultan's treasury. Following Egypt's example, the sultan established a few new secondary schools, and he founded official newspapers and a postal system.

In the 1830s Mehmet `Ali rebelled against the sultan, sending his son Ibrahim to invade greater Syria in 1831. Syria was a source of wood (in what is now Lebanon) and coal, and its people could be an important market for Egyptian factory-made textiles and other goods. Mehmet `Ali's government made many of the same reforms there as it had pursued in Egypt itself, but attempts to disarm and conscript the population resulted in widespread local revolts. When Mahmud II sent his army against the Egyptians in 1839, it was routed, and the Ottoman navy defected to Mehmet `Ali.

Mahmud II died shortly thereafter, his empire tottering. In 1840, when it seemed possible that Ibrahim's armies would march on Istanbul, the European Powers intervened. In 1840, the Treaty of London between the Egyptians and the Ottomans required an Egyptian pull-back, enforced by British military intervention. Because the Ottoman empire lay on the main routes to India, the British were always wary of any change in the Middle Eastern status quo that might block access to their richest colony. And as they did in China after the Opium War, they forced low tariffs on the Ottomans and Egyptians to ensure the sale of their own manufactured textiles.

The new sultan, Abdulmecid, continued the Tanzimat reforms, favored by the Europeans and a new class of salaried, educated bureaucrats and provincial landowners. These reforms put more power in the hands of civil officials and reduced the clergy's influence. Among Ottoman Christians and Jews, as well, their **millets**, or self-governing institutions dominated by clerics, were challenged by merchants and other laymen.

In 1839 Abdulmecid codified the reforms in the Rescript of the Rose Chamber, making all subjects equal before the law regardless of religion. Despite the last clause, non-Muslims remained second-class citizens whenever the Muslim **shariah** or canon law ruled. But in the sphere where civil law applied, all subjects were equal.

The Tanzimat reforms accomplished their main goal of re-establishing central government control in the Arab lands. An invasion force conquered Baghdad, bringing what is now Iraq back under the direct rule of Istanbul. Egypt had been contained. Local elites in Syria were likewise subdued. The new wealth of the Ottoman treasury that had been gained through cutting out intermediaries aided this process of centralization. In Europe, on the other hand, the Ottomans suffered important defeats. They lost Greece, and other Christian peoples of the Balkans, especially the Serbs, were restless. The French annexation of Algeria in 1831 signaled the onset of a newly aggressive European imperialism. Mahmud paid for many of his reforms and wars by debasing the Ottoman currency, causing inflation and urban unrest. The empire he bequeathed his successors was stronger than it had been, but increasingly weak in the face of advancing Europe.

Over this century and a half, then, several sultans and high officials made strenuous efforts to strengthen the imperial regime in the face of local resistance and foreign incursions. They transformed the inherited institutions significantly without abandoning the bases of imperial rule. These conservative reform efforts did not resolve fundamental problems, but they kept the empire alive until the end of the nineteenth century.

5.5 INDIA 1700/50–1850

In the period 1700 to 1850, India underwent dramatic changes in high politics but maintained key continuities at the local and provincial level. In the mid to late eighteenth century, the titular ruler of much of India was the Mughal, Shah `Alam II (r. 1759–1806). Yet the hollowness of his actual power epitomizes the way Indian politics at first decentralized and then found a new center in growing British hegemony. By this time the Mughal empire was no more than a convenient symbol, a banner under which increasingly independent provincial rulers operated so as to participate in its prestige and legitimacy. Like the Ottomans, but even more so, the center lost power while local powers, including the British, gained. Map 5.5 shows the early stages of British conquest of India.

Map 5.5 India in 1805

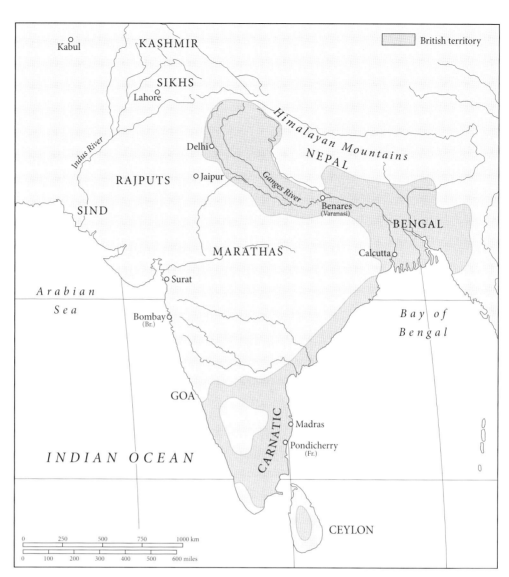

Regional Powers Divide India and Foreigners Intervene

If we surveyed the political scene from Delhi in the mid to late eighteenth century, what would we see? To the east, the Ruhilla Afghan tribes who had emigrated to India established small but militarily formidable principalities. In the southeast, Shi`ite-ruled Oudh refused to aid the Mughal emperor in the 1770s, and by 1819 had become a separate kingdom in its own right. Bengal in mid-century also had a Shi`ite governor or **nawab** who showed signs of becoming an independent prince. In the south, Hyderabad came to be ruled by a Sunni dynasty of "Nizams," descended from a Mughal governor who gradually became independent of Delhi. In another important southern province, Mysore, a Muslim dynasty became a major military power after displacing the Hindu ruling house.

In western and central India, the Hindu Marathas had established a powerful confederation. Although they challenged Mughal rule, they continued to use Persian, and still recognized fictive Mughal sovereignty. In the nearby north, leaders of the militant **Sikh** religion, which showed both Hindu and Muslim influences, successfully mobilized peasant clans in repeated revolts. Until about 1798, however, the Afghans prevented them from forming their own state. Further north, the Durrani Afghan state, established by a Sunni pastoral nomadic dynasty, repeatedly raided the fertile Panjab province, which it sometimes annexed. The Afghans' defeat of their rivals, the Marathas, in 1761 at Panipat, was only a pyrrhic victory. It stopped the Marathas from taking over the empire, but they remained powerful.

Since neither the Afghans nor the Marathas could provide political and military leadership, the weak center invited foreign intervention. Early in the century, the French had a chance to establish colonial rule in South India, but the British were determined to expel them. This eighteenth-century "World War" between Britain and France included conflicts both in India and in North America (known as the Seven Years' War). By 1756 the British forces in India had decisively defeated the French. They then faced a conflict with the nawab of Bengal, who fined them for what he saw as abuse of their trading privileges. Transferring forces from the south that had fought the French, the East India Company leader, Robert Clive then defeated the Bengali nawab's forces at Plassey in 1757. This victory marks the beginning of the British conquest of India.

The East India Company Conquers a Diverse Land

No cabinet in London, and no meeting of the general staff, ever planned the conquest of India. India was conquered by a private company! In 1600 the British East India Company (EIC) was given a charter granting it monopoly rights to promote trade in Asia. Like its predecessor, the Muscovy Company, and the rival Dutch East India Company, it combined the functions of exploration, warfare, and trade in an environment of constant competition. For governments, these armed trading companies were convenient ways to offload the costs of formal political rule. The abolition of the EIC's monopoly in 1834 marked the end of this colonial era and the opening of the new era of free trade. By then, the British controlled nearly all of the former Mughal empire.

The Indians did not give in without a fight, but their large armies lost to the smaller British forces. First the nawab of Oudh joined forces with the weak Mughal emperor to drive the British back out of their beachhead in Bengal, but the Mughal armies were badly defeated in 1764. The Mughals, so dominant for so long, had seen no need to make new guns or cannon. By the mid-1700s British muskets and artillery were far superior to the Indians'. It has been estimated that British-trained troops could fire three bullets for every one that an Indian musketeer could get off. Well-paid, well-drilled British troops fought loyally for a nation, while undisciplined Mughal hordes had no loyalty except to their paycheck. Mughal generals favored the cavalry, while the British made extremely effective use of the flintlock-armed infantryman.

After these defeats the Mughal emperor became little more than a British pensioner. He had to recognize the East India Company formally as his "divan" or revenue minister for Bengal. The former Mughal provinces had become either nominal vassals, or wholly independent. When the EIC refused to remit taxes to the center, even the fictions of empire crumbled. The British defeat of the Marathas in 1805 and capture of Delhi effectively ended the Mughal empire.

Political decentralization in India went much further than in the Ottoman empire. Although an earlier generation of historians used the misleading term "decline" for this period, we might better call it "the rise of the province." That is, some areas lost, but others benefited economically from protection by strong local states. Climate and warfare affected regions differently. Delhi was the most vulnerable to invasion. Sacked by Iranian invaders, its population fell from 400,000 to 100,000. Moreover, prolonged dry spells and droughts sometimes produced famine. This "Delhi dust bowl" cut tax receipts, which came from agriculture, weakened the Mughal king, and touched off peasant revolts.

Oudh, however, in the southeast, prospered when rainfall became abundant from 1750–1800. The nawabs, though gradually encircled by the British, held off major invasions and kept the peace. Lucknow, the capital, grew to 200,000 by 1800, partially offsetting Delhi's decline, and drawing off the cream of Delhi's poets, artists, historians, theologians, and mystics. The growth of these provincial Muslim capitals generated a cultural shift away from Iran and toward indigenous roots. For example, the nawabs of Lucknow switched their court language from Persian to the local North Indian language of Urdu or "Hindustani," a mixture of Persian vocabulary with what we would now call Hindi vocabulary and grammar. This language spread beyond the Muslim elite to many Hindu castes, like those who specialized in bureaucratic work, and even became a status symbol for upper-caste Hindus.

The extreme decentralization of Mughal India drew the East India Company deeper into alliances with some local nawabs and rajas against other local threats. Even though the Pitt Act of 1784 prohibited further territorial conquest (ineffectively), and many in Parliament saw EIC officials as corrupt and self-interested, the British government took advantage of the gains in trade and power created by the EIC governors in the field. Indian allies of the British were left alone once they gave up control of foreign policy and military affairs. What this jerry-built empire lacked in system, it gained in convenience.

The outbreak of the French Revolution in 1789 inaugurated "the first true world crisis since the Mongol invasions of the thirteenth century."[1] British and French world competition stimulated more aggressive conquests of South India by the adventurous governors-general of Bengal, Lord Cornwallis (1786–93) and Lord Wellesley (1798–1805). Cornwallis, in alliance with the Marathas and Hyderabad, defeated Tipu Sultan, the powerful nawab of Mysore. When Tipu Sultan rejected British leniency and made an alliance with the revolutionary French (going so far as to allow his subjects to call him "Citizen Tipu"), Lord Wellesley had him killed.

Hyderabad survived as a semi-autonomous princely state, as did part of Oudh. In the 1800s, the only rivals to British power left in India were the northwestern states of the Marathas, the Sikhs, and the Afghans. The Marathas, too, called on French aid, but the British exploited their disunity, smashing their army in 1803–05. By 1805 the EIC had a standing army of 155,000 troops, as big as many European armies. Lord Wellesley was called home for being too aggressive, but expansion continued. Successful but costly wars with Burma, the Sikhs, and the Afghans in the early nineteenth century gave the British an empire even larger than that of the Mughals, encompassing 2.2 million square miles and over 240 million people.

Colonial Administration Brings Profits, but Indian Peasants Lose

The EIC began as a trading company, but developed into a full-fledged colonial administration. It used its political control of Bengal to displace rival European trading companies and developed a salaried bureaucracy of British civil servants who were forbidden to trade privately. Private British merchants could engage in a wider range of trade than EIC merchants, but they had to pay customs duties, and were shut out of the company's lucrative monopolies in salt, opium, and saltpeter. They could, however, make profits in silk, grains, cotton, cloth piece goods, sugar, and indigo. The EIC monopoly of Indian-grown opium, sent east to pay for Chinese goods like tea and silk, meant that it no longer had to support its costly administration with silver and gold from Europe. Box 5.5 gives Karl Marx's analysis of the impact of British rule on India.

From 1814, as the East India Company lost its trade monopoly in every commodity but opium, it had to tax Indian agriculture to pay for the British administration. To collect its taxes, it had to alter the land system radically. In Bengal, full private property rights in land replaced the more ambiguous Mughal system. Now one landowner both collected revenue and paid the taxes. Under the Mughals, an official might have revenue rights, but local holders had customary rights and paid taxes. The Bengal "Permanent Settlement" of land rights imposed European ideas of landed property on a very different society. The British thought they were creating yeoman farmers, but they caused many peasants to lose their land to Bengali moneylenders and merchants, producing unhappiness and turmoil. Elsewhere in India, changes were less drastic. The British government officials governed more directly, with district commissioners collecting agricultural and land taxes from large numbers of small village holders. The system of administration worked out by the British relied heavily at the lower level on Indian clerks, translators, and other officials. Indian castes and clans who gained such positions used them to better their political and economic status, just as had happened under the Mughals.

British tax collection could be harsh. Over-taxation may have contributed to the horrible famine of 1770, when a third of the Bengali population died. In this case the British, however, were not alone to blame. The famine struck Muslim-ruled Oudh as well. Peasant rebellions against British exactions were frequent, but scattered. Easily put down, they did not pose a major threat to British control.

It seems indisputable that Britain benefited from its Indian empire, even if the government of India did not always pay for itself out of local tax receipts. In some periods India actually cost the British government millions of pounds. Offsetting this cost were the profits to the private sector, since India was a captive market for British goods, and the role of Indian opium in financing the China trade.

Britain emerged as by far India's largest export market. Although both Hindu and Muslim merchants founded some important firms in the first half of the nineteenth century, they were soon eclipsed by British capital. The import of British manufactured cloth, especially after the end of the Napoleonic Wars in 1815, damaged Indian textile-making, which was still largely done by hand on wooden looms, though Indian weavers and spinners hardly disappeared. Imported British manufactures cut into the core of the Indian handicraft market, so that artisans could only survive by making luxury goods or very coarse ones.

Most Indians continued in the first half of the nineteenth century to live their lives as their parents and grandparents had. The vast majority of Indians were agricultural workers living in villages. Though some cities grew, overall urbanization declined. With 13 to 15 percent of the population living in cities in 1700, India was less urbanized than China, Japan, or the Ottoman empire, and this percentage fell to 9.3 by 1881. The standard of living of the average peasant probably fell during the British period, in part because of the population explosion of the nineteenth century that put pressure on the land. Many Indians blame the British for destroying their chances for industrialization, but the overall effects of empire were mixed, and often less important than domestic changes.

Language and Cultural Change

The Indian elites adapted to their new conquerors. Muslim clans that sent their members from small towns to become courtiers continued this practice with the British, providing judges who applied Muslim law in Bengal. After 1790, when the EIC enforced only civil law, the Muslim elites gradually lost their privileged position. Disputes over personal status (marriage, divorce, inheritance), however, could still be settled according to Muslim or Hindu law. The cities offered new prosperity to some Hindu merchants, and moneylenders gained a new

Box 5.5 Karl Marx: "The Future Results of British Rule in India"

In this newspaper article Karl Marx, the German revolutionary theorist, predicts the impact of British colonialism on India. You may be surprised to learn that Marx saw a positive role for imperialism: The building of the railways and the unification of the continent, for him, destroyed the stagnant "Asiatic" despotism, and paved the way for an industrialized bourgeois society.

England has to fulfill a double mission in India: one destructive, the other regenerating the annihilation of old Asiatic society, and the laying the material foundations of Western society in Asia . . .

The British were the first conquerors superior, and therefore, inaccessible to Hindoo civilization. They destroyed it by breaking up the native communities, by uprooting the native industry, and by leveling all that was great and elevated in the native society. The historic pages of their rule in India report hardly anything beyond that destruction. The work of regeneration hardly transpires through a heap of ruins. Nevertheless it has begun.

The political unity of India, more consolidated, and extending farther than it ever did under the Great Moguls, was the first condition of its regeneration. That unity, imposed by the British sword, will now be strengthened and perpetuated by the electric telegraph. The native army, organized and trained by the British drill-sergeant, was the sine qua non of Indian self-emancipation, and of India ceasing to be the prey of the first foreign intruder. The free press, introduced for the first time into Asiatic society, and managed principally by the common offspring of Hindoos and Europeans, is a new and powerful agent of reconstruction. The Zemindari and Ryotwar themselves, abominable as they are, involve two distinct forms of private property in land – the great desideratum of Asiatic society. From the Indian natives, reluctantly and sparingly educated at Calcutta, under English superintendence, a fresh class is springing up, endowed with the requirements for government and imbued with European science. Steam has brought India into regular and rapid communication with Europe, has connected its chief ports with those of the whole south-eastern ocean, and has revindicated it from the isolated position which was the prime law of its stagnation. The day is not far distant when, by a combination of railways and steam-vessels, the distance between England and India, measured by time, will be shortened to eight days, and when that once fabulous country will thus be actually annexed to the Western world.

The ruling classes of Great Britain have had, till now, but an accidental, transitory and exceptional interest in the progress of India. The aristocracy wanted to conquer it, the moneyocracy to plunder it, and the millocracy to undersell it. But now the tables are turned. The millocracy have discovered that the transformation of India into a reproductive country has become of vital importance to them, and that, to that end, it is necessary, above all, to gift her with means of irrigation and of internal communication. They intend now drawing a net of railroads over India. And they will do it. The results must be inappreciable . . .

The introduction of railroads may be easily made to subserve agricultural purposes by the formation of tanks, where ground is required for embankment, and by the conveyance of water along the different lines. Thus irrigation, the sine qua non of farming in the East, might be greatly extended, and the frequently recurring local famines, arising from the want of water, would be averted. The general importance of railways, viewed under this head, must become evident, when we remember that irrigated lands . . . pay three times as much in taxes, afford ten or twelve times as much employment, and yield twelve or fifteen times as much profit, as the same area without irrigation . . .

I know that the English millocracy intend to endow India with railways with the exclusive view of extracting at diminished expenses the cotton and other raw materials for their manufactures. But when you have once introduced machinery into the locomotion of a country, which possesses iron and coals, you are unable to withhold it from its fabrication. You cannot maintain a net of railways over an immense country without introducing all those industrial processes necessary to meet the immediate and current wants of railway locomotion, and out of which there must grow the application of machinery to those branches of industry not immediately connected with railways. The railway-system will therefore become, in India, truly the forerunner of modern industry.

prosperity. The official language of the EIC until 1835 was Persian, which favored the Muslim intellectuals. British officials had to master Persian and other Indian languages, studying the classical tongues at an institute in England before coming out to India, or studying languages then spoken at Fort William in Calcutta and elsewhere in the subcontinent. But as long as the British remained dependent on Indian interpreters and specialists, Indians played a big role in shaping the empire.

After 1835 the EIC made English the official language of administration. The language used for interaction between the EIC and Indians became Urdu, which still favored Muslims, even though many Indians knew it as well. In the same year, Thomas Macauley issued his famous "Minute," or memorandum, detailing the benefits of an English education for Indians and urging that an attempt be made to recreate them as British gentlemen. His program was ultimately adopted, though only after opposition from the "Orientalists," those British who valued Indian languages and culture.

The new emphasis on English in education and the bureaucracy benefited Hindus, who until the 1880s were far more likely to seek such an education for their children. Only later did the Muslims try to catch up. By 1850 there were about 200 English-language schools in India enrolling some 30,000 pupils, though education represented only about 1 percent of the government budget.

Both Hindus and Muslims responded to the new foreign presence with calls for reform. A few Western-educated Hindu thinkers, such as Ram Mohan Roy (1772–1833), tried to shift the emphasis in Hinduism to high philosophical principles and away from what they saw as idol worship, caste identity, child marriage, and the burning of widows, or **sati** (a rare upper-caste custom practiced in some Hindu princely states among the aristocracy). Roy founded the Society of Brahma (Brahmo Samaj) in 1828. He served as diplomatic intermediary between Calcutta and Lucknow, and wrote some of his reformist theology in Persian. The Hindu, Muslim, and British worlds still strongly intersected in this period, before religious rivalries put an end to such syncretism.

Muslim reformers, especially those adhering to the Naqshbandi Sufi order, met the changed situation with calls for a return to the shariah or strict Muslim law. Shah ʾAbd al-ʾAziz of Delhi declared India under the British to be a "realm of war." This declaration was not meant to provoke hostile action against the British, but simply to make the statement that Indian Muslims no longer lived under a Muslim government. Some Muslims even welcomed this situation, which in Islamic law relieved them of the restrictions against charging bank interest on loans. Now they could compete with Hindu and Christian moneylenders and financiers. Many elite Muslims worked

against Hindu influences among Indian Muslims, and Muslim women were condemned for praying to the Hindu goddess Kali to cure their children of smallpox.

In Shiʾite-ruled Oudh, a clergy developed similar to the one in Iran, which used rational, scholastic approaches to reinterpret Islamic law and claimed the allegiance of the laity. Lithography and printing gave these literate elites new tools of communication and began spreading knowledge of Western sciences. Still, elite Hindu and Muslim calls for strict communal identities were thwarted at this time at the local level. In Lucknow, Hindus and Sunnis regularly joined in Shiʾite processions mourning the martyred family of the Prophet. It is doubtful that many illiterate commoners in villages or poor urban quarters had a strong communal identity in this period. The communal riots of twentieth-century India were products of later tensions; they did not have primordial roots.

Indian nationalists would later blame the British for destroying India's economy and inflicting on it stagnation and backwardness, much as Chinese nationalists attacked their "barbarian" Manchu rulers. These melodramatic accusations have some truth to them, but they simplify complex relationships. There was no united resistance to British rule, and many elites profited from collaboration with the new conquerors. The later nationalist movements grew out of the experience of empire, but neither China's nor India's society divided people rigidly between foreign rulers and native subjects.

5.6 WOMEN'S EXPERIENCE UNDER AGRARIAN PATRIARCHY

Except for the Russian empresses, no women emerged into public life in this period, but we now know quite a bit about their lives at home. Chinese women, elite and common, spent nearly all of their lives within family compounds, confined to their duties of cooking, minding children, and spinning and weaving cloth. The high Qing moral codes enforced more rigorous strictures on women than the late Ming, constantly preaching obedience to fathers, husbands, and sons. But as more elite women became literate, they developed extensive communication networks through letter writing and poetry circles. They could claim to be following orthodox Confucian doctrines at the same time as they educated themselves and displayed high aesthetic achievements. Even those who did not write classical prose showed their talents in the elaborate embroidered clothing that formed part of their dowry chest. Some male scholars also began to recognize women's special talents, as they espoused a cult of sentiment remarkably similar to European Romanticism. Jia Baoyu, the hero of *The Story of the Stone*, openly preferred women's conversation to his dull tutors. Lower on the economic hierarchy, women provided vital economic contributions to the household in textile production, which they could practice indoors despite their crippled feet. They could sell their cloth on the market for cash income, giving them wages approximately equivalent to that of male farm laborers. Even in the sphere of reproduction, women had more agency than we might assume. Chinese medical texts justified abortions to save the life of the mother, allowing women to control their fertility to some extent with herbal abortifacients.

Japanese women faced many of the same patriarchal restraints supported by Confucian orthodox teaching as their Chinese counterparts, although they did not bind their feet. They, too, were almost always confined to the household, but many peasant families supported the education of their daughters at rural schools and provided them with lavish clothing. Up to 10 percent of women gained some knowledge of the Japanese syllabic script and Chinese characters. In exceptional cases, some women escaped the bonds restraining them. Ema Saiko, one of Japan's finest poets and painters, developed her great talents with her father's support, and inspired many women disciples. Some new religious sects supported by the merchant class embraced women preachers. Jion-ni Kenka, a Buddhist nun, gave free lectures to men and women in Edo which attracted up to a thousand people. In both China and Japan, within the constraints of orthodoxy, extraordinary women could exploit opportunities open to them.

Likewise, only a few Russian women could escape from the pervasive power of the male-dominated institutions around them. Yet, they did improve their positions gradually. Peter the Great liberated elite women from the seclusion of the **terem**, or harem, in 1718, allowing them to join high court society and choose their marriage partners freely. Under a law of 1753, Russian women, unlike women in Western Europe, retained control of the property they had brought into a marriage throughout their whole lives and could bequeath it to their children when they died. Catherine pressed for broad education of women, founding the Smolny Institute for noble girls in 1764 and public schools for poorer women. A few remarkable women, like Nadezhda Durova, espoused the cause of freedom. She ran away from home in 1807, served in the Russian cavalry disguised as a boy, and published journals describing her distinguished military service. Mothers, wives, and daughters of leading male members of the intelligentsia played important supportive roles behind the scenes. Women political activists would soon throw themselves actively into the revolutionary movements of the late nineteenth century.

Conclusion The last 150 years of the Agrarian Age brought to fruition much of the potential of the Eurasian societies, before industrialism changed everything. A central theme of our story has been the progressive growth of the network of social interactions that allowed the co-ordination of human actions over wide expanses. The communication density of a society – determined by its trade and transport routes, its literacy, its agricultural productivity, and its government – had much to do with how well it used its available resources. These empires shared many features, although no generalization applies equally well to all of them. All except the Ottomans expanded the territory under their control; although the Mughals first fell into pieces and were collected together again under the British. China and Russia expanded the furthest, and even Japan moved north. As they expanded, the empires touched each other, eliminating most of the interstices occupied by nomads and tribal peoples. Treaties fixed boundaries and peoples in place under regularized rule, as bureaucrats replaced soldiers as the dominant players. Populations grew and moved into frontier areas (except in Japan and parts of the Ottoman domains). Internal trade networks linked regions together and facilitated the movement of people, goods, money, and ideas. Literacy rose to surprising levels, especially in East Asia, as high as 30 to 50 percent of the male population. Far fewer women, of course, were literate, and most remained confined to their households, but an elite did learn the fine arts of poetry, embroidery, and letter writing.

The rulers at the center all had trouble keeping these dynamic developments under control. Russia, China, and Japan generally became more centralized, as their bureaucracies aimed to penetrate, standardize, and make more visible the hidden practices of local custom, but local notables took power away from the sultans in Istanbul, and Mughal India fell completely apart, to be replaced by a new, more despotic foreign ruler. When possible, centralizing bureaucrats all mapped and measured their lands, and classified and counted their peoples, with more efficient methods of statecraft. Sporadic reform efforts in all the empires aimed to improve the flow of revenues toward the center, regularize local administration, and respond to the rising production of both agriculturalists and merchants. The Ottomans made more sustained, and more radical steps toward reform than the Chinese, Russians, or Japanese, but their goals were similar. None of them tried to undermine the basic system of rule; only to make it run more smoothly.

External pressure was only one factor in reform, and usually not the dominant one, but Western European traders and soldiers certainly grew more prominent around the continent. A chartered monopoly trading company conducted the conquest of India; Napoleon's armies had only a brief impact on Egypt, but the Ottoman openness to trade allowed significant commercial penetration; Russia voluntarily plunged into European continental politics and maritime trade. East Asians kept aloof as long as possible, until the global British push for open trade in the mid nineteenth century forced open China's ports, soon followed by the USA in Japan. On the whole, expanding empires and thickening communication networks across Eurasia substantially integrated the pre-industrial world.

Study Questions (1) Why were the Qing rulers so successful in expanding their empire in the eighteenth century, and so unsuccessful in responding to the Western imperial powers in the nineteenth century? Evaluate the impact of imperial leadership, official corruption, population growth, commercial prosperity, and scholarly discussions during this shift from expansion to decline.

(2) Although relatively isolated from world trade, Tokugawa Japan still grew economically and shared many common trends with the rest of the world. Which aspects of Tokugawa

social and economic change were unique to Japan, and which aspects paralleled those happening elsewhere?

(3) Russian expansion brought the empire vast new lands and peoples, but how well did Russian rulers use their new resources to develop the country? Did the reform programs of the tsars and intellectual elites make the country prepared to engage in the industrial world of the nineteenth century?

(4) What were the major causes of political decentralization in eighteenth-century India? Assess the comparative importance of domestic revolts, foreign invasions, and climate shifts.

(5) In what ways did the Ottoman elites attempt to meet the new European challenge from 1750 to 1850? What legal, administrative, military, and economic steps did they take?

(6) During the eighteenth century, China and Russia expanded, while the Ottoman empire and Mughal India lost central control and regional powers grew. Compare the consequences of expansion and regionalization for local agrarian producers, merchants, and foreign merchants in these areas.

Suggested Reading

China   XUEQIN CAO, *The Story of the Stone*. The vivid translation by DAVID HAWKES (Harmondsworth: Penguin, 1973) gives fascinating insight into Chinese family dynamics among the elite.

KANGXI, *Emperor of China: Self Portrait of K'ang Hsi*, trans. JONATHAN SPENCE (New York: Knopf, 1974). The emperor describes his life and achievements in his own words.

ROBERT B. MARKS, *Tigers, Rice, Silk, and Silt: Environment and Economy in Late Imperial South China* (Cambridge University Press, 1998). Marks closely analyzes environment, prices, and agricultural production.

PETER C. PERDUE, *Exhausting the Earth: State and Peasant in Hunan, 1500–1850* (Cambridge, MA: Harvard University Press, 1987). Perdue examines ecological change over the long term in one province.

WILLIAM T. ROWE, *China's Last Empire: The Great Qing* (Cambridge, MA: Harvard University Press, 2009). This is the best survey of the Qing dynasty.

Tokugawa Japan   TESSA MORRIS-SUZUKI, *The Technological Transformation of Japan from the Seventeenth to the Twenty-First Century* (Cambridge University Press, 1994). This is a broad survey of technological change.

Russia   YURI SLEZKINE, *Arctic Mirrors: Russia and the Small Peoples of the North* (Ithaca, NY: Cornell University Press, 1994). Slezkine's book is a fascinating discussion of Russian frontiers and ethnic identities.

RICHARD S. WORTMAN, *Scenarios of Power: Myth and Ceremony in Russian Monarchy* (Princeton University Press, 1995). Wortman insightfully traces imperial ritual over the entire tsarist period.

Ottomans and India   C.A. BAYLY, *Imperial Meridian: The British Empire and the World, 1780–1830* (London: Longman, 1989). This is a stimulating comparative analysis of British and other empires relying on Ibn Khaldun's principles.

Alan Mikhail, *Nature and Empire in Ottoman Egypt: An Environmental History* (Cambridge University Press, 2008). This is a highly original analysis of the resource flows underlying Ottoman rule.

Glossary

bakufu: The "tent government" of the Japanese military ruler, or shogun, with its headquarters first in Kyoto, then in Kamakura, and finally in Edo (Tokyo) under the Tokugawa regime.

banners: The military and political organization created by the Manchus to rule China in the seventeenth century. Banners included Manchus, Chinese, Mongolians, and other peoples in strictly disciplined hereditary units, each with its own distinctive flag.

corvée: Forced labor for the state: a form of human taxation imposed by autocratic regimes like absolutist France, Russia, China, and Japan.

daimyo: Noble lords of Japan, each of whom had his own landed estate, a castle, and armed retainers (samurai). In the Tokugawa period there were about 250 daimyo.

Dalai Lama: Title for the religious and political leader of Tibet, granted to the leader of the Gelugpa Buddhist sect by a Mongolian khan in the sixteenth century.

extraterritoriality: A provision of the unequal treaties imposed on China in the nineteenth century, comprising the right of foreigners to be tried in China by foreign courts.

khan: Title for a recognized leader of a nomadic tribal federation.

kokutai: The "national polity" of Japan, claimed by nationalists to be unique and superior to the rest of the world, because it is based on an unbroken imperial line that descend from the sun goddess.

kowtow: From Chinese "ketou," to prostrate oneself on the ground and knock one's head on the floor in acknowledgement of the superior authority of the emperor.

Kyodotai: Japanese ideal of a self-sufficient, harmonious, agrarian community, invoked by the Tokugawa government and Japanese nationalists of the twentieth century.

Maitreya: The appearance of the Buddha of the Future, worshipped by sects in China and Japan who expected the coming of a new world of prosperity and justice.

millets: In Ottoman Turkish, a way of referring to minority religious communities with their own internal governing institutions, recognized by the state. Recognized millets included Eastern Orthodox, Catholic, and Armenian Christians, as well as Jews.

mir: The Russian village community, which imposed collective tax obligations on all peasants and redistributed land to maintain equality within it.

nawab: Provincial Muslim governors in India, who became increasingly independent of the Mughal center during the eighteenth century.

Neo-Confucian: A system of philosophy, ethics, and political teachings developed by the scholar Zhu Xi in the twelfth century CE. It became the orthodox ideology of the Ming and Qing dynasties, enforced through the examination system.

Rechtstaat: German concept of a monarchy governed by law and a constitution. Reforming Russian ministers aimed at this ideal state, but could never put it into practice.

samurai: The armed warriors of Japan, each of whom usually owed military service to a lord, or daimyo.

sati (or suttee): A rare upper-caste Hindu custom requiring widows to burn themselves on their husbands' funeral pyres; target of suppression by British colonialists.

shariah: Muslim canon law based on interpretation of the Koran.

Shinto: Literally "Way of the Gods," a collection of local cults and nature worship considered to be the native religion of Japan, before the impact of Buddhism and Confucian teachings.

Sikh: Member of a new religion that grew up in the Panjab province during Mughal times. It originally resembled popular Hindu movements called bhakti, which emphasized ecstatic worship over somber ritual and promised even the little people salvation. The religion tended toward monotheism and some say it combines elements of Hinduism and Islam. Militant Sikhs instigated violent conflict in late Mughal times, during the eighteenth century.

Tanzimat: Literally "reorganization," this term refers to the whole range of military and civil reforms undertaken by the Ottoman sultans from about 1826 to about 1876.

terem: Russian word for the harem, which kept elite women in seclusion, until they were liberated by Peter the Great in 1718.

Triads: Sworn brotherhoods who supported the Ming dynasty of China against the Manchu conquest.

tsar: Title for the ruler of Russia, (derived from Roman "Caesar"), first used by Ivan III in the sixteenth century.

White Lotus: A Maitreyan Buddhist mass movement that caused rebellious outbreaks in China in the eighteenth and nineteenth century.

zaibatsu: Large financial combines that came to dominate Japanese economic production in the late nineteenth through mid twentieth centuries.

Note 1 Christopher Bayly, *Imperial Meridian: The British Empire and the World, 1780–1830* (London: Longman, 1989), p. 99.

6 The First Industrial Revolution and the origins of international inequality

Timeline	
1454	Gutenberg develops the printing press.
1560s	Four-wheeled wagons and coaches introduced and diffused in England.
1564	English Parliament authorizes the construction of the country's first private canal.
1624	Statute of Artificers in England offers patent protection to inventors.
1633	England's first turnpike act gives private toll-road owners the right to collect tolls in exchange for maintaining thoroughfares.
1688	Glorious Revolution restores Protestant monarchs to England and establishes the supremacy of Parliament.
1709	Abraham Darby uses coke – rather than charcoal – in the smelting of iron ore.
1712	Thomas Newcomen in Britain builds an atmospheric steam engine.
1760–1815	English Parliament issues acts of enclosure, making agriculture more efficient and forcing rural peasants into cities.
1760–1830	First Industrial Revolution: coal- and steam-driven industry, cloth factories, light industry, railroads, and telegraph lines.
1764	James Hargreaves invents the spinning jenny.
1765	James Watt modifies the Newcomen engine, making it more efficient.
1765–1808	Bourbon reforms in the Spanish empire discourage economic activity there by imposing new regulations, monopolies, and taxes.
1776–87	American Revolution, Articles of Confederation, Constitution.
1785	Steam-powered water frame and power loom allow a single worker to produce more thread than 100 had produced earlier.
1789–91	French Revolution.
1793	Eli Whitney invents the cotton gin.
1793–1812	Napoleonic Wars in Europe; Napoleon imposes new legal codes adopted in France in 1802–04 on French-occupied Europe.

1798	Thomas Robert Malthus publishes his *Essay on the Principles of Population as It Affects the Future Improvement of Society.*
1803	US Louisiana Purchase.
1807	Robert Fulton builds and successfully tests the *Clermont*, the first practical steamship.
1812	War between USA and Britain.
1814	Francis Lowell builds first factory using power looms in USA.
	George Stephenson builds the world's first steam-propelled intercity railway system.
1819	USA seizes Florida from Spain.
1820s–1840s	Extensive canal and railroad systems developed in the Netherlands.
1825	Erie Canal completed in USA.
1830	Manchester and Liverpool connected by rail.
1830–50	Massive laying of track in USA, England, and Western Europe.
1834	Zollverein reduces tariff barriers between German states.
1838	Chartist movement organized.
1842	Chadwick's *Report on the Sanitary Condition of the Labouring Population of Great Britain* estimates a life expectancy of 17 years in industrial Manchester.
1846	Repeal of the Corn Laws.
1846–48	Mexican–American War: USA annexes the northern half of Mexico.
1850–1929	Second Industrial Revolution: electrically powered, heavy industry, steel works, automobile factories, and modern assembly lines.

In 1799, at the age of 7, the orphan Robert Blincoe was removed from the St. Pancras poorhouse outside London and, along with other young boys and girls, sent by the municipal authorities to cotton mills in Nottingham in north central England. Concerned about the growing cost of welfare, the St. Pancras authorities sought to reduce expenses by sending orphans to work in cotton mills until the age of 21. As the cart carrying the young orphans approached the mill in Nottingham, Blincoe heard one of the assembled villagers remark, "God help the poor wretches."

The villager's pity was not misplaced. At 5 o'clock in the morning the young orphans were awakened and fed a breakfast of milk porridge and a scarcely digestible rye bread. Half an hour later boys and girls were at work at the factory standing without interruption until twelve noon and working a total of 14 hours a day, sometimes extended an additional hour or two. To encourage the orphans the manager told them "Do your work well and you'll not be beaten." After each of his repeated efforts to escape from the mill, Blincoe was severely beaten.

Although its long-term significance escaped him, Robert Blincoe was working in the very heart of the British Industrial Revolution. The labor of young orphans contributed to one of the most remarkable transformations in human history. While the Industrial Revolution was to bring great benefits for men and women all over the world, the price paid by Blincoe's generation of workers was a high one.

Before 1500, the main economic dividing line in the world ran between the subsistence economies of hunter-gatherers and semi-nomadic part-time cultivators, on one hand, and the more productive agricultural economies that produced surpluses sufficient to feed city-dwellers, including the courtiers and armies of their autocratic rulers. Even as late as 1700, neither England nor any other part of Europe yet stood out as economically more advanced than many other parts of the globe. In that year, the more developed coastal trading regions of Southern Europe, China, India, the Middle East, and West Africa as well as the Caribbean sugar islands probably had per capita incomes on a par with that of England.

Then, from 1700 to 1850, an extraordinary economic transformation took place. A small number of countries in the North Atlantic region achieved sustained **economic growth** (increase in GDP per capita) that left the rest of the world far behind. By

Figure 6.1 GDP per capita of the world and main regions (in 1990 international dollars)

YEAR / REGION	1	1000	1500	1820	2001
TODAY'S DEVELOPED REGIONS					
Western Europe	450	400	670	1,269	19,256
United States and Canada	400	400	400	1,233	26,146
Japan	400	425	525	675	20,413
Average Developed Regions	439	405	624	1,149	21,470
TODAY'S LESS DEVELOPED REGIONS					
Other Europe	400	400	597	803	5,811
Latin America	400	415	415	671	4,354
Asia (excluding Japan)	450	450	571	550	3,256
China	450	450	600	600	3,583
Other Asia	425	425	525	560	2,977
Africa	430	425	421	500	1,489
Average Developing Regions	423	424	525	560	3,464
WORLD AVERAGE	425	420	545	675	6,049

1850, Britain, the United States, and a handful of nations in Northwestern Europe (France, Germany, and the Low Countries) had reached heights of **productivity** (volume of production relative to resources) never before achieved. In that year, these modernizing countries (shown in Figure 6.1) were producing an annual per capita output of roughly 1,500 US dollars, nearly three times higher than any other world region and four to five times higher than the world's poorest regions. No societies in human history had ever been so productive.

Economic growth provoked massive demographic and social changes. Cities grew rapidly with migrants from the countryside. Many who moved had little choice, driven from the land by modernizing landlords who needed fewer hands. A propertyless urban proletariat, forced to adapt to the harsh discipline of the factory, inhabited the new industrial slums and mining towns. Children, like orphan Robert Blincoe, worked 12 to 14 hour days. Many industrial cities in this era were death traps, even more dirty and disease-ridden than ancient cities or medieval towns. Urban populations were unable to reproduce themselves. Life expectancy actually fell and infant mortality rates rose. Widespread malnutrition stunted growth. People actually grew shorter. For many of the people caught up in it, the First Industrial Revolution was an era of misery, malnutrition, disease, and premature death. Economic and technological progress came at a high price.

This chapter will:

- Describe the kind of evidence historians use to measure improvements or setbacks in the economy.

- Explain why the Dutch Republic and Britain became the first countries in the world to achieve sustained economic growth.
- Examine the key political, social, and economic conditions that came together to make Britain the leader in industrial technology in the eighteenth and early nineteenth centuries.
- Describe the spread of economic modernization to the United States and Northwestern Europe.
- Analyze the fall in living standards with rapid urbanization.
- Examine the transformation of family life and the role of women.
- Describe the first modern protests against the misery and exploitation of the new factory system.

6.1 MEASURING ECONOMIC GROWTH

To measure the economic success or failure of any society, historians need to know the answer to two questions: How productive are its people and how well are their needs being met? These questions can be difficult to answer, especially when the evidence is scattered and unreliable.

Understanding economic success or failure begins with measuring economic activity, that is, how much a society produces both in tangible goods as well as services (like transportation, merchandising, or education). The standard approach is to add up the market value of all the goods and services produced in a country in a single year. This is called the **gross domestic product** (GDP), Gross National Product (GNP), national income, total output, or some other term depending on exactly how the calculation is made. When GDP rises, the economy is getting bigger, producing more.

An increase in total production (GDP) is not the same as an increase in the productivity of the economy. The productivity of a nation's economy is usually measured by dividing GDP by population to get GDP per capita. Productivity only rises when an economy produces more goods and services per person, that is, when GDP per capita goes up. This is what economists call economic growth. In the long run, productivity has to rise for living standards to improve. People cannot consume more food, clothing, health care, or even luxury goods unless they live in a society that produces them or can trade local products to import them. In many places and times, however, productivity increases have chiefly benefited minorities of rulers, warriors, landowners, industrial magnates, or groups with scarce skills. Rising productivity is thus a necessary but not a sufficient condition for better living standards for all.

The productivity of an entire society can only rise when many individual enterprises – farms, factories, markets, service providers, shipping companies, and so on – find ways to become more productive or efficient. This means finding ways to produce more without using more labor, land, equipment, or raw materials. Increases in productivity are achieved mainly through improved technology – better machines or techniques of production. When productivity rises, the workers and resources no longer needed in the more efficient industry become available to produce something else. Between 1764 and 1802, for example, the amount of thread a single British worker could produce in a day increased more than a hundred times because of a series of labor-saving inventions. Cotton mills using the new technology produced far more thread and yarn of much better quality with fewer workers.

Improvements in the organization of production can also increase productivity through specialization and economies of scale. Two kinds of specialization occurred during the era of the Industrial Revolution: specialization within enterprises and specialization between regions. Enterprise specialization occurred when farms, trading companies, workshops, and eventually factories trained workers to perform specific tasks. Experience made each worker more adept and expert at his or her job than in enterprises where workers were expected to handle every possible task at one time or another. As the division of labor became more complex, output per worker and thus productivity rose. Eventually, entire enterprises began to specialize in a narrower range of products, those they could produce more efficiently (and thus more profitably). Similarly, entire regions began to specialize in specific kinds of farm and factory production.

Regional specialization, especially in agriculture, made it possible to exploit the unique qualities of local soil and climate to best effect. Factories were often built near supplies of raw materials and labor. **Economies of scale** occur whenever it costs less (per unit) to produce in larger quantities. In modern factories, first developed during the Industrial Revolution in England, output per worker was much higher than in smaller workshops, so it cost less to produce each yard of cloth or pound of iron.

Measuring Changes in Living Standards

Measuring trends in living standards is not as straightforward as it might seem. There is no universally accepted summary measure for the standard of living or physical well-being of human populations as there is for productivity. GDP per capita is a good measure of productivity, but it does not reveal much about how goods and services are distributed. If income distribution is unequal, living standards for most people may remain low even as GDP per capita increases. One common measure of human well-being is life expectancy, that is, how long people live. People who are better fed, clothed, and housed, with less strenuous jobs and better medical care in safer areas tend to live longer. For example, adult men in the United States in 1800 lived on average twenty years longer (roughly 55 versus 35 years) than Englishmen because the United States had cheaper food, higher wages, and fewer urban slums. Britain was closer to the norm, however. For most of human history, average life expectancy at birth seldom exceeded 30 to 40 years of age.

A second measure commonly used by archaeologists as well as historians is average height or stature. Individual height is partly controlled by genetic inheritance, but at the same level of **net nutrition** in childhood the average height of population groups is virtually identical across all races and ethnic groups. Net nutrition is equal to total nutrients consumed minus energy expended in warding off disease and in work or exercise. Populations that are well-fed and live in healthier environments grow taller than malnourished populations in disease-ridden or polluted areas. For example, white citizens of the United States had a 4-inch advantage over their English cousins in 1800. However, industrialization and the growth of city slums in the United States cut 3 inches off the height of native-born male adults in the United States between the generation born in the 1830s and that born in the 1880s.

Measuring productivity and welfare in the distant past can be difficult, because reliable and systematic data are often lacking.

Most governments did not begin doing economic surveys or national censuses until sometime in the nineteenth or twentieth century. For a few countries, historians have reconstructed GDP and life expectancy from partial data back to the eighteenth century or even earlier. Stature and other indicators of physical welfare, however, can be measured from skeletons, so archaeologists and historians are now able to compare past and present living standards, and to measure past trends in well-being, as never before.

For living standards to rise, economies have to become more productive (i.e. produce more goods and services per person). This is exactly what happened in the agricultural revolution that began in the Middle East after the last ice age, with the development of animal husbandry, and after the development of metallurgy, especially iron (see Volume 1, Chapter 1). In the First Industrial Revolution, productivity grew even more rapidly than in these earlier leaps forward. In most countries that lived through it, however, living standards initially fell or stagnated for decades. Not until the twentieth century did the majority of the people living in the industrial countries begin to experience the sustained improvements in living standards and well-being made possible by the Industrial Revolution.

6.2 WHY THE WEST BEFORE THE REST?

Historians have long debated and continue to debate why sustained economic growth began in Northwestern Europe and the United States (see Map 6.1). Until World War II, many historians and social scientists saw economic modernization as a uniquely Western achievement. For some, it "proved" that Northern Europeans and their New World descendants were racially or culturally superior to others. Asians, Africans, Middle Easterners, Native Americans, even Europeans from Southern and Eastern Europe did not have the capacity, it was argued, to think logically, solve complex scientific and technological problems, or manage large organizations – all indispensable for economic growth and industrialization. Others emphasized the importance of climate, religion, or culture, but still sought to explain why Westerners could and non-Westerners could never succeed economically (except under Western tutelage).

Since the premise of this question was false, the answers had to be wrong. By the end of the twentieth century, examples of economic modernization could be found on every continent. Every climate, race, and culture could point to economic successes comparable to the Industrial Revolution in Europe. The recognition that rapid modernization can occur in many once backward regions had two major effects on the debate about the causes of the original Industrial Revolution. First, it pushed

aside old-fashioned efforts to find the secret of the West's success in some deeply embedded genetic or cultural trait. Second, the question historians now seek to answer is a narrower one: What made it possible for Britain (joined soon by the United States and most of Northwestern Europe) to get a hundred-year head start on the rest of the world?

The answer to this question lies in a unique combination of positive developments that occurred first in Britain and then in the North Atlantic region generally in the era leading up to the First Industrial Revolution. By the eighteenth century, Britain and its settlement colonies in North America, along with several other European nations, shared four important prerequisites for economic modernization with the empires of Spain, China, India, and the Ottoman empire. These were:

- A stable and effective government.
- A productive agriculture capable of supporting increased urbanization.
- Abundant and accessible natural resources.
- An interest and capacity to engage in long-distance trade.

These characteristics were not unique to Britain and its colonies or Northwestern Europe in 1700. Most other prosperous regions of the world boasted all four. The Mughal regime in India faced more internal political problems than the others, Spanish and Ottoman agriculture may have been less productive, both the Ottomans and the Mughals lacked iron and coal, and the Chinese interest in foreign trade lagged behind the others. Nonetheless, these prosperous regions rivaled the British in meeting these necessary prerequisites for economic modernization.

How Sustained Economic Growth Got Started

These four achievements were necessary but not sufficient conditions for achieving sustained economic growth. The British and their American colonists possessed and their nearby neighbors in Northwestern Europe soon acquired three additional advantages that the great land-based empires did not have. These were:

- A set of institutions that made rulers obey laws that protected property-holders from confiscation and other arbitrary acts and made governments attentive to the interests of profit-seeking producers and merchants.
- A literate and thus more mobile and inventive population.
- An efficient internal transport system of canals, rivers, and paved roads that brought a major portion of each nation's population and natural resources into contact with both domestic and international markets.

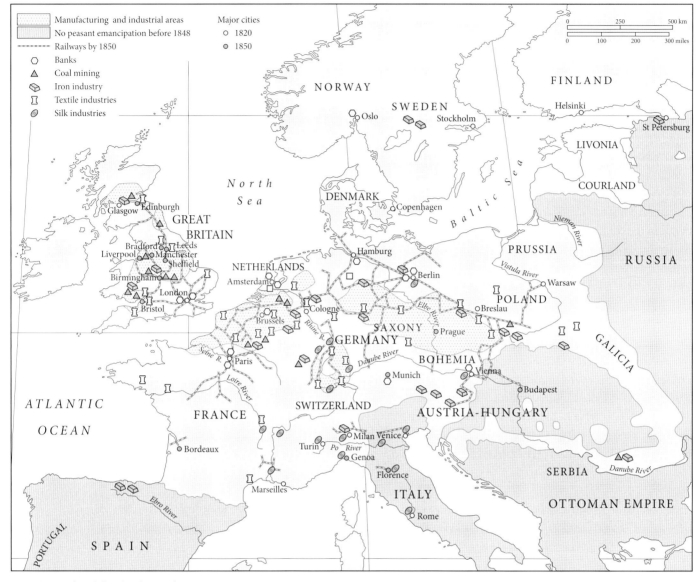

Map 6.1 Industrialization in Northwestern Europe

These three conditions did not exist outside the small circle of early modernizing countries in the North Atlantic. Many thinkers and even government officials in imperial Spain, late Ming China, Mughal India, and the Ottoman empire recognized the need for change and reform in the eighteenth century or even earlier, but every effort at reform in these countries failed. Reformers in all the great empires sought to modernize military forces, streamline administration, make tax collection more efficient, and promote useful and productive economic activities. Though sophisticated in organization and in their capacity to mobilize human and material resources across great distances, these governments never adopted the self-limiting features of the English parliamentary regime. Their economic goals always fell victim to other priorities. In the end, more effective armies supporting more efficient administrators in collecting ever

higher taxes discouraged entrepreneurial initiative and cut off economic advance. In many cases, reforms (like many of the Bourbon reforms in the Spanish empire between 1765 and 1808) actually discouraged economic activity by imposing new regulations, monopolies, and taxes.

Popular literacy in Britain and Northwestern Europe was first spread by dissident religious sects. Most European elites initially viewed popular literacy as a kind of vulgar pretension by inferiors who had no legitimate need to read books. Schooling was encouraged mainly by weak governments looking for support and religious institutions faced with stiff competition, because growing numbers of people found literacy valuable and insisted on having it.

Internal transportation along coastlines and up great rivers helped to unify most land-based empires. In the Spanish empire, communications stretched across the Atlantic Ocean. In China, the concentration of population along the Yellow and Yangtze rivers, and the construction of the Grand Canal that linked them in the sixth century, facilitated internal trade and communications. In all of these empires, however, only a tiny minority produced for distant markets and even fewer engaged in production for export. Most of the population of these empires lived too far from a river, canal, or seaport to benefit from trade with distant places. In contrast, virtually all of the British population in the late seventeenth century lived within 70 miles of the sea and within 30 miles of a navigable river or canal. The same was true for the Netherlands, Belgium, and the British colonies in North America. A major portion of the population of Northwestern Europe also lived near waterways or the sea.

Nonetheless, the more advanced areas of Spain, China, India, and the Middle East could have industrialized before Britain and Northwestern Europe and very nearly did so. The authorities could have diverted some tax revenues to patronize the development and use of new technologies (as they had done in the past), help finance new enterprises, improve internal transport systems, and mobilize workforces. This is exactly what happened later in a number of the countries that industrialized after 1850, including Germany, Japan, Russia, and China. In the eighteenth century, however, the reformers in these empires sought mainly to strengthen centralized authority, improve imperial finances, and modernize military forces. Economic modernization came later.

6.3 ECONOMIC MODERNIZATION IN HOLLAND AND ENGLAND

From ancient times to the eighteenth century, every period of economic advance seemed to end in disaster. In 1798, **Thomas Robert Malthus** (1766–1834), the brilliant English clergyman, wrote his famous *Essay on the Principles of Population as It Affects the Future Improvement of Society* to explain why this had happened throughout history. Malthus argued that population tended to grow geometrically while food production increased arithmetically. Only "vice and misery" kept population in check through warfare, disease, and famine. Living standards could never be kept above subsistence for long. Misguided efforts to improve the lot of the poor merely encouraged procreation and hastened the day when the food supply would fall below subsistence. Cycles of population increase followed by food crises condemned humankind to perpetual poverty. Small wonder Malthus inspired the description of economics as the "dismal science."

Malthus's observations seemed to be borne out by contemporary evidence. Seventeenth-century Europe appeared to be undergoing just the kind of long-term depression with attendant demographic pressures that Malthus had theorized. But two European countries did not suffer this decline. The Netherlands (or Dutch Republic) and Britain both escaped the cycle of expansion and decline that has been labeled the "Malthusian Trap." The English and Dutch economies continued to grow in the seventeenth century because of three mutually reinforcing and unprecedented revolutions in governance, in popular literacy, and in transportation.

Revolution in Governance

When England's **Glorious Revolution** of 1688 finally established the supremacy of the law and Parliament over the Crown, it guaranteed not only a more stable and representative government, but also a government more responsive than ever before to the needs of profit-seeking businessmen, landowners, tradesmen, merchants, shopkeepers, artisans, and manufacturers. After 1688, England had a government controlled by an elite of property-holders willing to write new laws and create new institutions to enrich themselves, their constituents, and, they believed, their nation as well. The Scottish moral philosopher, Adam Smith, provided a theoretical framework for limited government that is cited by economists to this day (see Box 6.1). The English government ceased to work primarily as a revenue machine for enriching the monarch, as in most of the rest of the world. Instead, the government respected citizens' property, refrained from levying overly burdensome taxes and forced loans, created courts that enforced business contracts (though not always impartially), aggressively promoted colonial expansion and overseas trade, and actively encouraged investment in transport facilities like ports and canals. Patent legislation, beginning with the Statute of Artificers (1624), protected inventors and assisted them in getting paid by those who used their inventions.

Parliamentary supremacy would not have worked so well, however, without the development of a unique judicial system that effectively protected individual rights and private property against government interference and abuse. The English common law formed the basis of the system. It consisted of an evolving body of principles derived originally from mixing Anglo-Saxon customs and Roman law. Over time, these principles and extensions of them came to be embodied in court decisions (precedents) respected by both Crown and Parliament. The common law thus created an environment in which citizens could feel free to pursue any moneymaking economic activity not expressly prohibited by Parliament. Moreover, common-law principles soon came to be applied to disputes between citizens over money, property, and contracts

Box 6.1 Ideological Foundations of Capitalism

Adam Smith (1723–90), a professor of logic at the University of Glasgow, is often cited as the founding father of modern economics. Smith published his monumental work *The Wealth of Nations* in 1776. The most cited passage of this work argued that individuals should be free to pursue private gain because in a capitalist economy the "invisible hand" of the market ensures that society will benefit:

As every individual endeavors as much as he can to employ his capital in support of domestic industry, and so to direct that industry that its produce may be of the greatest value; every individual necessarily labours to render the annual revenue of the society as great as he can. He generally, indeed, neither intends to promote the public interest, nor knows how much he is promoting it … he intends

only his own gain, and he is in this, as in many other cases, led by an invisible hand to promote an end which was no part of his intention. Nor is it always the worse for the society that it was no part of it. By pursuing his own interest he frequently promotes that of the society more effectually than when he really intends to promote it.

in increasingly uniform and predictable ways. The common law gave Britain an important advantage over other countries where arbitrary government, poorly defined property rights, and inefficient judiciaries made entrepreneurial activity more risky and thus more costly.

Holland achieved a revolution in governance comparable to England's when it proclaimed its independence from Spain in 1568. The Dutch Republic as it was then known (today the Netherlands), together with modern Belgium and Luxembourg, comprise what are still called the "Low Countries." When the northern predominantly Protestant and Dutch-speaking provinces revolted against Spanish rule, political power passed to self-perpetuating town councils dominated by prosperous merchants and a few of the larger landowners. The merchant oligarchs of the Dutch cities granted protections to individuals and their property similar to those in England. They also promoted the development of intensive agriculture, built an impressive network of canals to foster internal trade, pursued foreign trade opportunities aggressively, and aided local artisans and manufacturers.

Eventually, other countries adopted constitutional and judicial mechanisms to encourage profit-seeking economic activity similar to those pioneered in England and the Dutch Republic. The United States retained all of the key English institutions when it became independent. The French Revolution proclaimed, and Napoleon's invading armies imposed throughout Europe, new laws and legal codes designed to clarify property rights and protect citizens, especially propertied citizens, from arbitrary treatment. The legal systems of most of the contemporary capitalist world are modeled after either the English common law system (the United States as well as other former British colonies, such as Canada, Australia, New Zealand, India, Pakistan, Ghana, and Kenya) or the Napoleonic Codes

of 1802–04 (most of Western Europe, all of Latin America, former French and Portuguese colonies in Africa and Asia).

Revolution in Literacy

Protestantism and the printing press made Britain and the Netherlands the most literate societies in the world by 1700, with England's thirteen North American colonies and several other European countries (France, most of the north German states, and Sweden) not far behind. Protestant groups emphasized Bible reading. Catholic regions that bordered on predominantly Protestant areas followed suit. Literacy rates for women lagged behind those of men in most cases but schooling for girls rose steadily between 1700 and 1850. By 1800, more than 80 percent of all non-slave adults in the United States, 50 to 60 percent in Britain and the Netherlands, and 50 percent in France could read and write.

In Britain the government tolerated the spread of literacy and schooling, but did little to encourage it until the nineteenth century. Various Protestant sects helped to raise the desire of parents to see their children educated. By the late eighteenth century, however, only half of the nation's children (mostly boys) attended school. Two thirds of the children who did go to school attended for-profit private schools. Most of the rest received support from charitable societies and local churches. Many children learned a rudimentary version of the three R's from parents, relatives, or neighbors. Secondary schools were not widespread, though high quality "dissenting academies" spread widely in the eighteenth century. A disproportionate number of inventors and innovators during the British Industrial Revolution graduated from these institutions. Government support for schools did not become widespread until the late nineteenth century. Britain's revolution in government, which lowered the risks for entrepreneurs and encouraged their creativity, did little for education.

By contrast, the influence of dissenting Protestants in the thirteen British colonies in North America led to government support for primary schools, particularly in New England, though for-profit private schools predominated along with charity schools for the poor in the other colonies. The Southern slave colonies lagged in educating free white children and did nothing to educate slaves or Native Americans. In Northwestern Europe, literacy and schooling spread first in the Protestant Dutch Republic and northern Germany, then in Belgium and France. Here, too, private for-profit schools predominated, with church and charity schools for a minority of poor children. In Southern and Eastern Europe, literacy rates stayed well below the 30 percent threshold modern analysts consider minimal for economic growth until the late nineteenth or early twentieth century.

Literacy had three crucial effects on economic growth. First, literate people were likely to be more productive and efficient, even at relatively simple tasks. In England and the thirteen colonies, the apprenticeship system in many skilled crafts and the spread of on-the-job training in other occupations made literacy helpful, and often crucial, to raising productivity. Literate apprentices and workers could make lists, follow written instructions, learn more easily from the experience of others, send messages, and use arithmetic to keep track of output and costs.

Second, literacy made people more mobile, more likely to learn about distant opportunities and to move in search of better paying (and more productive) jobs. Educating women amplified this effect by making them less fearful of moving, even when they did not work outside the home.

Third, literacy and education encouraged people to change, to look for better ways to accomplish given tasks, to tinker and reorganize their work. While histories of the Industrial Revolution have tended to focus on a small number of key inventions and technological breakthroughs (like the spinning jenny, steam engine, and railroad), most of the gains in output per worker between 1700 and 1850 came from the thousands of untold improvements and micro inventions that multiplied throughout the economy. Sometimes referred to as **subinnovation**, this process could not have occurred on such a broad front in an illiterate population.

Transportation Revolution

After 1700, the British surpassed even the Dutch both in developing a superior road system and in canal-building. By 1730, Britain had nearly 900 miles of turnpikes, but this was still a small number compared to the 15,000 miles of

such roads created by over 500 Acts of Parliament during the "turnpike mania" in the 1750s. When the Industrial Revolution accelerated in the late eighteenth century, the British road system was the best in the world – ideal for transporting high value freight and people in a hurry.

The British invested even more in water transport. Navigable waterways (rivers plus canals) grew from 685 miles in 1660 to 1,160 miles in 1730 and 3,960 miles by 1830. At first the British concentrated on dredging channels and extending navigation on the country's extensive river system. As with the turnpikes, Parliament granted private companies the right to recoup their costs by charging tolls to shippers. Unlike the Dutch and other continental countries, however, they relied on private companies to finance and build the canals as well as to operate and maintain them. Acts of Parliament gave private companies the right to take property (with compensation), sell shares or borrow to raise funds, build canals along approved routes, and collect tolls. Most canals were built in the late eighteenth century and early nineteenth century. In addition to rivers and canals, the British also expanded coastal shipping, exploiting the country's unusually large number of natural harbors. England's extensive network of turnpikes, navigable rivers, and canals, together with its busy coastal trade, propelled the country forward. Eighteenth-century Britain had the most efficient and well-connected domestic market in the world.

No other country in the world could rival the English transportation network by the late eighteenth century. The Dutch, however, had developed an extensive system of canals in the seventeenth century, while the thirteen colonies and much of Northwestern Europe were able to rely on extensive river systems. Not until the extensive canal-building of the 1820s to 1840s and the construction of railroad lines beginning in the 1840s did the transport systems of these countries rival that of Britain.

How Did the British Get Ahead of the Dutch?

By 1700, the Dutch Republic had a government of laws that promoted private enterprise, a highly literate population, and a canal system rivaling that of England. Despite these parallels up to 1700, however, the British surged ahead during the eighteenth century. How did this happen?

The British had three main advantages over the Dutch. First, England had more people and more of the key natural resources, like iron and coal, needed for industry.

Second, the Dutch therefore continued to focus their efforts on the carrying trade, transporting mostly what others produced.

This strategy failed. The Dutch were drawn into a series of costly naval wars against powerful adversaries, including Spain, Portugal, and eventually even England. The other colonial powers succeeded in excluding Dutch merchants and shipping from their colonies. The Indian Ocean trade in luxuries, where the Dutch had forced aside the Portuguese, stayed small. Dutch trade and economic life stagnated from the 1670s until the middle of the eighteenth century. Dutch government, social life, and religious practice became defensive and conservative, looking to solve problems with monopolies, regulation, and stricter rules of conduct. This strategy also failed.

Third, just as the Dutch turned to enforcing Calvinist orthodoxy, England moved toward greater tolerance after the Glorious Revolution of 1688. The Dutch environment became less encouraging to innovation, just as the English were embracing experimentation and invention.

6.4 ECONOMIC REVOLUTION IN BRITAIN

Though no one alive in 1700 could see it clearly, England had managed to bring together all the essential elements needed to achieve an unprecedented increase in the productivity of its economy. The country had already experienced a fundamental political transition. It had a government that viewed profit-making business as respectable and beneficial, rather than an opportunity for predatory taxation. The English common law and the country's unwritten constitution, enforced by a still corrupt but increasingly independent judiciary, protected subjects' rights to engage in economic activity and to profit from their inventions without arbitrary government interference. Encouraged by the spread of literacy and official tolerance for diverse and even new ideas, and motivated by a practical curiosity as well as the lure of wealth and fame, Britons found or imported solutions to a host of difficult mechanical and technical problems. Better protected and educated than any other such group in the world, British landowners, merchants, artisans, shopkeepers, and profit seekers of all kinds put their money to work in ways that made the British economy ever more productive, aided by the best internal transport system, the largest merchant fleet, and one of the most productive agricultural systems in the world.

The British economy began growing steadily at a rate of perhaps half a percent per year a decade or two before 1700. Despite occasional panics and recessions and the disruptions of frequent wars, productivity rose year after year, decade after decade. At half a percent per year, GDP per capita will double in just over a century. This is approximately what happened in Britain between the 1680s and 1800. In the first

half of the nineteenth century, Britain's rate of economic growth rose to more than 1 percent per year. By 1850, GDP per capita had doubled again to a level four times higher than in 1700.

Growth in Agriculture and Trade

Even before industrial growth took off, Britain experienced an agricultural revolution in the eighteenth century that helped the economy grow. The British agricultural revolution involved enclosing arable open fields farmed by long-term tenants and converting them either to pasture for improved breeds of sheep and cattle or to the production of commercial crops, including fodder for animals. The enclosure movement actually began much earlier, but reached a peak in the enclosures ordered by acts of Parliament between 1760 and 1815. Agriculture became more efficient, producing more and more with fewer and fewer hands.

The displaced tenants and their families often had no choice but to migrate to urban slums in search of day laboring jobs or factory work. Population growth in this era made this problem even worse. The increases in unskilled (or country-skilled) workers seeking employment in the cities kept wages down and made investing in manufacturing all the more profitable. The Industrial Revolution might have been delayed or stopped altogether if Britain had lacked an urban workforce and the food to feed it.

The overseas commercial revolution that followed the discoveries of the fifteenth and sixteenth centuries helped set the stage, and then facilitated the Industrial Revolution in four main ways. First, it validated and reinforced the institutional changes that gave merchants and their interests a key role in government. Commercial success inspired the English government to push the reforms further and forced others to imitate, even if reluctantly. Second, expanding trade provided Europe with cheap foodstuffs and raw materials. This added calories to the diet of masses of consumers, supplied dyestuffs, cotton, and other inputs to industry, and in British North America secured strategic materials, like timber and pitch, for shipbuilding. Third, the commercial revolution made many merchants and producers rich, rich enough to invest in all manner of new enterprises, not only factories, but also farms, canals, and eventually railroads. Finally, the sheer magnitude of the transatlantic trade bred specialization and division of labor. Merchant firms and even entire ports specialized in the trade of a single product or region. Maritime insurance, commercial credit, warehousing and wholesale trading, accounting techniques, partnership contracts, news gathering and communications, and a host of other activities became more efficient.

The African slave trade and the sugar trade from the Caribbean constituted major components of the eighteenth-century commercial boom. Economic historians used to believe that this ugly chapter in Britain's global profit-seeking had little to do with stimulating or financing the Industrial Revolution. Recently, however, they have returned to the thesis of Eric Williams (1911–81), the historian and descendant of slaves who became the first prime minister of Trinidad and Tobago. Williams argued that slavery in the Caribbean and the United States played a pivotal role in British economic growth. Slave traders, sugar merchants, and absentee plantation owners in England invested their profits in the new industries. British factories exported their textiles and other products to Africa in exchange for slaves and to the Americas in exchange for slave-produced sugar, tobacco, and cotton. The Industrial Revolution would certainly have occurred without the profits and export markets provided by slavery, but might well have started later and taken longer to accomplish.

The First Industrial Revolution, 1760–1830

The Industrial Revolution in Britain was the first ever in the history of the world. This First Industrial Revolution built cloth factories and other light industries (shoes, paper, soap, leather goods, and beer) along with iron works, machine foundries, railroads, and telegraph lines. Coal fueled the First Industrial Revolution and its steam engines, along with traditional water and wind power.

No one knows exactly when the First Industrial Revolution began in Britain. Industrial output grew at about the same rate as the rest of the economy for most of the eighteenth century. In the 1760s, however, British inventors began producing a series of breakthrough technological innovations. The number of patents issued for new inventions rose from a record-setting 200 in the 1760s to 2,433 by the 1830s. Technological innovation became almost routine. By 1800, productivity in several branches of industry was rising so fast that manufacturing had become the main engine of economic growth. By 1830, industrial growth had transformed the country.

Even so, many historians have challenged the idea of an industrial revolution. Instead they argue that overall British economic growth in this era was not rapid by modern standards and that British industry did not grow much faster than the economy as a whole. Differing perspectives rather than facts may account for some of this debate. The First Industrial Revolution took a half-century or so to transform the English economy. Today this pace seems almost leisurely, even if the cumulative impact amounted to a huge and unprecedented transformation.

The most important technological breakthroughs of the First Industrial Revolution occurred in three areas:

- The development and refinement of the steam engine for use in mining, manufacturing, and transportation.
- The invention of machines to spin thread and weave cloth.
- The discovery of new methods to produce better iron more cheaply.

Of course, technological change occurred across a much broader range of industries and services as the Industrial Revolution advanced. The chemical industry, for example, developed bleaches and dyes for manufacturing textiles, key ingredients for making paper and leather goods, and explosives for mining and weapons. The technological breakthroughs that had the greatest impact on productivity, however, were steam engines, advances in thread- and cloth-making, and new techniques for producing cheap iron.

The Steam Engine

The steam engine dwarfed all the other technological breakthroughs of the First Industrial Revolution. Until its invention and refinement, all human economic activity depended on animal (including human) muscle power, wind, or gravity (falling water or weights) to move machinery. All of these energy sources were expensive and none was very reliable. Animals had to be fed and suffered from fatigue and injury, winds shifted by the minute or died, waterfalls dried up when rains failed. The steam engine made it possible to use heat to produce reliable, continuous motion at low cost.

Thomas Newcomen, blacksmith and ironworker in Dartmouth, England, designed the first atmospheric steam engine in 1705, hoping to power a pump that could drain water from mine shafts more reliably and efficiently than horses. The two key ideas embodied in the new machine were not new: steam to create a vacuum in a sealed chamber and a piston to operate a pump. Putting the two together was Newcomen's idea. He built a contraption that forced steam into one end of a cylinder (see Figure 6.2). The steam pushed a piston up. Then he cooled that cylinder by pouring cold water on it. The steam in the cylinder condensed into water, creating a vacuum. Air pressure then pushed the piston back down the cylinder. The up and down motion of the piston then operated a simple mechanical pump. After further tinkering and refinement, Newcomen put his steam-operated pump into operation in 1712.

The Newcomen machine consumed large quantities of coal and water, which made it practical to use in coal mines located near lakes and rivers, but difficult and costly to adapt to other locations and for other purposes. The Scotsman **James Watt**

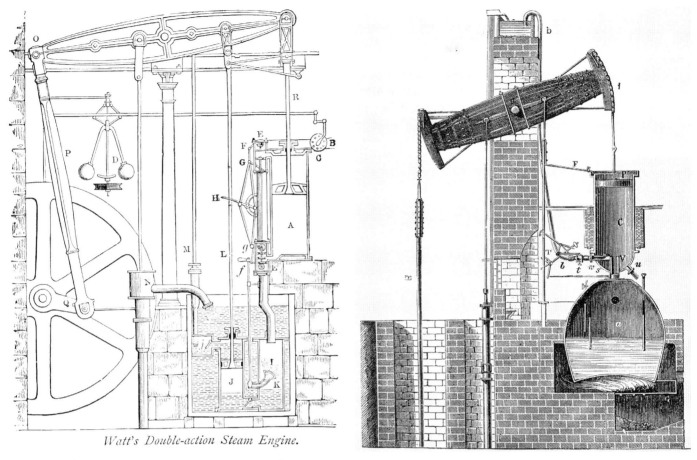

Watt's Double-action Steam Engine.

Figure 6.2 This diagram shows how James Watt modified Thomas Newcomen's steam engine by creating two chambers (one for the piston, the other for producing steam). The piston could be forced up by pumping steam into the piston cylinder, then moved back down with cool water from a condenser. The continuous movement of the piston made the difference. The illustration also shows the "steam digester," a forerunner of the steam engine, invented by French physicist and inventor Denis Papin in 1690.

made the two key modifications that turned the steam engine into a versatile and cost-effective industrial motor. In 1765 he built a machine with two separate chambers, one for the piston and the other for heating the water to make steam. Instead of alternately heating and cooling the same cylinder, the Watt machine made steam continuously in one chamber, from which controlled amounts were forced into the piston cylinder. As soon as this pushed the piston up, the piston cylinder could be water-cooled to create the vacuum and push it back down. Then, for the new cycle, steam from the chamber could be instantly forced into the piston cylinder again. It was not necessary, as it had been in the Newcomen machine, to reheat the piston cylinder all over again. This modification cut the fuel needed to run the Watt engine to less than a quarter of the amount needed by the Newcomen machine.

The second modification was equally ingenious: in 1782 Watt added a rotary mechanism and flywheel that converted the up and down motion of the piston into a smooth and continuous circular motion. Watt received a patent for his engine in 1769; it was first put to commercial use in 1776. Suddenly, it became feasible to substitute steam power for muscle, wind, and water.

As further refinements made steam engines ever more powerful and efficient, the new technology spread to manufacturing and transportation with spectacular effects on productivity. In manufacturing, the new spinning and weaving machines, first powered by water, eventually used steam engines to increase output dramatically.

Steam-powered Ships and Railroads

In transportation, steam engines were first adapted for use on ships. In 1807, the US entrepreneur **Robert Fulton** built and successfully tested the *Clermont*, the first practical steam-driven ship, which he steamed up the Hudson River against the current from New York City to Albany in only 33 hours. The new technology spread rapidly, incorporating improvements and

Figure 6.3 The Liverpool and Manchester Railway was the world's first scheduled twin-track inter-urban passenger railway. It began carrying passengers (and freight) between the port of Liverpool and the factory town of Manchester on September 15, 1830. The Age of the Railroad had begun.

LIVERPOOL AND MANCHESTER RAILWAY 1830

modifications with each new craft. Steamships were first used extensively for river navigation, especially in the United States on the Mississippi River and its tributaries. The first Atlantic crossing by a ship equipped with a steam engine (in addition to sails) was in 1818. The first all-steam vessel crossing was in 1826. Though fast and reliable, steamships were costly to operate because fuel took up much of the cargo space. Sailing ships continued to compete with steamships for slow-moving freight business for another half-century.

The Englishman **George Stephenson** (1771–1833) first adapted the steam engine to power railway wagons in 1814, but his first model featured a stationary engine that used long cables to pull coal wagons. In 1825, Stephenson installed and tested the world's first steam-powered locomotive on tracks used by animal trains to haul coal between Stockton and Darlington. Five years later, the first common carrier line opened between Liverpool and Manchester (shown in Figure 6.3), just as the first railroads in France and the United States opened using British-built locomotives. Though more expensive than water transportation, railroads were much cheaper than wagons pulled by animals. They carried bulky freight as well as passengers more quickly and reliably than wagons, barges, or ships. And unlike rivers and canals, railroads did not freeze over and shut down for months at a time in winter. Railroad construction took off in Britain and the United States in the 1830s and in the rest of Europe in the 1840s.

Railroads transformed space and time. Distances that once took weeks could now be managed in a day or two. Great expanses of land and rich mineral deposits once too far from a river, canal, or coastline to exploit profitably now came into reach. In countries lacking navigable rivers where canals could not be built (including much of Asia, Africa, Russia, and Latin America), the railroad had its greatest impact.

Textile Manufacturing

Textiles constituted the leading and largest consumer goods industry of the First Industrial Revolution for three reasons. First, in temperate climates, keeping warm requires some clothing for most of the year, so the potential demand for cheap cloth was high. Second, British (and some Belgian, Dutch, and French) textile artisans, mechanics, and inventors pioneered the development of new mechanical devices that enormously increased output per worker. Third, steam engines then made it possible to drive textile-manufacturing processes at unheard-of speeds, which increased productivity still more.

Until the Industrial Revolution, most of the world's population dressed, when they dressed at all, in animal skins and coarse homemade cloth. In temperate climates, woolen cloth predominated. In hotter climes, people used rough cotton fabrics. The great cloth-making industries of the pre-industrial world specialized in making cloth for clothing or tapestries for an elite clientele. In Europe common folk either raised sheep for wool or bought raw wool in a local market and processed it at home.

Processing raw materials into clothes required four steps. First, the raw fibers (wool, flax, linen, cotton) had to be cleaned and prepared. Raw wool was hardest of all to get clean. It had to be boiled in a solution of water and lye to get rid of dirt, fat, and oils. The work was so strenuous, filthy, and dangerous that in some parts of the world only slaves, forced laborers, or convicts did it. Once cleaned and dried, the dense masses of wool had to be pulled apart to remove other impurities. The wool was then dyed or bleached, dried again and fluffed or carded to make it pliable enough to work with. Second, the carded wool had to be twisted and shaped into yarn or coarse thread. Each of these steps required considerable skill to do well for wool as well as other fibers. Flax had to be cleaned, soaked, and softened before spinning, while cotton and especially silk tended to break and come apart. Making small amounts of thread took huge amounts of time. Third, the thread had to be woven by hand into cloth using a handloom, a time-consuming mechanical process that took days just to produce a single piece of fabric. The final step was to sew pieces of cloth together according to a pattern to produce a wearable item of clothing.

Technological breakthroughs beginning in the 1760s revolutionized three of the four steps required to turn raw fiber into clothing. By 1830 only the last step, that of making clothes from cloth, was still done mainly at home. Even the invention of the sewing machine in 1846 did not change this immediately. The revolution came first in cotton textiles, because the new mechanical devices worked best with cotton. The innovations were sparked by a series of early eighteenth-century improvements in weaving, especially the flying shuttle developed in 1733 that allowed one worker rather than two to operate a large loom. The ensuing increase in cloth production created a demand for more thread.

Experiments with many different devices and fibers from the 1730s to the 1760s finally yielded the **spinning jenny**, invented by **James Hargreaves** in 1764. This ingenious contraption replaced the spinning wheel, because it allowed a single operator to supervise a machine that produced eight to eleven threads instead of one. Refinements raised that number to between twenty and thirty.

However, thread produced in this way was too soft and weak to be used for the tough vertical threads (called the warp) required on most looms. In 1769 **Richard Arkwright** solved this problem with a machine called a spinning frame (later known as a water frame) or throstle, which used successive pairs of rollers pulling the cotton, each at a faster speed, while twisting it onto bobbins. Finally, in 1779, **Samuel Crompton** patented the **spinning mule**, a refinement to the water frame that made it possible to spin thread at high tension to produce a finer as well as stronger thread. The water frame with the Crompton mule quickly began producing thread of exceptional strength and consistency. Moreover, it could be operated by remote power. The first water frames used horses or water. By 1785, the first steam-powered water frame went into use. In less than twenty years, these new machines made it possible for a single worker to produce more thread than a hundred workers had produced earlier.

The next bottleneck turned out to be the supply of cotton. English factories could now produce immense quantities of good quality cotton thread so cheaply that cloth and clothing prices fell sharply and sales shot up. But cotton could not be grown in England. It had to be imported in bulk from warmer areas, like India, Egypt, Brazil, and the Southern United States. High quality long-fiber cotton that worked best on the new machines could be grown cheaply, but was costly to clean and pack for shipment by sea. **Eli Whitney** (1765–1825) in the United States solved this problem when he invented the cotton gin in 1793. This power-driven machine removed seeds, dirt, and other debris from the cotton and made it easy to pack it in bales for shipping. Whitney's cotton gin suddenly made large-scale cotton-growing on slave plantations a highly profitable business in the United States.

The last bottleneck in the textile industry began to dissolve after an amateur inventor with no trade experience, the Rev. **Edmund Cartwright**, invented a power loom in 1785. With various improvements and modifications into the 1820s, his invention transformed cloth-making from a painfully slow process, in which every thread had to be hand strung or woven, into a mechanized process in which a single worker could operate a dozen or more fast weaving machines. The English textile industry produced barely £500,000 worth of cloth per year in the 1770s. By 1800, output surpassed £5 million and continued to grow explosively for another twenty years. Though the new technology eventually revolutionized the production of wool, linen, and silk textiles as well, nothing could match the mass market for cotton thread and cotton cloth both at home and abroad.

Ironmaking

The transformation in ironmaking during the First Industrial Revolution came suddenly, after centuries of trial and error. Three key innovations helped to raise the quality, lower the price, and dramatically increase the output of the British iron industry between 1700 and 1850. The first was the discovery in 1709 by **Abraham Darby** at Coalbrookdale that coke made from coal could be used in place of charcoal in the smelting of iron ore. Heating coal under controlled conditions removed impurities and left coke. England had abundant coal, used mainly for home heating, but the country's forests were fast disappearing. Wood for making charcoal had become so expensive that it was driving up the cost of producing iron. It took decades, however, before further experimentation by trial and error refined Darby's discovery and made it possible to produce high quality iron with coke. The second major advance came with the discovery that coke worked best in larger furnaces. This inspired a series of improvements in furnace design that culminated with the adaptation of the Watt steam engine in 1776 to operate the bellows at John Wilkinson's huge furnace in Shropshire. The third great innovation came soon thereafter when **Henry Cort** patented in 1783 and 1784 a method of puddling and rolling the iron that greatly decreased the cost of making malleable, wrought iron.

These innovations in ironmaking made it possible by 1800 to produce a wide variety of tools, weapons, and other items of mass consumption more cheaply. They also led to the production of **capital goods** at lower cost. Capital goods consist of the machinery and equipment used to produce other products, such as spinning and weaving machines, steam engines, and blast furnaces. British iron production rose from 17,350 tons in 1740 to 125,079 tons on the outbreak of war with France in 1796. As new furnace designs and processing innovations took hold, iron production rose to 678,417 long tons by 1830. When railroad construction took off, iron production doubled in the 1830s and doubled again in the 1840s. By 1852, Britain produced a record 2,701,000 tons of iron, much of it in the shape of rails for new railroad lines as well as railroad cars and steam engines.

6.5 ECONOMIC GROWTH IN THE UNITED STATES AND NORTHWESTERN EUROPE

In 1800, GDP per capita in the United States and France stood at about 70 percent of the British level, still not much ahead of the more prosperous areas of Southern Europe, the Middle East, India, or China. Between 1800 and 1850, however, economic growth accelerated first in the United States and then in Northwestern Europe. By 1850, Britain's neighbors in the North Atlantic had joined the Industrial Revolution and, like Britain, leaped ahead of the rest of the world.

As the British economy grew, entrepreneurs and politicians in other countries sought to adopt and adapt the British innovations in technology and organization. The first to seek to

duplicate British advances were nearby rivals and former colonies: the United States and France, then Belgium, the Netherlands, and some of the German states. Merchants, scientists, spies, and travelers of all kinds reported on British developments and tried to duplicate them. British entrepreneurs meanwhile were even quicker to capitalize on mechanical or technological advances elsewhere.

British legislation attempted to impede the spread of industrialization to other countries and regions. Parliament outlawed the export of technical information, imposed heavy criminal penalties for industrial espionage, forbade emigration of skilled mechanics and others with knowledge of the new technologies until 1824, and banned the export of industrial machinery until 1843. Various laws prohibited the establishment of competing industries in Britain's growing colonial empire. Nothing worked. The technology of the First Industrial Revolution was relatively simple and easy to replicate. Technological information – plans, blueprints, instructions – could be understood by any literate individual with experience making or operating machinery. While many of the breakthrough inventions of 1760 to 1830 came from British workshops, a steady stream of adaptations and independent discoveries was also occurring in the United States and several other European countries.

Governance, Literacy, and Transportation

Duplicating the English success was not easy. The Industrial Revolution spread only to those countries that could replicate the conditions that had enabled the British economy to grow for so many decades beginning in the late seventeenth century. Only the United States fulfilled all those conditions, though several other countries in Northwestern Europe soon followed.

The United States inherited the protections of the English common law and made some of them explicit in a written constitution, though indigenous peoples and slaves of African descent were denied access to rights and protections as well as education. The new US government created a judicial system modeled after that of Britain and pursued policies aimed at encouraging productive private enterprise. The United States had also experienced a revolution in literacy comparable to that of Britain by the eighteenth century.

A long coastline and navigable rivers also gave the United States an efficient system of internal transportation even before it began building canals and railroads. After independence, turnpikes were created to link major towns, beginning in the 1790s. Then in the 1820s, a series of canals were built to connect the eastern states with the trans-Appalachian west. The first and most successful was the 363 mile Erie Canal, finished in 1825. By mid-century, the United States had built a total of 3,698 miles of canals. Then came steamships and railroads. Soon after Robert Fulton built the first successful steamship, river steamers began operating on the Mississippi River and its numerous tributaries. Railroad construction beginning in the 1830s helped to further unite the large country. By 1850, 8,879 miles of track had been laid with rails produced by the rapidly growing iron industry.

In Western Europe, only the Netherlands could boast a government that protected and encouraged private economic initiative as effectively as Britain in 1700. In most areas, absolutist monarchs reigned above the law, defending aristocratic privilege and making enterprise more costly and risky until after the French Revolution of 1789 when French armies precipitated the collapse of absolutist regimes throughout Europe.

High literacy rates and improved internal transportation systems also facilitated economic growth in Northwestern Europe. The Dutch had pioneered in both areas but were held back by the need to import crucial raw materials like coal and iron. Belgium, which had both, surged ahead. France and the German states had high literacy rates, but their relatively extensive river and canal systems missed important regions and resources.

Outside of the North Atlantic, conditions for economic growth did not improve. In most of Latin America, independence freed the Spanish and Portuguese colonies from trade monopolies and new constitutions imitated the French and US examples, but social and political strife complicated by international warfare postponed economic growth in most of the new countries for a half-century or more. Reform efforts in Qing China, Mughal India, and the Ottoman empire concentrated on futile attempts to restore vitality to old regimes by raising taxes and modernizing armies. Literacy and schooling remained confined to small elites and the lack of navigable rivers and canals in most areas kept internal transportation systems dependent on camels, mules, and wagons.

Economic Growth in the Thirteen Colonies

The economic development of the United States differed from the British pattern in three main ways. First, the thirteen colonies that declared their independence in 1776 had abundant and accessible natural resources. Land was relatively cheap, especially in the interior. Britain, in contrast, had plenty of coal and iron, but lacked timber, land, and a climate suitable for many agricultural products, such as sugar, tobacco, and cotton.

Second, the thirteen colonies lacked people to exploit their land and resources. With labor scarce and plenty of productive work to do, wages were higher than in Britain. The high wages attracted immigrants from Britain as well as other parts of Europe. Many English immigrants to the thirteen colonies came

as indentured servants. Too poor to pay for their passage by ship, they agreed to work for a fixed number of years (usually between three and seven) to repay the cost of their transportation.

Third, the scarcity of labor led many landowners in the Southern colonies to buy slaves to work on their tobacco, rice, and later cotton plantations. With the wages of free laborers so high, many plantations would not have been profitable without slaves. Most free immigrants then avoided the South, worried that the poor treatment slaves received would spill over into abuse of free laborers as well. By the time the colonies became independent with the Treaty of Paris in 1783, the new country was already divided between a Southern region with large numbers of slaves and the Mid-Atlantic and northern regions where free labor predominated.

The US economy expanded as immigrants arrived and set up new farms and enterprises. Productivity rose too. Though population increased at a fast 3 percent per year in the eighteenth century, the economy grew at 3.5 percent (0.5 percent per capita), as fast as Britain. GDP per capita nearly doubled. While still predominantly agricultural, the thirteen colonies had already begun to industrialize by the time they became independent. Their first industries developed mainly in the northern colonies to process agricultural, timber, and mineral products.

New England first specialized in saw mills producing lumber, potash, and pearlash made from burned timber and used in manufacturing soap and glass, naval stores like pitch, tar, and resin for ship-building, as well as fishing and whaling. The Mid-Atlantic colonies served as the colony's breadbasket (wheat and corn) and exported livestock as well as lumber products. In both regions, charcoal-burning blast furnaces for making iron developed in the eighteenth century to make tools, ploughs, household ironware, horseshoes, and a variety of other products.

Expansion of the US Economy

By the time of independence, the United States had already become the seventh-largest iron-producing nation in the world. US iron production caught up and passed Britain's in the 1820s. Textile production also developed rapidly late in the eighteenth century. In 1790, **Samuel Slater** set up the first US factory for spinning thread in Providence, Rhode Island. Power looms began revolutionizing cloth production with the establishment of **Francis Lowell**'s factory in Boston in 1814. By the 1820s, US manufacturing output already exceeded that of Great Britain.

Independence made it possible for the United States to develop its own economic policies without interference from London. The new republic adopted conservative financial and tax policies that promoted business, even though they benefited speculators and infuriated many veterans and farmers. A new constitution in 1787 strengthened the central government and provided it with adequate resources to govern effectively. The new republic maintained its neutrality during the European wars of 1793 to 1812 and profited as a neutral carrier, shipping supplies to all sides until it declared war on Great Britain near the end of the European hostilities in 1812. Tariffs on imported manufactured goods protected new industries from foreign, especially British, competition. Aggressive expansion quadrupled the national territory with the purchase of Louisiana from France (1803), the seizure of Florida from Spain (1819), and the annexation of the northern half of Mexico in the 1846–48 war, though the US invasion of Canada in the War of 1812 failed in its effort to annex the British colony. Improvements in transport and communications created a national market for manufactured goods and helped push the frontier ever further west. Settlers, backed by the federal government, pushed Native American populations aside and onto reservations, crushing resistance with relentless cruelty.

In the decades after the War of 1812 with Great Britain, US economic growth accelerated. In the Northeast, from Boston to Baltimore and west as far as Pittsburgh, a mixed economy of free farming and manufacturing production developed. Most of the farms stayed small, making more and more intensive use of the land to produce fruits, vegetables, and dairy products for the growing cities of the region. Manufacturing production grew rapidly, most of it to satisfy internal demand for consumer and construction goods. The industries of the Northeast exported their products not to foreign countries but to the agricultural South and Midwest within the United States.

The agricultural systems of the US South and Midwest differed sharply. The Southern states expanded production of cotton on slave plantations from the eastern seaboard to new territories acquired further west along the southern Mississippi and the Gulf of Mexico. The largest proportion of each year's cotton crop was exported to Great Britain. The British textile industry in turn exported its cloth throughout the world. British cotton textile output initially dwarfed that of the US industry, which produced mainly for the US home market. As US cotton manufacturing developed, however, the US industry became more efficient and competitive in world markets. Over time, a rising proportion of the cotton produced in the Southern states went to supply US factories in the Northeast.

Midwestern farmers from the Great Lakes south to Kansas and Nebraska produced grain and livestock for urban markets in the industrial Northeast. This region bought more of the output of the Northeast's industries than the South, because incomes were more equally distributed in the Midwest than in the South. Slave owners spent as little as possible on food and clothing for their chattel. In fact, slave children were often kept

undernourished and listless to save money and keep them out of trouble. Slave owners and overseers lived well, of course, but much of what they purchased came from abroad. In contrast, the dynamic inter-relationship between Northeastern industry and Midwestern farmers had a stronger effect on the nation's economic development.

Industrial Revolution in Northwestern Europe

As in the United States, British technology quickly spread to the European continent. By 1800, France and Upper Silesia (Germany) had adopted the Watt steam engine, while near the Silesian coal fields, coke-burning blast furnaces were already turning out iron. Spinning jennies and power-driven water frames also spread fast: By 1800, they were already working in new factories in Austria, France, Germany, Spain, and the United States. Power looms spread to continental Europe in the 1820s.

The most widely diffused innovations of the First Industrial Revolution, however, were steamships and railroads. Steamships began turning in record times for river transportation and even transatlantic voyages by the 1820s. Railroads spread out across landscapes in every part of the globe, beginning in the 1830s. In Northwestern Europe, they helped to create integrated national markets just as the new industries were developing. In France, with its substantial territory and large population, railroads played an especially important role. In the German states, railroads had to cross political boundaries but in doing so promoted both economic and eventual political unification.

In France, the fall of the *ancien régime* in the Revolution of 1789 put an end to the economic privileges of the nobility. Guilds and industrial regulation declined or disappeared entirely. Many noble families lost their lands to peasant uprisings that turned the country into a nation of small farmers. The Bourbon monarchy, restored after Napoleon's defeat in 1815, made gestures in the direction of compensation, but did little to restore land to its former owners. As a result, land and income were more evenly distributed in the French countryside than in Britain and migration to the cities occurred more gradually.

French industry, like that of the United States, developed more to serve the large domestic market than to export products to other countries. Cautious, family-owned companies and partnerships replaced the great magnates, tax farmers, and industrial monopolists bankrupted by the Revolution or Napoleon's wars. Like the United States, the French government promoted industrialization through protective tariffs that made competing British products more costly to consumers. The government also provided direct subsidies and other help, especially to large-scale enterprises that needed huge investments to start up, such as blast furnaces and railroads. In the 1820s, the French economy began growing again, enough to relaunch its delayed industrialization.

German industrialization also began in the post-Napoleonic era, centered as in France in regions accessible by water with abundant coal and iron such as Saxony, the Ruhr Valley, and the lower Rhine. The most important obstacle to German economic advance was political fragmentation. In 1789, Germany was composed of 314 independent territories, each with its own autocratic prince or governing oligarchy. Even after the Napoleonic occupations, which destroyed all but 30 of these mini-states, various and different constitutions and policies continued to be the norm. Three main barriers impeded German industrialization. First, with so many different jurisdictions, each with its own laws, taxes, and courts, no coherent policy of support for industrialization could be imposed. Second, fragmentation also impeded the development of a national market and of industries to serve the entire territory. The customs union or **Zollverein** created under Prussian leadership between 1819 and 1844 helped reduce tariff barriers among the German states, but not all joined. Third, serfdom in portions of eastern Germany blocked migration by rural workers from less to more productive occupations in the new industrial centers and hampered the development of a national labor market. Eliminating these obstacles only occurred with German unification under the Prussian Crown in 1871.

Except for Belgium, which had major deposits of coal and iron to exploit, no other country in Europe or elsewhere succeeded in launching a successful drive to industrialize in the first half of the nineteenth century. The Dutch economy revived in the second half of the eighteenth century, but lacking in natural resources, above all coal and iron, Dutch capitalists specialized in banking, shipping, and service industries. Spinning jennies spread to Austria, Italy, and Spain before 1800 and the power loom followed in the 1830s. Most of the new factories in these countries relied on water power. Steam engines, railroads, and blast furnaces came only after mid-century.

6.6 THE HUMAN COST OF INDUSTRIALIZATION

Economic growth with industrialization transformed societies. Rapid social, demographic, occupational, and cultural changes uprooted families, pushed them into crowded urban slums (like those shown in Figure 6.4), hurled them into factories full of grime and tension, and cast them aside to be buried in paupers' graves when they died of accidents and disease. In Britain, contemporary critics and later historians wrote of widespread family disorganization and abandonment, a generalized decline in health and nutrition levels, the traumatizing

Figure 6.4 One of the many New York City slum photographs of Jacob Riis (c. 1890). Riis and other reformers struggled to improve sanitation; squalor can be seen in the streets, washed clothes hanging between buildings. Like most cities, New York was not prepared for the huge influx of workers and immigrants that accompanied the Industrial Revolution. People crowded into already crowded houses. Rooms were rented to whole families.

Box 6.2 Death and Disease in Industrial Cities

Edwin Chadwick's famous *Report on the Sanitary Condition of the Labouring Population of Great Britain* (1842) offered a grim assessment of death and disease among the British working class:

After as careful an examination of the evidence collected as I have been enabled to make, I beg leave to recapitulate the chief conclusions which that evidence appears to me to establish.

First, as to the extent and operation of the evils which are the subject of this inquiry:

... That the various forms of epidemic, endemic, and other disease caused, or aggravated, or propagated chiefly amongst the labouring classes by atmospheric

impurities produced by decomposing animal and vegetable substances, by damp and filth, and close and overcrowded dwellings prevail amongst the population in every part of the kingdom, whether dwelling in separate houses, in rural villages, in small towns, in the larger towns – as they have been found to prevail in the lowest districts of the metropolis ...

Contaminated London drinking water containing various micro-organisms, refuse, and the like.

The high prosperity in respect to employment and wages, and various and abundant food, have afforded to the labouring classes no exemptions from attacks of epidemic disease, which have been as frequent and as fatal in periods

of commercial and manufacturing prosperity as in any others ...

That the annual loss of life from filth and bad ventilation are greater than the loss from death or wounds in any wars in which the country has been engaged in modern times.

That of the 43,000 cases of widowhood, and 112,000 cases of destitute orphanage relieved from the poor's rates in England and Wales alone, it appears that the greatest proportion of deaths of the heads of families occurred from the above specified and other removable causes; that their ages were under 45 years; that is to say, thirteen years below the natural probabilities of life as shown by the experience of the whole population of Sweden.

impact of factory discipline, high rates of alcoholism and crime, and increasing inequality. Women and children suffered disproportionately, with small children especially at risk.

At the same time, economic growth made it possible for a small number of merchants, bankers, factory owners, and other businessmen to accumulate immense fortunes and disproportionately rewarded a new middle class of shopkeepers, managers, skilled workers, and professionals (upper clergymen, lawyers, physicians, and the like). Altogether, however, these instant beneficiaries of economic modernization constituted less than a fifth of the population. Living standards for the majority stagnated or fell until late in the nineteenth or early in the twentieth century.

Living Standards

The overall effects of the Industrial Revolution on physical welfare can be seen in statistics on life expectancy. After rising in the eighteenth century, life expectancy stagnated at near 40 years of age throughout the North Atlantic economies until late in the nineteenth century. In some countries, like Britain and the United States, life expectancy actually declined in some decades. The appalling living and working conditions experienced by many city-dwellers accounted for most of this decline. Cities were always unhealthy places, but some of the urban slums of the Industrial Revolution proved to be even worse than the dark hovels of the ancient world. Manchester,

England, for example, became famous as the center of the British textile industry in the early nineteenth century, but earned even greater notoriety for the misery of its inhabitants. Edwin Chadwick's famous 1842 *Report on the Sanitary Condition of the Labouring Population of Great Britain* (quoted in Box 6.2) put the average age at death of "mechanics, labourers, and their families" in Manchester at 17 years of age.

Manchester was not alone. Throughout the industrializing world, average life expectancy declined in the early nineteenth century and stagnated until the twentieth. The chief cause was urbanization and the chief victims were infants and children. Industrial cities, especially the new industrial cities, packed people into slum tenements with no running water and no sewers or garbage collection. Disease ran rampant. Coal dust from countless smokestacks and chimneys filled the air, adding to the thick cotton dust that textile workers breathed into their lungs working 12–14 hour shifts. Box 6.3 quotes testimony on child labor in textile factories.

Health care, such as it was in the early nineteenth century, did not reach most working-class families. The most vulnerable in these conditions were children and the aged, but few lived long enough to suffer late in life. Infant and child mortality rates in British industrial cities in the first half of the nineteenth century reached extraordinary heights. In Manchester, according to Chadwick's report, 57 percent of all children died before their fifth birthday in the 1840s.

Box 6.3 Child Labor in Testimony to the Factories Inquiry Commission

The following are some typical testimonies concerning child labor gathered by the Factories Inquiry Commission of 1833.

Hannah Goode: *I work at Mr. Wilson's mill [in Nottingham, England]. I think the youngest child is about 7. I daresay there are 20 under 9 years. It is about half past five by our clock at home when we go in . . . We come out at seven by the mill. We never stop to take our meals, except at dinner.*

William Crookes is overlooker in our room. He is cross-tempered sometimes.

He does not beat me; he beats the little children if they do not do their work right. . . . I have sometimes seen the little children drop asleep or so, but not lately. If they are catched asleep they get the strap. They are always very tired at night. . . . I can read a little; I can't write. I used to go to school before I went to the mill; I have since I am sixteen.

Mrs. Smith: *I have three children working in Wilson's mill; one 11, one 13, and the other 14. They work regular hours there. We don't complain. If they*

go to drop the hours, I don't know what poor people will do. We have hard work to live as it is . . . My husband is of the same mind about it . . . last summer my husband was 6 weeks ill; we pledged almost all our things to live; the things are not all out of pawn yet . . . We complain of nothing but short wages . . . My children have been in the mill three years. I have no complaint to make of their being beaten . . . I would rather they were beaten than fined.

The high death rates and low life expectancy of urban populations during the Industrial Revolution would have rapidly depopulated cities like Manchester had new migrants not flowed into them from small towns and farms in a continuous stream. Why would people move to cities if they were so notoriously unhealthy?

At least three factors were at work. First, high unemployment rates, especially in recessions (like the "hungry 40s" in Britain), forced people to seek employment wherever they could find it. Second, urban wages were higher than in the countryside. Many migrants moved seeking better wages without anticipating that higher living costs would more than cancel out the apparent advantage. Third, mortality rates for adults were much lower than for children. Many migrants moved to urban areas before marriage made them aware of the risks that their children would face.

Because urban living and working conditions were so unhealthy, both children and adults needed to consume more food just to endure the stress of factory work and fight off disease. City populations thus experienced chronic malnutrition even when they managed to eat as much in the city as in the countryside. Malnutrition stunted the growth of people raised in urban areas. In the United States, where wages and living standards for the free population were higher than in Britain and the continent, the height of the native-born population began to decline with the cohort born in the 1790s and continued to decline into the 1830s. Adult men shrank by 3 inches from an average height of 5 feet 10 inches to 5 feet 7 inches (178 to 170 centimeters). The native-born population of the United States did not recover its late eighteenth-century stature until the

cohort born in the 1920s. A similar phenomenon occurred in Northwestern Europe. As each country commenced industrialization and urban populations increased, the average height of adults began to fall, not to recover in most cases until sometime in the twentieth century.

Urbanization and Social Change

Economic modernization also caused widespread and dramatic social change, first in Britain and then in the United States and Northwestern Europe. Urbanization itself represented an unprecedented transformation. In 1700, roughly 10 percent of the 5.8 million people in England and Wales lived in urban places. By 1850, the population had risen to 17.8 million with 60 percent in urban areas. The population of London rose from half a million to 2.7 million. The growth of industrial towns was even more spectacular. Glasgow, Liverpool, and Manchester rose from a few thousand souls in 1700 to over 300,000 by 1850. In the United States and in Northwestern Europe, a similar process occurred with a lag of two to five decades. New York City, for example, went from less than 20,000 in 1700 to nearly 700,000 in 1850. These cities accommodated their larger populations by allowing landlords to build block after block of cheap fire-prone wooden buildings full of tiny one-room apartments, most without heat, running water, adequate ventilation, or other amenities.

Urbanization and economic growth transformed family structure and gender roles. In the pre-industrial world and in rural areas, families usually worked together. Urban employment made that impossible. Men typically found employment

Box 6.4 Report on Women in the Coal Mines

British Parliamentary Papers of 1842 contain the following account of female labor in coal mines:

Girls [says the Sub-Commissioner J.C. Symons] regularly perform all the various offices of trapping, hurrying [Yorkshire terms for drawing the loaded coal corves], filling, riddling, tipping, and occasionally getting, just as they are performed by boys. One of the most disgusting sights I have ever seen was that of young females, dressed like boys in trousers, crawling on all fours, with belts round their waists and chains passing between their legs, at day pits at Hunshelf Bank, and in many small pits near Holmfirth and New Mills: it exists also in several other places . . .

On descending Messrs Hopwood's pit at Barnsley, I found assembled round a fire a group of men, boys, and girls, some of whom were of the age of puberty; the girls as well as the boys stark naked down to the waist, their hair bound up with a tight cap, and trousers supported by their hips. (At Silkstone and at Flockton they work in their shifts and trousers.) Their sex was recognizable only by their breasts, and some little difficulty occasionally arose in pointing out to me which were girls and which were boys, and which caused a good deal of laughing and joking. In the Flockton and Thornhill pits the system is even more indecent: for though the girls are clothed, at least three-fourths of the men for whom they "hurry" work stark naked, or with a flannel waistcoat only, and in this state they assist one another to fill the corves 18 or 20 times a day: I have seen this done myself frequently.

When it is remembered that these girls hurry chiefly for men who are not their parents; that they go from 15 to 20 times a day into a dark chamber (the bank face), which is often 50 yards apart from any one, to a man working naked, or next to naked, it is not to be supposed but that where opportunity thus prevails sexual vices are of common occurrence. Add to this the free intercourse, and the rendezvous at the shaft or bullstake, where the corves are brought, and consider the language to which the young ear is habituated, the absence of religious instruction, and the early age at which contamination begins, and you will have before you, in the coal-pits where females are employed, the picture of a nursery for juvenile vice which you will go far and wide above ground to equal.

in jobs that required greater strength – tending power looms, working on construction projects or in iron and machinery shops, loading freight on docks and in warehouses, taking unskilled day labor jobs, and the like. Many found what skills they had struggled to learn displaced by new machines. Handloom weavers after 1800, for example, faced increasing competition from power looms. In two decades, their wages dropped to a third of what they had once been. Periodic recessions threw them out of work for weeks and months at a time and forced them to watch their families go hungry. Conditions in the early factories, workshops, coal pits, and iron mines often left them injured, disabled, or exhausted. A large proportion of the urban workforce, perhaps 20 percent in early nineteenth-century Britain, was too chronically malnourished to work regularly.

Women worked mainly in domestic service, though a significant number took jobs in cotton mills tending spinning machines. Some even worked in the coal mines (see Box 6.4). While men found the long workdays exhausting and suffered disproportionately from injuries, women may have had an even more difficult time of it. Need forced them to work outside the home, but the wages they received represented only a fraction of men's earnings. Family support networks often disintegrated in moving to the city, coal dust filled the air and made it impossible to keep anything clean, children got sick constantly and many died young, and husbands deserted or fell disabled or dead from workplace accidents at alarming rates.

As working-class women struggled to feed their families and keep them together, a new cult of domesticity took root in the middle classes. Promoted by religious and cultural institutions, and eagerly supported by manufacturers that catered to new middle-class consumers, the ideal woman came to be defined as one who stayed home and out of the labor force, tending to the moral education of children, the contentment of husbands, and family expenditures for furniture, decoration, chinaware, clothing, food products, patent medicines, and other necessities. Domesticity thus sharply distinguished respectable middle-class women from the slum-dwellers. For working women, the Victorian cult of domesticity may have been the unkindest cut of all, as it deprecated their unavoidable (and underpaid) work as less valuable than the leisure of women whose husbands could afford to keep them at home.

Community and civic organizations scarcely existed in the new urban neighborhoods, though older cities with established churches and charities tended to do better than the new places. Skilled workers set up mutual aid societies, paying small amounts each week into a common insurance fund that helped widows and orphans or paid funeral expenses. Intellectuals, preachers, and reform politicians denounced the appalling conditions they witnessed and set up organizations to help the needy. Several Protestant denominations in England, such as the Methodists (a split-off from the Church of England), launched campaigns to re-convert slum-dwellers to Christianity and in the process called attention to governmental corruption and neglect.

Protest and Politics

Discontent with the conditions faced by urban populations during the First Industrial Revolution spawned new forms of protest and resistance. In Britain, strikes at cotton mills over wages, hours, harsh discipline, and abuse became common by the 1810s. In England and the continent, early nineteenth-century strikes often resembled village tax rebellions or the equally traditional bread riots of medieval towns. They often erupted more or less spontaneously in response to some particularly abusive behavior by an owner or supervisor, such as the firing of a co-worker or an arbitrary change in wages or working conditions. In time, however, workers organized unions to bargain with employers and linked their workplace and community grievances to local and national politics.

In Britain, workers spurred on by middle-class reformers and radicals took their protests into the political arena, but met obstacles at every turn. Many factory towns and industrial cities grew up on the site of small villages that had not been granted charters of self-government in the Middle Ages. Since Parliament made no general provision for the organization of city governments until 1835, many cities and towns like Manchester had no local authority to take responsibility for police, sanitation, water, and other public functions. Restrictions on the franchise excluded workers from voting even in towns and cities that had local governments.

When workers sought to protest conditions to the national government, they had no representatives to whom they could appeal. Parliament did expand the franchise in 1832 to admit the propertied middle class, but did not even consider giving the vote to propertyless workers. The 1832 law abolished or restructured "rotten" boroughs (parliamentary districts with few inhabitants that always "elected" pro-government

candidates) and increased representation for industrial towns, but denied the franchise to most of the people living in them. Worse yet, in 1834 Parliament passed a draconian New Poor Law that forced able-bodied but destitute men and their families into poorhouses, a punitive measure that was widely despised and resisted.

Not surprisingly, the textile factory towns of the Lancashire region that included Manchester became the center of strikes and protest movements that linked demands for the right to vote to workers' grievances against their harsh living and working conditions. The **Chartist movement**, organized in 1838, demanded that Parliament enact universal suffrage for adult men. Meetings, protest marches, strikes, and petitions throughout the 1840s forced Parliament to take up the issue of electoral reform again and again without success. Parliament did not enact anything like universal suffrage for men until 1884 (and even then, still excluded most men who did not own or rent property).

Parliament did pass legislation, however, that limited the working hours of children and women. These reform acts were poorly enforced and primitive by modern standards. Only children under 9 years of age were forbidden to work, for example. Parliament did repeal legislation that artificially inflated food prices with high tariffs on imported corn, meat, cheese, butter, and other products. The 1846 repeal of the **Corn Laws** and the passage of a new Customs Law that lowered other tariffs on food imports did more than any other legislation to improve British living standards.

Living and working conditions comparable to Britain's developed in the mining centers, mill towns and urban slums in the United States and Northwestern Europe as economic growth accelerated in the early nineteenth century. As in Britain, European governments in the other industrializing societies of Europe restricted the franchise to property owners until after 1850. As a result, social conflicts over working and living conditions in the first half of the nineteenth century frequently spilled over into political struggles against governments that excluded workers. In the United States, however, the 1787 Constitution gave voting rights to all free adult males in federal elections, though several states continued to impose property qualifications and other restrictions until later. Though most free men could vote (even non-citizens in many areas) and politicians often sought working-class support in the northern industrial cities, state governments and most city administrations sided with employers when strikes broke out. Democracy, many concluded, was not enough so long as economic power remained concentrated in the hands of wealthy owners and their allies.

Conclusion The First Industrial Revolution left a contradictory double legacy not only in Britain and the other early industrializing countries but also throughout the globe as it spread to other countries and continents. On the one hand, it bequeathed hugely important advances in technology, communications, and organization that made all human economic activity more productive. On the other, it left a legacy of greater inequality both within the industrializing countries and between them and the rest of the world. The history of the modern world was permanently shaped by this double legacy.

There is no question that the sustained economic growth that began in the late seventeenth century and continues today has vastly increased the productivity of the world economy. New technology and better organization have made it possible for people to become more and more productive. Improved communications made it easier and cheaper for the world's diverse regions to trade with each other to great mutual benefit. It is no accident that the most productive economies in history have usually been those best located to engage in trade with other regions. Without the economic growth of the past two to three centuries, modern life and living standards would be impossible.

From the beginning, however, economic growth has inspired protest and resistance – and not just from backward-looking people seeking to preserve outdated technologies and lifestyles. The First Industrial Revolution created or exacerbated three kinds of inequality, each of which remains a source of contemporary discontent.

First, *within* growing economies the gap between the income and living standards of the rich and the poor majority increased. Living standards for the majority actually deteriorated or stagnated, middle-class beneficiaries of economic advance were few in number, and a tiny minority made immense fortunes. In 1800, for example, the titled aristocracy of Great Britain on average stood 5 inches taller than the population as a whole; this difference worsened during the First Industrial Revolution and only began to diminish (to less than 1 inch today) in the late nineteenth century.

The economist Simon Kuznets (1901–85) argued that some increase in inequality could not be avoided in the early stages of industrialization, but claimed that this tendency was usually reversed in later stages by improved education and social programs such as retirement pensions. In the nineteenth century, however, many concluded that Karl Marx was right when he argued that mass misery and concentration of wealth could only be overcome through revolutions that would confiscate privately owned factories and other productive assets and turn them over to benevolent governments committed not to profit-making but to the welfare of all.

The second kind of inequality exacerbated by the Industrial Revolution occurred when the growing demand for raw materials and food in the industrializing countries provoked profit-seekers to enslave or otherwise exploit the inhabitants of less developed but resource rich areas. The most dramatic example was the slave trade that forced millions of Africans into slavery on New World plantations producing food and fiber for European consumers and factories. Conditions of near slavery also developed in mines and plantations on nearly every continent as the insatiable reach of European and US demand spread throughout the world.

Third, the Industrial Revolution created a new division in the world between rich and poor nations, between those that industrialized first and those whose economic growth began later, between the North Atlantic and the rest of the world. This new division of the world had far-reaching consequences. Five European countries (Belgium, France, Germany, Great Britain, and the Netherlands) plus the United States acquired the economic power and thus the military capacity to dominate the rest of the globe. The Spanish and Portuguese empires declined in the early nineteenth century as Latin America achieved independence, while the industrializing powers of the North Atlantic acquired new colonies and areas of influence and control. In some cases, the colonial or neocolonial power used its dominance to impede the development of industries or other activities that might compete with those back home. In most of the globe, even in colonial areas, economic growth began sometime in the late nineteenth or early twentieth century. This was too late, however, for most other countries to join the ranks of the developed world. With the exception of Japan and the Soviet Union, the less developed regions of the world did not begin to close this gap until late in the twentieth century.

Study Questions

(1) Distinguish between changes in productivity and changes in living standards. How are these measured?

(2) Why did sustained economic growth occur first in the "West" and not elsewhere?

(3) How would you distinguish between the necessary and sufficient conditions for economic growth?

(4) How did access to water transportation and later to railroads promote economic growth?

(5) Did slavery and the slave trade contribute to the Industrial Revolution?

(6) What happened to living standards in the Industrial Revolution?

(7) Why did workers protest during the Industrial Revolution?

Suggested Reading

DARON ACEMOGLU AND JAMES A. ROBINSON, *Why Nations Fail: The Origins of Power, Prosperity and Poverty* (New York: Crown Publishers, 2012). This key question is addressed here by political scientists turned historians.

ROBERT W. FOGEL, *The Escape from Hunger and Premature Death, 1700–2100* (Cambridge University Press, 2004). This is a classic work by Nobel laureate in economics on the history of living standards.

ERIC L. JONES, *The European Miracle: Environments, Economics, and Geopolitics in the History of Europe and Asia* (Cambridge University Press, 1981). This is an important work of synthesis on how Europe forged ahead of the rest of the world during the First Industrial Revolution.

JOEL MOKYR, *Enlightened Economy: An Economic History of Britain, 1700–1850* (New Haven, CT: Yale University Press, 2009). Mokyr's study is a major work on the role played by advances in science and scientific methods in driving the British economy ahead.

KENNETH POMERANZ, *The Great Divergence: China, Europe, and the Making of the Modern World Economy* (Princeton University Press, 2000). This comparative history analyzes when and how the West surged ahead of China after the eighteenth century.

PETER N. STEARNS, *The Industrial Revolution in World History*, 2nd edn. (Boulder, CO: Westview Press, 1998). This book is a global history of the spread of industrialization.

RICHARD STECKEL AND RODERICK FLOUD (eds.), *Health and Welfare During Industrialization* (University of Chicago Press, 1997). This is an excellent collection of essays by specialists working on diverse regions of the globe who show how living standards evolved from ancient times.

Glossary

Abraham Darby: Englishman (1678–1717) who developed a process for smelting iron ore with coke instead of charcoal. His method yielded iron castings thin, strong, and malleable enough to compete with brass.

capital goods: Machinery and equipment used to produce other products.

Chartist movement: A major British working-class movement for parliamentary reform in the late 1830s and 1840s. Its six major demands were universal manhood suffrage, equal electoral districts, vote by ballot, annually elected parliaments, payment of Members of Parliament, and the abolition of property qualifications for membership in Parliament.

Corn Laws: Regulations governing the import and export of grain in Britain since the twelfth century, which levied high tariffs on food imports, thus driving up the cost of living. A push for the liberalization of the grain trade, led by merchants from Manchester, finally led Parliament to repeal the Corn Laws in 1846. It was a major step toward free trade that also improved British living standards.

economic growth: A sustained increase in GDP per capita.

economies of scale: Cost savings per unit of output that result from producing in large quantities.

Edmund Cartwright: Prebendary of Lincoln cathedral in Lincolnshire, England (1743–1823), he produced the first wool-combing machine and the power loom, predecessor to the modern loom.

Eli Whitney: A Yale-educated engineer (1765–1825), he invented the cotton gin in 1793 and developed the mass production of interchangeable parts.

Francis Lowell: Member of a prominent Massachusetts family (1775–1817), he was first to process raw cotton into finished cloth in a single facility (1814).

George Stephenson: English inventor (1781–1848), a crucial pioneer of the steam locomotive, who built Stockton and Darlington Railway, the first public steam railway (1825). He went on to connect Liverpool and Manchester with the world's first passenger rail line in 1830.

Glorious Revolution: Parliamentarily sanctioned overthrow of King James II of England and accession of his daughter Mary II and her husband William III, Prince of Orange (1688). In restoring Protestant monarchs to the throne, Parliament also abolished the king's traditional power to suspend laws, asserted its right to meet frequently, and declared illegal the maintenance of standing armies during peacetime.

Gross Domestic Product (GDP): The total value of goods and services produced by an economy over a specified period of time, normally a year or a quarter. GDP per capita is often used to measure the productivity of a nation's economy.

Henry Cort: English ironmaster (1740–1800), inventor of the reverberating furnace, which uses circulating air to remove carbon from iron in a process called puddling.

James Hargreaves: English inventor (1720–78), said to have first imagined his masterpiece when his daughter Jenny played with a spinning wheel turned on its side. Hargreaves's spinning jenny significantly reduced the labor required to produce cloth by spinning many threads at once.

James Watt: Scottish inventor (1736–1819) of the dual-chamber steam engine, a 1765 modification of the Newcomen engine. Watt's invention powered the mills, distilleries, and waterworks that revolutionized the nineteenth-century world.

net nutrition: The total nutrients consumed minus energy expended in warding off disease and working.

productivity: Measure of how much a society (or firm) produces with the resources it has; for entire countries, economists usually look at GDP divided by population: gross domestic product per capita.

Richard Arkwright: A self-educated innovator and merchant in textiles (1732–92), he combined the new power-driven machinery of his day with a factory system of product assembly. In 1769 he patented the spinning frame.

Robert Fulton: American inventor, engineer, and artist (1765–1815) who made steamships workable (1807), designed inland waterways, and advanced naval technology.

Samuel Crompton: English inventor (1753–1827) whose spinning mule, invented in 1779, drew out and gave final spinning to cotton fibers, replacing hand-spinning.

Samuel Slater: A textile industrialist (1768–1835), born in England, who went on to be the father of the American cotton industry. His mill in Pawtucket, Rhode Island (1790), was the first successful one of its kind in the USA.

spinning jenny: See James Hargreaves.

spinning mule: See Samuel Crompton.

subinnovation: The thousands of untold improvements and micro inventions that multiply through a growing economy.

Thomas Newcomen: English ironmonger (*c.* 1664–1729) who invented the atmospheric steam engine, a precursor to the machines that would drive the Industrial Revolution. His first working model went into operation in 1712.

Thomas Robert Malthus: British economist and demographer (1766–1834) who theorized that population growth will always tend to outrun food supply. His thesis debunked the idea that population growth is always an indicator of national wealth, and led him to advocate limits on reproduction.

Zollverein: An important Prussian-led customs union established in 1834, including eighteen states in present-day Germany. It liberalized and simplified trade among its members.

7 The Age of Revolution

The American Revolution	
1756–63	Seven Years' War in Europe (whose North American theater is the French and Indian War).
1765–66	Passage and repeal of the Stamp Act, heightening antagonisms between Britain and the American colonies.
September 5, 1774	First Continental Congress.
October 1774	Provincial Congress meets in Concord, Massachusetts.
April 19, 1775	Battles of Lexington and Concord – the opening shots of the American Revolution.
January 10, 1776	Thomas Paine's *Common Sense* published.
July 4, 1776	Declaration of Independence adopted in Philadelphia.
September–October 17, 1777	Battle of Saratoga: British General Burgoyne surrenders his entire force to American General Horatio Gates.
November 15, 1777	Articles of Confederation adopted by Congress: creation of the United States of America.
October 19, 1780	British General Cornwallis surrenders at Yorktown.
September 3, 1783	Treaty of Paris between Great Britain and the USA, recognizing US independence.
May 1787	Constitutional Convention in Philadelphia.
July 13, 1787	Northwest Ordinance: principle of ultimate statehood for territories established, prohibition of slavery in the Northwest Territory, and land for public education.
June 1788	Ratification of the Constitution by New Hampshire, the ninth state. Constitution goes into effect.
August 20, 1794	Battle of Fallen Timbers, in which US forces defeat Native American tribes in Ohio.

| August 3, 1795 | Treaty of Greenville: Native American land claims resulting from the American Revolution are settled, mainly at the expense of Native Americans. |

The French Revolution

May 5, 1789	Estates General meets at Versailles.
June 20, 1789	With the Estates General suspended, delegates from the Third Estate band together and take an oath not to separate until France has a constitution.
July 14, 1789	Storming of the Bastille, longtime symbol of royal repression in Paris.
August 2, 1789	Declaration of the Rights of Man and Citizen.
September 3, 1791	Ratification of the French constitution of 1791.
April 20, 1792	In response to a declaration by Prussia and Austria, France declares war.
June 20–25, 1792	Flight of the king and his family, capture at Varennes, and return to Paris.
September 20, 1792	Prussian defeat at Valmy encourages revolutionary armies.
January 21, 1793	Execution of Louis XVI.
September 1793–July 1794	Reign of Terror; Robespierre dominates the Committee of Public Safety.
October 16, 1793	Execution of Marie Antoinette.
1796–97	Italian campaign of Napoleon Bonaparte; rise of Bonaparte's reputation.
November 9, 1799	Coup of 18 Brumaire: Napoleon executes *coup d'état* against the Directory.
May 18, 1804	Napoleon becomes emperor of France.
1812	Napoleon's disastrous Russian campaign.
April 1814	Napoleon abdicates.
May 3, 1814	The late king's brother, Louis XVIII, enters Paris.
September 1814–June 1815	Congress of Vienna.
March 20–June 22, 1815	The Hundred Days: Napoleon escapes from exile in Elba, lands in France, overthrows the government of Louis XVIII, and is defeated at Waterloo (June 18).

The Haitian Revolution

1787	French assembly votes suffrage to colonial whites.
September 1788	French Commission led by Léger Félicité Sonthonax arrives in Haiti. These commissioners are strongly influenced by revolutionary ideas.
August 22–23, 1792	Slave revolt begins.

August 29, 1793	French commissioner Sonthonax declares the abolition of slavery.
February 4, 1794	French National Convention declares the abolition of slavery in the French colonies.
May 1794	Toussaint L'Ouverture joins the republican side.
1797	Toussaint L'Ouverture makes himself dictator of Haiti.
1802	Napoleon sends an army to recapture Haiti.
June 1802	Toussaint L'Ouverture captured by treachery and deported to France.
January 1, 1804	Haitians under Jean-Jacques Dessalines defeat French army and proclaim the independence of Haiti.

The Latin American Revolutions

1807	Napoleon gets Spanish permission to send troops across Spain to invade Portugal; Spain joins invasion; Portuguese king and court flee to Brazil.
1808	Napoleon forces Spain's King Ferdinand (Fernando) VII to abdicate and imposes brother, Joseph Bonaparte, as new king; French army occupies Spain; Spanish resistance to French rule spreads to colonies.
1810	Hidalgo movement in Mexico; creoles overthrow Spanish officials and take control in the name of Ferdinand VII in Argentina, Colombia, Paraguay, and Venezuela; other colonies follow.
1811	Hidalgo movement defeated in Mexico, but guerrilla war continues; liberal Spanish Cortes (parliament) meets in Cádiz; colonies elect delegates.
1813	Cortes of Cádiz proclaims constitution of 1812; colonies underrepresented; Spanish troops retake Venezuela.
1814	Ferdinand VII restored to throne, abolishes constitution of 1812, and dissolves Cortes; Spanish army retakes Chile.
1816	Spain retakes Colombia; colonies mostly back under control of Spanish troops.
1818	San Martín invades Chile from Argentina.
1819	Simón Bolívar wins decisive victory over Spanish forces in Colombia at Boyacá.
1820	Military coup in Spain restores liberal constitution of 1812.
1821	Loyalist leader Iturbide in Mexico defects to rebels, Mexico independent; San Martín captures Lima; Portuguese King João IV leaves Brazil to return to Portugal.

| 1822 | João IV's son declares independence of Brazil, crowned as Emperor Pedro I; Simón Bolívar secures independence of "Gran Colombia" (Colombia, Ecuador, Venezuela). |
| 1824 | Battle of Ayacucho in Peru: Simón Bolívar decisively defeats Spanish in last key battle for Latin American independence; Bolivia soon to follow Peru; only Cuba and Puerto Rico remain colonies. |

Having struggled to acquire the fundamentals of reading, writing, and arithmetic, Thomas Paine (1737–1809), a collector of excise tax and a Methodist preacher in England, migrated to Britain's American colonies. In 1774 he arrived in Philadelphia seeking to make his living as an editor and freelance author but already with a radical political agenda. Early on, Paine denounced the slave trade and elaborated a specific plan for its abolition. His popular pamphlet, *Common Sense*, defended the American cause before public opinion in both Britain and the colonies. It was the first salvo in the career of a man who became the world's most radical polemicist. During the Valley Forge encampment, a bleak winter for the Revolution, Paine's popular *Crisis* rallied Americans, announcing "These are the times that try men's souls."

Once the American Revolution had succeeded, Paine returned to England and took up the defense of the French Revolution. In response to the English legislator Edmund Burke's celebrated polemic against the Revolution, Paine wrote *The Rights of Man*, one of the most widely read books of all time. Paine's pamphlets promoted a new republican writing style, a popular political language, accessible to the **artisan** (skilled manual worker) yet capable of expressing moral outrage and high seriousness. Mocking Burke's awe of tradition and popular reverence toward the British monarchy, Paine jibed: "A French bastard landing with an armed banditti and establishing himself King of England against the consent of the natives is, in plain terms, a very paltry rascally original. The plain truth is that the antiquity of English monarchy will not bear looking into." Reading these lines, many ordinary men and women in England, Ireland, Scotland, and Wales never looked at monarchy in quite the same way again.

Paine made revolutionary republicanism central to the fate of all humankind. He argued that the political revolution begun in America was a universal phenomenon that had spread to France and would soon sweep the entire world. In 1792 Paine asserted that "I do not believe that monarchy and aristocracy will continue seven years longer in any of the enlightened countries of Europe."

Fleeing England, where the success of his writing had made him feared by the government, Paine sought refuge in France where he had been awarded honorary citizenship and where he was elected to the new French assembly, the National Convention, although he spoke almost no French. In time the Anglo-American radical found himself in the uncomfortable position of being denounced as a moderate by French radical revolutionaries. As the Revolution reached its most militant phase, Paine escaped the guillotine only by lucky chance. American principles seemed outmoded in revolutionary France.

Later years demonstrated that Paine's pen was as brilliant as ever, although his eloquence found less favor. *The Age of Revolution* critiqued orthodox Christianity and his *Agrarian Justice* attacked dramatic inequalities in property ownership. These later works scandalized many of his American friends but they captured accurately enough the direction of change in the character of popular upheavals in the "Age of Revolution" as a single-minded focus on arbitrary rule gave way to social and cultural concerns.

The revolutions that spread throughout most of Old Regime Europe and the Western colonial world between 1789 and 1848 were the product of broad changes well underway in the preceding century:

- A new and growing capitalist economic system spread throughout the region based on expanded world trade, an international division of labor, and ultimately industrial development.
- A new kind of centralized state appeared with power undreamt of by earlier rulers, including the power to provoke resistance.
- A dramatic series of political upheavals swept much but not all of Old Regime Europe and the Americas; once revolutions had begun they developed a dynamic of their own, with outcomes unforeseen and often undesired by those who initially launched them.

- The political revolutions of this era provided unprecedented opportunities for previously excluded social and ethnic groups to participate in the political arena; even where old elites succeeded in recovering power, their privileges were no longer so secure; politics and social life had changed forever.

- By the end of the revolutionary era, socialism and cultural nationalism had become important forces in Western and Central Europe; they would play an even more important role in the future.

7.1 STATE TRANSFORMATION IN OLD REGIME EUROPE AND THE WESTERN COLONIAL WORLD

War molded the eighteenth-century state. Anglo-French military rivalry runs like a red thread throughout the century. An almost continuous series of wars led to repeated battles in the Americas, naval contests between British and French fleets in the West Indies, and land battles at Fort Duquesne, Louisbourg, Quebec, and Ticonderoga. Both countries were great mercantile powers, trading in the Atlantic and selling colonial items in home markets as well as in the Baltic and Mediterranean. They routinely used warfare to advance their commercial interests.

More single-mindedly focused on military power and territorial conquest, the major European political rivals of Britain and France were land-based agrarian empires – dynamically expanding militaristic states in Central, Eastern, and Southern Europe (see Map 7.1). The greatest of the German states, the growing kingdom of Prussia, was still a second-rank power. In Southern Europe, the Austrian Habsburgs were patiently rebuilding their empire with Hungarian, Romanian, and Slavic subjects. Its great eastward expansion in full swing, the Russian empire with its prodigious resources and vast size was the strongest of the military states.

European empire-builders claimed every inch of American ground, although indigenous resistance and rugged terrain made European states unable to enforce their claims over huge stretches of the continents. In their first centuries of conquest, European states had been more concerned with suppressing their competitors and extracting precious resources for war than with incurring the expense of duplicating European administrations. European states were determined that colonial economic resources benefit the colonizing power. American economies developed in tow of European metropoles.

The Collision of Empires Produces a Military Revolution in Europe

Refining tactics developed in the previous two centuries, Frederick II earned the title "the Great" on the battlefield. He owed his success to a mechanically perfected close order drill that enabled soldiers to march rapidly, to maneuver in formation over a battlefield, and to prime, load, and fire their muskets in a disciplined manner when faced with an attacking enemy. Box 7.1 elaborates in a little more detail on the character of this military revolution. Savage and relentless discipline taught new tactics to a soldiery recruited from landless laborers and poor peasants, reinforced by "volunteers" from captured enemies who were simply inducted into the army which had just conquered them. The king scorned his troops: "If my soldiers began to think, not one would remain in the ranks." Mass desertion was characteristic of such armies. During the Seven Years' War (1756–63), 70,000 troops fled Frederick's camps, a large number for a king who never commanded an army larger than 40,000 at any one time. Frederick's officers tried to keep his soldiers from passing through towns or villages where civilians might hide them. Marches at night or over mountainous terrain were avoided as providing too many opportunities for escape.

New European military techniques and intensified conflict increased the financial demands on states, making the smaller professional armies of the eighteenth century more costly than the larger armies of the seventeenth century. The near continuity of major wars between 1701 and 1815 and the need for thoroughly trained soldiers kept a substantial number of regular soldiers under arms. The cost of war grew because, fearful of desertion, officers could no longer follow the established military practice of allowing marching troops to forage the surrounding country; instead they met their needs by the more costly method of transporting supplies from the rear. In a pinch, monarchs supplemented their troops by purchasing the service of regiments of troops from such nurseries of military men as Switzerland or the smaller German states.

Powerful navies were essential to nations such as Britain, France, Holland, and Spain, with colonial possessions and investments in foreign trade. Although threatened by French seamanship and effectively challenged by a naval coalition during the American revolutionary war, Britain generally maintained its naval supremacy. Discipline in the British navy was as severe as in Frederick II's army. To obtain sailors during wartime, the British navy turned to "impressments," stopping commercial ships entering ports and forcibly enlisting their sailors. Desertion was also a problem for the British navy. Yet the extent of its commercial shipping and its many seaports made it relatively easy for the British navy to find sailors and gave it a decided advantage in naval warfare.

Map 7.1 Europe, 1715

Militias in the Atlantic World Militias (citizen soldiers called up in times of emergency) played a key role in the Americas. In the second half of the eighteenth century, the number of European soldiers stationed in the Americas increased but the need for fighting men grew even faster; everywhere in the Americas, militias and volunteer units were crucial to colonial warfare. In 1743 in Spanish Florida, militias recruited from both freedmen and slaves distinguished themselves in the colony's defense against British attack. During the War of the Austrian Succession (1740–48), American colonists mustered large numbers of militia-men and supplied the funds to arm and provision them for a successful attack on the French stronghold at Louisbourg.

Militias were most effective when defending their own home territory and often disappeared during the sowing or harvesting when labor was most needed on the farm. Faced with regular troops, militias often broke and ran, but they provided the building blocks for colonial armies. George Washington's construction of a professional army proved key to the colonists' ultimate victory, but militia and other volunteer forces produced many of the military leaders and troops for successful colonial revolutions, men such as Horatio Gates, Daniel Morgan, and George Washington himself. In Saint-Domingue, French colonial authorities recruited freed slaves into units that fought beside American rebels at the siege of Savannah in the American Revolution. Freedmen included leaders of the future Haitian rebellion, André Rigaud and Henri Christophe.

What Brings Military Victory? Money, Money, and Money The unceasing clash of armies was expensive. Brilliant military commanders such as Frederick II required money and lots of it.

Box 7.1 A New Military Discipline

Already in the early seventeenth century, military innovators such as Maurice of Nassau were developing new means of warfare that would have great impact on the costs and character of eighteenth-century warfare.

The technologies that increasingly transformed military life after 1600 made new demands on common soldiers. To be sure, the large-scale availability of musketry introduced a powerful weapon to the battlefield, but it only counted if it was fired. Loading and firing these weapons was not easy. It required getting powder, ball, and wadding into place and priming the gun while holding a lighted match. This was difficult enough but doing so while an enemy was

approaching, with murder in mind, made soldiers even more liable to error. Furthermore, in order to give soldiers time to prepare when faced with an approaching enemy, co-ordination was necessary, so that one line of soldiers would be firing while the next line was completing its preparations for firing and the line that had just fired was restarting the loading process. The near impossibility of aiming precisely only further increased the need for co-ordination. Military instructors wanted their troops to fire at the enemy, but aiming at a particular enemy took time, and muskets were highly inaccurate. If enough soldiers fired at the enemy they were sure to hit someone.

In order to make use of the new military technology, military instruction had to pay much more attention to discipline and maneuver. Soldiers had to be so familiar with the process of loading and firing that it seemed almost second nature to them; they would perform these actions automatically without thinking. In order to form into lines that could support one another, troops had to be drilled so that complicated maneuvers became automatic. The means used to inculcate this new discipline were harsh: rote practice and savage punishment for infractions. Always poorly paid, military life became much more highly disciplined.

In Britain, France, and the Netherlands, a sophisticated urban network based on the widespread monetization of the rural economy, the growth of manufactures, and a flourishing international trade, allowed rulers to impose taxes to raise military revenues. Persuasion was especially necessary in dealing with moneyed elites, for money could escape across borders more easily than landed wealth. The British Parliament's control over taxation, and mercantile influence in Parliament, limited though it was, also persuaded merchants that taxation was a good investment.

Neither persuasion nor coercion could extract large sums from Eastern Europe's relatively small and isolated towns or their weak merchant class. The major source of money income, the grain trade, mainly profited large landowners. Outside the surplus that landlords exported, serf-based agriculture was hardly commercialized. In place of negotiating with financiers, Eastern rulers had to win support from landed elites to get the required money and troops. A ruler could easily overawe a coterie of troublesome nobles but offending the nobility as a class invited serious trouble. Throughout Eastern Europe successful monarchs and landlords worked out broadly similar arrangements. Rulers expected male landlords and their sons to serve in royal bureaucracies and as officers in royal armies, recruiting their soldiers from their own estates and providing money to the royal treasury from their grain sales. In exchange, monarchs permitted landlords to govern the rural world. Although agrarian regimes differed in severity, landlords

passed on the tax burden by pressing the rural population harder and punished unruly males by forcing them into the ranks of the military.

France

France's problems stemmed from its in-between status. Both a continental and a colonial power, France needed a great fleet and a powerful regular army and depended for its revenues on merchants and landed aristocrats. **Tax farming** – a system wherein speculators estimated revenues, loaned monarchs money based on these estimates, and then collected revenues themselves – was a curse for the poorest and most vulnerable taxpayers. But it produced large sums of money for French monarchs in emergencies – and there were always emergencies.

French officials looked everywhere for money to pay debt. Taxes from which aristocrats were exempt were a major source of government revenue but, as the debt increased, the old tax structure was overlaid with new taxes levied on everyone equally and the French state turned to more rigorous audits that substantially increased revenues but often angered powerful nobles. It also sold offices to individuals who acquired a hereditary interest in the income they brought. As financial conditions worsened, French rulers repudiated past pledges of official exemption and demanded additional payments from such officials to maintain their privileges. In response, politically powerful taxpayers began to demand checks on arbitrary state action.

Figure 7.1 Front gate of the royal palace of Versailles. Begun as a rural retreat for Louis XIII in 1632, it was the center of French government from 1682–1789. One of its purposes was to overawe other European monarchs. Many did in fact try to imitate Versailles but none succeeded. It was also built to allow the king to keep watch on an always refractory nobility. Powerful monarchs like Louis XVI doled out offices to courtiers who attended them at Versailles. In October 1789 a band of Parisian women, accompanied by troops of the National Guard, marched on Versailles and forced the royal family to return to the king's Tuileries palace in Paris, putting the monarchy under the scrutiny of the people of Paris.

The fragmented structure of European states intensified the problems of tax collection. In 1700, even leaving their American empires aside, the principal continental European powers were all territorial conglomerates of geographically separate political units, each with its own laws, legal privileges, and assemblies, united under a common monarch. The territories of the relatively small Prussian kingdom were scattered across Central Europe. The French kingdom – the most centralized state of its time – was largely territorially contiguous, but contained sixteen separate representative estates, each with its own rights and privileges, and was crisscrossed with toll barriers.

The Rise of the Consolidated State

Over the course of the eighteenth century, European rulers sought to consolidate their kingdoms into territorially contiguous bodies with uniform laws, a common administration, and shared tax burdens. In the 1680s the French had paved the way with their division of their country into districts headed by **intendants**, regional administrative officials appointed directly by the king. Nothing symbolized the power of the new governmental order better than the palace of Versailles, erected between

1664 and 1719 by Louis XIV and Louis XV. It clearly established the superiority of the French monarchy; however powerful and wealthy, no aristocrat could possibly compete with Bourbon splendor (see Figure 7.1). The monarchs expected aristocrats who wanted powerful positions to come to Versailles. Louis XIV refused a highly remunerative position for a powerful noble with the simple sentence, "I do not know him." At Versailles the aristocrat could be watched, manipulated, and controlled by kings who sought to overawe the aristocrats who had so often in French history challenged monarchical power. Administration systems and palaces modeled on Versailles spread from Spain to Russia. Although European states attempted to increase their control over their colonies, none attempted to impose the same degree of centralization abroad as at home.

As states enlarged their administrative structures and powers to tax they also tightened their control over religion. State-supported churches existed almost everywhere and they performed many services that today belong to governments. Whether in Catholic Cuba, Anglican England, Congregationalist Massachusetts, Orthodox Russia, Presbyterian Scotland, or Lutheran Sweden, popular education, a measure of care for the destitute, and the maintenance of some civil records were typically clerical

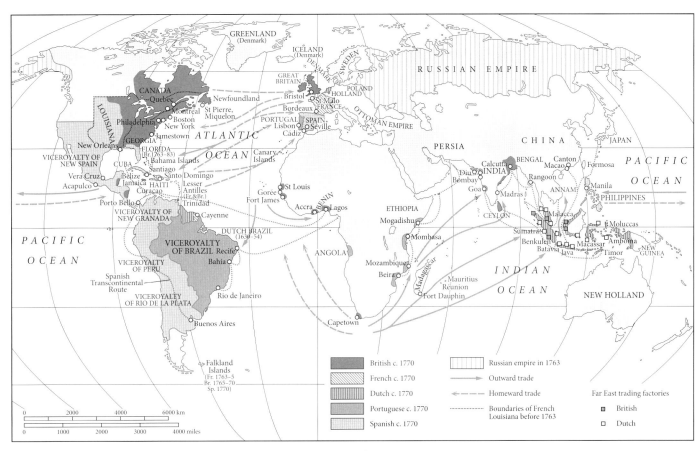

Map 7.2 Global trade patterns of the European states in the eighteenth century

responsibilities. In an era when church and state were so closely intermingled, states' determination to tighten their grip on religion followed naturally from their commitment to greater centralization. But by curbing the independent initiative of the clergy, centralizing states were undermining religious authority, one of the pillars of their own support.

Military conquest also added to tensions between states and established churches by increasing the numbers of disadvantaged religious minorities. Annexation and diplomatic negotiations gradually multiplied the situations in which kingdoms with established churches acquired territories of a different religion. In 1761, when British troops captured Quebec, British statesmen sought to win the French population's loyalty, and in 1774 the Quebec Act recognized Roman Catholicism as French Canada's established church. Inevitably, British acceptance of Catholicism in Quebec brought demands for greater tolerance for Catholics in England and Ireland.

Growth of Capitalism in Old Regime Europe and the Western Colonial World

Commerce and industry linked Old Regime Europe and the Western colonial world, forming a coherent trading region in which Americans were the chief customers for European finished goods, while Europeans were the chief consumers of American agricultural produce. An intercontinental division of labor transformed the Atlantic. Manchester workers put Barbadian sugar in their tea, Parisian intellectuals drank Brazilian coffee, and London bankers smoked Virginia tobacco and exchanged Peruvian silver for Asian silk, porcelain, and tea. American natives such as the potato and the tomato were growing in Ireland and Italy, and meanwhile European wheat, rye, and crabgrass thrived in Pennsylvania and along the Rio de la Plata. Map 7.2 gives a sense of the growing integration of this new global economy.

The growth of Atlantic trade enriched the coffers of many merchants but it also promoted the growth of a new labor force worldwide. In 1750 the populations of port cities, particularly Atlantic port cities – Amsterdam, Brest, Bristol, Cádiz, Dublin, Liverpool, and London – were growing rapidly. In part this growth was due to an increase in the number of maritime workers, sailors, longshoremen, and shipbuilders, but it also included those who catered directly to the maritime trades – sailmakers, ropemakers, and barrelmakers. Outside the port towns, many European workers involved in domestic industry labored in the countryside to produce the cutlery, tools, and cheap jewelry that along with cotton goods were staples of European trade. Labor force growth occurred not only in European port towns and rural domestic industries but wherever European trade touched ground, including ports and plantations all over the world. In 1753 the Dutch East India Company, including its military contingent, directly employed around 57,000 free and unfree workers – the great majority in Africa and Asia – and was the biggest international corporation of its age.

In the eighteenth century, European colonial powers continued to follow **mercantilist** policies, requiring their colonies to produce goods complementary to those of the colonizers and to provide captive markets for the products of metropolitan industry. The doctrine more or less accurately captured the spirit of military rivalry that dominated the period. European military protection was provided to the colonies that in return were expected to help support the colonizers' military machine. One favorite method for extracting colonial revenues was by taxing items of popular consumption: liquor and tobacco in the Spanish colonies and sugar and tea in British North America.

Labor: Free and Unfree Under mercantilism, a new international division of labor grew, one that brought Western European women and children to wage labor in factories while condemning many in the Americas and Eastern Europe to unfree labor in mines and fields. In a densely populated Western Europe, entrepreneurs increasingly found that the development

of a free labor market served their interests well. In a labor-scarce North America, capitalism adapted itself to different climates and political circumstances. In New England and the Mid-Atlantic colonies, a market-oriented small farming spread, with families providing most of the farm labor, hiring additional hands when needed. But in the American South, Brazil, much of the Caribbean, and parts of Spanish America, where labor-intensive crops such as sugar, tobacco, or cotton could bring large profits, capitalists accommodated themselves to slavery. Plantation slavery expanded at a rapid rate. Some societies with slaves were being transformed into slave societies, with enslaved plantation labor central.

For Russian serfs and American slaves, conditions declined after 1700 as they became increasingly integrated into the world economy. Chattel slavery had existed in the American world since the Spanish conquest of the Caribbean. Until the late seventeenth century, however, most slaves of African or indigenous origins were used as domestic servants, farm laborers, or urban artisans or workers. The conditions of temporarily indentured European servants had many similarities to those of African slaves. Nor was the slave's entry into American society entirely culturally traumatic. Many African slaves came from partially Christianized areas of Africa and were familiar with English, Portuguese, or Spanish language and cultural practices.

The character of slavery changed as plantation agriculture demonstrated its enormous profitability (see Figure 7.2). As demand increased, slave traders moved into the African interior to kidnap men and women who had little previous contact

Figure 7.2 At the beginning of the nineteenth century, slavery was a central feature of the Atlantic economy. By the end of the century it had been abolished nearly everywhere, although in some cases it was replaced by labor systems that significantly restricted laborers' rights. Great Britain was a pioneer of abolitionism; it was not legally prohibited there until 1833 but a series of judicial decisions between 1706 and 1772 effectively abolished slavery. Brazil was among the last states in the Atlantic world to abolish slavery (1885). In the USA slavery was only abolished by a great civil war (1861–65).

Box 7.2 Slavery and Freedom in the Eighteenth-Century Colonial World

In 1755 Olaudah Equiano, aged 10 years old, was captured by slave hunters in southeastern Nigeria and sold to English slave traders who in turn sold him to a Virginia planter, who resold him after a month to an officer in the British navy. Although the British officer promised to free Equiano at the end of the Seven Years' War for his service, the officer violated his promise and sold him into West Indian slavery.

Equiano's next master was Robert King, a Quaker merchant who promised to allow him to purchase his freedom for a fixed sum of money. Since many Quakers opposed slavery, his luck in being purchased by a Quaker merchant was a turning point in Equiano's life. While working as an able seaman for King, Equiano spent several years at sea. His visits with enslaved and free Africans in island commercial ports show how contacts could be maintained among fellow countrymen, sometimes at great distances.

Equiano was a good businessman and within a few years was able to acquire this relatively large sum. But would his master accept it? There was nothing but his master's word that he would honor the pledge; the master could just as well have confiscated the money and sold him to more brutal masters. Indeed, when he learned that Equiano had acquired such a large sum of money in a short time, his master did lament the prospect of losing so valuable a servant but, beseeched by Equiano and encouraged by the ship's captain, an Englishman who had befriended Equiano, the master finally honored his promise, accepted the money, and freed his slave.

Though his master had purchased him and participated in a slave system that Equiano held in horror, nonetheless Equiano felt a sense of obligation to his old master (similar to that felt by the Roman freedmen discussed in Volume 1, Chapter 6). In any case, he continued to man one of King's ships, even though this subjected him to frequent attacks by slave catchers who sought to kidnap him and re-enslave him. Ultimately Equiano settled down in London and became an articulate opponent of slavery. Equiano's devotion to the anti-slavery cause led to his association with London radicals and for a time he lived in the house of the celebrated English radical reformer Thomas Hardy. Equiano's memoirs are one of the few accounts, from the perspective of an African, describing his African homeland, his capture and enslavement, and his life as a seafaring slave and ultimately freedman.

---

with European religions or languages. The shipping of Africans across the Atlantic took a toll of millions of lives. The horrors of slavery and the slave trade seriously challenge the Enlightenment's own image of itself as an age of reason and growing humanity. Meanwhile, indentured servants refused to migrate to colonies to work under the oppressive conditions in sugar plantations. Plantation labor became the exclusive venue of coerced African slaves lacking familiarity with European ways and marked by their skin color. Box 7.2 discusses the life and writing of Olaudah Equiano. Captured by slave raiders in Africa, Equiano possessed real commercial ability and he was able to buy his freedom but liberty always remained precarious for freedmen and freedwomen. At best they were only secondary citizens and poorly positioned to defend their rights again slavers, who would kidnap and re-enslave them. The character of labor bondage changed in Europe as landlords increased production for Western European markets. Traditional Russian serfdom binding the cultivator to the land gave way to a slave-like system in which serfs became the possessions of masters who could buy and sell them and lose them in card games.

While capitalism and state centralization were important forces for social change, they confronted an incredible diversity of conditions across three continents. The resulting economic relations and state forms yielded different sets of grievances and opportunities for resistance. No wonder they would produce different outcomes when transformed in the revolutionary cauldron.

Political Culture of Old Regime Europe and the Western Colonial World

In the eighteenth century a philosophical movement, the **Enlightenment**, spread through the entire region, with significant consequences for the character of revolutions. The Enlightenment originated in the efforts of powerful rulers to dominate intellectual life as thoroughly as they did political life, in the need of governments for trained secular administrators, and in the growth of a literate capitalist middle class. It constituted a language and shared culture that brought men and women together across continents.

The great strength of Enlightenment thought was its appeal to diverse elite audiences. Great monarchs such as Louis XIV demonstrated French power not only on the battlefield but also by setting intellectual trends throughout Old Regime Europe. They founded national scientific academies and theaters and funded literary projects and books carried out by secular intellectuals who championed reason against tradition, secularism against religious intolerance, and science against superstition. The eighteenth century witnessed a growing demand from a middle-class public for accurate information about political affairs and the rise of a clandestine printing industry catering to this demand. Wealthy urban merchants and professional men joined with nobles in salons, coffee-houses, and scientific and literary societies to discuss the latest scientific and intellectual developments. Expanding from Moscow to Mexico City, freemasonry, a widespread secret society dedicated to mutual aid and fraternity, brought diverse elite groups, Catholics and Protestants, nobles and middle class, together in the name of good fellowship and secular morality. For many merchants and professional men, the thrill of belonging was heightened by contact with their social superiors. Heightened interpersonal contact between aristocrats and business and professional men also increased the possibility of aristocratic insolence and middle-class humiliation. In 1770 Antoine Barnave, a future revolutionary, was at the theater in Grenoble with his mother when their seats were demanded by the governor of the Dauphiné who wanted them for his friends. Barnave's mother refused to move and was carried out by soldiers.

By itself the Enlightenment did not produce revolution. Typically the Enlightenment's major spokesmen were dependent on government subsidies and they were usually dissatisfied with government allotments. Enlightened thinkers such as Benjamin Franklin, David Hume, Jonathan Swift, Voltaire, Adam Smith, Denis Diderot, Thomas Jefferson, and Jean-Jacques Rousseau represented a wide spectrum of political beliefs. Poets such as Alexander Pope and musicians such as Wolfgang Amadeus Mozart used their art to promote Enlightenment ideals. Some, such as Voltaire and Swift, were passionate critics of society while others, such as David Hume, were unexcitable; Hume did not allow his religious criticisms to be published until after his death. Freemasonry included Frederick II, the Prussian king who treated his troops like automatons, and Joseph Brant, the Native American leader who fought the American colonists on the frontiers, as well as the American revolutionaries Simón Bolívar and George Washington.

The Enlightenment Left a Profound Mark on the Age of Revolution The secular discourse of the Enlightenment enabled political ideas to pass easily across hitherto impermeable European religious and political boundaries; Voltaire read John Locke with the greatest reverence during his exile in England and spent time in the French-speaking court of Frederick II; the Scot David Hume befriended the Swiss-born Jean-Jacques Rousseau in Paris. The national and international networks of intellectual exchange served not only to spread Enlightenment ideas but also to create a public convinced that reason applied to political debate might result in worthwhile reforms. Communication was facilitated because French had replaced Latin by the eighteenth century as the language of civilized men and women. Scholars wishing to make an international name for themselves wrote in French. During the American Revolution, British officers communicated with German commanders in French.

In the last years of the Old Regime, fraternal societies grew rapidly and fostered the growth of an extraordinary spirit of **cosmopolitanism**, embracing thinkers of the caliber of Condorcet, Benjamin Franklin, Immanuel Kant, Anne-Robert-Jacques Turgot, and Voltaire. The German poet and playwright Friedrich Schiller asserted that "I write as a citizen of the world who serves no prince. At an early age, I lost my fatherland to trade it for the whole world." And Thomas Paine proclaimed that "my country is the world and my religion is to do good."

The Age of Revolution destroyed this embryonic spirit of cosmopolitanism as thoroughly as it destroyed so many other institutions and cherished beliefs of the Old Regime world.

7.2 THREE KEY REVOLUTIONS

Revolutions began amid conflicts among elites within existing institutions. As established governments and elite-controlled assemblies intensified their conflict, each sought allies, and the course of the revolution changed as new groups mobilized and joined the conflict. Overthrowing royal authority was easier than replacing it. Meeting with resistance, both revolutionaries and counter-revolutionaries frequently appealed to oppressed groups hitherto excluded from the political process. The entry of such groups as the Parisian crowd or Haitian slaves into the revolutionary process opened the way for social revolution. Predominantly political revolutions, as in the USA, occurred where victorious revolutionaries least involved excluded groups. Predominantly social revolutions, as in Haiti, occurred where victorious revolutionaries were largely composed of previously excluded groups. The French Revolution was as much a social as a political revolution.

The following sections analyze the origins and outcomes of these three major revolutions.

Colonial Revolution in British North America, 1774–95

In the short run, the Revolution in North America was the product of the growing disagreement between American colonists and their British governors over issues of taxation, but profound divisions within the British polity in the 1760s and 1770s facilitated the Revolution. Long the dominant force in British politics, the aristocratic Whigs' monopoly of power was broken by George III's determination to recruit both Whigs and their Tory rivals into his governments. The Whigs saw George III's strategy of forming coalitions above parties as threatening England's unwritten constitution and denounced the king's use of patronage and bribes to win parliamentary majorities as corrupt and despotic. American colonists who read Whig newspapers imported from London used the arguments advanced by the Whig opposition to justify their opposition to the king to a British audience.

The deeper roots of the Revolution can be traced to the end of the Seven Years' War (1756–63). The capture of Quebec in 1759 removed the military threat binding the colonies to Britain. Meanwhile the British government implemented centralization projects and new taxes deferred during the Anglo-French conflict. But colonial governments were struggling under the burden of debts incurred during the war, and their economies suffered from Britain's reduced demand for their agricultural goods and naval stores after the war's end.

British policy was not part of a despotic conspiracy, but it was designed to extract more revenue from the colonies and to increase imperial control. This goal inevitably involved restricting long-established colonial charters and legal concessions that Americans had come to regard as their rights. In 1765 Britain's passage of the Stamp Act drew a united colonial response. The act required stamps on legal documents as well as pamphlets, newspapers, and other items of popular consumption. Adding insult to injury, much of the act's revenue supported British garrisons whose task was to prevent colonists from occupying Native American lands west of the Appalachians.

Opposition to the tax led to the formation of patriotic parties throughout the socially and economically diverse colonies; patriots were able to appeal to both rich and poor, for all were subject to the tax. In Boston, the "Sons of Liberty" linked powerful merchants like John Hancock, ambitious lawyers like John Adams, and highly skilled master artisans like Paul Revere. Artisan participation brought contacts with poorer Bostonians such as the escaped slave and sailor Crispus Attucks. Artisans and sailors were the core of the crowds that intimidated applicants for the post of stamp tax collectors. The Stamp Act was repealed, only to be replaced by other unilaterally imposed measures of taxation such as the Townshend Acts. These again provoked popular protest that brought, in its turn, repression.

Britain's efforts to collect taxes from the sale of tea shipped to Boston and over which the government-controlled British East India Company enjoyed a monopoly provoked a boycott. A stubborn British governor refused to allow the tea to be returned and pressure grew. In December 1773 this led to the "Boston Tea Party" in which the Sons of Liberty boarded a tea ship and threw the tea into the harbor. It was a major step toward revolution (see Figure 7.3).

Figure 7.3 The Tea Party in Boston. On December 16, 1773, members of the Sons of Liberty, composed mainly of craftsmen, artisans, and journeymen, boarded a ship in Boston harbor and threw chests of tea into the bay. They were protesting the attempts of the British government to impose a tax on tea and other basic commodities. From Paris to Haiti, the slogan "No taxation without representation" rang through the Atlantic world. Events in Boston began a cycle of protest and revolution that produced American revolution.

THE "BOSTON BOYS" THROWING THE TAXED TEA INTO BOSTON HARBOUR.

Revolutionary Process In 1774 this cycle of taxation–resistance–repression led to the beginning of a **revolutionary process**. This begins when:

- At least two groups assert their right to rule.
- They effectively command the allegiance of substantial sections of the population.
- They mobilize force to assert their claims.

The Massachusetts governor, British General Gage, cancelled his convocation of the state's hostile legislature but it met anyway and constituted itself a "Provincial Congress" that levied taxes and solicited the allegiance of state militia units. Congress's assertion of supreme power was the first element of the revolutionary process. In April 1775, British troops marched into areas supporting the Congress in search of military supplies, meeting a small group of militiamen at Lexington. There the first shots of the American Revolution were fired. The Revolution had found its bayonets. This combination of alternative claimants to power – the British governor and the Massachusetts Congress, each asserting its exclusive right to rule, winning support, and commanding military force – marks the beginning of a revolutionary process.

The ways in which other groups in society respond to such claims constitutes the dynamic of the revolutionary process. The Massachusetts Provincial Congress took its case to the Second Continental Congress called to obtain redress of grievances and the restoration of harmony with Great Britain. Meeting in Philadelphia, the body convened colonists from the South, the Mid-Atlantic states, and New England who found they had many grievances in common. As conciliation failed and the military confrontation between British troops and American militia spread to New York City, the Congress proclaimed American independence on July 4, 1776.

While the conflict began with American political leaders and merchants challenging British authorities and mercantile privileges, the cause developed a more social aspect as each side adapted its policies to attract allies. The poor in Boston, New York, and Philadelphia, affected by naval impressments and consumption taxes, rallied to the Revolution. As the conflict deepened, everyone in the colonies was courted by one side or the other. Sometimes the decision of one group to support the Continental Congress led a rival group to opt for the British. The powerful landholders of the southern Hudson Valley supported the British while the northern landholders subject to Native American attack supported the Continental Congress; in both cases their tenants chose the opposite allegiance in the hope that their masters' defeat would mitigate a severe agrarian regime. After prolonged negotiations with the British, Ethan Allen and his Green Mountain boys rallied to the Revolution

in the hope that a new nation would recognize their land claims, disallowed by New York authorities. The backcountries of the Carolinas and the frontier areas of New York, equally suspicious of colonial elites and British rulers, were deeply divided.

As the conflict intensified, the British allied with indigenous peoples and offered to free the slaves of rebellious masters. However, Britain's alliance with Native Americans threatened loyalists almost as much as patriots and – in the critical case of New York – fear of Native American attacks made it easier for the American rebels to recruit soldiers. In the South, many slaves (up to one in four in South Carolina) sought British protection. But British promises of abolition were directed only to the slaves of rebel masters and were hampered by Britain's abiding commitment to slavery in its empire. Many escaped slaves were interned until the British authorities could determine their masters' political allegiances. Some British officers treated escaped slaves as war plunder and sold them to Caribbean masters. On balance, British threats of abolition led Southern loyalists, worried about slave revolts, to shift their allegiance to the rebels.

Britain's ability to provision its armies from 3,000 miles away demonstrated an unrivaled capacity and provided valuable experience for the wars of the French Revolution to come. Nevertheless, distance led to crucial failures of intelligence. The key defeat at Saratoga (1777) was the result of poor co-ordination. Subsequent British strategy alternated fatally between efforts to defeat American armies and attempts to rally loyalist "majorities" believed to exist in the Southern and Mid-Atlantic colonies. Driven by contradictory purposes, the British General Cornwallis stumbled into final defeat at Yorktown (1781).

While Yorktown marked the triumph of the rebellious colonies, a triumph recognized by the Treaty of Paris in 1783, a revolutionary dynamic continued on the new nation's western margins. British western administrators stubbornly resisted the concessions made by a distant English government and Native Americans fought against the seizure of their lands. The revolutionary process was not finally completed until the Battle of Fallen Timbers in 1794 and the Treaty of Greenville in 1795. These marked the defeat of Native American efforts to preserve land that they claimed as their own, land which they argued the British had no right to cede to the victorious colonists.

The most important outcomes of the American Revolution were political. First of course, from Savannah to Bangor and from the Atlantic to the Mississippi, a new independent state began to emerge. In 1787 at Philadelphia a new constitution constructed a federal state able to draw on the resources of the former colonies far more effectively than the previous British administration. The years between the ratification of the Articles of Confederation in 1781 and the adoption of the Constitution in 1787 revealed the weaknesses of confederation, and the new Constitution created a judiciary, an executive, and legislative assemblies with the power to regulate commerce and to levy and collect taxes – all features lacking in the old confederation. The Bill of Rights, a concession to the Constitution's opponents, committed the nation to protect local and individual rights. Ratification of the US Constitution by state conventions established the new nation's authority directly and not through the intermediary of state legislatures.

The revolutionary process set in motion a transformation of citizenship in the US: The modern word "citizen" originated in the Revolution. The extended conflict with Great Britain forced revolutionary elites to mobilize a modicum of popular support, setting in motion a wave of expansion of the electorate. By 1825, universal white manhood suffrage obtained everywhere but Louisiana, Virginia, and Rhode Island. Because of its record of loyalism to Britain, the Anglican church was disestablished in Virginia and most of the South.

Aside from the expansion of the electorate, the American Revolution produced other social changes. Popular suspicion of aristocratic privilege led to the repeal of state legislation favoring the inheritance of eldest sons. In areas of New York and Maryland, the confiscation of large loyalist landholdings benefited some tenants and squatters, although wealthy speculators profited most. The disputed land claims of Vermont farmers were recognized. Most importantly, the defeat of indigenous peoples led to the opening of the Northwest territories to colonization.

For other Americans, however, there was no transformation of political status, no new civic identity. For slaves in the American South, the Revolution brought no remedy, indeed the following decades saw the growing entrenchment of plantation slavery in the South. Most of the framers of the Constitution opposed slavery and hoped that it would be abolished but were hesitant to extend citizenships to Africans and saw no alternative to slaves as a workforce in the South's expanding plantation agriculture. Initially tormented by the existence of slavery, Southern statesmen such as Thomas Jefferson and James Madison yielded to acceptance as their republic grew and plantation agriculture became the lifeblood of the Southern economy. Nevertheless, the closing of the Northwest territories to slavery by the Articles of Confederation was enormously important for the future. Indeed, slaves' role in the revolutionary war and growing ideological opposition to slavery led to its abolition in key New England and Mid-Atlantic states.

Women were not among the principal beneficiaries of the Revolution, although women played an important role in supporting boycotts of British goods and supplying the troops.

In fact both revolutionary and loyalist women assumed new roles and unfamiliar burdens to preserve their families when their husbands were absent. Abigail Adams debated politics with her husband John Adams and his friends, but her celebrated admonition to her husband to "remember the ladies" was unavailing. Locally important women like Martha Ballard, a midwife in late eighteenth-century Maine, more or less ignored a political world which ignored them (Box 7.3). Whatever benefits women received as a group from the Revolution came in its aftermath when, worried about the post-revolutionary decline of republican fervor, politicians emphasized the need for mothers to inculcate civic interest in their sons. The ideal of the Republican Mother encouraged women's schooling, usually in new coeducational institutions.

Revolution in France, 1789–1815

The special significance of France in the Age of Revolution stems in part from its dual role in Europe. After a century of warfare on land and sea in which France had failed either to dominate Europe or to rival Britain outside Europe, its commercial and agricultural elites were increasingly unwilling to support far-flung military escapades. Revolution in France also began with disputes over taxation. With nobles and financiers and the king stalemated over how to deal with state debt, the king called a meeting of the traditional national representative body, the Estates General – which had not met since 1614. Customarily, this assembly was divided into orders or estates: The first estate was the clergy, the second the nobility, the third everyone else. The debate over the selection of delegates and the grievances discussed in local assemblies throughout France had a powerful politicizing effect, as did the furious controversies over methods of election.

Everyone expected the nobility to lead the assembly. But to everyone's surprise, the great majority of nobles elected were not the urbane and sophisticated **nobility of the robe**, men from wealthy families who had purchased their titles or earned them in the state bureaucracy, but the cruder and less polished **nobility of the sword**, men from obscure localities belonging to long-standing noble families claiming descent from military vassals. Within their estate meetings, they spent much of their time quarrelling among themselves – unable to distinguish political disagreement from personal reproach. At one point, someone suggested appointing teams of swordsmen and settling a major political dispute on the field of honor. The clergy too was divided between aristocratic religious authorities and rebellious parish priests.

More united, the third estate seized the initiative. On June 20, 1789, at the great palace of Versailles, a group of assembly

Box 7.3 Martha Ballard: A Midwife's Tale

In August of 1787 the framers of the US Constitution were still locked in struggle; the Constitution would not be signed for another month. Martha Ballard of Hallowell, Maine, took no note in her diary of these important events. She had more immediate concerns. She was a midwife who between August 3 and 27, as her biographer Laurel Thatcher Ulrich shows, "performed four deliveries, answered one obstetrical false alarm, made sixteen medical calls, prepared three bodies for burial, dispensed pills to one neighbor, harvested and prepared herbs for another and doctored her own husband's sore throat." Martha was

clearly an important and valued member of the Maine community where she lived. Yet she showed very little interest in politics. To be sure, in 1799 she attended a service to commemorate the death of George Washington, but did not bother to mention the march of young women through the community in honor of the dead president.

As a woman Martha Ballard was excluded from political participation: She could not vote, become a juror, or occupy a political office. Although disenfranchised, she still directed her very considerable energies into channels that promised more immediate rewards for her family

and community. As her biographer notes, "For Martha, politics was what men did at town meetings – necessary perhaps, but often troublesome and divisive."

Right up until her death in 1812, Ballard would continue to provide medical services to her community, rowing across the stormy Kennebec river at times that gave pause to local men and sitting up all night with patients only to go out again almost as soon as she had returned. Accepted as a colleague by some local medical men, an important local figure like Martha Ballard still lacked full citizenship.

members who feared that Louis XVI was planning to dissolve their assembly met in the old tennis court and constituted themselves a "National Assembly," vowing to remain together until they had created a new constitution. In practice the Assembly asserted sovereign power. Within a few weeks, armed National Guard militias formed in French cities, soldiers refused to fire on crowds, and on July 14, 1789, the Parisian populace stormed the infamous Bastille, the sinister old prison that towered over the popular districts of Paris (see Figure 7.4). A genuine revolutionary situation emerged as armed supporters mobilized to support the men who had taken the Tennis Court Oath.

Between 1789 and 1792, leading French politicians tried again and again to create a stable government. Even the execution of the king in 1793 did not end the conflict because the triumphant revolutionaries could not themselves agree upon a replacement. The Revolution's apogee came in 1793–94 as local rebellions against the national government swept the country while foreign armies invaded it. Attacked on all sides, the Assembly entrusted power to a handful of the most determined revolutionaries. These men, most prominently Maximilien Robespierre, mobilized the Revolution's supporters, crushed internal rebellion, and repelled invasion. The price the country paid was a bloody "Reign of Terror" when old associations and careless words sent men and women to the guillotine.

Recurrent disputes among revolutionaries over fundamental issues provided opportunities for previously marginal groups to influence political debates. In 1789 the king and his family had been forced to move from Versailles to Paris and

subsequently were followed to Paris by the new National Assembly. Henceforward both king and Assembly were subject to crowd pressure and intensified demand for social reform. Courting popular support, revolutionary authorities sought to regulate the price of bread and basic urban commodities.

Creating a Revolutionary Army The creation of a conscript army was one of the most important dimensions of the French Revolution. The reorganized French armies, composed of conscripts fighting alongside veterans, were more than a match for European armies of the Frederick II type. Swelled by volunteers fighting to defend their rights, revolutionary armies moved swiftly; their commanders had less fear that night marches or rough terrain would lead to mass desertions. Troops could be sent out to forage or skirmish in small units in expectation that they would return. These armies required songs, such as the *Marseillaise*, that could inspire them (see Box 7.4), for unlike Frederick's armies these depended on a sense of solidarity and citizenship. Military success was also strongly influenced by Old Regime military reforms carried out in response to defeat in the Seven Years' War; artillery pieces were made sufficiently mobile to accompany fast-moving revolutionary armies and new tactics deployed artillery in concentrated batteries, multiplying its effect. At the height of mass enthusiasm for the Revolution in 1790, the French government proclaimed the "levée en masse," by which they meant mass conscription (see Figure 7.5). As the results showed, French society was not yet so united around a common goal or identity as to be able to really enforce mass conscriptions, but revolutionary soldiers

Figure 7.4 With reform legislation stalled by the king, with rumors of a troop concentration around Paris, and with the dismissal of a reformist minister, a crowd began to march toward the Bastille. Intended to intimidate, the Bastille was a large ugly building looming menacingly over one of the principal popular quarters of Paris. Here lived the artisans and journeymen who would provide the future tinder for revolutionary Paris. Its fall marked the beginning of real revolution, when principled resistance to royal rule united with military force.

Box 7.4 La Marseillaise: The First National Anthem

When France declared war on Austria and Prussia in 1792, an army engineer, Claude-Joseph Rouget de Lisle (1760–1836), living in Strasbourg, was inspired to write a marching song. The song was initially entitled "War Song for the Army of the Rhine," but recruits from Marseilles took it up and brought it to Paris, where it became known as the "Marseillaise." On July 14, 1795, it became the French national anthem.

Banned under the Napoleonic empire and during the Bourbon restoration, it went underground, where it was taken up by republican sympathizers around the world. Over the years, it became a favorite among leftists of all stripes and socialists sang versions of it.

Ironically Rouget de Lisle himself was a moderate republican, jailed during the Terror.

Since then almost every nation has adopted a national anthem. From the American national anthem, which celebrates a battle in the War of 1812, to the Irish national anthem, simply titled "A Soldier's Song," to Monaco's anthem, which calls for the "proud fellows of the Civic Guard to listen to their commander's voice," war has been a major theme of national anthems.

La Marseillaise

Arise children of the fatherland,
The day of glory has arrived!
Against us tyranny has raised
The bloody standard,
Do you hear in our countryside
The bellows of ferocious soldiers?
They have come among us
To cut the throats of your children and comrades.

To arms, citizens,
Form your battalions,
Let impure blood
Water our furrows.

were quite far from the driven and coerced semi-prisoners of Frederick the Great.

In the hands of gifted generals, such as Napoleon Bonaparte, revolutionary armies repeatedly defeated the major European military powers. As revolutionaries fought among themselves, increased power accrued to successful military men. An exhausted France fell under the sway of Napoleon, who sought to reconcile aristocratic France to the Revolution by appointing

Figure 7.5 Levée en masse (literally "mass mobilization" or "mass uprising") refers to the conscription of all unmarried, able-bodied males between the ages of 18 and 25 into French armies or militia by the Convention of 1793. Of course the revolutionaries never really tried to induct everyone into the army but they did increase enlistment. Mass conscription provoked rebellion among populations unsympathetic to the Revolution but it also greatly increased the military resources available to defend France against the foreign armies that invaded it.

talented aristocrats to important positions. A string of brilliant Napoleonic military victories at Lodi, Marengo, and Austerlitz, combined with his sudden rise from obscurity, made Napoleon a hero to all young European men who felt that their own hidden talents were not appreciated. While Napoleon consolidated power in his own hands and halted the revolutionary process in France, his armies carried its reform politics to all those areas of Europe incorporated into the Napoleonic empire (see Maps 7.3 and 7.4), inspired dreams of national independence among Italian and Polish patriots, and forced other rulers to reorganize to meet the French challenge. No European ruler could ignore a revolution that produced victorious armies.

What Did the Revolution Accomplish? How did France change between the beginning of the Revolution in 1789 and the defeat of Napoleon in 1814? First, the Revolution created an even more centralized French state. Revolutionaries abolished the intermediary institutions of the old order, the semi-independent judicial institutions, tax farmers, charitable establishments, and provincial estates; France was departmentalized, districted, and communalized – divided into relatively homogeneous administrative districts. Under both the Terror and Napoleon, even when elected bodies remained at the departmental and arrondissement level, salaried full-time officials solely responsible to the central government usurped the real power. This new administrative structure extended the direct power of the central state into hitherto inaccessible village communes and imposed more and more obligations on mayors.

The strong new republic asserted claims on the civilian population that went far beyond those of the most thoroughgoing European absolutisms. Revolutionaries replaced a mélange of regional measures with the metric system. Determined secularists though they were, revolutionary legislators, like the monarchs before them, found it difficult to disentangle the many ties that bound church and state together. The Civil Constitution of the Clergy of 1790 was designed to harness the church to the same centralized direction as other public institutions in French society. Eventually in 1801 the Concordat, negotiated between Napoleon and Pope Pius VII, created a new framework for relations between the French state and the Catholic church, one in which the government could exert great influence but which also recognized papal supremacy in ecclesiastical matters. In 1798, the Jourdan-Delbrel law decreed universal military conscription for males.

The extensive new powers were justified politically by the state's assumption of vast new obligations to citizens and a complex extension of rights. At no time during the years between 1789 and 1814 was there a single category of citizenship to which everyone belonged. Nonetheless, even non-citizens were accorded some basic rights, and the Revolution's conception of basic rights grew as it radicalized and relied more heavily on popular support. In 1789, the Declaration of the Rights of Man recognized the rights to a fair trial, religious toleration, and freedom of the press. The constitution of 1791 introduced the categories of "active" and "passive" citizenship and, though the definitions expanded or contracted from one constitution to

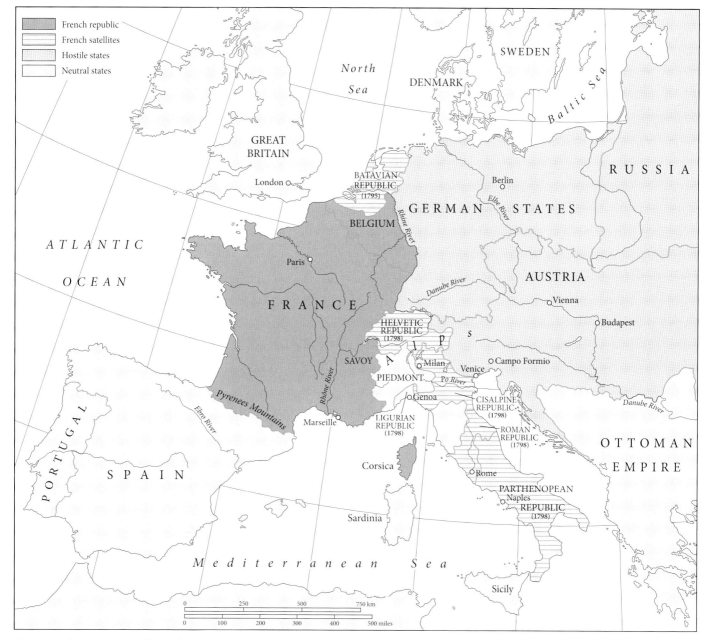

Map 7.3 The French republic and its satellites, hostile states, and neutrals in 1799

another, this basic distinction endured throughout the whole period. At its most restrictive, active citizenship, which gave its possessor the right to vote, applied to most male taxpayers. At its least, in the constitution of 1793, active citizenship belonged to most adult males.

Although the revolutionary legislators enacted divorce legislation and lifted some restrictions on property owning, French revolutionaries drew the line at extending citizenship to women. Women were considered by their very nature as incapable of citizenship and in the same category as children and the legally insane. Women's membership in the polity was mediated by their relationship to men. In 1791, Olympe de Gouges wrote a

"Declaration of the Rights of Woman," a feminist version of the celebrated "Declaration of the Rights of Man." In the streets of Paris and in some provincial cities a more popular feminism prevailed. Women formed republican clubs, submitted petitions demanding the right to vote, and swayed revolutionary societies by cheering or shouting down speakers from the galleries (see Figure 7.6). In 1793 a spokesman for the legislative majority stressed the role of women as mothers and the need for feminine modesty, and concluded that "It is not possible for women to exercise political rights." The revolutionary legislature then banned women's political clubs. The universal rights proclaimed in Paris did not extend to half the human race.

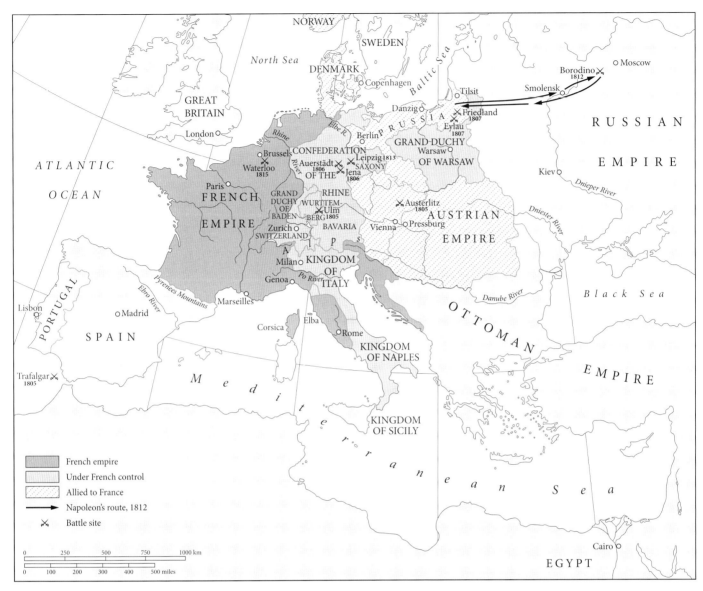

Map 7.4 Napoleonic Grand Empire

Figure 7.6 The French Revolution began with nobles and merchants asserting their rights against a tyrannical king. As the Revolution progressed, however, other groups followed this example and asserted their rights. Women replied to the rights of man with a demand for the rights of women. Parisiennes applauded speakers in patriotic societies and participated in crowd actions such as the march on Versailles. But most male revolutionaries refused to recognize women's rights and opposed women's suffrage.

The Revolution did have some important social consequences. Many legally privileged social statuses disappeared entirely. In 1790 titles of nobility were abolished and, in 1791, the corporations (which included groups which today would be called voluntary associations like professional or workers' organizations, but also some – like city councils – which we would designate "governmental organizations"). Between 1804 and 1811, a standardized legal system, tailored to the needs of a market society, was imposed on the entire country. The Napoleonic Codes ratified revolutionary legislation restricting legacies favoring the inheritance of eldest sons, but reversed most of the legal gains for women made during the Revolution and restored, indeed strengthened, the legal principle of male superiority. Sweeping changes also occurred in the countryside. While the Revolution had committed itself early on to the "abolition of feudalism," the terms on which it would be abolished remained a matter of negotiation until various waves of agrarian protest forced revolutionaries to grant terms more favorable to the rural population.

A new nationalist identity issued from the Revolution that claimed to be based on the popular will of the citizens who collectively formed the nation. The importance of citizens' popular identification with **civic nationalism**, a shared body of law and a common legislature – a political project that was not linguistic, racial, or cultural – was repeated and strengthened in the many public ceremonies that revolutionary propagandists used to educate the people.

Revolution in Haiti, 1790–1820

The Revolution in Saint-Domingue (later known as Haiti) reverberated throughout the Americas. The wealthiest colony in the Caribbean, the "Eden of the Western World" produced almost half of all the sugar and coffee consumed in Europe and the Americas; in the 1780s its foreign trade was greater than that of the USA.

The Revolution in Saint-Domingue began as a colonial revolution and, as in the British colonies, the imperial center had an important influence on its outbreak. Saint-Domingue was a colony of 500,000 African slaves, 40,000 whites, and 30,000 other people of color (*gens du couleur*). Despite its small size, Saint-Domingue's white population was deeply divided along class lines, with a small elite of rich planters and a mass of poor whites who had emigrated to Saint-Domingue, one of the few colonial outlets for France's surplus population. Alongside the white population were mulattos and freedmen who despite their wealth and slave owning were denied political rights in the colony.

Revolutionary turmoil in Saint-Domingue began with political crisis in France. From the moment that they heard of the call for elections to the Estates General, Saint-Domingue's whites demanded representation to put forward their grievances. In 1790 the revolutionary process in Saint-Domingue began with white males electing representatives to discuss their demands, foremost among them France's right to tax its colonial subjects. Echoing events in Massachusetts and France, the deputies from the three provinces refused to meet at the site set by the royal governor, instead declaring their own sovereignty and constituting themselves a "Colonial Assembly." Like the North American colonists, the Saint-Domingue Assembly called for "no taxation without representation."

A three-cornered fight quickly developed. One faction consisted of the royal governor, large planters, and merchants who supported limited reform; the second faction, the poor whites, demanded autonomy and representation; the third group were mulattos and freed slaves. The first two were bitterly opposed to each other. They agreed only on the need to forbid the people of colour and freedmen the political representation they demanded. In Paris, meanwhile, plantation owners organized a powerful lobby and quickly seized the initiative from such anti-slavery groups as the *Amis des Noirs*. Even though the French National Assembly did little for slaves, word began to filter back to Saint-Domingue – transmitted by sailors who loaded cargo as well as by inter-island traders – about the existence of French abolitionists and their efforts to curb white power in the colonies. What was one to make, many wondered, of France's newly adopted "Declaration of the Rights of Man," which read "men are born and remain equal in rights."

With the ruling elite sharply divided and the people of colour and freed slaves hopelessly alienated from either faction, slaves revolted. At the end of August 1791, to the sounds of drums and chants, slaves in the southern province revolted and their uprising spread rapidly. A reputed Voodoo priest was one of the insurrection's original leaders, and Voodoo ceremonies were associated with its early days. With elements drawn from Bantu, West African, and Christian tradition, the Voudon or Voodoo faith connected slaves from the disparate areas and peoples of Africa. By 1792, the insurrection seemed on the verge of being crushed as French concessions pacified those mulattos and freedmen who had been the slaves' allies. Professions of loyalty and Catholicism enabled the slaves to obtain shelter with the Spanish in Santo Domingo.

At this moment, Toussaint L'Ouverture, a freed slave, came to the fore. He had learned politics in a hard school where a wrong move could lead to a cruel death. He won Spanish respect while carefully watching French developments, until revolutionary commissioners newly arrived from France gave him his chance. Cut off from France by the outbreak of war, their own troops dying from tropical diseases, many planters negotiating for a British protectorate, and an imminent Spanish invasion threatening, the revolutionary commissioners decided in desperation to play a new card. In August 1793, without any authorization from France, they declared slavery abolished in large regions of Saint Domingue.

Abolition turned the tide. Rallying other slave commanders behind the demand for abolition, Toussaint L'Ouverture defeated British and Spanish invading forces between 1794 and 1798. Toussaint's victories were partly a consequence of the toll of tropical diseases spread among European soldiers. But tropical disease was nothing new and European commanders took high mortality into account in their military planning. What was new was the creation of disciplined armies of ex-slaves ready to take enormous casualties to defend their freedom.

While whites had massacred captured rebel slaves and individual slave commanders had in turn massacred whites, Toussaint sought to reconcile defeated white planters; to rebuild a shattered economy required business experience and international connections with the European mainland. Toussaint restored a gang system of sugar production only too reminiscent of slavery, although the workers themselves were paid a proportion of their earnings in cash. Still, Toussaint's efforts to conciliate the planters, his restoration of unfree labor, and his endorsement of colonial status, caused many to wonder about his intentions – all the more so because of his authoritarian style of leadership.

The French Return In the end, Toussaint's attempts at reconstruction were wrecked by Napoleon, who hoped to restore the island's economy so that its revenues would finance the revitalization and expansion of the French colonial empire. In 1800 he forced his weakened Spanish ally to concede its territory west of the Mississippi to France, thus greatly enlarging French colonial possessions. To finance colonial expansion, Napoleon sought to restore France's former treasure chest in Saint-Domingue. For Napoleon this meant restoring slavery. Keeping their intentions secret, French commanders securely established themselves before capturing Toussaint L'Ouverture by treachery. Initially, many of Toussaint's commanders, troubled by his policies, were willing to ally themselves with the French against Toussaint, who died a year later in a French jail.

France's efforts to restore slavery, however, rekindled mass resistance. Between 1802 and 1803, tens of thousands of French troops were unable to suppress the rising. After Napoleon's commander-in-chief, General Leclerc, died of yellow fever, his successor carried out an almost genocidal war against the black population, while the ex-slaves under Toussaint's successor Jean-Jacques Dessalines massacred whites. The efforts to put down the insurrection ended as European conflict resumed. In 1803 the French surrendered. On January 1, 1804, Dessalines declared Saint-Domingue's independence and restored its aboriginal name of Haiti, declaring "I have avenged America." Dessalines did not rule long. His assassination began a series of civil wars in which Haiti was divided temporarily into two separate states.

Besides the slave population of Saint-Domingue, the biggest beneficiary of Napoleon's defeat was the USA. His colonial scheme having failed, Napoleon sold French claims to the Louisiana territory to the USA and doubled the size of the American territory, undergirding that state's eventual rise to great power status.

The Saint-Domingue Revolution between 1790 and 1820 created an independent state dominated by military men, but the Haitian state proved much less able to mobilize resources than its French predecessor or than the USA. The new state's economy aimed at self-sufficiency and largely ceased to trade with the outside world. The turn toward autonomy had many causes. The new state nationalized the property of the white slavemasters and forbade non-citizens from acquiring Haitian property, which made it more difficult to attract capital. Foreign trade declined because slaveholding states in the Caribbean and the slaveholding USA feared the Haitian example and did not recognize the new state; France also refused to establish diplomatic relations. Perhaps the key reason for the turn toward autonomy was the refusal of the Haitian population to work in plantation agriculture. Haitian governments were finally forced to divide plantations and return to peasant agriculture. Many ex-slaves had engaged in small-scale agriculture in Africa and welcomed the return to small farms. Peasant agriculture in Haiti prospered and its small cultivators enjoyed a far better lot than under slavery. Agricultural production was consumed at home or bartered for goods; the system did not produce sufficient export revenues to support a strong Haitian state.

The expansion of citizenship in Haiti was an important revolutionary accomplishment and a profound social revolution as well, in the sense that little remained of the division of labor and the caste hierarchies existing before the Revolution. In 1790 the overwhelming majority of the population had been slaves; by 1820 slavery was totally abolished. Military men dominated the state itself. Women were largely excluded from public politics, although women such as Marie-Jeanne Lamartinière, who fought on the front lines with the besieged troops at Crête à Pierrot, were heroines of the liberation struggle.

Map 7.5 Latin America

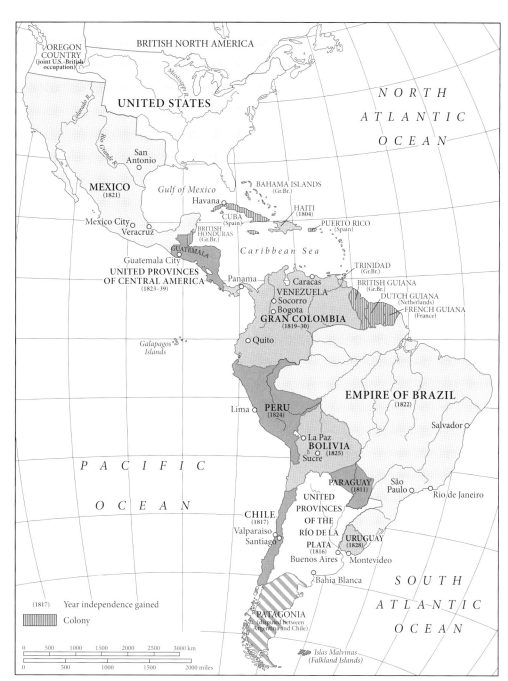

7.3 LATIN AMERICAN REVOLUTIONS, 1810–25

The New World colonies of Portugal and Spain moved rapidly toward independence after Napoleon's armies invaded Portugal with Spain's help in 1807 and then occupied most of Spain in 1808. The entire Portuguese court, including mad Queen Maria, her son and regent Prince João, and 10,000 courtiers, bureaucrats, and hangers-on escaped aboard forty-six ships and an escort of naval vessels conveniently supplied by Britain.

The Spanish court was less fortunate. Napoleon deposed Charles IV and his son Ferdinand and installed his own brother

Joseph Napoleon as Spain's new king. The collapse of legitimate authority in Spain provoked conflict in the Spanish colonies with competing groups claiming the right to govern in the name (and in the absence) of the king. By 1810, these conflicts exploded into civil war and social upheaval. When the fighting ended in 1825, Spain's vast empire had fragmented into more than a dozen (eventually nineteen) separate independent countries. Only Cuba and Puerto Rico remained yoked to Spain. In contrast, Portuguese Brazil managed to achieve a smoother and faster, if not bloodless, transition to independence as a single country. (See Map 7.5.)

Divisions and Discontents in the Colonies

As in the British colonies and in France, rising taxes provoked protests throughout the two empires. Beginning in the 1760s, both Spain and Portugal attempted to tighten administration, improve tax collection, and centralize power in the hands of the king. The Portuguese reforms, named after Sebastião José de Carvalho e Melo, 1st marquis of Pombal (Pombaline Reforms), like the Bourbon Reforms (named after the Spanish royal family) were unpopular in the colonies. In contrast to France and the British colonies, neither the Portuguese nor the Spanish Crown was required to submit requests for tax increases to representative assemblies. The flight of the Portuguese king to Brazil and the collapse of legitimate authority in the Spanish colonies created openings for the expression of discontent.

In the Spanish mainland colonies, as taxes, forced labor, and other exactions increased during the 1760s and 1770s, indigenous villagers rose up in dozens of small-scale rebellions against royal officials and tax collectors. Then, in 1780, a massive colony-wide uprising took place in Peru led by José Gabriel Condorcanqui, a descendant of Tupac Amaru, the last Inka ruler. He claimed that his goal was to restore the colony to Christianity by expelling Spanish officials and ending corruption and injustice. The death toll from fighting, massacres, and executions probably exceeded 100,000 – mostly indigenous rebels – in a population of less than 2 million.

In much of the Caribbean, a different dynamic was at work. The Haitian revolt erupted not when the colonial government was tightening its grip, but when it weakened. Slave revolts increased in number during periods of warfare when Europeans set about fighting each other and had fewer soldiers and militiamen to control or suppress the slaves. In Jamaica and Surinam, runaway slaves called **maroons** formed their own self-governing communities, raided plantations, and successfully resisted full-scale military expeditions sent to wipe them out. Eventually, the British and Dutch governments signed peace treaties agreeing to leave the maroons alone in exchange for an end to raiding and help (not always provided) in capturing future runaways. Between 1757 and 1814, thirteen major slave insurrections and eight significant maroon wars or uprisings erupted from northeastern Brazil to Venezuela on the mainland and throughout the Caribbean sugar islands.

The increasing polarization of colonial society during the eighteenth century made colonial elites more conservative. Wealthy **creoles** (people of European descent born in the Caribbean or Spanish America) objected to war-related tax increases and sabotaged efforts to dilute their grasp on local offices, but they could not protest too loudly for fear of opening a Pandora's box of lower-class resentments against themselves as well as

the colonial government. In the Spanish colonies, the independence revolutions did not begin with assemblies of citizens protesting against tax increases. Instead, the turmoil began with assemblies called to pledge loyalty to the king.

In Spain, resistance to Joseph Bonaparte became a national cause, supported by all social strata, though some court officials, notable grandees, and other elements of the elite collaborated with the French. The resistance was led by popular leaders who proclaimed their loyalty to Ferdinand VII (whose father had meanwhile managed a well-timed death) and called for the election of a **Cortes** (parliament) to rule in the king's absence. The Cortes met at Cádiz where the rebel government maintained a fragile hold on a small piece of national territory, aided by Spain's historic enemy Great Britain. Liberals who favored a constitutional monarchy, freer trade, and individual rights, dominated the proceedings and enacted a series of reforms that culminated in the adoption of a new constitution in 1812. Ferdinand VII, who hated constitutions almost as much as he hated his French jailers, watched and fumed in luxurious helplessness while these events unfolded.

Unlike Brazil, which never experienced a moment without an established government and monarch, the Spanish colonies suddenly found themselves adrift after 1808. Both Spaniards (politely called **peninsulares**) and creoles rejected appeals to pledge allegiance to Joseph Bonaparte. The peninsulares, whose ranks included most high officials, saw themselves as legitimate rulers, having been appointed prior to the French invasion. Wealthy creoles, on the other hand, tended to see the absence of the king as an opportunity to reverse the Bourbon reforms and take control in the name of "popular" sovereignty exercised through the **cabildos** (the town councils) of the colonial capital cities in which they outnumbered the peninsulares. All sides pledged devotion to Spain's legitimate king, the conveniently missing Ferdinand VII.

In Mexico City, with its large population of Spanish officials, merchants, and churchmen, the peninsulares struck the first blow. On the night of September 15–16, 1808, Spanish officials staged a *coup d'état*. They removed the viceroy from office for having made too many concessions to creole demands for autonomy. In doing so, however, they helped to close the door on a peaceful and orderly transition to a new regime and pushed the creole elite into clandestine plotting. On September 16, 1810, Fr. Miguel Hidalgo y Costilla, the parish priest of Dolores, a small town located two days' hard ride northwest of Mexico City, summoned his mostly indigenous and mestizo parishioners to the church in the town square and read a call (*grito*) to revolt. His call demanded the downfall of "bad government" but did not proclaim independence. Within days, the hundred or so rebels from Dolores had become an army of thousands.

The creole elite of Mexico City recoiled in horror at the popular following Hidalgo's call inspired. Leading creoles seized the government, summoned the colonial militia, raised new troops, and eventually defeated the rebels. Hidalgo and his principal lieutenants were tortured and executed, but others escaped capture to wage nearly continuous guerrilla warfare for another ten years.

In contrast to Mexico, the cabildos in the colonial capitals of all the main South American colonies (Caracas, Buenos Aires, Bogotá, Quito, Lima, Santiago de Chile) moved quickly in 1809–10 to seize control away from Spanish officials with the support of creole-dominated colonial militias. Had the Spanish Cortes meeting in Cádiz adopted a constitution granting a degree of home rule to the American colonies, a peaceful transition from empire to commonwealth might have been possible, at least for a time. Instead, the new "liberal" constitution of 1812 treated the colonies as virtual provinces of Spain to be governed from Madrid, and compounded the error by limiting their representation in the Cortes to far fewer deputies than much smaller and less populous provinces on the peninsula.

In 1814, after the defeat of Napoleon, Ferdinand VII returned to Madrid, abrogated the constitution, restored the absolute monarchy, and ordered the colonies to submit. By this time, what little chance there had been for compromise had disappeared. Most of the colonial "juntas" (ruling councils) had already declared for independence and became the nuclei for new governments. The colonial militias became national armies. Had Ferdinand not insisted on sending armies to subdue the colonies, the new regimes in the colonies might have evolved more or less peacefully into "constitutional oligarchies" dominated by creole elites. Instead, Spanish armies sent from Spain and troops raised locally by loyalist commanders suppressed the rebellions and reimposed Spanish authority temporarily in Mexico and Venezuela and dealt harshly with outbreaks in Peru, Colombia, and Chile. Central America and the Caribbean islands (Cuba, Santo Domingo, and Puerto Rico) remained continuously loyal to Spain. By 1816, the first phase of the Latin American independence struggles ended in nearly universal defeat of the insurgents and victory for Spain's traditionalist absolute monarch.

The Collapse of Spanish Rule, 1816–24

Then it all collapsed – not in one great battle, but slowly and inexorably, through eight years of violence, destruction, and upheaval from which emerged the independent republics of Spanish America. In the second phase of the independence revolts, three key developments favored the cause of Latin American independence:

- The rebel forces in Spanish America (but not in Brazil) became more socially inclusive and egalitarian, growing stronger as a result.
- Revolts by liberal-leaning officers in key military units in both Spain and Portugal in 1820 succeeded in wresting control from Ferdinand VII and João IV (crowned in Brazil in 1816 on the death of his mother).
- When new liberal governments took over in the two mother countries, creole elites who had supported the colonial regime as a bulwark against democracy and equality finally embraced independence.

During the independence wars, conflicts within the top strata of Spaniards and creoles created political opportunities for popular groups to push their way into politics. In the towns, mestizo traders, shopkeepers, artisans, and laborers joined crowds, signed up for militia duty, and sometimes even voted in new elections. In the mines, forced labor became unenforceable; workers ran off to war or back to their native villages and many mines closed. In the countryside, plainsmen and cowboys (*gauchos* in Argentina, **llanero**s in Venezuela), small proprietors (*rancheros* in Mexico), hacienda tenants and peons, indigenous villagers, and even slaves signed up or accepted conscription into the armies of both sides. In time, the rebels' key advantage won out. The rebels could proclaim the doctrines of citizens' rights and republican equality before the law. Loyalist commanders offered only better pay (most of the time) and the comfort of traditional symbols. As war dragged on, leaders on both sides found it more and more difficult to control their troops, but the breakdown of established institutions and practices inexorably favored the rebels.

In Venezuela, independence leader Simón Bolívar at first pledged not to disturb slavery and failed to form an alliance with the rough and illiterate llaneros of the interior. The independence forces suffered two major defeats as a result. Returning with a few hundred followers in 1817, Bolívar abandoned his alliance with the creole slave owners and merchants, sought help from llanero leaders, and offered freedom to slaves who deserted their masters to join his army. From Venezuela, Bolívar attacked Spanish forces in Colombia and Ecuador.

Meanwhile, an army of 5,000 that included 1,500 slaves promised manumission at the end of their enlistment as well as gauchos from the pampas, and a few Chilean volunteers (including independence advocate Bernardo O'Higgins) had managed to cross the Andes from Argentina into Chile in January 1817 – summer in the southern hemisphere, but still an incredible trek. Led by Argentine General José de San Martín, the army descended on the undermanned Spanish garrison defending Santiago. With Chile "liberated," San Martín began planning an invasion of Peru, where he eventually linked up with Bolívar's forces after seizing Lima in July 1821. By this time, the bulk of San Martín's army consisted of escaped slaves from the sugar plantations along the southern Peruvian coast. Throughout the Americas, growing popular support of and participation in the independence wars made victory possible, undermined the dominance of creole elites, weakened caste systems and slavery, and destroyed all hope for an untroubled restoration of colonial social hierarchies and political order.

Spanish efforts to suppress the independence revolts suffered a crippling blow within Spain itself. On January 1, 1820, a liberal revolt erupted in the army, led by the officers in a regiment awaiting shipment to the colonies in a great armada that Ferdinand had assembled to deal a final blow to the American insurgents. Led by Colonel Rafael Riego, the regiment voted to rebel against the government and demand restoration of the constitution of 1812. The revolt, which postponed the armada's departure indefinitely, spread to other military units and then to civilian groups first in Cádiz and then in the other cities. In March, the Madrid garrison joined the movement as rebel units marched toward the city. For the next three crucial years, Ferdinand VII lived as a virtual prisoner.

The new parliamentary government in Spain proclaimed the equality of citizens before the law and ordered elections in both Spain and the colonies, but refused to consider proposals for proportional representation or colonial autonomy. Since the creole elites in the colonies still loyal to Spain preferred inequality and home rule to liberalism imposed from Madrid, the restoration of the constitution of 1812 pushed this key group toward embracing independence – as the only way left to restore the colonial social hierarchy and elite rule. The most immediate and disastrous defection was Mexico, where the creole commander of the loyalist army, Agustín de Iturbide, negotiated a treaty with the independence guerrillas and proclaimed Mexico's independence in 1821. Even in the Andes, where elite support for Spain had been strongest, the events of 1820 hit hard. By August of 1823, when a French army sent by his cousin Louis XVIII freed Ferdinand VII and restored him to full power, it was too late. The independence armies united under Bolívar finally crushed the last of the Spanish armies high in the Andes at the Battle of Ayacucho on December 9, 1824.

Independence of Brazil

Brazilian independence occurred more swiftly and smoothly than in Spanish America, but not without bloodshed and protest. In 1820, a near revolution in Portugal forced King João IV, who preferred living in Rio de Janeiro, to call elections for a new Cortes. Liberals won the election and took two fateful steps.

First, they ordered João IV to return to Lisbon by April 1821 or lose his throne. He did so reluctantly, leaving his son Pedro behind to govern Brazil as "regent." And second, the Cortes abolished Brazil's status as a separate kingdom, divested Rio de Janeiro of its role as capital, and ordered the colony's separate provinces to resume their ancient subordination to the authorities in Lisbon. When the Cortes went further and demanded that Pedro also return to Portugal, the regent proclaimed Brazil an independent monarchy and had himself crowned as its first emperor, Dom Pedro I, in 1822, but the new monarch spent much of his reign struggling against slave rebellions and separatist revolts in the provinces.

Aftermath of Independence

After more than a decade of war and upheavals, most of Latin America achieved independence. In some ways, the new regimes fulfilled the hopes of the dissident creole elites who had begun the process with the single goal of wresting control from Spanish officials. The new nations denied citizenship to slaves, excluded Native American majorities, and discriminated against the poor, the illiterate, and women of all ranks and races. However, even in the 1820s, when 80 percent of the population was illiterate and lived in pre-railroad rural isolation, such regimes proved to be weak and prone to breakdown.

In most of Latin America, slaves rebelled or escaped with such frequency that slave systems began to disintegrate even before official proclamations of abolition. Slavery lasted longest in the few places (like Brazil and Cuba) where colonial governments had never been overthrown. Native Americans benefited from the abolition of caste distinctions and became legally equal to all other citizens. In the Andes, the new governments were so weak that they lacked the ability to tax and exploit indigenous populations. Weak governments had no choice but to grant de facto local autonomy to indigenous villages and their leaders. Gradually, in most of Latin America, the heavy burden of colonial institutions, taxes, monopolies, privileges, and exclusions began to dissolve. Not until after 1850, however, did liberalism and railroads end the region's political instability and economic stagnation.

7.4 EUROPE AFTER THE FRENCH REVOLUTION

Under the impact of struggles for civil rights and industrial development, the French revolutionary tradition underwent profound alteration: Two new revolutionary programs, cultural nationalism and socialism, emerged between 1815 and 1848 in Europe.

In contributing to social revolution, the impact of industrialization was indirect. It had its most dramatic effect in those areas where the legal code of the French Revolution struck down guilds, privileged monopolies, and corporations and where it abolished the legal jurisdiction of towns over their surrounding countryside. In Central and Western European cities such as Berlin, Düsseldorf, Paris, and Turin, subcontracting and domestic work increasingly threatened the livelihood of tailors, shoemakers, and cabinetmakers. By 1848, capital cities were tinderboxes, filled with skilled workers who possessed strong traditions of solidarity and organization and a growing sense of frustration and rage.

The countryside too was discontented. The abolition of communal control and customary rights over forest land, another result of French legislation, was an additional source of rural discontent in those heavily industrialized rural regions in the southeast of France, northern Italy, and portions of the Rhineland. Rights over woodland loomed large as the price of wood soared, due to the expansion of charcoal-based ironmaking and shipbuilding, and many villagers found it costly to purchase wood products that had formerly been theirs for the taking.

Economic crises in 1829 and in 1846–47 also produced both urban and rural anger. The wet, cool years of the 1840s spread potato blight and devastated the rye crops (see Box 7.5). In areas such as western and southern Ireland where urban industrial penetration of the country was minimal, government in the hands of landlords, and potatoes the major food of the laboring population, mass starvation resulted – but starving peasants were too concerned to find something to eat to engage in revolution. One of the consequences of the famine was to disperse hundred of thousands of impoverished Catholic Irish men and women throughout the English-speaking world. In this way the national tragedy of famine became a global phenomenon with consequences for the composition of the working classes around the world. More revolutionary were the effects of potato blight in areas of Northern Europe where peasants had been shifting from grain to potatoes, in northern France, Germany, the Netherlands, and Poland. Localities prevented mass starvation by purchasing and distributing wheat but the return of better times in 1848 revealed an impoverished peasantry desperate for land.

The second important factor working for revolution was the persistence and extension of state centralization and the associated continuing deprival of rights. Hierarchical centralization created by the Revolution and Napoleon and spread by French armies persisted. Restored governments in Western Europe typically kept most of the administrative apparatus left to them by the French.

The Napoleonic threat accelerated existing trends toward hierarchical centralization in nations that were never fully subjected to French rule. Despite the centralizing precedents of Frederick I in Prussia and of Maria Theresa and Joseph II in Austria, the restructuring of Prussia between 1807 and 1815

Box 7.5 The Irish Famine, 1846–51

One of the greatest famines in European history occurred in Ireland, at a time when the Industrial Revolution was transforming the British economy and spreading across portions of Europe. Famine refers to mass starvation stemming from a failure of food entitlements; it does not necessarily entail food shortage per se. In Ireland in 1846 and 1847 there was a genuine shortage of food, but hundreds and thousands could have been saved if Irish food resources had been used more efficiently. Most importantly, the food resources of the United Kingdom, of which Ireland was a component kingdom, were more than adequate to provide famine relief. That hundreds of thousands starved in a rich and powerful United Kingdom must be seen as the triumph of the principles of political economy over the demands of citizenship.

Even if its root causes were political, the magnitude of the Irish food crisis should not be underestimated. Over a five-year period, from the autumn of 1846 to the autumn of 1851, the potato blight *Phytophthora infestans* dominated the Irish countryside, hitting some areas in full strength year after year, striking some regions episodically, and ignoring other areas entirely. Convinced that local landlords should bear most of the burden of blight and worried that aid might undermine the work incentives of the Irish laboring classes, the British government attempted to keep its distance. Originally generous, private aid diminished as the famine persisted. Although all estimates are tentative, somewhere around a million Irish men and women died and more than two and a half million emigrated, transforming Ireland demographically.

The British commitment to free market principles did not flinch when confronted with famine in a portion of their kingdom which many Britons regarded with suspicion for political, religious, and cultural reasons. The price was a first-class disaster; this same policy of neglect would be adopted by British authorities in India, where it also produced catastrophe.

was modeled on Napoleonic France, as was the Austrian General Civil Code of 1811 and the administrative system installed in Austria's new Italian provinces, Lombardy and the Veneto. Although both Prussian and Austrian reformers imitated French reforms, a key difference remained. Where French reforms brought the central government into the daily lives of both the urban and rural populace, Prussian and Austrian reforms left large portions of the peasant world under the control of elite landowners. Starting from the top, Prussia imitated French centralized administration down to the county level in eastern rural regions, at which point it abandoned local administration to the rural elite, the Junkers. The Prussians also incorporated universal male military conscription into their reforms. But in France local authorities administered conscription, while in rural Prussia, basic military leadership of the conscripts remained in the hands of the local nobility. Their control of military conscription only increased the Junkers' local power. In the Austrian hereditary lands, centralization already penetrated to and included the county level, but some of the most important elements of the empire, such as the entire Hungarian kingdom, remained outside the system.

The military and political strength of the French state, revealed so clearly to European rulers in the preceding fifteen years – its ability to raise money, to conscript soldiers who fought valiantly, and to carry out financial and agrarian reforms – forced European monarchs to emulate their enemy; indeed, French occupation or the demands of war had already carried them far along the path during the Napoleonic period. Even as they adopted or extended state centralization wholesale, monarchs refused to voluntarily diminish their power by extending citizenship rights.

Because government centralization imposed an iron grid of uniformity on an extremely diverse and complex European society, centralizing monarchs made enemies in high places as well as low. Tensions were exacerbated by the territorial redistribution along France's eastern borders, designed at the Vienna peace conference to strengthen the region against French aggression (see Map 7.6). In these areas, populations subject to French rule for twenty-five years were given to foreign kings who lacked "traditional" legitimacy. The problems were deepened where the Vienna settlement increased religious divisions within existing states, as when it conceded devoutly Catholic portions of the Rhineland to the very Protestant Prussian king and the liberal Protestants of the Rhenish Palatinate to Catholic Bavaria.

Everywhere it was elites, mainly but not exclusively middle-class elites resenting centralized power over which they had little control, who led the public opposition that opened the

way for the great wave of revolutions that crested in 1848–51. The Vienna settlement's joining of rich small states to larger militarized monarchies which they were expected to financially support, caused discontent. In northern Italy, merchants complained about the prohibitive tariffs that cut their commercial links with France and tied them to stagnant Austrian markets and about the staggering debt accumulated fighting Napoleon and leading the European counter-revolution.

Due to French reforms, middle-class professionals, businessmen, and manufacturers were taxed with new efficiency. Increased taxes were spent on policies determined arbitrarily by kings and by court camarillas who spied on them and censored their books, as well as on an embittered clergy that would not forgive them their possession of church lands, purchased during the Revolution and the reign of Napoleon. Divided on many issues, the middle classes' affluence made them a dangerous opposition. They or their sons joined the many secret organizations that constituted an invisible opposition to established governments. Professional soldiers were another source of opposition. Military men, often of humble origin in France and Spain, were appalled to see armies given over to incompetent aristocrats. In the 1820s in Spain, military men, encouraged by local freemasons, frustrated by military defeat in South America, and discontented by the inability of the Spanish Crown to raise money for their pay, initiated a revolution to implement the constitution of 1812.

Together, regional opposition to centralization, middle-class hostility to absolutism, military discontent, and artisanal and peasant economic grievances provided the initiative that generated revolutions in 1820, 1830, and finally in 1848.

7.5 REVOLUTIONS, 1848–51

The revolutions sweeping continental Europe between 1848 and 1851 revealed the enduring and even deepening influence of the French Revolution on European politics (see Map 7.7). Opposition to absolutist rule was particularly explosive where groups had mastered the language of citizenship and nationhood and familiarized themselves with the tools for mobilizing masses on this basis.

The spread of both the political culture of citizenship and nationhood beyond the old revolutionary strongholds and their application to absolutist regimes in other contexts was one of the distinctive aspects of 1848. In that culminating year, revolution spread to commercialized areas of militarized monarchies that had never seen French rule; from Paris and Milan, the barricade form of protest and citizenship demands passed to Berlin and Vienna.

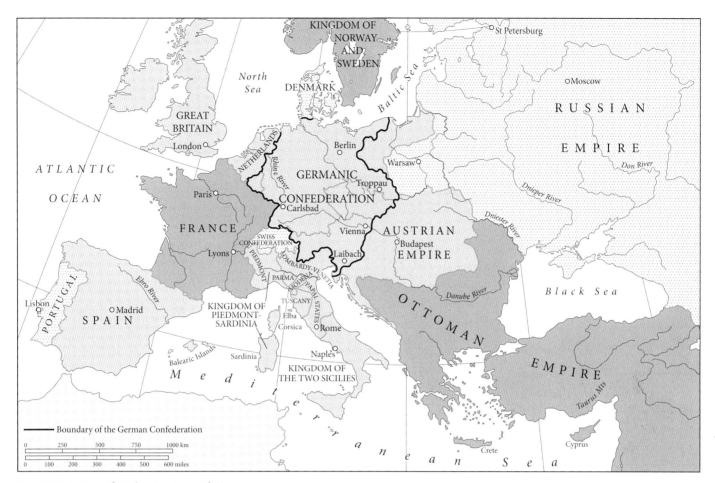

Map 7.6 Europe after the Congress of Vienna

While there was a great similarity to the opening of revolutionary situations in February and March of 1848, with barricades, the defection of National Guard troops, and the creation of provisional governments in capital cities, divergences quickly appeared as it proved difficult to resolve multiple power situations and new groups began to add their demands to the chorus of claims. To get a sense of these differences, it is helpful to examine the revolutionary process in two different arenas, the streets of Paris and the corridors of the Frankfurt Assembly.

Revolutionary Paris, 1848

Between 1815 and 1848 Paris was in the political vanguard of revolutionary Europe. In France alone, a significant section of politically active middle-class liberals, a minority certainly, was committed to democratic republicanism – to a government without a king and to something approaching universal manhood suffrage. In Paris, an artisanal working class, thrown into contact with these democratic republicans, began to assimilate their political ideals. These workers experimented with developing the core concepts of central state intervention, citizenship,

and nationality to put forward their own political demands. In the 1840s, the growth of trade unionism among highly skilled workers also threw workers into conflict with the state; trade unions were illegal and shared the shadows with political secret societies. Important in the politicization of the labor movement was the Société des Saisons, founded by that arch-conspirator, Auguste Blanqui. Predominantly middle-class, the society succeeded in recruiting workers to its ranks, even attempting to recruit foreign workers. In the 1840s, republican workers began to pay attention instead to socialist reformers such as Louis Blanc who championed the "right to work" as a new right of citizenship. On the edges of the republican labor movement a new reform-oriented socialist movement arose. In 1847, its short-lived foreign-worker affiliate, the League of Just, changed its name to the Communist League and commissioned Karl Marx and Friedrich Engels to write the *Communist Manifesto*.

New rights, never envisaged in 1793–96, were the focus of political struggles in Paris in the months after February 1848. The new "provisional government" of mostly middle-class political leaders found themselves faced with new demands from an organized working class that had its own leaders, its own

Map 7.7 Principal centers of revolution, 1848–49

organizations, and its own political program. These workers possessed leverage because many had joined the National Guard and acquired arms. At the same time, the army was demoralized, its embittered generals reticent to involve themselves in politics. The neutrality of the army and the deep divisions within the National Guard, split between workers and the lower middle classes, constituted an enduring dual power situation. From the opening days French workers demanded a "right to work." Their organized presence in the streets, and their determination to pressure the provisional government to recognize their demands, produced glaring divisions within the republican camp. Hastily called national elections gave very limited opportunity for political debate; in the countryside, peasants cast their ballots for familiar names, which usually meant members of the landed elite. As a result the new elected assembly that met in early May of 1848 had a monarchical majority. The new political environment foreclosed any further concessions to working-class pressures, while a trade depression, prolonged by the revolutionary turmoil, made workers desperate.

While consolidating its political hold, the government temporized, attempting to co-opt workers by enrolling them in "national workshops" and in a citizens' militia. The title "national workshops" came from a celebrated pamphlet by the socialist Louis Blanc. But instead of the state-funded collectives of skilled workers envisaged by Blanc, the national workshops turned out to be the traditional outdoor work gangs used by French governments in times of high unemployment. Workers felt betrayed but still depended on the national workshops for survival. In June of 1848, when the workshops in Paris were abolished by the reactionary legislature, they revolted and, with guns obtained from the National Guard, rebuilt their barricades. Here, the dual power situation, existing since February, finally reached its climax in armed conflict; an elite military unit recruited from the Parisian working classes subdued the revolutionary national workshop workers. Workers' defeat, in turn, paved the way for the rise of Louis Napoleon, the enigmatic nephew of Napoleon Bonaparte. Workers and peasants disillusioned by the shabby record of the republic sought refuge behind a glorious name. A few years after he became president of France in 1848 Louis Napoleon followed his uncle in sweeping away the remnants of the republic and assuming the imperial title (December 2, 1851), taking the name Napoleon III.

Frankfurt, 1848

Unlike in Paris, multiple claims to power did not dominate Frankfurt politics. Instead multiple claims to power occurred in cities such as Berlin and Vienna where national guards and civic militias confronted regular troops. Convened by German liberals, representatives of local revolutions gathered in Frankfurt to create a framework for unifying a fragmented German polity. With much of Germany swept by revolt, while the Frankfurt Assembly met to write a national constitution, governments in Prussia and Vienna were also drawing up constitutions for territories within the jurisdiction of the Frankfurt Assembly. Meanwhile, everyday administration and enforcement of the law remained in the hands of the traditional states that were gradually reacquiring their legitimacy.

While governments collapsed helplessly before an initial wave of revolution in March 1848, in some areas democratic movements were able to sustain the momentum better than others. Where ordinary people had little contact or experience with local government, it proved impossible to maintain the original radical impetus. For example, in East Prussia, the spiritual heart of the Prussian kingdom in eastern Germany where large landholders dominated local state government, the peasants' movement lacked organization and was intimidated by revitalized landlord groups. It soon collapsed into violent attacks on estates. By the end of 1848, most traces of radical sentiment had dissolved in the East Prussian countryside.

In rural western Germany the situation was quite different. In the Prussian Rhine provinces, small farms and commercialization dominated a countryside in close contact with towns and government administrators; this rich and prosperous territory lay hundreds of miles to the west of East Prussia and was surrounded by non-Prussian lands. In the Prussian Rhineland, political organization and state-centered protest were already familiar tools. While the first elections on May 1, 1848, brought a mixed delegation of religious figures and democrats, democratic sentiments gradually pervaded much of the countryside. By the time of the elections for the Prussian Assembly in January 1849, democratization had taken popular root, and the Rhineland sent a large number of democratic deputies.

The problems of building a democratic state were compounded and ultimately rendered impossible by the multiple linguistic and ethnic composition of the many small states represented at Frankfurt. Unlike in France, German reformers had to create a state as well as to revolutionize one. Out of the turmoil of the Frankfurt Assembly clearly emerged a new ethnic or cultural concept of nationalism. Just as workers in Paris took the framework of citizenship and rights and developed it in new directions, so politicians, influenced by the writings of German intellectuals, expanded the French concept of civic nationalism, the idea of the nation as a civic community, to **cultural nationalism**, the idea of the nation based on ethnicity and culture. In some ways, the idea emerged almost inevitably in places such as Germany, Italy, or Poland, where peoples with ancient ties and fairly similar languages found themselves partitioned across several states. Nationalist intellectuals such as Johann Gottfried von Herder and Johann Gottlieb Fichte in Germany, Giuseppe Mazzini in Italy, and Adam Mickiewicz in Poland believed that a popular identity based on language and culture gave their nation a historic destiny to occupy a central position in Europe. The difficulties with this position became readily apparent in a German Confederation with Czechs, Italians, Poles, and Slovaks inside its southern and eastern borders.

The democratic polity originally envisioned by many delegates encountered insuperable obstacles. Polish landowners exerted considerable influence in many areas of Posen and Silesia and, unlike Breton or Alsatian elites, they were committed to the restoration of a historically defined Polish kingdom that would include many ethnic groups within its borders. The presence of

Prussian deputies at the Assembly who as administrators had carried out harsh Germanization policies against the Poles certainly aroused Slavic suspicions. Developments in Bohemia, Moravia, and Slovakia were prophetic. To the Germans' surprise and consternation, Czechs from Bohemia and Moravia refused to participate in the elections for the Frankfurt Assembly and convened a Slavic Congress at Prague. Cultural nationalist movements, such as that of the Czechs, composed of priests, ministers, schoolteachers, local government officials, and shopkeepers who served as a nucleus for organizing those who shared a similar ethnic culture, first burst forth upon the public arena in 1848.

In the end, the eruption of new movements within the revolutions of 1848–51 – socialism in France and ethnic nationalism in the German Confederation and the Habsburg empire – broke up the unity of the revolutionary camp, set classes and nationalities fighting with one another, and paved the way for the return of monarchical armies. Appalled by socialist demands, middle-class republicans reconsidered their republicanism; confronted with Polish and Czech cultural nationalism, many German democrats turned toward a narrow German nationalism. Divisions within the revolutionary camp gave the monarchs their opportunity, and they subdued the divided revolutionaries with armies that had remained loyal. By and large, the multinational Austrian army and its officer corps held firm so long as they were not ordered to fire on members of their own nationality, but Russian help was needed to suppress the Hungarian army.

The revolutions of 1848–51 accomplished important changes. In their effort to pacify the peasants, rulers substantially transformed the organization of agriculture in Central and Eastern Europe. In the Austrian empire, the hated labor services were abolished, and in Prussia an ungenerous land redemption program abolished the remnants of feudalism. In both countries, most peasants freed from feudal ties quickly became dependent on wage labor for landowners. In the political arena, constitutionalism progressed. In Austria and Prussia, new constitutions that limited arbitrary power while giving the monarch wide powers remained in place – precariously. Not all of this political change was direct. In Holland, the sight of revolutions all around him and street demonstrations led the Dutch king to grant a constitution. Other changes were more prophetic. In France and Germany, the revolutions put universal manhood suffrage on the political agenda. Louis Napoleon's *coup d'état* and the subsequent referendum approving his usurpation of power also introduced new and ominous political methods into European politics. In great European cities, including Berlin, Venice, and Vienna, as in Paris, artisans and the urban middle classes had fallen out as artisans sought to win social reforms rather than concentrate on the constitutionalism that preoccupied the middle classes. Class hostilities would intensify throughout the rest of the century.

Conclusion Although its accomplishments were enormous, the Age of Revolution ended in a Europe where armies everywhere triumphed over insurrectionaries. In the Americas and the Caribbean there would be no return to colonial rule. In Europe, the revolutions' ebb left most of the continent transformed; centralized government and popular demands for citizenship rights shaped European politics through the modern era. The revolutions of 1848–51 failed to capture power, but there was no going back to Old Regime Europe. Thomas Paine was wrong in conceiving that universal revolution was sweeping the world and would be triumphant in his lifetime. Paine was wrong not only in his timing but in his idea that universal revolution was moving the world toward some fixed and determined point. Where they were successful, as in the USA and Haiti, revolutions took societies in very different directions from those anticipated by the people who initiated them. Revolutions generated such powerful dynamics that the national and social goals that originated during the revolutionary era would become central elements in shaping the political life, first of Europe, then of the world. Even today, just when the influence of the Age of Revolution seemed to have ended finally, it has risen up again, more forcefully and more unexpectedly than ever.

Study Questions (1) What is a "revolutionary process?" Pick any two revolutions in this chapter and compare and contrast the revolutionary processes at work.

(2) Compare the American, French, and Haitian Revolutions. What were their causes? What were their results? How do you explain the different outcomes of each revolution?

(3) How do you explain the outbreak of revolution all over *ancien régime* Europe and the Western colonial world in the years between 1776 and 1848? To what extent was a set of common underlying factors the cause of revolution? To what extent did revolutions once begun in one nation help to set off revolutions in other nations?

(4) Compare the Latin American revolutions of 1810–24 with either the US or the Haitian Revolution. What were the forces that brought about revolution? What were the results? Did these revolutions have more in common or were they more different? Explain.

(5) Compare the French Revolution of 1789–94 with one of the revolutions of 1848. What was new in 1848–51? How do you explain the differences between the two revolutions?

Suggested Reading DAVID ARMITAGE AND MICHAEL J. BRADDICK (eds.), *The British Atlantic World, 1500–1800* (New York: Palgrave Macmillan, 2002). This work takes a look at the Atlantic world that developed in North America and Britain.

IRA BERLIN, *Many Thousands Gone: The First Two Centuries of Slavery in North America* (Cambridge, MA: Belknap Press, 1998). Berlin's study is a magisterial overview.

LAURENT DUBOIS, *The Avengers of the New World: The Story of the Haitian Revolution* (Cambridge, MA: Belknap Press, 2005). Dubois is a leading Haitian historian.

BARBARA GRAYMONT, *The Iroquois in the American Revolution* (Syracuse University Press, 1972). Graymont studies the situation of the American Indians caught between colonists and imperialists.

PETER KOLCHIN, *Unfree Labor: American Slavery and Russian Serfdom* (Cambridge, MA: Belknap Press, 1987). This is a fascinating comparison of two labor-repressive regimes. They are more different than you might think.

PETER LINEBAUGH AND MARCUS REDIKER, *The Many-headed Hydra: Sailors, Slaves, Commoners, and the Hidden History of the Revolutionary Atlantic* (Boston, MA:

Beacon Press, 2000). These are essays on rebellion in the Atlantic world by leading scholars in the field. They are sensitive to the culture of the oppressed and the logic of capitalism.

Drew R. McCoy, *The Last of the Fathers: James Madison and the Republican Legacy* (Cambridge University Press, 1989). McCoy explores how Madison's attitudes toward slavery changed as he shifted from being a young rebel to a founding father.

Sidney Mintz, *Sweetness and Power* (New York: Viking, 1985). This is a classic study. Focusing on a single commodity, Mintz uses the history of sugar to explore the nature of colonial capitalism and its ties to European consumption patterns.

Mary Beth Norton, *Liberty's Daughters: The Revolutionary Experience of American Women, 1750–1800* (Ithaca, NY: Cornell University Press, 1980). Norton investigates what women got from the American Revolution.

Jack N. Rakove, *Original Meanings: Politics and Ideas in the Making of the Constitution* (New York: Random House, 1997). Rakove subjects the idea of establishing the "original meaning" of the founding fathers to withering criticism.

Glossary

artisan: Highly skilled manual worker who had served long apprenticeship. In some countries, artisans had recognized legal privileges and were the only workers licensed to work in their trade.

cabildos: Town councils in Spanish America.

civic nationalism: A sense of national identity based on a shared law and common political organizations.

Cortes (Portuguese): Portuguese parliament that passed liberal reforms and forced King João IV to return from Brazil in 1821.

Cortes (Spanish): Spanish parliament elected to govern and lead resistance when Napoleon imprisoned King Ferdinand VII; it passed liberal reforms and the 1812 constitution.

cosmopolitanism: Not bound by local habits or prejudices. Identification with all the people of the world.

creoles: People of European descent born in the Caribbean or Spanish America.

cultural nationalism: A sense of national identity based on a shared culture and usually a common language.

Enlightenment: An eighteenth-century intellectual movement that emphasized the importance of subjecting existing institutions, traditions, and ideas to the scrutiny of reason.

intendants: In France in the 1680s, regional administrative officials appointed directly by the central government. These officials would serve as a model for the eighteenth-century restructuring of regional administration throughout most of Europe and Spanish America.

llanero: Venezuelan plainsman or cowboy, similar to Argentine gaucho.

maroons: Escaped slaves who managed to live in remote areas and often created autonomous communities, raided plantations for supplies, and successfully resisted efforts to repress them.

mercantilism: The doctrine that it is the responsibility of the state to promote national industry, by government subsidy of home industry, by high tariffs, by increased foreign trade through monopolies, and by a balance of imports over exports and a resulting accumulation of bullion.

militia: A military force called out in emergencies and drawn from a population who are not professional soldiers.

nobility of the robe: French nobles from wealthy families who had purchased their titles or earned them in the state bureaucracy.

nobility of the sword: French nobles from long-standing noble families claiming descent from military vassals.

peninsulares: Latin American term for Spaniards.

revolutionary process: The dynamics of revolutionary encounters. A revolutionary process begins when at least two armed groups with some significant support claim the right to rule. It ends when one armed group has established its claim to rule.

tax farming: Financial speculators estimated tax revenues, loaned governments money based on these estimates, and then collected the revenues themselves.

Political systems, 1914

London
Paris

Chicago
New York

Mexico

Five largest cities *millions*

1. London
3. Paris
5. Berlin

| 7.419 | 4.767 | 4.55 | 2.185 | 2.071 |

2. New York
4. Chicago

1	Portuguese possessions
2	Spanish possessions
3	Dutch possessions
4	English possessions
5	French possessions
6	Russian possessions
7	German possessions
8	Italian possessions
9	Japanese possessions
10	USA possessions

PART III

1850–1914: Energy and empire

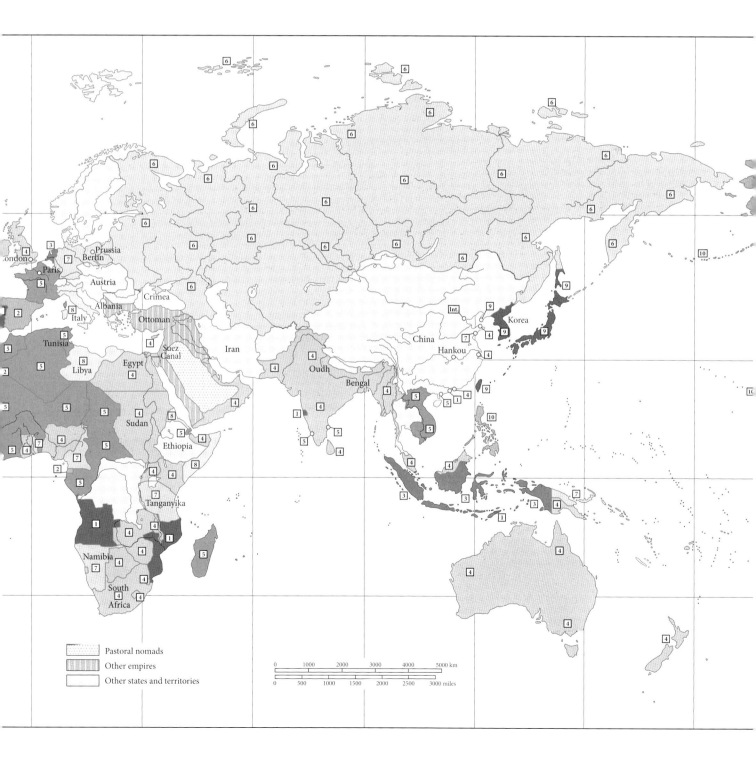

Pastoral nomads

Other empires

Other states and territories

London Paris Prussia Berlin Austria Crimea Albania Italy Ottoman Tunisia Libya Egypt Suez Canal Iran Oudh Bengal China Hankou Korea Int. Sudan Ethiopia Tanganyika Namibia South Africa Madagascar

0 1000 2000 3000 4000 5000 km

0 500 1000 1500 2000 2500 3000 miles

Africa	
1882	British occupy Egypt.
1884	Partition of Africa.
1899–1902	Second Boer War in South Africa.

Americas	
1861–65	American Civil War.
1867	Canada granted self-government, with Dominion status.
1890	Massacre of Sioux at Wounded Knee.
1901	First steel-framed building, Chicago.
1908	First Model T runs off the assembly line at Ford Motors.
1911	Mexican Revolution.

East Asia	
1850–64	Taiping Rebellion.
1899–1900	Boxer Rebellion.
1904–05	Russo-Japanese War.
1910	Japan annexes Korea.

Europe (including Russia)	
1861	Emancipation of the serfs in Russia.
1870–71	Franco-Prussian War.
1871	Unification of Germany. Paris Commune.
1883	Chancellor Bismarck of Germany passes first compulsory social insurance program.
1899	Captain Dreyfus convicted of treason.
1906	British naval battleship *HMS Dreadnought* launched, with 12-inch guns and powered by steam turbines.
1907	Marconi establishes the first commercial transatlantic radio communications service, between Clifden, Ireland and Glace Bay, Newfoundland.

Middle East	
1842–1918	Lifetime of Abdulhamid II, Ottoman sultan.
1869	Opening of Suez Canal.
1878	Ottoman empire recognizes the independence of Bulgaria, Montenegro, Romania, and Serbia.
1912–13	Balkan Wars.

South Asia	
1857–58	Indian Mutiny.
1885	Indian National Congress Party founded.

Between 1850 and 1914 both commerce and coercion expanded on a more global scale than ever before in human history. The technologies of the Second Industrial Revolution and the advance of the consolidated state powered this expansion. The Second Industrial Revolution was a North Atlantic revolution. The new centrality of Canada and the USA in the industrial order and the beginnings of industrial development in Japan were already laying the ground for a further shift toward the Pacific. Its technologies made possible the imperialist conquests characteristic of the era. At the same time, the model of the consolidated state that had emerged in the Age of Revolution spread throughout Europe and North America and then around the world. Existing states increasingly sought to unify and homogenize their national territories, while national minorities resisting such assimilation advocated the establishment of their own unified, homogeneous independent states. One important response to the expansion of industry and centralized state power was global popular protest. Worldwide protest evolved new forms and these innovative tactics showed similarities from Hankou to Chicago; in one guise or another, social movements spread throughout most of the world.

Between 1850 and 1914, in Western and Central Europe, North America, and Japan, a Second Industrial Revolution occurred whose impact on the daily life of men and women around the world was greater than that of the First Industrial Revolution. This revolution produced the large factory, the great corporation, and the factory worker, transforming steel production, machine construction, chemicals, and rubber. The Second Industrial Revolution depended heavily on fossil fuels, on coal and oil, and the geography of production and distribution were heavily affected by access to these resources.

Between 1850 and 1914 transportation and communication revolutions brought the world in closer contact. Within the world transformed by the Second Industrial Revolution, millions of rural men and women migrated to industrial cities, there to confront the problems of creating new routines of daily life and raising children in an urban environment. The large-circulation newspaper, the growth of a mass reading public, and the beginnings of the moving picture created a sense of belonging to a wider community among millions of people. The invention of the telegraph, underground cable, and telephone, the development of large-scale oceangoing steam-powered ships, and the enormous extension of railway tracks facilitated worldwide communication but also allowed states to strengthen their hold over the national territory. Economic conditions – both agricultural crisis in Europe and new demand for industrial and agricultural labor in the Americas, the Caribbean, and colonial Africa – encouraged migration on a transcontinental scale. European agriculturalists and laborers migrated to the Americas while Asians migrated to Africa and the Caribbean.

The technologies of the Second Industrial Revolution eventually increased the standard of living of European and North American workers but the dramatic growth of urban wage workers, a population that included both blue-collar and white-collar workers, brought immediate social problems. Mass unemployment took on new meaning in large cities inhabited by industrial workers. Old age and long-term sickness were threatening to the many new families dependent on the wages of the male household head. The long hours and terrible conditions of many small "sweat shops" in the great cities undermined the health of children and constituted a threat to succeeding generations.

The economic forces transforming the industrial world changed the worldwide balance of power. Europeans and Americans were constructing intercontinental empires on a scale unparalleled since the sixteenth-century Habsburgs. The adaptation of the new industrial technologies for military purposes allowed Europeans to project military power deep into the continental hinterlands of Asia and Africa. Technological revolution equipped Europeans with powerful new weapons that allowed them to consolidate their hold on India, to partition the African continent among themselves, and to make inroads on the previously inward-looking Chinese empire. Although aloof to Europeans, Chinese merchants had already established strong positions in Southeast Asia and the Pacific. While the Chinese state was in decline, Western powers were not able to make inroads there on anything like the scale of their advance into India.

The industrialized world of the Second Industrial Revolution also witnessed the expansion of powerful new consolidated states that intervened directly in the everyday lives of subjects who were becoming citizens. For the populations in the industrialized world, the expanding powers of the consolidated states had both negative and positive consequences. The implementation of conscription, increases in taxation, and higher food prices due to protectionist tariffs were unwelcome. Yet through social insurance, public health measures, and the provision of uniform legal codes, states also conferred benefits. Compulsory schooling promoted a common language, and culture could create the bases for national political culture, facilitating political discussion and debate. The same expanding state power that offered solutions to pressing problems also created new political dilemmas. Increased state intervention in the daily lives of the population met with the least appreciation where people felt that states were controlled by economically or socially hostile groups. Between 1850 and 1914 Europe and North America were moving in a democratic direction but practically every state excluded a majority of adults from the suffrage.

Centralizing states' efforts to impose a uniform culture and language on their citizens provoked hostile responses where large populations spoke different languages and prided themselves on their distinctive culture. Where populations did not speak the official language and share the predominant culture or religion, they often occupied peripheral positions in the economy and politics. Social and economic disability compounded cultural and linguistic disadvantage. States such as Argentina and the United States that had thrown off the colonial yoke during the Age of Revolution inherited not only rebellious autonomist regions but decentralized polities that limited central government authority. The American Civil War was only a preliminary stage in the construction of an American state able to intervene effectively in local affairs.

In the colonial world, nationalism developed out of anti-colonial struggles, and gradually nationalism and anti-colonialism melded together. Indigenous populations generally resisted European rule, just as they had resisted earlier efforts by non-European empire-builders. Initially, in the eyes of many colonial peoples, European conquerors did not seem too different from past conquerors who had been successfully assimilated into traditional cultures. While colonial people developed grievances against outside rule, the lack of standardized languages, diverse ethnic populations, and the lack of communication among regions led to the slow growth of national consciousness.

Certainly colonial powers did not use the same centralist techniques of nation-building in the colonies that they used at home. Despite rhetorics of imperial citizenship, the colonial peoples of the era of the Second Industrial Revolution never enjoyed the same rights as citizens as those of their European masters. European colonial authorities remained content with linguistic divisions within their empires and did not seek to extend the principles of universal education being introduced at home to colonial peoples; in some important cases, educational entitlements actually contracted under European rule. Most important, in an age of democratic expansion in Europe and the USA, democratic rights were seldom extended to colonial populations.

To the extent that states were integrated into world markets, carried out some form of elections, and were subject to consolidated authority, social movements emerged worldwide. Where attempts to instill the language and culture of dominant groups ran up against different languages and cultures, nationalist social movements were likely to appear. Where attempts at state centralization occurred within territorially separate regions without rights of citizenship, anti-colonial movements grew. Where centralized polities confronted linguistically and culturally homogeneous populations, social movements often focused on democratic reforms such as women's suffrage and economic reforms such as labor and social welfare struggles.

But such a summary ignores the full complexity and complicated array of social movements. Populist movements, Societies for the Abolition of the Slave Trade, and socialist movements developed as well as protectionist movements, Cow Protection Movements (India), and prohibition movements. However diverse, these movements developed most prolifically in the more democratic centralizing states. In the less democratic states, social movements were driven underground and sometimes developed in revolutionary directions. Nonetheless, social movements took root in every continent in the years before 1914.

8 The Second Industrial Revolution

Timeline	
1839–42, 1856–60	Opium Wars.
1851	Isaac Singer invents the continuous stitch sewing machine.
1853–56	Crimean War.
1853	Arrival of Commodore Perry in Edo Bay, Japan.
1859	First oil well drilled at Titusville, Pennsylvania.
1860	Félix Potin begins to build his grocery chain.
1861–65	American Civil War.
1861	Krupp begins arms production in Essen. Russia emancipates the serfs.
1862	Notts County formed: first professional soccer team in UK.
1863	Open-hearth steelmaking process developed by French Martin brothers based on German Siemens process.
1867	Russia sells Alaska to the USA.
1868	Cincinnati Red Stockings formed: first professional baseball team in USA.
1869	Opening of the Suez Canal, work of the French engineer Ferdinand de Lesseps.
1870–71	Franco-Prussian War.
1875	Bank Holiday introduced in UK.
1876	Battle of Little Big Horn: Sioux defeat US cavalry led by General G.A. Custer.
1879	Frozen meat from Australia enters British markets.
1882	USA bans Chinese migration.
1883–89	Construction of German welfare state: compulsory sickness insurance (1883), compulsory accident insurance (1884), compulsory old age insurance (1889).
1886	Battle of Adowa: Ethiopians defeat Italian army.

1888	Nikola Tesla patents his electric motor (manufactured by George Westinghouse).
1890	McKinley Tariff in USA.
1892	Méline Tariff in France.
	Rudolf Diesel patents his internal combustion engine.
1896	Henry Ford builds his first car.
1899–1902	Second Boer War in South Africa.
1899	First Hague Conference.
1907	Old age insurance in UK.
1911	National Health Act in UK provides health and unemployment insurance.

Cheap steel of high and uniform quality was the metal of the Second Industrial Revolution. Steel combined the hardness of cast iron with the pliancy of wrought iron and was more enduring than either. It made possible the launching of fleets of ocean liners and the building of skyscrapers in US cities. After a series of inventions, including the Bessemer process, reduced the cost of making low-grade steel, the major remaining obstacle to the production of cheap steel was the availability of suitable iron ore. Until the 1870s steelmaking required iron ore with a low phosphorus content – ores found in some British fields but rarely on the continent.

The solution to this long-standing technical problem was provided by two young amateurs, Sydney Thomas, a London police court clerk who studied chemistry, and his cousin Percy Gilchrist, a Welsh chemist. In 1878 Thomas presented a paper at the British Iron and Steel Institute suggesting that converters lined with limestone could remove phosphorus from ores and enable steelmakers to use the abundant continental deposits of ore in Belgium, France, Germany, and Sweden.

Word of the invention quickly spread to Germany where large industrialists, whose fortunes were based on coal mining and ironmaking, raced one another to England to acquire the license to use the new process. From its beginnings the Second Industrial Revolution would be a transnational process, occurring in many countries simultaneously. The Gilchrist-Thomas process enabled continental industrialists to use their abundant ore to produce cheap steel and by 1910 Germany was the largest European exporter of steel, replacing Britain which had occupied this position for a century.

Unlike the inventors of the First Industrial Revolution, neither Gilchrist nor Thomas ever attempted to use their processes on their own. They lived off the income from their patents. The Gilchrist-Thomas process marked the apogee – but also the end – of this tradition of amateur innovation and entrepreneurship that had prevailed in the First Industrial Revolution. The wave of innovation that followed was based on the discoveries of company-supported research laboratories and state-sponsored universities, and new inventions were to be put into effect by a new kind of industrial firm.

The age of the Second Industrial Revolution saw itself as an era of gigantism: great factories, huge population movements, enormous growth in the worldwide division of labor. The Second Industrial Revolution was a product of the introduction of new technologies but it involved a far more encompassing series of changes.

- Unlike the First Industrial Revolution, many of the technologies of the Second Revolution were enormously expensive and dependent on scientific research and educated technicians.
- The Second Industrial Revolution yielded a new kind of large-scale business enterprise that involved not only the integration of machine production but the development of marketing and distribution.
- In turn, the reorganization of marketing and distribution combined with the spread of a light industry opened the way for a revolution in consumer goods.
- The Second Industrial Revolution revolutionized communication and transportation, greatly reducing the costs of international interactions. Like the First Industrial Revolution, the effects of the Second Industrial Revolution were as much social as economic. It produced different types of worker: Not only the ranks of the industrial worker but those of the white-collar clerk and salesperson, as well as the sweated laborer, were swelled by the Second Industrial Revolution.

8.1 NATIONALISM AND INTERNATIONALISM

Unlike the case of the First Industrial Revolution where one nation, Great Britain, played the pioneering role, the key inventions of the Second Industrial Revolution emerged from the workshops and research institutes of several industrial nations. Map 8.1 shows the industrial regions of Europe scattered across the continent. Industrial regions in the German Ruhr or the French Pas-de-Calais looked a great deal more similar than did such regions compared to their surrounding rural districts. Indeed, the Second Industrial Revolution was truly intercontinental. In the 1880s and 1890s in Japan, the technologies of both the First and Second Industrial Revolutions were introduced simultaneously.

The age of the Second Industrial Revolution illustrates the complex relationship between nationalism and internationalism. At the very moment when technology was bringing the entire globe into contact, a terrible nationalist response was being prepared. Instead of seeing internationalism and nationalism as alternatives – the mistake of nineteenth-century politicians and philosophers – it is necessary to understand their profound linkage.

The word "internationalism" implies and takes for granted the existence of nations; it draws attention to the character of the relationships among nations.

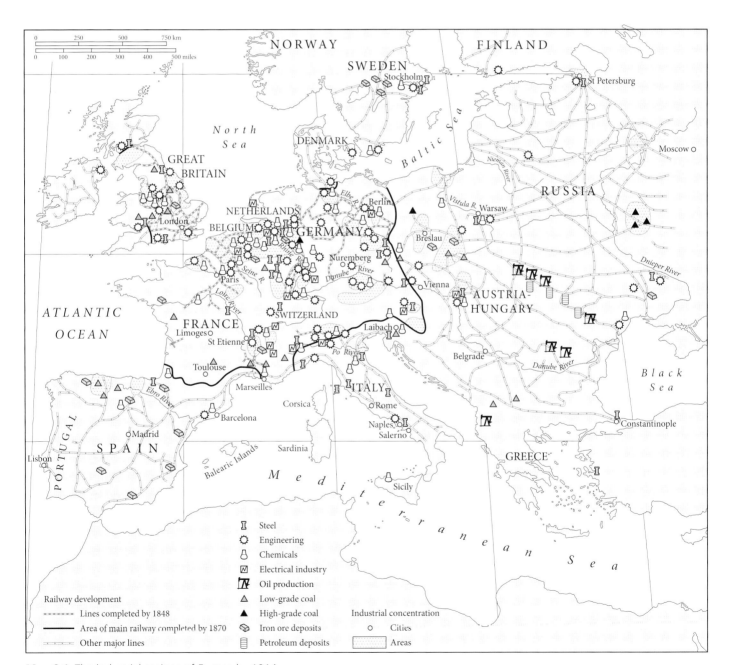

Map 8.1 The industrial regions of Europe by 1914

- Late nineteenth-century internationalism linked nations together on an unprecedented scale, yet states stood guard and exerted control over the points of linkage and this was the source of their strength.
- States protected both businessmen and workers from international competition.
- States molded the political cultures that shaped popular visions of international events.
- States shaped the course of international migration to accomplish their own purposes and to preserve existing ethnic majorities.
- States governed empires and refused to subordinate themselves to a larger imperial purpose.

In the age of the Second Industrial Revolution internationalism and nationalism were nourished by the same forces; they were twin products of technological and political change.

But a balance could not be sustained. The triumph of national rivalries over international connections in World War I set the twentieth century on its tragic course of economic disaster and renewed war.

8.2 TECHNOLOGICAL REVOLUTION AND NATIONAL ECONOMIES

Our view of factory and work life in the Second Industrial Revolution is still shaped by the novelists and popular writers who focused on the new technologies, the huge steel mills, and the multiplication of muscular male factory workers or miners. Great innovations dominated the age: Besides the revolution in steel manufacture this was the age of the internal combustion engine, cheap and practical electricity, petroleum and oil, the sewing machine, a transformation of industrial chemical production, and dramatically more efficient steam engines.

Besides these technological revolutions there was also an institutional revolution. A new type of businesses enterprise, the giant corporation, emerged during the Second Industrial Revolution. German and American firms that pioneered the way were managed by a hierarchy of full-time salaried executives, organized into separate units – factories, marketing, and research – each with its own management and independent resources. Thomas Edison's experimental facility at Menlo Park, New Jersey, was a forerunner of the university and corporate research centers that would produce the great industrial innovations of the future.

These firms profited enormously from their commitment to "vertical integration" in which a single producer controlled every step in the production process from obtaining raw material to producing the finished product. In 1879 in his Homestead Works, the US steel producer Andrew Carnegie not only consolidated control over separate manufacturing processes but centralized them, placing blast furnaces for converting iron ore to pig iron next to Bessemer converters for transforming pig iron into steel. In the 1890s Carnegie's steel company acquired property in the Mesabi ore fields and thus obtained control over its primary raw material. As mass production expanded, large firms also began to involve themselves with the marketing and distribution of their final products. In Japan, the long-established financial cliques, the **zaibatsu**, adapted themselves to the needs of industrialization, providing both the capital and the bureaucracies for organizing a new type of industry.

Large corporations were exceptionally powerful in Germany and the USA, the leaders and rivals in the electric and chemical industries. While France and Germany played an important role in the development of the automobile, the USA led in the mass production of automobiles. Germany and the USA also innovated in different economic sectors. Germany was a leader in rubber, rayon, and chemical products. The USA led in light, mass-produced machinery, including sewing machines, farm equipment, and cash registers. The machine products of heavy industry also promoted the growth of light industry and of food processing: Meatpacking, shoemaking, and brewing benefited from the development of cheap machinery. Profiting from the vast expansion of its railway network, the US steel industry expanded rapidly: In 1890 the USA took and long maintained the worldwide lead in both iron and steel production.

Factories in the Fields

The sudden growth of great factories produced serious problems of labor recruitment. Costs dictated that the large new factories had to be located not only in proximity to markets but near the huge quantities of coal and iron ore that they consumed. It was cheaper to bring workers to the resources than resources to the workers. As a result, steelworks grew up in largely agrarian regions of coal-rich Upper Silesia in the German Empire, or in the small towns of the Ruhr and the Saar, located between coal fields and iron ore deposits, or in locations like Chicago, at the transit point between the Great Lakes ore fields and the southern Illinois and western Pennsylvania coal mines.

When a pre-existing industrial labor force was not already in place, employers turned to the countryside. The giant factories were filled by peasants, rural outworkers, and small farmers from poorer agricultural regions of New England or eastern Germany marginalized by the development of cheaply transported grain. In other cases, employers recruited seasonal or temporary workers who planned to return to agriculture when they had accumulated enough money or to round out holdings they would receive from their parents. In still other cases, employers obtained workers from foreign countries, often from foreign peasant agriculture. The contribution of foreign migrants from rural areas to German and particularly to US industry was important. To find reliable workers, companies sent out recruiters, either to the countryside or to rival industrial areas. In 1910 in the Austro-Hungarian empire, Galician peasants might encounter recruiters from both German steel mills and US coal mines. Most frequently, fellow villagers who worked in urban industry returned or wrote to tell their fellows about their experiences and vouched for fellow villagers with their employers.

The growth of factories in the fields represented vast new conglomerations of social and political power. Unlike the textile factory of the First Industrial Revolution that might over-awe a village or small town, a steel works could dominate a city, an industry, a region. In 1912 one coal mining company in Germany's Ruhr Valley employed over 18,000 workers, but this was dwarfed by the more than 66,000 workers employed by the Krupp steelworks. In one lifetime, the number of industrial workers increased fantastically. In 1851 the German Ruhr region had around 14,000 coal miners, in 1913, 383,000 miners. In 1852 German Upper Silesia had 19,000 workers engaged in mining and smelting, in 1913, 194,000.

Steel magnates such as the American Andrew Carnegie, the Frenchman François de Wendel, and the German Friedrich Alfred Krupp presided over factory towns with tens of thousands of inhabitants. Typically, industrialists lived a public life of conspicuous consumption whose trappings were borrowed from the aristocracy. Given the great inequality existing in the English or Russian countryside, it is difficult to claim that the Second Industrial Revolution increased economic inequality. Subject to highly regressive taxes, the distribution of income during the Second Industrial Revolution in England was closer to that of the most polarized Third World countries than to modern England.

8.3 AN AGE OF FINANCE CAPITALISM

In the era of the Second Industrial Revolution, financiers and financial institutions took on new prominence. The convertors and hearths required by new steelmaking processes were already very expensive compared with the looms and spinning jennies of the First Industrial Revolution but the increasing vertical integration of steelmaking was more expensive still. Industrialists generally relied on powerful financiers. In Germany, large banks oriented toward industrial investment channeled the nation's savings to the development of the new economy. In the USA, in 1901 the great steelmaker Andrew Carnegie sold out to

J.P. Morgan's United States Steel Company. Morgan used his dominant position to encourage industrial integration and to prevent "cut-throat" competition in steelmaking. Financiers like Morgan facilitated the relatively free spread of capital across national borders.

The era of the First Industrial Revolution was marked by the lowering of worldwide tariffs as well as the expansion of world trade. Both liberal politicians like John Bright and liberal philosophers like Herbert Spencer expected that increased foreign trade would weaken the social power of bellicose landed aristocracies and tie people together so closely that state borders would have less and less meaning. In this new world, territorial disputes, one of the chief causes of war, would disappear.

These expectations were to be cruelly disappointed.

Why did Protectionism Become so Popular?

While world trade expanded rapidly, tariffs did not disappear, as states interceded to protect threatened groups. First to rally against free trade were European agriculturalists, mainly grain and meat producers. In the 1870s, sharply reduced transportation costs caused by the spread of railroads in the American Midwest, the Ukraine, and Canada poured cheap grain into European markets and, in the 1880s, the construction of refrigerator ships contributed frozen meat from Argentina and Australia. Unable to compete, many European agricultural populations, including independent peasants, small farmers, and aristocratic landlords, demanded protection. Soon they were joined by industrialists threatened by the accelerated industrialization of the German Empire and the USA. Unaccustomed to an ever more competitive international market, many French metal producers turned to protection – as did some British manufacturers. In general, industrial workers were opposed to protection, which meant higher prices for the workman's food. But increasingly, less skilled workers, the group most strongly affected by open international migration, began to demand migration restriction; such demands were directed against Jewish tailors in London, Chinese laborers in California, Italian harvest hands in Argentina.

In the late nineteenth century the cause of protectionism was not only embraced by losers in the competitive struggle but also by some of its winners. During the economically troubled years between 1877 and 1896, when profits plummeted, the great integrated factories that had driven so many smaller competitors out of business found themselves in danger. Having built new steel railways and rebuilt old railroads with steel, leading industrial concerns found themselves with huge plants and shrinking markets while financial and technical requirements demanded that companies must be kept working year round in good times or bad. Industrialists' social power ensured that their requests for assistance would be considered. Great powers such as France, Germany, and the UK lobbied client states in favor of national heavy industry. Indian railroad regulations privileged the higher quality but more costly British-made locomotives over lower quality, cheaper American products.

Some successful industrialists began to see tariff protection as a way of ensuring a reliable home market for themselves and, with their viability ensured, they would be able to compete more effectively in foreign and colonial markets. In 1891, American steelmakers played a key role in the passage of the protectionist McKinley Tariff. In France, organized industrialists in heavy industry did not originate the demand for protectionism, but in 1892 their rallying behind its banner ensured the triumph of the protectionist Méline Tariff. The greatest blow to the prestige of free trade doctrines came in 1902, in England in the heartland of free trade, when the Birmingham industrialist and former Liberal political leader Joseph Chamberlain publicly called for protectionism.

8.4 WHAT EXPLAINS THE INCREASED TIES BETWEEN STATES AND INDUSTRIALISTS?

In the 1850s and 1860s, states and heavy industry began to cooperate in many ways: States provided financial support and encouraged banks to help national firms participate in the development of railways and military hardware. On the European continent and in North America, almost everywhere except in Great Britain, states subsidized the development of railways, seen as necessary for improving government communications with provinces and for transporting troops. In the United States, the Civil War created a huge governmental demand for metal weaponry and uniforms. The growing use of mobile and heavy artillery in warfare further increased the military need for metalworking and climaxed with the introduction of the *Dreadnought*, launched in Britain in 1906. The Royal Navy was enormously proud of its new steel battleship but only slowly realized its dangers. The *Dreadnought* made the entire British battle fleet obsolete and cheaper German steel gave that country an advantage in the naval competition that ensued.

Just as the successes of the conscript armies of the French Revolution had forced absolutist monarchs to respond, so too Anglo-French victory in the Crimean War (1853–56), German military successes against the Habsburg Empire (1866) and France (1870–71), and Western victories in the Opium Wars forced rulers to pay attention to the connection between industrialization and military strength. With such examples before them, the Russian and Japanese empires came to realize the importance of industrialization. In part, Tsar Alexander II's decision to emancipate the serfs (1861) and subsequent efforts to reform peasant agriculture were motivated by the realization that a commercial agriculture might yield the taxes needed to promote industrial development and military modernization. US Commodore Perry's entrance into Edo Bay (1853) forced the same recognition on the Japanese government. Initially the government of the Meiji Restoration played a leadership role in building factories in areas that were considered military necessities, although later these factories were sold to businessmen.

The military costs of great power competition in Europe in the age of the Second Industrial Revolution imposed tremendous new financial burdens on governments. While contemporaries saw the British empire as the dominant power of the era, its naval planners realized that Britain could no longer afford to maintain its traditional naval supremacy. In the 1900s the rise of American naval power challenged British dominance in Latin America and the Caribbean, while the expansion of both American and Japanese naval power undermined Britain's position in the Pacific. Also, growing Russian economic and military strength threatened confrontations in the Near East and the Persian Gulf and so required Mediterranean naval power. These threats all came at a time when a slow rate of British economic growth made it more difficult to raise the necessary money to sustain British superiority and when the German emperor's decision to match or exceed British naval power produced a costly naval race. Gradually Britain's traditional commitment to naval supremacy declined into a grim determination to maintain an advantage over Germany.

8.5 HOW DID THE SECOND INDUSTRIAL REVOLUTION TRANSFORM THE LABOR FORCE?

The Second Industrial Revolution involved a more complicated set of changes than the simple rise of large factories, and the complexity of these changes becomes apparent if we look at the changing character of the labor force. The heavily muscled, bare-chested male worker, hammer in hand (see Figure 8.1), the semi-skilled industrial worker, who would become the basis of mass twentieth-century working-class politics, was only one component of the new labor force created by the Second Industrial Revolution. Even in terms of manufacturing, this stereotype was an inadequate portrait of the labor force, because it failed to account for the many young women working in light industry. But even more serious, such a stereotype excluded the rapidly expanding non-factory labor force. The factory hand,

THE SECOND INDUSTRIAL REVOLUTION ✳ 237

Figure 8.1 Foundry worker pouring steel.

white-collar worker, and sweated laborer were all equally products of the Second Industrial Revolution, each group having its own distinctive problems and concerns. Each contributed to the debate over social conditions.

Age, gender, race, national origin, marital status, and ethnicity figured prominently in all the job hierarchies and employment practices that developed before World War I. Nowhere was the importance of such factors of more consequence than among semi-skilled workers of the Second Industrial Revolution. Producer goods were the main terrain of semi-skilled workers but consumer goods industries often created a similar labor force, as was the case in automobiles, meatpacking, and shoe manufacture. The technologies of the Second Industrial Revolution often undercut the importance of highly skilled artisanal workers. Particularly in the USA with its great stock of unskilled immigrant workers, employers attempted to compensate for their lack of skilled workers with practices such as Taylorism designed to simplify work and replace skilled workers. Taylor's attitude toward the workman Schmidt (see Box 8.1) betrays a contempt for less skilled workers, but work in the new industries remained more demanding than Taylor claimed and it usually required substantial on-the-job training before workers reached maximum productivity. The new industrial worker is best described as "semi-skilled."

The great power accumulating in the hands of large employers in heavy industry enabled them to recruit a new labor force to their own specifications and, by and large, they made it in their own image, masculine. Smaller-scale factory employers such as those in light industry usually had less autonomy and were more

likely to employ women. Essentially employers, when they could, recreated the social inequalities existing in the home and in society at large. Women's and single migrants' participation in industry was limited to lower-paying, less skilled jobs for which demand fluctuated. The poorly paid, largely female and child labor force of the original factories of the First Industrial Revolution contrasts strikingly with the better-paid predominantly male labor force of the large factories of the Second Industrial Revolution.

Employers chose adult males partly because factory work was physically demanding but mostly to reinforce already existing patterns of inequality. Male manufacturers shared with male workers the feeling that married women would and should stay home to take care of children. Where it was available, working-class families usually sought work for both male and female children, although when families could afford it daughters, but never sons, were sometimes kept home to assist their mother in housekeeping. Exceptionally, in countries such as France or Japan, whose factories suffered from chronic labor shortage, women were employed in large numbers in manufacturing; in Japan women composed the majority of the factory labor force and married women played an important role within the French industrial workforce.

Workers and often their unions replicated existing social divisions within new industries and these divisions became self-sustaining. The masculine character of much industrial work promoted an ethic of fraternalism that flourished in predominantly or exclusively male clubs, bars, and cafes where masculinity and industrial work came to be associated.

Box 8.1 Scientific Management: Labor Relations in the Era of the Second Industrial Revolution

Frederick Winslow Taylor, the father of scientific management, came to Bethlehem Steel in 1899 with the intention of making a revolution in the workplace. Taylor claimed that by breaking down and analyzing the steps in the work process he could find the "one best way" of doing a task. He argued that more efficient work would benefit both worker and employer. One of the pillars of the Taylorist system was "piece work" in which a worker was paid according to how many units he or she produced. Many workers and trade unionists feared, with good reason, that Taylorism amounted to a pseudo-scientific procedure for upping piece-work requirements while lowering payments per piece. Taylor's record was mixed. Only when he began to focus on semi-skilled or unskilled workers

did he show the kind of results that fully pleased his employers. His attitude toward less skilled steelworkers rings clear:

The task before us, then narrowed itself down to getting Schmidt to handle 47 tons of pig iron per day and making him glad to do it ... Schmidt was called out from among the gang of pig-iron handlers and talked to somewhat in this way:

"Well, if you are a high-priced man, you will do exactly as this man tells you to-morrow, from morning till night. When he tells you to pick up a pig and walk, you pick it up and you walk, and when he tells you to sit down and rest, you sit down. You do that right straight through the day. And what's more, no back talk" ...

Now one of the very first requirements for a man who is fit to handle pig iron as a regular occupation is that he shall be so stupid and so phlegmatic that he more nearly resembles in his mental make-up the ox than any other type. The man who is mentally alert and intelligent is for this very reason entirely unsuited to what would, for him, be the grinding monotony of work of this character. Therefore the workman who is best suited to handling the pig iron is unable to understand the real science of doing this class of work. He is so stupid that the word "percentage" has no meaning to him, and he must consequently be trained by a man more intelligent than himself into the habit of working in accordance with the laws of science before he can be successful.

Unemployment

Although industrial workers might be dissatisfied with their wages and their long hours, often extending to ten or twelve hours, six days a week, workers' great fear was unemployment. The very idea of unemployment and efforts to register it was a creation of government statistical bureaus in this era. Of course, being out of work was not an invention of the Second Industrial Revolution but the idea of "unemployment" as a social category emerged as a result of state responses to the problems of the new factory labor force. Before the Second Industrial Revolution, the majority of adult workers composed part of what has been labeled an "economy of makeshifts" in which only the most skilled and highly paid workers had a really fixed occupational identity; the child laborers of the First Industrial Revolution often joined this economy of makeshifts when they were too old to work in the mills. Many a less skilled worker was a "jack of all trades," laboring seasonally in agriculture at planting or harvest time, assisting skilled construction workers, hauling or carting on demand, while occasionally turning to tinkering or trading. On the continent, some of these workers owned some land or at least had claims on landowning relatives who might tide them over in times of major scarcity. After years in urban labor, many workers had lost their ties to the countryside and

could not return to the country in times of crisis. Fear of unemployment was heightened by the bouts of unemployment that intensified in the years between 1900 and 1914.

Unemployment took on a new shape in the economy of the Second Industrial Revolution as a new and large labor force began to identify themselves as "metalworkers," "coal miners," and "clerks." Within industrial regions, job turnover in individual plants and mines was sometimes high, particularly among the young. Unlike the shifting and mobile casual labor force of the earlier period, however, workers often remained in an industrial occupation for most of their lives. Trained on relatively specialized machines in large factories, semi-skilled workers had much less opportunity to move long distances as part of their work than artisans. In bad times, when factory work contracted, workers remained near factories whose machines they had been trained to operate and close to former workmates who might inform them about new opportunities. These workers were the first to be identified as "unemployed."

Accidents

Accidents and industrial injuries were another concern of industrial workers. Working unprotected next to turning belts, moving wheels, or molten metal, and often manipulating huge pieces of metal, the workers of the Second Industrial Revolution were extremely liable to injury. The centralization of industry meant that work accidents were concentrated in certain localities where they strained local resources – and drew public attention. The effect of coal dust on miners' lungs and the daily toll of relatively routine underground accidents both took a far larger toll of miners' lives than did exceptional mining disasters, but the news of coal mining disasters, such as the 164 British miners killed in the Seaham explosion in 1880 or the 439 Welsh dead at Senghenydd in 1913, captured headlines and symbolized in the popular mind the problems of mining.

Old Age

Along with unemployment and industrial accidents, old age was another concern of working-class life; while the alternative was unattractive, long life posed problems that could rarely be answered in advance. Although mutual aid societies, where working men set up and administered their own savings funds, and commercial life insurance were spreading among workers in Britain and the USA, in so far as most workers put money aside, it was generally for funeral expenses or to tide them over periods of short-term illness or unemployment. Since fewer than half the male workers aged 20 would be alive at age 65 (in some European countries, far fewer), the incentive to put hard-won money aside for a problematic old age was less than compelling. Much depended on the ability and willingness of children to help their aged parents and on an elderly person's own continued ability to earn at least a meager income.

Most male workers probably expected and even hoped to die on the job, although they knew that as they passed their prime they would be less able to perform physically vigorous tasks and forced to seek less strenuous (and less well-paid) work. In coal mining and steelmaking, men were generally considered past their prime by the age of 40. Large companies often reserved less demanding tasks to reward faithful employees but the number of such tasks was limited. If all else failed and children were unable to provide sufficient aid, aged workers and workers' widows might end up in charitable institutions, or state-run poorhouses where elderly couples were separated from one another and sometimes lodged indiscriminately with the insane and the criminal population. Many elderly men and women preferred begging.

Why Did National Welfare States Emerge?

Modern welfare states first arose to deal with the problems of male industrial workers and their families. In the pre-World War I years compulsory national insurance, the core policy of the modern welfare state, was initially limited to sections of the industrial working class. The German Empire was the pioneer. Otto von Bismarck, the "Iron Chancellor" who had united the German state, created the framework for the first national welfare state. Bismarck hoped that social reform would capture working-class loyalty at a time when he was engaged in a bitter effort to suppress the German Social Democratic Party but he was also concerned to relieve the financial burdens placed on rural institutions by the return of aged and unwell workers to their agrarian roots. After prolonged resistance from the Reichstag, in 1883 Bismarck passed a compulsory sickness insurance bill, in 1884 compulsory accident insurance, and in 1889 compulsory old age insurance. Later, these programs were extended to white-collar workers. In 1906, after the sweeping Liberal victory, the UK passed its own legislation, most importantly a national insurance act in 1911 which included provisions for unemployment insurance, targeted exclusively to skilled industrial workers. By 1914, all the major European countries except Russia had compulsory accident insurance laws and even Austria-Hungary had old age pensions. Outside Europe, the USA and Japan remained significantly behind most industrialized European states in the development of the welfare state.

Why Did the White-Collar Labor Force Grow During the Second Industrial Revolution?

A revolution in distribution created a large market for the mass-produced commodities of the Second Industrial Revolution. The revolution in distribution multiplied the number of clerks, agents, engineers, and office workers and created a new white-collar labor force whose numbers increased in step with the factory workforce. The same large firms that hired large numbers of blue-collar workers in factories, employed **white-collar workers** in marketing and in the expanded offices of management. Where industrial workers possessed valuable skills, many white-collar workers prided themselves on their equivalent of a vocational high school degree. White-collar workers could be found in small-town railway stations and village schools but they were especially concentrated in the government agencies and business offices centered in the great cities whose population was exploding in the late nineteenth century. Berlin, London, New York, and Paris were cities in which white-collar workers were most at home.

In the first half of the nineteenth century much male white-collar professional training was imparted through an apprenticeship in which a young man learned skills such as accountancy, engineering, pharmacy, or the law from his employer. The professions might even be acquired informally. In the 1830s Abraham Lincoln considered blacksmithing but, borrowing books from a lawyer, he passed the bar exam on his own. In the second half of the nineteenth century, growing professionalization meant that many occupations such as accountancy, engineering, teaching, and law required formal education, and the growth of large firms decreased the likelihood that a young man might simply succeed his retiring employer. Already on the eve of World War I female typists who acquired their skills at business schools or at public schools were rapidly entering the white-collar workforce in Europe and the USA (but not in Japan). Although large numbers of women entered white-collar work, they were denied access to jobs that entailed promotion, and so were consigned to the lower ranks of the white-collar world.

The spread of the department store, co-operatives, grocery chains, and mail-order houses, and the expansion of branded, packaged consumer goods, further increased the number of white-collar workers at the expense of the small shopkeepers and small producers whose ownership of small amounts of property identified them as lower middle-class. After 1860 the Frenchman Félix Potin began to build a grocery empire of chain stores selling his own products made in his factory and stored in his warehouses on the edge of Paris. The Great Atlantic and Pacific Tea Company (A&P) and Woolworth both began selling groceries and novelties. Thomas Lipton's sale of standardized quarter-pound tea packages was the basis of his grocery empire. Big-city department stores catering to the middle classes, such as Paris's Bon Marché, New York's Macy's, and Chicago's Marshall Fields, were all products of the middle or late nineteenth century, as were the more popularly oriented mail-order houses such as Sears Roebuck. Among the most important international concerns were corporations that sold consumers products, such as the English Lever Brothers, the German Bayer (aspirin), the Swiss Nestlé, and the US Coca Cola.

On the edges of the white-collar world were domestic servants, the largest single category of wage worker in the great capital cities. These included both the full-time staff who lived with their families and the many more part-time house cleaners who might routinely work for several clients. Despite this close contact with better-off members of society, or perhaps because of it, many workers preferred factory to domestic labor. The expanding market for male laborers led to the departure from the household of all but the most highly skilled male workers, butlers and chauffeurs. Domestic service became predominantly women's work, often the work of ethnic and racial minorities who could not find work elsewhere.

White-Collar Workers or a New Middle Class? Were teachers, office workers, or engineers members of the working class or were they members of a new professionally trained middle class? Like industrial workers and unlike shopkeepers or small businessmen, they received wages. However, unlike industrial workers, they did not work with their hands, they were more educated, and their lifestyle in terms of dress and recreation was often closer to that of their employers or the lower middle-class shopkeepers than to those of industrial workers. German and English white-collar workers were initially excluded from the compulsory social insurance applied to industrial workers. In response to white-collar discontent, the German government created a social insurance program for them but was careful to create a program distinct from that created for industrial workers and with higher benefits. In some countries, such as France, schoolteachers began to organize unions to demand better pay and more autonomy, while in other countries such as Germany, teachers tended more to identify themselves as agents of the imperial state.

What was "Sweated Labor" and Why Did It Grow in the Era of the Second Industrial Revolution?

While the growing number of white-collar workers was often ignored by contemporaries, the presence of **sweated labor** was a repeated subject of discussion. Contemporaries tended to think of these impoverished workers as somehow survivors from a pre-industrial age rather than recognizing the plain fact that sweated labor was as much a product of the Second Industrial Revolution as the steel mill. Although some forms of sweated labor, particularly rural putting out, can be traced to pre-industrial times, and much of the transition to "ready made" clothing and furniture items belong to the first half of the nineteenth century, the spread of "subcontracting" in the garment trade, a favorite target of late nineteenth-century reformers, was a contemporary innovation. Sweated labor seemed pre-industrial only because it did not fit the model of industrial change exemplified by the great factories and costly concentrated machinery.

The rise of chain stores, mail-order houses, and department stores increased the market for "ready made" clothes and standardized household furnishings. Technological change had also transformed the organization of work in light industry producing consumer goods hitherto dominated by highly skilled workers. While the Carnegies and the Kruppses were consolidating every significant stage of the production process in their large factories, garment entrepreneurs were breaking up the production process and consigning each stage to a separate small "subcontractor." Such an organization of labor was possible because the new technologies that were transforming garment work, inventions such as the American Singer's sewing machine,

Figure 8.2 Sweated labor was work that paid little money, lasted long hours, and involved poor working conditions. Some sweated labor was done by adults in small shops but it was also done by women and children in cramped apartments and dank basements. The introduction of the sewing machine and an increased division of labor, employing subcontractors – especially in great cities like London, New York, and Paris – led to the spread of sweated labor.

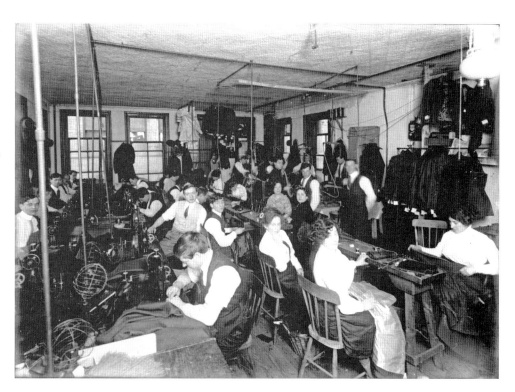

were relatively inexpensive (and could even be purchased on installment plans). In seasonal industries such as garments, where new fashions coincided with the elite social season, employers were particularly reticent to invest in costly machinery.

Meanwhile in fashion capitals London, New York, and Paris, a cheap labor market flourished among urban women and children whose own husbands and fathers were casual laborers with wages insufficient to support a family. The garment industry was exemplary of a new form of industrial organization that emphasized quick turnover, limited inventories, and adaptability and was associated with low wages, long hours, and poor working conditions. Reformers labeled this work "sweated labor." Some sweated labor was done in small shops like the Triangle Shirtwaist factory in New York in 1911. Although it styled itself a factory, it did not use mass production technologies but individual sewing machines. Doors were locked to prevent breaks or pilfering; locked doors were responsible for the death of 146 mainly young women workers when a fire broke out on the eighth floor. But much sweated labor was also done outside the shop, at home where garment work might be farmed out to mothers who worked with their children. After the 1890s, the migration of skilled Jewish garment workers, fleeing in response to pogroms and worsening conditions, provided a cheap skilled labor force in garment work; Jewish garment workers played an important role in London and Paris, but nowhere so much as in New York.

8.6 WHY DID A NEW CONCERN FOR SOCIAL QUESTIONS ARISE?

While great factories and the fiery steel hearths captured the attention of the late nineteenth-century public, some who looked more closely discovered more alarming aspects of industrial change. From conscience-stricken English society women, to crusading Catholic priests in Germany, to politically inclined, highly skilled artisanal workers in France, many of those who witnessed the expansion of urban "sweated industry" and the repressive environment of the factory towns became indignant. The disparity between the magnificent accomplishments of late nineteenth-century industry and the grinding poverty and repression that accompanied it were the basis of the so-called "Social Question," a question that seemed more urgent as the working classes were enfranchised and voted for socialist and labor parties.

Why Did Social Reform Movements Spread so Rapidly?

The plight of sweated laborers in the great cities won popular sympathy because it offended dearly held beliefs of the late nineteenth-century upper and middle classes as well the newly forming working classes. Mainstream nineteenth-century economic thought was resolutely individualist. Samuel Smiles's *Self Help* (1859) sold three quarters of a million copies in England before 1914 and was reprinted in Danish, French, and German. Smiles described the triumphs of resourceful and hardworking young men from impoverished backgrounds. Yet even stalwart advocates of individual initiative wondered whether stunted child laborers, undernourished and mutilated by accidents, could follow the high road to business success. Middle-class women who celebrated women's domestic role as nurturers and care givers and advocated making the home a refuge from the competitive world of business were shocked by the sight of mothers forced to work long hours to feed their family. In Britain imperialists were concerned about the high rate of military rejections in urban areas during the Boer War (1899–1902), Britain's war to consolidate its hold over a resource-rich South Africa.

Even though similar industrial and demographic transformations occurred in every country touched by the Second Industrial Revolution, workers everywhere turned to their individual states for help in dealing with the threats of industrial transformation and the problems of urban living. In the French Republic, the German Empire, the United Kingdom, and the United States, social reformers and labor movements appealed to governments to prevent "sweated labor." Concerned with working-class health, governments acted to prevent many of the worst abuses of technological innovation and market revolution. By 1914 laws prohibiting factory work for young children, regulating the hours of adolescent labor, and imposing restrictions on female labor had been legislated in most of North America and Western and Central Europe, although enforcement was still often weak and sporadic. Some feminists who fought for limiting child labor opposed restrictions on women's labor and this became an issue of contention.

Did Urbanization Promote Social Reform?

The urbanization of industrial work and accelerated growth of big cities in late nineteenth-century Europe made the regulation of urban sanitation and living conditions a concern not only of workers but of all social classes. Although products of poverty, contaminated water and contagious disease could kill anyone. In 1861 Prince Albert, the husband of Queen Victoria, died of typhoid fever, a waterborne disease, and one of the queen's daughters and one of her granddaughters died of diphtheria, a disease transmitted by human carriers (it turned out that the Windsor Palace water supply was contaminated). Medical advance contributed to the debate over the "Social Question" as reformers sought to implement new medical discoveries. Although Anglo-Americans were slow to accept his findings, Joseph Lister's work on the germ theory of disease and his stress on the importance of antiseptics enabled hospitals to become

something more than stopping points on the way to the cemetery. But medical progress was no panacea.

Many reformers came to the conclusion that state intervention was necessary to make cities safe. State intervention played an important role in improvements in sanitation: Regulating the production of food and medicine, enacting and enforcing urban sanitation regulations, setting specifications for building codes and building, and modernizing and maintaining sewer systems all contributed greatly to the prevention of killer epidemics and contagious diseases. Berlin, New York, and Paris all substantially improved their water supply during these years and this greatly decreased mortality due to cholera, dysentery, and typhoid.

As a result of medical discoveries, improved living standards, and state-enforced sanitation measures, a real improvement in life expectations occurred during these years. The effects of growing living standards can be seen in the growing heights of general populations. Height is an important indicator of well-being. Industrializing countries such as the USA and the UK recorded decreases in the height of populations in the early decades of the Second Industrial Revolution but heights began to rise again after 1890, as a result of the improved living standards of important sections of the labor force. But the record is not one of unalloyed progress. Late nineteenth-century medical discoveries, improved living standards, and state-mandated regulation had mixed success against the four greatest nineteenth-century killers, tuberculosis, pneumonia, diphtheria, and strokes. As a result of the development of an effective antiserum, diphtheria, the most common childhood killer, was waning already and on the road to eradication in the USA and the more industrialized European nations; in 1905 New Yorkers were encouraged when only 860 deaths occurred during a prolonged epidemic. Tuberculosis remained "the captain of all the men of death" but its killing power was also beginning its long-term gradual decline. Warmer clothes and better nutrition contributed to the decline in tuberculosis on the European continent. All the news on the mortality front was not good. Mortality due to strokes was unchanged and mortality rates for pneumonia somewhat increased.

Nevertheless, between 1850 and 1914 life expectations began a slow but steady increase in the industrializing nations of Europe and North America. Much of this improvement in life expectation was the result of decreasing infant and child mortality. In the German Empire, for example, between the 1870s and 1910–11 the life expectancy of newborn babies increased by about 11 to 12 years, from 38.5 to 50.7 for females and from 35.6 to 47.7 for males. The life of adult men and women also lengthened: In 1911 men and women who reached the age of 30 could expect to live four years longer than their parents in 1875. Life expectancy of those over 65 changed only slightly.

8.7 EVERYDAY LIFE AND POPULAR CULTURE

Fundamental changes in the most intimate aspects of ordinary life such as family size, recreational life, and gender roles occurred in countries and regions affected by the Second Industrial Revolution. At the same time a communications revolution lowered the cost of publishing and promoted the development of a mass circulation press. This revolution also allowed the press to cover international events on a practically up-to-the-minute basis. Despite the transnational processes shaping the labor force and the communications revolution that brought continents into close touch, a key feature of modern life in the industrialized world of the Second Industrial Revolution was the emergence of strong national political cultures that captured the allegiance of dominant ethnic groups.

While the Second Industrial Revolution affected popular life profoundly, it operated within the framework of pre-existing popular culture and beliefs. Everywhere workers defended their own institutions – families, neighborhoods, and local taverns – that gave them a sense of their own identity and value. At the same time, the new working classes developing in rapidly expanding urban areas had different everyday experiences from their parents and grandparents. These experiences provided the raw material for the molding of a popular culture that differed from that of their pre-industrial predecessors yet remained distinctively working-class.

How Did the Transformed Working Classes Live in the City?

In the great cities as in the factory towns, the new working classes lived in their own distinctive areas. In contrast to the highly skilled artisanal working classes – old city-dwellers who lived in distinctive occupational concentrations within the city center – factories needed space and were established on the outskirts of the cities or in separate urban communities where land was cheap. Although mass urban transportation in the form of buses, trams, and trains was developing in the late nineteenth century, these were typically confined to the middle classes and better-paid white-collar workers; factory workers could not afford them. The new white-collar labor force also fled to the more prosperous urban peripheries. When they could, workers chose the housing most accessible to their factory jobs, but often they had to reside in working-class suburbs of the city, areas with affordable rent, and to make their way to the factory as best they were able. The presence of a nearby factory inevitably changed the character of the whole adjacent suburban area, usually for the worse, as workers sought to divide up existing housing to create

affordable housing or as small-scale contractors built shoddy housing to take quick advantage of demand. Anxious to cut corners, builders seldom gave much thought to sanitation systems and urban authorities sometimes ignored sanitary problems or lacked sufficient authority to take proper measures. Figure 8.3 shows rows of tight-packed, quickly constructed houses built for London workers. In 1910, as today, central Paris was an elegant tourist city of broad avenues and dazzling lights, but few tourists ever visited the working-class suburbs with their unpaved roads, inadequate water supplies, lack of gas and electricity, and nonexistent public schools.

The departure of the most stable working-class families to the suburbs accelerated the deterioration of the old city centers of longtime working-class settlement. The remaining workers were often casual laborers such as dockers who lived near the wharves of Hamburg, London, Liverpool, New York, and Rotterdam. Growing as a result of the expansion of international trade, dock work demanded strong muscles, but it depended on the availability of ships that needed to be unloaded, and a period of rough weather could result in weeks without work. Dock laborers were generally hired by the job from crowds of men who assembled near the dockyards; the fierce competition meant that dock work was everywhere among the lowest paid of adult male employments. The fluctuating character of dock work exposed the men's incomes and those of the families dependent upon them to the chance of weather or to the favoritism of foremen; the resulting uncertainty of the male breadwinner's wage exposed his family to the perils of "sweated labor."

How Did the Second Industrial Revolution Affect Men and Women?

A distinctive feature of the new family economy of both the factory worker and sweated laborer was the tighter demarcation of male and female spheres of activity. Adult males were often away from home as much as ten or twelve hours a day for six days a week. Male absence was often increased by the development of a work-based masculine culture in which workers, sometimes men from the same plant or shop, sometimes from the same working-class neighborhood, assembled on Saturday nights in working-class cafes or taverns. Between 1850 and 1914, throughout much of Europe, working-class consumption of alcohol and patronage of bars and taverns increased greatly, largely because improved income allowed workers to afford to drink and because distillers aggressively sought out locations in working-class neighborhoods, in close proximity to factories. The importance of male hangouts was more than recreational. They were the milieu in which unemployed workers learned about job opportunities and

Figure 8.3 Working-class housing in London offered little space and unsanitary living arrangements. Laws generally ignored working-class housing.

workers discussed politics. Continental police spies patronized them faithfully to gauge popular opinion.

Not all pubs and cafes excluded working-class wives nor were pubs and cafes everywhere the primary institutions of working-class recreational life. Accompanied by their husbands, working-class women were often familiar figures at neighborhood cafes and bars that had a less raucous atmosphere than the drinking places located next to factories. As working-class incomes improved, during these years many bars and cafes even began to incorporate musical entertainment designed to cater to married couples. The late nineteenth-century music halls, cafe concerts, and beer gardens were the purveyors of a new form of popular entertainment that appealed to a broad popular audience of men and women. Millions of English men and women whistled and hummed music hall tunes such as "My Old Man Said 'Follow the Van,'" (see Box 8.2) and "Tipperary" while the sad Parisians of Toulouse-Lautrec's "Moulin de la Galette" provide another perspective on cafe life. In the Scandinavian countries and to a lesser extent in Great Britain, temperance societies might serve the same purpose as taverns, cementing social ties formed in the workplace and giving workers a chance to discuss political events in private. Although the temperance movement had little effect on American ethnic workers, US temperance activity and legal restrictions on alcohol consumption led to declining American liquor consumption from its peak in the first half of the nineteenth century.

Together, work and recreation influenced the character of family life. With fathers away at work, young working-class sons and daughters knew "Mum" more intimately, for they observed her day-to-day role in the household economy. While Dad connected his sons to the world of work and future employment, Mum connected sons and daughters to the neighborhood world presided over by married women like herself who minded each other's children, tended one another's sick, and passed along information, including possibly sometimes birth control material. Although there were parallels in the life courses of working-class men and women, overall men's life course usually offered more freedom and autonomy.

Why Did a General Decline in Fertility Occur During the Years of the Second Industrial Revolution?

In the late nineteenth century, a silent revolution, one of the most important in modern world history, began among working-class and middle-class families in Western and Central Europe and the USA (see Figure 8.4). Basically, married women went from bearing five to eight children over the course of their childbearing years and instead bore one to four. Not only was fertility diminished but it was concentrated into a shorter and usually earlier period of a married woman's childbearing years. Between 1870 and 1914, many of the major industrializing nations underwent a rapid fertility decline in which fertility

Box 8.2 "My Old Man Said, 'Follow the Van'": Marie Lloyd and the Music Hall

"My Old Man Said, 'Follow the Van'" was a well-known music hall song. It described a working-class family's night-time flight from their apartment in order to avoid paying back rent and the plight of a child lost in the family's departure. It was perhaps the best-known song of Marie Lloyd, "Queen of the Music Hall." Born in London in 1870, the eldest of nine children, Marie Lloyd's life coincided with the height of the music hall. In 1922 she collapsed on tour. Her funeral was attended by large crowds of Londoners who remembered her songs and identified with the situations and characters in them. By the time of her death, silent movies and the radio had begun to displace the music hall. Marie Lloyd's death marks its end.

We had to move away
'Cos the rent we couldn't pay,
The movin' van came round just after dark;
There was me and my old man
Shoving things inside the van,
Which we'd often done before, let me remark . . .

My old man said, "Follow the van,
And don't dilly-dally on the way!"
Off went the cart with the home packed in it,
I walked behind with my old cock linnet.
But I dillied and dallied, dallied and dillied,
Lost the van and don't know where to roam.
I stopped on the way to have the old half-quartern,
And I can't find the way home.

Figure 8.4 Births in selected European countries, 1860–1910 (per thousand population).

	Germany	England and Wales	France	Russia
1860	36.4	34.3	26.2	49.7
1870	38.5	35.2	25.9	49.2
1880	37.6	34.2	24.6	49.7
1890	35.7	30.2	21.8	50.3
1900	35.6	29.6	21.3	49.3
1910	29.8	26.2	19.6	45.1

descended well below previously prevailing birth rates and never returned to them. Countries that witnessed this fertility decline before 1914 included England and Wales, Germany, Italy, the Scandinavian countries, and the USA. A major exception among industrialized countries was France, which had undergone a similar fertility decline in the late eighteenth century.

The causes of fertility decline were various and not all of them were a product of the Second Industrial Revolution. Although popular culture sentimentalized childhood, young children always imposed a burden on working-class and lower middle-class families. Over the course of the nineteenth century the financial burdens of child-raising increased considerably faster than family income. In many regions, the huge factories of the Second Industrial Revolution made child labor superfluous, and the increased enactment and enforcement of schooling laws denied an important source of income to many families, including the families of small shopkeepers, who used their children as shop assistants. Instead of contributing money and services to the household, children became an expense, especially for better-off working-class and lower middle-class families who began to contribute toward the vocational training of sons and daughters to become clerks or schoolteachers.

Also, as infant and child mortality rates improved, married couples lowered their estimate of the number of children they must conceive so that at least one would survive to care for them in their old age – an important consideration in an age in which the welfare state was only beginning. The support of working children had long been the mainstay of aged urban workers. Although it was becoming earlier, the relatively late age of marriage in Western and Central Europe, late twenties for men, mid twenties for women, and the early age for beginning work, between 12 and 14, meant that most young men and women stayed at home for a decade or more, contributing to their parents' household and tending to their parents' needs.

The growth of feminist movements (discussed in Chapter 9) led women to assert their own right to control their fertility, while the spread of education and increased literacy facilitated the spread of birth control material, even in states such as France, where the dissemination of birth control materials was illegal. In some countries, contraceptives replaced coitus interruptus as the major technique of fertility control.

Why Did the Power of Organized Religion Decline in Industrial Europe?

Although many churchmen were opposed to any form of birth control, the hold of religion among urban working-class populations in Europe was declining. Religious affiliation was often weakened by the rapid growth within suburb and city center of areas with largely working-class populations. The absence or weakness of religious establishments in rapidly growing European cities created an environment in which anticlerical or antireligious sentiments could flourish. The major life transitions, birth, death, and marriage, still demanded commemoration with religious rites but such services were no longer readily available and often were more costly and required more effort than in the village.

"Established churches," official government-supported churches, such as the Anglican church in England, the Catholic church in France, the Lutheran church in Sweden, or the Orthodox church in Russia, found it particularly difficult to adapt to the new demographic and social trends. They had developed a traditional hierarchy based on long-enduring territorial divisions and frequently needed government approval to change established patterns of religious expenditure and institutional organization. The unfamiliarity of many powerful clergymen with the realities of industrial labor and their fear of political radicalism did not make them vigorous champions of missionary activity. Many working-class families had the feeling, not that they had left the church, but that their church had left them. In the USA the working-class break with religion was slighter than in most European countries. The late nineteenth-century USA no longer possessed established churches, and decentralized Protestant religious groups found it easier to adjust to urbanization. In turn, at least after migrant groups had securely established themselves, Catholicism, Lutheranism, and Eastern European Orthodoxies often became symbols of ethnic identity.

By the late nineteenth century, some churchmen within all denominations had begun to recognize the reality of a Social Question and were attempting to compensate for decades of neglect. Anglican clergymen were prominent in the establishment of settlement houses in London slums. In many regions of Europe and North America, Protestant clergymen became leaders in almost all areas of social reform. Pope Leo XIII's 1891 encyclical, **Rerum Novarum** ("of new things" in Latin), marked a significant turn toward addressing social issues and encouraging Catholics to involve themselves in social reform.

At the very moment when the clergy began to concern themselves with popular urban religion, the framework of popular social life was secularizing. Once centered around religious celebrations, saints' days, holy days, and Carnival (days immediately preceding Lent), European recreational life was yielding to activities following a secular calendar, with singing societies, cycling clubs, and football. States were creating secular holidays that commemorated national history or that served national purposes. In 1880 French republicans created Bastille day, July 14, to celebrate the foundation of the republican state. In 1870 the British Parliament instituted an official Bank Holiday, requiring employers to give their workers four days off a year: the bill's sponsor explained that the national holiday would benefit bank clerks whose only days off were on Christmas and Good Friday.

In the development of popular recreation, England set the pace and the continent followed. Formerly elite recreations such as cricket, rugby, and soccer, which originated at elite schools such as Eton and Rugby, became popular, spreading to the working classes. They became national sports not only in the UK but in Australia, Canada, Jamaica and the British Caribbean, and South Africa and to a lesser extent in India. Many of the best-known English football clubs developed from working men's societies during the 1880s as cities began to subsidize grounds and sponsors began to charge admissions. By the 1890s professional football teams predominated, crowned in 1904 by the formation of the International Association Football Federation. Interestingly the USA followed its own path. At the same time that football, rugby, and cricket were emerging in England, baseball, basketball, and American football were developing in the USA. Figure 8.5 shows an early baseball game.

Why Did a Popular Press Grow and What Impact Did It Have?

In both Europe and North America, a growing popular audience followed their favorite teams in the newspapers. Although a mass press had its origins in France, Great Britain, and the USA in the 1830s and 1840s, the expansion of literacy greatly enlarged the reading public. By 1914 every nation in Europe and North America had at least perfunctory compulsory elementary school attendance laws in place. Implementation was another matter but by 1914 in France, the German Empire, and Great Britain

Figure 8.5 As the labor movement proved more successful in bettering working conditions, workers began to have more time to spend on leisure activities. Games like soccer, baseball (pictured here), and cycling grew in popularity and spread throughout the nation and even the world. Both workers and middle classes, who disagreed on so many things, could unite to back their local team.

almost everyone under age 60 could read and the figures were almost as high for Japan. In Austria, although the variation among regions was great, about 75 percent of the population was literate, in Italy 60 percent, and in Russia 40 percent. In the USA, education was the affair of states and regional variation was great; the US South long remained an area in which popular education lagged, and in the 1880s and 1890s popular education in the great cities was overwhelmed by the presence of non-English-speaking migrant children. In response, reformers accused urban systems that neglected to enforce the compulsory schooling laws of failing to accomplish their mission of "Americanizing" immigrants.

Widespread literacy in a standardized language was the foundation not only for the expansion of a mass press but for the formation of a mass national political culture. The development of a mass press accelerated in the second half of the nineteenth century. Steam presses enabled daily papers to reduce their costs so that workers could afford to purchase them, while English and French laws severely restricting a mass press were repealed or modified. In 1900 the American *New York World*, the English *Daily Mail*, and the French *Petit Parisien* had a daily circulation of 1 million. Even in countries like Germany where a mass press did not fully develop, the cheapened cost of printing enabled specialized groups such as the socialists and the Catholics to publish newspapers. For the first time, newspapers were able to provide current coverage of international events. As late as 1841,

news of President William Henry Harrison's death in Washington, DC took three months and twenty days to reach Los Angeles, but in 1901 news of President William McKinley's shooting in Buffalo reached California within minutes. From 1867 on, the development of cables made possible rapid communication across the Atlantic. By 1914, submarine cables linked all the continents.

Political leaders were quick to take advantage of mass newspapers to mold a national political culture with ceremonies such as Victor Hugo's funeral in 1885, the commemoration of the fourth century of Columbus' discovery of America in 1892, and the celebration of Queen Victoria's Diamond Jubilee in 1897, events of unprecedented splendor designed to awe newspaper readers throughout the country. Readers thrilled to stories of their nation's explorers in Africa and Asia. Newspaper reports from the Boer War were followed with fascination by ordinary English men and women who had never left their native town. Spontaneous popular celebrations occurred when news reached London of the relief of the Boer siege of British troops in Mafeking (May 17, 1900), although the extent of the enthusiasm was exaggerated by later writers. Governments quickly realized the need to influence the reporting of such political events. From almost the beginning of the Boer War in 1899, the British postmaster-general forbade the sending of coded telegrams from any location in Africa south of Aden and announced the imposition of censorship.

Figure 8.6 Proletarians of the world unite! This Viennese poster illustrates the socialist vision of racial and gender equality in a classless world. It represented one popular view of the world in the late nineteenth and early twentieth centuries – but not the only popular one.

Who Resisted the Nationalist Appeals of Centralized States?

Attempts to construct a national political culture inevitably spurred resistance. Wars that consolidated nations, such as the Franco-Prussian War of 1870–71, also incorporated minorities into the new nation. Chapter 10 will discuss how popular movements not only resisted but shaped the character of political culture; but the limitations to their influence are just as important as their successes. The strength of the national political culture in the late nineteenth century is best demonstrated in the parties that most resisted it. Socialists criticized existing states and stressed the similar situation of all workers, yet socialists depended upon states to carry out their own most cherished ideals. In France and Germany, a socialist movement with its own labor press developed that emphasized class divisions within nations. As

illustrated in Figure 8.6, Socialists prided themselves on their internationalism. In the years after 1889 they constructed a socialist international supported by the large socialist parties that developed in those industrial areas of Europe where workers possessed the right to organize. But however international their rhetoric, socialist parties remained primarily national parties organized for electoral purposes. Although socialist propaganda adapted itself to regional languages and minority tongues, the standardized national language was generally the preferred socialist vehicle. Socialists' idealistic internationalism contrasted with their practical efforts to involve workers actively in national politics. Revolutionary socialists and anarchists might denounce such efforts as "reformist" but there was no practical alternative to states as instruments for changing workers' lives.

Besides the socialists, ethnic nationalists, as we shall see in Chapter 9, also opposed the integration of cultural minorities into a majority political culture. The mass press written in a standard national language was opposed by ethnic nationalists who demanded the teaching of the native language in schools in areas where minorities predominated. In the German Empire, Austria-Hungary, and the Russian empire, schoolteachers, clergymen, and small shopkeepers who were members of minority groups led the opposition to the imposition of majority languages. Such opposition was all the more powerful in Austria-Hungary, eastern Germany, and western Russia where national ethnic minorities were the regional majority. In response to the development of national newspapers, minorities developed their own newspapers, readily accessible to rural and urban dwellers who spoke Czech, Estonian, Serbo-Croat, Polish, or Ukrainian. While criticizing existing states, they demanded autonomy or national independence for their ethnic group; in effect they wanted their own state with its own national political culture.

When the war broke out most people rallied around their rulers, their identification with the state in which they lived proving more important in shaping popular political outlooks than the common patterns of work and daily life shared by workers and their families, or those of language and tradition embodied in minority nationalisms. As the war continued and its toll grew, however, attitudes changed.

8.8 WHY DID THE ERA OF THE SECOND INDUSTRIAL REVOLUTION PRODUCE MASS MIGRATION?

New technologies of transport, an expanding international economy, and shifts in worldwide political power resulted in great increases in intercontinental migration but also changes in the character of migratory flows. Between 1850 and 1914, the steamship and the locomotive propelled a transport revolution. New inventions, such as the introduction of the screw propeller and the construction of more fuel-efficient boilers, increased the speed of travel while decreasing its cost. The effect of improved steamships was dramatic: In 1867 the average sailing vessel journey between Europe and America was forty-four days, but a steamer could make the trip in fourteen days; by 1900 the trip was down to a week. Meanwhile competition among carriers reduced the cost of a round trip so that workers could commute to seasonal employment. In 1869 the opening of the Suez Canal almost halved the trip between the UK and India. On land, the railroad brought a similar revolution, and by 1914 the basic railway network had been constructed in India, the USA, and Western and Central Europe (although not in Canada or Russia). By then the automobile had become an item of mass consumption in the USA.

While the First Industrial Revolution urbanized England – in 1851 the majority of the population of England and Wales was urban – the Second Industrial Revolution accelerated the urbanization of the European continent; by 1900 Belgium and Holland had also become predominantly urban and the German Empire was on the verge of becoming so. While the decline in urban mortality rates contributed modestly to urban population increase, mass migration from small towns and rural regions was the driving force behind the huge growth in the urban population.

Throughout Europe, rural migrants who had regulated their day by the rising and setting of the sun were subjected to clock discipline. The year based on the seasons, with its heavy concentration of work in spring and summer and its abbreviated winter workdays, gave way to the homogeneous calendar of monotonous weeks and months. Rural dwellers who had decided on the crops that they would grow, estimated the labor involved, and apportioned their labor over the agricultural season, now followed the orders of foremen and supervisors. In their factory towns, rural migrants often found themselves living next to friends and neighbors from their own village and region but they also found themselves living next to enclaves of strangers from distant regions of their own country and migrants from other European countries.

Intercontinental migration was a major factor in creating new transnational relations. In the years between 1850 and 1914, two distinct circuits of mass migration emerged: an inter-state circuit and an intra-colonial circuit. Each involved millions of people. Although they exerted a heavier hand on the imperial circuit, states played a key role in determining what groups went where.

Voluntary migration predominated in migration to Europe and from Europe to the Americas, South Africa, and Australasia.

"Voluntary" migration indicates that the decision to emigrate and the choice of a destination were made by migrating individuals or families. Many migrants might have preferred to remain at home with their families and fellow villagers if they could have had a decent prospect of winning security on the land. Although an increasing proportion of English migrants began to come from industrial cities, the great proportion of continental migrants were from agriculture. Hard times in European nations swelled the migrant flow, particularly when conditions were booming in foreign lands.

Even in the European circuit not all migration was voluntary. After the 1890s, many Russian Jews fled to escape pogroms or induction into a repressive Russian army. Not all European migrants entered free labor markets in the Americas. Italian migrants to Brazil, Canada, and the American South, and Chinese and Mexican migrants to the American west coast, often borrowed money from private or government agents and were compelled to work off their loan under extremely harsh working conditions.

European peasants and rural day laborers were major contributors to European and North American factories and mines. Also prominent among migrant destinations were the settler states, the so-called **Dominions** of the British empire – Australia, New Zealand, Canada, and South Africa – often referred to significantly as the "white Dominions." These were self-governing components of the empire where masses of British migrants had settled, where English was widely spoken, and where British culture from rugby to "English literature" were enshrined in the school curricula. British cultural hegemony was vigorously contested by the Québécois in Canada and the Boers in South Africa as well as by indigenous peoples, but in the period before 1914 English-speakers were the dominant groups within these settler states. The existence of powerful English-speaking communities in these countries proved especially attractive for many British migrants.

What Were the Characteristics of Migration During this Period?

The distinctive feature of market-driven voluntary migration during the Second Industrial Revolution was the expansion of return migration. Of the Polish and Italian migrants to the USA, perhaps 30–40 percent returned. In the first circuit, the major migrant destinations were the emerging economic giants, Germany and the United States, and the migrants themselves typically hard-pressed peasants. Before 1850, transatlantic migration was usually a one-way trip; in the period 1850–1914, return migration became common, and many Italian and Spanish farm laborers migrated seasonally to the Argentine pampas. Italian

and Polish male migrants to the United States were disproportionately young males who expected to, and often did, return
home. Returning migrants often brought with them new ideas
and consumption standards.

Although migration in the world of independent states was
largely voluntary, states acted to encourage migration and to
shape the direction of migratory flows. Prominent British economists such as John Stuart Mill argued that emigration might be a
solution to the problem of unemployment, and many local
municipalities and private charitable institutions followed his
counsel. In bad times, British municipalities had long subsidized
the migration of unemployed workers and their families. British
welfare institutions, both public and private, lay and religious,
encouraged the migration of children entrusted to their care to
Canada and Australia. The extent to which such state-aided
migration was voluntary at all is questionable in the case of the
80,000 children under the age of 14 that British welfare agencies
sent to Canada between 1865 and 1924 to become agricultural
and domestic servants.

Migration restriction was one of the characteristics of sovereign states, and the USA and the British Dominions exerted their
prerogative to favor dominant racial and cultural groups. Both
the USA and the Dominion settler states prevented large flows of
non-white migrants whose migration became feasible as a result
of the transportation revolution. Having long prohibited African
migration, by 1882 a series of US laws had banned Chinese
migration, and later Japanese migration. Canada also banned
Chinese migrants but only in 1908 did it close the door to Indian
migrants, a harder task since Indians were fellow members of the
British empire. Australia too established its "whites only" policy
in the same period.

In Britain both private and public emigration societies encouraged emigration within the empire. They were concerned that
during the nineteenth century most British emigrants chose the
United States as their destination. Such migrants were regarded
as lost to the British empire, while migrants to the empire were
regarded as strengthening imperial ties with Australasia, Canada,
and South Africa. Efforts to redirect migration seem to have been
at least somewhat successful. Between 1900 and 1914 almost a
half of British emigrants went to the British empire.

The second great migration circuit between 1850 and 1914
involved unfree non-white labor in colonial regions. Indian
and Chinese indentured laborers were recruited to work in
plantation labor in South Asia, South Africa, and the Caribbean. Such indentured labor may best be described as "unfree
wage labor" – a condition under which workers were paid
wages, but the nature and terms of their labor seriously limited
their personal freedom and their informed participation in
markets.

What Were the Characteristic Features of Asian Migration to Africa and the Caribbean?

The same declining transportation costs that enabled Irishmen
and Italians to pay their way to the USA enabled British officials
and planters to bring Indian and Chinese laborers to the
Caribbean. This migration was a direct result of the abolition
of slavery and of new demands for plantation labor. Faced with
the prospect of emancipation in the late 1830s, planters in the
British Caribbean responded in different ways. In some cases,
such as Barbados, plantation owners reorganized production to
create a self-reproducing although impoverished labor force, but
in most cases they were unable to do so.

To restore the profitability of their Caribbean possessions,
British imperial officials turned to indentured servitude, "coolie
labor," initially Africans from Sierra Leone and St. Helena, but
later, and more successfully, laborers from the North Indian
provinces and still later from South India and China. Prodded
by the Colonial Office, the Indian government passed legislation
allowing emigration to Mauritius (1842), Jamaica, British
Guiana, and Trinidad (1844), St. Lucia (1856), and Grenada
(1858). While prospective migrants were informed about the
terms of the indenture contract, they were almost always ignorant of the repressive techniques used by Caribbean colonial
administrations. At first, emigrants were bound for three years,
but later to longer periods; the terms of indenture and the nature
of its enforcement grew measurably harsher over time.

The conditions dictating Asian decisions to migrate were often
a good deal more compulsory than those of late nineteenth-
century Europeans. The Indians came from areas of India where
British taxation had increased pressure on an already exploitative
native order, and migrant flows were related to the ebb and flow
of famine conditions. British Indian authorities tried to promote
the emigration of women to stabilize the Indian presence but a
greater than two to one male/female emigrant ratio remained
typical. About 30 percent of the emigrants eventually returned to
India and many became small traders and merchants; as a result,
the Indian plantation labor force relied upon continued migration for its survival. In the end, Indian labor recruited within the
empire proved indispensable in supplying a labor force in British
Guiana and Trinidad. Large numbers of Indian laborers were
also exported to Burma and Malaya.

In their search for unfree labor, colonial authorities also
turned to a China swept by popular uprisings provoked by the
pressure of resources stretched to the limits. One of the terms of
the treaty that settled the **Opium Wars** (1839–42, 1856–60),
opening Chinese markets up to Western intervention, was an
insistence that Europeans be able to recruit Chinese workers for
colonial labor. British planters imported Chinese laborers to

Malaya and Burma and the Dutch to the Dutch East Indies. In Malaya and Burma, however, Chinese families migrated and became a major component of the nations' populations.

Working conditions among indentured Asian male laborers were reminiscent of the "sweated laborers," the women and child laborers of the European and American slums, but within Europe and North America states intervened to limit and restrict the sweated labor of workers who were considered citizens. In the Caribbean and South Africa, imperial states promoted forms of indentured labor that resembled sweated labor (although they tried to restrict its "excesses") and they enacted and enforced laws that limited indentured laborers' citizenship rights and restricted their mobility within the local economy.

The recruitment of indentured Asians to unfree labor in Britain's African and Caribbean colonies proved a serious source of internal grievance within Asian sending nations. In China, the imperial government found itself under particular pressure to reverse this policy and, since China still possessed some vestiges of sovereignty, it was able to do so. The migration of Chinese indentured servants declined precipitously in 1866 after the negotiation of an Anglo-French-Chinese convention regulating the emigration of migrants; planters felt that the terms negotiated were too favorable to the Chinese.

But the issue of indentured laborers proved most explosive in India because it highlighted the fundamental disparities in imperial civil rights between the self-governing Dominions and the non-self-governing colonies. Indentured Asian labor became important not only to the future of the British Caribbean but to the future of Britain's new South African colonies. In 1903, with the intercession of Lord Milner, the High Commissioner of South Africa, the South African mining industry requested the freedom to recruit over 100,000 indentured servants from India to join the existing settled Indian population. At the same time, the South African government stipulated that these indentured servants would not be allowed to stay in South Africa after their commitments were completed. George Curzon, viceroy and governor-general of India, refused. His refusal was based on waves of dissatisfaction sweeping British India due to the treatment of indentured servants already in South Africa as well as the obstacles placed in the way of Indian shopkeepers establishing themselves in South Africa.

A leader of this agitation was a young Indian lawyer living in South Africa since 1893, Mohandas Gandhi. Gandhi's experience of racial and social inequality within the empire was an early step in his evolution toward demanding Indian independence. Despite Britain's claims to exert a standard imperial justice throughout the empire, the self-governing Dominions frequently imposed discriminatory laws against the non-self-governing colonies, which were denied the right to control their own migration.

8.9 THE NEW IMPERIALISM

Another aspect of the new alliance between consolidated states and capital was the growth of a new imperialism, discussed in Chapter 9. The gigantism of the factories and machines of the Second Industrial Revolution seem to have inspired a sense of collective megalomania among Western statesmen. Leading British statesmen and high officials talked of a "United Empire" or a "Greater Britain" that in some versions would bring together the "Anglo-Saxon" nations of North America and Australasia into a world federation. In other versions of this dream, Britain would integrate its Asian and African colonies into an imperial economy surrounded by tariff barriers. British statesmen were hardly the only dreamers of world empire. Not content with Germany's effective domination of the European continent, German political geographers such as Friedrich Ratzel began to talk about the battle for the "World Island" (Eurasia) and argued that healthy nations required territorial expansion (see Box 8.3). Such wild imaginings, which ignored actual political realities, created a climate that promoted the onset of war. After becoming the foremost land power, the German Empire and its young Kaiser entered the race to become the world's foremost naval power, a policy leading inexorably to conflict with Britain.

The maddest of all these schemes, those of the Belgian monarch Leopold II, actually came true! Taking advantage of determination on the part of the great powers not to let a major rival control the heart of Africa, Leopold ultimately became the independent personal ruler of a Congo Free State many times larger and more populous than his Belgian kingdom. Once in control, Leopold ruthlessly exploited the native population in an effort to increase rubber production. Millions of Africans died in support of his dreams of unlimited power and yet the Congo continuously hovered on the edge of bankruptcy.

What Explains the Successes of the New Imperialism?

These wild and tragic dreams were partly inspired by the armaments revolution rooted in the new industrial technologies. Suddenly European armies acquired overwhelming superiority on land. The division of Africa in the 1880s among the European powers exhibited the new military power of European states. Within ten years almost the whole of the continent was divided up by European powers. Since the seventeenth century, ocean-going European warships had been superior to those of the non-European world, but until the second half of the nineteenth century, European armies' victories were mostly confined to defending fortified sites of their own selection. Unless supported by native rulers, European armies found colonial land war risky,

Box 8.3 Friedrich Ratzel and Geopolitics

Friedrich Ratzel (1844–1904) was a leading German political geographer of the late nineteenth century. Like his contemporaries Halford J. Mackinder in England and Alfred Thayer Mahan in the US, Ratzel articulated a series of geographical principles intended to provide a basis for national policy. Ratzel described nations in biological terms and applied Darwinian principles of competition to national rivalries. In his view, nations were subject to natural processes such as growth or decay and the ultimate fate of a nation depended on its ability to expand territorially. The following is an excerpt from an essay by Ratzel, published in 1896:

Political geography regards each people as a living body extending over a portion of the Earth's surface ... The peoples are constantly agitated by internal movements, which are transformed into external movement whenever a portion of the Earth's surface is occupied afresh, or one formerly occupied is surrendered ... a people resembles a fluid mass slowly ebbing and flowing ... as a rule (such movements) take the form of encroachment and usurpation, or small territories, with their inhabitants, are annexed to larger ones ...

Since the area of states grow with their civilisation, people in a low state of civilisation are naturally collected in very small political organizations, and the lower their condition the smaller are the states ... A people is an organic body which in the course of its history is fixed more and more firmly in the soil on which it lives. As the individual contends with the virgin soil until he has converted it into cultivated land, so a people struggles with its territory and makes it ever more and more its own by shedding its sweat and blood on its behalf, until the two cannot even be thought of apart.

especially when confronted with large non-European armies. At the end of the eighteenth century in India, superior British military organization enabled British armies to defeat armies many times larger than themselves. But Indians soon adopted British military techniques and by mid-century British and Indian armies were fighting on a basis of near equality. Muskets, gunpowder, and even heavy artillery were well within the technological reach of powerful Asian and African rulers.

The military innovations of the Second Industrial Revolution could not be easily manufactured outside Europe and North America because they depended on a whole series of highly complicated and costly industrial technologies; to pay for them required large sums of ready cash. The first significant change in the mid-nineteenth-century military balance was the introduction of the armed steamboat that enabled Europeans to project their powers internally along rivers. The first Opium War (1839–42) revealed the new military capacity of Western powers. The Chinese were not brought to the bargaining table by the rout of their oceangoing fleet but negotiated when the British sent a battleship up the Yangtze River directed toward the heart of imperial power.

Military innovations, originating in European military rivalries, further accelerated the European lead; by the 1880s European regular troops were able to penetrate into the non-riverain interior of colonial countries without losing their military advantages. In the 1850s and 1860s the invention of the breech loader enabled gunmakers to construct rifles that were fast, accurate, tough, and impervious to the weather, and in the 1870s the

repeater rifle spread. Soon the French chemical industry contributed smokeless powder, which dramatically increased rifle efficiency. Within a few years, Europeans had acquired a functional machine gun, the Maxim gun, light enough for troops to carry in the field.

Of course colonial armies were not guaranteed success. In 1876 at Little Big Horn, General Custer was defeated by Amerindians who possessed not only greater numbers but superior weapons, purchased illegally in Canada. In 1886, at Adowa, the Abyssinian emperor, Menelik, an experienced general, familiar with European weaponry, defeated an invading Italian army composed largely of recent conscripts. But the most decisive weapons, the armed steamboats, Maxim guns, and heavy artillery were beyond the budget of most indigenous groups. The most serious colonial rebellion of the late nineteenth century was mounted by the South African Boers, who could pay hard cash for weaponry imported through Holland.

At the same time, Europeans discovered ways of combating endemic diseases that had constituted as effective a barrier to European conquest as indigenous armies. If disease had been a key weapon in the European conquest of the Americas, disease fought on the side of the indigenous populations of West and Equatorial Africa. Although mortality rates were extremely variable, again and again as many as one half to three quarters of Western military units might die when exposed to tropical climates. After 1850 the death rates of European troops declined dramatically. The knowledge that they could maintain healthy troops in tropical areas was a prerequisite for the division of

Box 8.4 Civilized Warfare: Only for the Civilized? The Hague, 1899

In 1898 Nicholas II, tsar of Russia, circulated a statement to ambassadors and ministers from other countries resident in St. Petersburg, calling for a conference to promote peace and to limit armaments spending. The conference met at The Hague in the Netherlands on May 18, 1899. Among the topics considered by separate commissions was "the laws and customs of warfare." At an early meeting of this commission, the Swiss General Künzli put forward a proposal to "prohibit projectiles which aggravate wounds and increase the sufferings of the wounded." Künzli specified that one of the targets of his proposal was the British

"dumdum" bullet. Named after the armory in India where it was manufactured, the dumdum was a soft-nosed small arms bullet that expanded upon contact and left a gaping hole in its victim.

The British general, Sir John Ardagh, demurred. Drawing a distinction between civilized warfare and savage warfare, he argued that different rules should apply to each. Ardagh explained that in "civilized warfare a soldier wounded by a ball of small caliber retires to an ambulance and advances no longer: but that in war against savages the case is very different; although penetrated two or three times, the savage does not

summon hospital attendants, he does not stop marching forward, and before you had time to explain to him that he is in flagrant opposition to the decisions of the Conference of The Hague, he cuts off your head."

Ardagh's distinction horrified a Russian member of the commission. The Russian speaker, M. Raffalovich, felt that Ardagh's distinction was "contrary to the humanitarian spirit which rules this end of the Nineteenth Century."

Such attitudes increased the brutality of the colonial military and antagonized local populations.

Africa. Improvements in the mortality of Westerners in the tropics were only marginally due to medical discoveries, although the expansion of the production of quinine, long known as effective against malaria, was an important step in many areas. More important than medicine were the cumulative experiences of seasoned colonial commanders in parts of India and the Caribbean where troop mortality had previously been so high. When malaria attacked, officers moved their troops to the highlands to recover their strength. At the first sign of cholera or yellow fever, commanders marched their troops out of barracks and camped them in the distant countryside. Commanders did not know that they were moving their soldiers away from malaria-carrying mosquitoes and water contaminated with cholera, only that such actions reduced troop mortality.

What Explains the Support for New Imperialism in the Colonizing Nations?

In Africa and Southeast Asia the "new imperialism" witnessed the replacement of informal spheres of influence and covert power by outright annexation and claims to full sovereignty. As British and French businessmen had always known, direct rule is considerably more expensive than exerting informal influence and it inevitably produced anti-colonial social movements. In compensation, however, European administrators' enforcement of European law in colonies gave a new security to international financiers and merchants. Part of the problem for financiers was that when they invested large amounts of money

outside the European and North American circle of independent states, dangers of political instability and national insolvency arose. The experience of English industrialists in Latin America, particularly in Argentina and Peru, underlined the dangers encountered by bankers in situations where they lacked political leverage. Not so much the search for fabulous profits, but the same longing to protect existing investments that backed protectionism in European and American core states, also supported imperialism.

If businessmen longed for a secure investment environment, military men saw empire as invaluable for maintaining military assets. For the British military, imperialism helped maintain a strong navy in an age when Germany threatened to dominate the continent. To remain a great power, Britain required naval supremacy and the ports, coaling stations, and advanced communications that were the fringe benefits of imperialism. British military plans also depended upon Canadian, South African, Australian, and New Zealand troops and colonial ships and, indeed, the Dominions mobilized impressively when war did come in 1914. Although they often balked at the cost of colonies, costs they shared with the general taxpayer, businessmen supported colonial administrations that gave them privileged access to resources or privileged markets. In other areas, such as cable-laying, security was used to justify reliance on British companies.

Conservative social reformers saw empire as a way of regenerating British society and as a way of addressing the "Social Question." The empire could serve as a reservoir for the unemployed, and imperial tariffs might enable British workers to maintain a high-wage economy against American and German competition. Some British social reformers hoped to create an "imperial race" capable of ruling a mighty empire. Inspired by the application of Darwinian theories to state competition, they saw imperial success as a demonstration of Anglo-Saxon genetic superiority; such racist beliefs were shared by many imperialists in France, Germany, and the USA. Although missionaries often criticized the actions of colonial authorities, many leading Catholic and Protestant religious figures viewed imperialist advance as a way of promoting Christianity and as part of a Western religious mission to "civilize" the non-Western world.

Support for imperialism came from many sources in European society. Businessmen saw colonies as a source of protection, military men saw colonies as a military resource, social reformers saw colonies as rich lands that needed populating by the poor. Even France with its declining population justified its possession of Algeria in these terms. For many white-collar workers and hard-driven unskilled workers, imperialism was an exciting adventure story told in the daily newspapers. No one strand dominated the drive toward imperialism. Yet at the center of the imperial cause were wealthy businessmen and aristocrats who did not judge imperialism by solely economic or political criteria. They were bankers and businessmen who enjoyed important positions in the political establishment of their nation. For them, imperialism was both profitable and sound military and state policy.

What Were the Weaknesses of the New Imperialism?

Late nineteenth-century "empires" were fundamentally different from past empires. To one degree or another, late nineteenth-century empires were combinations of (more or less) consolidated "**metropoles**" characterized by effective centralized administration, citizenship rights and duties, and national consciousness, joined with subordinate "colonial states" having a significantly lower level of centralization and citizenship rights and duties, and more limited identity. In 1914, all the leading states and many secondary and tertiary powers, such as Belgium, Denmark, and Holland, were new empires in the sense of our definition.

Despite their impressive military superiority, the structure of these new empires, amalgamations of core and colonial states, made them highly unstable. Metropoles demanded that empires benefit metropole groups, and such requirements inevitably undermined imperial solidarity. Co-option of local elites into an imperial ruling elite had often been one of the secrets of successful imperial rule. To one degree or another, all the European empires attempted such co-option, but self-governing metropoles placed severe restrictions on the extent of this. Metropole politicians demanded that the colonies be open for migrants from the metropole and that the higher levels of imperial administration remain in the hands of metropole citizens. If colonial elites were not integrated equally into colonial empires, neither were the empires integrated into the metropoles. Even the most democratic of metropole politicians did not seek the unification of empire based on the thoroughgoing extension of democracy and a common representative assembly based on population. No key metropole leader sought to impose compulsory public education in the colonies, much less education in the standardized national language. The case of Algeria was exemplary. Though in principle a part of the French nation with representatives in the French assembly, the French policy of "association" essentially meant that the overwhelming majority of the Algerian population remained subjects with their own separate institutions, not equal citizens.

Conclusion The age of the Second Industrial Revolution was an age of huge tools, large factories, mass migration, and great cities. It was also an age of grand dreams, provoked in part by the record and scope of the accomplishments of industry. Seemingly sober businessmen contemplated a great imperial state uniting Britain and its colonies into a single self-governing political unit, governed by a parliament in London. Workers in the urban slums imagined uniting all the world's workers into a single socialist commonwealth where workers would democratically control industry.

The Second Industrial Revolution was an age of internationalism. Unlike the First (British) Industrial Revolution, the technologies of the Second Industrial Revolution were transcontinental, invented by Britons, Americans, Austrians, Germans, Italians, and Serbs. Similarly its great plants were located all across North America and Europe, particularly in regions that were transport hubs or had access to coal and iron ore. Great corporations arose that employed not only semi-skilled workers who manufactured the products but also white-collar workers who adopted the technologies and compiled the accounts and who also sought to advertise and distribute the products.

It was an age of class formation and class conflict. In this era capitalism and militarism established close relations. Great industrialists like Carnegie, Krupp, and Schneider presided over factory towns and dominated local politics. In the first half of the nineteenth century these men would have been advocates of free trade but this was no longer the case. The great steel plants needed to operate continuously to be profitable and industrialists often supported tariffs that would ensure them a reliable, steady market, enabling them all the better to operate in the more risky world of international competition. Industrialists worked closely with the military, which was a main consumer of its products. It was also the age when the great socialist parties of Europe were first constructed. Growing socialist electoral strength led many to think that the triumph of socialism was inevitable.

It was a world of relentless gender hierarchy. These new continuously operating factories employed workers who could expect to spend their entire working lives in the same factory. After an initial period of rapid job turnover, these workers settled down as heads of household. Males were the usual heads of industrial households because employers routinely gave better-paying jobs to males. Partly they did so because images of paternalism were pervasive at almost every level of the industrial hierarchy. But they also did so because the replication of existing gender divisions within the new hierarchies enabled them to perpetuate an inequality that was profitable to businessmen. Employers did not have to justify wage differentials or defend job assignments when gender would do this for them.

While many young women worked in industry, most abandoned work to care for children. Such inequality in both factory and household led to the creation of two very different social worlds. A male world of absentee fathers was better-paid and had the money to patronize the bars and taverns that were the framework of male workers' social life. Side by side with this was the female world of household and neighborhood where the sick were cared for and the children raised.

It was a world of consolidated states that intervened to defend their citizens, but outside the stable industrial economy there was also a world of sweated labor that only gradually became subject to state regulation. Sweated labor referred to forms of industrial employment characterized by small shops and home production where work was done in an unsanitary environment, with low wages and long hours. All the workers' worlds that we have surveyed – blue-collar or white-collar – were responses to technological change but technology did not determine everything in the formation of the industrial workforce. Over the course of the nineteenth century, coalitions of workers and social reformers passed laws and appointed inspectors who had great success in diminishing the number of sweated laborers.

State intervention developed dramatically in this era. Increasingly coalitions of workers and middle-class reformers acted to protect workers or at least skilled workers against the risks of accident, old age, and unemployment. Growing socialist and labor parties were often important in these reforms. Such parties celebrated their commitment to internationalism every May Day after 1889 but these parties also encouraged workers to register and vote and to demand reforms from the existing state. Increasingly these workers began to see citizenship as a status that conferred privilege.

States played a key role here too. They closed their borders to some migrants. They encouraged their emigrants to take some directions rather than others. They regulated conditions in some colonies but not in others. Migration was another characteristic feature of this age. In proportion it was the greatest age of migration the world has yet seen. Two great streams of migration were dominant. There was a migration path connecting Europe to North and South America: This path was usually dominated by free white populations who often intended to migrate permanently even when it became economically feasible to travel back and forth. The other stream connected India and China to parts of Africa and the Caribbean: Many who traveled this path were unfree, often indentured, and were not encouraged to stay when their indenture ended.

This last world was also the world of imperialism. Here consolidated states that were democracies ruled foreign colonial states devoid of democracy. Developments in health care helped make imperialism possible. Over time military men learned practical techniques for dealing with cholera, malaria, and yellow fever. At the same time they developed new weaponry, such as the Maxim gun, that was too costly for most colonial peoples and terribly effective in dealing with massed groups of soldiers.

The world of the Second Industrial Revolution was certainly a world of vision but many of its visions were more like nightmares. Germans demanded "living room" and Britons talked of world empire. The world of the Second Industrial Revolution was certainly a world of international industry, global migration, and growing citizenship. It was also a world of militarism, class conflict, gender hierarchy, and imperialism. Unfortunately it was the latter that won and the result was a great war.

Study Questions

(1) The era of the Second Industrial Revolution witnessed the spread of industry and an increase in world trade. Yet while international forces were strong, national forces remained vigorous and ultimately helped produce World War I. Explain why both internationalism and nationalism were so strong in this period.

(2) The Second Industrial Revolution dramatically changed the organization of industry. Compare the industrial changes produced by the First and Second Industrial Revolutions. Which do you think were more important? Which had the greatest influence on European social and political life?

(3) The Second Industrial Revolution also transformed the character of the labor force. Discuss how the labor force changed and its implications for European society and politics. While discussing the impact of labor force change on European society and politics, you might also discuss whether European society and politics had any impact on industrial change.

(4) The era of the Second Industrial Revolution coincided with a dramatic upsurge in imperialist activity on the part of industrial nations. What was the relationship between industrialization and imperialism?

(5) Some have claimed that the Second Industrial Revolution transformed popular life and culture. Do you agree? Describe the most significant changes during this period and explain their relation (or lack of relation) to the Second Industrial Revolution. Compare popular life and culture of the era of the Second Industrial Revolution with that of some past period that we have studied. Compare it with today. Was popular life and culture closer to modern-day practices or to that of the earlier period that you identified? Explain yourself.

Suggested Reading

EDWARD BERENSON, *The Trial of Madame Caillaux* (Berkeley: University of California Press, 1992). Berenson portrays French society on the eve of World War I.

ALFRED D. CHANDLER, *Scale and Scope: The Dynamics of Industrial Capitalism* (Cambridge, MA: Belknap Press, 1990). This is a magnificent study of the evolution of business organization in Great Britain, Germany, and the United States in the age of the Second Industrial Revolution and beyond.

JONATHAN CONLIN, *Tales of Two Cities: Paris, London and the Birth of the Modern City* (Berkeley: Counterpoint Press, 2013). Conlin explores how Paris and London contributed to the rise of the modern city.

WILLIAM CRONON, *Nature's Metropolis: Chicago and the Great West* (New York: W.W. Norton, 1992). Cronon covers relations between city and country in the era of the Second Industrial Revolution.

ADAM HOCHSCHILD, *King Leopold's Ghost: A Story of Greed, Terror, and Heroism in Colonial Africa* (Boston: Houghton Mifflin, 1999). This book tells of the almost unbelievable cruelty of Belgian rule.

ANDREW LEES and LYNN HOLLEN LEES, *Cities and the Making of Modern Europe, 1750–1914* (Cambridge University Press, 2007). Two accomplished urban historians provide an overview of the subject.

JOHN MERRIMAN, *The Red City: Limoges and the French Nineteenth Century* (New York: Oxford University Press, 1985). Merriman traces the roots of worker militancy in a French provincial town.

CARL SCHORSKE, *Fin-de-Siècle Vienna: Politics and Government* (New York: Knopf, 1979). The intellectual splendor of a ramshackle empire is conveyed in Schorske's study.

JAY WINTER and JEAN-LOUIS ROBERT, *Capital Cities at War: London, Paris, Berlin, 1914–1919* (Cambridge University Press, 1997). This is a well-balanced, comprehensive comparison of life in London, Paris, and Berlin under the stress of war.

Glossary

Dominions: Between 1867 and the early twentieth century, a country within the British empire that possessed autonomy but still owed allegiance to the British Crown. Canada was the first Dominion but was followed by Australia, New Zealand, and South Africa.

metropole: The core state, typically more or less consolidated, from which colonial rulers governed loosely centralized colonies.

new imperialism: The end of the eighteenth and the beginning of the nineteenth century had witnessed a great wave of European colonialism. The late nineteenth century witnessed another great wave and this second wave is referred to as the "new imperialism." It included the division of Africa at the Congress of Berlin in 1878 and was characterized by increasing tension between Britain and Germany.

Opium Wars: Chinese consumers were not attracted by Western products but Western consumers wanted Chinese goods. There was a market in China for Indian opium and Britain fought two wars, in 1839–42 and 1856–60, to keep this market open when Chinese authorities sought to ban opium.

Rerum Novarum: An encyclical letter by Pope Leo XIII in 1891 indicating the Catholic church's concern with the results of industrialization. Condemning socialism, the pope encouraged Catholics to form trade unions and moderate social reforms.

sweated labor: The House of Lords Select Committee of 1888–89 first defined sweated labor as characterized by (1) an unduly low rate of wages; (2) excessive hours of labor; and (3) insanitary state of the house in which the work is carried out.

white-collar workers: Salaried or professional workers who do not perform manual labor.

zaibatsu: Name given to a handful of huge modern-day Japanese industrial concerns. With some exceptions they originated as financial cliques in the Meiji period (1868–1912).

9 States and social movements

Timeline	
1824–90	Interest associations and trade unions legalized in most Western European countries.
1846–48	Mexican–American War: USA takes New Mexico, Arizona, and California, in addition to earlier annexation of Texas (1845).
1848	Karl Marx and Friedrich Engels publish the *Communist Manifesto*. First US women's rights convention, Seneca Falls, New York. Revolutions, all at least partly reversed, in Austria, Bohemia, France, Germany, Italy, Hungary, and Switzerland, with temporary flourishing of social movements in those countries and wide repercussions elsewhere.
1850–90	Manhood suffrage enacted and strikes legalized in most Western European countries.
1850–64	Taiping Rebellion in China.
1865	End of Civil War in USA, with freeing of all remaining slaves.
1867	First discovery of diamonds in South Africa. Beginnings of the industrialization of Mexico.
1871	Paris Commune.
1876–1910	Rule of General Porfirio Díaz, whose regime was called the Porfiriato.
1885–86	New wave of strikes in USA.
1886	First discovery of gold in South Africa; another rich industry begins. Haymarket Massacre in Chicago; major wave of strikes in USA.
1894–95	First Sino-Japanese War: China is badly beaten.
1899–1902	Second Boer War in South Africa.
1899–1900	Boxer Rebellion in China.
1910	Revolution overthrows Porfirio Díaz in Mexico, but begins years of turmoil.
1912	Fall of China's Qing dynasty, beginning of revolution, with civil wars until 1949.
1914–18	World War I.

During the 1880s, foreigners often compared China's central Yangtze port of Hankou to Chicago. Similar in size to Chicago with around 1.7 million inhabitants, it also occupied a Chicago-like central position in China's commercial networks. At the end of April 1883, rumors of an impending invasion and uprising started an exodus of Hankou residents. It also caused a shutdown of all businesses except the pawnshops where people traded precious goods for the cash to get them out of town. On May 3, troops called to the city found a drunken, boastful conspirator in a brothel. Following leads the loquacious braggart provided, officials unraveled preparations for a blood-bath in Hankou and two nearby cities. The uprising was sched-uled to start the very next day. Authorities declared martial law, closed opium dens and brothels, expelled Buddhist nuns from their convents (selling some of them at auction as concubines), and began a vast search for members of the conspiracy. Vigilant and violent in their tracking down of suspects, Chinese authori-ties eventually executed nearly 200 people for involvement in the plot.

The thwarted rebellion's nerve center lay in a well-knit regional network linking Buddhist opponents of China's national regime. Drawing on centuries-old religious traditions, they hoped to start a nationwide movement that would topple the **Manchu** ruling dynasty (the Qing dynasty established by Manchurian nomadic warriors in 1644) and purify China's corrupt public life. Although Qing authorities managed to nip this conspiracy in the bud, they had good reasons to worry. Both before and after 1883, religiously inspired critics of the regime repeatedly allied themselves with its other opponents and tem-porarily took over cities or whole regions. Forces of the **Taiping Rebellion** (a civil war against the Qing dynasty in the 1850s and 1860s), seeking to establish a heavenly kingdom in China, had for example taken and retaken Hankou repeatedly between 1852 and 1856, leaving the city depopulated and in ruins. Within thirty years after 1883, furthermore, a more secular but equally committed group of revolutionaries actually overturned the Chi-nese empire and established a republic. Ideologically informed struggle was serious business in China between 1850 and 1914.

It was also serious business in Chicago, USA. As Hankou's dissidents were preparing their abortive rising, Chicago's workers were participating in one of America's greatest popular mobilizations ever. The 1870s in the United States had brought massive strikes and the formation of multiple labor parties. They had also brought new forms of unionism, including the Federation of Organized Trades and Labor Unions in the United States and Canada (who recruited skilled craftsmen) and the fast-growing Knights of Labor. Unlike the conventional organization of specialized guilds in skilled crafts, the Knights assembled a wide variety of workers – skilled and not so skilled – in chapters that varied greatly in composition according to local circumstances. They opened their doors to women, including all-female chapters, in 1881. The Knights even enrolled some anarchists, who proposed to dissolve the state and let workers take control of capital. In 1884 the Federation of Organized Trades announced a campaign for an eight-hour working day at a Chicago convention. The federation planned to begin its campaign with a general strike on May 1 – May Day – 1886. At first American anarchists boycotted the campaign as a diversion from true revolution. When they recognized the eight-hour day's popularity with workers, however, they joined the movement.

After widespread strikes on the railroads and in other indus-tries during 1885 and early 1886, 300,000 US workers laid down their tools in the May Day general strike. At meetings all over the country, fiery orators denounced capitalist greed and demanded the eight-hour day. In Chicago, 40,000 strikers went out. Saturday, May 1 (then a regular working day in the USA) passed peacefully. But on Tuesday night, May 4, the final speaker at a workers' street meeting in Chicago's Haymarket Square was anarchist Samuel Fielden. Box 9.1 gives some sense of the anarchist rhetoric that rallied Chicago workers at this time. (See also Figure 9.1.) Fielden was ending his militant remarks when a police detachment marched onto the scene and ordered the crowd of 200–300 people to disperse. As Fielden stepped down from the wagon on which he had been standing, someone – probably an anarchist – threw a dynamite bomb in the midst of the police. Police immediately began firing revolvers into the crowd. According to the most reliable witnesses, only police and the single bomb-thrower used lethal weapons. Sixty-seven police were wounded, seven of them fatally. Most of their wounds came from each other's bullets. Very likely thirty or forty members of the crowd also received bullet wounds, and seven or eight of them died.

Anti-radical action then flared up across America. Historians speak of the later 1880s as one of America's greatest Red Scares. The Chicago police arrested and interrogated hundreds of sus-pected radicals, most of them European immigrants. A Chicago grand jury indicted ten well-known anarchists, including Fielden. None of them, it later turned out, had killed anyone. Most of them, in fact, had not even been at the meeting when the bomb exploded. Realizing that they could not make a conspiracy charge stick unless they identified the bomb-thrower and con-nected the accused men with him, prosecutor and judge argued instead that anarchists' general advocacy of violence to over-throw government had directly caused the policemen's deaths. Making that argument, they charged the ten anarchists with murder.

Two of the ten men under indictment escaped from Chicago never to be caught, but the remaining eight received murder

Box 9.1: The Background of the Haymarket Massacre

During an 1886 strike at the McCormick Harvesting Machine Company, Chicago police shot at a group of strikers, killing six of them. That night, anarchist August Spies distributed a printed circular headed "WORKINGMEN! TO ARMS!" It said:

Your masters sent out their bloodhounds – the police – they killed six of your brothers at McCormick's this afternoon. They killed the poor wretches, because they, like you, had courage to disobey the supreme will of your bosses. They killed them because they dared ask for the shortening of the hours of toil. They killed them to show you "Free American citizens" that you must be satisfied and contented with whatsoever your bosses condescend to allow you, or you will be killed!

You have for years endured the most abject humiliations; you have for years suffered immeasurable iniquities; you have worked yourselves to death; you have endured the pangs of want and hunger; your children you have sacrificed to the factory lords – in short, you have been miserable and obedient slaves all these years. Why? To satisfy the insatiable greed and fill the coffers of your lazy thieving masters! When you ask him now to lessen your burden, he sends his bloodhounds out to shoot you, to kill you!

If you are men, if you are the sons of your grandsires, who have shed their blood to free you, then you will rise in your might, Hercules, and destroy the hideous monster that seeks to destroy you.

To arms, we call you, to arms!
YOUR BROTHERS

The next day, anarchists and workers gathered at Chicago's Haymarket Square to protest the McCormick shootings. When police arrived to break up the meeting, someone threw a bomb, police fired back, and fourteen or fifteen people died. Police soon arrested August Spies, who was hanged for inciting murder.

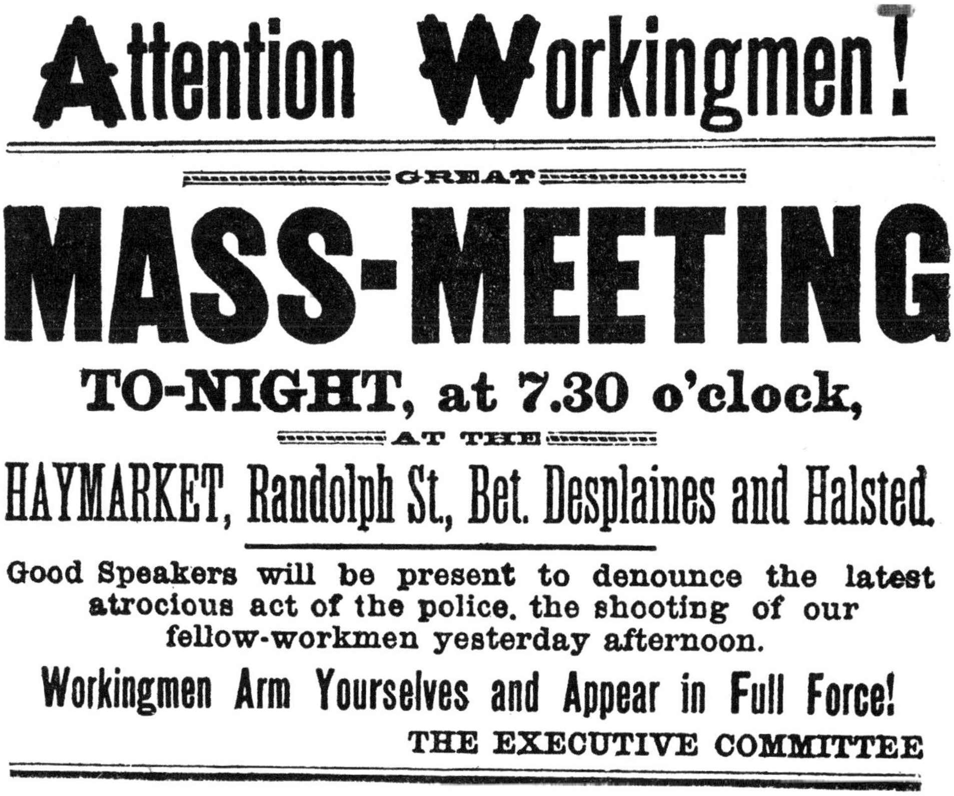

Figure 9.1 Poster advertising a mass-meeting of workers on the evening after the Haymarket Square incident of May 4, 1886.

convictions. One of the eight killed himself in jail with a dynamite-charged cigar. Four of them hanged, and three went to prison until the governor of Illinois, convinced of their innocence, pardoned them seven years later. As an organization, the Knights of Labor had nothing to do with the Haymarket meeting. They had kept their distance from anarchists and direct-action radicals. Although they had marched on May Day for the eight-hour day, for example, they had consistently refused to join marches led by revolutionaries' red flags. They also publicly condemned the Haymarket bombing. Nevertheless, the nationwide anti-labor action that began in 1886 drove them and other radical groups into rapid decline. The craft-centered American Federation of Labor (successor to the Federation of Organized Trades) became the leading American labor organization for decades to come. Less skilled American factory workers had no one representing them at a national scale until the 1930s.

In both Hankou and Chicago, citizens organized actions that threatened the state, and government authorities stepped in vigorously to crush dissent. Even these brief summaries, however, point to differences between the Chinese Qing empire and the North American republic. In China, the regime's opponents aimed directly at the ruling dynasty, drawing on a great tradition of religiously tinged rebellion. In the United States, some radicals did attack government officials – anarchist Leon Czolgosz, for example, assassinated US president William McKinley in 1901 – but in general American anarchists and labor activists of the late nineteenth century defined their enemy as big capital, treating unsympathetic government officials as lackeys of capitalists.

Enemies of the Chinese regime prepared their attacks underground, organizing secret societies rather than public associations. Unlike their American contemporaries, they did not carry on their work through strikes, meetings, marches, petitions, pamphlets, and similar public displays of their program. In China, urban workers rarely struck against their employers before the twentieth century. Explicitly political strikes came even later. In contrast, American workers were staging general strikes, and battling public authorities as they did so, well before 1886. Like religiously inspired Chinese conspirators, it is true, American labor organizers sometimes created secret societies; the Knights of Labor themselves had started out in secret before going public. Like the Knights of Labor in their prime, however, North American workers' organizations mostly acted publicly, backed political candidates, and sought recognition as serious political actors. Even anarchists generally conformed. They employed the familiar means of meetings, marches, demonstrations, pamphlets, petitions, electoral campaigns, strikes, and statements to the press.

Once Chinese authorities identified a threat, furthermore, they stepped in ruthlessly without visible public opposition. American authorities, in contrast, usually acted in the face of open criticism from their opponents. When forced to choose, to be sure, most American government officials lined up on the side of capital. Red Scares like that of 1886 only reinforced the opposition of government to organized labor. Nevertheless, even the anarchists' prosecution of 1886 aroused wide public opposition in the United States. The mayor of Chicago, who had attended most of the fateful Haymarket meeting, actually testified on behalf of the defendants. Both China and the United States were divided deeply in the 1880s, but much more of the division entered regular American public politics.

Comparison of China and the USA in the 1880s makes it easier to see that the world's political regimes vary along two different dimensions. One dimension runs from relatively undemocratic to relatively democratic regimes. The other runs from low-capacity to high-capacity governments. A regime is a **democracy** to the extent that it (1) maintains broad, equal citizenship across different categories of gender, race, ethnicity, and locality; (2) gives citizens significant voice with respect to control over governmental personnel, policies, and resources; and (3) protects citizens from arbitrary action by government agents. In these terms, by comparison with all the world's regimes of the 1880s, China had a relatively undemocratic, the USA a relatively democratic regime. The "relatively" matters: In the 1880s, American women had no vote and little independent political standing of any kind, while Jim Crow institutions were increasingly excluding black Americans from any political rights. The treatment of Chicago's anarchists itself makes clear that American protections from arbitrary action had serious limits.

Low-capacity governments exercise little control over the people, resources, and activities currently available within their territories. **High-capacity** governments exercise extensive control over those people, resources, and activities. Despite its vast territory and its vulnerability to rebels, the Chinese state of the 1880s maintained remarkable influence over most of its population most of the time; it operated a relatively high-capacity government. The American national state of the time covered a similarly large territory. But it had lower capacity, partly because it faced so many competing jurisdictions at the national, state, and local level, partly because so much of its territory still consisted of frontier, wilderness, Indian territory, or thinly governed rural areas. During the late nineteenth century, the Chinese state was losing some of its capacity without becoming significantly more or less democratic. The American state, in contrast, was gaining capacity while inching toward slightly greater democracy.

This chapter asks how such changes in the character of the world's states between 1850 and 1914 interacted with changes in popular politics, especially the forms of politics we call social movements. It answers that:

- Increases in state capacity generally made states more central to ordinary people's politics, polarizing people more sharply into supporters and opponents of existing regimes, while increases in democracy, where they occurred, provided new incentives and opportunities for ordinary people to engage in national politics.
- Where heavy industry grew up, capitalists acquired an interest in stable labor supplies and stable governments, which favored the growth of three-way bargaining among capital, labor, and state officials, which in its turn promoted legalization and institutionalization of labor unions, strikes, and collective bargaining.
- **Social movements** became much more common forms of popular politics between 1850 and 1914.
- Where state capacity and democracy rose together, social movements became more prominent vehicles for popular politics than elsewhere.
- Nevertheless, in colonial territories and other areas maintaining strong contacts with Western democracies, social movement tactics also became more prominent means of making claims.
- Authorities commonly responded to social movements at first through resistance and repression, but they rapidly learned to bargain selectively with those social movement leaders and organizations whose demands were more compatible with existing structures of power.

9.1 GROWTH OF STATE CAPACITY

Between 1850 and 1914, the world as a whole saw notable increases in state capacity, but only minor democratization. Rather than advancing bit by bit like population growth or urbanization, democratization commonly occurs in waves, responding to major political crises. After each wave, some recession toward less democratic regimes usually occurs. The first such bursts occurred in Europe and North America during the late eighteenth century and again around the revolutions of 1848. At a world scale, the years around World War I, the aftermath of World War II, the postwar withdrawal of European powers from most of their colonies, and the breakup of the Soviet Union all brought surges of democratization, followed by partial recession to less democratic regimes. In countries as far-spread as the British Isles, the United States, and Argentina, the period from 1850 to 1914 brought some extension of voting rights and other democratic reforms. Still, the world as a whole did not reach 1914 much more democratic than it had been after the revolutions of 1848.

For state capacity, the story was different. Several world-wide trends converged to increase the control of states over populations, activities, and resources within their territories. Although rapid urbanization increased short-run threats to existing systems of political control, in the longer run it concentrated people in places where routine patrolling and surveillance by governmental forces became feasible. Similarly, the growth of factories, offices, and other large workplaces first challenged capitalists' ability to manage workers, but eventually facilitated bureaucratic co-ordination of work. Once that happened, government officials could control workers by controlling their firms. Labor unions did not provide sturdy shields against governmental control because they were generally publicly visible, organized firm by firm, and dependent on governmental enforcement of their rights. A series of changes, in contrast, advanced the capacity of rulers to monitor, regulate, and redistribute resources within their territories: (1) creation of effective national armies and police forces; (2) extension of new technologies of communication and transportation; (3) creation of centralized systems for information-gathering and taxation; (4) regularization and expansion of colonial rule; and (5) establishment of working agreements between capitalists and state authorities.

In many countries, increasing state capacity occurred through a shift from indirect to direct rule. Before the nineteenth century, systems of indirect rule prevailed through much of the world. Rulers conceded great autonomy to regional strongmen – they were almost always men, not women – in return for the strongman's delivery of taxes, goods, labor, military means, and political compliance. Indirect rule made big empires possible, but it always limited the central state's capacity. By 1914 direct rule had become much more common throughout the world. Central administrations extended from national capitals into local communities through state-run armies, post offices, service organizations, and much more. Two contradictory processes countered each other: On one side, long-distance labor migration produced huge flows from country to country and continent to continent. On the other, states spent increasing energy fixing people into place by means of censuses, passports, surveys, policing, political surveillance, and personal taxation. On balance, states gained power more than migrants evaded their control.

These changes had strong implications for popular politics, our main focus in this chapter. Democratization in high-capacity states created new opportunities for social movements. It facilitated their ability to co-ordinate actions over larger spaces, the small clandestine discussion groups that constituted the core of popular politics in repressive states giving way to national social movements that proudly displayed the breadth of their membership. It further enabled social movements to focus their attention and concentrate their actions on state or national capitals or government centers where they could exert maximum influence. When and where democratization occurred, it gave relatively powerless but well-organized people greater opportunities to intervene in issues on which they had previously had little say: state guarantees of welfare, military policy, taxation, and much more. Workers, for example, rarely held the upper hand, but they did gain rights to organize, assemble, strike, and support candidates who would forward their interests. Democratization also provided new means and occasions for speaking up. Legalization of political parties, special-interest associations, labor unions, public meetings, and petitions offered expanded means for otherwise powerless people to make their views known. Elections, referenda, legislative assemblies, public hearings, and similar occasions all generated public discussion and displays of differing opinions. Banners, badges, and signs broadcasting support for groups or programs became standard features of public occasions.

Increased state capacity had further effects on popular politics. Whether or not the regime was relatively democratic, rising state capacity increased the salience of national actions and issues to everyday politics. In relatively undemocratic regimes, it increased the state's presence in everyday life, made the extent of local and regional rulers' collaboration with national regimes more crucial to the welfare of ordinary citizens, and increased the incentives either to make private deals with representatives of national authorities or to join opposition movements. Worldwide networks of radicals and nationalists, many of them exiled from their native countries, began collaborating and communicating ideas. In more democratic regimes, increased state capacity raised the stakes of national politics and provided new opportunities for popular groups that could gain both recognition and the power to use state capacity in support of their own interests. Women, farmers, industrial workers, military veterans, and other interest groups became increasingly familiar actors on the national scene.

9.2 THE RISE OF SOCIAL MOVEMENTS

Before the nineteenth century, ordinary people of Western Europe and North America often spoke out on behalf of their interests. They spoke out by jeering unpopular officials or cheering popular ones, attacking price-gouging merchants, publicly shaming wife-beaters, driving workers who violated local rules out of town seated backward on donkeys or fence rails, tarring and feathering strike-breakers, breaking the windows of malefactors' houses, and other relatively direct forms of action. They occasionally joined large-scale rebellions against landlords, tax collectors, marauding mercenaries, or corrupt authorities. But they did not mount social movements of the kind that became common during the nineteenth century.

Social movements centered on campaigns in support of or opposition to publicly articulated programs by means of associations, meetings, demonstrations, petitions, electoral participation, strikes, and related means of co-ordinated action. They provided an opportunity to offer a sustained challenge to powerful figures and institutions without necessarily attacking them physically. They said, in effect, "We are here, we support this cause, there are lots of us, we know how to act together, and we could cause trouble if we wanted to." In the British Isles, for example, by the 1820s popular leaders were organizing effective social movements against the slave trade, for the political rights of Catholics, and for freedom of association among workers. In the United States, anti-slavery was becoming a major social movement not much later. American workers' movements proliferated during the first half of the nineteenth century. By the 1850s social movements were starting to displace older forms of popular politics through much of Western Europe and North America.

Throughout the world since 1850, social movements have generally flourished where and when contested elections become central to politics. Contested elections promote social movements in several different ways (see Box 9.2). First, they provide a model of public support for rival programs, as embodied in competing candidates; once governments have authorized public discussion of major issues during electoral campaigns, it becomes harder to silence that discussion outside of electoral campaigns. Second, they legalize and protect assemblies of citizens for campaigning and voting. Citizens allowed to gather in support of candidates and parties easily take up other issues that concern them. Third, elections magnify the importance of numbers; with contested elections, any group receiving disciplined support from large numbers of followers becomes a possible ally or enemy at the polls. Finally, some expansion of rights to speak, communicate, and assemble publicly almost inevitably accompanies the establishment of contested elections. Even people who lack the vote can disrupt elections, march in support of popular candidates, and use rights of assembly and communication.

Once social movements existed, they became available for politics well outside the electoral arena. Movements for moral reform such as temperance – opposition to the sale and public consumption of alcohol – sometimes swayed elections. American anti-alcohol activists formed a Prohibition Party in 1869. But temperance advocates also engaged in direct moral

Box 9.2 How Contested Elections Promoted Social Movements

In the more democratic Western countries, social movements and contested national elections for officials and representatives both flourished after 1850. One reason that they flourished together was that the creation of parties, platforms, candidates, and election campaigns provided opportunities for people to take up issues such as citizens' rights, social welfare, and working conditions. Genuinely contested elections promoted social movements in several different ways:

(1) Like official holidays, elections and campaigns usually involved public assemblies from which it was difficult for authorities to exclude non-voters; those assemblies then became privileged occasions for the public voicing of claims.

(2) They provided a model of public support for rival programs, as embodied in competing candidates; once governments authorized public discussion of major issues during electoral campaigns, it became harder to silence that discussion outside of electoral campaigns.

(3) Elections magnified the importance of numbers; with contested elections, any group receiving disciplined support from large numbers of followers became a possible ally or enemy at the polls. Social movements used demonstrations, public meetings, petitions, and associational memberships to broadcast their numbers.

(4) Candidates often had incentives for displays of popular support, including support from non-voters; such displays fortified the claim to represent "the people" at large, and to command wider support than one's electoral opponents.

(5) To the extent that voting districts were geographical, both campaigns and polls offered opportunities for injecting local and regional issues – issues of social movements – into the public discussion.

(6) Visible legal divisions between those who did and did not have the right to vote (for example, men and women) promoted claims by the excluded for rights denied, as they made exclusion dramatically evident.

intervention by organizing religious campaigns, holding public meetings, circulating pledges of abstinence, and getting educators to teach the evils of alcohol. In both Great Britain and the United States, the Salvation Army (founded in London, 1865) carried on street crusades against alcohol and for the rescue of alcoholics without engaging directly in electoral politics. American agitator Carrie Nation got herself arrested thirty times during the 1890s and 1900s as she physically attacked bars in states that had passed, but not enforced, bans on the sale of alcohol. Social movements expanded with electoral politics, but soon operated quite outside the realm of parties and elections.

Anti-slavery action in the United Kingdom and the United States illustrates the social movement's rise. Mobilization against slavery and increasing salience of national elections – with slavery itself an electoral issue – reinforced each other in the two countries. The timing of anti-slavery mobilization is surprising. Both the **abolition** of the slave trade and the later emancipation of slaves occurred when slave-based production was still expanding across much of North and South America. The Atlantic slave trade fed captive labor mainly into production of sugar, coffee, and cotton for European consumption. North and South American slave labor provided 70 percent of the cotton processed by British mills in 1787 and 90 percent in 1838. Although slave production of sugar, coffee, and cotton

continued to expand past the mid nineteenth century, transatlantic traffic in slaves reached its peak between 1781 and 1790, held steady for a few decades, then declined rapidly after 1840.

Outlawing of slavery itself proceeded fitfully for a century, from Haiti's spectacular slave rebellion (1790 onward) to Brazil's grudging emancipation (1888). Argentina, for example, outlawed both slavery and the slave trade in its constitution of 1853. Between the 1840s and 1888, then, the Atlantic slave trade was disappearing and slavery itself was ending country by country. Yet slave-based production of cotton and other commodities continued to increase until the 1860s. How was that possible? Increases in slave-based commodity production depended partly on rising labor productivity and partly on population growth within the remaining slave population. Slavery did not disappear because it had lost its profitability. Movements against the slave trade, then against slavery itself, overturned economically viable systems.

How did that happen? Although heroic activists sometimes campaigned publicly against slavery in major regions of slave-based production, crucial campaigns first took place mostly where slaves were rare but beneficiaries of their production were prominent. For the most part, anti-slavery support arose in populations that benefited no more than indirectly from slave production. The British version of the story begins well before 1850, in 1787 to be exact. British Quakers, Methodists, and other anti-establishment Protestants joined with more secular advocates of working-class freedoms to oppose all forms of coerced labor. A Society for the Abolition of the Slave Trade, organized in 1787, co-ordinated a vast national campaign, an early social movement.

Manchester

At first glance, the central role of Manchester, the Industrial Revolution's first great metropolis, in that campaign looks strange. Textile production in Manchester depended heavily on cotton produced by slaves in the Americas. But in Manchester, both masters and workers believed in the superiority of free over slave labor, despite disagreeing over what sorts of freedom workers should enjoy. In 1788, Manchester's citizens sent to Parliament a petition against the slave trade endorsed by a reported 10,639 citizens, about two thirds of the adult male population. Even at the risk of paying more for cotton produced by free labor, they agitated for the end of slavery. During the winter of 1787–88 abolitionists organized multiple public meetings in the city, typically leaving a copy of the petition in place for signature or endorsement with an X after the meeting.

Manchester's initiative set the city against the leaders of Liverpool, the main port through which slave-produced cotton entered England. In the name of economic progress and property rights, Liverpool's leaders objected to anti-slavery activism. Manchester's example, however, had the wider resonance in Great Britain. Perhaps 100,000 people throughout England put their names to abolitionist petitions in 1787–88. At the same time, other associations, public meetings, and petition drives were agitating for parliamentary reform as well as for repeal of restrictions on the political rights of Catholics and of Protestant Dissenters (Baptists, Methodists, and other non-members of the government-backed Anglican church).

Britain and the Rise of the Social Movement

During the next two decades, British activists rounded out the social movement repertoire with two crucial additions: the lobby and the demonstration. Lobbying began literally as talking to Members of Parliament in the lobby of the Parliament building on their way to or from sessions. Later the word became generalized to mean any direct intervention with legislators to influence their votes. British activists also created the two forms of demonstration we still know today: the disciplined march through streets and the organized assembly in a symbolically significant public space, both accompanied by co-ordinated displays of support for a shared program. Of course all the forms of social movement activism had precedents, including public meetings, formal presentations of petitions, and the committees of correspondence that played so important a part in American resistance to royal demands during the 1760s and 1770s. But between the 1780s and the 1820s British activists created a new synthesis. From then to the present, social movements regularly combined associations, meetings, demonstrations, petitions, electoral participation, lobbying, strikes, and related means of co-ordinated action.

Within Great Britain, Parliament began responding to popular pressure with partial regulation of the slave trade in 1788. By 1806 abolition of the slave trade had become a major issue in parliamentary elections. In 1807 Parliament declared illegal the shipping of slaves to Britain's colonies. From that point on, British activists demanded that their government act against other slave-trading countries. Great Britain then pressed for withdrawal of other European powers from the slave trade. At the end of the Napoleonic Wars in 1815, the major European powers except for Spain and Portugal agreed to abolition of the trade. Under economic and diplomatic pressure from Britain, Spain and Portugal withdrew reluctantly from officially sanctioned slave trading step by step between 1815 and 1867. From 1867 onward, only outlaws shipped slaves across the Atlantic.

Soon after 1815, British activists were moving successfully to restrict the powers of slave owners in British colonies, and finally – in 1834 – to end slavery itself. Although French revolutionaries outlawed both the slave trade and slavery throughout France and its colonies in 1794, Napoleon's regime restored them ten years later. France did not again abolish slavery and the slave trade until the revolution of 1848. With Brazil's abolition of slavery in 1888, legal slavery finally disappeared from Europe and the Americas. Backed aggressively by state power, British social movement pressure had brought about a momentous change.

9.3 ANTI-SLAVERY AND AMERICAN FEMINISM

The North American version of the struggle passed through a civil war. Great Britain's outlawing of the slave trade after 1808 effectively removed that issue from North American public politics. But slave-based production flourished, especially in the American South. In the United States, an abolitionist movement formed in the 1820s and gained strength into the 1860s. It formed in company with movements for women's rights, temperance, and religious renewal. Feminist leaders Lucretia Mott and Elizabeth Cady Stanton, for example, both came from upper New York State, but they first met at London's World Anti-Slavery Convention of 1840. A single woman, Mott was a New England Quaker then living in Philadelphia. She had founded the first United States Female Anti-Slavery Society. Her home was a stop on the "underground railroad" along which slaves escaped to Canada and freedom. The well-educated daughter of a judge, Stanton was born in western New York State, married an abolitionist leader, and eventually settled with her growing family in the small city of Seneca Falls, New York.

Mott and Stanton renewed their acquaintance in 1848. Along with several other like-minded women, they issued a call to a women's rights conference the same summer (see Box 9.3). To their surprise, some 300 women and men came to Seneca Falls, New York for that congress. The United States women's suffrage movement had begun.

Many of the same women who supported suffrage also opposed slavery. A major representative of that combination was the black preacher Sojourner Truth (1797–1883; see Figure 9.2). Born as the slave Isabella Van Wagner in Ulster County, New York, she gained freedom when New York State abolished slavery in 1827. At that point 30-year-old Isabella left her husband and father of her five children, underwent a religious conversion, but continued to work as a cook as she gained fame preaching the Gospel. In 1843 she changed her name to Sojourner Truth. With support from famous figures such as Harriet Beecher Stowe, author of *Uncle Tom's Cabin*, she became a fixture on the abolitionist-feminist lecture circuit. Her dictated autobiography, first published in 1849 as the *Narrative of Sojourner Truth*, sold widely as testimony on the evils of slavery. As reported by her friend Marius Robinson, she ended her talk at an 1851 women's rights convention in Akron, Ohio with the declaration:

I cant read, but I can hear. I have heard the Bible and learned that Eve caused man to sin. Well if woman upset the world, do give her a chance to set it right side up again. The lady has spoken about Jesus, how he never spurned woman from him, and she was right. When Lazarus died, Mary and Martha came to him with faith and love and besought him to raise their brother. And Jesus wept – and Lazarus came forth. And how came Jesus into the world? Through God who created him and woman who bore him. Man, where is your part? But the women are coming up, blessed be God, and a few of the men are coming up with them. But man is in a tight place, the poor slave is on him, woman is coming on him, and he is surely between a hawk and a buzzard.

As it worked out, American women did not actually get the right to vote in national elections until passage of the nineteenth constitutional amendment in 1920. Yet women's participation in nineteenth-century promotion of suffrage, temperance, and anti-slavery movements made female reformers prominent figures in American politics. Even more so than in Great Britain, American social movement activism forced anti-slavery onto initially reluctant national politicians. Great lobbying and petitioning campaigns of the 1830s preceded formation of explicitly anti-slavery Liberty and Free Soil parties during the 1840s and emergence of an anti-slavery majority within the new Republican Party of the 1850s.

A rough alliance brought together Northeastern activists who stressed the dignity of free labor and Western activists who more directly combated the threat of slave-based production's expansion into frontier regions. The alliance faced fierce opposition from Southerners who increasingly elaborated theories of states' rights, white superiority, slaves as property, and sacred Southern tradition. The two sides treated each other with growing suspicion, contempt, and violence. The Southern-backed Fugitive Slave Act (1850) required United States marshals to seize

Box 9.3 Elizabeth Cady Stanton Speaks Up for Women's Rights

At the Seneca Falls, New York, women's rights conference of 1848, feminist leader Elizabeth Cady Stanton gave a speech echoing the American Declaration of Independence. The conference passed a resolution declaring that it was the *duty* of women themselves "to secure to themselves their sacred right to the elective franchise." The Declaration of Sentiments signed in Seneca Falls by sixty-eight women and thirty-two men included these words echoing Stanton's speech:

We hold these truths to be self-evident: that all men and women are created equal; that they are endowed by their Creator with certain inalienable rights; that among these are life, liberty, and the pursuit of happiness; that to secure these rights governments are instituted, deriving their just powers from the consent of the governed. Whenever any form of government becomes destructive of those ends, it is the right of those who suffer from it to refuse allegiance to it, and to insist upon the institution of a new government, laying its foundation on such principles, and organizing its power in such form, as to them shall seem most likely to effect their safety and happiness ... Such has been the patient sufferance of the women under this government, and such is now the necessity which constrains them to demand the equal station to which they are entitled.

I SELL THE SHADOW TO SUPPORT THE SUBSTANCE.
SOJOURNER TRUTH.

Figure 9.2 Isabella Baumfree was born in Ulster County, New York. She escaped slavery with her young daughter and took the name Sojourner Truth in 1843. She was an abolitionist and a champion of women's rights.

escaped slaves even if they arrived in states that had abolished slavery. From that point on, the marshals' capture of slaves in Massachusetts or New York regularly brought crowds to the rescue.

On February 15, 1851, for example, arrest of Shadrach, an escaped slave who had become a waiter in a Boston coffeehouse, called out Bostonians en masse. They broke into the jail, freed Shadrach, and spirited him off to freedom in Canada. Three years later, escaped slave Anthony Burns had less luck. Arrested in Boston on a pretext, he ended up in jail, awaiting shipment back to Virginia and slavery. After large meetings on the evening of May 26, 1854, some 50,000 people led by well-known Boston abolitionists gathered at the courthouse to free Burns, but the

marshal's troops held them off; one of the troops died in the attack. The authorities called in heavily armed detachments from the army, navy, and marines. They took Burns through a crowd estimated at 200,000 people, loaded him on a US revenue cutter, and sent him back to Virginia with several escorting naval vessels. The Massachusetts legislature came close to impeaching the judge who authorized calling out military force to deport Anthony Burns.

Violence occurred on both sides. On January 6, 1861, W.J. Weiss wrote his mother from Mississippi:

> Mob law *reigns supreme. Let me recount some of the deeds of horror I have witnessed. Last week I was at the steamboat landing on the Mississippi River. A Gentleman there who was a native of Ohio was waiting for a boat to go up the river. While there he remarked that he would soon be in a free state. He was closely questioned, and found to entertain principles not compatible with the Southern institution. He was seized, crowded into an empty pork barrel, and headed up tight and was then rolled into the river. Three men, natives of some Northern state, were hung two weeks ago.*

At this point, Mississippi, Florida, Alabama, Georgia, Louisiana, Texas, Virginia, Tennessee, Arkansas, and North Carolina were in the process of seceding from the United States; on February 4 they would form the Confederate States of America. The Civil War was starting. At war in 1862, Abraham Lincoln issued his Emancipation Proclamation, ending slavery – but almost entirely in the Confederacy! – starting in January 1863. After the war ended in 1865, the thirteenth amendment to the US Constitution wrote the prohibition of slavery into fundamental law.

9.4 WORKERS, PARTIES, UNIONS, AND STRIKES

Although women and men have worked since the beginning of human time, the period from 1850 to 1914 brought organized workers into national politics as never before. Trade unions, workers' parties, and strikes all became major vehicles for pressing labor's demands on capital and the state. Western Europe and North America set widely influential models for workers' mobilization. But elsewhere in Europe, in Latin America, in East Asia, and wherever big industry grew up, workers' collective action began to figure importantly in national politics.

The Second Industrial Revolution and Democratization

As Chapter 8 showed in detail, the Second Industrial Revolution made capital-intensive production and large workplaces much more prominent across the industrial world. Growth of heavily capitalized industries such as factory textile production, metalworking, and mining promoted large-scale workers' action in three ways. First, much more so than with earlier forms of production, such industries assembled many workers doing similar things in large workplaces. That promoted communication and recognition of common interests. Second, they formed company towns, dense working-class neighborhoods, and gathering places where workers not only interacted with each other but formed significant political constituencies. Third, they gave capitalists themselves interests in securing stable, reliable workforces, protection for their increasingly expensive industrial plants, and workers' representatives with whom they could bargain. Employers varied enormously in how much they used rewards and how much they used threats, but on balance their heavy investment in buildings, equipment, and raw materials sensitized them to workers' demands. They needed steady workers to keep their machines operating steadily.

Large legal obstacles stood in the way. Well into the nineteenth century, many European and American workers who were technically free actually worked under long-term contracts as apprentices or indentured servants. Western governments generally treated hiring as a private contract. As a result, workers who left the job without advance notice or refused to follow their employers' orders ran the risk not only of losing their accumulated wages but also of being fined or jailed for breach of contract. Workers who resisted collectively or made joint demands ran the further risk of prosecution for conspiracy. Legal restrictions on free speech, assembly, and association made it more difficult for workers to organize in the first place. Only where workers put strong collective pressure on employers and governments did the law finally begin to change.

Political Rights

In Western Europe, a standard package of rights emerged from long struggles among workers, capitalists, and governments – rights to organize, to assemble, to speak, to vote, to bargain collectively. Figure 9.3 lists the dates of five such landmarks in eleven Western European countries. In the United Kingdom (England, Wales, Scotland, and Ireland), Parliament responded to a great wave of worker mobilization that followed the end of the Napoleonic Wars by conceding the rights of workers to form associations for mutual benefit and public interests in 1824. The parliamentary committee recommending the change argued that while in principle laws against "conspiracy" applied equally to employers and workers when either side combined to affect wages, hours, or working conditions, in fact magistrates never

prosecuted employers, and "Prosecutions have frequently been carried on, under the statute and the common law, against the workmen, and many of them have suffered different periods of imprisonment for combining and conspiring to raise their wages, or to resist their reduction, and to regulate their hours of working." Following parallel arguments, Belgium and Norway adopted similar measures in 1830 and 1839. The other eight countries followed, usually in the wake of political crises, from 1848 to 1890.

The same countries passed the threshold at which half or more of adult males had voting rights between 1848 and 1912. Italy, the last to create a unitary central state, also came latest in both freedom of association and voting rights. Female suffrage generally lagged behind. One cluster of countries granted women equal voting rights with men during or shortly after World War I. But Belgium, France, Italy, and Switzerland all waited until after World War II. In general, nineteenth-century workers' rights meant the rights of male workers. Women had to battle their way toward equal treatment.

With some restrictions, trade unions (including those rare trade unions that organized women) became legal along with other popular associations in the United Kingdom from 1824 onward. Similar authorizations of trade unions occurred elsewhere in Western Europe between 1839 and 1890. The right to strike came later. In fact, workers had collectively withdrawn their labor from European shops for a long time before the nineteenth century. Authorities had often looked the other way when workers went on strike, and employers had often preferred collective bargaining to mass firing or calling in troops. But Western European workers only acquired legal protection for a collective declaration that they were striking on behalf of specific demands between 1839 and 1921. Three quarters of all the legalizations in Figure 9.3 occurred between 1848 and 1909. For Western Europe, those were the heady decades of expansion in workers' political rights.

In the very process that gave workers and other common people political rights, nineteenth-century Western European countries also created new police forces. Before the nineteenth century, private guards, game wardens, local constables, posses, militias, and regular armies had done whatever policing occurred in Western Europe. Bounty-hunters and thief-catchers also tracked down criminal suspects for posted rewards. During the nineteenth century, however, salaried police forces operating in uniform under civilian control began to take over policing of cities and some rural areas. Fear of crime in fast-growing cities provided one spur to the creation of specialized police forces. But concerns about public order provided another.

Once ordinary people had the right to assemble and organize, once it became difficult or even illegal to send in regular

Figure 9.3 Timing of popular and workers' rights in Western Europe.

Country	Year of First Legalization:				
	Interest Association	Manhood Suffrage	Female Suffrage	Trade Union	Strike
Austria	1867	1907	1919	1870	1918
Belgium	1830	1893	1949	1866	1921
Denmark	1849	1849	1918	1849	1849
France	1884	1848	1945	1884	1864
Germany	1869	1871	1919	1869	1918
Italy	1890	1912	1946	1890	1890
Netherlands	1855	1896	1922	1855	1872
Norway	1839	1898	1915	1839	1839
Sweden	1864	1909	1921	1864	1885
Switzerland	1848	1848	1971	1848	1848
United Kingdom	1824	1885	1928	1824	1875

Manhood Suffrage: When at least 50 percent of adult males first had voting rights

Female Suffrage: When adult females acquired equal voting rights with adult males

troops simply because people were demonstrating or striking, authorities created specialized police forces. They hired men (before the twentieth century, they were always men) whose job was not only to patrol streets looking for drunkards and criminals, but also to contain or disperse crowds that got out of hand. They put police in uniform to mark them off from the general population and advertise their presence. Just as police facilitated their daily work on the beat by creating networks of informers and collaborators, they dealt with crowd control in part by infiltrating dissident organizations, bargaining out parade routes with leaders of protests, and calling out extra forces to police elections, public ceremonies, mass meetings, and major strikes.

France

A closer look at France fills out the picture. Eighteenth-century France had a variety of forces responsible for public order, but nothing like a national urban police force. Nor did any force specialize in patrolling workers' disputes. Although authorities often failed to intervene in industrial conflicts, strictly speaking workers' assemblies, organizations, and strikes were illegal. Under the Revolution, France's Le Chapelier Law of 1791 forbade both employers and workers to organize against each other. The law specifically denied workers the rights to appoint a president, secretaries, or syndics, to keep records, to make decisions or

deliberate, or to regulate their purported common interests, or to make among themselves agreements for the concerted refusal of work, or for supplying at a fixed price the efforts of their industry or labor.

Later legislation under the Revolution and Napoleon made the penalties much more serious for workers than for employers. Napoleon's administrators required workers to carry passbooks recording their work records, and to leave the books in their employers' hands as long as they held their jobs. Since workers could not get new jobs without passbooks, that meant they could not quit work except with their employers' permission. Even with permission, workers ran the risk that employers' negative comments in the book would keep new firms from hiring them.

Under Napoleon, the state set up two separate national police forces – **gendarmes** who patrolled highways and rural areas, regular police for urban areas. Gradually the regular police took over from municipal constables and other local forces across the country. They kept close watch on workers and sent regular reports on workers' organizations (both legal and illegal) to Paris. After multiple workers' insurrections, a law of 1834 increased the government's ability to break up workers' associations and meetings. As France industrialized from the 1840s onward, however, the government gradually relaxed its restrictions. In each case, concessions to workers followed a cycle of labor unrest, repression, and subsequent relaxation.

The revolution of 1848 provided an opening for widespread action by workers and established manhood suffrage, only to see the new empire created by Louis Napoleon in 1852 cut back both sets of rights.

In 1864, nevertheless, the French empire granted a limited right to strike. In 1868, it became legal for workers to hold public meetings without prior authorization from the government. Later the same year an imperial edict permitted trade unions to organize, just so long as they had their rules approved by authorities, deposited minutes of their meetings with the authorities, and allowed police observers to attend. After another revolution in 1870, the Paris Commune of 1871, and settling of a new republic into place during the later 1870s, France finally legalized trade unions fully in 1884. The authorization in the 1884 law ran: "Occupational unions, appropriately constituted on the basis of the prescriptions of the present law, may establish themselves freely for the consideration and protection of their economic, industrial, commercial and agricultural interests." The "prescriptions of the present law" meant mainly giving governmental authorities a copy of the union statutes and a list of its officers – not of its members. These provisions cemented the toleration of unions and strikes that had been building since 1864. Strikes rose quickly after 1864, mounting in wave after wave to great peaks on either side of World War I. By then, strikes had become standard bargaining tools for workers in single plants, in whole industries, and sometimes over large parts of the national industrial or agricultural workforce.

From its founding, the low-capacity US state tolerated both strikes and workers' organizations. As the Red Scare of the 1880s tells us, however, it tolerated them uneasily and with varying degrees of latitude. During the 1890s, in fact, the US government put legal impediments in the way of organizing industrial (rather than craft) unions. The USA did not remove those impediments until the 1930s. Still, during the latter half of the nineteenth century the United States became one of the industrial world's most strike-prone countries. After American railroads suddenly cut the wages of their employees by 10 percent in the summer of 1877, one of the century's largest and bloodiest strike waves swept over railroad junctions in West Virginia, Maryland, Pennsylvania, New York, New Jersey, Ohio, Indiana, Illinois, and Missouri. Strikers battled both federal troops and the railroads' private armies as non-strikers attacked railroad property. Some ten people died in Baltimore, twenty-five in Pittsburgh, forty or fifty in Chicago. In Chicago, a crowd of 20,000 heard a fiery speech by anarchist Albert Parsons, who nine years later would be one of the four men executed for his alleged participation in the Haymarket bombing.

The year before Haymarket, the Knights of Labor led another major railroad strike in 1885, actually winning reinstatement of fired workers and restoration of lost wages. Including the general strike of 1886, the mid-1880s brought the greatest wave of strikes the United States had experienced up to that time. The next peaks of strike activity arrived in the early 1890s, around 1903 and, especially, just after World War I. In terms of strikes per million non-agricultural workers, the United States never again reached its rates of 1877 to 1919. But American strikes got larger. In terms of sheer numbers of strikers, the USA remained one of the world's most strike-prone countries into the 1960s.

South African Workers' Struggles

The experience of South Africa shows that other industrializing parts of the world also experienced a rise in strikes between 1850 and 1914. European adventurers discovered diamonds along South Africa's Orange River in 1867. Within three years, 5,000 prospectors, both black and white, were digging and sifting for diamonds in the region; by 1872, 20,000 whites and 30,000 blacks were working the surface. Not long after, geologists and entrepreneurs began squeezing out the small operators by digging deep mines. They usually employed white workers to run their underground operations and black workers to do the heavy labor. Other adventurers found gold in the region called Witwatersrand in 1886. The two finds started one of the world's greatest mining rushes. The city of Kimberley grew up rapidly as the diamond capital, the city of Johannesburg as the headquarters for gold. By the end of the nineteenth century, South Africa was producing a majority of the world's traded diamonds and more than a quarter of its gold. To the present, South Africa has remained a major producer of diamonds and gold. From the start, the segregated workforce included both white and black workers. Blacks generally received the more dangerous, less autonomous, and more poorly paid forms of work. In 1911, white gold miners averaged almost twelve times the annual wages of their black co-workers. Most African mine laborers signed on for term contracts, returning to rural villages at the ends of their contracts or when white managers fired them. Only after World War I did black workers begin finding jobs in South Africa's urban manufacturing.

South Africa's first major strike occurred in its diamond mines – with both black and white miners taking part – during 1884. Gold miners followed with their own strikes during the 1890s. As mining expanded feverishly and made enormous profits for South African capitalists, labor shortage gave workers temporary leverage. Mine owners attempted to hold down wages and check strikes by importing more docile workers from China. A cartoon in the *South African News* of 1903 showed a paunchy, pin-striped mining magnate reacting to the dramatic resignation of Great Britain's minister for the colonies by declaring: "I am Hoggenheimer – *the* Hoggenheimer. Your resignation bores me; your fiscal rot bores me; everything bores me just now except Chinese labour." More than 60,000 Chinese workers arrived between 1904 and 1907, but even that measure did not stop white and black miners. After a populist party won the 1907 election, in fact, the South African government deported all Chinese miners.

Mine owners continued to substitute cheaper black labor for white where they could, thus pitting whites against blacks. Major strikes of white miners ensued in 1907, 1913, and 1914, with strikers demanding not only better working conditions but also exclusion of black workers from some semi-skilled jobs. A railway strike of 1914 attracted widespread support from workers in other industries. As in France, great peaks of strike activity bracketed World War I. In France, South Africa, and elsewhere, tightening of political controls and moving of workers into military service or government-supervised war production during the war years temporarily depressed strike activity. Despite South Africa's racially divided workforce, strikes remained major means of working-class action among both blacks and whites from that point onward. Throughout the world of concentrated industry, strikes became focal points of workers' struggles after 1850.

9.5 NATIONALIST AND REVOLUTIONARY MOVEMENTS

As state capacities expanded during the nineteenth century, who ran the state and how became more pressing questions for people who had to live in its shadow. Two different responses to those questions took the forms of nationalist and revolutionary movements. A state is a political organization, but a nation is a group of people who share a common origin, history, and cultural heritage. Some states are multinational; Canada is a case in point. Many self-identified nations lack their own states; American Indian tribes provide multiple examples. Although various kinds of attachment to one's own nation have existed since the beginning of history, the nineteenth century generated far greater nationalist movements than ever before. Nationalism's central doctrines claimed that nations should match states: Nations should have their own states, and states should have their own nations.

Those claims encouraged people who shared linguistic, religious, cultural, and historical ties but did not occupy states of their own to demand new, separate states; we can call

that program **bottom-up nationalism**. But the basic program of matching nations to states also encouraged people who already ran existing states to impose their own linguistic, religious, cultural, and historical traditions on everyone who lived within those states; we can call that program **top-down nationalism**. With top-down nationalism, authorities claimed that loyalty to the nation – as they defined the nation – should override loyalties of religion, locality, friendship, and kinship. Although bottom-up and top-down nationalism obviously struggled with each other, they also fed each other. The more minorities within existing states demanded autonomy, the more their rulers insisted on the priority of their own linguistic, religious, cultural, and historical traditions. The more state authorities attempted to impose uniform linguistic, religious, cultural, and historical traditions on their whole populations, however, the more those minorities that were relatively organized and self-conscious resisted.

Over the period from 1850 to 1914, top-down nationalism gained ground, but bottom-up nationalism grew more vociferous. Top-down nationalism gained as large states gobbled up small ones, built standardized education systems, gave priority to national languages, celebrated triumphal versions of their histories, and recruited officials who would serve rulers' interpretation of the national interest. Top-down nationalism also gained as Western countries expanded colonial rule in Africa, Asia, and the Pacific. Top-down nationalism even gained in former colonial empires, as rulers of newly independent countries in Latin America, Asia, and Southern Europe launched programs of nationalization, complete with suppression of their own minorities. Top-down nationalism prevailed, for example, through most of Spain's former colonies in Latin America. Although the bulk of the population sprang from African or indigenous American origins, Spanish language and European ways became standards for schooling and public life. In all parts of the world, however, this expansion of top-down nationalism generated a counter-current of bottom-up nationalism: Croats resisting Hungarian hegemony in their part of the Austro-Hungarian empire, Slavs resisting Greek hegemony in a Greece recently separated from the Ottoman empire, Zulus fighting off European control in South Africa, indigenous peoples seeking to retain shreds of sovereignty throughout the Americas, Indians struggling to re-establish some sort of power in the face of British rule.

Revolutionary movements differed significantly from nationalist movements. They argued that the wrong people were running existing states, and ought to be replaced forcefully. They sought to seize control of those states, and run them differently. Revolutionary movements varied greatly in their

Box 9.4 Friedrich Engels Voices Marxist Optimism

Early in 1848, Karl Marx and Friedrich Engels published the *Manifesto of the Communist Party*, a ringing call for workers to unite on behalf of revolution. It began: "A spectre is haunting Europe – the spectre of Communism." Although the European wave of revolutions in 1848 went down to defeat, they established models of revolutionary mobilization and representative government that inspired later generations. Marx died in London in 1883. Seven years later, Engels wrote a new preface to the *Manifesto* for the German edition of 1890. It ended:

"Working men of all countries, unite!" But few voices responded when we proclaimed these words to the world forty-two years ago, on the eve of the first Paris Revolution in which the proletariat came out with demands of its own. On September 28, 1864, however, the proletarians of most of the Western European countries united to form the International Working Men's Association of glorious memory. True, the International itself lived only nine years. But that the eternal union of the proletarians of all countries created by it is still alive and lives stronger than ever, there is no better witness than this day. Because today, as I write these lines, *the European and American proletariat is reviewing its fighting forces, mobilized for the first time, mobilized as* one *army, under* one *flag, for* one *immediate aim: the standard eight-hour working day, to be established by legal enactment, as proclaimed by the Geneva Congress of the International in 1866, and again by the Paris Workers' Congress in 1889. And today's spectacle will open the eyes of capitalists and landlords of all countries to the fact that today the working men of all countries are united indeed.*

If only Marx were still by my side to see this with his own eyes!

---

programs for state capacity. At one extreme, anarchists argued that revolutionaries should reduce state capacity to a minimum, thus eliminating the power of ruling classes to exploit ordinary people and freeing ordinary people to create their own voluntary forms of association. At the other extreme, some utopians wanted high-capacity states that would implement national programs of enlightenment, justice, and prosperity. In between, most revolutionaries resembled the followers of Karl Marx – Marxists – in arguing that some form of state power would be necessary for a long time to come, but that representatives of the common people should hold state power.

Marxists and other revolutionaries organized internationally. The period from 1850 to 1914 brought the high tide of revolutionary internationalism. Socialist, communist, and anarchist revolutionaries all hoped to bring all the world's workers, regardless of nationality, into a single alliance against capital and existing state power. That alliance, they claimed, would smash the power of capital and bring about the rule of oppressed people everywhere. The socialist First International (1864–76) and Second International (1889–1916) brought together radicals from much of Europe and North America. Box 9.4 provides a quote from Marx's collaborator, Friedrich Engels, writing in an optimistic vein. There was reason. By 1912, the Second International had members from all European countries, the USA, Canada, and Japan. Local and national chapters of revolutionary movements communicated constantly, sent emissaries to each other, and held international congresses. But World War I shattered worker internationalism, as national union federations and labor parties generally collaborated with their governments' war efforts.

Nationalist and Revolutionary Movements Combine

Nationalist and revolutionary movements sometimes combined. Giuseppe Mazzini (1805–72), for example, centered his revolutionary career on creating a united, independent Italian state in the interest of its common people. He collaborated closely with revolutionaries in Switzerland, France, and England as well. Similarly, the Revolutionary Alliance led in China by Sun Yixian combined a program of economic collectivism with fierce opposition to Manchu rulers. After a failed attempt at revolution in 1895, one of Sun Yixian's followers declared before dying by torture that "the Manchu-Qing, the robbers of Manchuria, conquered our country, stole our land, killed our ancestors, seized our sons and daughters . . . if we do not now exterminate the Manchus, it will be impossible to restore the Chinese race." A revolutionary coalition including Sun Yixian's forces did overthrow the Manchu-origin Qing dynasty in 1912. At that moment Sun Yixian himself was in Denver, Colorado organizing support for his movement among overseas Chinese. He rushed back to take charge. With the revolution, his follower's words of 1895, seditious then, became retroactively patriotic.

China's history between 1850 and 1914 offers us an opportunity to look more closely at the interplay of states, workers, nationalism, revolutionary action, and social movements at large. After China, we can then turn to Mexico and Argentina for contrasting experiences during the same period.

9.6 WORKERS AND SOCIAL MOVEMENTS IN CHINA

China is doubly interesting because during the nineteenth and twentieth centuries an old, distinctive political system interacted ever more closely with intrusive Westerners. Westerners established major commercial enclaves in China, sent religious missionaries in large numbers, and tried strenuously but unsuccessfully to control Chinese politics. Europeans and Americans had forced China into treaties opening up Shanghai, Ningbo, Fuzhou, Amoy, Hong Kong, and Guangzhou in 1842, then added another thirty major cities to the list one by one over the next sixty years. As a result, Chinese elites had more contact with Westerners in China than Western elites had with Chinese in the West.

There were exceptions, for example the Chinese emigrants who flocked to California during the gold rush that began in 1849, supplied a significant share of the labor for building America's railroads, but later suffered sharp discrimination in the United States. (Two of Sun Yixian's uncles had gone to California in the gold rush, another uncle and a brother went to Hawaii, and he himself emigrated briefly to Hawaii in 1879.) Between 1850 and 1914, nevertheless, no part of the West had a Chinese presence comparable to the Western presence in Shanghai, where large European and American settlements featured houses, shops, and factories in Euro-American style.

Industrializing Shanghai became a major magnet for migrants from large parts of China. Broadly speaking, skilled workers came from the south to work in seaport trades and craft shops, while peasants from the north moved disproportionately into work such as rickshaw pulling, construction labor, and lower-level factory jobs. Women and men alike migrated in well-defined streams, sometimes singly and sometimes as families, but in Shanghai they moved into gender-segregated jobs. Like migrants in other parts of the world, workers from all regions of China arrived in smaller streams linking particular places of origin with particular workplaces and trades. Worker organization reflected that reality; for the most part, Shanghai's workers built their organizations around native places. That form of organization inhibited some kinds of collective action, but promoted others. On one side,

fragmentation into native-place groups hindered organization of workers across whole classes or industries. On the other, it integrated most workers into well-knit networks of familiar people who could act together within their own spheres. In 1853–55, for example, guilds of workers from the south spearheaded a rebellion that took over Shanghai for eighteen months.

The same organizations dominated strike activity. If skilled male workers from the south predominated in the higher levels of labor organizations, they did not monopolize collective action. Of the thirty-three strikes recorded in Shanghai between 1895 and 1910, in fact, relatively unskilled women workers – especially silk spinners – carried out twenty-five. In Shanghai, most nineteenth-century strikes occurred in the course of resistance to wage cuts, speed-ups, and other management attempts to get more work for less money. By the early twentieth century, however, Shanghai's workers were regularly striking for higher wages, better working conditions, and control over hiring. In 1911, for example, Cantonese woodworkers in the shipyards struck for higher wages and for exclusion of lower-paid workers from Ningbo; they won on both counts. With the great revolution of that year, the new government guaranteed workers the right to associate and abolished the stringent penalties for striking enacted by the Qing regime. Labor organizations multiplied and either formed or affiliated with political parties.

Between then and World War I, workers began forming coalitions that crossed the barriers of localities and trades. They spoke the language of class conflict; in 1912, a skilled workers' league in a Shanghai arsenal declared that "Craftsmen are like laborers and the arsenal is like a capitalist. The laborers must escape from the stranglehold of the capitalist." In Shanghai and other Chinese industrial centers, organized workers were participating widely in local struggles and national political movements by the time of World War I.

The Boxer Rebellion

Nationalist movements also attracted considerable support in China. Japan defeated China swiftly in the war of 1894–95, which put Taiwan under Japanese control until 1945. That military humiliation stimulated nationalist movements for resistance to foreigners and for reform of China's institutions. Anti-Christian mobilizations occurred repeatedly during the 1890s. The **Boxer Rebellion** provides a case in point. Observers misnamed the insurgents because one of their central rituals involved calling down a popular god, going into trances, and dancing dizzily while waving swords in a parody of combat. During the rebellion, a poster put up in Beijing announced that:

The supernaturally assisted Boxers ... have only arisen because devils have plagued the North China Plain. They have urged people to believe in Christianity, which is to usurp Heaven. They do not respect the gods or Buddhas, and are forgetful of their ancestors. These men have no principles in their human relationships ... The rain does not fall. The ground has dried up. All this has happened because the Christian churches have put a stop to the workings of Heaven. The gods are angry, and the immortals vexed ... If you want to drive away the devils, it will not take much effort. Pull up the railway lines! Smash the great steamships! ... Once all the devils have been slaughtered, the great Qing dynasty will enjoy a peaceful ascendancy.

The Boxers did not rebel against the regime, but acted against the foreigners they saw as undermining the regime. They described themselves as true patriots. Box 9.5 gives a Chinese government official's description of the Boxers' entry into Beijing. In 1900, Boxer forces besieged foreign embassies in Beijing. An international force including Americans drove them out and imposed heavy reparations on China; it was the first time American troops ever fought on Chinese soil.

After the Boxer Rebellion, urban Chinese activists increasingly adopted the standard means of social movements: associations, meetings, demonstrations, petitions, electoral participation, and politically oriented strikes. In 1905–06, Chinese activists carried on a widespread and relatively effective boycott of American goods in response to mistreatment of Chinese immigrants in the USA. The revolution of 1911 brought together several of these currents: anti-foreign, anti-Qing, and pro-reform. It also weakened the central state's capacity. Map 9.1 gives a sense of the breakup of the Chinese empire then underway. Warlords and separatists seized power in many parts of China. Not until the communist revolution of 1949 did a new regime succeed in taking over the whole of China.

9.7 MEXICAN STRUGGLES, 1850–1914

China lost Taiwan (1874) and Korea (1885) to the expanding Japanese empire during the nineteenth century, and suffered Russian occupation of Manchuria after the Boxer rising. When Japan roundly defeated Russia in their war of 1904–05, Japanese forces took over part of Manchuria. The treaty ports also established a serious foreign presence in China. Still, most of China escaped foreign colonialism. Central and South America had a very different experience, largely conquered by Europeans after 1500, mostly integrated into European colonial administrations, but forming a great many independent countries and self-governing colonies during the nineteenth century. Mexico and Argentina offer contrasting pictures of postcolonial experience between 1850 and 1914. Mexico represented the northern end, Argentina the southern end, of Spain's colonial empire. But with early nineteenth-century independence, the two countries moved in rather different directions, with Mexico deeply affected by its adjacency to the United States, and Argentina establishing extensive, independent relations with Europe.

As Napoleon seized control of Spain in 1808, the Spanish imperial province of New Spain – Mexico, the rest of Central America, plus the Spanish Caribbean – began to stir with demands for independence. After plentiful bloodshed and oscillation, Mexico became definitively independent in 1820. At that point, the new country occupied not only its present territory, but also Texas, New Mexico, Arizona, and California. By 1850, Mexico had passed through another thirty years of war, including devastating wars with US-backed Texans (1836) and the United States itself (1846–48). In those wars and the coerced sale of a substantial strip along the new border (1853), Mexico lost the northern half of its former territory.

For the next sixty years, military leaders and regional strongmen usually ruled the country, often engaged in fighting each other, and spent a significant part of their energy holding

Box 9.5 The Boxers' Arrival in Beijing

A Chinese official gave this sympathetic description of the arrival of Boxer rebels in Beijing in 1900:

Tens of thousands of Boxers (tuan-min) have come from all parts in the past few days. Most seem to be simple country folk who make their living by farming.

They have neither leaders directing them nor potent weapons. They provide their own traveling expenses and eat only millet and corn. Seeking neither fame nor fortune, they fight without regard for their own lives and are prepared to sacrifice themselves on the field

of battle. They come together without prior agreement, a great host all of one mind. They wish only to kill foreigners and Christians and do not harm the common people. From this perspective, it seems that they are fighting for righteousness.

Map 9.1 China: foreign possessions and spheres of influence about 1900

down resistance and revolt by indigenous people. Nevertheless, a broad political division grew up between Liberals (who generally opposed church power and tried to promote capitalist development) and Conservatives (who generally aligned themselves with the church, the military, and great landlords). Liberals managed to establish manhood suffrage in 1857, although they maintained indirect elections to federal offices. They also dissolved landholding Indian communities and nationalized church property. Under the war-shaken Liberal regime of Benito Juárez, much of this land moved rapidly into the hands of Juárez supporters. As the regime delayed repayment of its international debts, a European task force invaded (1861). Although the other European powers withdrew, French troops toppled Juárez and installed Archduke Maximilian of Bavaria as emperor (1864). Maximilian lasted until 1867, when Liberal armies defeated his forces. Maximilian died before a Mexican firing squad.

Military struggles for power continued until General Porfirio Díaz seized power in 1876, imposing a dictatorship (known

in Mexico as the Porfiriato) that lasted until 1910. During that long regime, railroads, mines, commercial agriculture, and small-scale manufacturing all increased Mexico's involvement in the international economy, especially in trade with the United States. Railroads first linked Mexico and the USA in 1885. American investments began pouring into Northern Mexico, and American financiers developed heightened interest in the Mexican government's policies.

Economic expansion did not produce democratic politics. Díaz built up the central state's capacity, and diminished the power of local communities. In the countryside, Díaz established a brutal force of marshals called the *rurales*. Under Díaz, both exploited workers and dispossessed Indian villagers engaged intermittently in violent resistance. Peasants of Tomochic, Chihuahua state, rebelled in 1892 against government seizure of their land, declaring that they would follow God's law instead of the government's. The government lost more than 500 troops in putting down their rebellion. On the whole, nevertheless, workers, peasants, and Indian communities lost political ground under the Porfiriato.

Some opposition to the regime did begin to form in Northern Mexico among commercial farmers, small capitalists, clandestinely organized workers, and revolutionaries based across the border in the United States. About 250 strikes (inspired in part by returned migrants who had worked with radicals in the USA) occurred during the Porfiriato. They faced forceful repression. American volunteers and *rurales*, for example, put down the Cananea strike of 1906, while the army and police joined *rurales* in killing 200 strikers at Río Blanco (1907). Porfirio Díaz did not tolerate open opposition.

Priding himself on his modern ideas, nevertheless, in 1908 Díaz promised to allow the formation of opposition parties, never expecting anyone to take him seriously. But in 1910 Francisco Madero, a landowner from the north, challenged Díaz in the election. When Díaz had him imprisoned, Madero called for the Mexican people to rise up against the dictator, touching off armed revolt around the country. Anti-Díaz forces united temporarily to overthrow the regime. Madero became president in 1911.

That did not settle the unrest. In the central Mexican state of Morelos, large plantation owners dominated small farmers. Since the 1880s, they had expanded their mechanized plantations, exporting cane and beet sugar to take advantage of the global trade boom. By the 1900s, Morelos, Hawaii, and Puerto Rico were the most modern sugar producers in the world. But intense competition forced the plantation owners to continue to expand their operations, squeezing out independent farmers with political and economic pressure. Díaz, a creature of the planter class, gave them special tax breaks, and built the railroads that brought their crops to foreign markets.

Emiliano Zapata

With Díaz's downfall, the villagers of Morelos elected Emiliano Zapata (1879–1919) to defend their interests (see Figure 9.4). Zapata led an agrarian revolution in Morelos to protect his people, the small farmers. He soon turned hostile to Madero and the federal forces in Mexico City, who refused to recognize the power of his farmers' movement. General Victoriano Huerta, Madero's military commander, launched an invasion of Morelos. Meanwhile, Pancho Villa (1878–1923) led a turbulent group of drifters, marauders, railroad laborers, and refugees in his own separate movement in the north, at times raiding US territory.

Unable to quell internal rebellions, Madero soon lost support from radicals, the professional military, the wealthy, and the United States. In the course of a 1913 rebellion, the US

Figure 9.4 Emiliano Zapata was the leader of a Mexican agricultural rebellion that stressed the localism and provincialism so characteristic of peasant revolutionaries. Radical demands for the redivision of the land combined with a deep suspicion of the state.

ambassador authorized President Madero's murder and Madero's replacement by Victoriano Huerta. In 1914, US forces occupied the city of Veracruz, forcing General Huerta into exile. The revolution had split into three factions who could not cooperate with each other: Venustiano Carranza, representing the centralizing government in Mexico City, Villa's rovers in the north, and Zapata's agrarian rebels in the south. Federal forces invaded Morelos in 1916, but Zapata organized guerrilla warfare to drive them out. He was killed in an ambush in 1919, but his followers continued his agrarian program. In 1920, when Carranza was overthrown by Alvaro Obregon, in alliance with the **Zapatistas** (supporters of Zapata's movement), the farmers of Morelos gained genuine power in the central government and a commitment to defend their lands against encroachment. In 1934 Mexico, unlike the rest of Latin America, enacted genuine land

Box 9.6 The First Zapatista Declaration (1911)

Emiliano Zapata of Mexico's Morelos State led peasant land occupations and distributions during the revolution that began in 1910, overthrowing the long-term dictator Porfirio Díaz. When revolutionary leader Francisco Madero became president and resisted land reform, Zapata issued the Plan of Ayala (November 28, 1911), calling for a more radical revolution. After repeated internal struggles and repeated interventions by the United States, in 1917 Mexico finally adopted a constitution including land redistribution among its many reforms. Zapata then maintained armed resistance to the new regime's rightward drift, until the government lured him into a fake meeting and had him killed in 1919, at the age of 40. One paragraph of the many complaints against Madero in the 1911 Ayala Plan ran thus:

Taking into consideration that the so-often-repeated Francisco I. Madero has tried with the brute force of bayonets to shut up and to drown in blood the pueblos who ask, solicit, or demand from him the fulfillment of the revolution's promises, calling them bandits and rebels, condemning them to a war of extermination without conceding or granting a single one of the guarantees which reason, justice, and the law prescribe; taking equally into consideration that the President of the Republic Francisco I. Madero has made of Effective Suffrage a bloody trick on the people, already against the will of the same people imposing Attorney José. Pino Suárez in the Vice-Presidency of the Republic, or Governors of the States designated by him, like the so-called General Ambrosio Figueroa, scourge and tyrant of the people of Morelos, or entering into scandalous co-operation with the científico party, feudal landlords, and oppressive bosses, enemies of the revolution proclaimed by him, so as to forge new chains and follow the pattern of a new dictatorship more shameful and more terrible than that of Porfirio Díaz, for it has been clear and patent that he has outraged the sovereignty of the States, trampling on the laws without any respect for lives or interests, as has happened in the State of Morelos, and others, leading them to the most horrendous anarchy which contemporary history registers.

In January 1994, a self-styled Zapatista Army for National Liberation captured four towns in the state of Chiapas in declared opposition to the Mexican government's participation in the North American Free Trade Agreement of 1992. Led by the mysterious Subcomandante Marcos, the new Zapatistas issued their own radical Lancandona Declaration, named for the nearby jungle but clearly adopting the model of the Ayala Plan.

reform, protecting agrarian communities and dismantling large plantations. Box 9.6 sketches out elements of a Zapatista political program.

Weak-state Mexico produced many a revolutionary rising between 1850 and 1914. But social movements in the form of special-purpose associations, public meetings, demonstrations, petitions, and sustained campaigns did not occur. Those standard accompaniments of competitive elections and democratic politics did not even start to glimmer in Mexico until after World War I.

9.8 STATES AND SOCIAL MOVEMENTS IN ARGENTINA

Like South Africa, Argentina took shape as a European colony, but a colony much less closely controlled by its colonial power than twentieth-century South Africa. Spain began conquering substantial parts of southern South America in 1516, only twenty-four years after Columbus' first voyage to the Caribbean. For two centuries, Spain drew massive supplies of gold and silver from South America, but did relatively little to encourage trade or manufacturing in its colonies there. By the later eighteenth century, nevertheless, the two major ports on the River Plate, Montevideo and Buenos Aires, had become important exporters of hides and beef from the cattle ranches in their hinterlands. In 1776, the Spanish Crown established a new viceroyalty of the River Plate based in Buenos Aires and covering much of what we now know as Argentina, Uruguay, Paraguay, and Bolivia, plus a significant chunk of today's Peru. After repeated struggles as French forces invaded Spain, in 1810 a group of local people in Buenos Aires threw out the Spanish viceroy and declared independence. Over the next ten years, the new masters of Buenos Aires fought off royalist forces, but lost Paraguay, Uruguay, and Bolivia to new independence movements. From the 1820s onward, a separate Argentina occupied something like

Map 9.2 Latin America in the first half of the twentieth century

its present territory. Within that territory, however, struggles for political and military control continued for almost a century. The thinly settled country divided roughly into three sorts of region: a commercial and industrial sector centered on the dominant port of Buenos Aires, extensive cattle ranching in the Buenos Aires hinterland, and areas of Indian settlement further away. Buenos Aires already served as a major port for export of silver and raw materials under Spanish rule. It remained the country's major connector with Europe (especially Great Britain)

during the nineteenth century. British capital came to dominate Argentine markets later in the century. Until the demise of slavery, Argentina's cattle farmers shipped hides to Europe, but made a significant part of their money by salting beef for the feeding of slaves elsewhere in Latin America.

Before 1850, almost all of today's Argentina south of Buenos Aires plus about a quarter of the north – well over half the country's present area – still counted as Indian land. Even in the country's upper half, European-origin people continued to battle Indians just as ruthlessly as their US contemporaries. Within the Spanish-speaking population, divisions ran deep as well. On one side, merchants and manufacturers of Buenos Aires generally sought to impose the city's authority on the whole country. On the other, regional leaders and ranchers tried to maintain a federal system or full independence from the capital.

Juan Manuel de Rosas (1793–1877), a provincial leader, invaded Buenos Aires with his federalist forces in 1829, establishing an Argentine Confederation. His dictatorship survived until 1852, when a new civil war ousted him. (Rosas died in English exile twenty-five years later; his remains lay in a Southampton cemetery until the semi-revolutionary Argentine government of 1989 brought them back to Buenos Aires as a gesture of reconciliation between civilians and the military.) In the following year, Rosas's successors established Argentina's first formal constitution. Among other things, the constitution decreed universal manhood suffrage. Serious state consolidation, often modeled on political structures already long established in the province of Buenos Aires, then began. During the 1860s, Argentina finally began laying down the organization and infrastructure of a national state: army, treasury, national currency, government securities, judiciary, customs service, postal service, newspapers, railroads, national elections, political parties. State forces started pushing aggressively into Indian territories. Central state capacity began to rise.

Creation of national governmental institutions did not end Argentine strife. Within a nominally republican constitution, democratic institutions remained fragile. Despite manhood suffrage for Argentine citizens, mass immigration meant that many residents lacked citizenship, electoral participation among citizens remained narrow, full-fledged political parties did not exist, patron–client politics prevailed, and military leaders could always send their troops to the polls as a bloc. Public politics regularly splintered into warring factions; battles between national army units and regional militias over the disputed election of 1880, for example, left a reported 3,000 dead. At the edges of European settlement, Argentine rulers fought fierce Indian resistance to encroachment by cattle ranchers. The ranchers, to be sure, considered the Indians they were displacing to be savages, rustlers, and marauders. Like many US presidents of the nineteenth century, General Julio Roca made his reputation as an exterminator of Indians, especially during his so-called "conquest of the wilderness" in southern Argentina during 1879. The bloody election of 1880 won Roca the Argentine presidency.

International wars, civil wars, and armed rebellions continued into the 1890s, but through the combat a shaky Argentine state survived. Argentina survived in part because its economy was expanding, with Buenos Aires a more and more indispensable co-ordinator of national economic life. Despite military turmoil, during the later nineteenth century Argentina became a major exporter of wool, flax, grain, and beef to world markets, as a significant manufacturing sector began to grow up in and around Buenos Aires. The number of manufacturing firms rose from under 3,000 in 1853 to 23,300 in 1895 and 48,800 in 1914. In place of the River Plate's mudflats, Buenos Aires's authorities dug a major deepwater port during the 1890s. Immigration sped up, especially from Italy and Spain; between 1871 and 1914 almost 6 million immigrants arrived in Argentina, and more than 3 million stayed, in a country whose total population only reached 4 million in 1895. Starting in the 1860s and greatly accelerating in the 1880s, British investment pumped capital into Argentina.

Rise of the Argentine Social Movement

Until the late nineteenth century, Argentina saw little of the social movement politics that already prevailed in Western Europe and North America. In 1889, nevertheless, Buenos Aires students formed an organization called the Youth Civic Union (Unión Cívica de la Juventud) to oppose government policies. The organization soon attracted non-student followers and evolved into a general Civic Union. In 1890 the Union staged a Buenos Aires demonstration with 30,000 participants. Later that year a popular militia aligned with the Union attacked government forces in a failed rebellion, only to discover that major politicians who had encouraged the attack had behind its back made a deal to change the government. The 1890s brought organization-based popular politics onto the national scene, but against a distinctive Argentine background of military and strongman politics.

Between 1890 and 1914, associational life flowered in Argentina. A broad, semi-conspiratorial movement of people who called themselves Radicals connected numerous local middle-class political clubs with a hierarchy of party committees. They adopted standard social movement means, including mass meetings and demonstrations. Several anarchist federations organized workers in the Buenos Aires region. In addition to their own demonstrations on such occasions as May Day and New Year's Day, anarchists originated half a dozen general strikes in and around Buenos Aires between 1899 and 1910. When they threatened to sabotage festivities for the centennial of Argentine independence in 1910, however, the government began arresting anarchists as vigilantes and smashed their meeting places. Meanwhile, socialists who distinguished themselves sharply from the anarchists initiated standard social movement campaigns for working-class credit, housing, education, divorce, women's suffrage, and an eight-hour day. Their Socialist Party, founded in 1894, brought together workers with professionals and some small manufacturers. By the time the party elected its first member of Argentina's Chamber of Deputies in 1904, social movement politics had taken firm root in the country.

Conclusion   All the countries this chapter has visited engaged with Western imperialism in one way or another. By 1850, the United States, Mexico, and Argentina had all wrestled themselves free of European colonial masters. Argentina never became much of a colonial power, and Mexico practiced all of its colonialism internally. Between 1850 and 1914, however, the United States began gathering colonies of its own, especially colonies from the newly disintegrating Spanish empire. China lost only peripheral territories to colonial control, but Western powers including the United States established multiple enclaves in its coastal regions and tried repeatedly to turn the Chinese economy to Western ends. Great Britain made serious inroads in South Africa during the wars of the French Revolution, and made strenuous efforts to take over the whole country during the 1870s. But both black Africans and Dutch-origin Boers resisted mightily for another thirty years. South Africa nevertheless became a major British colony after the Boer War of 1899–1902, with full-fledged imperial status from 1910 (see Map 9.3). Great Britain and France were already becoming two of the world's imperial powers in 1850, and both extended their empires well into the twentieth century.

In each of these cases, changes in the state resulted in part from the variable relationship to imperialism. Throwing off imperial rule left the United States, Mexico, and Argentina with fragmented polities; they only made their ways to the more centralized states of 1914 through multiple internal wars and the hard-fought success of centralizing movements. Interaction with Western powers weakened the Chinese state, and left it in warring factions after the revolution of 1911. British intervention directly created the new South African state of 1910. Historians are still debating the effects of imperial conquest on France and Britain – after we deduct the costs of empire, for example, did it actually bring net profits to the home countries? But imperial expansion surely produced more extensive, higher-capacity states in the two imperial countries.

Social movement experience differed accordingly. Anti-slavery movements pitted metropolitan activists against their own colonial interests in Great Britain and France. In the United States, anti-slavery activism set one section of the metropole against another. In the colonies, social movement tactics made it possible for anti-colonial organizers to use the techniques of metropolitan politics against their imperial masters. Yet in all our countries, as electoral politics became more salient, associational life freer, workers better organized, and policing more regular, social movement forms such as public meetings, petitions, demonstrations, and lobbying loomed larger and larger in popular politics.

Growth of states and social movements did not exhaust the world's politics between 1850 and 1914. The American Civil War both transformed the American polity and disrupted world trade in cotton and textiles, with repercussions from England to Argentina. European colonial expansion reached fever frenzy during those years. Growth of international markets for manufactured and agricultural goods gave tariffs, customs barriers, and freedom of the seas new political importance. International wars grew fiercer, with World War I becoming history's most destructive conflict up to that point. Western countries, Japan, and some European colonies edged modestly toward democracy, providing models for later democratization. Not just revolutionary movements, but modernizing revolutions occurred in China, Russia, Mexico, France, and elsewhere. Both the Ottoman and Austro-Hungarian empires began to disintegrate. Much more political change was occurring than state formation and social movement proliferation.

Still, the formation of high-capacity states and the expansion of social movement politics made big differences to human lives between 1850 and 1914. Strong states could oppress and exploit people more effectively, but under democratic conditions they also provided the means for common people to seize new benefits. Mass public education, railroads, urban

Map 9.3 South Africa, early twentieth century

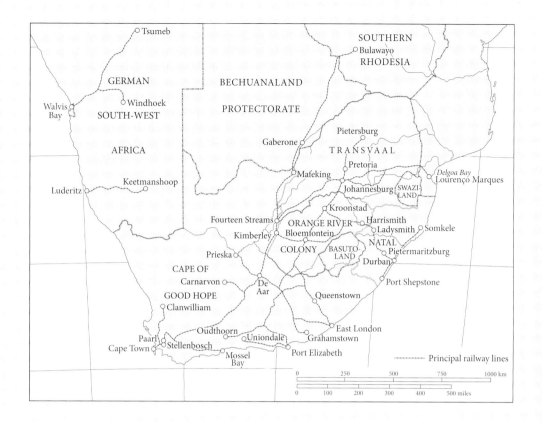

water systems, social insurance, postal and telegraph services, hospital construction, parks, and police protection all depended at least in part on high-capacity governments. Social movements offered a new kind of popular voice different from armed rebellion, passive resistance, and patronage politics. In significant parts of the world, they promoted the abolition of slavery, city planning, governmental protection of workers' rights, and popular participation in national decision-making. Although as of 1914 New Zealand, Australia, and Finland were alone in granting full voting rights in national elections to women, elsewhere women were mobilizing widely, using social movement methods as they did so. In Europe and the Americas, women were effectively demanding reform with regard to employment, working conditions, marriage, and property as increasingly they called for the vote as well. The twentieth century became the great age of popular social movements and of states that responded to them.

Study Questions

(1) Name two important differences between the popular politics of China and the United States around 1900. What explains the differences?

(2) How did increases in state capacity affect popular politics across the world as a whole between 1850 and 1914? Use two countries to back up your argument.

(3) Why, where, and when did social movements become standard forms of politics between 1850 and 1914?

(4) How did competitive national elections promote social movements? Give examples.

(5) Who advocated the end of the slave trade and of slavery itself? How, when, and where?

(6) Why did the creation of uniformed, salaried police forces and the legalization of industrial strikes tend to occur in the same periods, country by country?

(7) Name at least one major difference in the histories of the French, Argentine, and South African regimes between 1850 and 1914, then spell out the implications of the difference for popular politics in the three countries.

Suggested Reading

CARLOS A. FORMENT, *Democracy in Latin America, 1760–1900,* vol. I: *Civic Selfhood and Public Life in Mexico and Peru* (University of Chicago Press, 2003). Forment gives incomparable detail on associational life and popular politics in two contrasting countries, with strong implications for the rest of Latin America.

JOHN MASON HART, *Revolutionary Mexico: The Coming and Process of the Mexican Revolution* (Berkeley: University of California Press, 1987). Hart explains how the twentieth-century Mexican regime emerged from decades of revolutionary struggle.

NICHOLAS N. KITTRIE AND ELDON D. WEDLOCK, JR. (eds.), *The Tree of Liberty: A Documentary History of Rebellion and Political Crime in America* (Baltimore, MD: Johns Hopkins University Press, 1986). This is an unparalleled collection of primary documents on repression, rebellion, and protest in North America from 1496 to 1985.

DAVID MONTGOMERY, *Citizen Worker: The Experience of Workers in the United States with Democracy and the Free Market During the Nineteenth Century* (Cambridge University Press, 1993). This study explores how American workers coped and organized in a time of industrialization and expanding capitalism.

ELIZABETH J. PERRY, *Challenging the Mandate of Heaven: Social Protest and State Power in China* (Armonk, NY: Sharpe, 2002). A close observer of China past and present studies contentious connections between successive states and their citizens in that great country.

DAVID ROCK, *Argentina, 1516–1987* (Berkeley: University of California Press, 1987). This is a standard account of a complicated history from European colonization to twentieth-century political change.

LEONARD THOMPSON, *A History of South Africa* (New Haven, CT: Yale University Press, 1990). From before Europeans arrived to the height of the anti-Apartheid struggle, the history of what became South Africa overflows with confrontations of states and citizens.

CHARLES TILLY, *Social Movements, 1768–2004* (Boulder, CO: Paradigm Press, 2004). Tilly's book is a century-by-century history of social movements throughout the world, with special reference to connections between social movements and democracy.

Glossary

abolition(ism): In the United Kingdom and the United States, the campaign to abolish slavery, from the 1780s to the 1860s.

bottom-up nationalism: Claims by a population under the jurisdiction of a given state to be a distinct nation and therefore to deserve autonomy, independence, or a special form of rule.

Boxer Rebellion: Popular anti-Western movement in China, 1899–1900, which also accused the (Manchu) Chinese Qing regime of being foreign.

democracy: The combination of relatively broad and equal citizenship; effective citizens' voices with respect to governmental personnel, resources, and activities; and protection of citizens, especially members of minorities, from arbitrary action by agents of government.

gendarmes: In France and other countries that adopted the French style of policing, the police force specializing in patrolling highways and rural areas.

high-capacity: High-capacity governments exercise extensive control over their people, resources, and activities.

low-capacity: Low-capacity governments exercise little control over their people, resources, and activities.

Manchu: Nomadic warriors, originally from Manchuria, who conquered China in 1636–44, and established the Qing dynasty (1644–1912), which nineteenth- and twentieth-century Chinese nationalists often treated as foreign domination.

social movement: A campaign in support of or opposition to publicly articulated programs by means of associations, meetings, demonstrations, petitions, electoral participation, strikes, and related means.

Taiping Rebellion: China's religiously inspired anti-foreign attacks and mass mobilizations of the 1850s and 1860s. It constituted a massive civil war against the Qing dynasty.

top-down nationalism: Claims by rulers to define and impose the national interest and the proper national culture.

Zapatistas: Name for followers of Emiliano Zapata in Mexico (1911–19), later borrowed by activists in Chiapas, Mexico (1994–).

10 Nationalism and anti-colonialism

Timeline	
1832	Giuseppe Mazzini (1805–72) founds Young Italy organization.
1837	Invention of the telegraph. Some dispute exists about the actual inventors and the initial patent holders. The Englishmen William Fothergill Cooke and Charles Wheatstone (1837) and the American Samuel F.B. Morse (1837) have good claims. The Russian Baron Schilling von Carstatt (1832) would have been a contender had the tsar not cancelled his contract. Such disputes give a good sense of the international scientific competition going on in this era. It was a great age for international patent lawyers.
1848	Revolutions shake several countries in Europe, including Italian- and German-speaking regions. Babi revolts in Iran.
1849	Short-lived Roman Republic, led by Mazzini and Garibaldi, is established in February and overthrown in July.
1853–56	Crimean War pits Russia against an alliance of France, Britain, and the Ottoman empire.
1856	Treaty of Paris ends Crimean War. The Black Sea is demilitarized, and the Ottoman empire is guaranteed integrity by France and Britain. Ottoman Reform Decree makes Christians and Muslims equal under the law in this empire. British government of India annexes the kingdom of Oudh.
1857–59	Great Rebellion ("Mutiny") in India. British reassert power through military. British government rule supplants East India Company administration.
1860–61	Giuseppe Garibaldi allies with Genoese ruler Victor Emmanuel to overthrow the Kingdom of Naples and Sicily. Kingdom of Italy proclaimed.
1864	Prussian war against Denmark over Danish claims to duchies of Schleswig and Holstein. Duchies are gained jointly by Prussia and Austria. The two begin to fight over control of these territories.

1866	Austro-Prussian War. Prussia wins, gains Hanover, Nassau, Hesse-Kassel, Schleswig-Holstein, and Frankfurt am Main. Prussian ally Kingdom of Italy annexes Venetia from Austria.
1869	Suez Canal is completed.
1870–71	Franco-Prussian War. Prussia wins.
1870	All People's Association founded in Bombay. Napoleon III of France deposed. Beginning of Third Republic in France. Kingdom of Italy annexes Rome. Pope Pius IX declares himself prisoner in the Vatican.
1871	Treaty of Frankfurt ends Franco-Prussian War. Germany gains Alsace-Lorraine. German-speaking principalities south of the Main join Prussian-dominated German Empire.
1876	The Indian Association founded in Calcutta. First Ottoman Constitutional Revolution. Sultan Abdulaziz overthrown by popular revolt. Abdulhamid II succeeds to throne. First Ottoman parliament is elected and a constitution crafted. Egypt declares bankruptcy, overwhelmed by interest payments on loans contracted from Europe. Queen Victoria crowned Queen-Empress of India.
1877–78	Russo-Turkish War. Russia wins.
1878	Sultan Abdulhamid II puts constitution on hold and reverts to absolute monarchy.
1879	European powers depose Ottoman viceroy of Egypt, Isma`il.
1881–82	Movement for parliamentary rule in Egypt. Among leaders is Col Ahmad `Urabi.
1881	France invades Tunisia and makes it a colony.
1882	Britain invades Egypt, makes it a "protectorate" until 1922. European colonial "Scramble for Africa" begins.
1885	Indian National Congress holds its first annual convention. Sir Charles Gordon and other Europeans killed by forces of the Mahdi in Khartoum, begining British war of conquest in the Sudan.
1886	German colony of Tanganyika established (in what is now Tanzania).
1888	German insensitivity provokes riots among Muslim townspeople in Tanganyika.
1889	Dissident Committee for Union and Progress ("Young Turks") founded in Ottoman empire.
1898	Kitchener and Anglo-Egyptian army defeat Mahdist forces at Omdurman in the Sudan. Marks beginning of British colonial period in that country.
1904–07	Uprising in Southwest Africa (Namibia) against German colonialism. Germans put it down with concentration camps and machine gun fire.

1905–07	Maji Maji uprising in southeast Tanganyika against German colonialism. Persian Constitutional Revolution in Iran. Parliament established.
1905	The British partition Bengal province into (largely Muslim) West Bengal and (largely Hindu) East Bengal, provoking nationalist rallies and boycotts.
1907	Counter-revolution by Iranian Muhammad Ali Shah, absolutism re-established.
1908	Young Turk Revolution in Istanbul. Return of constitution and parliament.
1909	Muhammad Ali Shah overthrown and constitutional regime reinstated in Iran. Sultan Abdulhamid II deposed after he attempts to lead a counter-revolution. Party of Union and Progress dominates Ottoman parliament from 1909–11. John Morley, Secretary of State for British India, allows the majority of members of the central and provincial legislative councils to be elected by propertied Indians (Morley-Minto Reforms).
1911	Bengal is reunited.
1912–1913	Balkan Wars. Ottomans lose Crete and Balkan territory. Albania created.
1912	Italy forcibly annexes Libya from the Ottoman empire.
1913	Military coup by Young Turk officers in Istanbul.
1914	Young Turk officers take Ottoman empire into World War I on side of Germany.

The life of Ana Maria Ribeiro di Garibaldi illustrates for us the changing nature of national identities in the mid nineteenth century. Born into a family of fishermen in 1817 in Morinhos, a small town on the coast of Brazil, she married another village fisherman named Manuel in 1835. It was apparently not a happy marriage. Only four years later, a rebel ship showed up off the shore of Morinhos. The captain caught sight of her and rowed to shore, saying "You will be mine." She got in the rowboat and went off with him for the rest of her life.

The captain was Giuseppe Garibaldi, a failed revolutionary who had been involved in a revolt in Piedmont (what is now northwestern Italy). Sentenced to death, he fled, arriving in South America in 1836. He became a mercenary for a small state, Rio Grande del Sul, which was trying to secede from Brazil. So it was that he was captaining the Rio Pardo schooner when it stopped off Morinhos in 1839. During the following year, the Brazilian navy closed in on him, and he left the service of the rebel state, which seemed increasingly doomed.

He and Anita then drove a herd of cattle to Montevideo and tried to enter civilian life without much success. They probably married in 1842. She maintained that Manuel had died, but many have cast doubt on this claim. She was in any case accepted as Garibaldi's wife, and she bore him several children. Three lived. In 1842, Giuseppe took command of the Uruguayan navy

and fought an Argentine dictator. In 1843 at Montevideo he organized the Red Shirts, an Italian division. He even defended Montevideo itself some years later.

In 1848 revolution broke out in several parts of the Italian peninsula, as it did in many European capitals. Giuseppe at first offered his services to the pope, if the latter would agree to lead a movement for Italian unification. The pope rejected this offer. The Garibaldis, accompanied by eighty Red Shirts, then hastened to Rome that year to support the new Roman Republic created by revolutionaries there. The republic could not hold out, however. The Austrian and papal armies closed in. The Garibaldis and its other partisans were forced to retreat, heading for the countryside. At a farmhouse near the village of Guiccioli di Mandrioli not far from Ravenna, Anita Garibaldi died. Historians dispute whether she died from the simple exhaustion of the battle and the withdrawal, or whether she was giving birth to a fifth child when the end came. Garibaldi went on to play a key role in the creation of the Kingdom of Italy in the early 1860s, as we will see. Anita, a Brazilian-born woman from a fishing village, married an Italian who first tried to help create a new state carved out of Brazil. Then they defended Uruguay from the Argentine dictatorship. In the end, Anita risked and then lost her life for the sake of the short-lived Roman Republic. Her "national" identity and loyalties changed every few years during her dramatic life, and she broke many taboos in forcefully pursuing a vision of liberty and national realization.

This chapter explores:

- The emergence of nationalism as a way of thinking about a society, in contrast to earlier monarchic, imperial, or clan-based conceptions, and the forms of colonialism that spurred nationalist reactions.
- The various and sometimes coinciding forces that could promote nationalism, including international political intrigue, bottom-up worker and peasant nationalism, and top-down leadership by political elites.
- The nineteenth-century communications revolution that made co-ordinated nationalist campaigns increasingly viable.
- The development of nationalism in a range of geographical areas, including Italy, Germany, the Ottoman empire and its Turkish heartland, Iran, and Japan.

10.1 NATIONALISM AS A WAY OF IMAGINING SOCIETY

In the modern period new forms of political organization emerged that radically reshaped the world's states. In the eighteenth century most of the world was ruled by various sorts of monarch, from paramount chiefs to emperors. They reigned over a number of different kinds of polity: clan, oligarchy, kingdom, and empire. Their realms were most often ethnic and linguistic patchworks and their troops were loyal to the monarch rather than devotees of a single nation. Their bureaucracies were usually limited, and personalities often played a bigger role than regulations and routine. The populace consisted of subjects of the king, not citizens. These subjects might have a special affection for the members of their ethnicity or the region where they were born and raised, but that region formed only one part of a larger realm over which the monarch presided. The religion to which the monarch adhered enjoyed special prerogatives and adherents of other faiths were often disadvantaged. Most people (especially women) were illiterate, with the exception of relatively small elites of aristocrats, bureaucrats, merchants, clergymen, and the better-off urban guildsmen. The languages of literacy tended to owe their primacy to religion (Latin, Arabic, Sanskrit) or bureaucratic tradition (Persian, Mandarin Chinese, Ottoman Turkish), or both. Bureaucrats often wrote in a special script that was impenetrable to ordinary readers. Local languages were seldom written, were not used in schooling, and had no state backing. They therefore were not standardized across

dialect, and were less uniform languages than a range of local usages. Most subjects were peasants, and agriculture was the major source of income for the agrarian state. City-dwellers formed a small proportion of the population. From time to time, a few republics or city-states arose, but these were so exceptional as to seem peculiar before the late eighteenth century.

Nations and Empires

In the course of the seventy years after 1850, most of the kingdoms and empires of the world were replaced by nation-states or colonial empires, and virtually the only monarchies that survived were ones that became constitutional in character. A widely accepted definition of **nationalism** is Ernest Gellner's dictum that it is the principle which holds that the political and national unit should be congruent. This is a good definition of the goals of nationalism as long as we remember that it states a political program rather than describing reality; that is, both the "political unit" and the "national unit" had to be made with struggle over time. Various writers conceived of the "national" unit in a multitude of ways. Historian Eric Hobsbawm has argued that the revolutionary-democratic idea of the "national" (as in the United States and France) extended the nation to all citizens, regardless of their original ethnicity, religion, or language, as long as they accepted the requirements of loyalty to the nation and made an effort to learn the majority language. Nineteenth-century Germans and some others, however, tended to think of the national unit as a dominant ethnicity. Thus, some nationalists believed that a distinct and exclusive "people" formed the basis for the nation. In 1815 Ernst Moritz Arndt argued that the fortunate Germans are an original people because they are not bastardized by alien peoples, they have not become "mongrels." It is important to note that in fact, modern science has demonstrated that all peoples have extensively intermarried with others all through history, and all are "mongrels." In the nineteenth century, however, races as separate blood-lines were thought by many to be a valid scientific category. German nationalists thus strove to see that the German-speaking peoples were encompassed by a single state. They had some successes, as we will see, in uniting various small principalities. But they failed in their comprehensive goal, since Austria and Switzerland remained separate from Germany, and significant German-speaking populations continued to exist in Eastern Europe and even on the Volga.

Two main sorts of actor have sought to shape nations, as Charles Tilly has argued. There are elite nationalists who seek to establish nation-states from the top down, as happened in nineteenth-century Japan or Germany. There are also popular groups, including peasants and workers, who seek a national identity as a framework for greater justice and equality, from the bottom up. Both kinds of process are important to most nationalisms, though one or the other tends to predominate.

If nationalism imagines a "national unit" and then tries to erect a single "political unit" around it, **colonialism** does the opposite. Colonialism was the project of one nation-state ruling over other peoples, depriving them of their own state, for military, strategic, or economic gain. It is often forgotten that nineteenth-century nationalism and colonialism went hand in hand. Paradoxically, the French were among the earliest to overthrow their monarch and establish a nation-state, but they then went on to alternate between empire and monarchy for decades, all the time building up a world empire in Africa and Asia. Thus, even when it gave up having an emperor in 1871, France was until the mid-1960s an imperial republic with many overseas possessions ruled by de facto viceroys.

Forms of Colonialism

Many nineteenth-century thinkers believed that there were "advanced" and "primitive" peoples. The advanced or civilized peoples deserved not only their own consolidated state but also to rule over the less advanced peoples. The colonized were thought of as juveniles who were incapable of ruling themselves as yet, and who needed to be tutored by the colonizing state, perhaps for a very long time. When Japan modernized and emerged as a military and diplomatic equal with Europe (underlined by its 1905 defeat of Russia), it sought colonies in Taiwan and Korea. Some colonies were merely administered, in a sort of bureaucratic colonialism. Others were part of a project of **settler colonialism**, so that, for instance, hundreds of thousands of French moved to Algeria. These settlers typically were awarded the choice land and came to occupy the highest economic and highest status niches in the colonized land. Although the direct economic benefit to the ruling country of the colony was sometimes small (and sometimes colonies cost more money to run than they generated for the colonizing government), the indirect benefits could be large. For instance, businesses of the colonizing country often had a captive market free from the competition of businesses based in other countries. British firms had a huge advantage in British India, and Dutch concerns had special privileges in the Dutch Indies. If we figure in the profits of private business and the strategic advantages, most colonial enterprises made economic and political sense. Economics was only one issue. Much of the impetus to colonialism was rooted rather in a quest for prestige or in rivalries with other great powers.

The colonized peoples over time tended to develop their own grievances and new social classes who imagined new national units (such as "India" or "Kenya"), for which they wanted to construct political units. They had the extra burden, however, of first throwing out the colonial state, which was often well entrenched, militarily superior, and backed by settlers from the imperial center. Anti-colonial struggles were often characterized by an implicit nationalism, but most often they began as expressions of discontent with the colonizer rather than as well-developed aspirations to a nation-state. In the colonial world, as well, there were popular forces, such as peasant revolts or artisan strikes, working for a national identity from the bottom up, and elite nationalists (landlords, bankers, wealthy politicians) who sought a nation that they could rule.

Revolutions in Communications and Technology Promote Nationalism

Nationalist movements were often aided by the nineteenth-century revolution in communications and transportation technology. Although printing was by the mid nineteenth century of old standing in Europe and East Asia, the 1800s often witnessed increases in popular literacy and an expansion in the quantity of newspapers and other politically oriented printed material. Roughly a third of Chinese could read and write at a basic level in the mid nineteenth century, and about half of the Japanese. The rates in Western Europe were often even higher, and grew through the century. Even in areas such as the Middle East and the Indian subcontinent, where printing had not been adopted on any significant scale before the nineteenth century and where, therefore, literacy rates were very low in world terms, there was a significant expansion of schooling and of the newspaper audience in the course of the century.

The rise of the telegraph and the building of telegraph lines throughout Europe and Asia, and even the laying of lines on the seabed across oceans, connected peoples in new ways and gave them tools for organizing. The first nationwide political protest in Iran, the 1891–92 revolt against the award to a British company by the shah (king) of a monopoly on the marketing of Iranian tobacco, was in part made possible by the ability of protesters in various cities to send telegrams to one another, co-ordinating their protests. Elsewhere, the railroad also increased links and mobility among people. This nineteenth-century version of the information revolution enabled new forms of political organization, such as nationwide political parties, to emerge from grassroots political action. In some countries industrialization aided the construction of nationalist movements, moving formerly isolated peasants into cities, giving them the opportunity to organize on the shop floor, and giving them nationwide political interests that often differed from those of the factory owners and government bureaucrats. Some have argued that economic markets helped create nations, but the preponderance of the evidence suggests instead that national markets, like national languages, are mainly fostered once the state has already been created. High rates of industrialization and urbanization affected the form of nationalist and anti-colonial movements, but were not pre-requisites for them.

10.2 ITALY

Italian unification was made possible by all three of the forces so far discussed, including international intrigue, bottom-up worker and peasant nationalists, and top-down elite politicians. The Italian experience inspired many nationalists in dozens of lands. The peninsula we now call Italy was a hodgepodge of smaller states, monarchies, the Papal States, and republics, with parts ruled by the French and Austro-Hungarian empires. In the northwest was the kingdom of Piedmont, which neighbored France and had border disputes with that state over Nice. The northeast was dominated by Austro-Hungary and the Venetian Republic. The south and the island of Sicily formed the Kingdom of Naples. As we have seen, since the 1820s, some intellectuals such as Giuseppe Mazzini (1805–72) had imagined a united Italy based on geography and broad linguistic and cultural heritage, and had spread this idea to statesmen, adventurers, and whoever among the public would listen to them (see Box 10.1). Among the visionaries Mazzini had inspired was another Giuseppe, Giuseppe Garibaldi (1807–82), originally a merchant seaman. We have heard about Garibaldi, who played an important but ultimately failing role in the revolution of 1848, in the vignette about his wife Anita at the beginning of this chapter.

The kingdom of Piedmont had a constitution and an elected national assembly that evolved through the 1850s into a parliament, so that its new king, Victor Emmanuel II, became a constitutional monarch. He had a reputation for standing up to the Austrians that was perhaps undeserved (the Austrians were easy on him because they saw him as a preferable alternative to urban radicals in places like Genoa, whom the king had actually had bombarded). Victor Emmanuel's image as an enlightened, constitutional ruler willing to champion Italian causes attracted to him the loyalty of Garibaldi and other radicals, who had earlier been staunch republicans. Great powers diplomacy and conflicts helped unleash a crisis in the late 1850s, but these schemes intersected with severe social discontents among Italy's peasants and workers and with the equally imaginative plotting of revolutionaries such as Garibaldi (who had returned to the peninsula).

Napoleon III and the Making of Modern Italy

In 1858–59 France's emperor, Napoleon III – a nephew of the great Napoleon – conspired with Piedmont to draw Austria into a war that could be portrayed as the fault of the Habsburgs in European public opinion, with an eye to pushing the Austrians out of the peninsula altogether. Piedmont would be much strengthened, and the whole area would become a French sphere of influence. The scheme aimed at consolidating the region into four kingdoms, among which Piedmont would be the strongest. Garibaldi was recruited to the plot and accepted Victor Emmanuel II as his leader. Despite some initial setbacks, the scheme worked. After some skirmishes and threats of a European peace conference, Austria demanded that Piedmont be disarmed. Victor Emmanuel refused. Austria invaded in April 1859. In May, Napoleon III came to the aid of Piedmont. In the summer of 1859 the French troops, brought to the front with new efficiency by railroad, and their Piedmontese allies succeeded in detaching the region of Lombardy from the Habsburgs, but then were forced to make a truce. Victor Emmanuel reluctantly accepted the armistice, which did not secure for him the end of the Habsburg presence in the region, since the French were not willing to pursue the war further and he was too weak to do so on his own.

Popular Revolt and the Making of Modern Italy

Piedmontese prestige grew so much because of the Austrian defeat that it gained enormous influence in the duchies of central Italy, which suffered popular revolutions in 1859. By early 1860 Piedmont was able to annex them, gaining French support for this move by giving up Nice and Savoy to France. In April of 1860, a popular uprising began on the island of Sicily in the Kingdom of Naples, and Garibaldi was persuaded by Piedmont officials to lead a small force of about 1,000 men to intervene on behalf of the popular forces. The peasant rebels, aided by Garibaldi's guerrillas and his experience in this sort of war, were able to defeat a much larger army of 25,000 men who vainly fought to retain the island for the king of Naples. Despite opposition from the conservative Piedmontese prime minister and from the French and British, but possibly with the secret encouragement of King Victor Emmanuel II, Garibaldi was able to cross from Sicily to the peninsula with over 3,000 men. There they joined up with peasant rebels who overthrew the king of Naples and handed the kingdom to him as its "dittatori" (civilian ruler). These events forced Victor Emmanuel to take more aggressive action, with all its risks, than he would have preferred. He sent his armies into the Papal States and annexed everything but the French-occupied city of Rome, then met Garibaldi in

Box 10.1 Giuseppe Mazzini: On Nationality

In "Europe: Its Conditions and Prospects" (1852) Giuseppe Mazzini presented a nationalist manifesto:

There are in Europe two great questions; or, rather, the question of the transformation of authority, that is to say, of the Revolution, has assumed two forms; the question which all have agreed to call social, and the question of nationalities. The first is more exclusively agitated in France, the second in the heart of the other peoples of Europe. I say, which all have agreed to call social, because, generally speaking, every great revolution is so far social, that it cannot be accomplished either in the religious, political, or any other sphere, without affecting social relations, the sources and the distribution of wealth; but that which is only a secondary consequence in political revolutions is now the cause and the banner of the movement in France. The question there is now, above all, to establish better relations between labour and capital, between production and consumption, between the workman and the employer . . .

It is probable that the European initiative, that which will give a new impulse to intelligence and to events, will spring from the question of nationalities. The social question may, in effect, although with difficulty, be partly resolved by a single people; it is an internal question for each . . . The question of nationality can only be resolved by destroying the treaties of 1815, and changing the map of Europe

and its public Law. The question of Nationalities, rightly understood, is the Alliance of the Peoples; the balance of powers based upon new foundations; the organisation of the work that Europe has to accomplish . . .

It was not for a material interest that the people of Vienna fought in 1848; in weakening the empire they could only lose power. It was not for an increase of wealth that the people of Lombardy fought in the same year . . . They struggled, they still struggle, as do Poland, Germany, and Hungary, for country and liberty; for a word inscribed upon a banner, proclaiming to the world that they also live, think, love, and labour for the benefit of all. They speak the same language, they bear about them the impress of consanguinity, they kneel beside the same tombs, they glory in the same tradition; and they demand to associate freely, without obstacles, without foreign domination, in order to elaborate and express their idea; to contribute their stone also to the great pyramid of history. It is something moral which they are seeking; and this moral something is in fact, even politically speaking, the most important question in the present state of things. It is the organisation of the European task. It is no longer the savage, hostile, quarrelsome nationality of two hundred years ago which is invoked by these peoples . . .

[The nationality of the princes was] founded upon the following principle:

Whichever people, by its superiority of strength, and by its geographical position, can do us an injury, is our natural enemy; whichever cannot do us an injury, but can by the amount of its force and by its position injure our enemy, is our natural ally, is the princely nationality of aristocracies or royal races. The nationality of the peoples has not these dangers; it can only be founded by a common effort and a common movement; sympathy and alliance will be its result. In principle, as in the ideas formerly laid down by the men influencing every national party, nationality ought only to be to humanity that which the division of labour is in a workshop – the recognised symbol of association; the assertion of the individuality of a human group called by its geographical position, its traditions, and its language, to fulfill a special function in the European work of civilisation.

The map of Europe has to be remade. This is the key to the present movement; herein lies the initiative. Before acting, the instrument for action must be organised; before building, the ground must be one's own. The social idea cannot be realised under any form whatsoever before this reorganisation of Europe is effected; before the peoples are free to interrogate themselves; to express their vocation, and to assure its accomplishment by an alliance capable of substituting itself for the absolutist league which now reigns supreme.

Naples. The adventurer greeted him as the first king of Italy and turned southern Italy and Sicily over to him. The conservative Piedmont model of constitutional monarchy, with a parliament elected only from a wealthy sliver of the population, was imposed on the new united Italy in the place of Mazzini's vision of a radical, egalitarian republic. Map 10.1 gives an overview of the making of the Italian state, which will be dissussed in detail.

The romantic nationalists constructed a story about Italy's "Resurgence" (**Risorgimento**) around these events in which the

Map 10.1 The unification of Italy

nation had existed from of old and had only now been restored to unity and political autonomy. In fact, of course, there had been no such thing as an Italian "nation," and it was the new Italian state, formalized in 1861, that undertook to create one. What we now call Italy has seldom been a united political unit in history. Before the mid nineteenth century, important parts of the peninsula were ruled for long stretches by the French and the Austrians. Local city-states and kingdoms governed only small geographic areas. The north was far more urbanized and dependent on handicrafts than the largely rural south, so that styles of life differed enormously throughout the peninsula. There was no single "Italian" language: Only 2.5 percent of the population could read and write standard Italian. Rather, there were many dialects, most of them not written. People from Florence in the north could not necessarily understand people from Sicily in the far south. Moreover, the distinction between languages and dialects is itself not definitive. If France, for example, had managed to incorporate a large part of the Italian

peninsula into itself, teaching the children French in school, they would have become French just as did the Corsicans (who speak a dialect of Italian at home). Only once a single state unified the Italian peninsula politically from 1861 was Italian standardized as a language of bureaucracy, schooling, and the press, and an Italian-speaking people with allegiance to an Italian nation-state gradually created. It is the interaction of peoples and states that creates nations. One does not begin with relatively homogeneous "nations."

10.3 BISMARCK AND THE MAKING OF THE GERMAN EMPIRE

As in Italy, politics and warfare involving the great powers played an essential role in the process of state-making in Germany, which came to be unified in the years 1866–71. The radical and populist elements that contributed to the making of

Map 10.2 The unification of Germany

Italy, however, were largely absent in the German experience, where there were no peasant revolutions that overthrew local kings. The making of Germany was a largely top-down affair, and, indeed, raised some anxieties among many ordinary folk.

Northeastern Germany or Prussia, ruled by William I and his arch-conservative prime minister, Otto von Bismarck, defeated Austria in a war of 1866, in part because of its greater industrial and technological development. The breech-loading rifle played an important role in this war, since it allowed soldiers to reload without standing up and stuffing the muzzle with powder and shot, which had exposed them to enemy fire in the past. Despite this victory, Bismarck, fearing French intervention, did not occupy any Austrian territory. Many of the smaller German-speaking principalities had allied with Austria, and although Bismarck did not annex them at that time, he did move against Frankfurt, Schleswig-Holstein, and a few other small principalities, and established a "North German Confederation" that

lasted for four years. Bismarck also concluded secret treaties with the southern states of Bavaria, Württemberg, and Baden. Map 10.2 gives an overview of the unification of Germany.

Relations between this expanded Prussian power and France became increasingly frosty, as France began to fear that an expansionist Germany would reach to the French border and pose a threat to France itself. There were also tensions between the two over Luxembourg. At one point Bismarck leaked the news of his secret treaties with the southern principalities, and from all accounts the prospect of unification with militaristic, authoritarian, and bureaucratized Prussia was very unpopular among the people of the south. The nationalist ideology assumed that all speakers of German would want to live under the same state, but in reality their attitude depended a great deal on what sort of state they thought they were joining.

Conflicts between Germany and France over the succession to the Spanish throne embroiled the two in a war in 1870–71 that ranged 800,000 troops from Prussia and its allies against about half that many Frenchmen, such that the latter were defeated despite having better arms. In the wake of the Franco-Prussian War, the German Empire emerged, unifying a number of principalities into a single polity. Some, such as Bavaria, were allowed to retain substantial autonomy in some spheres, such as control of rails and telegraph, and its own diplomatic service, and even kept their own local dynasties.

After 1871 the German Empire began a process of rapid industrialization, but even more than in Italy politics remained dominated by conservative elites such as the landholding Junkers and the new business magnates such as the Krupps. The Junkers were middle to large landholders in the east of the country, often with some aristocratic background, and formed the bulk of the Prussian military. The need of the German Empire for unity in the face of continued powerful challenges from European rivals drove high Protestant officials to initiate a campaign (the *Kulturkampf*) against Roman Catholicism in 1871–87, in which Jesuits were expelled and monasteries closed. The process of unification had added largely Catholic regions to the country in the south, and the German center was unsure of its control there. The Catholic church resisted this assault in subtle ways. The *Kulturkampf* ultimately faded away. The struggle demonstrated the ways in which nationalists were frequently intolerant of other possible power centers, such as institutionalized world religions. Popular enthusiasm for a united Germany was generated by civil society organizations such as the supporters of the German navy, who had active and well-subscribed clubs. Despite Bismarck's attempt to prevent them, important leftist and workers' movements developed. Struggles among these new social classes and ideologies helped forge a German identity within the framework of the Empire.

10.4 OTTOMANISM

The Ottomans are a good example of imperial nationalism, where empires of a polyglot character sought a modern, overarching political identity. The Ottoman empire, as with most already existing empires, was a patchwork of regions and peoples. Its possessions included much of the Arabic-speaking world, but it gradually lost most North African possessions to Western colonial powers. It retained the Hijaz (Western Arabia), Greater Syria, and Baghdad and Basra. In religion, less than 10 percent of Egyptians were Coptic Christian. Perhaps 15 to 20 percent of the inhabitants of Palestine were Eastern Orthodox Christians. In both cases, the remainder were largely Sunni Muslims. Maronite Christians, members of a Uniate church of Roman Catholicism, predominated in what is now Lebanon,

but that region also had many Shi`ite Muslims and other religious minorities. Kurds lived in eastern Anatolia and north of the Fertile Crescent (Kurdish is an Indo-European language related to Persian). Eastern Anatolia was also the homeland of hundreds of thousands of Christian Armenians. Armenians spoke their own language, which was also Indo-European in character. Christians predominated in the Ottoman Balkans in Southeastern Europe, though Bosnia-Herzegovina, Albania, and Bulgaria had substantial Muslim populations, as did Thrace near nineteenth-century Greece.

The official language of the Ottoman empire was a form of Turkish, also called Ottoman (in Turkish: Osmanli). It served as the language of members of the Ottoman elite, no matter what their ethnic or social origins. The vast majority of Ottoman subjects did not speak it, however. It was little studied in the Arabic-speaking provinces except by local provincial officials and high elites. Village Turks would not have understood the high-flown Arabic and Persian words. (At this time, the very word "Turk" referred to villagers, not to the Ottoman aristocrats.) The Christians of Bulgaria and Serbia seldom learned it. The Ottoman empire was loosely united by loyalty to the sultan in Istanbul, by a vast bureaucracy of tax collection, by the provision of some services, and by military garrisons that dotted the realm. Christian Ottoman intellectuals, inspired by the example of Greece and (later) Italy, often began dreaming of pulling away from the empire to form a new nation based on religion and language. Such movements arose in the Danubian Principalities (what is now Romania), in Serbia, and in Bulgaria. They were supported strongly by the Russians, since many of these peoples were Slavs or belonged to the Eastern Orthodox church of which the tsars saw themselves as champions.

In the early 1850s tensions grew between the Russians and the Ottomans. In 1850, the Ottomans granted concessions to the French with regard to Latin rite Christians in Jerusalem and its environs, then under Ottoman rule. Tsar Nicholas I (r. 1825–1855) wanted similar concessions for the Greek Orthodox Christians in the Holy Land. He also demanded that the Ottoman sultan, Abdulmecid, recognize Russia as protector of all the Ottoman subjects who belonged to the Eastern Orthodox branch of Christianity, and offered him political support against France. The Ottomans refused the offer, partially at the urging of Great Britain's diplomats, who were zealous in keeping Russian influence out of the Middle East. The Ottoman empire contained the major routes to India from Britain, and London viewed it as a reliable friend. The British wanted no Russian influence in Istanbul.

In July of 1853 the Russians began occupying the Principalities. The Ottoman prime minister, Mustafa Resit Pasha, was bent on resisting this Russian aggression. By late October of

1853, Ottoman troops had crossed the Danube and begun engaging the Russians. The conflict drew France and Britain in, and they declared war on Russia in March of 1854. French and British forces began gathering in Gallipoli in support of the Ottomans. Nicholas I, seeing this development, sought a compromise by handing the Principalities over to Austria, but this move proved unacceptable to the Ottomans, French, and British. They did not wish to provoke a European war by marching on the Austrians. They therefore hit on the idea of attacking Russia itself, not via the Balkans but in the Crimean peninsula, Russian territory on the Black Sea that lacked a rail link. From September 1854, when allied landings took place near the Russian port of Sevastopol, a number of difficult battles were fought, and allied troops suffered horribly from the harsh winter. In September 1855, the allies finally occupied Sevastopol. By February of 1856, the warring parties had gathered in Paris for a peace conference. The Treaty of Paris, signed March 29, 1856, stipulated that all sides would withdraw from territories conquered during the war. Ottoman territorial integrity was affirmed, but the Principalities would be guaranteed some autonomy. In turn, the sultan would agree to protect the rights of non-Muslims in the empire. The Black Sea was militarily neutralized.

As a result of these negotiations, Sultan Abdulmecid issued his Reform Decree in 1856, affirming that all Ottoman subjects were equal under civil law. Classical Islamic law had given non-Muslims the status of second-class citizens, so this decree in some sense dethroned Islam as a basis for the Ottoman state. In the subsequent generation, Ottoman officials and intellectuals attempted to construct a new pan-imperial identity, which they called **Ottomanism** (Osmanlilik). They tried to reimagine the empire not only because of European pressure over the status of Christians, but because it had become clear to the Istanbul ruling elite that there was a real danger of the sultan's Christian subjects in the Balkans pulling away to form their own states. This attempt to construct an Ottoman ideology had some successes, though it did not always work out the way the sultans intended. Muslim artisans, already hurt by imports of manufactured goods from Christian Europe, were outraged at their Christian neighbors putting on new airs, and in 1860 they rioted and massacred several thousand Christians in Damascus. The Ottoman state, however, remained committed to the promises of 1856, and actually hanged prominent Muslim notables for their role in this affair.

In 1876, as a result in part of the empire's financial difficulties, revolutionaries overthrew Sultan Abdulaziz, who committed suicide. They induced the new sultan, Abdulhamid II, to agree to elections for a parliament, which then hammered out a constitution. The parliamentary representatives of the lower house were elected from throughout the empire, serving as a short-lived symbol of Ottomanism. In 1877–78, however, another war broke out between Russia and the Ottomans. It was provoked by the heavy-handed Ottoman suppression of a rebellion in Bulgaria in 1876. Ottoman troops killed 15,000 people in one incident, and these actions became known as the "Balkan massacres" in Christian Europe. Tensions rose again with Russia, and the Russians attacked in 1877. This time the Russians advanced ruthlessly through the Balkans to approach Istanbul itself. Although France and Britain had earlier pledged to protect the Ottomans from such Russian aggression, they were reluctant to be viewed as supporting the perpetrator of the Balkan massacres. The Serbians now declared their independence and sent troops to support the Russians. Ironically, during this war many massacres were committed against Muslims in the Balkans by Russia and her local allies. By the early winter of 1878 the Russians were poised to take over the Ottoman empire altogether, a prospect that finally impelled French and British diplomatic intervention. In the peace treaty signed in Berlin on March 3, 1878, Montenegro, Serbia, and Romania were granted independence. Most of Bulgaria became an autonomous vassal state with its own prince, though nominally under Ottoman sovereignty. Part of this territory remained under direct Ottoman rule until Bulgaria claimed it by force in 1885.

The Ottoman empire became a largely Muslim power with the effective loss of so many of its Balkan possessions. In the wake of this defeat, the Ottoman sultan, Abdulhamid II, dismissed parliament for good and suspended the constitution, arguing that an absolute monarchy (Russia) had defeated a democratic Ottoman empire, proving that absolute monarchy is superior. He then attempted to promote **pan-Islamism**, a conception of identity that would unite Muslims against further European encroachments. He also began claiming to be not only a sultan, but also a caliph (a sort of Muslim pope), not a station the Ottoman emperors had previously enjoyed. The impossibility of creating true unity between the Sunni Ottomans and the Shi`ite Iranians, however, blunted the success of this movement, though the idea proved especially attractive to Indian Muslims under British rule. It also had some supporters among the Central Eurasian Muslims conquered by the Russian empire, a fast-growing population. In the end, neither Ottomanism nor pan-Islamism proved sturdy enough identities to keep the Ottoman empire intact.

Abdulhamid II's restoration of royal absolutism in 1878 ushered in three decades of political conservatism. Although it did expand substantially, the Ottoman economy made relatively little progress toward industrializing, remaining largely agricultural, and suffering from substantial balance of trade deficits (that is, the Ottomans imported more from trading partners such as Italy, Austria, France, and Great Britain than they sold to them). Over time, persistent balance of trade deficits tend to weaken a country's economy. Workers, merchants, and farmers nursed grievances over their economic situation. The sultan's political conservatism and his hatred of democracy did not prevent his government from continuing to improve the empire's economic infrastructure, however. New civil schools were established with modern curricula. Railroads were laid that linked the heartlands of the empire with distant regions such as Baghdad and the Arabian peninsula. Modern military academies produced well-educated junior officers.

Some of the junior officers, especially army physicians, grew to hate Abdulhamid II for the ways in which they felt he was keeping the Ottoman empire backward. They became known as the **Young Turks**. One Young Turk thinker, Ziya Gökalp, developed ideas of **pan-Turkism**, asserting that the "Turks" were a single race. He initially dreamed of uniting them all (including Central Eurasians such as Uzbeks and Kazakhs) under one government. The symbol of the pan-Turkists was the she-wolf, which had been worshipped by the tribal Turks before their conversion to Islam. (Nationalism and neo-paganism have often gone hand in hand.)

By 1908 the Young Turks or Committee of Union and Progress were in a position to demand that the sultan restore the parliament, and he agreed. Astonished Ottomans read in the newspapers those forbidden words, "liberty" and "patriotism," and "parliament." In the spring of 1909 Abdulhamid II attempted to stage another counter-coup, but this time important artillery units sided with the Young Turks, and he was deposed. For three years, parliamentary politics became the norm in the Ottoman empire.

The civilian and the military wings of the now Party for Union and Progress did not agree on policy. Christian Ottomans in the Balkans never fully accepted the idea of an Ottoman nationalism in which they could be full partners, and they pulled away. Some Arabic-speaking Ottomans were disturbed by the dominance of Turkish and Turkish-speaking officials, even though this dominance was of long standing. More Balkan Christians broke away in 1912–13. Italy forcibly annexed Ottoman Libya in 1911–12. Traditional Arab leaders in western Arabia (the Hejaz), used to a good deal of local autonomy, were unhappy about the tighter grip on the region gained by Ottoman governors through the railroad and rapid troop transport. The attempt to create an overarching Ottoman nationalism from the elements of the old empire, which would satisfy Turkish-speakers, Arabic-speakers, and Eastern Europeans, and would keep Christians in the empire, had been a distinct failure. A democratic framework might have convinced some groups to try to work within an Ottoman system, but the inability of the new political parties to accept defeat, and the dominance of the military, made the second experiment in Ottoman democracy short-lived. In 1913 the military wing of Union and Progress led by Enver Pasha staged a coup. This military junta took the Ottomans into World War I on the German side, and when the French and British defeated Istanbul, they carved the empire up into the states now found in the Middle East. Map 10.3 shows the remains of the Ottoman state after 1918.

10.5 IRAN

Iran had been one of the three great Muslim empires of Asia in the early modern period, as we saw, its economy driven by the silk trade. In the nineteenth century it was reduced to a buffer zone between the Russian and British empires. Russia and Britain competed for territory in Central Eurasia, with the Russians conquering what is now Uzbekistan, Kazakhstan, and other territories. The British advanced north from their base in India, invading Afghanistan more than once. In the end, Iran and Afghanistan were maintained as territories that separated the two expanding empires, helping ensure that they could avoid a major war by simply not sharing a common border. Iranians lost their primacy in the silk trade in part because of silkworm disease, and they turned to cash crops such as cotton, tobacco, and opium. In response to the increasing dominance over Iran by Britain and Russia, the Iranians attempted to move from ramshackle empire to modern nation. Unlike the French, who appealed to reason and universal secular values in fashioning their modern nationalism, many Iranians called on Shi`ite Islam as a key aspect of their identity. The conflict between secularism and religion, so central to the twentieth-century Middle East, played out in original ways in Iranian nationalism.

The Turkic Qajar dynasty had come to power in Iran in the late 1700s. A form of what has been called "tribal feudalism" prevailed, with the Iranian army heavily dependent on the participation of pastoral nomads, who were perhaps half of the population of about 5 million in 1800. The Qajar state formed small ministries and established relatively weak control over the Iranian plateau. It was badly defeated by Russia in the Caucasus in 1813 and 1828. In 1844–52 the country was roiled by the messianic Babi movement, led by Ali Muhammad

Map 10.3 Ottoman territorial losses

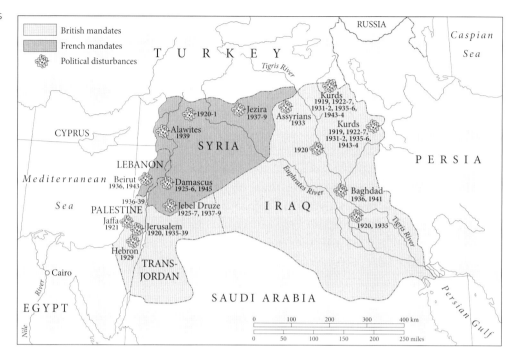

Shirazi, who claimed to be the Mahdi or promised one of Islam. He was executed in 1850 and as a result some of his followers attempted to assassinate the king, Nasir al-Din Shah, in 1852. The shah survived, and brutally suppressed the movement, which had been remarkable for spreading throughout the country and provoking uprisings in a number of small towns. Iran's population is estimated to have gone from being half pastoral nomadic in 1800 to only a quarter pastoralist in 1900, with three quarters sedentary in villages and towns. The total population doubled from about 5 million to about 10 million. (Most Middle Eastern countries have experienced rapid population growth in the past two centuries, which has contributed to political instability.)

Even insular Iran witnessed some reforms. In the early 1850s a reformist prime minister, Amir Kabir, established the first polytechnic college, where modern subjects were taught alongside European languages. In the late nineteenth century a modern middle class grew up of import-export merchants, intellectuals, journalists, and landlords who grew cash crops for the world market (cotton, silk, rice, grain, and opium). Many had their children educated in Istanbul, Bombay, or Europe. They increasingly wanted a greater say in government affairs. A few intellectuals, influenced by European thought, began conceiving of Iran as an ancient nation that went back to the Achaemenids (the history of which was being recovered in greater detail in the late nineteenth century). These radicals

denounced Arabs and Islam as having inflicted backwardness and superstition on the great Iranian nation, and they began praising the old Zoroastrian religion or arguing for secularism. They were at this time, the late nineteenth century, a very small minority.

Constitutional Revolution in Iran

In 1905–11 the Constitutional Revolution broke out in Iran. Its champions believed, as did the Ottoman constitutionalists of 1876 and 1908, that absolute monarchy was making the country weak and opened it to European political dominance (since the king or shah often needed foreign loans and curried favor with imperial nations like Russia, Great Britain, and even Belgium). Interestingly, remnants of the old Babi movement who had become intellectuals or journalists played a small but significant role in this revolution. Its main proponents, however, were the great merchants and the modern intellectuals, along with some more progressive Shi`ite clergymen. Its opponents included conservative clergymen like Fazl Allah Nuri, as well as the aristocracy. Conservative Shi`ite clergymen believed that only God's commands as revealed in the Koran could form a basis for law, and that a parliament representing the people had no standing.

Muzaffar al-Din Shah (r. 1896–1907) granted the constitution and allowed a parliament to be elected. In a compromise, the constitution did permit a council of Shi`ite clergymen to review laws passed by parliament to ensure they did not contradict Islamic law. But the council was never actually seated, and the clergy generally lost power at this time. The new king, Muhammad Ali Shah, who was enthroned early in 1907 after his father's death, increasingly disliked the constitutional restraints. In 1908 he abolished parliament and suspended the constitution, executing many constitutional activists.

A revolt broke out, centered in Tabriz, that by the following year took Tehran and chased the autocratic shah out of the country, putting a child ruler on the throne. In 1909, parliament was recalled and the constitution restored. This victory came at the cost, however, of greatly weakening the central government on the eve of World War I. The project of fashioning an Iranian nation was still only beginning. The literacy rate was very low. A quarter of the country was still made up of pastoral nomads. Only about half the population spoke Persian at home. The central government, even after the Constitutional Revolution, made little investment in mass education. Still, many of the images and metaphors developed by the makers of the Constitutional Revolution had a strong nationalist overtone, and Iran had moved from tribal feudalism to constitutional monarchy. Newspapers proliferated and flourished, with much less censorship. Something like a national feeling began to be expressed in some quarters.

10.6 JAPAN

Japanese nationalism came in response to international pressures, which intensified in the second half of the nineteenth century. Conflicts with the United States over whaling and trade led to the famous naval mission of Commodore Matthew C. Perry to Japan, which arrived in Edo Bay on July 2, 1853. Commercial agreements with the USA followed, including the Perry Convention of 1854 and the Harris Treaty of 1858. Russia, and then other European powers, sought similar treaties. These ended the long policy of national closure, whereby Japanese society had been closed off to the outside world in the early modern period. The way in which the Tokugawa ruler was viewed as having had to give in to the demands of foreigners weakened his prestige inside Japan and set the stage for a serious challenge to his rule.

Many members of the Japanese elite began to feel that their country had fallen behind the rest of the world and that serious changes were needed. A group of anti-foreign notables in Choshu, some of whom had been to Western Europe, began challenging Tokugawa rule. The shogun came under increasing

pressure from the European powers in the 1860s, helping unite the Japanese, who began fearing his apparent weakness. In 1867–68 the Choshu group of samurai and others, often supported by commoners such as merchants, helped restore power to the emperor, who had been a mere figurehead under the Tokugawa shogunate for hundreds of years. The Meiji emperor's forces conquered the capital Edo, renaming it Tokyo (the Eastern Capital).

The Choshu and other officials emerged as key to creating the new imperial Japanese state. They ended many feudal practices, destroyed the power of the samurai nobles and subjected them to the central state, and created a modern army that had a powerful place in civilian politics. Their slogan was "Enrich the country, strengthen the military!" A powerful navy was in particular part of the program of the restorationists, paralleling developments in Germany. There was another parallel. We have seen that the German Empire persecuted Roman Catholicism, suspicious of its monasteries and Jesuits as being more loyal to a world religion than to the new nation-state. In the same way, the new Meiji government gave special privileges to the Shinto religion, which it valued as native to Japan and as centered on emperor-worship. For the first few years the government kept in place the long-lived ban on Christianity. In 1868–70, it persecuted the Buddhist monks just as Bismarck had bothered the Jesuits, closing many monasteries and temples and even destroying some priceless buildings and scriptures. Buddhism had been closely associated with the old samurai ruling class of the Tokugawa period, another reason it was mistrusted. Although active hostility to Buddhism thereafter died down, the episode shows again the ways in which centralizing nation-states favor religious identities that they perceive to be compatible with national identity.

Calls for a legislature had been part of the movement for the restoration of the emperor, and he pledged it in his 1868 charter oath, saying "Deliberative councils shall be widely established and all matters decided by public discussion." As among the Ottoman constitutionalists, many felt that British power in particular stemmed from its constitutionalist form of government, which they sought to emulate. After decades of political experimentation and popular struggles for political participation, the emperor promulgated a conservative German-influenced constitution in 1889 and elections were called for parliament in 1890. More than 1,000 candidates ran for 300 seats, but the property requirements limited the electorate to about 450,000 landowners. Members of parliament could introduce legislation and had to give their consent to the budget. They could freely discuss political affairs, so that the scope for political dissent widened.

The Japanese constitution, however, gave much more power to the emperor than was common in Western European constitutional monarchies, and politics remained authoritarian despite the enthusiasm of many urban businessmen and intellectuals for a more British-inspired model. The Japanese emperor was nevertheless among the few nineteenth-century sovereigns gladly to grant a constitution and a parliament with real budgetary and legislative power. As we have seen, the Ottoman rulers were forced into taking a similar step in 1876, but Abdulhamid II abolished it only two years later. Most constitutions in Asia came about only after a revolutionary political struggle, as in Iran and China, and decades later than in Japan. Those constitutions, however, typically left the monarch with fewer powers than those enjoyed by the Japanese emperor.

The school system was revamped and nationalist ideas were stressed in the curriculum, though a lot of schooling remained private. The government taxed agriculture to gain surpluses it could use in promoting industrialization, though free market capitalism was modified when a handful of great business concerns (*zaibatsu*) emerged in such a way as to limit competition.

Extensive military reforms allowed Japan to defeat China over influence in Korea in 1894–95. Japan also gained control of Taiwan, and then pulled off the remarkable feat of triumphing over Russia in 1905. The hopes of nationalists and anti-colonialists throughout Asia and Africa were raised by the defeat of a Western power at the hands of an Asian one. By 1910 Japan had annexed Korea. Not only had the "national unit" of Japan been put under the rule of the "state unit," but Japan had also emerged as a colonial power that was increasingly recognized as on an equal footing with those of Western Europe. By 1911 the unequal commercial treaties enacted with foreign states had been revoked and Japan was at long last at liberty to extend protection to its infant industries. Japanese nationalism mixed a call for revival of ancient institutions and cultural forms that were "native" to the islands (the emperor, Shinto religion) with vigorous attempts to import the best in organizational and technological innovation from the North Atlantic powers. It thus helps demonstrate how a nationalist rhetoric of roots and authenticity can mask a thoroughgoing borrowing of foreign models and practices.

10.7 ANTI-COLONIAL MOVEMENTS

European naval and military technology, advances in economic organization, and bureaucratic skills had allowed European powers to penetrate African and Asian trade from the 1500s. Most such powers did not actually try to hold a lot of territory until, as we have seen, the British East India Company began conquering inland India from 1757 forward. The British gradually expanded into Nepal, Burma, and Malaya in Asia. The French invaded Algeria in 1830 and spent decades putting down revolts and establishing French rule. They also encouraged the immigration into Algeria of thousands of French settlers. And they colonized Vietnam, Cambodia, and Laos in Southeast Asia.

From the 1880s, the European colonial powers engaged in what has been called a "Scramble for Africa." As Map 10.4 shows, the greater part of Africa was divided among the colonial powers within a few years. Debt crises in Tunisia and Egypt began the serious movement of Europe into the continent. The French took Tunisia in 1881, and the British conquered Egypt in 1882. The British were then drawn into the Sudan by political instability further up the Nile Valley. The French, alarmed at British inroads into the Sahel region just south of the Sahara, expanded their conquests. France ultimately ruled much of North and West Africa above what became British Nigeria, whereas the British became the predominant power in East and southern Africa. The search for raw materials fueled much of this conquest, as with the Belgian conquest of the Congo. This dark and exploitative side of European colonialism in Africa was memorialized by British-Polish novelist Joseph Conrad in his novella *The Heart of Darkness*. Other colonial adventures appear to have had little economic justification, but to have reflected rivalries between Britain and France, or the desire of military "men on the spot" to make their mark. The men on the spot were the local colonial officers and officials, many of whom launched wars of conquest without much in the way of authorization from London and Paris, and if they were successful the imperial center usually backed them. The Scramble for Africa led to the incorporation of the vast majority of the peoples of that continent into British, French, Belgian, Italian, and German colonial empires between 1880 and World War I. Older Portuguese colonies already existed.

In the period 1850–1914, peoples in colonial states reacted in many ways to the increased domination of European colonial empires, which ultimately came to rule hundreds of millions of the world's inhabitants. Some sought to prepare the way for their political autonomy from the imperial center, either through ordinary political activities (founding parties, agitating for changes in law) or through violent revolt. Neither was successful in this period, but these movements did often create institutions or symbols and memories that had a long-term impact. Of course, many peasants or craftsmen who revolted did so for local reasons and in hope of redress of particular grievances, rather than in a bid to overthrow the rule of the foreigners altogether. It should also be remembered that because of the overwhelming superiority of Western arms and military tactics in this period, the vast majority of colonial subjects most often felt they had no choice

Map 10.4 Africa in 1914

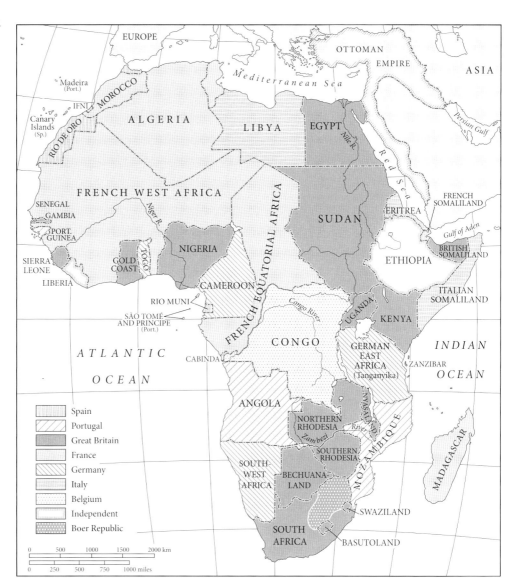

but to find ways of collaborating with European rule. Indeed, many colonial armies, as in India, were staffed primarily with local enlistees, and Europeans formed the higher corps of officers.

On the other hand, the vigorous history of peasant and urban revolts in the colonial world is often forgotten, given the longevity and seeming stability of many colonial states. For example, French Algeria, taken from the Ottomans in 1830, was the site of constant and serious tribal and Islamic Sufi revolts through the 1880s, and even thereafter tribes and peasants occasionally rose up. The Dutch in Indonesia had to fight the Muslim people of Aceh almost constantly from 1873–1908. In this chapter a few select extended accounts will be given to illustrate these sorts of struggle.

India

Among the largest colonies in Africa and Asia was India, and it frequently served as a bellwether. The term "Indian" comes from the Indus River, and in the nineteenth century most of the peoples we now call "Indian" would have referred to themselves as "Hindustani" or Hindvi, without regard to caste or religion. There was as yet, however, no "Indian nation" and such terms are more a convenience for us in thinking about history than a reflection of the identities most important at the time. In the late 1850s, the Indians launched the Great Rebellion against British rule, called the "Mutiny" by British colonial historians. We have already seen the significant changes wrought in Indian life by the advent of British rule. Most Indians found ways of accommodating themselves to these new European overlords, but peasant revolts remained endemic in some provinces. These revolts occurred all over the subcontinent, including the south (where the Muslim Moplahs rebelled from 1849–52), the center (where Bhils and other pastoralist castes had frequently rebelled), and Bengal (where in the late 1850s the dislocations caused by the growth of indigo planting caused peasant uprisings). There were a number of small mutinies by units of the Bengal army in various places.

The Great Rebellion The Great Rebellion did not affect most of British India, with little sign of significant revolt in the south at Madras or the west at Bombay. The oldest British bastion, Bengal, was largely unaffected, and Europeans remained safe throughout at Calcutta, which they were able to use as a port to bring in by sea from Great Britain the men and arms that ultimately prevailed. Rather, the most serious episodes of the revolt occurred in the areas called the Northwest Provinces and Oudh (nowadays this is the Indian province of Uttar Pradesh). The epicenters were the cities of Delhi, Lucknow, and Kanpur.

Much of this region was ruled in the eighteenth century by the **nawab** (provincial ruler) of Oudh or Awadh, a Mughal province that gradually became a state in its own right. In 1801 the British unilaterally annexed more than half of this area from the nawab, on the pretext that he had fallen behind on the tribute the British claimed he owed them. This annexed region, the northern parts of which had an unusually large concentration of Muslims, was renamed the Northwest Provinces. The nawab of Oudh continued to rule a substantial area, now surrounded by the British on three sides and bordering Nepal and the Himalayas to the east. This dynasty belonged to the Shi`ite branch of Islam and had its origins in Iran, and a powerful Shi`ite ruling class formed around it in the capital city, Lucknow. The majority of the Muslim population, however, remained Sunni, and these predominated in the army. Other Sunnis were medium landlords or urban and village artisans. Muslims, however, formed only about 10 percent of Oudh's population. The rest were Hindu. Almost all villagers were Hindu, as were a number of very large landholders, called "rajas." Hindu holy men of various sorts wielded great moral authority.

In the mid-1850s, a major conflict erupted among the three religious groups. In the city of Faizabad near Lucknow was located a temple to the Hindu monkey god Hanuman. Many Sunni Muslims believed that the temple rested on the foundations of an old mosque that Hindus had torn down. Fiery Sunni clergymen in Oudh's small towns preached vengeance in 1855, leading to a Muslim attack on the Hanuman temple that was repulsed by Hindu holy men and retainers of the rural magnate Raja Man Singh. News of this Muslim–Hindu riot spread throughout Oudh, and a movement began of Sunni Muslim shopkeepers and artisans, who formed a sort of vigilante militia and began marching toward Faizabad. They demanded that their Muslim government intervene to punish the Hindu holy men. The king of Oudh, Wajid Ali Shah, wavered as to what action he should take. Although relatively broadminded, as most Oudh rulers had been, he had no sympathy for Hindu claims to

all land they said had been trodden by their monkey god. He favored building a mosque up against the Hanuman temple, so that there would be one building with two separate entrances and no connecting corridor between the two places of worship within. The British, however, objected that such a course of action would likely lead to further bloodshed between Hindus and Muslims. They worried that the Hindu majority might rise up and overthrow the king, and that in any such Hindu–Muslim disturbances, the losers would flood as refugees into nearby British territory as destitute refugees. The danger of Hindu–Muslim violence spreading from Oudh into the Northwest Provinces and even Bengal was also ever-present in their minds. The British therefore pressured Wajid Ali Shah simply to put down the Sunni Muslim militias marching on Faizabad. The Oudh ruler worried, however, that a majority of his army was Sunni, and they might not obey. In the end, he assembled some Shi`ite units, and called upon Shi`ite large landlords such as Mahmudabad, and these put down the militant Sunnis.

These events helped convince the then governor-general, Lord Dalhousie, that Oudh was misruled and unstable, and a threat to the order of British India. Dalhousie also coveted the rich agricultural regions in Oudh and the extra revenue that taxes on them would yield to the East India Company. In February of 1856, therefore, Dalhousie unilaterally annexed Oudh to the British empire and dethroned its monarch. In so doing he breached a long-term alliance with Oudh that went back to the late 1760s. Many Oudh subjects were outraged as the British marched into Lucknow and the former king was forced to go to Calcutta to plead with Dalhousie to reconsider. He was unsuccessful, and planned to go to London to seek redress from Queen Victoria herself, but the Rebellion broke out before he could embark, trapping him and his entourage in Calcutta.

The British now had direct rule of all the territory between the Bay of Bengal and Peshawar in the north, including Bengal, Bihar, Oudh, the Northwest Provinces, Delhi, and the Panjab. They were no longer seriously afraid of any outside power, though the Russian advances in neighboring Central Asia to the north would cause some anxiety in Calcutta in the succeeding decade. British officials therefore began behaving more aggressively toward local Indians, whether elites or peasants and soldiers. As they took over Oudh, they began informing old elite families that tax-exempt land grants from the former king would now be taxed, and some lands that had been bestowed, like medieval fiefs, on a temporary basis would be taken away altogether. British high-handedness about land settlement in Oudh alarmed not only rural landlords but also urban dwellers who had landed wealth, such as the Muslim and Hindu clergy. The great landlords, such as the raja of Mahmudabad and Raja Man Singh, it should be remembered, were something like barons, and had their own private armies, which had seen action in the 1855 events. Upsetting them about the security of their holdings was unwise.

The British military that held these northwestern territories was called the Bengal army, because most of the units had been originally formed in that province. But over time a significant number of recruits had come to be from clans based in Oudh, and many of these troops, including Hindus, were upset about the annexation of their home province. Many were apprehensive about the future, since they either had small landholdings, or had relatives who did, or retained ties as clients with a large landlord. This anxiety manifested itself in a concern that the British, by their high-handed intervention in the Indian political, property, and social systems, might be planning to wipe out local Indian identity altogether. Suspicions formed among the troops that the British were plotting to steal their "caste" or ethnic identities from them, leaving their souls stripped bare and open to then being converted to Christianity, the alien religion of the foreign conquerors.

These suspicions were fueled by a number of new policies. The British had earlier avoided posting local Indian recruits too far from home. By this time, however, they needed troops in Burma, and they formally announced that these troops, called sepoys from the Persian word for soldier (*sipahi*), would be posted abroad at will. Many Hindus believed that crossing deep or "black" water was morally wrong and resulted in their defilement, their loss of "caste," and they feared that the British might force them into such a state. Another important development of the mid-1850s was the introduction of the 1853 **Enfield rifle**. This weapon could be loaded while a soldier lay down, which was a great advantage over the old muzzle-loading muskets. The rifle used a cartridge of greased paper, and one end was meant to be bitten or torn off to expose the gunpowder for easier firing. In British culture greased paper was not problematic, but grease derives from animal fat, typically beef or pork, and the former is considered unclean by Hindus while Muslims are ritually polluted by the latter. The Hindu and Muslim sepoys therefore began resisting the use of the new bullets, declining to bite them or to tear them with their hands, since either sort of contact would defile them. British officers often considered this resistance mere superstition, or worse, a form of insubordination, and some imposed harsh and humiliating punishments on sepoys who refused to employ the new bullets.

Just as most revolutions are really a set of simultaneous but separate revolts in different places by different people, so the Great Rebellion in India had several major players. These included the mutineering troops of the Bengal army, of course. But they were joined by the old displaced Muslim and Hindu ruling class, by urban artisans who rioted in their support, and

by peasant warriors of the great barons of the interior. The mutiny itself was begun in the northern city of Meerut on May 19, 1857, by men from a unit harshly punished for their refusal to bite the unclean Enfield cartridges. Soldiers and rioters invaded the British compound and massacred both officers and their civilian dependents.

The revolt then spread along the major rivers, up to Delhi and down to Lucknow and Kanpur. In Delhi the mutinying troops massacred many British and succeeded in getting the last king of the old Mughal dynasty, Bahadur Shah II, then about 80 years old, to become the figurehead of the revolt. In Lucknow one of the deposed old nawab's young sons was chosen as the new nawab of Oudh, and his regents, in alliance with radical Sunni clergy and Hindu great landlords and their retainers, became extremely powerful. Lucknow's artisans joined in the attack on the British cantonment and played a vigorous role in the Rebellion. Hindu warriors from the countryside also swarmed into the city and emerged as an important political force. In nearby Jhansi, the rani or queen who had been deposed by the British joined in the revolt with her Hindu supporters.

The British were initially repulsed and lost control of much of the area between Bihar and the Panjab. They continued to have clandestine allies along the Ganges and Jumna rivers, however, and were able to maintain shipping and telegraph contact between Calcutta and Delhi. News of the massacres of British women and children inflamed British public opinion in London and infuriated the remaining British soldiers in the subcontinent. The specter of "black" Indians attacking "white" British women was offensive to the British not only because of the gruesomeness of the crimes but because such attacks violated their ideas about race and gender. Indians were seen as inherently inferior to the British, and were not welcome in British clubs. Their actions were seen not only as heart-rending but as impudent, as defiling white women who ought to have been above them, and as bringing into question the manliness of British colonial officers and soldiers who should have been able to protect the women. In this way of thinking, the women were helpless, and needed white men to protect them. Many a British charge during the subsequent war began with invocations of the memory of Indian massacres of British women.

The British launched a counter-offensive, importing masses of new recruits and sophisticated arms and artillery from London. Even then, many of their battles were hard-fought, and they only defeated the rebels over a period of many months. Henry Havelock's September 1857 attempt to "relieve" Lucknow and protect the British trapped there resulted in his own forces being pinned down, and he in turn had to be relieved by Colin Campbell's force in November. The Sikh troops of the Panjab remained loyal to the British under Sir Henry Lawrence. They spearheaded the reconquest of Delhi. The ferocity of British retaliatory massacres against Indians, whether civilians or combatants, more than repaid the slaughters in the cantonments early in the Rebellion, though this British harshness is not prominent in popular histories of the "Mutiny."

Although they had regained North India by summer of 1858, and deposed the last Mughal king, the British continued to face guerrilla action in the eastern marches and hills until well into 1859. The Great Rebellion was a mainly North Indian affair, and involved a number of distinct social groups who rallied around revived symbols of older forms of local Indian polity, nawabs, ranis, and even an elderly Mughal emperor who had more experience of writing poetry than ruling. The rebels were filled with anxiety by aggressive British policies with regard to taxation and toward their landholdings, toward their religious sensibilities, and (in the case of urban artisans threatened by British imports) toward their livelihoods. Their inability to cobble together a state that could resist the British probably had less to do with their will or organizational and fighting abilities than with the overwhelming superiority of British arms, especially state of the art artillery newly imported from Britain.

British Responses to the Mutiny As a result of the Rebellion, the British government took direct control of India, making the governor-general a viceroy and displacing the East India Company. In 1876 Queen Victoria was crowned "Queen-Empress," that is, queen of Great Britain and empress of India. British administrators became far more cautious about annexing princely states or heavily taxing agricultural areas, and shifted more of the tax burden to the cities. It has been argued that relatively high taxes on urban merchants and professionals, while seemingly a safe choice in the 1860s, set the stage for increasing tensions between them and the British government in later decades. Rural and urban rebellions of the sort that erupted in 1857 continued to take place on a smaller scale. Alongside these protests, a new sort of politics grew up, pursued by British-educated lawyers, businessmen, and intellectuals. They founded political parties and created the beginnings of a parliamentary life, and ultimately contributed to the success of the ideological task in which the rebels of 1857 had failed, that of imagining a viable political form for an India independent of British rule.

In the aftermath of the revolt, the new Crown government of India paid special attention to improving the information and transportation infrastructure of the subcontinent, having learned the military value of the telegraph lines and regretting that less than 500 miles of railway track had been laid by the late 1850s. By 1900, 25,000 miles of rails crisscrossed the entirety of India,

and old trading routes such as the "Grand Trunk Road" from Peshawar down to Calcutta were given new expression as rail lines. The rails contributed to the growth of the Indian economy, though their economic usefulness was sometimes impaired because they were laid with an eye to moving troops quickly to potential hot spots. By the 1880s, there was a similar number of miles of telegraph line. Newspapers flourished, though often, as under Viceroy Lord Lytton, these were subject to harsh censorship, while at other times a more liberal press policy was enacted. India remained largely agricultural, and the importance of cotton, spinning, and weaving continued, but new factories were established, especially in Bombay Presidency. Significant investments were made in India by British entrepreneurs. The opening of the Suez Canal in 1869 cut thousands of miles off the journey between India and England (see Figure 10.1), vastly reducing costs and time, but this change sometimes benefited Britain more than India. The colonial authorities often gave British imports special tariff breaks, hurting local Indian producers.

The British, convinced that too much interference in local beliefs had contributed to the revolt, retreated from cultural projects in India. They pressured Christian missionaries and their supporters to back off previous ambitious plans and become more low key. They became less willing to intervene in Indian customs. The proportion of British soldiers in the 200,000-man Indian army was raised to about one third, and local recruits were sought especially from groups that had remained loyal during the Rebellion. Rural magnates in Oudh, known as **taluqdars**, were given back their confiscated land and made into pillars of the new establishment.

Intellectuals, often lawyers and often from elites such as the priestly Brahmin caste, the Parsi or Zoroastrian business magnates, or the Muslim Sayyid caste, emerged as an important cultural and political force. In 1870, the All People's Association was founded in Bombay, and its founders worked for Hindu reform and for greater equity for Indian colonial subjects of the empire. In 1876 the Indian Association was founded in Calcutta by a highly educated Bengali who had faced discrimination in the British civil service and been dismissed over a trivial matter. Sir Sayyid Ahmad Khan, fearful that Muslims were falling behind Hindus in securing influential government jobs because of an antipathy to English, helped found the Aligarh Muslim University, which trained Muslims in modern subjects and languages and produced much of that community's political elite.

In 1885, seventy-three representatives gathered in Bombay for the first annual convention of the Indian National Congress. In the succeeding years Congress passed many resolutions aimed at improving the lot of Indians, including protests at the high military expenditures of the British government of India, and

Figure 10.1 The Suez Canal greatly reduced the time of the sea route from Europe to India. A one-way trip from Bombay to London became two months shorter. It made it much easier for Britain to sustain its empire and illustrated the communications revolutions transforming the late nineteenth- and early twentieth-century world.

OPENING OF THE SUEZ CANAL PROCESSION OF SHIPS.

though these had little direct effect, the organization gradually became a vehicle for nationalist ideas and aspirations. One of the Congress militants, B.G. Tilak (1856–1920), called in the early twentieth century for a boycott of British goods. Box 10.2 gives an idea of Tilak's nationalism and tactics. For ordinary Indians, most of them village farmers, rapid population growth tended to offset any economic gains, and it was difficult for most of them to see how they benefited from British rule, which at times became quite harsh. The population grew rapidly from around 186 million in 1800 to about 285 million in 1900 in the entire Indian subcontinent, but because of high growth rates in the rest of the world, its proportion of the world population had fallen from about a fifth in the eighteenth century to only about 17 percent.

In 1905 through about 1912, India erupted with protests that foreshadowed the rise of a thoroughgoing Indian nationalism. The immediate cause was an administrative plan put forward to partition Bengal, which was seen by the government of Viceroy Lord Curzon as unmanageably large. The partition created a Muslim-majority eastern province, and would have robbed the Hindu Bengalis of their majority in the west, as well, by including other ethnicities. The Hindu intellectuals spearheaded protests against what looked like a divide and rule tactic, which spread throughout the colony and ended in a vigorous movement to boycott British textiles and made clothing. The boycott led to a 25 percent drop in such imports, and greatly aided local Indian industries, as the more politically aware insisted on the "made in India" label. In many provinces, governors responded

to the protests harshly, setting aside civil liberties, enacting decrees that severely punished newspaper articles seen as seditious, and putting down protests with the jackboot. Several Congress politicians were jailed for a time, and a more radical wing of younger Congress politicians emerged. A split also emerged between Hindus and Muslims, since Muslim leaders were not unhappy about the Bengal partition. They were worried about being reduced to a permanent, impotent minority in an India with elections where the majority ruled, since they were widely scattered and formed only 25 percent of the population. They agitated for separate electorates, to ensure their votes had weight.

Ultimately, in 1909, more liberal elements of the British administration, led by Secretary of State John Morley, instituted changes in the Indian legislative councils both at the center and in the provinces. They allowed a majority of members to be elected by propertied Indians. From 1910 the largely elected legislative council members began being able to question government officials, debate the budget, and even propose legislation themselves. India became a strange mixture of colony and republic. In 1911, Bengal was reunited, though the Muslims were granted separate electorates. The first wave of modern political protest, involving parties, the press, urban street action, economic boycotts, and demands for legislative representation, had proven relatively successful, even though the tiny propertied class of English-educated Indians was the main beneficiary at first. Ironically, this movement depended heavily on the

Box 10.2 Bal Gangadhar Tilak Seeks Indian Independence

A split gradually developed in the Indian National Congress, founded in 1885. The original founders were gradualists, desiring ultimate independence of Britain. A more militant tendency soon developed, however, which wanted immediate self-rule. The more militant faction was led by Bal Gangadhar Tilak (1856–1920). He urged a boycott of the British in his 1907 speech "Address to the Indian National Congress."

Two new words have recently come into existence with regard to our politics, and they are Moderates and Extremists. These words have a specific relation to time, and they, therefore, will change with time. Every new party begins as Extremists and ends as Moderates. The sphere of practical politics is not unlimited. We cannot say what will or will not happen 1,000 years hence – perhaps during that long period, the whole of the white race will be swept away in another glacial period. We must, therefore, study the present and work out a program to meet the present condition.

. . . One thing is granted, namely, that this government does not suit us. As has been said by an eminent statesman – the government of one country by another can never be a successful, and therefore, a permanent government. There is no difference of opinion about this fundamental proposition between the old and new schools. One fact is that this alien government has ruined the country. In the beginning, all of us were taken by surprise. We were almost dazed. We thought that everything that the rulers did was for our good and that this English government has descended from the clouds to save us from the invasions of Tamerlane and Chingis Khan, and, as they say, not only from foreign invasions but from internecine warfare, or the internal or external invasions, as they call it . . . We are not armed, and there is no necessity for arms either. We have a stronger weapon, a political weapon, in boycott. We have perceived one fact, that the whole of this administration, which is carried on by a handful of Englishmen, is carried on with our assistance. We are all in subordinate service. This whole government is carried on with our assistance and they try to keep us in ignorance of our power of cooperation between ourselves by which that which is in our own hands at present can be claimed by us and administered by us. The point is to have the entire control in our hands. I want to have the key of my house, and not merely one stranger turned out of it. Self-government is our goal; we want a control over our administrative machinery . . . The Englishman knows that they are a mere handful in this country and it is the business of every one of them to befool you in believing that you are weak and they are strong.

This is politics. We have been deceived by such policy so long. What the new party wants you to do is to realize the fact that your future rests entirely in your own hands. If you mean to be free, you can be free; if you do not mean to be free, you will fall and be for ever fallen . . . but if you have not the power of active resistance, have you not the power of self-denial and self-abstinence in such a way as not to assist this foreign government to rule over you? This is boycott and this is what is meant when we say, boycott is a political weapon. We shall not give them assistance to collect revenue and keep peace. We shall not assist them in fighting beyond the frontiers or outside India with Indian blood and money. We shall not assist them in carrying on the administration of justice. We shall have our own courts, and when time comes we shall not pay taxes. Can you do that by your united efforts? If you can, you are free from tomorrow. Some gentlemen who spoke this evening referred to half bread as against the whole bread. I say I want the whole bread and that immediately. But if I can not get the whole, don't think that I have no patience.

I will take the half they give me and then try for the remainder . . . This is the way in which a nation progresses, and this is the lesson you have to learn from the struggle now going on.

---

extensive communications and transportation revolution built in the colony by the British after the Great Rebellion, making use of the telegraph, railroads, newspapers, and the newly literate middle strata that the British had proudly sought to create from about 1835. Unlike the 1857 rebellion, these changes could not be rolled back with a few good artillery units.

Egypt

The Indian events demonstrate the ways in which colonial subjects sometimes mobilized for significant change, even though they may have accepted and co-operated with foreign rule most of the time. In other parts of the world, we see the phenomenon of informal colonialism, wherein European merchants, business people, and consuls penetrated societies that appeared to enjoy political independence. This informal colonialism could also provoke movements of popular protest. Egypt, for example, was a vassal state of the Ottoman empire. It had its own local dynasty, called khedives and founded by Mehmet `Ali Pasha, and its own bureaucracy, army, and police. Yet it paid tribute to Istanbul every year, and recognized the sovereignty of the sultan. Egypt in the 1850s suffered from a relatively bad economy, though it was helped slightly by the building of the first railway, between Alexandria and Cairo, which was completed in 1858. The beginnings of a population explosion also bedeviled the province, since per capita income would remain low if there were more and more persons among whom the limited agricultural production would have to be divided.

The American Civil War and the Egyptian Cotton Economy
The outbreak of the American Civil War, however, helped enrich Egypt enormously in the 1860s under the khedive Isma`il (r. 1863–79). The US North blockaded the South, which had supplied 80 percent of the cotton for England's factories, producing a cotton famine. The British desperately looked elsewhere, to Egypt and India in particular. Egypt was favored with a natural strain of long-staple cotton that was suited to the factories of Great Britain, and with the price soaring, Egyptians began exporting large quantities of this cash crop from their Mediterranean port of Alexandria. Cotton was gold, and the Egyptian state benefited a great deal from the taxes it imposed on this cash crop. The government bureaucracy was able to expand, along with the army and the police, and thousands of students began going to state schools.

Isma`il launched voyages of exploration up the Nile, and ultimately sent colonial armies of conquest into East Africa as far as Uganda, dreaming of making Egypt an imperial power in its own right. The government laid hundreds of miles of railroad track and put in an extensive network of telegraph lines and a steamship postal delivery system. This Egyptian information revolution for the first time allowed rapid and easy exchange of news up and down the Nile Valley. Initially the state benefited most from this change, as when Isma`il's modern river navy was able to respond quickly to a messianic peasant uprising in 1863 in Upper Egypt, easily putting it down. The Egyptian government allowed a French concern to build the Suez Canal, which became the major route between Europe and its colonies in the East, and suddenly made Egypt among the more strategically important places in the world. Seeking to be accepted as a European-style monarch, Isma`il initiated a Chamber of Delegates in 1866, which was initially appointed and made up mainly of large landlords who were intended to do little more than advise the khedive. Over time, however, they began being

elected, and began thinking of themselves as a real parliament, desiring more say over the government budget. Thinking that the new cotton wealth would continue to come in, the Egyptian viceroy borrowed great sums from European bondholders and banks, paying exorbitant fees and interest by European standards.

The end of the Civil War in the USA, however, contributed to a cotton bust, so that the late 1860s were a time of economic retrenchment. Although prices rose again in the early 1870s, Egypt had become over-committed, and increasingly could repay the loans only by overtaxing the peasants, beating them and forcing them to turn over livestock and crops in such quantities that their ability to produce the next year was imperiled. In 1876, Egypt formally defaulted on its loans and even sold to the British, for a pittance, its stake in the Suez Canal to raise cash. The European states and financial concerns responded by establishing the Debt Commission and putting one Frenchman and one Englishman on the Egyptian cabinet to oversee the budget and ensure that the debt servicing continued to be paid. Egyptians were the most indebted people in the world, per capita, and conditions in the countryside became desperate.

In 1876, as well, the Egyptian government instituted Mixed Courts that applied elements of European law in matters such as property rights, and for the first time lenders were able to foreclose on Egyptian peasants who fell into arrears in paying off their debts. Previous Egyptian custom had required that peasants be given time to come up with the money. Since most moneylenders were Greeks or other Christians, anti-Christian, anti-European sentiment began to fester in the countryside, especially where many peasants had lost their land. The Mixed Courts functioned to reassure European investors and expatriates that Egyptian law would be just, but most lower-class Egyptians found them quite the opposite.

In the late 1870s Egypt suffered from drought. Because the rains did not fall abundantly upriver in East Africa, the Nile was low and did not flood its banks by much, depriving the topsoil of needed silt (which acted like natural fertilizer). Egypt also suffered from another fall in cotton prices, and finally from famine that killed thousands. Rapid population growth after 1850 may have contributed to the problems, since the number of Egyptians rose from about 3.8 million in 1800 to about 8 million in 1880, leaving peasants with ever smaller plots of land in each generation. Some Egyptians and immigrant Syrians agitated for a stronger parliament and for an end to European financial control, and by winter to spring of 1879, Isma`il had thrown in his lot with them, in hopes of using the great discontent in the country to gain some independence from the encroaching Europeans.

The European powers were outraged. Their consuls, who were based in a new part of Alexandria and had begun to function almost like a senate in their own right, met and decided to depose Isma`il. They did so in June of 1879, bringing his son, Tawfiq, into Cairo as Ottoman viceroy, with the support of Sultan Abdulhamid II in Istanbul. The agitation against creeping European infringements on the rights of Egyptians in their own country did not cease, however. In summer of 1879 the fiery Muslim activist Sayyid Jamal al-Din "al-Afghani" (who was actually from Iran but had lived in Afghanistan) attracted huge crowds when he spoke at mosques against informal European colonialism and on behalf of the downtrodden common folk. He was expelled from the country in August, but his disciples continued to agitate for his causes. Many private newspapers began being founded in the 1870s, as the printing revolution took hold in Egypt several centuries after it had in East Asia and Europe. The readership of these newspapers, who came to number tens of thousands in the early 1880s, learned about the outside world and European politics. The readers included the 10,000 Egyptians who had graduated from state schools under Isma`il and formed a new intellectual class. The illiterate also heard the news. Schoolboys at shops or in village coffeehouses would even read out to local audiences reports about the latest speech on Egyptian affairs given by the British prime minister.

Because of the need to service Egypt's debts to European concerns, the bureaucracy and army were shrunk and salaries were paid quite late. Egyptians in this period of limited resources began thinking of themselves as a set of distinct ethnic groups in competition for the limited resources. Arabic-speaking Muslim Egyptians formed the majority, and they often came to resent the Egyptian Coptic Christians who had a disproportionate role in the bureaucracy, as well as immigrant Syrian Christians and some 100,000 Europeans of all social classes who had been drawn to the country by the white gold rush of the cotton trade. Many of the Europeans were ruffians, and violence between them and Egyptians in the towns became common. Whereas formerly Muslims might not much differentiate among themselves, now local Arabic speakers began also resenting the Ottoman elite, made up of big landlords, military men, and high bureaucrats who spoke Ottoman Turkish and had their origins in Anatolia, Eastern Europe, or the Caucasus.

The officer corps was dominated by the Ottoman Egyptians, mainly of Turkish, Albanian, or Circassian extraction. These groups were at the top of Egyptian society, but many of them did not even speak Egyptian Arabic well. Egypt was still a vassal state of the Ottoman empire, and Egyptians were subjects of the sultan. Ottoman officials and their families settled in Egypt formed the upper class. The military academy was closed to local Egyptians. Some Egyptians had served long and honorably enough to have risen into the officer corps from the ranks. The financial crisis, however, made it difficult for the Egyptian government to think about expanding the officer corps or letting new groups into it who were not from one of the upper-class Ottoman ethnicities that then dominated it. The government determined to keep Egyptian recruits only for short periods, closing off any hope of further Arabic-speaking soldiers being promoted to officer rank. The Egyptian junior officers were outraged, and joined with the medium and large peasants and many of the intellectuals and urban guild members in becoming radicalized. Through 1880 and into the summer of 1881, many activists agitated for new parliamentary elections, and they were supported by Egyptian officers such as Colonel Ahmad `Urabi. Viceroy Tawfiq reluctantly agreed to hold elections, and the Chamber of Deputies met in the fall of 1881 and began hammering out a constitution. The members of this parliament also began demanding oversight over the budget, as with most parliamentary bodies in the world. This move was opposed by Britain and France for fear that the Chamber of Deputies might be unwilling to continue to allot fully half of Egypt's budget to servicing the debts to European concerns. Tawfiq acquiesced in `Urabi's popularity, promoting him to general and appointing him minister of war.

Riots in Alexandria France and Britain became increasingly worried about anti-European sentiment and about the dangers they saw to European investments in Egypt, as well as to the continued payment of the debt servicing. Ironically, these two democratic states were unprepared to trust the democratic process in Egypt, and they tended to downplay the populist roots of the increased social activism, seeing `Urabi as little more than leader of a would-be military junta. In late May of 1882, they sent warships into Alexandria harbor and presented an ultimatum to the viceroy that he dismiss `Urabi as minister of war. Tawfiq gladly gave in and did so. The mood turned ugly in Alexandria, which had a large European population of Greeks, Italians, Maltese, French, and British. On June 11 a riot broke out between Egyptians and Europeans, in which several hundred Egyptians were killed and about fifty Europeans (the latter for the most part had firearms, which the Egyptians did not). This riot was quelled late in the day by the government, but it was too late. The European press, often depending on European expatriates in Alexandria who had substantial investments in the country, represented this event as an unprovoked massacre of Europeans by Muslim mobs. The French saw that events were hurtling toward a military intervention and withdrew, having their hands full in recently annexed Tunisia and increasingly unsatisfied that the British were being fair to Egyptian grievances. In Great Britain, on the other hand, the press reports had drummed up a war fever and members of Parliament were demanding action. The killing of European civilians reminded them painfully of the 1857 revolt in India.

On July 11 the British navy bombarded Alexandria and forced `Urabi and his troops to withdraw from the city. The shells and departing vandals set fires that virtually destroyed this rich cotton port. Artisans and peasants joined in the revolt in fair numbers. A national convention was held in late July attended by the great men and the members of parliament. They issued a decree deposing Viceroy Tawfiq as a creature of the Europeans. A new common-law cabinet was formed that gave `Urabi charge of its revolutionary military. Those opposed to Tawfiq were influential in much of the area south of Alexandria. In August Sir Garnet Wolseley and his troops, many of them from India, were landed near the Suez Canal, and they took that part of Egypt, protecting British access to India. They then gradually marched on Cairo. In early September they met `Urabi's forces at Tell al-Kabir near the capital, and after initially being rebuffed, were able by dint of superior weaponry and tactics to defeat the Egyptian army, after which they marched into Cairo, where they took `Urabi and other revolutionaries prisoner.

**Aftermath of the `Urabi Revolt** The `Urabi revolt could not be called a nationalist one. The leaders had maintained that they remained loyal Ottoman subjects, ignoring the sultan's opposition to their movement. They did not want a separate nation-state, but rather more regional rights and more equitable treatment for Arabic-speaking Muslims. Their most pressing goal was to roll back the informal colonization of their land by European economic interests, immigrants, and imperial consuls. A regional, elected parliament responsive to the Egyptian middle and upper classes was their tool of choice.

The British restored Tawfiq to his title, but in fact transformed Egypt into yet another British colony in all but name. To respect continued Ottoman claims, Egypt was termed a "protectorate." The British were then drawn into the Sudan where, just as they were taking Egypt, a messianic uprising had broken out, led by a Sufi mystic named al-Mahdi or the "promised one." As with the Babi movement in Iran, he appealed to Muslims who felt modernity was threatening their world, and that only a divinely inspired leadership could restore it to balance.

This revolt was fueled in part by resentment against the changes in Sudanese society made by the Egyptian bureaucracy and army, especially by Egyptian attempts to outlaw the slave trade. Many Sudanese clans and guilds had grown wealthy from trading slaves. These, along with other clans, joined the Mahdi in hopes of establishing a Muslim revivalist state that would block such foreign-inspired modernist intrusions and expel the Egyptians and other foreigners. Prime Minister Gladstone was

against imperial expansion and had not been happy about being led by circumstances to intervene in Egypt. He did not wish to commit troops to the Sudan, even to escort out of Khartoum endangered European expatriates. He did agree to send an old Egyptian hand, Charles Gordon, in hopes that he could find a way to get them out. In the event, however, the Mahdi's forces besieged and took Khartoum and killed Gordon and other Europeans in 1885. Thereafter the British feared that their position in Egypt itself might be threatened if they did not take action, and they initiated a long war against the Mahdi and his successors. Major General Sir Herbert Kitchener and his Anglo-Egyptian army of 26,000 men finally won this struggle in 1898 at Omdurman, where they defeated the Mahdist leader, Abd Allah. Thereafter the Sudan too became a British colony. The Mahdist uprising somewhat resembled the 1857 revolt in India, with its attempt to re-establish older forms of authority and social organization that were threatened by modern colonialism.

The British proconsul or colonial overlord of Egypt, Lord Cromer, established British control of the Nile Valley and lowered taxes in the countryside in order to win over the landlords and peasants. British land laws and the continued importance of agricultural capitalism centered on cotton allowed a small number of elite Egyptian families to build up huge hacienda estates. Egypt became England's cotton farm. Cromer insisted on paying down the debt, which he did. The combination of lower taxes and faithful debt servicing left very little for government funding of areas such as education. Cromer, who began in the Indian civil service, observed in one memorandum that educating so many Indians had probably been a mistake, probably referring to the rise of the anti-colonial Congress Party there. In the early twentieth century, a new generation of Egyptian intellectuals was led by Ahmad Lutfi al-Sayyid, who founded a newspaper dedicated to educating Egyptians for eventual independence as a separate state. Before 1914, however, such thinkers from the upper strata of professionals and large landlords thought in terms of working within the British empire for a distant goal.

Africa

As part of the post-1882 Scramble for Africa, the Germans behaved with incredible harshness in Namibia and established quasi-military rule over what is now Tanzania. Resistance to the massive wave of colonization in this period depended primarily on alliances among clan chieftains and other local leaders such as religious figures, threatened with being swept aside by new, colonial forms of authority and organization. The African polities, however, tended to be small and regional, and were internally divided as well as often divided against one another. Large European empires could come in and make deals with dissatisfied vassals or could set two enemies to fighting and then step in to pick up the pieces. The Europeans, being relatively wealthy and powerful, were attractive as partners for some local elites willing to collaborate with them. In many areas of Africa, villagers were virtually stateless, and so open to conquest. In some instances, as in the Ivory Coast in West Africa, the isolated, rural, stateless villagers put up strong and extended resistance to European conquest (in this case by the French).

Some of these dynamics are visible in the German African empire. Bismarck's Germany established a colony in what is now Tanzania, then known as Tanganyika, in 1886. The Germans claimed the rural hinterland outright, but negotiated a "lease" of the coast and its port towns from the sultan of Zanzibar, the recognized ruler of the largely Muslim coastal areas. German insensitivity provoked riots by Muslim townspeople in 1888. The German Empire intervened militarily to put them down. In subsequent decades, aggressive German investment, railroad-building, and appropriation of land spurred the coffee and rubber industries, but some policies made many local people furious. In 1905–07 those in the southeast showed their fury over being deprived of what they thought of as their traditional rights in the land by mounting what was called the Maji Maji uprising. It was led by a messianic prophet, Kinjikitile Ngwale, who claimed to be able to provide his followers with holy water that would make them immune to the bullets of the colonizers. The Germans defeated the movement, but changed some policies, such as moving away from a heavily military administration to a more civilian one.

On the other side of Africa, in the southwest, the Germans established another colony, Southwest Africa (now Namibia). They employed divide and rule tactics against the bushmen and brought in German settlers. Copper and diamonds came to be important primary commodities. The smooth establishment of imperial German control was interrupted in 1904–07 by a major uprising. Unlike in Tanganyika, the German response in this area was marked by almost unheard of cruelty, with some populations rounded up and put in concentration camps and other rebellious villagers shot en masse or hanged in large numbers. In the course of putting down this rebellion of Africans, the German army used a newly invented weapon, the automatic machine gun, with deadly effectiveness (often against villagers who lacked firearms). In some ways, such colonial wars proved a practice arena for World War I in Europe.

Other such sporadic rebellions were mounted in British and French colonies, as well. Africans, clearly, were unable to throw off imperial rule at that time. Africans suffered in any attempt to oppose the Europeans in the nineteenth century from the relatively small size of the polities dotting the continent, from low literacy, and from the multiplicity of languages spoken. The opportunities for propagandizing the masses were limited to oral media such as gossip and song (which sometimes could be somewhat effective, as the uprisings show). Superior European weaponry, tactics, information, and organization allowed these local units to be defeated and absorbed, however loosely, into new colonial frameworks. These new colonies, it should be remembered, ruled the same underlying kin and village groupings as the chieftains they displaced. They depended heavily on the co-operation of key elites drawn from them. Ironically, the very processes of colonialism helped spread identities that ultimately allowed more effective resistance to it. The French, without meaning to, gave new impetus to the spread of Islam in West Africa by their road-building, which allowed Muslim merchants and missionaries to travel more quickly and efficiently. Colonial languages such as French and English allowed elites to link up with one another politically in an area that might otherwise have been linguistically fragmented.

Conclusion It has been argued that nationalism is above all an act of the imagination. We can speak of it in a situation where large numbers of persons can identify with their fellow countrymen and countrywomen, as a single political community on a specific territory with a common government. Groups that come to support a nationalist vision (intellectuals, businessmen, workers, peasants) typically create a mythic history that enshrines the nation as somehow eternal, despite its recent origins in fact, and despite the ethnic and political diversity that reigns beneath the national umbrella. They spread a single standardized language. They set up a countrywide school system that teaches literacy and loyalty to the state. Nationalism depends heavily on the techniques of modern identity-making. The railroad, the telegraph, the steamship, the museum, the anthem, the leading newspaper, and the best-selling novelist are all key to the formation of this feeling of national belonging. The conscript army that throws village boys from all over the country together under often extreme conditions is sometimes overlooked as a significant vehicle of patriotic feelings.

The economic competition among nations fostered by industrialization often did more to increase national solidarity than to divide the population into warring workers and industrialists (contrary to what Marx thought at the time). This point leads us to underline that nationalism was not only an ideology of internal unity. It often arose in part because of what were perceived as external threats. French Emperor Napoleon III's overbearing domination of much of Europe ironically helped foster both Italian and German nationalism, and his policies of colonial subjugation in North Africa provoked revolts on the part of Algerians. The French nationalism of the secularizing Third Republic after 1870 owed much to competition with a newly united and militarily powerful Germany. Ottoman attempts to create an imperial nationalism that might appeal to its diverse populations were both inspired by and provoked by fear of the success of Italian and French nationalisms based on the idea of the nation-state. Such aristocratic nationalisms failed in the long run.

Industrialization and scientific advance spurted in nineteenth-century Europe, giving European armies and commercial groups a marginal advantage over most of the peoples of the other continents. It is often forgotten how slim the margin of victory often was in colonial wars. Of course, in some initial encounters, as with the first Anglo-Afghan War in the 1840s or the rebellion of 1857 in India, the Europeans were massacred. Still, the margin was fairly consistent.

Under colonialism, the development of nationalism was complicated. Colonial regimes seldom pursued mass education in a single language, preferring instead to train cadres of elites in the colonial language so as to allow them to staff the lower colonial bureaucracy and military ranks. They had no incentive to attempt to standardize a local language or to impose it on the entire population. Whereas those in Garibaldi's united Italy came to speak and read standard Italian, India retained sixteen major languages and dozens of smaller ones through two hundred years of British colonialism in the subcontinent, with English coming to be the language of the highly educated and powerful throughout the region. Despite the attempts of postcolonial India and Pakistan to promote Hindi and Urdu respectively, neither has yet become a truly national language with near-universal dominance. The French in Algeria probably actually plunged that population into more illiteracy in Arabic than had been common in the early nineteenth century, removing state support for Koran schools. Likewise, the British in Egypt deliberately avoided developing institutions of mass education, seeking to train only a small group of Egyptian intellectuals in English to staff their colonial bureaucracy. Colonial newspapers were often heavily censored, and they were of little use for spreading nationalist consciousness. Weak Old Regime states such as Qajar Iran or the Two Kingdoms of Sicily and Lombardy in the Italian peninsula were often ineffective in suppressing dissident intellectuals and peasants, whereas colonial regimes tended to be far more efficient in breaking up such networks.

For these reasons and others, anti-colonial movements in the nineteenth century tended to be deprived of the major means of nation-making. Unable to manufacture a linguistic ethnicity through gaining control of the state, they were forced to resort to other claims of legitimacy. In some instances, they hearkened back to precolonial forms of authority, whether the Mughal empire in India or Sufi messianism in the Sudan. In other cases they appealed to instruments of modernity, such as the modern army or the parliament, as in Egypt's `Urabi revolution. While later nationalists often took inspiration from them, these movements did not aim at the creation of an independent nation-state on the Italian model, but rather at the restoration of indigenous forms of government, including empire, that did not ground sovereignty in a single territorially based nation. By the eve of World War I, however, some Egyptian, Algerian, and Indian intellectuals had begun thinking in terms of the nation and representative institutions, and begun working for independence. Colonialism retarded some aspects of nation-making, but in providing an easy target and obvious enemy for anti-imperialists, it often allowed a mobilization of grievances that could easily take on a nationalist tinge.

Study Questions (1) "Peoples" existed, speaking a broadly similar language and living in particular territories, before 1800. Why do most social scientists not consider them "nations" in that period? What are the key attributes of the nation-states that emerged in the course of the nineteenth century?

(2) Many people consider language and race to be "natural," commonsense categories. The author of this chapter argues, however, that both language and race are artificial ideas. Do you agree or disagree, and why?

(3) What were the communications and infrastructure breakthroughs that made it possible for states to transform their citizens into members of a common nation?

(4) What sorts of discontent produced the great anti-colonial uprisings and movements, such as those in Egypt, India, and German-ruled Africa? What forms of collective action did the rebels use to fight the colonizer? Why did they tend to fail in the nineteenth and very early twentieth century?

(5) Some movements for national unification were primarily waged by the laboring and middle classes, while others were mainly pursued by ruling elites. Discuss the examples above, showing the difference between these two different paths to nation-building.

Suggested Reading BENEDICT ANDERSON, *Imagined Communities: Reflections on the Origin and Spread of Nationalism*, rev. edn. (London: Verso, 2006). Anderson's image of state as "imagined community" is powerful and widely influential. He presents a variety of explanations of state formation.

ROGERS BRUBAKER, *Citizenship and Nationhood in France and Germany* (Cambridge, MA: Harvard University Press, 1992). This is a striking comparison between very different varieties of citizenship in France and Germany.

ERNEST GELLNER, *Nationalism*, 2nd edn. (Ithaca, NY: Cornell University Press, 2009). Gellner emphasizes the role of states in forging nations.

Andrew Gordon, *The Modern History of Japan: From Tokugawa Times to the Present*, 2nd edn. (New York: Oxford University Press, 2008). Gordon's comprehensive survey, well written and highly original, is a good introduction to modern Japanese history.

E.J. Hobsbawm, *Nations and Nationalism since 1780: Programme, Myth, Reality*, 2nd edn. (Cambridge University Press, 2012). Hobsbawm's book is a classic Marxist critique of nationalism, analyzing it as false consciousness.

Afaf Lutfi Sayyid-Marsot, *A Short History of Modern Egypt* (Cambridge University Press, 2007). This is a concise history of the economic, social, and industrial history of modern Egypt by a leading authority in the field.

Anthony Smith, *Nations and Nationalism*, 2nd edn. (Ithaca, NY: Cornell University Press, 2009). Smith explores nationalism as rooted in the early modern period and based on pre-existing conditions.

Ian Talbot, *India and Pakistan (Inventing the Nation)* (London: Arnold, 2000). In this account of national identity formation in the non-Western world, Talbot explores differences and similiarities.

Glossary
colonialism: The project of one nation-state ruling over other peoples, depriving them of their own state, for military, strategic, or economic gain.

Enfield rifle: In 1853 the Enfield rifle became standard issue for the British army. It was the first muzzle-loading rifle with interchangeable parts used by the British army. Its use of beef and pork fat to lubricate the rifle provoked religion-based resistance among Hindu and Muslim troops in India and was one cause of the Great Rebellion of 1857.

nationalism: The principle that holds that the political and national should be congruent, that ethnicity and territorial boundaries should coincide.

nawab: Honorific title for the princely ruler of Oudh. Originally a semi-autonomous province of the Mughal empire, it was moving toward independence.

Ottomanism: The attempt to construct a pan-imperial identity within the Ottoman empire. Following the Reform Decree of 1856 by Sultan Abdulmecid, the law now affirmed that all Ottoman subjects were equal under law.

pan-Islamism: A political movement advocating the unity of Muslims under one Islamic state – often a caliphate – or an international organization similar to a European Union with Islamic principles.

pan-Turkism: A term used, beginning in the 1880s, by Turkic nationalists to assert the existence of a Turkic nation. Today any pan-Turkic nationalist would include on a list of pan-Turkic peoples most of the population of Azerbaijan, Kazakhstan, Kyrgyzstan, Turkey, Turkmenistan, and Uzbekistan.

Risorgimento: A term (in Italian "rising again") for the reunification of Italy. It was much used by Italian nationalists to suggest that an Italian nation that went back to the time of the Romans was being revived and reborn with the formation of an Italian state in nineteenth-century Italy.

settler colonialism: Settler colonies were often based in climates and environments similar to those of the European sending region. By making the best land available to Europeans, colonial governments facilitated the mass migration of Europeans to settle in colonial areas.

taluqdars: Large landowners in British India. Although the precise definition varied from province to province, they were charged with collecting taxes, enforcing law and order, and providing military support. As British control over India expanded, British authorities were forced to deal with these magnates. The British tended to see the taluqdars as akin to feudal lords in the West and announced the end of tax-exempt land grants and even threatened to seize some of their land. This was one of the underlying grievances of the Great Rebellion of 1856.

Young Turks: A political reform movement in the early twentieth-century Ottoman empire that sought to establish a constitutional monarchy and modernize the state.

Wars between 1914 and 1945

Ireland
London
Normandy Paris
New York

Midway
Pearl Harbor

Mexico

Five largest cities *millions*

1. New York

3. Tokyo

5. Berlin

| 12.588 | 8.099 | 6.37 | 6 | 4.339 |

2. London

4. Paris

PART IV

1914–1950: Wars and revolutions

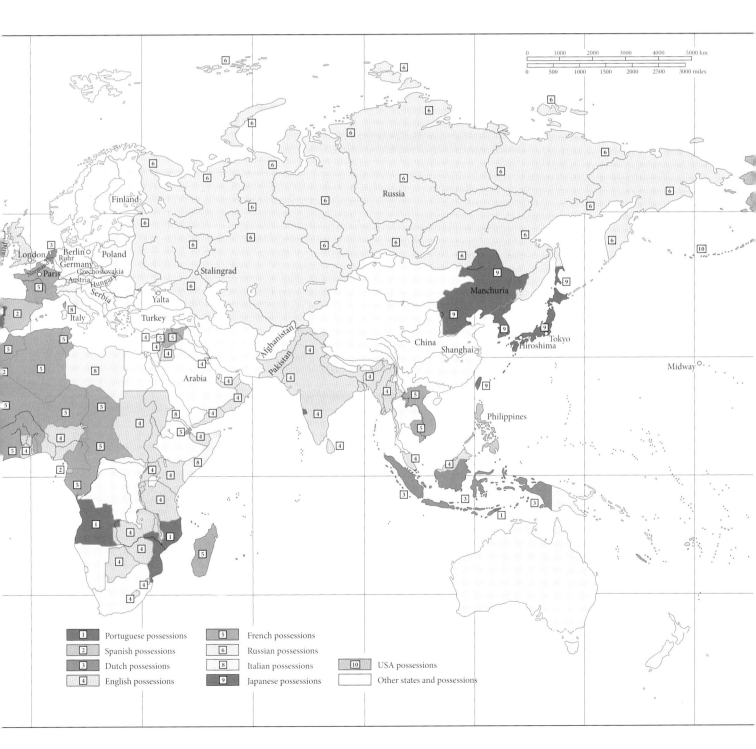

Europe (including Russia)	
1905	First Russian Revolution.
June 28, 1914	Archduke Ferdinand assassinated, leading to World War I on July 28, 1914.
1917	Bolshevik Revolution begins.
November 11, 1918	End of World War I.
1919	Paris Peace Conference, leading to Treaty of Versailles.
1919–33	Weimar Republic in Germany.
1920	League of Nations created in Geneva.
1921	New Economic Policy begins in Russia.
1924	Death of Lenin.
1933	Hitler becomes German chancellor.
1938	Munich Agreement signed.
1939	Molotov–Ribbentrop Pact of non-aggression between Germany and Soviet Union.
September 1, 1939	Germany invades Poland, beginning World War II.
December 7, 1941	Surprise Japanese attack at Pearl Harbor brings USA into World War II the next day.
May 7, 1945	Germany surrenders, ending World War II in Europe.

East Asia	
1905	Russo-Japanese War.
1910	Japan annexes Korea.
1912	End of Qing dynasty. Taisho emperor takes Japanese throne.
1919	May Fourth Movement in China.
1926	Guomindang begins its military Northern Expedition in China, leading to reunification of the country in 1928.
1930	Assassination of Hamaguchi.
1931	Japanese invasion of Manchuria. Manchuria Communist Party establishes Jiangxi Soviet.
1934–35	Long March of Chinese Communist Party to Yan'an province.
1937	Marco Polo Bridge Incident begins Second Sino-Japanese War.

Middle East	
1912	Ottoman empire loses First Balkan War.
1917	Balfour Declaration supports Jewish homeland in Palestine.
1923	Ottoman empire dissolved. Treaty of Lausanne recognizes creation of independent Turkey.

South and Southeast Asia	
1914	Gandhi returns to India from South Africa.
1919	Amritsar massacre in India.
1920	Gandhi launches boycott of British goods.
1922	Gandhi arrested.
1925	Reza Khan declared shah of Persia.

Americas	
1910	Mexican Revolution begins.
1913–21	US presidency of Woodrow Wilson.
April 1917	USA enters World War I.

1920	US Congress rejects League of Nations.
	Nineteenth Amendment brings about women's suffrage in USA.
1931	Stock market crash leads to beginning of Great Depression.
1933–45	US presidency of Franklin D. Roosevelt.
1933	First Hundred Days of New Deal.

The main theme of this part is the collapse and partial restoration of the liberal, capitalist, and imperial orders that allowed Europeans to dominate most of the world. For Europeans, the nineteenth century was a time of unprecedented prosperity and power. Their mastery of the new industrial technologies had given them direct control of over half of the world's peoples and huge influence over the rest. The great global linkages created by the European empires drew in commodities and labor from all over the world to create the products that went out to consumers everywhere. The USA, too, enjoyed its Gilded Age of wealth and empire, and Japan was rising quickly to join the elite club of great powers. It seemed that this machinery of expanding production and power could continue indefinitely. Many predicted, in the words of the historian Arnold Toynbee, the coming of an age of universal peace, wealth, and justice, an "earthly paradise."

It was not to be. The Great War which broke out in 1914 destroyed the international imperial order, devastating all the European societies far beyond anyone's expectations. Worse was to come. The brief, precarious stability of the 1920s fell apart in the 1930s under the impact of a savage world depression and the rise of a new, vicious mass movement: fascism. The world plunged into a new global war even more destructive than the first.

Politics, especially the politics of war and mass mobilization, dominate the story of the early twentieth century more than any other theme. War magnified the power of governments over their peoples, but also increased the claims of subjects on their states. Governments could not step back and leave markets alone, nor could they expect free trade by itself to bring peace and prosperity. Economic integration alone was not enough to draw the world together. Driven by geopolitical conflict, empires and nation-states could use the immense resources generated by industrial technologies for the purpose of political and cultural domination, just as easily as for peaceful trade. Large human collectivities, mobilized by mass communication technologies, came to see each other as irreconcilable enemies, not sharers in mutual gain. We can see now what was not obvious at the time: that the great capitalist empires harbored major contradictions. Their inability to resolve their differences nearly brought down the entire liberal democratic capitalist order once and for all.

The liberal imperial system of the late nineteenth century was unable to adjust to the rise of new powers and the decline of old ones. As Germany and Japan increased their economic strength, they followed the tried and true pattern of seeking colonies and competing for resources with the leading powers, Britain and France. As the Austro-Hungarian, Ottoman, and Chinese empires weakened, the stronger powers fought over the spoils. Two great coalitions emerged: Britain, France, and Russia (the Allies) versus Germany and the Austro-Hungarian and Ottoman empires (the Central Powers). China, Japan, and the USA later joined the Allied powers. Slavic nationalists, seeking freedom from Austro-Hungarian rule with Russian backing, touched off the spark that exploded into global conflict.

Crisis for European imperial powers, however, meant opportunity for others. Revolutionary socialism, in the new, centralized, organizational form developed by Lenin, took power in Russia in 1917 and sought to transform fundamentally the major economies of the world with a new program of international proletarian revolution. Colonized peoples, galvanized by the victory of Japan over Russia in 1905 and Lenin's appeals, stepped up their resistance to imperial rule. Indians under Gandhi's leadership launched major civil disobedience movements to drive the British out. But despite initial high hopes, the socialist revolution did not spread beyond Russia, and in the colonial world only tiny Ireland gained its independence through revolution and civil war. Eastern and Southern Europeans forged new nations out of the wreckage of the old empires, and China finally put itself together as a united nation in 1928, but the British and French still maintained their overseas empires, or even expanded them, in modified form.

The most dynamic new mass movement of the interwar years was fascism, a new form of social movement that grew out of wartime conditions. Its ideology of militarism, cult of the leader, aggressive imperial expansion, and social repression promised to restore stability to a turbulent world. Fascists, originating in Italy under Mussolini in the 1920s, took power in Germany and Spain in the 1930s, and had strong influence in China, Japan, and elsewhere as world economic depression deepened. Once again, the liberal economic system and political order failed to respond effectively. Fearful of another horrible war, and ideologically hostile to the Soviet Union, Europeans took no co-ordinated steps to check Hitler's determination to dominate the continent. The United States, likewise, after brief intervention in World War I, withdrew from active involvement in world affairs, doing nothing effective to resolve European economic crises, stop Japan, or defend China. World War II grew out of the failures to solve the issues of political power and structural inequality that generated World War I.

Except for Indochina (modern-day Cambodia, Laos, and Vietnam), East and Southeast Asia were not under European colonial control. For this reason, major turning points occurred at different times than in Europe. Europeans and Americans date the climactic events of the twentieth century as 1914 (the onset of World War I), 1929 (the beginning of the world depression), and 1939 (the initiation of World War II in Europe with Hitler's invasion of Poland). For East Asians, more significant dates are 1905 (Japan's victory over Russia), 1911 (the collapse of the Qing empire), 1928 (the reunification of China), and 1931 (Japan's invasion of Manchuria). Still, East Asians shared in the same processes as the rest of the world: the fall of empires, the rise of nations, the rise and fall of liberal free market economies, the failed struggle for democracy, the rise of militarized nationalism and fascism, and the ejection of colonial powers.

To some extent, East Asians also participated in the European conflict: 100,000 Chinese workers helped the French during World War I; Japan joined the Allies against Germany in World War I in order to take over Germany's colonies in the East. The depression years of the 1930s caused militarism to flourish in Japan, while the Bolshevik Revolution inspired revolutionary activists in China and elsewhere. On the other hand,

East Asia had two special features: first, the remarkable rise of Japan to the ranks of a true global power, including colonies, the only non-Western nation to make this step; and second, the reconstruction of China from a vast empire into an even more populous nation-state with nearly the same boundaries as the empire it replaced, inspired by a revolutionary ideology and party organization adopted from the Soviet Union.

Both revolutionary nationalism and imperialism were originally Western products, but they took on fundamentally new and distinctive characteristics when transmitted to East Asia. Like Europeans, who could not successfully defend liberal polities or a free trade order against challenges by militarized, protectionist, and expansionist states, East Asians also abandoned most of the basic features of liberalism, but militarism in East Asia did not produce the mass mobilization or violent racism seen in fascist Europe, and the anti-colonial drive of East Asia gave its world war features not found in the old imperial powers of the West.

The world in the nineteenth century had been united as never before by the power of industrial technology and imperial domination. It was a highly unequal world, where only a small elite held power, but most of the population benefited from general economic growth. In the first half of the twentieth century, the world divided into hostile blocs, each convinced of its own superiority and each determined to destroy the other. No one really benefited from the conflict; even the winners suffered terrible devastation. Why the human community, despite its great scientific and technological advances, could not prevent the most savage descent into barbarity in world history remains the baffling mystery of our age.

11 The Great War and world revolutions, 1914–1921

Timeline	
June 28, 1914	Bosnian nationalist Gavrilo Princip assassinates Austrian archduke in Sarajevo.
July 28, 1914	Austria declares war on Serbia, followed during the next week by Germany on Russia, France, and Belgium, Great Britain on Germany, and many others.
October 29, 1914	Ottoman empire enters the war against Russia.
December 1914	By the end of the year, naval warfare is wide-ranging, trench warfare is intense in Belgium and France (Western Front), air warfare is intensifying between France, Germany, and Great Britain; great movement on Eastern Front; British, French, Japanese, and Australian forces attack German colonies in Africa, Asia, and the Pacific.
May 7, 1915	German submarines sink British ocean liner *Lusitania* off Irish coast, with 1,195 dead, including 139 Americans.
1916–17	Russia's military defeats stir desertions, strikes, and political opposition to regime.
1916	Start of Arab rebellions against Ottoman empire.
January 22, 1916	American president Woodrow Wilson initiates unsuccessful proposals for general peace settlement, calling it "peace without victory."
April 24–29, 1916	Easter Rebellion in Ireland, vigorously repressed by the British.
March 12–16, 1917	Fall of tsarist regime in Russia's February Revolution (according to the old Russian calendar), rule of coalition Provisional Government.
April 6, 1917	United States declares war on Germany, followed by numerous others (USA also declares war on Austria-Hungary on December 7).
November 7, 1917	Bolshevik Revolution (known as October Revolution according to old Russian calendar) begins in Russia and overthrows Provisional Government.

March 3, 1918	Russians sign Treaty of Brest-Litovsk with the Central Powers, abandoning Transcaucasia, Finland, Estonia, Latvia, Lithuania, Ukraine, and Poland.
1918	Truces and surrenders end major hostilities throughout the war zones; numerous changes of government and declarations of independence.
1918–19	Worldwide spread of influenza, killing millions, especially those connected by war. Revolutions and civil wars in Afghanistan, Arabia, Austria, China, Finland, Germany, Hungary, Italy, Mexico, Russia, Turkey, and elsewhere.
January 18, 1919	Paris Peace Conference opens in Versailles; main peace treaty (Treaty of Versailles) signed on June 28.
1919–39	Multiple disputes over boundaries established in Versailles settlement. Ethnic hatreds flourish in the Balkans and Central Europe. For much of the interwar period, the terrorist Internal Macedonian Revolutionary Organization (IMRO) possesses its own army. Its assassinations and murders keep Bulgarian, Greek, and Macedonian ethnic sensitivities alive in the Balkans. In 1938 when Hitler marches into Czechoslovakia, Hungarian and Polish troops occupy portions of their fellow small state, eager to eat the scraps that Hitler throws them.
1919–22	Intermittent civil war in Ireland, ending with creation of the Irish Free State, but Northern Ireland still attached to the United Kingdom.
1919	Formation of International Labor Organization and International Commission for Air Navigation under the League of Nations, as well as the International Federation of Red Cross Societies and the Communist Third International (Comintern). US Senate rejects Treaty of Versailles.
1920	Official establishment of the League of Nations.
1921	USA makes separate peace with Austria and Germany.
1922	Washington Conference creates multiple treaties and sets quotas for navies.

World War I was a true world war. The war's impact was felt everywhere, including, as the case of Kas Maine shows, the British colonies. Kas Maine reached his twentieth birthday in 1914. Born of a black sharecropping family near the Harts River in South Africa's Transvaal region, Kas left a deep impression on researchers in the University of Witwatersrand's Oral History project who interviewed him repeatedly between 1979 and his death aged 91 in 1985. He enchanted interviewers with his complicated life and his almost total recall of its vivid details. By 1914, the able, articulate Kas had learned to read and write English while acquiring fair fluency in Afrikaans, the Dutch-based language spoken by most of South Africa's white farmers. He had also antagonized one white landlord sufficiently to force Kas's whole family to move to another farm, done several stints as a construction laborer or cook, and sent money home for his father to buy him the livestock he would eventually need in order to marry and establish his own household.

The Afrikaans-speaking **Boers**, farmers descended from Dutch settlers, had lost a bloody war with their English-speaking neighbors between 1899 and 1902. It was no trifling colonial conflict: Great Britain sent 450,000 men to conquer the previously independent Boer republics, and put 120,000 Boer women and children into the world's first concentration camps. The chastened Boers then settled grudgingly into coexistence with the British as citizens first of separate British colonies, then of a unified, self-governing British Dominion like Canada or Australia. Black Africans paid a large price for the coexistence of Boers and British. The white minority turned the black majority into subjects, not citizens. With no vote and little voice, blacks suffered from an increasingly repressive regime. In 1913, for example, South Africa's Native Land Act barred black land ownership in 87 percent of the Dominion's territory, outlawed sharecropping in areas of high white demand for black wage labor, and backed up efforts of white employers in those areas to force blacks into low-wage work.

For major landlords, mine owners, builders, and manufacturers, cheap black wage labor proved a bonanza. State backing may actually have given South Africa's big employers a more profitable deal than outright slavery would have provided: Slaveholders, after all, must feed and clothe their slaves as well as keeping them employed in off seasons. Low-wage employers did neither. South Africa's poorer white farmers, however, also typically depended on black labor but lacked the cash for wage payments. For that reason, authorities usually looked the other way when white landlords or tenants made verbal contracts with black sharecroppers. Black sharecroppers, they knew, could never get their side of those contracts enforced in white courts. Black sharecropping families like the Maines therefore lived a precarious, migratory existence. In good times with co-operative white farmers, they could build up their flocks and sell agricultural products on their own while supplying goods and services to the farmers. In bad times, however, they could only survive by finding supplementary employment elsewhere. They always ran the risk of sudden expulsion from the land they occupied.

The South African world of stark, government-enforced racial inequality seems a long way from the Europe of 1914. But the outbreak of World War I (as people called it once World War II began) strongly affected the life of Kas Maine. The German colony of South West Africa (now Namibia) lay to the northwest of South Africa. Afrikaans-speaking South Africans often voiced sympathy for the colony's German-speaking white settlers. Many Boers aligned themselves against the British, on the German and Austro-Hungarian side of the split that was opening in Europe. During 1914, Boers on the construction team for which Kas was working started to return home in preparation for a new rebellion against British authorities. When Great Britain and Germany declared war on each other in August 1914, the English contractor for Kas's road gang dismissed all his workers. Instead of returning to the farm, Kas and a cousin went to work in the diamond fields. Kas gave up, however, after a few weeks of heavy digging. He then returned to his family, but found them caught up in a new civil war among the whites.

When the South African government agreed to invade South West Africa on behalf of the British empire, a number of South Africa's senior Boer military officers defected and formed rebel armies. Eventually about 12,000 volunteers joined them. Those armies recruited Boers in the Maine family's region, requisitioned horses and cattle from the flocks tended by the family, and interrupted agricultural trade so severely that the family sent out its younger members, including Kas, into various forms of poorly paid wage work. Even that expedient faced war-driven trouble, since the war reduced the world market for South African diamonds, drove down their prices, and shrank the opportunities for work in the mines.

Whether as a consequence of the war or otherwise, the war period also brought replacement of a relatively easy-going Afrikaans-speaking farm manager by a hard-driving, efficiency-minded English-speaker. The new manager's demands drove the Maines off to another farm. Although the worldwide influenza epidemic of 1918 (itself facilitated by the war) spared Kas, it killed several members of his family. Those were hard times. By war's end, a grown-up Kas was splitting his time between diamond-mine wage labor and farm work, accumulating cattle so he could marry, and moving into his long life as sharecropper, herbalist, blacksmith, cattle-breeder, and jack of many other trades.

The effects of European war on South Africa's rural interior tells us how connected the world of 1914 had become. Because the previous century of commercial and imperial expansion had spread European and North American influence to all parts of the globe, very few corners escaped the impact of World War I. In South Africa, we can see the war affecting world markets, altering local economies, spreading disease, and generating armed rebellion. Elsewhere, the **Great War** (as people of the time commonly called it) strengthened some governments, undermined others, redrew the map of colonies, redirected international migration, spurred revolutions, and left a number of countries in ruins. The years from 1914 through 1921 proved a major pivot in world history.

This chapter considers the Great War as a worldwide series of events, tracing its influence over social, political, and economic changes throughout the world. Those changes emphatically include revolutionary movements in Russia and elsewhere. Here are the chapter's main points:

- By 1914, a century of imperial and capitalist expansion had extended the influence of European and North American events through the whole world; for that reason, Europe's first general war in a century almost immediately stirred deep responses on every continent.

- War mobilization generally strengthened the powers of states over their citizens in the short run, bringing large numbers of younger men into national armed forces and significant parts of the remaining population, including women, into war production.
- Most states drew major organized elements within them – including labor, capital, churches, and civic organizations – into the war effort, often on promises of postwar rewards. The hardships of war led groups to increase their demands for relief when states began to lose their wars as well as when wartime controls ended.
- As a consequence of these processes and of direct conquest by other European powers, Europe's major remaining continental empires – Russian, German, Austro-Hungarian, and Ottoman – all disintegrated during and after the war.
- Meanwhile, imperial powers on the winning side – notably Great Britain, France, Belgium, Japan, and the United States – consolidated or expanded their control in overseas territories.
- During this period, the United States moved rapidly toward world political and economic dominance.

The turbulent years from 1914 to 1921 therefore brought the world into very different conditions from those that had prevailed before the Great War.

11.1 WHY WAR HIT HARD

As Chapters 8 to 10 have demonstrated, between 1850 and 1914 a kind of globalization without the name was tightening connections among different parts of the world. Booming world trade shipped out manufactured goods from Europe, North America, and Japan as well as agricultural products from the Americas, Australia, and New Zealand in return for raw materials and precious objects from poorer regions. Capitalists from Europe and North America were likewise investing widely in Latin America and Asia. We have seen India, for example, becoming a hugely important market for British manufactures as well as a source of cotton, jute, tea, and other agricultural products for British consumption.

Communications and transportation accelerated, with telegraph, telephone, radio, railroads, automobiles, aircraft, steamships, and standardized times all playing their parts. Mass migration moved 20 million Chinese into Southeast Asia, 10 million Russians into eastern and southern reaches of the

growing Russian empire, 3 million or so Indians to destinations in Africa and the Americas, 9 million Japanese into Southeast Asia and the Pacific region, and a full 30 million Europeans to the Americas plus another 3 million to Britain's Pacific territories. These increasing, unequal ties generated dependency, resistance, and turmoil in poorer parts of the world, but they simultaneously increased the sensitivity of people everywhere to threats and opportunities emerging from Western countries.

European Powers Extend their Influence

Major powers also extended their influence by means of war, conquest, and military intervention. European empires – especially the British – continued their expansion over much of the earth. While tsarist Russia was separated from Britain and France by the Channel and the North Sea (both exposed to submarines), as Map 11.1 shows, the German and Austro-Hungarian empires enjoyed an advantageous position at the heart of Central Europe adjacent to one another. Both the United States and Japan joined the imperial game, with the USA acquiring Hawaii, the Philippines, Guam, and Puerto Rico, while throwing its weight around increasingly in Central America and the Caribbean. Meanwhile, Japan took over Formosa (now Taiwan), Korea, and parts of Manchuria. Colonizing powers did not merely conquer powerless peoples, however; they often competed with each other militarily. They competed with each other for control of colonies, for access to markets, and for security of their trade routes.

British forces intervened repeatedly in the eastern Mediterranean and the Near East, for example, because the Suez Canal (which became British property in 1875) provided a major transport link among Britain, the Mediterranean, India, and Indian Ocean ports. The Crimean War (1853–56) aligned Britain, France, and the Ottoman empire against Russian expansion into Ottoman territory, while another war broke out between Russia and the Ottomans in 1877–78. After 1890, the First Sino-Japanese War (1894–95), the Spanish–American War (1898), the Russo-Japanese War (1904–05), the Tripolitan War (1911), and two Balkan Wars (1912 and 1913) all involved competition among major powers for control over colonial territories.

New Technologies of War and Social Mobilization

Through these conflicts, the means of war were becoming more destructive. Between 1850 and 1914, Western armed forces first began using breech-loading (rather than muzzle-loading) artillery, immense steel cannon, magazine rifles, machine guns, nitroglycerine, poison gas, submarines, trucks, tanks, airplanes, dirigibles, steel-plated ships, railroad transport, and communication by radio and telegraph. Military expenditures rose across the Western world. Most dramatically, Germany and Britain staged a race to build the world's most formidable navy, Germany and France another race to build the world's most formidable army. Competition among Western states – plus Japan – accelerated after 1905, with even Russia building military strength in reaction to the battering it received in its war with Japan.

Social technology figured centrally in the increasing destructiveness of war. The idea of a fully mobilized "nation in arms" had already formed in France under the Revolution and Napoleon, but it became a much more widespread reality in Europe after 1870. Military budgets rose dizzily. Armies swelled and military conscription became more general. In most countries the military actually lost political independence as civilian administrators, revenue services, bankers, arms suppliers, and professional politicians became more crucial to the success of rearmament. In compensation, military leaders received command of enormously more lethal instruments of destruction.

The combination of increasing economic integration, accelerated communication, mass migration, colonial expansion, colonies as stakes of war, increasingly destructive armaments, and widespread domestic mobilization for war efforts magnified the effects of regional conflicts on the rest of the world. When Japan and Russia fought for influence in Korea and Manchuria, for example, not only enfeebled China but also all the Western powers that had been investing in East Asian trade found their interests seriously threatened. All of them reacted. In the other direction, conflicts within Europe rapidly spread elsewhere as colonies, clients, and allies became involved directly or indirectly. That happened in World War I.

Domestic Participation in War

Within war-making countries, furthermore, the soaring costs and expanded participation of mobilization for war produced deep domestic effects. Large-scale wars always increase governmental demands for military goods, services, manpower, and the money to pay for them. They usually produce substantial expansion in the size and power of governments. The immense scale of twentieth-century military organization simply multiplied those age-old effects of mobilization for war. In addition, the recruitment of huge armed services from the general population created direct connections between national governments and their citizenry. Mass armies created governmental connections not just with troops themselves, but also with families of those troops. In the longer run, troops and families acquired claims on governments, especially in the cases of families that lost breadwinners temporarily or permanently. Wartime conditions transformed the position of many women, who ran households while their husbands were at war, or who obtained industrial jobs for the first time. To a lesser extent, governments also accumulated obligations to workers who moved into war industries and other forms of support for the war effort. Governments typically imposed new controls over consumption, exchange, population movement, and political expression, all in the name of pursuing the war. Rationing of food and essential goods, for example, involved unprecedented governmental intervention in household life. Explicitly or implicitly, all governments promised compensating rewards when the war ended.

Enthusiasm Fades as the War Lengthens

A fascinating dynamic emerged. At the start of a war effort, even previously dissident populations generally collaborated; in some cases, as illustrated in Figure 11.1, mass street rallies expressed support for the war effort, although this was not true everywhere. Despite the flourishing of worker internationalism and pacifism across the Western world after 1870, for example, European and American workers rapidly lined up with the war aims of their own governments in 1914. Even the German Social Democrats, pledged by their membership in the Socialist International to oppose any war among the International's members, instantly joined the German war effort by suspending strikes and supporting military appropriations. But enthusiasm for war declined in almost every combatant country as the conflict ground on. It sometimes turned to outright opposition. Military and civilian dissidence rose the longer a country's participation in the war endured, the greater the war's cost to the military and civilian populations, the more the prospect of a country's defeat increased, and therefore the greater the likelihood that the postwar government would default on its wartime commitments. By May and June 1917, for example, France's beleaguered soldiers were widely refusing orders to enter high-risk combat; military courts gave 554 of them death sentences, and authorities actually executed 49 of them.

These effects varied greatly from country to country. At one extreme, the United States entered the war late (1917) at relatively low domestic cost, and emerged from the war with a strengthened government. (Even in the USA, however, antiwar socialists continued to receive visible support during the elections of 1917, with mayoral candidates gaining 22 percent of the vote in New York City, 25 percent in Buffalo, 34 percent in Chicago, and 44 percent in Dayton, Ohio.) At the other extreme, Russia called up 5 million troops rapidly in 1914 without great resistance, but by 1916 was facing massive strikes on the home front coupled with widespread desertions and mutinies on the battlefront. In 1917, Russia's February and October revolutions overthrew two governments in a row. Between the extremes

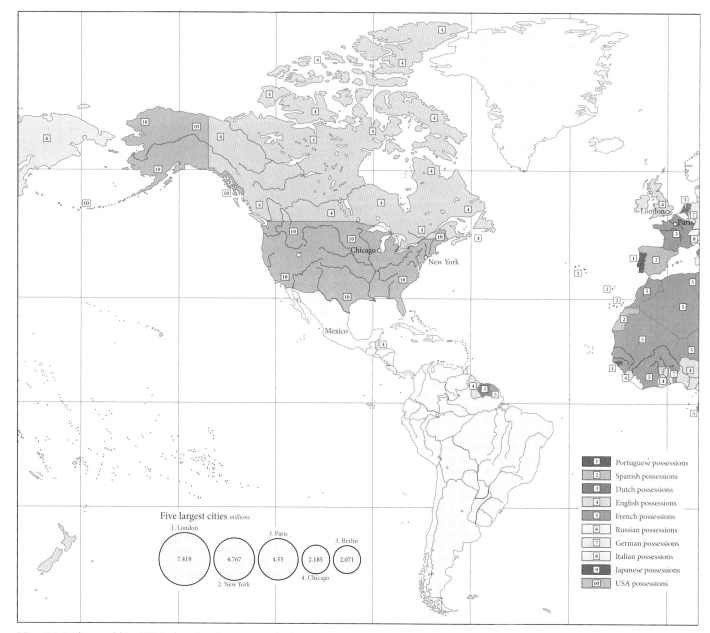

Map 11.1 The world in 1914, showing European colonies

marked by the United States and Russia, most belligerent governments eventually encountered significant resistance to their demands during the war, and major anti-governmental mobilizations as the war ended. In 1917 something like 1.4 billion of the world's 1.6 billion people lived in countries or colonies at war. For that reason, few people anywhere escaped the strong domestic effects of war mobilization.

11.2 THE GREAT WAR

Writing in 1923, Winston Churchill – no pacifist! – summed up World War I:

No truce or parley mitigated the strife of the armies. The wounded died between the lines: the dead mouldered into the soil. Merchant ships and neutral ships and hospital ships were sunk on the seas and all on board left to their fate, or killed as they swam. Every effort was made to starve whole nations into submission without regard to age or sex. Cities and monuments were smashed by artillery. Bombs from the air were cast down indiscriminately. Poison gas in many forms stifled or seared the soldiers. Liquid fire was projected upon their bodies. Men fell from the air in flames, or were smothered, often slowly, in the dark recesses of the sea. The fighting strength of armies was limited only by the manhood of their countries. Europe and large parts of Asia and Africa

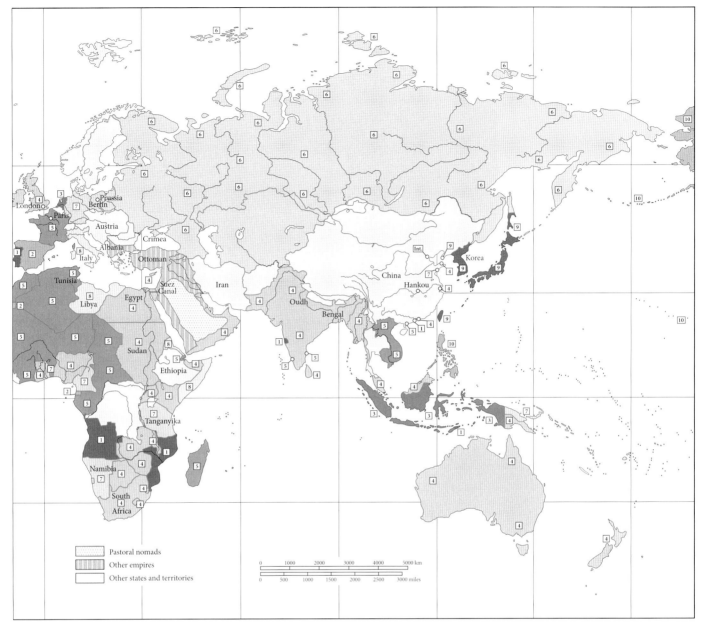

Map 11.1 (cont.)

became one vast battlefield on which after years of struggle not armies but nations broke and ran. When all was over, Torture and Cannibalism were the only two expedients that the civilized, scientific, Christian States had been able to deny themselves, and these were of doubtful utility.

How did such a terrible conflict begin? To understand the interconnections of 1914 to 1921, we must reject two common suppositions about human affairs: (1) that big events must have big, unitary causes; and (2) that most things happen to people because someone wants them to happen. World events from 1914 to 1921 challenge both those suppositions. Events of those years rumble with sudden cascades and unintended

consequences. But they also show us how intense international connections channeled and amplified the effects of open conflicts once they occurred.

Grand Alliances

As earlier chapters have shown, the major European powers spent much of the nineteenth century chipping away at the Ottoman empire. They did so partly by direct incorporation of former Ottoman territory but mostly by creating independent states aligned with one or more of the European powers. Greece, Serbia, Romania, Montenegro, and Bulgaria all became independent in the process. But the Ottomans, Russia, and

Figure 11.1 Despite all the prewar talk about the determination of the labor and socialist movements to oppose war or even to turn war into revolution, the majority of European workers and even labor and socialist leaders rallied around the national flag when war was declared. As the number of dead began to rise, popular attitudes began to change in many countries.

Austria-Hungary continued to vie for superiority in the Balkans, with other European powers pushing and shoving when they could. At the same time, Germany, France, Britain, and Italy were competing for political and economic dominance on two other flanks of the Ottoman empire, in North Africa and in the Near East. Meanwhile, the newly independent states tried to build up their own security and annex adjacent territories. War between Greece and Turkey (1896), Austria's annexation of Bosnia and Herzegovina (1908), war pitting Bulgaria, Serbia, and Greece against the Ottoman empire (1912), and a second war of Serbia, Greece, Romania, and the Ottomans against Bulgaria (1913) all resulted from regional jockeying for power and land in the Balkans. The Ottoman empire was losing ground, furthermore; the conflict of 1913, for example, carved an independent Albania from a corner of the empire.

Two great alliance systems formed. Germany and the Austro-Hungarian empire shared a common German-speaking ruling class and nobility with family connections. The Ottoman empire joined them to gain allies against Russia. Later Bulgaria joined them to make up the Central Powers. France and Russia had long-standing common interests in restraining Germany, and Britain finally joined them, forming the core of the so-called Entente – "understanding" in French – which as it accumulated new members during World War I became known as the Allies. (See Map 11.2.) During the years before 1914, members of the

Central Powers and the Entente competed in building up their armed forces and making war plans. Both sides projected quick victories based on the combination of vastly increased firepower with the mobility provided by railroads and automobiles. By and large, neither general staffs nor anyone else recognized that trucks, machine guns, magazine rifles, and barbed wire had greatly increased the capacity of troops to dig in and hold defensive positions. Soon after the start of World War I an elaborate system of trenches, with fortresses, dugouts, and barbed wire rose up from Switzerland in the south to Belgium in the northwest (see Figure 11.2). The machine gun and heavy artillery dominated the battlefront. It took generals a long time and many lives to recognize that quick offensives alone could not win wars. Devastating **trench warfare** dragged on in Europe for four years.

By the time a Bosnian nationalist assassinated the Austrian Archduke Franz Ferdinand, heir to the Austrian throne, and his wife Sophie in Austrian-annexed Sarajevo, Bosnia, on June 28, 1914 (see Figure 11.3), battle lines were already drawn. The Austrians accused Serbia of backing the assassin. Their German allies assured Austria-Hungary of military support in the event of war against Serbia. After a month of frenzied international negotiations, Austria-Hungary declared war on Serbia. Almost immediately Austria's ally Germany declared war on Russia, France, and Belgium, launching an invasion of Belgium on its

Map 11.2 Europe in 1914

way into France. Great Britain replied by going to war with Germany. Almost as soon, Montenegro declared war on Austria and Germany, Austria on Russia, and Serbia on Germany. Within five days, all the major European powers, plus some minor states, had joined the war. Most of them mobilized very rapidly. Invaded France, for example, called up 2.9 million reservists during the first two weeks of August 1914.

Drawing in the Colonies

Soon Europe's colonial powers were recruiting troops from their overseas dependencies. An astounding 1.2 million Indians volunteered for service in British imperial armies; 800,000 joined combat units, while 400,000 more went to work as laborers in war zones. Even in racially oppressive South Africa, 17,000 black soldiers joined a so-called Native Labor Contingent in East Africa, while another 25,000 went to France. Eventually China – not a colony, but much beholden to Europeans and

Americans – sent 140,000 laborers to dig trenches in France. Non-white volunteers did not generally receive equal treatment, however. About 16,000 black men from the British West Indies, for example, served in the war, and more than 1,200 died. Yet British authorities made sure that they fought outside the European theater, typically enforcing racial segregation, providing them with inferior services, and assigning them to heavy labor. With few exceptions, Caribbean black troops who did serve in Europe worked as servants, laborers, and ammunition carriers. The war effort drew massively on imperial connections, but generally maintained existing divisions within empires.

Ground Wars and Navies

A month after their invasion, German forces had occupied France's major northeastern regions of coal and heavy industry while pushing within 60 miles of Paris. France's government fled to the relative safety of Bordeaux on September 2. With aid from

Figure 11.2 Trench warfare on the Western Front: A war of lightning movement (which everyone had expected) quickly turned into a trench war (which no one had expected). War in the trenches with its mud, barbed wire, poison gas, and long-distance cannon was not the romantic combat that men had envisaged in 1914.

the British Expeditionary Force, French troops pushed back German armies 30 miles or so along most of the front, but then settled into fierce trench warfare on French territory. (A reassured French government returned to Paris in December 1914.) That was the Western Front. Russians fought Germans, Austrians, and (later) Bulgarians along the Eastern Front, advancing for a time well into Austria-Hungary.

War at sea ranged much more widely, from the Falkland Islands (Malvinas) off Argentina eastward to the North Sea and westward across the Pacific. Entente forces, including those of Japan, also invaded German colonies throughout the world. A rough division of strategies emerged at sea: Germans engaged chiefly in mine-laying, shore bombardment, and submarine warfare, while the British dominated open seas and transported troops great distances for invasions of territories controlled by the Central Powers. German sinking of British ships carrying

American goods and passengers nudged the United States toward war with Germany.

Ground war in Europe finally brought down the Central Powers – Germany, Austria-Hungary, and Bulgaria – not to mention Russia, allied with the eventual winners but knocked out by heavy war losses and revolution. Nevertheless, naval warfare mattered enormously. It mattered not only as a site of battle but also as a determinant of troop movements, of supply lines, and of incentives to join the war. At the war's beginning, Great Britain had armed itself mainly for naval warfare: The British Expeditionary Force sent to the continent in August 1914, for example, had only 476 field guns, while the British Grand Fleet already carried 1,560 pieces of artillery. The Force traveled with 950 trucks and 250 cars, for a total of perhaps 50,000 horsepower, while the Grand Fleet sailed on 3 million horsepower.

Entry of the Independent Nations

Figure 11.4 charts entries of independent states into World War I. Elements of the British empire and colonies of other European states generally joined the conflict with their respective mother countries. Later entries into the war (notably those of Bulgaria on the Central Powers side, Italy and Romania on the Entente side) often depended on threats to the latecomers' territory or promises of territorial gain at war's end. The United States, under President Woodrow Wilson, first tried to broker a peace settlement. When Germany declared unrestricted submarine warfare and British intelligence provided evidence of German designs on the United States, however, the US declared war in April 1917.

American pressure brought in Panama, Cuba, Brazil, and China as well. (Guatemala, Nicaragua, Costa Rica, Haiti, and Honduras, all under strong US influence, joined the hostilities in 1918.) Just at the same time as the USA entered, Russia coincidentally, beset by revolution, began to exit; Germans and Russians concluded an armistice in December 1917. War continued on the Western Front, in the Balkans, in the Near East, and across the seas, but the Eastern Front fell silent as previously subject territories began escaping from the defeated Russian empire. In the Treaty of Brest-Litovsk (March 3, 1918), Russia gave up its claims on Poland, Ukraine, Lithuania, Latvia, Estonia, Finland, Georgia, Armenia, and Azerbaijan.

A Calendar of the War

Here is a rough calendar of the war and its aftermath.

1914 After assassination of the Austrian Archduke Franz Ferdinand in Sarajevo, Austria went to war with Serbia, with Germany soon joining Austria by declaring war on

Figure 11.3 The assassination of a Habsburg prince and his wife in an Austrian province that most Europeans could not find on the map was the origin of World War I. Six men had been assigned to assassinate Franz Ferdinand but, for one reason or another, two missed their chance. The third assassin succeeded because he had stopped in a deli. Upon emerging he found the imperial couple's car backing up toward him.

Year	Central Powers	Entente/Allies
1914	Austria, Germany, Turkey	Serbia, Russia, France, Belgium, Great Britain, Montenegro, Japan
1915	Bulgaria	Italy, San Marino
1916		Portugal, Romania
1917		USA, Panama, Cuba, Greece, Siam, Liberia, China, Brazil
1918		Guatemala, Nicaragua, Costa Rica, Haiti, Honduras

Figure 11.4 Entries of belligerents into World War I.

Russia and invading Belgium on the way to France. Great Britain rapidly declared war on Germany and sent troops to France. German and Anglo-French armies fought in northeastern France. British, French, and German pilots began air raids on enemy territories. Austrian forces moved into Serbian and Russian territory in the south while Russians invaded German lands to the north. Turkish and German ships bombarded Russia's Black Sea ports, Turkish troops invaded Russian positions in Georgia, while Britain tightened its hold over Cyprus and Egypt. British naval forces battled Germans in the North Sea and the South Atlantic, as German ships shelled England's east coast. In several parts of Africa, French and

British forces invaded German colonies. (South African troops, for example, invaded German South West Africa and took it over by July 1915.) With British help, the Japanese attacked German possessions in China and the Pacific.

1915 Trench warfare continued in France and Belgium, as air raids and air battles intensified. Germans made their first dirigible raids on England. German armies advanced against Russia in the north, while Austro-German forces pushed the Russians far back in the south. British and French forces landed and fought in the straits approaching Istanbul, but withdrew by year's end. The Ottoman empire began deporting and killing Armenians, who rebelled and (with help from a Russian invasion) temporarily held the city of Van. Ottoman armies battled British forces in Arabia. A German submarine's sinking of the liner *Lusitania* off Ireland (with 139 of its 1,195 dead passengers American) brought the USA closer to entering the war. Italy did enter the war, attacking Austrian territory between the Adriatic and the Alps, as Serbian and Montenegrin armies seized positions along the Adriatic. Bulgaria likewise entered the war, joining the Austrians and Germans in invasions of Serbia, Albania, and Montenegro.

1916 Lethal trench warfare (including Verdun and the Somme) continued in France. The ten months of the Battle of Verdun (Figure 11.5) produced almost a million casualties. Meanwhile British forces used tanks for the first

Figure 11.5 The Battle of Verdun was one of the longest and deadliest battles in world history. It lasted from February to December of 1916 and incurred somewhere around 1 million casualties, including about 377,000 French and 337,000 Germans. At the end of the battle the situation on the ground remained roughly what it had been at the outset.

time. British air power began to outmatch German strength in the air, but dirigible raids on England continued, and Germans made their first airplane attack on London. German naval warfare advanced under and on the sea, including bombardment and raids against shipping along British and Scottish coasts. Russia launched a counter-offensive in Poland, but it stalled. Romania joined the war by invading Transylvania, but suffered invasion and occupation of its heartland, Wallachia, by Austro-German armies. Entente forces blockaded and threatened Greece, suspected of collusion with the Central Powers, then advanced into Macedonia. War continued in Arabia, including a major revolt of Arabs against Ottoman rule, as well as in Palestine, Mesopotamia, and Persia. After a German submarine landed Roger Casement, a nationalist leader, on the Irish coast, a small group of nationalists rose up in Dublin for one week in the Easter Rebellion.

1917 Canadian, British, and French forces made advances against German lines in France and Belgium, as the air war intensified. German submarine attacks reached their peak. The USA declared war on Germany and (eventually) Austria-Hungary. American pilots quickly joined the fighting, and an American expeditionary force was organized for transfer to Europe. Despite their revolution, Russians undertook one last offensive in Poland, but lost badly to German armies in the Baltic before the new Bolshevik rulers arranged a ceasefire. French and British

troops invaded Greece, forced a regime change, and brought the new regime in as an ally. Austro-German armies drove back the Italians. British armies advanced against the Ottomans in the Near East. Meanwhile, emissaries of the Austro-Hungarian emperor (who had succeeded to the throne in 1916) were conducting secret peace talks with the French and British governments.

1918 German offensives drove deep into France. By midyear, however, British and French forces (increasingly reinforced by Americans) were counterattacking, invading Belgium, northeastern Russia, the Caucasus, Bulgaria, and the Near East. From August onward, the Allied armies were driving German forces back from France and Belgium. After Allied forces invaded Romania with promises to drive out the Central Powers, Romanians re-entered the war on the Allied side. Italians conquered Albania, as Czech, Yugoslav, Polish, Hungarian, and Romanian leaders all declared independence of the disintegrating Austro-Hungarian empire. Austria-Hungary surrendered (November 3), followed by Germany (November 11).

1919 Leaders of the "Big Four" Allied powers, excluding Russia and China – Britain, France, Italy, and the United States – met in April in Versailles, outside of Paris, to draw up peace treaties defining a new international order. They signed the treaty on June 28, but ultimately the US Senate and the Chinese government rejected it.

Seen as a football match or a free-for-all, World War I has the appearance of a last-minute comeback on the Allied side. Although the Ottoman empire was visibly losing ground by late 1916, Austria-Hungary, Bulgaria and, especially, Germany seemed to be punishing their enemies severely until the beginning of 1918. The departure of revolutionary Russia from the war cost the Allies a major player. Before 1918, only very astute observers could see that the balance of air power was shifting to the Allies, that Austrian and German industrial capacity was breaking, that supplies and troops from the United States were bringing crucial new energy to the Allied effort, and that the

Allies' superior sea power was enabling them to encircle their foes despite the persistent menace of German submarines.

11.3 IMPACTS OF WORLD WAR I

Redrawing the Map

In postwar settlements that stretched from 1917 to 1920, the victorious powers redrew the European map. The map of Europe in 1919 (see Map 11.3) looked very different from that of 1914

Map 11.3 Europe after 1919

(see Map 11.2 above). Russia's Baltic, Polish, and southwestern territories became independent states. Germany ceded Alsace-Lorraine to France while losing other territories to Belgium, Poland, and international control. In place of the Austro-Hungarian empire the map makers put a new Yugoslav federation, Czechoslovakia, a greatly diminished Hungary, and a shrunken Austria. Italy gained Alpine and Adriatic regions previously held by Austria. Romania gained handsomely at the expense of Hungary. The Ottomans lost even more badly, giving up almost all their territories outside of Anatolia except for the segment of Europe closest to Istanbul. Not all these arrangements stayed in place long. As we shall see, for example, a revolutionary Russian state reconquered some regions that had declared independence as imperial Russia lost the war. But by 1920 the great powers had laid down a European map that differed greatly from the political geography of 1914. That map would remain more or less constant until World War II.

Population Losses

In a cooler look at the outcome, no team won. The whole world bled, especially the European world. Figure 11.6 presents rough figures for combat casualties among the major belligerents of World War I. In absolute terms, Germany topped the list with more than 6 million killed and wounded. But proportionate to its size France, a battleground for most of the war, bled more than the rest: Around 11 percent of the entire French population died as a result of combat between 1914 and 1918. France called up more than three quarters of all its men aged 15 to 49; one out of six among those mobilized died in the war. Although the 300,000 Americans killed or wounded sounds like a huge number, it amounted to less than 1 percent of the American population.

The table in Figure 11.6 omits deaths among other participants in the war, including at least 177,000 for Romania, 165,000 for Serbia and Montenegro, 62,000 for Bulgaria, 60,000 for French colonies, 54,000 for Australia, 53,000 for Canada, 17,000 for New Zealand, 35,000 for Belgium, and nearly 60,000 for India. Altogether, about 10 million people, overwhelmingly Europeans, died in the battles of World War I. In addition, uncounted millions of civilians died from bombardment, torpedoes, mines, malnutrition, or disease caused more or less directly by the war. In Europe alone, the war produced the equivalent of 300 billion dollars (US dollars of 1918) in property damage.

Effects on Men and Women

As it proceeded, such a huge war deeply affected the populations of Europe and European colonies, whether or not they participated directly in the military effort. Consider the United Kingdom, for which historians have assembled exceptionally good documentation. In England and Wales, about 55 percent of all men aged 15–49 served in the armed forces, in Scotland about 49 percent, even in rebellious Ireland more than 14 percent. While 6 million men eventually served in British military units, by 1918 another 3 million people – both men and women – were working directly for the state in war industries. Many adult women who had been barred from jobs in heavy industry now entered the factory (see Figure 11.7). Overall, the British state mobilized something like a fifth of its entire population directly into war service. Most families had at least one member participating directly in the war effort.

In the United Kingdom, domestic effects went far beyond direct employment by the state. Departure of men for war and war industry opened up jobs for women. Country people moved rapidly into urban employment. Imposition of rationing equalized distribution of food and fuel across social classes as government attention to public health improved conditions for poor people. As an unexpected result, living conditions actually

Figure 11.6 Troops killed and wounded among major belligerents in World War I (thousands).

Killed and Wounded as Percent

Country	Killed	Wounded	of Total Population around 1910–11
Austria-Hungary	1100	3620	9.7
France	1327	3044	11.2
Germany	2037	4247	9.7
Great Britain	723	2122	6.3
Italy	578	947	4.4
Ottoman Empire	804	400	6.1
Russia	1811	4050	3.6
USA	114	206	0.3

Killed: dying in combat, dying later of combat wounds, or missing in action

Figure 11.7 Women working in the railyard. Labor shortage during the war led to the employment of many women and the discovery that women could perform many tasks previously considered male. In the immediate postwar years problems inevitably arose when so many women lost their jobs to returning male veterans.

improved for the British working classes. Life expectancy increased during the war over the civilian population as a whole.

Such positive effects of war for the civilian population did not occur everywhere. In Germany, for example, public services and food supply disintegrated as the war turned against German forces in 1916. Germany's civilian population suffered almost as much as Germany's battered troops. Everywhere, however, World War I disrupted families, caused large shifts of population, and produced deep interventions of government in routine social life. Belligerent states generally restricted civil liberties and increased repression of dissidents; in May 1917, for example, France executed twenty-three civilian antiwar activists as traitors. Even the United States, late to enter the war and much less hard-hit by death and destruction than its European allies, imposed controls on civilian food supplies, took over the railroads, banned alcohol production (well before Prohibition), and brought 4.8 million men and women into military service by 1918.

Influenza: A Global Disease Spread by War

Another huge effect of World War I swept across the entire globe, but soon disappeared from stories that people told about the war. It was **influenza**, the "flu." People often think of the flu as little worse than a bad cold, but the disease kills. Influenza results from a family of viruses that infect both humans and animals, mutate quickly from one season to the next, move from person to person through casual contact, and sometimes appear suddenly in fiercely fatal forms. The 1918 variant was the fiercest of recorded human history. In Box 11.1 Edmund Wilson describes his experience with the disease on the Western Front.

Across the world, the influenza epidemic of 1918 killed around 40 million people – four times the whole war's combat deaths (see Map 11.4). In most cases, victims died horribly, drowning in their lungs' congestion, within four or five days after first showing the fever, sore throat, and headache that are flu's typical early symptoms. The victims often turned blue or purple before dying. The new flu arrived suddenly and killed quickly. It spread through the world in three waves: a relatively mild attack in March–April 1918, a monumental assault in August–November 1918, and a final serious recurrence in February–April 1919. London's medical authorities, for example, recorded 16,520 deaths from influenza in the year from June 1918 to May 1919, with almost three quarters of them coming in the fall of 1918. The infection's peak coincided with the war's end. In fact, street celebrations at the armistice surely helped spread the fatal infection.

War did not cause the newly virulent virus, but connections created by war spread it from continent to continent. Even today, close to a century later, medical historians are not sure exactly where, when, and how the illness began. Yet they recognize it as not just an epidemic but a **pandemic** – a rapid, worldwide spread of disease. In the United States, the first reported flu victim was company cook Albert Gitchell at the US Army's Fort Riley, Kansas, who arrived at the infirmary with a "bad cold" on March 11, 1918. By that week's end, 500 soldiers at Fort Riley had the flu. About the same time, 36 American cavalrymen in a detachment on its way to Europe fell ill, and 6 died. Another epidemic struck the seacoast town of San Sebastián, Spain (only 30 miles from the French border and, with Spain neutral, a welcome escape from the war zone) around the same time. Nearly all governments tried to conceal the seriousness of the outbreak; only the Spanish press made it public. Much to the irritation of Spaniards, publicity for San Sebastián's local outbreak attached the name "Spanish flu" to the whole pandemic. The spring wave of flu made many people sick in the United States, France, Great Britain, Germany, China, and Japan, but caused relatively few deaths.

Box 11.1 Edmund Wilson Sees Influenza Close Up

American author Edmund Wilson (1895–1972) served in the US army during World War I, working in a hospital unit before transferring to military intelligence. In his autobiographical book *A Prelude*, published in 1967, he reported his experience:

Before I had left Vittel, the flu epidemic of 1918 had taken, I think, as heavy a toll of our troops as any battle with the Germans had done. The hospitals were crowded with flu patients, many of whom died. I was in night duty and on my feet most of the time.

The other night orderly was an elderly undertaker, who went around in felt slippers, with a lantern and a kind of nightcap on his head. He knew just how to handle dead bodies. We would put them on a stretcher and carry them down to a basement room, where we sometimes had to pile them up like dogs. They were buried in big common ditches. This was much the busiest time in our hospitals. We never had a chance to think – though doctors and nurses also died – about catching the disease ourselves. When the worst of it was over, I did collapse, although I had not caught the flu.

Map 11.4 World distribution of influenza, 1918

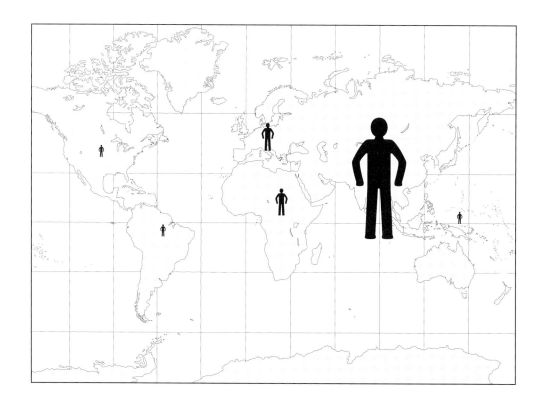

The flu returned with a vengeance, however, in the fall of 1918. American military installations were the first to report its return. By concentrating soldiers in barracks, military authorities unwittingly encouraged the spread of the virus. The disease spread from military ports, including the inland port of Chicago; the regions hardest hit centered on Boston, Baltimore, Chicago, New Orleans, San Francisco, and Seattle. The harborside installation to which new navy recruits reported in Boston recorded multiple cases at the end of August, with deaths more than 60 per day at nearby Fort Devens in September. Additional cases broke out at a navy school hosted by Harvard University (in Cambridge, just across the river from Boston) the same month. A detachment of sailors from Boston brought the disease to the Philadelphia Navy Yard on September 7, and it spread from there. A few days after 200,000 people gathered in Philadelphia on September 28 for a Liberty Loan parade, the city's authorities reported 635 new flu cases; on the single day of October 10, 759 Philadelphians expired from flu. Altogether, the flu epidemic of fall 1918 killed at least 13,000 people in Philadelphia. During the month of October alone, 195,000 Americans died of influenza. More than a quarter of all Americans came down with the disease. It killed more than 700,000 of them – six or seven times as many Americans as died in combat during World War I.

Yet the USA accounted for no more than a sixth of the world's deaths from flu in 1918. Europe, India, China, Japan, the Pacific, the Caribbean, northern South America, and parts of Africa all suffered seriously. A number of British warships stopping for fuel and supplies in Freetown, Sierra Leone, during late August and early September carried the epidemic to sea; on the navy ship *Africa*, for example, three quarters of the crew of 779 came down with the flu not long after leaving port there, and 51 of them died. India may have received the hardest blow, 5 million deaths or more. India suffered especially because so many of its doctors were serving with the British army.

Causes of the Pandemic Because it took time for doctors and officials to recognize the mysterious new disease and because war-ravaged zones did not keep meticulous death records, the pandemic's precise geography will forever remain uncertain. Whether the war zones of Russia, the Mediterranean, the Balkans, and the Near East suffered as badly as their Western European neighbors we cannot know for sure. But the general correspondence between involvement in World War I and exposure to the new plague jumps out from the maps of illness. During the Paris peace talks of April 1919, US President Woodrow Wilson himself collapsed and almost died of influenza.

All of the currently competing hypotheses about the 1918 flu's origins are consistent with the idea that it spread through connections made or reinforced by war:

- Recurrence and spread of a virus that had already appeared intermittently in the European war zone before 1918.
- Spread of the virus from a region of South China in which it had long been endemic by Chinese laborers who in 1916 traveled to France for trench-building.
- Initiation in the United States, perhaps in a move from pigs (which are vulnerable to a closely related virus) to humans who already carried a version susceptible to genetic modification.

Whatever the pandemic's origins, its deadly virus circulated through the world by means of connections made more intensive and vulnerable by a world war.

War and National Politics

Long before the influenza epidemic, war was reshaping domestic life within each belligerent country. Massive movement of men into military service, expansion of war industry, resulting shifts of employment and residence within the civilian workforce, rising taxation, governmental borrowing, and growth of governmental controls over information, population movement, and strategic materials, cumulated into huge rearrangements of previously existing routines. In the process, every government that joined the war abridged some freedoms, but also made new commitments to segments of its citizenry. Most obvious was large-scale borrowing, which tied the financial futures of those who bought war bonds and other government securities to the future financial capacities of their governments (Figure 11.8). In addition to financial commitments, governments commonly forced no-strike agreements on crucial groups of workers, induced manufacturers to shift into war production, and reoriented service institutions such as universities toward the war effort, all on the assumption or explicit promise of rewards after the war.

The families of women and men in military service, furthermore, required some support while their family members were gone, some commitment to help families of the killed and wounded, and some assistance in readjustment when demobilization finally came. In these ways, the majority of each belligerent country's population, however favorable or unfavorable they were to the war before it began, acquired a strong stake in the government's future capacity to meet its commitments. News from the war front thus struck with triple impact: first, as information about the prospects that family members and friends would return from war intact; second, as an indication of the likelihood that an intact government would survive to meet its obligations; and third, as a signal of the chances that the home territory itself would come under attack or occupation.

Obviously the relative weight of these three impacts varied enormously from country to country and period to period. Except for German submarines and the flu epidemic, American citizens on the US mainland had relatively little direct contact with the war. The war's primary effects within the USA occurred through the central government's great expansion, the significant (if mainly temporary) movement of previously excluded women and blacks into industrial jobs, and the impact of military service on servicemen's families. French people, in contrast, lived war more or less directly from the first day to the last.

Great Britain lay between the USA and France: suffering no invasion, but sending troops across the Channel almost immediately, mobilizing for a huge war effort, having a revolutionary leader delivered to Ireland by German submarine, and experiencing direct German attacks by ship, airplane, dirigible, and submarine. Still other areas began the war far from military action, but found the war drawing them in. Arabia and the Near East provide telling examples: They began the war as Ottoman territory, but by 1915 French and British forces had promoted a series of struggles for regional power that left the area in civil war well past the armistice. In South Africa, Kas Maine's experience has shown us how military mobilization, civil war, flu, and disruption of world markets transmitted the war's effects all the way to rural areas in colonies far from Europe.

Figure 11.8 What exactly were governments selling? Although some countries relied on bonds more than others, everywhere bonds were used to finance the war effort. In defeated nations, governmental collapse often resulted in the repudiation of bond obligations and the impoverishment of the defeated population.

Coups, Revolutions, and Civil Wars

Figure 11.9 identifies countries that experienced military coups, revolutionary situations, or civil wars for each year from 1914 through 1921. A **military coup** occurs when elements of existing armed forces depose a national executive or put a new executive in place. A revolutionary situation occurs when domestic opponents of an existing regime control at least one major city, region, or governmental institution within a recognized state's territory for a month or longer. A civil war occurs when at least two organized armies drawing troops from a recognized state's population battle each other within the state's territory for a month or longer. The three often overlapped; a revolutionary situation became a civil war when dissident forces organized their own army and started to battle units of the national army or when segments of the existing army broke off to join the opposition. Coups that spun out of control likewise started civil wars. Throughout the period, military coups and

Figure 11.9 Military coups, revolutionary situations, and civil wars in the world, 1914–21

Year	Countries and Colonies with Coups, Revolutionary Situations and/or Civil Wars
1914	China, Dominican Republic, Haiti, Libya, Mexico, Peru, South Africa
1915	Arabia, China, Haiti, Iran, Mexico, Poland, Portugal, South Africa
1916	Arabia, China, Dominican Republic, Ethiopia, Honduras, Iran, Ireland, Mexico, Ottoman Empire, Poland
1917	Arabia, China, Costa Rica, Cuba, Estonia, Ethiopia, Iran, Mexico, Poland, Portugal, Russia
1918	Arabia, Austria-Hungary, China, Finland, Germany, Haiti, Iran, Portugal, Russia
1919	Afghanistan, Arabia, China, Costa Rica, Egypt, Germany, Haiti, Honduras, Hungary, Ireland, Korea, Latvia, Peru, Portugal, Russia
1920	Arabia, Bolivia, China, Germany, Iraq, Ireland, Italy, Mexico, Russia, Turkey
1921	Arabia, China, Guatemala, India, Iran, Italy, Morocco, Paraguay, Turkey

Military Coup: Elements of existing armed forces depose national executive, put new executive in place.
Revolutionary Situation: Domestic opponents of an existing regime control at least one major city, region, or governmental institution within a recognized state's territory for a month or longer.
Civil War: At least two organized armies drawing troops from a recognized state's population battle each other within the state's territory for a month or longer.

small-scale civil wars were concentrated in the countries of the Caribbean and Central America that lay in the zone of US influence. As Chapter 9 showed, Mexico broke into revolution in 1910, and lived in political turmoil through the decade. (Mexico's revolution started a new twentieth-century trend of extensive participation by rural people in major revolutions.) Post-revolutionary China continued in political crisis throughout the period, with warlords battling the national government unceasingly. Arabia, stirred to anti-Ottoman revolt by British and French backing, then continued in local wars over the right to rule. South Africa we have already seen generating a Boer–British civil war in 1914 and 1915 before a British force definitively crushed the Boers. We have likewise seen Irish nationalists in open rebellion against British rule in 1916, 1919, and 1920.

Two other important patterns appear in the table in Figure 11.9. First, World War I belligerents that were losing badly tended to break into revolutionary situations and civil war. Russia offers the most momentous example, but Austria-Hungary, Germany, and the Ottoman empire clearly qualify. (Bulgaria, the remaining member of the defeated Central Powers, approached civil war in 1918 and 1919, but an authoritarian peasant-based regime took over from 1919 until a coup overturned it in 1923.) Second, instead of subsiding as wartime tensions declined, large-scale civil strife rose as the war ended. The peak of coups, revolutionary situations, and civil wars arrived in 1919, as belligerents were returning to peacetime regimes.

11.4 RUSSIAN REVOLUTIONS

Russia's revolutions reverberated further than the rest. Ever since 1905, the 300-year-old tsarist empire had been in ferment. In the 1890s, radical intellectuals organized political parties to demand a constitutional monarchy. Japan's defeat of Russia further stimulated demands for a representative assembly. On January 22, 1905, known as "Bloody Sunday," police in St. Petersburg killed 130 workers at a peaceful demonstration, arousing tremendous public outrage. From October 20–30, workers in St. Petersburg staged a massive general strike, and created their own council, known as the **soviet**, to represent them. Tsar Nicholas II then had to accept an elected assembly, known as the Duma. The Duma struggled to enact reforms in the teeth of the tsar's opposition; in this frustrating period, radical revolutionaries gained while liberal democrats declined. At the same time, Russia grew closer to Britain and France, and more hostile to Germany and Austria-Hungary. The Balkan crisis drew Russia unwillingly into war, but it enabled the tsar at first to rally national support. Yet he quickly alienated his people by rejecting co-operation with the Duma, instead listening mainly to his wife and the mad monk Rasputin. He listened to other ministers, too, but they gave him contradictory advice. The Russian bureaucracy was paralyzed. Early victories by Russian armies soon turned into stalemate and demoralization.

When World War I began, the Russian empire included the territories we now know as Finland, the Baltic states, Belarus,

Ukraine, and eastern Poland. Its long western borders joined those of its enemies, Germany and Austria-Hungary. The Eastern Front's major battles of 1914 to 1916 took place mainly in Polish territory and the Baltic region. Significant defeats in the south (Galicia and Bukovina) during 1915 made Russian military vulnerability more visible. In 1916, German forces promoted uprisings against Russian rule and announced creation of an independent Polish state. As Russian armies retreated, soldiers deserted in growing numbers, workers increasingly went on strike, and public opposition to the tsarist regime swelled.

Petrograd's Workers Lead the Revolution

Before the war, St. Petersburg served as Russia's capital and major link to Western Europe via the nearby Baltic. At the war's start, the tsar changed his capital's name to Petrograd (Peter's City), which sounded less German to him than St. Petersburg. Petrograd's ungrateful citizens, however, spearheaded opposition to the tsar's regime. In early 1917, the city's workers mounted huge strikes, which soon led to a general mutiny of the capital's troops who refused to repress a demonstration in support of International Women's Day (see Figure 11.10). Many saw this first revolution as a spontaneous movement that contrasted with the Bolshevik Revolution that followed. Leon Trotsky, the leader of the second revolution that led the Bolsheviks to power, disagreed (see Box 11.2). Spontaneous or not, in the wake of the so-called February Revolution, the radical movement picked up speed. In March, the Duma answered an imperial order to dissolve by establishing a provisional government. Tsar Nicholas abdicated in favor of his brother Michael, who soon abdicated as well, so there was no tsar at all at the top. All this happened against a background of strikes, street fighting, and factional maneuvering. In Petrograd about 1,500 people died, more than half of them soldiers on one side or the other. The Duma set in place a provisional government of liberals and conservatives, but soon faced determined opposition from a Petrograd soviet (council) of workers' and soldiers' deputies. The soviet and the Duma were supposed to work together, but the soviet organized committees in factories and army units that began to act as a counter-government.

Leftist social democrats bulked large in the soviets and the committees, but an earlier split had produced two rival parties within social democracy: the relatively accommodationist **Mensheviks** (meaning "minority") and the more radical **Bolsheviks** ("majority"). The Bolsheviks gained strength day by day. By that time, a first revolutionary situation (undermining of the tsar) had given way to a second (struggle between the Provisional Government and its soviet-based opposition). All this happened in March 1917 (February in the old Russian calendar). During April and May, radical leaders such as Leon Trotsky and V.I. Lenin (see Figures 11.11 and 11.12) began returning to Russia from exile. Lenin's call for a seizure of power by the soviets led by the Bolsheviks struck many as absurd but gradually the majority of Bolsheviks swung behind their leader. The revolutionary situation mutated rapidly as Bolsheviks organized opposition to the Provisional Government and the Mensheviks within it. Parallel soviets organized in Moscow and elsewhere, including army units, factories, and peasant communities across the land. A number of former left Mensheviks, including Trotsky, joined the Bolsheviks. Nevertheless, a spontaneous uprising undertaken against Lenin's orders failed in July 1917, sending Lenin back into exile and Trotsky to prison.

Figure 11.10 Women's march in St. Petersburg. Many marchers, particularly women textile workers, also went out on strike and they were joined by metalworkers in large factories such as the Putilov iron works (shown here). Judging by the photo, what was the proportion of men and women in the protest at the Putilov works? Why would women be likely protestors in a Russia dissatisfied with war? Why might international women's rights be the spark for revolution?

Box 11.2 Leon Trotsky Denies the "Spontaneity" of the February Revolution

One of the major leaders of the Bolshevik Party, president of the Petrograd Soviet, a crucial figure in the Bolshevik Revolution of October 1917, organizer of the Red Army, and loser in the struggle for power with Stalin that followed Lenin's death, Leon Trotsky wrote a great history of the revolution during his Mexican exile. Against the idea of a spontaneous insurrection against the tsar in March 1917 (February in the Russian calendar of the time), Trotsky's *History of the Russian Revolutions* objects:

But if the Bolshevik Party could not guarantee the insurrection an authoritative leadership, there is no use talking of other organisations. This fact has strengthened the current conviction as to the spontaneous character of the February revolution. Nevertheless the conviction is deeply mistaken, or at least meaningless.

The struggle in the capital lasted not an hour, or two hours, but five days. The leaders tried to hold it back; the masses answered with increased pressure and marched forward. They had against them the old state, behind whose traditional façade a mighty power was still assumed to exist, the liberal bourgeoisie with the State Duma, the Land and City Unions, the military-industrial organizations, academies, universities, a highly developed press, and finally the two strong socialist parties who put up a patriotic resistance to the assault from below. In the party of the Bolsheviks the insurrection had its nearest organization, but a headless organization with a scattered staff and with weak illegal nuclei. And nevertheless the revolution, which nobody in those days was expecting, unfolded, and just when it seemed from above as though the movement was already dying down, with an abrupt revival, a mighty convulsion, it seized the victory.*

Figure 11.11 Leon Trotsky (1879–1940) was, with Lenin, a principal leader of the Russian Revolution. Trotsky had long been an opponent of Lenin within the Russian socialist party, but in 1917 Lenin and Trotsky united, based on their agreement that Russia required a socialist-led revolution. Trotsky became the head of the Red Army but was later exiled and eventually assassinated by rival socialist Bolshevik leader Joseph Stalin.

The "October" Revolution of November 6–7, 1917

The surviving government itself split over how to deal with the Bolsheviks. When the newly appointed prime minister, Alexander Kerensky, dismissed hard-line commander-in-chief Lavr Kornilov, the dismissed commander tried unsuccessfully to execute a coup. Kornilov's threat from the right impelled Kerensky to switch direction, releasing the imprisoned Bolsheviks and calling for Petrograd's workers to save the revolution. From that point onward, the Bolsheviks and their allies the peasant-based Social Revolutionaries gained strength steadily. When

Figure 11.12 Vladimir Lenin (1870–1924) was the leader of the Bolshevik Party, originally a faction of the Russian socialist party. Returning from exile after the February revolution, Lenin argued that the Bolsheviks should establish a government based on soviets (councils of workers and peasants). In 1917 Lenin became head of the Council of People's Commissars and head of the USSR (Union of Soviet Socialist Republics).

Kerensky again tried to shut down the Bolshevik newspaper *Pravda* ("Truth") and arrest Petrograd's radical leaders on November 5, Trotsky and the Bolsheviks returned to open resistance. On November 6 and 7, Bolsheviks and Social Revolutionaries drove out the Provisional Government and seized power. John Reed, an American socialist, sympathetic to the Bolshevik cause, describes the seizure of power in Box 11.3. Lenin emerged from hiding in the Petrograd suburbs to join Trotsky in leading the new regime. Kerensky fled to organize resistance at the front, his magnificent touring sedan protected by a car from the American embassy flying an American flag. The events of November 6 and 7 constitute the centerpiece of the Bolshevik Revolution – called "the October Revolution" because in Russia at the time the calendar was thirteen days behind Europe's so the events took place on October 24–25.

Late on November 7, a turbulent meeting of the National Congress of Soviets in Petrograd endorsed the Bolshevik coup, but with bitter dissent in its midst. The workers' and soldiers' soviets found themselves being cut out from central power, while peasants had hardly any voice at all. In power, the Bolsheviks faced serious challenges. The war went on, as independence movements and counter-revolutionary armies began forming across much of the empire. Trotsky led the organization of a Bolshevik-dominated military force, the Red Army. At the same time, the new government was trying to collectivize industry, land, and capital. Collectivization meant confiscating private property and handing it over to workers' and peasants' soviets under strict control of communist party cadres. This policy of "War Communism" gave the new government productive resources, but it alienated small businessmen, peasant landowners, and industrial workers. Meanwhile, peasants themselves were seizing land from large estates or their own communities. In largely peasant Russia, November elections for a constituent assembly produced a large majority for the Social Revolutionaries, not the Bolsheviks. When that assembly met in January 1918, Red troops dissolved it immediately. The Bolsheviks had essentially driven out their Social Revolutionary partners, and seized sole control of the central government.

Domestic Consequences of the Russian Revolution

Soon after taking power, Trotsky was bargaining out peace terms with the Central Powers at Brest-Litovsk (now in Belarus, near the Polish border). Between the opening of talks (December 3, 1917) and the treaty signing (March 3, 1918), Russia lost imperial territories in Poland, the Ukraine, Estonia,

Box 11.3 John Reed Reports the October Revolution

American radical journalist John Reed, whose *Ten Days That Shook the World* offered his eye-witness account of the October Revolution, attended Petrograd's Congress of Soviets of Workers' and Soldiers' Deputies on November 7:

But suddenly a new sound made itself heard, deeper than the tumult of the crowd, persistent, disquieting – the dull shock of guns. People looked anxiously towards the clouded windows, and a sort of fever came over them. Martov, demanding the floor, croaked hoarsely, "The civil war is beginning, comrades! The first question must be a peaceful settlement of the crisis. On principle and from a political standpoint we must

urgently discuss a means of averting civil war. Our brothers are being shot down in the streets! At this moment, when before the opening of the Congress of Soviets the question of Power is being settled by means of a military plot organized by one of the revolutionary parties –" for a moment he could not make himself heard above the noise, *"All of the revolutionary parties must face the fact!*

"The first vopros *(question) before the Congress is the question of power, and this question is already being settled by force of arms in the streets! . . . We must create a power which will be recognized by the whole democracy. If the Congress wishes to be the voice of the*

revolutionary democracy it must not sit with folded hands before the developing civil war, the result of which may be a dangerous outburst of counter-revolution . . . The possibility of a peaceful outcome lies in the formation of a united democratic authority . . . We must elect a delegation to negotiate with the other Socialist parties and organizations . . ."

Always the methodical muffled boom of cannon through the windows, and the delegates, screaming at each other . . . So, with the crash of artillery, in the dark, with hatred and fear, and reckless daring, new Russia was being born.

Finland, Moldavia, Latvia, Lithuania, Georgia, Armenia, and Azerbaijan, some to local rebellions, others to pressure from the Central Powers. Forces from the Central Powers, moreover, soon invaded different parts of the Russian periphery. Civil war continued into 1920. But a reorganized Red Army, led by Trotsky, eventually reclaimed most of the empire's old territory (see Map 11.5). The army did not win back Finland, Poland, or the Baltic states. But it did build up to a mighty force of 5 million men by 1920. Under Trotsky, in collaboration with Lenin, Bolsheviks (by then known as the Communist Party) penetrated and controlled the armed forces. They controlled the civilian government which demobilized the army during the 1920s. Centered on the Communist Party, it incorporated many military veterans into a system of control far more centralized than the tsars had ever managed.

After 1917, civil war and an Allied blockade strangled Russia's industrial production; the number of manufacturing workers sank from 3.6 million in 1917 to 1.5 million in 1920. Rebuilding the agrarian economy, Lenin then instituted the so-called New Economic Policy (NEP): In return for relaxing central controls over agricultural production and permitting peasants to market their surplus, the government imposed a grain tax to feed the non-agricultural population. NEP promoted an economic revival. The revival lasted past Lenin's death in 1924 (see Chapter 12).

International Consequences of the Russian Revolution

Russia's revolutions generated other international wars, civil wars, and revolutionary situations in the former empire's space. Germany dominated Latvia, Lithuania, and Estonia until the end of World War I, when the Soviet Union unsuccessfully tried to retake them. Lithuania soon went to war with Poland over disputed territory. After the armistice, Poland itself sought to conquer adjacent territories that had once belonged to Polish kingdoms. Poland's claims produced not only a war with Lithuania (1919–20) but also a shorter war with the Soviet Union (1920). Finland split into civil war between Whites and Reds in 1918, but with German aid the Whites drove out the Reds. In 1919, Finland and the Soviet Union conducted a brief war over predominantly Finnish-speaking regions that had remained with Russia, but no territory changed hands. All the Baltic states, including Finland, started programs of democratization and land reform, only to swing right again during the 1920s. Two sorts of struggle intersected: between adjacent powers over placement of international boundaries; and within those boundaries for control of postwar regimes.

The Soviet Union failed in its program of exporting proletarian revolution immediately to the industrialized world and from there to everywhere else. It was not for want of trying. During 1918, with Soviet encouragement, communist parties emerged in

Map 11.5 Russian Civil War, 1918–21

Germany, Poland, Hungary, Austria, the Netherlands, Finland, Latvia, and Greece. In 1919, Lenin and the Bolsheviks founded the Communist International (Comintern), which set standards for communist parties throughout the world. Soon allies everywhere were organizing. The American Communist Party (of which John Reed was a founding member) first formed in 1919, the Communist Party of Great Britain in 1920, and the French Communist Party the same year. China's Communist Party held its founding session in July 1921. Often new communist parties regrouped previously existing radical organizations, but just as often their creation produced a split between them and non-communist socialist organizations. For most of the sixty years following 1921, for example, rivalry between communists and socialists dominated the politics of France's left.

11.5 MORE EUROPEAN REVOLUTIONS, REBELLIONS, AND CIVIL WARS

Hungary

Outside of the former Russian empire, revolutionary bids for state power proliferated as World War I ended. Hungarian Bela Kun had fought against Russia for the Austro-Hungarian empire. While a prisoner of war in Russia, however, he became a Bolshevik. Returning to shattered Hungary in November 1918, he founded a communist party. In March 1919 a coalition of communists and socialists formed a Soviet Republic with Kun at its head. The new government began a vast program of collectivization. Civil war soon challenged the new regime. By

August 1919, Czech, Romanian, and Hungarian counter-revolutionary armies drove out the collectivists and installed a reactionary government under Admiral Horthy. During 1919, a similar sequence played out in Vienna for Austria: a temporary communist-socialist seizure of power, followed by military opposition, overthrow, and seating of a conservative regime.

Germany

Germany behaved differently. As the war was ending in October and November 1918, sailors mutinied against orders to fight the British. In emulation of the Russians, workers and soldiers organized councils, then supported socialist bids to create republics in Bavaria and elsewhere. On November 9, the imperial cabinet declared the Empire ended, handing the government over to a socialist coalition. The emperor fled to Holland. Soon all the hereditary rulers of states within the German Empire abdicated, leaving a federal republic as the Empire's successor. Within the socialist camp, a split opened up between the governing coalition (which advocated a gradual approach to socialism) and factions further left (which sought a Soviet-style seizure of power). Crushing of a left-wing (Spartacist) revolt in January 1919 led to the arrest and murder of Spartacist leaders Rosa Luxemburg and Karl Liebknecht.

As a constituent assembly met at Weimar, communists made new attempts to seize power by force in Berlin and elsewhere, but failed. In the Bavarian capital Munich, however, a left-wing coalition actually established a short-lived Soviet Republic of Bavaria during April 1919, only to be overrun by federal troops at the month's end. During the next two years, the fledgling German government faced armed challenges from three directions: renewed attempts by socialists to establish revolutionary rule; competing attempts by monarchists to restore something like the old regime; and secessionist rebellions along the French and Polish borders. The Weimar Republic entered the 1920s polarized between right and left.

Ireland

Ireland never created anything like a Soviet Republic, but it moved into a revolutionary situation during and after World War I. Ireland followed a nationalist path to revolution. At first the Irish people collaborated with the war effort. To be sure, Ulster's Protestants collaborated much more enthusiastically than the rest of the Irish population. The prewar Ulster Volunteer Force, a Protestant paramilitary unit opposed to Irish Home Rule established in 1913, joined the British army en masse. Meanwhile, the British maintained 20,000 troops and police in the rest of the island to check popular militias of largely Catholic

republicans (advocates of an Irish Republic) that started forming in 1914. Still, serious opposition to the British cause did not crystallize until the war had been going on for almost two years. The abortive Easter Rebellion of 1916, planned with the help of exiles and Irish Americans in New York, supported by German agents, backed by German bombardment of the English coast, and suppressed brutally by British troops, slowed the cause of Irish independence temporarily. Nevertheless, Irish nationalists began regrouping in 1917.

Except for the Protestant representatives of Ulster, Irish MPs withdrew from the United Kingdom's Parliament in reaction to the adoption of military conscription for Ireland in April 1918. Returned MPs led the organization of opposition back home. In December 1918, Irish nationalists won southern Ireland's votes in a parliamentary election handily, with thirty-four of the sixty-nine successful candidates elected while in prison. The newly elected MPs decided to form their own Irish parliament instead of joining the UK assembly. On meeting in January 1919, they chose Éamon de Valera, then still in prison, as their parliamentary president. De Valera soon escaped from prison, but after four months of activity in Ireland, left for the USA to rally political and financial support among Irish Americans.

Soon the British government was actively suppressing Irish nationalist organizations. Nationalists themselves mobilized for resistance and attacked representatives of British authority. By the end of 1919, Ireland reached a state of civil war. The British painfully established military control, but also began negotiating with Irish representatives. Within two years, the negotiations led to an agreement: partition of Northern Ireland from the rest, and Dominion status similar to that of Canada and South Africa for a newly created Irish Free State outside of Ulster. Although hard-line Irish republicans refused to accept the settlement and raised an insurrection in 1922, the arrangement lasted in roughly the same form until the 1930s.

Italy

Hungarian, German, and Irish revolutions emerged directly from World War I. In different variants, they followed the cycle of mobilization for war, governmental commitments, governmental failure, resistance, and postwar demands that Russia displayed in extreme form. With a delay, the same pattern fits Italy. Italy ended the war nominally on the winning side. But the Italian government ended the war militarily discredited, deep in debt, battered by 1.5 million casualties, almost none of its territorial aims fulfilled, and challenged by a large socialist opposition. Workers mobilized as the war ended, producing a huge strike wave in 1919 and 1920. During 1920, a lockout in metal-working factories incited a far-reaching innovation: seizure of the premises by their workers, evolving into demands for socialization of their industries. Italians called these events the occupation of the factories. Americans who later adopted the Italian tactic called it the **sit-down strike**, while French workers dubbed it the strike in place (*grève sur le tas*).

Italian labor did not rise unopposed, however. In 1919, a growing nationalist movement led by Benito Mussolini (drawn especially from veterans and workers) announced themselves as the **fascist** alternative to the socialists. Between the end of 1919 and March 1921, Fascist Party membership doubled from 40,000 to 80,000, reaching 222,000 by August 1921, and 322,000 by May 1922. The fascists became shock troops of opposition to socialist workers, sustaining a low-level civil war with socialists and workers up to the fascist seizure of national power in 1922 (see Chapter 12).

Elsewhere, civil wars and revolutionary situations likewise showed the effects of World War I, but more indirectly or in different ways. Arabia and the Near East, we have already seen, plunged into rebellion and civil war. Struggle intensified as soon as the Allies loosened the Ottoman empire's grip and began intervening in the new states that started to emerge under European influence.

Afghanistan's story was more complicated. Although Afghanistan's northern border touched the Russian empire, before World War I Russia had accepted Afghanistan as a zone of British influence. During the war, the British-run government of India continued to subsidize and intervene in the Afghan regime. As the war ended, an Islamic nationalist movement arose in opposition to the British connection. Its members assassinated Afghanistan's collaborating ruler, raised a rebellion against the ruler's son, and appealed to Indian Muslims to join them in throwing off British rule. The son survived. In 1921, the new ruler began following an old political precept: The enemy of my enemy is my friend. He allied the regime with the Soviet Union as a counterweight to British influence while moving toward alliances with Muslim Turkey and Persia at the same time.

11.6 END OF SOME EMPIRES, EXPANSION OF OTHERS

World War I and its peace settlements had a paradoxical effect on empires. Within Europe and the Near East, the great territorial empires disintegrated. Outside of the region, in contrast, Europe-centered empires in some respects gained strength. The Russian, German, Austro-Hungarian, and Ottoman empires had all incorporated multiple territorial units with various systems of rule under the headship of hereditary monarchs. As the last few chapters have shown, of course, the four empires had been moving in different directions before World War I. The Russian empire rapidly incorporated non-Russian people, the Austro-Hungarian continued to acquire heterogeneous territories at a more modest pace, the German Empire consolidated its power mainly in already German-speaking regions, while the Ottoman empire was dwindling toward a Muslim core divided between Arabs and Turks. As of 1914, nevertheless, all four empires still grouped multiple distinctive regimes under single monarchs.

All four empires had, furthermore, ruled indirectly in a number of regards: They conceded considerable autonomy to regional lords (themselves often hereditary) just so long as those lords delivered taxes, military support, and political compliance to the center. That is what it means to call them "empires" rather than simply calling them big states. Those systems of imperial rule disappeared during and after World War I. Their enemies, especially the United States, warred against them in the name of liberating captive nations. Some of their successor states adopted federal organizations, but all of them created more centralized systems of relatively uniform direct rule. Despite the great powers' deliberate formation of multi-ethnic states in Yugoslavia, Czechoslovakia, and Romania, postwar states increasingly organized top-down nationalism: making regional cultures conform to a national model, building loyalty to a single tradition and collective self-definition, subordinating minorities to the majority. In postwar settlements, the great powers promoted the model of self-determination by using regional plebiscites widely when assigning frontier populations to one state or another.

All over the former imperial zones, small-scale struggles broke out immediately after the war in which newly named leaders of newly entitled nationalities tried to incorporate adjacent peoples of similar ethnic origin or to extend the boundaries of their new states. Czech troops, for example, fired on German-speakers in the areas of Czechoslovakia closest to Austria who voiced demands to be annexed to Austria, while Romanians and Ukrainians fought a small war over their borderlands. Even the Soviet Union, which began to recognize titular nationalities within its component republics after 1921, gave priority to Russian as the country's common language and insisted on loyalty to the communist-run Soviet state. In all these regards, the imperial model lost ground within Europe after World War I.

Yet the war's outcome strengthened European imperial power outside of Europe. To be sure, Germany lost almost all of its colonies in the peace settlement, and the Ottoman empire shrank to a Turkey without colonies. Within the British empire, wartime mobilization and war service promoted greater autonomy in India, South Africa, Ireland, and the colonies where Europeans had displaced or overwhelmed the indigenous people. But the Belgian, French, and British overseas empires not only gained de facto control over a number of former German colonies, but also began more intensive economic exploitation of such existing colonies as (Belgian) Congo and (British) Malaya. The Congo shipped copper and diamonds to Belgium while Malaya shipped tin, rubber, palm oil, and spices to Great Britain. France tried seriously, if unsuccessfully, to integrate its North African colonies into its metropolitan structure.

11.7 INDIA'S STRUGGLES, 1914–22

Within European colonies, World War I likewise altered economies and public politics. India provides a telling example. After a stop in England to organize an Indian corps for war service, Mahatma Gandhi returned to India from his twenty-year South African sojourn in 1914. He had become a veteran organizer of non-violent opposition in South Africa. Back in India, Gandhi supported the British war effort, which sent Indian troops to Europe, Mesopotamia, Palestine, Egypt, and East Africa. (The wide dispersal of Indian troops probably helps explain India's enormous vulnerability to the influenza pandemic of 1918.) But he also played a crucial part in expanding the political role of the Indian National Congress Party and in forging its alliance with the All-India Moslem League. The Hindu–Muslim coalition often worked uneasily, since Muslim activists generally opposed dismantling the Ottoman empire (still the world's leading Muslim power). In 1915, indeed, a conspiratorial Muslim group sought German support for an uprising in India and Afghanistan.

As the war ground on, the Congress and the League began demanding an elected Indian legislative assembly as a first step toward self-government. In 1916 they even agreed on a program Indian nationalists had previously resisted: separate earmarked electorates for Muslim voters. Recognizing the need for concessions, the British cabinet member responsible for Indian affairs declared a new policy in Parliament on August 20, 1917:

The policy of His Majesty's government, with which the Government of India are in complete accord, is that of the increasing association of Indians in every branch of the administration, and the gradual development of self-governing institutions, with a view to the progressive realization of responsible government in India as an integral part of the Empire.

But "gradual" meant different things to British legislators and Indian nationalists. In parallel with European events, the war's end brought an increase in popular mobilization. Gandhi led a campaign of strikes, demonstrations, and passive resistance. The colonial government struck back with repression. Authorities arrested Gandhi in April 1918 for violating an order to keep his organizing efforts out of the Panjab region. A low point arrived in April 1919, when a British general ordered his troops to fire on a large protest meeting in Amritsar, Panjab. As troops blocked the only exit from the meeting place, their volleys killed 379 demonstrators and wounded 1,200 more. The government then compounded its problems by declaring martial law and imposing severe punishments on participants that included public whipping and forced crawling through the streets. Widespread indignation in both India and Great Britain accelerated the introduction of moves toward self-government – or at least greater inclusion of Indians in the government of India.

The promise of inclusion split the Congress Party, with Gandhi's group bitterly opposing Britain's partial measures. In 1920, Congress launched a major campaign of non-co-operation with British authorities and boycott of British goods. Indians rallied around the watchwords *satyagraha* (holding to the truth), *ahimsa* (non-violence), *hartal* (boycott), and *swaraj* (home rule), each of which had multiple religious, moral, and political overtones. The program included resignation from public office, non-participation in elections, withdrawal from school, and avoidance of law courts. It also involved spectacular actions such as a monster bonfire of foreign cloth, which Gandhi lit in Bombay (August 1921). Gandhi heavily promoted the wearing of homespun cotton cloth to replace foreign imports, and publicized images of himself spinning his own clothing. He gathered support from leading writers like Leo Tolstoy in Russia, who shared many of his ideals.

Meanwhile, militant Muslims organized their own campaign to maintain the Ottoman sultan (emperor) as leader of the world's Muslims, restore the Ottoman empire as it was in 1914, and re-establish Muslim control of all the faith's holy places in the Near East. The predominantly Hindu Congress hesitantly backed their Muslim allies' program. Although Gandhi and his followers insisted on non-violence, in many parts of India people attacked landlords, moneylenders, and officials. Muslim attacks on Hindu landlords, in fact, led to wider Hindu–Muslim battles, and repeated splits in the movement for self-government. As conflicts escalated in 1922, the colonial government imprisoned Gandhi, thus cutting short a great, turbulent civil disobedience campaign. Mass campaigns later revived, however, up until India's independence.

11.8 THE RISING POWERS: GREAT BRITAIN, JAPAN, AND THE UNITED STATES

All things considered, among major belligerents of World War I Japan, Great Britain, and the United States emerged with the least damage. Their political regimes survived the war, their colonial possessions remained in hand, and their industrial capacities had actually expanded since 1914. Yet all three of them experienced their own versions of war mobilization, wartime commitments, and postwar demands. In the process, furthermore, the international balance of power shifted strongly toward the United States, and secondarily toward Japan. Before World War I, the British empire had clearly qualified as the world's greatest political and economic power. From 1918 onward, Britain felt a growing challenge from the United States in both regards. Japan did not yet compete on even terms with either one, but it was rapidly becoming Asia's premier independent power. In 1922 a crucial conference in Washington, DC, confirmed the new standing by setting these caps on tonnage in major warships:

Great Britain 525,000 tons

United States 525,000 tons

Japan 315,000 tons

France 175,000 tons

Italy 175,000 tons

The United States did not step into its more powerful international position gracefully. American President Woodrow Wilson announced his Fourteen Points as a program to guarantee world peace. This program would ensure the independence of new nations and replace imperial treaties with collective security pacts and a new international organization, the League of Nations. The US Senate, however, led by isolationists suspicious of involvement in world affairs, not only blocked US membership in the League, but also refused to ratify the Versailles peace treaty. (Irish emigrants' opposition to any collaboration with Great Britain in a general peace settlement also made both issues political hot potatoes in the USA.) Nevertheless, the financial and political reconstruction of postwar Europe involved extensive US intervention. US President Herbert Hoover, for example, made his international reputation by organizing relief and food supply in Europe after the war. He also established the American Relief Administration, which contributed to relieving the famines in Russia in 1921–22.

Each of the three leading countries experienced new domestic demands as the war ended, and met at least some of them. In Japan, war-induced rice shortages and high prices generated anti-governmental mobilization by consumers and workers through much of the country in 1918. In 1919 the Diet (national legislature) held back a strong popular bid for manhood suffrage to replace tax payment restrictions that kept industrial and agricultural workers from voting. Under pressure from nationwide demonstrations, the Diet finally enacted a reform doubling the electorate, but falling short of manhood suffrage. Japanese workers also produced a great wave of strikes in 1919. About the same time, rebellions against military rule in colonized Korea persuaded the Japanese government to install a civilian administration. Like other countries, in short, Japan went through a turbulent cycle of demands and concessions as the war ended.

Even more visibly than Japan, Great Britain went through a cycle of wartime co-operation between capital and labor, followed by postwar mobilization. Organized workers grumbled at wartime controls and losses of real wages, but still accepted no-strike agreements in war industries. As the war ended, however, they began to act collectively. While about 300,000 workers went on strike before war began in 1914, for example, nearly a million struck in 1918 and an average of 2 million per year in 1919 and 1920. Union membership doubled from about 4 million to 8 million between 1914 and 1920. In that process, the Labour Party became a major independent actor in British politics.

Payoffs came soon: After several great postwar rounds of strikes, the government made new wage settlements with coal miners and increased unemployment benefits for the large number of people left without work by postwar demobilization. Great Britain also passed a new Reform Act in 1918, expanding the electorate to all men 21 or older with six months' residence and all women 30 or older living in established households. The same legislation installed the principle of equal constituency size; British politicians argued for the reform as just compensation for popular participation in the war. Postwar reforms included creation of a new Ministry of Health, pension increases, raised salaries for teachers, and subsidies for housing construction. Not that labor simply had its way. Business interests blocked a tax on capital that organized labor, faced with the problem of paying off the government's war debts, backed enthusiastically. A Liberal–Conservative coalition, furthermore, soon froze the Labour Party out of government.

Despite its lesser involvement in World War I, the United States felt the war's impact deeply. The war affected the USA in two different ways: through the familiar cycle of mobilization, demobilization, and claim-making; and through momentous expansion of American power on the international scene. Like their counterparts elsewhere, American workers generally collaborated with the war effort – despite considerable anti-British agitation on the part of Irish Americans and great division among German Americans. Local committees approved by the government tracked down shirkers from military service and attacked

German religious pacifists with vigilante mobs. To make up for war-induced labor shortages, employers recruited unprecedented numbers of women and blacks. Black migration from the rural South to urban centers such as Detroit greatly accelerated. In the United States, unlike the European pattern, strikes continued through the war. In the Red Scare years of 1919–20, employers and conservative politicians blamed postwar turmoil on Soviet communist agitation. In fact, most strikes had other causes. Although a bitter steel strike tied up the industry in 1919 and 1920, the peak year for American strikes between 1914 and 1921 actually arrived in 1917. A remarkable 438 strikes started in the first full month after the USA entered the war.

Organized women – few of them industrial workers – had a visible impact on American public politics. Feminists had been campaigning actively for suffrage and for prohibition of alcohol consumption (deemed a curse to families) since around 1890. Temperance policies gained some support during the war due to stereotypes of Irish people as hard drinkers, of Germans as distillers, brewers, and swillers of beer, and of both as un-American. To save grain, the government itself placed extensive limits on alcohol during the war. In 1918, anti-alcohol campaigners drove the Eighteenth Amendment to the US Constitution, prohibiting public sale and consumption of alcohol, through Congress; by January 1919, the necessary three quarters of states had ratified the amendment.

Female suffrage took a bit longer. From the entry of Wyoming into the Union with universal suffrage (1890), a number of individual states had extended the vote to women. Activists waged successful campaigns for suffrage in the states of Washington (1910) and California (1911). They also put women's suffrage on the agenda of national political parties. Feminist leaders Carrie Chapman Catt and Nettie Rogers Shuler later recalled the 1916 convention of the Democratic party:

Amid tense excitement the roll call by States was ordered on the minority report. And now something else never before seen in a party convention happened. The women with the yellow ribbons produced roll-call forms and began jotting down each vote as it was cast. Said the New York Times: "The sight of them had a most unnerving effect upon the delegates. It was like the French convention of the Revolution, gallery ruled, and the women with the roll-call blanks, noting the way they voted, suggesting the knitting women of the Reign of Terror.

The national suffrage campaign swelled, until the National American Woman Suffrage Association claimed 2 million members in 1917. The US government finally adopted the Nineteenth Amendment – female suffrage – in 1920. As a fairly direct result of women's votes in the election of the same year, Congress passed two feminist measures: establishing government programs for child care (the Sheppard-Towner Act of 1921) and retaining US citizenship for American women who married foreigners (the Cable Act of 1922).

Another legislative act of 1921, however, displayed American ambivalence toward the rest of the world. The immigration law of that year drastically cut back arrivals from overseas by establishing annual quotas for immigrants from each country corresponding to 3 percent of the total of citizens from that country already resident in the USA as of the 1910 census. That measure privileged immigration from Northwestern Europe, and discriminated against the rest of the world. Yet at the same time the USA was flexing its muscles through most of that same world. Despite the US refusal to sign the peace treaties and join the League of Nations, the American government and American businessmen involved themselves heavily in reorganizing postwar European finances, regulating rearmament on a world scale, seeking control over oil supplies, and entering European markets. Du Pont, General Electric, General Motors, Ford, and other big American corporations prospered by selling to the American market, but they increasingly entered markets abroad. Although the much larger United States had already equaled Britain's industrial production around 1880, it first matched Britain's share of world trade around 1920. It had already become the world's greatest military power, and was bidding for leadership in science as well. The American Century, as Henry Luce of *Time* magazine later called it, had begun.

Conclusion While the American Century had begun, it took time for Americans and non-Americans to realize it. Starting in August 1914, the great killing machine chugged on, but an increasing number of contemporaries realized that the war had essentially become a stalemate. Only American entry into the war in 1917 produced Allied victory in 1918. Although the emergence of an industrialized USA and a revolutionized USSR profoundly altered the nature of world politics, it took a long time for peoples and diplomats to realize the consequences. Recognition of the fundamentally new shift in power was long delayed because the postwar USA did not want to become involved with European and world politics and because the postwar USSR was excluded from them. At war's end the hatred of conflict was so great that almost no one could contemplate it.

Whether contemporaries realized the significance or not, the Great War produced new levels of human destruction and created tectonic shifts in global power, far beyond anyone's expectations. It had begun as a conflict between two imperial alliances contending for influence in Southern Europe. It ended with the collapse of the losing alliance – the Germans, Austro-Hungarians, and Ottomans – as well as the Russian empire, and a massive wave of social revolutions and nationalist resistance across Eurasia. Its indirect effects spread to all the continents. Britain and France held their ground, but their imperial grip weakened, and the United States and Japan emerged with substantial economic and political gains, while China began its arduous path toward national unity. Geopolitical power shifts were also linked to mass movements, as politicized citizens demanded more from winning and losing states alike to compensate for their sufferings during the war. Even though no one wanted any further conflict, putting a stabilized capitalist order back together proved to be an impossible task. The socialist wave receded, but new mass movements continued to shake the world. Hopes for peace in the immediate postwar period turned out to be tragic illusions.

Study Questions (1) Describe and explain the major changes in South African political life produced by World War I.

(2) After its initial reluctance, what brought the United States into the Great War?

(3) What connection existed between the Great War and the influenza pandemic of 1918–19?

(4) In what ways did the Great War promote the Russian revolutions of 1917?

(5) Where and how did the Great War promote democratization?

(6) What accounts for the great concentration of rebellions, revolutions, and civil wars from 1917 to 1921?

(7) World War I destroyed empires and societies, but it also strengthened the central power of many states. Which nations gained power because of the war, and which lost the most? What determined their gains and losses?

Suggested Reading PETER ENGLUND, *The Beauty and the Sorrow: An Intimate History of the First World War* (New York: Knopf, 2011). This is a history of World War I based on a collection of memoirs from all the combatant nations, including much material on the home front.

JOHN KEEGAN, *The First World War* (New York: Random House, 1998). Keegan, a specialist in military history, knows how to portray the gritty realities of war and place them in their political context.

Gina Kolata, *Flu: The Story of the Great Influenza Pandemic* (New York: Touchstone, 2001). A skilled science writer tells the dramatic story of the 1918 virus that killed more people than died in the battles of World War I.

John Reed, *Ten Days That Shook The World* (New York: International Publishers, 1926). This is a vivid evocation of the early days of the Russian Revolution by an American journalist who participated in it.

Aviel Roshwald, *Ethnic Nationalism and the Fall of Empires: Central Europe, Russia and the Middle East, 1914–1923* (London: Routledge, 2001). World War I and its aftermath profoundly altered the political maps of Europe and the Middle East, including the assignment of ethnic groups and names to countries. Roshwald shows how and why.

Sidney Tarrow, *The Language of Contention: Revolutions in Words, 1688–2012* (Cambridge University Press, 2013). Tarrow explores the power of words in building social movements and in challenging them.

Charles Tilly, *European Revolutions, 1492–1992* (Oxford: Blackwell, 1993). This work places the revolutions of 1914–21, especially the Russian Revolution, in historical perspective, and analyzes their regular connections with war.

Leon Trotsky, *The History of the Russian Revolution*, trans. Max Eastman (London: Victor Gollancz, 1965). Trotsky's book is a brilliant evocation and analysis of Russia's revolutions of 1917 by a Bolshevik who led and lived them day by day.

Charles Van Onselen, *This Seed is Mine: The Life of Kas Maine, a South African Sharecropper, 1894–1985* (New York: Hill & Wang, 1996). This is the surprising story of a black South African, compiled from years of interviews.

Jay Winter and Jean-Louis Robert (eds.), *Capital Cities at War: Paris, London, Berlin, 1914–1919* (Cambridge University Press, 1997). Winter and Robert describe how the civilian populations of major European cities participated in, experienced, and reacted to the Great War as it wore on.

Glossary

Boers: Used generally for Afrikaans-speakers of European origin in South Africa (from old Dutch word for "peasant").

Bolsheviks: The more radical wing of the Russian Social Democratic Party in 1917 (Russian: "majority").

fascists: Italian nationalist and anti-socialist movement led by Benito Mussolini, which seized power in 1922.

Great War: How World War I was known until the Second World War began.

influenza: Viral disease that killed millions worldwide in 1918–19.

Mensheviks: The more moderate wing of the Russian Social Democratic Party in 1917 (Russian: "minority").

military coup: Takeover of a government by a group from its own military forces (also known as a *coup d'état*).

pandemic: Rapid worldwide spread of a disease (in contrast to local epidemics).

sit-down strike: Workers take over their workplace instead of picketing outside (also known as a factory occupation or strike in place).

soviet: In Russia, a governmental council, usually elected.

trench warfare: Infantry and artillery battles fought from deep trenches, typical of the Western Front in World War I.

12 Twentieth-century social revolutions, 1922–1939

Timeline	
1920–22	Indian leader Mohandas Gandhi launches Non-Co-operation Movement.
April 25–October 12, 1920	War between Poland and the USSR.
December 6, 1921	Irish representatives sign a treaty granting Ireland Dominion status as an Irish Free State. Northern Ireland retains its right to opt out of the new state.
1921	New Economic Policy in USSR concentrates socialization on the largest enterprises and allows leeway to peasants and small businesses.
April 16, 1922	Treaty of Rapallo between Germany and the USSR, in which each renounces financial and territorial claims upon the other, to the concern of other European nations.
January 11, 1923	French and Belgian troops occupy the Ruhr.
1925	Locarno Conference and Treaties.
July–October 1926	Victory of Stalin over the left-wing opposition of Leon Trotsky.
1927	Guomindang troops led by Chiang Kai-shek take offensive against warlords but also slaughter communists in Shanghai and other Chinese cities.
1928	Kellogg–Briand Pact, signed by most nations, renounces the use of war to resolve disputes.
October 1, 1928	Beginning of the first Five Year Plan, the USSR's policy of ruthless industrialization.
1929–31	British Labour government in power.
October 29, 1929	Stock market crash in New York: beginning of the Great Depression.

May 11, 1931	Failure of the Austrian Creditanstalt: Great Depression spreads to Europe.
1932	Election of Franklin Delano Roosevelt as President of the USA. Roosevelt calls for a "New Deal for the American people."
January 30, 1933	Adolf Hitler comes to power in Germany as chancellor.
February 27, 1933	Reichstag Fire: Hitler uses the pretext of the burning of the Reichstag to expel communists and effectively become dictator.
December 1, 1934	Assassination of Stalin's ally Sergey Kirov provides pretext for the beginning of the Great Purge in which millions of Soviet citizens are imprisoned and executed.
March 7, 1936	Germany renounces the Locarno Treaties and reoccupies the Rhineland.
June 1936	Great wave of strikes results in the Matignon Accords, a major concession to French labor.
June 5, 1936	Popular Front government under Léon Blum formed in France.
July 17, 1936	Beginning of the Spanish Civil War.
March 12–13, 1938	German invasion and annexation of Austria.
September 29, 1938	Munich Agreement permits German annexation of portions of Czechoslovakia.
March 1939	Destruction of the Czechoslovakian state.
March 28, 1939	Franco's troops take Madrid, bringing about end of the Spanish Civil War on April 1.
September 1, 1939	Germany attacks Poland.

Lu Xun (1881–1936), China's most famous modern writer, was born in the small market town of Shaoxing, near Shanghai. In 1901 he went to Japan, intending to become a doctor. In his medical school class, he saw a slide of apathetic Chinese bystanders watching the execution of a Chinese man by Japanese soldiers during the Russo-Japanese war of 1905. Shocked by their passivity, he concluded that China's most deadly disease afflicted the spirit, not the body. He returned to China, resolving to become a writer to rouse his people from their deadly slumber. In "Call to Arms," his first short story collection, he described with great sympathy and insight the foibles of ordinary Chinese folk following time-honored customs, nearly oblivious of the worldwide crisis that surrounded them. In "Diary of a Madman," whose title is borrowed from the Russian writer Nikolai Gogol, the writer suddenly realizes that the basic principle of China's classic civilization is "eat people." Ah Q, Lu Xun's most famous character, blithely walks to his own execution without ever knowing why he joined the cause of revolutionary nationalism. Lu Xun and his colleagues particularly stressed the need to free women from the straitjacket of traditional morality so that they could participate actively in making the new nation. Lu Xun organized the League of Left Wing Writers to mobilize Chinese writers in the service of revolutionary nationalism. Lu Xun's mood constantly oscillated between high hopes and black despair. He died in 1936, hoping for China's national unification based on radical social revolution, defying his own repressive government and the imminent threat of Japanese invasion.

Bertolt Brecht (1898–1956), Germany's most famous modern playwright, also attempted to mobilize writers for political ends. In the vibrant culture of the Weimar Republic, his poems and plays attracted young Germans who mocked the repressive piousness of the Kaiser's Reich and looked for liberation in social transformation. In *The Threepenny Opera* (1928), with his collaborator, the brilliant jazzy song writer Kurt Weill, Brecht described capitalism as little different from a criminal enterprise, and in the stunning song "Pirate Jenny" a bitter waitress expresses her rage by daydreaming about a pirate king who will kill all her male oppressors. Brecht and Weill had to flee Germany when the Nazis took power, ending up in Los Angeles, where radical German émigrés mingled awkwardly with Hollywood moguls. Brecht returned after the war to East Germany to conduct his own dramatic troupe with socialist government support.

Both Brecht and Lu Xun left artistic works that evoke powerfully the mixed moods of the 1920s and 1930s, fluctuating between utopian ideals and black despair, urges for radical change clashing with brutal militarism, repression, and war. Both absorbed cultural elements from all over the world: Brecht and Weill mixed American jazz, British music hall songs, and Chinese opera techniques; Lu Xun drew on Russian and Eastern European writers, Chinese poets, and the Japanese vocabulary of modernity. They created new languages to express the extravagant hopes and violent moods of their time.

The years between 1922 and 1939 witnessed the failure of the World War I peace settlement, the massive collapse of the world economic order and the contraction of world trade, and the beginning of the most devastating war in human history. The period began with great hopes and high expectations for champions of liberal democracy and capitalist economic principles. In 1922, liberal democracy dominated the European and North American political scene and was advancing in many areas of the world, with democratic elections held in such disparate areas as Turkey and Japan. China's new democratizing nationalist government reunited most of the country by 1927, and Germany's new Weimar democracy seemed to have attained stability. Behind a wall of radical rhetoric the USSR was turning inward, preoccupied with its efforts to industrialize. In 1928 influential and experienced liberal statesmen united to declare an end to the use of war for political purposes.

Such misty dreams soon evaporated. By 1939, liberal democracy had been overthrown by military dictators and ousted by fascists in Germany. Militarists controlled Japan. Looking less like democrats than apprentice fascists, China's Nationalists become more repressive as they mobilized for war. Even in such democratic bastions as the UK and France, liberal leaders looked weak and indecisive, no longer sure that history was on their

side. An increasingly large proportion of the world's population lived under authoritarian rule. Nearly everywhere the move toward more democracy, integration, and social equality, so powerful in the early and mid 1920s, was reversed by dictatorship, militarism, and nationalism in the 1930s. This chapter looks at how liberal democracy, so triumphant after World War I, seemed on the verge of collapse by 1939. Here are the main trends of these two decades:

- The early 1920s saw expansion of liberal democracy, with strong legislatures elected according to principles of universal manhood suffrage and expansion of women's political rights.
- But almost from the beginning, crises struck Italy, Germany, the newly formed Eastern European states, and Japan, where newly enfranchised citizens confronted economies disorganized by war or wracked by ethnic conflict.
- Worse followed. The Great Depression of 1929 created political crises that wiped away, even reversed, the liberal democratic achievements of 1919, spreading into a global crisis as liberal economic policies of belt-tightening proved unavailing. After 1929, the global economy contracted, protectionism became the order of the day, and the world careened toward war.
- In the 1930s, many states joined together into self-sufficient blocs; the success of militarized economies expanding under heavy government control undermined the liberal faith in government non-intervention, pacifism, and free trade. Both fascist Germany and communist USSR seemed to deal with economic crisis better than the UK or France. In Asia, fascism and communism attracted much greater support than liberal democracy, especially because they promised to free colonized nations from the liberal imperial powers. The USA, under Roosevelt's New Deal was a relatively exceptional example of liberal democrats' use of government intervention to defend market capitalism.
- At the international level old-established liberal democracies as well as the newly created democracies responded weakly to anti-democratic challenges. The liberal powers failed to prevent the Japanese invasion of Manchuria in 1931 (the real beginning of World War II), the Italian invasion of Ethiopia in 1935, or the intervention of Germany, Italy, and the USSR in the Spanish Civil War from 1936 to 1939.
- By 1939, three distinctive ideologies had emerged, liberal democracy in Britain, France, and the United States, fascism in Italy and Germany, and communism in the USSR. China was divided by civil war between communists and nationalists, and fascists and communists had significant support in some leading liberal democracies. Colonial peoples wrestled with these choices but their view was

usually tempered by the knowledge that liberal democratic principles often applied only to Europe and North America; it did not extend fully to the colonies. The late 1930s saw a dramatic realignment of these divisions. By the end of 1939, it looked as if both Hitler and Stalin, fascism and communism, had joined forces to destroy liberal democracy.

12.1 THE YEARNING FOR PEACE; THE FEAR OF REVOLUTION

World War I's unprecedented slaughter profoundly affected almost every European household in the combatant nations. For many survivors, the war brought an enormous loss of faith in the existing order. Although the wartime experience intensified emotions among all the combatants, it did not unify postwar populations. Many on the left blamed the war on greedy munitions makers, prideful monarchs, and imperialist rivalries. Others on the right felt that the loss of fathers, brothers, and sons could only be given significance by pursuing the nationalist goals for which their kin had died. Whatever their rhetoric, the prospect of war filled the citizens of democratic states with horror. And not only the citizens of democratic states. In 1938 in the months preceding the Munich crisis, when Hitler was threatening war over Czechoslovakia, the German dictator was upset by the downcast spirit of crowds at a Berlin military review.

While war terrified most Europeans, a small minority regarded it with nostalgia. Drafted at early ages, schooled in the trenches, and suddenly demobilized and returned jobless to the streets, some young veterans longed for the only life they had known. They joined irregular military formations, the source of so much gratuitous violence in postwar Europe. In Germany, the military and the right-wing socialists recruited disbanded soldiers, the **Freikorps**, to defend against radical revolution or to fight Polish nationalists who were occupying land and asserting territorial claims within the disintegrating empires. In Italy, former elite troops, the **Arditi**, swelled the ranks of Mussolini's street fighters. Even the British government recruited auxiliary forces, freed from the stringencies of normal military discipline, to wage a vicious secret war against Irish nationalists.

Irregular troops joined the fight against communist revolution – a threat that emerged with particular force in the years between 1918 and 1920. The German Freikorps murdered socialist leaders Rosa Luxemburg and Karl Liebknecht after a failed rising in 1919. For a while, even well-informed commentators like the French prime minister, Georges Clemenceau, believed that the wave of revolution that began in the Russian empire in 1917 might sweep through a desolate and defeated Germany,

Austria, and Hungary, perhaps cresting in the invasion of a class-divided France and Italy. Fear that the Red Army might march through a Europe of mutinous and disintegrating armies increased anxiety about workers' unrest. Such visions were no mere fantasy. Communist revolution threatened Germany in 1919, and the Red Army, having repulsed a Polish attack, marched on Warsaw in 1920. Polish troops with French advisors only barely prevented a Red Army advance into Central Europe.

Fearing revolutionary contagion, European liberal democracies and the USA refused to recognize the Soviet regime. In 1922 Weimar Germany outraged the British and French by signing the Treaty of Rapallo with the Soviet Union, in which the Soviet Union gave up its demands for reparations and moved toward normal commercial and diplomatic relations. One reason that Britain and the USA excluded Russia, clearly a great power, from routine diplomatic affairs was that the UK only diplomatically recognized the USSR in 1924 and the USA in 1933. The threat of communist revolution was never far from the thoughts of appeasement-minded statesmen like Neville Chamberlain. Liberal democracies tolerated first Mussolini and then Hitler because they feared that strong measures against the fascists might cause these governments to collapse and so benefit communists.

Non-Europeans often saw the war differently. For some, the war brought economic opportunity. While British and French industries concentrated on producing military goods, Japan replaced them in the Asian markets for consumer goods and took over Germany's territories in China. For others the war offered political inspiration. In India news of the Irish Easter Rebellion in 1916 against British rule and the subsequent Irish War of Independence provided encouragement. For still others the war only intensified their despair. The Chinese, who sent over 100,000 workers to support the French war effort behind the lines, demanded without avail the renunciation of unequal treaties and restoration of their territorial sovereignty.

12.2 DEMOCRATIZATION AND NATIONALISM

Democracy made giant strides in the war's immediate wake. As the war lengthened and grew more bloody, wartime leaders promised social reform or democratization to keep the soldiers fighting. The popular revolutions that ended the war all called for democratization, and the new American President Woodrow Wilson (in office from 1913 to 1921) and the victors at Versailles praised it. As conditions for joining the new League of Nations, the new European nations formed in the war's aftermath promised to provide equal protection for all citizens without distinction of birth, nationality, language, race, or religion. Austria, Germany, and Turkey became republics and adopted democratic constitutions. Universal manhood suffrage finally came to the United Kingdom in 1918. British women received a measure of suffrage in 1918 and equal suffrage in 1928, and US women won the right to vote in 1920. Between 1918 and 1922 women obtained the suffrage in many other countries, including British East Africa, Germany, India, and Palestine. The figure of the "modern woman," who had not only political rights but personal autonomy and sexual freedom, attracted much comment in many nations. Would the newly enfranchised women destroy the family and traditional morality, or would they become informed, engaged citizens who strengthened the nation? (See Box 12.1.)

In the 1920s, as democracy advanced outside Europe and North America, it took on different meanings for colonized peoples than for their rulers. For the imperial powers, democratization usually meant greater participation in decision-making by both domestic and colonized peoples, but under the assumption that colonies would be maintained into the foreseeable future. To obtain support for the war effort, administrators had promised varying degrees of self-government. In India, as in the rest of the colonial world, nationalists read the writings of Woodrow Wilson and Vladimir Lenin and embraced their calls for self-determination.

India

The Indian National Congress, an organization containing both Hindus and Muslims, began to challenge British rule in the years after World War I. At the same time, the notorious Amritsar massacre of 1919, in which a British general massacred hundreds of peaceful protestors, inflamed Indian anger (see Chapter 11). The 1919 Government of India Act provided a larger role for elective councils. Laws restricting the press were repealed and the ranks of the Indian army were "Indianized." While the act was frustrated by the independent Indian princes and disrupted by the Muslim League, which was beginning its evolution toward separatism, the British in India acknowledged the eventual goal of Indian independence. The Indian National Congress rejected these steps as inadequate, but other Indians agreed to work with the new representative system. Returning to India from South Africa during the war, the young London-trained lawyer Mohandas Gandhi launched a **Non-Co-operation Movement** based on principled non-violence that shook British rule in 1920–22.

The Middle East

India was not alone; a democratic wave swept the colonial world. In 1925 British authorities approved a constitution for Egypt, a country Britain had occupied since 1882. New nations emerged

Box 12.1 Men and Women in the 1920s and 1930s: From Liberation to Repression

The postwar period promised to liberate women from their restricted routines of housekeeping, reproduction, and sexual subordination. The war discredited pious moralists, especially those who glorified service to family and nation, and the collapse of empires released pent-up frustration. Nora, the heroine of Henrik Ibsen's play *A Doll's House*, had already stormed out of her house in 1879. When her husband told her she was violating her "sacred duty" to him and her children, she replied defiantly, "I've another duty just as sacred: my duty towards myself." Chinese feminists took up her cry in the 1920s to escape Confucian patriarchy, joining revolutionary movements or even endorsing "free love." In the US, women crusaders

against drunken men who neglected their families in favour of saloons forced passage of laws banning alcohol, but Prohibition brought widespread defiance by men and women alike. Flappers, bathtub gin, the Charleston, F. Scott Fitzgerald, carefree playboys and playgirls found their echoes in England's Bloomsbury set and the disturbing "mobo" and "moga" (modern boy and modern girl) of Japan. After getting out of jail for sending birth control information through the mail, Margaret Sanger opened her first clinic in New York City in 1923 to educate young women in family planning. She lectured to large audiences in Asia, Europe, and Africa. Advertisers also promoted the independent woman, the consumer who

chose her household products wisely, or the seductive cigarette smoker.

The 1930s pushed women back into the home, or into the streets, and hurt the pride of men and women alike. The gaunt sharecropper's wife, the blonde Aryan beauty with chubby children, the Russian tractor girl, the militant Chinese guerrilla warrior, replaced the self-indulgent youth of the Jazz Age. Work and war, not pleasure and freedom, took charge of the images of popular culture. But the realities of economic hardship and famine could make their lives even worse, forcing women into prostitution and selling their children. Lu Xun asked skeptically, "When Nora walked out the door, where did she go?" The 1930s left many women with few alternatives.

in the Middle East, like Iraq, made of three provinces formerly part of the Ottoman empire. The British occupied Baghdad in 1919, and in 1920 gained a "mandate" to justify temporary control. In the Great Arab Revolt of 1920, Iraqis besieged British garrisons, initiating the Arab independence movement. In 1924 the Iraqi national assembly ratified a constitution for Iraq. Under King Faisal, Iraq gained independence and admission to the League of Nations in 1932.

The mandate system failed in Palestine, another Ottoman province, because the British, in the Balfour Declaration of 1917, had committed themselves to making Palestine a "national home for the Jewish People." The Arab majority in Palestine rioted against a new wave of Jewish immigrants and refused to approve a new constitution. As clashes between Arabs and Jews continued, Arabs demanded an end to land sales to Jews and Jewish immigration, while Jews rioted against British restrictions. When a British commission proposed partition of Palestine into two states in 1937, most Jews reluctantly accepted it, but a Pan Arab Congress overwhelmingly rejected the idea. The British gave up on a partition that satisfied no one. Many of the seeds of the modern Middle East conflict had already sprouted in the interwar years.

12.3 NATIONALISM AND IMPERIALISM IN EAST ASIA

The Versailles Conference inspired Chinese nationalists who hoped that Wilson's principles might end the era of unequal treaties and ward off a menacing Japan. China was now a nation and not an empire; and almost 2,000 Chinese workers had died in France helping the Allies during the war. Chinese expected to recover Germany's leasehold territories in Shandong. But Great Britain, France, and Italy, in order to get Japanese naval support against Germany, had signed a secret treaty supporting Japan's claims on Shandong. At Versailles, Woodrow Wilson supported the secret treaty. Chinese delegates at Versailles faced strong pressure to go along, especially since the warlord government of Beijing depended heavily on Japanese financial support. On May 4, 1919, infuriated by the great powers' abandonment of the noble principles of self-determination, young students and intellectuals rallied in the streets of Beijing and Shanghai to protest the betrayal of their nation to foreign interests. Soon merchants, workers, and urban people all over China joined them, denouncing Japanese aggression and Western imperial hypocrisy. By blockading the delegates in their hotel in Paris, Chinese students prevented the delegates from signing the treaty. This "May Fourth Movement" marks the symbolic beginning of mass Chinese nationalism.

May Fourth came to mean much more than a single day's demonstration. It developed into an all-out effort by China's

young educated class to create a new society based on Western models. They eagerly read new magazines filled with translations of all kinds of foreign ideas. In foreign journals they discovered socialism, through Japanese translations of Russian and German texts, and began to organize the small but growing working classes in the cities. Sun Yat-sen (1866–1925), the founder of China's nationalist movement and the first president of the Chinese republic, himself endorsed socialism as one of his Three People's Principles, but, disillusioned with the West's response, he turned to the Soviet version. Lenin had appealed to all colonized peoples to rebel against Western imperialism. A humiliated China now began to see itself as a "semi-colony," or even, in the words of Li Dazhao, one of the founders of the Chinese Communist Party, a "proletarian nation."

Of all the major powers, Japan gained the most from World War I. While the Europeans fought each other, Japan expanded its exports and sought to create a powerful position for itself in China. By declaring war on Germany, the Japanese acquired its possessions in the Shandong peninsula. The Japanese then presented the Chinese with the Twenty-One Demands, a set of secret agreements that would have given Japan a dominant position in most of coastal China and special control in Manchuria. Japan had learned the rules of the imperial game well: It aimed to replace European influence at the expense of a weakened China. When the demands leaked out, furious Chinese protest backed by the British and Americans forced the Japanese to withdraw the most extreme provisions, but these demands exposed both Japanese ambitions and Chinese weakness.

While China disintegrated, Japan was emerging as a premier power in the Pacific, a rising empire, but also one evolving in a liberal democratic direction. The reign of the Taisho emperor (1912–26) symbolized a new political direction, quite different from the authoritarian, elitist state of the Meiji era. The emperor himself was physically weak, and often ill, but more important, party politicians gained power in battles against the bureaucratic and military figures of the Meiji state. In 1918 Hara Kei, master of pork barrel politics and the supreme master of parliamentary maneuvers, formed the first stable party government in Japan's history, one which was able to challenge the most powerful of elite interest groups. He gained passage of a bill to build narrow-gauge railroad tracks throughout the Japanese countryside in the teeth of opposition from military interests, who wanted large-gauge railroads to facilitate the movement of troops onto the continent. In 1925 Japanese elections were carried out according to universal male suffrage. It seemed that the people were gaining influence.

But **Taisho democracy** turned out to be quite limited. The emperor still reigned supreme, and military ministers acted independently of parliamentary control. Most significantly, even the most popular political parties never rejected colonies or imperial adventures. Japan was an "imperial democracy" in two senses: It had a divine emperor supervising a parliamentary state, and a mass public that supported Japan's increasing power in Asia. Japan still looked for opportunities to expand its economic power and geopolitical influence, but in the 1920s it chose cultural, economic, and diplomatic means over military ones.

12.4 LIBERAL DEMOCRACY AND ITS PROBLEMS IN THE 1920S

The expansion of democracy in the wake of World War I and the formation of new nations from collapsed empires created an unparalleled political situation. Millions of new citizens came to the polls and voted, often for new political parties. Most voters endorsed liberal democracy, but many of them elected socialists and communists. In Italy, the election of 1922 witnessed the first appearance of the fascists; in a variety of countries from Ireland to Egypt, nationalists made a substantial showing.

Liberal democrats shared a number of basic principles, but the application of each of these principles posed problems:

- Liberal democrats argued that the principle of the **self-determination of nations** (the right of ethnic minorities within larger nations to claim on political independence) was indispensable to democracy in Europe, but could not satisfactorily explain why it was inapplicable outside Europe, in the colonies.
- They advocated free markets and the gold standard to preserve fiscal responsibility. This meant balanced budgets and austerity, if necessary, to preserve the value of a currency, even at the cost of social unrest. At a time when Europe was potentially filled with millions of unemployed men who knew how to use weapons, austerity had its problems.
- They maintained that international order should be protected by collective security guarantees among democratic nations and preserved by disarmament agreements. Yet what should they do to enforce these norms against nations who violated them?
- Each of the fundamental liberal principles promised a more attractive, peaceful, and prosperous world, but each of them ran into severe contradictions. Self-determination, the gold standard, and collective security all proved to have fatal flaws.

Liberal democrats believed, for example, that democracy should be the organizing principle for the new nations of Europe. New regimes adopted anthems and flags, established schools, and organized police forces and national armies. Despite the pledges they had given at Versailles, the nation-building enthusiasm of national leaders often brought them into conflict with ethnic minorities such as the Germans in Czechoslovakia's Sudetenland or the Hungarians in western Romania. Increasingly, nationalism in Eastern Europe turned against Jewish minorities. Nationalists competed with Jews, who composed a disproportionate portion of the urban population of Eastern European cities like Budapest, Kiev, Minsk, and Vilna. Assertive nationalist politicians from peasant backgrounds often espoused traditional anti-Semitic prejudices. These new urban middle classes demanded government jobs and university positions for themselves, not for minorities such as the Jews, whom they regarded as "stateless" foreigners.

Liberal democrats advocated the self-determination of nations – but in practice applied these principles only to the defeated nations of Europe. Partly responding to Wilson's Fourteen Points, the victorious powers carved up the Ottoman, Austro-Hungarian, and German empires according to criteria roughly based on cultural identification. But Wilson in 1918 acted as the military leader of the Allied coalition, not, as he had originally hoped in 1915, as an independent mediator. The call for self-determination contributed to the breakup of the German and Austro-Hungarian empires (and to the Russian empire which in some sense was a defeated power) but it could not be used against victors. Alsace-Lorraine, the French province incorporated into Germany in 1870–71, would become French no matter what the Alsatians wanted.

Despite elections in 1921 that showed that the vast majority of the Irish electorate favored independence, Woodrow Wilson's principles were not applied there. An Irish Free State emerged in 1922 from a civil war led by the militant nationalists in the Sinn Féin movement. This new state had significantly limited sovereignty and it did not include six northern Irish counties. Diplomatic factors were as important as military factors in the Irish state's creation. In the critical years between 1916 and 1922, Britain looked to the USA for support and co-operation during the war and an Anglo-American treaty of mutual defense was a major goal of British policy after the war. A powerful Irish American lobby favoring Irish independence, the Friends of Irish Freedom, with 175,000 members and associates, emerged during the war. British politicians sought to avoid actions in Ireland that might be used by the Irish American propaganda mill, and such considerations limited the application of the most severe repression. His American citizenship probably prevented the execution of Éamon de Valera, a leader of the 1916 rebellion, later president of Ireland and a central figure in twentieth-century Irish politics.

Neither did the Versailles drafters apply the principle of self-determination consistently to the defeated Germans. The treaty incorporated substantial German minorities living adjacent to

Germany into the new Czechoslovakian state because they considered the mountainous Sudetenland a useful military borderland. Also Poland incorporated German minorities in the northeast so as to give the country an opening to the sea. Selective application of the principle of self-determination to benefit the war's winners generated accusations of hypocrisy and stoked hatreds that would plague the succeeding decades.

Neither did the self-determination of nations apply to the German colonies in Africa and the successor states of the Ottoman empire; the emergence of independent states in these areas would have challenged the British and French colonial orders. Under the guise of "tutelage," Britain and France used the League of Nation's mandate system to divide the German colonies and the Ottoman empire among themselves. In Africa, Britain got Tanganyika and German Southwest Africa and France got the German Cameroon; in the Middle East, France got Syria and Britain got Palestine, Transjordan, and Iraq. In these regions, liberal principles looked like an excuse for winning empires to divide the spoils of losing empires. No wonder the Japanese felt entitled to their share in Asia.

Before 1914, liberals had believed in free trade, balanced budgets, and limited government, but the demands of total war had forced all the major powers to institute some measure of economic planning, violating basic liberal principles, while inflation and disruption of trade destroyed national currencies. At the end of the war, financiers reacted against planning and tried to restore the prewar golden age, when the solid British pound, based on gold, underwritten by the Bank of England, guaranteed stable currency values. They called it a "return to normalcy." In 1925, the British made the pound freely convertible to gold, re-establishing the international gold standard. Soon most of Europe followed suit. The prestige of gold, however, covered up economic weaknesses. The French, after rampant inflation, could only set the franc at one fifth of its prewar value. The return to a gold standard administered by British bankers ignored the fact that much of Britain's gold reserves had flowed to the USA, and Britain and France were heavily in debt to the USA. In reality, the health of the European financial system depended on the health of the US economy, not on its gold supplies. If the American prop fell, the entire liberal economic order would collapse.

Interwar liberal democrats also believed in collective security and mutual disarmament. They established the League of Nations in Geneva in 1920 to pursue these goals. According to liberal democratic theory, the democratic community of nations would intervene to sanction aggressors who threatened war. The League's early days were difficult. Woodrow Wilson, its chief promoter, could not convince the American Senate to approve US participation. In 1923, France tried to go it alone, seizing Germany's industrial heartland, the Ruhr Valley, to enforce German payment of **reparations** (compensation to the victors for the cost of World War I). This failed disastrously, provoking German inflation and gaining France nothing but German resentment and international condemnation. France then realized the advantages of working through collective agreements. After the establishment of a workable provision plan for reparations and the signing of the Locarno Treaty in 1925, in which Germany accepted its western borders, the international scene favored peace initiatives. Germany's entry into the League of Nations in 1926 raised fleeting hopes that international organizations might guarantee peace, expressed in the Kellogg–Briand Pact of 1928 outlawing war as an instrument of national policy. All the major powers endorsed this lofty principle; the only flaw was that they refused to support sanctions against violators.

Japan also participated actively in global initiatives for peace. Japan joined the League of Nations and participated in the Washington Naval Conference of 1921–22 and the London Naval Conference of 1930, the last successful effort to limit arms expansion. Foreign Minister Shidehara resisted pressure to build up military forces, relying instead on collective diplomacy to ensure Japan's commercial and security interests. Japan agreed to cut its naval expenditures, provided that the two dominant naval powers, Britain and the United States, promised not to build fortifications in the western Pacific. On the other hand, the Japanese strongly opposed another promise of the Washington Conference, to restore tariff autonomy to China, because this would limit their access to Chinese markets. Even though Japanese investments expanded in Manchuria and the rest of China, Chinese resentment of Japanese commercial penetration repeatedly burst out in anti-Japanese boycotts. The policy of peaceful expansion yielded Japan good will from Western powers, but only limited results in China.

In sum, liberal principles gained a great deal of support in the 1920s, both from governmental leaders and from publics looking for a way out of incessant economic struggle and war. Each of the liberal principles appealed in the abstract to urbanized middle classes, but each of them faced difficult challenges from internal contradictions and alternative visions of the world. Socialism, in both its parliamentary and revolutionary versions, still posed a familiar challenge, but fascism, the newly emergent mass movement, threatened liberals and socialists alike.

12.5 ALTERNATIVE VISIONS: SOCIALISTS, COMMUNISTS, AND FASCISTS

The liberal program appealed to middle classes, but it left out many others. They looked to different political movements to serve their needs. The three most prominent were democratic socialists, revolutionary communists, and fascists.

Committed to democratic reformist politics, democratic socialists surged in the 1920s. Democratic socialists, like communists, favored government intervention and control of the economy, but placed a high value on democracy. At least initially, democratic socialists also tended to support the League of Nation's emphasis on collective security. They shared with the liberals a faith in parliamentary institutions and international diplomatic organizations, but tried to push their governments into greater concern for social welfare and controlling the economy. They still insisted on the class character of socialism: Mass politics should serve primarily the interests of the working class. This insistence gave socialists a strong sense of social identity but also cut them off from many middle-class liberals who shared their moral concern about capitalism's limitations.

For much of the twentieth century, democratic socialists struggled to reconcile class appeals and reformist goals. In the 1920s democratic socialists not only took part in governments but for the first time led them. German Social Democrats became the largest single party in the 1919 elections and participated in government with the Catholic Center Party and liberal Democratic Party until forced out of government by a center-right coalition in 1930. The British Labour Party came to power in alliance with Liberals for a brief interlude in 1924–25 and again in 1929–31. In France a coalition government led by a socialist, Léon Blum, came to power in 1936.

During their brief heyday, however, these socialists did not demonstrate effective economic or political leadership. The British Labour government of 1929–31 could not devise an economic policy for confronting economic crisis. The Labour Chancellor of the Exchequer, Philip Snowden, endorsed orthodox political economy more strongly than the liberal economist John Maynard Keynes or the US president, Franklin Roosevelt. Léon Blum's government began serious social reforms which gathered immense enthusiasm from French workers, expressed in the great wave of strikes which followed his election. Unfortunately, despite an opening round of extensive reforms, Blum, too, proved unable to solve the problems of the Depression. The French far-right targeted Blum's "Popular Front" government and the communists who participated in it, adopting the slogan "Better Hitler than Blum." Democratic socialists, torn between radical reform and compromise, attacked from the left and the right, sank in the stormy crosscurrents of the period.

12.6 SOVIET COMMUNISM: DOMESTIC REFORM AND WORLD REVOLUTION

In the early 1920s, the communists were the energetic and militant face of socialism, and liberal democrats feared them.

To be sure, while a few sparks of revolution still flared up in such unlikely places as Bulgaria in 1923, the great revolutionary conflagration that seemed underway at war's end had diminished. Only in China did there seem real opportunities for revolution. Still, despite intensive Western efforts, including armed intervention by British, French, Japanese, and US troops, the Russian Civil War had ended in 1922 with communists in power. From the moment they took power in 1917, the Bolsheviks had seen the immediate future as something like a coin toss. Either heads or tales: Heads, and the Allies or the tsarist armies would win and use their military power to crush the communists. Tales, and the Soviet armies would march triumphantly through Europe greeted by revolutionary workers who had overthrown their own capitalist regimes. Against all odds, however, the coin landed on its edge. The revolution did not spread, yet a communist government survived in the USSR.

Survival in a capitalist world required major policy changes. Presiding over a fractious Communist Party, Lenin realized that the wartime policy of War Communism – which often amounted to little more than confiscation – had profoundly alienated the rural population during the Civil War. In 1921 Lenin persuaded his party of the need for a radical change of course. His government inaugurated the **New Economic Policy** (NEP) to pursue moderate policies toward small business and the peasantry. The original purpose of NEP was to use the market economy to restore a Russian economy battered by both foreign and civil war. NEP restored the economy, but at the cost of increasing the number and wealth of rich peasants who opposed the regime. Rich peasants, called **kulaks** (the Russian word for "fist"), flourished in the late tsarist period as the rural commune dissolved. The upheavals of the revolution reduced their income, but NEP allowed them to revive, although poorer peasants detested them as greedy entrepreneurs. Rival Bolsheviks furiously debated the future of NEP, while Lenin suffered a series of strokes that disabled him until his death in 1924. At the time of his death, Soviet communists were divided between rightists and leftists; it is important to remember, though, that these divisions were based on the Soviet context; anywhere else in the world at that time, both rightist and leftist communists would have seemed extreme left-wing radicals. Rightist communists like Nikolai Bukharin, a sophisticated economic theorist, argued for continuing the NEP indefinitely, allowing for slow economic growth based on consumer spending and light industry. In contrast, leftist communists like Leon Trotsky, the charismatic orator and military organizer, argued for an end to NEP's indulgence of the kulaks, and in favor of increased government-sponsored industrialization.

Behind the scenes, consolidating organizational support, appointing his followers to key positions, and antagonizing neither Bukharin or Trotsky, was the dull but sinister General Secretary, Joseph Stalin, silently biding his time while Lenin lay dying. Lenin's death precipitated a struggle for supreme power that Stalin won. Ultimately Stalin expelled Trotsky from Russia, then started the process of collectivization, forced draft industrialization, and tyrannical centralization that marked the Soviet Union for decades to come.

Initially the Soviet communists had embraced internationalism. In 1922 tsarist Russia became the Union of Soviet Socialist Republics (USSR or Soviet Union; see Map 12.1). The Soviet Union claimed to be a federation of socialist republics, embodying the principle of self-determination of nations. Although for most of its history the USSR was actually ruled from Moscow in a highly centralized fashion, the division of the USSR into separate state-based territorial units would bear significantly on its fate as the regime began to dissolve after 1989.

The Communist International, or Comintern, founded in 1919, was the device intended for leading the world revolution. Contrary to Marx's expectations, the communist revolution had succeeded in the economically backward tsarist empire, not in the industrially advanced European countries. Soviet communists argued that an exclusive focus on the industrial working classes led socialists to underestimate the possibility that workers could lead peasants to revolt in backward countries. Such revolts might then trigger revolutions in advanced nations and spread the world revolution, ultimately fulfilling Marx's predictions. For example, with Russia's agricultural resources and Germany's industrial power, a real socialist order might be constructed. This attention to less developed states gave the new movement an appeal to those who sought to develop backward countries.

Partly because of its attention to less developed nations, the newly founded Communist International almost from the start had stronger international affiliations than the old socialist international. Many Latin American socialists joined the communist movement. While only the Chilean Communist Party enjoyed mass support, communist parties were founded in Mexico (1919), Argentina (1921), Brazil (1922), and Cuba (1925). Communist parties also spread to the Middle East and Asia, in Indonesia (1920), Persia (1920), China (1921), Egypt (1924), and India (1924).

Despite these advances, the Communist International harbored a basic contradiction: Was it really designed to spread revolution or to defend the national interests of the Soviet Union? In the early years of the revolution this produced

Map 12.1 Union of Soviet Socialist Republics

tension, as when in 1923 the Soviet Union established normal diplomatic relations with the German government, while actively supporting the German revolutionaries who were trying to overthrow it.

Eventually Soviet leaders like Stalin came to believe that the preservation of the USSR was the chief priority. If communist parties in advanced countries could only prevent their governments from strangling the fledgling socialist state in its cradle, Soviet communists would build socialism in the USSR, without financial aid from advanced economies. It was easy to see that such a strategy required a harsh and dictatorial rule to extract from the peasantry the resources necessary to build a socialist state.

Stalin's China Catastrophe

By the time the smoke cleared in 1921, it became clear that, except in the USSR, the revolutionary wave had crested and revolution was no longer the order of the day. Only in China did there seem to be a revolutionary opportunity. In 1911, with the collapse of the empire and the establishment of a republic, warlords had torn apart the country. Sun Yat-sen, unable to defeat the warlords by himself, looked to the new communist state for aid.

Comintern agents helped to found the Chinese Communist Party in 1921, when a grand total of thirteen delegates, including the young teacher Mao Zedong (1893–1976), met on a boat on a lake in Zhejiang. By 1923 the party had at most 300 members, far too small to take any leading role in politics. Since only Sun Yat-sen's Nationalist Party was in a position to unify the new nation, the Comintern ordered the Chinese communists to join the nationalist Guomindang and work from within it. Sun Yat-sen did not oppose this; he was hostile to communism, but he needed Soviet aid. He accepted communists as members and initiated a thorough reorganization of the Guomindang. At the same time, the Soviets created a military academy at Whampoa, down the river from Canton, to train a new army motivated by nationalist revolutionary ideology. The young student Zhou Enlai (1898–1976), just returned from France, took over Whampoa's political education department. The commandant of Whampoa, however, was Chiang Kai-shek (1887–1975), who had just come back from military training in Moscow. He was very suspicious of the communist presence in the Guomindang, but like Stalin, he kept his distance from intra-party debates, and he cultivated the loyalty of military men.

Under the cover of this alliance, called the first United Front, Guomindang factions and communists maneuvered for support. Sun Yat-sen's death in 1925, like Lenin's in 1924, left the future of both revolutionary movements uncertain. The crux of the Chinese revolution came when Chiang Kai-shek launched his new army on the successful Northern Expedition. Trotsky warned against putting trust in Chiang and joining the Guomindang, and sought to arm Shanghai workers. In contrast, Stalin's policy was to win Chiang as an ally in the hope that Nationalist China might be a valuable partner for the USSR. As Chiang's dedicated, politically indoctrinated troops defeated the warlord armies, they approached Shanghai, center of the Chinese working class, where communists had built a significant labor movement. They represented a patriotic, revolutionary mass movement of their own. How should communists respond to the Guomindang advance – as allies or enemies?

Stalin instructed Chinese communists to disarm the workers, respect the United Front, and welcome Guomindang troops into the city. Instead, showing their militancy, Shanghai workers launched a general strike and armed insurrection to oust the warlords while waiting for the Guomindang army to reach Shanghai. Chiang, meanwhile, had made deals with wealthy industrialists who feared labor unrest, and leaders of the underworld, like the Green Gang, who specialized in strike-breaking. On April 12, 1927, he used these paramilitary thugs together with his new army to repress the communist unions, killing and arresting hundreds. The communist movement was broken in Shanghai, its principal stronghold. By the end of 1927 Chiang had suppressed communist uprisings in Canton and other major cities, driving the communists into the countryside and, so it seemed, into oblivion.

The China catastrophe crucially affected political developments in the Soviet Union, inflaming the dispute over Lenin's legacy. Trotsky led the leftist opposition that condemned such wholehearted alliances with the Nationalists. Generally it was acknowledged that Stalin's China policy had proved disastrous but it was Trotsky who lost the inner-party struggle. A powerful revolutionary movement had been crushed and there were no others in the field. Many Soviet communists now saw no alternative to a strategy of building socialism in one country. Although both sides drew on arcane citations from Marxist classics and abstruse theories of Chinese economic development, the real issue was the role of the USSR in a stabilizing world. Trotsky was a brilliant polemicist, but after the Chinese failure, few could see serious prospects of revolution anywhere. Also, through his control of the organizational department of the Party, Stalin had staffed the bureaucracy with cadres more interested in their careers than in world revolution. Stalin turned to strengthening the Soviet Union alone, which he interpreted as building up his own dictatorial power over the Party and promoting industrialization at breakneck speed. In 1929 Stalin expelled Trotsky from the USSR.

By the end of the 1920s, revolutionary socialism seemed to have run its course. Only the Soviet Union survived, and it was no worker's paradise. Mao Zedong and his small band of rural comrades seemed to have no future.

12.7 THE RISE OF FASCISM

Fascism was a product of World War I, born in Italy. Its creator was the bombastic former socialist journalist Benito Mussolini. Unlike the majority of his socialist comrades, Mussolini became a vociferous supporter of the war, promoting the virtues of manliness, discipline, violence, and submission to an absolute leader (Il Duce). The fascists' celebration of violent action gathered appeal in a chaotic Italian political environment, where all males voted for the first time in 1919. No one knew whether the old, elitist Italian liberal regime could survive the new era of mass politics. The Catholic "Popolari" Party, the predecessor of a later Christian Democracy, brought many Catholics who had boycotted the secular republic into the electoral system and this threatened existing interests. Workers went on strike in massive numbers and occupied factories, while socialists announced the imminent onset of revolution, rejecting all compromise with the liberals. In the midst of all this turmoil, Mussolini promised to restore order quickly and ruthlessly. He dramatically announced his March on Rome for October 1922.

The traditional politicians attempted to use the fascists to retain their political control. Mussolini gained success in the end not from force of arms or popular frenzy but from the complicity of the Italian king, Victor Emmanuel III. The king, fearing that suppressing a popular right-wing movement might remove a powerful tool against the socialist and communist left, persuaded Mussolini to accept the premiership. In the end Mussolini did not march into Rome but came in a sleeping car.

Because of the tacit support of the monarchy, many dismissed Mussolini as a mere figurehead for traditional conservative groups. They overlooked the most important feature of fascism, its modern character. Unlike traditional strongmen and military dictators, fascism was a popular movement that depended on mobilizing its supporters in the streets. This mobilization included assembling huge crowds to hear Mussolini speak, as well as the strong-armed squadrons that beat up socialists and communists in the streets of Rome and Turin and in the countryside. Mussolini introduced on a national level many of the basic fascist symbols: black shirts, the Roman salute, and assemblies filled with flags and uniformed men. Mussolini even shaped fascist dress. His muscled followers who attacked socialists and communists were called the "black shirts." Following this model, Hitler created his "brown shirts." Figure 12.1 shows a Nazi version of a fascist gathering. A rush on shirt colors ensued: Spanish fascists wore blue shirts, Romanians green shirts, and Americans silver shirts. Irish fascists were late in the game and had to be content with blue shirts. Actually Mussolini took many basic fascist symbols from the Symbolist poet Gabriele D'Annunzio who for four years ruled the city of Fiume on the Adriatic coast, proudly proclaiming its nationalist devotion.

Figure 12.1 Nazi rally at Nuremberg. German fascists drew on a common repertoire of right-wing tactics, designed to identify followers in public parades and to display publicly, in the street, their popular support. Fascists developed special salutes, wore distinctive uniforms, and adopted recognized insignia. Many Nazi tactics were first developed by the Italian fascists D'Annunzio and Mussolini.

Mussolini stole D'Annunzio's tactics and adopted them for a nationwide political movement.

Despite his mass appeal, Mussolini included the old elites in his new order. Most importantly, he settled the long-standing dispute with the Vatican, which had never accepted the Italian nation-state. He negotiated the **Lateran Pact** with the pope, establishing Vatican City as the pope's independent domain, and giving the pope large financial subsidies and concessions that included religious instruction in schools, in exchange for papal recognition of the Italian state. In gratitude, the papacy turned a blind eye to his repression and ultimate suppression of the Catholic Party formed to represent Catholic interests in the Italian democracy.

Mussolini, a brilliant political tactician, brought unprecedented numbers of people into political life. He seemed to have created a dynamic, new Italy, but what exactly were his principles? As a socialist, he claimed to support workers' rights, but he helped employers smash strikes and backed rural landowners who suppressed peasant movements. On the other hand, the fascist state was not simply a capitalist tool. Its grandiose projects of expansion, invoking imperial Rome, demanded resources from industrialists, shopkeepers, workers, and peasants alike. Many have classified fascism and communism together as "totalitarian" anti-liberal movements, but this categorization is not very useful. Fascism did not have the systematic ideology of Marxism; it was a chameleon-like movement that encompassed widely varying social and political programs under vague slogans of militarism and violence. Everywhere, however, fascism included street violence and the determination to prevent popular democratic protest in the streets. Fascism's' struggles to control the street made it too a modern movement.

12.8 ECONOMIC UNDERCURRENTS OF THE 1920S: OMINOUS SIGNS

In the 1920s, Mussolini's fascism seemed an anomaly, a curious exception to the swelling liberal democratic tide. After turbulent beginnings in 1918 and 1919, the mid-twenties were a new era of hope and opportunity, a restoration of "normalcy," the awkward term coined by US President Warren Harding (1921–23). But even this period showed signs of serious underlying economic problems. Three fundamental economic contradictions created the crisis that allowed fascism to become the dominant political movement of the 1930s:

- Dislocations and overproduction stimulated by the war.
- The unsettled issue of German reparations.
- The reluctance of the USA to take responsibility for a world economy that it dominated.

Wartime Overproduction Leads to Bust

The war seriously disorganized the European economic system. In many areas, it encouraged overcapacity, including huge investments in munitions plants and the coal and ore fields to supply them. With access to the continent seriously restricted, the British also greatly expanded ship production. To replace raw materials unavailable due to the British blockade, the German chemical industry spent huge sums to develop artificial substitutes for materials such as nitrate, petroleum, and rubber. The end of the war left a great surplus of metalworks, coal, and ships and a plethora of expensive synthetic chemical products. The Japanese, too, experienced wartime boom and bust, but for somewhat different reasons. They had profited greatly during the war from the absence of European competition. Exports boomed, fueling rapid inflation and causing rice riots in 1918. In 1920 the boom ended, the Japanese stock market crashed, and the Japanese economy never really revived for the rest of the decade.

Around the world, agriculture generally did not share in the great prosperity of the 1920s. Like the Japanese, farmers producing export crops suffered from overproduction. Between 1914 and 1918, with so many peasants enrolled in European armies and needing to be fed, farmers in the Americas and Australasia increased production, putting marginal lands into cultivation. After the war, European peasants returned to their farms, adding their output to that of American grain. The prices of grains decreased relative to the prices of industrial commodities. These declining terms of trade helped urban consumers but damaged farmers' incomes. Many American farmers had borrowed heavily to buy land and machinery, but falling prices forced them into bankruptcy. Big agribusinesses bought up failed farms, trying to turn them into factories in the fields. Hybrid corn, one of the first successes of biotechnological research, greatly boosted yields and the profits of seed companies. They succeeded too well, creating more grain surpluses than the USA or the world economy could absorb. While large companies profited, millions of farmers had to abandon their family lands for the cities.

Japanese agriculture also failed to prosper, even though its scale and technology changed little. Landlords lived well at the expense of masses of impoverished tenants, but tenants began to organize to demand better conditions. Thousands of rent disputes broke out every year. Chinese peasants did somewhat better, despite the depredations of warlords, landlords, and rapacious local governments. They, too, organized peasant unions to defend themselves. Seeing these peasant unions, Mao Zedong in 1927 extravagantly prophesied that the peasantry would rise "like a mighty storm, like a hurricane, a force so swift and violent that no power, however great, will be able to hold it back." He was wrong, for the time being.

The festering agricultural crisis undermined liberal ideals from both above and below. In the colonial world, surpluses of plantation commodities crippled colonial economies. Demand for raw materials such as copper and rubber had also grown during the war and decreased dramatically upon its end. As reserves of agricultural commodities accumulated, producers sought to establish international marketing agreements to restrict trade. US President Herbert Hoover (1929–33), however, vetoed a bill providing for the government to stabilize prices by buying surplus goods and selling them abroad. He would not abandon liberal principles to help poor farmers. These economic conditions created masses of discontented farmers around the world, who saw capitalists profiting while they suffered and the government did nothing. They were eager recruits for fascist pro-agrarian appeals.

Reparations Drag Down the World Economy

Who would pay for the war? Long after the war was over, this question reverberated throughout Europe and North America, roiling national politics and frightening investors. The big answer to the question was clear from the start: everyone. Politicians in the victorious nations long tried to avoid this basic truth. US voters were told that Britain and France must repay the debts that they had incurred, regardless of their postwar financial condition. British and French voters were told that a defeated Germany would pay for the war. In 1918, Sir Eric Geddes told a crowded assembly, "The Germans, if this Government is returned, are going to pay every penny; they are going to be squeezed as a lemon is squeezed until the pips squeak. My only doubt is not whether we can squeeze hard enough, but whether there is enough juice."

Sir Eric did not say where Germany, whose citizens died of starvation in the hundreds of thousands during the Armistice in 1918–19, would get the money to pay reparations. The Reparations Committee report of 1921 set an extremely high figure, calculated to keep Germany weak. The only way Germany could pay for the war was to earn money through exports on the world market, but large increases in German exports would threaten jobs in victor nations. Given the overproduction problems of the postwar period, no one wanted to give the enemy Germans a hand.

The seeming intractability of the reparations issue intensified the difficulties of German economic recovery, and these were magnified by the economic crisis provoked by the French occupation of the Ruhr. Together they produced an extreme inflation in 1923 that destroyed the German mark. As Germans ran to bread stores with wheelbarrows full of money, prices multiplied by the thousands, millions, and trillions. Germany had to default on its reparations, despite French and Belgian threats to collect them by force. For the short term, in 1924, US bankers and investors provided Germany with loans to pay the French and British, who then used this money to pay the debts that they had contracted to the USA, the USA refusing to forgo the 10 billion dollars owed to it by the Allies. This circulation of money did not restore a solid economic foundation in the long term, but it did allow Germany to create a new currency and restore its factories, and allow France to rebuild the eastern provinces of Alsace and Lorraine that the Germans had occupied and pillaged. This situation was further complicated by the French occupation of the Ruhr in 1923–25; the German government financed the opposition to the occupation by letting the presses run and creating massive inflation. The German inflation destroyed the savings of the middle class, making them good recruits for fascism.

The USA Will Not Save the World Economy

Clearly, by the mid-1920s the stability of the European economic order depended on the USA. Unfortunately, the USA depended on no one. This was the third great weakness of the 1920s economy. The overwhelming power of the US economy first emerged in the wake of World War I. In 1929 the USA produced over 42 percent of total world production, more than the total of the next five industrial nations combined. Although the USA was the premier exporter and importer, foreign trade made up a much smaller percentage of its national income than for any other industrialized nation. Except for strategic raw materials, the USA was virtually independent of world trade. The USA refused to acknowledge its great growth in industrial capacity during the war and the relatively small damages in economic and human resources that the USA had suffered relative to other combatants. Given its superiority in so many areas, it was surprising that American small businesses protected themselves against foreign competition by winning passage of the Fordney–McCumber Tariff in 1922. Habitually a debtor nation, the USA had now become the world's foremost creditor. Having lent money to its allies during the war, the USA expected to collect after the victory. This hard-line position showed no mercy to bankrupt farmers who lost their farms, or bankrupt European economies trying to recover from war.

The strong US economic position was based on an important expansion of the US consumer market in the 1920s. The dramatic growth of construction, automobile, and radio industries, financed by cheap loans, spread prosperity throughout the country. In 1928 Herbert Hoover campaigned on the slogan, "Two chickens in every pot, two cars in every garage." The reference to "Two cars in every garage" would have provoked laughter in any

Box 12.2 The Sounds of an Era

From the brothels and bars of New Orleans and Chicago came a new music that transformed world culture. Louis "Satchmo" Armstrong (1901–71), the brilliant African American trumpeter, electrified audiences with his brash, exciting sound; the composer and band leader Duke Ellington (1899–1974), clarinetist Benny Goodman, and singers like Billie Holiday developed the new musical style of jazz. In one early definition, "Jazz is rag-time, plus 'blues,' plus orchestral polyphony," or as a player put it, "Jazz is when you play what you feel." Jazz came from many traditional African American sources, like marches, spirituals, blues, and field hollers, but its improvisational style and syncopated rhythms marked a new urban culture. Most of the great jazz artists were African American, but the music was open to anyone. It attracted large crowds of all races in the great cosmopolitan cities of the world. Americans, Frenchmen, Germans, Japanese, Russians, and Chinese all flocked to dance halls and night clubs. We call the twenties the Jazz Age, meaning creativity, pleasure, nightlife, and smoldering sexuality. The USA expressed contradictions in Prohibition, speakeasies, bathtub gin, the Charleston, F. Scott Fitzgerald. Shanghai likewise.

Jazz spread even further because of new technologies: the record player (patented 1896], and especially, radio. Guglielmo Marconi invented radio in 1895, but the first commercial broadcasting station, KDKA, started in 1920 in Pittsburgh, Pennsylvania. Newspapers and pulp novels could only reach literate people, but with radio, writers, speechmakers, and performers could broadcast their voices instantaneously to millions. The telephone connected one person to another interactively; radio was one-way communication from a single person to millions of others. Radios sold rapidly in the new consumer culture. In 1939 there were 27 million sets in the US and 9 million sets in Britain. Politicians quickly exploited radio for their purposes. Hitler used it to broadcast his speeches and announce his demands. Roosevelt's "Fireside Chats" projected a warm, reassuring image to the traumatized victims of the Depression.

As the lively 1920s turned into the grimmer 1930s, music and technology served new ends. The jazz musicians continued their work, but they suffered economically like everyone else. Marching songs replaced dancing as the emblems of the decade. Bertolt Brecht wrote the United Front Song for the international brigades fighting in Spain:

And just because he's human
He'd like just a crust of bread to eat.
He wants no bosses over him, and no
slaves under his feet.
March right, march left, march right,
march left
To the work that you must do.
Join in the workers' United Front, for you
are a worker too.

But the Nazis had their own version. Storm troopers belted out the Horst Wessel Song, in honor of a student martyr:

Flag high, ranks closed,
The SA marches with silent solid steps,
Comrades shot by the red front and
reaction
March in spirit with us in our ranks.
The street free for the brown battalions,
The street free for the Storm Troopers,
Millions, full of hope, look up at the
swastika.
The day breaks for freedom and for bread.

Film, the other great mass communication technology, also created new forms of entertainment and politics. Films reshaped mass understanding of history, much more powerfully than books. D.W. Griffith's classic silent film, *The Birth of a Nation* (1915), told the story of the Civil War and Reconstruction in a brilliant montage from a Southern, pro-Ku Klux Klan perspective. Charlie Chaplin, from the left, hilariously satirized industrial labor in *Modern Times* (1936). Two great documentary films powerfully sum up the conflicts of the interwar period: Ernest Hemingway and Joris Ivens's *The Spanish Earth*, a gripping documentary of the Spanish Civil War, and Leni Riefenstahl's *Triumph of the Will*, a celebration of Nazi mass meetings, disturbing because it is so effective. Films, like radio, sent strong political messages to mass publics; they also provided escape from the miseries of the Depression, and documented the war, when it came.

other country of the world. In the USA this was still only a vision, but a credible one. To the astonishment of foreign visitors, some workers did own cars, financed on credit. Henry Ford's assembly line, the envy of socialists and capitalists alike, churned out Model T cars by the millions (see Figure 12.2). In 1924 a Model T cost only 294 dollars, half of its price in 1912. By 1929 there were 26.5 million registered cars in the USA. Cars demanded steel, paint, tires, oil, and roads, and travelers needed motels and fast food. All these industries of the 1920s created a distinctive American way of life, radically different from that of the rest of the world. Electric appliances saved labor and provided more leisure time; radios and films provided

Figure 12.2 The Ford Model T (1908–27) was the first automobile produced on an assembly line with completely interchangeable parts and so the first car affordable for many working-class Americans. The production methods introduced by Ford were widely adopted by many manufacturers.

entertainment and, most important, advertising to generate new consumer demands. Consumer spending rose, fueling industrial production, which created more jobs, which created more income for further spending. Those with extra income could get rich quick by investing in the booming stock market. The only flaw was that it was built on the assumption that American growth would continue indefinitely into the future and that European markets would return to prewar conditions. When would the bubble burst?

12.9 THE GREAT DEPRESSION

The **Great Depression**, the greatest crisis in the history of capitalism, marks the turning point from the optimism of the mid-twenties to the despair of the thirties. The crisis began with the stock market crash: On Black Tuesday, October 29, 1929, the stock market lost almost as much as the cost of US participation in World War I. The crash, however, only accelerated an economic decline that had already begun; it alone could not have caused such a long depression.

The precarious basis for US prosperity was indeed part of the problem. Consumer spending had shot upward while farm incomes declined and the average US worker's income only increased slowly. The stock market crash toppled an already dangerously expanded accumulation of debt. Still, panics had happened before, and recovery had come quickly. No one expected that the US economy would not recover its 1929 level

for ten years, that unemployment would reach over 12 million people, or that GDP would drop by 50 percent. Such a huge collapse was unprecedented.

US depression brought on European crises. As the US economy plunged, unforgiving American bankers began to call in their loans to Austrian and German banks. In May of 1931 the great Austrian bank, the Creditanstalt, hovered near bankruptcy. Believing their own economy invulnerable, French bankers refused to provide loans to save the bank. When the Creditanstalt collapsed, the crisis spread to Germany, forcing German financiers to abandon the gold standard and freeze foreign accounts. With Austria and Germany abandoning the gold standard, speculators turned to Britain, the world center of gold transactions. Such a precipitous demand for gold exhausted British reserves, forcing the British to abandon the gold standard in September 1931. Britain's decision shocked orthodox economists around the world. Within the next year a host of nations followed Britain in abandoning the gold standard. Unfortunate Japan had pursued a tight fiscal policy throughout the 1920s in order to get back to the gold standard at the prewar rate. Japanese financiers triumphantly returned to gold in January 1930. Global deflation then devastated Japanese exports. When Japan left gold the next year, the value of the yen dropped by half.

Still, the Depression did not affect all nations equally. Unemployment, already high in the UK during the 1920s, merely intensified in the 1930s. France remained above the crisis until 1932. Neither the UK nor France, however, suffered the catastrophic mass unemployment that hit the USA and Germany in the early thirties. When Franklin Delano Roosevelt declared in his 1932 inaugural address, "I see one third of a nation ill-housed, ill-clothed, ill fed," he was probably close to actual estimates. Newspaper stories about the slaughter of young pigs and the burning of corn crops underscored the irony of an economy in which increasing agricultural production led to hunger. The even higher German unemployment rates had greater impact because the post-World War I inflation had already exhausted the resources of many German families. First hyperinflation, then depression: a perfect recipe for destroying a liberal state.

With the traditional system for regulating international commerce in ruins, nations turned toward protectionism. Even the UK, the great historical champion of free trade, adopted protectionist measures in 1932 for itself and most of its empire. Against the advice of almost every American economist, the Smoot–Hawley Tariff of 1930 raised US tariffs even higher than the Fordney–McCumber. In 1933 the new US president, Franklin Roosevelt, greeted a World Economic Conference assembled to prevent such tariff wars with the devastating news that he was raising US tariffs still higher.

The Depression quickly spread outside Europe, inflicting further hardship on agricultural economies which had only struggled through the 1920s. As US consumers deferred purchases of automobiles and radios, the world market for rubber and tin also collapsed. Large quantities of rubber and sugar appeared on markets in which demand was already declining. The result was utter catastrophe for plantation commodities, hurting sugar growers in the Caribbean and the Dutch East Indies, coffee growers in Africa, rubber workers in Malaya and Vietnam, jute growers in Bengal, and silk weavers in China.

12.10 THE COLLAPSE OF LIBERAL DEMOCRACY; SOCIALIST AND FASCIST ALTERNATIVES

Faced with severe economic collapse, liberal democracy crumbled. Within a few years, dictatorships established themselves throughout the new nations of Central and Southern Europe. In Yugoslavia conflicts between Croats and Serbs and the ongoing agrarian crisis led King Alexander to declare himself dictator. After 1934 in Bulgaria, military men and Tsar Boris dominated government. In 1936 in Greece, General Metaxas carried out a *coup d'état*. In Eastern and Central Europe only Czechoslovakia retained a flourishing democracy. In 1936 General Francisco Franco attempted to overthrow a recently elected democratic government, touching off the Spanish Civil War.

In Latin America, dictators returned as the prices of basic commodities and raw materials fell. In Brazil, the fall of coffee prices supported the Vargas dictatorship. In Argentina, collapsing prices in beef, corn, hides, wheat, and wool helped restore the old conservative oligarchy to power. In 1932, military coups shook Chile, although elections returned by the end of the year.

Liberal democracy was an early casualty of the Great Depression in Japan. The debacle of the gold standard allowed clever Japanese bankers, aided by politicians, to double their money by selling yen for dollars before the devaluation and buying them back a year later. The rest of the public despised these corrupt financial cliques, or *zaibatsu*, who profited from others' misery. They found the military much more honorable. Fanatical nationalists, with a strong base in the armed services, also castigated liberals for signing the international arms control treaties that undermined Japan's security. The intense agrarian depression led many Japanese in the countryside to feel that the islands were poor because they were overpopulated: They left to settle Manchuria (see Figure 12.3). In the new protectionist world, Japan, scarce in natural resources, had to ensure its own supplies. If it could not get raw materials by trade, it needed to carve out its own territorial sphere on the continent. These pressures accelerated Japan's advance into China.

More imaginative approaches to dealing with economic crises emerged in the USA and Sweden; in both countries pragmatic social reformers amended time-honored principles to save liberal democracy from revolution. In the USA the election of Franklin Delano Roosevelt (1933–45) created a new attitude toward governmental intervention. The main message of Roosevelt's first inaugural address contrasted strongly with the message of his predecessor Herbert Hoover (1929–33). Hoover, a cautious engineer, tried to devise responses to the Depression, but basically believed that government could do no more to solve an economic crisis than it could exorcise a "Caribbean hurricane by statutory law." Roosevelt was convinced that government must play a larger role, but he had no particularly clear idea of what to do. He pledged a "New Deal" for the American people without specifying exactly what it meant. During its "First Hundred Days," the Roosevelt administration initiated a whirlwind of unprecedented policy initiatives. They included everything from reforms of the banking system, limiting speculation and insuring depositors, to the repeal of Prohibition, incentives for farmers to cut back production so as to raise prices, the great electrification project of the Tennessee Valley Authority, aid to the unemployed, protection for workers, and great public works projects. Yet Roosevelt in principle believed in a balanced budget and did not sympathize with labor unions. When the US economy began to improve as a result of his spending, Roosevelt moved to restore a balanced budget in 1937, sending the economy back into recession in 1938. His New Deal did not end the Depression, but it did radically

Figure 12.3 Japanese advance in Manchuria, 1931. The Japanese military took the initiative in starting the war in Manchuria and, when the invasion proved successful, the government was entirely helpless.

change the response of the federal government to major crises. People expected action, not laissez-faire.

In Sweden, a coalition of the Social Democrats and the Farmers' Party came to power in 1933. Like Roosevelt, but unlike British Labour or French socialists, Swedish socialists were willing to go into debt to provide work for the unemployed. Co-operatives spread throughout the country, mitigating some of the Depression's worst effects on farmers. A dramatic expansion of social services, including free prenatal care and social insurance, helped to preserve Swedes from the worst effects of economic crisis.

12.11 SOCIAL EFFECTS OF DEPRESSION

For socialists and communists, the Great Depression vindicated Marx's economic prophecies, yet the Depression paralyzed the left nearly as much as the liberal democrats. Rising unemployment, it turned out, did not automatically make workers more militant; it often made them more passive as they could no longer afford their union dues or socialist newspapers. Apathetic workers tolerated the conservative rule of Baldwin and Chamberlain in the UK and Daladier in France. In Weimar Germany, on the other hand, radical groups on the right and the left engaged in street battles over control of working-class organizations. These violent divisions undermined efforts to unite workers against conservative governments. The New Deal reforms in the USA, by contrast, galvanized mass organizing by labor unions to put pressure on Roosevelt to enact further progressive policies. The victory of the French Popular Front in 1936 produced a great general strike, although after a period of important reforms the Popular Front soon lost its steam.

The Depression not only marginalized unions and socialist parties, but also individual workers. The crisis swelled the numbers of hoboes, beggars, and tramps – males, young and old, who survived through charity, casual labor, and petty crime. No wonder that the image of disheveled unkempt men traveling the roads and roaming the cities came to symbolize the Depression (see Box 12.3). The Depression hit working males especially hard, creating the highest unemployment in such typical male bastions as construction, metalworking, steel, coal mining, and shipbuilding. In Europe's great industrial regions, employers had frequently given these men the steadier, higher-paying jobs as part of a "family household economy" in which adult male household heads were given the more stable jobs.

Box 12.3 Hoboes, Migrants, Refugees, and Armies: People on the Move

A well-known US Depression song runs thus:

Once I built a railroad, made it run,
Made it race against time.
Once I built a railroad, now it's done.
Buddy, can you spare a dime?
Once I built a tower to the sun,
Brick and rivet and lime.
Once I built a tower, now it's done.
Buddy, can you spare a dime?
Once in khaki suits – gee, we looked swell!
Full of that Yankeedoodleedum!
Half a million boots went slogging
through Hell,
And I was the kid with the drum!
Say, don't you remember, you called me
Al?
It was Al all the time.
Say, don't you remember? I'm your pal!
Buddy, can you spare a dime?

The nineteenth-century global industrial order stimulated huge waves of migration. By the millions, people left their villages to find work in the great cities, crossing oceans by steamship and continents by railway: 50 million Europeans left the continent for the Americas, 30 million Indians and Chinese went to Southeast Asia and the USA, and 20 million Chinese went to Manchuria, Korea, and Japan. Many, like the Jews of Russia and Eastern Europe, fled pogroms and oppression, but many others simply looked for a better life. The empires recruited contract laborers to grow plantation crops in the tropics to feed growing demands for coffee, sugar, and cotton.

The crises of the twentieth century restricted some of this labor migration, but put new kinds of people on the move, against their will. US immigration quotas cut back immigration from over a million per year to less than 200,000 by 1924. The Depression completely cut off the inflow, and even drove many migrants back home. Canada, however, took up some of the slack, tripling its immigration rate. Within the USA, now the laborers came from within the country, especially from African Americans moving out of the segregated South. Asians, however, continued to flood into Southeast and Northeast Asia at even higher rates.

Within Europe, over 5 million people moved because they had to, not because they wanted to. Soldiers marched to the battlefronts because they had to follow orders. Military forces ejected civilians from their homes, by destroying them through bombing, or by deporting them under enemy occupation. The end of World War I brought large-scale "cleansing" of ethnically mixed regions, like the "exchanges" of Greek and Turkish populations between Turkey and Greece and the expulsion of Polish miners from the Ruhr to France. When World War II began, entire governments moved long distances, like the Russians who retreated from German attack beyond the Volga River, and the Chinese Nationalists and Communists, who carried their industries and universities into the interior to escape the Japanese.

Even in the USA, which escaped the direct impact of war, Depression and war heightened mobility. Men without jobs turned to begging in the streets or riding the rails; the Dust Bowl drought forced families to head west by the thousands. In John Steinbeck's classic novel *The Grapes of Wrath*, published in 1939, the Joad family lament their humiliation when debt forces them to abandon their farm for the roads, and express their feeling of comfort when they join fellow migrants in a relief camp:

"We're Joads. We don't look up to nobody. Grampa's grampa, he fit in the Revolution. We was farm people till the debt. And then – them people. They done somepin to us. Ever' time they come seemed like they was a-whippin' me – all of us. An' in Needles, that police. He done somepin to me, made me feel mean. Made me feel ashamed. An' now I ain't ashamed. These folks is our folks – is our folks. An' that manager, he come an' set an' drank coffee, an' he says, 'Mrs. Joad' this, an' 'Mrs. Joad' that – an' 'How you gettin' on, Mrs. Joad?'" She stopped and sighed. "Why, I feel like people again."

The tramp, the homeless woman, and the urban beggar replaced the images of ambitious immigrants arriving at Ellis Island to start a new life.

The fateful decision to leave one's home and family could bring the adventurous migrants a better life; it could also mean starvation and death. Like the other trends of this period, migration forced people to extremes.

In the USA, nature added to economic misery by inflicting severe drought in the western plains from 1930–36. Farmers themselves had made it worse by clearing marginal lands during the boom years without regard for irrigation. "Rain follows the plow," they said, but nature did not listen. This "Dust Bowl" disaster uprooted hundreds of thousands of families, who flocked to California as migrant laborers, more victims of economic and environmental mismanagement.

The Depression's full impact on women is harder to measure. European fertility declined during the economic crisis. European women labored disproportionately in the temporary and part-time occupations, such as domestic service, whose unemployment escaped the official records. Those with white-collar jobs generally kept them. Still, when they did lose their jobs, women workers almost always received lower benefits than males. When their husbands were out of work, they had to work harder at home to economize on expenses. The Depression undermined the gains in personal rights which they had made during the 1920s. European right-wing politicians and some left-wing politicians sought to ban married women from work on the theory that the husband was the natural provider. Such efforts succeeded in the civil services, particularly threatening women schoolteachers, who frequently had to conceal their marital status.

Communist movements basked in the reflected glory of the USSR, whose continued economic advance in these desperate times inspired many in the West. Even in the USA, the Communist Party gained support. Yet the USSR mirrored the triumph of national interest over internationalist principles represented by the growth of protectionism in the capitalist world, except that for it, internationalism meant not free trade but world revolution. The triumph of Stalin and his slogan of "Socialism in One Country" in 1927 at the Fifteenth Communist Party Congress represented the victory of Russian nationalism. Now the economic and political interests of the USSR explicitly came before the promotion of world revolution. In Stalin's view, building socialism in a backward country like Russia could only be done by force. He would tolerate no dissent, neither outside the party nor within it. In mass purges of the 1930s, he executed hundreds of thousands of Soviet citizens, including almost all of the Bolshevik companions of Lenin, as "Trotsko-Bukharinite agents of Fascism." Box 12.4 gives a taste of the extraordinary rhetoric of the Moscow Trials. It was patently false but many in the West supported Stalin not because they believed it but because in a Europe of advancing fascism they needed to have hope.

Nonetheless, the first Five Year Plan, proclaimed in 1928, marked out for the USSR a very different path from that followed by Western nations. Going far beyond Roosevelt, Stalin announced comprehensive, systematic planning of industrial production under autocratic governmental control. Factory managers had to meet quotas decided by the state, or else they were shot; workers who worked overtime to fill production quotas got medals, but little pay. The Five Year Plan achieved an enormous economic expansion; much of it occurred east of the Urals, in regions of Russia that were not exposed to foreign invasion. Peter the Great, who started the Russian iron industry in the Urals, would have been proud to see the massive new steel city of Magnitogorsk, in the empty Kazakh steppe, built into a huge industrial establishment. The human toll of Soviet industrialization was high, and the frenzied efforts to fulfill impossible quotas resulted in enormous waste, but efficiency was not Stalin's goal. He wanted a powerful state based on large-scale heavy industry, the core of a modern economy, at whatever cost in human life.

Despite real industrial progress, the Soviets were weak in the countryside, where three quarters of the population lived. The Bolsheviks had taken power as a workers' party in alliance with the peasant party. Lenin had approved this proletarian–peasant alliance, but he, like all Marxists, distrusted peasants. They were too attached to their own family farms to understand the collective consciousness of the working class, and agriculture was a backward form of production. Yet all the Bolsheviks knew that the peasants provided the only possible resources for industrialization. During the NEP, the kulaks had prospered from selling crops in the flourishing free markets. Bukharin thought that by taxing the kulaks and preserving markets, the Soviet Union could gradually accumulate the capital needed for industrial investment, but Stalin saw the kulaks as enemies of the Soviet state. He insisted on confiscating the kulaks' property and turning all the land into collective property. The Soviet collectivization campaign, a coercive imposition on the peasantry, met strong resistance. Not only rich kulaks, but many ordinary farmers killed their cattle, dumped their milk, and hid their grain stores rather than give them to the alien state. Stalin responded by deporting or starving to death about a million kulak families. By 1937, the state owned all of the land, but agricultural production had plummeted. A great famine struck the Ukraine in 1932–33. Stalin succeeded by brute force in suppressing peasant resistance to the regime and gaining control of the agricultural surplus, at the price of dealing a blow to Soviet agriculture from which it never recovered (see Figure 12.4).

12.12 NAZISM

Meanwhile, the victory of fascism in Germany utterly transformed world politics. Germany, the greatest industrial power in Europe, with the most powerful military tradition,

Box 12.4 The Moscow Trials

In 1934 the mysterious assassination of Sergey Kirov, Leningrad Communist Party head and Stalin ally, began a series of show trials that culminated in the three great purge trials of 1936–38 known as the "Moscow Trials." The Moscow Trials did not mark the triumph of Stalin – he had already defeated all his enemies and firmly grasped the reins of power. It did mark the "liquidation" (a polite Stalinist term for execution) and imprisonment of the greater part of the revolutionaries who had led the Russian Revolution and built the Red Army. At these trials, Lenin's closest friends and collaborators confessed to being spies, engaging in terrorist acts, and deliberately wrecking socialist efforts. While the charges were preposterous and disapproved by a committee chaired by the American philosopher John Dewey, many observers wanted to know why tough, hardened revolutionaries confessed. Much sophisticated theorizing went into analyzing their motives. Current research suggests the confessions were produced by sustained torture and threats to family members as well as

promises that lives would be spared. Stalinist prisons were much more severe than those of the tsars and the confessions reveal the ability of modern states not only to kill but to dehumanize and degrade those whom they regard as enemies. Revolutionaries who did not succumb to torture and confess were simply shot. While prominent Soviet leaders appeared at the trials, many hundreds of thousands of people, many of them communists, were also executed as counter-revolutionaries, and several million were sent to prison camps where they were destined to die.

The excerpted confession that follows is that of V.F. Shangovich (1897–1938). He joined the party in the early days of the revolution and spent time in a Polish prisoner-of-war camp after being captured during the Russo-Polish War. He was First Secretary of the Belorusian Communist Party at the time of his arrest.

Citizens, Judges, I do not intend to say anything in my defence. I have committed loathsome, vile and heinous crimes against the country and the people, and

I perfectly realize that I must fully answer for them before the proletarian Court. I have betrayed my country, and as a traitor, I deserve no mercy.

For a long period, ever since 1921, I was a Polish spy and carried on espionage activities on behalf of the Polish intelligence service ... Guided by the direct instructions of the "bloc of Rights and Trotskyites" and of Rykov and Bukharin personally, on the one hand, and by the orders of the Polish General Staff, on the other ... I undermined agriculture, destroyed horses, deprived collective farmers of household land, muddled the planning of crop areas and endeavoured, from provocateur motives, to incense the collective farmers against the Soviet government ...

I am fully responsible for the creation of a terrorist group. Against the leadership of the Party and the government.

I do not want in my last plea to dwell on all my vile and treacherous activities and the treacherous activities of my accomplices who are sitting here in this dock.

I do not plead for clemency, Citizens Judges, because I am not fit to plead for it.

came under the absolute control of the genius and madman Adolf Hitler. His personality made German National Socialism, or Nazism, unlike any other form of fascism. Hitler, like other fascists, had an impressive ability to appeal to many audiences. Dressed in his conservative blue business suit, Hitler could persuade Germany's industrialists that he had their interests at heart. Dressed in his paramilitary uniform, he could convince the most militant of the rank-and-file street fighters that he was one of them. As a war veteran, he spoke with conviction about military strategy, though he knew little about it. Hitler managed to harness a conservative German military and political establishment to extraordinarily reckless purposes, destroying Germany in the process.

Hitler's anti-Semitism, however, gave Nazi ideology a visceral hostility to Jews not found in the Italian fascist movement. Amalgamating crank beliefs common to the early twentieth-

century right, Hitler found support in the anti-Semitic writings of the American industrialist Henry Ford, the English imperialist Houston Stewart Chamberlain, and the French theorist of racial types, Joseph de Gobineau. In the paranoid view of Hitler and his supporters, all the critical problems of twentieth-century capitalism – poverty, economic instability, socialist movements – were explained by a single sinister figure, the Jew. Only eliminating the Jews from Europe – first by deportation, later by extermination – could bring justice to the world.

The real question, though, is not Hitler's personality but how such a madman became head of the most powerful European state? Once again, World War I and the Great Depression provide the basic answer. Without a lost war and a depression, Hitler would not have come to power. His first effort at leading a revolt, the Munich "Beer Hall Putsch" of 1923, quickly fizzled, and the elections of 1924 and 1928 seemed to demonstrate that

Figure 12.4 Russian agricultural workers in the 1930s. The introduction of collectivization in Soviet agriculture was a great disaster. Many Russian agriculturalists possessed some claims to land and regarded collectivization as a state seizure of their property. They responded by killing their livestock and failing to plant new crops. Mass starvation was sometimes the result.

the Nazis were losing all influence. Until the end of the 1920s, the Nazis seemed to be only a crude, loud fringe group.

Yet right-wing extremists found fertile soil in Weimar Germany's turbulent society. As the economy had ominous undercurrents, so did German politics. General commitment to the democratic ideals of Weimar was quite weak. Weimar's tolerant atmosphere allowed many political movements to grow: too many to allow a stable government to last for long. Voters and politicians careened from election to election, making and unmaking coalitions every few years in response to unending crises: reparations, military occupation, inflation, strikes, socialist demonstrations, right-wing counter-demonstrations, etc. Frightened of left-wing revolution, the German establishment longed for the undemocratic "golden era" of the Kaiser. Judges and police officials treated right-wing lawbreakers far more leniently than left-wingers. Even centrist politicians refused to accept sincerely the Versailles Treaty as a framework for negotiation. Many still clung to the myth that the German army had not been defeated in the field but had been "stabbed in the back" by treacherous socialists. German businessmen repelled by Hitler's crude anti-Semitism still worked closely with the Nazis. Conservative politicians had contempt for Hitler but thought they could use the Nazis to achieve their political goals and discard them when they no longer needed them. They underestimated Hitler's abilities and ignored the risks.

And yet, the political left also shares responsibility for Hitler's success. The moderate Social Democratic Party, closer in political beliefs to liberal democracy than to communism, concentrated on rallying workers, making little effort to appeal to the Protestant small farmers and small businessmen affected by the Great Depression. These people felt that they lacked a spokesman in German politics. The Nazi poster in Figure 12.5 captures the feelings of many middle-class and even working-class Germans: They had nowhere else to go. They were among the first to rally to the Nazis. The moderate leaders of the Catholic Center Party, challenged internally by right-wingers and by the secessionist Bavarian Peoples' Party, minimized their commitment to democracy and retreated to a narrow concern for Catholic interests.

German communists too share the blame. Between 1928 and 1933 the Soviet Communist Party turned against the NEP and began policies of mass collectivization and rapid industrialization. The forced speed with which these measures were carried out led to much waste in industry but absolute disaster in agriculture; when the government attempted to seize the kulaks' possessions, many responded by killing their animals or destroying their property. Russian agriculture has never recovered from this destruction.

The Soviet government responded with terror and political hysteria, considering anyone who hesitated as an enemy. The extremism of Soviet internal politics soon translated into Soviet foreign policy. Following Stalin's theory of **social fascism**, the communists proclaimed that German socialists were just as dangerous to German workers as the fascists, indeed more

Figure 12.5 Our last Hope, Hitler. This poster captures the desperation of many Germans that led them to vote for the Nazis.

dangerous. Moderate socialists and liberal democrats with all their compromising and negotiating confused the workers. Deprived of the obfuscations of moderate socialists, a fascist victory would allow the communists the opportunity to confront the fascists directly and accelerate the onset of communist revolution. This was a fateful delusion. In the 1925 election, communists insisted on running their own candidate instead of rallying round the Center Party candidate supported by all other republican parties, including the Social Democrats. The result was a runoff which brought the conservative militarist, Paul von Hindenburg, to the German presidency.

The commitment of ordinarily sober German businessmen to far-right parties, the ineffective politics of the centrist parties, and communist intransigence polarized German society. Violent attacks by Nazis on socialists and communists, taking Mussolini's tactics to a new extreme, stimulated violent responses by workers' groups, but this degeneration of political debate into street fighting undercut Weimar's liberal democratic principles.

The elections between 1930 and 1932 show increasing polarization between extreme right and extreme left with all the centrist parties losing. Politics was also polarized as both communists and fascists increased their percentage of the electorate (see Figure 12.6). Hitler could never gain a majority, but he could convince conservative elites that he was the only one capable of stopping socialism. In November 1932, Hitler and the National Socialists did not win a majority, but advisors around President Hindenburg urged the old man to appoint Hitler as chancellor under the belief that they could use Hitler for their own purposes.

Becoming chancellor in January 1933, Hitler quickly outmaneuvered Hindenburg's advisors. Calling immediately for new elections, Hitler skillfully used an effort to burn down the German parliament, the Reichstag, to rally the right and to win a narrow absolute majority for the National Socialists and their allies. With an effective majority, Hitler excluded the elected communists from the Reichstag and, opposed only by the Social Democrats, passed an enabling law that made him dictator. In 1934 upon Hindenburg's death, Hitler made himself both chancellor and president.

Once possessed of dictatorial power, Hitler adopted his own distinctive approach to curing depression. Hitler impressed Germans and the world in his early years with his domestic successes. His government put people to work, but in contrast to Roosevelt and the Swedish Social Democrats, most of his spending focused on rearmament. In contrast to Stalin's Five Year Plan, National Socialist expenditures did not create new factories or increase overall productive capacity so much as they restored Germany's productive capacity and diverted it to armament. But this spending drive meant heavy debts. In 1937, the banker Hjalmar Schacht, the architect of German economic policy, resigned, warning that Germany could not afford to incur further debts. Hitler, however, knew who would pay Germany's debts: the peoples that he conquered. That meant challenging the collective security system designed to contain Germany in its current borders.

12.13 TOWARD THE SECOND WORLD WAR

In those powerful states where liberal democracy still survived, such as France, the UK, and the USA, political leaders seemed incapable of taking a stand to defend threatened states and the principles of collective security enshrined in the League of Nations. Liberal democracies, militarily dominant in 1918, were on the defensive in the 1930s. How did this happen? First and foremost, the searing experience of World War I had made

Figure 12.6 Elections to the Reichstag: percentage of vote for major parties, 1924–33.

	1924	1924	1928	1930	1932	1932	1933
	May 4	Dec. 7			July 31	Nov. 6	
Social Democrats	20.5	26.0	29.8	24.5	21.6	20.4	18.3
Communists	12.6	9.0	10.6	13.1	14.6	16.9	12.3
Center Party	13.4	13.6	12.1	11.8	12.5	11.9	11.7
Democrats	5.7	6..3	4.9	3.8	1.0	1.0	.8
People's Party	9.2	10.1	8.7	4.5	1.2	1.9	1.1
Nationalists	19.5	20.5	14.2	7.0	5.9	8.8	8.0
National Socialists	6.5	3.0	2.6	18.3	37.4	33.1	43.9

democracies extremely reluctant to go to war. The spirit of appeasement grew out of the trenches. Eventually, the dramatic and public failure of appeasement rallied democratic populations to the war effort. Still, save for the appeasers there might have been no war or at least a very short one, with German fascism quickly destroyed. Appeasers negotiated, delayed, and made concessions: anything to avoid war.

Temporizing with the Japanese wounded the authority of the League; temporizing with the Italians killed it. In 1931 Japan sought to annex a resource-rich Manchuria that could absorb colonists and reliably supply raw materials. The UK was utterly unprepared to deal with Japan, and the USA refused to do more than deny official recognition to Japan's conquests. It continued to ship vital raw materials to Japan, and it did not build up its Pacific fleet. In October 1935 Italy invaded Ethiopia. Italy's brutal invasion of Ethiopia, its use of poison gas, and the heroic resistance of the Ethiopian army helped mobilize opinion in democratic nations against Italian fascism. But despite an initially strong British condemnation and call for League sanctions, Italian invasion posed difficult political problems, for both British and French politicians hoped to use Mussolini to restrain Hitler. The relentless pursuit of Mussolini illustrated the Anglo-French hope that war could be avoided through diplomacy or, if it could not be avoided, fought cheaply without bringing the USSR into the field. As a result, the UK followed a contradictory policy of sanctions which denied the Italians everything but the oil shipments that Mussolini most desperately needed. Just as with Japan, such a policy antagonized the dictator without stopping him.

After Hitler's assumption of power in 1933, liberal democratic attention focused on Germany, the major threat to world order. Hitler's experiences in World War I and his years of involvement in street politics had taught him how to combine military and political power to exploit the weaknesses of democratic decision-making. Hitler's rearmament focused not on large, slow armies, but on modern weapons, like tanks and planes, that allowed for quick displays of power. Initially, Hitler complained about plausible grievances, like German humiliation by Versailles and the mistreatment of German minorities in Eastern Europe. Those who had come to recognize flaws in the Versailles settlement granted that he had a case. Hitler chose his targets in advance and notified the world of his actions suddenly in radio talks. Confronted with the need for quick responses and aware that large-scale war might result, Western politicians hesitated. Once his acts had been allowed to stand, Hitler then followed up with promises of future moderation. Faced with his effective combination of propaganda and lightning fast military mobilization, liberal democrats made concessions to German fascists. They had refused to make similar concessions to German democrats because Germany had not mobilized such military force before.

Taking advantage of liberal democratic weaknesses, Hitler's political and military strategy achieved extraordinary successes, changing the map of Europe by intimidation and threats. By renouncing the Treaty of Versailles in 1935 and remilitarizing the Rhineland in 1936, he first moved toward restoring German sovereignty within its 1919 borders. Next, through the annexation of Austria in March 1938 and the Sudetenland in September 1938, he incorporated German minorities left outside Germany's borders by the Treaty of Versailles. Confused liberals could only stand by and watch as German majorities in Austria and the Sudetenland enthusiastically greeted the troops. Hitler effectively attacked British, French, and US hypocrisy in promoting the "self-determination of nations" while denying all Germans their right to live under a single Reich. His Third Reich promised to surpass the glory first attained by Charlemagne, then by Bismarck's Second Empire.

Hitler reached his diplomatic high point at the Munich Conference of September 1938, when through a combination of threats and promises he persuaded Britain and France to abandon their pledges to defend Czechoslovakia. Germany was allowed to annex a portion of Czechoslovakia, the Sudetenland, in exchange for Hitler's pledge that this was "his last territorial claim in Europe." Neville Chamberlain, the British prime minister who negotiated the Munich settlement, announced that he had obtained "peace in our time" (see Figure 12.7). Great crowds enthusiastically greeted French and British statesmen returning from Munich, although the French prime minister, Édouard Daladier, already realized the shameful nature of the Munich Agreement. Liberal democratic illusions were quickly shattered. While many Europeans thought that the restoration of its sovereignty to Germany and the incorporation of German minorities into a new German state were legitimate goals, no one accepted Hitler's annexation of the Czech rump state in March 1939 (see Map 12.2). This territory was composed almost entirely of Slavs and had never been part of pre-1919 Germany. Hitler now revealed his real aims, which had never been a secret: He regarded Slavs as inferior people who deserved only to be enslaved and occupied by Germans, who needed **Lebensraum** (living space) to make themselves into the master race. The Poles were next.

Map 12.2 Central Europe, 1939

Figure 12.7 The German dictator, Adolf Hitler, greeted by British prime minister Neville Chamberlain in Munich, 1938. The agreement forged at this conference was intended in Chamberlain's words to "bring peace in our time." The disillusion would be swift and cruel.

Finally the British and French realized that war was inevitable. Hitler's occupation of Czechoslovakia created a pro-war majority committed to standing by Poland. When Hitler invaded Poland in 1939, he was genuinely surprised that the UK and France declared war, given their previous betrayal of Czechoslovakia and the Treaty of Versailles. Moreover, the German army had become much stronger after the year's delay, so those who feared war had reason to be even more apprehensive. Logically speaking, an early stand against Hitler would have prevented the destructive war, but it took time to create a consensus. Britain came around first; France was more divided but a majority opted for war; the USA still embraced isolationism.

12.14 THE ALLIES: UNPREPARED FOR THE DEMANDS OF WAR

As politicians discovered the insatiability of Hitler's demands, they also discovered their lack of preparedness for war. In the

1920s, politicians in Britain and France had slashed military spending. In part, of course, this was a natural reaction to the bloated war budgets of 1914–18, the commitments made to restore damaged areas of France, and the promise to make Britain "a land fit for heroes." It is easier to understand the reluctance to arm in the 1920s than in the 1930s. Why were the democracies so slow to respond to the clear threat of fascist aggression? The following factors held them back:

- A typical liberal commitment to balanced budgets, holding down military spending.
- A reluctance to abandon the international arms limitation treaties of the collective security era.
- Shock at the very high cost of new military technologies, especially air power.
- Competitive protectionism, which prevented economic alliances and led countries to make individual deals with the fascist nations.
- Lingering anti-communism, excluding the Soviet Union from the anti-fascist alliance.
- US disengagement from responsibility for Asian or European security.

In short, the weaknesses of the liberal regimes apparent in the 1920s limited their response to military mobilization by Japan and Germany.

British and French commitment to balanced budgets hindered spending for rearmament. The British navy, once the pride of the empire, had gravely declined. At the Washington Naval Conference of 1921–22, Britain for the first time in centuries accepted the idea of naval parity with another power, the United States. It also accepted ratios with Italy and Japan. Naval limitation forced many skilled workers to leave the industry. Their absence seriously constrained British ability to build ships quickly. The relationships established in Washington among the great naval powers made it difficult for Britain to confront the Japanese navy while retaining any credible threat in its home territory in the North Atlantic. The futile symbolic action of the USA against Japanese aggression in China made the British particularly reluctant to support the imposition of sanctions by the League of Nations when Britain, the main sea power, would have to enforce them. (See Map 12.3.)

Britain's concern to preserve the dominance of its much weakened navy in the North Atlantic also damaged its efforts to stand against Hitler. For example, in March of 1935, in response to Hitler's announcement of the formation of a German air force, a military formation forbidden by the Treaty of Versailles, Britain, France, and Italy formed the Stresa Front. Unfortunately the Front was broken by British efforts to protect its naval position. In May 1935, when Hitler offered to guarantee

Map 12.3 Japanese territorial gains: East Asia on the eve of World War II

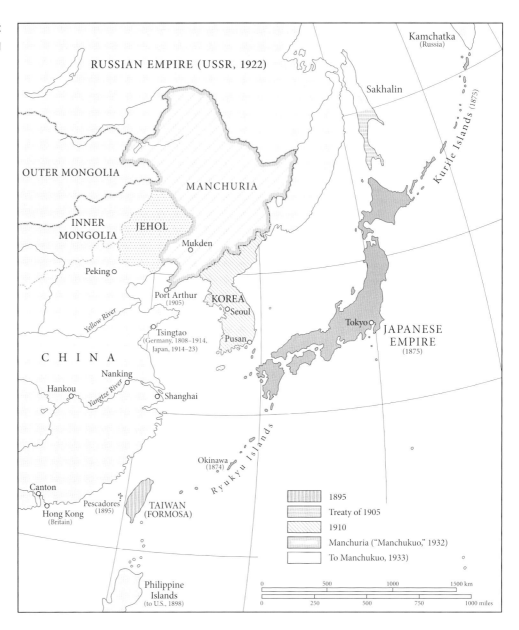

RUSSIAN EMPIRE (USSR, 1922)

Kamchatka
(Russia)

Sakhalin

Kurile Islands (1875)

OUTER MONGOLIA

MANCHURIA

INNER
MONGOLIA

JEHOL

Mukden

Peking

Port Arthur
(1905)

KOREA

Seoul

Tokyo

JAPANESE
EMPIRE
(1875)

Yellow River

Tsingtao
(Germany, 1808–1914,
Japan, 1914–23)

Pusan

C H I N A

Nanking

Hankou

Yangtze River

Shanghai

Okinawa
(1874)

Ryukyu Islands

Canton

Pescadores
(1895)

Hong Kong
(Britain)

TAIWAN
(FORMOSA)

▦	1895
▨	Treaty of 1905
▧	1910
▤	Manchuria ("Manchukuo," 1932)
☐	To Manchukuo, 1933)

0   500   1000   1500 km

0   250   500   750   1000 miles

Philippine
Islands
(to U.S., 1898)

that the Germans would not rebuild a fleet more than one third the size of the British navy, the British abandoned its Stresa allies and rushed to accept.

At the same time as they protected their traditional naval forces, military leaders realized that the nature of warfare had changed: They needed air power. The Spanish Civil War had revealed that bombers could devastate cities. Unlike sea power, the Allies had no supremacy in aircraft, a costly new military expenditure. By 1938 Britain was spending more on its air force than on its fleet.

The protectionist response to the crisis of the Great Depression changed interwar diplomacy. In the 1920s, France had struggled to unite the countries surrounding Germany on its east and south into a **Little Entente** whose members had a common political interest in restraining Germany's efforts to renegotiate Versailles. The disappearance of the gold standard changed state relations in Eastern Europe and the Balkans. In a protectionist era, governments, not businessmen, negotiated international trade. As Germany rearmed, agriculture responded sluggishly to the need for increased production and food prices began to rise. Furthermore Germany needed strategic raw materials such as bauxite, chrome, lead, zinc, and oil. Even nationalist Germans concluded that German rearmament required an abandonment of the National Socialist commitment to economic autarchy, and access to Eastern European resources. Germany offered irresistibly high prices for Eastern European raw material imports in a glutted world market.

Figure 12.8 Pablo Picasso's "Guernica" was a great artist's response to the bombing of the Spanish Basque town of Guernica by rebellious generals. This was one of the first attempts to subdue a population by aerial bombardment and, at the time, produced widespread indignation. By the end of World War II such bombing would be a commonplace, used by all powers.

The Munich Agreement turned the movement of Eastern European states toward Germany into an all-out race. The Anglo-French position throughout all of Eastern and Southern Europe collapsed. Before World War I, Eastern Europe and the Balkans had already been closely tied to German markets. Now, these nations competed to strike favorable deals, giving Hitler greater appreciation of the importance of Eastern European riches to the German economy. In *Mein Kampf*, his autobiography written in prison in the 1920s, Hitler had already expressed his intentions of moving east. This expansion became an urgent necessity after 1938.

Finally, reflexive anti-communism played a major role in the failure to resist dictatorial aggression. The Spanish Civil War of 1936–39 was the first test of the possibility of international co-operation against fascism, and a preview of the war to come. The democracies failed it. General Francisco Franco led a rebellion against the legally elected Spanish government, which called on international support for its defense. But the liberal Spanish government also had the support of socialists and even anarcho-syndicalists, who pushed for social revolution. The British prime minister, Stanley Baldwin, and other conservative elites preferred Franco's military rule to a new outbreak of revolutionary upheaval. Léon Blum's socialist gov-ernment in France was too torn by division to intervene. British-led efforts at collective non-intervention only starved the republicans of support. Only the USSR supported the republican government, strengthening the small Spanish Communist Party and recruiting fighters from outside Spain, the "International Brigades," to defend Spanish democracy. Anarchists, communists, socialists, and dedicated liberals, including famous writers like Ernest Hemingway and George Orwell, converged on the Spanish cockpit from around the world. Along with them also came dedicated Communists, determined to use the conflict to prevent a fascist victory in

Spain. Meanwhile, fascist Italy and Germany sent military aid and advisors to Franco's rebels. The appearance of the Soviet-backed International Brigades further frightened British statesmen, making them loath to aid either side. When German bombers devastated the small town of Guernica, ruthlessly using air power to terrorize civilians, Pablo Picasso immortal-ized the atrocity in a famous painting (see Figure 12.8). Guernica appalled the world, but it did not save Spain. Franco won, and ruled as a dictator until his death in 1975. In the course of the war, 700,000 died in battle, 30,000 were executed or assassinated, and 15,000 were killed in air raids. A new style of war had begun. The Japanese massacre of the Chinese civilians in Nanjing in 1937 only confirmed the fact.

In late 1938, as the inevitability of war became clear, Western leaders began to pursue the possibility of an alliance with the Soviet Union. They did so with extreme half-heartedness, however, sending third-rate negotiators who were instructed to proceed slowly. Western negotiations with Stalin foundered on the inability of Westerners to persuade their Polish ally to allow Soviet troops to move through Poland. Fundamentally, negoti-ations foundered on Western hesitation at the prospect of a Soviet alliance, and the belief that a Hitler–Stalin pact was inconceivable. But the inconceivable happened.

In August 1939, the news of a German–Soviet alliance aston-ished the world. Hitler and Stalin agreed to partition Eastern Europe between them. Everyone realized that it meant the out-break of war. Remembering World War I, Hitler had always feared a two-front war. His agreement with Stalin allowed Germany to turn its full force to the west.

Stalin's decision to deal with Hitler remains strategically inex-plicable. Britain and France were unlikely to allow Germany to march across Poland to fight the USSR: Neither the UK nor France could allow a single power to dominate Eurasia from the Rhine to Siberia. The chance that Germany would long tolerate a

USSR that Hitler had so often denounced was also minimal. Nonetheless, the visceral anti-communism of the UK and France allowed the fate of the world to rest in the hands of dictatorial megalomaniacs.

Many astute observers underestimated Soviet power. The purges had decimated the Soviet high command and Soviet setbacks in the invasion of Finland seemed to suggest the weakness of the Soviet army. Had they been consulted, the Japanese who had fought the Soviets in Siberia could have testified to the fighting ability of the Red Army. Boosted by the great increases in productive capacity of the Five Year Plans, the Soviet Union was, unknown to most European military men, already a pre-eminent power. The alliance between Germany and the USSR thus represented a great potential threat to liberal democracy. In September 1939 the future of liberal democracy in all of Eurasia literally hung in the balance.

Conclusion

Between 1918 and 1939 communists, liberal democrats, and fascists contended for control over the European continent. The year 1919 witnessed the failure of the great revolutionary wave begun in Russia in 1917. After 1919 the revolutionary tide receded, leaving the USSR as the sole communist state. The failure of German and Hungarian revolutions in 1919 marked the end of an era when it had looked as if Soviet-inspired revolution might spread through Europe. Increasingly during the 1920s the USSR was preoccupied with internal politics and remained on the periphery of the world political stage.

While communist revolution failed in the immediate postwar years, liberal democracy advanced in giant strides across the continent. In some countries, European liberal democracy's commitment to free market policies and ethnic rights were never solidly institutionalized, but almost everywhere rulers paid it lip service. Although some political leaders in Central and Southern Europe embraced liberal democracy wholeheartedly at Versailles, democratic constitutions were known to be a quick way to Woodrow Wilson's heart. Many political leaders adopted more nuanced views when they returned home.

In 1922 Italy became the first fascist country. The advance of radical socialists and reformist Christian political parties within a newly democratic Italy and a great increase in worker militancy frightened Italian elites and provided the backdrop to Mussolini's rise. The fascist movement first came to prominence due to its attacks on labor militants. Italian fascists further benefited from popular horror at the losses their nation had suffered during the war and the feeling that the liberal democracies had betrayed them. Although Italy had benefited from the dismantling of the Austro-Hungarian empire, its main rival, Italian nationalists were infuriated by their failure to acquire territory in the southern Alps and eastern Adriatic promised by the Allies.

While the 1922 accession to power of Mussolini was a serious warning, the Great Depression in 1929 marked the turning of the tide against liberal democracy. In the 1930s, faced with massive unemployment, the newly established liberal democracies in Central and Southern Europe collapsed – with the single exception of Czechoslovakia. In Spain, civil war led to the establishment of the reactionary Franco dictatorship. This last was particularly disheartening for liberal democrats because of the failure of liberal democratic France and Britain to stand by one of their own. In contrast, Mussolini and Hitler provided abundant aid to Franco. In Britain poverty was becoming endemic in many of the old coal mining regions and factory towns where the First Industrial Revolution had been born. For a while the French Popular Front, a coalition of left and center-left political parties, offered hopes but, after an initial round of reforms, the movement fractured.

In the 1930s both communists and fascists began to attract new attention. To desperately unemployed Europeans of the era, communists emphasized that there was no unemployment in the USSR, while fascists, particularly in Germany, declared that somehow the Jews were responsible for it all. Liberal democrats seemed unable to provide a vigorous response to dictators and to the left-wing and right-wing social movements that challenged liberal democracy. In 1933 Adolf Hitler's Nazi party took power in Germany, the largest industrial power in Europe. Some claimed that, except for very wealthy nations like the USA, liberal democracy was not a doctrine for hard times. With the signing of the Hitler–Stalin pact in 1939 it looked as if fascists and communists had joined together to defeat liberal democracy. To many, that European liberal democracy was finished.

Study Questions

(1) Compare the ideals of liberal democrats, democratic socialists, communists, and fascists. Why did liberal democrats and democratic socialists fare so poorly during the Great Depression? Why did fascists and communists have such appeal?

(2) The UK and France emerged in 1919 as the pre-eminent world powers. Germany seemed to have been utterly crushed. Yet within twenty years Germany not only restored its power but expanded it so that it threatened the entire world. What explains this amazing turn of events? What were the forces in Germany's rise?

(3) Liberals had high hopes for reconstructing a new world order in the wake of World War I, and so did revolutionary socialists. Yet both of them failed, and neither could stop their most dangerous enemies, the fascist parties. What were the weaknesses of each movement?

Suggested Reading

WILLIAM SHERIDAN ALLEN, *Nazi Seizure of Power: The Experience of a Single German Town, 1930–1935* (Chicago: Quadrangle Books, 1965). This is a classic account of how the Nazis took power in a German town.

JULIAN JACKSON, *The Politics of Depression in France, 1932–1936* (Cambridge University Press, 1985).

The Popular Front in France: Defending Democracy, 1934–1938 (Cambridge University Press, 1988). Jackson is a foremost student of interwar France, and a judicious historian in a field filled with controversy.

IAN KERSHAW, *The Nazi Dictatorship: Problems and Perspectives of Interpretation*, 4th edn. (Oxford University Press, 1995). This study discusses and critiques various interpretations of Nazism.

CHARLES P. KINDLEBERGER, *The World in Depression, 1929–1939* (Berkeley: University of California Press, 2013). This is the classic account of the primary factors that caused financial markets to crash in the 1930s: panic, contagions, and the lack of a stable international economic structure. It has important implications for the world after 2008.

MICHAEL SEIDMAN, *Workers Against Work: Labor in Paris and Barcelona During the Popular Fronts* (Berkeley: University of California Press, 1991). Seidman's comparative study provides insight into the left in Spain and France. Today when the Popular Front is mentioned we think of France but contemporaries were just as likely to think of Spain.

PHILIP SHORT, *Mao: A Life* (New York: Henry Holt, 1999). This is a useful biography of Mao's life, incorporating much new material.

LEWIS H. SIEGELBAUM, *Stakhanovism and the Politics of Productivity in the USSR, 1935–1941* (Cambridge University Press, 1988). Siegelbaum describes the promotion of intensive use of capital and labor in the Soviet Union, as represented by the cult of Sergei Stakhanov, a Russian miner who became famous for exceeding his allotted quota for coal production.

HUGH THOMAS, *The Spanish Civil War* (New York: Harper & Row, 1977). Thomas's book is a classic history of the Spanish Civil War.

Glossary

Arditi: A term used for front-line fighters during the First World War (Italian: "fearless ones"). These war volunteers organized themselves after World War I and were recruited by Italian fascists to form the nucleus of the fascist squads that made fascism a movement dominating the Italian street.

Freikorps: After the First World War, the German military encouraged the formation of private armies designed to fight ethnic minorities and the threat of Soviet invasion (German: "Free Corps"). Later they were used against the left within Germany.

Great Depression: Beginning in 1929 in the United States, the Depression spread gradually throughout the entire world. It was the greatest downturn in the history of capitalism and was only finally ended by spending for the coming world war.

kulaks: Russian term for prosperous peasants. The Soviet government's claim that it was battling opposition from prosperous peasants was really only a cover-up for a massive confiscation of peasant produce and repression of those who resisted.

Lateran Pact: Treaty signed in 1929 between Mussolini and Pope Pius XI. Essentially the papacy recognized the legitimacy of the Italian state (and Mussolini) and in return received Vatican City, an independent enclave within Rome, and a variety of concessions, including religious instruction in schools.

Lebensraum: Term used by the Nazi party as a political slogan (German: "living space"). It summed up Nazi claims that Germany was overpopulated, that national power required large amounts of territory, and that space must be created, mainly in Eastern and Southern Europe, for German settlement.

Little Entente: In 1920–21 Czechoslovakia, Romania, and Yugoslavia signed a series of treaties that constituted an alliance to protect themselves against irredentist claims by Germany, Hungary and Bulgaria. France promoted this alliance and also pledged its support to each of the nations.

New Economic Policy: First announced in 1921, the NEP was a move toward moderation which gave the USSR time to recover from an era of war, revolution, and civil war. Socializing reforms were mainly confined to the largest enterprises and great economic leeway was given to peasants and small businesses.

Non-Co-operation Movement: Launched by Gandhi as a non-violent movement in 1920, it called for boycotting foreign goods, schools, law courts, legislatures, and military recruitment. Although meeting with great success, the movement inspired a growing number of violent uprisings against British rule, popular riots, and also confrontations between Hindus and Muslims. Appalled by the growing violence, Gandhi began to rein in the movement in 1922.

reparations: Compensation that the Treaty of Versailles required Germany to pay to compensate for the damages it had inflicted in World War I.

self-determination of nations: Woodrow Wilson's call for a world in which minority populations concentrated in contiguous territory within larger nations would have the right to determine their own destiny.

social fascism: Communist interpretation (originating in Soviet internal politics) of foreign politics. Stalin, having defeated the left-winger Trotsky, attacked the communist right-winger Bukharin. Stalin claimed that fascists like Mussolini and Hitler were not the main danger in the 1930s but the socialists who were "objectively" supporters of fascism and misled the working classes. The decision of the communists to oppose the socialists, instead of uniting with them to fight Hitler, helped bring Hitler to power.

Taisho democracy: Term used to describe a period of party-dominated politics in Japan when liberal and radical ideas spread.

13 World War II and the collapse of empires, 1931–1950

Timeline	
1931	Manchurian Incident: Using an attack that it had staged as a pretext, the Japanese army seizes the Chinese province of Manchuria.
1937	The Marco Polo Bridge Incident leads to renewed conflict between Japan and China.
September 1, 1939	Poland invaded by Germany.
September 7, 1939	Under the terms of the Molotov–Ribbentrop Pact, the USSR invades Poland from the east.
May 10, 1940	Beginning of Battle of France: France overrun by German army.
June 22, 1940	France signs armistice.
July 10–October 31, 1940	Battle of Britain: Germany fails to obtain air superiority over British skies (a prerequisite for an invasion). Air war over Britain winds down as Germany concentrates its resources against the USSR.
June 22, 1941	Germany invades USSR.
November 16, 1941	Russian offensive stops German advance just outside of Moscow.
December 7, 1941	Japan cripples US fleet in surprise attack at Pearl Harbor; USA declares war on Japan the next day.
December 11, 1941	Germany and Italy declare war on USA.
December 1941–March 1942	Japanese armies seize the Philippines, the Dutch East Indies, Burma, and Malaya.
January 20, 1942	Wannsee Conference: German leaders meet to plan the extermination of the Jewish people.

June 4–7, 1942	Battle of Midway: US fleet turns back Japanese fleet. The momentum shifts in the Central Pacific.
January 1943	Soviet troops cut off German army at Stalingrad. The defeat of the Germans before Stalingrad is a turning point of the war.
June 6, 1944	Allied troops land at Normandy Beach. The western invasion to defeat the Germans is begun.
February 4–11, 1945	Roosevelt, Churchill, and Stalin meet at Yalta to plan the final defeat and occupation of Germany.
May 7, 1945	Germany surrenders.
August 6, 1945	Atomic bomb dropped on Hiroshima.
August 8, 1945	USSR declares war on Japan.
August 14, 1945	Japan surrenders.
August 17, 1945	Dutch East Indies declares independence and becomes Indonesia; the Netherlands acknowledges this, after four years of armed struggle, on December 27, 1949.
October 24, 1945	Foundation of the United Nations.
November 20, 1945–October 1, 1946	Nuremberg trials.
August 14–15, 1947	Independence for India and Pakistan.

In 1939 Mémé Santerre worked with her husband Pépé as a farm laborer in a sugar refinery with a farm attached in the Nord region of northeastern France. She had little in common with Faye Lazebnik, a young photography student living with her family in a small eastern Polish town, roughly half of whose population was Jewish.

But World War II would change both of their lives. In 1939, as a result of the Molotov–Ribbentrop Pact, the Soviet Red Army occupied eastern Poland after the German army had stunned the world with its rapid defeat of Poland. The Soviet regime deported some of the town's wealthiest citizens to Siberia and restricted the religious life of both Jews and Christians but daily life went on. For prisoners of war, the Germans generally applied the Geneva Conventions. In 1940 Mémé fled her French village as the German armies rushed through in their lightning defeat of France. Having been strafed by enemy planes along her route, and with no place to go, she and Pépé returned home to find a German officer in charge of the farm and refinery where they worked. Captain Schmidt, the officer in charge, was an authoritarian Bavarian farmer who shared Pépé's love of horses. Rationing, which drove neighbors to desperation, did not bother the impoverished Santerres, long accustomed to a meager diet.

Still, Mémé was constantly aware of the possibility of violence. The house of a Jewish factory owner in town was requisitioned and he disappeared. Betrayed by an informer as a leader of the Resistance, their old boss was arrested, tortured, and sent to a concentration camp. Allied planes destroyed the refinery, killing three workers. In the last days of the war, as American troops headed toward the Nord, an attempt was made on the German commander's life. The Germans retaliated by rounding up twenty-one village men and machine-gunning them; Pépé would surely have been shot if he had not been working in the barn with Schmidt's prized horses. After the war Mémé picked up the threads of her life and looked forward to the new social security laws passed in France in the immediate postwar years.

The German invasion of the USSR on June 22, 1941 affected Faye Lazebnik far more profoundly. That day, the Germans seized control of her town. Amid a reign of terror, interspersed with brutal murders, the Jewish population of the town was segregated into a barbwire-bounded ghetto. On August 13, 1942, all those who had not died or escaped were marched to a field and shot. Only five families were spared because the Germans needed the skills of family members; at the very last moment, the Germans decided also to spare Faye, whose skills as a photographer were deemed important, but not her family. She soon escaped to join the partisans, the Soviet-led irregular forces that were resisting the Germans.

Acting as a nurse, working as a photographer, and fighting with the partisans gave Faye a way of dealing with her family's death. Still she was continually surprised by the anti-Semitism that she discovered among her Polish and Russian fellow partisans whose ranks were swelled by Jews fleeing the Holocaust but also by Soviet soldiers who escaped from prisoner of war camps. In these camps, located mostly in eastern Germany, millions of Russian soldiers were worked or starved to death. More partisans were recruited as the Germans destroyed everything in their wake, killing civilians, Jewish and non-Jewish, in mass in their supposed war against partisans. In December 1942 the Germans found themselves forced to retreat from Faye's village; as they left they herded all the remaining inhabitants, 5,000 gentiles, into a barracks and set it on fire, killing all those who tried to escape.

After the war Faye sought to leave Eastern Europe. For her, residence in this area felt "like living in a cemetery." After considerable efforts, she and her husband Morris migrated to Canada.

Both Mémé Santerre and Faye Lazebnik lived an eventful war. All war is horrible, but Faye Lazebnik's war, the war on the Eastern Front, was on a scale and of a cruelty quite different from Mémé Santerre's on the Western Front. As these cases show, World War II was actually several different wars, with different politics and different human experiences in various theaters. In order to understand its character, it is necessary to see it from different perspectives.[1]

The Second World War cast a long shadow over the second half of the twentieth century. In contrast with the Versailles settlement, the peace settlement in Europe after World War II lasted. No major European war broke out for the rest of the twentieth century. Until the breakup of the USSR in 1991, the major outlines of the postwar settlement remained intact. World War II and the immediate postwar era reshaped the world dramatically:

- In contrast with the First World War, the Second World War bore much more heavily on civilians and prisoners of war than on actual combatants. Breaking with nineteenth-century conventions in favor of humane treatment of prisoners of war and civilians, the war marked a turn toward an age of ethnic cleansing, genocide, torture, and mass murder.
- The character of the war varied regionally. In Western Europe, liberal democracies clashed with fascism. In Eastern Europe, fascist and communist dictatorships fought each other, while in Asia and Africa the authoritarian states, Germany and Japan, fought old established colonial empires.
- Some anti-colonial movements, like the Indians, avoided contact with the Japanese but continued anti-colonial protests during the war; others, like the Vietnamese and Chinese, fought against the Japanese invaders; and still others, as in the Dutch West Indies or the Indian National Army, collaborated with the Japanese to throw off the colonial yoke. Everywhere, the war accelerated the pace of anti-colonialism.
- While the USSR played the most crucial role in defeating Germany, US forces played a important role in Europe and a decisive role in Asia. The military position at the war's end shaped the postwar settlement. The presence of Soviet armies in Berlin, Prague, and Warsaw gave the USSR dominance in Eastern and Central Europe. US predominance in the Pacific gave it an almost exclusive role in the administration of Japan.
- The war left some nations newly united, and others sharply divided. Divided nations, from East and West Germany to North and South Korea, generated violent conflict in the postwar period, particularly when such divisions overlapped with ideological divisions in the Cold War.
- The extraordinary wartime alliance between the Western capitalist democracies and the communist USSR hardly survived the war. The war divided Europe into a capitalist Western Europe dominated by the USA and a non-capitalist Eastern Europe controlled by the USSR. After the war, both sides grew rapidly under radically different economic systems, building on institutions created during the war.

13.1 WORLD WAR II: AN OVERVIEW

World War II took more lives, inflicted more pain and suffering, and destroyed more property than any war in human history. It was more truly a world war than World War I; although the Americas remained largely outside the war zone, fierce fighting ranged over Africa, Eurasia, and Oceania; major battles were fought around Midway Island in the Central Pacific, at Wuhan on the Yangtze in China, at Imphal in Burma, at El-Alamein in Egypt, at Stalingrad in the Soviet Urals, and outside Caen in France. After an initial period of remarkable successes, the Axis powers, principally Germany, Italy, and Japan, were defeated by the Allied powers, mainly Great Britain, France, the USA, China, and the USSR.

Both of the great coalitions that fought the war had severe internal tensions. Churchill, Roosevelt, and Stalin made an odd threesome. Churchill was determined to preserve the British empire, which Roosevelt opposed. Roosevelt sympathized with

Stalin's security goals for Russia but electoral considerations committed him to an independent Poland. Moreover it seemed ironic that a war begun to defend Poland from foreign (German) control should end with foreign (Russian) control. Churchill thought it a joke to consider Chiang's China a great power; Roosevelt shared most Americans' instinctive sympathy for Chinese, derived from a century of missionary and trade relations. Stalin distrusted and misunderstood capitalist democracies and was bitter about what he considered the slow emergence of a second front in Western Europe. Yet the coalition survived until victory. The USA ended up sending more than 11 billion dollars' worth of armaments to the USSR. Churchill noted that the only thing worse than fighting with allies was fighting without them.

On the Axis side, despite formal agreements emphasizing the unity of the Axis powers, the Japanese and Germans operated almost totally independently. There was no exchange of technology or strategic co-ordination. The Japanese were slow to accept the importance of radar, despite German pressure. They had a common powerful enemy in the USSR, but the Japanese did not share with the Germans important information about the strength of the Red Army. Defeats in serious border skirmishes in Manchuria and Outer Mongolia in 1938 and 1939 had shown the Japanese the power of the Red Army but they largely concealed these defeats from Hitler. The German attaché in Tokyo learned of Pearl Harbor while walking his dog.

The lack of a co-ordinated Axis policy toward the USSR also caused strategic problems. While the USSR did not declare war on Japan until 1945, the war between Germans and the USSR hindered Japanese mobilization at crucial moments. Throughout 1942 and 1943 the Japanese army remained on the Soviet borders, ready to seize Central Asian land if the Soviet Union collapsed before the German onslaught. This prevented Japan from fully concentrating its forces on the USA in the Pacific.

Four Major Theaters of Conflict

Very important battles were fought in the Mediterranean, North Africa, the Indian Ocean, and Burma, but the largest conflicts centered on four key theaters: Western Europe, Eastern Europe and Russia, North China, and the Pacific. Each theater had its own history and affected the daily life of ordinary people differently.

When did World War II begin? For Europeans and their colonial empires, the war broke out in Europe in September 1939 when Hitler invaded Poland. For Americans, the war began with the Japanese attack on Pearl Harbor on December 7, 1941. For Asians, however, the war had already begun to emerge in 1931 with Japan's invasion of Manchuria, and it escalated into a full-scale war with China in 1937. Map 13.1 shows the Asian theater. Unlike in World War I, in World War II it was a major theater of the war.

13.2 THE ROAD TO WAR: ASIAN BEGINNINGS

The origins of the Asian war were in 1931, the year that Japanese army officers, after planting a bomb on a Japanese train to provide a pretext, took over Manchuria and declared it an independent state, Manchukuo. They put the deposed Chinese emperor, Pu Yi, on the throne. Despite their efforts, no one recognized Japan's act, but no one seriously opposed it. The League of Nations condemned Japan, which withdrew from the League, but it exacted no economic sanctions.

The Japanese officers in Manchuria acted independently of their government in Tokyo, but they soon gained official and popular support at home. Economic depression made Manchuria look attractive for settlement; Manchuria had many of the industrial raw materials essential for Japan's economic growth; and China looked much too weak to assert effective control. Japan feared that Russia would move into this power vacuum if Japan did not move first. Some radical ideologues promoted the Manchurian Incident as the first step toward a united pan-Asian federation that would drive out Western imperialism. They did not aim for a wider war, but hoped to stabilize their position on the Asian continent by negotiating a truce with the Nationalist government of China.

Although among the victors in World War I, many Japanese leaders saw themselves as defending their own security in a hostile world by taking power over a weakened Chinese regime, developing the economic resources of their colonies in Korea and Manchuria, and leading the rest of Asia in a united campaign against Western colonialism.

Who Were the Chinese Nationalists?

China in 1931, however, was not like the China of 1915 or 1919, whose government had allowed Japanese expansion, despite popular protest. The Nationalist government claimed to represent a united nation determined to oust both Western and Japanese powers from China's territory. It defined China's sovereign territory in grand terms, as nearly the maximal extent of the Qing empire, including Manchuria, Taiwan, Hong Kong, Mongolia, Xinjiang, and Tibet. Except for acknowledging Mongolia's independence, no Chinese government has ever given up these demands.

Chiang Kai-shek's government ruled from its capital in Nanjing (or Nanking) from 1927 to 1937, a period known as the "Nanking decade." It was a time of high hopes and great

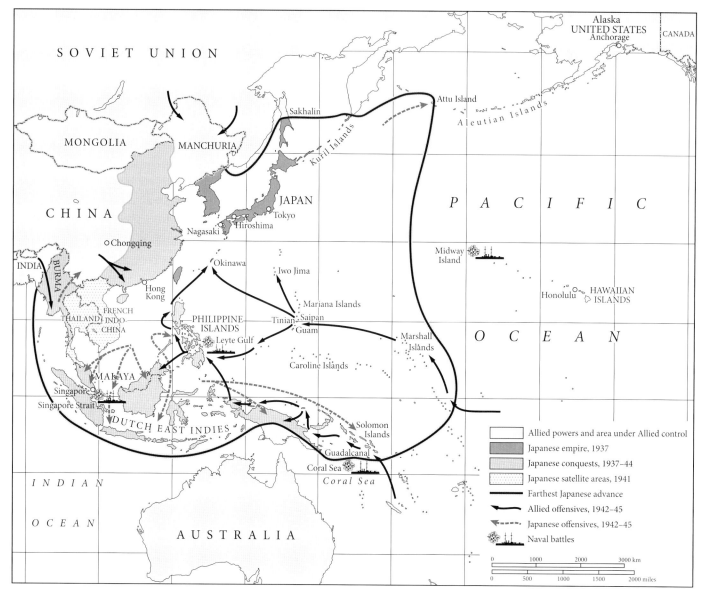

Map 13.1 World War II in Asia and the Pacific

disappointments. Having crushed the communists in Shanghai and other major cities, Chiang pursued a relentless campaign to wipe them out of their rural strongholds too. With German military advisors, he besieged the communist base area in Jiangxi with a series of encirclement campaigns, until he forced the Communist Party to flee to the barren northwest. At the same time, China's industry grew at a rapid rate, aided by economic planners who copied fascist models. Some 80 percent of government spending went to the military. In 1934, Chiang signed a secret treaty to trade Chinese ore for iron, steel, and weapons factories from Germany. Chiang even had his own Brown Shirt organization and secret police. He launched a "New Life" movement to "militarize the life of the Chinese people" and "nourish their capacity to endure hardship." His militarized, authoritarian state seemed to have brought stability.

Yet Chiang's regime also aroused great discontent. Industrialists prospered with government orders, but workers' efforts to strike were savagely repressed and writers censored. China's peasants suffered the most. The Depression cut textile exports, hurting the large number who produced for world markets, but natural disasters were even worse: The great Yangtze River floods of 1931 drove 14 million people from their homes, and famine struck the north. Chiang's regime, based on Shanghai capitalists and lower Yangtze landlords, conducted no serious agrarian reform. Sun Yat-sen's Three People's Principles, which included "people's welfare," now looked like nothing but empty rhetoric. As Chiang failed to respond forcefully to the Japanese takeover of Manchuria, instead sending his best troops to root out the communists in the south, critics attacked his failure to defend China's territory and called for unity against the Japanese threat.

The Rise of Chinese Communism

Meanwhile, the Communist Party had established the Jiangxi Soviet in the mountains of Jinggangshan, a remote mountainous area in southern central China. There, Mao finally had a chance to try out his heretical ideas about the ability of peasants to support a revolutionary national movement. His government enacted radical land reform, giving poor peasants enough land to live on for the first time in their lives, and in return, enrolled their sons in the Red Army, led by the great commander Zhu De. Through literacy campaigns and constant propaganda, Mao and his urban comrades connected the great cause of China's national unification with the local concerns of remote peasant villagers. But the Jiangxi Soviet had to struggle constantly for survival against Chiang's relentless pressure. Mao, too, had German military advisors, former communists, who told him to hold still and bolster his defenses.

In 1935–36, once again defying conventional wisdom, as Chiang's fifth encirclement campaign closed in, Mao uprooted his entire army and took off across some of China's most inaccessible territory on the famous Long March. Fighting off Nationalist attacks all the way, losing 100 percent of their original strength while gaining new recruits, Mao's peasant soldiers crossed the jungles of Southwest China, the deep gorges and high plateaus of Tibet, and the deserts of the northwest to arrive at Yan'an in Northern Shaanxi. There they established a second socialist base area, on very different principles from the first.

Yan'an was so poor that it had almost no landlords, and all the wealthy had fled long ago. The communist social revolution took a moderate form here, encouraging poor and middle peasants to join together. Those who had tenants could keep them, as long as their rents were moderate. Everyone was encouraged to work together on an equal basis to form a new kind of solidarity directed against Chiang's bourgeois regime and Japan's imperial aggression. Mao's Red Army acted very differently from the warlord armies the peasants were used to: The soldiers taught the peasants to read, they paid for their food, and they put the doors back on peasants' houses after using them for beds. Mao's Communist Party also looked very different from Stalin's. While Mao argued that peasants could be the agrarian spearhead of social revolution, Stalin had just finished massacring and deporting peasants who resisted collectivization.

Yet Mao would not have survived in Yan'an either, without the Japanese intervention. Chiang Kai-shek continued to press for the extermination of the communists: The Japanese, he said, were only a disease of the skin; the communists were a disease of the heart. In 1936, Chiang flew to Xi'an to pressure the warlord Zhang Xueliang to support his anti-communist campaign, but the warlord, whose father had been assassinated by the Japanese in Manchuria, had listened sympathetically to communist appeals for unity. Zhang surrounded Chiang's compound with his troops; while Chiang prepared to die, Zhang brought in the communist negotiator Zhou Enlai to set terms for a new United Front against Japan. Under heavy nationwide pressure, Chiang had to agree.

This extraordinary "Xi'an Incident," a turn of events as surprising as the Molotov–Ribbentrop Pact, completely changed the terms of the Asian conflict: Now a nominally united China faced an isolated Japan, and refused to compromise. Unlike in 1931, the Marco Polo Bridge Incident of 1937, which started the all-out China war, was not a Japanese plot; it was a small skirmish outside Beijing which drew in large armies on both sides. Now the clash between a united China and a desperate Japan was inevitable.

Thus the road to war in Asia had many twists and turns. No single dictator or master plan drove events: A concatenation of pressures and events drove Chiang Kai-shek and the Japanese militarists into a war that neither of them really wanted.

13.3 THE WAR IN EUROPE

In contrast with the complexities of the Sino-Japanese war, the war in Europe was begun by Adolf Hitler. As described in Chapter 12, Hitler brought together a disparate coalition of traditional army officers, storm troopers, industrialists, and Nazi Party officials to serve his megalomaniac dreams. German fire was fueled by humiliation over defeat in World War I and hostility to a postwar settlement perceived as unfair. The war that Hitler started followed paths blazed by a century of conservative German nationalists but Hitler pursued these traditional conservative policies beyond their wildest dreams. Instead of economic hegemony in Eastern Europe, he sought complete domination; instead of pushing back Russia (either soviet or tsarist), he sought to destroy it; instead of stoking the anti-Semitism that promoted discrimination, he perpetrated the Holocaust. Hitler's racism may not have been new but the ferocity with which he pursued it was. Racism became the central organizing principle of the new order.

Aside from the extremism of Hitler's new order, the most modern element of the Nazi movement was its methods. Essentially Hitler built a fascist social movement. Unlike traditional conservatism that confined its appeals to the elite, Hitler took an ultra-conservative program and shaped it to build a mass movement; the Nazi rallies at Nuremberg illustrate the popular appeal of Nazi organizations (see Figure 13.1).

Figure 13.1 Nazi rally.

The Western Front: Short Conflict, Long Occupation

Battle on the Western Front ended quickly in 1940, not to resume until 1944. Germany's defeat of France spectacularly demonstrated its mastery of a new form of warfare, the **Blitzkrieg** or "lightning war." France fell in two months, May and June 1940, confounding its reliance on the "impregnable" Maginot line. Against the advice of his general staff, Hitler put his faith in a group of young, ambitious German tank commanders. Tanks like those in Figure 13.2 were key weapons in the new warfare. Rather than assaulting the Maginot line, they went around it through Belgium, co-ordinating vast, rapid maneuvers of tanks and airplanes over difficult terrain. The tank commanders' plan involved high risks. Had the French early on discovered the extent of the German presence in the Ardennes, they could have inflicted a serious, perhaps decisive defeat on the Germans. The French, paralyzed by class divisions among the officers and unfamiliarity with new technologies, were helpless. This risky but entirely successful action reinforced Hitler's confidence that his own military judgment was superior to that of the traditional military men.

By contrast, Britain's first military achievement was only a successful retreat. British troops, stranded on the Belgian coast, managed to evacuate themselves from Dunkirk without severe casualties. After the retreat, Churchill oriented the nation toward a defensive strategy, telling the House of Commons, "We shall fight on the beaches, we shall fight on the landing grounds, we shall fight in the fields and in the streets, we shall fight in the hills; we shall never surrender." Churchill realized that there was little that Britain could do in 1940 to seriously challenge German power. It is said that during his House of Commons speech he whispered: "And we'll fight them with the butt ends of broken beer bottles because that's bloody well all we've got!" Rather he used his magnificent rhetorical talents to keep up morale while waiting for something to happen. Figure 13.3 illustrates the British response to the German challenge.

In the **Battle of Britain**, in July–October 1940, the Royal Air Force defeated a major German air offensive against a shifting variety of British targets, denying Germany the air supremacy necessary for a cross-Channel invasion that could have knocked Britain out of the war. Winston Churchill called the British performance "their finest hour." Churchill provided masterly leadership at a time of extreme British crisis.

On the Western Front, the combatants followed some rules of civilized conduct toward prisoners of war and non-Jewish citizens. German reprisals for Resistance attacks were savage but grew worse as the German position deteriorated. Hitler's long-standing commitment to negotiating – at least temporarily – a settlement with the UK was one motivation for the Germans' relatively civilized behavior toward captured Western prisoners of war. German atrocities such as the murder of American prisoners at Malmedy and of Canadian troops on the Normandy beachheads cannot be compared with the treatment of Red Army prisoners on the Eastern Front. After the fascist actions

Figure 13.2 German Tanks of the 1st Armored Division on the Western Front, 1939. These tanks would lead the invasion of France in 1940.

Figure 13.3 This famous cartoon by celebrated cartoonist, David Low, underlined the great achievement of Winston Churchill: forging an effective coalition of Labour, Liberal, and Conservative parties to carry out the war.

ALL BEHIND YOU, WINSTON

in the Spanish Civil War, however, bombing civilians from the air no longer counted as an atrocity for either side. The doctrine of **strategic bombing** justified destruction of non-military targets to break civilian morale.

In Western Europe, convinced that mainstream conservative leaders could most effectively divert industrial and human resources to German purposes, Hitler looked for collaborators. He found most enthusiastic co-operation from Vichy France, under the World War I hero Marshall Pétain. Seeking to win German favor, the anti-Semitic Vichy regime in France hunted down Jews and German emigrants to France with genuine enthusiasm. In areas under their direct administration, the Germans repressed any sign of popular politics, ruthlessly tortured and murdered members of the Resistance, and executed innocent people – as many as 30,000 hostages in France. In Germany, homosexuals were targeted. As Allied armies closed in from both the east and the west, conditions became more difficult in the German-occupied areas. Dutch men and women starved when food was diverted to German populations.

Many Europeans, including the French Resistance, still fought back, despite the cost. In France, where the issue has been studied, it seems that civilian co-operation with the Germans, even the co-operation of anti-Semites, decreased as the news spread that arrested Jews were doomed. In the latter days of the war, as it became clear that the Nazis might lose, resistance and terrorist reprisals increased. Resistance activity helped the Anglo-American-Canadian landings. In those areas of Europe run by the Germans and their collaborators, the Jewish experience was always grim, but was not everywhere the same. Everywhere in occupied Western Europe in 1942 and 1943, people were ordered to turn over Jews, Roma or Sinti ("gypsies"), and German political refugees to the authorities. Jews were the major victims of these government roundups. In German-occupied Poland and the Ukraine, German troops found willing collaborators. In Mussolini's Italy and Admiral Horthy's Hungary, both fascist states and German allies, but not aggressively anti-Semitic, the Jewish population largely remained untouched until late in the war when the Germans intervened directly or established regimes more fully compliant to their will.

Even though they fought to end German rule, the Western European nations and the USA bear some responsibility for the Holocaust, due to their prewar policies. Many Jews living in France and the Benelux nations had fled Nazi persecution in Germany or the conquered territories in the east. When they sought to flee the continent, the UK and the USA denied them entry or permanent residence. High unemployment made the USA and the UK reluctant to accept foreign migrants, but some key US Congressmen and State Department officials were openly anti-Semitic. Increasingly, the small number of Jews who succeeded in fleeing the European continent found refuge in British Palestine. Concerned about Arab opinion, the British authorities sought to discourage immigration, but nonetheless the Jewish population of the region grew. In the years after the war, the swelling tide of immigration formed the basis for the creation of the Jewish state of Israel in 1948.

D-Day, the invasion of Western Europe, finally came on June 6, 1944, with a combined amphibious assault on the Normandy coast by 2.2 million British, American, French, and Canadian forces. German troops in the east were already reeling from Soviet advances, and the time and place of the invasion had been successfully kept secret. D-Day, the subject of numerous books and films, still came too late to save the Jews of Europe. Unexpectedly, Allied forces had to hold off a strong German counterattack, the Battle of the Bulge, in December 1944, and they did not cross the Rhine until March 1945. Although even very early on the Soviets benefited significantly from the drain on German forces in the west, particularly air forces, the decisive battles in the European war took place on the Eastern Front in 1942 and 1943 before the very substantial US aid had begun to arrive in quantity.

The Eastern Front: Long Conflict, Occupation, Atrocities

Hitler authorized Operation Barbarossa, the invasion of the Soviet Union, on December 18, 1940, and the invasion began on June 22, 1941. He expected Blitzkrieg tactics to work in the enormous spaces of the east as in the more confined west. He also expected Slavs, in his view inferior people, to be worse fighters than the Western Europeans, and their hostility to communism to make them support German "liberation." Map 13.2 shows the expansion of the Eastern Front produced by the invasion of the USSR.

Despite the enormous losses inflicted on the Russians by Stalin's refusal to believe that Hitler was preparing to attack him, the Soviet Union was better prepared, better outfitted, and more highly motivated than anyone had expected. The Russian Civil War had familiarized Soviet military men with the importance of a war of movement and the problems of transporting large numbers of men and equipment over great spaces. Ironically, military strategies elaborated by generals whom Stalin had shot in the purges were instrumental to Soviet victory. Also, the heavy tanks, the T-34s and KV-1s, that were just beginning to roll off Soviet assembly lines were superior to anything that the Germans possessed or projected. The Russian army of peasant and worker recruits fought valiantly. Although suffering huge casualties, they nonetheless inflicted blows on the German war machine. The people of Leningrad endured a 900-day siege, and never surrendered. The Germans had not expected to need winter clothes. By surviving until the winter, the Soviets blunted the edge of the Blitzkrieg strategy. In December 1941, Stalin learned from a Russian spy that Japan would send its forces against the USA, not Russia. This knowledge allowed him to bring back his Siberian troops to push the Germans back from Moscow. The crucial turning point of the entire war took place in the streets of **Stalingrad**, on the Volga River, in the winter of

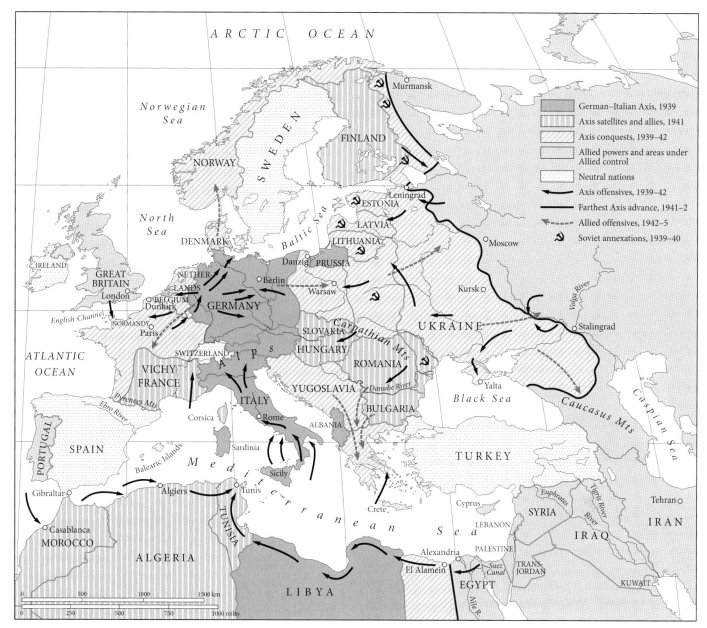

Map 13.2 World War II in Europe and North Africa

1942–43. Hitler refused to retreat, even as his armies were encircled. From this point onward, the Soviets pushed Hitler back, with bitter, tough fighting.

The Soviets defeated the German armies because in some respects the Five Year Plan had succeeded: Now they had enough industrial resources east of the Urals to supply a long conflict. In his determination to win the war, Stalin had made an accommodation with the Orthodox church and apparently given up revolutionary ideals. Many of the old army men who were incompetent but Stalinist sycophants were replaced by men of gennine ability. He glorified the generals who fought Napoleon, and Alexander Nevsky, who had fought the Teutonic knights in the thirteenth century.

By spring of 1944, the Soviets recovered the frontiers of the tsarist empire, including the Baltics and Poland. By early 1945 they turned south into Romania and Hungary, and took the rest of Poland. Before the Western powers had crossed the Rhine, the Soviets were nearing Berlin. The toll of Soviet casualties and the occupation of Eastern Europe by tough and experienced Soviet troops confronted Europeans with new political problems.

Occupation, Extermination, and Racial War In Eastern Europe and Russia, anti-Semitism, racial antagonism, anti-communism, and the confrontation of two ruthless dictators created a nightmare land of murder and cruelty. German concentration camps and death camps in Eastern Europe collected Jews from all over the continent. In 1941, mass murders of Jews by Lithuanians and Ukrainians, themselves victims of German aggression, only compounded the horror of the German advance. At the **Wannsee Conference** of January 20, 1942, top Nazi officers decided on extermination as the "final solution" to the Jewish question. The large Jewish populations of Hungary, Poland, Romania, and the Western USSR were their chief target. Notorious death camps, like Auschwitz (see Figure 13.4), worked prisoners to death, and killed them directly with Zyklon-B gas in "shower rooms"

(see Box 13.1). Major German industrialists, like Krupp steel and I.G. Farben chemicals, produced these modern instruments of human destruction. From 5.5 to 6 million Jews perished in the Holocaust, up to 80 percent of the total Jewish population of Europe.

Jews suffered by far the most, but they were not alone. Eastern Europe was the scene of a unilaterally declared race war. The Nazis, led by the monstrous Heinrich Himmler and his SS troops, intended to drive out the inferior Slavs from Eastern Europe to make way for German settlement, or *Lebensraum*. Germany temporarily needed conquered Poland's labor power, but it attempted to destroy the country's elite, murdering tens of thousands of Polish intellectuals, journalists, and teachers. The Nazis applied the same policy toward the Soviet Union, with fateful results. Initially, many Soviet ethnic minorities, Baltic peoples, Ukrainians, and Byelorussians, repressed by Stalin, greeted the invading Germans as liberators, but brutal German occupation provoked Soviet-supported guerrilla warfare.

In 1941 Stalin announced that "If they [the Germans] want a war of extermination, they shall have one." But the Germans were not Stalin's only targets. The Soviets settled many scores during the war. Near the Katyn Forest, in Poland, the Soviets slaughtered 15,000 Polish military men and administrators who had surrendered to them in 1939. Germans who discovered the graves of this **Katyn massacre** in 1943 cynically used the massacre to publicize Stalin's brutality. Retreating Soviet troops killed large numbers of Baltic peoples and deported Chechens, Crimean Tatars, Kalmyks, and Volga Germans whose loyalty they suspected.

Germany not only made war against the Slavs as a people but against communism in particular. When they invaded the USSR, German troops were explicitly instructed to murder political commissars – communist officials attached to Red Army units to watch over the behavior of military men whose loyalty to the soviet cause was doubtful – but actually any captured Red Army soldier became a candidate for execution. Of 5.5 million Soviet prisoners of war, over 3.5 million died in captivity. Hundreds of thousands of Soviet soldiers were deliberately starved to death, machine-gunned en masse as they marched into captivity, or died of a combination of overwork, starvation diets, and inadequate housing.

In Germany itself, foreign workers also had a hard lot; true to the Nazi racial code, Slavs were treated worst and Northern Europeans best, but living conditions for all foreign workers declined precipitously as the war continued, and many died. In the end, as Allied troops closed in on Germany, the country's government even turned on its own population. Exemplary punishment of fleeing teenagers and elderly men who refused suicidal orders to stand and fight marked the last weeks and days of the war around Berlin.

Figure 13.4 Auschwitz was one of the many camps in Eastern and Central Europe which were the site of the Jewish genocide during World War II. Genocide is the systematic destruction of all or part of a racial, ethnic, religious, or national group. The word was coined by Raphael Lemkin in a 1944 book and is rooted in the words *genos* (Greek for family, tribe, or race) and *-cide* (Latin for killing). The practice of genocide is not new but the scale and scientific methods used to carry it out made the Jewish genocide, practiced in such places as Auschwitz, unique. For many Western thinkers, the Jewish genocide challenged basic assumptions of progress and modernity.

Box 13.1 Victims of the Holocaust

A French doctor described what he saw at one of the crematoria used to kill Jews at the extermination camp of Auschwitz-Birkenau:

It is mid-day, when a long line of women, children, and old people enter the yard. The senior official in charge . . . climbs on a bench to tell them that they are going to have a bath and that afterward they will get a drink of hot coffee. They all undress

in the yard . . . The doors are opened and an indescribable jostling begins. The first people to enter the gas chamber begin to draw back. They sense the death which awaits them. The SS men put an end to this pushing and shoving with blows from their rifle butts beating the heads of the horrified women who are desperately hugging their children. The massive oak double doors are shut. For two endless minutes one can hear banging on the walls

and screams which are no longer human. And then – not a sound. Five minutes later the doors are opened. The corpses, squashed together and distorted, fall out like a waterfall . . . The bodies, which are still warm, pass through the hands of the hairdresser, who cuts their hair, and the dentist, who pulls out their gold teeth . . . One more transport has just been processed through No. IV crematorium.

13.4 JAPAN'S CHINESE QUAGMIRE

On July 7, 1937, a small skirmish outside of Beijing drew Japan and China into an all-out war that neither side wanted. Japanese officers had hoped to negotiate a compromise with China, allowing them control over Manchukuo (see Box 13.2) and influence over North China, but Chiang and Mao refused anything but total Japanese withdrawal. Chiang at first offered stiff resistance against Japan's invasion. He threw his best German-trained troops against the Japanese at Shanghai, losing 250,000 men killed or wounded, 60 percent of his army, but he had to retreat up the Yangtze river by November. Defeated troops mixed with refugees on a chaotic retreat to Nanjing, whose local warlord abandoned the city with no preparations for its defense. Whole Chinese cities evacuated in panic at the news of Japanese advance.

Japanese troops occupied Nanjing in December. For the next seven weeks, they systematically raped, looted, tortured, and executed large numbers of the defenseless civilian population. Western residents in the city looked on aghast. The causes of the Nanjing massacre remain obscure, and the total number killed unclear, but probably over 100,000 Chinese died. Japanese exasperation at unexpected military resistance, contempt for the local Chinese, and a deliberate effort to terrorize the Nationalist government into submission are only part of the explanation. The terror campaign failed, as Chiang withdrew up the Yangtze to Chongqing, above the Yangtze River gorges, protected by high mountains from invasion. There he held out until the end of the war.

Meanwhile, the communist guerrillas expanded their reach through the North China countryside, leaving Japanese occupying forces isolated in major cities and along railroad lines. In the south, the communist New Fourth Army also gained support. The Chinese Communist Party and the Nationalists preserved the United Front in name only. They did not co-ordinate their resistance. In 1940 communist forces attacked the Japanese in the north with over one hundred regiments, but failed to drive them out. The Japanese responded with the "Kill all, burn all, destroy all" campaign, burning thousands of villages, eliminating animals, crops, and people. But Chiang, fearing the gains in prestige by the communists, ordered the New Fourth Army into an ambush to destroy its power. For all practical purposes, the United Front had ended.

The Japanese achieved lightning victories, but they could not endure a long war. They controlled the wealthy eastern half of China, but only at the cost of large military occupation forces: over 1 million men, who faced continuing resistance, and they were running out of strategic materials like oil and rubber. With the fall of France in 1940, Japan moved into Indochina. Its entry into the Tripartite Pact with Germany and Italy in 1940 only alienated Britain and the USA. Although the USA had tried to stay out of the war in Asia, Roosevelt realized that he could not allow Japan access to the resources of the imperial possessions in Southeast Asia. In July 1941, he froze Japanese assets. Last minute negotiations broke down when the Japanese refused to withdraw from China in exchange for trade relations.

13.5 WAR IN THE PACIFIC: LIGHTNING EXPANSION, LOOMING DEFEAT

Despite the growing tension, the Japanese attack on Pearl Harbor, on December 7, 1941, took the USA completely by surprise. The Japanese achieved a brilliant tactical victory,

Box 13.2 A Chinese View of Manchukuo

Jung Chang, in her family memoir *Wild Swans*, describes the experiences of her mother as a schoolgirl under Japanese rule in Manchuria:

The pupils were educated to be obedient subjects of Manchukuo. One of the first songs my mother learned was:

Red boys and green girls walk on the streets,
They all say what a happy place Manchukuo is.
You are happy and I am happy,
Everyone lives peacefully and works joyfully free of any worries.

The teachers said that Manchukuo was a paradise on earth. But even at her age my mother could see that if the place could be called a paradise it was only for the Japanese. Japanese children attended separate schools, which were well equipped and well heated, with shining floors and clean windows. The schools for the local children were in dilapidated temples and crumbling houses donated by private patrons. There was no heating . . .

When local children passed a Japanese in the street, they had to bow and make way, even if the Japanese was younger than themselves . . . The pupils had to bow elaborately to their teachers every time they met them . . .

As part of their education, my mother and her classmates had to watch news-reels of Japan's progress in the war. Far from being ashamed of their brutality, the Japanese vaunted it as a way to inculcate fear. The films showed Japanese soldiers cutting people in half and prisoners tied to stakes being torn to pieces by dogs. There were lingering close-ups of the victims' terror-stricken eyes as their attackers came at them. The Japanese watched the eleven- and twelve-year-old schoolgirls to make sure they did not shut their eyes or try to stick a handkerchief in their mouths to stifle their screams. My mother had nightmares for years to come.

---

sending ships and planes across thousands of miles of empty ocean in total radio silence. In any larger perspective, however, the attack was a terrible mistake. It united the USA and overcame very strong popular desires to remain above the fray and outside the conflict. Churchill was exultant: "So we had won after all! . . . How long the war would last or in what fashion it would end no man could tell, nor did I at this moment care . . . We should not be wiped out. Our history would not come to an end . . . Hitler's fate was sealed. Mussolini's fate was sealed. As for the Japanese, they would be ground to a powder. All the rest was merely the proper application of overwhelming force."

In the wake of Pearl Harbor, the Japanese soon ousted General MacArthur from the Philippines, took Hong Kong and Malaya, and took over the Dutch East Indies. They captured the supposedly "impregnable" British naval base at Singapore from the rear, by land.

The British defense of Singapore was bungled, but it also reminds us again of how the war looked different to peoples in the West and those in Asia. In Europe, Britain and France publicly championed democracy and universalism against Hitler's fascism and racism. In Asia and Africa, however, Britain and France pursued undemocratic policies that were thoroughly racist although not so murderous as those of the Nazis. On the outskirts of Singapore, on the eve of battle against the attacking Japanese, Indian officers who had come to defend the colony were forbidden to use swimming pools and tennis courts open to white British officers.

For Asians tired of such colonial attitudes, Japan's quick defeat of Western-led armies seemed to offer a new chance to restructure Asian politics. Japan's rapid succession of victories seemed to mark the end of empire. In campaigns of dazzling speed, the Japanese closed the Burma Road, the only lifeline of supplies to the Nationalists in Chongqing. (Later, American and Chinese pilots reopened supply lines by flying them from lower Burma "over the hump" of the high mountains of Southwest China.) The Japanese seized the Pacific islands of Wake, Guam, and the northern half of New Guinea, establishing hegemony in the western Pacific. Throughout Southeast Asia, they promoted the ideology of a Greater East Asia Co-Prosperity Sphere, to unite the colonized peoples of Asia against Western imperialism. The expanded Japanese empire seemed to have a new future.

Japan's ascendancy was brief. Roused from its reluctance to intervene in Asia by Pearl Harbor, the USA mobilized its overwhelming Pacific forces. At the Battle of Midway, in June 1942, US naval forces won a great naval victory, restoring the balance of power in the Pacific and recapturing the initiative in the Central Pacific. Tough, grinding battles by marines on the Pacific islands gradually brought US forces closer to the Japanese islands. The fierce resistance by Japanese soldiers convinced American commanders that the Japanese were fanatical warriors who would never accept defeat. Taking Iwo Jima cost over 19,000 American casualties, but put bombers within 750 miles of Yokohama. By mid-1944, US bombers were close enough to begin firebombing raids on Japanese cities (see Figure 13.5).

Figure 13.5 Many rightly associate mass bombing with the nuclear attacks on Hiroshima and Nagasaki, but the firebombing of many Japanese cities anticipated nuclear war. On May 29, 1945, in little over an hour the so-called "Great Yokohama Air Raid" destroyed 42 percent of the city of Yokohama and killed thousands of its citizens.

13.6 THE WAR IN CHINA: NATIONALISTS AND COMMUNISTS

The war at sea in the Pacific was a straight conflict between the USA and Japan. The war on land in China was much more confused. No less than five different governments ruled parts of China: the Japanese occupation army, the Nationalist and communist governments, and two puppet regimes. US troops and air force played primarily advisory roles. The two primary anti-Japanese leaders, Chiang Kai-shek and Mao Zedong, pursued completely different military and political strategies.

Mao's Strategy

Mao and his leading general, Peng Dehuai, believed that they would gain mass support by continuing active operations against the Japanese, even at the cost of tremendous losses in men and weaponry. Despite savage Japanese reprisals, they continued to blow up railroad tracks, ambush Japanese patrols, and gain resources from the northern Chinese countryside. They also supported the Yan'an base area by smuggling supplies across the battle lines. Yan'an became a miniature model for a future socialist society, based on dedication to the nationalist anti-Japanese cause. Unlike the Jiangxi Soviet, Yan'an policy did not stress sharp class struggle: all groups from poor peasants to "enlightened landlords" could participate, and there would be

no major redistribution of land, only lowered rents. By damping down class struggle and stressing national resistance, Mao made himself the pre-eminent national leader while Stalin still supported the Nationalists as the main anti-fascist military force. Stalin had little faith in a peasant guerrilla army, but Mao defied his orders to collaborate with Chiang, knowing that Chiang was out to destroy him. Mao's distinctive style of revolutionary nationalist mobilization based on peasant forces was forged in the Yan'an years. At the same time the dissemination of pictures of Mao and his identification with the larger movement were tactics promoting the identification of the whole movement with the leader (see Figure 13.6). Relations between the USA and the communists were not helped by the American ambassador's continual mispronunciation of the communist leader's name as "Moose Dung."

Chiang's Strategy

Chiang, by contrast, saved his resources for the inevitable civil war to come. He expected, correctly, that once the USA entered the war, it would defeat Japan on its own. After Pearl Harbor, Chiang resisted active military campaigning, infuriating his American advisor, General "Vinegar Joe" Stilwell. Stilwell, who had long experience in China, knew that Chinese troops, when properly trained and led, could fight hard, but Chiang refused to stamp out corruption in his administration and rejected military

Figure 13.6 This widely distributed photo shows Mao Zedong talking to adoring peasants in Yan'an province in the 1930s; already by then Mao had become the "star" of Chinese communism. In 1933, to escape Nationalist encirclement, Mao and his army left Jiangxi province on a march (actually several marches) that covered around 6,000 miles, ending in Yan'an province in 1935. Mao's agricultural program found greater success in Yan'an than in Jiangxi. This so-called "long march" became a mythic experience for Chinese communists; the inner corps of Chinese Communist Party leadership was formed there.

plans that forced him to commit his valuable remaining troops. He much preferred the plans of the dashing air force commander, Claire Chennault, who promised to bomb Japanese installations with his private air force, the Flying Tigers, leaving Chinese soldiers unscathed. Chennault's bombing only provoked another Japanese offensive in 1944 that drove Nationalist forces out of South China.

The War and the Nationalists

The Japanese occupation of the lower Yangtze Valley cut off the roots of the **Guomindang** (GMD). The cities here, like Shanghai, Nanjing, and Ningbo, had been the center of Nationalist power and tariffs on foreign trade the main source of government finance. Japanese invasion, by driving the Nationalists into unfamiliar Sichuan, increased their dependence on local warlords and deprived them of commercial revenue. From 1945 to 1948, Chiang printed huge quantities of unbacked banknotes, causing a financial crisis that wrecked the Nationalist currency, the yuan, ruining the savings of average workers on fixed incomes, but offering great profits to speculators. Military inaction and financial incompetence made even the most ardent anti-communists lose faith in Chiang's regime.

Chiang's regime in Chongqing lost its morale during these dispiriting years of inaction. The bureaucracy was mired in corruption, army officers stole from their troops, and peasants starved under mismanagement while war profiteers prospered. Chinese draftees deserted in droves. Strict Nationalist censorship prevented exposure of the Nationalist regime's many weaknesses: its inefficiency, factional rivalry, embezzlement of foreign aid, and poor military leadership. Foreign journalists and US State Department representatives, however, saw clearly the decay in Chongqing, but Chiang had strong supporters in the USA, like Henry Luce, publisher of *Time* magazine, and his missionary allies. Chiang was on the cover of *Time* magazine ten times, and he and Madame Chiang were Man and Wife of the Year in 1937. Except for Gandhi and Deng Xiaoping, no other Asians have had such prominence.

The War and the Communists

The USA did send an observer mission to Yan'an, which was greatly impressed by the contrast with Chongqing. In Yan'an, the military observers found dedication, genuine national spirit, and real contact between the government and the local population. Most of them missed the less savory aspects of Yan'an's government: Mao had raised himself to supreme leader, conducted "rectification campaigns" to stamp out all criticism, and preserved his goal of complete revolutionary transformation of China after the end of the war. He, too, prepared for the oncoming civil war, but by mobilizing peasants and soldiers in guerrilla warfare and indoctrinating them with revolutionary nationalist ideology. Morale and political organization, not advanced weaponry, were his tools of victory. Mao's guerrillas, however, could only harass, not drive out Japanese troops. Ultimately, neither the Communist Party nor the Nationalists could defeat Japan. Only US military power could do that.

13.7 JAPAN'S FAILED EMPIRE IN ASIA

Japan's anti-colonial ideology initially attracted enthusiastic recruits, especially among Indians. After the fall of Singapore, many Indian prisoners of war who had fought in the British army joined an Indian National Army (INA) under Japanese direction. This army, led by the Indian nationalist Subhas Chandra Bose, fought to liberate India from British rule. Inadequate supplies of food and weapons and Japanese assertions of racial superiority, however, humiliated Bose's INA. Japanese officers, for example, did not have to salute any INA officers but all INA officers had to salute all Japanese officers.

In China, Korea, the Philippines, and other occupied countries, the Japanese army forced sexual slavery on native women. It established official brothels where "comfort women" were compelled to give sexual services to Japanese soldiers. The army's exploitation of these women destroyed their ability to have children or normal families. The bitterness created by Japan's military policies, and the refusal of the Japanese government to provide compensation, still obstructs friendly relations between Japan and other Asian countries.

In Pacific battlegrounds, Japan's harsh warrior code cost the Japanese heavily. Japanese leaders encouraged resistance to the last man in the mistaken belief that a demonstration of total commitment would intimidate and terrorize the US enemy. In Pacific conflicts such as Tarawa, Iwo Jima, and Saipan, hopelessly outnumbered Japanese troops died in human wave charges or followed their commanders in committing suicide for their emperor, yelling "banzai" (ten thousand years) in his honor. Of the approximately 5,000 Japanese troops on Tarawa in the Gilbert Islands, only one officer and sixteen enlisted men survived. By fighting and dying almost to the last man, Japanese troops actually made the US conquest easier, removing the onerous burden of provisioning, guarding, and transporting large numbers of prisoners of war. Such fierce resistance encouraged the strategy of "island hopping": avoiding the most well-defended Japanese islands and concentrating on strategically valuable ones, ultimately leaving the most powerful and best fortified positions to "rot on the vine" far from Japanese supply lines.

Atrocities, Technology, and Vengeance

On every continent World War II continued the trend toward lowering of standards of human behavior begun by World War I. It inured many civilians and military men to the idea of mass murder, torture, and brutal treatment on a colossal scale.

Japan had already outraged the world with its massacres of Chinese. Atrocities against Americans led to full-blooded calls for vengeance. The surprise attack on Pearl Harbor and the notorious "Bataan Death March" of captured American and Filipino prisoners triggered old images of the "Yellow Peril" in American minds. US wartime propaganda was at least as racist as the Japanese. Much war propaganda presented all Japanese as a people with little regard for human life and as automaton followers of their leaders.

Toward the end of 1944, as US forces approached ever nearer to the Japanese home islands, the Japanese employed **kamikaze** tactics, recruiting suicide bombers to crash planes filled with explosives into US ships. This new tactic took a heavy toll of US ships, but it started too late in the war to have any effect on its outcome. Fierce resistance encouraged fierce attacks. At times American military men suggested that some strange quirk of the Asian mind encouraged recruitment. But as Box 13.3 shows, the motivation of many kamikazes was not that different from American volunteers for dangerous assignments. Moreover, when given positions, such as human torpedoes, where they could change their minds, many did. General Curtis Le May, who played an active role in the firebombing of Dresden, devised a new strategy of mass destruction in accord with the doctrine of "strategic bombing," attacking not military targets but civilian morale, with a new ferocity. Jellied napalm – a fiery substance that adheres to surfaces on contact – was first used in Japan. The bombing of Tokyo on March 10, 1945, was deliberately designed to create a fire storm to incinerate its wooden houses. At least 125,000 inhabitants of Tokyo were killed, 40 percent of the city destroyed, and a million people left homeless. Tokyo was only the first of a series of firebombing attacks on Japanese cities that paved the road toward Hiroshima.

The Japanese suicidal defense of Okinawa between April and June of 1945 led military men to argue that the large casualties of a land invasion must be avoided by the use of nuclear weapons. By mid-1945, Japan was prostrate, militarily and psychologically. Its leaders, unable to break from total loyalty to what they saw as the emperor's will, refused to surrender unless the position of the emperor was guaranteed, but the only terms the USA would accept were total surrender. The bomb dropped on Hiroshima on August 6, 1945, killed 80,000 people almost instantaneously. The bomb dropped on Nagasaki killed 40,000 more. (See Box 13.4.) These

Box 13.3 Japan's Human Torpedoes

Yokota Yutaka, 16 years old at the time of the Pearl Harbor attack, volunteered to serve in the Japanese navy as a human pilot of a torpedo, responding to an appeal from his middle school commander: "Your Motherland faces imminent peril. Consider how much your Motherland needs you. Now, a weapon which will destroy the enemy has been born. If there be any among you who burn with a passion to die gloriously for the sake of their country, let them step forward."

There's an old expression, "Bushido is the search for a place to die." Well, that was our fervent desire, our long-cherished dream. A place to die for my country. I was happy to have been born a man. A man of Japan.

When he was not able to carry out his suicide mission, because the fuel line on his torpedo failed, he cried bitter tears of disappointment: He believed after the war that the torpedoes had sunk many American ships.

Kozu Naoji, another torpedo pilot, had a different point of view:

It was horrible to contemplate death in a torpedo. Many young men charged into the enemy and died during the war ... If everything went well for them, and the battleship that was their target was close, looming in front of them, at least they could count the seconds to impact: "Three, two, one ..." Then, as long as they kept their eyes open, they'd know the moment of their deaths!

But the torpedo wasn't like that. You're underwater. You can't look out. You've already determined your course, peering through the periscope. You submerge. You run full speed at the estimated enemy position. From the moment you commence your attack, you see nothing ... You keep thinking , "Now. Now. Now!" But you never know when that moment will come. "Time's elapsed," you realize. You missed the target. You come to the surface. You search again for the enemy. You realize you passed astern ... In reality, hardly one ever hit an enemy ship ... The verification of all American ships lost during the war has long been completed. According to their records, torpedoes claimed just three ships sunk or heavily damaged.

I didn't see myself throwing my life away for the Emperor, nor for the government either, nor for the nation. I saw myself dying to defend my parents, my brothers and sisters. For them I must die, I thought.

Box 13.4 Noiseless Flash: The Discovery of a New Disease

In 1946 journalist John Hersey published his famous account of Hiroshima in *The New Yorker*, describing radiation sickness:

At exactly fifteen minutes past eight in the morning, on August 6, 1945 ... the atomic bomb ... flashed above Hiroshima ... the unprecedented disease ... had three stages ... The first stage had been all over before the doctors even knew they were dealing with a new sickness ... It killed ninety-five percent of the people within a half mile of the centre, and many thousands who were farther away ...

The second stage set in ten or fifteen days after bombing. The main symptom was falling hair. Diarrhoea and fever, which in some cases went as high as 106, came next. Twenty-five to thirty days after the explosion, blood disorders appeared ... If the fever remained steady and high the patient's chances for survival were poor. The third stage was the reaction that came when the body struggled to compensate for its ills. In this stage many patients died of complications such as infections of the chest cavity.

terrible bombs, combined with the USSR's declaration of war, finally ended Japanese resistance (see Figure 13.7).

After the war, in the wake of the enormous world outcry produced by the discovery of the Nazi death camps, the victorious Allies held trials to provide a legal framework for defining and punishing war crimes. Of particular importance in formulating a legal basis for punishing these mass murders were the Nuremberg trials.

The **Nuremberg trials**, held from November 20, 1945 to October 1, 1946, indicted twenty-one individuals and the central

Figure 13.7 On August 6, 1945, the US Air Force dropped the first atomic bomb on the city of Hiroshima, followed three days later by a bomb on Nagasaki. So far these remain the only uses of atomic weapons in warfare. In Hiroshima, within two to four months, somewhere between 90,000 and 166,000 died of the bomb's effects, roughly half on the first day. The timing of the bombing was unfortunate. The USSR declared war on Japan on August 8 and the combined hostility of the USA and the USSR convinced Japanese political leaders that their cause was hopelessly lost; they had already decided upon surrender.

Nazi institutions – the Gestapo, the Nazi Party, the SS, Cabinet, and General Staff – for crimes against peace, war crimes, and crimes against humanity (see Figure 13.8). Eleven of Germany's highest rulers were condemned to death, eight imprisoned, and two acquitted; lesser courts continued to search for and punish war criminals, although the search became less scrupulous as the Cold War intensified. The Tokyo trials were much less convincing, as the Japanese leaders to a man concealed their activities in order to spare the emperor. Few missed the irony: If the emperor himself was innocent, as the American Occupation authorities claimed, how could any one else be convicted? Nevertheless, twenty-five major leaders were indicted, and seven condemned to death; 900 other Japanese were executed for mistreating prisoners of war.

After World War II, as after World War I, there were those who hoped that some good could come from so much evil. In 1948, the UN Universal Declaration of Human Rights, for which Eleanor Roosevelt lobbied heavily, announced a list of ideals to which all nations of the world could subscribe, including freedom of speech, rights of political activity, and economic and social welfare. The UN Commission on Human Rights would publicize and enforce them. Even though nearly all nations endorsed these principles, putting them into practice has been difficult, and interpretations of the principles vary a great deal.

Figure 13.8 The Nuremberg trials, 1946. The trials included the first prosecutions for "crimes against humanity": a new legal and moral code?

13.8 TOTTERING COLONIALISM

In Asia, the USA and the Japanese fought over the remnants of the great Western colonial empires: the Philippines, French Indochina, the Dutch East Indies, and British India, Burma, and Malaya. In Asia and the Middle East, whether colonies were conquered by the Axis powers or remained in the possession of Allied colonial administration, the anti-colonial cause advanced (see Map 13.3).

India's Road to Independence

Views of Winston Churchill (1874–1965) in the USA and India illustrate how different the war looked from a Western democratic perspective and an Asian anti-colonial perspective. After Pearl Harbor, Americans admired Churchill – son of an aristocratic, politically engaged father and an American mother – as a gritty conservative who had united his nation. He had vigorously opposed German aggression while many British and European conservatives apologized for Hitler. In May 1940, speaking to the House of Commons for the first time as prime minister, Churchill proudly confessed: "I have nothing to offer but blood, toil, tears and sweat." From the doorman to the duchess, his eloquence rallied Britons.

To Indians, Churchill looked very different. Serving as both officer and journalist on the Indian Northwest Frontier in 1896–97, he picked up a romantic conception of the British

imperial role. In the early 1930s, Churchill led a ferocious campaign against parliamentary efforts to grant limited autonomy to India, publicly scoffing at Indians' capability for self-rule. When the British viceroy met with Gandhi in 1931, Churchill expressed his scorn that any British official would meet with a "half-naked fakir." A fakir was a Hindu ascetic who lived by begging; at times Gandhi had dressed as a fakir. In November 1942, Churchill famously declared: "I have not become the King's First Minister in order to preside over the liquidation of the British Empire." Nevertheless, he knew that Britain needed Indian soldiers to combat Germans in the Middle East, to fight in Southeast Asia, and to ward off the immediate Japanese threat to India from nearby Burma.

Mohandas Gandhi (1869–1948) stood at the center of the struggle for Indian independence in both the interwar and postwar periods. Although capable of strange imaginative flights, Gandhi knew how to appeal to two very disparate audiences: British liberal politicians and a mass Indian public. Educated as a lawyer in London and politically active in South Africa, Gandhi knew the British elite well. Schooled in Indian religious philosophy, Gandhi likewise spoke a religious language that many Indians, especially Hindus, could understand. He excelled in finding issues that could appeal to the Indian masses. His 1930 campaign against the salt tax demonstrated his tactical ability. The salt tax, a small levy, irritated all Indians, so it provided a common issue. By leading a march to the sea to obtain untaxed salt, defying British law with civil disobedience,

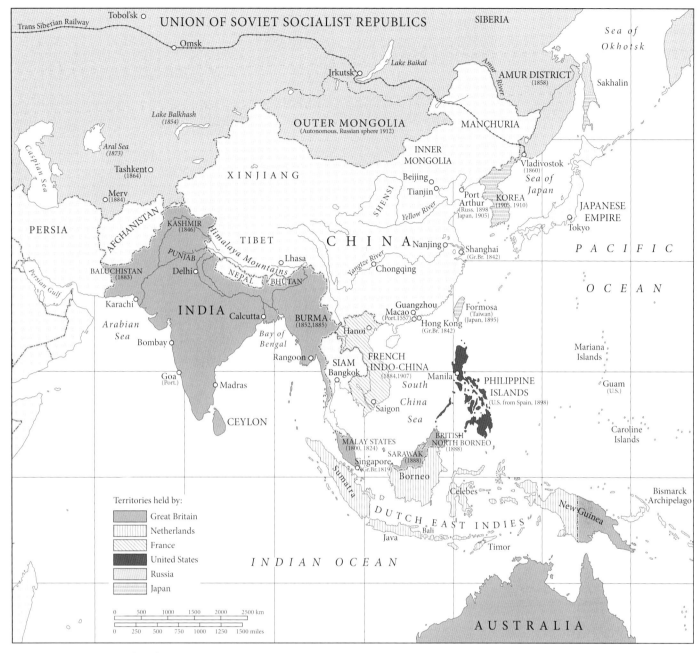

Map 13.3 East Asian colonial territories, 1840–1940

Gandhi made headlines all over the world. He countered nationalists who endorsed violence with a deeply felt commitment to pacifism. He worked effectively with the meticulous Congress Party leader, Jawaharlal Nehru (1889–1964; see Figure 13.9). Neither man, however, had great familiarity with Muslim leaders or their constituencies. Although the Congress Party claimed a secular nationalist ideology that included all religious and ethnic groups equally, the Hindu majority membership threatened the Muslims' influence. The British, by favoring certain Muslim groups in the colonial period, in order to balance the local power of the Hindu majority, had exacerbated communal tensions between the two religious groups. These tensions boded

ill for future Muslim–Hindu relations. Mohammad Ali Jinnah, Gandhi's contemporary and leader of the Muslim League, could not accept Congress Party claims to represent all Indians. By 1938, the League and the Congress Party had agreed to go their separate ways.

Given no notice of Britain's initial declaration of war, Gandhi and the Congress Party were deeply suspicious of British intentions. Churchill's assumption of leadership hardly inspired Indian trust, even though most of Churchill's cabinet members were drawn from a Labour Party that supported Indian independence. The dramatic Allied military defeats early in the war made British concessions to Indian nationalists appear

Figure 13.9 Jawaharlal Nehru (1889–1964) and Mohandas K. Gandhi (1869–1948), the unlikely pair that led the fight for Indian independence. Indian freedom was won by Gandhi's popular appeal, Nehru's negotiating skills, and the strategic vision they shared.

desperate, not magnanimous. The defeat of British troops in Burma by smaller Japanese forces in 1942 shook British prestige. Gandhi described British concessions as a "post-dated check on a failing bank." A leading Labour leader, Sir Stafford Cripps, went to India to rally Congress support with promises of immediate postwar independence, but suspicion and memories of disappointed expectations after World War I dogged his mission.

Unfortunately, Cripps was not able to guarantee a united India that would include all Muslims as well as the princely states that had been incorporated into British India. While Indian nationalists were committed to a united India, the Muslim League demanded a separate state, to be called Pakistan. In wartime India, faced with nationalist opposition, British leaders were concerned that a strong stand against an independent Muslim state might encourage Muslim disaffection. At the same time, British failure to scotch the idea of a separate state only encouraged Muslim aspirations.

Unlike the situation during the First World War, both Gandhi and the Congress Party were not prepared to postpone demands

for independence to support the war effort. In fact, many thought that independence could be forced from an empire in crisis. The Congress Party, supported by Gandhi, began to prepare for the "Quit India" campaign of massive civil disobedience. One prominent Congress Party leader, Subhas Chandra Bose, did in fact join with the Japanese and even worked to create an Indian military contingent fighting with the Japanese (INA). But the Japanese did not prove particularly responsive to Bose and Indian political leaders avoided any commitment to the Japanese. The colonial government responded vigorously to this challenge. Relying on a policy of repression and concession – imprisoning major leaders of the Congress Party and Gandhi as well as promising postwar independence – the British authorities managed to keep India in the war. The Indian army itself and the Indian police force remained loyal to British rule, yet many of the young men recruited to the army during the war took seriously British pledges of postwar independence.

Keeping India in the war, however, brought mass famine to Bengal in 1943. This famine was not a simple product of bad harvests or low yields. Its origins were political. By occupying Burma, the Japanese closed off a rice trade that had long supplied Bengal, while the area's grain reserves supplied troops preparing for the British offensive in Burma. Farmers had taken loans before the harvest, committing their crops to moneylenders. When the harvest declined, they could not pay off their loans and feed themselves. They died in the millions because they lacked resources to acquire their own food. Focused on the war effort, the British did nothing to help them. They even confiscated boats that could import grain, fearing their use by Japanese invaders. Helpless peasants could not rebel against British rule, but Indian leaders lost all faith in colonial benevolence.

With the end of the war in Asia, India confidently expected independence. Loyal sailors staged mutinies demanding it. The triumph of the Labour Party in the 1945 elections ousted the imperialist Churchill, giving Britain a leadership more sympathetic to independence. Britain's close ally and vital financial backer, the USA, also urged Britain to decolonize. Pressured from all sides, British officials decided to concede independence as soon as possible, but they had no solution to the Muslim–Hindu divide. Hasty negotiations based on the limited suffrage of the 1946 elections provided a very inadequate basis for dividing India and Pakistan. The vacillations of the Hindu maharaja ruling Kashmir, a majority Muslim region on the border between the two states, would leave a bitter bone of territorial contention between the two nations. But growing communal violence made the separation of India and Pakistan inevitable. In 1948, shortly after independence, the last hopes of a unified India collapsed with the assassination of Gandhi by a Hindu nationalist fanatic. In the partition, at least 10 million people were forced to migrate, to leave India to settle in Pakistan or vice versa, while over a million were killed in communal violence.

Southeast Asia

By breaking the aura of invincibility that had gradually accumulated around Europeans over the preceding century, Japan's sudden attacks dealt a serious blow to colonialism. The Japanese often inflicted brutal treatment on Europeans to break their complacent aura of superiority, but they discredited themselves as colonial liberators by treating native Asian peoples with equal brutality.

Modern Indonesia grew out of the Dutch East Indies after Japanese occupation in 1941. In the 1920s, young nationalists like Achmed Sukarno (1901–1970) founded the Indonesian Nationalist Party (PNI) to unite millions of people scattered across thousands of islands into a single nation. The Dutch suppressed the movement, exiling its leaders to remote outer islands, but the idea survived. The Japanese sought to mobilize the Indonesian population, particularly the Javanese, by organizing mass associations for indoctrination in the principles of the Co-Prosperity Sphere, and by training militia for its defense. The Japanese particularly appealed for support to secular nationalist and Muslim elites. Sukarno willingly recruited Indonesians for the Japanese war effort. His goal was to build popular associations that for the first time linked all the islands together.

Using these organizations, the charismatic Sukarno made himself a natural leader of a multilingual state still searching to establish a national identity. Java, Bali, Sumatra, Borneo, Aceh, Timor, and the Spice Islands had never been under a single administration until the arrival of the Dutch. Unlike mainland Asia, they had no large empires as models of national unity, nor a common language. Sukarno, fluent in Javanese, Sundanese, and Balinese, had also learned Arabic from his reading of the Koran. Educated in Dutch, he studied English, French, German, and later Japanese. His multilingual, multicultural abilities served as the unifying force for Indonesia, entirely centered on his own personality. Sukarno also played an important role in creating and promoting the modern Indonesian language, derived from the trading language used by Malays and other seafaring peoples among the islands.

Little fighting occurred in the Dutch East Indies during the war. When Japanese rule suddenly collapsed in August 1945, Indonesian nationalists quickly stepped in to declare independence. British troops attempted to support the return of the Dutch regime but backed down before a powerful wave of nationalist protest. The "youth" movement that swept Indonesia toward the end of 1945 marked the death knell of the old colonial state. Suddenly the Indonesian nationalists had acquired a mass base, which they never had under Dutch rule. It still took another four years before the Dutch finally conceded independence. Unlike India or China, Indonesia achieved independence without major civil wars or hostile divisions. It was a new nation forged out of thousands of small pieces around a single charismatic leader; ethnic, political, and religious conflicts would come later.

13.9 DIVIDED NATIONS: CIVIL WAR FOLLOWS ON WORLD WAR

With the surrender of Germany in May 1945 and Japan's surrender in September 1945, the victorious Allied coalition prepared to divide up the postwar world. The Axis powers were totally defeated. Hitler committed suicide in his bunker; Mussolini was removed from national power in 1943 and executed by partisans in 1945; the Japanese emperor, Hirohito, survived in place, but several top officers committed suicide as US forces occupied the Japanese islands. The unlikely coalition of the USA, Britain, and the Soviet Union quickly broke apart because it could not resolve these major issues:

- The relationship between the communist and liberal democratic blocs after the liberation of Europe.
- The future of decolonized nations.
- The reintegration of the world economy.

The Atlantic Charter tried to present a new liberal democratic program. Issued by Roosevelt and Churchill in 1941, it announced the liberal democracies' aims. They endorsed self-determination of nations, equal economic opportunity, free access to raw materials, disarmament of aggressors, and fair labor standards. Their declaration conspicuously ignored the Soviet Union's role in the postwar peace. The Yalta Conference in February 1945 did bring together Stalin, Roosevelt, and Churchill to plan the postwar occupation of Germany. Yalta, however, excluded Chiang Kai-shek, whose government looked increasingly ineffective, and said nothing about the future of Poland. With Soviet armies closing in on Berlin and moving into Eastern Europe, Stalin set up a puppet government in Poland against strong protest from Roosevelt and Churchill. They had to agree, since at that time they counted on Soviet entry into the Pacific war. Figure 13.10 shows a picture of Churchill, Roosevelt, and Stalin at Yalta. Roosevelt looks wan and aged – symptoms of the stroke that would kill him in a few months.

Yalta implicitly recognized a Soviet sphere of influence determined by military front lines, but Roosevelt still hoped for co-operation from Stalin after the end of the war. He expected to tame the communist threat by including the Soviet Union in a new international organization, the United Nations. Unlike the ineffective League of Nations, the United Nations had a Security Council of the major Allied powers – Britain, France, the USA, the Soviet Union, and China – and gave veto power to the Big Three – the USA, Britain, and the Soviet Union.

Several months later, relations with the Soviets changed sharply for the worse. Roosevelt's death in April left his vice president, Harry Truman, responsible for the most fateful decision of the war: the decision to drop two atomic bombs on Japan. Successful detonation of a nuclear weapon on July 16, 1945, in the New Mexico desert gave Truman the opportunity to end the war in the Pacific without Soviet participation and without large expected losses from an American invasion of the Japanese islands. The sudden surrender of Japan removed the need to yield to Soviet demands. Meanwhile, Stalin had secured his buffer zone in Eastern Europe by installing communists or their sympathizers in power in Soviet-occupied areas. Hope of co-operation dimmed.

The Partition of Germany

At Yalta, Stalin, Roosevelt, and Churchill agreed to a temporary division of Germany into four zones, under British, American, French, and Soviet administration, but they could not agree on

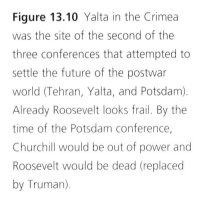

Figure 13.10 Yalta in the Crimea was the site of the second of the three conferences that attempted to settle the future of the postwar world (Tehran, Yalta, and Potsdam). Already Roosevelt looks frail. By the time of the Potsdam conference, Churchill would be out of power and Roosevelt would be dead (replaced by Truman).

Germany's ultimate future. The aims of the allied powers quickly diverged. Determined to resist Russian expansion, the USA decided to rebuild western Germany's productive capacity, while the Soviets dismantled the eastern zone's industries for their own uses. Stalin expected to collect half of the 20 billion dollar reparations bill from the whole of Germany, but Truman cut the Soviet share back to only what was left in the Soviet zone. As the US, British, and French consolidated their zones, with a separate currency, the Soviets created their own separate administration. The Soviets blockaded divided Berlin (1948–49) to prevent the incorporation of its western zones, but a massive Allied airlift defeated this effort. Two separate states, the Federal Republic of Germany in the west, and the German Democratic Republic in the east, emerged by 1949, and Berlin, deep within the eastern zone, remained a divided city.

China's Civil War, 1945–49

Japan's sudden surrender led both Nationalists and communists to quickly move out from their isolated bases to seize the wealthy eastern half of the country. On paper, Chiang seemed to have all the cards. Chiang still had a huge army of 2.7 million men, equipped with modern American tanks and planes. Mao had about 1 million peasant soldiers mainly armed with guns and trucks. They first fought over Manchuria, the heavy industrial heartland built by the Japanese. The USA sent marines into Manchuria to accept the Japanese surrender and flew in Chiang's soldiers to occupy the province. Even Stalin threw his support to Chiang and backed his regime in exchange for concessions. Soviet troops plundered much of Manchuria's industry, but left large stockpiles of weaponry for the communists. Lin Biao, however, moved his Eighth Route Army more quickly than Chiang's and with much greater co-ordination. From his base in Harbin, Mao gained resources from administering a major industrial city. He also sent teams of cadres into the countryside to carry out radical land reform, confiscating all holdings of the Japanese and their collaborators. In 1944, throughout North China, behind Japanese lines communists had begun to reallocate land by holding mass meetings of peasants to attack the landlords who had not been able to flee. Probably a million landlords lost their lives in this phase, but peasants who had held no land at all gained a new livelihood, thanks to the Communist Party. Mao, by creating a more equal rural society, now had enthusiastic recruits for his military campaign.

Chiang, unfortunately, had learned nothing from the war with Japan. He dispersed his troops to garrison the great cities of North and coastal China, leaving the countryside to the communists. He carried out no land reform, and continued to rely on former warlords, collaborators, and the discredited local elites.

Soon, the communists deployed the same guerrilla tactics against the Nationalists that they had used against the Japanese, this time with even greater success. Lin Biao then announced a shift from guerrilla warfare to open confrontation with Nationalist forces. US efforts to mediate a peaceful coalition government ended in failure. By the end of 1947, Lin Biao's troops in Manchuria had broken the strength of Nationalist garrisons infected with "apathy, resentment, and defeatism." In 1948 communists held nearly all of the North China countryside, took Manchuria's major cities, and gained a major victory at Xuzhou, a key railroad junction 200 miles from Nanjing, in a 65-day battle with over half a million troops on both sides. They took Tianjin in January 1949; Beijing surrendered on January 31. Central China fell quickly in the next three months, as Chiang retreated to Taiwan. On October 1, 1949, in Beijing, in front of the great Qing imperial palace gates, Mao announced the founding of the People's Republic of China. Chiang's government maintained its rule over Taiwan as the successor to Sun Yat-sen's Republic of China, still claiming to be the only legitimate government of China as a whole.

Korea and Vietnam

Rival nationalist and communist currents also swept over Korea and Indochina, producing hostile, divided nations even more unstable than those in Germany, South Asia, and China. The Japanese and the French had suppressed nationalist movements in these two smaller states for so long that they burst out with intense force when the colonial rulers were gone.

The Allies had agreed that Japan must abandon its conquests on the Asian continent, but left the terms for its withdrawal extremely vague. Who would accept the surrender of Japanese troops, and who would establish the first local administration? In Manchuria, Nationalists, the Communist Party, Soviets, and Americans all played confusing roles. The USA and USSR tried to make Korea's position clearer. An agreement, hastily negotiated in the very last days of the war, entrusted the USSR with accepting Japanese surrender above the 38th parallel of the Korean peninsula, the USA below that parallel. Initially, the USA attached little importance to the portion of Korea it governed, leaving the hated Japanese to enforce order. For a brief period in 1945, Koreans themselves took charge. Popular committees led by nationalists of many political inclinations replaced Japanese power all over the peninsula. Soon, both superpowers installed their own leaders regardless of Korean opinion.

Kim Il-sung versus Syngman Rhee The Soviets chose Kim Il-sung, known as a nationalist guerrilla fighter who had conducted several small campaigns against the Japanese in

Manchuria. Soviet backing gave him the ability to oust his rivals in the Soviet zone in return for professing loyalty to Stalin. Kim Il-sung fully endorsed the communist ideology of Stalin and Mao, but he remained a staunch nationalist, determined to reunite Korea on his terms soon. The USA picked Syngman Rhee, an American-educated politician who had spent the war in Washington, DC. Few in Korea knew him. Under US sponsorship, he established a dictatorship in South Korea based on exiles and Japanese collaborators. He, too, fully intended to reunite Korea, with US backing, in the near future. By 1948, the USA ended its occupation of Korea, leaving the two hostile nationalist leaders to confront each other.

Ho Chi Minh In Indochina, Japan's invasion of French colonial territory allowed a revolutionary nationalist movement to gain victory. Under French rule, a series of nationalist movements had organized briefly and been quickly suppressed. Vietnam thus differed from Burma and Indonesia, where the Japanese had supported local nationalists against colonial rule and helped them to create resistance armies. Vietnamese nationalist organizations and leaders could only survive outside Indochina, in places like China, Japan, Thailand, or France. This favored communist revolutionaries who could take advantage of international contacts. Ho Chi Minh founded his Revolutionary Youth League in Canton in 1925 to prepare the way for the Indochinese Communist Party in 1930. He followed Comintern instructions, but he also watched the Chinese communists closely. He created his own soviet, the Nghe Tinh Soviet, in 1931 in a remote border area, but it lasted less than a year. Ho was sent to prison in Hong Kong for two years. Like Mao, at almost the same time, Ho realized that Vietnam's revolutionary potential lay mainly in the countryside. Unlike Mao, Ho had no rival Nationalist Party to contend with; the VNQDD, the equivalent of China's Guomindang, had also been crushed by the French.

As in China, the Japanese gave Ho the breathing space to expand his movement to become the dominant nationalist movement of Indochina. They took over the colony after the fall of France in 1940. As French troops fled, the Vietnamese began their anti-colonial struggle with attacks on remaining French garrisons. They formed the Viet Minh in 1941 to co-ordinate all groups, both popular and elites, in anti-colonial resistance. As it became clear that Japanese rule would not lead to Vietnam's independence, but only another military occupation, the Viet Minh turned against Japanese forces. General Vo Nguyen Giap, who had been to Yan'an, created the military forces that defended the Viet Minh base area near the Chinese border. In 1944–45, partly because of Japanese reprisals, a major famine struck the north, in which nearly 2 million people died. Ho and the Viet Minh gained great credit by using their guerrilla forces to deliver relief to starving peasants.

After the liberation of Paris in 1944, Japanese forces drove out the remnants of French administration, attempting to create another puppet regime like Manchukuo under the old emperor, Bao Dai. But with Japan's surrender, the puppet regime collapsed, and Ho Chi Minh declared a provisional government in the north. Ho had made himself the undisputed leader of Vietnam's anti-colonial mass movement, but France refused to give up its colonies. With reluctant American support, they sent troops back to recapture Indochina.

Although determined to maintain their independence, the Vietnamese showed considerable flexibility in confronting the problems of postwar Indochina. For a while, a large Chinese Nationalist army stumbled through the country, which the Vietnamese had to avoid confronting directly. Many other social groups, including Buddhists and Catholics, saw the Viet Minh as a nationalist umbrella that could accommodate their interests. The Viet Minh even suggested their willingness to accept some form of autonomy within a French federation, but the French refused. Soon a full-fledged war against the French developed, that would end only with French defeat in 1954.

In summary, where national divisions coincided with Cold War divisions, as in Korea, Germany, Vietnam, and China, postwar political settlements were especially explosive, but the atrocities following the partition of India indicate that religious antagonism could just as easily drive men to murder each other.

13.10 ECONOMIES AND SOCIETIES DURING THE WAR AND AFTER

World War II, even more than World War I, demanded total mobilization of its populations. Everywhere, a great deal of economic production had to be diverted to service giant war machines, and civilians bore the heavy burden of war production. The war greatly transformed the relationship between states, societies, and economies in three ways:

- It expanded the role of government in the economy, in liberal, fascist, and communist countries alike.
- It created new jobs and social roles for women, as active producers beyond the household.
- It fostered new forms of co-operation between governments, universities, and businesses that created new technologies for military and civilian use.

Many of these social changes endured beyond the war to shape the era of postwar boom.

Mobilizing Resources for War

Despite their exaltation of state power, fascist and communist countries trailed the liberal democratic UK in mobilizing resources for war. Between 1941 and 1945, of all the major wartime powers the UK easily mobilized the largest percentage of its gross national product for war expenditures. After Britain came the USSR; the Soviet accomplishment is most remarkable, however, because the Soviet standard of living was so much lower than that of the UK. The Soviet prison camps were not very productive and war expenditures put many Soviet citizens on the brink of starvation. Neither Germany nor Japan was as successful in extracting resources from its native population although both, and particularly Germany, relied heavily on conscript and forced labor for industrial production. Partly as a result of the ongoing war in China, the Japanese standard of living was already low in 1941 and the pressure produced by wartime expenditures cut even further into living standards. Until almost the very end of the war, the USA was behind both the UK and the USSR in proportion of GNP, but the US GNP was so much greater than any other nation's that US war expenditures exceeded those of the other combatants.

Although fascists and communists praised economic planning, here too the liberal democracies, the UK and the USA, were more successful. The USA had been the state most hostile to economic planning, but Roosevelt brought about a radical change. He established the War Production Board in 1942 to direct civilian production toward war needs. By 1943 war production was 40 percent of the GNP. This meant, for example, shutting down civilian automobile production and using its resources (steel, rubber, glass, etc.) for the military. A key limitation on the Allies' production was the loss of raw materials from their colonies, especially rubber, nearly all of which came from Southeast Asia. This desperate need inspired the mobilization of scientists to serve the war effort by developing synthetic rubber. By 1944, the USA could supply 90 percent of its rubber synthetically. US plants, building on their experience with mass production, turned out huge numbers of tanks, planes, ships, and artillery shells, far beyond what any other country could produce.

Women at Home and at Work

The large military demand, however, threatened to drive up prices and create scarcities of civilian goods. Federal taxes increased sharply to restrict consumer demand, and sales of war bonds soaked up savings, but price freezes and ration coupons were also necessary. Wages rose with inflation, but labor unions were not allowed to strike. The Office of Price Administration recruited local women's groups to police shopkeepers to make sure that they followed price guidelines and did not cheat consumers. These women sent in piles of bread wrappers to Washington to expose merchants who shortchanged consumers. They became political activists not just as voters but also as consumers.

The war brought new roles for women everywhere. The UK, the USSR, and the USA relied heavily on women workers. Many of them obtained relatively high-paying jobs for the first time in their lives, since they had to fill the slots left empty by young men at the front. They earned new respect for their skills in what had been exclusively male occupations. "Rosie the Riveter" in the USA symbolized the new image of women as tough industrial workers. Stalin also put women to work, as communist ideology promoted the equality of men and women in the labor force. The guerrilla war in China depended heavily on women shouldering an equal burden with men; even in the Nationalist areas, women took up jobs as clerks and textile factory workers that took them out of confined households. Governments determined to mobilize their entire population behind the war effort had to include men and women alike.

Yet wartime ideologies contained contradictions too. Fascists in Germany and Japan had insisted that a woman's primary role was in the home; they rejected the unsettling freedom of women from the household that the 1920s had brought. Still, as German and Japanese wartime fortunes declined and their sources of forced labor diminished, both nations began to encourage female employment. A million Japanese women had to work by government order, but they also had to be "the warm fountainhead which protects the household, assumes responsibility for rearing children, and . . . supports the front lines." In important ways the ability of the great powers to mobilize their resources was constrained by choices made in the early days of the war. For example, Nazi Germany desperately needed to conscript female labor after 1938, but this policy contradicted Nazi ideological principles on marriage and motherhood that aimed to remove women from the workforce and increase the birth rate. The Germans relied on the Nazi Party to build a network of local volunteers who would attempt to enforce local safety regulations and provide educational services for civilians. In contrast, Japan incorporated preexisting local organizations in constructing its neighborhood associations. The close long-standing ties of neighbors in Japan made it more difficult to uncover slacking or eligible women workers than the system based on party loyalism in Germany. In fact, relatively fewer women went to work in Japan than in Germany, the USA, Britain, or the Soviet Union, despite severe labor shortages. The ideology of keeping women at home undermined the needs of the war.

The War and Racism in the USA

The war not only exposed racism among the colonial powers but it also exposed US racism; in a war widely regarded as a struggle between Western democracy and Nazi racism, US wartime treatment of African Americans and Japanese Americans was shameful. Although they fought loyally for their country, African Americans who were drafted or volunteered were outraged by the segregation prevalent in the US army. In 1940 on the eve of the war the army had just five African American officers, three of them chaplains. In 1942 African American leader A. Philip Randolph, outraged by US failures to treat black soldiers equally, threatened protests. Although his protests did not succeed in integrating the army, they produced real benefits, principally the incorporation of African Americans into the war industries on an equal footing. This provided much higher wage-earning opportunities in expanding US war industries in the northern USA than most African Americans were able to earn elsewhere. Massive riots in summer of 1943 in Detroit, a city producing for the war effort, indicated that many Americans, even in the more liberal north, were not yet willing to accept racial equality.

Unfortunately there was no silver lining to the treatment of Japanese Americans. Panicked by unfounded accusations of collaboration, the USA interned west coast Japanese American citizens in camps. While many young Japanese Americans volunteered to serve in Europe and fought there with great bravery, even the US Supreme Court upheld internment policies.

Amid the Rubble

In all of the major combatant nations, save the USA, ordinary civilians were exposed to war as they generally had not been in World War I. London had been bombed during World War I but the air war that occurred in 1940 was on an altogether different scale. In November of 1942 the long-range bombers began to take a toll on German cities and in November 1943 on Japanese cities. Under the bombs, living conditions in urban areas became increasingly trying for those who survived, especially in industrial cities, which were the targets of repeated bombings. In Germany and Japan, as in England, efforts were made to disperse children into the countryside – efforts that were generally unsuccessful either because rural people were unused to urban youngsters or because urban children felt most comfortable in their old neighborhoods even when the environment had grown deadly. Everywhere many youngsters returned home when they could. Their elders were not that much different. Despite the incredible pounding in British, German, and Japanese cities, surviving workers, often women workers, continued to climb out from the ruins and find their way to work in factories that were often largely in shambles (see Box 13.5). These "rubble women" put their homes and workplaces back together brick by brick. In Berlin and Tokyo, as in London and Stalingrad, the human capacity for routine and survival defeated all efforts at strategic bombing designed to destroy civilian morale.

Box 13.5 Cities Under Bombardment: Capitals in Wartime

World War II drew civilians into war more deeply than any previous war, because of technological advance and moral regression. Air power, now fully developed as a military weapon, allowed every country's bombers to devastate its enemy population. Over the course of the war, the line between civilian and military targets eroded into nothing. The key target for bombing was the morale of industrial workers, not the factories themselves. Except for the USA and France, all the capital cities of the major belligerents suffered from bombardment and siege. Paris was spared because France surrendered quickly; London endured the Blitz for a few months in 1940, but was saved by the Royal Air Force. Leningrad was under siege for nearly three years, as millions starved. US and British air forces began firebombing German cities in 1942. They created a successful firestorm over Hamburg in July 1943, destroying 80 percent of its buildings and killing 30,000 inhabitants. By the end of the war, every major German city was in ruins. Yet for the most part, strategic bombing failed to break civilian morale. German workers kept up industrial production stubbornly throughout the bombing.

Chiang Kai-shek and Mao reached relative safety from bombing only by withdrawing deep into the Chinese interior, but the millions of Chinese left under Japanese occupation suffered executions, lootings, rapes, and reprisals. When US bombers could reach the Japanese islands, they deliberately targeted the wooden cities with firebombing, so as to inflict the maximum number of casualties. They only spared the historic city of Kyoto, the emperor's ancient home, because they thought wanton destruction of Japan's cultural heart would inspire even more desperate resistance. All sides ruined more of human culture than ever before in history, because of a fatal conjuncture of technology and ideologies of unlimited mass destruction as a legitimate tool of warfare.

Amid the ruins, states managed to husband resources and keep war production going. The fascist countries claimed to be creating a new economic order, requiring strong state control of the economy, but without the class struggle fostered by socialism. Japanese economic bureaucrats created Control Associations that brought together heads of the major *zaibatsu* (financial combines) with bureaucrats to allocate raw materials and set prices. They rejected free markets, promoting an ideology of harmony based on Japan's unique "national polity," or **kokutai**. In this vision, the Japanese people's hearts throbbed with a single beat in the service of the divine emperor, to defend the empire abroad and social order at home. The Japanese, in their own minds, had a unique historical mission because of their unbroken imperial line. In fact, Japan's new economic order was not very different from other fascist plans, and much of its implementation did not look too different from Roosevelt's New Deal. The demands of wartime mobilization forced radically different political systems to converge with each other.

Chiang Kai-shek's Nationalist government also endorsed industrial planning. Although he had lost the key industrial bases of China – the heavy industry of Manchuria and the light industry of Shanghai – Chiang's economic ministries drew up plans to replace their losses by allocating scarce materials to designated plants in the interior. Mussolini's ideology of rapid modernization and regeneration of national spirit through military mobilization appealed to many in Chiang's regime too. In some ways, Chiang's Nationalists resembled the European fascists, but the Chinese and Japanese authoritarian militarists only looked like fascists from the top down. Neither of them could create a genuine mass organization, a political party that could assemble enthusiastic masses to salute all-powerful leaders.

Economic Planning

Nor was real economic planning, as opposed to their paper plans, at all coherent. Japan's planners were torn between the demands of protecting agriculture, the source of the army's soldiers, and the need to accommodate *zaibatsu* interests, and between the demands of the overseas empire and the cost of keeping up morale at home. Chiang's feuding ministries never developed a coherent economic plan that came anywhere near Stalin's Five Year Plan, or even the US War Production Board. Germany itself also never pulled its economy together behind a single focus. Stalin's Five Year Plans, in spite of tremendous waste, still did provide his armies with the heavy industrial goods that they needed, at the cost of devastating sacrifices by civilians. But ironically, the most effective economy at planning for both civilian and military needs was the capitalist USA.

Despite its incoherencies and inadequacies, the model of economic development guided by a bureaucratic state proved

its merits during the war, and survived it. Japan's postwar boom showed great continuities with its wartime experience: Even the same people came back to the same ministries, transformed by their shift from military to civilian clothing. China's Nationalist planners on Taiwan seized the chance to carry out many of the projects that had not been possible on the mainland. They, in turn, built on what Japan had already developed on the island to serve its colonial empire. The Koreans also used the Japanese infrastructure. Much of what we call the Asian developmental model originated in the Pacific war.

Harnessing Science to the Chariot

The war also demonstrated the success of a radically new idea: promoting scientific and technological advance under government leadership. Here again, the democracies proved more successful than the fascists or communists. Germany had been the world's leading scientific nation in the 1920s, but the Nazis drove the most talented Jewish scientists to escape abroad. Hitler invested energy in supporting bizarre theories of "racial science," but neglected physics, which he regarded as a "Jewish science." His military leaders supported research into missiles but not nuclear physics. The two technologies that most vitally affected the war, radar and the atomic bomb, were products of the USA, building on German prewar achievements. The Office of Scientific Research and Development (OSRD), led by the engineer Vannevar Bush, established the Radiation Laboratory project at MIT. Radar proved to be the crucial method of countering German submarine warfare, keeping shipping lanes safe across the Atlantic.

The second great American military project, the Manhattan Project, began with Vannevar Bush's leadership but came under tight military control. The demonstration of a successful chain reaction in December 2, 1942, by Enrico Fermi under the football stadium of the University of Chicago showed that an atomic bomb was technically possible. Producing the bomb required an immense industrial mobilization, bringing together army and air force officers, scientists, and technicians to create a sufficient supply of fissionable uranium and plutonium, some of the scarcest and most toxic elements on the planet. Physicists who had fled Hitler's dictatorship worked under tight military security in complete isolation at Los Alamos until they successfully tested the first atomic bomb on July 16, 1945. Hitler's vicious ideology inspired the scientists with a desperate urge to save the democratic world with a weapon of mass destruction. Scientists could no longer pretend to be disinterested seekers for truth. They never had been, but now they worked enthusiastically for the security interests of a state that protected them. We have not escaped these insidious and complex ties between state security, scientific research, and technologies of destruction established in the war years.

Conclusion This chapter covers one of the shortest time periods in this textbook, but it was an era of unprecedented violence and political competition among contending social systems and political ideas. In the 1920s and 1930s communism, liberal democracy, and fascism captured the allegiance of millions of people in the world's most powerful states. Between 1939 and 1945 these states went to war. At the beginning, it looked as if the USSR and Nazi Germany had come together with the goal of destroying liberal democracy. In fact this coalition proved unsustainable and a coalition between liberal democracy and communism defeated the fascist states. The quest for large amounts of lands and the unexploited resources of the east proved more tempting for fascists than a move west. Also Hitler was convinced that the USA and the USSR could never work together. At the beginning of the war both the Allies and the Axis greatly underestimated Soviet strength. And willingness to fight. At a great cost in human life the Soviets constructed a powerful war machine.

Another important factor in Allied victory was that the warmaking power of both liberal democracies and the Soviets proved far more formidable than anyone had expected. For all their devotion to war preparation, the Germans did not excel in war production. German weapons were characteristic of German tools in general: more precise and well tooled, but often requiring higher skills to operate than American weapons, and less susceptible to mass production. In fact the capitalist USA proved more able to mobilize resources than either Germany or the Soviet Union and its wealth was much greater than either one. The amazing productivity of the USA made possible the rapid construction of a warmaking regime. For example, the naval dockyard needed experts in ship construction but also required steel. American industry could provide both in large numbers. American aircraft carriers required steel and American wealth enabled the USA to invest in new technologies such as the atomic bomb and to devote more attention to areas such as code breaking.

The end of the war witnessed the total defeat of the chief fascist powers and the relegation of fascism to the peripheries of the world political spectrum. The immediate postwar period witnessed the appearance of a reinvigorated but chastened liberal democracy. Looking at how communism had expanded gave many liberal democrats in the West a feeling that communist victory was almost inevitable. Clearly a dominant issue of the postwar era would be whether communism and liberal democracy could coexist and, if they could, the terms of their coexistence. With the appearance of the atomic bomb and its acquisition by the Russians, it became clear to all that failed coexistence might result in world catastrophe.

Study Questions (1) In June 1942 the Axis powers, Germany, Italy, and Japan, seemed to dominate Eurasia and the Pacific. Yet less than three years later, they were utterly defeated. What were the two or three biggest factors in their defeat? Explain.

(2) Compare and contrast the character of World War II on the European Western Front and the European Eastern Front. How did soldiers experience the conflict? How did ordinary people who were noncombatants? Explain these differences.

(3) Compare and contrast the character of World War II in Europe and in Asia. How did most Western and Eastern Europeans see the conflict in their region? How did most Asians see the conflict in their region? Explain.

(4) Despite military assistance from the USA and even a measure of Soviet support, Chiang Kai-shek lost the Chinese civil war to Mao Zedong. Explain the factors that contributed to Mao's triumph and Chiang's defeat. In your view, how important were the effects of World War II on the outcome? Explain.

(5) Pick two nations and compare and contrast their wartime mobilization on the home front in World War II. How did this affect the outcome of the war? What were the similarities between the nations you have chosen? What were the differences? How do you explain the differences?

(6) In the early post-World War II years, India and Indonesia received independence. Compare and contrast the independence struggles of India with Indonesia. How did wartime events bear on these struggles?

Suggested Reading

MICHAEL BURLEIGH AND WOLFGANG WIPPERMANN, *The Racial State, 1933–1945* (Cambridge University Press, 1991). This is a fascinating argument about the uniqueness of the Nazi state, stressing the centrality of racism.

ISTVÁN DEÁK, JAN T. GROSS, AND TONY JUDT (eds.), *The Politics of Retribution in Europe: World War II and Its Aftermath* (Princeton University Press, 2000). This interesting essay collection deals with the punishment of collaborators in various European countries after World War II.

JOHN W. DOWER, *War Without Mercy: Race and Power in the Pacific War* (New York: Pantheon, 1997). Dower discusses racist propaganda used by both Japan and the USA in mobilizing populations during the war and how this propaganda affected the conduct and outcome of the war.

CAROLYN EISENBERG, *Drawing the Line: The American Decision to Divide Germany, 1945–1949* (Cambridge University Press, 1996). This is an important study of the decision to divide Germany after World War II.

GEOFF FIELD, *Blood, Sweat, and Toil: The Remaking of the British Working Class During the War* (Oxford University Press, 2012). Geoff Field takes a new look at the role of class on the British home front, helping us understand the swing left in Britain in the immediate post-war years.

RAUL HILBERG, *The Destruction of the European Jews*, rev. edn. (New York and London: Holmes & Meier, 1985). A classic study of the Holocaust, this monumental tome is a good place to start. The updated edition gives a good sense of the work in the field.

MELVYN P. LEFFLER, *A Preponderance of Power: National Security, the Truman Administration, and the Cold War* (Stanford University Press, 1992). This is an important study of the origins of the Cold War.

ALAN S. MILWARD, *War, Economy, and Society, 1939–1945* (Berkeley: University of California Press, 1979). This is a helpful study of the war mobilization.

NORMAN NAIMARK, *The Russians in Germany: The History of the Soviet Zone of Occupation, 1945–1949* (Cambridge, MA: Belknap Press, 1995). This book is an important study of the Russians in East Germany. It was an inauspicious beginning, one from which East Germany never recovered.

Glossary

Battle of Britain: The fall of France in June 1940 left Britain without major allies. German military men unanimously concurred that air dominance over the English Channel was a prerequisite for an invasion of Britain. Beginning on July 10, the German air force began a campaign designed to destroy the British air force. August 18 marked the high point of the attack. German losses incurred in August were unsustainable at a time when they were preparing the invasion of the Soviet Union. Secret technologies such as radar have been claimed as key elements of British victory. In fact, from the beginning the Germans had underestimated the size of the British air force, the quality of its planes, and the training of its pilots. The intense daylight bombing declined after October 31.

Blitzkrieg: German for "lightning war." The idea was originated by British military theorist Liddell Hart, and taken up practically by German General Heinz Guderian. It involves use of armored columns for a deep thrust in a narrow front. It was instrumental to the success of German armies in their invasions of Poland and France.

Guomindang (GMD): Nationalist and democratic movement founded by Sun Yat-sen in 1911. (It is sometimes transliterated as the Kuomintang or KMT, and usually translated as the Chinese Nationalist Party.) It rallied Chinese patriots both in the mainland and in the diaspora. After Sun's death in 1925, it divided between left and right and came under the control of a dictatorially minded military man, Chiang Kai-shek, who massacred Chinese communists in 1927. This massacre widened the differences between the Guomindang and the Chinese Communist Party, ultimately bringing on a civil war, which the CCP won in 1949.

kamikaze: Japanese for "divine wind." In World War II, it signified an aircraft filled with explosives and crashed into an enemy ship. The Japanese turned to the use of kamikazes in 1944 after the naval war had already been lost. At first the kamikaze pilots were volunteers but later it became compulsory.

Katyn massacre: In 1940 after the collapse of Poland under attacks from Germany in the west and the USSR in the east, the Soviets slaughtered thousands of Polish army officers who had surrendered to them. In 1943, in an act of stunning hypocrisy, the Germans uncovered the graves and offered them to the world as a sign of Soviet barbarism. Since the USSR was instrumental to Allied success, dealing with the Katyn incident posed problems for the Western allies and the exiled Polish government in London.

kokutai: Japan's unique national polity, national character, or national essence.

Nuremberg trials: The Nuremberg trials, held from November 20, 1945 to October 1, 1946, were a series of trials and tribunals held by the Allies after World War II. The most famous was the trial that began on November 20 and prosecuted some of the most prominent leaders in Nazi Germany's economic, political, and military life. The International Military Tribunal (IMT) charged by the Allies with conducting the trial indicted defendants for violation of the rules of war, including war crimes and crimes against humanity. Twelve of the accused were sentenced to death, and many others were given long prison terms.

Stalingrad: The Battle of Stalingrad (August 1942–February 1943) was a devastating German defeat on the Eastern Front in an effort to capture a strategic city named after the Soviet dictator. The surrender of General von Paulus's Sixth Army was a heavy blow to German morale. It was the turning point of the Second World War.

strategic bombing: Bombing directed at civilian targets for a strategic purpose. It was a policy decriminalized by the war as all the major combatants adopted it. At the time, strategic bombing was often contrasted with precision bombing, but the dichotomy is a false one. No bombers of this era had high standards of accuracy and civilian populations suffered large casualties even when not targeted.

Wannsee Conference: Mass killings of Poles, Jews, and Russian soldiers captured by the German army had accompanied the German armies' advance through Eastern Europe. The Wannsee Conference, held in a Berlin suburb on January 20, 1942, was the first announcement to important Nazi leaders of a co-ordinated policy of genocide. Doomed groups – initially the Jews were singled out – were to be transferred to the east where they would be either worked to death or killed outright. A second portion of the conference was devoted to a scheme to kill millions of people in Eastern Europe to make way for German settlements. The course of the war did not permit the implementation of this second stage.

Note 1 Serge Grafteaux, *Mémé Santerre: A French Woman of the People* (New York: Schocken Books, 1985), and Faye Schulman, *A Partisan's Memoir: Woman of the Holocaust* (Toronto: Second Story Press, 1995).

Cold War conflicts

Five largest cities *millions*

1. Tokyo

3. Mumbai   5. New York

35.47   20.69   20.04   19.58   19.39

2. Mexico City   4. São Paulo

New York

Mexico City

São Paulo

Paris

Portugal

Senegal

Ghana   Biafra

PART V
1950–2000: Global threats and promises

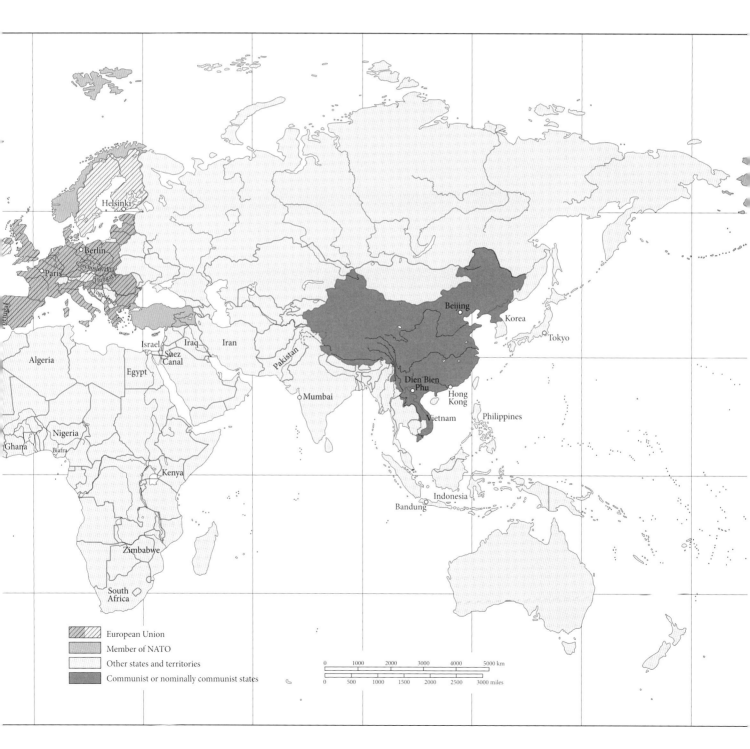

European Union

Member of NATO

Other states and territories

Communist or nominally communist states

Africa	
1957	Independence of Ghana.
1962	Independence of Algeria.
1967–70	Nigerian Civil War.
1975	Independence of Mozambique and Angola.
1994	Nelson Mandela elected president of South Africa.

Americas	
1954	US Senate censors Senator Joseph McCarthy.
1955–69	Civil Rights Movement in USA.
1959	Fidel Castro seizes power in Cuba.
1961	Failure of Bay of Pigs invasion of Cuba.
1964	President Lyndon Johnson announces a "War on Poverty."
1967	Murder of Che Guevara.
1968	Student revolts in USA and Europe.
1973	Overthrow of Salvador Allende, president of Chile.
1980	Ronald Reagan elected president of the USA.

Europe (including Russia)	
May 7, 1945	Surrender of Germany.
1947	Marshall Plan announced.
1949	Formation of North Atlantic Treaty Organization (NATO).
1957	Treaty of Rome establishes European Economic Community.
1989	Fall of Berlin Wall; communism collapses in Eastern Europe.

South Asia	
1947	Independence of India and Pakistan.
1968	Tet Offensive in Vietnam.
1973	The last American combat troops leave Vietnam.

East Asia	
1949	Mao announces foundation of the People's Republic of China.
1950–53	Korean War.
1958	Mao launches Great Leap Forward.
1972	Nixon's visit to China.
1976	Tiananmen Square protests.

World War II left Eurasia in ruins, and two huge continental superpowers, the USA and the USSR, dominating the world. Of the two, the USA had by far the bigger economy and superior military force. The wartime alliance of the two powers did not last long: Within two years, they had begun a bitter global conflict, the Cold War. Because both sides had nuclear weapons, this war threatened to exterminate humanity itself. Fortunately, the conflict quickly stabilized in Europe, dividing it into two spheres of influence, and both powers stepped back from nuclear confrontation over Cuba. But in the rest of the world, local upheavals threatened to draw in the superpowers, making each civil war and rebellion in the Third World a test of the superpowers' "credibility."

The two most destructive wars took place in Korea and Vietnam. In neither one did either superpower gain total victory. Korea remains a divided nation, and in Vietnam revolutionary nationalists successfully expelled French colonialists, their Vietnamese collaborators, and their American supporters. The Soviet Union, emboldened by American defeat, moved into Afghanistan, but faced its own Vietnam there. By 1980, the superpowers no longer seemed to dominate the world.

Despite the superpower confrontation, the postwar world economy grew at an unprecedented rate for thirty years. Europe, the USA, and Japan grew the most rapidly, knitting together the capitalist bloc with even closer ties of capital, labor, and culture. The socialist bloc, led by the Soviet Union, East Germany, and China, also grew rapidly under the discipline of Five Year Plans. Ties within each bloc grew tighter, until China split from the Soviet Union in the 1960s, while trade between the blocs was quite limited. Both blocs depended heavily on new sources of energy, particularly oil, to drive their rapid industrial growth. The USA and USSR were fortunate in having large supplies of oil, but they also depended heavily on Middle Eastern supplies, giving this region new prominence in world geopolitics. By the 1970s, global growth slowed, stimulating attacks on the liberal welfare states by free marketeers, and efforts at reform in the socialist bloc.

Two major trends – decolonization and the rise of East Asia – offset the division of the world in two. The European powers could no longer maintain their colonial empires, but it took thirty years for them to realize it. The British almost immediately gave South and Southeast Asians independence, and the Dutch pulled out of Indonesia, but the French fought on to the bitter end in Indochina and Algeria. Africans created dozens of new nations. The first colonizer was the last to go, when Portugal gave up its African colonies in the 1970s. Formal colonialism did not really end until blacks took power in the white settler regimes of Rhodesia (Zimbabwe) and South Africa. Nelson Mandela's election as president of South Africa in 1994 ended the era of direct white political domination of non-white peoples. The collapse of the Soviet Union in 1991 also meant the end of an empire, or at least the decline of an empire, since a number of fledging nations remain within its current boundaries. Only China remained as a major nation-state inheriting an empire's territory.

Although the USA and USSR tried to draw the newly independent nations into their alliances, many of them sought to keep their distance and create a non-aligned bloc. Yet many of the former colonies depended heavily on their imperial masters for markets and investment capital. Latin America also still relied on the USA as it had before. The new nations of Africa faced serious crises of political stability, environmental stress, overpopulation, and poverty. Their colonial rulers had prepared them badly for independence, but most of the new governments seriously mismanaged their economies, as well.

At first unnoticed, the rise of East Asia to global economic significance drastically changed the shape of the world economy. Japan led the way, growing at a rate of nearly 10 percent per year from 1955 to 1973, soon followed by South Korea, Taiwan, and Hong Kong. China joined the East Asian boom in the 1980s, as did many countries in Southeast Asia. By 1992, six East and Southeast Asian countries produced 25 percent of world GDP, while the six leading Western countries produced 33 percent.

East Asian dynamism began to restore the region to the economic prominence it had once held in 1500, or 1800. Even though World War II left sharp ideological divisions between the two Koreas, the mainland and Taiwan, and China and Japan, economic growth promised to overcome them. An integrated East and Southeast Asian region began to look like a real possibility.

The Middle East also riveted world economic and political attention, because of conflict, not integration. The withdrawal of British and French power left sharp divisions that generated unending wars: the Arab-Israeli conflict, civil war in Lebanon, the Iran–Iraq War, the Gulf War, and US invasion of Iraq among them. The unquenchable demand for oil by the industrial powers gave the Arab monarchies and dictatorships new wealth and power. Some profits went into state-led development projects; a lot went into militaries and bureaucracies. The Iranian revolution launched a new wave of revolutionary movements based on Shi`ite Islam; fundamentalist Sunni movements gained support across the region. By the end of the century, Islamists had failed to gain power anywhere else, but they remained a serious challenge to secular governments everywhere within the region.

By the 1980s, the simple dichotomies of the Cold War began to erode, and from 1989 to 1991 the bipolar division of the world ended with the great reforms in the Soviet Union, the destruction of the Berlin Wall, and the liberation of Eastern Europe. Yet the former Soviet republics and most of the freed Eastern European nations could not compete on open world markets. Their economies contracted catastrophically. In Russia, the elites of the Soviet period stole most of the country's natural wealth.

In addition, global economic growth began to slow, and inequality between rich and poor nations drastically increased. The growing, mobile world population put new stresses on the planet: Global warming, addictive drugs, and new epidemic diseases like AIDS piled on to familiar plagues like malnutrition, contaminated water, drought, and famine. The complexity of global problems made some long for the simplicities of the Cold War era; for them, the new War on Terror provided an answer. Others put their faith in the free market alone, or in technology. Tremendous advances in information technology and biotechnology could bring knowledge to everyone and end many major diseases. The same technologies could support terrorist war or the concentration of powerful resources in the hands of a few. The major problems of the new millennium will test the ability of the privileged elites to reduce the huge gap between them and the rest. Yet the power of organized states to act is decreasing, challenged by markets, non-governmental organizations, criminals, and drug smugglers, among others. High uncertainty marks the future.

14 Cold wars and hot wars: economic boom and slowdown, 1950–1985

Timeline	
June 5, 1947	Announcement of the Marshall Plan of economic aid for a war-shattered Europe.
June 1948	Yugoslav leader Tito breaks with the USSR – the first communist leader to break with Stalin and survive.
1948–49	Berlin Airlift. In response to USSR blockade of West Berlin, the USA and the UK undertake to provision the city by air. The airlift lasts from June 1948 to May 12, 1949, when the Soviets lift the blockade.
October 1949	The People's Republic of China is officially proclaimed in Beijing by the Chinese Communist Party after its victory in the civil war.
1950–53	Korean War – a direct military confrontation between US and communist forces. North Korea invades South Korea. US, Korean, and Chinese troops are involved in large-scale battles. Armistice ending the war leaves borders roughly unchanged.
1951	End of US occupation of Japan.
March 5, 1953	Death of Soviet dictator Joseph Stalin.
May 1954	Defeat of the French at the Battle of Dien Bien Phu; France begins to withdraw from Vietnam.
October 1956	Troops of the USSR invade Hungary to suppress a popular rebellion against communist rule.
October–November 1956	The Egyptian government nationalizes the Suez Canal. Britain, France, and Israel invade Egypt to protect the canal. Pressure from the USA and USSR forces them to withdraw.
March 1957	Treaty of Rome establishes the European Economic Community, forerunner of the European Union.
January 2, 1959	Fidel Castro and his guerrilla army enter Havana and overthrow government of dictator Fulgencio Batista.

August 1961	Beginning of the construction of the Berlin Wall separating East and West Germany.
October 14–28, 1962	Cuban missile crisis: Premier Khrushchev of the USSR secretly sends long-range nuclear missiles to Cuba. USSR and USA hover on the brink of nuclear war.
February 27, 1963	Chinese Communist Party openly criticizes USSR. Public emergence of the Sino-Soviet split.
June 5, 1967	Outbreak of the Six Day War. Israel defeats Egypt, Jordan, and Syria, and occupies the Sinai, the Golan Heights, the Gaza Strip, and the West Bank Territories.
August 20, 1968	USSR invades Czechoslovakia under the pretext of defending socialism, and overthrows reformist socialist government of Alexander Dubček.
February 21–28, 1972	Richard Nixon visits communist China. Joint communiqué announces negotiations to renew formal diplomatic relations.
January 1973	Paris Peace Accords. USA and North Vietnamese negotiators sign a ceasefire allowing the USA to withdraw from South Vietnam.
1973–75	Helsinki Accords. A series of agreements signed by the USSR, the USA, Canada, and twenty-three other European states recognizes the existing borders in Eastern Europe and also pledges to respect human rights, creating a Helsinki Watch Commission to monitor violations.
1975	South Vietnamese government and most of the rest of Southeast Asia falls to North Vietnamese offensive.
February 1979	Islamic Revolution in Iran overthrows the shah and establishes Ayatollah Khomeini as leading figure.

In 1959 Richard Nixon (1913–1994), vice president of the USA, traveled to the USSR to accompany Nikita Khrushchev (1894–1971), Soviet premier, to the opening of an exhibition on the American home. The contrast between the two men was striking. Khrushchev came from a peasant background, had supported the purges of the 1930s, and was a close associate of Joseph Stalin. He had commanded troops in the Battle of Stalingrad and had previously been First Secretary of the Russian Communist Party.

Except for military service, Nixon too had spent his life in politics. Serving in the South Pacific during the war, he had been elected to the House of Representatives and Senate from California. He had come to national prominence in 1948 as a member of the House Un-American Activities Committee and had played a leading role in the investigation of whether a former State Department official, Alger Hiss, had been a secret communist and passed government papers to the Soviets. The committee's findings were inconclusive but Hiss was later convicted of perjury.

As they wended their way through the exhibition, Khrushchev and Nixon, followed by reporters, fell into debate that grew more intense, stopping in front of a section of the show devoted to the American kitchen; the debate that followed became known as the "kitchen debate." Nixon invited the Soviet premier to look round and observe "a house, a car, a television set – each the newest and most modern of its type we can produce." Nixon noted that while the USSR might be ahead of the USA in regard to missile thrust, the USA was superior in color television. Kitchen technology and color television were important because, Nixon explained, "in America, we like to make life easier for women . . . easier for housewives." Khrushchev scoffed that "your capitalistic attitude toward women does not occur under Communism." Nixon reiterated that the suburban home outfitted with the latest technology, presided over by a stay-at-home housewife, would triumph over superior Soviet weaponry. In the entire debate relatively little attention was given to democracy. Khrushchev emphasized equality: "In Russia, all you have to do to get a house is to be born in the Soviet Union. You are entitled to housing." Nixon responded with a doctrine of consumerism: that "Diversity, the right to choose, the fact that we have 1,000 builders building 1,000 different houses is the most important thing."

Khrushchev concluded with a prophecy. "In another seven years, we'll be at the level of America and after that we'll go farther."[1]

The issues raised in the "kitchen debate" run through the decades of the Cold War when differences in world outlook, personality, and state interest intersected to make the conflict seem irreconcilable. Already by the end of 1947, after two and a half years of attempted accommodation, the two great super-powers that had emerged from the war in Europe, the USA and the USSR, found it impossible to reconcile their differences. They could not agree over the future status of Germany, over Soviet sponsorship of the communist dictatorships spreading through-out Eastern Europe, over the terms of US loans to the USSR, or over terms for controlling nuclear weapons. Many, both within and without Europe, wondered how long the prevailing order could survive when the strongest states had such irreconcilable differences? Would a nuclear World War III follow on the heels of World War II?

At the same time it proved impossible to work out a compromise in China where the communist forces led by Mao Zedong were visibly winning a civil war with Chiang Kai-shek's Nationalists. China was not yet a superpower but was an obvious future candidate for this position. How would the USA respond to a communist China? How would a communist China respond to a capitalist USA? What attitude would the USSR take toward another communist country? More than four decades of tension and hostility followed – the so-called "Cold War." Starting out in Europe and East Asia, by its end it was threatening to engulf Latin America and Africa. It reached its apogee in the Cuban missile crisis of 1963 when the USA and the USSR were on the brink of nuclear war.

While the Cold War years saw the very existence of humanity threatened, they also coincided with the largest global economic boom in modern history, and in many regards it was a period of remarkable social stability, particularly in Europe and America.

For about thirty years (1944–1973) both capitalist and socialist blocs enjoyed unprecedented economic growth. Japan surged to become one of the world's leading economic powers. An isolated China followed a different path. Initially the triumphant Chinese communists began to rebuild an economy shattered by decades of foreign and civil war, but subsequently Mao Zedong's policies, labeled "The Great Leap Forward" (1958–61) and then the "Cultural Revolution" (1966–76), returned the economy to chaos at a toll of millions of lives.

The central themes of this chapter are:

- The rise of Cold War Europe and the two great military, political, and economic blocs that emerged from World War II.
- A look at the effects of extraordinarily rapid economic growth between 1944 and 1973 in Europe (both East and West) and, beginning somewhat later, in East Asia (Japan and the four "Asian tigers": Hong Kong and Singapore, South Korea and Taiwan).
- The breakup of Cold War divisions, commencing in 1960 with the Sino-Soviet split and US President Richard Nixon's 1972 visit to the People's Republic of China. This meeting began the ending of China's diplomatic and economic isolation and saw a reinvigoration of the Pacific economy.
- The concurrent slowdown of global economic growth in Europe and North America in the mid-1970s and how it sharpened existing social tensions while revealing new social cleavages.
- Starting in the mid-1960s, new political divisions grew alongside traditional socialist and communist movements, based on gender, lifestyle, and ethnicity, while anti-migrant movements consumed the far right. More recently, right-wing popular movements have re-emerged outside the existing party system, with similarities to the fascist movements that seemed utterly vanquished in 1945.

14.1 LOST OPPORTUNITIES?

An earlier generation of historians emphasized the early postwar years, 1945–48, as a period of lost opportunity for reaching an agreement between the USA and USSR. Certainly the years between 1945 and 1948 were years of extraordinary fluidity. During these years a communist, Ambroise Croizat, was a French minister of labor; a moderate socialist, Edvard Benes, president of communist-controlled Czechoslovakia; a monarch, King Michael, occupied the throne of communist-controlled Romania; and the Southeast Asian communist leader, Ho Chi Minh, worked for the CIA.

Box 14.1 The "New" Cold War History: How We Know What We Know

In the wake of the collapse of communist regimes in the USSR and Eastern Europe and the softening of Chinese communism, many government archives in these countries began to appear in the 1990s, making available previously inaccessible records and memoirs. In response, even Western governments made available some new documents. While releases of communist government documents have, at least up till the present, seldom been comprehensive and clearly regulated, the material that has appeared has forced historians to reconsider views held when only Western archival materials were open to public scrutiny. In the following passage, John Lewis Gaddis, a leading historian of the Cold War, reflects on the proliferation of scholarly studies based on newly released material.

What seems most striking now about this "old" Cold War history are not the disagreements that took place among its practitioners but rather its common characteristics. It showed little of the detachment that comes from following, not reflecting, a historical epoch. It gave one side disproportionate attention: whether crucial or complementary, most of this scholarship focused on the United States, its allies, or its clients. It neglected the fact that two superpowers dominated the post-1945 world; that each often acted in response to what the other had done; and that third parties responded to – but sometimes manipulated – each of them.

The "new" Cold War history will be multi-archival, in that it will at least attempt to draw upon the record of all major participants in the conflict. It will abandon the asymmetry that provided clinical detail on the public and behind-the-scenes behavior of western leaders, but little beyond speculation when it came to backstage maneuvering within the Marxist-Leninist world. It will thus be a truly international history, affirmative action for the "second" as well as for the "first" and "third" worlds.

We know a lot more today about the origins of the Cold War than twenty years ago. Box 14.1 discusses the bases for this new history. New sources have led to new interpretations. Our new history relies on sources from both sides of the conflict. As a result historians, grounded in Soviet as well as in Western archives, have become more skeptical about the chances of reaching accord in the 1940s. For one, the bogey of a communist menace gave the American military and politicians a convenient scapegoat for justifying increased military budgets. For another, Joseph Stalin dictated Soviet policy and his suspicion of Western political leaders was ingrained; nothing the USA could have done would have won his trust. He was conscious of Soviet weakness and felt that the weaker the Soviet state, the less it was possible to make concessions and actually show weakness.

14.2 THE POSTWAR WORLD

The unconditional surrender of Germany (May 7, 1945) and of Japan (August 14, 1945) found the Eurasian continent in chaos. Over 50 million had died, including 6 million Jews, murdered because of their religion or ethnicity. The roads were clogged with an estimated 30 million refugees, plus workers forcibly recruited to work in German-occupied territory. In Asia, 4 million Japanese soldiers and civilians remained in China trying to find a way home, and millions of Chinese displaced by civil war and the Japanese bombing of Chinese cities took to the roads.

Besides the war's human toll, massive bombing had inflicted extensive damage to urban housing, railroad yards, and bridges all over Europe. Armies in retreat routinely destroyed factories. Actually, despite the pictures of great devastation in European cities shown in papers and magazines, Allied bombing had been considerably more effective in destroying housing and public buildings than in crippling German industry: German arms production remained almost unimpeded until the very last months of the war. There remained a great deal of capacity within European industry and this offered hope for the future. Still, living standards and production plummeted at the war's end, as businessmen and politicians hesitated to undertake the costly task of reconversion and reconstruction until they knew more about the terms of the postwar settlement. Many Europeans felt like the French peasant who announced that he would not replant his apple trees if his orchard was only going to become a battleground for the Russians and the Americans.

After World War II, the old European-dominated world order had visibly collapsed. Exhausted by the costs of war and eager to embark upon a program of social reform, Great Britain, which had just brought the Labour Party to power, was desperately soliciting American loans. It could not afford to play its traditional role in the Near East of holding off Russian advance. In France, a large, well-organized Communist Party threatened to take power at the election booth, yet conservative French governments stubbornly insisted on reasserting French colonial rule.

Another former power, Germany, was out of the power game entirely. Having perpetrated almost incomprehensible horrors, it was divided into sectors administered by Britain, France, the USA, and the USSR. Despite the rhetoric, none of the Allies genuinely favored German reunification.

Many people in both Moscow and Washington expected that economic crisis would follow the end of World War II just as after World War I. The great Austrian economist Joseph Schumpeter foresaw disaster for capitalism, a view shared by Soviet dictator Joseph Stalin. They were spectacularly wrong.

14.3 THE USA, 1945–50: POWERFUL, WEALTHY, AND SUSPICIOUS

In fact the end of World War II witnessed the longest and most substantial period of prosperity in modern economic history. The center of this remarkable economic growth was the USA, unquestionably a superpower. The rapid demobilization of the US army, from 12.5 million servicemen in 1944 to 1.3 million in 1948, and dramatic cuts in military spending signaled Americans' desire to return to civilian life. Despite demobilization, only the USA could project military power worldwide. As master of the world's sea lanes, with its air force of heavy bombers, and its possession of bases around the world, the USA could deploy its forces widely. Its possession of the atomic bomb secured the USA an unparalleled bargaining position at least until the USSR obtained the bomb in 1949.

The American war experience was unique. Over 400,000 Americans died, the nation's highest number of fatalities in any conflict except for the Civil War. Some of the battles in the South Pacific were blood baths, with defeated Japanese troops ending the battle with a final suicidal charge; 6,800 American troops were killed at Iwo Jima and 12,000 in the Okinawa campaign. But the US mainland escaped attack, except for a temporary occupation (1942–43) of several desolate and inaccessible Aleutian islands and two small bombings in Oregon, unknown until discovered by forest rangers.

In contrast with all the other principal players, the USA ended the war much stronger than before. The war finally ended the unemployment that had plagued the USA since the Great Depression. Women, African Americans, and Latinos increased their participation in the industrial labor force, although with females usually receiving lower wages than males. The war encouraged the further mechanization of industry and many Americans acquired new technical skills. Wages doubled during the war. Although rationing and price-fixing limited purchasing power, they created a deferred demand that would contribute to growth in the immediate postwar years.

In almost every respect the US economy towered over the world economy. In 1945 the USA possessed half of the world's manufacturing capacity and produced more than a third of its goods. It had two thirds of the world's gold reserves and owned half the world's shipping. While the USA was the world's largest exporter, exports were a relatively small proportion of American Gross National Product. Although other countries needed US products, it did not badly need many foreign products, except for a handful of strategic goods, such as oil, rubber, and metal ores.

Broad-based American economic strength, backed by the eagerness to spend money accumulated during the war, prepared the basis for a new consumerism that for decades symbolized "Americanism" to the rest of the world. This image of Americans did not originate entirely in the postwar period. The automobile had already become an item of mass consumption in the prewar years. During the war Europeans were astounded to discover that ordinary GIs could repair cars. But America's love of the car took deeper root as Americans searched for the latest models; in the mid-1950s almost as many cars were scrapped as rolled off the assembly line each year. As Richard Nixon pointed out in the "kitchen debate," a particular feature of the postwar US world was the spread of private housing. Spurred on by the expansion of automobile sales and later by the construction of a new interstate highway system, suburbs mushroomed, as first the middle and then the working classes left old urban ethnic enclaves. In the late 1940s, Americans became the first mass audience for television.

The post-World War II period also witnessed profound changes in American family life. First of all, cresting in 1956, there was a fertility increase, the "baby boom," that extended to every female age cohort in the reproductive years. Partly this was the result of fertility deferred during the war when couples had put off having children. But it was also the result of postwar prosperity and the expansion of factory jobs that paid high wages to male workers. The generation that came of age during and after World War II had the highest percentage of marriages of any after World War II: 96.4 percent of women and 94.1 percent of men married. Many American couples whose parents had had two children, now had three or four children.

At a time when many Americans were having children, others were going to college. While college education remained an elite privilege in Europe and Asia, the US GI Bill of 1944 opened college education to many young veterans who would have been ineligible in the prewar years. Sending so many young people to college instead of to work prolonged the time of "adolescence" (a newly coined word) and helped to create an independent youth culture. Young white suburban teenagers with spending money constituted a rapidly expanding market for clothes and music. Teenage musical fashions often alarmed parents. Beginning in 1954, the hip gyrations of teen idol Elvis Presley shocked the elder generation – and parental disapproval increased his appeal to the young. Blue jeans and rock and roll emerged to became universal symbols of a new youth culture.

Racism

Western Europeans who contemplated their new American ally read and watched movies that featured America's fast cars, new houses, and fashionable clothing. But popular media typically ignored the racism that characterized so many aspects of American life. Legally enforced segregation in the South did not start to collapse until outlawed by the Supreme Court in 1954, but exercising the right to vote for many African Americans disenfranchised by discriminatory laws and voting practices in the American South was much more difficult. As late as 1955 the murder of a young African American in Mississippi drew national and international attention: Emmett Till was beaten, mutilated, and murdered for whistling at a white woman. His killers, though well known in the community, walked free. World War II accelerated the great migration of African Americans to northern cities, where they encountered the informal segregation of housing, creating and expanding northern black ghettos.

Anti-Communism

America's ferocious and visceral anti-communism also disturbed thoughtful Western Europeans. In the mid-1930s and mid-1940s, communists won some sympathy in the USA by championing the labor movement and rallying Americans against fascism, but while many Americans admired Soviet wartime heroism, they remained deeply suspicious of the Soviet Union. Americans of Slavic, Hungarian, and Romanian background watched in horror as communist dictators took over their homelands. Soviet recruitment of spies among American communists and their supporters inevitably compromised the communist cause. The American communists Ethel and Julius Rosenberg were executed in 1953 for giving nuclear secrets to the Soviets. The outbreak of the Korean War (1950–53), in which US troops confronted North Korean communist armies, heightened American fears of internal subversion and external attack.

For many Europeans the paranoid American fear of communism crystalized in the personality of Senator Joseph McCarthy who attacked the film industry, the State Department, and even the army as nests of communist spies, finally earning a formal rebuke from the Senate. Loyalty oaths and blacklists ruined careers of actors, teachers, and government officials. The CIA secretly sponsored leading anti-communist artists as part of a "war for cultural freedom." Seeing communism in a McCarthyite light as a worldwide conspiracy radiating from Moscow oversimplified world politics, making it impossible to see, for example, the nationalism that divided Chinese, Russian, and Vietnamese communists. The US refusal to recognize the People's Republic of China compounded the possibilities of misunderstanding and miscommunication.

14.4 THE USSR, 1945–50: LAND OF DREAMS

The USSR was the other great superpower. Strategic location contributed to its superpower status. The Soviet state dominated Central Europe, bordered the oil fields of the Middle East, and could get resources from Manchuria through its Chinese ally. It possessed a large army, experienced and well-armed, with the capacity to overrun Western Europe before the USA could mobilize fully its military resources.

Another aspect of Soviet power rested in its ideological appeal and postwar prestige. Around the world there were men and women who looked at the USSR as the embodiment of their own most cherished goals. Some were willing to sacrifice for it, a very few even to spy for it. In many of the newly independent countries of Asia and Africa, communists' claims to have found a way to modernize backward economies through state-controlled planning aroused interest and won sympathy. Communism had transformed a weak Russian empire that had collapsed before the German onslaught in World War I into a powerful state that played the leading role in defeating Germany in World War II; the Soviet army accounted for roughly two thirds of the German troops killed in the war.

The Red Army's enormous size has been used to explain Soviet victory. Certainly the ability to quickly mobilize replacements after so many troops had been lost in the early days of the war was an important factor in Soviet success but it is only one reason. In crucial areas such as tank production, some Soviet tanks were technically superior to the Germans. In the first part of the war the Soviet T-34 medium tank and later the KV heavy tank were considered a generation ahead of their opponents. The tsarist empire had produced some of the greatest European scientists but its intellectual elite was stretched very thin. Soviet universities and institutes were broader and more deeply rooted in their society. In 1945 when Stalin demanded a crash program to develop a nuclear weapon, he succeeded in getting one in five years. Espionage played a contributory role here but a sophisticated and diverse scientific climate was necessary to translate cryptic drawings and haphazardly accumulated plans into a working weapon.

Soviet victory came at a terrible price. Much of the war on the Eastern Front was fought on Russian territory. The crucial battles of Stalingrad and Leningrad were fought in and around major Russian cities that were largely destroyed in the process. Ordinary citizens died in unprecedented numbers. Although it will always be a matter of dispute, current Russian estimates suggest that somewhere around 26.6 million people were killed in the war, 8.6 million of them soldiers. As Khrushchev well knew during the "kitchen debate," wartime casualties made the Soviet workplace a woman's world. In 1945 adult women outnumbered men by nearly three to one and women and teenagers bore the brunt of manual and factory labor. In stark contrast to American prosperity, the terrible winter of 1946–47 caused misery throughout all of Europe but people actually starved to death in the USSR.

The postwar period disappointed Soviet citizens who had hoped to receive new freedoms after the defeat of Germany. For many the Soviet military advance into Central Europe had been a revelation. Taught that they were liberating oppressed farmers, Soviet troops were stunned to discover Central European prosperity and plenty. Rumors that the hated Soviet collective farms would be abolished and currency reforms enacted that would favor consumers proved only rumors. Instead Stalin's growing paranoia resulted in a return to repression. Despite its role in rallying Russians against the Germans, the Orthodox church again became a target of atheist propaganda. The "Doctors' Plot" of 1952 with its claims of a Jewish conspiracy was particularly ominous. Up to his death in March 1953, Stalin subjected even the most loyal Party members to humiliation and terror. At a time when Soviet foreign minister Vyacheslav Molotov doggedly defended Stalinist policies in New York, his own beloved wife was in a Soviet jail.

Within a year of Stalin's death his successors had instituted a "collective leadership." Stalin's successors were determined not to return to the years of purge and terror. A symbol of Stalin's terror, Lavrentiy Beria, the head of the secret police, was arrested and executed. The brutal and economically inefficient prison camps that held hundreds of thousands of prisoners began to empty, a move hastened by a series of camp revolts. Although less brutal and bloody, nothing fundamental changed in the character of the regime.

14.5 THE ONSET OF THE COLD WAR

In a 1947 speech, former British prime minister Winston Churchill noted that: "From Stettin in the Baltic to Trieste in the Adriatic, an iron curtain has descended over Eastern Europe . . . it is unlikely to be raised in our lifetime" (the phrase

"iron curtain" came from the Nazi propagandist Joseph Goebbels). Map 14.1 shows Cold War Europe. Soviet manipulation of elections in Poland in 1947, installation of docile communist leaders, and expulsion of the head of the popular Polish Peasant Party confirmed Churchill's pessimistic view of Soviet intentions.

The **Marshall Plan**, first announced by the American Secretary of State George Marshall on June 5, 1947, was another step toward the Cold War. It marked a major US effort at reconstructing a shattered Western European economy, an investment of 12.5 billion dollars over the next four years. It was a radical shift from America's tightfisted isolationism after World War I. Many Soviets felt that having borne the brunt of the war they deserved some economic relief. But as Marshall enlarged his plan, he raised his sights to promote extensive international trade among participating nations. The American emphasis on free trade was anathema to the closed economy and tightly guarded borders of the Soviet state. The USA probably did not expect the USSR to participate or that it would allow the communist-controlled European nations to participate. Now two separate economic blocs confronted each other across an "Iron Curtain."

Differences over the future of Germany intensified suspicions between the USA and the USSR. Neither country was interested in reunifying Germany, but as the Cold War intensified both countries competed to win German allegiances for fear that, if one did not do so, the other would. As a result the USA and the UK went on to rebuild the industrial economy in the Western sectors of Germany that they controlled and the Soviets in the Eastern sector.

The Berlin Airlift (June 1948–May 1949) was another step toward Cold War. Essentially the Soviets closed off all land access to the city and insisted that Berlin rely on its communist-controlled hinterland for its provisioning, thus forcing the economic integration of East Berlin into the Soviet sector. Western Europeans universally condemned this contravention of previous agreements and many, frightened by what they saw as Soviet aggression, actually sympathized with suffering Berliners who not too long before had been targets of Allied bombs. The blockade and airlift accelerated the formation of the North Atlantic Treaty Organization (NATO) in April 1949, joining Western European nations and the United States in an anti-Soviet military alliance. Western nations, considering how to bring German resources to bear in a conflict with the Soviet Union, encouraged the announcement in Bonn of a constitution for a West German State, the German Federal Republic. In August 1949, the Soviets surprised the world by successfully detonating an atomic bomb, breaking a monopoly that the Americans had expected to last for several more years. The

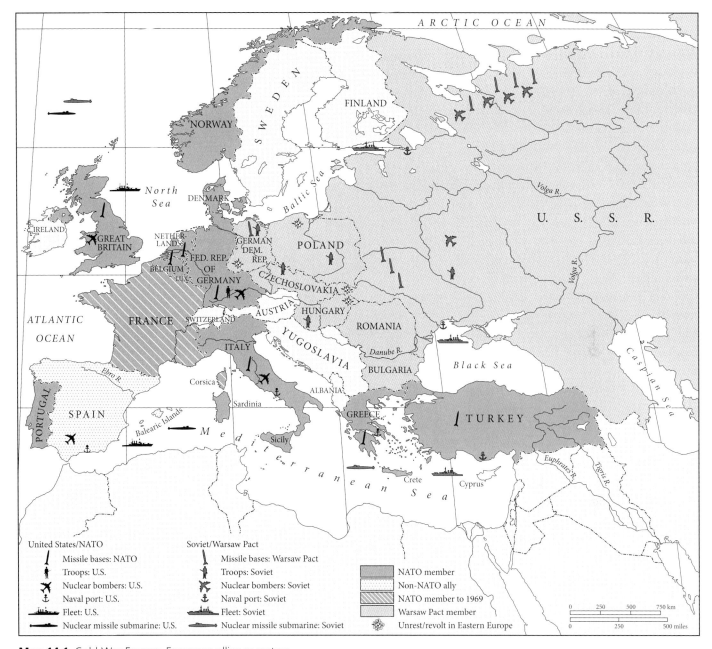

Map 14.1 Cold War Europe: European alliance system

Soviets in turn recognized the communist regime in East Germany, the German Democratic Republic.

By 1949 the basic political structures of Cold War Europe were in place.

14.6 THE OCCUPATION OF JAPAN

The onset of the Cold War marks a turning point in the history of modern Japan. The USA excluded the USSR from any role in the nation's administration. In Japan as in Eastern Europe, the issue of who had boots on the ground at war's end was decisive

in determining who ruled. American General Douglas MacArthur set occupation policy.

At the war's end the Japanese people were thoroughly disillusioned. They had sacrificed heavily for the war effort yet they had been constantly deceived about the war's course. The USA appointed General Douglas MacArthur as Supreme Commander of the Allied Powers (SCAP); he sought to take advantage of this disenchantment to build a more democratic Japan. The new Japanese constitution was a democratic and pacifistic document. The emperor renounced his divine status, women won the suffrage, and Japan renounced the use of military force. The new army, the "Self-Defense Force," was kept very small.

A whole host of reforms was proclaimed early on. Unions were legalized and labor standards were instituted. Land reform was begun. Occupation authorities set out to dismantle the monopolistic conglomerates, the *zaibatsu*, which played a powerful role in the Japanese economy. They freed labor leaders and other radical politicians from prison. Soon, however, the Japanese themselves pushed further, staging large strikes, and even demanding that the emperor be held responsible for the war.

In another context Japanese strikes and demonstrations might not have alarmed occupation authorities but in an era of growing Cold War tension it caused concern. The year 1948 marked a turning point. Before then American rulers had seen their task as one of democratizing Japan and undermining traditional authorities. As the Cold War intensified the occupiers began to re-envision their role as one of restoring order and preventing the spread of communism. Midway through their campaign to dismantle the *zaibatsu*, the occupation authorities reversed position and sought to encourage them again. Now the occupation attacked radicals, imposed censorship, and returned to office many bureaucrats from wartime ministries. The emperor would not be tried as a war criminal, and his responsibility during the war would be carefully concealed. Japan lost its colonies, but paid no reparations. It became a firm ally of the USA, allowing large American bases to be established in Japan. Japan's initial economic advance came from exporting to the wide-open American market. The bureaucrats who had guided wartime production turned to the production of civilian goods: Machinery to make small trucks was retooled for compact cars, sales for motorcycles boomed, and electronic design became a Japanese specialty.

Japanese Economic Miracle

By the end of the occupation in 1952, a Japanese **economic miracle** was well underway. Japan bounced back quickly from wartime destruction, but then it continued to grow at remarkably fast rates for the next three decades. Between 1955 and 1970 Japan's average growth rate was over 9 percent. Protected by the US nuclear umbrella, Japan devoted all its investment to economic growth in export industries. Consumption was kept down while the government supervised investment policies. After the repression of radical activity in 1948, Japanese industrialists reinforced and strengthened the paternalistic policies that emphasized the values of company loyalty and discouraged mobility. In return workers gained large bonuses at the end of every year from company profits with guaranteed lifetime employment and early retirement. These features lent Japanese capitalism a special form, one that was extraordinarily successful in bringing Japan to the top of the economic ladder in a few decades. The origins of this "Japanese miracle" lie in the special

wartime conditions that fostered guided economic development, and the unique status of Japan as dependent ally in Cold War Asia.

14.7 COLD WAR EUROPE: EAST AND WEST

Although the fortunes of the USA and the USSR and their allies in the Cold War ebbed and flowed, the political and social structures hastily constructed following World War II endured for nearly fifty years (see Map 14.2). Their lasting strength came from a political consensus within individual nations based on an analysis of the interwar years and a determination to avoid repeating these mistakes. The Allied victory represented a triumph, not only for one set of nations, Britain, the USA, and the USSR, over another set, Germany and Italy, but a victory for the forces within each nation committed to state intervention and greater social equality. Social Catholics, socialists, and communists triumphed over traditional free marketers, conservatives, and fascists. During the prewar years, Christian Democratic parties had often been parties of the center-right, but after the war they generally took a sharp left turn; the far right that had for long dictated policy in these parties was in retreat and the collaboration of some of the Catholic hierarchy with the Nazis put traditionalists on the defensive.

In contrast to World War I, the years after World War II did not bring a threat from a revolutionary left. Militant workers did not dispute workplace decision-making with engineers or managers. Armed and experienced in combat, often organized by communists, clandestine **resistance** groups opposing the Nazis or Japanese and their collaborators had from the beginning mobilized around themes of patriotism, social reform, and national unity. At war's end they increased their power in government and administration but were in no position to rouse the masses to social revolution. In Eastern Europe, the Red Army prevented workers' committees from seizing control of industries as German troops and collaborating employers fled. Stalin had little tolerance for spontaneous popular action of any kind. In Eastern Europe, if there was to be a revolution, it would be from the top down.

14.8 REPRISALS

In 1945 all of the countries that had been occupied by the German armies confronted the problems of collaboration. In occupied states, many had used German power to revenge themselves upon their interwar opponents. Politically, collaborators were most likely to come from the right, particularly the far

Map 14.2 Cold War Europe: the states of Europe and the Soviet Union

right. But among their ranks were also Marcel Déat, the pacifist-socialist philosopher, and Jacques Doriot, once the communist mayor of Saint-Denis, a working-class suburb on the outskirts of Paris. At the war's end, resistance fighters emerged to settle scores. After an outburst of executions, the treatment of collaborators moderated quite dramatically. Even in Eastern Europe, where reprisals were most severe, many collaborators who now endorsed communist policies remained unpunished. Driven by the need to reconstruct their economies and to re-establish political order, governments punished only the most prominent and bloody collaborators, the rightist militia leaders who tortured resistance leaders, the concentration camp guards, the intellectuals who publicly wrote praising Hitler, and the politicians who extolled collaboration. They generally overlooked the government administrators, judges, and businessmen whose daily actions quietly sustained the German administration in the occupied countries.

Postwar governments, concerned with restoring national unity, glossed over the wartime experience of most citizens, emphasizing the generalized sufferings of the entire nation rather than the wholly disproportionate losses suffered by minority groups, the Jews in particular. East Germany decorated its military cemeteries with monuments dedicated to "the victims of fascism and militarism." Not Germans but Nazis were the culprits. When asked who won the war, a young East German visitor to the Buchenwald memorial replied: 'Why, we did of course.' It would take decades before Europeans, in many cases the grandchildren of the war generation, were prepared to take a close look at collaboration and at the anti-Semitism that had inspired it in many nations.

As the victorious Russian army marched toward Germany there was a significant breakdown of military discipline, intensified by calls for revenge against all Germans by important Russian military and intellectual figures. The Russian poet Ilya

Ehrenburg's much publicized chants of hate for all things German reinforced Marshal Zhukov's orders of January 1945, proclaiming: "Woe to the land of the murders . . . We will get our terrible revenge for everything." Soviet generals did very little to prevent the mass rapes that followed the fall of Berlin. Soviet toleration of such actions had political ramifications. Soviet brutality doomed German communists' efforts to win the support of women – the great majority of voters in a population bled by wartime losses – and contributed to their third-place showing in traditionally "Red Berlin" in key elections in October 1945.

14.9 A NEW EUROPEAN CONSENSUS

No More Mass Unemployment

The experience of the interwar years and the victory of the Allied powers led governments in Eastern and Western Europe to forge a new collectivist consensus. First and foremost, the postwar governments were determined at whatever cost to avoid the unemployment that had fed fascism. To do this, from the very beginning new governments allocated large portions of their budgets to investment even though such heavy commitments threatened national bankruptcy. In 1946 the Marshall Plan helped Western European nations finance growth without further depressing living standards, facilitating democratic growth.

Government intervention in the economy accelerated industrial development greatly in both the capitalist West and the communist East. The number of industrial workers expanded rapidly in France and Italy as well as in Poland and Czechoslovakia. While Western European workers raised their living standards greatly, Eastern European workers also shared in this prosperity. Eastern Europe was catching up with Western Europe. In 1913, the per capita GNP of Eastern European nations was 57 percent of Western Europe's; in 1938, 61 percent; but in 1973 it was 82 percent.[2] Per capita GNP, however, is a poor measure of consumer welfare, particularly in "command economies" like those in the USSR and Eastern Europe. These governments were better at constructing steel and chemical plants and producing tanks than at distributing consumer goods. They fixed prices for housing, clothing, and food at low levels, but often produced goods of poor quality.

A Working-Class Presence

Besides government intervention to promote growth, a second key element of the postwar consensus was the incorporation of working-class parties and trade unions into the political order. As working-class parties – socialists in Western Europe and communists in Eastern Europe – became parties of government, they played an active role in promoting state intervention and industrial growth. Communist governments in Eastern Europe and the USSR proudly claimed to be parties of the industrial working class, and special privileges, including access to higher education, were conceded to individuals of proletarian background. Nikita Khrushchev's background as a poor peasant and then a skilled metalworker was a ticket to advancement. In Eastern Europe strikes were entirely repressed. In France, the Communist Party leader Maurice Thorez boasted of his coal mining origins and the Party closely monitored its own working-class composition. Western European socialist parties rallied to the idea of a **mixed economy**, characterized by state planning alongside private enterprise. In Western Europe strikes decreased (the exceptions here were Britain, France, and Italy). Western European socialists were typically supported primarily by trade unions and working-class organizations but the force of electoral politics often led them to adopt broader identities. In 1959 the annual meeting of the German Social Democratic Party, the party of Marx, not only repudiated nationalization but also rejected the use of the revolutionary term "comrade."

Male Industrial Workers Get Security

A third result of the new political consensus established after World War II was the determination to address the problems of male workers and their dependents. The images of men tramping the streets looking for work was one of the enduring legacies of the 1930s. From 1945 to 1960, the European welfare state expanded as it never had before. Basic medical care was widely extended. The British Labour Party government created a vastly more egalitarian society, and French coalitions of socialists, communists, and Christian Democrats established a modern welfare state. Even Eastern European states granted old age pensions to agricultural and industrial workers and, in the 1960s, free medical care. This was an impressive accomplishment for still weak economies. In 1956 Hungarian leaders put in power by the Red Army after suppressing a working-class rebellion instituted a particularly generous welfare state. This **goulash communism** with its combination of authoritarian politics and receptivity to consumerism, partly financed by the USSR, was seen a way to gain public support and avoid further upheavals.

Gender and the Construction of the European Welfare State

In many European countries, for the first time, male workers no longer expected to work until they were physically unable. They could retire with benefits at a specified age, often 65. Sometimes retirement was even compulsory in order to give young workers a chance (Japan set its mandatory retirement age at 55). These plans were not initially very financially generous, but still they increased the number of male retirees. In industrialized Western Europe, the percentage of males aged 65 and over who were economically active fell from 50–60 percent in 1930 to roughly one third in 1950.

While male workers won real security, their wives often did not. Many welfare states linked benefits to employment patterns. They rewarded continuous employment and skill, the classic attributes of male labor, and penalized discontinuous labor and unskilled work, characteristics of female labor. In much of Western Europe, social entitlements mainly cover employment and its attendant risks. Welfare states pay little attention to the risks of single motherhood, which include lack of access to male wages and the need to combine paid and unpaid labor. Similarly welfare states have ignored or underestimated the burden of caring in which one private individual, usually a woman, tends a sick relative, spouse, or child.

Gender inequality was even worse in those countries that pursued familistic policies that sought to counteract interwar fertility decline and to replace wartime losses. Familistic welfare policies achieved only very modest advances in increasing the population, but in supporting subsidies for childbearing and wage supplements and other privileges for large families, capitalist France and communist Romania reinforced the image of women's social role as childbearers. The German state's commitment to "subsidarity" explicitly rewarded traditional family values and encouraged mothers to stay at home.

Freer Trade and Transnational Communities

A fourth aspect of the consensus was a new reliance on multinational co-operation and close military co-operation. Breaking with the interwar policy of protectionism, the two superpowers sought to impose transnational economic and military unions on the blocs that they controlled: NATO and the European common market in the West, and the Warsaw Pact and COMECON in the East. American influence was not so powerful as Soviet influence, and Western Europeans enjoyed considerable freedom of maneuver, including the right to say no. They resisted most US efforts to encourage expansion of free trade, accepting only those measures which had serious support within the nation. Founded in 1951, the nucleus of the current European Union (EU), the European Coal and Steel Community of France, Germany, Italy, and the Benelux nations, survived because it responded to important interests within member states. After initial hesitation, the UK decided that it belonged with a Europe that had by then evolved into a European Economic Community (EEC). In 1973 it was finally admitted and British entry set off another round of admissions that included Ireland, Denmark, and Greece. Western European states also joined the World Bank and **GATT** (General Agreement on Tariffs and Trade, intended to encourage the reduction of trade barriers), a system that underwrote a new era of expanding trade; this network left out Eastern European states. The Soviet Union created its own economic community, called **COMECON** (Council for Mutual Economic Assistance), imposing a significant division of labor in Eastern Europe, but trading among Eastern European states without Soviet participation was generally discouraged. Map 14.3 shows the economic division of Europe during the Cold War. By the 1960s, Soviet fiat was not what it used to be: Romania broke with the USSR when Soviet planners tried to force it to concentrate on agriculture.

14.10 INCREASING SOCIAL EQUALITY AND THE END OF THE EUROPEAN PEASANTRY

The results of the post-World War II changes and the rise of a collectivist political consensus were greater social equality and accelerated economic growth; the expansion of a relatively well-paid industrial working class and the decline of an impoverished rural population encouraged equality, as did pensions and health care. In the UK, for example, the share of total household income of the top 1 percent fell from 61 percent in 1923 to 23 percent in 1974; in Sweden, from 50 percent in 1920 to 21 percent in 1975. The expropriation of industry and landholdings dramatically decreased social inequality in Eastern Europe. The new, more modest social elites of managers, party leaders, and military men still had higher incomes than workers, and special access to high-class housing and summer homes. Within Soviet and Eastern European factories, wage differentials narrowed significantly.

Economic expansion began the final stage of the millennial history of peasant Western Europe. As older urban workers retired and urban factory jobs expanded, young peasants left for the cities and factories. In Western Europe a commercialized agriculture that produced a few cash crops replaced the small independent farmer whose consumption was largely based on what was produced at home. Many Eastern European governments undertook a more drastic solution to peasant poverty and attempted to collectivize agriculture. Collectivization was rarely successful though, and often had the perverse consequence of preserving backward conditions in agriculture. In some countries, such as Poland, reformists faced with the immensity of the task abandoned collectivization, leaving an impoverished peasant sector that survives today.

Map 14.3 Economic division of Europe during the Cold War

Member of the European Economic
Community (Common Market) 1986

Member of Council for Economic
Assistance (COMECON)

Foreign Migrants Replace Rural Migrants in the Building of the Labor Force

Economic growth and European prejudices created a new marginal group to replace the peasantry as a source of poorly paid unskilled work: migrant workers (see Figure 14.1). Europeans are much more accustomed to emigrating than to receiving immigrants. The transition between sending and receiving intercontinental migrants occurred with great suddenness in the years immediately following World War II. In the wake of economic growth after the war, labor shortages in the successfully industrialized countries drew in migrants from across Europe and then from further afield. Migrants from current or former colonies often took precedence. Foreign

migration into the leading European industrial countries, Britain, France, East Germany, West Germany, and Italy, was actually only a larger version of the end of the peasantry described above, for many foreign immigrants were themselves small-plot peasants or landless laborers, first from Portugal, Spain, and Italy, later from North Africa and Turkey. Legal provisions to protect them from exploitation often were not enforced.

European countries had no desire to attract permanent immigrants from different cultural or racial backgrounds. West Germany explicitly declared that only people of Germanic background and culture could claim citizenship. It welcomed immigrants of German ethnicity fleeing from East Germany and lands claimed by Poland as well as much more distant relatives, such as the centuries-old established German

1870–1913	1914–1949	1950–1973	1974–1998
-13,993	-3,662	+9,381	+10,898

Figure 14.1 Net migration from Western Europe, 1870–1998 (in thousands, negative sign means outflow).

minorities in Romania and the USSR. All other migrants, labeled **guest workers**, had only temporary status. British and French impulses to limit migration by different races and cultures were not so different from those of the Germans but complicated by their continuing imperial ties. Attempting to restore empires shaken by war, the UK and France emphasized the mutually beneficial character of imperial membership; this seemed scarcely the time to revoke the time-honored right of imperial citizens to enter the metropole.

In the British empire, the right of non-white migrants to reside in the imperial motherland was easiest to maintain so long as it was little used. As early as 1948, the voyage of the *Empire Windrush*, a ship containing Jamaican migrants, panicked the Labour government because it raised the prospect of boatloads of non-white migrants establishing themselves permanently in the UK. Terror of non-white migration overcame the government's fear of labor shortage. Just when British officials were actively recruiting laborers from "first class people" who would be "of great benefit to our stock" in displaced person camps and among Italian coal miners, the government was using informal channels and a variety of pretexts to discourage migration from non-white colonies. Sir Harold Wiles, Deputy Permanent Undersecretary at the Ministry of Labour, pronounced that the "early training and way of life" of "coloured workers born abroad . . . must make it more difficult for them to settle down with British born workers." It is ironic that the racial categories that contemporaries judged so reprehensible when used by the Nazis were deemed acceptable when used by Western officials only a few years after the terrible experience of World War II. French policy shared the same basic concerns as British but was further complicated by the status of Algeria, the great majority of whose inhabitants were disenfranchised second-class citizens, although the country was formally incorporated into France.

Of course people migrated for a variety of reasons. Sometimes they had no choice. In the last days of World War II the fractious German minority in Czechoslovakia was expelled under circumstances which resulted in the deaths of hundreds of thousands men, women, and children. Azeris, Kalmyks, and Chechens were all Soviet minorities suspected of disloyalty and forcibly resettled within the USSR toward the end of World

War II. The US internment of its Japanese citizens was also an example of forced migration.

14.11 THE EASTERN BLOC: BACKED BY THE RED ARMY

Although there were many similarities between Eastern and Western Europe in both the interwar and postwar eras, the East was different in one fundamental way. Communism came to most of Eastern Europe with the Red Army. Initially, after the war, liberal democrats, peasant parties, and socialists shared power with communists, but as the Cold War developed, communist parties, backed up by the Red Army, ousted their former allies, and the Red Army never fully departed until communism in Eastern Europe collapsed.

Hungarian Revolution

The year 1956 marked a turning point in the history of Soviet communism. On February 25, the Soviet premier, Nikita Khrushchev, gave a secret talk at the Twentieth Congress of the Communist Party of the USSR, denouncing Stalin as the creator of a "cult of personality" and a dictator and murderer. This speech shocked many in the communist movement, where idolizing Stalin had been de rigueur. At least one Eastern European communist official is said to have died of a heart attack while listening to the speech, although most of the Russians and Eastern Europeans in the room must have known at least some of the truth about Stalin. After all, many of the Russians present were the executors of these policies. In the months that followed, the speech led to a spiritual crisis, particularly in the West, as many once loyal members exited communist parties. For others in Eastern Europe the exposure of Stalin seemed to present new political opportunities. Having repudiated Stalin, perhaps the party would repudiate his methods and policies? In Hungary a communist leader, Imre Nagy, sought to divert investment from heavy industry to consumer goods and to pay attention to peasant grievances but his reformist efforts caused dissent with the Hungarian Communist Party and led to confrontations with Moscow. As Hungarian communists moved to withdraw from the Warsaw Pact, the Soviets acted decisively. In early November 1956, Soviet armies invaded the country and brutally suppressed a popular insurrection. One of the most poignant aspects of the Hungarian Revolution was its overtly working-class character (see Box 14.2). Workers' committees, modeled on Russian soviets of 1917, were the basic institutions of the rebellion and the right to strike was among its foremost demands.

Box 14.2 The Hungarian Revolution: Setting Up the Budapest Central Workers' Council

In 1956 in communist Hungary, student unrest and anti-Russian rioting led to the appointment of a communist reformer, Imre Nagy. On October 30, Nagy promised free elections and an end to dictatorship; a few days later he repudiated the Warsaw Pact binding Hungary to an alliance with the USSR. At this point Soviet troops, which had been evacuating the country, returned and Imre Nagy was replaced by János Kádár. After Kádár proved unable to negotiate a settlement on Soviet terms, fierce fighting followed in which thousands were killed. Nagy was imprisoned and then executed in 1958.

One of the interesting aspects of the Hungarian Revolution was the important role played by workers in the protests and the emphasis placed on workers' councils. Using traditional working-class forms of protest and methods of organization, workers attempted to change a government that claimed to represent

the working class. The bloody repression of the revolution marked the end of popular efforts to reform communist regimes until the Prague Spring of 1968.

The following account is by Miklós Krassó, a young philosophy student who later fled to the West:

The general strike began immediately and the workers' councils were set up completely spontaneously, at first on an improvised basis. They often started with the workers refusing to allow the Party secretary into the factory premises and then setting up councils to run things ...

It was extraordinary to see how identical the demands were: freedom of parties to operate, withdrawal of Russian troops, withdrawal from the Warsaw Pact, neutrality, the right to strike and so on.

[After travelling around] I returned to Ujpest to see what was happening to the workers' council there, to which I had

earlier been elected ... After listening to the discussion there, I came to the idea of creating a central workers' council. I drafted a proclamation and when the meeting ended I put my proposal to the revolutionary workers' council.

The proclamation simply said that at the moment there is dual power in the country: the Kádár government is just there on paper, it's non-existent. There are only two powers: one is the Russian armed forces, and the other is the Hungarian people and in the first place the Budapest working class ... we must create a central workers' council.

They accepted it ... I was to present the plan to the meeting of workers' council delegates ... The meeting was to be at the Ujpest town hall, but when we arrived it was surrounded by Russian tanks and the members of the Ujpest council had all been arrested the previous night (as I learned later, many of them were hanged).

The Hungarian Revolution led communist parties in Eastern Europe to secure their political legitimacy. Stigmatized as Russian lackeys, the parties followed the lead of the Soviet Union, then undergoing its own nationalist revival, by stressing connections to their own national tradition. The East German regime assiduously sought to demonstrate that its commitment to the culture of Bach, Beethoven, Goethe, and Mozart was more genuine than that of its West German rival. An East German scholar proclaimed that "only the defeat of the German Imperialists with the smashing of German fascism through the armies of the Socialist Soviet Union cleared the way for a genuinely objective evaluation and appreciation of Bach."[3]

14.12 ROCK AROUND THE BLOC

Soviet communists also sought to portray themselves as defenders of Russian culture from American "cultural barbarism." At first, they saw the enemy as American "wild jazz," but soon

perceived a far more serious threat: rock and roll. Communist youth were initially told to beat up youths who "danced alone" or grew long hair, but finally, in 1961, the Soviet Union decided to fight fire with fire. The All-Union Congress of Ballroom Dancing introduced a whole series of new dances, including the "progulka," a shuffle step, and the "druzhba," with "swift dynamic movements ... certain to attract the attention of the youth." And yet, astonished adult communists discovered that many party youths waited until their elders had departed from Saturday night socials and then put on records by Bill Haley, Elvis Presley, and later the Beatles, even dancing the decadent "Twist."[4]

Eastern European communists failed to appreciate that economic growth was creating an independent youth culture that, as in the West, might generate its own social critique. But this rigidity alienated the young – the "Twist" was less an unthinking imitation of American culture than the battle cry of a new social group, not only the birth of a youth culture but the birth of a new, larger vision of society, including white-collar workers and professionals. Succeeding generations of Eastern European youth continued to look to American and British music and even to create their own rock groups based on Western models. Although young teens occasionally rioted to protest repression, they were usually granted a certain leeway; they might be the sons and daughters of the Communist Party elite.

Stalin's successors abandoned mass murder; dissident writers were now sent to prisons or asylums. Leaders like Khrushchev knew that reforms were needed, especially in agriculture, but did not know how to bring about change. To encourage more efficient output from the collective farms, he allowed farmers working in collectives to plant their own private plots on their own time and sell their produce on markets. At the same time, he launched massive clearance of ecologically fragile lands in Central Asia for cotton production that failed dramatically and produced a Russian dust bowl. In 1964 Khrushchev's conservative colleagues, fearing the impact of his "harebrained schemes" on the Party's grip on power, arranged to have him ousted, but he retained his apartment in Moscow and his vacation cottage on the Black Sea. Stalin would have put a bullet in his head. His successors, including Leonid Brezhnev, who ruled from 1964 to 1982, and the other septuagenarian and octogenarian males who set policy after Khrushchev's deposition, took no more risks. Brezhnev's last years, when an aged, mortally ill president refused to relinquish power, were pervaded by a spirit of stagnation and decay. In 1968 similar attempts at political and economic reform by Czechoslovak communists led by Alexander Dubček resulted in another Red Army intervention to oust reformers.

This unparalleled period of sustained economic growth brought the **Americanization** of Western Europe. Even though their opposition was sometimes tongue-in-cheek (see Box 14.3), Europeans were often worried about the spread of American institutions. They feared Americanization as a menace in which crass commercialism would corrupt more traditional and more refined European values. Certainly by the late 1960s, millions of Western European workers and even some Eastern European workers possessed color televisions of the kind that Richard Nixon boasted about during his so-called "kitchen debate." Almost everywhere in Western Europe, the extension of school years, a declining demand for child labor, and a growing prosperity that found its way into teenagers' pockets supported an adolescent culture of blue jeans and rock and roll music adopted from American and British teenagers. The cheap, portable transistor radio gave teenagers the freedom to listen to their own music anywhere and anytime they wanted and the cheap motorcycle gave them expanded mobility. Beginning in 1963 with "She Loves You," the long-haired but well-coifed Beatles followed Elvis Presley among adolescent heros; in 1965 came the raunchier Rolling Stones. While John Lennon's "Imagine" was a paean to socialist and pacifist ideals, the Stones' "I Can't Get No Satisfaction" articulated a more explicitly sexual rebellion.

Box 14.3 The American Challenge: Coca-Colonization

In the years after World War II, as living standards improved many European writers and intellectuals began to worry about the threat of "Americanization" – the fear that American consumerism and popular culture would undermine old established European values and traditions. A prime symbol of this American menace was Coca-Cola. In 1950, a proposal to ban Coca-Cola was put forward in the French legislature with support from both the left and the right. An American newspaperman believed that the true purpose of the legislation was only too evident:

You can't spread the doctrines of Marx among people who drink Coca-Cola. The

dark principles of revolution and a rising proletariat may be expounded over a bottle of vodka on a scarred table, or even a bottle of brandy; but it is utterly fantastic to imagine two men stepping up to a soda fountain and ordering a couple of cokes in which to toast the downfall of their capitalist oppressors.

Frenchmen were equally aware of the issues at stake. A French writer commented:

Conquerors who have tried to assimilate other peoples have generally attacked their languages, their schools, and their religions. They were mistaken. The most vulnerable point is the national beverage. Wine is the most ancient feature of

France. It precedes religion and language; it has survived all kind of regimes. It has unified the nation.

The debate over Coca-Colonization continues up to the present. But whether under US auspices or not, a consumer revolution swept Western Europe in the 1950s and 1960s that greatly increased the living standards of the ordinary Western European and made shopping, department stores, supermarkets, and malls a part of ordinary life all over Western Europe. And the left was not completely wrong: Communist May Day marches did decline because French workers used the holiday to drive their families to vacation in the countryside.

In fact the 1960s did mark the beginning of a major transformation of sexual attitudes. In 1960 the American Federal Drug Administration approved the use of the pill for birth control. This change coincided with larger demographic transformations, a rise in the age of marriage and a rise in the single population and those "never marrying." Throughout most of Europe fertility began or began anew its slow but continuous decline. In the mid-1960s a new "second wave" feminism appeared. In contrast with the "first wave feminism" of the late nineteenth and early twentieth centuries which focused on rights, this new feminist wave emphasized a range of social, class, family, and cultural issues. The gender biases within welfare states became prime targets of this movement. Within this feminist wave a powerful movement for gay rights emerged.

While new movements grew, some old movements declined. The growth of consumerism weakened some traditional working-class institutions. Co-operatives that had thrived on selling cheap food and clothing were frequently unable to adjust to changing working-class tastes and went into a decline. Television undercut the neighborhood solidarity of the pub or cafe. New housing projects in the suburbs siphoned young working-class families from traditional working-class neighborhoods that were abandoned to the old and the migrants. In Paris the traditional May Day march declined as workers got in their cars and drove south for the holiday.

14.13 THE COLD WAR HEATS UP IN ASIA

By 1950 the victory of the Chinese communists in the Civil War confronted Stalin with almost as many problems as it did Truman. Stalin never accepted the communist leader Mao Zedong's idea of a socialist revolution based on the peasantry as truly Marxist, but he recognized the propaganda advantage of putting the world's most populous nation in the socialist column and also a nation with which he shared a very long border (see Map 14.4). When Mao visited Moscow in December 1949–January 1950 to negotiate a Sino-Soviet treaty, he was surprised and angry to discover that Stalin intended to preserve provisions, first acquired by tsarist Russia, that gave Russia extraterritorial powers in portions of China. The Chinese succeeded in modifying many of these, but the Soviet Union retained control over the port of Dalian and, in a secret agreement, the Chinese permitted Soviet infringements on Chinese sovereignty in the northeast. But Mao did win what seemed like an important concession: at least limited support in any confrontation with the USA. In the new treaty, the Soviet Union promised to support China in a war with Japan or "any nation allied with her" and offered modest aid for Chinese development.

Boding ill for its future, the Sino-Soviet alliance failed its first test. Stalin encouraged China to invade Taiwan, the island stronghold for the retreating Nationalist troops, but he also agreed to a proposal of the North Korean leader Kim Il-sung for the invasion of South Korea. Kim had promised Stalin that an impoverished south ruled by an unpopular Syngman Rhee would rise to support a Northern invasion. Stalin persuaded Mao to support Kim's invasion of South Korea without committing the USSR to the battle. As it turned out, the USA did fight, Stalin gave no military support to Mao, South Koreans did not come running to Kim, and Mao was unable to take Taiwan. China and North Korea lost their aggressive gambles.

The Korean War

The USA had not included Korea within its security perimeter, but when North Korea invaded South Korea on June 25, 1950, Americans felt that the invasion could not be allowed to stand. At first, the Northern troops advanced almost unopposed through the peninsula. Taking advantage of a Soviet boycott, the USA won UN support to fight the Northern invasion. US General Douglas MacArthur boldly landed on the coast at Inchon far in the rear of the North Korean armies, severing their supply lines in the process. The USA deployed the Seventh Fleet to defend Taiwan, making a Chinese invasion impossible.

As the North Koreans retreated, American policymakers debated. Having cleared the fleeing North Koreans from the south, should they follow them into the north and attempt to unify the nation? General MacArthur assured Washington that it had nothing to fear from China. Most American foreign policy experts agreed that so long as they did not enter Chinese territory they need not fear Chinese action. They failed to appreciate Chinese fears. Mao saw America's invasion of North Korea and support for Taiwan as signs that the USA intended to roll back the Chinese revolution. When he turned to Stalin for aid, Mao discovered to his consternation that Stalin refused to provide support, even the limited air cover he had promised in Moscow, although later he did provide some assistance to North Korea. China sent large numbers of poorly armed but enthusiastic "volunteers" to support the fleeing North Koreans. The Chinese and the North Koreans both suffered massive casualties, and after seesaw fighting, in 1953 the battle line finally stabilized very close to the 38th parallel, its original starting point.

By 1953 the basic structures of Cold War Asia were in place.

China Goes It Alone

In the 1950s and early 1960s China moved to isolate itself from the world. The Soviet alliance and the Korean War seemed to

Map 14.4 The People's Republic of China

close off the possibility of working with the West, but Stalin's deception during the Korean War fueled Chinese hostility toward its putative ally. Denied access to Western resources and provided with only very modest Soviet help, Chinese efforts to modernize a largely agrarian country confronted insuperable obstacles. If Mao felt betrayed by Stalin, he had even less respect for Khrushchev's efforts to promote "peaceful coexistence" with the West in an era of nuclear weapons. In 1955 China began its own nuclear program with Soviet support but, increasingly leery of a nuclear China, Khrushchev now reneged on his part of the agreement. In 1960 he abruptly summoned home all Soviet advisors, and tore up the blueprints for hundreds of industrial plants. China's sole ally was tiny Albania. The war of words grew bitter. Mao accused Khrushchev of being a "running dog of imperialism" and Khrushchev called the Chinese lunatics who would incinerate the world in a nuclear holocaust. In 1969 Chinese and Soviet troops clashed along their border in Manchuria.

14.14 CUBAN REVOLUTION

The most serious crisis of the Cold War originated with the Cuban Revolution and the penetration of Cold War divisions into Latin America. After several years of guerrilla warfare against the brutal dictator Fulgencio Batista, revolutionaries led by Fidel Castro triumphed in Cuba in 1959. The young revolutionaries who took power included communists, but Castro was by no means a communist himself, and in fact the Cuban Communist Party had not supported the revolutionaries. But Castro and his fellow rebels were unafraid to carry out reforms that challenged the powerful US corporations that dominated Cuba's sugar exports and oil refining. But the Cuban Revolution occurred in the context of the Cold War. Seeing a chance to cultivate a friend in Latin America, the USSR signed a trade agreement with Cuba promising to sell it cheap oil. When US and British refineries in Cuba rejected the Soviet oil, Castro took them over. The USA responded by stopping further purchases of Cuban sugar. Castro then nationalized US corporations as the USA announced a commercial boycott and severed diplomatic relations. Khrushchev noted how many in Latin America cheered on the Cubans.

On the American side, Cuba represented a test of the strategy of "rollback," the use of force to overthrow established communist governments. Almost as soon as the Castro regime had taken power, the US began encouraging counter-revolutionary Cubans to overthrow it. When John F. Kennedy became president in 1960, he found that the outgoing Eisenhower administration had worked out a scheme for a Cuban invasion led by exiles in Miami. Despite doubts, Kennedy allowed the invasion to proceed. In April 17–19, 1961, the invasion failed utterly on the beaches of the Cuban **Bay of Pigs**. Victory over the USA reinforced Fidel Castro's position in Cuba and greatly increased his standing among the Latin American left and among anticolonial movements around the world. Shortly thereafter, Castro announced publicly that he was a Marxist and that the Cuban government would make efforts to spread communist revolution through guerrilla warfare to the colonial world. The Soviet Union also increased its economic and military aid. It promised to buy Cuba's entire sugar crop at prices above the world market as long as the USA imposed its boycott. This would prove an expensive commitment for a weak Soviet economy.

Looking at Cuba, Khrushchev might also have been thinking about West Berlin, for in the early 1960s the success of West Berlin revived Soviet fears. A thriving capitalist enclave inside the Soviet bloc, West Berlin drew in skilled workers and professionals escaping from a repressive East Germany. After vainly attempting to intimidate the USA and the Western powers into abandoning the city, in August 1961 East German authorities began building a wall around West Berlin to cut it off from the surrounding Eastern zone. "The Wall" effectively stopped East Germany's manpower drain but also constituted an ongoing reminder that East Germany, the most prosperous of the communist states, could not hold its labor force except by force.

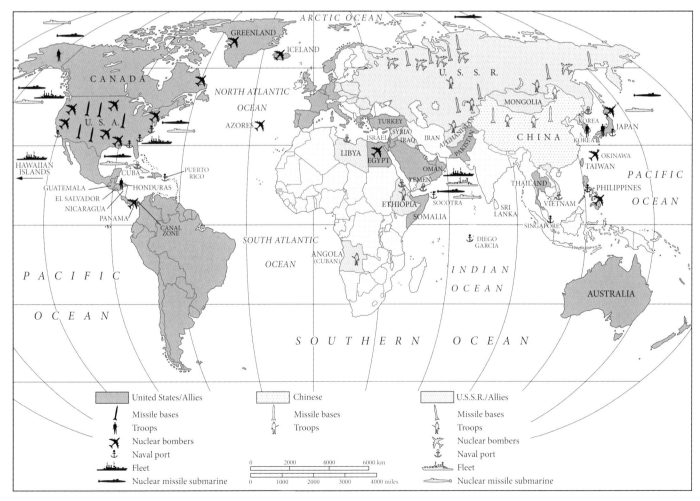

Map 14.5 The global Cold War in the 1950s and 1960s

Cuban Missile Crisis

In any case, Khrushchev developed a secret plan to install nuclear missiles in Cuba and erase the Soviet Union's lag in the development of intercontinental ballistic missiles. Perhaps Khrushchev thought that in the end, Cuban missiles might be exchanged for the end of the Western presence in Berlin? Meanwhile, the Soviets assured the USA that military aid to Cuba was purely defensive. When US reconnaissance flights spotted the Soviet nuclear missiles just before they became operational, the greatest crisis of the Cold War began.

Several alternatives were presented to Kennedy: Some advised an immediate air attack on the missiles, while others favored recognizing their presence as an accomplished fact. After the failure at the Bay of Pigs, Kennedy excluded the possibility of tolerating the missiles. At that moment the world was nearer nuclear war than anyone knew, for Soviet troops in Cuba were deployed with (though not formally authorized to use) tactical nuclear weapons. A mistake by a Soviet colonel or an American pilot could well have begun a nuclear holocaust. On October 22, 1962, Kennedy announced a naval "quarantine" of Cuba to prevent the landing of any offensive weapons. (Kennedy used the term "quarantine" because "blockade" was recognized in diplomacy as an act of war.) At that very moment, a convoy of Soviet ships filled with powerful nuclear missiles was heading toward Cuba. Responding to Kennedy's television address, the Soviet government rejected the US challenge. On radio or television, millions of Americans followed minute-by-minute reports of the ships' progress as they approached the blockade zone. Within hours of the projected naval confrontation, the Soviets backed down. Short of nuclear war, there was no way that the USSR could defend Cuba, only 90 miles away from the USA but thousands of miles away from the USSR, and American superiority in intercontinental ballistic missiles gave pause. In the end, in return for the removal of nuclear missiles from Cuba and pledges not to reinstall them, the Soviets received an American promise not to invade Cuba and, as a secret codicil, a promise to remove US Jupiter missiles from Turkey after the crisis had wound down.

In the eyes of the world the USSR had visibly backed down when challenged. Castro felt betrayed. The Soviets, determined never to be forced to back down again, began to channel enormous resources into constructing a huge nuclear arsenal that finally reached a state of **MAD**, an apt title for the condition of Mutually Assured Destruction, in which full-scale use of weapons of mass destruction by both superpowers would result in the complete annihilation of both sides.

But the revelation of how quickly a conflict could turn nuclear had a sobering effect on both Americans and Soviets. The great crisis over Cuba began slow steps toward the easing of tensions. Having achieved nuclear parity, both sides turned more attention to arms control and disarmament. In 1963 the USA and the USSR ratified a Nuclear Test Ban Treaty, followed by Strategic Arms Limitation Talks (SALT) treaties in the 1970s, culminating in the Helsinki Accords of 1973–75. The Helsinki Accords ratified the division of Europe, but also included provisions for human rights, allowing dissenters in the Eastern bloc to invoke the treaty for international support.

Preventing the Spread of Cuban-Style Revolution

After the Cuban Revolution, the USA feared the spread of communism in its hemisphere. John F. Kennedy, who had labeled Latin America the "most dangerous area in the world," launched the "Alliance for Progress," sometimes billed as a "Marshall Plan for Latin America." Per capita spending levels, however, were far greater in Europe than in Latin America. Kennedy's successor, Lyndon Johnson, gave it lower priority. Still, Latin American involvement in the Cold War did bring it more US aid. During the 1960s Latin America received 18 percent of US foreign aid, double what it had received under Eisenhower.

Kennedy was determined there would be no more Cubas. Toward that end, the US government sponsored military assistance and training programs that successfully prevented guerrilla victories but also inhibited democratic development. Guerrilla movements were founded in almost every Latin American country but by 1978 it was clear that almost all had failed to bring popular revolution. While Castro-type revolutions were defeated, the right-wing forces unleashed by US aid took a toll of democratic regimes. Overthrowing the democratic reformist government of Jacobo Arbenz in Guatemala, supporting the military coup against Salvador Allende's elected socialist government in Chile, arming terrorist paramilitary forces against the Nicaraguan Sandinistas, or doing little to stop murderous "disappearances" of critics in Argentina, gave the USA a reputation as being an anti-democratic force in the region.

14.15 VIETNAM: THE TRIUMPH OF REVOLUTIONARY NATIONALISM

Just as American leaders were successfully confronting their Soviet counterparts over Cuba, the USA was becoming involved in what would prove a losing struggle in South Vietnam.

By 1945 the Vietnamese communist leader Ho Chi Minh had become a legendary figure in Indochina. Vietnamese nationalists were awed by a man who had fought for national independence at the Versailles Conference in 1919. Anti-colonial rebellion and long traditions had managed to create a strong sense of a single Vietnamese nation. Outside of China, Vietnam was the only anti-colonial movement that managed to build an efficient, disciplined regular army. The long anti-French struggle promoted the development of talented military leaders such as Vo Nguyen Giap, whose forces moved easily between routine guerrilla warfare and traditional combat. In March 1954, at the remote mountain outpost of Dien Bien Phu, Giap demonstrated the astonishing ability of his army in regular combat, when his troops, aided by local peasant conscripts, carted heavy artillery up steep mountain trails, besieged a garrison of 12,000 French troops, and forced them to surrender.

Defeat at Dien Bien Phu spelled the end of French rule in Indochina (the French administrative unit that included Cambodia, Laos, and Vietnam), but it did not bring national union. At the 1954 Geneva conference, Vietnam was provisionally divided between a communist-controlled north and a non-communist south, preparatory to national elections to reunify the country. But as France left, the USA took its place, determined to prevent South Vietnam from going communist. While earlier American regimes had seen Indochina as a victim of French imperialism, President Eisenhower saw it as part of a global communist plot for domination: If Vietnam fell, other countries would soon fall like "a chain of dominoes."

Short of keeping it non-communist, however, the USA had no clear plans. At first, America's man in South Vietnam was Ngo Dinh Diem, an authoritarian nationalist similar to Chiang Kai-shek, but also a devoted Catholic in a predominantly Buddhist nation. Unfortunately, Diem lacked both democratic inclinations and basic political skills. He rejected open nationwide elections, knowing that Ho Chi Minh would surely win. The 1956 election was not a bit fairer than those carried out in Poland in 1952 or East Germany in 1954. Diem's intolerance of Buddhists, and the notorious corruption of his brother-in-law Ngo Dinh Nhu and wife Madame Nhu, alienated non-communist nationalists in the South. In reply, the North Vietnamese government created the National Liberation Front (NLF), which won support from bankers, lawyers, and Buddhists who rallied against the Diem dictatorship. In 1963 when Buddhists began to set themselves on fire in the streets of Saigon in protest, President Kennedy approved Diem's overthrow and assassination by Saigon generals. But Diem's successors had even less legitimacy and competence.

When Lyndon Johnson succeeded to the presidency after Kennedy's assassination, he decided to send combat divisions to Vietnam, using a confused confrontation in the Gulf of Tonkin to gain Congressional approval. As demand for troops increased, Johnson reinstituted the draft. But as troops levels mounted, it became clear that the American public was unwilling to make large personal sacrifices to win in Vietnam. Military and civilian planners' hopes that superior US technology might win a war of attrition proved illusory. Vietnamese dictators did not inspire American sacrifice.

US Escalation Proves Unavailing

Ultimately the Vietnamese proved better able to sustain a long attrition than the USA. The USA draft drew on a youth population that had developed a striking degree of autonomy and cohesion. Dramatic increases in draft levels for a war whose purpose was never very clearly articulated increased antiwar activism in American universities, marked by teach-ins and large marches on Washington. US antiwar activism was transmitted to Europe through the same cultural channels as American enthusiasm for the Beatles.

Together the NLF and the North Vietnamese People's Army of Vietnam constituted a truly formidable force. The NLF mobilized a diverse coalition in South Vietnam, while the North Vietnamese army drew on the resources and strict discipline of an authoritarian communist regime. The Tet Offensive beginning on January 30, 1968, the turning point of the war, took a terrible toll of South Vietnamese lives and almost destroyed the NLF, but it was an enormous political victory. During the Tet lunar holiday the NLF launched attacks in more than 100 cities all over South Vietnam. For an American public constantly reassured that its military leaders could see "the light at the end of the tunnel," the offensive was a mortal blow to US government credibility. US military requests for over 200,000 more troops for Vietnam inevitably involved the nation in an extended debate that drove President Johnson from office. American boasts that their enemies were suffering enormous losses were true but overlooked the deep commitment of the Vietnamese to their nationalist war effort. After the war, an American general told Giap that his army had never defeated US troops in direct combat. Giap replied, "That is true, but it is also irrelevant." Political will, not body counts, determined the war's outcome.

Johnson's successor, Richard Nixon, and his Secretary of State, Henry Kissinger, used a mixture of fierce bombing of the North, widening of the war to Cambodia and Laos, and great power pressure to bring the North Vietnamese to the bargaining table, but they were only able to win breathing space for a graceless exit, signing the Paris Peace Accords in January 1973 and abandoning the hapless South Vietnamese troops to their fate, leaving Cambodia in the hands of genocidal maniacs. In Cambodia, US bombing of the border with Vietnam had driven soldiers and refugees further west, causing the fall of Cambodia to the Khmer

Rouge, Cambodian communists with a genocidal mentality. They killed up to one third of Cambodia's population before the Vietnamese drove them out. Illegal US bombing of Cambodia bears heavy responsibility for this catastrophe.

Ironically, the reunification of Vietnam disappointed many of those who had fought so hard for its creation. Instead of genuine unification, the North Vietnamese installed their own officials in the South, making only token appointments among the South Vietnamese who had participated in the national liberation struggle. The new Vietnamese government had no real solutions for developing a country that had suffered almost unparalleled

destruction of people and property. In the 1980s and 1990s, however, as China reformed its economy and rejoined the world, the Vietnamese cautiously followed.

The unraveling of the Cold War in Asia began when Richard Nixon stunned his closest allies, Japan and Taiwan, by announcing suddenly that he intended to visit Beijing the following year with the intention of normalizing US relations with the People's Republic of China (PRC). Nixon's announcement was a response to efforts by the USSR in the late 1960s to expand its naval presence worldwide. In the vacuum created by American internal division, the Brezhnev regime sought to imitate the

Map 14.6 Cold War conflicts in Asia

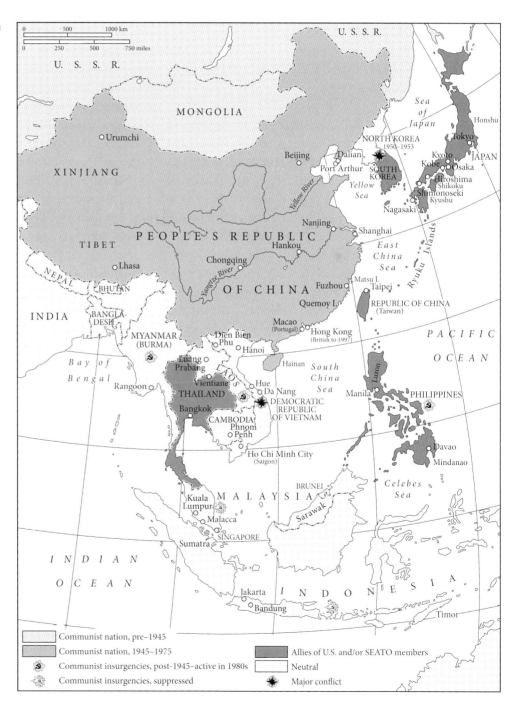

USA in being able to project its power over the entire globe. The Soviet invasion of Afghanistan in late 1979 suggested that the Soviets no longer felt checked by US military strength.

Ultimately the USSR's invasion of Afghanistan proved more similar to the US involvement in Vietnam; guerrillas aided by US weaponry engaged the Soviet army and its puppet government in a long guerrilla war that neither side could win. Meanwhile behind the facade of Soviet military strength, the USSR was falling seriously behind in both economic and military technology. The Soviet economy found itself increasingly shackled by its commitments to the Eastern European countries and Cuba, whose economies were in even worse shape. By the early 1980s neither the USA nor the USSR felt like a superpower.

14.16 THE END OF THE ECONOMIC MIRACLE IN EUROPE

In 1974, after three decades of dynamic growth, unemployment reappeared in Europe. Unemployment was heavily concentrated in the depressed rural regions on the Western European periphery and in the European rust belt of declining steel mills and coal mines. Governments that tried to relieve unemployment with deficit spending, however, touched off rampant inflation. "Stagflation," a new economic concept, meaning economies plagued by both slow growth and inflation, became the watchword of the 1970s. The oil crisis of 1973, begun by the embargo set by the Organization of Petroleum Exporting Countries (OPEC), raised the price of a vital commodity, affecting the entire economy. The economic crisis that began in the 1970s marked the end of three decades of steady decline in social inequality, eroded the consensus in favor of state planning in both Western and Eastern Europe, and fatally undermined liberal Keynesian policies in the United States.

Resurgent free marketeers argued that stagflation came from prodigal spending by postwar welfare states and the political leverage of working-class parties. Their solution, adopted by parties as diverse as British Conservatives and French Socialists, was to trim welfare state costs, reduce trade barriers, and engage in global economic competition. Although the collapse was sudden, the system had been slowly undermined for years. Only a few years after the end of World War II, Christian parties abandoned their radical commitment as conservative forces reasserted control or prompted collapse. Reminiscent of the post-World War I years, the radical upsurge of the 1960s raised questions of workplace control in France and Italy and challenged the hierarchical character of state intervention; this in turn helped bring about the revival of neo-fascist groups in both countries. In Eastern Europe, bureaucratic centralized planning proved increasingly unable to raise living standards, but efforts to introduce more flexible socialist planning were abandoned after Eastern European and Russian troops invaded Czechoslovakia in 1968.

In Western Europe in the 1980s, the abandonment of commitments to full employment and the return to the free market commitment to price stability coincided with profound changes in industrial and economic structures. Technological evolution no longer rewarded large plants and assembly lines as before. Traditional resource endowments of coal and iron ore were exhausted or no longer loomed so significant in industrial production. But opening national markets to increased foreign trade on such an extensive scale cost European governments a significant amount of control over their own economies. In most European countries increased exposure to international markets resulted in increased unemployment in traditional heavy industries, while often benefiting the more technologically advanced economic sectors. In the good times, unemployment decreased, but in bad times, such as the deep recession of the 1980s, unemployment soared and the level of unemployment was higher at the end of each succeeding economic cycle. As in the interwar period, these developments undermined labor solidarity, favoring white-collar workers and some strata of skilled blue-collar workers at a time when the position of the mass of industrial workers was under attack.

Although mass unemployment returned, the social consequences were not the same as in the interwar years. While union demands were restrained by international competition, male workers were not thrown into the streets. Despite cutbacks, post-World War II welfare states protected adult males and families with male household heads. But the social policies that preserved the adult white male native industrial working class from marginality exposed other groups to grim poverty and the social marginalization inevitably resulting from immiseration.

Migrant laborers took the brunt of the pain. During economic recession in the 1970s many European politicians responded to popular demand and imposed restrictions on new migration; even though Europeans refused to accept many of the jobs in manual labor performed by migrants, a great wave of anti-migrant measures swept Western Europe. The legislation produced unexpected results. Accelerating a trend already under way, migrant laborers who had established themselves in European countries began to send for their families in fear that family members would themselves soon be denied the right to migrate. Migrant children newly settled in Europe were at an educational disadvantage; they often found legal bars to their employment and confronted ethnic prejudice. As a result they swelled the ranks of the unemployed, spurring further anti-migration sentiments as politicians pointed to migrants in the welfare ranks.

Within one lifetime, a migrant community that had one of the highest labor force participation rates in Europe became a group with one of the lowest. Anti-immigrant actions were not unique to the West; in the 1980s these sentiments were expressed openly throughout Eastern Europe. Migrant workers were vulnerable to demagogic attacks, because few could vote and they had few mainstream political supporters.

The turn toward financial austerity, the expansion of international trade and the resulting increase in unemployment, the declining number of industrial workers, and the weakening of labor movements also led European governing coalitions to attach less importance to the political incorporation of organized labor. In the UK Margaret Thatcher's government (1979–90) attacked the trade unions head on. She brought down inflation, but raised unemployment to 14 percent, unprecedented in the postwar period. Her defeat of the miners' strike in 1981 marked a new relationship between British government and the labor movement, one that continued even when the Labour Party returned to power. Trade unions retained more political influence in such bastions of organized labor strength as Sweden and Germany, but even there membership declined. Reformers called for socialist parties to seek support from single-interest social movements such as feminists, ecologists, or gay rights movements.

Increasingly, European leftist parties have begun to reorient their recruitment toward newly emerging movements, organizing demonstrations and mass actions. Ecology, feminist, and gay rights movements have won successes in the USA and Western Europe because they represent new and growing constituencies. The US Civil Rights Movement was widely followed in Western Europe and provided one model of organization and political tactics for many feminists and gays. In the 1970s and 1980s there has been a revival of nationalist movements and a rapid spread of anti-migrant movements.

Conclusion   The abandonment of the commitment to full employment and the growing marginalization of organized labor in both Western and Eastern Europe in the 1980s, and the persistence of a welfare state that protected some but not all, marks the end of the postwar period. The collapse of communism in Eastern Europe and the Soviet Union as well as the reorientation of China toward capitalism are all part of this dramatic reorientation in social policy. The renewal of a free market capitalism that seemed on its last legs in 1945 has generated new kinds of capitalist growth: heavily focused on specific new technologies, very prone to boom and bust speculation, and generating much greater inequality than the postwar decades saw.

The rise of new social movements represents a distinctive feature of the present period; new issues have emerged, such as a feminism opposed to the gendered character of welfare states created in the post-World War II period. While both old groups such as migrants and trade union organizations are being marginalized, once marginal groups such as nationalists and newly arising groups such as feminists are mobilizing to win political rights.

From the 1980s on, realignments made Europe's political world much more complex than the simple black and white polarities of the Cold War. "Left" and "right" lost their original meanings when socialists endorsed pro-capitalist investment and rightists called for the breakup of national states. Europeans now shared in the great consumer culture that began in the United States, but they feared American hegemony in the world. The sharp boundaries of the Cold War world, and the boundaries between Europe, Russia, and the Middle East, have blurred over. With the end of Cold War, simplicity has also gone. New times demand new solutions.

Study Questions   (1) In the years following World War II, the Cold War gripped Europe. Discuss the differences between the regions on either side of the "Iron Curtain." Where did they differ? What did they have in common? How do you explain the European origins of the Cold War?

(2) Local leaders in Asia and in South America and the Caribbean sought to use the enmity between the USA and the USSR to promote their own interests. Such efforts presented dangers as well as opportunities. Discuss both dangers and opportunities. Who benefited most? Who least?

(3) The Cold War looked quite different in Asia than it did in Europe. Compare and contrast the two. Why did the Asian Cold War turn deadly while the European Cold War supported a frozen peace?

(4) By the end of the 1970s, political commentators were already discussing the end of a Cold War consensus in Western Europe. Discuss the unraveling of this consensus. What changed? Why?

Suggested Reading   Thomas J. Christensen, *Useful Adversaries: Grand Strategy, Domestic Mobilization, and Sino-American Conflict, 1947–1958* (Princeton University Press, 1996). This is an excellent study of the role of US anti-communism and the China lobby in keeping the Cold War going.

Victoria de Grazia, *Irresistible Empire: America's Advance through Twentieth-Century Europe* (Cambridge, MA: Belknap Press, 2005). De Grazia has written a remarkable study of European reaction to American advertising, marketing, and merchandising in twentieth-century Europe.

John W. Dower, *Embracing Defeat: Japan in the Wake of World War II* (New York: W.W. Norton, 1999). This is a comprehensive and very readable study of how Japan responded to defeat.

ALEKSANDER FURSENKO AND TIMOTHY NAFTALI, *One Hell of a Gamble: Khrushchev, Castro, Kennedy, and the Cuban Missile Crisis, 1958–1964* (New York: W.W. Norton, 1997). This multi-source study presents the most up-to-date version of the Cuban missile crisis, the high point of the Cold War. It suggests that we were even closer to a nuclear confrontation than was realized at the time.

JOHN LAMBERTON HARPER, *The Cold War* (Oxford University Press, 2009). Harper challenges established views that American resolve won and argues that the USSR more or less did itself in.

AKIRA IRIYE, *The Origins of the Cold War in Asia and the Pacific* (New York: Columbia University Press, 1977). This is a classic study of the origins of the Cold War in Asia.

MELVYN LEFFLER, *A Preponderance of Power: National Security, the Truman Administration, and the Cold War* (Stanford University Press, 1992). The authors look at the strengths and weaknesses of Cold War diplomacy as it passed from an era of economic hegemony to one of rearmament. This work is definitive and readable.

HENRY ROUSSO, *The Vichy Syndrome: History and Memory in France since 1944* (Cambridge, MA: Harvard University Press, 1991). This book studies collaboration in France and French memory of collaboration. Rousso has been at the vanguard of studies of Vichy and collaboration and the discovery of French complicity.

SAM TANENHAUS, *Whittaker Chambers: A Biography* (New York: Random House, 1997). This highly readable treatment casts a lot of light on Cold War America and helps explain the sense of an internal communist threat.

HERMAN VAN DER WEE, *Prosperity and Upheaval: The World Economy, 1945–1980* (Berkeley: University of California Press, 1986). This is a good overview of the world economy in a critical period.

Glossary

Americanization: Combination of commercialism and improved living standards that occurred in post-World War II Europe. Many Europeans were concerned that it would vulgarize European culture and society.

Bay of Pigs: Failed attempts to overthrow Fidel Castro by American-trained Cuban exiles who invaded at the Bay of Pigs in April 17–19, 1961. Begun under the Eisenhower administration, the action was carried out by the Kennedy administration. The threat of US invasion increased Fidel Castro's concern about his administration's security and led the USSR to seek to reassure him by moving Soviet missiles to Cuba.

COMECON: Council for Mutual Economic Assistance, established by Stalin in 1949 to encourage economic planning and co-ordination in Soviet-dominated Eastern Europe. Surprisingly, the socialist-dominated Eastern bloc was less successful in co-ordinating inter-state economic activities than capitalist Western Europe.

economic miracle: Term used to describe the thirty years after the end of World War II in Japan and Western Europe. While many in 1945 pessimistically predicted the kind of economic chaos that followed World War I, in fact these years witnessed the longest period of sustained growth in the history of capitalism.

GATT: General Agreement on Tariffs and Trade. Established by the UN in 1948, its purpose was to encourage the reduction of tariffs, remove trade barriers, and establish a worldwide economic forum.

goulash communism: Term for attempts to reconcile communist domination of political society with orientation toward consumerism. It began with economic reforms in Hungary in 1968.

guest workers: Term used to describe migrants to Europe who had only temporary residence rights.

MAD: Mutually Assured Destruction was the Cold War strategic doctrine that world peace depended on the superpowers having enough nuclear weaponry to destroy one another in an armed confrontation. The doctrine's acronym, MAD, appealed to its critics.

Marshall Plan: US program of economic assistance for a battered post-World War II Europe. It was announced by US Secretary of State George Marshall in 1947 and came into operation as the European Economic Recovery Program (1948–52). Under strong pressure from the Stalinist USSR, Eastern European nations refused to participate in the Marshall Plan. This was an important step in the beginnings of the Cold War.

mixed economy: The integration of state planning with private enterprise. It was used extensively in post-World War II Western European planning.

resistance: Underground movements that fought against collaborationist or fascist regimes in German-occupied Europe or Japanese-occupied Asia. Resistance movements engaged in sabotage, prisoner of war recovery, and intelligence gathering.

Notes
1 On the "kitchen debate" see Elaine Tyler May, *Homeward Bound: American Families in the Cold War Era* (New York: Basic Books, 1988).
2 I.T. Berend, *Central and Eastern Europe, 1944–1993* (Cambridge University Press, 1996), p. 188.
3 Alan L. Nothnagle, *Building the East German Myth: Historical Mythology and Youth Propaganda in the German Democratic Republic, 1945–1989* (Ann Arbor: University of Michigan Press, 1999), p. 71.
4 Timothy W. Ryback, *Rock around the Bloc: A History of Rock Music in Eastern Europe and the Soviet Union* (New York: Oxford University Press, 1990).

15 Decolonization, democratization, and civil wars, 1950–1980

Timeline	
1946	Philippines gains independence from USA.
1947	India and Pakistan become independent of Britain. At least half a million die in partition.
	In October, Indian troops land in Kashmir, and fight Pakistan for it until 1949.
1948	India asserts control over Hyderabad.
	Britain withdraws from Palestine. Israel declares independence and wins 1948 war; 700,000 Palestinians are displaced.
1951	Prime Minister Mosaddegh of Iran nationalizes Iranian petroleum, provoking a crisis with Britain and the United States.
1952–56	Mau Mau rebellion in Kenya.
1952	Young Officers coup in Egypt.
1953	American Central Intelligence Agency overthrows Prime Minister Mosaddegh in Iran and restores shah to the throne.
1954	Colonel Gamal Abdel Nasser comes to power in Egypt (rules until 1970).
	National Liberation Front begins movement for Algerian independence.
1955	Sukarno's party wins elections in Indonesia.
	Non-Aligned Movement leaders meet in Bandung, seeking to avoid alliances with either the USA or the Soviet Union.
	Baghdad Pact groups Middle East countries with USA and UK against communism.
1956	Abdel Nasser of Egypt nationalizes the Suez Canal, provoking a brief war with France, Britain, and Israel; the USA forces them to withdraw.
1957	Ghana led to independence from Britain by Kwame Nkrumah.

1958	Indonesia nationalizes Dutch property.
	Iraqi officers' coup against the British-installed monarchy in Baghdad.
	Rioting French colonists invade office of Algeria's governor-general, demanding Algeria be made permanently part of France and that General Charles de Gaulle become president. He returns to power.
	De Gaulle of France offers Overseas Territories option of remaining in the French Community or seeking total independence.
1959–61	Great Famine in China results from Mao forcing farmers into communes.
	United Arab Union between Egypt and Syria; falls apart in 1961.
1960	Rebellion of French colonists in Algeria collapses for lack of military support.
	Korean leader Syngman Rhee forced out of office by student riots. Succeeded by military strongman General Park Chung-Hee.
	Madagascar and West African Republic opt for complete independence from France; Nigeria becomes independent of Britain.
	Senegal, Mali, and Guinea leave West African Republic to become independent states.
	Léopold Senghor elected president of Senegal; rules until 1981.
1962	Algerian independence; Ahmed Ben Bella becomes president.
1963	Ayatollah Khomeini leads protests against the regime of the shah in Iran.
	Kenya becomes independent of Britain.
	Sukarno of Indonesia declares himself President for Life.
	Korean–Japanese Peace Treaty.
1965	Korean economy begins to take off.
	General Suharto overthrows Sukarno and begins pogrom against communists.
	Ferdinand Marcos becomes president of the Philippines.
	Second war between India and Pakistan, over Kashmir.
	General Houari Boumedienne comes to power in a coup in Algeria and rules until 1978.
1966	Great Proletarian Cultural Revolution begins in China.
1967	Nigerian civil war over attempt of Biafra to secede.
	Six Day War ranges Egypt, and Syria against Israel; Israel wins easily, conquering the West Bank and Gaza.
1968	Baath Party coup in Iraq.
1970	Anwar El Sadat comes to power in Egypt.
1973	October Arab-Israeli War; oil boycott of West.
1974–75	Fascist government in Portugal is overthrown, and Portuguese colonies in Africa are granted independence.
1975–77	Indian Prime Minister Indira Gandhi declares "Emergency" and assumes dictatorial powers. She is defeated in 1977 elections.

1976	Zhou Enlai and Mao Zedong both die, ending an era of far left rule in China. Morocco annexes former Spanish Sahara, sparking war of resistance.
1978–79	Islamic Revolution overthrows the shah in Iran.
1978	Camp David Peace Accords between Israel and Egypt.
1979–80	British Rhodesia becomes independent as Zimbabwe under Robert Mugabe.
1979	Deng Xiaoping launches Four Modernizations campaign, kicking off China's streak of impressive economic growth.
1982	Israeli invasion of Lebanon.
1983	Shi`ite radicals in Lebanon bomb US embassy and marines barracks.
1984	Indian Prime Minister Indira Gandhi is assassinated by Sikh separatists; succeeded by son Rajiv Gandhi.
1986	Corazon Aquino wins elections in the Philippines; corrupt former president, Ferdinand Marcos, flees into exile.
1989	China's government crushes student protests at Tiananmen Square. Indian Prime Minister Rajiv Gandhi is assassinated by Tamil separatists.
1990–94	Apartheid regime is dismantled in South Africa, and blacks win right to vote; Nelson Mandela is elected president.
1997	Hong Kong returns to Chinese rule after a century and a half as a British colony.
1998	General Suharto steps down; democracy comes to Indonesia.

The lawyer Nelson Mandela (1918–2013) spent twenty-five years in jail for organizing against the South African **apartheid** regime, but in 1994 he was elected president of South Africa. The young Mandela was an activist against the racist policies of the white regime; only later in life did he endorse non-violent political action. In his inauguration speech, he called for the "healing of wounds" and an end to the "pernicious ideology and practice of racism and racial oppression." His Korean counterpart, Kim Dae-jung (1925–2009), also spent time in jail under military rule, but as prime minister pursued policies of democratization and reconciliation with his colonial rulers, the Japanese. Both won the Nobel Peace Prize.

Other anti-imperial leaders took different paths. Mao Zedong (1893–1976) and Kim Il-sung (1912–94) strongly endorsed violent struggle, isolating their countries from the world. Ho Chi Minh (1890–1969) and his Viet Minh nationalists successfully fought off both the French and the Americans during a thirty-year struggle. The bloody contest between Palestinians and Israelis continues today, despite intensive efforts at mediation. The struggle to rid the world of imperial domination has led to many unpredicted outcomes, and it is not yet over.

Before the beginning of World War II, about a third of humankind lived under some form of European or Japanese colonial rule. That war permanently altered world governance in many ways, and after it was over, pressures for change mounted. The USA in the Cold War often pushed the older powers to give up their colonies. Domestic politics in countries such as Great Britain and France often made continued colonial rule abroad difficult to justify, since much of the public was unwilling to shoulder its burdens any longer. In the colonies, subjects often were no longer willing to collaborate with European rule. Nationalist movements seeking independence grew, encompassing politicians, businessmen, and the middle and working classes. Since European colonialism had functioned with relatively few troops and civil servants, this loss of co-operation was often fatal.

The colonial states enacted strong central administration and government censorship. When the Europeans went away, some new governments simply kept these laws on the books. They used their strong states to plan important parts of the economy, as in India, although they did not go as far as the Soviet Union or China. Ironically, the authoritarian policies of Europe's conservative politicians gave postcolonial leaders the levers of control to practice state socialism when the colonies became independent.

Elsewhere, as in Burma, Korea, Indonesia, Egypt, Iraq, Pakistan, and much of sub-Saharan Africa, decolonization gave the military an opportunity to come to power. Colonial practices often strengthened the military and weakened civilian institutions such as political parties. As one of the few well-organized and long-standing institutions, the military often had key advantages over civilian politicians. Young officers were often caught up in a spirit of nationalism. Contemptuous of the corruption of politicians, they were convinced that they could do a better job.

Postcolonial leaders also attempted to recover "national" assets from imperial powers. Nasser seized the Suez Canal in 1956; Iran attempted to nationalize the Anglo-Iranian Oil Company in the 1950s; Indonesia nationalized Dutch property in 1958; Zaire (the former Belgian Congo) took over its copper mines. The nationalization and embargo of oil sales by OPEC (the Organization of Petroleum Exporting Countries) in 1973 followed the same pattern.

The colonial era left a bitter legacy of cultural conflict. Middle-class, educated elites who knew the language of the former colonial power favored secular government. The poor and the working classes, resenting the dominance of these colonially educated elites, responded to appeals of local ethnic or religious forces against them. Ethnic differences were not simple personal choices of identity; they were embedded in strong organizations of mutual aid, local power, and economic activity. These social foundations raised the stakes of ethnic and religious conflict, making them life-and-death struggles.

World War II spurred decolonization by showing that non-Europeans could stand up against imperialists. The Japanese had supplanted European powers in much of Southeast Asia, taking the Dutch East Indies (which became Indonesia) away from The Hague, Vietnam from Paris, and Malaya from London. The Nazi satellite government of Vichy France could not firmly control all its colonies. The evils committed in the name of a third German "empire" or Reich gave the colonial enterprise a bad name. Indonesian nationalist Achmed Sukarno wondered why it was wrong for Germany to rule Holland, but all right for Holland to rule the East Indies. Although Great Britain retained India during the war, politicians eager for independence launched a "Quit India" movement that the British only countered by jailing large numbers of people. A prominent Indian dissident, Subhas Chandra Bose, even went over to the Japanese and fought alongside them against the British in Burma (See Chapter 13).

The European powers had maintained colonies for many reasons, not limited to economic benefit. Some colonies were very profitable, others were not. It would be hard to demonstrate that the British benefited in any significant way from possession of the territory that snaked along the Gambia River in West Africa in the midst of surrounding French colonies. The British had even at one point attempted to hand over the Gambia to the French, but British officials wanted something, at least, in return, and the French were unwilling to offer anything. Sometimes,

colonies had been acquired by ambitious military men on the ground in Africa or Asia, or to forestall a strategic victory for a European rival. India had often cost the government of Great Britain more to run than it brought in, in taxes, though the long-term economic benefits to British private commerce of having such a captive market may have offset public losses. In contrast, Malaya's tin and rubber became extremely lucrative for Britain, amounting to a significant proportion of its gross income, and so relinquishing that colony was an unpleasant prospect for London. Likewise, the British earned more from taxes on the Anglo-Iranian Oil Company than the Iranian government received in royalties on its own petroleum. Iran was in any case an independent country not formally under British rule, though the south of the country was a recognized British sphere of influence. The case of Iran shows that imperial sorts of benefit could be garnered without administering territory.

Chapter 14 discussed the international aspects of the Cold War, and the economic developments within the capitalist and socialist blocs, the USA, Europe, and Japan, and the Soviet Union. This chapter looks at the world beyond the two super-power blocs, including former colonies and the special experience of China. These are the main themes:

- One of the strongest drives of the postwar period was the determination of colonized peoples to gain independence.
- Colonial states left the independent nations a legacy of contention. On one hand, new nations could take over colonial institutions to create strong authoritarian regimes.
- On the other hand, botched or incomplete decolonization has bequeathed the twenty-first century many of its most pressing diplomatic and military challenges, including Kashmir, Taiwan, and the Israeli–Palestinian struggle.
- Language, ethnicity, and religion figured prominently in all these postcolonial struggles, as forces both for division and for unity. Economic ideologies of the Cold War masked deeper social identities.

15.1 THE KOREAS AND THE IMPLICATIONS OF DECOLONIZATION

Chapter 14 discussed Korea's position as a battleground of the Cold War. Here we discuss domestic developments in the two Koreas as two dramatically different consequences of decolonization. Map 15.1 illustrates the Cold War in Asia.

Decolonization often led to new partitions of formerly united territories, and to civil wars or wars between two successor states to the same colonial government. Sometimes such conflicts came about because colonialists had created "countries" like Nigeria that threw together peoples who had little in common with one

Map 15.1 Cold War in Asia 1945–75

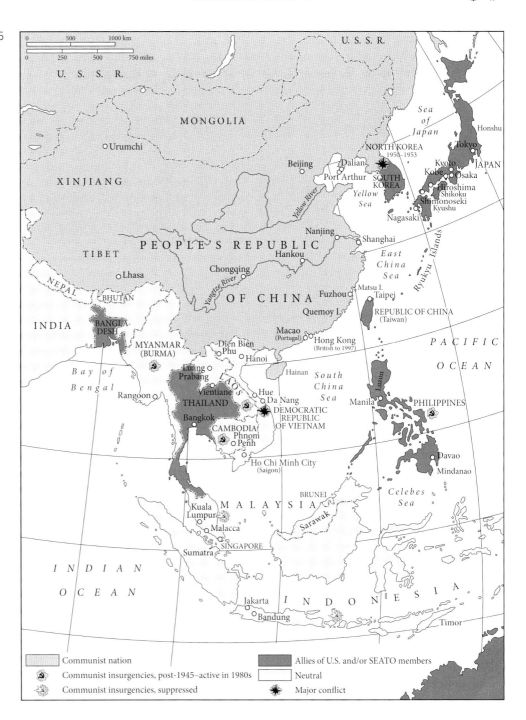

Communist nation
Communist insurgencies, post-1945–active in 1980s
Communist insurgencies, suppressed
Allies of U.S. and/or SEATO members
Neutral
Major conflict

another. Koreans, however, had always seen themselves as one people, even before Japanese colonial rule. This strong sense of unity made the division of the country even more painful.

Japan had left a significant infrastructure behind. Unlike most colonial powers, Japan wanted to develop Korean industry rapidly in order to serve Japanese military needs. It built railroads, developed ports and mines, and brought a monetized economy to the Korean countryside. It promoted the economic integration of the country. North Korea, which concentrated mainly on industrial production for its military, built on these colonial policies. Kim Il-sung (r. 1948–94) pursued political and economic policies

similar to those of Mao Zedong but even more extreme. He developed a cult of personality, demanding absolute obedience, and constructed a command economy on a Stalinist model. Heavy industry alone, especially military production, got all the state investment, while Korean peasants forced into collective farms barely survived. In the 1950s and 1960s, North Korea grew faster than the South, but the heavy pressure on agriculture exhausted its resources. Kim Il-sung's extreme policy of **juche**, or "self-reliance," led to North Korea's near total isolation from the world. Even the Chinese, their closest allies, had only limited access to the country. When severe famine struck, Kim's regime refused foreign aid, just as China did in the 1959–61 famine. Under Kim Jong-il (r. 1994–2011), Kim Il-sung's son, North Korea became dependent on Chinese oil shipments, South Korean and Japanese food shipments, and its only valuable export: weapons, including nuclear components. From its colonial experience, the North Korean leadership only drew negative lessons: hostility to all foreign powers, at immense economic cost.

Japanese colonial policies shaped the development of Korea in a different way. Protestant Christian missions had attracted many converts, especially from entrepreneurial families, who grew wealthy by using Japanese capital for industrial development. In the South, the Japanese had encouraged the commercialization of agriculture and the development of markets, but the colonial administration had also usurped a great deal of land. South Korean leader Syngman Rhee (1875–1965), himself a Methodist minister, could draw supporters from these commercially minded evangelicals. But unlike most elite rulers in Southeast Asia or Latin America, he also pursued a fairly successful program of land reform, made easy because the Japanese had put so much land under government control. South Korea thus escaped the kind of landlordism that plagued countries like Pakistan, where the concentration of landed wealth in the hands of a few very wealthy families created large numbers of impoverished farm workers and day laborers. These impoverished workers could not buy many consumer goods, so there was little demand for light industrial production. South Korea also put heavy emphasis on mass literacy and technical education, on the Japanese model, creating a large class of skilled workers and technicians who could adopt the newest technology.

South Korean small and mid-sized firms multiplied in the 1950s, boosting light industrial output, while the large industrial cartels, or **chaebol** (the Korean equivalent of Japanese *zaibatsu*) pioneered investment in heavy industries like steel and shipbuilding with the world's most advanced technology.

By 1965 the economy took off, producing impressive rates of annual growth in the 7–10 percent range for decades thereafter. South Korean peasants went to cities and went into small business in large numbers, in part because the USA provided food aid and so drove down agricultural prices. Extended families were broken up, making way for more individualism. Educational institutions proliferated, and nearly universal literacy was attained. Per capita income increased a hundred-fold between 1960 and 1990. By the end of the century South Korea had emerged as the world's twelfth-largest economy, with a GDP nearly as large as India's in the 1990s, but with a population of only 46 million people. The only other postcolonial countries in the top thirty were the other East Asian powerhouses, Taiwan and Hong Kong. The capital, Seoul, grew from about 1 million to about 10 million in our period. Women campaigned for and gained more political and economic rights. On the dark side, the *chaebol* dominated heavy manufacturing, with government support. They were plagued by **crony capitalism** (a small business elite with strong influence on government policy) and corruption.

South Korea accomplished all this economic progress while suffering from cycles of political unrest and military dictatorship. Student riots forced Syngman Rhee out of office in 1960. General Park Chung-hee ruled the country from the 1960s through to his assassination in 1979. After he forced through an unpopular peace treaty with Japan in 1963, Japanese businesses poured investment into South Korea, aiding the take-off. The USA also provided billions of dollars of civilian and military aid. By the late 1980s, the South Korean business and military elites finally joined the students in taking a dim view of military rule, and the country made a transition to democratic elections. Kim Dae-jung, the determined campaigner for human rights, winner of the Nobel Peace Prize for 2000, had spent years in jail under Park's dictatorship. As prime minister, he began to promote more friendly relations with Japan, culminating in a visit by the Japanese prime minister. Only then did South Korea finally outgrow the Japanese colonial heritage of military administration.

South and North Korea represent two extreme ends of the spectrum of decolonization. The northern half's leaders nursed their grudges, insisted on eliminating foreign influence, and drove their country into famine and isolation. The southerners, still no friends of the Japanese, overcame their bitter legacy, adapted many of the colonial institutions to their own purposes, and prospered under the American and Japanese wings.

15.2 FOUR CHINESE WORLDS: THE MAINLAND, TAIWAN, HONG KONG, AND SINGAPORE

The two Chinas, the mainland and Taiwan, also went in different economic directions, but began to converge by the end of the century. Mao had won the civil war in 1949 by claiming to be the genuine source of resistance to Japanese invasion. The surviving Nationalist leadership fled to Taiwan, where they still claimed to be the only legitimate government of all of China. Hong Kong and Macao remained the last colonial enclaves, under British and Portuguese rule, until 1997 and 1999 respectively.

Taiwan

The mainlanders arriving in Taiwan in 1949 were refugees, a defeated army, and a discredited government. At first, sharp tensions grew between the mainlanders and the indigenous

Box 15.1 Land Reform: The Key to Development?

All the newly independent countries had primarily agricultural economies, and quite unequal ownership of land. Upon independence, against resistance from landed elites, many governments enacted substantial land reform. Others did not. Effective land reform after independence strongly affected the societies' economic growth, educational levels, and degrees of democratization.

The governments that carried out land reform could be authoritarian nationalists, as in Taiwan, South Korea, and Egypt, military occupiers, like the USA in Japan, modernizing monarchs, as in Iran, national socialists, as in Iraq, or revolutionary socialists, as in China and North Korea. In Japan, Taiwan, and South Korea, successful land reform broke the power of landlords, giving economic influence to small farmers who engaged actively with rural markets. They sold their crops to growing urban populations and provided the demand for urban consumer products. East Asia boomed because of their production and consumption. Eventually, the prospering small farmers and urban

marketers demanded an end to undemocratic rule. It arrived in Taiwan and South Korea in the 1980s. On the other hand, in Middle Eastern regimes that broke down old landed elites, like Egypt and Iraq, the state took away most of the gains to small farmers and invested them in war, leaving the societies undemocratic and markets underdeveloped.

Marxist regimes distrusted peasant farmers as inherently "petty bourgeois." They gave them land to mobilize them, but soon took it back. The Chinese communists conducted land reform in the 1940s before they took power, but in the 1950s they collectivized landholding, inflicting on the peasants heavy extraction, restriction of mobility, and famine. Only in the 1980s did the Chinese small farmer re-emerge as the bedrock of dynamism for the Chinese economic miracle. The North Korean leaders never accommodated peasant needs, and North Korean peasants still face famine today. Vietnam never had the extremes of Chinese collectivization, but has not completely undone it either.

Where land reform did not occur, investment in education was low, and social tensions remained. Land reform was a key element of the Kennedy administration's Alliance for Progress in Latin America, but for the most part it failed to happen. Only Mexico, which had its own social revolution in the early twentieth century, and Cuba in the 1960s significantly overturned the rural social structure. High polarization between extreme wealth and extreme poverty still plagued the region, undercutting prospects for growth. The same was true of the Philippines, where Corazon Aquino's remarkable electoral victory still failed to challenge dominant landed elites. In India, the rural and working classes turned to ethnic and Hindu nationalist parties to express their hostility to the secular, urban elites who had failed to address their needs.

In sum, land reform did not solve all problems of decolonization, but putting resources in the hands of small farmers usually had positive effects on political and economic development.

Taiwanese, a Chinese-speaking population that had seen peace and prosperity under Japanese colonial rule. The ruthless suppression by Chiang's troops of an anti-Nationalist uprising of the local population on February 28, 1947, still rankles relations between the Nationalist immigrants and the local Taiwanese. Jiang Jingguo (r. 1972–88), however, son of Chiang Kai-shek, reoriented the government away from the hopeless reconquest of the mainland toward domestic economic growth. Taiwan, like Korea, built on its Japanese colonial infrastructure to become a new export powerhouse, first producing simple clothing like sandals, underwear, and umbrellas, then moving up the technology ladder to motor scooters and finally computers. Here, too, land reform and universal education were a key element in raising the lower level of the population, while a huge emigration of talent to US universities, at first a heavy brain drain, later brought back high-technology skills. Despite

political insecurity, including threats of invasion by Beijing, Taiwan prospered by shifting from military to economic goals under the US security wing. (Box 15.1 describes the progress of land reform in other countries of the world in the postwar period.)

Hong Kong

Hong Kong, ruled by the British until 1997, played a key intermediary role between the mainland and the outside world: When mainland China opened up, Hong Kong boomed; when the mainland cracked down, Hong Kong took in its brightest refugees. Chinese commercial talent that fled the mainland in 1949 built up Hong Kong into a major center for capital investment, while the British protected capital with property laws and an honest civil service.

Singapore

Singapore, like Hong Kong a small city-state, shook off colonial rule and profited from doing so. Under the former socialist Lee Kuan Yew (r. 1959–90), it took on the role of intermediary port in Southeast Asia, profiting as a trans-shipping and investment center. Although formally a democracy, Lee's government was effectively a single-party state and it repressed dissent, promoting a stern Victorian message of discipline and cleanliness combined with respect for multiple cultural identities. Singapore held its mixed population of Chinese, Indians, Malays, and British together under a paternalistic and highly pro-capitalist government, which made English the national language. For all its peculiarities, the Singapore solution worked for Singapore.

Mainland China

Mainland China, 350 times the size of Singapore, faced somewhat different problems. For the first decade of his rule, Mao followed the Stalinist model of building up heavy industry under state control and extracting agricultural surplus from the peasantry through collectivization. The Chinese collectivization campaign was far less damaging in its early stages than Stalin's brutal seizure of property in the 1930s; Mao had learned from Stalin's mistakes. His cadres convinced most peasants that they could modernize their small-scale production by joining larger collectives under Party guidance. But the combined pressure of rapid industrialization and agricultural modernization drove the economy into a crisis in the late 1950s. The growth of agricultural output began to slow down. The Party had to either reduce investment in heavy industry so as to let the peasants rest, or drive peasant living standards down to keep industry going. Lenin had chosen the first course with the New Economic Policy; Stalin chose the second course in his collectivization campaign.

Mao knew about the Soviet dilemma, but he thought that his party could find a new way out: China could "walk on two legs" by simultaneously promoting industry and agriculture together on giant **communes** of up to 50,000 people. During this Great Leap Forward, peasants would sleep in barracks, work intensively on huge collective plots, and make steel in their backyard furnaces. China, in Mao's vision, would overtake British steel production in fifteen years.

This time, Mao's utopian dreams brought catastrophe. The communes disrupted the delicate balance of the agrarian economy so much that nature rebelled, and the backyard steel turned out to be worthless. In the Great Famine of 1959–61, over 30 million out of China's 660 million people starved or died, the largest man-made famine in history. Mao still could not openly

admit defeat; he purged the great General Peng Dehuai, who spoke out against him on behalf of the starving peasants; but he had to allow more pragmatic figures, like Deng Xiaoping (1904–97), to "put him on the shelf" in an honored position, but out of real power. From 1962 to 1966, the Chinese economy recovered, as Deng Xiaoping allowed peasants to have private plots and sell goods on the market. Pragmatic planning by economic experts took precedence over "red" cadres.

Mao, however, plotted revenge against his own Party, which he saw as having abandoned the revolutionary struggle. In 1966, he launched the Great Proletarian Cultural Revolution to attack the "small handful of cadres in power who had taken the capitalist road." Its main supporters were China's high school and college students, educated to have unquestioning faith in Mao, and in Mao's wife, Jiang Qing, who made herself the dictator of cultural life. Students waved the Little Red Book of quotations from Chairman Mao, put dunce caps on experienced communist organizers, and paraded professors and Party people, beating and shouting at them in public, causing many to commit suicide or go insane. Meanwhile, Jiang Qing reduced China's entire cultural repertory, past and present, to seven revolutionary operas personally approved by herself.

Mao thought that all this anarchy would produce a new revolutionary spirit: "To rebel is good," he pronounced. But soon, the student Red Guard groups fought each other over the correct interpretation of the Red Book, political order broke down in the cities, and serious economic disruption threatened the country. Only Premier Zhou Enlai (1898–1976), still loyal to Mao, could keep the government going, and he, too, became a target of Jiang Qing and the most radical Red Guards. In the end, to save China from total collapse, Mao had to allow the People's Liberation Army to take over, and he sent millions of Red Guards down to the countryside to "learn from the peasantry." There, the pampered urban students mostly learned the misery of peasant life; many could not come back home for over ten years.

Mao's last years were a time of secret plots, anxiety, and confusion. Lin Biao, the new leader of the People's Liberation Army, had been designated as Mao's successor, but he died in a plane crash in 1971 trying to escape to Mongolia after supposedly plotting a coup. Mao began the opening of China to the USA by meeting Nixon and Kissinger in Beijing; his wife and her radical supporters looked with alarm on the new moderation and opening of the country to the outside world. Zhou Enlai's death on January 8, 1976, genuinely saddened most Chinese, who saw him as the primary force of stability; students and workers brought wreaths and poems in his honor to Tiananmen Square, the central political space in Beijing, but the radicals cleared the square and beat up those present, claiming that this was a "counter-revolutionary incident." They blamed Deng

Xiaoping for instigating it. On Mao's death on September 9, however, the radicals quickly lost power, and Deng Xiaoping established his position as China's paramount leader. The radicals, including Jiang Qing, were put on trial as the Gang of Four and held responsible for nearly all the tragic waste of China's lost decade, 1966–76. Mao's role, as the fifth member, went unmentioned in Party documents.

In 1979, Deng launched a campaign for **Four Modernizations** (agriculture, industry, national defense, and science and technology), encouraging workers and students to develop their technological skills and peasants to grow what they wanted on their fields, and sell the surplus for profit. The remnants of collective farming vanished in all but name, and China's agricultural output soared. Students found their way back from the countryside; many of them, disillusioned with revolutionary activism, put their youthful zeal into business, and got rich. President Jimmy Carter (in office 1976–80) normalized US relations with China, opening the door to massive trade and investment, while Taiwan had been ejected from the United Nations in 1971. From the early 1980s, the Chinese economy grew at the extraordinary rate of 10 percent a year. Mainland China had joined the East Asian miracle.

Yet economic growth once again generated political tensions. In the late 1980s, college students, intellectuals, and workers began to resist the power of the Communist Party. The Party-state still held on to the "towering heights" of the economy, the heavy industrial enterprises that employed millions of workers. These inefficient colossi could not compete in a global market, and their workers did not profit from the new economy's growth. The corruption of Party officials, who taxed and collected bribes from every possible source, outraged everyone. Deng supported economic liberalization, but firmly rejected any political change that would limit Party power. But it took the death of the admired reformer Hu Yaobang, who had been dismissed from power by Deng, and the visit of Mikhail Gorbachev to Beijing in 1989, to ignite revolt. Students once again gathered in Tiananmen Square to memorialize the death of a leader, as they had done in 1976. Their demands were vague, but they wanted an end to corruption, freedom to study and choose their careers, and recognition of their political rights. Workers in the square raised more radical demands for the right to strike and higher wages.

The Party, divided between hard-line conservatives and reformers, still under the thumb of the aging Deng Xiaoping, delayed its response as mass demonstrations grew. Students went on a hunger strike, deeply impressing the urban population. The crowd at the square grew to about a million people. On June 3–4, 1989, the Chinese army brutally suppressed the movement, killing or wounding thousands of protesters in Beijing. Some other cities may have had even worse massacres, but in Shanghai the capable Party secretary Jiang Zemin kept things quiet.

The Tiananmen Square incident raised many questions about China's troubled relationship to the West. Americans, Europeans, and the thousands of Chinese students studying abroad strongly supported the chances for individual advancement opened up by the reform movement. The conservative leadership, and many others inside the country, however, feared social disorder. They called the Tiananmen movement nothing but "turmoil," blaming it on imperialist agitation.

Since Deng Xiaoping's death in 1997, China has conducted three uncontested successions to leadership, with the rise of Jiang Zemin (r. 1997–2003), followed by Hu Jintao in 2003, and Xi Jinping in 2013. Jiang restored relations with the USA, visiting President Clinton, and continued Deng's market reforms, but he did not introduce democracy. Hong Kong returned to Chinese control in 1997 with many misgivings about whether Beijing would allow its special society to flourish. The USA relaxed political pressure on China by "delinking" human rights and trade, and the economy continued to grow, fueled by exports to the USA and heavy investment from the USA, Japan, and Europe. China's entry into the World Trade Organization made it a full member of the world economic and political community. From a weak, impoverished, decaying empire in 1900, a victim of full-fledged imperialist attack from all sides, it has emerged as one of the great powers again, certain to exert enormous influence in the future.

15.3 SOUTHEAST ASIA: THE PHILIPPINES AND INDONESIA

All of Southeast Asia, except for Thailand, fell under colonial rule, beginning with the Portuguese in the seventeenth century, and ending with the British, French, and the USA in the late nineteenth century. An extraordinarily diverse region of island archipelagoes, continental agrarian bureaucracies, jungles, forests, and tribal peoples, it contained all the world's major religions – Islam, Christianity, Buddhism, and Confucianism – and nearly all of its ecological zones. Colonial domination and the struggle against it gave its peoples some common experiences, though divisions between the rival movements were usually not as sharp as in East Asia (Vietnam included). Cold War rivalries and democratization movements each displayed particular features in different countries.

The Philippines: Three Colonial Rulers, One Dictator, then Democracy

The Philippines had three distinct colonial experiences, beginning with the Spanish empire in 1521, the American era of 1898–1942, and then a brief period of Japanese rule. Although the Japanese conquered the Philippines in 1942, by 1943 they had declared it "independent." They installed a collaborationist regime that largely consisted of old elite Filipino families, of mixed Chinese, Spanish, and local Filipino heritage. Ensconced as great landlords, merchants, and professionals, they outlasted the Japanese occupation to prosper when the USA reconquered the islands and scheduled them for independence in 1946. The transition to independence in the Philippines was less violent than that of Korea, China, or Vietnam: no civil war or political division ensued. Like many other postcolonial states, however, the independent Philippines fell short of expectations. President Ferdinand Marcos, democratically elected in 1965, instituted a dictatorship in the 1970s and early 1980s. While dedicated to modernization from above that somewhat challenged the old landlord elite, the Marcos regime pursued a policy of crony capitalism, delivering enormous wealth into the hands of friends and relatives of the president. Unlike Korea, however, the close alliance of government and capitalist classes did not direct investment into efficient economic growth. The Philippines had not undertaken a serious land reform program to undermine the old elites and create a new middle-class interest group. In addition, the Muslim minority in the largely Catholic Philippines agitated for independence and sometimes mounted open rebellions, only to be harshly repressed.

The country had to wait for political liberalization in the 1980s before "people power" challenged the entrenched elite. Corazon Aquino, the widow of an assassinated senator who had opposed Marcos, symbolized not only populist discontent with capitalist dictatorship but also the increasingly public role of Filipina women, who had entered professions such as nursing in large numbers and many of whom had substantial experience as guest workers in the Persian Gulf and the USA. Aquino won the elections in 1986, despite Marcos's fraud and repression, while the IMF imposed strict financial controls, forcing the country into a debt crisis. When the USA refused to back him, Marcos fled into exile. The people had won, but recovering the millions Marcos had stolen proved difficult, and Aquino did not really challenge the elite she came from. The Philippines, with a weak state, entrenched corruption, and continued instability, grew slowly and fitfully through the 1990s. It remained a nation, just barely.

Indonesia After Independence: Dictatorship, Repression, Fragmentation

Building a new nation in the Indonesian archipelago was no easy task, either. Indonesia, the world's most populous Muslim country, also contains Hindus, Chinese, and Christians, and its Muslims are divided into many distinct ethnic and ideological

groups. The military emerged as a strong institution working to ensure national unity at the cost of some repression. It quashed the Communist Party and the Islamic parties, and often put the Chinese merchant class in a precarious position.

The Partai Nasional Indonesia (PNI), led by Achmed Sukarno (r. 1945–67), won the first countrywide general elections, held in 1955. His platform of "Five Principles" (**Pancasila**) promoted belief in God, humanitarianism, national unity, democracy, and social justice. Like Sun Yat-sen's Three People's Principles, they evoked noble ideals in very unspecific language, avoiding the systematic ideology of capitalism or communism. The visit of the American president John F. Kennedy even seemed to give American backing to his efforts (see Figure 15.1). Sukarno's Principles became influential in the **Non-Aligned Movement**, including Egypt and India, which met in the Indonesian city of Bandung in 1955 and attempted to create an independent bloc in the emerging Cold War order. Zhou Enlai also attended, from China, supporting the effort of these nations to avoid being drawn into tight alliances with either the Soviet Union or the United States during the Cold War.

In the Indonesian elections of 1955, the Islamic parties and Communist Party also did well, getting 18 percent and 16 percent of the seats respectively. Indonesia had become a country of mutually hostile ethnic groups, institutions, and political parties, but divisions had not quite reached the stage of war. Sukarno (1901–70) took advantage of this disunity, and may also have genuinely been frightened by it. Speaking of the need for "Guided Democracy" in tones reminiscent of Sun Yat-sen and Chiang Kai-shek, he became increasingly authoritarian. He tried to play the right-wing army off against the Communist Party, alarming the USA when he got too close to the latter.

In 1963, Sukarno declared himself "President for Life." In the meantime, the Communist Party, with 2 million members, had acquired affiliations with trade unions and other institutions that accounted for 9 million people. As Sukarno tried to juggle the contending parties, right-wing officers feared a communist takeover. In 1965, General Suharto (r. 1967–98) overthrew Sukarno, beginning a crackdown on the communists in which an estimated half a million or more people, including many Chinese, were killed.

The Asian financial crisis of 1997 brought the Indonesian economy near to collapse, forcing Suharto to step down in 1998, as Indonesia began experimenting with parliamentary democracy for the first time since the mid-1950s. The economy hardly recovered at all until 2003. Although the left had by then been much weakened, Islamic parties re-emerged as major players. Some small Islamist groups became implicated in terrorism and an alliance with al-Qaeda, but the mainstream Islamist parties were not violent and were willing to compete

Figure 15.1 US President John F. Kennedy and Indonesian President Sukarno.

for power in parliament. Paramilitary forces committed atrocious massacres in East Timor to prevent its independence when the Portuguese left, but failed to recover the territory. Indonesia is now a parliamentary democracy, and its economy has grown quickly in the last decade, but it faces national breakdown, under threat from strong secessionist movements in Aceh, radical Islamists with international ties, anti-Chinese lynch mobs, ecological devastation, and institutionalized corruption.

Indonesia's odyssey shows that it is difficult to turn a colonial administration into a unified nation-state when only military force holds its diverse building blocks together. Its national identity may survive the turmoil of democratization, but none of the older ideologies – capitalist, Marxist, or Pancasilist – seems adequate for its new challenges.

15.4 INDIA AND PAKISTAN

The date of Indian and Pakistani independence was set for midnight on August 15, 1947. A little over one sixth of the military and civil service of British India went to Pakistan. The new, Muslim-majority state included two wings, West Pakistan and East Pakistan. West Pakistan consisted of the provinces of Panjab, Sindh, Baluchistan, and the Northwest Frontier Province. East Pakistan contained the eastern portion of the old Indian province of Bengal, which was now partitioned. Although the assets of old British India were to be distributed proportionally to the new states, other social goods could not be shared. Almost all the advanced sectors of the British Indian economy, including factories, remained on the Indian side. West Pakistan was largely agricultural and illiterate. East Pakistan, too, mainly a peasant society, had grown the raw agricultural goods, such as jute, which were processed in West Bengal factories.

As the date of partition approached, and as communal riots continued, panic gripped the Hindus and Muslims of the Panjab and of the United Provinces. Some 10 million frantic persons emigrated from their homes, often with little more than the clothes on their backs, to a new country they hoped would be more hospitable. Urdu-speaking Muslims from the Gangetic Plain headed for Karachi. They came to be 10 percent of the population of West Pakistan. Millions of urban Hindus and Sikhs fled the major city of Lahore, since it had been given to Pakistan.

Communal riots and hysteria spurred such exchanges of populations, but well-organized communalist parties also provoked some emigrations in order to consolidate their hold on certain communities, even if it meant targeting their own people. As tempers flared, mobs attacked the emigrants on the road or in their railway cars. It is estimated that between half a million and a million people were slaughtered during the partition.

Trains arrived at the stations full of bloody corpses, and women were raped and killed in the fields.

Exchange of populations, whether peaceful or violent, often occurred during decolonization. Three quarters of a million Palestinians fled or were expelled from Israel in 1948 as the British Mandate of Palestine broke down, and 850,000 Jews fled or were expelled from Arab lands, of whom 644,000 settled in Israel. Greeks and Turks "exchanged" nearly a million people at the end of the Ottoman empire. A million Europeans left Algeria as a result of the revolution that gave that country independence in 1962, and the French colonial authorities are estimated to have been responsible for the deaths of a million Algerians in the period before they finally granted independence. The India–Pakistan atrocities stand out for the scale of movement, the deliberate fostering of hatred by organized parties on both sides, and the unwillingness of the British to do anything to stop them.

In South Asia, two large and important provinces remained in dispute. The Muslim ruler of Hyderabad in South India ruled over a Hindu majority. At first he wanted to join Pakistan, then sought independence. Jawaharlal Nehru, India's first prime minister (in office 1947–64; see Figure 15.2), gave him a year to come to terms with joining India, and in September 1948 sent troops in a "police action" to take control of Hyderabad by force. It became the Indian province of Andhra Pradesh. The other princely states were also absorbed by India, for the most part voluntarily. In Kashmir, a northern province at the foothills of the Himalayas, the situation was reversed. A Hindu Raja, Hari Singh, ruled over a largely Muslim population. Singh initially favored joining India, but Nehru made such a move conditional on his promoting into power the popular Muslim Kashmiri leader, Sheikh Abdullah, with whom the raja had poor relations. Hari Singh therefore considered seeking independence, while his people largely desired to join Pakistan. Since tens of thousands of them had just served in World War II, they could organize local militia to oppose Hindu dominance. Some of these veterans joined peasants in rebelling against their Hindu landlords, while Pushtun "holy warriors" (mujahidin) crossed into Kashmir from Pakistan to aid them.

On October 27, 1947, Indian troops landed in Srinagar, apparently at the request of Raja Hari Singh. Pakistan rejected this move, on the grounds that it violated the earlier standstill agreement, and fought back. Fighting continued into 1949, when an armistice was signed. Pakistan had about a third of Kashmir when hostilities ceased, and its front line became known as the "Line of Control." The rest was under Indian rule. In 1949, Nehru forced Raja Hari Singh to turn over power to the Muslim leader Sheikh Abdullah, apparently hoping that this move would mollify Kashmiri Muslims and keep them in the Indian union.

Figure 15.2 Nehru inherits the Gandhi legacy.

The referendum stipulated by High Commissioner Mountbatten and the UN Security Council was never held.

The unsettled status of Kashmir has plagued the subcontinent and world peace ever since. Pakistan and India went to war over it again in 1965, and fought a smaller engagement at Kargil in 1999. From the late 1980s, Kashmiri Muslims began an insurgent movement, which India attempted to repress with military force. In winter and summer of 2002, India and Pakistan, by then nuclear states, nearly went to war on two separate occasions, in part over Pakistani fighters infiltrating Kashmir to target Indian police and troops on behalf of Kashmiri separatists.

Not only did Hindus and Muslims fight each other; Muslims also fought Muslims. Pakistan could not hold its western and eastern wings together, because Bengalis in the east resented the dominance of the Panjabi ethnic group. In 1971, East Pakistan seceded, declaring itself the independent country of Bangladesh, provoking a bloody civil war. India intervened on the side of Bangladesh, ensuring its independence. Pakistan shrank to encompass only its Indus Valley provinces. Although both East and West Pakistan had been largely Muslim, ethnic and linguistic differences emerged as more important than religious commonalities.

The South Asian Economic Boom, or Lack of It

Most of the Indian subcontinent in 1950 consisted of small villages. Illiteracy was high by world standards. The multilingual and multi-ethnic states posed difficulties for national integration. Some large cities had small but significant industrial sectors, but factory workers constituted a small minority of Indian and Pakistani workers. Out of these common conditions, India and Pakistan developed differently. Map 15.2 shows the states of South Asia. Pakistan's governments never succeeded in instituting significant land reform, though some Pakistani leaders, such as General Ayoub and Prime Minister Zulfiqar Ali Bhutto, took small steps in that direction. Pakistan therefore remained a country dominated by large landlords, who had no interest in seeing their peasants educated. As late as 1980, three quarters of Pakistanis lived in rural areas, and only 24 percent were literate. Only 5 percent of women could read and write at a basic level. Although its social statistics improved in the late twentieth century, Pakistan's rapid rate of population growth made it impossible for the country to raise living standards substantially. By 2000, Pakistan had over 148 million people, and the population was still growing at 2.7 percent each year. The rich yields of the Panjab Plain and Indus valleys cushioned the country in most years from the worst effects of its lack of real development.

The government put most of its money into the military, and little into public education. Pakistan inherited from British India a highly professional civil service and military, along with a political tradition of big landlord domination, but no real experience of grassroots democracy. The country's workers were constrained by laws that hurt unions. Agricultural workers were even forbidden to unionize. Pakistan's civilian politicians found it impossible to stand up to the officers of the professional Pakistani army, who continually intervened in politics. Generals frequently took power, though eventually they returned to the barracks. These serial coups left political parties and their traditions weakened.

Given the vast gulf that separated the small wealthy elite from the common peasant or urban laborer, Pakistani politicians were constantly tempted to appeal to Islam as a common basis of identity. The Islam that came to be used for this political purpose was not the tolerant, mystical Sufism of the Panjabi and Sindhi villagers or the secular Islam of the upper middle classes, however, but the rigid, fundamentalist legalism favored by the urban lower middle-class and newly educated. The major party pushing the implementation of strict religious law was the

Jamaat-i Islami. Although it sometimes found powerful patrons, as with the dictator General Zia ul-Haq (r. 1977–88), the Jamaat-i Islami and similar parties never did very well at the polls when it contested elections, through the twentieth century. Most Pakistanis were traditionalist Muslims, valuing the intercession of saints, rather than fundamentalists who gauged religious belief by strict adherence to religious law.

India was even more diverse than Pakistan, with a population that grew to over a billion in the course of the second half of the twentieth century. Unlike Pakistan, it avoided dissolution and retained a parliamentary system of government for the most part, with a short period of "emergency rule" in the late 1970s. Nevertheless, powerful secession movements arose among Sikhs in the Panjab, Muslims in Kashmir, and speakers of Dravidian languages in the south. All were harshly put down. Gandhi's and Nehru's Congress Party, which had played such a key role in winning the country's independence, dominated the four decades after independence. Prime Minister Jawaharlal Nehru was succeeded by his daughter Indira Gandhi (no relation to the Mahatma), who was in power most of the time until her assassination by Sikh separatists in 1984. Her son, Rajiv Gandhi, served as prime minister from that time until his own assassination at the hands of Tamil separatists in 1989.

Nehru's policies stressed democratic elections at both the provincial and federal level, and religious tolerance. He refused to allow the substantial Muslim community that remained in India after partition to be branded disloyal. Although Hindus constituted some 85 percent of Indians, the state sought to treat all religious groups even-handedly. The Congress Party had a strong socialist tendency, though it was also supported by India's powerful industrialists. Nehru pushed through an effective land reform law in the 1950s, which ended the power of the very large landlords and helped create a rural middle class of farmers with medium-sized farms. Still, dominant rural castes continued to be much wealthier than other villagers, and the ballot box gave most Indian peasants relatively little real political clout, and almost no claim on economic resources.

The Indian state under the Congress Party was, however, committed to some kinds of social equality. In universities and the civil service, a program of affirmative action was adopted for the "scheduled castes" or what traditional Hindus would see as outcastes, and tribal groups. Women were also able to make great progress under Congress rule. About one quarter of the economy came to be accounted for by the vast public sector, and the government made it difficult to take currency out of the country. Importing and exporting required numerous permits and onerous paperwork. A powerful government planning commission made much economic policy. The state had a monopoly on radio and television (a policy continued from the colonial

Map 15.2 South Asia

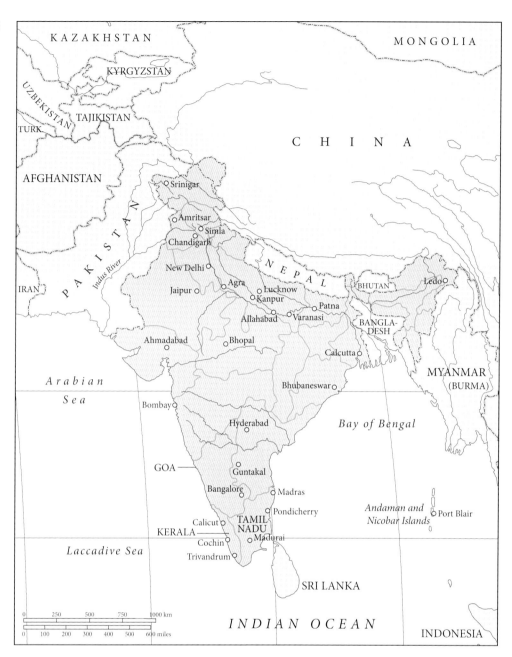

approach to radio), and there was no private media competition. The government could thus always get its views out to the public. Congress economic policies were not very successful, resulting in average economic growth of only 3 percent per year, the same as the population growth rate.

In the 1970s, Indira Gandhi attempted to centralize most power in her own hands, making herself virtual dictator during the "Emergency" of 1975–77. To her surprise, when she called elections at the end of this two-year period of one-woman rule, the Indian electorate turned her out of office. Although she was able later to return as prime minister, the Congress lock on political power was fatally weakened. Hindu nationalist parties

such as the Bharatiya Janata Party were gaining in popularity, especially among upper-caste Hindus in the northern Hindi belt, who felt threatened by Congress affirmative action policies toward the scheduled castes.

Just as Islamic nationalism ultimately emerged among the strongest political forces in Pakistan, so Hindu nationalism began supplanting secular socialism as the most important political tendency in India in the late twentieth century. More extreme Hindu nationalists considered non-Hindu Indians such as Muslims, Sikhs, and outcastes to be second-class citizens, and violence against Muslims became increasingly common. Hindu nationalism also proved attractive for lower middle-class Indian men who knew little English and felt locked out of politics by the largely English-speaking Congress elite.

In some sense, religiously based politics served as a second wave of decolonization in India and Pakistan, helping displace from power elites who had gained their cultural capital by learning colonial languages and administrative techniques, and who had inherited an essentially colonial state apparatus from foreigners. Religious politics often also served as a way for lower middle-class men, threatened with losing their dominant position because of the secular state's education of women, to put women back in a subordinate position. Both traditional Islam and traditional Hinduism require women's subservience to men. A similar movement occurred in postcolonial Algeria, where a French-speaking national elite came to be challenged by Arabic-speaking Islamists from the **casbahs**, or old city quarters. Gender politics was also important in Algeria, as we shall see.

15.5 AFRICA

France and Britain were committed to holding on to their colonial possessions in Africa far more fervently than in most other parts of the world. Map 15.3 shows colonial possessions in Africa. Only a bloody decade-long war convinced the French to pull out of Algeria. Britain faced violence as well, though on a smaller scale, in Kenya. Most determined of all, however, were the Portuguese, who had gained African colonies in the heyday of their greatness as a seagoing power. Postwar Portugal, poor and ruled by a fascist government, needed the income from its colonies.

From 1945 to 1955, France and Britain first attempted to reformulate colonialism as a development project. European colonial powers had often not been much interested in social and economic development of their African possessions. The Belgian monarchy had notoriously seen the Congo as little more

Map 15.3 Colonial possessions in Africa

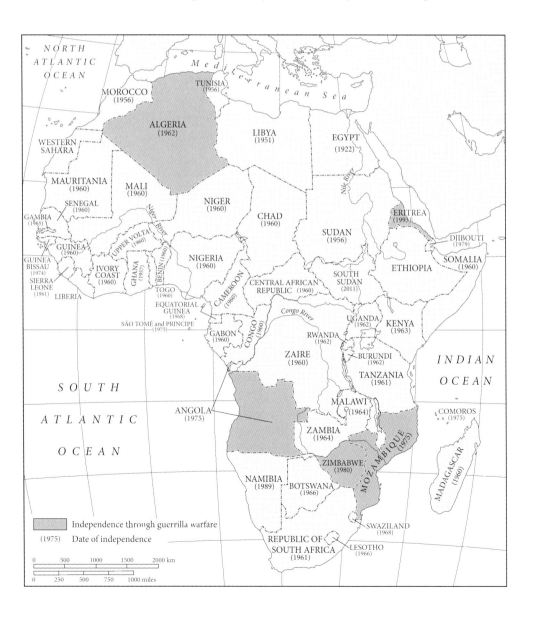

than an opportunity for plunder. The French and British built roads and railways and made infrastructural investments to ensure control, not to improve the lives of the colonized. Colonial administrators developed a new attitude after 1945.

Postwar French politicians, thinking that they might be able to retain the empire by ruling less harshly and by incorporating more Africans into French politics, met in Brazzaville, French Congo, in 1944, to plan the future. They divided their African subjects at that point into only two categories: "moderns" (**évolués**), meaning Western-educated, and peasants. This classification ignored the millions of traders, artisans, and urban workers in Africa. To address peasant discontent, the French reluctantly agreed to abolish forced labor after five years. They were still not convinced African peasants could be induced to work as hard for wages. To deal with the concerns of the moderns, they decided to allow some Africans to vote in French elections.

In 1946 France made some of its possessions, mainly in the Caribbean, into Overseas Departments, which had the same administrative status as the departments or provinces in France itself. The other colonies, designated Overseas Territories, could elect delegates to the French National Assembly. At that time, France ruled 60 million colonial subjects and only 40 million Frenchmen, but the Overseas Territories only got twenty seats in the assembly, a tiny number given the imbalance of populations.

Even so, many Francophone African politicians got their start by serving in the French National Assembly in the late 1940s. Among them was the poet Léopold Senghor, of what later became Senegal. Senghor fought against the Nazis in the French army, then was captured and released in 1942. He then joined the underground French Resistance to German occupation. Elected to the French National Assembly, Senghor emerged as among the foremost poets of **négritude**, an identification with "blackness" that transcended particular languages, cultures, or places of birth. Other more radical poets saw négritude as a call to avoid complete assimilation to French culture, and to take pride in the black heritage. Senghor and other like-minded African members of parliament, such as his colleague Lamine Guèye, pressed successfully for an immediate end to forced labor in the colonies.

They also agitated for an end to the distinction between national citizens and imperial subjects, though here they met greater resistance, since the French empire was based on this distinction. Any change in status could make the French themselves a minority in a large multicultural state. Since the postwar French state guaranteed health services and wage levels to its citizens, citizenship for Africans would also oblige the state to raise the African standard of living to French levels. Despite

their frustrations, Senghor and the West Africans worked through parliamentary institutions, but other Africans were more radical. In many ways events in Madagascar proved more prophetic than those in West Africa. Local politicians in that French territory mounted a nationalist uprising in 1947 that lasted until 1949, and was only suppressed by the French with much bloodshed.

By 1956 lawmakers had given up on trying to incorporate their colonies directly into France, except for Algeria. They gave each colony the authority to administer most of its own local affairs, under French supervision, with French control over foreign affairs. Free elections with universal voting rights were held in 1956 in the territories, but the results affected only the government of the colonies. France had given away so many administrative rights to the "subjects," while denying them significant economic aid, that the subjects wondered why they needed the French at all.

In 1958, when General Charles de Gaulle (president from 1959–69) began the Fifth Republic, he gave the Overseas Territories the option of remaining in something called the French Community or of opting for independence. The members would have representation at the level of the Community for matters of higher education, court administration, foreign policy, and defense. Many territories voted to remain in 1958, only to begin rethinking the issue immediately. Madagascar, for instance, became autonomous within the French Community in 1958, but opposition politicians managed to win support for complete independence in 1960.

Likewise, in West Africa, Léopold Senghor had spent his life working for a synthesis of black African culture and French civilization, and he argued strongly for remaining in a French framework in 1958. But by 1960 the West African public decided to break with France and seek independence. The territories had at first attempted to form federations, but by 1960 these had broken up. Senegal, Mali, and Guinea became independent countries. Algeria joined the roster of the independent former colonies in 1962.

Senghor was president of Senegal from 1960–81, but his earlier aspirations had been to see a broader French Community where Africans were equals with Parisians. Failing that, he had wanted to see a large West African federation that could carry on French African civilization on a major scale. In the end, he served as the president of a small postcolonial state. Rather than continuing to participate in French economic progress, Senegal was cut loose by France and left with a stagnating peanut-growing agricultural economy. Senghor was at least able to exercise his idealism in the direction of ensuring Senegal did not become a mere dictatorship, as did a number of other former French colonies.

By the mid-1960s, French decolonization was largely complete with the exception of a few Pacific and Caribbean islands and French Guiana in South America. The postwar experiment in extending France had ended. France and its colonies were now foreign countries, and France had no further formal responsibilities for them. Yet France continued to interfere in the affairs of its former colonies, using foreign aid and military intervention to prop up those it saw as friendly and punish those who adopted a strong anti-imperialist stance. The administrative divisions established by the empire had fostered localism, leaving former French West Africa divided into many small, poor states rather than united in a more viable and powerful larger federation. Many leaders of the new states, such as Sékou Touré in Guinea, continued authoritarian French traditions. For example, he forbade strikes by labor unions on the grounds that they harmed the new nation. Even without direct control, French imperial influence continued.

The British empire never even considered trying to incorporate the former colonies into the United Kingdom. Its officials nevertheless also saw themselves as having a duty to develop the remaining colonies in Africa into modern societies. Just as Churchill had done with regard to Palestine and India, politicians in London continued to underestimate how strongly the colonized desired independence. Many British colonial officials, on the other hand, were more realistic. For instance, those in the Gold Coast (which became Ghana) recognized the nationalist movement of Kwame Nkrumah as a serious force from the time it mounted strikes in the late 1940s. They worked to give more executive authority to African ministers and accepted Ghana's independence in 1957. Nkrumah, a committed African nationalist, hoped his country's experience would begin a vast process of decolonization in the continent. Although he represented the aspirations of many Ghanaians for independence, Nkrumah also demonstrated authoritarian tendencies, abolishing political parties as soon as he became president of an independent state. In Box 15.2, Nkrumah describes his vision of a united African continent that could contend with the wealthy imperial countries of the world.

Nigeria symbolized all that went wrong with colonialism: It allowed a country with a large, literate population and great potential wealth to fall apart into destructive war. The British engaged in a complex set of negotiations with Nigerians through the 1950s, addressing questions of the relationship of the central government to the three major regions and the relationship of those regions to one another. In 1960 they granted independence to a federal government that attempted to balance the interests of its major ethnic groups. The Muslims of the north were populous but not very well educated. The east had a literate population, and many easterners got jobs in the bureaucracy in Lagos, the capital. The west had a thriving economy supported by the cocoa trade.

The British inadvertently reinforced regional and ethnic rivalries at the same time as they attempted to subordinate them to the center. They thus set the stage for conflicts between Christians and Muslims, between various tribes, and between speakers of various languages. These ethnic conflicts provoked a civil war in 1967, when the province of Biafra in the south attempted to secede. The central government inflicted famine on Biafra to prevent its secession. The country's ethnic rivalries made unified rule difficult, opening the way to a series of military governments. On the other hand, Nigeria benefited from the discovery and exploitation of petroleum resources, which give ethnic groups an incentive to remain in the federation. Still, with the tenth largest population in the world (over 100 million people), its GDP in 2000 was only 36 billion dollars, below fiftieth in the world ranking.

The British were less enthusiastic about relinquishing Kenya on the east coast of the continent. This reluctance derived in part from the existence of a small but significant white settler population there, which had taken land around Nairobi from local groups such as the Kikuyu. Three major anti-colonial forces arose in the late 1940s and through the 1950s in Kenya. One was the Kenya African Union, led by Jomo Kenyatta, a political activist, journalist, and anthropologist trained at the London School of Economics. The KAU was a modern political party like the Congress in India, organized to run the country whenever the British left. The second force was the Asian immigrant middle class, consisting of shopkeepers and professionals, who allied with Kenyatta in seeking a peaceful transition to independence. The third was the most troubling. It consisted of the **Mau Mau** movement among the Kikuyu, which vehemently protested the ways in which British colonial modernity had hurt poorer members of that tribe. In particular, urban squatters resented loss of access to village land, and consequent loss of what they thought of as the requirements for adult manhood. This radicalized section of the population, which had been hurt by modernization, began agitating against British rule. From 1952 to 1956 they waged a violent campaign of assassination and communal attacks.

The British colonial administration, which thought of itself as bringing modernity to Africa, deeply resented what they saw as the barbarism of the Mau Mau, with its initiation rituals and devotion to returning to the ancestral ways of the Kikuyu tribe. They were also alarmed at the deaths of white settlers. The Mau Mau killed over 100 Europeans and 2,000 Kenyans loyal to Britain. The British replied with massive force, killing 11,000 rebels and relocating 20,000 Kikuyu as a counter-insurgency

Box 15.2 Kwame Nkrumah: "I Speak of Freedom," 1961

Kwame Nkrumah (1909–72) was the leader of Ghana, the former British colony of the Gold Coast and the first of the European colonies in Africa to gain independence with majority rule. Until he was deposed by a *coup d'état* in 1966, he was a major spokesman for modern Africa.

For centuries, Europeans dominated the African continent. The white man arrogated to himself the right to rule and to be obeyed by the non-white; his mission, he claimed, was to "civilise" Africa. Under this cloak, the Europeans robbed the continent of vast riches and inflicted unimaginable suffering on the African people. All this makes a sad story, but now we must be prepared to bury the past with its unpleasant memories and look to the future. All we ask of the former colonial powers is their goodwill and co-operation to remedy past mistakes and injustices and to grant independence to the colonies in Africa … It is clear that we must find an African solution to our problems, and that this can only be found in African unity. Divided we are weak; united, Africa could become one of the greatest forces for good in the world. Although most Africans are poor, our continent is potentially extremely rich. Our mineral resources, which are being exploited with foreign capital only to enrich foreign investors, range from gold and diamonds to uranium and petroleum. Our forests contain some of the finest woods to be grown anywhere. Our cash crops include cocoa, coffee, rubber, tobacco and cotton.

As for power, which is an important factor in any economic development, Africa contains over 40% of the potential water power of the world, as compared with about 10% in Europe and 13% in North America. *Yet so far, less than 1% has been developed. This is one of the reasons why we have in Africa the paradox of poverty in the midst of plenty, and scarcity in the midst of abundance.*

Never before have a people had within their grasp so great an opportunity for developing a continent endowed with so much wealth. Individually, the independent states of Africa, some of them potentially rich, others poor, can do little for their people. Together, by mutual help, they can achieve much. But the economic development of the continent must be planned and pursued as a whole. A loose confederation designed only for economic co-operation would not provide the necessary unity of purpose. Only a strong political union can bring about full and effective development of our natural resources for the benefit of our people.

The political situation in Africa today is heartening and at the same time disturbing. It is heartening to see so many new flags hoisted in place of the old; it is disturbing to see so many countries of varying sizes and at different levels of development, weak and, in some cases, almost helpless. If this terrible state of fragmentation is allowed to continue it may well be disastrous for us all.

There are at present some 28 states in Africa, excluding the Union of South Africa, and those countries not yet free. No less than nine of these states have a population of less than three million. Can we seriously believe that the colonial powers meant these countries to be independent, viable states? The example of South America, which has as much wealth as, if not more than, North America, and yet remains weak and dependent on outside interests, is one which every African would do well to study.

Critics of African unity often refer to the wide differences in culture, language and ideas in various parts of Africa. This is true, but the essential fact remains that we are all Africans, and have a common interest in the independence of Africa. The difficulties presented by questions of language, culture and different political systems are not insuperable. If the need for political union is agreed by us all, then the will to create it is born; and where there's a will there's a way.

The present leaders of Africa have already shown a remarkable willingness to consult and seek advice among themselves. Africans have, indeed, begun to think continentally. They realise that they have much in common, both in their past history, in their present problems and in their future hopes. To suggest that the time is not yet ripe for considering a political union of Africa is to evade the facts and ignore realities in Africa today.

The greatest contribution that Africa can make to the peace of the world is to avoid all the dangers inherent in disunity, by creating a political union which will also by its success, stand as an example to a divided world. A Union of African states will project more effectively the African personality. It will command respect from a world that has regard only for size and influence. The scant attention paid to African opposition to the French atomic tests in the Sahara, and the ignominious spectacle of the UN in the Congo quibbling about constitutional niceties while the Republic was tottering into anarchy, are evidence of the callous disregard of African Independence by the Great Powers.

We have to prove that greatness is not to be measured in stockpiles of atom bombs. I believe strongly and sincerely

Box 15.2 (*cont.*)

that with the deep-rooted wisdom and dignity, the innate respect for human lives, the intense humanity that is our heritage, the African race, united under one federal government, will emerge not as just another world bloc to flaunt its wealth and strength, but as a Great Power whose greatness is indestructible because it is built not on fear, envy and suspicion, nor won at the expense of others, but

founded on hope, trust, friendship and directed to the good of all mankind.

The emergence of such a mighty sta-bilising force in this strife-worn world should be regarded not as the shadowy dream of a visionary, but as a practical proposition, which the peoples of Africa can, and should, translate into reality. There is a tide in the affairs of every people when the moment strikes for

political action. Such was the moment in the history of the United States of America when the Founding Fathers saw beyond the petty wranglings of the separate states and created a Union. This is our chance. We must act now. Tomor-row may be too late and the opportunity will have passed, and with it the hope of free Africa's survival.

move designed to get them away from Mau Mau influence. In the aftermath, the British increasingly turned to what they thought of as modern Kenyan politicians, such as Kenyatta. They granted the country independence in 1963. Kenyatta went on to establish a one-party state in Kenya. Despite political authoritarianism and high rates of population growth, Kenya managed to grow impressively on the economic front for a while, at an average of 6 percent per year after independence, but by the 1990s it was making little progress.

Most African countries were independent by 1970, with the exception of white settler regimes in Rhodesia (now Zimbabwe) and South Africa, and of the Portuguese possessions. Liberation movements in Mozambique and elsewhere tied down the Portuguese army. By 1974, high-level officers were publicly arguing that these liberation movements could not be put down by sheer force. In 1974 the fascist government in Portugal collapsed at the hands of an officers' coup. They led Portugal toward democracy at home, and in 1974–75 the new government granted independence to Lisbon's colonies in Africa.

The white settler regimes of the former British colonies of Rhodesia and South Africa were the last to fall (in 1979–80 and 1990–91 respectively). After a long guerrilla war against the small white minority, Rhodesia became Zimbabwe, led by Robert Mugabe, who won the first national election where blacks could vote as equals. South Africa, which had three times as many English and Dutch settlers proportionately, held out longer. The African National Congress had fought against white rule since the early twentieth century. Ultimately, all of Africa gained independence. But the continent struggled with more than its fair share of civil wars, ethnic strife, droughts, epidemics such as AIDS, and political repression in the postcolonial period. Some of these problems were heritages of the colonial period, while others sprang from local conditions.

15.6 THE MIDDLE EAST

By the twentieth century, European incursions had broken up the region into nearly thirty separate states, many of them small and with few economic prospects. Map 15.4 shows the territories of the modern Middle East. Algeria, Tunisia, Syria, Lebanon, and most of Morocco spent the first half of the twentieth century under French rule. The British ruled Egypt directly until 1922, and Iraq as a mandate until 1932, but kept intervening in both countries until the mid-1950s. The British Mandate of Palestine lasted until 1948, and they dominated the Persian Gulf until 1969. In the Middle East and North Africa, unlike elsewhere, the British and French followed similar policies. Both relinquished their Levantine possessions, but elsewhere sought to regain and prolong their dominance.

Many of the long-running struggles in the modern Middle East originated in the colonial era. In 1976 Morocco annexed the former Spanish Sahara, putting down local resistance, in order to undo French and Spanish division of territory. The conflict between Israelis and Palestinians, which still roils the entire Middle East, goes back to British policies in World War I. Lebanon's civil strife in the late 1950s and its long civil war from 1975 to 1989 derive from the French creation of the country. France detached the territory from Syria in a bid to create a pro-French, Christian-dominated satellite in the Middle East. Iraq claimed Kuwait as an Ottoman successor state, trying to undo British secret treaties with the emir of Kuwait which had given him independence. These claims touched off the Gulf War of 1990–91.

The Israeli–Palestinian Conflict

Between 1950 and 1980, Israel and the Arab states fought three major wars in which decolonization played an important role.

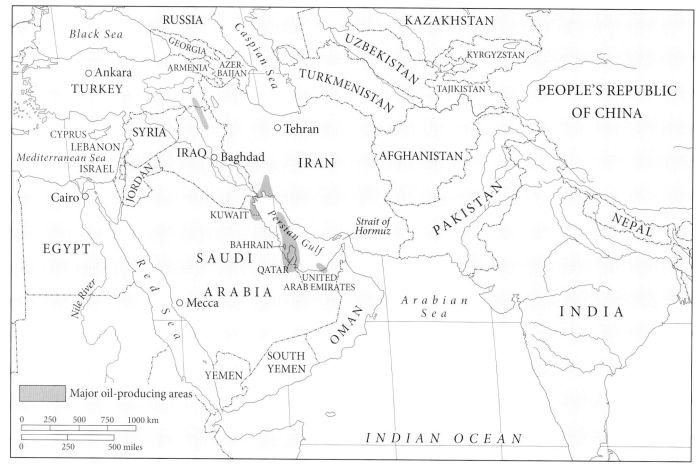

Map 15.4 Modern Middle East

Map 15.5 shows the geography of this conflict. Both sides sought to redress the contradictory policies of the British Mandate of Palestine. The British had vacillated in their support of the rise of a Jewish state. In the 1920s and early 1930s, the British had allowed and even encouraged the immigration of hundreds of thousands of Jews to Palestine. After the outbreak of the Great Revolt among Palestinians in 1936–39, the British grew more cautious and limited Jewish immigration. In 1947, a civil war between the 1.3 million native Palestinians and the more than 580,000 largely immigrant Jewish colonists in the Mandate of Palestine broke out, as Britain withdrew. In that war, over 700,000 of the 873,000 Palestinians living in the areas that became Israel fled or were expelled. In response to the establishment of Israel and the plight of the Palestinians, mobs and communalist organizations in Arab countries such as Tunisia, Yemen, and Iraq increasingly targeted synagogues or Jewish communities. As a result, most Middle Eastern Jews fled to Israel, seeing much of their wealth taken by the governments that neglected to protect them. Only Morocco, Iran, and Turkey retained small but significant Jewish communities. This exchange of populations resembles on a smaller scale what

happened between India and Pakistan at the partition the year before, though with only a fraction of the loss of life witnessed in South Asia.

The main Arab powers more often sought their own national interest than that of the Palestinians. In the first Arab–Israeli war, Egypt attempted to annex Gaza and the Negev, and succeeded in getting the former. Jordan's leaders took the West Bank, including much of Jerusalem, having made a secret deal with the Israelis behind the scenes. The Zionists emerged from the war with a state, Israel. The Israeli prime minister, David Ben-Gurion (in office 1948–54, 1955–63), quickly announced that the displaced Palestinians would not be readmitted to the territories controlled by Israel. They had lost their homes, land, and property permanently. Israel enacted a law of return, specifying that any Jew anywhere in the world had the right to immigrate to the new country of Israel. In this respect, Israel acted like European countries such as Ireland, Germany, and Italy, which favored immigration from people of the same ethnic origin. From an Israeli point of view, Israel had been forced to absorb the hundreds of thousands of Jews that were forced to flee their homes in the Middle East, and it was only fair for "the

Map 15.5 Arab–Israeli conflict

Arabs" to absorb the displaced Palestinians. Palestinians, in contrast, remained mere refugees in Jordanian-ruled territory, Lebanon, Syria, and Egypt. Many, dreaming of going home, chose to live in squalid refugee camps, while others lacked the money to get out. The Jordanian, Egyptian, and Syrian economies, plagued by relatively low rates of economic growth, could not assimilate the Palestinian refugees. They remain in the camps today.

Western observers and pan-Arab intellectuals who speak of "the Arabs" ignore the fact that the Arabic-speaking countries often have little in common with one another. Their dialects differ almost as much as Italian does from Spanish, and the way of life of a Jordanian tribal shepherd differs enormously from that of an Egyptian peasant on the Nile. The former colonies or Mandates quickly developed an effective national identity, often based on long-standing regional sentiments. The political systems differ as well. Jordan is a monarchy, for example, while Syria was a republic. Lumping "the Arabs" together makes no more political sense than calling all speakers of Romance languages "Latins."

Thus, despite speaking a dialect of Arabic, Palestinians were not easily absorbed by their new hosts. Egypt and Jordan, pursuing their own state interests, did not offer them a rump state in Gaza and the West Bank. Gaza, cut off from its traditional markets in Palestine and Jordan and unable to develop lucrative new ones with Egypt, sank into poverty. The Jordanian political and military elite tended to come from a Bedouin, East Bank background, and viewed the Palestinians with suspicion. Christian-dominated Lebanon denied them citizenship. Only about 15 percent of Palestinians were Christian, with the majority being Muslim. Had they become Lebanese citizens, they would have given the Lebanese Muslims a decisive majority of the population, which was already fairly evenly divided, with the Muslims growing faster because of larger family size. Lacking citizenship, Palestinian refugees in Lebanon were reduced to permanent outcast status, denied access to economic, educational, and political opportunities. The decolonization of the Mandate of Palestine meant a new state for the Zionist movement, but disaster for the dispossessed Palestinians.

The Suez Crisis of 1956: Egypt's Victory

The war over the Suez Canal, the next landmark in the decolonization of the Middle East, drew in the British and French as well as Egyptians, Syrians, and Israelis. Militant Arab nationalist regimes in postcolonial Egypt and Syria rejected Israel's right to exist. In turn, Israeli hawks wanted to annex more land, such as water-rich southern Lebanon, and were in no hurry to make peace.

In 1952, a group of military men styling themselves the Young Officers made a coup in Egypt. They felt that corrupt officers and officials had sold out the Egyptian soldiers fighting in Palestine/ Israel in 1948, often selling good equipment on the black market instead of sending it to the front. They viewed the weak King Farouk as a pro-British playboy misusing the country's resources. They saw the dominant Wafd Party as a tool of the British, as it only served the interests of pro-British big landlords. First, as in Korea and Taiwan, the military government

undertook significant land reform, ending landlordism and allowing a rural middle class to emerge.

By 1954, Colonel Gamal Abdel Nasser (r. 1954–70) emerged as the military leader of Egypt. He dissolved civilian political parties, including the powerful Muslim Brotherhood, a secretive fundamentalist movement that had sometimes resorted to terrorism. When a member attempted to assassinate him, Nasser outlawed the Brotherhood, jailing many members and forcing others underground. But both Nasser and the Brotherhood rejected British dominance of Egypt, represented by the Suez Canal. The canal, built by an ambitious Egyptian viceroy in 1869, had been sold to the British in 1876. The Egyptian public increasingly demanded the British give up control of this key Egyptian resource.

At first, Britain negotiated with Nasser, pledging to withdraw its military from Egypt by June of 1956, but thereafter, Egypt's relations with the West deteriorated. Nasser gravitated to the Non-Aligned Movement and refused to shun the communist bloc. He bought weapons from Czechoslovakia in 1955, in part because the USA, which tilted toward Israel, declined to sell him weaponry. In May of 1956, Nasser recognized China. The fiercely anti-communist Eisenhower administration, seeing any willingness to deal with the communists as a betrayal, was furious. The USA, Britain, and the World Bank then denied Nasser funding for his large hydroelectric dam at Aswan.

When the original deadline passed without a British withdrawal, Nasser nationalized the Suez Canal, intending to use tolls on its traffic to finance the building of the Aswan Dam. In Box 15.3 he describes his rejection of joint ownership of the canal. Nasser's nationalization of the canal was unacceptable to the British government and to French and British stockholders in the Suez Canal Company. The Conservative prime minister, Anthony Eden, compared Nasser to Mussolini, and feared that Nasser sought to cut off Europe from Middle Eastern oil (though there was no reason to think Nasser intended to do this).

Eden and the French planned to invade Egypt and take back the canal, but they ran into strong opposition from the USA and the USSR at the UN. They therefore secretly turned to Israel, backing a plan for an Israeli invasion of Egypt that would allow Franco-British forces to come into the Canal Zone as peacekeepers between the two belligerents. Nasser's popularity throughout the Arab world and his support for Palestinian guerrillas threatened Israel's position, as did his blockade of the Gulf of Aqaba, denying Israeli ships passage through the canal.

The Israeli assault on October 29, 1956 took the Sinai peninsula, easily defeating Egyptian forces. France and Britain, in accordance with the plan, offered to secure the Suez Canal region so as to separate the two sides. When Nasser turned them down, they sent in troops. The three attackers won the war, but they

Box 15.3 Nasser Denounces the Proposal for a Canal Users' Association

Speech by President Nasser of the United Arab Republic, September 15, 1956:

In these decisive days in the history of mankind, these days in which truth struggles to have itself recognized in international chaos where powers of evil domination and imperialism have prevailed, Egypt stands firmly to preserve her sovereignty. Your country stands solidly and staunchly to preserve her dignity against imperialistic schemes of a number of nations who have uncovered their desires for domination and supremacy.

In these days and in such circumstances Egypt has resolved to show the world that when small nations decide to preserve their sovereignty, they will do that all right and that when these small nations are fully determined to defend their rights and maintain their dignity, they will undoubtedly succeed in achieving their ends ...

I am speaking in the name of every Egyptian Arab and in the name of all free countries and of all those who believe in liberty and are ready to defend it. I am speaking in the name of principles proclaimed by these countries in the Atlantic Charter. But they are now violating these principles and it has become our lot to shoulder the responsibility of reaffirming and establishing them anew ...

We have tried by all possible means to cooperate with those countries which claim to assist smaller nations and which promised to collaborate with us but they demanded their fees in advance. This we refused so they started to fight with us. They said they will pay toward building the High Dam and then they withdrew their offer and cast doubts on the Egyptian economy. Are we to declaim

[disclaim?] our sovereign right? Egypt insists her sovereignty must remain intact and refuses to give up any part of that sovereignty for the sake of money.

Egypt nationalized the Egyptian Suez Canal company. When Egypt granted the concession to de Lesseps it was stated in the concession between the Egyptian Government and the Egyptian company that the company of the Suez Canal is an Egyptian company subject to Egyptian authority. Egypt nationalized this Egyptian company and declared freedom of navigation will be preserved.

But the imperialists became angry. Britain and France said Egypt grabbed the Suez Canal as if it were part of France or Britain. The British Foreign Secretary forgot that only two years ago he signed an agreement stating the Suez Canal is an integral part of Egypt.

Egypt declared she was ready to negotiate. But as soon as negotiations began threats and intimidations started ...

Eden stated in the House of Commons there shall be no discrimination between states using the canal. We on our part reaffirm that and declare there is no discrimination between canal users. He also said Egypt shall not be allowed to succeed because that would spell success for Arab nationalism and would be against their policy, which aims at the protection of Israel.

Today they are speaking of a new association whose main objective would be to rob Egypt of the canal and deprive her of rightful canal dues. Suggestions made by Eden in the House of Commons which have been backed by France and the United States are a clear violation of the 1888 convention, since it is impossible to

have two bodies organizing navigation in the canal ...

By stating that by succeeding, Abdel Nasser would weaken Britain's stand against Arab nationalism, Eden is in fact admitting his real objective is not Abdel Nasser as such but rather to defeat Arab nationalism and crush its cause. Eden speaks and finds his own answer. A month ago he let out the cry that he was after Abdel Nasser. Today the Egyptian people are fully conscious of their sovereign rights and Arab nationalism is fully awakened to its new destiny ...

Those who attack Egypt will never leave Egypt alive. We shall fight a regular war, a total war, a guerrilla war. Those who attack Egypt will soon realize they brought disaster upon themselves. He who attacks Egypt attacks the whole Arab world. They say in their papers the whole thing will be over in forty-eight hours. They do not know how strong we really are.

We believe in international law. But we will never submit. We shall show the world how a small country can stand in the face of great powers threatening with armed might. Egypt might be a small power but she is great inasmuch as she has faith in her power and convictions. I feel quite certain every Egyptian shares the same convictions as I do and believes in everything I am stressing now.

We shall defend our freedom and independence to the last drop of our blood. This is the staunch feeling of every Egyptian. The whole Arab nation will stand by us in our common fight against aggression and domination. Free peoples, too, people who are really free will stand by us and support us against the forces of tyranny.

lost the peace. They had launched the attack on the eve of the US presidential campaign without informing President Eisenhower. Eisenhower feared that the European imperialists' unpopular move would push African and Asian peoples into supporting communism, and even lose the Middle East to the Soviet Union. He forcefully insisted that the three nations withdraw, threatening economic reprisals if they resisted. United Nations peacekeeping forces separated the Egyptians and Israelis.

Nasser's political victory emboldened anti-imperialists and alarmed the Western powers. Arab nationalists gave the United States little or no credit for its intervention, instead praising the Soviet Union for criticizing "the tripartite aggression" at the United Nations. Nasser thereafter grew increasingly close to the Soviet Union, and dreamed of a greater Arab state. Syria joined Egypt in the United Arab Republic for a brief period, but by 1961 the Syrians, fearing Egyptian domination and Nasser's turn to socialism, pulled out.

Defeats for Arab Nationalism, 1967–73

Nasser's brash nationalism was crushed in the 1967 Six Day War, when Israel handily defeated Egypt's military forces and took back the Sinai Peninsula. In that war, the Israelis also captured the West Bank from Jordan, the Gaza Strip from Egypt, and the Golan Heights from Syria. Over a million Palestinians came under Israeli rule, and high rates of population growth turned them into over 3 million by the end of the twentieth century.

After this defeat, Nasser offered to resign, but a burst of popular support allowed him to remain in office until his death in 1970. His successor, Anwar El Sadat, moved audaciously to break Egypt's political logjam. He launched the 1973 October War against Israel's forces in the Egyptian Sinai, in which the Egyptian army succeeded in crossing the Suez Canal and pushing the Israelis back before they regrouped. The United Nations intervened to impose a ceasefire. Egyptians saw the war as a victory, even though Israeli forces successfully riposted and threatened Cairo, the capital.

During the war, the Organization of Petroleum Exporting Countries (OPEC) imposed an oil embargo on the West because of its support for Israel. The success of the embargo, organized by Sadat, led to a wave of oil nationalization moves in the Persian Gulf. OPEC thus made strong claims for indigenous ownership of petroleum resources and for the right to use monopoly tactics to set prices and seek political advantage. The great increase in petroleum prices in the 1970s that resulted from these moves transferred massive amounts of wealth from the industrialized economies to the major oil producers, making Saudi Arabia into a financial giant and transforming Iraq into a major military power.

Having brandished the oil weapon, Sadat pursued Egypt's interests, not the Palestinians'. In 1978 he concluded the Camp David Accords with Israel, establishing peace between the two countries in return for Israeli withdrawal from the Sinai. But Egypt's separate peace with Israel did not resolve the fate of the Palestinians. Israelis debated fiercely what to do with the newly occupied territories. Rightists wanted to incorporate them into Israel permanently, but that raised the possibility that the Arab population in Israel would come to equal or outnumber the Jews. Israel had been founded by the Zionist movement as a Jewish state. Most Israelis supported a settler movement that began founding Jewish settlements around Jerusalem, in Gaza, and in the parts of the West Bank closest to Israel. Israeli doves were willing to give up a good deal or all of the West Bank and Gaza if it would lead to peace, but for most of the 1970s and 1980s Palestinian political movements refused to negotiate with Israel. From the 1990s, movement began toward a bi-national solution, with a Palestinian state in the West Bank and Gaza, but the negotiations were dogged by terrorism against Israeli civilians by radical Palestinian factions, and by harsh Israeli reprisals and military occupation. The decolonization of the British Mandate of Palestine still disturbed regional and world politics at the end of the twentieth century.

Iraq

In 1958, the USA and Britain suffered another major blow. Iraqi officers overthrew the monarchy that the British had installed in the 1920s. The Baghdad Pact of 1955 grouped Iraq, Turkey, Iran, and Pakistan with the UK in an anti-communist security organization. Nasser opposed the Baghdad Pact as a reassertion of Western colonialism in the region. The new nationalist Iraqi military regime withdrew from the Baghdad Pact, undertook successful land reform, and promoted urbanization and higher literacy. At the same time, the Communist Party in Iraq grew to half a million members.

Alarmed at the officers' alliance with communists, the United States secretly supported the rival Baath Party. This movement, which dreamed of a one-party state that would distribute wealth among the Arab people, had some similarities to populist or fascist movements. After a botched coup in 1963, in 1968 the Baathists overthrew the officers, banned the communists and repressed Muslim political figures, especially among the Shi`ites. In the 1970s it achieved impressive economic progress, promoting industrialization and education, and raising living standards. In 1979, however, a long-time Baath activist named Saddam Hussein came to power in a bloody internal coup. Ambitious and ruthless, he launched wars against Iran (1980–88) and then Kuwait (1990–91), and brutally suppressed his own people. The

USA, which supported Saddam Hussein in the 1980s against Iran, ultimately turned against him and removed him from power in coalition with the United Kingdom in 2003. In fifty years, Iraq had cycled from a colonial mandate to a radical nationalist state and back to Anglo-American occupation.

Algeria

For a while, Algeria served as the most powerful symbol of decolonization in the Middle East, and perhaps the Third World in general. In the late 1950s the country had a population of about 10 million native Algerians, and another million European colonists. The colonists had taken the best land and controlled the modern sectors of the economy, living in European-style city quarters built away from traditional neighborhoods.

From about 1954 a group of young men began issuing leaflets in the name of the National Liberation Front (known as FLN for its French initials), calling for the restoration of Algeria's sovereignty. They would employ two tactics: diplomacy abroad, and guerrilla warfare at home. By staging uprisings in provincial towns, they provoked the French into arresting large numbers of non-violent nationalists, pushing them into the radical camp. In summer of 1955 the FLN began killing European settlers, provoking executions of innocent Muslims. By 1956, the FLN had won over much of rural Algeria, though the French still had command in major cities like Algiers. Hard-line governor-generals supported French colonists' demands for harsh repression. The French sent 500,000 troops to Algeria to attempt to take back territory captured by the rebels. In 1957, the FLN began a campaign of urban terrorism targeting the colonists, but specialized French counter-subversion teams broke this ring up, using torture to extract information from captured bombers. The FLN had to again concentrate on the rural areas, where it drew deep support from the grass roots.

In May of 1958, the French settlers themselves turned violent, attacking the offices of the governor-general, insisting that Algeria become permanently part of France, and demanding the return of General Charles de Gaulle to power. De Gaulle, a hero of the French Resistance, had withdrawn from politics during the Fourth Republic of 1944 through 1958 because he felt the government lacked a strong executive. As the colonists desired, he came back to power in 1958, creating the Fifth Republic with himself as a powerful president. He even allowed Muslim Algerians to vote on the new French constitution. The majority of voters approved its provisions making Algerians into French citizens. The Algerian crisis thus reshaped French politics.

The FLN, losing both the military and political struggle, continued to press its claims from exile, while Eisenhower pressured de Gaulle to relinquish Algeria. The USA feared that a long, drawn-out anti-colonial struggle could push the Algerians to become communists, and that French repression and widespread use of torture was giving the West a poor image in the Third World. Many of the French public were also dismayed at the hard-line tactics used in the Battle of Algiers. In September 1959 de Gaulle backed down, declaring that the Algerians had the right to make their own decisions about their fate.

The French colonists, alarmed, mounted an uprising early in 1960, hoping for support from right-wing generals. The officer corps remained loyal to de Gaulle, however, and the rebellion collapsed. The French began negotiations with the Algerian provisional government in exile, and in a referendum held in 1962, 6 million Algerians, virtually the entire electorate, voted for independence. Ahmed Ben Bella became the new president. The Algerian civil war had cost the lives of several hundred thousand Algerians and 10,000 French soldiers, but Algeria was one of the few anti-colonial movements to settle a conflict by elections.

Independent Algeria symbolized the aspirations of many peoples in Asia and Africa, but its new government was plagued by authoritarianism and factionalism. The FLN excluded the communists from power, and Ben Bella quickly emerged as a dictatorial figure who was committed to confiscating the property of the million French settlers who remained in the country. Faced with a choice between becoming Algerian citizens and risking being marginalized as foreign nationals, the colonists left in droves.

In 1965, General Houari Boumedienne staged a coup and ruled until his death in 1978, making Algeria a military dictatorship. Boumedienne abolished parliament, damaged agriculture by attempting to collectivize it, and nationalized French petroleum and gas companies, ensuring that energy revenues came directly into the hands of the state. A new class of wealthy Algerians grew up, who worked in government and who had access to petroleum revenues. Although independent Algeria attempted to "Arabize," promoting Arabic as the national language and teaching it in schools, the wealthier sections of the population continued to speak French and to attempt to ensure that their children had a French education.

In the 1970s, a sharp gap divided the secular French-speaking elite, with its special access to petroleum wealth, and the poor, Arabic-speaking youths of the traditional city quarters or the countryside, who had few prospects. Algeria's high rate of population growth put heavy pressure on inadequate government services. By the 1980s, the poorer, Arabic-speaking population increasingly turned to Muslim fundamentalist parties. The economy stalled badly in the second half of the 1980s, hurt by low petroleum prices and the poor performance of inefficient state-owned industries. By the 1990s the conflict between Muslim fundamentalists and secularists had turned into a full-scale civil war, in which radical Muslims assassinated intellectuals and targeted modern-looking women, and government troops raided pro-fundamentalist villages. The government won out, though much of the population remained sullen. Some radicalized fundamentalists turned to global terrorism, joining groups affiliated with the al-Qaeda terror network. Algeria's postcolonial identity crisis thus spilled over into Europe and North America. (In 2000 an Algerian Islamist terrorist attempted to come into the USA from Canada in order to blow up the Los Angeles airport.) Algeria's sharp decline from postcolonial model to repressive militarism illustrates the all too common alienation of elites of independent nations from the people they rule.

Iran

Iran moved into the American sphere of influence in the late 1950s, after the USA forced Soviet troops to withdraw from its northern border. US officials remained anxious, because the Iranian Communist Party, called Tudeh, or "Masses," had a significant following among intellectuals and some industrial workers. The US had difficulty, as usual, distinguishing between nationalist and communist movements.

Iran Demands Its Oil The Iranian elections of 1950 centered on Iran's petroleum resources, which had been developed by the British Anglo-Iranian Oil Company. The British government, however, made more in taxes on the AIOC than the Iranian state received for its own oil. Iranians regarded the last agreement with the British, made in 1933, as entirely too generous to the Westerners, giving Iranians only about a third of the royalties. US petroleum companies had come into the Persian Gulf, and the Arabian American Oil Company (ARAMCO) offered the Saudi Arabian government a 50–50 split on petroleum profits. Iranians increasingly wanted the same deal, but the British adamantly refused to revise their agreement.

Frustration with British intransigence angered many members of the Iranian parliament. The results of the 1950 elections strongly favored the nationalists, led by Mohammad Mosaddegh. In the spring of 1951, the Iranian parliament passed an Oil Nationalization Act. They felt that if the British would not negotiate in good faith, then the Iranian nation would simply reclaim its own property, recompensing the AIOC for equipment and other assets. Since the independence of Pakistan and India had deprived Britain of its strategic dominance in the region, the Iranians had little fear of a military response. The shah or king, Mohammad Reza Pahlevi (r. 1941–79), felt obliged to appoint Mosaddegh prime minister.

Mosaddegh is Ousted by US Pressure Mosaddegh headed a powerful coalition, with three wings: secular nationalists, mainly from the middle and upper classes, including many graduates of Iran's expanding high school and university systems; religious Shi`ites, who opposed foreign domination because they feared it would weaken traditional Islam; and leftists, including communists, who were anti-British and pro-Soviet. Together, these three forces made up the National Front.

At the beginning of the nationalist movement, the USA had been sympathetic to Iranian complaints about being gouged by the British terms, and jealous of British oil companies' competitive advantage. But Iran's nationalization of the oil industry frightened the Americans, because the idea might catch on elsewhere. Even though the leftists formed a minority element in the National Front, Mosaddegh's alliance with the Communist Party also alarmed Washington.

The British first took the dispute to the International Court at The Hague, which ruled that it had no jurisdiction. The decision implied that Iranian petroleum was a domestic Iranian resource, giving the parliament a right to nationalize it. The Anglo-Iranian Oil Company then led a worldwide boycott of Iranian oil, maintaining that the Iranians had stolen the company's property. US petroleum companies joined the boycott. The Iranians' new national petroleum company managed to produce some oil, but could only sell it to a few consumers. The inability to market petroleum, Iran's major export, threw Iran into economic crisis, and the Truman administration no longer honored its promises of development loans.

The USA put enormous pressure on the conservative shah, who deeply disliked the nationalist movement. In the summer of 1952, he attempted to replace the prime minister, but an outpouring of popular support made him bring Mosaddegh back. The Eisenhower administration now saw Mosaddegh as a stalking horse for communist domination. Eisenhower and the US Central Intelligence Agency (CIA) agreed to a plan for a coup drawn up by British intelligence (MI6).

Economic and political disarray in Iran made the coup possible. Leftist support for Mosaddegh had weakened, and some of the more radical Shi`ite clerics were also unhappy with his moderate secularist policies. Massive street protests forced the shah to go into exile, but the crowds were getting out of control, scaring shopkeepers and other middle-class voters. Mosaddegh's crackdown on demonstrations angered the Tudeh Party, which decided to withdraw its support completely. CIA field officer Kermit Roosevelt, a distant relative of the former president, spread around large sums in dollars to buy a crowd that marched against the prime minister on August 19. These anti-Mosaddegh demonstrations were supported by some of the more radical Shi`ite clerics and by right-wing military officers. The Iranian left refused to call out its supporters in counter-demonstrations. The army moved in and arrested the prime minister, bringing back the shah. Mosaddegh spent the last three years of his life under house arrest.

In the end, the Iranians got the 50–50 split on oil revenues they had wanted. Shah Mohammad Reza Pahlevi came back as an absolute monarch, instituting a capitalist dictatorship. He banned most political parties and declined to hold free and fair multi-party elections. He built up a massive secret police apparatus that spied on many ordinary Iranians. He favored crony capitalism, throwing lucrative contracts and business licenses to his favorites and making some of them into billionaires. A thousand families came to control much of the country's wealth. Government policies favored large, modern industries over smaller traditional ones, and favored cities over the rural areas. The USA maintained military installations in the country, mainly using Iran as a listening post in gathering intelligence on the Soviet Union. The shah showed off his lavish spending on a royal style of life, creating discontent among the desperately poor, who lived in shantytowns without sewerage service. He also favored secular Iranian nationalism, glorifying the country's Zoroastrian past at ancient Persepolis more than its Muslim culture. His modernizing policies, like land reform, hurt the Shi`ite clerics.

In 1963 Ayatollah Ruhullah Khomeini led protests against the shah's regime on a religious holiday. The shah put down these protests, the most serious since 1953, exiling Khomeini first to Turkey and then to Najaf in Iraq. From exile, Khomeini denounced the shah's materialism, his subservience to Western interests, and the corruption of Iranian life by Western culture. A clever politician, Khomeini gained support from university students and the new middle class. He did not stress his more conservative sentiments, such as opposition to the vote for women.

Ayatollah Khomeini Leads a Theocratic Revolution During the 1960s the shah's dictatorial rule became increasingly unpopular, although on the surface he seemed unbeatable. He modernized the country from above, multiplying the number of high school and university graduates and creating a new middle class of nurses, technicians, and other white-collar workers. These intellectuals cared about press censorship and privacy and detested the shah's secret police, the dreaded SAVAK. The shah's neglect of the agricultural sector caused large numbers of villagers to migrate to urban shantytowns where they became construction workers. As devoted Shi`ite Muslims, they supported the clerics. So too did many traditional shopkeepers, moneylenders, and artisans in the country's covered bazaars. The modernizing shah deeply disliked the bazaar and the mosque, which he saw as obstacles to progress.

In the 1970s Iran both benefited from and suffered from the oil price shock. In the years after 1973, as petroleum prices grew four-fold, Iran's annual income from oil grew from about 500 million dollars in 1964 to 5 billion in 1974 and 20 billion in 1976. The country seemed to be getting rich. In fact, the sudden growth of petroleum revenues caused many problems. The new wealth made the Iranian currency more valuable, but that hardening of the currency in turn made Iranian exports more expensive for neighbors like Pakistan and India, which could no longer afford to buy as many raisins, pistachios, and handmade goods. The decline in exports harmed many ordinary agricultural and handicraft laborers. The sudden influx of money into the economy also caused inflation. The shah blamed the rapid rise of prices on the greediness of shopkeepers, whom he treated harshly, with fines and imprisonment. Consumers nevertheless had to pay more and more for everyday purchases.

The government soaked up the oil wealth, but did not share it with the people, fearing even higher inflation if it pumped the money directly into the economy. Its neglect left laborers, consumers, and shopkeepers unhappy and added to the university students and graduates who disliked his authoritarianism, and the clerics and religious Shi`ites who disliked his secularism.

Most Iranians also bore a grudge against the United States, which had reinstalled the shah on the throne in 1953, helped train his secret police, and backed him diplomatically and economically. In 1978 popular demonstrations against the shah's rule broke out across the country. The regime's attempt to repress them only produced martyrs and bigger demonstrations the next time. Frightened of a repeat of 1953, the shah put pressure on the Iraqi government to expel Khomeini, who had large numbers of audio cassettes of his sermons against the shah smuggled into the country. Khomeini left for Paris, where, ironically, he had much more access to the world press, including the BBC. When popular unrest again forced the shah out of the country, Khomeini came back to Tehran in triumph on February 1, 1979. He and his fellow clerics quickly took control of the revolution. They crafted a new constitution that put most power in the hands of a supreme religious jurisprudent, with a much weaker prime minister and parliament. A referendum on the Islamic republic in spring of 1979, which did not allow secret ballots, passed overwhelmingly.

Although Iran had become a theocracy, some of the new leaders hoped to re-establish relations with the USA. More radical revolutionaries, still angry over Washington's support for the shah, wanted to prevent any rapprochement. In the fall of 1979, Shi`ite and leftist radicals held Americans hostage at the US embassy in Tehran. By the time of their release early in 1981, the US government and the Islamic Republic of Iran were open enemies. Khomeini launched a campaign of political repression, killing over 10,000 dissidents and jailing thousands more. Millions died in the Iran–Iraq War, launched by Saddam Hussein.

Iran backed Shi`ite radicals in Lebanon who were determined to end the Israeli occupation of southern Lebanon begun in 1982 and to push American influence out of that country. Shi`ite population growth, and smaller Christian families in addition to extensive Christian emigration, had reversed the relative importance of the Shi`ite and Christian populations in the country by the 1980s. Shi`ite radicals bombed the US embassy in Beirut in April of 1983, killing 63, and then bombed a US marines barracks that October, killing 242. A similar operation killed 58 French troops. Shi`ite groups also took stray Americans hostage and hijacked US airliners. Americans ceased being major targets in Lebanon only after the Iran-Contra operation, in which high officials of the Reagan administration secretly sold Iran weapons in return for Iranian pressure on radical Shi`ites in Lebanon to let US hostages go.

From a radical Shi`ite point of view, both the Islamic Revolution in Iran and the anti-US actions of Shi`ite radicals in Lebanon were a form of late decolonization. Although the USA had not formally occupied either country, it exercised vast influence on both governments through financial and diplomatic pressure. This kind of control can be called "neocolonialism," or domination without direct occupation. The idea of using Islamic rhetoric and slogans as a way of mobilizing the masses against Western dominance was not new, having being employed in nineteenth-century India. What was new was the level of popular involvement in politics, and the high levels of literacy and urbanization in Third World countries, which made Islamism a far more effective tool than in the past. Khomeini's success in opposing the USA would inspire not only Shi`ite movements, but also Sunni radicals such as those in al-Qaeda. Al-Qaeda members hated the Shi`ite branch of Islam, but they modeled some of their rhetoric and tactics on those of Khomeini and the Shi`ite radicals of 1980s Lebanon.

Conclusion

The colonial period of the eighteenth, nineteenth, and early twentieth centuries powerfully shaped the destinies of more than a third of humankind. The process of decolonization was equally influential in making the contemporary world. The colonial enterprise had many motivations: a desire for control of strategic territory, a desire to exploit economic resources, military men's desire for national glory, and competition among colonial powers.

In all cases, successful colonial conquest depended on the superior military might, better weaponry, and more efficient military and administrative organization of the colonizer. Conversely, it also depended on low rates of urbanization, literacy, and industrial organization among the colonized, and on the willingness of locals to collaborate. Many Indian landlords, moneylenders, and traders were entirely willing to co-operate with British rule in India, because they saw it as an even-handed source of stability that benefited their social classes. Most of Africa and Asia in the eighteenth and nineteenth centuries had a weak sense of national identity, and elites had no objection to serving foreign masters.

After World War II most of the factors that had enabled colonialism disappeared. The exhausted British and French publics no longer wanted to bear the burden of empire. The Nazis had given the conquest of other peoples a bad name. The rise of Japanese power had challenged myths of innate Western superiority. The colonial experience had produced large numbers of politicians and intellectuals fluent in the languages and customs of the colonizers, and no longer willing to accept the superiority of the metropole. They, along with a budding class of industrialists and entrepreneurs, decided not to co-operate with the colonial administrators. Box 15.4 describes the impact of the reverse migrations of colonial peoples to their imperial metropoles on globalization.

Most colonies had large enough urban and literate populations (even if this modern sector remained a minority in largely rural countries) to mount significant strikes and demonstrations that threatened the economic viability of the colonial apparatus. They were socially and politically mobilized as never before. As colonial powers seldom completely controlled the countryside, rural revolts could work in tandem with urban ones. Eventually the colonial powers themselves realized that ruling a whole country for its resources was more costly than controlling its trade through multinational corporations. Neocolonial influence replaced direct colonial rule.

To be sure, political developments after independence failed to fulfill the idealism of the anti-colonial activists, but this disillusionment was itself part of decolonization. It turned out that the colonized were neither inferior nor superior to the colonizers. All were fallible human beings. Some had better organization, technology, or resources, that is all.

Study Questions

(1) Achmed Sukarno of Indonesia compared Dutch colonial rule of the East Indies (later Indonesia) to Nazi German rule of Holland itself during World War II. Is this comparison reasonable? Why or why not?

(2) What was the impact of the Cold War and the US fight against communism on decolonization and its aftermath? Pay special attention to the Koreas and Indonesia.

(3) How did religious identities affect decolonization and postcolonial attempts to create new states? Pay special attention to Indonesia and India and Pakistan.

(4) The French colonies experimented with three possible routes to decolonization. One was for all colonial subjects to become French citizens. Another was large confederations of former colonies. The third was smaller, independent, postcolonial nation-states. The last option won out. For what reasons was it more successful than the first two plans?

Box 15.4 The Empires' Peoples Come Back

As people from the former colonies returned to the metropole, they created hybrid cultures and new diasporas that contributed to globalization. Substantial numbers of South Asians migrated to the United Kingdom after World War II. By the end of the twentieth century, there were about a million Hindus, Sikhs, and Buddhists, and nearly 2 million Muslims in the UK. Large numbers of Jamaicans and others also came from the Caribbean former colonies. Although they included entrepreneurs and shopkeepers, the South Asians were largely working-class. The rise of large Indian and Pakistani communities led to occasional race riots, and to complaints of discrimination by Hindus and Muslims in a country dominated by Anglican Christians. At the same time, a taste for Indian food and South Asian music spread among the British population.

Throughout the twentieth century, some North Africans headed back to France. After 1975, French law permitted the immigration of a worker's family, encouraging immigrants to settle. French attempts to limit the influx of foreign labor in the late 1970s and early 1980s failed. By the end of the twentieth century, Muslims constituted about 7 percent of the French population. They mainly came from Algeria and other North African countries, though others derived from West Africa. Previous immigrants to France had usually been European Catholics, such as Polish mine workers. Many French considered the Muslim and African immigrants harder to assimilate.

As demand for labor in the slow-growing French economy fluctuated, many immigrants were thrown out of work. Poor North African slums grew up, especially in the south around Marseilles, and in some parts of Paris and other cities. Many children from immigrant Algerian families grew up knowing only French slang and no Arabic, and many knew little of Islam. On visits to Algeria, these children were often insulted, the unveiled girls being viewed as loose women and the boys as having lost their culture. In France itself, right-wing French nationalists following racist politician Jean-Marie Le Pen raised alarms about the French being overwhelmed by foreigners. The rise of radical Islamism added fear of terrorism to racial prejudice, when Muslim radicals set off bombs in Paris. Most Algerian immigrants to France, however, were law-abiding and simply seeking a better life for themselves and their families. France by the late twentieth century was no longer made up only of secularists, traditionalist Catholics, and Jews (about 2 percent of the population). It had added Muslims as a major population, and they expanded the meaning of what it was to be French.

Elsewhere in the world, too, migrants and stranded minorities from fallen empires suffered discrimination and abuse. Koreans in Japan, Russians in Central Asia, Chinese in Vietnam, and Hispanics in the USA, for example, were often singled out by the dominant groups, seen as politically suspicious, excluded from citizenship for reasons of language or heritage, and sometimes deported en masse. On the other hand, immigrants added new elements which often blended with their host societies, enriching and enlivening their cultures. Now you can find sushi at truck stops in the USA and Filipina brides in Japanese villages. The contradictions of hybridity seep into majority and minority populations in every culture.

(5) How did colonialism end in Algeria? Compare and contrast events there with those in Egypt under Nasser.

(6) Nationalists everywhere thought that freedom from colonial domination would bring their countries a new era of peace and prosperity. More often than not, they were very disappointed. What went wrong?

Suggested Reading Tony Chafer, *The End of Empire in French West Africa: France's Successful Decolonization?* (Oxford and New York: Berg, 2002). This is the fullest and most perceptive account in English of how France tried to create a French Union in post-war West Africa but was forced in the end to allow the formation of many new states. He attends not just to elite actions but also to history from below.

Clive Christie, *A Modern History of Southeast Asia: Decolonization, Nationalism and Separatism* (London: Tauris, 1996). Christie traces the genesis and outcome of ethnically based separatist movements in the region before and after World War II and explains why larger nationalist projects won out.

Frederick Cooper, *Africa Since 1940: The Past of the Present* (Cambridge University Press, 2002). A major theorist of decolonization, Cooper sketches out how colonial states were constructed to extract resources for the metropole and how that affected the struggles of workers and nationalists to erect independent countries.

James D. Le Sueur (ed.), *The Decolonization Reader* (New York: Routledge, 2003). This is a collection of key essays on the process whereby the global south gained independence in the post-war period, including a range of historiographical debates.

Ian Talbot, *India and Pakistan* (London: Arnold, 2000). Talbot avoids assuming that identities are essential or primordial, but rather examines how they were constructed in South Asia in the light of new communications technologies and political movements.

Glossary

apartheid: White South African policy of strict racial segregation and whites-only rights to vote and hold political power.

casbahs: Old city quarters in North African cities.

chaebol: South Korean industrial cartel (corporate semi-monopoly).

communes: Production units in China combining large-scale agriculture with heavy and light industry.

crony capitalism: A form of capitalism in which a small elite of related business families earns large profits and exerts strong influence over government economic policies. Many commentators have seen it as a prime source of corruption and a major obstacle to Third World development.

évolués: (French: "evolved.") According to French colonial ideology, these were Western-educated "natives" capable of being "modern" persons.

Four Modernizations: Deng Xiaoping's program in China to promote agriculture, industry, national defense, and science and technology.

Jamaat-i Islami: Pakistani Muslim fundamentalist party.

juche: North Korean policy of extreme national self-reliance.

Mau Mau: Movement among members of Kikuyu tribe in Kenya to return to tribal ways, rejecting Western culture; it resulted in rebellion against British rule.

négritude: Senegalese poet and politician Léopold Senghor's theory of an identification with "blackness" that went beyond individual cultures or places.

Non-Aligned Movement: Founded in 1961 in Belgrade, it represented an attempt by a group of nations, mainly post-colonial nations, to create a middle position in the emerging Cold War order, independent of both the USA and the USSR. Among its earliest members were leaders from India, Indonesia, Egypt, Ghana, and Yugoslavia. The organization was never able to play the mediating role that its founders wished for and the decline of the Cold War left it with an uncertain role in world politics.

Pancasila: The "Five Principles" of President Sukarno in Indonesia: belief in God, humanitarianism, national unity, democracy, and social justice.

16 Globalization, inequality, and disintegration of states, 1980–2050

Timeline	
1979	Chinese prime minister, Deng Xiaoping, begins policy of "reform and opening up" – the liberalization of the Chinese economy.
1980	Strikes in shipyards in Gdansk, Poland. Rise of Polish Solidarity trade union.
1985	Mikhail Gorbachev (b. 1931), Soviet reformer, becomes General Secretary of the Soviet Communist Party in 1985 and head of state in 1988.
1987	World Health Organization launches Global Program on AIDS/HIV.
December 7, 1988	Gorbachev announces to the UN General Assembly a new Soviet policy of non-intervention in internal affairs of Eastern European members of the Warsaw Pact. USSR military domination of Eastern Europe is effectively ended.
1989	Term "Washington Consensus" coined to refer to a policy agreement among International Monetary Fund, the World Bank, and the US Treasury to impose free market policies on countries seeking aid from these institutions.
February 1989	USSR leaves Afghanistan.
March–April 1989	General elections in USSR of new Congress of People's Deputies are first relatively free Soviet elections.
April–June 1989	Tiananmen Square protests for democratic reforms in China.

November 9, 1989	Introduction of new travel rights in East Germany creates a political crisis in the East German state; the state begins to collapse.
August 2, 1990–February 28, 1991	Gulf War: Iraqi strongman Saddam Hussein annexes Kuwait but is expelled by US-led coalition forces.
August 1991	*Coup d'état* against Gorbachev's reforms fails; beginning of collapse of Soviet Union.
December 1991	Dissolution of the USSR; fifteen former republics declare themselves independent states.
1995	World Trade Organization created in Geneva; established on the foundations of the General Agreement on Tariffs and Trade (GATT), it has increased powers to mediate trade disputes and to enforce adherence to existing agreements.
November 30, 1999	"Battle of Seattle": Massive protests oppose meeting of World Trade Organization in Seattle, Oregon. Protestors denounce "globalization."
2001	China admitted into WTO and bids successfully for Olympics.
September 11, 2001	Al-Qaeda, an Afghanistan-based terrorist group, carries out attacks on US Pentagon and New York World Trade Center, killing almost 3,000.
2001	US-led coalition invades Afghanistan.
March 20, 2003	US-led NATO coalition invades Iraq, capturing Baghdad and overthrowing Saddam Hussein's regime on April 9.
May 1, 2004	Poland enters European Union.

Events of the year 1989 astonished the whole world. The usually sober 200-year-old political yearbook *Annual Register* began its 1989 edition with these breathless words:

> *If 1988 saw peace breaking out in various parts of the world, 1989 was even more remarkable as the year in which the Iron Curtain was lifted in Europe, with a rapidity which left most pundits gasping. Not only was the infamous Berlin Wall thrown open to divided German people; also, one by one, the East European communist regimes which had sustained the post-1945 continental divide succumbed to the irresistible forces of awakened democracy. That this historic transformation occurred in the bicentenary year of the French Revolution has a symbolism which appealed to many.*

Early in 1989, the Soviet Union withdrew its last official armed forces from Afghanistan, where it had been battling American-backed military forces for nine years. In other events of that vibrant, violent year, Chinese troops suppressed pro-democracy uprisings in Beijing and many other cities, a South African president who pledged to end white racial domination took office, his government ended years of South African opposition to the independence of neighboring Namibia, and Iran's religious leader pronounced a death sentence *in absentia* against author Salman Rushdie for his book *Satanic Verses*.

On the American side, United States forces invaded Panama to depose its military ruler, who had earlier collaborated in American action against Latin American leftists. Meanwhile an

Figure 16.1 Selected headlines from the *New York Times*, 1989.

2/15	(Moscow): Last Soviet Soldiers Leave Afghanistan After 9 Years, 15,000 Dead and Great Cost
2/19	(Warsaw): Solidarity May Win 40 Percent of Parliament
3/17	(Moscow): Soviets Savor Vote in Freest Election Since '17 Revolution
5/4	(Beijing): Urging Chinese Democracy, 100,000 Surge Past Police
5/17	(Beijing): A Million Chinese March, Adding Pressure for Change
6/4	(Beijing): Troops Attack and Crush Beijing Protest; Thousands Fight Back, Scores are Killed
6/8	(Warsaw): Warsaw Accepts Solidarity Sweep and Humiliating Losses by [Communist] Party
6/16	(Budapest): Hungarian Who Led '56 Revolt is Buried as a Hero
10/1	(Hof, West Germany): More Than 6,000 East Germans Swell Tide of Refugees to the West
10/25	(Helsinki): Gorbachev in Finland, Disavows Any Right of Regional Intervention
11/10	(Berlin): The Border Is Open; Joyous East Germans Pour Through Wall; Party Pledges Freedoms, and City Exults
11/10	(Sofia): Bulgarian Chief Quits After 35 Years of Rigid Rule
11/15	(Prague): Unease in Prague; A Soviet Warning on Foot-Dragging is Given to Prague
11/20	(Prague): 200,000 March in Prague as Calls for Change Mount
11/25	(Prague): Prague Party Leaders Resign; New Chief, 48, Surprise Choice; 350,000 at Rally Cheer Dubcek
11/26	(Budapest): Hungarians Hold First Free Vote in 42 Years, Shunning a Boycott
11/28	(London): Unease Fills Western Allies over Rapid Changes in East
12/3	(Valletta, Malta): Bush and Gorbachev Proclaim a New Era for U.S.-Soviet Ties
12/7	(Moscow): Lithuania Legalizes Rival Parties, Removing Communists' Monopoly
12/8	(Mexico City): Castro Says He'll Resist Changes Like Those Sweeping Soviet Bloc
12/24	(Bucharest): Rumanian Army Gains in Capital but Battle Goes On
12/29	(Prague): Czechoslovakia: Havel, Long Prague's Prisoner, Elected President

American jury convicted Marine Lieutenant Colonel Oliver North of tampering with documents and lying to Congress about an affair in which (with backing from the highest levels of the American government) he helped sell arms secretly to Iran and divert the money to American-backed counter-revolutionary troops in Nicaragua. Overall, the year produced political realignments on a scale we usually only see at the ends of major wars.

In fact, 1989 did mark the termination of a major war: the Cold War, traced in Chapter 14. Newspaper headlines from 1989 in Figure 16.1 tell a remarkable tale. The long standoff

between the United States and the Soviet Union ended as Soviet satellite states broke away from their alliance and the Soviet Union itself began to fragment. How did that happen? The Afghan civil war made a big difference. In 1979, Soviet assistance to Afghanistan's left-leaning military coup seemed like just one more Cold War confrontation, but it proved crucial. As the United States poured in support for a variety of Afghan rebels, the Soviet military suffered a frustrating and humiliating stalemate.

The Soviet Union's withdrawal of its troops from Afghanistan in the late 1980s occurred as one step in Soviet leaders' attempts to cut losses, reform government, and revive the national economy. Liberalizer Mikhail Gorbachev became head of the Soviet Communist Party in 1985. Gorbachev soon began promoting **perestroika**, a shift of the economy from military to civilian production, toward better and more abundant consumer goods, and in the direction of higher productivity. He also moved hesitantly into a program of **glasnost**, an opening up of public life: releasing political prisoners, accelerating exit visas for Jews, shrinking the military, reducing the Soviet Union's external military involvement, and ending violent repression of demands for political, ethnic, and religious autonomy. Gorbachev was still a dedicated socialist. His goal was to strengthen the Soviet Union through reforms, not destroy it. But destroy it he did, by unleashing a process of state disintegration driven by the private interests of its own cadres: Soviet Communist Party officials.

Gorbachev's reforms generalized and liberated national markets. That meant reducing state involvement in production and distribution of goods and services. As a result, the central state's capacity to deliver rewards to its followers declined visibly from one month to the next. In response, officials and managers engaged in a sort of run on the bank: wherever they could divert fungible assets to their own advantage, they increasingly did so. They started stealing from the state. The more one person stole, the more reason the next person had to steal before no assets remained.

Opportunism channeled by the old regime's own institutions undid the regime. Russia's communists had long dealt with non-Russian regions by co-opting regional leaders who were loyal to their cause. The regime had integrated such leaders into the Communist Party, recruited their successors among the most promising members of designated nationalities, but trained them in Russia and accustomed them to doing business in Russian. Candidates for regional leadership made long stays in Moscow under close supervision. The ones who proved smart, tough, and reliable went back to run their homeland's Communist Party. The system had the strength of putting regional leadership in the hands of people from the region. The system's strength also proved to be its downfall. Widespread popular demands for guarantees of religious and political liberties arose in 1987. But disintegration really began during the next two years, as nationalist and nationalizing leaders rushed to seize assets and autonomy that would fortify their positions in the new regime. Most of the people who came to power in the Soviet Union's successor states had already held important positions under the Soviet regime. But even politicians who had long served as party functionaries began portraying themselves as independents, reformers, or nationalists. Many of them actually succeeded.

As the USSR disintegrated, accordingly, both regional power-holders and their rivals suddenly acquired strong incentives to distance themselves from the center. Most of them started recruiting popular followings. Ambitious regional leaders established credentials as authentic representatives of the local people, urged special treatment for their own nationalities within territorial subdivisions of the USSR they happened to occupy, and pressed for new forms of autonomy. In the republics on the Baltic Sea in the north and along the USSR's western and southern tiers, like the Ukraine and Azerbaijan, new nationalists capitalized on the possibility of special relations with kindred states and authorities outside the Soviet Union: Sweden, Finland, Turkey, Iran, the European Union, and NATO. Those cross-border relations offered more political leverage and economic opportunity than the Soviet Union itself could provide.

Ethnic segmentation, economic collapse, undermining of the old regime's powers, and Gorbachev's principled refusal to engage in the old regime's customary vigorous, violent repression transformed public politics. Among other things, they opened opportunities for right-wing movements. Many observers and participants feared that the military, intelligence, and Party establishment would try to reverse the flow of events, by ousting Gorbachev and recentralizing control. History proved them right. In August 1991, a self-identified Emergency Committee sequestered Gorbachev. The committee's coup, however, failed, as Boris Yeltsin, political boss of the Russian Republic (and shortly to be president of the Russian Federation, 1991–99), led the resistance in Moscow. Over the next four months Yeltsin sought to succeed Gorbachev. He proposed to take power not as Party secretary but as chief of a confederation maintaining a measure of economic, military, and diplomatic authority over its component states. Even that effort ended with the dissolution of the Soviet Union into an ill-defined association to be called the Commonwealth of Independent States. The Baltic states refused to join, while other soviet republics began rushing toward the exit. The Soviet Union was no more.

Once the Soviet regime collapsed, Russian nationalists within Russia (including the opportunistic nationalist Yeltsin) faced a fierce dilemma. Lenin and Stalin had set up the Soviet Union as a confederation of republics, each of which contained a dominant nationality: Russians, Ukrainians, Armenians, Uzbeks, and many others. Yeltsin now claimed to take over the right of Russians to rule the Russian Federation, including millions of non-Russian minorities. Russia supported the Soviet Union's founding principle that titular nationalities should prevail in each republic. On the other hand, it vigorously criticized the treatment of Russians outside the Russian Federation as second-class minorities. Estonia, Lithuania, Ukraine, and Kazakhstan, for example, all contained millions of self-identified Russians. Those numerous Russians had suddenly become members of minorities – sometimes very large minorities – in newly independent countries. They faced unpalatable choices: assimilate to the titular

Map 16.1 Post-Cold-War Europe, 2000

nationality (by, for example, learning Estonian), accept lesser forms of citizenship, or emigrate. The Russian Federation posed as their protector. Unsurprisingly, newly independent neighbors often accused the Russian Federation of imperialism.

Fairly soon, the great Western powers agreed to contain Russia by drawing its former satellites selectively into Western political and economic circuits. They tried to secure the enormous resources of former Soviet territories, for example the huge oil reserves of Azerbaijan in and around the Caspian Sea. Led by the United States, the great powers unilaterally ended the Cold War. It formally ended by agreement between President Bush and Boris Yeltsin in February 1992. (See Maps 16.1 and 16.2.)

Although the calendar said otherwise, the collapse of the Soviet Union and the Cold War's termination also closed the twentieth century. It closed a short, intense century of imperialism, world wars, and socialist–capitalist struggle. It opened a new century of globalization, Asian resurgence, nationalism, civil war, and – at least temporarily – capitalist world domination. This chapter reviews the pivotal years after 1980 and looks forward speculatively to the new century's midpoint: 2050. Here are the chapter's main points:

- The human world has globalized repeatedly over the last 100,000 years, at each major expansion in the scale of trade, political power, or religious faith. The most recent previous round of globalization featured expanding European political and economic influence between 1850 and 1914. Since 1980, the relative importance of Asians and Americans has increased visibly.

- In the current phase of globalization, worldwide networks of capital, communication, science, and crime figure more prominently than ever before.

- These trends are undermining the sorts of high-capacity state that ruled most of the world between 1750 and 1950. As a result, emerging forms of economic, political, and social organization defy state control more than most organizations did over the previous two centuries.

- Unequal distribution of access to capital, communications, science, and coercion promotes sharpening inequality among world regions. The twenty-first century's major political challenges center on that inequality and its consequences.

Map 16.2 The former Soviet Union after its breakup in 1991

Any such reading of the future entails significant risks. It could go wrong in many different ways. But it will gain value from careful reflection on humanity's previous history. Despite what many commentators say, globalization did not begin with the internet in the 1990s. Let us first look back at the earlier phases of globalization, to see which features of our time are old, and which are new.

16.1 WAVES OF GLOBALIZATION

Since the movement of humans out of Africa some 50,000 years ago, humanity has globalized repeatedly. Any time a distinctive set of social connections and practices expands from a regional to a transcontinental scale, some **globalization** is occurring. Each time an existing transcontinental set of social connections and practices fragments, disintegrates, or vanishes, some deglobalization occurs. Only when the first sort of process is far outrunning the second does it clarify matters to say that humanity as a whole is globalizing. On balance, the period since 1980 qualifies. Although trends such as resurgent nationalism and civil war point toward deglobalization, internationalization of capital, trade, industrial organization, communications, political institutions, science, disease, atmospheric pollution, and crime have produced a net movement toward globalization.

Over the long run of human history that this book surveys, globalization has taken three related forms: first, increased co-ordination and interdependence of important activities at a world scale; second, spread of ideas, techniques, and forms of organization from one population and place to another; third, migration of specific connected populations, with their particular ways of life, across the globe. As an example of the first form, when Mongol empires covered much of Eurasia during the thirteenth and fourteenth centuries CE, trade, military formations, and religious communication expanded. The second form includes rapid conversion of millions to Christianity, Buddhism, Islam, and other religions as priests and proselytizers traveled across the worlds accessible to them. The third form includes the Aryan move into India, or the Arab seafarers who went to Southeast Asia. All three of these forms of globalization covered much of Eurasia, but globalization deeply involving all the world's major populated regions only began with European and Ottoman colonization and conquest after 1500. Then we see huge flows of slaves out of Africa, along with migrants out of Asia and Europe into the Pacific and the Americas.

Globalizing processes vary in their relative emphasis on trade, political power, and cultural transformation. Chinese, Armenians, Jews, and India's Gujaratis built commercial networks that spanned the world without backing from big political structures. Strong commitments to fellow merchants from the same home town or family bound them together. Religious faiths have used the sword to convert, but more often they use persuasion to substitute one set of commitments for another, as when Islamic Sufi preachers demonstrated magical powers to Central Eurasians and Southeast Asians. Europeans, Ottomans, Mongols, and Chinese often used large armies to spread their influence. In their purest forms, commercial globalization produces markets and merchants, political globalization produces empires, and religious-cultural globalization produces cultural communities. All major surges of globalization have mixed these forms in varying proportions.

Three Waves: The First Wave

The half-millennium since 1500 has seen three main waves of globalization. The first arrived right around 1500, driven by the simultaneous expansion of Europeans across the Atlantic and Pacific, the Ottoman empire in Eurasia, and Chinese and Arab merchants into the Indian Ocean and Pacific. The Ottomans extended their control into Southern Europe, North Africa, and the Near East, while Western Europeans were building commercial and territorial empires in Africa, the Pacific, and the Americas. Meanwhile, seafaring Muslim merchants (most of them not Ottoman) continued to connect Africa, the Near East, and Indian Ocean ports. In Asia, European and Muslim commercial activity interacted with China's energetic expansion into Southeast Asian coastal trade under the Ming empire (1368–1644). Ottoman expansion ended in the late seventeenth century, and Muslim merchants were partly displaced by Europeans across the Indian Ocean and the Pacific, but Europeans and Chinese kept the first post-1500 globalizing process going into the twentieth century. Europeans began colonizing the more temperate zones of their empires in Africa, the Americas, and the Pacific; Chinese migrants by the millions likewise moved into Southeast Asia, the Pacific, Central Eurasia, and Manchuria. Here are two signs of the world's increasing connectedness: By the late sixteenth century large amounts of silver mined in South America were ending up in Chinese treasuries, and large quantities of Chinese porcelain found their way to Istanbul.

The Second Wave

The second major wave after 1500 overlapped with the first. Remember the furious boom of long-distance migration between

1850 and World War I: 3 million Indians, 9 million Japanese, 10 million Russians, 20 million Chinese, and 33 million Europeans. During this period, international trade, capital, and human flows reached unmatched heights, especially across the Atlantic. Railroads, steamships, telephone, and telegraph lowered their costs and sped them up. Massive movements of labor, goods, and capital made prices of traded goods more uniform across the world and reduced wage gaps among the globalizing countries, particularly Japan, Western Europe, and the richer countries of North and South America. On the other hand, globalization's second wave increased disparities in wealth and well-being between those beneficiaries and everyone else. Except for settler colonies like Australia and New Zealand, European colonies did not generally share in the prosperity. The profits from colonial exports went only to a small elite.

Migration, trade, and capital flows slowed between the two world wars, but as Europe and Japan recovered from World War II, a third surge of globalization began. This time, intercontinental migration accelerated less than between 1850 and 1914. Fewer economies felt acute labor shortages, and labor unions organized more effectively to bar immigrant competition. As a consequence, long-distance migration bifurcated into relatively small streams of professional and technical workers, on one hand, and large numbers of servants and general laborers, on the other. Because differences in wealth and security between rich and poor countries were widening visibly, potential workers from poor countries made desperate attempts to migrate into richer countries, either permanently or for long enough to earn substantial money for their return home. Whole industries grew up to facilitate illegal, semi-legal, and legal but brutal forms of migration into richer countries.

Flows of goods and capital reached record heights. Many of those flows occurred within firms, as multinational companies spanned markets, manufacturing sites, headquarters, and sources of raw materials in different countries. But international trade among countries and firms also accelerated. Goods produced in East Asia, Western Europe, and North America became available almost everywhere in the world. At the same time, political institutions, communications systems, technology, science, disease, pollution, and criminal activity all took on increasingly international scales. The third wave of post-1500 globalization is moving ahead with full force as you read this book.

The Third Wave: Asia Rises, Industry Disperses

The waves of 1850–1914 and of today differ conspicuously. Despite imperial outreach and the rising importance of Japan, nineteenth-century expansion centered on the Atlantic, first

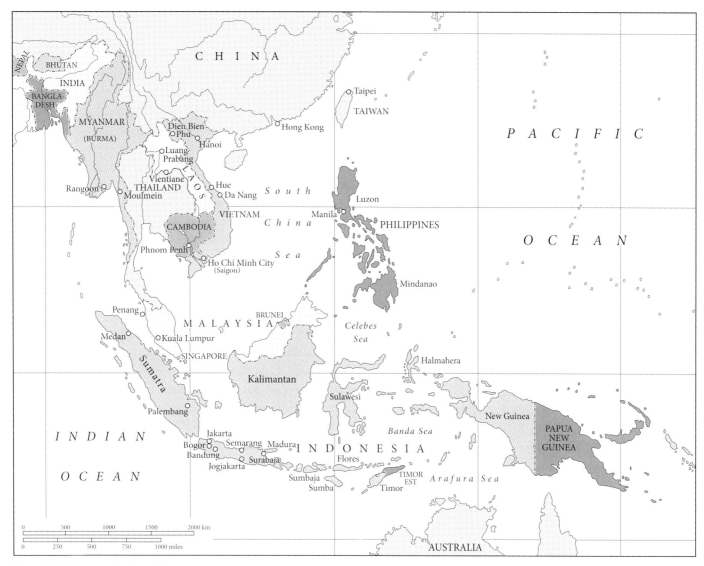

Map 16.3 Modern Southeast Asia

benefiting the major European states, then increasingly favoring North America. Its twentieth- and twenty-first-century counterpart involves Asia much more heavily. As sites of production, as objects of investment, and increasingly as markets, China, Japan, Korea, Taiwan, India, Pakistan, Bangladesh, Indonesia, Malaysia, Singapore, Thailand, the Philippines, and other Asian countries participate extensively in global growth. (See Map 16.3.)

Globalization of the 1980s took a sharp upward turn because of one critical shift: the opening of China to the world. The bipolar Cold War world had confined most trade, human, and cultural flows within the contending blocs, and made the Third World a ground of competition between them. With China's opening and the Soviet Union's collapse, far more interchange developed across the old battle lines.

Another difference: Nineteenth-century economic expansion depended heavily on coal and steel. As a consequence, capital and

workers flowed especially to a limited number of smokestack regions, producing the characteristic grimy concentrations of industrial cities along waterways and rail lines. By the late twentieth century, oil, natural gas, hydroelectric generators, and nuclear reactors had largely displaced coal as sources of power in the world's richer regions. High-tech industries like electronics and pharmaceuticals depend on important clusters of scientific and technical expertise such as the zone south of Paris and Silicon Valley, California. But these industries, unlike the concentrated coal and steel factories, can easily subdivide production according to the availability of labor and markets, dispersing production sites around the world. Service and information industries push even further in the same direction: low-wage clerks in South India, for example, process information for firms based in New York and London, with fiber-optic cable and satellite connections transmitting data instantly in both directions.

16.2 GLOBALIZATION CAN STRENGTHEN STATE POWER, OR UNDERMINE IT

Nineteenth-century globalization consolidated states. It augmented their control over resources, activities, and people within their boundaries as it increased their regulation of flows across those boundaries. In the process, uneasy but effective working agreements emerged among governments, capital, and labor at the national scale. Organized labor, organized capital, organized political parties, and organized bureaucrats fought hard, but made deals. Those bargains eventually turned states from free trade toward protection of industries that combined large labor forces with extensive fixed capital. Chemical, steel, and metal-processing industries led the way. The current variety of globalization, in dramatic contrast, undermines the central power of most states, freeing capital to move rapidly from country to country as opportunities for profit arise. Post-1980 states also cannot contain accelerated flows of communication, scientific knowledge, drugs, arms, gems, or migrants across their borders.

Not all states and state activities weakened at the same rate, of course. The United States gained military and economic power as the Soviet Union collapsed and US markets became more desirable targets for the whole world. Many states continue to regulate education, welfare, transportation, and a wide variety of other domestic activities for which they had begun to take serious responsibility during the nineteenth century, but many US politicians advocated privatization of many functions, including railroads, postal services, and even prisons. The power of most states to shield their systems of taxation and expenditure from international pressures has declined.

At the same time, non-governmental and supra-governmental organizations have escaped at least partially from control by any particular state. The newly powerful non-state organizations include multinational corporations, world financial institutions, the United Nations, political compacts such as the European Union, military alliances such as the North Atlantic Treaty Organization (NATO), and international activist groups such as Doctors Without Borders. An irony appears: The United States sponsored or at least supported the initial formation of many such transnational organizations. In their early phases the USA often bent them to its national interests. Yet as the twenty-first century began, even the United States, the world's greatest financial and military power, could not simply order these organizations around. Sometimes it simply chose to ignore them, often at heavy cost. But despite isolationist reactions, the USA kept looking for allies.

The Washington Consensus and its Discontents

Here is a case in point that illustrates the far-reaching effects of the new globalization. At the end of World War II, the same rich countries that sponsored the formation of the United Nations – including the USA – created an International Bank for Reconstruction and Development (IBRD) to help rebuild war-torn economies. Over the half-century following the war, the IBRD evolved into the World Bank. The World Bank now lends money and finances development programs in poorer countries worldwide. A complementary international organization, the International Monetary Fund, intervenes in financial markets, lending large sums of money to rescue countries from currency crises, but forcing them to join the international system. A third big institution, the World Trade Organization (formed in 1995, taking over administration of the General Agreement on Tariffs and Trade formed by the great powers after World War II) negotiates agreements to promote international trade.

In collaboration with financiers and central banks of capitalist countries, the three powerful organizations fashioned the so-called **Washington Consensus**: a set of directives, called **structural adjustment**, telling poorer countries to open up their economies for investment and trade while reducing their governments' intervention in economic life. Structural adjustment included reducing or privatizing government services, removing protections from local industries, and opening economies to foreign capital. The idea was simple: increased investment and a market-driven international division of labor would promote economic growth, and thus benefit everyone in the long run. In the short run, however, structural adjustment often increased unemployment, raised food prices, allowed foreigners to purchase cheaply raw materials needed by the country, and replaced local managers with foreigners. Box 16.1 gives a summary of the principles of structural adjustment.

Whatever short-run damage it inflicted, structural adjustment did attract foreign capital. Financial experts classify capital flows from rich to poor countries into four kinds: (1) official flows, either as government-backed direct aid or long-term loans; (2) private flows as bank loans with strict terms for repayment; (3) portfolio investments giving rights to dividends but not to managerial power; and (4) **foreign direct investment**: establishing, buying into, or buying up firms in poor countries. Between 1990 and 1999, official flows from rich to poor actually declined, but the other three all rose significantly. Most remarkable was foreign direct investment (FDI), which gave outside capitalists power within local economies. FDI soared from about 15 billion dollars in 1990 to about 185 billion dollars in 1999. To be sure, that total still looked puny compared with the roughly 2.5 trillion dollars of foreign money already invested in industrial economies,

Box 16.1 The Washington Consensus

During the 1980s and 1990s, major capitalist powers, including the United States, generally agreed on a set of reforms for developing economies that people called the "Washington Consensus." It included these elements:

- Fiscal discipline.
- Redirection of public expenditure toward education, health, and infrastructure investment.

- Broadening the tax base and cutting marginal tax rates.
- Market-determined, positive, and moderate interest rates.
- Competitive exchange rates for national currencies.
- Trade liberalization, which involved replacement of protective tariffs by low, uniform tariffs.

- Openings to foreign direct investment.
- Privatization of state enterprises.
- Abolition of regulations impeding entry into national markets, restricting competition within them – with exceptions for protection of personal safety, the environment, consumers, and financial institutions.
- Legal security for property rights.

---

including the American economy. Very poor countries, like most African countries, furthermore, got little FDI: a mere 10 billion of the total. Still, the share of new money going outside the existing industrial powers was rising fast. Venture capital from the United States, Japan, Great Britain, Germany, France, the Netherlands, and other capitalist countries began flowing into poorer economies even more rapidly than during the nineteenth century. More than ever before, the globalization of the late twentieth century centered on flows of investment capital.

Challenging the Washington Consensus

A small handful of countries, however, defied the Washington Consensus, and did extraordinarily well. Instead of opening markets universally, they restricted foreign access to special high-tech enclaves. Instead of pulling the government out of the economy, they targeted investment to particular sectors and industries with subsidies, export controls, and regulations. They often had military or one-party governments, but their industrial policies were directed by engineers and economic technocrats. They were authoritarian **developmental states** (featuring direct governmental intervention to promote economic growth) that realized that the key to economic growth was no longer material resources but *knowledge*, so they heavily supported mass education and research and development.

The reason such heavy state intervention did not lead to stagnation was reciprocity: in return for government favors, the chosen industries had to perform, by meeting high targets for export growth and technological progress. Japan set this pattern of "administrative guidance" in the 1960s, and South Korea, Taiwan, Hong Kong, and Singapore followed in the 1980s. Thailand, Indonesia, and Malaysia have now advanced significantly, and China and India are imitating the East Asian tigers' successes. Elsewhere, a few countries like Turkey, Argentina, Brazil, Mexico, and Chile have

adopted similar policies. Together, these countries, not including Hong Kong and Singapore, have raised their share of world manufacturing GDP from 5 percent to 17.4 percent between 1965 and 1995. Their manufacturing output has grown at an average rate of 9 percent a year for thirty years, while the advanced North Atlantic countries have grown at only 3.3 percent.

At first, bankers and international officials took the postwar economic expansions of Japan, South Korea, Taiwan, and Singapore as proof that their adjustment plans worked well. They ignored the fact that in all these East Asian countries, the governments took an active role in promoting development. During the 1990s, however, widespread popular protests against structural adjustment, chaos in post-socialist economies, and increasing evidence of impoverishment in already poor parts of the world gave capitalist leaders pause. Experts began to argue that market connections alone did not guarantee economic growth. They disagreed over the relative importance and relationships of political institutions, property rights, welfare provisions, education, health, stimuli for technological innovation, and other forms of infrastructure. But they tended to agree that market integration would only work its wonders in the presence of extensive supporting institutions. The success of the Asian developmental states, which had built on strong bureaucracies, native market economies, and respect for widespread education, showed that market integration was no magic recipe: in fact, it was not even the most important one. History mattered more.

16.3 POVERTY

Poverty Persists Despite World Capital's Promises

Box 16.2 summarizes the shifting views of a powerful international financial institution, the World Bank, on priorities for economic development from 1991 to 2003. Earlier, the World

Box 16.2 The World Bank Changes Focus

The World Bank, a powerful worldwide financial institution based in Washington, DC, issues an annual report on the world economy, with special emphasis on prospects for economic development. The Bank began organizing its annual report thematically in 1991. Titles of reports from 1991 to 2003 give an idea of the great lender's changing preoccupations:

1991: The Challenge of Development
1992: Development and the Environment

1993: Investing in Health
1994: Infrastructure for Development
1995: Workers in an Integrating World
1996: From Plan to Market
1997: The State in a Changing World
1998: Knowledge for Development
1999: Entering the Twenty-First Century
2000/2001: Attacking Poverty
2002: Building Institutions for Markets
2003: Sustainable Development in a Dynamic World

During the early years, annual reports centered on capital investment and return, with special attention to poor countries and post-socialist regimes. Then they moved dramatically away from the assumption that integration into world markets would more or less automatically promote capitalism and development toward the view that market capitalism required extensive institutional underpinnings, including property rights and the rule of law.

Bank displayed confidence that plugging economies of poor countries directly and rapidly into world markets would start them moving toward economic growth. As socialist regimes collapsed, World Bank reports recommended the same treatment for post-socialist economies: Plug them in and watch them take off. As late as 1996, the annual report titled *From Plan to Market* introduced some reservations about instant transitions without adequate supporting institutions, but still more or less equated "reform" with adaptation to world markets for capital and commodities. Later reports began to doubt the value of abrupt exposure to world markets. Haunted by the collapse of many post-socialist economies and the failure of many development efforts elsewhere, they still advocated market integration, but only when coupled with measures to ease transitions into full competition.

Now, development reports stressed the importance of infrastructure, including social infrastructure: not only schools, roads, and technologies, but also reliable governments, responsible public officials, human rights, and social security. The preface to the 1999 World Bank report, *Entering the Twenty-First Century*, declared that:

Development thinking has evolved into a broad pragmatism, realizing that development must move beyond economic growth to encompass important social goals – reduced poverty, improved quality of life, enhanced opportunities for better education and health, and more. Experience has also taught that sustainable progress toward these goals requires integrated implementation and must be firmly anchored in processes that are open, participatory, and inclusive. In the absence of a strong institutional foundation, the outcomes of good policy initiatives tend to dissipate.

The 2000/01 report began, "Poverty amid plenty is the world's greatest challenge." It noted that, of the world's 6 billion people, almost half lived on less than 2 dollars per day, and a fifth on less than 1 dollar per day, with 44 percent of the extremely poor living in South Asia – Pakistan, India, Bangladesh, Myanmar (formerly known as Burma), Sri Lanka (formerly known as Ceylon), and nearby areas. The gap between incomes in the twenty richest and twenty poorest countries had doubled since 1960. In Latin America, South Asia, sub-Saharan Africa, and post-socialist countries as a whole, the proportion of very poor people rose rapidly during the 1990s. The world as a whole grew richer, but the number of poor people expanded rapidly. Unequal distribution of globalization's costs and benefits caused that troubling disparity. (See Maps 16.4, 16.5, and 16.6.)

Poverty and Inequality

Notice the case of East Asia in Figure 16.2. In 1960, the region contained 38 percent of the world's population, but only received 13 percent of the world's commercial income. By 1999, East Asia had lost slightly in its share of world population as South Asia and sub-Saharan Africa experienced more rapid population growth. But by then East Asia had come up to a full quarter – 25.9 percent – of the world's commercial income. Meanwhile, North America, Western Europe, Eastern Europe, and sub-Saharan Africa were losing market shares despite relatively rapid economic growth in the first two.

Figure 16.3 provides a rough picture of the resulting gaps among world regions in 2000. Despite the increasing importance of mobile financial capital, personal income still corresponded broadly to industrial production in the year 2000. We can therefore read the

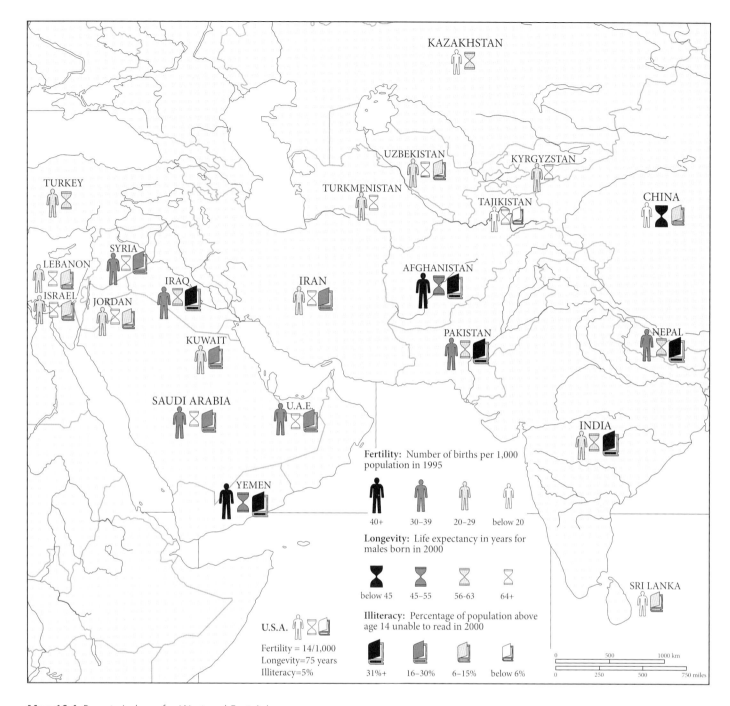

Map 16.4 Poverty Indexes for West and East Asia

graph as a comparison of regions in terms of population and wealth. It shows startling inequalities. North America had only 5 percent of the world's population but 30 percent of the world's industrial production. At the other extreme, Africa had 13 percent of world population and a mere 2 percent of industrial production. Asia (including the rich economies of Japan, South Korea, Taiwan, and Singapore) stood in between, with a full 61 percent of world population and only 26 percent of industrial production. If we compared these figures with an even worldwide distribution of wealth, they would mean that inhabitants of North America had six times their share of the wealth, Asians less than half their share, Africans less than a sixth of their share.

Country-by-country disparities, of course, ran even larger. National income per capita is a peculiar statistic for three reasons: First, it averages over the entire population – men, women, and children of all ages – regardless of whether they are earning money. Second, how well it describes the economic situation of most people depends on how equally income is distributed; medium per capita income plus high inequality means many poor people. Third, income figures exaggerate

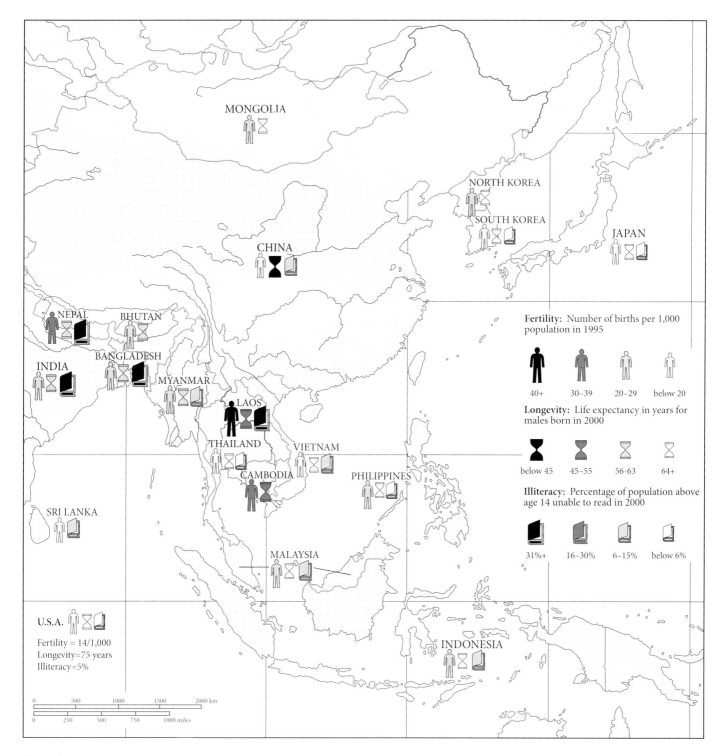

Map 16.4 (*cont.*)

differences between rich and poor countries because in poorer regions as a whole people produce a larger share of goods and services outside of the market; national income accounts generally undercount non-market goods and services. Nevertheless, big international differences in per capita income reliably indicate large disparities in overall conditions of life.

Compare Switzerland, whose annual income per person is more than 38,000 dollars, with Sierra Leone, whose average inhabitant

receives 130 dollars per year – about 36 cents a day per person. The differences are huge. They make it easier to understand why most people in such countries as Sierra Leone have no hope of ever acquiring goods most Western Europeans and North Americans take for granted. They have no prospect of buying automobiles, televisions, or expensive prescription drugs.

A poor man in Kenya interviewed by researchers working for the World Bank put it this way: "Don't ask me what poverty is

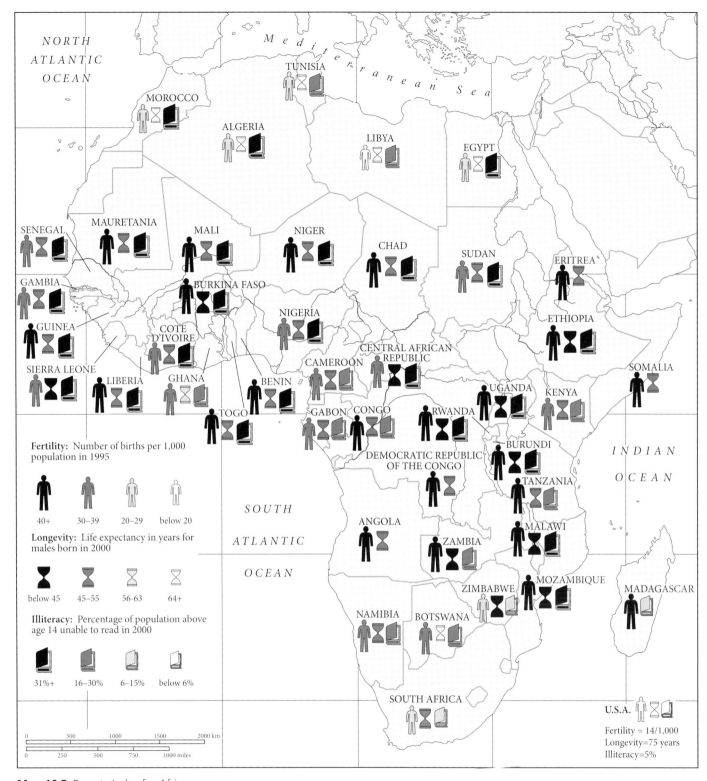

Map 16.5 Poverty Index for Africa

because you have met it outside my house. Look at the house, then count the number of holes. Look at the utensils and the clothes I am wearing. Look at everything and write what you see. What you see is poverty." Members of a discussion group in Ecuador described poverty thus: "Certainly our farming is little; all the products, things bought from stores, are expensive; it is hard to live, we work and earn little money, buy few things or products; products are scarce, there is no money and we feel poor. If there were money . . ." Poor people live with shortages of basic necessities as well as of the luxuries that most people in rich countries consume every day. To be poor in a poor country is to be surrounded by many others who share your misery, and only occasionally to encounter someone rich. To be poor in a rich country is to see close up what others have and you do not.

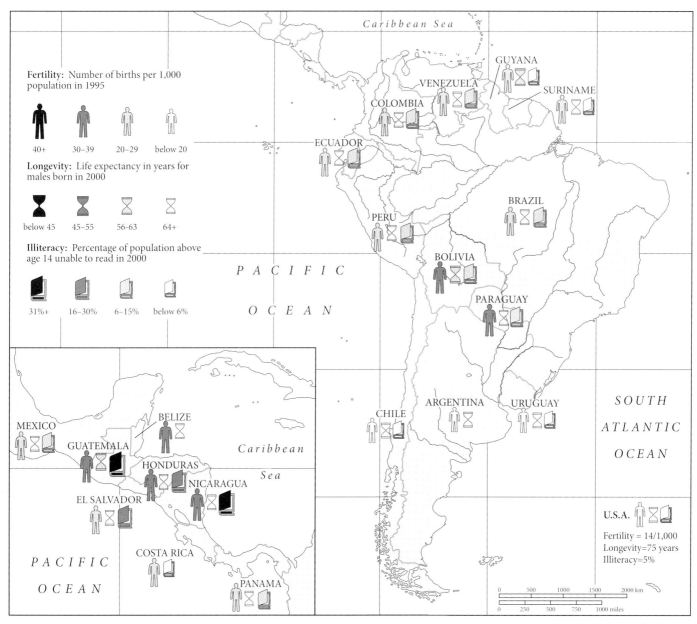

Map 16.6 Poverty Index for Latin America

Poverty is Not Only Less Money

Still, we should avoid thinking that money alone makes the difference. Figure 16.4 shows that national income correlates with a number of other advantages, but by no means perfectly. In the table, the highest income countries are Norway, Japan, and the United States, in that order. The lowest income countries are Niger and Bangladesh. In the table's two poorest countries, income per capita runs no more than a dollar a day, as compared with Norway's 90 dollars per day per person. How many people actually live above or below these national averages depends, however, on the inequality of income distribution. On the list, South Africa, Mexico, Niger, Turkey, and the United States top the other countries in their degrees of income inequality. Japan, the Czech Republic, and Norway have relatively low income

inequality, which means that higher shares of their populations benefit from the national prosperity. The table shows that Japanese, Czech, and Norwegian citizens gain from the greater equality of income distribution: they enjoy high rates of school enrollment for their children and significantly lower infant mortality than other rich countries such as the United States.

High average income by itself, then, does not guarantee extensive schooling or low infant mortality. Take another comparison: Australia, the Czech Republic, and France all had lower per capita incomes than the United States in 1999, but their babies more often survived their first years. Even in fairly prosperous countries with advanced medical facilities, provision of health care for poor people increased the overall population's life expectancy.

Region	1960		1970		1980		1990		1999	
East Asia	13.0%	38.0%	19.5	38.3	21.8	38.0	25.9	37.1	25.9	35.9
Australia/New Zealand	1.7	0.5	1.6	0.5	1.5	0.5	1.5	0.5	1.6	0.5
North America	35.1	7.9	30.6	7.4	29.2	6.8	29.2	6.2	29.8	6.1
South/Central America	5.8	8.2	5.7	8.8	7.0	9.3	5.6	9.5	5.8	9.7
Western Europe	40.5	12.4	38.7	10.9	36.4	9.5	33.5	8.1	32.3	7.7
Eastern Europe	N/A	N/A	N/A	N/A	N/A	N/A	N/A	N/A	N/A	N/A
Sub-Saharan Africa	1.3	6.8	1.3	7.2	1.2	7.8	1.0	8.8	1.0	9.4
Middle East/N. Africa	1.2	4.0	1.3	4.2	1.7	4.5	1.7	4.9	1.7	5.1
South Asia	1.3	22.0	1.3	22.7	1.2	23.8	1.5	24.8	1.9	25.7
World	100.0	100.0	100.0	100.0	100.0	100.0	100.0	100.0	100.0	100.0

East Asia: China, Hong Kong, Indonesia, Japan, South Korea, Malaysia, Philippines, Singapore, Taiwan, Thailand

North America: Canada, United States

South/Central America: Argentina, Bolivia, Brazil, Chile, Colombia, Costa Rica, Dominican Republic, Ecuador, El Salvador, Guatemala, Haiti, Honduras, Jamaica, Mexico, Nicaragua, Panama, Paraguay, Peru, Trinidad-Tobago, Uruguay, Venezuela

Western Europe: Austria, Belgium, Denmark, Finland, France, Germany, Greece, Ireland, Israel, Italy, Luxembourg, Netherlands, Norway, Portugal, Spain, Sweden, Switzerland, United Kingdom

Eastern Europe: N/A

Sub-Saharan Africa: Benin, Botswana, Burkina Faso, Burundi, Cameroon, Central African Republic, Chad, Rep. of Congo, Congo Dem. Rep., Côte d'Ivoire, Gabon, Ghana, Kenya, Lesotho, Madagascar, Malawi, Mauritania, Mauritius, Niger, Nigeria, Rwanda, Senegal, South Africa, Tanzania, Togo, Uganda, Zambia, Zimbabwe

Middle East/North Africa: Algeria, Egypt, Morocco, Saudi Arabia, Sudan, Syria, Tunisia, Turkey

South Asia: Bangladesh, India, Nepal, Pakistan, Sri Lanka

Figure 16.2 Regional percentage of world gross national product and population, 1960–99.

Figure 16.3 Gaps among world regions in 2000.

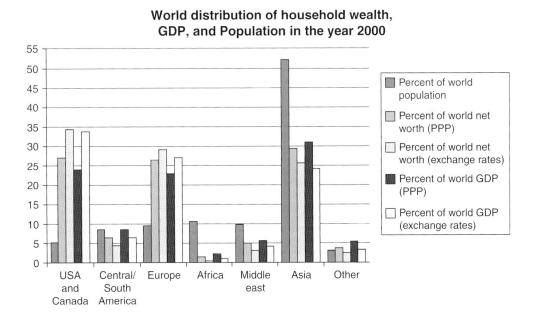

World distribution of household wealth, GDP, and Population in the year 2000

Legend:
- Percent of world population
- Percent of world net worth (PPP)
- Percent of world net worth (exchange rates)
- Percent of world GDP (PPP)
- Percent of world GDP (exchange rates)

Among poorer countries, the data also show that relatively equal access to health care saves babies' lives. Infant mortality means the proportion of babies that die within their first year of life. On vastly less per capita income, China manages much lower infant mortality than Mexico, South Africa, or Turkey. China does so by spreading its meager health resources more evenly, and by investing heavily in public health. When poverty, inequality, and low public expenditure on health combine, they usually produce lower levels of schooling and much higher rates of death among the newborn. In these terms, citizens of Niger had the worst of

Figure 16.4 Indicators of well-being for selected countries, 1980–99.

Country	GNP per Capita[1] 1999	Income Inequality[2] 1990s	Percent of Age Group Enrolled in School Primary 1980	Primary 1997	Secondary 1980	Secondary 1997	Infant Mortality per 1,000 births[3] 1980	1998	Public Expenditure on Health as Percent of GDP[4] 1990–1998
Australia	20050	35.2	100	100	81	96	11	5	5.5
Bangladesh	370	33.6	60	75	18	22	132	73	1.6
China	780	40.3	84	100	63	70	42	31	2.0
Czech Rep.	5060	25.4	95	100	93	100	16	5	6.4
France	23480	32.7	100	100	94	99	10	5	7.1
Indonesia	580	36.5	89	99	42	56	90	43	0.6
Japan	32230	24.9	100	100	93	100	8	4	5.9
Jordan	1500	36.4	73	68	53	41	41	27	3.7
Mexico	4400	53.7	98	100	67	66	51	30	2.8
Niger	190	50.5	22	24	7	9	135	118	1.3
Norway	32880	25.8	99	100	84	98	8	4	6.2
S. Africa	3180	59.3	68	100	62	95	67	51	3.2
Turkey	2900	41.5	81	100	42	58	109	38	2.9
USA	30600	40.8	90	100	94	96	13	7	6.5

[1] Gross National Product/population, in US dollars

[2] Gini index: 0 = perfect equality, 100 = complete inequality

[3] Deaths of children less than 1 year old in year/1,000 live births in same year

[4] GDP = Gross Domestic Product

all worlds: extremely low per capita income, high income inequality, and very small public expenditure on health. In 1998, a newborn infant in Niger was thirty times as likely to die within a year as a newborn Japanese. Only a small minority of those who survived their first year of life in Niger were likely to complete primary school, much less to attend high school.

Science and the Internet will not Equalize the World

International inequality extends well beyond income, schooling, and life expectancy. From the perspective of people in the wealthier North American and European countries, for example, the internet looks like a great equalizer, connecting everyone with everyone else. After all, in 2000 the United States led the world with 160 internet-connected computers per thousand people; Finland followed closely with 125 connections per thousand, and Iceland came next with 100. Iceland, those numbers mean, had one computer connected to the Internet for every ten people. Over the world as a whole, the internet had an estimated 378 million users.

The total seems immense, but stop to think: it represented only 6 percent of the world's population in 2000. Inverted, the figure means that 94 percent of humanity then lacked access to the internet. The USA, Canada, Western Europe, Japan, and South Korea accounted for something like nine tenths of all the world's internet users. Less than one person in a thousand was surfing the internet in South Asia and sub-Saharan Africa. Since connection to the internet does, as advertised, provide rapid access to vast quantities of information and millions of people, the net effect of the internet's impressive expansion has been to increase information inequality across the world. Most likely, computer-based communication will continue to divide the world sharply into informational rich and poor for decades to come.

Similar stories apply to other forms of globalization: seen from centers of influence, it looks as though the entire world is globalizing. Seen from the edges, penetration of global influence is highly selective. At least in the short and medium runs, it increases inequalities. Scientific advances, for example, are having profound effects on medicine, communications, agriculture, and manufacturing. But those effects concentrate very heavily in already rich countries. To take a simple indicator, the only countries registering ten or more patents per million population in 1997 were Japan, South Korea, Australia, Canada, the United States, the Nordic countries, and the countries of Western Europe less Spain and Portugal. Their technological advantages over the rest of the world were actually increasing.

Or take advances in medicine. As the HIV virus spread globally during the 1990s and early twenty-first century, Western pharmaceutical companies started creating drugs that greatly prolonged and improved the lives of HIV victims. But the virus continues to kill in Africa. In 2000, an estimated third of all Botswana's women aged 15–24 and a sixth of all the men in the same age range carried the virus. (In the typical pattern of AIDS epidemics, a relatively small number of sexually active men infect a larger number of their sexual partners, whether female or male. As a result, where heterosexual transmission of HIV prevails, many more women than men become infected.) The hardest-hit countries – Botswana, South Africa, Zimbabwe, Zambia, and other African regions further north – have neither the financial means nor the delivery systems to get life-saving drugs to their ailing populations.

16.4 NEW INDUSTRIAL GEOGRAPHY: THREE REGIONAL SHIFTS

Nevertheless, globalization has been transforming the world's economic and political geography. During the period after 1980, three major shifts deserve attention: breakup or transformation of all the major socialist regimes; movement of a number of regional economies into production and export of high-tech goods; and the overall rise of Asia and the Pacific as sites of economic and political power. In addition to the Soviet story we told earlier, socialist breakup and transformation included the disintegration of Yugoslavia. It also involved the cautious but quite successful movement of China toward production for world markets, notably that of North America.

High-Technology Industry

The new regional specialization in niches of high-tech production shows up in the list of countries having at least 10 percent of their manufacturing exports in high-tech products as of 1998:

Australia, Austria, Canada, China, Costa Rica, Denmark, Finland, France, Germany, Hungary, Indonesia, Ireland, Israel, Japan, Kyrgyz Republic, Malaysia, Mexico, Netherlands, Norway, Philippines, Russia, Singapore, South Korea, Sweden, Switzerland, Thailand, United Kingdom, United States.

Beside the old industrial countries on the list, we find ex-socialist states such as Hungary (21 percent of manufacturing exports

high-tech), the Kyrgyz Republic (16 percent), and Russia (12 percent). We also find up-and-coming low-wage manufacturers of Central America and the Pacific. A regional, rather than national, list would include coastal India and parts of South America's southern cone as well. In such industries as electronics, international firms based in the major industrial powers have been seeking out entrepreneurs who can supply disciplined low-wage workers for production of high-tech components. The entrepreneurs are showing up increasingly outside the traditional centers of manufacturing.

Goodbye State Socialism

By 2000, China was the only big country still calling itself socialist, and even China was making mighty efforts to sell its goods in capitalist markets across the world. Mixed economies with strong unions, extensive public services, broad social safety nets, and serious restraints on capital still existed in Scandinavia, the Netherlands, and a few other places. But after 1989, centralized state socialism with planned economies, government-supervised production, and restricted private property almost disappeared as a major alternative to capitalism. Four massive changes produced that rapid shift: China's own impressive example; rapid defection of citizens from socialist institutions in the more industrialized state socialist countries; collapse of economic co-ordination among countries within the Soviet bloc; and striking opportunism in the less industrialized post-socialist regimes.

Immense China – 1.3 billion people in 2000 – has created a surprising combination of state socialist discipline and market enterprise. The Chinese Communist Party remained in charge, huge armed forces played significant parts in public life, and central planning still applied across much of the national economy. The regime quickly put down dissent. The May–June headlines in Figure 16.1, for example, included the bloody repression of a democracy-seeking student movement in Beijing and elsewhere. This much looks like the standard picture of the more backward state socialist regimes in the 1980s: central controls, widespread repression, aging industrial facilities, and economic stagnation.

But China has undertaken a split strategy. Remember the history of China's coastal regions; they have served for centuries as bases for trade and migration through much of the Indian Ocean and Pacific. After 1980, the Chinese government began stimulating industry in those regions, opening them to foreign investment, and giving them freedom from the tight economic controls prevailing elsewhere in China. The extreme case was Hong Kong, the former British colony that returned to China in 1997. Under British rule, Hong Kong became a major Asian center of capitalist enterprise, with the advantage of fairly easy access to the Chinese mainland. As it acquired Hong Kong, the Chinese central government installed political control, but it allowed Hong Kong's merchants and manufacturers to maintain their extensive ties with world markets. Hong Kong's population continued to prosper, with per capita income in the vicinity of Australia, Canada, and Denmark.

In terms of economic expansion, the mixed strategy worked remarkably well. Between 1990 and 2000, economic production grew by these percentages across the world:

Canada 2.9	Mexico 3.1
China 10.3	Russia 8.8
India 6.0	USA 3.4
Japan 1.3	World 2.6

Russia was recovering from the near-collapse of its economy around 1990, especially by stepping up sales of oil and natural gas. For that reason, its high rate of growth during the 1990s does not necessarily forecast future expansion. From the viewpoint of economic growth, China was the big success story. In the early twenty-first century, the big question is not whether China's economy will continue to grow, but whether the country as a whole will gradually come to resemble the world's major capitalist countries, or create a new sort of relation between economics and politics.

Meanwhile, other former state socialist regimes were exiting from their old political and economic arrangements in different directions. Long before 1989, dissidents in the more industrialized regimes called for political and economic freedoms. As part of his liberalization, Gorbachev announced that the Soviet Union would no longer send troops to back threatened sister regimes. At the same time, the economic division of labor that the Soviet communists had established within the Soviet Union and its Eastern European satellites began to fall apart; shrinking of the Soviet military, for example, caused widespread unemployment in the Polish textile factories that had produced uniforms for Soviet soldiers.

In Poland, the trade union movement called Solidarity challenged national communist leaders from 1980 onward, suffered a martial law crackdown in 1981, but came back with major strikes in 1988 and successful demands for national elections in 1989. The elections actually ousted the Communist Party from power and brought Solidarity in as leader of the governing coalition. In Hungary, the governing Communist Party began fragmenting in 1988, and even the fragments lost power in the elections of 1990. In East Germany and Czechoslovakia, thousands of people took to the streets against their regimes in 1989, and the communists soon left power. By 2000, Poland and Hungary were struggling to establish market economies and democratic politics, East Germany had become the poorer eastern provinces

of the German Federal Republic, and Czechoslovakia had split into the Czech Republic and Slovakia.

All these post-socialist countries were integrating more or less successfully into the capitalist economy and democratic politics of Western and Central Europe. The less industrial socialist regimes of Bulgaria and Romania likewise made efforts to establish post-socialist niches in the new Europe. Dirt-poor Albania (which had maintained fierce isolation from the Soviet bloc despite its own version of state socialism) fragmented politically and continued in economic turmoil.

These transformations of Eastern Europe significantly affected the other substantial Balkan socialist entity: the Yugoslav federation. The death of Marshal Tito (1980) left a divided succession, but did not break the country into its components. But as Soviet satellites began moving away from socialism after 1989, Yugoslavia's most industrialized republic, Slovenia, began establishing closer ties to Western Europe, especially Austria and Germany. The independence of Slovenia in 1990 started a cascade of demands for autonomy and independence elsewhere in Yugoslavia, notably in Croatia, Bosnia-Herzegovina, Montenegro, Macedonia, and the Serb-controlled but predominantly Albanian-speaking region of Kosovo. As Serbia sought to re-establish its dominance within what remained of the federation, intermittent civil war broke out across much of the country. At the start of the twenty-first century, the economic and political future of the former Yugoslavia remained very uncertain.

The Soviet Union itself began splintering soon after 1989. By 1991, the USSR's Baltic provinces (Estonia, Latvia, and Lithuania) gained independence with Western support, and late-blooming nationalists were leading separatist movements in Ukraine, Belarus, Moldova, the Caucasus, and Central Asia. (Armenia, Georgia, and Azerbaijan split off from the USSR in the Caucasus, while newly independent Central Asian republics included Tajikistan, Uzbekistan, the Kyrgyz Republic, Turkmenistan, and Kazakhstan.) In most of these regions, authoritarian leaders who had once been Communist Party functionaries came to power. Their general combination of poverty with dependence on exports of agricultural products or raw materials such as oil and natural gas made their external economic relations somewhat easier to control than in the case of highly industrialized economies. On the whole, the new rulers played nationalist cards, insisting on giving priority to their own national groups – Tajik, Uzbek, and so on – and suppressing opposition in the name of national development. So far, export-oriented industrial centers like that of the Kyrgyz Republic remain rare in post-Soviet territory except for parts of the Baltic and the western Russian Federation. Nevertheless, post-socialist states in general figure importantly in the twenty-first-century redrawing of the world's industrial map.

The Rise of Asia and the Pacific

The new industrial geography has fundamental implications for the future. For most of the last 10,000 years, the principal centers of world economic activity and political power have lain in or immediately around Asia, the Indian Ocean, and the Pacific. After 1500 CE, Western Europe and North America became dominant through the first two waves of globalization we have reviewed. But the third wave is shifting dominance back toward Asia and the Pacific. Australia, Japan, South Korea, and Taiwan had already achieved world prominence by 2000.

At that point, tiny Singapore and Hong Kong had become wealthy industrial and commercial centers. Coastal China was becoming a manufacturing zone of world significance. Elsewhere in the region, Malaysia, Indonesia, the Philippines, and coastal India were all creating specialized industrial sectors tied closely to the major Asian industrial powers and exporting to the whole world. Outside of Australia, China, Japan, and South Korea, countries of the Asia-Pacific region were mostly adapting technologies developed elsewhere. During the 1990s, the region's economies proved quite vulnerable to withdrawal of venture capital by speculators based in Europe and America. But collectively they were beginning to compete with the powerhouse economies of Europe and North America.

Nevertheless, economic expansion occurred quite unequally within Asia. East Asian countries stood out from the rest. As compared to most other countries outside of Western Europe and North America, they managed high rates of saving and reinvestment. They invested heavily in education, including female education. They stressed education in science and technology. Although they had made their earlier headway by gaining privileged access to North American and Western European markets, they soon adopted more general strategies of entering international markets with well-crafted and attractively priced precision products – small automobiles, personal computer components, stereo systems, and more. China combined this high-tech strategy with another strategy that became common elsewhere in Asia: moving into low-wage industries (notably apparel and housewares) and competing directly with manufacturers of similar products in higher-wage countries. Outside of Japan, South Korea, Taiwan, Singapore, and coastal China, indeed, Asia's expanding economies were growing chiefly either by attracting low-wage manufacturing or by exporting oil to richer countries.

Asia had another less visible but crucial asset: its trading **diasporas**. International networks of entrepreneurs who share cultural heritage have figured importantly in economic connections over almost all the history this book has surveyed, from the Assyrians of 2000 BCE onward. Such diasporas matter because their members communicate effectively over great distances and often create institutions sustaining credit and trust for high-risk enterprises. Entrepreneurs from India's Gujarat region, for example, have sustained trade between South Asia and Africa for centuries. More recently, they have moved actively into North America. Gujaratis now own the majority of North American motels, and are heavily involved in other varieties of North American business. Estimates of South Asian overseas net worth across the world run from 150 to 300 billion dollars.

On an even larger scale, the 50 million ethnic Chinese outside of China include a number of diasporas, commonly identified with one mainland coastal region or another. Ethnic Chinese have organized economic activity throughout the Pacific. They have also been entering European and North American business with greater and greater success. In 1997 alone, for example, Taiwanese firms invested in fifty-five European manufacturing projects, forty-four of them in the computer industry. Asian diasporas are laying down networks through which expanding Asian economies will spread their influence far outside their home regions.

Politically as well as economically, Asia and the Pacific have been flexing their muscles. In 2000, more than half the world's people lived in China, India, Indonesia, Pakistan, Bangladesh, Japan, the Philippines, South Korea, Thailand, or Myanmar. China's people alone made up a fifth of the entire world's population. According to United Nations demographers, Asia contained 56 percent of world population in 1950, topped 60 percent by 2000, and was likely to remain close to that level in 2050 despite declining birth rates. As of 2000, most Asia-Pacific countries had not yet translated their demographic heft into political or military power. But China, India, and Pakistan possessed nuclear weapons. With 3 million troops under arms, China fielded the world's largest army by far. Its army, furthermore, was playing a major part in developing the economy, running some 15,000 business enterprises and 50,000 factories on its own authority. Combining demographic, economic, and political potential, Asia and the Pacific will surely weigh much more heavily in world affairs by 2050 than they did in 2000.

By 2000, North Americans were already seeing ample evidence of the shift toward Asia and the Pacific. Within Canada and the United States, population was moving rapidly toward the Pacific coast, with Vancouver, Seattle, and Los Angeles increasingly becoming central ports by air and sea as well as major manufacturing centers. Asian communities were growing and prospering up and down the coast. East Asian automobiles and electronic devices had long since become everyday items, as Japanese and Korean firms built plants worked mainly by North American labor. Students from East and South Asia flocked to North American universities, with many of them ending up as leading members of North American professions. Nurses from the Philippines made up substantial minorities of American hospital nursing staffs. The crucial next phase will begin when some of these flows reverse – when, for example, young American-trained professionals regularly go off to Asia for further training or regular careers. By 2050, we can reasonably expect that to be happening in many fields.

16.5 DARKER SIDES OF GLOBALIZATION: ENVIRONMENTAL DEVASTATION AND DRUGS

Many of the same unequal global connections that transfer wanted goods and services across the world also deliver commodities that few people desire.

Pollution

Global warming provides an obvious example. The world's rich countries use far more fuel for transportation, manufacturing, and heating than poor countries do. Fuel use inevitably produces atmospheric emissions of gases. As a consequence of fuel consumption, carbon dioxide, methane, and other greenhouse gases are entering the atmosphere, magnifying the sun's heating effect on the planet. As a result, polar ice is melting and sea levels are rising throughout the world. Low-lying settlements such as those in Bangladesh face the threat of greater and greater flooding. So far, rich industrial countries have contributed most to global warming through exhaust from their factories, houses, buildings, and motor vehicles. But because poorer industrializing countries generally consume higher-emission fuels, the balance is changing. In 2013 China surpassed the United States as the world's largest polluter (but just barely).

Air and water pollution resulting from manufacturing, transportation, agricultural effluents, and human waste operate on smaller scales than global warming, but they likewise occur in part as results of globalization. Poor parts of the globalizing world are now urbanizing much more rapidly than rich parts of the world, with the result that people in those regions suffer increasingly from such urban diseases as bronchial asthma, tuberculosis, cholera, and lead poisoning. We have already seen, furthermore, how global connections facilitated the world's influenza pandemic of 1918 and the spread of AIDS through Africa and Asia after 1990. AIDS devastates sexually active segments of populations and their children so rapidly, in fact, that it could easily obliterate economic growth in the hardest-hit African countries.

Where plugging local resources into world markets works all too well, the process likewise has a dark side. Once surveyors discover new deposits of oil, for example, they can almost always find international firms eager to drill and pump. But when that happens fast, it defaces the landscape, displaces the local population, attracts polluting tankers or pipelines, and rarely produces benefits for the bulk of the people in the oil-producing region. Although national treasuries and high officials have fattened on the proceeds, expanded oil production in Nigeria has left 70 percent of the population below the income threshold of a dollar per day. Oil is not alone. Lumbering of Indonesia's lowland trees (including those officially in national parks) is proceeding so fast that one of the world's richest forests is on its way to extinction: Specialists estimate that 65–80 percent of the once fabled lowland forests of Sumatra have already been lost to farmers. In Indonesia, international logging firms collude with local officials to split the profits from ignoring the future, and back up their collusion with violence against anyone who tries to stop them.

The Drug Trade: An Even More Unwanted Consequence of Globalization

Other unhappy traffics likewise result at least partly from globalization: intercontinental shipment of prostitutes, illegal arms trading, traffic in mercenary soldiers, financing of military rebels with diamonds, kidnapping for extortion and profit, forcible recruitment of child soldiers, taking of slaves, and illegal immigration. Consider the international trade in hard drugs as one of the better-documented cases in point. We have already seen Westerners promoting the opium trade in China during the nineteenth century. But the recent scale and profitability of illicit drugs outshadow earlier versions of the trade. During the late 1990s, experts in the United Nations estimated that international drug trafficking amounted to 8 percent of all world trade. Let us concentrate on cocaine and heroin, which generate greater global connections than cannabis, hallucinogens, barbiturates, and amphetamines. Like most other illicit trades at the global scale, cocaine and heroin pass mainly from very poor to richer parts of the world. They enrich criminal entrepreneurs in the richer regions and their agents in poor regions.

Box 16.3 identifies two crucial facts about commerce in cocaine and heroin at the twentieth century's end. First, cultivators of the original crops receive no more than trivial shares of the proceeds: 1 dollar in 2,500 of the street price for cocaine, 1 dollar in 25,000 of the street price for heroin. (Compare the markup with oil, which at the gas pump sells for roughly 40 times its price leaving the ground.) Only very poor peasants have much to gain by producing the raw materials. Second, the markups get larger and larger as the drug approaches its distant consumers; the final wholesalers at destination make the big money. As a result, eradication of the original crops faces severe limits as an anti-drug policy: profiteers further down the supply line have powerful incentives and means to search out new growers as the old ones give up their crops.

Three major zones produced the great bulk of commercialized opium and coca at the twentieth century's end. At that point, Afghanistan produced about 2,800 tons of opium per year. Myanmar came a close second with more than 2,500 tons. Delivered as powdered heroin to New York streets, according to the figures in Box 16.3, the two regions' annual production would be worth about 1.4 trillion dollars. Coca came largely from the highlands of Bolivia, Peru, and Colombia. Colombians also grew opium poppies, but on nothing like the Afghan scale. In the spring of 2001, Afghanistan's Muslim rulers told United Nations officials that they were eradicating the country's opium crop; if that had actually happened, we might have expected heroin production to increase in both Myanmar and Colombia, if not in adjacent areas as well. As Western forces drove out the ruling Taliban, however, they disrupted trade routes, but gave new freedom to poppy growers, drug merchants, and warlords who profit from them. The trade is so lucrative that intermediaries will certainly make energetic searches for new growers before giving up the business.

As with other globalized products, a well-defined international division of labor has formed. Cocaine goes primarily to dealers, and then to users, in North America, with a secondary circuit through the Caribbean to Western Europe. Cali, Medellin, Miami, New York, Chicago, Los Angeles, Jamaica, and Trinidad all play significant parts in the cocaine network. Heroin flows from the Afghan region especially to Europe (both Eastern and Western), with Istanbul, Moscow, Palermo, Naples, and Addis Ababa significant centers of redistribution. Heroin from Myanmar and elsewhere in Southeast Asia often passes through Bangkok, Singapore, or Hong Kong on its way to Australia and the United States, while another circuit leads through Mauritius to Italy. A shift in the major sites of production would not destroy these distribution networks, but it would alter their relative importance.

In addition to the ruined lives of many users, the trade in heroin and cocaine produces a series of deleterious side effects. It provides income for criminal networks that may invest their proceeds in legitimate businesses, but also commonly deal in prostitution, gambling, and other illicit trades. It finances civil wars, as both right-wing and left-wing forces discover they can tax producers and distributors. It promotes money laundering on a colossal scale, which in turn supports tax-sheltered banking centers like those that dot the Caribbean map. It encourages the purchase of protection from government officials, and sometimes their direct participation in drug sales. According to the Paris-based Geopolitical Drug Observatory, the roster of states in which parts of the government or significant numbers

Box 16.3 Prices of Cocaine and Heroin

The following tables show the prices of cocaine and heroin at different stages of production and distribution in 1999 (US dollar value)

Cocaine Produced in Bolivia, Peru, or Colombia

Farmer sells 200 kg of coca leaves (enough for 1 kg of base paste) to local dealer	$200
Local dealer converts into 1 kg of paste, sells to intermediary	$350
Intermediary purifies and sells 1 kilo of base cocaine to exporter	$500
Courier buys 1 kg of hydrochloride of cocaine from Colombian exporter	$2,500
Wholesaler in Miami sells 1 kg to courier	$14,000
New York wholesale price	$30,000
Paris wholesale price	$40,000
Wholesale price in Copenhagen, Moscow, or Riyadh	$150,000
Retail price of cut cocaine	$500,000

Heroin Produced in Pakistan

Dealer buys 1 kg of opium from farmer	$60
Laboratory buys opium from dealer	$80
Wholesaler buys processed heroin from laboratory	$3,000
Price at Pakistani border	$5,000
Wholesale price in Turkey	$12,000
Wholesale price in Netherlands	$50,000
Retail price of heroin on the street	$150,000

of officials profit from the drug trade includes Albania, Azerbaijan, Cambodia, Colombia, Equatorial Guinea, Gambia, Mexico, Morocco, Myanmar, Nigeria, Pakistan, Paraguay, Peru, Poland, Russia, Suriname, Syria, Thailand, Turkey, Ukraine, and Uzbekistan. Note the division of labor: consumers and principal financial beneficiaries in wealthy countries, producers in poor countries, political profiteers mostly in between. The drug trade offers a paradigm for the darker sides of globalization (see Box 16.4).

16.6 FUTURE INEQUALITIES: EXPLOITATION AND HOARDING

Let us step back in order to look further into the future. In the short run of 1980–2000, globalization was widening inequalities between rich and poor parts of the world despite the resurgence of East Asia and the Pacific. Where might we expect world inequality to be in 2050? Over the long run of human history, we have witnessed two overlapping processes generating inequality among whole categories of people – men and women, different ethnic groups, citizens of different countries, and so on. The first is *exploitation*, the second *opportunity hoarding*. Exploitation occurs when members of one category capture a value-producing resource, enlist the labor of people from another category in producing value from that resource, but give the laborers less than the value they have added. Thus mine owners get miners to dig underground, but pay the miners much less than the value of the coal they bring to the surface.

Opportunity hoarding occurs when members of a category capture a value-producing resource, use their own effort to produce value from that resource, but exclude members of other categories from the resource. Thus pharmaceutical companies develop life-saving drugs, then protect their profits from sale of those drugs through secrecy, patents, and coercion of distributors. The two inequality-generating processes overlap in such arrangements as serfdom, where landlords reserve the best land for themselves, maintain monopolies over marketing agricultural products, grant subsistence plots to cultivators, and commandeer labor from their serfs.

Control of Land Has Been the Main Source of Inequality for Millennia

For most of human history, large-scale inequality between members of different social categories has depended chiefly on control of land, backed by coercive force. The overall human shift from hunting and gathering to settled agriculture, beginning some ten thousand years ago, had two profound effects. First, it magnified distinctions based on control over land. Second, it augmented the ability of networks combining coercive force with well-connected hierarchies to seize and hold land. Pastoral people, slash-and-burn farmers, and pure hunter-gatherers have great trouble establishing continuous control over land – among other reasons, because they do not create sedentary military forces. Exceptions such as Mongol empires generally depended on terrifying force to extract tribute from agricultural populations that *did* possess land. Settled cultivators

themselves created specialized institutions for control of land. Exploitation, in these circumstances, included such arrangements as slavery, serfdom, feudal exaction, rack-renting, and sharecropping. Opportunity hoarding grew up with exclusive rights to superior land, pastures, forests, fisheries, wild game, and minerals.

Almost everywhere, categorical divisions by gender and age differentiated control over land and its related resources. The fact that warriors were almost exclusively male simply reinforced that very general principle. But such divisions as race, ethnicity, caste, religion, and lineage grew up in part as causes, and in part as consequences, of inequality with respect to control over land and coercive means. They figured directly as causes when conquerors used such divisions to establish advantage-yielding differences from the conquered. They figured as effects when divisions by race, ethnicity, caste, religion, and lineage emerged from boundaries created by exploitation and opportunity hoarding. Thus the now profound division between Hutu and Tutsi in Rwanda grew from a fuzzy nineteenth-century boundary between culturally similar but mainly agricultural Hutu and mainly pastoral Tutsi, a boundary greatly sharpened and reinforced by German, then Belgian, incorporation of the less numerous Tutsi into their systems of colonial rule.

In land-based systems, exploitation and opportunity hoarding commonly co-exist, and often reinforce each other. In many peasant economies, for example, local landlords operate exploitative systems in which tenant households owe them dues, services, and labor on the landlord's domain for which the peasants receive little or no compensation. But peasant households themselves hoard the opportunities afforded them by the land they lease or own, the cattle and tools they have accumulated, and the claims on others embedded in ties of kinship, neighborhood, and religious solidarity. Landless laborers typically occupy the worst positions within such systems, extensively exploited by landowners, and excluded from rights based on full membership in the peasant community.

Our own era has diminished the centrality of land in the generation and maintenance of inequality. Over the world as a whole, nevertheless, control of land – and its auxiliary, coercive means – has by no means dissolved as a foundation of exploitation and opportunity hoarding. Consider testimony from members of a poor (but by no means the poorest) village family in India's northern province of Uttar Pradesh. The family are Harijan, formerly known as Untouchables. Life histories from patriarch Ram Dass and his extended family show vividly not only how much inequalities in land ownership dominate local life but to what degree central governments still depend upon collaboration of small and medium landlords to keep the rest of the population in check. Ram Dass comments on how Thakurs,

Box 16.4 Global Tourism, Global Migration, and Child Labor

One constant theme of this book has been human movement. Globalization has always put large numbers of human beings into motion. Their reasons for leaving home can be personal, but they reflect larger trends. Some willingly leave, and some are forced. Wars of expansion bring soldiers into conquered lands; the chaos following the collapse of empires and defeat in war forces refugees to take to the roads. Other involuntary movements include the imposition of ethnic cleansing, deportation, confinement in concentration camps, kidnapping and sale into bondage, and children sent into distant areas by their families. The scale of these movements has expanded dramatically since the 1980s.

Globalization's effects on the flow of human beings in recent years have penetrated all countries, all economic levels, all genders, and all ages. Many of the flows are unregulated, and highly exploitative; some are beneficial to both sides. All seem to go beyond what any individual nation-state can control.

Many laborers leave home for economic reasons. Some stay permanently in their new countries, eventually acquiring rights of citizenship, while others, categorized as "temporary labor," never achieve stability, even if they live in their country for many years. Migrant labor can include the wealthy, cosmopolitan jet-setters supervising international investments for large multinational corporations, or the great masses of construction workers who flock to the oil-rich Middle East countries. The declining cost of air fares plus the increasingly global reach of capital investment stimulate the construction of new production facilities across the globe, attracting workers from many poor countries. Large countries like India and China also promote great increases in internal migration by focusing development efforts on key-point cities and regions. Booming cities like those on China's east coast attract over 100 million unregistered migrants from the poorer interior. Unlike the Depression-era migrants, these great human flows have taken place during a time of global economic growth. Poorer, stagnant regions are drained of their most vigorous people while the boom towns can keep wages low because of the intense competition for jobs and the insecurity of the new migrants.

Other people move around for cultural motives: to explore new places and learn about other parts of the world. Global tourism, growing at 7 percent per year worldwide, is one of the world's most rapidly growing industries. One sign of the close attention paid to the culture industry is the expansion of World Heritage Sites. A committee of the United Nations began designating these sites in 1978. They now number over 800. The majority are in Western Europe, but a substantial number are found in Latin America, the Caribbean, and Asia. Designation as a World Heritage Site requires local governments to make special investments in restoration and repair, but the governments attract international capital investment and technical expertise for cultural projects. The sites can then become major sources of economic growth as tourist development expands. Visitors to the temple complex of Angkor Wat in Cambodia, for example, bring in a substantial amount of Cambodia's GNP. Cambodia, a desperately poor, war-torn, agricultural country, has found its best chance for development in the display of its cultural heritage to foreign visitors.

Child labor, however, is another key element of global tourism. Children produce most of the carpets sold in India and Pakistan to foreign tourists, and they help make the fashionable clothing sold in Western boutiques. Children serve drinks on beaches and work in tourist hotels for low wages. In the worst cases, children provide sexual services for global travelers. Child labor makes possible large profits for export industries like textiles and fish processing. The children usually come from poverty-stricken regions of the country and many are sold into bondage by their parents, who are trapped by indebtedness. In other words, deepening impoverishment of one region goes hand-in-hand with rapid growth in other regions, tied closely by international networks of capital and human beings.

Global adoption networks also show how closely cultural changes are linked to human flows. Couples in advanced industrial countries often put off child-bearing so that the women can advance themselves at an equal pace with men in the workplace. This is a result of technologies of birth control combined with rising opportunities for women. Conversely, in China for example, the single-child-per-family policy combines with a constant preference for boys to create a surplus of boys at birth, rising rates of infanticide, and abandonment of female children at orphanages. New technologies for detecting the sex of the child before birth and elective abortion created these trends. Yet those girls who survive in orphanages now find parents abroad from families who have delayed childbearing. So it is now common to see entire planes full of hopeful parents heading to China and returning with baby girls in their arms. The female orphans of China have joined the ranks of other world travelers set in motion by global change.

higher-caste village landlords, came into their own after Nehru's reforms eliminated zamindari overlords:

Apart from the Thakurs, everyone was poor before zamindari abolition. Some of the Banias [traders] did have money from business. The middle castes were also poor, though not as poor as us Harijans. And even up to now, the richest are the Thakurs, then the middle castes, and the poorest are the Harijans! The Thakurs had all the advantages earlier: they were rich, they were educated, they had land, and they had us Harijans to be their slaves. So it is not surprising that still today they are the lords and we are still poor.

In India as a whole, distinctions by religion, caste, and gender reflect long histories of conquest, exploitation, and opportunity hoarding, but now serve to solidify and justify current inequalities with respect to land. A majority of the world's population still lives in systems where land ownership looms large.

But Machines Have Been Replacing Land Around the World

Nor need we reach far back into the histories of today's wealthy states to find similar conditions. As Westerners built centralized states with standing armies, after all, they continued to restrict military service to males, to tie full citizenship to military service, and to impose restrictions on suffrage and office-holding based on landed property-holding. But in the world's richer regions, starting a few hundred years ago, inequality began to spring increasingly from control over machines and raw materials for machines. At first, a balance between land and machines prevailed, because landlords and merchants who supplied wool, cotton, flax, and silk to machine operators actually dominated their own territories as textile production expanded. Since vital raw materials included fuel and metals, furthermore, people who controlled land containing those precious materials continued to prosper. But, step by small step, ownership of machines became an ever more prominent basis for exploitation and opportunity hoarding.

Divisions within machine production were articulated deeply and widely, with categorical distinctions having no logically necessary connection to the labor process. It became standard to package work relations in jobs, and to allocate those jobs by gender, age, race, ethnicity, and other social criteria. Stories grew up to explain and justify such job segregation, often alleging natural differences among categories in capacity and propensity for certain kinds of work. Categorical differences in availability and qualifications, however, actually resulted largely from the existence of segregation. What had been men's work (for example, telephone switchboard operation) quickly became

women's work without much change in routines, for example, which means that natural differences did not matter much. As in land-based systems of exploitation and opportunity hoarding, categorically differentiated relations to machine production became the basis of deep inequalities over social life as a whole.

The Future

What can we expect in the future? First, machine-based systems of inequality will continue to spread throughout the world for another half-century or more. It will take a long time before India, China, Africa, Latin America, and other relatively rural parts of the world accomplish full shifts to economies – and inequalities – based on control of machine power. If they do. After all, it is conceivable that substitution of machines for labor power will accelerate so rapidly in already mechanized economies that the export of low-wage machine work to poor countries will lose its current attractiveness. Similarly, poor countries might become significant sites for manufacturing only in those industries where machine production reaps great advantages from proximity to raw materials or to low-wage consumers. In service industries, we might find the most routine forms of data-processing farmed out to low-wage workers in poor countries, but headquarters and high-wage work remaining in major cities of rich countries. We face the frightening prospect of exclusion at a world scale: increasingly deep division between a minority segment living with machine-based inequality and a majority segment condemned to land-based inequality.

Finance, Information, and Science May Replace Machine Dominance, for a Few Still, three newly prominent bundles of value-producing resources show some signs of displacing control over machines from its world dominance of the last few centuries. The first is financial capital – by no means a new element in the world economy, but one whose volume and volatility now lend enormous power to those who control it. Small, well-connected networks of financiers can batter whole national economies by shifting their investments from site to site.

The second is information – as old as the world, but newly prominent with the spectacular expansion of electronic communication. Information includes media of communication such as newspapers, magazines, radio, television, telephones, and the internet itself. Despite the internet's ubiquity, electronic information is even easier to hoard than money, machines, and land; all it takes is tight electronic controls over who has access to files and communication.

The third, science, looms larger by the day. In the form of pharmaceutical development, genetic engineering, bio-mechanical computing, microelectronics, medical diagnostics, telecommunication, geophysical mapping, and astrophysical exploration, scientific innovation produces possibilities of control, hence of inequality, exceeding all its predecessors.

Financial capital, concentrated information stores, and scientific expertise all currently remain under control of small networks of persons, compared to the world population as a whole. Each has expanded with extensive systems of opportunity hoarding, which yield increasing advantages to those who live within those systems. To what extent they form bases for exploitation remains more controversial. Remember that by exploitation we mean the process by which those who control a resource enlist the labor of others in production of value by means of that resource, and yield to those others less than the value added by their effort. Opponents of foreign direct investment regularly warn against the exploitative power of financial capital in just such terms. Critics of marketing surveys, credit information pooling, and government information systems levy parallel charges against concentrated information stores. Fears of big science likewise rest on ideas that it will take away more than it gives. At least in principle, all three could serve as bases of exploitation as well as opportunity hoarding.

Inequality Will Not Decline: Education and Coercion Will Dominate Their impact on inequality will still depend on two other factors we have encountered before: their integration with categorical differences, and their relation to concentrated means of coercion. Although financial capital, information, and science have incorporated existing distinctions by gender, age, race, ethnicity, and religion to some degree, so far the largest gap fostered by these emerging bases of inequality separates people with qualifying technical educations from everyone else: MBAs, law degrees, computer science degrees, doctorates, and the like. Of course each arena has its heroic tales of people who succeeded without certification: college dropouts who made billions as investors or internet entrepreneurs, and so on. Not since the Chinese mandarins, nevertheless, have specially educated people played so prominent a part in world affairs, and received rewards so definitively separating them from their neighbors.

The second factor is connection between these competing bases of inequality and organized concentrations of coercion. Through most of human history coercive means remained relatively fragmented, dispersed among communities, warlords, thugs, bandits, pirates, mercenaries, feudal retainers, religious organizations, and private armies, despite the occasional formation of an empire. Over the last few centuries, humanity performed the surprising feat of placing its major concentrations of coercive means under the control of national governments. The cost was increasingly bloody international warfare. But it brought the benefit of reduction in domestic mayhem – more so in other Western countries than in the United States.

In our own time, that trend seems to be reversing. Civil war, guerrilla war, genocide, mass political killing, gun-running, and even mercenary activity have been rising irregularly since World War II. The US State Department's count of international terrorist incidents from 1968 through 2001 provides one indication. The international terrorist incidents in the count include those in which a group based outside a given country attacked targets within that country. It is in fact, like all attempts to define "terrorism," an inconsistent definition, excluding relatively contained civil wars such as that of Sri Lanka, but including Arab and Israeli attacks on each other as well as domestic attacks of the Red Army Faction (or Baader-Meinhof Gang) in Germany, the Red Brigades in Italy, and the Japanese Red Army. It certainly includes the crashing of aircraft into the Pentagon and the World Trade Center on September 11, 2001. Those attacks proved that the United States was vulnerable to terror as deadly and spectacular as that occurring in distant countries. Still, they marked an enormous exception: During the twenty-first century, flagrant acts of terror, national or international, have been concentrated heavily in poor countries with weak states.

Year-to-year variation in the frequency of such events depends especially on fluctuations in bombing. Minor spurts occurred during the 1970s, which included the Munich Olympic Village attack of 1972. But the high point came in the five years from 1984 through 1988. After then, terrorist attacks fell off irregularly but substantially. Bombing, armed attacks, and hostage-taking all became more common during the peak years. Then all – especially bombing – declined. Although ups and downs occurred from year to year, international terrorist incidents were still becoming less frequent as the twenty-first century began. Since 2014 terrorist attacks have increased again but their shape and extent have begun to change. Some terrorist groups such as "Islamic State" in Iraq and Syria have begun to evolve into armies with the intention of forming states. Others, like al-Qaeda, have an international scope, with units in many areas of the world (see Figure 16.5).

Other evidence concerning armed conflicts across the world places the post-1945 peak of interstate and civil wars around 1992. National liberation movements played an increasingly prominent part in terrorism and civil wars as the overall frequency of incidents decreased after then. From the early 1990s onward, civil war and genocide became the world's leading sources of violent deaths on a large scale. Genocide is systematic

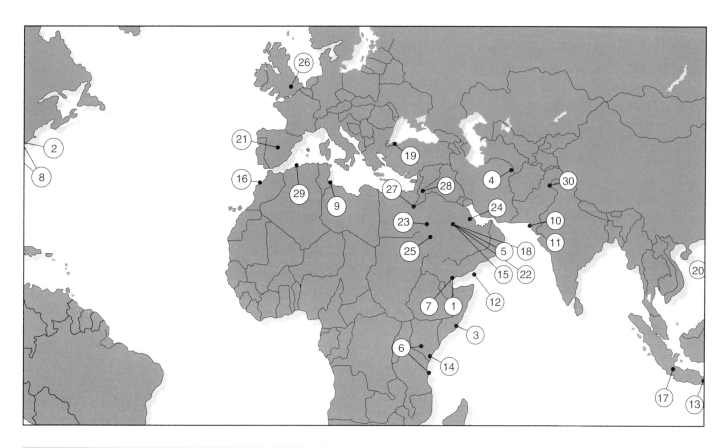

	Date		Location	Description	Number killed[†]
1	**1992**	December	Aden, Yemen	Hotel bombing	2
2	**1993**	February	New York	World Trade Center bombing	6
3		October	Mogadishu, Somalia	Ambush of US forces	18
4	**1994**	June	Mashad, Iran	Shia shrine bombing	27
5	**1995**	November	Riyadh, Saudi Arabia	Truck bomb	7
6	**1998**	August	Kenya and Tanzania	US embassies bombed	301
7	**2000**	October	Aden, Yemen	*USS Cole* bombing	17
8	**2001**	September	New York, Virginia and Pennsylvania	9/11 attacks	3,000 approx.
9	**2002**	April	Djerba, Tunisia	Synagogue bombing	21
10		May	Karachi, Pakistan	Hotel bombing	10
11		June	Karachi, Pakistan	US consulate bombing	11
12		October	Yemen coast	*Limburg* oil tanker bombing	1
13		October	Bali, Indonesia	Nightclub bombings	202
14		November	Mombasa, Kenya	Hotel bombing	15
15	**2003**	May	Riyadh, Saudi Arabia	Expatriate compound bombing	35
16		May	Casablanca, Morocco	Multiple bombings	45
17		August	Jakarta, Indonesia	Hotel bombing	16
18		November	Riyadh, Saudi Arabia	Car bombs	17
19		November	Istanbul, Turkey	Synagogues bombed	57

(*cont.*)

	Date		Location	Description	Number killed[†]
20	**2004**	February	Philippines	Ferry bombing	116
21		March	Madrid, Spain	Train bombings	191
22		April	Riyadh, Saudi Arabia	Government building bombing	3
23		May	Yanbu, Saudi Arabia	Refinery attack	5
24		May	Khobar, Saudi Arabia	Expatriate compound attack	22
25		December	Jeddah, Saudi Arabia	US consulate attack	5
26	**2005**	July	London	Underground/bus bombings	56
27		July	Sharm el-Sheikh, Egypt	Resort bombings	88
28		November	Amman, Jordan	Hotel bombing	63
29	**2007**	April	Algiers, Algeria	Car bombs	33
30	**2008**	June	Islamabad, Pakistan	Danish embassy bombing	6

Sources: Press reports; Congressional Research Service

[*] Later information unavailable

[†] Including perpetrators

Figure 16.5 Active sites of al-Qaeda groups

extermination of one ethnic category's members by killers from another ethnic category. Rwanda's anti-Tutsi genocide of 1994, in which hundreds of thousands of Hutu took part, killed more people than any other single episode of the 1990s; half a million people may have died in Rwandan massacres that year. (The dead included not only Tutsi, but also Hutu who did not collaborate fully with the killing.)

The Rwandan genocide only represented the most extreme and unequal form of ethnic conflict. Coupled with muscular nationalism (the force-backed demand for a state dominated by members of a single ethnic or national category), ethnic conflict became the early twenty-first century's greatest source of political killing.

The swelling of bottom-up nationalist claims during a period of globalization surprised many Western analysts. Like those who thought that simply plugging low-income economies into world markets would stimulate those economies to take off, many optimists thought that Western models of democracy and public order would spread rapidly through the globalizing world. In fact, some democratization did occur. Freedom House, a respected American organization that monitors and rates the world's states for political liberty or its absence, divided countries into the following categories:

free: Maintaining a high degree of political and economic freedom and respecting basic civil liberties.

partly free: Enjoying more limited political rights and civil liberties, often in a context of corruption, weak rule of law, ethnic strife, or civil war.

unfree: Denying citizens basic rights and civil liberties.

As Figure 16.6 shows, over most of the period from 1981 through 2000, Freedom House counted around a third of the world's people as living under unfree regimes. The proportion rated as living under free regimes rose slowly from 1981 to 1991, but then took a nose dive as India slipped into the partly free category. India's return to a free rating in 1999 (as a coalition government including Hindu nationalists came to power through regular elections) boosted the number of people rated as free by a billion. Over the entire period, the proportion of the world's population that Freedom House rated as unfree declined from 42.5 to 35.5 percent, while the free percentage rose modestly from 35.9 to 38.9. What happened mostly, then, is a move of unfree regimes toward limited political rights and civil liberties. That move often occurred under pressure from great powers, international organizations, and neighboring regimes.

The shift was coupled, however, with an increase in violent struggles over who would run those regimes. Earlier chapters (especially Chapters 9 and 10) showed how the top-down nationalism of such countries as France stamped in place a model identifying states with particular national cultures. That same top-down nationalism then incited bottom-up nationalism in the names

Year under Review	Free	Partly Free	Not Free	World Population
Mid-1980	1,613.0 (35.90%)	970.9 (21.60%)	1,911.9 (42.50%)	4,495.8
Mid-1981	1,631.9 (35.86%)	916.5 (20.14%)	2,002.7 (44.00%)	4,551.1
Mid-1982	1,665.1 (36.32%)	918.8 (20.04%)	2,000.2 (43.64%)	4,584.1
Mid-1983	1,670.7 (36.00%)	1,074.8 (23.00%)	1,917.5 (41.00%)	4,663.0
Mid-1984	1,671.4 (34.85%)	1,117.4 (23.30%)	2,007.0 (41.85%)	4,795.8
Mid-1985	1,747.2 (36.27%)	1,121.9 (23.29%)	1,947.6 (40.43%)	4,816.7
Mid-1986	1,842.5 (37.10%)	1,171.5 (23.60%)	1,949.9 (39.30%)	4,963.9
Mid-1987	1,924.6 (38.30%)	1,205.4 (24.00%)	1,896.0 (37.70%)	5,026.0
Mid-1988	1,992.8 (38.86%)	1,027.9 (20.05%)	2,107.3 (41.09%)	5,128.0
Mid-1989	2,034.4 (38.87%)	1,143.7 (21.85%)	2,055.9 (39.28%)	5,234.0
Mid-1990	2,088.2 (39.23%)	1,485.7 (27.91%)	1,748.7 (32.86%)	5,322.6
Mid-1991 (a)	1,359.3 (25.29%)	2,306.6 (42.92%)	1,708.2 (31.79%)	5,374.2
Mid-1992	1,352.2 (24.83%)	2,403.3 (44.11%)	1,690.4 (31.06%)	5,446.0
Mid-1993	1,046.2 (19.00%)	2,224.4 (40.41%)	2,234.6 (40.59%)	5,505.2
Mid-1994	1,119.7 (19.97%)	2,243.4 (40.01%)	2,243.9 (40.02%)	5,607.0
Mid-1995	1,114.5 (19.55%)	2,365.8 (41.49%)	2,221.2 (38.96%)	5,701.5
Mid-1996	1,250.3 (21.67%)	2,260.1 (39.16%)	2,260.6 (39.17%)	5,771.0
Mid-1997	1,266.0 (21.71%)	2,281.9 (39.12%)	2,284.6 (39.17%)	5,832.5
Mid-1998 (b)	2,354.0 (39.84%)	1,570.6 (26.59%)	1,984.1 (33.58%)	5,908.7
Mid-1999	2,324.9 (38.90%)	1,529.0 (25.58%)	2,122.4 (35.51%)	5,976.3
Mid-2000	2,465.2 (40.69%)	1,435.8 (23.70%)	2,157.5 (35.61%)	6,058.5
Mid-2001	2,500.7 (40.79%)	1,462.9 (23.86%)	2,167.1 (35.35%)	6,130.7
Mid-2002	2,717.6 (43.85%)	1,293.1 (20.87%)	2,186.3 (35.28%)	6,197.0
Mid-2003	2,780.1 (44.03%)	1,324.0 (20.97%)	2,209.9 (35.00%)	6,314.0
Mid-2004	2,819.1 (44.08%)	1,189.0 (18.59%)	2,387.3 (37.33%)	6,395.4
Mid-2005	2,968.8 (45.97%)	1,157.7 (17.93%)	2,331.2 (36.10%)	6,457.7
Mid-2006	3,005.0 (45.97%)	1,083.2 (16.57%)	2,448.6 (37.46%)	6,536.8
Mid-2007	3,028.2 (45.85%)	1,185.3 (17.95%)	2,391.4 (36.21%)	6,604.9
Mid-2008	3,055.9 (45.72%)	1,351.0 (20.22%)	2,276.3 (34.06%)	6,683.2
Mid-2009	3,088.7 (45.49%)	1,367.4 (20.14%)	2,333.9 (34.37%)	6,790.0
Mid-2010	2,951.9 (42.95%)	1,487.0 (21.63%)	2,434.2 (35.42%)	6,873.2
Mid-2011	3,016.6 (43.29%)	1,497.4 (21.49%)	2,453.2 (35.21%)	6,967.2
Mid-2012	3,046.2 (43.29%)	1,613.9 (22.93%)	2,376.8 (33.78%)	7,036.8
Mid-2013	2,826.9 (39.72%)	1,822.0 (25.60%)	2,467.9 (34.68%)	7,116.8

(a) The large shift in population figures is due to India's change in status from Free to Partly Free.
(b) The large shift in population figures is due to India's change in status from Partly Free to Free.

Figure 16.6 Percentage of the world's people living under unfree regimes.

of groups that did not belong to those national cultures. Plenty of nineteenth-century political struggles centered on claims to represent the nation, and thus on attempts to take state power from others in the nation's name. The success of many such struggles opened a new path to political power for leaders who could either secede from an existing regime in the name of a distinct nation or seize control of an existing state in the people's name.

After World War II, decolonization brought a new wave of nationalist claims. Those claims were often even more far-fetched than those of nineteenth-century nationalists, since leaders of ethnically heterogeneous colonies whose boundaries had been formed through military conquest by colonizers regularly claimed to represent unified nations. Because great powers and the United Nations continued to honor such nationalist claims, they multiplied as the Cold War ended, socialist federations disintegrated, and the advantages of being recognized as authentic national leaders increased.

What advantages? Despite the hardships often imposed on poor countries by economic globalization and structural adjustment, those who ran states that were integrating more fully into the world economy and polity usually gained far more benefits than those who did not run the same states. What Freedom House calls a "context of corruption" refers indirectly to that fact. In different parts of the world, recognition as legitimate rulers of a state could bring foreign aid, loans, military assistance, contracts with multinational firms, bribes, and jobs for the group in power. In Europe, it could mean candidacy for membership in NATO and the European Union. In the Americas, it could mean US loans, military assistance, investment, and market openings.

In addition, state power gave religious, linguistic, and ethnic groups opportunities to strike at their rivals and enemies. Where adjacent states stand to gain influence by installing rulers of similar ethnic, religious, or linguistic identity in their neighbors, the incentives to nationalism increase. Put together, the model of states as national, the rewards to recognized rulers, and the power to suppress rivals stimulated nationalist struggles for power in a large minority of the world's states. What looks at a distance like mindless hatred of one group for another actually has a strong political rationale.

More sinister rationales for claiming state power also sometimes prevail. To run your own state establishes a claim to collect from illegal, semi-legal, or dangerous enterprises on your own territory. In Sierra Leone, Liberia, and Zaire in the 1990s and early twenty-first century, for example, access to diamonds has allowed mining entrepreneurs and aspiring rulers to turn their shared military power into great wealth. Analysts of the bloody conflict that has pitted various military forces against Russian authorities in Chechnya, on the Russian Federation's southwest border since the secession of Georgia in 1991, have plausibly but contradictorily described the struggle as:

- A claim of a unified indigenous people to independence.
- A bid by nearby Muslim powers to extend their influence into a predominantly Muslim section of Russia.

- A fight over control of oil drilled in or passing through Chechnya.
- An attempt to create a zone where criminal enterprises could flourish.

Each description contains an element of truth, but none of them alone captures the conflict's complexity. Chechnya's struggles intertwine rivalries among warlords, nationalists, Muslim activists, and criminals.

In Colombia, Mexico, Peru, Afghanistan, and Myanmar, the drug trade offers similar opportunities. It also provides good reasons for local rebels, whatever their announced political programs, to keep the central state and the international community at arm's length. In both Colombia and Chechnya, hostage-taking for ransom has become a vicious political art form, and a major source of financial support for paramilitary forces. Not all such forces are demanding independence or state power in the names of oppressed nations. But the stakes of civil war and rebellion resemble each other across a wide range of regional conflicts. Far from being protests against globalization, furthermore, most of them feed on new opportunities offered by globalization. In that sense, globalization has promoted the rise of what outsiders call ethnic conflict, religious fanaticism, and even genocide.

Despite often being incited by outside states or by paramilitary shadows of existing states, on the whole these homicidal activities are escaping the system of state control over concentrated coercion that grew up between 1750 and 1950 or so. To the degree that international flows of drugs, arms, oil, gas, military expertise, and precious stones come under the influence of those who already dominate financial capital, information banks, or scientific knowledge, whole new forms of inequality could form, with disastrous consequences for humanity as a whole. Sound historical understanding of these complex processes, intelligently applied, can reduce the likelihood of such tragic outcomes.

Conclusion This chapter has described four significant trends of the last twenty-five years which will most likely continue at least until 2050, barring total catastrophe: the unprecedented pace of globalization, driven by advanced technologies of communication and transportation and by the mobility of capital; the rise of Asia to economic and political status rivaling the USA and Europe; the undermining of nation-states as the predominant arena for regulating political and economic activity; and rising inequality within and between major regions and states of the world. Many privileged people around the world have gained a great deal from the new globalization, but more nefarious characters like drug lords and terrorists have also done well. Large populations, particularly in the failed states of the world, however, have seen their livelihoods decline, forcing many of them to leave for new homes. None of these trends is brand new; each has its antecedents, but their combination and rapidity signal the onset of a new era. The persistence, and even aggravation, of poverty and environmental crisis indicates that the transition to this new global era will not be smooth.

Study Questions (1) What war ended in 1989, and how?

(2) What part did nationalism play in Boris Yeltsin's rise to power?

(3) Compare the three main waves of globalization since 1500.

(4) What are the most prominent forms of globalization, and what mixture of them has prevailed since 1945? When and how has globalization strengthened states? When and how has it weakened them?

(5) How did the Washington Consensus affect poor countries?

(6) How and why did the World Bank's position on conditions for economic growth change after 1990?

(7) What sorts of inequality matter most for the quality of life, and why?

(8) How, and how successfully, did communist China promote economic growth during the 1990s?

(9) What is the dark side of globalization, and how does it connect with the bright side?

(10) Is control over land becoming more or less important as a basis for inequality across the world? How and why?

Suggested Reading MANUEL CASTELLS, *End of Millennium* (Malden, MA: Blackwell, 2000). This is a wide-ranging survey of major world trends, linking them to the creation of a new network society based on information flows.

TYLER COWEN, *Creative Destruction: How Globalization is Changing the World's Cultures* (Princeton University Press, 2002). Cowen presents a lucid, energetic, persuasive statement of the view that in music, literature, cinema, cuisine, and the visual arts, expanding markets promote diversification, rather than stultifying uniformity.

MARLIES GLASIUS, MARY KALDOR, AND HELMUT ANHEIER (eds.), *Global Civil Society 2002* (Oxford University Press, 2002). This yearbook reports the latest on worldwide non-governmental organizations and social movements.

ULF HANNERZ, *Transnational Connections: Culture, People, Place* (London: Routledge, 1996). This study focuses on what close-up observation reveals about how globalization works at the small scale.

Alf Hornborg, *The Power of the Machine: Global Inequalities of Economy, Technology, and Environment* (Walnut Creek, CA: AltaMira, 2001). Hornborg describes how unequal trade across the world depletes the environment.

Mary Kaldor, *New and Old Wars: Organized Violence in a Global Era* (Cambridge: Polity, 2013). Kaldor explores how modern international institutions have shaped the character of national rebellion.

James N. Rosenau, *Distant Proximities: Dynamics Beyond Globalization* (Princeton University Press, 2003). Rosenau discusses what a world without strong states would look like.

Joseph Stiglitz, *Globalization and its Discontents* (New York: W.W. Norton, 2002). A Nobel Prize winner and former World Bank chief economist surveys the accomplishments and (mostly) misdeeds of international agencies, especially the International Monetary Fund.

Glossary

developmental states: States in which governments intervene directly and deeply into the national economy to promote growth.

diasporas: International networks of entrepreneurs who share family or cultural ties, facilitating credit and commercial trust.

foreign direct investment: Commitment of capital by financiers from one country to the ownership or management of enterprises in another country.

glasnost: (Russian: "openness.") Relaxation of central controls over the Soviet Union's public life during the later 1980s.

globalization: Increase in the scale and impact of transcontinental connections among persons, groups, and organizations.

perestroika: (Russian: "restructuring.") Attempt to modernize the Russian economy and move away from central planning during the later 1980s.

structural adjustment: Integration of national markets into the international economy, and policy changes that promote such integration.

Washington Consensus: Principles of economic development generally accepted by major capitalist states and financial institutions during the 1980s and 1990s. These primarily involved opening up economies to foreign investment and reducing state management of economies.

CONCLUSION

We conclude with a discussion of two critical issues: global terrorism and global warming. Both of them threaten to harm huge numbers of people, and both have roots far back in the human past. The greatest recent terrorist threat, that of al-Qaeda, derives directly from the imperial domination of the Middle East in the nineteenth and twentieth centuries, but al-Qaeda's supporters find their inspiration in the founding of Islam in the seventh century. Yet only the globalization of the late twentieth century made al-Qaeda's actions possible.

Global warming is a more subtle, but equally dangerous trend which, if nothing is done to avert it, will bring catastrophe to hundreds of millions of vulnerable people. It is a direct result of global industrialization since the nineteenth century. Scientists have carefully documented the warming of the planet over the past century, but the nations of the world have so far only taken very small steps to address this vital threat to human existence.

GLOBAL TERRORISM

On September 11, 2001, members of the terrorist group al-Qaeda hijacked four transcontinental airliners taking off from Boston's Logan airport. They crashed two of them into the two World Trade Center towers in New York City (see Figure 1). The explosion of the gasoline in the airplanes incinerated the twin towers and their occupants. The third plane crashed into the Pentagon. Passengers on the fourth plane, probably intended for the White House, brought it down in a field in Pennsylvania. Nearly 3,000 people died in these attacks. The boldness of the al-Qaeda attacks stunned and horrified the world. Never before had so many civilians been killed by a deliberate attack on American soil. President George W. Bush vowed to make a War on Terror the theme of his administration.

Many commentators claimed that September 11 opened a new era in world history. They argued that terrorist groups were waging a new kind of warfare with new goals. The Bush administration relied on this argument to justify unprecedented concentration of power in the hands of the president, defiance of international agreements, and new intrusions into Americans' civil rights. By claiming that history did not matter, the Bush administration invoked a state of "exception," putting the US government beyond the control of international powers or domestic constitutional restraints.

In fact, the terrorists of September 11 carried on a pattern of violence in the service of political ends that has developed since World War II. The predominant trends in collective violence over the past sixty years have been the increasing ratio of civilian to military casualties, the rising proportion of paramilitary organizations, and the shift from inter-state wars to civil wars. Although the targets and organizers have changed, however, those who use violence still use it for recognizable goals. They are not simply fanatics, but militants willing to attack civilians to reach specific political ends.

Nearly all regions of the world have suffered extensive violence from paramilitary groups and civil wars. The US State Department counted 300 to 500 terrorist attacks occurring around the world annually from 1980 to 2002. Armed conflicts raged in many parts of Africa and places like Colombia, Chechnya, Kosovo, Nepal, Peru, Sri Lanka, and Tajikistan through the 1990s. Decolonization increased the number of independent countries, thus increasing the

C.1 The attack by the al-Qaeda militants on the twin towers of New York City's World Trade Center in 2001 shocked the world, particularly Americans, into recognizing the power of global terrorism to use modern technologies, like airplanes, to inflict mass destruction on civilian populations.

targets for dissidents, and many of the new countries could not control security within their territories. The USA and Soviet Union also sponsored domestic resistance to the regimes allied against them in the Cold War, promoting legal and illegal arms shipments around the world. The global diaspora of peoples combined with global transportation and communication networks linked emigrants to political movements within their home countries. Al-Qaeda stood out not by its willingness to use terror, but by its ability to strike at the financial and military capitals of the United States.

Al-Qaeda recruited young men willing to kill themselves in a jihad, or holy war, against Western civilization. Osama bin Laden, the guiding genius of the al-Qaeda organization, openly attacked Western societies as "crusaders" who were intent on destroying Muslim societies around the world. He called on all Muslims to unite against Western infidels in support of his terrorist activities:

I say that the events that happened on Tuesday September 11 in New York and Washington are truly great events by any measure, and their repercussions are not yet over ... [Economic damage will reach] no less than $1 trillion by the lowest estimate, due to these successful and blessed attacks. We implore God to accept those brothers within the ranks of the martyrs, and to admit them to the highest levels of Paradise.[1]

The Bush administration first responded by attacking Afghanistan, ruled by the fundamentalist Islamist group called the Taliban, which had given shelter to bin Laden and his supporters. Supported by a group of warlords and dissident ethnic groups, the American forces invaded Afghanistan, overthrew the Taliban, and installed a new government headed by Hamid Karzai, an Afghan in exile in the USA.

The Bush administration next focused its sights on Saddam Hussein, the dictatorial ruler of Iraq. George W. Bush senior, in 1990, had sent US forces to invade Iraq when Hussein attempted to seize Kuwait. He quickly drove back the Iraqi army, but he left Hussein in power, fearing that the breakup of the country would help Iran. An international boycott of Iraqi oil sales was intended to ensure that Hussein could not obtain the revenues to rebuild his army and weapons programs. The boycott inflicted heavy damage on Iraqi society, causing many to die from lack of proper medical care. European nations pressed to allow "oil for food" sales that would direct revenue solely toward humanitarian needs in Iraq. They thought that Hussein could be contained through economic pressure.

George W. Bush junior, however, seemed to be convinced that Saddam Hussein supported al-Qaeda's terrorist activities, even though there was no evidence of any contact between them. He also claimed that Saddam Hussein had active plans to construct weapons of mass destruction (WMD), including nuclear, chemical, and biological weapons, but no convincing intelligence information supported this conclusion. After the Gulf War, inspectors from a United Nations special commission were sent to ensure that Saddam Hussein dismantled all his major weapons programs, but hard-liners in the US government still suspected that he was concealing WMD activities. When Hussein expelled the UN inspectors, suspicions grew. Under heavy pressure from the USA and European nations, Hussein agreed to readmit the inspectors to Iraq. The inspectors, struggling against Iraqi obstruction, reported that they had found no evidence of active weapons programs. These reports satisfied European nations (except for Great Britain), but the Bush administration rejected them.

In March 2003, the US government, defying the majority opinion of European nations and much of the rest of the world, launched an attack on Iraq. It easily defeated Saddam Hussein's armies. Very few Americans died in the invasion, while over 25,000 Iraqi civilians died. But it has not created a viable Iraqi state, much less the model of democracy that it proclaimed as its goal.

Bin Laden himself and his organization, al-Qaeda, had spread across the world, beyond the reach of a single nation-state. They drew support from many regions. It was not until May 2, 2011, that bin Laden was tracked down and killed in Pakistan by American special forces. There were strong indications that his presence in Pakistan was due to support from factions of the Pakistani intelligence forces.

The USA demonstrated that it could use its overwhelming military superiority to destroy hostile regimes, but it had much less success in putting the devastated countries back together. As of 2014, Afghanistan still holds together loosely, but a confederation of warlords runs most of the country, while the US-backed government controls only the area around the capital in Kabul. Even the existing pro-US government has become increasingly insubordinate given the prospect of US withdrawal and the imminent possibility of having to go it alone. The cultivation of opium poppies rose 64 percent in 2004 to 4,200 tons per year; 40 percent of its GDP comes from drug trade profits, and it supplies more than 75 percent of the world's heroin and more than 95 percent of European demand. Efforts by the US military and Afghan government to eradicate opium were almost totally ineffective, because farmers received no significant support to help them convert to other crops. The Afghan state and economy would collapse without the world drug trade.

Iraq is now sharply divided between warring factions of Sunni and Shi`ite Muslims, while the Kurds in the north stand firmly for their own autonomy. The Taliban and al-Qaeda still operate on the poorly controlled borders of Afghanistan and Pakistan, many other Muslim insurgents have flocked to Iraq to attack American forces, and the religious parties control key security forces of the Iraqi government. The Iraqi constitution made Islam the religion of the state, bringing Iraq close to becoming an Islamic republic like Iran. But the weak central government had little control over many regional leaders, and the minority Sunni Muslims

C.2 George Bush sent American armies into Iraq to overthrow Saddam Hussein, based on the false conviction that Hussein was developing weapons of mass destruction. The American occupation of Iraq exacerbated conflict between Sunni and Shi`ite militant groups, one of which destroyed this prominent mosque in 2006.

rejected the new constitution because it gave them little say. Oil exports, which Bush's advisors had claimed would finance the cost of the war, dropped from 2.8 million barrels per day before the war to 1.8 million barrels per day. Guerrilla fighters successfully instigated increasing hostility between Sunnis and Shi`ites by blowing up revered Shi`ite mosques (see Figure 2) and staging continual attacks on local politicians and police, and cutting off Baghdad from much of its fuel and electricity. The USA, with 130,000 troops in the country, suffered over 2,000 casualties by the third year of occupation, and Iraq showed no signs of becoming a stable nation-state. It, too, joined the long list of failed states created since the end of the Cold War.

Many critics have argued that the invasion of Iraq diverted US strength away from substantial efforts to contain the al-Qaeda terrorist organization. Many of the al-Qaeda leaders have been arrested or killed by European, Pakistani, and other national security forces. On the other hand, Muslim opinion in the Middle East has turned sharply anti-American, generating further support for radical Islamist attacks on the West. Revelations of torture of Muslims by American soldiers at the prison of Abu Ghraib have discredited US claims that they were bringing a more humane and democratic order to the Middle East. The radical Islamist group Hamas, dedicated to eliminating the state of Israel, won popular elections in Palestine in 2006, replacing the secular organization al-Fatah, which had been negotiating for peace. Muslim immigrants facing heavy discrimination and unemployment in France staged large riots in 2005 after two young boys in an impoverished Paris suburb were electrocuted while fleeing police. Ultimately 9,000 cars were burned along with many day care centers and public buildings; the rioting lasted over three weeks and spread to 274 towns. The most extreme commentators predicted an unending "clash of civilizations" between Islamic peoples and the West, arguing that the religious principles of Islam were completely incompatible with Western principles of liberal democracy and capitalism.

Understanding the predicament of the USA and its allies facing Middle Eastern terrorism requires a longer historical perspective. Did September 11, 2001, really change the course of world history? Of course, it is too soon to tell what all the ramifications of the event will be. We can, however, ask how much the terrorist attacks came out of longer-term developments of the twentieth century. In this sense, the September 11 attacks were not entirely unanticipated. Their impact also varied greatly in different regions of the world.

For many years, al-Qaeda had been planning attacks on the USA itself. The first open terrorist attacks by al-Qaeda, in 1998, blew up the American embassies in Kenya and Tanzania, leaving over 200 dead, mostly Africans. An effort to blow up the World Trade Center towers in 1993 was stopped, but the radical Islamic terrorists did not give up their plan. In short, many people in the intelligence and military communities of the USA knew well the danger of al-Qaeda, but they failed to co-ordinate their activities well enough to get adequate information about it. The astonishing lack of US specialists in the government who had linguistic or cultural knowledge of Afghanistan, Iran, or many other Middle Eastern countries greatly hindered US efforts to penetrate secretive organizations in these societies. Americans' false sense of security and general lack of interest in foreign affairs left them ignorant of important developments in the Middle East.

The Cold War first spawned al-Qaeda and the USA contributed to its foundation. Al-Qaeda was not an unknown organization in 2001. Osama bin Laden created it in the late 1980s, on the border between Pakistan and Afghanistan. Its primary source of recruits was the war against the Soviet occupation of Afghanistan, which began in 1979. The American CIA, co-operating with intelligence agencies in Pakistan, sent substantial support to the mujahidin, guerrilla fighters against Soviet forces. Al-Qaeda was one of these Islamist militant groups. They undermined Soviet control of the Afghan countryside and generated popular support in the country, forcing the Soviets to withdraw in 1989. After the Soviets left, however, the USA and other Western powers did little to help rebuild Afghanistan. The country fell under the control of rival warlord factions until the Taliban took over much of the country. Americans generally forgot about this remote region of the world.

The industrialized world's addiction to oil further fueled Middle Eastern conflict. When Iraq invaded Kuwait, the primary American concern was Saddam Hussein's threat to dominate the supply of oil from the Middle East. Saudi Arabia agreed to allow American troops to be stationed on its soil in aid of the Gulf war. Radical Islamists attacked the Saudis for being so weak as to require foreign, non-Muslim military aid. Osama bin Laden, as a Saudi citizen expelled from the country, began issuing his first public statements in 1994, attacking the Saudis for corruption and weakness in the face of Western military power. He appealed to all members of the Muslim community, the *umma*, to unite to throw out Western imperial power from the Middle East. In his view, jihad was a defensive war to respond to centuries of oppression of Muslims by Western powers. Blaming colonial rule by Britain and France, Israeli domination of the Palestinians, and the US-led boycott of Iraq for having caused the death of millions of innocent Muslims, he called for Muslims to respond in kind: "We aren't terrorists in the way [the Americans] want to define the term, but rather because we are being violated in Palestine, in Iraq, in Lebanon, in Sudan, in Somalia, in Kashmir, in the Philippines, and throughout the world."[2] Al-Qaeda also grew out of politicized Islamist movements which had begun in the early twentieth century. The Muslim Brotherhood, founded by the Egyptian teacher Hasan al-Banna in 1928, and the Jamaat-i Islami party of Pakistan, established in 1941, argued that their societies should strictly follow Islamic law, or shariah, and this Islamic society could only be created through social and political action. They promoted rebellions against existing Islamic states, which they regarded as corrupt, and attacked the conservative clerics, the ulama, for being subservient to these weak and immoral states. Bin Laden was deeply influenced by courses he took in Saudi Arabia from Muslim Brotherhood teachers.

Osama bin Laden took full advantage of modern media communications. By granting video interviews to the independent Arab television station Al Jazeera, he spoke directly to the masses of the Muslim world. Al-Qaeda's members fully exploited the opportunities offered by globalization: They used credit cards and online reservations to travel freely across borders; they used internet networks and cell phones to communicate with each other; and they sent funds around the world using both the most modern electronic networks and the very personal financing services of Middle Eastern "honey shops." They cleverly exploited the openness of global society to evade efforts of intelligence agencies to track them. Their "base" in Afghanistan only provided trained new recruits, but their organization was truly global, like the capitalism they attacked. Many of the participants had college degrees from Western universities. Osama bin Laden studied management and economics at a modern university in Saudi Arabia, and showed substantial skill at managing his family's construction company. He applied the same talents to running his terrorist organization.

Finally, the deficiencies of regional states aided al-Qaeda. The three Islamic states of Saudi Arabia, Iraq, and Pakistan have long connections with American and European security interests. Saudi Arabia, because of its enormous oil wealth, enjoys special attention from American administrations. Yet Saudi Arabia is a monarchy based on a strict form of Islam known as Wahhabism, which limits the roles of women, forbids alcohol, and rejects corrupting influences from the West. Osama bin Laden and many of his supporters, as Saudis who knew of the temptations offered by Western luxuries, aimed to drive out all American influence from Saudi Arabia and from the holiest places in the Middle East.

Iraq was ruled by the secular Ba'ath party from 1964. Saddam Hussein rose to power as a modernizing autocrat dedicated to increasing the wealth and power of his state. He used his oil revenues to build up a powerful military force, but also to promote education, literacy, and urbanization. When the Iranian Islamic Revolution threatened his regime, he invaded Iran, beginning the eight-year-long Iran–Iraq War. Western powers supported Saddam Hussein in order to prevent the Iranian revolution from spreading further. Until he overstepped his bounds by invading Kuwait, Saddam Hussein was seen as a valuable balancing and modernizing force in this key region of the oil-producing gulf.

Pakistan, an Islamic state constructed after South Asians won independence from Britain, used its position in the Cold War to draw on US and European support in return for functioning as a counter-balance against India, suspected of being too favorable to the Soviet Union. After the Sino-Soviet split, China also leaned to Pakistan's side. But Pakistan suffered from corrupt politicians, inadequate economic policies, overpopulation, and lack of education, and it had no oil revenues to finance its growth. The secular democratic reformer Benazir Bhutto won a popular election and ruled from 1988–90 and 1993–96, but opposition politicians ousted her on charges of corruption. General Pervez Musharraf took power from the civilian politicians by military coup in 1999. He found himself heavily challenged by Islamists, while his intelligence and military bureaucracies promoted the Islamic mujahidin in Afghanistan. Pakistan also supported Islamic militants fighting for the recovery of all of Kashmir from India. Pakistan was a fragile state constructed out of the remains of the old British Raj, surviving as a secular military dictatorship increasingly under pressure from rising Islamic movements. Musharraf joined the US war against al-Qaeda, but he remained an uncertain ally.

In sum, al-Qaeda's terrorist activities drew support from global communication networks, unequal world economic growth, the heavy dependence of the industrialized world on oil, and the weaknesses of Middle Eastern and South Asian states. Their decentralized, far-flung organization was perfectly adapted to the new world of global networks. Even though bin Laden's rhetoric invoked the community of seventh-century Islam, his organization was deeply embedded in the modern world.

GLOBAL WARMING AND ENVIRONMENTAL CRISIS

In 2001 the United Nations Intergovernmental Panel on Climate Change issued its third report, in Arabic, Chinese, English, French, Russian, and Spanish. The panel found that the amount of carbon dioxide in the atmosphere had increased by more than 30 percent since pre-industrial times and was still increasing at an unprecedented average rate of 0.4 percent a year. Carbon dioxide is a "greenhouse gas," meaning that it absorbs infrared radiation from the planet's surface, preventing it from being reflected back into space. Increasing concentrations of greenhouse gases cause the average temperature of the planet to rise, bringing serious and irreversible effects on the global climate. Including other greenhouse gases, like methane, raised the rate of increase to 1 percent per year. The primary causes of increases in greenhouse gases were deforestation and human consumption of fossil fuels. Emissions from industrial plants and automobiles had caused the concentration of carbon dioxide in the atmosphere to rise sharply, like a "hockey stick," since the industrial age began in the late nineteenth century. The famous hockey stick graph has been used in many discussions of climate change (see Figure 3).[3] Later reports in 2007 and 2014 confirmed the existence of rapid temperature change, and showed that human-induced global climate change has begun to have increasingly severe effects on the health of all human and natural systems.

The 2001 panel estimated that if carbon dioxide concentrations doubled, which would take seventy years at current rates, global temperature would rise by 1.5 to 4.5 degrees centigrade. By comparison, global mean temperature has risen only 5 to 6 degrees centigrade since the last glacial maximum. A rise in temperature of 2.5 degrees centigrade would make the globe as warm as it was in the age of the dinosaurs.

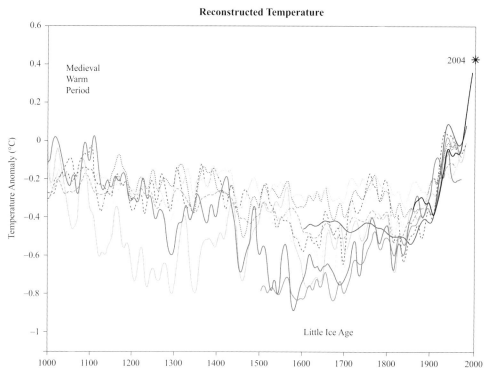

C.3 This graph (famous as the "hockey stick") reconstructs global temperatures over the past thousand years, based on numerous readings from ice cores, tree rings, and other natural data. It shows definitively the unprecedented rise in global temperatures resulting from human industrial activity since the mid nineteenth century.

C.4 Mount Kilimanjaro in Tanzania is located only about 180 miles away from Olduvai Gorge, a central site for the origin of the modern human species. Global warming, a consequence of human productive activity, is eliminating the snows of this great mountain, and may well lead to the end of the human species itself.

The evidence for global warming has accumulated for two decades, especially from researchers who bore into polar ice caps and glaciers on high tropical mountains, from studies of ancient forests buried in the tundra, from layers of sediment in prehistoric bodies of water, and also from mathematical models. In the case of ice cores, scientists have analyzed the concentration of carbon dioxide in bubbles trapped in ice cores, and estimated temperatures from levels of snowfall and dust found in the ice layers. The long-term climatic record shows clear correlations between carbon dioxide concentrations and global temperature extending back for 150,000 years. Temperatures have fluctuated within a modest range for many millennia, but temperature can also change rapidly in geological terms, by several degrees in a few decades. In the last hundred years, however, carbon dioxide concentrations have risen to unprecedented levels. It is natural to conclude that global temperature will soon rise to levels never seen before in the history of our species.

The melting of polar ice caps and warming of the ocean would increase the total volume of sea water, endangering the majority of the world's population who live in coastal areas. The average rate of human-induced sea level rise is up to 1 millimeter per year. By the year 2100, average sea level could rise by 1.6 feet worldwide, but storms and tidal waves would also increase in frequency. In the worst case, the West Antarctic ice sheet could slide into the sea, raising sea levels by over fifteen feet, flooding all existing ports, and putting much of Florida and Louisiana, for example, under water.[4] In addition, warmer seas provide more energy for tropical storms, whose incidence and severity has noticeably increased. In continental regions, global warming generally means increased incidence of drought. Warming decreases soil moisture, harming crop growth. Extreme weather events, like heavy rainstorms, cyclones, and dust storms, could also increase.

In 2005, the scientist James Hansen told the American Geophysical Union that "the Earth's climate is nearing, but has not passed, a tipping point beyond which it will be impossible to avoid climate change with far-ranging undesirable consequences."[5] Lonnie G. Thompson, a climatologist who has drilled cores in the glacial ice of mountains around the world, from China to Peru to Africa, announced in February 2001 that the famous snows of Mount Kilimanjaro (see Figure 4), the highest mountain in Africa, would disappear within twenty years and that there was no hope of saving them. The snows of Kilimanjaro first appeared 11,700 years ago, just about the same time as hunter-gatherers in the Middle East began to learn how to plant and cultivate seeds in the soil. They originated agrarian civilization, the story that opens this book. Global warming, at the rate it is going, would put extreme stress on humankind's fundamental food supplies.

Scientists have discovered that humankind has for the first time begun to change substantially the climatic conditions which make all life possible. Some argue that the "Holocene" geological era of the last 12,000 years has ended, and a new era, the "Anthropocene," has begun. The consciousness of such dramatic human effects on the entire planet has led many people to realize that all of us share responsibility for human and non-human life as part of a single global community. The images of the planet viewed from space by orbiting satellites reinforces this sense of a common human fate (see Figure 5 below).

The increasing weight of scientific evidence stimulated the US Environmental Protection Agency and the United Nations Environment Programme to try to create a global consensus to discuss policies to address the political and social implications of global warming. The UN reports describe increasingly severe strains on basic resources supporting human survival, especially in the poorest countries of the world.[6] Supplies of land, water, fish, and forest have shrunk rapidly, placing many people on the brink of disaster. To make things worse, the rate and severity of natural disasters have steadily grown. On average 211 million people suffered natural disaster every year in the 1990s compared to 147 million in the 1980s.

C.5 Satellite images of planet Earth give us humans a global perspective, which dramatically illustrates that we are all bound together on a single physical object with one interconnected natural ecosystem.

The Reagan and Bush administrations in the USA, however, backed by oil, gas, and other industrial interests, strongly resisted any measures that would limit the use of their energy resources, or attempt to turn energy consumption toward solar power. Other alternatives to energy sources generating greenhouse gases have also faced resistance. Hydropower, for example, requires building large dams, and nuclear power brings high risks of radiation and nuclear weapons proliferation. The United States, until recently the largest producer of greenhouse gases, has refused to limit energy use in any way that would slow its rate of economic growth. China, the second largest producer, heavily dependent on coal, endorses the scientific evidence for global warming, but refuses to stop building further inefficient coal-powered plants without substantial international aid.

Is there any chance that the major nations of the world will work together to limit the impact of global warming? The Montreal Protocol of 1987 offered some hope. This global agreement was designed to limit the production of chemicals that reduce concentrations of ozone in the atmosphere. Scientists had discovered that chlorofluorocarbons (CFCs) and other gases produced by aerosol spray cans and supersonic transport (SST) airplanes cause the expansion of "ozone holes." Over Antarctica, scientists had observed huge declines in the concentration of ozone. It had dropped up to 40 percent from the 1960s to the 1980s. Global decreases ranged from 1.7 to 6.2 percent in the northern hemisphere. Without ozone, ultraviolet rays from the sun would severely damage humans and animals. In the Montreal Protocol, twenty-four industrial nations, including the USA, agreed to phase out the use of CFCs in order to protect human health. The USA and many European countries agreed to ban the use of CFCs in aerosols, and US concerns about ozone led to severe restrictions on landing rights for European SST airplanes at US airports. The United Nations Environment Programme led the negotiations that resulted in this landmark international treaty, the first in which major industrial nations committed themselves to preventing major global atmospheric change. Despite intensive opposition from industrial producers, who denied the scientific evidence, a consensus formed that nation-states must act to preserve the global environment even at the cost of economic growth.

In 1992, the Rio Conference brought together many nations to respond to the world's increasing environmental stress. The term "sustainable development" became an almost universal catchphrase expressing the desire to ensure that economic growth would not endanger the health of future generations. In the Kyoto Protocol of 1997, 180 nations, including Canada, the European Community, Japan, and Russia, agreed to limit the production of greenhouse gases on the model of the Montreal Protocol. They pledged to make "demonstrable progress" in reducing greenhouse gas emissions by 2005, and to reduce them by 5 to 8 percent below the level of 1990 by the years 2008–12.[7] The US Congress, however, rejected the Kyoto Protocol, seriously undermining its effectiveness. Carbon dioxide emissions from major industrial powers continued to rise with no effective limits, while developing countries like China and India, which were exempt from the Kyoto Protocol restrictions, rapidly increased their coal consumption to fuel industrial growth.

Direct evidence of the impact of global warming soon appeared. In August 2005, Hurricane Katrina struck the city of New Orleans with devastating force, putting much of the city underwater and forcing the evacuation of hundreds of thousands of people. Climatologists have good evidence that the increasing strength of tropical storms in the Caribbean is closely related to global warming. Although global warming did not directly cause the great tidal wave, or tsunami, which struck the coastal regions of South and Southeast Asia in December 2004, the tsunami exposed the extreme vulnerability of everyone who lives along the coastlines of major oceans. Global warming raises sea levels everywhere, making these people particularly at risk. Entire island communities could disappear.

Global warming and its associated environmental crises have sources that stretch back many centuries. From the sixteenth to eighteenth centuries, humans around the world moved into sparsely populated frontier regions, extracting valuable resources in order to enrich the states that sponsored them and the merchants who traded in global markets. Forests, grasslands, animals, minerals, fish, and birds all dropped sharply in number under the pressure. The nineteenth and twentieth centuries increased the pressure on resources, since industrialization insatiably required supplies of raw materials and energy. European industrial empires plundered the colonies in search of their resources, while people of the Americas rapidly exploited abundant lands and jungles. After decolonization, the independent states of Africa and Asia continued to attack nature in pursuit of rapid development. Ideas of "sustainable development" only began to gain support at the end of the twentieth century, when it became clear that the existing rate of growth could not continue forever. Evidence of global warming and knowledge of eventual exhaustion of oil supplies brought some to realize the need for new directions of economic growth, supported with new technologies, but these reformers face powerful resistance from defenders of the established coal- and oil-fired industrial regime. The environmental activists have attracted increasing public support, but they have so far made only limited progress in ensuring sustainable development for the entire planet.

There is now a greater global consciousness of the fragility of all the achievements of human society in the face of environmental change. Environmental movements are active in nearly every country in the world. New technologies may provide the answers to excessive energy consumption: lightweight cars, alternative fuels, recycling, solar power, among others. Some visionary engineers even foresee means to pull carbon out of the air and bury it in the sea to offset the continued production of greenhouse gases. Technical solutions exist, but the collective political will to shift human productive energies toward coexistence with nature, instead of war on it, has not yet won out.

Whether the nation-states of the world can take collective action against global problems still depends heavily on the three themes of this book: unequal power relationships among humans in states and societies; commercial and cultural links between the world's peoples; and the particular kinds of social life which divide us into separate societies and cultures, but also unite us around shared concerns of family, religion, art, and the preservation of human life.

Like global terrorism, global warming emerged in the late twentieth century as a worldwide phenomenon that seriously threatens the survival of the human race. The inability of the world's nations to respond effectively to it raises ominous fears about the long-term future of human civilization. Yet these phenomena were not sudden products of the late twentieth century; they emerged from longer trends and structures. Historical analysis cannot predict specific events, but it can help to show how long-term processes, based in power, commerce, and social life, create the conditions for major catastrophic events that radically alter human experience. For this reason, the study of world history may help guide us in understanding major trends of the future.

Suggested Reading   OSAMA BIN LADEN, *Messages to the World: The Statements of Osama Bin Laden* (New York: Verso, 2005). This is a complete collection of bin Laden's speeches, video interviews, and writings.

MARK BOWEN, *Thin Ice: Unlocking the Secrets of Climate in the World's Highest Mountains* (New York: Henry Holt, 2005). Bowen's book is a gripping account combining mountaineering adventure with a description of the science of global change derived from ice cores.

Tɪᴍ F. Fʟᴀɴɴᴇʀʏ, *The Weather Makers: How Man is Changing the Climate and What it Means for Life on Earth* (New York: Atlantic Monthly Press, 2005). This book is an elegantly written survey of the effects of global warming on human and natural life.

Jᴏʜɴ F. Rɪᴄʜᴀʀᴅs, *The Unending Frontier: An Environmental History of the Early Modern World* (Berkeley: University of California Press, 2003). Richards describes the global clearance of forests and oceans from 1500 to 1800.

Oʟɪᴠɪᴇʀ Rᴏʏ, *The Failure of Political Islam* (Cambridge, MA: Harvard University Press, 2001). Roy's study is a very insightful analysis and history of the rise of political Islamist movements.

Cʜᴀʀʟᴇs Tɪʟʟʏ, "Violence, Terror, and Politics as Usual." *Boston Review*, 27 (Summer 2002), 21–24. Tilly's article analyzes terrorism as part of general trends in collective violence over the past century.

Notes

1 Osama bin Laden, *Messages to the World: The Statements of Osama bin Laden* (New York: Verso, 2005), pp. 112–13.

2 Bin Laden, *Messages to the World*, p. 111.

3 The term "hockey stick" was coined by the climatologist Jerry Mahlman to describe the pattern shown by the Mann, Bradley, and Hughes 1999 research paper reconstructing historical temperatures. The metaphor envisages a graph that is relatively flat to 1900 as forming an ice hockey stick's "shaft," followed by a sharp increase corresponding to the "blade."

4 Bowen (see Suggested Reading) cites Michael Oppenheimer, "Global Warming and the Stability of the West Antarctic Ice Sheet," *Nature*, 393 (May 1998), 325–32.

5 Excerpted in "The Tipping Point," *New York Review of Books*, January 12, 2006, p. 18.

6 The UN has published Global Environmental Outlook reports in 1997, 1999, and 2002 (www.unep. org/geo/geo3). This was initiated in response to reporting requirements of Agenda 21 (begun at the Rio de Janeiro conference of 1992).

7 David G. Victor, *The Collapse of the Kyoto Protocol and the Struggle to Slow Global Warming* (Princeton University Press, 2001).

INDEX